THE
CAMBRIDGE
FACTFINDER

THE
CAMBRIDGE
FACTFINDER

Edited by
DAVID CRYSTAL

CAMBRIDGE
UNIVERSITY PRESS

Published by the Press Syndicate of the University of Cambridge
The Pitt Building, Trumpington Street, Cambridge CB2 1RP
40 West 20th Street, New York, NY 10011-4211
10 Stamford Road, Oakleigh, Victoria 3166, Australia

First published in 1993
Revised edition first published in 1994

Typeset by Flairplan Phototypesetting Ltd, Ware, UK, Prestige Typographics Ltd, Bury St
Edmunds, UK and Desktype Image Creation Ltd, Cambridge, UK

Printed in Great Britain at The Bath Press, Avon

A catalogue record for this book is available from the British Library

Library of Congress cataloging-in-publication data available

ISBN 0 521 471249 hardback
ISBN 0 521 469910 paperback

ABOUT THIS BOOK

The Cambridge Factfinder contains more facts than any other book of its kind. We also believe it is much easier to use than other such books. What might seem at first the most simple of books – a collection of bits of information for use in the home, at school or in the office – is actually the product of much hard thinking about how best to organize the information, and, indeed, what the nature of this information is.

What is a fact?

> Something that has really occurred or is actually the case; something certainly known to be of this character; hence a particular truth known by actual observation or authentic testimony, as opposed to what is merely inferred, or to a conjecture or fiction; a datum of experience, as opposed to the conclusions which may be based upon it.

This definition, one of the longest in the *Oxford English Dictionary*, gives a hint of the difficulty involved in saying what exactly counts as a 'fact' and thus of the difficulties facing any editor who has to decide what should be included in a book of them. At first glance, the answer is obvious: there are facts about objects and animals (what are the characteristics of *X*?), people (who is *X*?), places (where is *X*?), and times (when did *X* happen?), and these facts can be numerical (how many *X*? how often did *X* happen?), verbal (how to describe *X*?), and tabular (how to classify *X*?).

At second glance, the situation becomes more complicated (and more interesting). There are facts about fictions (*X* in mythology or literature) and fictions about facts (disputes over the longest or largest *X*). There are situations where we cannot decide whether something is fiction or fact (the changing politics of country *X*). There are near-facts (estimates of *X*), transient facts (world records about *X*), qualified facts (the majority of *X*), arguable facts (the most important *X*), politically biased facts (the growth or decline of *X*), and contrived facts (neat classifications of *X*). A factbook must not ignore these awkward and marginal cases, but having included them it must always remember to warn readers if 'there's something they should know' before swallowing a 'fact' whole. Examples of this advice are given on p. 42 (about longest rivers) and p. 406 (about saints' days). Many bitter arguments (such as those that arise out of a disputed answer in a quiz game) could be avoided if more attention were paid to this issue.

What isn't a fact?

On the other hand, certain notions are not part of a factbook. Definitions of words, for example, really have no place. It is a fact that Memphis and its necropolis is a World Heritage Site (p. 45). However, if you don't know what a necropolis is you had best look the word up in a dictionary. Nor do explanations of concepts have any place in a factbook. If, to continue the example, you are unclear about who would be buried in a necropolis, you had better look this up in an encyclopedia. A factbook is not intended to do the job of a glossary, a manual, or a textbook.

Nor is a fact a single, isolated piece of information. An enquirer may have a single question in mind, and want a single fact for an answer, but any factbook worth its salt should show how this enquiry fits into a broader frame of reference. No fact exists in isolation. Everything is part of a pattern. It is therefore important to show the pattern. A factbook should say to a reader: 'You asked about X, and here's the answer – but don't forget there's also Y and Z, which can help you understand X further. And, while you're here, have a look at Y and Z anyway, as they're interesting too.' A good factbook, once entered, should put questions in perspective, and also be difficult to leave. There should be a strong temptation to stay awhile, and browse. In *The Cambridge Factfinder*, the organization of information into fields of meaning, sequenced logically, and grouped hierarchically, provides both motivation and means. If the job is done well, answering factual questions proves to be the least trivial of pursuits.

Selecting the facts

A factbook could, in theory, be any size, from a few dozen to thousands of pages. Whatever the size, two considerations are paramount. There should be a balance between the various areas of knowledge covered; and there should be a pragmatic principle at work by which the editor tries to answer those questions that readers are most likely to ask.

Balance is relatively easy to achieve, by devising a scheme that works systematically through the various well-recognized domains of enquiry. In *The Cambridge Factfinder*, this is handled by starting with the most general perspective (the Universe) and finding a coherent path (one of many possible) through physical, biological, historical, geographical, and social domains.

Justifying the selection within each domain is less simple, and any editor has to fall back on the well-tried principle that 'one can please all of the people some of the time ...' In the present case, the task was much aided by the experience of running the *Cambridge Encyclopedia* Datasearch project since 1990. This project enables readers of the *Encyclopedia* to interrogate its database to obtain further information about topics that interest them. By keeping a record of the types of enquiry, it has proved possible to develop a sharpened sense of the kinds of things people want to know about. Examining the question-lists of innumerable pub quiz competitions, and other such games, has provided a further dimension.

Finding your way about

A factbook should be as accurate and as up-to-date as the state of knowledge permits, and *The Cambridge Factfinder* team has made every effort to ensure that these criteria are met. Full use has been made of the database compiled for *The Cambridge Encyclopedia*, which is continually being updated. The comprehensive coverage of the *Encyclopedia* has helped to guarantee the breadth of the present project; and the many specialized reference books in the Cambridge list have proved to be of great value in developing the project's depth of detail. Directly or indirectly, over 250 experts have been involved in generating the information that the *Factfinder* contains.

But it is no use having marvellously up-to-date and accurate facts if readers cannot find them. Critical to the success of any factbook, therefore, is an appropriate means of information retrieval. This is where most factbooks fall down. They may advertise that there are 'hundreds of thousands of facts' within their covers, but if it proves impossible to find the answer to a simple question without having to spend several minutes combing through the pages, the factbook has to be judged a failure. The solution is simple: proper indexing, with a preparedness to set aside sufficient space so that the project gets the index it deserves.

There are, broadly speaking, two ways into a factbook, and both are represented in *The Cambridge Factfinder*:

- One way suits the person who is interested in a general area of knowledge, and who wishes to explore it systematically. This person may not have a specific question in mind, only a vague uncertainty or need for clarification. Often a precise question does not become apparent until a range of possible answers has been presented. Such enquirers need a thematic guide to the factbook, where the various types of information are presented conceptually, with as much logical order relating the concepts as it is possible to impose. The logic underlying *The Cambridge Factfinder* is shown on p. ix. Using this information, it should be possible to 'home in' quickly on a broad area, and then to focus on a chosen topic.

- The other way suits the person who does have a precise question in mind – a who, a what, a when, a where. For this person, a thematic approach is of relatively little value. If you wish to find out a fact about the *gull*, for example, you want to be able to go immediately to wherever in the book this item is located, and not waste time searching for it unfruitfully under such a heading as *sea birds* (it is in fact a shore bird). Similarly, under which heading would you look for information about a particular thing or person? (Does the *Tay Bridge* appear under Communications, Scotland, or UK? Is *Leonardo da Vinci* under sculptors, architects, or painters?) All of this uncertainty is avoided through the expedient of an in-depth letter-by-letter index, with appropriate cross-references to handle alternative points of entry. Thus, in the index to this book, *Tay Bridge* is under *T* and *Leonardo da Vinci* is under *L* (with cross-references from *D* and *V*). The headings are there, too (*bridges* under *B* etc.), as an alternative route to themes and sub-themes. The index of *The Cambridge Factfinder* is far and away the most comprehensive ever prepared for a book of this kind, and it is space well used.

In short, the opening pages present in a thematic way the various fields or systems of information dealt with in this book. The closing pages present in an alphabetical way the items those systems contain. This dual perspective has been called, in lexicography, an 'index-to-system' approach, and it is the first time that it has been used to its full potential in a factbook. Such an approach adds coherence, increases speed of item look-up, makes the information more accessible, and promotes flexibility by providing alternative routes to answering a question. I hope that, after using the book, this is an opinion that readers will share.

Acknowledgement

A book of this kind is the product of thousands of person-hours of preparatory editorial and design work. I have had the privilege of working with a team of in-house editors – Paul James, Kendall Clarke, Pauline Graham, and Alyson Jones – who have had the onerous task of compiling the bulk of the tabular material, and an in-house designer – Geoff Staff – who has had the unenviable task of supervising the transition from edited copy to printed page. Their contribution to *The Cambridge Factfinder* has been fundamental, and it is a pleasure to have this opportunity to acknowledge it.

David Crystal

Editor
David Crystal

Illustrators
David Brogan
George Kilgour
John Marshall
Joanna Cameron
European Map Graphics Ltd

Cartography
European Map Graphics Ltd

Design
Sally Jeffery

AREAS OF KNOWLEDGE

This page shows how *The Cambridge Factfinder* is divided into broad areas of knowledge. Also indicated (in roman numerals) are the pages where you will find a much more detailed breakdown of each section in the Table of Contents which follows. For really specific queries, you should use the Index at the back of the book.

TABLE OF CONTENTS

Table of contents

Table of contents

Table of contents

Table of contents

Table of contents

THE UNIVERSE

THE COSMOS

Star distances

Star	Distance (l y)[a]
Proxima Centauri	4.24
Alpha Centauri A	4.34
Alpha Centauri B	4.34
Barnard's Star	5.97
Wolf 359 (CN Leonis)	7.80
Lalande 21185	8.19
UV Ceti A	8.55
UV Ceti B	8.55
Sirius A	8.67
Sirius B	8.67
Ross 154	9.52
Ross 248 (HH Andromedae)	10.37
Epsilon Eridani	10.63
Ross 128 (Fl Virginis)	10.79
L 789–6	11.12
GX Andromedae	11.22
GQ Andromedae	11.22
61 Cygnus A	11.22
61 Cygnus B	11.22
HD 173739	11.25
Epsilon Indi	11.25
Tau Ceti	11.41

[a] l y = light years.

Star magnitudes

Star	Common name	Magnitude	Distance (l y)[a]
Alpha Canis Majoris	Sirius	−1.47	8.7
Alpha Carinae	Canopus	−0.72	98
Alpha Centauri	Rigil Kentaurus	−0.29	4.3
Alpha Boötis	Arcturus	−0.04	36
Alpha Lyrae	Vega	0.03	26
Alpha Aurigae	Capella	0.08	45
Beta Orionis	Rigel	0.12	815
Alpha Canis Minoris	Procyon	0.34	11
Alpha Orionis	Betelgeuse	0.50 (v)	520
Alpha Eridani	Achernar	0.50	118
Beta Centauri	Hadar	0.60 (v)	490
Alpha Crucis	Acrux	0.76	370
Alpha Aquilae	Altair	0.77	16
Alpha Tauri	Aldebaran	0.85 (v)	68
Alpha Scorpii	Antares	0.96	520
Alpha Virginis	Spica	0.98	220
Beta Geminorum	Pollux	1.15	35
Alpha Piscis Austrini	Fomalhaut	1.16	23
Beta Crucis	Mimosa	1.20 (v)	490
Alpha Cygni	Deneb	1.25	1600
Alpha Leonis	Regulus	1.35	85

[a] l y = light years.
(v) = variable.

The constellations

Latin name	English name	Latin name	English name	Latin name	English name
Andromeda	Andromeda	Cygnus	Swan	Pavo	Peacock
Antlia	Air Pump	Delphinus	Dolphin	Pegasus	Winged Horse
Apus	Bird of Paradise	Dorado	Goldfish	Perseus	Perseus
Aquarius (Z)	Water Bearer	Draco	Dragon	Phoenix	Phoenix
Aquila	Eagle	Equuleus	Little Horse	Pictor	Easel
Ara	Altar	Eridanus	River Eridanus	Pisces (Z)	Fishes
Aries (Z)	Ram	Fornax	Furnace	Piscis Austrinus	Southern Fish
Auriga	Charioteer	Gemini (Z)	Twins	Puppis	Ship's Stern
Boötes	Herdsman	Grus	Crane	Pyxis	Mariner's Compass
Caelum	Chisel	Hercules	Hercules	Reticulum	Net
Camelopardalis	Giraffe	Horologium	Clock	Sagitta	Arrow
Cancer (Z)	Crab	Hydra	Sea Serpent	Sagittarius (Z)	Archer
Canes Venatici	Hunting Dogs	Hydrus	Water Snake	Scorpius (Z)	Scorpion
Canis Major	Great Dog	Indus	Indian	Sculptor	Sculptor
Canis Minor	Little Dog	Lacerta	Lizard	Scutum	Shield
Capricornus (Z)	Sea Goat	Leo (Z)	Lion	Serpens	Serpent
Carina	Keel	Leo Minor	Little Lion	Sextans	Sextant
Cassiopeia	Cassiopeia	Lepus	Hare	Taurus (Z)	Bull
Centaurus	Centaur	Libra (Z)	Scales	Telescopium	Telescope
Cepheus	Cepheus	Lupus	Wolf	Triangulum	Triangle
Cetus	Whale	Lynx	Lynx	Triangulum	
Chamaeleon	Chameleon	Lyra	Harp	Australe	Southern Triangle
Circinus	Compasses	Mensa	Table	Tucana	Toucan
Columba	Dove	Microscopium	Microscope	Ursa Major	Great Bear
Coma Berenices	Berenice's Hair	Monoceros	Unicorn	Ursa Minor	Little Bear
Corona Australis	Southern Crown	Musca	Fly	Vela	Sails
Corona Borealis	Northern Crown	Norma	Level	Virgo (Z)	Virgin
Corvus	Crow	Octans	Octant	Volans	Flying Fish
Crater	Cup	Ophiuchus	Serpent Bearer	Vulpecula	Fox
Crux	Southern Cross	Orion	Orion		

Z = zodiac constellation.

The northern sky

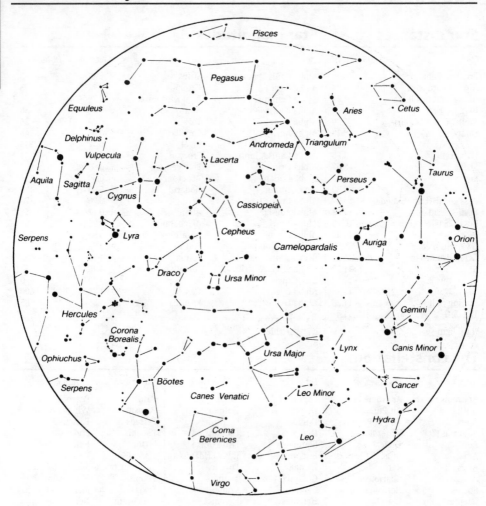

'Alpha' stars within constellations[a]

Name	Constellation	Name	Constellation	Name	Constellation
Achernar	Eridanus	Ankaa	Phoenix	Fomalhaut	Piscis Austrinus
Acrux	Crux	Antares	Scorpius	Hamal	Aries
Acubens	Cancer	Arcturus	Boötes	Kaïtain	Pisces
Al Giedi	Capricornus	Arneb	Lepus	Kitalpha	Equuleus
Al Rijil	Centaurus	Atria	Triangulum Australe	Markab	Pegasus
Aldebaran	Taurus	Betelgeuse	Orion	Men	Lupus
Alderamin	Cepheus	Canopus	Carina	Menkar	Cetus
Alkes	Crater	Capella	Auriga	Mirphak	Perseus
Alkhiba	Corvus	Castor	Gemini	Phakt	Columba
Alnair	Grus	Choo	Ara	Polaris	Ursa Minor
Alphard	Hydra	Cor Caroli	Canes Venatici	Praecipua	Leo Minor
Alphekka	Corona Borealis	Deneb	Cygnus	Procyon	Canis Minor
Alpheratz	Andromeda	Diadem	Coma Berenices	Rasalgethi	Hercules
Altair	Aquila	Dubhe	Ursa Major	Rasalhague	Ophiuchus

[a]'Alpha' denotes the brightest star in a constellation.

The southern sky

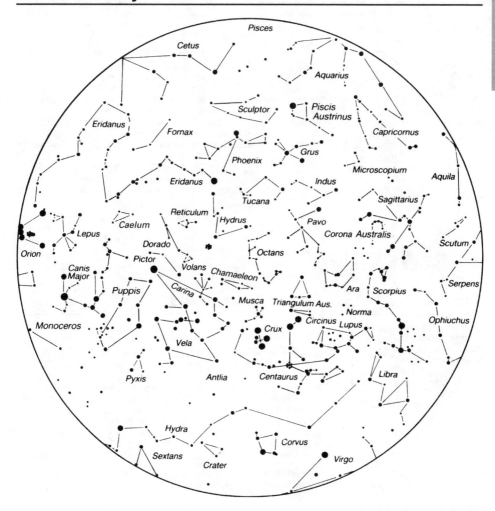

Name	Constellation	Name	Constellation	Name	Constellation
Rasalmothallah	Triangulum	Shedir	Cassiopeia	Thuban	Draco
Regulus	Leo	Sirius	Canis Major	Unukalhai	Serpens
Rukbat	Sagittarius	Spica	Virgo	Vega	Lyra
Sadalmelik	Aquarius	Svalocin	Delphinus	Zubenelgenubi	Libra

^a'Alpha' denotes the brightest star in a constellation.

Meteor showers

Name	Dates of maximum	Hourly rate
Quadrantids	3–4 Jan	100
Lyrids	21–2 Apr	10
Eta Aquarids	5–6 May	35
Delta Aquarids	28–9 Jul	20
Perseids	12–13 Aug	75
Orionids	22 Oct	25
Taurids	4 Nov	10
Leonids	17–18 Nov	10
Geminids	13–14 Dec	75

Historic comets

Name	First seen	Period of orbit (years)	Date of last perihelion[a] passage
Arend-Roland	1957	not known	8 Apr 57
Mrkos	1957	not known	1 Aug 57
Humason	1962	3 000	14 May 62
Ikeya	1963	not known	21 Mar 63
Ikeya–Seki	1965	879.88	21 Oct 65
Tago–Sato–Kosaka	1969	420 000	21 Dec 69
Bennett	1970	1 680	20 Mar 70
Kohoutek	1973	75 000	28 Dec 73
Kobayashi–Berger–Milon	1975	not known	5 Sep 75
West	1976	500 000	25 Feb 76
Halley	240 BC	76.1	9 Feb 86

[a]'Perihelion' refers to the position of the closest approach to the Sun of an object in an elliptical orbit.

THE SOLAR SYSTEM

The Sun

Age 4 500 000 000 years
Diameter 1 392 000 km/864 950 mi
Mass 2×10^{30} kg
Mean density 1.4 g/cm^3
Luminosity 3.9×10^{27} kW
Effective surface temperature 5 770 K/ 5 496.8 °C
Average orbital velocity 107 210 kph/ 66 620 mph

Solar eclipses 1994–9

Date	Extent of eclipse	Visible from parts of[a]
10 May 1994	Annular[b]	Mid-Pacific, N America, N Africa
3 Nov 1994	Total	Indian Ocean, S Atlantic, S America, Mid-Pacific
29 Apr 1995	Annular[b]	S Pacific, S America
24 Oct 1995	Total	Middle East, S Asia, S Pacific
9 Mar 1997	Total	C & N Asia, Arctic
26 Feb 1998	Total	Mid-Pacific, C America, N Atlantic
22 Aug 1998	Annular[b]	Indonesia, S Pacific, Indian Ocean
16 Feb 1999	Annular[b]	Indian Ocean, Australia
11 Aug 1999	Total	N Atlantic, N Europe, Middle East, N India

[a] The eclipse begins in the first area named. [b] In an annular eclipse a ring-shaped part of the Sun remains visible.

Planetary data (1)

Planet	Distance from Sun maximum (million km)	maximum (million mi)	minimum (million km)	minimum (million mi)	Sidereal period[a]	Axial rotation (equatorial)	Diameter (equatorial) (km)	Diameter (equatorial) (mi)
Mercury	69.4	43.0	46.8	29.0	88 d	58 d 16 h	4 878	3 031
Venus	109.0	67.6	107.6	66.7	224.7 d	243 d	12 104	7 521
Earth	152.6	94.6	147.4	91.4	365.26 d[b]	23 h 56 m 4 s	12 756	7 927
Mars	249.2	154.5	207.3	128.5	687 d	24 h 37 m 23 s	6 794	4 222
Jupiter	817.4	506.8	741.6	459.8	11.86 y	9 h 50 m 30 s	142 800	88 800
Saturn	1 512	937.6	1 346	834.6	29.46 y	10 h 14 m	120 000	74 600
Uranus	3 011	1 867	2 740	1 699	84.01 y	16–28 h[c]	51 000	31 600
Neptune	4 543	2 817	4 466	2 769	164.79 y	18–20 h[c]	49 500	30 800
Pluto	7 346	4 566	4 461	2 766	247.7 y	6 d 9 h	2 300	1 430

[a]'Sidereal period' refers here to the period of revolution around the Sun with respect to the stars.
[b] Precisely 365 d 5 h 48 m 46 s.

[c] Different latitudes rotate at different speeds.
y: years d: days h: hours m: minutes s: seconds
km: kilometres mi: miles.

The universe

Planetary data (2)

Mercury
Atmosphere hydrogen, helium, neon; *satellites* 0; *features* lunar-like crust, crustal faulting, small magnetic field.

Venus
Atmosphere carbon dioxide; *satellites* 0; *features* shrouded in clouds, 70% rolling plains, 10% highlands, 20% lowlands, craters.

Earth
Atmosphere nitrogen, oxygen; *satellites* 1; *features* liquid water oceans filling lowland regions between continents, permanent ice caps at each pole, unique in supporting life, magnetic field.

Mars
Atmosphere carbon dioxide; *satellites* 2; *features* cratered uplands, lowland plains, massive volcanic regions.

Jupiter
Atmosphere hydrogen, methane; *satellites* 16; *features* covered by clouds, craters, volcanic features, dark ring of dust, magnetic field.

Saturn
Atmosphere hydrogen, helium; *satellites* 18 (the exact number is not yet determined, but could be 18 or more); *features* several cloud layers, magnetic field, thousands of rings.

Uranus *Atmosphere* methane, helium, hydrogen; *satellites* 15; *features* clouds, layers of mist, magnetic field, c. 11 rings.

Neptune
Atmosphere methane, hydrogen; *satellites* 2; *features* unable to detect these telescopically from Earth.

Pluto
Atmosphere methane; *satellites* 1; *features* unable to detect these telescopically from Earth, thought to be partially covered with frozen methane.

The 'asteroid belt' is found mainly in a large series of orbits lying between Mars and Jupiter.

Planetary satellites

	Year discovered	Distance from planet (km)	Distance from planet (mi)	Diameter (km)	Diameter (mi)
Earth					
Moon	–	384 000	238 000	3 476	2 155
Mars					
Phobos	1877	938 000	583 000	27	17
Deimos	1877	2 346 000	1 458 000	15	9
Jupiter					
Metis	1979	128 000	79 000	40	25
Adrastea	1979	129 000	80 000	24	15
Amalthea	1892	181 000	112 000	270	168
Thebe	1979	222 000	138 000	100	60
Io	1610	422 000	262 000	3 650	2 260
Europa	1610	671 000	417 000	3 104	1 950
Ganymede	1610	1 070 000	665 000	5 260	3 270
Callisto	1610	1 883 000	1 170 000	4 800	3 000
Leda	1974	11 100 000	6 900 000	20	12
Himalia	1904	11 480 000	7 134 000	186	116
Lysithea	1938	11 720 000	7 283 000	40	25
Elara	1905	11 740 000	7 295 000	80	50
Ananke	1951	21 200 000	13 174 000	30	19
Carme	1938	22 600 000	14 044 000	40	25
Pasiphae	1908	23 500 000	14 603 000	50	30
Sinope	1914	23 700 000	14 727 000	40	25
Saturn					
Pan	1990	134 000	83 000	10	6
Atlas	1980	138 000	86 000	40	25
Prometheus	1980	139 000	86 000	100	60
Pandora	1980	142 000	88 000	100	60
Epimetheus	1980	151 000	94 000	140	90
Janus	1966	151 000	94 000	200	120
Mimas	1789	186 000	116 000	390	240
Enceladus	1789	238 000	148 000	500	310
Calypso	1980	295 000	183 000	30	19
Telesto	1980	295 000	183 000	30	19
Tethys	1684	295 000	183 000	1 050	650
Dione	1684	377 000	234 000	1 120	700
Helene	1980	378 000	235 000	15	9
Rhea	1672	527 000	327 000	1 530	950
Titan	1655	1 222 000	759 000	5 150	3 200
Hyperion	1848	1 481 000	920 000	480	300
Iapetus	1671	3 560 000	2 212 000	1 460	910
Phoebe	1898	12 950 000	8 047 000	220	137
Uranus					
Miranda	1948	130 000	81 000	480	300
Ariel	1851	191 000	119 000	1 160	720
Umbriel	1851	266 000	165 000	1 170	730
Titania	1787	436 000	271 000	1 580	980
Oberon	1787	583 000	362 000	1 500	950

A further ten satellites at distances of 50 000–86 000 km/31 000–53 400 mi, and with diameters of 15–170 km/9–106 mi, were discovered in 1986.

	Year discovered	Distance from planet (km)	Distance from planet (mi)	Diameter (km)	Diameter (mi)
Neptune					
Triton	1846	355 000	221 000	2 720	1 690
Nereid	1949	5 510 000	3 424 000	300	190

A further six satellites at distances of 48 000–118 000 km/29 800–73 300 mi, and with diameters of 50–400 km/31–248 mi, were discovered in 1989.

	Year discovered	Distance from planet (km)	Distance from planet (mi)	Diameter (km)	Diameter (mi)
Pluto					
Charon	1978	20 000 000	12 500 000	1 200	745

The near side of the Moon

NORTH

J Herschel
Mare Frigoris
Endymion
Mare Humboldtianum
Aristottes
Plato Alps
Atlas
Sinus Roris
Jura Mts
Eudoxus
Hercules
Sinus Iridum
Lacus Somniorum
Mare Imbrium
Sinus Iridum
Posidonius
Cleomedes
Archimedes
Mare Marginis
Palus Putredinis
Mare Serenitatis
Aristachus
Mare Crisium
Palus Somnii
Erastosthenes
Oceanus Procellarum
Mare Vaporum
Kepler
Sinus Aestuum
Mare Tranquillitatis
Mare Undarum
Copernicus
Mare Smythii
Mare Spumans
Sinus Medii
Grimaldi
Mare Fecunditatis
Theophilus
Langrenus
Mare Nubium
Ptolemaeus
Albategnius
Alphonsus
Mare Nectaris
Fracastorius
Arzachel
Catharina
Petavius
Mare Humorum
Piccolomini
Purbach
Palus Epidemiarum
Walter
Schickard
Maurolycus
Janssen
Tycho
Mare Australe
Longomontanus
Maginus
Clavius

SOUTH

The lunar 'maria'[a]

Latin name	English name	Latin name	English name
Lacus Somniorum	Lake of Dreams	Mare Serenitatis	Sea of Serenity
Mare Australe	Southern Sea	Mare Smythii	Smyth's Sea
Mare Crisium	Sea of Crises	Mare Spumans	Foaming Sea
Mare Fecunditatis	Sea of Fertility	Mare Tranquillitatis	Sea of Tranquillity
Mare Frigoris	Sea of Cold	Mare Undarum	Sea of Waves
Mare Humboldtianum	Humboldt's Sea	Mare Vaporum	Sea of Vapours
Mare Humorum	Sea of Humours	Oceanus Procellarum	Ocean of Storms
Mare Imbrium	Sea of Showers	Palus Epidemiarum	Marsh of Epidemics
Mare Ingenii	Sea of Geniuses	Palus Putredinis	Marsh of Decay
Mare Marginis	Marginal Sea	Palus Somnii	Marsh of Sleep
Mare Moscoviense	Moscow Sea	Sinus Aestuum	Bay of Heats
Mare Nectaris	Sea of Nectar	Sinus Iridum	Bay of Rainbows
Mare Nubium	Sea of Clouds	Sinus Medii	Central Bay
Mare Orientale	Eastern Sea	Sinus Roris	Bay of Dew

[a]'Maria' refers to the lowland areas of the moon flooded by lava 3.5 thousand million years ago.

The far side of the Moon

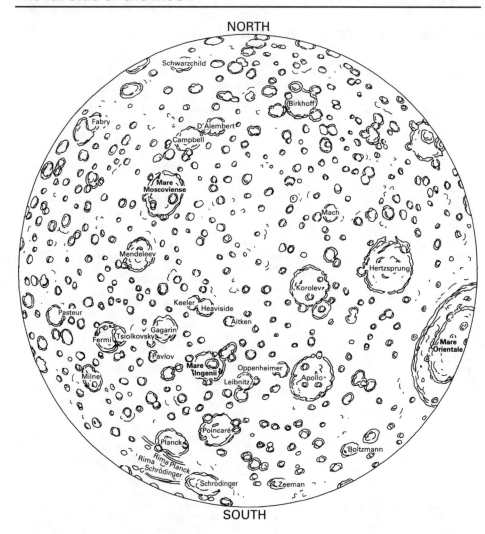

Lunar eclipses 1993–2000

Date	Extent of eclipse	Time of mid-eclipse	Where visible
4 Jun 1993	Total	13.02	Pacific, Australia, SE Asia
29 Nov 1993	Total	06.26	N and S America
25 May 1994	Partial	03.32	C and S America, part of N America, W Africa
15 Apr 1995	Partial	12.19	Pacific, Australia, SE Asia
4 Apr 1996	Total	00.11	Africa, SE Europe, S America
27 Sep 1996	Total	02.55	C and S America, part of N America, W Africa
24 Mar 1997	Partial	04.41	C and S America, part of N America, W Africa
16 Sep 1997	Total	18.47	S Africa, E Africa, Australia
28 Jul 1999	Partial	11.34	Pacific, Australia, SE Asia
21 Jan 2000	Total	04.45	N America, part of S America, SW Europe, W Africa
16 Jul 2000	Total	13.57	Pacific, Australia, SE Asia

The universe

SPACE EXPLORATION

Major space astronomy events/missions

Name of event/mission	Country/agency	Year of launch	Event description
Sputnik 1	USSR	4 Oct 1957	First Earth satellite
Sputnik 2	USSR	3 Nov 1957	Biosatellite
Explorer 1	USA	31 Jan 1958	Discovery of Earth's radiation belts
Luna 1	USSR	2 Jan 1959	Escaped Earth gravity; discovery of the solar wind
Vanguard 2	USA	17 Feb 1959	First Earth photo
Luna 2	USSR	12 Sep 1959	Lunar impact
Luna 3	USSR	4 Oct 1959	First lunar photo (hidden side)
TIROS 1	USA	1 Apr 1960	Weather satellite
Transit 1B	USA	13 Apr 1960	Navigation satellite
ECHO 1	USA	12 Aug 1960	Communications satellite
Sputnik 5	USSR	19 Aug 1960	Orbited animals
Vostok 1	USSR	12 Apr 1961	First manned orbital flight (Yuri Gagarin)
Mercury	USA	20 Feb 1962	First US manned orbital flight (John Glenn)
Mariner 2	USA	26 Aug 1962	Venus flyby
Mars 1	USSR	1 Nov 1962	Mars flyby
Vostok 6	USSR	16 June 1963	First woman in orbit
Ranger 7	USA	28 Jul 1964	First close-up TV pictures of lunar surface
Mariner 4	USA	28 Nov 1964	Mars flyby pictures
Voskhod 2	USSR	18 Mar 1965	First spacewalk (AA Leonov)
Venera 3	USSR	16 Nov 1965	Venus impact
Luna 9	USSR	31 Jan 1966	Lunar soft landing; first picture from the lunar surface
Gemini 8	USA	16 Mar 1966	Manned docking
Luna 10	USSR	31 Mar 1966	Lunar orbiter
Surveyor 3	USA	17 Apr 1967	Lunar surface sampler
Cosmos 186/188	USSR	22/28 Oct 1967	Automatic docking
Zond 5	USSR	14 Sep 1968	Animals in lunar orbit
OAO 2	USA	1968	First orbiting astronomical observatory
Apollo 8	USA	21 Dec 1968	Manned lunar orbit
Apollo 11	USA	16 Jul 1969	First person on the moon (Neil Armstrong)
Copernicus	USA	1970	First far-ultraviolet observatory
Venera 7	USSR	17 Aug 1970	Venus soft landing
Mars 2	USSR	19 May 1971	Mars orbit
Mars 3	USSR	28 May 1971	Mars soft landing
Pioneer 10	USA	3 Mar 1972	Jupiter flyby; crossed Pluto orbit; escaped Solar System
Skylab	USA	1973	High-resolution images of solar corona in X-rays
Pioneer 11	USA	6 Apr 1973	Saturn flyby
Mariner 10	USA	3 Nov 1973	First detailed picture of Mercury
Venera 9	USSR	8 Jun 1975	Venus orbit; first picture of Venusian surface
Apollo/Soyuz	USA/USSR	15 Jul 1975	First manned international co-operative mission
Viking 1, 2	USA	Aug/Sep 1975	First pictures taken on the Martian surface
Voyager 1, 2	USA	Aug/Sep 1977	First images of Jupiter, Saturn, Uranus, and Neptune
IUE	USA/UK/ESA	1978	First international space observatory
ISEE C	USA	12 Aug 1978	Comet intercept
STS 1	USA	12 Apr 1981	First launch of *Columbia* space shuttle
STS 6	USA	4 Apr 1983	First launch of *Challenger*
Soyuz T 9	USSR	27 Jun 1983	Construction in space
STS 9	USA	28 Nov 1983	First flight of the ESA spacelab
STS 41 D	USA	30 Aug 1984	First launch of *Discovery*
STS 51 A	USA	8 Nov 1984	Recovery of satellites 'Westar 6' and 'Palapa B2'
Vega 1	USSR	15 Dec 1984	Halley flyby
STS 51 J	USA	3 Oct 1985	First launch of *Atlantis*
Giotto	ESA	1986	First high-resolution image of Halley's nucleus
STS 26	USA	29 Sep 1988	First launch after *Challenger* disaster
Magellan	USA	5 May 1989	Global radar map of Venus
STS 34	USA	18 Oct 1989	*Galileo* launch
Muses A	Japan	24 Jan 1990	Two satellites placed in orbit round the moon
STS 31	USA/ESA	24 Apr 1990	Launch of Hubble Space Telescope
STS 41	USA/ESA	6 Oct 1990	Launch of *Ulysses*; first flight above the solar poles
STS 37	USA	5 Apr 1991	Launch of Compton Gamma Ray Observatory

(ESA = European Space Agency)

Satellite launch centres

Country	Launch base	Organization responsible	First launch
USA	Cape Canaveral	US Air Force/NASA	31 Jan 1958 (Explorer 1)
	Kennedy Space Center	NASA	9 Nov 1967 (Apollo 4)
	Vandenberg AFB	US Air Force/SAMTO/NASA	28 Feb 1959 (Discoverer 1)
	Wallops Island	NASA Goddard Space Flight Center	16 Feb 1961 (Explorer 9)
USSR (now CIS)	Kapustin Yar, or Volgograd cosmodrome	Ministry of Defence/Academy of Sciences/Intercosmos	16 Mar 1962 (Cosmos 1)
	Plesetsk, or Northern cosmodrome	Ministry of Defence/Academy of Sciences	17 March 1966 (Cosmos 112)
	Tyuratam Leninsk, or Baikonur cosmodrome	Ministry of Defence/Academy of Sciences	4 Oct 1957 (Sputnik 1)
Australia	Woomera Range	WRE/British DTI/ELDO	29 Nov 1967 (Wresat)
China	Jiuquan SLC	Ministry of Defence/MOA	24 Apr 1970 (SKW1/Tungfanghung)
	Xichang SLC	MOA	29 Jan 1984 (STW1)
France	Guianan Space Centre at Kouru	CNES/ESA/Arianespace	10 March 1970 (Dial)
	Hammaguir/Colombia Bechar	CIEES/CNES	26 Nov 1965 (A1 'Asterix')
India	SHAR/Sriharikota Range	ISRO	18 Jul 1980 (Rohini RS1)
Italy	San Marco platform	CRA/University of Rome	26 Apr 1967 (San Marco 2)
Japan	Kagoshima Space Centre	ISAS/University of Tokyo	11 Feb 1970 (Ohsumi)
	Tanegashima Space Centre	Nasda	9 Sep 1975 (ETS1/Kiku)

Under construction in the 1990s

Brazil	Alcantara Launch Centre	Ministry of Aeronautics/COBAE/CTA	planned for mid 1990s
Sweden	Esrange, Kiruna	Swedish Space Corporation	during the late 1990s

International space launchers

The major launch vehicles in use and some of their important predecessors. The data refer to lift capacity (given in kg/lb, in most cases to the nearest hundred) and year of launch.

LEO: low Earth orbit (c.200 km/125 mi)
GEO: geosynchronous Earth orbit (36 000 km/22 500 mi)
ETO: elliptical transfer orbit (intermediate between LEO and GEO)

CIS

Cosmos	*Cyclone*	*Soyuz/Molniya*	*Proton*	*Cosmos*	*Energia*
500 kg/1 800 lb to LEO (1964)	4 500 kg/10 000 lb to LEO (1966)	7 300 kg/16 000 lb to LEO 1 600 kg/3 500 lb to ETO (1960)	18 900 kg/41 600 lb to LEO 1 600 kg/3 500 lb to GEO (1965)	16 000 kg/35 000 lb to LEO (1985)	100 000 kg/ 220 000 lb to LEO (1987)

International space launchers (continued)

China | **India** | **Japan**

Long March 1
225 kg/500 lb
to LEO
(1970)

Long March 2
1 900 kg/
4 200 lb
to LEO
(1975)

Long March 3
900 kg/
2 000 lb
to GEO
(1984)

SLV-3
45 kg/100 lb
to LEO
(1980)

MU-3
180 kg/400 lb
to LEO
(1971)

N-2
700 kg/
1 500 lb
to GEO
(1981)

H-1
300 kg/700 lb
to LEO
(1986)

European Space Agency

Ariane 1
1 700 kg/3 700 lb
to ETO
(1979)

Ariane 3
2 400 kg/5 200 lb
to ETO
(1984)

Ariane 4
4 200 kg/9 200 lb
to GEO
(1987)

Ariane 5
6 500 kg/14 300 lb
to GEO
(c.1995)

United States of America

Scout
800 kg/400 lb
to LEO
(1960)

Delta
1 700 kg/3 700 lb
to LEO
(1960)

Scout
270 kg/600 lb
to LEO
(1979)

Space Shuttle
24 400 kg/53 700 lb
to LEO
(1981)

Pegasus
455 kg/1 000 lb
to LEO
(1990)

Taurus
1 450 kg/3200 lb
to LEO
(1992)

Delta II - 6925
3 990 kg/8 780 lb
to LEO
(1989)

Delta II - 7925
5045 kg/11 100 lb
to LEO
(1990)

International space launchers (continued)

Atlas
1 700 kg/3 700 lb
to LEO
(1963)

Atlas E
820 kg/1 800 lb
to LEO
(1974)

Atlas I
5 580 kg/12 300 lb
to LEO
(1990)

Atlas II
6 395 kg/14 100 lb
to LEO
(1991)

Atlas IIA
6 760 kg/14 900 lb
to LEO
(1991)

Atlas IIAS
8 390 kg/18 500 lb
to LEO
(1993)

Titan 3B
3 900 kg/8 600 lb
to LEO
(1966)

Titan 34D
13 600 kg/30 000 lb
to LEO
(1984)

Titan II SLV
1 905 kg/4 200 lb
to LEO
(1988)

Titan III
14 515 kg/32 000 lb
to LEO
(1989)

Titan IV
17 700 kg/39 000 lb
to LEO
(1989)

THE EARTH

HISTORY

The developing world

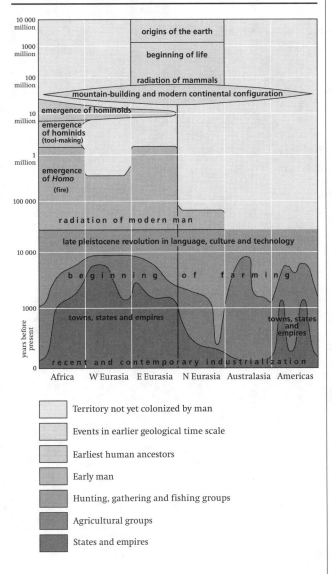

Africa   W Eurasia   E Eurasia   N Eurasia   Australasia   Americas

	Territory not yet colonized by man
	Events in earlier geological time scale
	Earliest human ancestors
	Early man
	Hunting, gathering and fishing groups
	Agricultural groups
	States and empires

Major ice-age periods

A schematic presentation of the major glacial periods (black) in the Earth's history. It is likely that a number of glaciations occurred within each epoch. Note the change in scale on the time axis at 1 000 million years ago.

The Earth

Geological time scale

Eon	Era	Period	Epoch	Million years before present	Geological events	Sea life	Land life
Phanerozoic	Cenozoic	Quaternary	Holocene	0.01	Glaciers recede. Sea level rises. Climate becomes more equable.	As now.	Forests flourish again. Humans acquire agriculture and technology.
			Pleistocene	2.0	Widespread glaciers melt periodically, causing seas to rise and fall.	As now.	Many plant forms perish. Small mammals abundant. Primitive humans established.
		Tertiary	Pliocene	5.1	Continents and oceans adopting their present form. Present climatic distribution established. Ice caps develop.	Giant sharks extinct. Many fish varieties.	Some plants and mammals die out. Primates flourish.
			Miocene	24.6	Seas recede further. European and Asian land masses join. Heavy rain causes massive erosion. Red Sea opens.	Bony fish common. Giant sharks.	Grasses widespread. Grazing mammals become common.
			Oligocene	38.0	Seas recede. Extensive movements of Earth's crust produce new mountains (eg Alpine–Himalayan chain).	Crabs, mussels, and snails evolve.	Forests diminish. Grasses appear. Pachyderms, canines, and felines develop.
			Eocene	54.9	Mountain formation continues. Glaciers common in high mountain ranges. Greenland separates. Australia separates.	Whales adapt to sea.	Large tropical jungles. Primitive forms of modern mammals established.
			Palaeocene	65	Widespread subsidence of land. Seas advance again. Considerable volcanic activity. Europe emerges.	Many reptiles become extinct.	Flowering plants widespread. First primates. Giant reptiles extinct.
	Mesozoic	Cretaceous	Late / Early	97.5	Swamps widespread. Massive alluvial deposition. Continuing limestone formation. S America separates from Africa. India, Africa and Antarctica separate.	Turtles, rays, and now-common fish appear.	Flowering plants established. Dinosaurs become extinct.
		Jurassic	Malm / Dogger / Lias	144 / 163 / 188	Seas advance. Much river formation. High mountains eroded. Limestone formation. N America separates from Africa. Central Atlantic begins to open.	Reptiles dominant.	Early flowers. Dinosaurs dominant. Mammals still primitive. First birds.
		Triassic	Late / Middle	213 / 231	Desert conditions widespread. Hot climate slowly becomes warm and wet.	Ichthyosaurs, flying fish, and crustaceans appear.	Ferns and conifers thrive. First mammals, dinosaurs, and flies.

Era / Eon	Period	Epoch / Stage	Date (million years)	Geology	Sea life	Land life
		Early	243	Break up of Pangea into supercontinents Gondwana (S) and Laurasia (N).		
			248			
Palaeozoic	Permian	Late	258	Some sea areas cut off to form lakes. Earth movements form mountains. Glaciation in southern hemisphere.	Some shelled fish become extinct.	Deciduous plants. Reptiles dominant. Many insect varieties.
		Early	286			
	Carboniferous	Pennsylvanian	320	Sea-beds rise to form new land areas. Enormous swamps. Partly-rotted vegetation forms coal.	Amphibians and sharks abundant.	Extensive evergreen forests. Reptiles breed on land. Some insects develop wings.
		Mississippian	360			
	Devonian	Late	374	Collision of continents causing mountain formation (Appalachians, Caledonides, and Urals). Sea deeper but narrower. Climatic zones forming. Iapetus ocean closed.	Fish abundant. Primitive sharks. First amphibians.	Leafy plants. Some invertebrates adapt to land. First insects.
		Middle	387			
		Early	408			
	Silurian	Pridoli	414	New mountain ranges form. Sea level varies periodically. Extensive shallow sea over the Sahara.	Large vertebrates.	First leafless land plants.
		Ludlow	421			
		Wenlock	428			
		Llandovery	438			
	Ordovician	Ashgill	448	Shore lines still quite variable. Increasing sedimentation. Europe and N America moving together.	First vertebrates. Coral reefs develop.	None.
		Caradoc	458			
		Llandeilo	468			
		Llanvirn	478			
		Arenig	488			
		Tremadoc	505			
	Cambrian	Merioneth	525	Much volcanic activity, and long periods of marine sedimentation.	Shelled invertebrates. Trilobites.	None.
		St David's	540			
		Caerfai	590			
Proterozoic (Precambrian)	Vendian		650	Shallow seas advance and retreat over land areas. Atmosphere uniformly warm.	Seaweed. Algae and invertebrates.	None.
	Riphean	Late	900	Intense deformation and metamorphism.	Earliest marine life and fossils.	None.
		Middle	1300			
		Early	1600			
	Early Proterozoic		2500	Shallow shelf seas. Formation of carbonate sediments and 'red beds'.	First appearance of stromatolites.	None.
Archaean	Archaean (Azoic)		4600	Banded iron formations. Formation of the Earth's crust and oceans.	None.	None.

STRUCTURE

The Earth

Age 4 500 000 000 years
Area 509 600 000 km²/197 000 000 sq mi
Mass 6.0 × 10²⁴ kg
Land surface 148 000 000 km²/57 000 000 sq mi (c.29% of total area)
Water surface 361 000 000 km²/140 000 000 sq mi (c.71% of total area)
Circumference (equator) 40 076 km/24 902 mi
Circumference (meridian) 40 000 km/24 860 mi
Diameter (equator) 12 757 km/7 927 mi
Diameter (meridian) 12 714 km/7 900 mi
Period of axial rotation 23 h 56 m 4.0996 s
Lithosphere 80 km/50 mi thick
Thickness of upper mantle 700 km/430 mi
Thickness of lower mantle 2 200 km/1 370 mi
Thickness of outer core 2 250 km/1 400 mi
Radius of inner core 3 480 km/2 160 mi
Density of core 13.09 g/cm³
Temperature at core 4 500 °C

The structure of the Earth

Earth's crust composition

This pie chart shows percentages of the most abundant elements in the Earth's crust.

a Oxygen 46.6%

b Silicon 27.72%

c Aluminium 8.13%

d Iron 5.0%

e Calcium 3.63%

f Sodium 2.83%

g Potassium 2.59%

h Magnesium 2.09%

i Other elements 1.41%

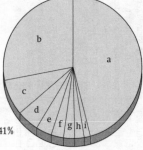

Mineral composition of rocks

Mineral component (%)	Granite	Basalt	Amphibolite	Schist	Shale	Sandstone	Limestone
Quartz	30			32	17	97	3
Alkali feldspar	60	5				1	1
Plagioclase	5	45	42	18			
Pyroxene		40					
Amphibole			50				
Olivine		5					
Biotite	4			5	7		
Muscovite				38	1	1	
Magnetite	1	5	3	3	1	1	1
Staurolite				2			
Clay minerals					80		1
Calcite					1	1	94

Type of rock spans the rock-type columns.

Chemical composition of rocks

Oxide component (%)	Granite	Basalt	Amphibolite	Schist	Shale	Sandstone	Limestone
SiO_2	70.8	49.0	49.3	63.3	62.4	94.4	5.2
TiO_2	0.4	1.0	1.2	1.4	1.1	0.1	0.1
Al_2O_3	14.5	18.2	16.9	17.9	16.6	1.1	0.8
Fe_2O_3	1.6	3.2	3.6	3.6	3.2	0.4	0.3
FeO	1.8	6.0	6.8	2.6	2.1	0.2	0.2
MgO	0.9	7.6	7.0	1.6	2.5	0.1	7.9
CaO	1.8	11.0	9.5	1.9	1.7	1.6	42.6
Na_2O	3.3	2.5	2.9	1.3	0.9	0.1	0.1
K_2O	4.0	0.9	1.1	3.1	3.0	0.2	0.3
H_2O	0.8	0.4	1.5	2.6	5.2	0.3	0.7
CO_2					1.0	1.1	41.6

Type of rock spans the rock-type columns.

Mohs scale of hardness

Friedrich Mohs (1773–1839) introduced a simple definition of hardness, according to which one mineral is said to be harder than another if the former scratches the latter. The Mohs scale is based on a series of common minerals, arranged in order of increasing hardness.

Mineral	Composition	Simple hardness test	Hardness
Talc	$Mg_3Si_4O_{10}(OH)_2$	Crushed by finger nail	1
Gypsum	$CaSO_4 \cdot 2H_2O$	Scratched by finger nail	2
Calcite	$CaCO_3$	Scratched by copper coin	3
Fluorite	CaF_2	Scratched by glass	4
Apatite	$Ca_5(PO_4)_3F$	Scratched by penknife	5
Orthoclase (feldspar)	$KAlSi_3O_8$	Scratched by quartz	6
Quartz	SiO_2	Scratched by steel file	7
Topaz	$Al_2SiO_4F_2$	Scratched by corundum	8
Corundum	Al_2O_3	Scratched by diamond	9
Diamond	C		10

World minerals map

Rare metals
Nb Niobium
Ta Tantalum
U Uranium

Precious metals
Gold
Platinum
Silver
Diamonds

Light metals
Al Aluminium
Ti Titanium

Chemical and fertilizer minerals
B   Borax
F   Fluorite
P   Phosphate (rock)
K   Potash
S   Sulphur
Ap Apatite

Ferro-alloy metals
Cr Chromium
Co Cobalt
Mn Manganese
Mo Molybdenum
Ni Nickel
W   Tungsten
V   Vanadium

Other industrial minerals
Asb Asbestos
Cly China clay
Mgs Magnesite
Mi Mica
Tc Talc

Iron

Base metals
Sb Antimony
Cu Copper
Pb Lead
Hg Mercury
Sn Tin
Zn Zinc

Arctic Circle
Tropic of Cancer
Equator
Tropic of Capricorn

22

Continental drift

240 million years ago
The single supercontinent *Pangea* is formed, with a single superocean, *Panthalassa*.

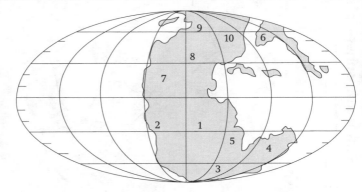

120 million years ago
Tethys, a broad gulf, divides Pangea into two huge landmasses: *Laurasia* in the north; *Gondwana* in the south.

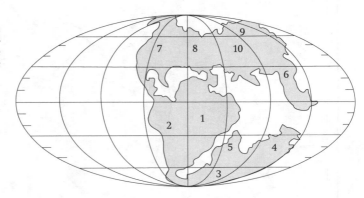

60 million years ago
Laurasia and Gondwana have split to begin to form the continents as we know them today.

Major lithospheric plates

Pacific Plate

Philippine Plate

Indo-Australian Plate

Eurasian Plate

Iranian Plate

Arabian Plate

Hellenic Plate

African Plate

Scotia Plate

South American Plate

Caribbean Plate

Cocos Plate

Nazca Plate

North American Plate

Divergent plate

Convergent plate

Earthquake distribution

Distribution of earthquakes
in depth ranges:
- 0–100 km / 0–62 mi
- 0–700 km / 62–435 mi

Major earthquakes

All magnitudes on the Richter scale[a]

Location	Country	Year	Magnitude	Deaths
Cairo	Egypt	1992	5.9	500
Erzincan	Turkey	1992	6.2	2 000
Uttar Pradesh	India	1991	6.1	1 000
Georgia	USSR	1991	7.2	100
Hindu	Afghanistan/			
Kush Mts	Pakistan	1991	6.8	1 300
Cabanatuan,				
Luzon	Philippines	1990	7.7	1653
Caspian Sea				
area	Iran .	1990	7.7	40 000
Moyobamba	Peru	1990	5.8	90
Carpathian Mts	Romania	1990	6.6	70
Luzon Island	Philippines	1990	7.7	1 600
San Francisco	USA	1989	6.9	100
Armenia	USSR	1988	7.0	25 000
Mexico City	Mexico	1985	8.1	7 200
Naples	Italy	1980	7.2	4 500
El Asnam	Algeria	1980	7.3	5 000
Tabas	Iran	1978	7.7	25 000
Tangshan	China	1976	8.2	242 000
Guatemala City	Guatemala	1976	7.5	22 778
Kashmir	Pakistan	1974	6.3	5 200
Managua	Nicaragua	1972	6.2	5 000
Tehran	Iran	1972	6.9	5 000
Chimbote	Peru	1970	7.7	66 000
Anchorage	USA	1964	8.5	131
Agadir	Morocco	1960	5.8	12 000
Ashkhabad	USSR	1948	7.3	19 800
Erzincan	Turkey	1939	7.9	23 000
Chillan	Chile	1939	7.8	30 000
Quetta	India	1935	7.5	60 000
Gansu	China	1932	7.6	70 000
Nan-Shan	China	1927	8.3	200 000
Kanto	Japan	1923	8.3	143 000
Gansu	China	1920	8.6	180 000
Avezzano	Italy	1915	7.5	30 000
Messina	Italy	1908	7.5	120 000
Valparaiso	Chile	1906	8.6	20 000
San Francisco	USA	1906	8.3	500
Calabria	Italy	1783		50 000
Lisbon	Portugal	1755		70 000
Calcutta	India	1737		300 000
Hokkaido	Japan	1730		137 000
Catania	Italy	1693		60 000
Shemaka	Caucasia	1667		80 000
Shensi	China	1556		830 000
Chihli	China	1290		100 000
Cilicia	Turkey	1268		60 000
Corinth	Greece	856		45 000
Antioch	Turkey	526		250 000

[a]The Richter scale is a logarithmic scale, devised in 1935 by geophysicist Charles Richter, for representing the energy released by earthquakes. A figure of 2 or less is barely perceptible, while an earthquake measuring over 5 may be destructive. More relevant as a measure of earthquake strength is the intensity, for which the modified Mercalli scale is widely used.

Earthquake severity

Modified Mercalli intensity scale (1956 revision)

I Not felt; marginal and long-period effects of large earthquakes. II Felt by persons at rest, on upper floors or favourably placed. III Felt indoors; hanging objects swing; vibration like passing of light trucks; duration estimated; may not be recognized as an earthquake. IV Hanging objects swing; vibration like passing of heavy trucks, or sensation of a jolt like a heavy ball striking the walls; standing cars rock; windows, dishes, doors rattle; glasses clink; crockery clashes; in the upper range of IV, wooden walls and frames creak. V Felt outdoors; direction estimated; sleepers wakened; liquids disturbed, some spilled; small unstable objects displaced or upset; doors swing, close, open; shutters, pictures move; pendulum clocks stop, start, change rate. VI Felt by all; many frightened and run outdoors; persons walk unsteadily; windows, dishes, glassware break; knick-knacks, books, etc, fall off shelves; pictures off walls; furniture moves or overturns; weak plaster and masonry D crack; small bells ring (church, school); trees, bushes shake visibly, or heard to rustle. VII Difficult to stand; noticed by drivers; hanging objects quiver; furniture breaks; damage to masonry D, including cracks; weak chimneys broken at roof line; fall of plaster, loose bricks, stones, tiles, cornices, also unbraced parapets and architectural ornaments; some cracks in masonry C; waves on ponds, water turbid with mud; small slides and caving in along sand or gravel banks; large bells ring; concrete irrigation ditches damaged. VIII Steering of cars affected; damage to masonry C and partial collapse; some damage to masonry B; none to masonry A; fall of stucco and some masonry walls; twisting, fall of chimneys, factory stacks, monuments, towers, elevated tanks; frame houses move on foundations if not bolted down; loose panel walls thrown out; decayed piling broken off; branches broken from trees; changes in flow or temperature of springs and wells; cracks in wet ground and on steep slopes. IX General panic; masonry D destroyed; masonry C heavily damaged, sometimes with complete collapse; masonry B seriously damaged; general damage to foundations; frame structures, if not bolted, shift off foundations; frames racked; serious damage to reservoirs; underground pipes break; conspicuous cracks in ground; in alluviated areas sand and mud ejected, earthquake fountains, sand craters. X Most masonry and frame structures destroyed with their foundations; some well-built wooden structures and bridges destroyed; serious damage to dams, dykes, embankments; large landslides; water thrown on banks of canals, rivers, lakes, etc; sand and mud shifted horizontally on beaches and flat land; rails bent slightly. XI Rails bent greatly; underground pipelines completely out of service. XII Damage nearly total; large rock masses displaced; lines of sight and level distorted; objects thrown into the air.

Note Masonry A Good workmanship, mortar and design; reinforced, especially laterally, and bound together using steel, concrete etc; designed to resist lateral forces. Masonry B Good workmanship and mortar; reinforced, but not designed in detail to resist lateral forces. Masonry C Ordinary workmanship and mortar; no extreme weakness like failing to tie in at corners, but neither reinforced nor designed against horizontal forces. Masonry D Weak materials, such as adobe; poor mortar; low standards of workmanship; weak horizontally.

Major volcanoes and eruptions

Name	Location	Height (m)	Height (ft)	Major eruptions (year/s)	Last eruption (year)
Aconcagua	Argentina	6960	22831	extinct	
Ararat	Turkey	5198	18350	extinct	Holocene
Awu	Sangihe Is	1327	4355	1711, 1856, 1892	1968
Bezymianny	Russia	2800	9186	1955–6	1984
Coseguina	Nicaragua	847	1598	1835	1835
El Chichón	Mexico	1349	4430	1982	1982
Erebus	Antarctica	4023	13200	1947, 1972, 1986	1991
Etna, Mt	Italy	3236	10625	122, 1169, 1329, 1536, 1669, 1928, 1964, 1971, 1986	1992
Fuji	Japan	3776	12388	1707	1707
Galunggung	Java	2180	7155	1822, 1918	1982
Hekla	Iceland	1491	4920	1693, 1845, 1947–8, 1970	1981
Helgafell	Iceland	215	706	1973	1973
Hudson	Chile	1740	5742	1971, 1973	1991
Jurullo	Mexico	1330	4255	1759–74	1774
Katmai	Alaska	2298	7540	1912, 1920, 1921	1931
Kilauea	Hawaii	1247	4100	1823–1924, 1952, 1955, 1960, 1967–8, 1968–74, 1983–7, 1988, 1991	1992
Kilimanjaro	Tanzania	5930	19450	extinct	Pleistocene
Klyuchevskoy	Russia	4850	15910	1700–1966, 1984	1985
Krakatoa	Sumatra	818	2685	1680, 1883, 1927, 1952–3, 1969	1980
La Soufrière	St Vincent	1232	4048	1718, 1812, 1902, 1971–2	1979
Laki	Iceland	500	1642	1783	1784
Lamington	Papua New Guinea	1780	5844	1951	1956
Lassen Peak	USA	3186	10453	1914–15	1921
Mauna Loa	Hawaii	4172	13685	1859, 1880, 1887, 1919, 1950, 1984	1987
Mayon	Philippines	2462	8084	1616, 1766, 1814, 1897, 1968	1978
Nyamuragira	Zaire	3056	10026	1921–38, 1971, 1980, 1984	1988
Paricutín	Mexico	3188	10460	1943–52	1952
Pelée, Mont	Martinique	1397	4584	1902, 1929–32	1932
Pinatubo	Philippines	1758	5770	1391	1991
Popocatépetl	Mexico	5483	17990	1920	1943
Rainer, Mt	USA	4392	14416	1st-c BC, 1820	1882
Ruapehu	New Zealand	2796	9175	1945, 1953, 1969, 1975	1986
St Helens, Mt	USA	2549	8364	1800, 1831, 1835, 1842–3, 1857, 1980	1987
Santorini/ Thera	Greece	556	1824	1470 BC, 197 BC, AD 46, 1570–3, 1707–11, 1866–70	1950
Stromboli	Italy	931	3055	1768, 1882, 1889, 1907, 1930, 1936, 1941, 1950, 1952, 1986	1990
Surtsey	Iceland	174	570	1963–7	1967
Taal	Philippines	1448	4752	1911, 1965, 1969	1977
Tambora	Sumbawa	2868	9410	1815	1880
Tarawera	New Zealand	1149	3770	1886	1973
Unzen, Mt	Japan	1360	4462	1360, 1791	1991
Vesuvius	Italy	1289	4230	79, 472, 1036, 1631, 1779, 1906	1944
Vulcano	Italy	502	1650	antiquity, 1444, 1730–40, 1786, 1873, 1888–90	1890

Major tsunamis

Tsunamis are long-period ocean waves produced by movements of the sea floor associated with earthquakes, volcanic explosions, or landslides. They are also referred to as *seismic sea waves*, and in popular (but not technical) oceanographic use as *tidal waves*.

Location of source	Year	Height (m)	(ft)	Location of deaths/damage	Deaths
Sea of Japan	1983	15	49	Japan, Korea	107
Indonesia	1979	10	32	Indonesia	187
Celebes Sea	1976	30	98	Philippine Is	5000
Alaska	1964	32	105	Alaska, Aleutian Is, California	122
Chile	1960	25	82	Chile, Hawaii, Japan	1260
Aleutian Is	1957	16	52	Hawaii, Japan	0
Kamchatka	1952	18.4	60	Kamchatka, Kuril Is, Hawaii	many
Aleutian Is	1946	32	105	Aleutian Is, Hawaii, California	165
Nankaido (Japan)	1946	6.1	20	Japan	1997
Kii (Japan)	1944	7.5	25	Japan	998
Sanriku (Japan)	1933	28.2	93	Japan, Hawaii	3000
E Kamchatka	1923	20	66	Kamchatka, Hawaii	3
S Kuril Is	1918	12	39	Kuril Is, Russia, Japan, Hawaii	23
Sanriku (Japan)	1896	30	98	Japan	27122
Sunda Strait	1883	35	115	Java, Sumatra	36000
Chile	1877	23	75	Chile, Hawaii	Many
Chile	1868	21	69	Chile, Hawaii	25000
Hawaii	1868	20	66	Hawaii	81
Japan	1854	6	20	Japan	3000
Flores Sea	1800	24	79	Indonesia	400–500
Ariake Sea	1792	9	30	Japan	9745
Italy	1783	?	?	Italy	30000
Ryukyu Is	1771	12	39	Ryukyu Is	11941
Portugal	1775	16	52	W Europe, Morocco, W Indies	60000
Peru	1746	24	79	Peru	5000
Japan	1741	9	30	Japan	1000+
SE Kamchatka	1737	30	98	Kamchatka, Kuril Is	?
Peru	1724	24	79	Peru	?
Japan	1707	11.5	38	Japan	30000
W Indies	1692	?	?	Jamaica	2000
Banda Is	1629	15	49	Indonesia	?
Sanriku (Japan)	1611	25	82	Japan	5000
Japan	1605	?	?	Japan	4000
Kii (Japan)	1498	?	?	Japan	5000

Recent hurricanes

A hurricane (H) is an intense, often devastating, tropical storm which occurs as a vortex spiralling around a low-pressure system. Wind speeds are high – above 120 kmh/75 mph. Hurricanes originate over tropical oceans and move in a W or NW direction in the northern hemisphere, and SW in the southern hemisphere, losing energy as they reach land. They are also known as *typhoons* in the western N Pacific and *cyclones* in the Bay of Bengal.

Name	Location	Year	Deaths	Damage (US $bn)	Name	Location	Year	Deaths	Damage (US $bn)
H Andrew	S Florida	1992	30	7.3	H Alicia	N Texas	1983	18	2.0
H Iniki	Kauai, Hawaii	1992	3	1.0	H Allen	S Texas	1980	235	0.3
H Bob	NE USA	1991	17	1.5	H David	Florida	1979	2400	0.3
Cyclone	Bangladesh	1991	200 000		H Frederic	Alabama, Mississippi	1979	31	2.3
H Hugo	S Carolina	1989	49	7.0					
H Gilbert	Caribbean, Mexico	1988	318	5.0	H Eloise	NW Florida	1975	100	0.49
					H Carmen	Louisiana	1974	1	0.15
H Joan	Caribbean	1988	216		H Fifi	Honduras, C America	1974	10 000	1.0
H Elena	Mississippi, Alabama, NW Florida	1985	2	1.25	Cyclone Tracey	Darwin, Australia	1974	65	1.0
H Gloria	E USA	1985	15	0.9	H Agnes	E Coast, USA	1972	122	2.1
H Juan	Louisiana	1985	12	1.5	Cyclone	Bangladesh	1970	300 000	0.086
H Kate	Florida	1985	16	0.3					
Cyclone	Bangladesh	1985	11 000						

ATMOSPHERE

Layers of the atmosphere

The composition of dry air at sea level

Gas	Volume (%)
Nitrogen (N_2)	78.08
Oxygen (O_2)	20.95
Argon (Ar)	0.93
Carbon dioxide (CO_2)	0.031
Neon (Ne)	0.0018
Helium (He)	0.000 52
Krypton (Kr)	0.000 11
Xenon (Xe)	0.000 008 7
Hydrogen (H_2)	0.000 05
Methane (CH_4)	0.000 2
Nitric oxide (NO)	0.000 05
Ozone (O_3)	0.000 002 (winter) 0.000 007 (summer)

CLIMATE

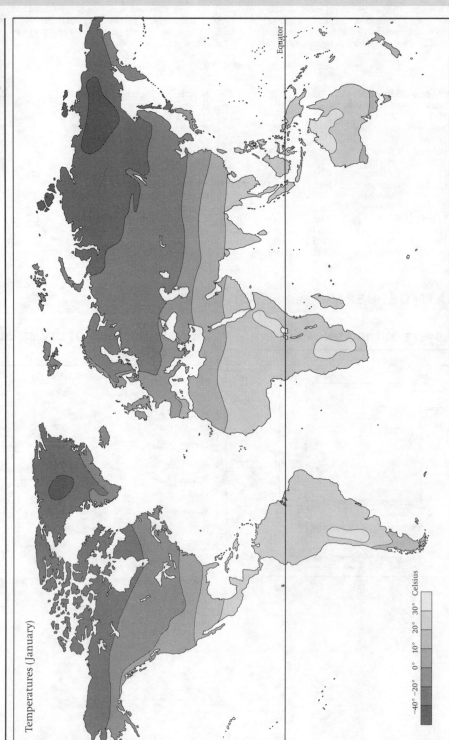

Temperatures (January)

Equator

-40° -20° 0° 10° 20° 30° Celsius

The Earth

World temperatures

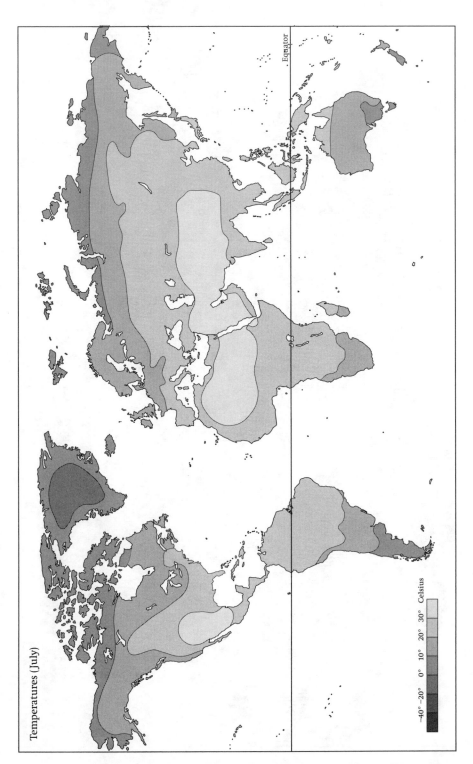

Temperatures (July)

-40° -20°   0° 10° 20° 30° Celsius

Equator

World precipitation

0   100 300 500 1000 2000 3000 5000 mm

Meteorological records

Hottest place	Dallol, Ethiopia	34°C / 94°F (annual mean)
Coldest place	Pole of Cold, Antarctica	−58°C / −72°F (annual mean)
Driest place	Arica-Antofagasta, Pacific coast, Chile	0.1 mm / 0.004 in (annual mean rainfall)
Wettest place	Tutenendo, Columbia	11770 mm / 463.5 in (annual mean rainfall)
Windiest place	Commonwealth Bay, George V Coast, Antarctica	320 kmh/231 mph (maximum wind speed)

Cloud types

Depressions

Plan view of the six idealized stages in the development and final occlusion of a depression along the polar front in the northern hemisphere. Stage 4 shows a well-developed depression system and stage 5 shows the occlusion. The cross-section is taken along the line AB in stage 4. The cloud types are:

Cb – cumulonimbus;
As – altostratus;
Ac – altocumulus;
Cs – cirrostratus;
Ns – nimbostratus;
Ci – cirrus.

Meteorological sea areas

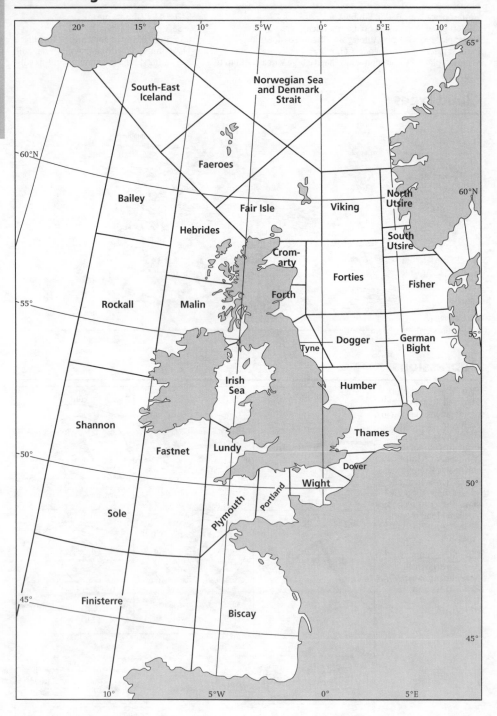

The Earth

Wind force and sea disturbance

Beaufort number	Wind speed		Wind name	Observable wind characteristics
	(kmh)	(mph)		
0	<1	<1	Calm	Smoke rises vertically
1	1–5	1–3	Light air	Wind direction shown by smoke drift but not by wind vanes
2	6–11	4–7	Light breeze	Wind felt on face; leaves rustle; vanes moved by wind
3	12–19	8–12	Gentle breeze	Leaves and small twigs in constant motion; wind extends light flag
4	20–8	13–18	Moderate	Raises dust, loose paper; small branches moved
5	29–38	19–24	Fresh	Small trees begin to sway
6	39–49	25–31	Strong	Large branches in motion; difficult to use umbrellas
7	50–61	32–8	Near gale	Whole trees in motion; difficult to walk against wind
8	62–74	39–46	Gale	Breaks twigs off trees; impedes progress
9	75–88	47–54	Strong gale	Slight structural damage caused
10	89–102	55–63	Storm	Trees uprooted; considerable damage occurs
11	103–17	64–72	Violent storm	Widespread damage
12–17	>118	>73	Hurricane	

Sea disturbance number (Beaufort)	Average wave height		Observable sea characteristics
	(m)	(ft)	
0 (0)	0	0	Sea like a mirror
0 (1)	0	0	Ripples like scales
1 (2)	0.3	0–1	More definite wavelets
2 (3)	0.3–0.6	1–2	Large wavelets; crests beginning
3 (4)	0.6–1.2	2–4	Small waves becoming longer; fairly frequent white horses
4 (5)	1.2–2.4	4–8	Moderate waves with longer form; many white horses; some foam spray
5 (6)	2.4–4	8–13	Large waves forming; more white foam crests; spray
6 (7)	4–6	13–20	Sea heaps up; streaks of white foam blown along
6 (8)	4–6	13–20	Moderately high waves of greater length; well-marked streaks of foam
6 (9)	4–6	13–20	High waves; dense streaks of foam; sea begins to roll; spray affects visibility
7 (10)	6–9	20–30	Very high waves with overhanging crests; generally white appearance of surface; heavy rolling
8 (11)	9–14	30–45	Exceptionally high waves; long white patches of foam; poor visibility; ships lost to view behind waves
9 (12–17)	14	>45	Air filled with foam and spray; sea completely white; very poor visibility

SURFACE

World physical map

Major ocean-surface currents

Cold ocean currents
Warm ocean currents
Seasonal drift

The Earth

Continents

Name	Area		% of total	Lowest point below sea level			Highest elevation		
	(km²)	(sq mi)			(m)	(ft)		(m)	(ft)
Africa	30 970 000	11 690 000	20.2	Lake Assal, Djibouti	156	512	Kilimanjaro, Tanzania	5 895	19 340
Antarctica	15 500 000	6 000 000	9.3	Bently subglacial trench	2 538	8 327	Vinson Massif	5 140	16 864
Asia	44 493 000	17 179 000	29.6	Dead Sea, Israel/Jordan	400	1 312	Mt Everest, China/Nepal	8 848	29 028
Oceania	8 945 000	3 454 000	6	Lake Eyre, S Australia	15	49	Puncak Jaya, Indonesia	5 030	16 500
Europe	10 245 000	3 956 000	6.8	Caspian Sea, Russia	29	94	Elbrus, Russia	5 642	18 510
North America	24 454 000	9 442 000	16.3	Death Valley, California	86	282	Mt McKinley, Alaska	6 194	20 320
South America	17 838 000	6 887 000	11.9	Peninsular Valdez, Argentina	40	131	Aconcagua, Argentina	6 960	22 831

Oceans

Name	Area		% of total	Average depth		Greatest depth		
	(km²)	(sq mi)		(m)	(ft)		(m)	(ft)
Arctic	13 986 000	5 400 000	3	1 330	4 300	Eurasia Basin	5 122	16 804
Atlantic	82 217 000	31 700 000	24	3 700	12 100	Puerto Rico Trench	8 648	28 372
Indian	73 426 000	28 350 000	20	3 900	12 800	Java Trench	7 725	25 344
Pacific	181 300 000	70 000 000	46	4 300	14 100	Marianas Trench	11 040	36 220

Major island groups

Name	Country	Sea/Ocean	No. of islands	Main islands	Area		Inhabitants
					(km²)	(sq mi)	
Aeolian	Italy	Mediterranean	7	Stromboli, Lipari, Vulcanö, Salina	90	30	10 208 (1981)
Åland	Finland	Gulf of Bothnia	6 080	Eckerö, Lemland, Vardö, Lumparland	1 500	570	23 239 (1983)
Aleutian	USA	Pacific	150	Andreanof, Adak	18 000	6 800	11 942 (1990)
Alexander	Canada	Pacific	11 000	Baranof, Prince of Wales	na	na	32 586 (1980)
Andaman	India	Bay of Bengal	300+	N Andaman, S Andaman	8 300	3 200	279 111 (1991)
Azores	Portugal	Atlantic	9	São Miguel, Flores	2 300	900	241 794 (1991)
Bahamas	Bahamas	Atlantic	700	New Providence, Grand Bahama	13 900	5 400	254 685 (1991)
Balearic	Spain	Mediterranean	5	Mallorca, Menorca, Ibiza	5 000	1 900	702 770 (1991)
Bismarck	Papua New Guinea	Pacific	2 000	New Britain, New Ireland, Admiralty Island	49 700	19 200	397 000 (1992)
Bijagos	Guinea-Bissau	Atlantic	15	Orango, Formoza, Caravela, Roxa	50	30	25 713 (1979)
Canary	Spain	Atlantic	7	Tenerife, Gomera, Lanzarote, Las Palmas	7 300	2 800	1 456 474 (1991)
Cape Verde	Cape Verde	Atlantic	10	Barlavento group, Sotavento group	4 000	1 500	386 000 (1991)

Name	Country	Sea/Ocean	No. of islands	Main islands	Area (km²)	(sq mi)	Inhabitants
Caroline	USA	Pacific	680	Yop, Pohnpei, Truk	1300	500	97 400 (1983)
Channel	UK	English Channel	4	Guernsey, Jersey, Sark, Alderney	200	80	145 000 (1986)
Commander	Russia	Bering Sea	4	Bering, Medny	1800	700	na[a]
Comoros	Republic of Comoros	Mozambique Channel	4	Grand Mohore, Anjouan, Moheli, Mayotte	1900	700	503 000 (1990)
Cook	New Zealand	Pacific	15	Palmerston, Rarotonga, Mangaia	240	90	17 900 (1992)
Cyclades	Greece	Aegean	c.220	Andros, Mikonos, Paros	2600	990	95 083 (1991)
Dodecanese	Greece	Aegean	12	Rhodes, Kos	2700	1000	145 071 (1981)
Falkland	UK	Atlantic	200	W Falkland, E Falkland, S Georgia	12 200	4700	2 121 (1991)
Faroe	Denmark	Atlantic	22	Strømø, Østerø	1400	540	478 000 (1990)
Fiji	Fiji	Pacific	844	Viti Levu, Vanua Levu	18 330	7080	744 000 (1991)
Galapagos	Ecuador	Pacific	16	Santa Cruz, Santiago	7800	3010	9 785 (1990)
Gotland	Sweden	Baltic	2	Gotland, Fårö	3140	1210	57 383 (1991)
Greenland	Denmark	N Atlantic, Arctic	2	Greenland, Disko	2 175 600	840 000	55 533 (1991)
Hawaiian	USA	Pacific	8	Hawaii, Oahu	16 760	6470	1 083 000 (1991)
Hebrides	UK	Atlantic	10+	Lewis, Skye, Mull		na	44 344 (1981)
Indonesia	Indonesia	Pacific	13 677	Java, Sumatra	1 900 240	735 810	184 796 000 (1992)
Ionian	Greece	Aegean	7	Kerkira, Levkas	2300	890	184 796 (1991)
Japan	Japan	Pacific	1000+	Honshu, Hokkaido, Kyushu, Shikoku	370 000	145 000	123 156 678 (1991)
Juan Fernandez	Chile	Pacific	3	Mas a Tierra, Santa Clara	180	70	516 (1982)
Kuril	Russia/Japan	Pacific	56	Shumsu, Iturup	15 600	6000	15 000 (1970)
Laccadive	India	Arabian Sea	27	Laccadive, Amaindivi	30	10	51 681 (1991)
Lofoten	Norway	Norwegian Sea	5	Hinnoy, Austvagoy	1420	550	26 241 (1970)
Madeira	Portugal	Atlantic	4	Madeira	790	310	263 306 (1991)
Malaysia	Federation of Malaysia	Pacific/ Indian	20 000	Borneo, New Guinea, Sumatra	329 750	127 280	18 630 000 (1992)
Maldives	Republic of Maldives	Indian	1190	Male	300	120	226 000 (1991)
Malta	Republic of Malta	Mediterranean	5	Malta, Gozo	320	120	360 000 (1992)
Mariana	Common-wealth of Mariana Islands	Pacific	14	Saipan, Tinian, Rota	470	180	43 345 (1990)
Marquesas	France	Pacific	10	Nukultiva	1190	460	8 000 (1992)
Marshall	Marshall Islands	Pacific	1200+	Bikini	180	70	50 000 (1992)
Mascarene	France	Indian	3	Réunion, Mauritius, Rodrigues	na	na	1 475 700 (1982)
Melanesia		Pacific	na[a]	Solomon, Bismark, Fiji, New Guinea	540 000	210 000	4 677 000 (1986)

Major island groups (continued)

Name	Country	Sea/Ocean	No. of islands	Main islands	Area (km²)	(sq mi)	Inhabitants
Micronesia		Pacific	na[a]	Caroline, Gilbert, Marshalls, Kiribati	3 270	1 260	358 700 (1986)
New Hebrides	Republic of Vanuatu	Pacific	72	Espiritu Santo	14 760	5 700	152 000 (1992)
Newfoundland	Canada	Atlantic	na[a]	Prince Edward	405 720	156 650	568 474 (1991)
New Zealand	New Zealand	Pacific	4+	North, South	268 810	103 760	3 434 950 (1991)
Nicobar	India	Bay of Bengal	300+	Great Nicobar	8 300	3 200	279 111 (1991)
Novaya Zemlya	Russia	Arctic	5	North, South	81 300	31 400	400 (1983e)
Orkney	UK	North Sea	20	Mainland, Ronaldsay	980	380	19 710 (1992e)
Philippines	Republic of the Philippines	Pacific	7 100	Luzon, Mindanao, Samar	300 680	110 680	63 609 000 (1992e)
Polynesia		Pacific	na[a]	Hawaii, Tonga, Kiribati, Easter, Samoa	17 200	10 700	61 480 000 (1990)
Queen Charlotte	Canada	Pacific	150	Prince Rupert	9 800	3 800	5 316 (1991)
São Tomé and Príncipe	Republic of São Tomé & Príncipe	Atlantic	2	São Tomé, Príncipe	970	370	124 000 (1991e)
Scilly	UK	English Channel	140	St Mary's, St Martin's	20	10	2 000 (1992e)
Seychelles	Republic of Seychelles	Indian	115	Mahé, La Digue	450	170	68 700 (1992e)
Shetland	UK	North Sea	100	Mainland, Unst	1 400	550	22 640 (1992e)
Society	France	Pacific	2	Tahiti	1 500	590	165 000 (1992e)
Solomon	Solomon Islands	Pacific	6+	New Georgia, San Cristobal	27 560	10 640	329 000 (1992e)
South Orkney	UK	Atlantic	2	Coronation, Laurie	620	240	uninhabited
Sri Lanka	Republic of Sri Lanka	Indian	2	Sri Lanka, Mannar	65 610	25 200	17 464 000 (1992e)
Taiwan	Republic of China	China Sea/Pacific	na[a]	Taiwan	36 000	13 900	20 727 000 (1992e)
Tasmania	Australia	Tasman Sea	5+	Tasmania, King Flinders, Bruny	67 800	26 200	452 851 (1991)
Tierra del Fuego	Argentina/ Chile	Pacific			73 700	28 500	69 450 (1991)
Tristan da Cunha	UK	Atlantic	5	Gough, Inaccessible, Nightingale	100	40	350 (1990e)
Tuamotu	France	Pacific	80	Rangiroa, Hao, Fakarava	800	320	11 500 (1992e)
Tuvalu	Tuvalu	Pacific		Funafuti Atoll, Nanumea	30	10	9 500 (1992e)
Virgin	USA	Caribbean	50+	St Croix, St Thomas	340	130	101 809 (1990)
Virgin	UK	Caribbean	36	Tortola, Virgin Gorda	150	60	16 644 (1991)
Zanzibar	Tanzania	Indian	3	Zanzibar, Tumbatu	1 600	640	400 000 (1991e)

[a]na – data not available.

Considerable variation will be found among sources giving area estimates for island groups, because of the difficulty in deciding where the group boundary line should lie. All estimates above 100 km²/sq mi have been rounded to the nearest 10, and all above 1 000 km²/sq mi to the nearest 100.

Largest seas

Name	Area[a]	
	(km²)	(sq mi)
Coral Sea	4 791 000	1 850 200
Arabian Sea	3 863 000	1 492 000
S China (Nan) Sea	3 685 000	1 423 000
Mediterranean Sea	2 516 000	971 000
Bering Sea	2 304 000	890 000
Bay of Bengal	2 172 000	839 000
Sea of Okhotsk	1 590 000	614 000
Gulf of Mexico	1 543 000	596 000
Gulf of Guinea	1 533 000	592 000
Barents Sea	1 405 000	542 000
Norwegian Sea	1 383 000	534 000
Gulf of Alaska	1 327 000	512 000
Hudson Bay	1 232 000	476 000
Greenland Sea	1 205 000	465 000
Arafura Sea	1 037 000	400 000
Philippine Sea	1 036 000	400 000
Sea of Japan	978 000	378 000
E Siberian Sea	901 000	348 000
Kara Sea	883 000	341 000
E China Sea	664 000	256 000
Andaman Sea	565 000	218 000
North Sea	520 000	201 000
Black Sea	508 000	196 000
Red Sea	453 000	175 000
Baltic Sea	414 000	160 000
Arabian/Persian Gulf	238 000	92 200
Gulf of St Lawrence	238 300	92 000

Oceans are excluded.
[a]Areas are rounded to nearest 1 000 km²/sq mi.

Largest islands

Name	Area[a]	
	(km²)	(sq mi)
Australia	7 692 300	2 969 200
Greenland	2 175 600	830 780
New Guinea	790 000	305 000
Borneo	737 000	285 000
Madagascar	587 000	227 600
Baffin	507 000	196 000
Sumatra	425 000	164 900
Honshu (Hondo)	228 000	88 000
Great Britain	219 000	84 400
Victoria, Canada	217 300	83 900
Ellesmere, Canada	196 000	75 800
Celebes	174 000	67 400
South I, New Zealand	151 000	58 200
Java	129 000	50 000
North I, New Zealand	114 000	44 200
Newfoundland	109 000	42 000
Cuba	110 860	42 790
Luzon	105 000	40 400
Iceland	103 000	40 000
Mindanao	94 600	36 500
Novaya Zemlya (two islands)	90 600	35 000
Ireland	70 280	27 100
Hokkaido	78 500	30 300
Hispaniola	77 200	29 800
Sakhalin	75 100	29 000

[a]Areas are rounded to the nearest three significant digits.

Largest lakes

Name/location	Area[a]	
	(km²)	(sq mi)
Caspian Sea, Iran/CIS	371 000	143 240[b]
Superior, USA/Canada	82 260	31 760[c]
Aral Sea, Kazakhstan	64 500	24 900[b]
Victoria, E Africa	62 940	24 300
Huron, USA/Canada	59 580	23 000[c]
Michigan, USA	58 020	22 400
Tanganyika, E Africa	32 000	12 350
Baikal, Russia	31 500	12 160
Great Bear, Canada	31 330	12 100
Great Slave, Canada	28 570	11 030
Erie, USA/Canada	25 710	9 920[c]
Winnipeg, Canada	24 390	9 420
Malawi/Nyasa, E Africa	22 490	8 680
Balkhash, Kazakhstan	18 300	7 000[b]
Ontario, Canada	19 270	7 440[c]
Ladoga, Russia	18 130	7 000
Chad, W Africa	10 000–26 000	4 000–10 000
Maracaibo, Venezuela	13 010	5 020[d]
Patos, Brazil	10 140	3 920[d]
Onega, Russia	9 800	3 800
Rudolf, E Africa	9 100	3 500
Eyre, Australia	8 800	3 400[d]
Titicaca, Peru	8 300	3 200

[a]Areas are given to the nearest 10 km²/sq mi. The Caspian and Aral Seas, being entirely surrounded by land, are classified as lakes. [b]Salt lakes. [c]Average of areas given by Canada and USA. [d]Salt lagoons.

Largest deserts

Name/location	Area[a]	
	(km²)	(sq mi)
Sahara, N Africa	8 600 000	3 320 000
Arabian, SW Asia	2 330 000	900 000
Gobi, Mongolia and NE China	1 166 000	450 000
Patagonian, Argentina	673 000	260 000
Great Victoria, SW Australia	647 000	250 000
Great Basin, SW USA	492 000	190 000
Chihuahuan, Mexican	450 000	175 000
Great Sandy, NW Australia	400 000	150 000
Sonoran, SW USA	310 000	120 000
Kyzyl-Kum, Kazakhstan/Uzbekistan	300 000	115 000
Takla Makan, N China	270 000	105 000
Kalahari, SW Africa	260 000	100 000
Kara-Kum, Turkmenia	260 000	100 000
Kavir, Iran	260 000	100 000
Syrian, Saudi Arabia/Jordan/ Syria/Iraq	260 000	100 000
Nubian, Sudan	260 000	100 000
Thar, India/Pakistan	200 000	77 000
Ust'-Urt, Kazakhstan/Uzbekistan	160 000	62 000
Bet-Pak-Dala, Kazakhstan	155 000	60 000
Simpson, C Australia	145 000	56 000
Dzungaria, China	142 000	55 000
Atacama, Chile	140 000	54 000
Namib, SE Africa	134 000	52 000
Sturt, SE Australia	130 000	50 000
Bolson de Mapimi, Mexico	130 000	50 000
Ordos, China	130 000	50 000
Alashan, China	116 000	45 000

[a]Desert areas are very approximate, because clear physical boundaries may not occur.

Highest mountains

Name	Height[a]		Location
	(m)	(ft)	
Everest	8850	29030	China–Nepal
K2	8610	28250	Kashmir–Jammu
Kangchenjunga	8590	28170	India–Nepal
Lhotse	8500	27890	China–Nepal
Kangchenjunga S Peak	8470	27800	India–Nepal
Makalu I	8470	27800	China–Nepal
Kangchenjunga W Peak	8420	27620	India–Nepal
Llotse E Peak	8380	27500	China–Nepal
Dhaulagiri	8170	26810	Nepal
Cho Oyu	8150	26750	China–Nepal
Manaslu	8130	26660	Nepal
Nanga Parbat	8130	26660	Kashmir–Jammu
Annapurna I	8080	26500	Nepal
Gasherbrum I	8070	26470	Kashmir–Jammu
Broad-highest	8050	26400	Kashmir–Jammu
Gasherbrum II	8030	26360	Kashmir–Jammu
Gosainthan	8010	26290	China
Broad-middle	8000	26250	Kashmir–Jammu
Gasherbrum III	7950	26090	Kashmir–Jammu
Annapurna II	7940	26040	Nepal
Nanda Devi	7820	25660	India
Rakaposhi	7790	25560	Kashmir
Kamet	7760	25450	India
Ulugh Muztagh	7720	25340	Tibet
Tirich Mir	7690	25230	Pakistan
Muz Tag Ata	7550	24760	China
Communism Peak	7490	24590	Tajikistan
Pobedy Peak	7440	24410	China–Kyrgyzstan
Aconcagua	6960	22830	Argentina
Ojos del Salado	6910	22660	Argentina–Chile

[a]Heights are given to the nearest 10 m/ft.

Highest waterfalls

Name	Height[a]		Location
	(m)	(ft)	
Angel (upper fall)	807	2648	Venezuela
Itatinga	628	2060	Brazil
Cuquenan	610	2000	Guyana–Venezuela
Ormeli	563	1847	Norway
Tysse	533	1749	Norway
Pilao	524	1719	Brazil
Ribbon	491	1612	USA
Vestre Mardola	468	1535	Norway
Roraima	457?	1500?	Guyana
Cleve-Garth	450?	1476?	New Zealand

[a]Distances are given for individual leaps.

Deepest caves

Name/location	Depth	
	(m)	(ft)
Jean Bernard, France	1494	4900
Snezhnaya, Russia	1340	4397
Puertas de Illamina, Spain	1338	4390
Pierre-Saint-Martin, France	1321	4334
Sistema Huautla, Mexico	1240	4067
Berger, France	1198	3930
Vqerdi, Spain	1195	3921
Dachstein-Mammuthöhle, Austria	1174	3852
Zitu, Spain	1139	3737
Badalona, Spain	1130	3707
Batmanhöhle, Austria	1105	3626
Schneeloch, Austria	1101	3612
GES Malaga, Spain	1070	3510
Lamprechtsofen, Austria	1024	3360

Longest rivers

Name	Outflow	Length[a]	
		(km)	(mi)
Nile–Kagera–Ruvuvu–Ruvusu–Luvironza	Mediterranean Sea (Egypt)	6690	4160
Amazon–Ucayali–Tambo–Ene–Apurimac	Atlantic Ocean (Brazil)	6570	4080
Mississippi–Missouri–Jefferson–Beaverhead–Red Rock	Gulf of Mexico (USA)	6020	3740
Chang Jiang (Yangtze)	E China Sea (China)	5980	3720
Yenisey–Angara–Selenga–Ider	Kara Sea (Russia)	5870	3650
Amur–Argun–Kerulen	Tartar Strait (Russia)	5780	3590
Ob–Irtysh	Gulf of Ob, Kara Sea (Russia)	5410	3360
Plata–Parana–Grande	Atlantic Ocean (Argentina–Uruguay)	4880	3030
Huang Ho (Yellow)	Yellow Sea (China)	4840	3010
Congo (Zaire)–Lualaba	Atlantic Ocean (Angola–Zaire)	4630	2880
Lena	Laptev Sea (Russia)	4400	2730
Mackenzie–Slave–Peace–Finlay	Beaufort Sea (Canada)	4240	2630
Mekong	S China Sea (Vietnam)	4180	2600
Niger	Gulf of Guinea (Nigeria)	4100	2550

[a]Lengths are given to the nearest 10 km/mi, and include the river plus tributaries comprising the longest watercourse.

The Earth's largest drainage basins

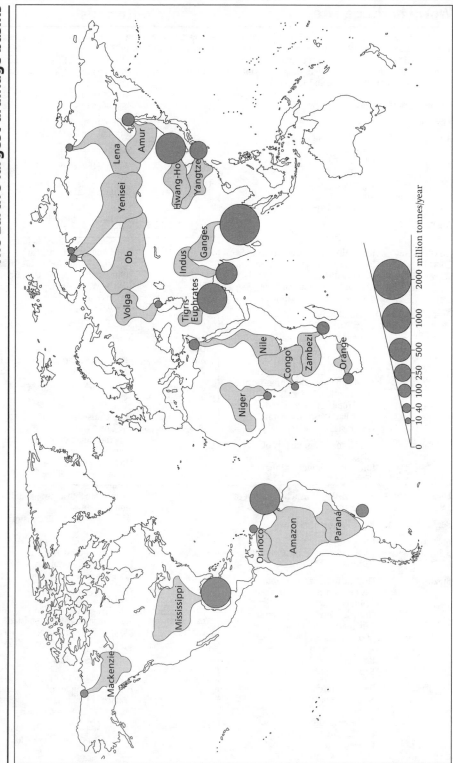

2000 million tonnes/year

0   10 40 100 250 500   1000

Mackenzie

Mississippi

Orinoco

Amazon

Paraná

Niger

Nile

Congo

Zambezi

Orange

Tigris-Euphrates

Volga

Ob

Yenisei

Lena

Amur

Hwang-Ho

Yangtze

Indus

Ganges

World heritage sites

A world heritage site is a site (natural or cultural) recognized by the international community (in the shape of the World Heritage Convention founded by the General Conference of UNESCO in 1972) as possessing universal value, and thus coming under a collective responsibility. A country nominates a site to the Convention, and a decision on whether to include it in the world heritage list is made by a 21-member international committee. There are now 378 sites – 276 cultural, 87 natural, and 15 mixed – in 86 states.

Contracting state	Name of property
Albania	Butrinti
Algeria	Al Qal'a of Beni Hammad
	Tassili n'Ajjer
	M'Zab Valley
	Djemila
	Tipasa
	Timgad
	Kasbah of Algiers
Argentina	Los Glaciares
	Iguazu National Park
Argentina and Brazil	Jesuit Missions of the Guaranis: San Ignacio Mini, Santa Ana, Nuestra Señora de Loreto and Santa Maria Mayor (Argentina), ruins of São Miguel das Missões (Brazil)
Australia	Kakadu National Park
	Great Barrier Reef
	Willandra Lakes Region
	Tasmanian Wilderness
	Lord Howe Island Group
	Australian East Coast Temperate and Sub-Tropical Rainforest Parks
	Uluru National Park
	Wet Tropics of Queensland
	Shark Bay, Western Australia
	Fraser Island
Bangladesh	The Historic Mosque City of Bagerhat
	Ruins of the Buddhist Vihara at Paharpur
Belarus/Poland	Belovezhskaya Pushcha/Białowieza Forest
Benin	Royal Palaces of Abomey
Bolivia	City of Potosi
	Jesuit Missions of the Chiquitos
	Historic city of Sucre
Brazil	Historic town of Ouro Preto
	Historic centre of the town of Olinda
	Historic centre of Salvador de Bahia
	Sanctuary of Bom Jesus do Congonhas
	Iguaçu National Park
	Brasilia
	Serra da Capivara National Park
Bulgaria	Boyana Church
	Madara Rider
	Thracian tomb of Kazanlŭk
	Rock-hewn churches of Ivanovo
	Ancient city of Nessebar
	Rila Monastery
	Srebarna Nature Reserve

Contracting state	Name of property
	Pirin National Park
	Thracian tomb of Sveshtari
Cambodia	Angkor
Cameroon	Dja Faunal Reserve
Canada	L'Anse aux Meadows National Historic Park
	Nahanni National Park
	Dinosaur Provincial Park
	Anthony Island
	Head-Smashed-In Buffalo Jump
	Wood Buffalo National Park
	Canadian Rocky Mountains Parks (Burges Shale, previously inscribed on the World Heritage List, is part of this site)
	Quebec (historic area)
	Gros Morne National Park
Canada and United States of America	Kluane National Park/Wrangell–Saint Elias National Park and Preserve, and Glacier Bay National Park
Central African Republic	Parc national du Manovo-Gounda Saint Floris
China (People's Rep. of)	Mount Taishan
	The Great Wall
	Imperial Palace of the Ming and Qing Dynasties
	Mogao Caves
	The Mausoleum of the First Qin Emperor
	Peking Man Site at Zhoukoudian
	Mount Huangshan
	Wulingyuan scenic and historic interest area
	Jiuzhaigou Valley scenic and historic interest area
	Huanglong scenic and historic interest area
Colombia	Port, fortresses and group of monuments, Cartagena
Costa Rica/ Panama	Talamanca Range – La Amistad Reserves/La Amistad National Park
Côte d'Ivoire	Tai National Park
	Como National Park
Croatia	Old city of Dubrovnik
	Historical complex of Split with the Palace of Diocletian
	Plitvice Lakes National Park
Cuba	Old Havana and its fortifications
	Trinidad and the Valley de los Ingenios

Contracting state	Name of property
Cyprus	Paphos
	Painted churches in the Troodos region
Czech Republic	Historic centre of Prague
	Historic centre of Český Krumlov
	Historic centre of Telč
Dominican Republic	Colonial city of Santo Domingo
Ecuador	Galapagos Islands
	City of Quito
	Sangay National Park
Egypt	Memphis and its necropolis – the Pyramid fields from Giza to Dahshur
	Ancient Thebes with its necropolis
	Nubian monuments from Abu Simbel to Philae
	Islamic Cairo
	Abu Mena
El Salvador	Joya de Caren archeological site
Ethiopia	Simen National Park
	Rock-hewn churches, Lalibela
	Fasil Ghebbi, Gondar Region
	Lower valley of the Awash
	Tiya
	Aksum
	Lower valley of the Omo
Finland	Old Rauma
	Fortress of Suomenlinna
France	Mont-Saint-Michel and its bay
	Chartres Cathedral
	Palace and park of Versailles
	Vézelay, church and hill
	Decorated grottoes of the Vézère Valley
	Palace and park of Fontainebleau
	Château and estate of Chambord
	Amiens Cathedral
	The Roman theatre and its surroundings and the 'Triumphal Arch' of Orange
	Roman and romanesque monuments of Arles
	Cistercian abbey of Fontenay
	Royal Saltworks of Arc-et-Senans
	Place Stanislas, Place de la Carrière and Place d'Alliance in Nancy
	Church of Saint-Savin sur Gartempe
	Cape Girolata, Cape Porto and Scandola Nature Reserve in Corsica
	Pont du Gard (Roman aqueduct)
	Strasbourg – Grande Ile
	Paris, banks of the Seine
	Cathedral of Notre-Dame, former Abbey of Saint-Remi and Tau Palace, Cathedral of Reims
	Bourges Cathedral
Germany	Aachen Cathedral
	Speyer Cathedral
	Würzburg Residence with the court gardens and Residence Square
	Pilgrimage church of Wies

Contracting state	Name of property
	The Castles of Augustusburg and Falkenlust at Brühl
	St Mary's Cathedral and St Michael's Church at Hildesheim
	Roman monuments, cathedral and Liebfrauen-Church in Trier
	Hanseatic city of Lübeck
	Palaces and parks of Potsdam and Berlin
	Abbey and Altenmünster of Lorsch
	Mines of Rammelsberg and the historic town of Goslar
	Town of Bamberg, Maulbronn Monastery complex
Ghana	Forts and castles, Volta, Greater Accra, Central and Western Regions
	Ashante traditional buildings
Greece	Temple of Apollo Epicurius at Bassae
	Archaeological site of Delphi
	The Acropolis, Athens
	Mount Athos
	Meteora
	Paleochristian and Byzantine monuments of Thessalonika
	Archaeological site of Epidaurus
	Mediaeval city of Rhodes
	Archaeological site of Olympia
	Mystras
	Delos
	Monasteries of Daphni, Hossios Lukas, and Nea Moni of Chios
	Pythagoreion and Heraion of Samos
Guatemala	Tikal National Park
	Antigua Guatemala
	Archaeological park and ruins of Quirigua
Guinea and Côte d'Ivoire	Mount Nimba Strict Nature Reserve
Haiti	National History Park – Citadel, Sans Souci, Ramiers
Holy See	Vatican City
Honduras	Maya site of Copan
	Rio Platano Biosphere Reserve
Hungary	Budapest, the banks of the Danube with the district of Buda Castle
	Hollokö
India	Ajanta Caves
	Ellora Caves
	Agra Fort
	Taj Mahal
	The Sun Temple, Konarak
	Group of monuments at Mahabalipuram
	Kaziranga National Park
	Manas Wildlife Sanctuary
	Keoladeo National Park
	Churches and convents of Goa
	Khajuraho group of monuments
	Group of monuments at Hampi
	Fatehpur Sikri

World heritage sites (continued)

Contracting state	Name of property
	Group of monuments at Pattadakal
	Elephanta Caves
	Brihadisvara Temple, Thanjavur
	Sundarbans National Park
	Nanda Devi National Park
	Buddhist monuments at Sanchi
	Humayun's Tomb, Delhi
	Qutb Minar and its monuments, Delhi
Indonesia	Komodo National Park
	Ujung Kulon National Park
	Borobudur Temple compound
	Prambanan Temple compound
Iran	Tchogha Zanbil
	Persepolis
	Meidan Emam, Esfahan
Iraq	Hatra
Ireland	Archeological ensemble of the Bend of the Boyne
Italy	Rock Drawings in Valcamonica
	The Church and Dominican convent of Santa Maria delle Grazie with 'The Last Supper' by Leonardo da Vinci
	Historic centre of Florence
	Venice and its lagoon
	Piazza del Duomo, Pisa
	Historic centre of San Gimignano
Italy/Holy See (each according to its jurisdiction)	Historic Centre of Rome, the properties of the Holy See in that city enjoying extraterritorial rights, and San Paolo fuori la Mura
Japan	Buddhist monuments in the Horyu-ji area
	Himeji-jo
	Yakushima
	Shirakami-Sanchi
Jordan*	Old City of Jerusalem and its walls
	Petra
	Quseir Amra
Lebanon	Anjar
	Baalbek
	Byblos
	Tyr
Libyan Arab Jamahiriya	Archaeological site of Leptis Magna
	Archaeological site of Sabratha
	Archaeological site of Cyrene
	Rock-art sites of Tadrart Acacus
	Old town of Ghadamès
Macedonia, (Former Yugoslav) Republic of	Ohrid Region with its cultural and historical aspect and its natural environment
Madagascar	Tsingy Bemaraha Strict Nature Reserve
Malawi	Lake Malawi National Park
Mali	Old towns of Djenné
	Timbuktu

Contracting state	Name of property
	Cliff of Bandiagara (Land of the Dogons)
Malta	Hal Saflieni Hypogeum
	City of Valetta
	Megalithic temples of Malta
Mauritania	Banc d'Arguin National Park
Mexico	Sian Ka'an
	Pre-Hispanic city and national park of Palenque
	Historic centre of Mexico City and Xochimilco
	Pre-Hispanic city of Teotihuacan
	Historic centre of Oaxaca and archaeological site of Monte Alban
	Historic centre of Puebla
	Historic town of Guanajuato and adjacent mines
	Pre-Hispanic city of Chichen-Itza
	Historic centre of Morelia
	El Tajin, Pre-Hispanic City
	Whale Sanctuary of El Vizcaino
	Historic centre of Zacatecas
	Rock paintings of the Sierra de San Francisco
Morocco	Medina of Fez
	Medina of Marrakesh
	Ksar of Aït-Ben-Haddou
Mozambique	Island of Mozambique
Nepal	Sagarmatha National Park
	Kathmandu Valley
	Royal Chitwan National Park
New Zealand	Te Wahipounamu – South West New Zealand (Westland/Mount Cook National Park and Fiordland National Park, previously inscribed on the World Heritage List, are part of this site)
	Tongariro National Park
Niger	Aïr-Ténéré Reserve
Norway	Urnes Stave Church
	Bryggen
	Røros
	Rock drawings of Alta
Oman	Bahla Fort
	Archaeological sites of Bat, Al-Khutm, and Al-Ayn
Pakistan	Archaeological ruins of Moenjodaro
	Taxila
	Buddhist ruins of Takht-i-Bahi and neighbouring city remains at Sahr-i-Bahlol
	Historical monuments of Thatta
	Fort and Shalamar Gardens in Lahore
Panama	The fortifications on the Caribbean side of Portobelo-San Lorenzo
	Darien National Park

* The Old City of Jerusalem was annexed by Israel in 1967, but this claim has not been recognized by the UN.

Contracting state	Name of property	Contracting state	Name of property
Paraguay	Jesuit Missions of La Santisima Trinidad de Parana and Jesus de Tavarahgue		Old town of Segovia and its aqueduct
Peru	City of Cuzco		Churches of the Kingdom of the Asturias
	Historic sanctuary of Machu Picchu		Santiago de Compostela (Old Town)
	Chavin (archaeological site)		Old town of Avila with its extra muros churches
	Huascaran National Park		Mudejar architecture of Teruel
	Chan Chan Archaeological Zone		Historic city of Toledo
	Manu National Park		Garajonay National Park
	Rio Abiseo National Park		Old town of Cáceres
	Historic centre of Lima		The Cathedral, the Alcazar and the Archivo de Indias, in Seville
Philippines	Tubbataha Reef Marine Park		Old city of Salamanca
	Baroque churches of the Philippines		Poblet Monastery
Poland	Kraków's historic centre		Archeological ensemble of Mérida
	Wieliczka Salt Mine		Royal Monastery of Santa Maria de Guadalupe
	Auschwitz Concentration Camp		The Route of Santiago de Compostella
	Historic centre of Warsaw		
	Old city of Zamość	Sri Lanka	Sacred city of Anuradhapura
Portugal	Central zone of the Town of Angra do Heroismo in the Azores		Ancient city of Polonnaruva
	Monastery of the Hieronymites and Tower of Belem in Lisbon		Ancient city of Sigiriya
	Monastery of Batalha		Sinharaja Forest Reserve
	Convent of Christ in Tomar		Sacred city of Kandy
	Historic centre of Evora		Old town of Galle and its fortifications
	Monastery of Alcobaça		Golden Temple of Dambulla
Romania	Danube Delta	Sweden	Royal Domain of Drottningholm
	Biertan and its fortified church		Birka and Hovgården
	Monastery of Horezu		Engelsberg Ironworks
	Churches of Moldavia	Switzerland	Convent of Saint Gall
Russian Federation	Historic centre of Saint Petersburg and related groups of monuments[a]		Benedictine convent of Saint John at Müstair
	Khizi Pogost[a]		Old city of Berne
	Kremlin and Red Square in Moscow[a]	Syrian Arab Republic	Ancient city of Damascus
	Historic monuments of Novgorod and surroundings		Ancient city of Bosra
	Cultural and historic ensemble of Solovetsky Islands		Site of Palmyra
	The White Monuments of Vladimir and Suzdal		Ancient city of Aleppo
	Trinity Sergius Lavra in Sergiev Pasad	Thailand	Thungyai-Huai Kha Khaeng wildlife sanctuaries
Senegal	Island of Gorée		Historic town of Sukhothai and associated historic towns
	Niokolo-Koba National Park		Historic city of Ayutthaya and associated historic towns
	Djoudj National Bird Sanctuary		Ban Chiang archaeological site
Seychelles	Aldabra Atoll	Tunisia	Medina of Tunis
	Vallée de Mai Nature Reserve		Site of Carthage
Slovakia	Vlkolinec		Amphitheatre of El Djem
	Banská Stiavnica		Ichkeul National Park
	Spissky Hrad and its associated cultural monuments		Punic town of Kerkuane and its necropolis
Slovenia	Skocjan Caves		Medina of Sousse
Spain	The Mosque of Córdoba		Kairouan
	The Alhambra and the Generalife, Granada	Turkey	Historic areas of Istanbul
	Burgos Cathedral		Göreme National Park and the rock sites of Cappadocia
	Monastery and site of the Escorial, Madrid		Great Mosque and hospital of Divrigi
	Parque Güell, Palacio Güell and Casa Mila, in Barcelona		Hattusha
	Altamira Cave		Nemrut Dag

World heritage sites (continued)

Contracting state	Name of property
	Xanthos-Letoon
	Hierapolis-Pamukkale
Ukraine	Kiev: Saint Sophia Cathedral and related monastic buildings, and Lavra of Kiev-Pechersk
United Kingdom	The Giant's Causeway and Causeway Coast
	Durham Castle and Cathedral
	Ironbridge Gorge
	Studley Royal Park including the ruins of Fountains Abbey
	Stonehenge, Avebury and associated sites
	The castles and town walls of King Edward in Gwynedd
	Saint Kilda
	Blenheim Palace
	City of Bath
	Hadrian's Wall
	Palace of Westminster, Abbey of Westminster, and Saint Margaret's Church
	Henderson Island
	The Tower of London
	Canterbury Cathedral, Saint Augustine's Abbey, and Saint Martin's Church
United Republic of Tanzania	Ngorongoro Conservation Area
	Ruins of Kilwa Kisiwani and ruins of Songo Mnara
	Serengeti National Park
	Selous Game Reserve
	Kilimanjaro National Park
United States of America	Mesa Verde
	Yellowstone
	Grand Canyon National Park
	Everglades National Park
	Independence Hall
	Redwood National Park
	Mammoth Cave National Park

Contracting state	Name of property
	Olympic National Park
	Cahokia Mounds state historic site
	Great Smoky Mountains National Park
	La Fortaleza and San Juan historic site in Puerto Rico
	The Statue of Liberty
	Yosemite National Park
	Chaco Culture National Historical Park
	Monticello and University of Virginia in Charlottesville
	Hawaii Volcanoes National Park
	Pueblo de Taos
Uzbekistan	Itchan Kala[a]
	Bukhara
Venezuela	Coro and its port
Vietnam	The complex of Hué monuments
Yemen	Old walled city of Shibam
	Old city of Sana'a
	Historic town of Zabid
Yugoslavia	Stari Ras and Sopocani
	Natural and culturo-historical region of Kotor
	Durmitor National Park
	Studenica Monastery
Zaire	Virunga National Park
	Garamba National Park
	Kahuzi-Biega National Park
	Salonga National Park
Zambia/Zimbabwe	Victoria Falls/Mosi-oa-Tunya
Zimbabwe	Mana Pools National Park, Sapi, and Chewore Safari Areas
	Great Zimbabwe National Monument
	Khami Ruins National Monument

[a]The nominations related to these cultural sites were submitted in 1989 by the USSR.

National Parks in England and Wales

Name (Date of designation)	Location	Area (km²)	(sq mi)
Brecon Beacons (1957)	Powys, Dyfed, Gwent, Mid Glamorgan	1351	522
Dartmoor (1951)	Devon	954	368
Exmoor (1954)	Somerset, Devon	693	268
Lake District (1951)	Cumbria	2292	885
Northumberland (1956)	Northumberland	1049	405
North York Moors (1952)	North Yorkshire, Cleveland	1436	554
Peak District (1951)	Derbyshire, Staffordshire, South Yorkshire, Cheshire, West Yorkshire, Greater Manchester	1438	555
Pembrokeshire Coast (1952)	Dyfed	584	225
Snowdonia (1951)	Gwynedd	2142	817
Yorkshire Dales (1954)	N Yorkshire, Cumbria	1769	683

National Parks in the USA

Park (Date authorized)	Location	Area (ha)	(ac)
Acadia (1916)	SE Maine	15770	38971
Arches (1929)	E Utah	29695	73379
Badlands (1929)	SW South Dakota	98461	243302
Big Bend (1935)	W Texas	286565	708118
Biscayne (1968)	SE Florida	72900	180128
Bryce Canyon (1923)	SW Utah	14502	35835
Canyonlands (1964)	SE Utah	136610	337570
Capitol Reef (1937)	S Utah	97895	214904
Carlsbad Caverns (1923)	SE New Mexico	18921	46755
Channel Islands (1938)	S California	100910	249354
Crater Lake (1902)	SW Oregon	64869	160290
Denali (1917)	S Alaska	1645248	4065493
Everglades (1934)	S Florida	566075	1398800
Gates of the Arctic (1978)	N Alaska	2854000	7052000
Glacier (1910)	NW Montana	410188	1013595
Glacier Bay (1925)	SE Alaska	1569481	3878269
Grand Canyon (1908)	NW Arizona	493059	1218375
Grand Teton (1929)	NW Wyoming	125661	310516
Great Basin (1986)	E Nevada	31206	77109
Great Smoky Mountains (1926)	SW North Carolina, SE Tennessee	210550	520269
Guadalupe Mountains (1966)	W Texas	30875	76293
Haleakala (1916)	Maui Is, Hawaii	11956	28655
Hawaii Volcanoes (1916)	Hawaii Is, Hawaii	92745	229177
Hot Springs (1832)	C Arkansas	2358	5826
Isle Royale (1931)	NW Michigan	231398	571796
Katmai (1918)	SW Alaska	1792810	4430125
Kenai Fjords (1978)	S Alaska	229457	567000
Kings Canyon (1940)	E California	186211	460136
Kobuk Valley (1978)	N Alaska	692000	1710000
Lake Clark (1978)	S Alaska	987000	2439000
Lassen Volcanic (1907)	N California	43047	106372
Mammoth Cave (1926)	C Kentucky	21230	52452
Mesa Verde (1906)	SW Colorado	21078	52085
Mount Rainier (1899)	SW Washington	95265	235404
North Cascades (1968)	N Washington	204277	504781
Olympic (1909)	NW Washington	370250	914890
Petrified Forest (1906)	E Arizona	37835	93493
Redwood (1968)	NW California	44280	109415
Rocky Mountain (1915)	C Colorado	106762	263809
Sequoia (1890)	E California	162885	402488
Shenandoah (1926)	N Virginia	78845	194826
Theodore Roosevelt (1947)	W North Dakota	28497	70416
Virgin Islands (1956)	St John, Virgin Islands	5947	14695
Voyageurs (1971)	N Minnesota	88678	219128
Wind Cave (1903)	SW South Dakota	11449	28292
Wrangell-St Elias (1978)	SE Alaska	3297000	8147000
Yellowstone (1872)	Idaho, Montana, Wyoming	898350	2219823
Yosemite (1890)	E California	307932	760917
Zion (1909)	SW Utah	59308	146551

The Earth

THE ENVIRONMENT

CLIMATE

The climate system

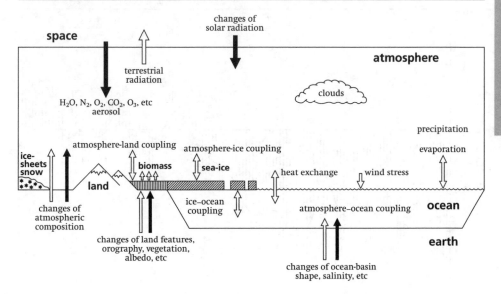

Schematic illustration of the climate system components and interactions (from Houghton, J.T. (ed), 1984, *The Global Climate*; Cambridge University Press).

Climate alterations produced by cities

Element	Compared to rural environs	Element	Compared to rural environs
Contaminants		Snowfall: inner city	5–10% less
Condensation nuclei	10 times more	Snowfall: lee of city	10% more
Particulates	10 times more	Thunderstorms	10–15% more
Gaseous admixtures	5–25 times more		
		Temperature	
Radiation		Annual mean	0.5–30°C/0.9–54°F more
Total on horizontal surface	0–20% less	Winter minimums (average)	1–2°C/1.8–3.6°F more
Ultraviolet: winter	30% less	Summer maximums	1–3°C/1.8–5.4°F more
Ultraviolet: summer	5% less	Heating degree days	10% less
Sunshine duration	5–15% less		
		Relative humidity	
Cloudiness		Annual mean	6% less
Clouds	5–10% more	Winter	2% less
Fog: winter	100% more	Summer	8% less
Fog: summer	30% more		
		Wind speed	
Precipitation		Annual mean	20–30% less
Amounts	5–15% more	Extreme gusts	10–20% less
Days with less than 5 mm/0.2 in	10% more	Calm	5–20% more

Temperature change

Global-mean combined land-air and sea-surface temperatures, 1861–1989, relative to the average for 1951–80

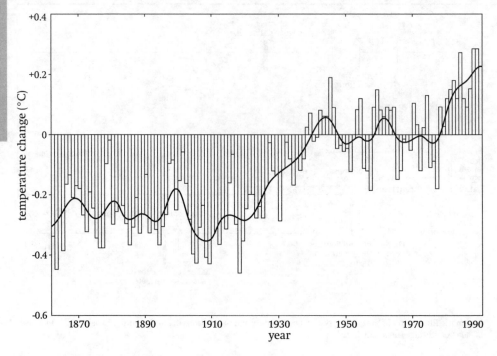

Global mean surface temperature during the last 120 years

Changes of maximum (day-time) and minimum (night-time) temperatures

United States of America

South-eastern Australia

China

The greenhouse effect

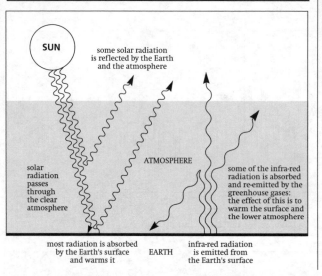

Greenhouse gases

The contribution from each of the human-made greenhouse gases to the change in radiative forcing from 1980 to 1990. The contribution from ozone may also be significant, but cannot be quantified at present.

POLLUTION

Pollutants and the ecosystem

Pathways of pollutants and other substances in ecosystems.

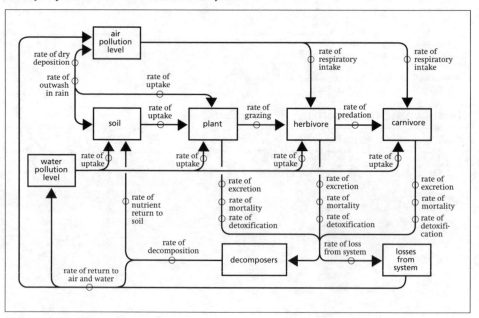

Carbon dioxide

Carbon-dioxide emissions from energy use, selected OECD* countries, 1971–89[a].

	Carbon (million tonnes)							
	1971	1975	1980	1985	1986	1987	1988	1989
Canada	97.3	113.6	130.0	120.6	118.8	122.8	131.1	135.5
USA	1239.5	1274.7	1410.0	1364.8	1359.1	1413.3	1463.9	1480.0
Japan	225.6	261.8	272.0	260.4	257.9	252.6	280.2	288.0
Australia	48.8	56.4	66.0	66.4	66.3	70.2	71.0	76.3
New Zealand	4.5	5.4	5.0	6.7	6.9	7.0	7.5	7.9
Austria	15.1	15.1	17.0	16.5	16.7	17.1	16.7	17.0
Belgium	36.8	36.5	39.0	31.1	32.0	32.5	33.0	33.6
Denmark	17.5	16.1	18.0	18.3	18.2	18.6	17.7	16.2
Finland	15.0	15.6	19.0	17.3	17.7	19.6	17.8	18.4
France	129.9	130.7	144.0	112.7	108.7	108.8	106.1	110.8
Germany	291.9	279.6	304.5	291.4	294.7	292.6	289.3	281.9
Greece	8.5	11.8	15.0	18.2	18.0	19.5	20.9	22.7
Iceland	0.5	0.5	0.0	0.5	0.5	0.5	0.5	0.6
Ireland	6.3	6.1	7.0	7.3	7.7	8.0	7.9	8.1
Italy	97.7	102.4	112.0	105.4	106.8	111.3	112.4	117.3
Luxembourg	3.9	3.4	3.0	2.6	2.6	2.5	2.5	2.7
Netherlands	46.8	48.3	53.0	49.8	51.9	52.7	53.3	53.5
Norway	7.5	7.6	9.0	8.8	10.2	9.6	8.8	10.6
Portugal	5.7	6.9	8.0	8.8	9.7	9.8	10.5	13.0
Spain	36.7	48.1	57.0	56.4	57.4	57.6	58.5	63.2
Sweden	27.4	26.9	25.0	22.8	22.8	22.2	22.1	21.4
Switzerland	11.9	11.2	12.0	12.4	13.1	12.4	12.6	12.1
Turkey		24.2	28.0	35.8	38.6	41.3	39.8	43.8
UK	188.5	171.7	169.0	160.5	163.3	165.7	164.9	164.0
North America	1336.8	1388.3	1540.0	1485.4	1477.9	1536.1	1595.0	1615.5
Australia	53.3	61.8	71.0	73.1	73.2	77.2	78.5	84.2
OECD* Europe	960.2	962.7	1039.5	976.6	990.6	1002.3	995.3	1010.9
EU	870.2	861.6	925.5	862.5	871.0	879.6	877.0	887.0
OECD*	2575.9	2674.6	2922.5	2795.5	2799.6	2868.2	2929.0	2998.6
World [b]	4379.7	4811.5	5528.4	5801.9	5900.0	6080.8	6255.9	

[a] Anthropogenic carbon-dioxide emissions from energy use only. Oil held in international marine bunkers is included. Quantities are assigned to the country in which these bunkers are situated. Oil and gas for non-energy purposes are excluded.
[b] World emissions estimated using a simplified method compared to that used for OECD countries.
* Organization for Economic Cooperation and Development (see note on page 73).

Geographic distribution of carbon emissions

Geographic distribution of the emissions of carbon from combustion of fossil fuels in 1980.

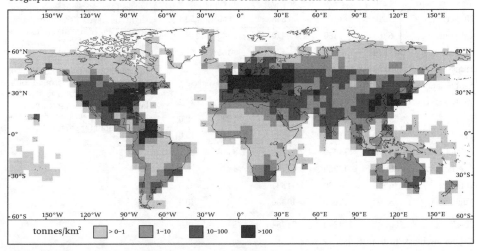

Changes in greenhouse-gases pollution

Concentrations of carbon dioxide and methane after remaining relatively constant up to the 18th-c, have risen sharply since then due to human activities. Concentrations of nitrous oxide have increased since the mid-18th-c, especially in the last few decades. CFCs were not present in the atmosphere before the 1930s.

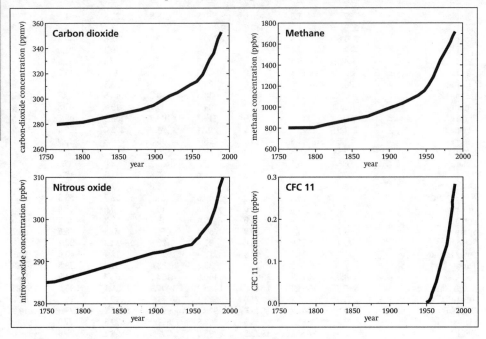

Acid-rain damage to forests in Europe

Country	Forest expanse		Extent of damage[a]		
	(km²)	(sq mi)	(km²)	(sq mi)	(%)
Finland	194 000	74 880	67 900	26 210	35.0
Norway	83 330	32 160	4 100	1 580	4.9
Sweden	265 000	102 290	10 600	4 090	4.0
West Germany	73 230	28 270	38 240	14 760	51.9
Netherlands	3 090	1 190	1 548	600	50.1
Belgium	6 160	2 380	1 110	430	18.0
Luxembourg	820	320	423	160	51.6
France	150 750	58 190	2 796	1 080	1.85
Switzerland	12 000	4 630	4 320	1 670	36.0
Austria	375 400	144 900	9 600	3 700	24.2
Italy	63 630	24 560	3 180	1 230	5.0
East Germany	29 000	11 190	3 500	1 350	12.0
Poland	86 770	33 490	22 730	8 770	26.2[b]
Czechoslovakia	46 000	17 760	12 500	4 820	26.1
Hungary	16 700	6 450	1 837	710	11.0
Yugoslavia	95 000	36 670	10 400	490	10.9
Totals	1 500 880	579 340	194 784	75 190	12.9

Figures given date to August 1986.

[a] Four classes of damage are generally recognized, viz. slight damage, medium to serious damage, critical damage with trees actually dying, and complete damage with trees dead (conforming to needle/leaf loss of 11–25%, 26–60%, 61–90%, and 91–100%). In West Germany as of late 1985, 32.7% of trees showed slight damage (63% of damaged area), 17% medium to serious damage (32.8%), and 2.2% critical or complete damage (4.2%).

[b] In late 1986 the Polish Academy of Sciences estimated around 50%. Extensive forest damage has also been reported in western parts of the former Soviet Union, but no statistical details are available.

Acid-rain concentrations

Concentrations in acid precipitation, selected areas, 1980–91.

pH

Country	Areas	1980	1985	1986	1987	1988	1989	1990	1991
Canada	Great Lakes	4.40	4.23	4.20	4.31	4.33	4.31	4.34	4.32
USA	Great Lakes	4.45	4.54	4.52	4.52	4.51			
Japan	Tokyo		5.00	5.00	5.50	4.70	4.60	4.60	
Austria	Illmitz	4.47				5.30			
Belgium	Bruxelles	5.96	5.26	5.15	5.68	4.84	4.81	5.12	
	Offagne		5.61	5.29	5.84	5.23	5.03	4.47	
Denmark	Tange	4.43	4.48	4.66	4.54	4.80	4.52	4.41	4.53
Finland	Uto, Ahtari, Virolahti	4.63	4.46	4.49	4.54	4.52	4.45	4.54	4.56
France	Vert-Le-Petit	4.58	4.64	4.99	4.54	4.90			
	Carpentras	5.30	5.70	5.50	4.90	5.40	6.10		
Germany	Rheinland	4.20	4.40	4.40	4.50				
	Deuselbach	4.36	4.42	4.46	4.55	4.46	4.64		4.55
Iceland	Irafoss	5.22				5.32			
Ireland	Valentia	4.63				5.39			
Italy	Ispra				5.07	4.23	4.68		
Luxembourg	National								
Netherlands	National	4.46	4.71	4.68	4.62	4.66	4.63	4.70	
	Limburg	5.04	5.02	4.88	4.83	4.98	4.96	5.00	
	N Holland	4.34	4.76	4.49	4.24	4.54	4.76		
Norway	National	4.36	4.41	4.36	4.45	4.38			
	Birkenes	4.16	4.24	4.26	4.38	4.25	4.27	4.37	
	Skreadalen	4.54	4.48	4.51	4.54	4.55	4.56	4.61	
Portugal	Braganca	6.22	5.30		5.10	5.50	5.50	5.60	
	Faro	6.70	6.70						
Spain	La Cartuja					6.22			
	Roquetas					6.38			
Sweden	Rorvik	4.20	4.22	4.20	4.30	4.30	4.20	4.30	4.30
	Goteburg		4.27	4.50	4.50				
Switzerland	Duebendorf					4.58	4.58	4.64	4.52
	Payerne			4.94	4.90	4.88	4.78	5.11	5.13
UK	Inverpolly	4.70	5.30	5.22	5.10	4.87	5.00	4.90	4.82
	Eskdalemuir	4.24	4.72	4.69	4.68	4.63	4.79	4.71	4.70
Czech Republic	Praha-Libus			4.72	4.28	4.49	4.40	4.89	4.44
Slovak Republic	Bratislava	4.19	4.44	4.63	4.49	4.58	4.51	4.90	5.67
Hungary	National		4.77	4.77	4.77	4.77			
Poland	Suwalki	4.45	4.52	4.41	4.50	4.65	4.40	4.40	4.27

SO^{2-}_4 (mg/l)

Country	Areas	1980	1985	1986	1987	1988	1989	1990	1991
Canada	Great Lakes	3.61	2.65	2.57	2.52	2.49	2.49	2.36	2.52
USA	Great Lakes	2.65	2.09	2.28	2.18	2.29			
Japan	Tokyo		2.30	3.30	3.20		3.13	3.70	
Austria	Illmitz	6.03				4.26			
Belgium	Bruxelles	5.13	6.51	6.12	5.88	5.13	5.73	5.70	
	Offagne		4.62	3.78	3.12	2.67	2.94	3.51	
Denmark	Tange	2.91	3.92	3.03	3.48	3.18	3.54	2.76	3.69
Finland	Uto, Ahtari, Virolahti	4.12	3.67	3.93	3.30	3.57	2.20	2.51	2.74
France	Vert-Le-Petit	5.24	4.38	4.17	4.59	3.06			
	Carpentras	5.65	5.16	5.73	5.91	5.15	2.75		
Germany	Rheinland		5.48	4.93	6.30				
	Deuselbach	3.33	3.33	2.65	2.52	2.55	2.68	2.18	2.43
Iceland	Irafoss	0.93							
Ireland	Valentia	1.86				1.20			
Italy	Ispra				4.03	4.98	3.90	3.41	
Luxembourg	National					4.02			
Netherlands	National	6.16	5.43	5.59	4.61	4.06	4.65	4.70	
	Limburg	8.06	7.29	7.35	5.91	6.65	6.46	6.40	
	N Holland	7.65	7.16	7.05	7.16	7.86	11.06		
Norway	National	3.69	2.94	3.03	2.22	2.49	2.70	2.13	
	Birkenes	1.44	1.77	1.59	1.41	1.23	1.29	1.17	
	Skreadalen	1.60	1.00			0.86	0.73	0.74	
Portugal	Braganca	1.90	1.00						
	Faro								
Spain	La Cartuja					3.81			
	Roquetas								
Sweden	Rorvik	3.52	4.29	4.98	3.90	4.29	3.96	3.75	3.36
	Goteburg	9.59	7.97	6.09	4.74				
Switzerland	Duebendorf						3.54	2.67	2.98
	Payerne			2.58	1.86	1.98	3.75	2.28	2.63
UK	Inverpolly	1.30	0.91			0.76	0.59	0.54	0.69
	Eskdalemuir	2.50	1.49	1.50	1.41	1.57	1.37	1.22	1.26
Czech Republic	Praha-Libus			11.57	8.76	8.74	8.76	6.48	7.57
Slovak Republic	Bratislava	13.29	9.06	11.28	8.43	7.95	8.91	8.13	12.30
Hungary	National		4.28	4.28	4.28	4.28			
Poland	Suwalki	5.25	5.55	5.25	4.89	4.38	4.50	4.68	

NO_3 (mg/l)

Country	Areas	1980	1985	1986	1987	1988	1989	1990	1991
Canada	Great Lakes	2.59	2.24	1.99	2.17	2.11	2.44	1.86	2.17
USA	Great Lakes	1.60	1.33	1.40	1.41	1.45			
Japan	Tokyo		1.20	2.20	2.50		1.92	2.99	
Austria	Illmitz	2.83				2.75			
Belgium	Bruxelles	5.30	3.10	3.10	3.10	3.28	2.97	3.76	
	Offagne		2.92	2.92	2.30	2.26	2.26	2.57	
Denmark	Tange	1.72	3.01	2.25	2.04	2.26	2.61	1.90	2.57
Finland	Uto, Ahtari, Virolahti		2.56	2.52	2.04	2.48	2.17	2.08	1.91
France	Vert-Le-Petit	3.69	4.11	3.85	4.47	4.13			
	Carpentras	2.47	1.61	1.83	3.26	2.81	1.61		
Germany	Rheinland								
	Deuselbach		2.49	1.99	2.15	2.16	2.54	1.90	2.49
Iceland	Irafoss					0.44			
Ireland	Valentia					0.44			
Italy	Ispra				2.01	3.85	2.11	2.67	
Luxembourg	National								
Netherlands	National	3.08	2.81	3.27	2.98	2.40	2.80	2.50	
	Limburg	4.24	3.44	3.52	3.19	3.75	3.81	4.10	
	N Holland		3.34	2.66	3.06	4.16	2.01		
Norway	National	2.52	2.57	2.66	1.90	2.57	3.36	2.08	
	Birkenes	0.93	1.42	1.28	1.24	1.24	1.24	1.02	
	Skreadalen	0.21	0.30			0.04	0.08	0.17	
Portugal	Braganca	0.21	1.21						
	Faro								
Spain	La Cartuja					2.83			
	Roquetas					1.02			
Sweden	Rorvik	3.03	3.49	3.76	2.52	3.54	3.50	2.79	3.10
	Goteburg	3.33	4.46	5.26	4.29				
Switzerland	Duebendorf						3.36	2.61	3.39
	Payerne			1.68	1.59	1.64	3.14	1.99	2.77
UK	Inverpolly	0.37	0.56	0.50	0.59	0.55	0.45	0.44	0.58
	Eskdalemuir	1.24	0.93	0.86	1.00	1.06	1.02	0.87	0.93
Czech Republic	Praha-Libus			5.48	4.17	5.13	4.31	4.18	5.24
Slovak Republic	Bratislava	3.78	3.92	4.75	3.70	4.36	4.49	4.05	3.92
Hungary	National		3.28	3.28	3.28	3.28			
Poland	Suwalki	2.17	2.61	2.88	2.52	2.61	2.30	2.48	

The environment

Traffic pollution

Road traffic volumes: total vehicles, selected OECD* countries, 1970–89.

Vehicle km (thousand millions)

	1970	1975	1980	1981	1982	1983	1984	1985	1986	1987	1988	1989
Canada	125.9	171.4	205.5	201.8	204.2	204.1	202.4	201.0	206.8	216.5	220.8	225.1
USA	1787.3	2104.1	2418.6	2425.4	2538.2	2634.1	2745.2	2840.0	2937.2	3072.9	3243.0	3307.4
Japan	226.0	286.3	389.1	394.7	402.6	408.9	415.5	447.0	465.0	471.1	511.8	520.7
Australia	79.0	98.0	114.7	118.8	125.2	128.7	132.7	137.5	139.9	144.2	148.6	152.9
New Zealand	13.2	15.7	16.5	16.7	17.6	19.0	18.2	18.6	19.3	20.4	20.9	21.5
Austria	21.9	30.1	35.4	35.9	36.1	36.4	37.7	38.3	39.4	49.7	51.9	54.2
Belgium	33.3	38.3	45.8	46.3	46.8	46.5	46.8	47.1	48.2	49.7	51.4	52.2
Denmark	23.0	25.3	26.3	26.6	26.3	27.2	28.3	29.7	31.6	33.3	34.9	36.0
Finland	19.3	24.4	26.8	27.3	28.2	29.1	29.9	31.2	32.4	34.3	36.5	38.7
France	208.0	260.7	298.0	309.0	313.0	318.0	321.0	328.1	345.0	376.0	399.0	414.0
West Germany	234.2	279.9	340.8	326.5	337.8	341.0	350.8	351.1	375.1	396.1	416.5	427.0
Greece	9.2	13.3	20.4	21.6	23.2	24.9	26.6	28.6	30.4	32.2	34.2	36.0
Iceland	0.7	1.0	1.2	1.2	1.3	1.4	1.4	1.5	1.6	1.7	1.8	1.7
Ireland	10.7	12.1	18.5	19.0	17.6	17.7	18.3	18.8	19.3	19.9	21.1	23.0
Italy	146.4	184.6	226.6	235.2	248.7	239.5	247.9	257.8	265.0	278.7	286.1	297.2
Luxembourg	1.5	1.7	2.2	2.3	2.3	2.4	2.5	2.5	2.8	2.9	3.0	3.1
Netherlands	48.3	55.7	70.3	69.9	68.9	71.7	74.2	74.4	78.2	82.2	87.4	89.4
Norway	10.7	14.7	16.6	16.6	17.2	17.6	18.2	19.5	20.6	21.2	21.2	21.2
Portugal	9.4	15.5	21.2	23.2	24.8	26.4	27.7	27.9	29.4	30.4	31.6	32.8
Spain	35.1	55.5	74.6	72.0	73.2	73.9	75.8	75.1	82.6	85.9	92.8	100.0
Sweden	35.1	41.6	44.2	44.3	44.7	46.0	46.9	48.0	50.7	52.6	59.0	60.8
Switzerland	25.0	30.5	36.8	38.4	39.6	40.6	41.2	42.3	43.3	44.4	45.1	47.5
Turkey	6.1	13.4	14.8	15.3	16.0	16.8	18.6	19.1	19.0	20.9	22.3	23.4
UK	178.9	206.0	241.7	245.2	252.4	257.9	268.3	274.0	285.0	310.7	327.5	356.7
Yugoslavia	10.8	20.9	29.5	30.8	32.3	33.2	34.4	33.0	34.8	35.6	36.1	36.9
North America	1913.2	2275.6	2624.1	2627.2	2742.3	2838.2	2947.6	3041.1	3144.0	3289.4	3463.8	3532.6
Australia	92.1	113.7	131.3	135.5	142.8	147.7	150.9	156.1	159.2	164.6	169.5	174.4
OECD*	3288.3	3979.8	4706.7	4733.2	4905.9	5029.7	5196.3	5359.1	5567.7	5847.8	6168.5	6342.9

Traffic volumes are expressed in thousand millions of kilometres travelled by road vehicles. The average number of kilometres travelled each year by road vehicles was multiplied by the number of motor vehicles in use.
*Organization for Economic Cooperation and Development (see note on page 73).

Pesticide pollution

Consumption of pesticides, selected OECD* countries.

	Year	Active ingredients (tonnes) Pesticides total	Insecticides	Fungicides	Herbicides	Other pesticides
Canada	1990	33716	2262	2512	26414	2528
USA	1991	370918	79450	66738	224730	
Japan	1985	83056	45018	18662	19416	
Austria	1986	6069	500	2426	3053	90
Belgium	1989	9664	1313	2626	5307	400
Denmark	1991	4660	146	146	1426	2896
Finland	1991	1742	69	146	1375	152
France	1991	96374	7096	55565	33713	7060
West Germany	1990	33146	1525	10985	16957	3679
Greece	1989	8151	2844	1925	3031	300
Hungary	1989	25950	2806	10452	9622	3000
Iceland	1983	5	1	2	2	
Ireland	1991	1915	162	535	1097	121
Italy	1989	91078	10744	57088	10566	12680
Netherlands	1989	19146	745	4052	3330	11019
Norway	1990	1184	19	153	965	46
Poland	1989	20620	1065	7206	11875	474
Portugal	1988	21570	2700	12870	5000	1000
Spain	1989	134150	52754	29011	20342	32043
Sweden	1991	1837	19	723	1054	41
Switzerland	1989	2423	153	1112	925	200
Turkey	1991	28220	10412	5599	7191	5000
UK	1982	40300	1480	4780	28100	5900

*Organization for Economic Cooperation and Development (see note on page 73).

Amount of waste generated

Amounts of waste generated, by source, selected countries.

Amount (thousand tonnes)

	Year	Municipal	Industrial	Energy production	Agriculture	Mining	Demolition wastes	Dredge spoils	Sewage sludge	Others
Canada	1990	16000		12400	14000	1052990	9000	7540	500	
USA	1990	177500	7080000	1093039	165821	1541850	34692		11454	
Japan	1985	50441	132304	27748	62690	26017	57886		2001	63492
Austria	1990	4783	31801	1150	880	21	18309	111	365	
Belgium	1988	3410	27000	1069			680	4805	687	2830
Czech Rep	1987	2600	39604	25774	451	533373	2677	23071	2750	
Denmark	1985	2430	2304	1532			1747		1263	
Finland	1990	3100	10160	950	23000	21650	7000	3000	1000	150
France	1990	20320	50000		400000	100000			600	9800
Germany	1990	27958	81906	29598		19296				
Greece	1990	3000	4304	7680	90	3900				
Hungary	1989	4900	45000		62000				30000	493
Iceland	1990	80	135							
Ireland	1984	1100	1580	130	22000	1930	240		570	860
Italy	1991	20033	34710				34374		3428	
Luxembourg	1990	170	1300				5240		15	
Netherlands	1990	7430	7665	1553	19210	391	12390	17500	320	
Norway	1990	2000	2000		18000	9000	2000		100	
Poland	1990	12806	58732	17845		67284			1000	
Portugal	1990	2538	662	165		202				15
Slovak Rep	1987	1901	22602	3128	942	4276	5977		1041	497
Spain	1990	12546	13800		112102	70000	22000		10000	
Sweden	1990	3200	13000	625	21000	28000	1200		220	3850
Switzerland	1990	3000	1000				2000		260	
Turkey	1989	19500								
UK	1990	20000	56000	13000	80000	107000	32000	21000	1000	15400
Yugoslavia	1989		7164		20597					
OECD*		408000	1300000							

*Organization for Economic Cooperation and Development (see note on page 73).

Industrial and hazardous waste

Industrial waste, hazardous and special waste, total amount generated by type.

Amount (thousand tonnes)

	Year	Chemical waste	Non-chemical waste	Total	Hazardous and special waste[a]
Canada	1980		196	61000	3290
USA	1986	105400		760000	238327
Japan	1985			312271	666
Austria	1983	525	12733	13258	400
Belgium	1989			26700	915
Denmark	1988			2400	112
Finland	1987			10500	230
France	1989			50000	3000
West Germany	1987	10218	51206	61424	14210
Greece	1989	423	3881	4304	423
Ireland	1984			1580	20
Italy	1989			39978	3640
Luxembourg	1990			1300	742
Netherlands	1988	624	6063	6687	1500
Norway	1989	2186			200
Portugal	1987	530	133	662	165
Spain	1987			5108	1708
Sweden	1980	500	3500	4000	500
Switzerland	1989				400
UK	1989			50000	2220
Yugoslavia	1989			7164	
OECD*	1989			1430000	303000

[a]The total amount of special waste is 18 million tonnes.
*Organization for Economic Cooperation and Development (see note on page 73).

Water pollution

Water quality of lakes, annual mean concentration of phosphorus and nitrogen, selected lakes, 1970–1990.

Country	Lake	Total phosphorus (mgP/l)					Total nitrogen (mgN/l)				
		1970	1975	1980	1985	1990	1970	1975	1980	1985	1990
Canada	Ontario	0.022	0.022	0.017	0.011	0.009	0.226	0.283	0.308	0.572	0.218
	Erie	0.017	0.023	0.011	0.012			0.278	0.163		
USA	Cayuga (NY)	0.020	0.020				0.370	0.510			
	W. Twin (Ohio)	0.150	0.100				1.930				
Japan	Biwa (N)		0.008	0.009	0.007	0.007	0.190	0.290	0.270	0.260	0.290
	Biwa (S)		0.027	0.017	0.020	0.022	0.450	0.530	0.330	0.360	0.380
	Kasumigaura		0.040	0.080	0.060	0.074		1.200	1.000	1.200	1.200
Austria	Mondsee		0.029	0.025	0.014	0.010					
	Ossiachersee		0.015	0.010	0.016	0.034					
Denmark	Knud Soe	0.060	0.050	0.030	0.025	0.030		1.780	3.000	2.900	2.270
Finland	Paeaejaervi	0.013	0.014	0.010	0.014	0.013	0.900	1.150	1.350	1.100	1.200
	Paeijaenne	0.010	0.011	0.009	0.008	0.007	0.500	0.460	0.460	0.510	0.900
	Yli-kitka		0.005	0.006	0.007	0.008		0.180	0.170	0.260	0.230
Germany	Bodensee	0.044	0.082	0.083	0.066	0.033	0.730	0.790	0.880	0.940	0.980
Hungary	Terto-to				0.140	0.170				1.280	2.120
	Balaton		0.030	0.010	0.020	0.030		1.140	0.930	0.780	0.480
Ireland	Ennel		0.089	0.029	0.032	0.017		0.270	0.470	0.340	0.467
	Derg		0.025	0.020	0.060	0.042		0.840	1.200	1.260	0.806
Italy	Maggiore		0.026	0.036	0.019				0.770		
	Como		0.068	0.078	0.052		0.640	0.710	0.800	0.800	
	Garda		0.009	0.020	0.011		0.310	0.300	0.390	0.350	
	Orta			0.011	0.006		13.000	9.620	9.500	7.110	
Netherlands	Ijssel		0.350	0.350	0.300	0.180		4.025	4.385	4.140	3.950
Norway	Mjoesa	0.010	0.010	0.009	0.007	0.007	0.400	0.400	0.500	0.432	0.382
	Randsfjorden			0.004		0.006			0.514		0.460
Portugal	Ria de Aveiro			0.015	0.026						
Spain	Castrejon			5.790	4.805	3.158					
	Alcantara		0.387	0.428	0.141	0.251		1.341	2.864		
Sweden	Maelaren	0.029	0.024	0.034	0.031	0.028	0.918	0.735	0.708	0.859	0.637
	Vaettern	0.008	0.007	0.009	0.006	0.007	0.514	0.568	0.625	0.681	0.730
Switzerland	Leman	0.104	0.082	0.090	0.073	0.058			0.660	0.730	0.709
	Constance	0.055	0.078	0.077	0.066	0.039		0.861	0.900	0.930	0.970
Turkey	Kurtbogazi			0.110	0.200	0.030			0.430	0.360	0.280
	Sapanca			0.030	0.030	0.040			0.942	0.617	0.370
	Altinapa			0.030	0.150	0.130			1.550	0.549	1.810
UK	Neagh		0.095	0.108	0.115	0.096			0.480	0.475	0.773
	Lomond			0.009	0.009	0.003			0.300	0.290	0.200

Consequences of water pollution

Cultural or accelerated eutrophication caused by sewage and nitrate fertilizer run-off into lakes.

D = death of the lake

a = eutrophication from heavy nitrogen pollution

b = eutrophication from moderate nitrogen pollution

c = natural eutrophication

biological productivity per unit volume of lake

age of the lake

DEFORESTATION

Forests of the world: areas and carbon stocks

Forest type	Area		Carbon stocks in plants (thousand million tonnes of carbon)	Carbon stocks in detritus and soil (thousand million tonnes of carbon)
	(millions km²)	(millions sq mi)		
Tropical forests (both evergreen, and in primary form)	8.6	3.3	202	288
Temperate-zone forests	8.2	3.2	65	161
Boreal forests	11.7	4.5	127	247
Woodland and shrublands	12.8	4.9	57	59
Rest of Earth's land surface	103.3	39.9	109	720
Totals	144.6	55.8	560	1475

World distribution of various types of forest

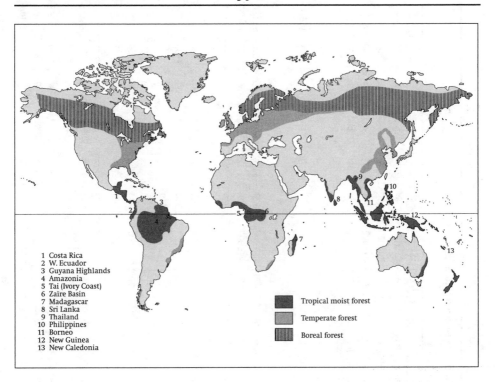

1 Costa Rica
2 W. Ecuador
3 Guyana Highlands
4 Amazonia
5 Tai (Ivory Coast)
6 Zaïre Basin
7 Madagascar
8 Sri Lanka
9 Thailand
10 Philippines
11 Borneo
12 New Guinea
13 New Caledonia

Tropical moist forest

Temperate forest

Boreal forest

Forest depletion and growth

Depletion and growth of forests in selected countries, 1970–89

Country	Harvest 1970	Harvest 1980	Harvest 1985	Harvest 1989	Losses 1970	Losses 1980	Losses 1985	Losses 1989	Total 1970	Total 1980	Total 1985	Total 1989	Growth 1970	Growth 1980	Growth 1985	Growth 1989	Intensity 1970	Intensity 1980	Intensity 1985	Intensity 1989
	Annual depletion (1000 m³)												Annual growth (1000 m³)				Intensity of use (harvest/annual growth)			
Canada	121400	158800	143700	156000		24600	143800	138100		181100	287500	294100		305300	338000	363400		0.52	0.43	0.43
USA	397372	402923	482522		113976	115902	129918		511320	518824	612440		67516	736780	763851		0.59	0.55	0.63	
Japan	65996	42932	42067	38554	390	2100	1286	1050	66386	45032	43353	39604			115500				0.36	
Australia	13700		16300												42000				0.39	
New Zealand	8478	10776	9626											5000	17556			2.16	0.55	
Austria	15100	15200		13408				3178				16586		19298			0.81	0.78		
Belgium	3200		2800												5000				0.56	
Denmark	2109	2138	2249	2163									1935	2851			1.09	0.75		
Finland	51990	53740	48880	48869	6710	5960	6320	6257	58700	59700	55200	55127	57150	62800	68380	73522	0.91	0.86	0.71	0.66
France	32300	34380	35000	37000	16700	18500	37700	37000	49000	52880	72700	74000		64500	74700	76500		0.53	0.47	0.48
West Germany	28196	30327	31219	31819			14550	353			45769	32172	34000		42000		0.88		0.71	
Greece	35000		2900												3600				0.81	
Ireland	380	527	953		2	7	53		382	534	1006		1903	2370	2710		0.20	0.22	0.35	
Italy	6942	7712	9383		200	200	250		7142	7912	9633		13070	12080	11667		0.53	0.64	0.80	
Luxembourg			1500				140								1000					
Netherlands	1200																0.98	0.87		
Norway	8500	9100	9400	11800	1100	1400	1800	2000	9600	10500	11200	13800	14500	15700	16600	18300	0.59	0.58	0.57	0.64
Portugal	10700	9500	2435			1840	8602				11037				7000				0.35	
Spain	6192	7661	9512	11529										16674	24000			0.46	0.40	
Sweden	63600	53000	59600	59000	8000	8000	4500	5300	71600	61000	64100	64300	78700	81700	97200	99200	0.81	0.65	0.61	0.59
Switzerland	4210	4690	4410	4800											6000		0.91		0.74	
Turkey	17789	23243	18124	14500					17789	23243	18124	14500	22135	22135	22135	22135	0.80	1.05	0.82	0.66
UK	3600	4660	5170	6505					3000	4660	5170	6505	5700	10720		15415	0.63	0.43	0.47	0.42
Yugoslavia	14797	19149	22428	21540	4625	4470	4844	3568	18283	23619	27272	25108	21088	29351	29351	29351	0.70	0.65	0.76	0.73

Mean annual percentage change in forest and woodland area, 1974–84

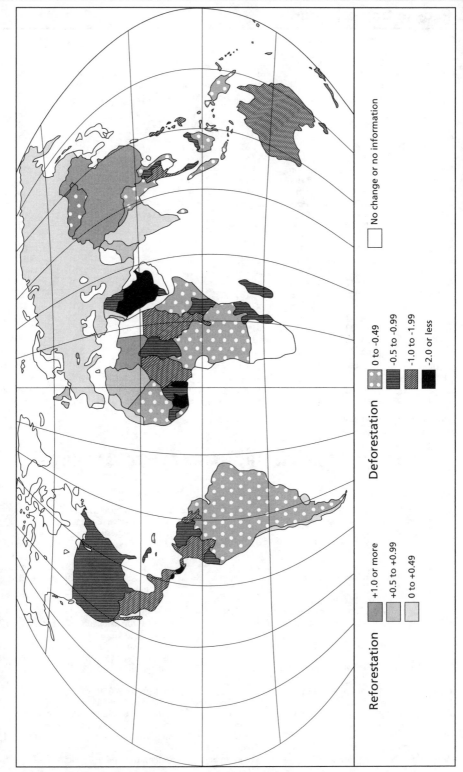

Reforestation

+1.0 or more

+0.5 to +0.99

0 to +0.49

Deforestation

0 to -0.49

-0.5 to -0.99

-1.0 to -1.99

-2.0 or less

No change or no information

Trade in tropical wood

Trade in tropical wood, selected OECD* countries, 1990.

	Imports of cork and wood from				Total		
	Africa (1000 US$)	Latin America (1000 US$)	Far East (1000 US$)	Oceania (1000 US$)	(1000 US$)	per capita (US$)	% of total imports
Canada	366	4958	14008		19332	0.7	2.8
USA	7304	194866	110337	19	312526	1.2	9.2
Japan	41312	11504	2273440	117021	2443277	19.8	27.8
Australia	43	1481	100465	6368	108357	6.3	30.5
New Zealand	427		7234	3134	10795	3.2	39.0
Austria	5587	285	11513	11	17396	2.3	3.1
Belgium	35692	5031	112670	446	152839	14.8	17.9
Denmark	4736	2459	15509		22704	4.4	4.5
Finland	5550	1014	2615		9179	1.8	3.0
France	300701	15984	136453	15	453153	8.0	39.3
West Germany	133666	16123	200003	76	349868	5.5	16.3
Greece	49100	174	227		49501	4.9	19.7
Iceland	41	135	138		314	1.2	1.5
Ireland	39545	8119	3083		50747	14.5	34.9
Italy	296261	30726	129784		456771	7.9	17.9
Netherlands	47590	11223	266190		325003	21.7	28.2
Norway	5657	2650	5267		13574	3.2	4.8
Portugal	132939	6709	3123		142771	14.5	61.0
Spain	252133	37368	27630		317131	8.1	33.1
Sweden	3961	1897	5083		10941	1.3	2.8
Switzerland	5633	647	1898		8178	1.2	2.3
Turkey	36512	68	2722		39302	0.7	29.8
UK	56935	78651	165429	713	301728	5.3	12.0
North America	7670	199824	124345	19	331858	1.2	8.1
OECD* Europe	1411239	219263	1089337	1261	2721100	6.5	18.7
EU	1348298	212567	1060101	1250	2622216	8.0	21.0
OECD*	1460691	432072	3594821	127803	5615387	6.7	20.2

*Organization for Economic Cooperation and Development (see note on page 73).

RECENT NOTABLE ENVIRONMENTAL DISASTERS

Date	Event	Location	Consequence
1957	Fire in Windscale plutonium production reactor. Ignited three tonnes of uranium	Cumbria, UK	Spread of radioactive material throughout Britain. Official death toll 39, but this is strongly contested.
1970	Collision of the tanker *Othello*	Tralhavet Bay, Sweden	17640000–29400000 gallons of oil spilled.
1971	Overflow of water storage space at Northern States Power Company's reactor	Monticello, Minnesota, USA	50000 gallons of radioactive waste dumped into Mississippi River. Contamination of St Paul water system.
1972	Collision of the tanker *Sea Star*	Gulf of Oman	33810000 gallons of oil spilled.
1974	Explosion of container of cyclohexane	Flixborough, UK	28 deaths.
1975	Fire at Brown's Ferry reactor	Decatur, Alabama, USA	$100 million damage. Cooling water level lowered significantly.
1976	Leak of toxic gas TCDD	Seveso, Italy	Topsoil had to be removed in worst contaminated areas.
1976	Grounding of the supertanker *Urquiola*	La Coruña, Spain	Spillage of 29400000 gallons of oil.
1977	Well blow-out at Ecofisk oil field	North Sea	Spillage of 8200000 gallons of oil.
1977	Fire on the *Hawaiian Patriot*	Northern Pacific	Spillage of 29106000 gallons of oil.
1978	Grounding of the Cyprus tanker *Amoco Cadiz*	Portshall, France	Spillage of 65562000 gallons of oil. Pollution of 160 km/99 mi of French coast.
1979	Uranium released from secret nuclear fuel plant	Erwin, Tennessee, USA	Approximately 1000 people contaminated.
1979	Collision of *Burmah Agate*	Galveston Bay, Texas	Spillage of 10700000 gallons of oil.

Date	Event	Location	Consequence
1979	Release of radioactive steam after water pump breaks down	Three Mile Island, Pennsylvania, USA	Pollution by radioactive gases. Partial core meltdown in reactor.
1979	Blowout in Ixtoc oil well	Gulf of Mexico	176 400 000 gallons of oil spilled.
1979	Collision of the *Atlantic Empress* and *Aegean Captain*	Trinidad and Tobago	88 200 000 gallons of oil spilled.
1980	Chemical spill due to Sandez factory fire	Basel, Switzerland	Rhine polluted for 200 km/124 mi.
1983	Fire on the *Castillo de Beliver*	Cape Town, South Africa	Spillage of 73 500 000 gallons of oil.
1983	Blow-out in Nowruz oil field	Persian Gulf	Spillage of 176 400 000 gallons of oil.
1984	Union Carbide pesticide plant leaks toxic gas	Bhopal, India	Death of 2 352 people officially. Unofficially, an estimated 10 000 died.
1986	Explosion of nuclear reactor	Chernobyl, Ukraine	Official death toll 50. Radioactive cloud spread across Europe contaminating farmland. Long-term effects on inhabitants of surrounding areas are not yet ascertainable.
1987	Abandoned radiotherapy unit containing radioactive material leaks	Goiana, Brazil	Radioactive contamination affected 249 people.
1988	Accident at water-treatment works resulting in aluminium sulphate being flushed into local rivers	Camelford, Cornwall, UK	Local people suffer from stomach and skin disorders. Thousands of fish killed.
1989	Grounding of the tanker *Exxon Valdez* on Bligh Reef	Prince William Sound, Alaska, USA	Spillage of 10 080 000 gallons of oil; 1 170 km/1 162 mi of Alaskan coastline polluted. More than 3 600 km²/1 390 sq mi contaminated. Thousands of birds and animals killed.
1989	Explosion in hull of Iranian supertanker *Khark 5*	Atlantic Ocean, north of Canary Islands	Spillage of 19 000 000 gallons of crude oil and 370 km/230 mi oil slick, almost reaching Morocco.
1991	Break-up of the Greek tanker *Kiriki*	Cervantes, W Australia	Spillage of 5 880 000 gallons of crude oil and pollution of conservation and fishing areas.
1991	Oil fields set alight by Iraqi forces during the Gulf War	Kuwait	Spillage estimated between 25 000 000–130 000 000 gallons. Air pollution and potential increase in acid rain.
1992	Grounding of the Greek oil tanker *Aegean Sea*, with subsequent fire	La Coruña, Spain	Spillage of an estimated 16 000 000 gallons of crude oil, creating a slick 19 km/12 mi long and 2 km/1 mi wide and causing contamination of 80 km/50 mi of Spanish coastline. Serious pollution of sealife and clam and oyster fisheries.
1993	Break-up of the tanker *Braer* on the rocks of Pitful Head	Shetlands, Scotland, UK	Spillage of 26 000 000 gallons of oil. Slick contained to 180–270 m/200–300 yd, but serious pollution of fishing grounds and fish farms, as well as sea animals and birds.

FLORA AND FAUNA

Threatened species

Threatened animal species in selected OECD* countries (early 1980s).

Country	Mammals	Birds	Reptiles	Amphibians	Fishes
Mediterranean countries					
France	58(57)[a]	155(58)	19(39)	18(53)	20(27)
Italy	13(13)	60(14)	24(52)	13(46)	70(14)
Spain[b]	53(53)	142(37)	20(41)	18(78)	12(9)
European non-Mediterranean countries					
Austria	38(46)	121(60)	[c]	[c]	54(59)
Denmark	14(29)	41(22)	0(0)	3(21)	17(10)
Finland	21(34)	15(7)	1(20)	0(0)	4(7)
West Germany	44(47)	98(22)	9(75)	11(58)	40(23)
Hungary	14([c])	83([c])	4([c])	1([c])	2([c])

Flora and fauna

Threatened species (continued)

Country	Mammals	Birds	Reptiles	Amphibians	Fishes
Netherlands	29(48)	85(33)	6(86)	10(67)	11(22)
Norway	10(14)	28(10)	1(20)	1(20)	c
United Kingdom	26(51)	51(26)	2(33)	2(33)	18(49)
North America					
Canada	6(6)	10(2)	2(6)	2(4)	15(2)
United States	35(8)	69(6)	25(7)	8(4)	44(2)
Oceania					
Australia	40(13)	36(5)	8(1)	6(4)	c
New Zealand	14(21)	16(6)	7(19)	c	3(0)

[a] Numbers given are total numbers of threatened species in each taxonomic group. Numbers in parentheses are the threatened species expressed as a percentage of the total number of species known to exist in a particular country.
[b] Data for Spain refer to peninsular Spain and the Balearics only.
[c] Estimates not available. 'Threatened' refers to the sum of the number of species in both 'endangered' and 'vulnerable' categories, which are roughly analogous to US 'endangered' and 'threatened' categories, respectively.
* Organization for Economic Cooperation and Development (see note on page 73).

Extinction of birds and mammals

Species and subspecies of mammals and birds extinct since 1600.

Location	Mammals	Birds	Location	Mammals	Birds
Continents			New Zealand	0	16
Africa	11	0	Chatham	absent	5
Asia	11	6	Lord Howe	0	8
Australia	22	0	Norfolk	absent	6
Europe	7	0	Cebu (Philippines)	0	11
North America	22	8	Bonin, Ryukyu	0	10
South America	0	2	Other	0	21
Total	73	16	Indian Ocean		
			Madagascar	1	2
Pelagic	1	0	Christmas	3	0
			Mascarenes	0	14
Islands			Seychelles	0	2
Continental			Atlantic Ocean		
Africa	0	2	West Indies	22	15
Asia	4	0	Other	1	5
Australia	0	2	Mediterranean	2	1
North America	4	3			
Oceanic			Total: all islands	41	155
Pacific Ocean					
Galapagos	4	0	Total: all locations	115	171
Baja California islands	0	8			
Hawaii	0	24			

This tabulation omits numerous island birds believed to have become extinct after 1600 but known only from recently reported subfossil bones.

Threatened plant species

Country/region	Species	Rare and threatened taxa	Extinct taxa since 1700	Endangered taxa
Australia	25 000	1716	117	215
Europe	11 300	1927	20	117
New Zealand	2 000	186	4	42
South Africa	23 000	2122	39	107
USSR	21 100	653	~20	~160
United States (continental)	20 000	2050	90	?
Worldwide[a]	250 000	25 000	5050	15 000[b]

[a]Estimated from various sources.
[b]Includes 4 000 species from Pacific coastal Ecuador and 3 000 from Atlantic Coastal Brazil.

Tropical marine areas under threat

Habitat	Reason
Mangroves	
Niger River delta, Nigeria	Exploited for timber, fuel, fodder, and urban expansion.
Kenya and Tanzania	Cleared for fuelwood, building materials, and tourist resorts.
Indus River mouth, Pakistan	Overexploitation for fuel, fodder, and building material.
Sundarbans, India and Bangladesh	Overexploitation for fuel, fodder, timber, and fishponds.
Malaysia and Gulf of Thailand	Destruction for fish and shellfish ponds and agricultural land.
Philippines	Destruction for timber, tannin, fuelwood, and fish and shellfish ponds.
Indonesia	Massive destruction for logging and woodchip industries, fish and shellfish ponds, and for building materials and fuelwood.
Queensland, Australia	Town and tourist development.
US south coast, Texas to Florida	Over-development of coastline for urban expansion, resorts, and housing estates. Also used as rubbish dumps.
Panama	Cleared for fish and shrimp ponds.
Ecuador	Cleared for fish and shrimp ponds.
Caribbean	All mangrove stands disturbed. Main threats: tourism and coastal land development.
Seagrasses	
East Africa	Under threat from heavy sedimentation of shallow coastal waters caused by erosion of agricultural lands.
Southeast Asia	Under threat from loss of mangroves, coastal development, urban expansion, and bucket dredging for tin.
Caribbean and Gulf of Mexico	Under threat from dredge and fill operations, loss of mangroves, coastal development for tourism, and oil production.
Coral reefs	
East Africa	Coral mining for building materials, blast fishing, tourist trade, and sedimentation.
The Gulf	Oil and industrial pollution, and sedimentation.
Thailand and Malaysia	Tourist resorts, bucket dredging for tin, and over-fishing.
Philippines	Blast fishing, coral mining, collection for tourist trade, and use of poisons.
Southern Japan—Ryukyu Archipelago	Destroyed by coastal development and sedimentation.
Indonesia	Destroyed by blast fishing, coral mining, tourist trade, and coastal development.
South Pacific	Tourism, and sedimentation from coastal development.
Wider Caribbean	Collection for tourist trade, coastal development, mangrove destruction/sedimentation, and damage by boat anchors.

CONSERVATION

Protected areas – national parks

National parks, selected OECD* countries, 1990.

	Number of sites	Total size		Territory	Protected area per 1000 inhabitants	
		(km²)	(sq mi)	(%)	(ha)	(ac)
Canada	237	309 529	119 478	3.1	1179.2	2913.8
USA	59	202 320	78 095	2.2	81.3	200.9
Japan	15	12 991	5 014	3.4	10.6	26.2
Australia	339	275 551	106 363	3.6	1639.5	4 051.2
New Zealand	11	21 011	8 110	7.8	628.5	1 553.0
Finland	17	3 541	1 367	1.0	71.3	176.2
France	5	2 613	826	0.5	4.7	11.6
West Germany	1	131	50	0.1	0.2	0.5
Greece	8	526	203	0.4	5.2	12.8
Iceland	3	1 801	695	1.7	711.9	1 759.1
Ireland	3	225	87	0.3	6.4	15.8
Italy	3	1 259	486	0.4	2.2	5.4
Netherlands	1	54	21	0.1	0.4	0.9
Norway	17	19 102	7 272	5.9	451.9	1 116.6

Conservation

Protected areas – national parks (continued)

	Number of sites	Total size (km²)	(sq mi)	Territory (%)	Protected area per 1000 inhabitants (ha)	(ac)
Portugal	2	994	384	1.1	9.6	23.7
Spain	9	1 228	474	0.2	3.2	7.9
Sweden	15	5 892	2 274	1.3	69.4	171.5
Switzerland	1	169	65	0.4	2.5	6.2
Turkey	11	1 944	750	0.2	3.5	8.6
UK	1	41	16		0.1	0.2
Yugoslavia	17	4 055	1 565	1.6	17.0	42.0
OECD*	758	860 922	332 315	2.7	103.5	255.7
World	1 392	3 092 274	1 193 618	2.3	58.4	144.3

* Organization for Economic Cooperation and Development (see note on page 73).

Environmental programmes

CLIMAP	Climatic Applications Project (WMO)
COADS	Comprehensive Ocean Air Data Set
GAW	Global Atmospheric Watch
ERBE	Earth Radiation Budget Experiment
ERS	Earth Resources Satellite
GEWEX	Global Energy and Water Cycle Experiment
GMCC	Geophysical Monitoring of Climatic Change
ICRCCM	Intercomparison of Radiation Codes in Climate Models
IGAC	International Global Atmospheric Chemistry Programme
IGBP	International Geosphere-Biosphere Programme
ISCCP	International Satellite Cloud Climatology Project
JGOFS	Joint Global Ocean Flux Study
SAGE	Stratospheric Aerosol and Gas Experiment
TOGA	Tropical Ocean and Global Atmosphere
WCRP	World Climate Research Programme
WOCE	World Ocean Circulation Experiment

Multilateral conventions concerning the environment

No.	Subject	Type[a]	Place and date	No. of OECD country signatures	No. of OECD ratifications or accessions	Entry into force
	Sea pollution					
1–1	Prevention of pollution of the sea by oil (OILPOL)	Conv.	London, 1954	15	19	26 Jul 1958
1–2	Limitation of liability of owners of sea-going ships	Conv.	Brussels, 1957	14	15	31 May 1968
1–3	Pollution of the North Sea by oil	Agr.	Bonn, 1969	8	8	9 Aug 1969
1–4	Civil liability for oil pollution damage (CLC)	Conv.	Brussels, 1969	15	19	19 Jun 1975
1–4a	Protocol to amend No. 1–4	Prot.	London, 1984	10	3	pending
1–5	Intervention on the high seas in case of oil pollution (INTERVENTION)	Conv.	Brussels, 1969	18	17	6 May 1975
1–5a	Protocol to No. 1–5 (substances other than oil)	Prot.	London, 1973	8	14	30 Mar 1983
1–6	Cooperation against pollution of the sea by oil	Agr.	Copenhagen, 1971	4	4	16 Oct 1971
1–7	International fund for compensation for oil-pollution damage (FUND)	Conv.	Brussels, 1971	12	15	16 Oct 1978
1–7a	Protocol to No. 1–7 (FUND)	Prot.	London, 1976	3	11	pending
1–7b	Protocol to No. 1–7 (FUND)	Prot.	London, 1984		2	pending
1–8	Prevention of marine pollution by dumping from ships and aircraft	Conv.	Oslo, 1972	20	20	7 Apr 1974
1–9	Prevention of marine pollution by dumping of wastes and other matter (LDC)	Conv.	London, Mexico, Moscow, Washington, 1972	22	21	30 Aug 1975
1–10	Prevention of pollution from ships (MARPOL)	Conv.	London, 1973	11	5	pending
1–10a	Protocol to No. 1–10 (MARPOL PROT) (segregated ballast)	Prot.	London, 1978	8	15	2 Oct 1983

The environment

No.	Subject	Type[a]	Place and date	No. of OECD country signatures	No. of OECD ratifications or accessions	Entry into force
1–11	Protection of the marine environment of the Baltic Sea	Conv.	Helsinki, 1974	4	4	3 May 1980
1.12	Prevention of marine pollution from land-based sources	Conv.	Paris, 1974	13 (+EU)	11 (+EU)	6 May 1978
1–13	Protection of the Mediterranean Sea against pollution	Conv.	Barcelona, 1976	5 (+EU)	5 (+EU)	12 Feb 1978
1–13a	Protocol to No. 1–13 (dumping from ships and aircraft)	Prot.	Barcelona, 1976	5 (+EU)	5 (+EU)	12 Feb 1978
1–13b	Protocol to No. 1–13 (pollution by oil/cooperation in emergency cases)	Prot.	Barcelona, 1976	5 (+EU)	5 (+EU)	12 Feb 1978
1–13c	Protocol to No. 1–13 (protection against land-based sources)	Prot.	Athens, 1980	4 (+EU)	2 (+EU)	17 Jun 1983
1–14	Limitation of liability for maritime claims (LLMC)	Conv.	London, 1976	8	8	1 Dec 1986
1–15	Law of the Sea	Conv.	Montego Bay, 1982	24 (+EU)	1	pending
1–16	Protocol concerning Mediterranean specially protected areas	Prot.	Geneva, 1982	4		pending
1–17	Cooperation in dealing with pollution of the North Sea by oil and other substances	Agr.	Bonn, 1983	8	(+EU)	pending
1–18	Protection and development of the wider Caribbean region	Conv.	Cartagena, 1983	4 (+EU)	0	pending
1–18a	Protocol to No. 1–18 (oil spills)	Prot.	Cartagena, 1983			pending
1–18b	Protocol to No. 1–18 (specially protected areas and wildlife)	Prot.	1990			
1–19	Protection of the natural resources and environment of the South Pacific	Conv.	Noumea, 1986		3	pending

Nuclear

No.	Subject	Type[a]	Place and date	No. of OECD country signatures	No. of OECD ratifications or accessions	Entry into force
2–1	Third-party liability for nuclear energy	Conv.	Paris, 1960	16	14	1 Apr 1968
2–1a	Protocol to No. 2–1.	Prot.	Paris, 1982	17	13	7 Oct 1988
2–2	Liability of operators of nuclear ships	Conv.	Brussels, 1962	5 (+EU)	2	pending
2–3	Supplementary to No. 2–1 (third-party liability for nuclear energy)	Conv.	Brussels, 1963	13	11	4 Dec 1974
2–3a	Additional protocol to No. 2–3	Prot.	Paris, 1982	13	10	pending
2–4	Banning nuclear weapons tests in the atmosphere, outer space, and under water	Conv.	Moscow, 1963	23	23	10 Oct 1963
2–5	Prohibition of nuclear weapons on the sea-bed, ocean floor, and sub-soil	Conv.	London, Moscow, Washington, 1971	22	22	18 May 1972
2–6	Civil liability in maritime carriage of nuclear material	Conv.	Brussels, 1971	10	8	15 Jul 1975
2–7	Early notification of a nuclear accident	Conv.	Vienna, 1986	22	8	27 Oct 1986
2–8	Assistance in the case of a nuclear accident or radiological emergency	Conv.	Vienna, 1986	21	4	26 Feb 1987
2–9	Joint protocol relating to the application of the Vienna Convention and the Paris Convention	Prot.	Vienna, 1988	15	1	pending

Flora and fauna

No.	Subject	Type[a]	Place and date	No. of OECD country signatures	No. of OECD ratifications or accessions	Entry into force
3–1	Preservation of fauna and flora	Conv.	London, 1933	6	4	14 Jan 1936
3–2	Regulation of whaling	Conv.	Washington, 1946	7	17	10 Nov 1948
3–3	Conservation of the living resources of the South-East Atlantic	Conv.	Rome, 1969	6	7	24 Oct 1971
3–4	Wetlands of international importance especially as waterfowl habitat	Conv.	Ramsar, 1971	13	22	21 Dec 1975
3–5	Protection of world cultural and natural heritage	Conv.	Paris, 1972	17	17	17 Dec 1975
3–6	Antarctic seals	Conv.	London, 1972	8	7	23 Nov 1972
3–7	Polar bears	Agr.	Oslo, 1973	4	4	26 May 1976
3–8	Fishing and conservation of the living resources in the Baltic Sea	Conv.	Gdańsk, 1973	4	EU	28 Jul 1974

Multilateral conventions concerning the environment (continued)

No.	Subject	Type[a]	Place and date	No. of OECD country signatures	No. of OECD ratifications or accessions	Entry into force
3–9	International trade in endangered species	Conv.	Washington, 1973	17	20	1 Jul 1975
3–10	Future multilateral cooperation in the North-West Atlantic fisheries	Conv.	Ottawa, 1978	6 (+EU)	3 (+EU)	1 Jan 1979
3–11	European wildlife and natural habitats	Conv.	Bern, 1979	18 (+EU)	17 (+EU)	1 Jun 1982
3–12	Conservation of migratory species of wild animals	Conv.	Bonn, 1979	13 (+EU)	12 (+EU)	1 Nov 1983
3–13	Conservation of antarctic marine living resources	Conv.	Canberra, 1980	9 (+EU)	9 (+EU)	7 Apr 1982
3–14	Biological diversity	Conv.	Rio de Janeiro, 1992	22 (+EU)	1	pending
Air pollution						
4–1	Long-range transboundary air pollution	Conv.	Geneva, 1979	21 (+EU)	21 (+EU)	16 Mar 1983
4–1a	Protocol to 4–1 on the reduction of sulphur emissions or their transboundary fluxes by 30%	Prot.	Helsinki, 1985	13	12	2 Sep 1987
4–1b	Protocol to 4–1 concerning the control of emissions of nitrogen oxides or their transboundary fluxes	Prot.	Sofia, 1988	14	4	pending
4–2	Transfrontier cooperation	Conv.	Madrid, 1980	9	11	22 Dec 1981
4–3	Protection of the ozone layer	Conv.	Vienna, 1985	17 (+EU)	23 (+EU)	1 Jan 1989
4–4	Protocol to 4–4	Prot.	Montreal, 1987	17 (+EU)	23 (+EU)	1 Jan 1989
Rhine pollution						
5–1	Protection of the Rhine against pollution	Agr.	Bonn, 1963	5 (+EU)	5 (+EU)	1 May 1965
5–2	Rhine chloride pollution	Conv.	Bonn, 1976	4	4	1985
5–3	Protection of the Rhine against chemical pollution	Conv.	Bonn, 1976	5 (+EU)	5 (+EU)	1 Feb 1979
Miscellaneous						
6–1	International carriage of dangerous goods by road (ADR)	Agr.	Geneva, 1957	14		29 Jan 1968
6–2	Restriction of use of detergents	Agr.	Strasbourg, 1968	9	10	16 Feb 1971
6–2a	Protocol amending No. 6–2	Prot.	Strasbourg, 1983	5	3	1 Nov 1984
6–3	International liability for damage caused by space objects	Conv.	London, Moscow, Washington, 1972	15	22	17 Aug 1972
6–4	Nordic environmental protection	Conv.	Stockholm, 1974	4	4	5 Oct 1976
6–5	Prohibition of military use of environmental modification techniques	Conv.	Geneva, 1977	19	11	5 Oct 1978
6–6	Protection of workers against air pollution, noise and vibration (ILO 148)	Conv.	Geneva, 1977		6	11 Jul 1979
6–7	Control of transboundary movements of hazardous wastes and their disposal	Conv.	Basel, 1989			
6–8	Civil liability for damage caused during carriage of dangerous goods by road, rail, and inland navigation vessels (CRTD)	Conv.	Geneva, 1990			

[a] Abbreviations: Agr. – Agreement; Conv. – Convention; Prot. – Protocol.

Waste-recycling activities

Recovery rates, selected countries, 1975–1989.

Percentage (%)

	Paper and cardboard				Glass				
	1975	*1980*	*1985*	*1989*	*1975*	*1980*	*1985*	*1987*	*1989*
Canada		18.0	18.0	23.0		12.0	12.0		
USA	15.4		20.0		2.9		8.0		
Japan	39.6	48.1	49.6			35.3	47.2	54.4	
Australia			31.8				17.0		
New Zealand			19.0				53.0		
Austria		30.0	36.8			20.0	38.0	44.0	
Belgium	8.7	14.7				33.0	42.0	39.0	
Denmark	28.4	25.6	31.3	29.7		8.0	53.9	55.0	
Finland	29.0	35.0	39.0	40.0		10.0	21.0	25.0	
France	31.7	37.0	41.3	45.7		20.0	26.0	26.1	28.5
West Germany	34.2	33.9	43.6	43.0	7.7	24.0	35.5	39.4	42.3
Ireland	22.0	15.0				8.0	7.0	8.0	
Italy						20.0	25.0	38.0	
Netherlands	42.0	45.5	50.3	58.4		41.0	53.0	62.0	55.2
Norway	23.8	21.9	21.1	23.2					10.0
Portugal		38.0					10.0	14.0	
Spain		38.1	44.1				13.1	22.0	
Sweden	30.0	34.0	40.0				20.0		22.0
Switzerland		38.0				36.0	46.0	47.0	
UK	28.0	29.0	27.0	27.0		5.0	12.0	14.0	18.0

* Much of the data in this section comes from the Organization for Economic Cooperation and Development (OECD).
OECD Europe refers to all EU member countries of OECD, plus Austria, Finland, Iceland, Norway, Sweden, Switzerland, and Turkey.
OECD refers to all members of OECD Europe, plus Canada, US, Japan, Australia, and New Zealand.

NATURAL HISTORY

Natural history

CLASSIFICATION OF LIVING ORGANISMS

It has been estimated that between 3 million and 20 million different kinds of organism are alive in the world today. Large numbers of other organisms have become extinct, and some of these are preserved as fossils. Most modern schemes of classification of living organisms are based upon the pioneering work of the Swedish biologist Carl von Linné (in Latin, Carolus Linnaeus; 1707–78), who established the practice of *binomial nomenclature*, by which all organisms are given two names, traditionally printed in italics. The first name is that of the *genus*, and is common to a group of closely related organisms. The second is that of the *species* and is unique to a particular type of organism. Higher levels of classification show a hierarchy of relationships. These are illustrated here using the human species as an example.

Classification of the human species

Taxonomic level

Kingdom	Animalia	(animals)
Phylum (division)[a]	Chordata	(chordates)
Subphylum	Vertebrata	(vertebrates)
Class	Mammalia	(mammals)
Order	Primates	
Family	Hominoidea	(hominids)
Genus	*Homo*	
Species	*sapiens*	

[a] In classifiying plants, fungi and bacteria, the term *division* is used rather than *phylum*.

The five kingdoms

While almost all modern systems of classification use the same basic taxonomic system, there are several different ways of grouping living organisms together. This book uses the popular Whittaker system, which divides the living world into five kingdoms.

Kingdom	*Members of kingdom*
Prokaryotae*	Monera, or bacteria
Protoctista	Algae, protozoans, slime moulds
Fungi	Mushrooms, moulds, lichens
Animalia	Animals
Plantae	Plants

*The kingdom Prokaryotae is sometimes given to include the viruses. Other systems describe viruses as being outside normal systems of classification.

ANIMALS

The animal kingdom is usually divided into about 30 phyla, which differ enormously in size and are listed here in order of primitive to advanced.

Classification of animals

Phylum	Common name/examples	No. of species	Comments
Placozoa	*Trichoplax adhaerens*	1	The only species in the phylum, this is the simplest animal known. No tissues, organs, or symmetry.
Porifera	Sponges	10000	All aquatic: vast majority in sea-water, 150 in fresh water. No tissues, organs, or symmetry.
Cnidaria	Coelenterates; *hydra;* true jellyfish; corals; sea anemones	9500	Nearly all marine. Radially symmetrical with tissues and organs; have stinging cells (nematocysts) on tentacles.
Ctenophora	Comb jellies; sea gooseberries	90	Aquatic; transparent.
Mesozoa	Mesozoans	50	Small, worm-like organisms.
Platyhelminthes	Flatworms; flukes; tapeworms	15000	Ribbon-shaped and soft-bodied; the least complex of the animals that have heads.
Nemertina	Ribbon worms or proboscis worms	900	Characteristic feature is long, sensitive anterior proboscis, used to explore the environment and capture prey.
Gnasthostomulida	Jaw worms or gnasthostomulids	80	Microscopic marine worms.
Gastrotricha	Gastrotrichs	400	Aquatic microscopic animals with cilia on their bodies.

Classification of animals (continued)

Phylum	Common name/examples	No. of species	Comments
Rotifera	Rotifers or wheel animals	2000	Aquatic microscopic animals with their anterior end modified into a ciliary organ called a *corona*, the beating of which resembles a rotating wheel.
Kinorhyncha	Kinorhynchs	150	Small worm-like marine animals.
Loricifera	Loriciferans	10	Tiny marine animals whose abdomen is covered by a girdle of spiny plates called a *lorica*.
Acanthocephala	Spiny-headed worms	600	Gut parasites of vertebrates, usually of carnivores.
Entoprocta	Entoprocts	150	Small marine animals, mostly sedentary, living in colonies attached to rocks, shells, algae, or other animals.
Nematoda	Nematodes or roundworms	>80000	Unsegmented, more or less cylindrical worms which occur free-living in all types of environment, and also as parasites of plants and animals. It has been estimated that there may be as many as 1 million species of nematode in the world (ie vast numbers of undiscovered species). In terms of numbers of individuals, nematodes are the most abundant group of multicellular animals.
Nematomorpha	Horsehair worms; hair-worms; Gordian worms	240	Very long, thin worms which are parasitic in insects and crustaceans as juveniles, and free-living in water as adults.
Ectoprocta	Ectoprocts	5000	Small aquatic animals, mostly colonial.
Phoronida	Horseshoe worms; phoronids	10	Marine worms with as many as 1500 hollow tentacles. Live in tubes which they secrete and strengthen with sand or shell fragments.
Brachiopoda	Lamp shells	335	Bottom-living marine animals with shells with two valves. They thrived during the Palaeozoic era – more than 30000 extinct species have been described.
Mollusca	Molluscs, including snails, slugs (gastropods), clams, mussels, oysters (bivalves), octopus, squid (cephalopoda)	110 000	The second largest phylum of animals, molluscs live in aquatic or moist environments, are soft-bodied, and are usually protected by a calcareous shell which is secreted by a fold of the body wall called the *mantle*.
Priapulida	Priapulids	10	Small carnivorous marine worms.
Sipuncula	Peanut worms	>300	Unsegmented marine worms, which live in crevices or are burrowing.
Echiura	Spoon worms	140	Unsegmented marine worms, which burrow in marine deposits.
Annelida	Annelids, including earthworms, leeches, ragworms	8900	Worms with a well-developed coelom, and with the body divided up into a number of more or less similar segments. Terrestrial, freshwater, or marine.
Tardigrada	Water bears; tardigrades	380	Minute animals which live in films of water around mosses and other low terrestrial features. Four pairs of stubby legs armed with terminal claws.

Phylum	Common name/examples	No. of species	Comments
Pentastoma	Tongue worms	70	Parasitic worms in the respiratory passages of air-breathing vertebrates. They have a chitinous cuticle which is periodically moulted to allow growth.
Onychophora	Velvet worms; onychophorans	80	Soft-bodied, segmented animals with many paired but unjointed legs. Confined to humid tropics.
Arthropoda	Arthropods, including crustaceans (shrimps, barnacles, woodlice, crabs), scorpions, mites, ticks, spiders, insects, centipedes, millipedes	>2 000 000	By far the largest animal phylum, with more species than all the other phyla combined (more than 800 000 species of insects alone have been described; some zoologists think there may be as many as 10 million). Arthropods are segmented animals with paired, jointed appendages on some or all of their body segments.
Pogonophora	Beard worms	100	Extremely slender, gutless, tube-living marine worms.
Echinodermata	Echinoderms, including starfish, sea urchins, sea cucumbers	6 000	Marine, mostly bottom-dwelling animals, usually displaying five-fold symmetry. The fluid-filled tube feet are used for locomotion and feeding.
Chaetognatha	Arrow worms	>100	Small, slender, torpedo-shaped marine planktonic animals which are voracious carnivores.
Hemichordata	Hemichordates	90	Small soft-bodied animals which inhabit shallow U-shaped burrows in sandy or muddy sea bottoms.
Chordata	Mammals; birds; amphibians; reptiles; fish; plus a small number of invertebrates	45 000	The best known phylum of Animalia, containing all the species which, in the minds of many, are considered 'animals'. Chordates are distinguished by having (i) the walls of their pharynx, at some stage in their life cycle, perforated by gill clefts; (ii) a hollow dorsal nerve cord; (iii) an axial cartilaginous rod – the *notochord* – lying immediatedly beneath the nerve cord. Most chordates have backbones and are called *vertebrates*, but two of the three subphyla are small *invertebrate* groups.

Animal records

Size
This table shows the largest species in the animal kingdom, plus some others of particular interest. Unless otherwise stated: (i) *largest* means bulkiest and heaviest; (ii) the size given is the largest size regularly attained by the species, not that of individual 'record-holders'.

Species		Dimension	Size (m)	(ft)	Comments
Mammals					
Cetacea	Blue whale (*Balaenoptera musculis*)	Length	35.0	115	The largest and longest-living mammal, and the largest animal ever known.
	Sperm whale (*Physeter catadon*)	Length	25.0	82	The largest-toothed mammal and the largest marine carnivore[a].
Marine carnivores	Sperm whale (see above) Southern elephant seal (*Mirounga leonina*)	Length	6.0	20	The largest seal.

Animals

Animal records (continued)

	Species	Dimension	Size (m)	(ft)	Comments
Ungulates	African elephant (*Loxodonta africana*)	Height	3.2	10.5	The largest land mammal.
	Giraffe (*Giraffa camelopardalis*)	Height	5.5	18.0	The tallest land mammal.
Terrestrial carnivores	Kodiak bear (*Ursus arctos middendorffi*)	Length	2.4	7.8	The largest land carnivore.
	Indian tiger (*Panthera tigris tigris*)	Length	3.15	10.3	The largest member of the cat family.
Primates	Eastern lowland mountain gorilla (*Gorilla gorilla graueri*)	Height (standing)	1.88	6.2	The largest and tallest primate[b].
Rodents	Capybara (*Hydrochoerus hydrochoerus*)	Length	1.4	4.6	The largest rodent.
	Coypu (*Myocastor coypus*)	Length	0.9	2.9	
Marsupials	Red kangaroo (*Megaleia rufa*)	Height	2.15	7.1	The largest marsupial.
Birds	Ostrich (*Struthio camelus*)	Height	2.75	9.0	The largest and tallest bird.
Reptiles	Estuarine or saltwater crocodile (*Crocodylus porosus*)	Length	4.8	15.7	The largest reptile.
Snakes	Anaconda (*Eunectes murinus*)	Length	8.5	27.8	The largest snake.
	Reticulated python (*Python reticulatus*)	Length	10.0	32.8	The longest snake.
Lizards	Komodo monitor (*Varanus komodoensis*)	Length	2.25	7.4	The largest lizard.
	Salvadori monitor (*Varanus salvadori*)	Length	4.75	15.6	The longest lizard.
amphibians	Giant salamander (*Andrias davidianus*)	Length	1.2	3.9	The largest amphibian.
Fishes					
Marine	Whale shark (*Rhincodon typus*)	Length	13.0	43.0	The largest marine fish.
Freshwater	Sturgeon (*Acipenseridae* spp.)	Length	5.0	16.4	The largest freshwater fish.
	European catfish (*Siluridae* spp.)	Length	4.0	13.1	
Molluscs	Atlantic giant squid (*Architeuthis dux*)	length	17.0	56.0	The largest mollusc and the largest invertebrate.
	Pacific giant octopus (*Octopus dofleini*)	length	10.0	32.8	
Crustaceans					
Marine	Giant spider crab (*Macrocheira kaempferi*)	Claw span	2.7	8.8	The largest crustacean.
	North Atlantic lobster (*Homarus americanus*)	Length	1.06	3.5	The heaviest crustacean.
Freshwater	Crayfish (*Astacopsis gouldi*)	Length	0.6	1.9	The largest freshwater crustacean.
Worms	Bootlace worm (*Lineus longissimus*)	Length	40.0	131.0	The longest worm.
Jellyfish	Arctic giant (*Cyanae capillata arctica*)	Diameter	2.2	7.2	The largest jellyfish.
		Length of tentacles	35.0	115.0	
Insects	Goliath beetle (*Scarabaeidae* spp.)	Length	0.11	0.4	The largest insect.
	Queen Alexandra's birdwing (*Ornithoptera alexandrae*)	Wing-span	0.28	0.9	The largest butterfly.
Spiders	Goliath bird-eating spider (*Theraphosa leblondi*)	Leg-span	0.25	0.8	The largest spider.

[a] Discounting the filter-feeding baleen whales (eg the blue whale) which feed on small crustaceans such as krill.

[b] Humans (*Homo sapiens*) regularly exceed this height. In fact, the tallest recorded human, Robert Pershing Wadlow (1918-40), who measured 2.72 m/8.9 ft at his death, is probably the tallest ever primate.

spp. = species

Weight

	tonnes
Blue whale	120
Sperm whale	50
Right whale	50
Whale shark	43
Basking shark	40
African elephant	6
White shark	5
Elephant seal	4
Hippopotamus	3
Manta ray	3
White rhinoceros	2
Moonfish	2
Saltwater crocodile	1.5
American bison	1.5
Leatherback turtle	0.8
Kodiak bear	0.74
Gorilla	0.35
Anaconda	0.23

Speed in the air

Mammals	km/h	mph
Bat	20–50	12–30

Birds
Diving

	km/h	mph
Peregrine falcon	360	220
Golden eagle	300	185

Horizontal flight	km/h	mph
Swift	200	120
Teal	120	75
Oystercatcher	100	60
Swan	90	55
Duck	85	53
Partridge	84	52
Pheasant	60	35
Crane	50	30
Gull	40	25
Crow	40	25

Fish

	km/h	mph
Flying fish	90	55

Insects

	km/h	mph
Dragonfly	75	45
Hawkmoth	50	30
Hoverfly	14	9
Bumblebee	11	7

Speed in water

Mammals

	km/h	mph
Dolphin	64	40
Killer whale	55	34
Sea lion	40	25

Birds

	km/h	mph
Penguin	40	25

Reptiles

	km/h	mph
Leatherback turtle	35	22

Fish

	km/h	mph
Sailfish	110	68
Swordfish	90	55
Blue shark	70	44
Tuna	70	44
Salmon	40	25
Trout	37	23
Pike	33	20

Speed on the ground

Mammals

	km/h	mph
Cheetah	110	68
Roe deer	98	61
Antelope	95	59
Lion	80	50
Red deer	78	48
Hare	70	44
Horse	69	43
Zebra	65	40
Greyhound	60	35
Giraffe	50	30
Wolf	45	28
Elephant	40	25

Birds

	km/h	mph
Ostrich	50	30

Reptiles

	km/h	mph
Crocodile	13	8
Mamba	11	7

Mammals

Order	Family	Common name/examples	No. of species	Distribution of order	General characteristics of order
Monotremes	Ornithorhynchidae	Platypus	1	Australia	Lay eggs from which young are hatched.
	Tachyglossidae	Echidna (spiny anteater)	2		
Marsupialia	Didelphidae	Opossums	65	Australia, S and C America	Premature birth of young and continued development outside the womb.
	Thylacinidae	Tasmanian wolf	1		
	Dasyuridae	Native cats; marsupial mice	48		
	Myrmecobiidae	Numbat	1		
	Notoryctidae	Marsupial moles	2		
	Peramelidae	Bandicoots	22		
	Thylacomyidae	Burrowing bandicoots	20		
	Caenolestidae	Rat opossums	7		
	Phalangeridae	Phalangers; cuscuses	15		
	Burramyidae	Pigmy possums; feathertail gliders	6		
	Petauridae	Gliding phalangers	25		
	Macropodidae	Kangaroos; wallabies	47		
	Phascolarctidae	Koala	1		
	Vombatidae	Wombats	4		
	Tarsipedidae	Honey possum	1		
Insectivora	Erinaceidae	Hegdehogs; gymnures	14	Europe, N and S America, Asia, Australia	Active mainly at night; do not need to rely on vision for orientation.
	Talpidae	Moles	22		
	Tenrecidae	Tenrecs	20		
	Potamogalidae	Otter shrews	3		
	Chrysochloridae	Golden moles	11		

Mammals (continued)

Order	Family	Common name/examples	No. of species	Distribution of order	General characteristics of order
	Solenodontidae	Solenodon, almiqui	2		
	Soricidae	Shrews	291		
	Macroscelididae	Elephant shrews	28		
	Tupaiidae	Tree shrews	15		
Chiroptera	Pteropodidae	Old World fruit bats; flying foxes	154	Europe, N and S America, Asia, Africa, Australia	Insectivorous; nocturnal; migrate annually to and from summer roosts and winter migration sites; use echolocation for orientation; order defined by true flight.
	Rhinopomatidae	Mouse-tailed bats	3		
	Emballonuridae	Sheath-tailed or sac-winged bats	50		
	Nycteridae	Slit-faced or hollow-faced bats	13		
	Megadermatidae	False vampires	5		
	Hipposideridae	Old World leaf-nosed bats	60		
	Rhinolophidae	Horseshoe bats	70		
	Noctilionidae	Bulldog bats	2		
	Mormoopidae	Insectivorous bats	9		
	Phyllostomatidae	American leaf-nosed bats	120		
	Desmodontidae	Vampire bats	3		
	Natalidae	Funnel-eared bats	4		
	Furipteridae	Smoky bats	2		
	Thyropteridae	Disk-wing bats	2		
	Myzopodidae	Old World sucker-footed bats	1		
	Vespertilionidae	Common bats	290		
	Mystacinidae	New Zealand short-tailed bats	1		
	Molossidae	Free-tailed bats	90		
Rodentia	Aplodontidae	Mountain beaver or sewellel	1	Europe, Asia, N and S America, Africa, Australia	One pair of upper and lower incisors which grow throughout life; broadly herbivorous; gnawing mechanism; clawed digits.
	Sciuridae	Squirrels; chipmunks; marmots	250		
	Cricetidae	Field mice; deer mice; voles; lemmings; muskrats	560		
	Muridae	Old World rats and mice	450		
	Heteromyidae	Mice; pocket mice; kangaroo rats	75		
	Geomyidae	Pocket gophers	40		
	Zapodidae	Jumping and birch mice	10		
	Dipodidae	Jerboas	25		
	Spalacidae	Mole rats	3		
	Rhizomyidae	Bamboo rats; African mole rats	18		
	Octodontidae	Octodonts; degus	7		
	Echimyidae	Spiny rats; rock rats	40		
	Ctenomyidae	Tuco-tucos	26		
	Abrocomidae	Abrocomes or chinchilla rats	2		
	Chinchillidae	Chinchillas; viscachas	6		
	Capromyidae	Hutias; coypus	10		
	Dasyproctidae	Pacas; agoutis	13		
	Dinomyidae	Pacarana or Branick's paca	1		
	Caviidae	Cavies; guinea pigs; maras	12		
	Hydrochoeridae	Capybaras	2		
	Erethizontidae	New World porcupines	8		
	Petromuridae	Rock or dassie rat	1		
	Thryonomyidae	Cane rats	2		
	Bathyergidae	Blesmols or African mole rats	9		
	Hystricidae	Old World porcupines	15		
	Castoridae	Beavers	2		
	Anomaluridae	Scaly-tailed squirrels	7		
	Ctenodactylidae	Gundis	8		
	Pedetidae	Cape jumping hare or springhaas	1		
	Gliridae	Dormice	20		
	Seleveniidae	Jumping dormouse	1		

Order	Family	Common name/examples	No. of species	Distribution of order	General characteristics of order
Edentata	Myrmecophagidae	Anteaters	3	S and N America	Reduced dentition; long sticky tongue; powerful clawed forefeet.
	Bradypodidae	Tree sloths	5		
	Dasypodidae	Armadillos	20		
Lagomorpha	Ochotonidae	Pikas	14	Asia, N America, Europe, S Africa, S America, Australia	Herbivorous; well-developed incisors which grow continuously from roots; elongation of the limbs distally.
	Leporidae	Hares; rabbits	46		
Carnivora	Canidae	Dogs; foxes; wolves; jackals	35	Europe, Asia, N America, S America, Africa, Australia	High level of intelligence; highly developed sense of smell; varied dentition; well-developed carnassials.
	Ursidae	Bears; giant panda	7		
	Otariidae	Eared seals; walrus	15		
	Procyonidae	Raccoons; coatis; lesser panda	15		
	Mustelidae	Weasels; otters; skunks; badgers; mink	65		
	Phocidae	Earless seals	20		
	Felidae	Cats	35		
	Viverridae	Civets; mongooses; genet	70		
	Hyaenidae	Hyenas	4		
Cetacea	Balaenidae	Right whales	3	S America, Africa, N America, Europe, Asia, Antarctica, Australia	Breathe through blowholes; tapered body; develop young internally and give birth at sea; long breeding period; hearing is major sense; migrate seasonally.
	Eschrichtiidae	Grey whales	1		
	Balaenopteridae	Rorquals; humpbacks	8		
	Platanistidae	River dolphins	4		
	Delphinidae	Dolphins; killer whales	30		
	Phocoenidae	Porpoises	6		
	Monodontidae	Beluga; narwhal	2		
	Physeteridae	Sperm whales	3		
	Hyperoodontidae (formerly Ziphiidae)	Beaked whales	15		
	Stenidae	Long-snouted dolphins	4		
Proboscidea	Elephantidae	African elephant, Asian elephant	2	Africa, Asia	Bulky bodies and elongated snout; each toe has heavy hoof nail; no canine teeth; herbivorous.
Sirenia	Dugongidae	Dugong	1	Australia, S America, Africa	Herbivorous; totally aquatic; torpedo-shaped bodies; tough, almost hairless skin; body contains much fat.
	Trichechidae	Manatees	3		
Perissodactyla	Equidae	Horses; asses; zebras; donkeys	7	Africa, Europe, Asia	Herbivorous; high-crowned grinding teeth.
	Tapiridae	Tapirs	4		
	Rhinocerotidae	Rhinoceroses	5		
Artiodactyla	Tragulidae	Chevrotains	4	Asia, Africa, C and S America	Ruminants; herbivorous; cloven-hoofed; moderately large brain; migrate seasonally.
	Antilocapridae	Pronghorn	1		
	Giraffidae	Giraffe; okapi	2		
	Cervidae	Deer	35		
	Bovidae	Cattle; goats; sheep; antelopes; gazelles	110		
	Camelidae	Camels; llamas	4		
	Suidae	Pigs	8		
	Tayassuidae	Peccaries	3		
	Hippopotamidae	Hippopotamuses	2		

Animals

Mammals (continued)

Order	Family	Common name/examples	No. of species	Distribution of order	General characteristics of order
Primates	Lemuridae	Lemurs	14	Africa, Asia,	Omnivorous; multi-
	Cheirogaleidae	Dwarf lemurs; mouse lemurs	4	S America	purpose dentition;
	Indriidae	Indris; sifaka; avahi	4	(man is	large brain; body
	Daubentoniidae	Aye aye (lemur)	1	distributed	position upright;
	Lepilmuridae	Sportive lemurs	2	worldwide)	five-digit hands and
	Galagidae	Galagos	7		feet; stereoscopic
	Lorisidae	Lorises; pottos; bushbabies	12		vision.
	Tupaiidae	Tree shrews	17		
	Tarsiidae	Tarsiers	3		
	Callitrichidae	Tamarins; marmosets	15		
	Cebidae	New World monkeys	30		
	Cercopithecidae	Old World monkeys	72		
	Hylobatidae	Gibbons; siamang	7		
	Pongidae	Great apes: gorilla, chimpanzee, orangutan	10		
	Hominidae	Man	1		

Length of pregnancy in some mammals

Animal	Gestation period[a]	Animal	Gestation period[a]	Animal	Gestation period[a]
Camel	406	Hamster	16	Pig	113
Cat	62	Hedgehog	35–40	Rabbit	32
Cow	280	Horse	337	Rat	21
Chimpanzee	237	Human	266	Reindeer	215–45
Dog	62	Hyena	110	Seal, northern fur	350
Dolphin	276	Kangaroo	40	Sheep	148
Elephant, African	640	Lion	108	Skunk	62
Ferret	42	Mink	50	Squirrel, grey	44
Fox	52	Monkey, rhesus	164	Tiger	105–9
Giraffe	395–425	Mouse	21	Whale	365
Goat	151	Opossum	13		
Guinea pig	68	Orangutan	245–75		

[a]Average number of days.

Classification of birds

This table uses the Voous taxonomic sequence running from what are supposed to be the most primitive families to the newest ones.

Order	Family	Common name/ examples	No. of species	Distribution of family	General characteristics of order
Struthioniformes	Struthionidae	Ostrich	1	Africa	The ostrich is the world's largest living bird. Swift-running, flightless and gregarious; ground-nesting; feeds on vegetable matter.
Rheiformes	Rheidae	Rheas	2	S America	Swift-running, flightless ground-nesting birds which feed on vegetation and insects. Ostrich-like with short wings and no tailfeathers.
Casuariiformes	Casuariidae	Cassowaries	3	Australia	Large, flightless, running
	Dromaiidae	Emu	1	and adjacent islands	birds with three toes and rough, hair-like plumage.

Order	Family	Common name/ examples	No. of species	Distribution of family	General characteristics of order
Apterygiformes	Apterygidae	Kiwis	3	New Zealand	Small-eyed, flightless, tailless birds with vestigial wings. They nest in burrows; are mainly nocturnal, insectivorous, and forest-dwelling.
Tinamiformes	Tinamidae	Tinamous	45	S and C America	Terrestrial, ground-nesting birds which can fly but do so rarely. They have patterned plumage; feed on vegetation; and live in grassland, brush, and forest.
Sphenisciformes	Spheniscidae	Penguins	16	Antarctica, Australia, Africa, S America	Black-and-white, flightless, aquatic birds. They nest in burrows or on the ground and are good swimmers, living off fish, squid, and crustacea. Walk upright or glide on their stomachs. Specially adapted feet feature a highly efficient heat-exchange mechanism to ensure survival in cold climates.
Gaviiformes	Gaviidae	Divers or loons	4	N America, Eurasia	Black and brown diving birds which breed on inland lakes and nest on the ground. They eat mostly fish, and winter on sea coasts. Clumsy on land, their legs are adapted for swimming and diving.
Podicipediformes	Podicipedidae	Grebes	20	Africa, Europe, Asia, Australia, N and S America	Large grey and brown short-winged diving birds with partly webbed feet. They eat fish, and nest on the water. They inhabit freshwater lakes in the summer and sea coasts in winter. Some are migratory.
Procellariiformes	Diomedeidae	Albatrosses	14	Seas worldwide	Generally long-winged, partly webbed-toed seabirds which feed on fish and nest on isolated islands and cliffs. Some species discharge oil in self-defence.
	Procellariidae	Petrels; fulmars; shearwaters	55		
	Hydrobatidae	Storm petrels	20		
	Pelecanoididae	Diving petrels	4		
Pelecaniformes	Pelecanidae	Pelicans	7	All continents	Diverse order of diving birds, found in marine and freshwater coastal habitats worldwide. They nest on cliffs or in trees; have a diet of mostly fish; and are generally web-toed.
	Sulidae	Gannets; boobies	9	N Atlantic, S Africa, Australasia, tropical oceans	
	Phaethontidae	Tropicbirds	3	Tropical oceans	
	Phalacrocoracidae	Cormorants	29	Worldwide	
	Fregatidae	Frigatebirds	5	Tropical oceans	
	Anhingidae	Darters	4	N and S America, Africa, Asia, Australasia	

Classification of birds (continued)

Order	Family	Common name/ examples	No. of species	Distribution of family	General characteristics of order
Ciconiiformes	Ardeidae	Herons; bitterns	60	Worldwide except northernmost America and Eurasia	Upright, wading birds with specialized bills. Their toes are sometimes webbed and the middle claw is often serrated, or pectinate, for preening.
	Scopidae	Hammerhead	1	SW Arabia, Sub-Saharan Africa	
	Balaenicipitidae	Whale-headed stork	1	Africa	
	Ciconiidae	Storks	17	N America, Eurasia	
	Threskiornithidae	Spoonbills; ibises	31	Worldwide	
	Phoenicopteridae	Flamingos	5	Tropical zones	
Anseriformes	Anatidae	Ducks; geese; swans	147	Worldwide except Antarctica	Marsh-dwelling waterbirds which eat mostly vegetation and nest on the ground.
	Anhimidae	Screamers	3	S America	
Falconiformes	Cathartidae	Vultures (New World)	7	Americas	Birds of prey, or *raptors*. Expert fliers, they have hooked beaks and talons; and are generally large, heavily feathered birds with excellent eyesight and good hearing.
	Sagittariidae	Secretary-bird	1	Sub-Saharan Africa	
	Pandionidae	Osprey	1	Worldwide	
	Falconidae	Falcons; caracaras	60	Worldwide except Antarctica	
	Accipitridae	Kites; Old World vultures; harriers; hawks; eagles; buzzards	217	Worldwide except Antarctica	
Galliformes	Megapodidae	Megapodes	9	E Indies, Malaysia, New Guinea, Australia	The Galliformes, or gamebirds, have short, rounded wings, ill-adapted for sustained flight. They have large feet and claws, and are usually omnivorous in diet. The male plumage is often brilliant. Many are endangered owing to habitat destruction and over-hunting.
	Cracidae	Guans; curassows; chachalacas	42	Americas	
	Tetraonidae	Grouse	16	Eurasia, Americas	
	Phasianidae	Pheasants; quail; partridge	180	Worldwide, except N Eurasia and S America	
	Numididae	Guineafowl	7	Sub-Saharan Africa	
	Meleagrididae	Turkeys	2	N and S America	
Gruiformes	Mesitornithidae	Mesites	3	Madagascar	Diverse order of ground-feeding birds, generally with brown or grey plumage and long, rounded wings.
	Turnicidae	Buttonquails; hemipodes	16	Sub-Saharan Africa, China, Australia, Philippines, Mediterranean	
	Pedionomidae	Plains wanderer or collared hemipode	1	Australia	
	Gruidae	Cranes	15	All continents except S America and Antarctica	
	Aramidae	Limpkin	1	Americas	
	Psophiidae	Trumpeters	3	S America	
	Rallidae	Rails	129	Worldwide	
	Heliornithidae	Finfoots	3	Tropical America, tropical Africa and SE Asia	
	Rhynochetidae	Kagu	1	New Caledonia	
	Eurypygidae	Sunbittern	1	S America	
	Cariamidae	Seriemas	2	S America	
	Otididae	Bustards	22	Africa, Eurasia, Australia	

Natural history

Order	Family	Common name/ examples	No. of species	Distribution of family	General characteristics of order
Charadriiformes (Sub-order Charadrii)	Jacanidae	Jacanas or lily-trotters	7	Americas, Africa, SE Asia, N Australia	Diverse order of mostly small to medium-sized shorebirds and seabirds.
	Rostratulidae	Painted snipe	2	S America, SE Asia, Australia	They generally have long, narrow wings, except for
	Haematopodidae	Oystercatchers	6	All continents	auks whose shorter wings
	Charadriidae	Plovers; lapwings	62	Worldwide	can act as paddles
	Scolopacidae	Sandpipers	81	All continents	underwater.
	Recurvirostridae	Avocets; stilts	7	All continents	
	Phalaropodidae	Phalaropes	3	N Eurasia, N America	
	Dromadidae	Crab plover	1	Indian ocean coastlines	
	Burhinidae	Stonecurlews or thick-knees	9	All continents except N America	
	Glareolidae	Pratincoles; coursers	17	Eurasia, Africa, Australia	
	Thinocoridae	Seed snipe	4	S America	
	Chionididae	Sheathbills	2	Antarctica and sub-Antartic islands	
(Sub-order Lari)	Stercorariidae	Skuas; jaegers	6	Worldwide	
	Laridae	Gulls	45	Worldwide	
	Sternidae	Terns; noddies	42	Worldwide	
	Rynchopidae	Skimmers	3	Tropical Africa, SE Asia, eastern N America, C and S America	
(Sub-order Alcae)	Alcidae	Auks	22	Northern hemisphere seas	
Columbiformes	Pteroclididae	Sandgrouse	16	Africa, S Europe, Asia	Small to medium-sized arboreal and terrestrial
	Columbidae	Pigeons; doves	300	Worldwide except Antarctica	birds with thick, heavy plumage.
Psittaciformes	Psittacidae	Parrots; lories; cockatoos; lovebirds; macaws; budgerigars	330	All continents except Antarctica	The parrots have zygodactyl toes: two pointing forward, and two backward, enabling them to climb and hold objects. They have strong, hooked bills – (with mobile upper mandible) used for cracking nuts, holding things and climbing – as a 'third foot'. Often colourful, they nest in trees and on ledges and have a largely vegetarian diet.
Cuculiformes	Musophagidae	Turacos	22	Sub-Saharan Africa	Diverse order of arboreal and terrestial birds. Many
	Cuculidae	Cuckoos; anis; roadrunner; coucals	128	Worldwide	cuckoos are brood parasites, relying on other species to raise
	Opisthocomidae	Hoatzin	1	S America	their young.
Strigiformes	Strigidae	Owls (typical)	124	Worldwide except Antarctica	The owls are nocturnal raptors found in grassland and woodland habitats,

Classification of birds (continued)

Order	Family	Common name/ examples	No. of species	Distribution of family	General characteristics of order
	Tytonidae	Barn owls	10	Worldwide except C Asia, New Zealand and Antarctica	usually nesting in cavities. Their large, forward-facing eyes peer out of a facial disc and give them binocular vision. Owls can turn their heads in either direction more than 180°, and also have acute hearing.
Caprimulgiformes	Caprimulgidae	Nightjars or goatsuckers	70	Open habitats in temperate and tropical regions	These are generally insectivorous. Some hibernate and many are migratory. They have wide, gaping mouths with hooked beaks, large eyes and short legs with weak feet. Many species are two-coloured, featuring grey and red phases.
	Podargidae	Frogmouths	12	SE Asia, Australia	
	Aegothelidae	Owlet-nightjars	8	Australia, SE Asia	
	Nyctibiidae	Potoos	5	S America	
	Steatornithidae	Oilbird	1	S America	
Apodiformes	Apodidae	Swifts	80	Worldwide	Aerial birds that depend on their flying skills for food. Swifts are insectivorous and migratory. While on the wing they feed, mate, collect nest material, drink, and even, in some species, pass the night at high altitudes. Hummingbirds feed on nectar, supplemented with insects.
	Hemiprocnidae	Crested swifts	3	SE Asia	
	Trochilidae	Hummingbirds	320	Americas	
Coliiformes	Coliidae	Mousebirds or colies	6	Sub-Saharan Africa	These acrobatic, highly social birds live in scrub and bushes, feeding on fruit and vegetation – often becoming agricultural pests.
Trogoniformes	Trogonidae	Trogons	35	America, Asia, Sub-Saharan Africa	Colourful, sedentary, arboreal birds that feed on fruit and insects. They nest in tree cavities and termite mounds.
Coraciiformes	Alcedinidae	Kingfishers	87	Worldwide	The three anterior toes on these birds are united, an adaptation for perching and tree-climbing. Many are brightly coloured, some are social. All nest in cavities, digging holes in, for example, earth banks or rotten trees.
	Todidae	Todies	5	W Indies	
	Momotidae	Motmots	8	S America	
	Meropidae	Bee-eaters	24	Africa, Eurasia, Australia	
	Leptosomatidae	Cuckoo-roller	1	Madagascar, Comoros Islands	
	Coraciidae	Rollers	16	Africa, Eurasia, Australia	
	Upupidae	Hoopoe	1	Africa, Eurasia	
	Phoeniculidae	Woodhoopoes	6	Sub-Saharan Africa	
	Bucerotidae	Hornbills	45	Sub-Saharan Africa, SE Asia	

Order	Family	Common name/ examples	No. of species	Distribution of family	General characteristics of order
Piciformes	Galbulidae	Jacamars	15	S America	These birds are zygodactylous (see Psittaciformes). Colourful and arboreal, they feed on vegetation and insects, and nest in holes.
	Bucconidae	Puffbirds	30	S America	
	Capitonidae	Barbets	76	Americas, Sub-Saharan Africa, SE Asia	
	Indicatoridae	Honeyguides	15	Sub-Saharan Africa, Himalayas, SE Asia	
	Ramphastidae	Toucans	40	S America	
	Picidae	Woodpeckers; piculets; wrynecks	200	Worldwide	
Passeriformes (Sub-order Eurylaimi)	Eurylaimidae	Broadbills	14	Africa, Asia	Around 5200 species, well over half of all birds, belong to the order Passeriformes, the perching birds or passerines. The order includes the most familiar garden birds – tits, chickadees, robins and sparrows – as well as other species found in virtually all land habitats. No passerine is a true water bird, though the dippers come close. Most are small or medium-sized birds (the largest species are the raven and the Australian lyrebird). The perching feet have four well-developed, separate toes. These are very vocal, singing birds. The male is often more brightly coloured than the female. Most are opportunistic feeders, being dependent on high-energy foods such as seeds and insects. Monogamy is the norm.
(Sub-order Menurae)	Menuridae	Lyrebirds	2	SE Australia	
	Atrichornithidae	Scrub-birds	2	W and E Australia	
(Sub-order Tyranni)	Furnariidae	Ovenbirds	220	C and S America	
	Dendrocolaptidae	Woodcreepers	48	S America	
	Formicariidae	Antbirds	230	S America	
	Tyrannidae	Tyrant flycatchers	375	Americas	
	Pittidae	Pittas	29	Africa, SE Asia, Australia	
	Pipridae	Manakins	53	S America	
	Cotingidae	Cotingas	65	S America	
	Conopophagidae	Gnateaters	9	S America	
	Rhinocryptidae	Tapaculos	29	S America	
	Oxyruncidae	Sharpbill	1	S America	
	Phytotomidae	Plantcutters	3	S America	
	Xenicidae	New Zealand wrens	4	New Zealand	
	Philepittidae	Sunbird asities	4	Madagascar	
(Sub-order Oscines)	Hirundinidae	Swallows; martins	74	Worldwide	
	Alaudidae	Larks	75	All continents	
	Motacillidae	Wagtails; pipits	54	Worldwide	
	Pycnonotidae	Bulbuls	120	S Asia, Africa	
	Laniidae	Shrikes	69	N America, Africa, Eurasia	
	Campephagidae	Cuckoo-shrikes	72	Africa, Australia, S and E Asia	
	Irenidae	Leafbirds	14	S and E Asia	
	Prionopidae	Helmet shrikes	9	Sub-Saharan Africa	
	Vangidae	Vanga shrikes	13	Madagascar, Comoros	
	Bombycillidae	Waxwings; silky flycatchers	8	N Eurasia, S America	
	Dulidae	Palmchat	1	S America	
	Cinclidae	Dippers	5	N Africa, Eurasia, W America	
	Troglodytidae	Wrens	60	NW Africa, Eurasia, N and S America	
	Mimidae	Mockingbirds	30	Americas	
	Prunellidae	Accentors	13	N Africa, Eurasia, S Asia	

Classification of birds (continued)

Order	Family	Common name/ examples	No. of species	Distribution of family	General characteristics of order
	Subfamilies of the family Muscicapidae				
	Turdidae	Thrushes	305	Worldwide	
	Timaliidae	Babblers	252	Africa, S Asia, Australasia, N America	
	Sylviidae	Warblers (Old World)	350	Worldwide	
	Muscicapinae	Flycatchers (Old World)	155	Australasia, Old World	
	Malurinae	Fairy-wrens	26	Australia, New Guinea	
	Paradox- ornithinae	Parrotbills	19	Asia, Europe	
	Monarchinae	Monarch flycatchers	133	Sub-Saharan Africa, S Asia, Australasia	
	Orthonychinae	Logrunners	20	SE Asia, Australia	
	Acanthizinae	Australian warblers	65	SE Asia, Australasia	
	Rhipidurinae	Fantail flycatchers	39	SE Asia, Australasia	
	Pachycephalinae	Thickheads	46	SE Asia, Australasia	
	Paridae	Tits	46	Africa, Eurasia, N America	
	Aegithalidae	Long-tailed tits	7	Eurasia, N America	
	Remizidae	Penduline tits	10	Africa, Eurasia, N America	
	Sittidae	Nuthatches	21	N America, Eurasia, N Africa, Australia	
	Climacteridae	Australasian treecreepers	8	Australia, New Guinea	
	Certhiidae	Holarctic treecreepers	5	Eurasia, Africa, N America	
	Rhabdornithidae	Philippine treecreepers	2	Philippines	
	Zosteropidae	White-eyes	85	Sub-Saharan Africa, S and E Asia, Australasia	
	Dicaeidae	Flowerpeckers	50	SE Asia, Australasia	
	Pardalotidae	Pardalotes or diamond eyes	5	Australia	
	Nectariniidae	Sunbirds; spiderhunters	116	Old World tropics, Africa to Australia	
	Meliphagidae	Honeyeaters	169	Australasia, S Africa	
	Ephthianuridae	Australian chats	5	Australia	
	Subfamilies of the family Emberizidae				
	Emberizinae	Old World buntings; New World sparrows	281	Worldwide except SE Asia and Australasia	
	Catambly- rhynchinae	Plush-capped finch	1	S America	
	Thraupinae	Tanagers; honeycreepers	233	Americas	
	Cardinalinae	Cardinals and grosbeaks	37	S America	
	Tersininae	Swallow tanager	1	S America	
	Parulidae	Wood warblers	119	Americas	
	Vireonidae	Vireos; pepper shrikes	43	Americas	
	Icteridae	American blackbirds	94	Americas	
	Subfamilies of the family Fringillidae				
	Fringillinae	Fringilline finches	3	Eurasia, Canary Islands	
	Carduelinae	Cardueline finches	122	Worldwide except Australia	

Order	Family	Common name/ examples	No. of species	Distribution of family	General characteristics of order
	Drepanidinae	Hawaiian honeycreepers	23	Hawaiian Islands	
	Estrildidae	Waxbills	124	Africa, S Asia, Australia	

Subfamilies of the family Ploceidae

	Family	Common name/ examples	No. of species	Distribution of family	General characteristics of order
	Ploceinae	True weavers	95	Africa, S Asia	
	Viduinae	Widow birds	10	Sub-Saharan Africa	
	Bubalornithinae	Buffalo weavers	3	Sub-Saharan Africa	
	Passerinae	Sparrow weavers; sparrows	37	Africa, Eurasia	
	Sturnidae	Starlings	106	Africa, Eurasia, Australia, New Zealand	
	Oriolidae	Orioles; figbirds	28	Africa, Eurasia, Australia	
	Dicruridae	Drongos	20	Sub-Saharan Africa, S Asia, N and E Australia	
	Callaeidae	New Zealand wattlebirds	3	New Zealand	
	Grallinidae	Magpie larks	2	Australia	
	Corcoracidae	Australian mudnesters	2	E Australia	
	Artamidae	Wood swallows	10	SE Asia, Australia	
	Cracticidae	Bell magpies	9	New Guinea, Australia	
	Ptilonorhynchidae	Bowerbirds	18	New Guinea, Australia	
	Paradisaeidae	Birds of paradise	43	New Guinea, Australia	
	Corvidae	Crows; magpies; jays	113	Worldwide	

Incubation and fledgling periods

Bird family	Incubation period (days)	Fledgling period (days)
Hole nesters		
Bee-eaters	20	23
Hornbills	35	46
Kingfishers	22	29
Owls	30	30
Rollers	18	28
Swifts	20	44
Open nesters		
Anis	13	11
Cuckoos	12	22
Passerines	13	13
Pigeons	15	17
Turacos	17	28
Seabirds		
Wandering albatross	78	280
Fulmar	49	49
Gannet	44	90
King penguin	53	360
Adelie penguin	33	51
Giant petrel	59	108
Storm petrel	41	63
Shag	30	53
Common tern	23	30
Sandwich tern	23	35

Wingspans

Common name (Latin name)	Length (m)	(ft)
Wandering albatross (*Diomedea exulans*)	3.5	11.5
Marabou stork (*Leptoptilos dubius*)	3.3	11.0
Andean condor (*Vultur gryphus*)	3.2	10.5
White pelican (*Pelicanus onocrotalus*)	3.1	10.0
Lammergeier (*Gypaetus barbatus*)	2.7	9.0
Mute swan (*Cygnus olor*)	2.3	7.5
Crane (*Grus grus*)	2.3	7.5
Golden eagle (*Aquila chrysaetos*)	2.2	7.2
White stork (*Ciconia ciconia*)	2.1	7.0
Grey heron (*Ardea cinerea*)	1.9	6.0
Northern gannet (*Sulla bassana*)	1.8	5.9
Canada goose (*Branta canadensis*)	1.8	5.9
Greater flamingo (*Phoenicopterus ruber*)	1.65	5.4
Herring gull (*Larus argentatus*)	1.6	5.2
Osprey (*Pandion haliaetus*)	1.6	5.2
Barn owl (*Tyto alba*)	0.9	3.0

Natural history

Animals

Life-history features

Species	Maximum recorded age (years)	Annual adult mortality (%)	Age of first breeding (years)	No. of eggs	Body weight (g)	Body weight (oz)
Blue tit	10	70	1	12–14	11	0.4
European robin	13	52	1	4–6	18	0.6
Song sparrow	8	44	1	4–6	30	1.0
House sparrow	12	50	1	3–6	30	1.0
European starling	20	50	1–2	4–6	80	3.0
American robin	10	48	1	4–6	100	3.5
European blackbird	20	42	1	3–5	80–110	3.0–4.0
Barn swallow	16	63	1	4–6	20	0.7
Common swift	21	15	2	2–3	36–50	1.0–2.0
Tawny owl	18	26	2	2–4	680–750	24.0–26.5
Mourning dove	17	55	1	2	140	5.0
Woodpigeon	16	36	1	2	450–550	16.0–19.0
Atlantic puffin	22	5	4	1	350–550	12.0–19.0
Black-legged kittiwake	21	14	4–5	2–3	300–500	10.5–17.5
Herring gull	36	6	3–5	3	750–1 250	26.5–44.0
Curlew	32	26	2	4	575–800	20.0–28.0
Redshank	17	31	1–2	4	110–155	4.0–5.5
Lapwing	23	32	1–2	4	200–300	7.0–10.5
Avocet	25	22	2–3	4	250–400	9.0–14.0
Pheasant	8	58	1–2	8–15	900–1 400	32.0–49.0
Kestrel	17	34	1–2	4–6	190–240	6.5–8.5
Buzzard	26	19	2–3	2–4	550–1 200	19.0–42.0
Osprey	32	18	2–3	2–3	1 200–2 000	42.0–71.0
Mallard	29	48	1–2	9–13	850–1 400	30.0–49.0
Tufted duck	15	46	1–2	8–11	550–900	19.0–32.0
Eider	18	20	2–3	4–6	1 200–2 800	42.0–99.0
Barnacle goose	23	9	3	3–5	1 400–1 600	49.0–56.5
Mute swan	22	10	3–4	5–8	10 000–12 000	353.0–424.0
Grey heron	25	30	2	4–5	1 600–2 000	56.5–71
White stork	26	21	3–5	3–5	3 000–3 500	106.0–123.5
Shag	21	16	3–4	3–4	1 750–2 250	62.0–79.0
Short-tailed shearwater	31	5	5–8	1	530	19.0
Royal albatross	36	3	8–10	1	8 300	293.0
Yellow-eyed penguin	18	10	2–4	2	5 200	183.5

Reptiles

Order	Family	Common name/ examples	No. of species	Distribution	General characteristics of order
Chelonia	Dermatemydidae	Central American river turtle	1	C America, Mexico	Aquatic and terrestial reptiles – turtles, terrapins and tortoises. These have a rigid body shell comprising a dorsal carapace and a ventral plastron, into which most species draw their head and legs for protection. The jaws are beaked, without teeth.
	Chelydridae	Common and alligator snapping turtles	2	N and S America	
	Kinosternidae	Mud and musk turtles	21	Tropical regions	
	Testudinidae	Tortoises	40	All continents except Australia	
	Platysternidae	Big-headed turtle	1	SE Asia	
	Emydidae	Common turtle	76	Abundant in northern hemisphere	
	Cheloniidae	Sea turtles	5	Worldwide	
	Dermochelyidae	Leatherback turtle	1	Worldwide	
	Carettochelyidae	New Guinea plateless turtle	1	New Guinea	
	Trionychidae	Soft-shell turtles	20	All continents except S America and Australia	
	Pelomedusidae	Side-necked turtles	14	Africa, S America	

Order	Family	Common name/ examples	No. of species	Distribution	General characteristics of order
	Chelyidae	Snake-necked turtles	31	Australia, S America	
Rhynchocephalia	Sphenodontidae	Tuatara	1	New Zealand	Primitive nocturnal reptile, feeds on snails, worms, occasionally small lizards and birds.
Squamata (Sub-order Sauria)	Gekkonidae	Geckos	650	Worldwide	The Squamata are a large and very diverse order comprising three suborders, Sauria (lizards), Serpentes or Ophidia (snakes), and Amphisbaenia (worm lizards). This order contains the great majority of living reptiles. Lizards vary in size from a few centimetres (some geckos) to about 3 m/10 ft in length (the Komodo dragon). They feed as herbivores, insectivores or as predators of small vertebrates. The skull is made up of several separate mobile elements (a form of modification known as cranial kinesis). Limbs may be reduced in burrowing forms.
	Pygopodidae	Flap-footed lizards	15	Australia, New Guinea	
	Dibamidae	Burrowers	3	Philippines, Vietnam, New Guinea	
	Iguanidae	Iguanas	600	N and S America, W Indies, Galapagos, Fiji, Madagascar	
	Agamidae	Agamid lizard	300	Tropical regions worldwide	
	Chameleontidae	Old World chameleons	85	Africa, W Asia, India	
	Scincidae	Skinks	800	Worldwide except polar regions	
	Cordylidae	Girdle-tailed lizards	50	S Africa, Madagascar	
	Lacertidae	Old World terrestrial lizards	150	Europe, Asia, Africa	
	Teiidae	Whiptail lizards	200	Tropical regions	
	Anguidae	Glass lizards; alligator lizards; galliwasps	67	Americas	
	Anniellidae	California legless lizards	2	California	
	Xenosauridae		4	Mexico, China	
	Helodermatidae	Gila monster lizard; bearded lizard	2	N America, Mexico	
	Varanidae	Monitor lizards	30	Tropical regions	
	Lanthanotidae	Earless monitor lizard	1	Borneo	
	Xantusiidae	Night lizards	12	C America, Cuba	
(Sub-order Serpentes)	Typhlopidae	Blind snakes; worm snakes	200	Tropical regions	Snakes have no limbs, have long, cylindrical scaly bodies, lidless eyes and highly mobile jaws (cranial kinesis). They eat animals (or eggs), killing by suffocation, by biting, or by venom, and cannot chew. They moult there skin several times each year.
	Letotyphlopidae	Slender blind snakes	40	N and S America, SW Asia, Africa	
	Xenopeltidae	Sunbeam snake	1	India	
	Uropeltidae	Shieldtail snakes	50	S Asia	
	Boidae	Pythons; boas; woodsnakes	60	Tropical regions	
	Acrochordidae	Wart snakes	2	Australia, E Indies, SE Asia	
	Colubridae	Terrestrial, arboreal and aquatic snakes	>1 500	Worldwide	
	Viperidae	Vipers; rattlesnakes; moccasins	180	Europe, Asia, Africa, not Australia	
	Elapidae	Cobras; mambas; coral snakes	170	Asia, Africa, N and S America	
	Hydrophiidae	Sea snakes	50	Indian and Pacific oceans	

Animals

Reptiles (continued)

Order	Family	Common name/ examples	No. of species	Distribution	General characteristics of order
(Sub-order Amphisbaenia)	Amphisbaenidae	Worm lizards	100	Africa, C and S America, SE Asia and Seychelle Islands	Small, limbless burrowing lizards with concealed eyes and wedge-shaped skulls to aid with digging. They eat small animals.
Crocodilia	Alligatoridae	Alligators; caiman	7	S America, Africa, Asia,	Small to very large (7 m/23 ft) carniv-
	Crocodilidae	True crocodile	13	Australia	orous, amphibious reptiles. Heavy
	Gavialidae	Gavial or gharial	1	India	cylindrical body armoured with bony plates; elongated snout; webbed toes; powerful tail; mainly nocturnal.

Amphibians

Order	Family	Common name/ examples	No. of species	Distribution	General characteristics of order
Trachystomata		Sirens	3	N America	Aquatic, eel-like amphibians; no hindlimbs; forelimbs tiny; without external eyes or ears.
Gymnophiona		Caecilians	160	C and S America, Africa, SE Asia, Seychelle Islands	Caecilians are limbless, worm-like subterranean amphibians with annuli (rings) along length of body.
Urodela or Caudata	Hynobiidae	Asiatic salamanders	30	N Asia (from Ural Mountains to Japan and Taiwan)	The tailed amphibians salamanders and newts. Adults aquatic or terrestial, occasionally arboreal;
	Cryptobranchidae	Giant salamanders; hellbenders	3	N America, China and Japan	eggs and larvae primitively aquatic.
	Sirenidae	Sirens; dwarf sirens	3	SE United States, Mexico	Feed on slow-moving invertebrates (worms,
	Proteidae	Olm	1	Balkan peninsula	slugs and snails).
	Necturidae	Mud puppies	5	N America	
	Amphiumidae	Congo eels	3	SE United States	
	Salamandridae	Salamanders and newts	42	Europe, N Africa, Middle East, S Asia, N America	
	Ambystomatidae	Mole salamanders; axolotl	33	N America	
	Plethodontidae	Lungless salamanders	210	Americas, S Europe	
Anura	Leiopelmatidae	Primitive frogs	4	New Zealand, N America	The frogs and toads. Tail absent; hind-
	Discoglossidae	Fire-bellied toads; midwife toads	8	Europe, Asia, N America, Philippines	limbs enlarged for jumping. Adults aquatic or terrestrial,
	Rhinophrynidae	Burrowing toad	1	C America	occasionally arboreal
	Pipidae	Tongueless frogs	14	Africa, S America	or burrowing. Eggs

Order	Family	Common name/ examples	No. of species	Distribution	General characteristics of order
	Pelobatidea	Spadefoots	59	Europe, Asia, N America, Australia	and larvae (tadpoles) typically aquatic, but reproductive
	Myobatrachidae	Terrestrial, arboreal and aquatic frogs	95	New Guinea, Australia, South Africa	strategies vary. Largely insectivorous. (Smooth wet-skinned
	Rhinodermatidae	Mouth-breeding frog	1	S America	species of Anura are
	Leptodactylidae	Terrestrial neotropical frogs	650	Americas, Caribbean	usually known as frogs, rough dry-
	Bufonidae	True toads	235	Worldwide	skinned species as
	Brachycephalidae	Terrestrial toads	2	Brazil	toads, but there is no
	Dendrobatidae	Arrow-poison frogs	70	C and S America	technical difference
	Pseudidae	Fully aquatic frogs	5	S America	between the two.)
	Centrolenidae	Leaf frogs	60	C and S America	
	Hylidae	Tree frogs	400	Worldwide	
	Ranidae	True frogs	850	Worldwide	
	Sooglossidae	Terrestrial frogs	3	Seychelle Islands	
	Microhylidae	Narrow-mouthed frogs	230	Africa, Asia, N and S America, Australia	

Fishes

There have been many different systems of fish classification, and today there is still much debate about taxonomy. Most systems divide the world of fishes into three: the jawless fishes, the cartilagenous fishes and the bony fishes. This table lists some of the best-known types of fish.

Order	Common name/ examples	No. of species	Distribution	General characteristics of order
Class Agnatha (*jawless fishes*)				
Cyclostomata	Lampreys	30	Cool, fresh, and coastal waters of all continents, except Africa	Eel-shaped body; well-developed dorsal and caudal fins; horny teeth; feed on the blood of other fishes; only breed in fresh water.
	Hagfishes	30	Cold, marine bottom waters; equatorial oceans	soft-skinned; nearly cylindrical; eyes vestigial, covered by skin; feed on dead or moribund fishes or invertebrates; locate food by scent; only breed in marine water.
Class Chondrichthyes (*fishes with a cartilage skeleton*)				
Selachii	Sharks	>200	Tropical and temperate zones; particularly New Zealand, S Africa	Large group of predatory fishes belonging to nineteen separate families; streamlined bodies; highly sensitive sense of smell; attacks on humans very rare, usually occur in water warmer than 21°C (70°F); an exception, however, is the white shark, which is also the most dangerous; others include hammerheads (very mobile using rudder effect of head), tiger and sand sharks; largest are the whale and basking sharks.

Fishes (continued)

Order	Common name/ examples	No. of species	Distribution	General characteristics of order
Batoidei	Rays; skates; stingrays	>300	All oceans from tropical to temperate latitudes	Bottom dwellers, preying on other animals on sea floor; differ externally from sharks having gill openings confined to lower surface; eyes on dorsal surface; many armed with thorns, tubercles or prickles; stingrays live in shallow, coastal waters; if provoked, will lash back their tails; electric rays are sluggish, stun invertebrates and fishes by shocks produced from electric organs. Skates lie on bottom, often partially buried; rise in pursuit of prey, particularly herring; trap victims by swimming over them and settling upon them; their egg cases ('mermaid's purses') are often washed ashore.

Class Osteichthyes *(fishes with a bony skeleton)*

Order	Common name/ examples	No. of species	Distribution	General characteristics of order
Dipnoi	Lungfishes	6	Freshwater; Australia, Africa, N America	Voracious, eating aquatic animals, including own species; most grow to substantial size; sac-shaped, pneumatic organs that lie along alimentary tract, whose structure and function are like primitive lungs of amphibians.
Acipenseriformes	Sturgeons	25	Marine and freshwater; Europe, Asia, N America	Braincase mostly cartilaginous; ground feeding by dragging tactile, whisker-like barbels over bottom; toothless mouth with protractile lips surrounded by taste buds; food fish for humans, source of caviar.
	Paddlefishes	2	Marine and freshwater; China and N America	Braincase mostly cartilaginous; feed by straining plankton through gill system; elongated, paddle-shaped snout composed entirely of cartilage, measuring one-third of the total body length.
Polypteriformes	Bichirs or reedfishes	11	Tropical swamps and rivers in C Africa	Inhabit edges of streams and flood plains, concealed by day, forage for worms, insect larvae, small fishes by night.
Elopiformes	Bonefishes	4	Coastal and deep waters of warm oceans	Specialized bottom feeders; grubs with snout for worms and shellfish which they crush with rounded palatal teeth.
	Tarpons	2	Warm coastal waters Atlantic	Fast-swimming predator; swim bladder lung-like, partially compartmented, highly vascularized; obligate air breathers, can die from asphyxiation if prevented from reaching surface.
	Ladyfish	6	Warm coastal waters circumtropical	Fast-swimming predators; appear to 'roll' at sea surface apparently for intake of air; open duct to swim bladder when air is taken through mouth.

Order	Common name/ examples	No. of species	Distribution	General characteristics of order
Anguilliformes	Eels	>500	Marine and freshwater; of Europe and N America; some in shallow water or deep sea	Elongate, cylindrical body form; carnivorous until maturity; morays and congers inhabit rock crevices, others form vast colonies of individuals in tropical reef areas; return to sea to spawn.
Clupeiformes	Herrings	190	Virtually worldwide in marine waters, and in many bodies of freshwater	Teeth usually absent or weakly developed; single schools of herring estimated to include many millions.
	Anchovies	200	Widespread in surface coastal waters of tropical and temperate seas; a few anadromous (returning to fresh water to spawn)	Snout projects beyond very wide mouth; upper and lower jaws usually armed with rows of minute teeth; found in large schools, some spreading over 100 m/330 ft, contracting to writhing sphere of thousands of fishes only a few metres across at approach of a predator.
Osteoglossiformes	Bony tongues	6	Freshwater; rivers and lakes, turbid waters or regions with dense aquatic vegetation	Strongly-toothed jaws; large mouth; well-developed swim bladder; some species, upper portion of ear (for balance) completely separated from lower part (for hearing).
	Freshwater butterfly fish	1	Freshwater; Africa	Greatly expanded wing-like pectoral fins (behind gills) which are used for short flights to the air, either to escape predators or to catch insects.
Salmoniformes	Salmons; trouts; chars; smelts; graylings; whitefishes	150	Widespread, marine or freshwater. Salmon common in N Atlantic; return to freshwater to breed	Trim, fusiform body; powerful caudal (tail) muscles; commonly migrate upstream to spawn; very important food fishes.
	Pikes; mudminnows	10	Freshwater; northern hemisphere	Long bodies; dorsal and anal fins positioned posteriorly, adipose fin absent.
Ostariophysi	Carps; minnows; barbs; suckers; loaches	3500	Fresh to brackish waters: Africa, S and C America, Eurasia	Small to medium-sized fishes; upper jaw protractile, jaw teeth usually absent. Body covered in scales.
	Catfishes	2500	Low saline, brackish freshwater or marine	Order of small to very large freshwater fishes; oral incubation of eggs by some species; most active at night or under conditions of reduced light.
Characiformes	Tetras; darters; piranhas	>1300	Freshwater: S and C America, Africa	Mostly small, colourful fishes; upper jaw projectile, jaws bearing teeth; of prime importance in aquarium trade.
Paracanthopterygii	Toadfishes	45	Primarily marine, mainly tropical and temperate shallow waters along continental coasts; occasionally freshwater	Generally have two dorsal fins; nine venomous species restricted to coast and rivers of C and S America.
	Trout-perches	8	All freshwater; N America	Live under conditions of dim light; can be found in clear water of the Great Lakes at depths of about 64 m/210 ft.
	Codfishes	800	Primarily marine, shallow-water, some deep-sea types, worldwide distribution; particularly N Atlantic	Largest of order, growing to about 2 m/6.5 ft in length and attain weights that may exceed 90 kg/ 200 lb; migrate over long distances, gathering in late winter and early spring to spawn, each species goes to particular area.

Fishes (continued)

Order	Common name/ examples	No. of species	Distribution	General characteristics of order
Atheriniformes	Flying fishes	50	Surface marine waters, worldwide	Surface fishes of the open ocean where they breed; capable of leaping or skipping on surface to escape predators; tail (caudal) fin usually asymmetrical, lower lobes longer than body so while out of water lower lobe vibrates as a scull driving fish along.
	Needlefishes; garfishes	25	Mostly temperate and tropical marine; a few freshwater	Pelagic (inhabiting the open ocean); predatory habit highly developed; long, formidable toothed jaws elongated into strong-toothed beak; breed near shore.
	Cyprinodonts	500	Tropical and subtropical distribution, including hot springs of Africa and America	Diminutive; many important as experimental animals in biological research; among hardiest of fishes, some surviving in rigorous environments, including water temperatures in hot springs approaching coagulation point of protoplasm.
Gasterosteiformes	Sticklebacks	11	Fresh, brackish, and marine waters of northern hemisphere	Small, scaleless fishes; short jaws armed with sharp teeth; body more nearly fusiform (tapered at both ends).
	Tube snout	1	NE Pacific Ocean	Elongated, slender, cylindrical body, tipped by prolonged snout; small toothed mouth has hinged upper jaw; scale-less body armoured with series of embedded bony plates.
	Sea horses	24	Widely distributed; marine	Bony rings instead of scales; use coiled tail to grip seaweed and other plants/objects; propulsion by means of dorsal fin (midline of back); tiny pectoral fin used for steering; rise or settle to another depth by changing air volume within the bladder.
Scorpaeniformes	Scorpion fishes; rockfishes; redfishes; turkeryfishes; gunards	330	Tropical, temperate, and northern seas	Live on coral or rocky bottom; many possess remarkable degree of concealing coloration and shape; dorsal fin spines long and numerous; head spiny; body scaly; some with venom glands on fin spines.
Perciformes				The largest group of fishes, comprising about 7 000 species in 150 families.
	Perches	125	Freshwater temperate species	Possess numerous short, fine, pointed teeth; prefer quiet waters; pike-perches semi-migratory, prefer quiet, running waters.

Order	Common name/ examples	No. of species	Distribution	General characteristics of order
	Tunas	40	Open waters of tropics and warm seas of world	May travel across entire Pacific Ocean from California coast to Japan, or reverse, to spawn; one of the larger predatory perciforms; carnivorous; well-developed vascular system under skin, associated with sustained high-speed swimming and a body temperature a few degrees higher than surrounding water.
	Marlins	7	Worldwide in warm seas	Greatest game fishes of the ocean; black marlin is the largest at 900 kg/2 000 lb.
Pleuronectiformes	Flatfishes	2	Indo-Pacific and Africa	Asymmetrical; found in depths up to 1 000 m/3 300 feet, most occur on continental shelf in less than 200 m/650 ft of water; swim by undulating movement of body and fins; lie on bottom, generally covered by sand or mud, with only eyes protruding; eyes can be raised, lowered and moved independently.
	Flounders	300+	Marine and freshwater, tropic and temperate seas	Either right-eyed (dextral) or left-eyed (sinistral); asymmetrical; feed primarily on crustaceans, other bottom invertebrates and small fish; when feeding lie motionless and then pounce on close prey.
	Soles	100+	Tropic and temperate seas, some freshwater	Asymmetrical; strongly compressed; eyes, usually small, on one side (dextral); mouth curved downward; caudal fin with numerous rays.
Tetraodontiformes	Box fishes	25	Prominent around coral reefs, open sand and grassy flats; worldwide	Carapace closed behind anal and usually behind dorsal fin; no ventral keel; blow jet of water out of mouth onto sand bottom to expose burrowing invertebrates.
	Puffer fishes	7	Prominent around coral reefs, open sand and grassy flats; worldwide	Poisonous flesh, at least during certain seasons of year; most of highly poisonous substance contained in viscera; flesh can be eaten if professionally cleaned.
	Ocean sunfishes	3	Prominent around coral reefs, open sand and grassy flats; tropical and subtropical oceans worldwide	Massive, crushing jaws and teeth; feed extensively on soft-bodied invertebrates, such as jellyfishes.

Insects

Order	Common name/ examples	No. of species	Distribution	General characteristics of order
Collembola	Springtails	2 000	Worldwide	Blind, primitively wingless insects with entognathous mouthparts (ie contained within an invagination of the head). They leap by means of a forked springing organ on the underside of the abdomen.
Diplura	Diplurans	660	Worldwide	Small, slender, blind, whitish insects, with entognathous mouthparts; found in damp soil, under logs and stones.

Animals

Insects (continued)

Order	Common name/ examples	No. of species	Distribution	General characteristics of order
Protura	Proturans	120	Worldwide	Primitively wingless; white; blind; no antennae; reduced mouthparts; found under bark, stones or rotting vegetation.
Thysanura	Bristletails; silverfish	600	Worldwide	Primitive wingless insects found amongst decaying wood etc, in human habitations, and in association with ants and termites; feed on fungi, lichens, algae, pollen, or decaying vegetable matter.
Ephemeroptera	Mayflies	2 000	Worldwide, except Antarctica	Some species carnivorous, but majority are herbivorous. Life cycle consists of four stages. Nymph can live for 2 weeks to 2 years; the adults are winged and non-feeding, living from 2 to 72 hours, during which time they mate.
Odonata	Dragonflies; damselflies	5 000	Worldwide	Carnivorous, often brightly coloured; aquatic larvae; adults have powerful predatory mouthparts and two pairs of richly veined wings. Larvae feed on aquatic larvae, tadpoles, worms, and small fishes; adults on flying insects.
Orthoptera	Grasshoppers; locusts; crickets	24 000	Worldwide	Wings, when present, number four; chewing mouthparts; mostly plant feeders. Hindlimbs usually specialized for jumping; many species produce sounds by rubbing together forewings. Of immense economic importance.
Phasmida (Phasmoptera)	Stick insects; leaf insects	2 500	Tropical areas	Arboreal; nocturnal; feed on plant juices; camouflage and mimicry highly developed.
Blattaria	Cockroaches	3 700	Worldwide	Depressed body; long legs; forewings hard or leathery; hindwings membranous, but may be reduced or absent. Typically live on the ground, under stones, or in litter and wood debris. Some are household pests.
Embioptera	Webspinners	200	Tropical regions	Inhabit extensive galleries or labyrinths of silk on bark, litter, moss, lichens, or within the soil. Body slender; legs short; females and some males wingless.
Zoraptera	Zorapterans	20	Tropical regions	Tiny insects resembling slender termites.
Dermaptera	Earwigs	1 500	Worldwide	Feed as scavengers or predators with large pincers variously used for predation, defence, courtship, and grooming. Wings frequently reduced or absent.
Mantodea	Mantids; mantises	1 800	Tropical and subtropical areas	Predatory insects in which body shape is highly adapted for camouflage; head very mobile, eyes large; in some species female eats male headfirst during copulation.
Isoptera	Termites or white ants	2 000	Europe, Australia, Asia, N America	Cellulose-eating, social insects that construct nests which vary in size from a few centimetres to several metres. Caste system includes morphologically distinct soldiers and workers.
Phthiraptera	Sucking lice (Anoplura); biting lice (Mallophaga); booklice and barklice (Psocoptera)	3 400	Worldwide	Parasites of birds or mammals; eyes reduced or absent; reduced antennae; mouthparts mandibulate or piercing.

Natural history

Order	Common name	No. of species	Distribution	General characteristics of order
Thysanoptera	Thrips	5 000	Tropical regions	Fringed wings, bristles on body wall; mouthparts specialized for piercing and sucking. Feed on plant juices, fungi, spores, pollen, or body fluids of other arthropods. Some species hibernate in winter in cold climates.
Homoptera	Cicadas; hoppers; whiteflies; aphids; scale insects	45 000	Worldwide	Plant feeders with mouth parts adapted for sucking plant sap; wings number two or four when present. Many are crop pests.
Hemiptera	True bugs	35 000	Worldwide	Sucking mouthparts adapted to pierce plant or animal tissue; most species terrestrial, a few aquatic; well-developed compound eyes; scent glands usually present. Many are crop pests.
Neuroptera	Alderflies; dobsonflies (Megaloptera); lacewings (Plannipennia); snakeflies (Raphidiodea)	4 500	Worldwide	Biting mouthparts; two pairs of similar wings. Alderflies and dobsonflies have aquatic larvae. Snakeflies arboreal, characterized by elongate and highly mobile thorax.
Trichoptera	Caddisflies	7 000	Worldwide	Moth-like; wings covered with hairs; long antenna; large compound eyes; larvae almost exclusively aquatic.
Lepidoptera	Butterflies; moths; skippers	138 000	Worldwide	Two pairs of wings, covered by dustlike scales; four stages of life; day-flying; herbivorous; complete metamorphosis occurs (larvae are caterpillars). Adults typically with slender, coiled, sucking proboscis.
Coleoptera	Beetles; weevils	250 000	Worldwide	Two pairs of wings, front pair modified into horny covers; antennae variable; large compound eyes; mouthparts adapted for chewing; hard outer skeleton; complete metamorphosis.
Hymenoptera	Ants; bees; sawflies; wasps	130 000	Worldwide except polar regions	Pollinators of wild and cultivated flowering plants; some species have complex social organization; complete metamorphosis; four membranous wings; mouthparts adapted for chewing and sucking; larvae usually maggot-like.
Strepsiptera	Stylopids	400	Worldwide	Parasites of other insects; male winged, female wingless and larvae-like.
Mecoptera	Scorpion flies	450	Mostly tropical, subtropical areas	Inhabit moist forests feeding on nectar or preying on other insects.
Diptera	True flies	150 000	Worldwide	Forewings membranous, hindwings modified as minute club-like balancing organs (halteres). Feed on plant and animal juices or other insects; two wings; sucking mouthparts; some pupae aquatic. Many are disease vectors, though many are also beneficial as pollinators.
Siphonaptera	Fleas	1 750	Worldwide	Wingless; parasitic; mouthparts adapted to piercing and sucking; larvae elongated and often enclosed in cocoons. Feed mainly on mammals, but also some birds. Disease vectors.

PLANTS

Classification of plants

Phylum	Common name/examples	No. of species	Comments
Bryophyta	Liverworts (*Hepaticae*); hornworts (*Anthocerotae*); mosses (*Musci*)	24 000	Small plants living in moist habitats (their sperm must swim through water to reach their eggs). Reproduce by spores.
Psilophyta	Whiskferns	12	Simple vascular plants lacking true roots and, in some species, leaves. Reproduce by spores.
Lycopodophyta	Club mosses	1 000	Small, terrestrial or epiphytic (ie grow on other plants); needle or scale-like leaves arranged spirally on stem. Reproduce by spores.
Sphenophyta or Equisetophyta	Horsetails; scouring rushes	20	Primarily found in moist, muddy habitats; stems creeping underground and producing erect annual or perennial stems with tiny leaves whorled into sheaves around stem. Jointed hollow stems and rough, ribbed texture caused by the mineral silica. Reproduce by spores.
Filicinophyta or Pteridophyta	Ferns	12 000	Vascular plants which reproduce by spores; stems mostly creeping, large leaves (megaphylls) with branching veins. The most complex, diverse and abundant of the plant phyla that do not form seeds.
Cycadophyta	Cycads	100	Evergreen perennial shrubs or trees with stems that are usually unbranched but thickened by some secondary growth. Palm-like or fern-like compound leaves; they contain symbiotic cyanobacteria in special roots.
Ginkgophyta	Ginkgo; maidenhair tree	1	Native to China but cultivated worldwide, the ginkgo is a tall tree with deciduous fan-shaped leaves; the only living descendant of a once-large group.
Coniferophyta or Pinatae	Conifers	550	By far the most familiar of the gymnosperms (plants having naked seeds); usually evergreen shrubs or trees with simple needle-like leaves, spirally arranged. Commercially important for timber, pulp, turpentine, and resin products.
Gnetophyta	Gnetophytes (cone-bearing desert plants)	70	Cone-bearing desert plants. Resemble flowering plants in many ways; were once thought to be a link between conifers and angiosperms.
Angiospermophyta or Magnoliophyta	Angiosperms; flowering plants	>230 000	The dominant land vegetation of the Earth, including nearly every familiar tree, shrub, or garden plant that produces flowers and seeds. Characterized by the aggregation of sexual reproductive structures with specialized shoots (flowers), which typically comprise four kinds of modified leaves: sepals, petals, stamens (male organs), and carpels (female organs).

World vegetation map

Mountain vegetation
Tundra
Boreal forest
Conifer forest
Mixed forest, mid-latitudes
Broadleaf forest
Mediterranean scrub
Steppe
Savannah
Tropical rain forest
Monsoon forest
Dry tropical scrub and thorn forest
Desert vegetation
Sub-tropical forest

Flowering plants

Natural history

Common name	Latin name	Height (cm)	(in)	Colour
Annuals and biennials				
Baby's breath	Gypsophila	30–45	12–18	White, pink
Begonia	Begonia	15–45	6–18	Pink, white, red
Black-eyed Susan	Thunbergia	120–300	47–118	Yellow
Busy Lizzie	Impatiens	15–30	6–12	White, pink, red, orange, mauve
Canterbury bell	Campanula	45–75	18–30	Purple, white
Chrysanthemum	Chrysanthemum	45–60	18–24	Yellow, red, white
Corn cockle	Agrostemma	75	30	Pale lilac
Cornflower	Centaurea	30–75	12–30	Blue, pink
Dahlia	Dahlia	30–60	12–24	White, red, yellow
Daisy	Bellis	8–15	3–6	White, pink, red
Flower of an hour	Hibiscus	60	24	Cream
Forget-me-not	Myosotis	15–30	6–12	Blue
Foxglove	Digitalis	90–150	35–59	Purple
Godetia	Godetia	20–60	8–24	Pink, orange
Heliotrope	Heliotropium	45	18	White, dark blue, purple
Hollyhock	Althea	90–150	35–59	Pink
Larkspur	Delphinium	30–120	12–47	White, pink, red, blue
Morning glory	Ipomoea	180–360	71–142	Blue, purple, red
Nasturtium	Tropaeolum	30–180	12–71	Yellow, orange
Pansy	Viola	15–25	6–10	Violet, yellow
Petunia	Petunia	15–45	6–18	Pink, red ,blue, white
Phlox	Phlox	15–45	6–18	Pink, red, white, yellow
Poppy	Papaver	15–90	6–35	Red, pink, white
Pot marigold	Calendula	15–30	6–12	Yellow, orange
Snapdragon	Antirrhinum	90–120	35–47	Crimson, scarlet
Sunflower	Helianthus	60–300	24–118	Yellow
Sweet alyssum	Alyssum	8–15	3–6	White, purple, lilac, pink
Sweet pea	Lathyrus	30–240	12–94	Orange, crimson
Sweet William	Dianthus	30–60	12–24	White, red
Wallflower	Cheiranthus	20–60	8–24	Crimson, white, purple, orange, cream
Bulbs				
Begonia	Begonia	30–45	12–18	Pink, yellow, white, cream
Bluebell	Scilla	8	3	Blue, purple
Crocus	Crocus	8–10	3–4	White, purple, yellow
Cyclamen	Cyclamen	8–15	3–6	Red, pink, white
Daffodil	Narcissus	15–30	6–12	Yellow, white
Freesia	Freesia	15	6	White, red, yellow, pale blue
Hyacinth	Hyacinthus	8–15	3–6	Yellow, white, blue, pink, violet, red
Iris	Iris	15–30	6–12	Blue, yellow, white, purple
Lily of the valley	Convallaria	20	8	White
Snowdrop	Galanthus	13	5	White
Star of Bethlehem	Ornithogalum	15–30	6–12	White
Sword lily	Gladiolus	90–125	35–49	Yellow, red, pink, peach, orange
Tulip	Tulipa	20–80	8–31	Red, yellow, white, purple, peach
Border perennials				
Campion	Lychnis	90	35	Red, pink
Chinese bellflower	Platycodon	15–30	6–12	White, pink, pale blue
Clematis	Clematis	90–125	35–49	Blue, white
Columbine	Aquilegia	60–90	24–35	Yellow, red, blue
Crane's-bill	Geranium	45	18	Violet, pink
Lady's mantle	Alchemilla	45	18	Yellow
Lamb's ear	Stachys	45	18	Lilac, pink
Lupin	Lupinus	90–125	35–49	Pink, lilac, white, blue
Michaelmas daisy	Aster	60–125	24–49	Pink, white, crimson, blue
Peony	Paeonia	60	24	White, pink, red
Primrose	Primula	15–60	6–24	Yellow, red, lilac
Red hot poker	Kniphofia	75–155	30–61	Orange–red
Solomon's seal	Polygonatum	60–90	24–35	Cream
Speedwell	Veronica	45–155	18–61	Blue, pink, white
Violet	Viola	10–15	4–6	Violet, white, lilac, pink

Shrubs

Common name	Latin name	Height (cm)	Height (in)	Colour
Azalea	Rhododendron	180	71	Pink, red, white, yellow
Bay laurel	Laurus	610	240	Yellow
Broom	Genista	210	83	Yellow
Butterfly bush	Buddleia	250	98	Purple, white, mauve
Camellia	Camellia	180–250	71–98	Red, pale pink, white, bright pink
Fatsia	Fatsia	300	118	White
Firethorn	Pyracantha	370	145	Red, yellow
Fuchsia	Fuchsia	180	71	Red
Gorse	Ulex	180	71	Yellow
Heather	Erica	20–60	8–24	White, purple, yellow
Holly	Ilex	1500	590	Red
Honeysuckle	Lonicera	210–300	83–118	Pink, cream
Hydrangea	Hydrangea	90–150	35–59	Pale blue, white, pink, purple
Japonica	Chaenomeles	120–90	47–75	Red, white
Jasmine	Jasminum	300	118	Yellow
Lavender	Lavandula	90	35	Blue
Lilac	Syringa	370	145	Purple, white, lavender, lilac
Magnolia	Magnolia	150–610	59–240	White, red
Myrtle	Myrtus	300	118	White
Oleaster	Elaeagnus	230–300	90–118	White
Periwinkle	Vinca	20–5	8–10	White, blue
Rhododendron	Rhododendron	180	71	Red, purple, pink, white
Silk tassel bush	Garrya	275	108	White
Veronica	Hebe	30–300	12–118	Blue, white
Viburnum	Viburnum	180–300	71–118	White, pink, red, blue
Winter sweet	Chimonanthus	275	108	Yellow

Trees

Common name	Latin name	Varieties	Height (m)	Height (ft)
Alder	Alnus	Common; Italian; golden leaf	20	65
Antarctic beech	Nothofagus	False beech	12	39
Ash	Fraxinus	Common; raywood; manna	18	59
Avocado	Persia	americana; drymifolia	18	59
Bamboo	Bambusoidae	Dendrocalamus strictus; Bambusa arundinacea	36	118
Baobab	Andansonia	digitata; gregorii	9–12	29–39
Beech	Fagus	Dawyck; fern-leaved; weeping; copper; golden	30	98
Birch	Betula	Silver; Swedish	10	33
Coconut palm	Cocus nucifera	Coconut palm	30	98
Cypress	Chamaecyparis	Lawson cypress	30–6	98–118
Elm	Ulmus	Wych; Dutch; English; weeping; Chinese	27–36	88–118
False acacia	Robinia	frisia; pseudoacacia	18	59
Flame tree	Delonix regia	Flame tree	15	49
Flowering cherries	Prunus	Ornamental almond; ornamental plum; ornamental peach; ornamental cherry	6–12	20–39
Flowering crab	Malus	John Downie; golden hornet; Japanese; Montreal beauty; profusion; Van Eseltine; lemoinei	6–15	20–49
Golden rain	Laburnum	Common; scotch; vosii	4	13
Gum	Eucalyptus	Gum; snow gum	15	49
Handkerchief	Davidia	involucrata	15	49
Hawthorn	Crataegus	monogyna; Paul's scarlet; crusgalli; orientalis; prunifolia	4	13
Hazel	Corylus	Common; aurea, corkscrew; filbert; giant; purpurea	3–9	10–29
Honey locust	Gleditsia	Sunburst; elegantissima	7	23
Hornbeam	Carpinus	Common	12	39
Horse chestnut	Aesculus	Red; common	18	59
Indian bean	Catalpa	Indian bean; aurea	6	20
Judas	Cercis	Judas; white Judas	4	13

Plants

Trees (continued)

Common name	Latin name	Varieties	Height (m)	(ft)
Juniper	*Juniperus*	*communis; virginiana; sabina; chinensis; phoenicea; horizontales; thuinfera*	3-6	10–20
Larch	*Larix*	European; golden	24–30	79–98
Lime	*Tilia*	Common; large-leaved; American	24–7	79–88
Mango	*Mangifera indica*	Mango	18	59
Maple	*Acer*	Field; Norway; purple Norway; sycamore	6–9	20–9
Mountain ash	*Sorbus*	Rowan; Joseph rock; Swedish whitebeam	15	49
Mulberry	*Morus*	Black mulberry	6	20
Oak	*Quercus*	English; sessile; Turkey; red; holm; willow	24	78
Ornamental pear	*Pyrus*	*pendula*	6	20
Palm	*Palmae*	Sugar; cohune; *palmyra*; silver; coconut; *carnaulsa*; doum; coco de mer; date; royal; cabbage	20	65
Paulownia	*Paulownia*	*tomentosa*	7	23
Pea	*Caragana*	*pendula*; dwarf	4	13
Pine	*Pinus*	Scots; Corsican; Austrian; Monterey	18–36	59–118
Plane	*Platanus*	London plane	24	79
Poplar	*Populus*	White; grey; *aurora*; *Italica*; aspen	24	79
Pride of India	*Koelreuteria*	*paniculata*	6	20
Sweet chestnut	*Castanea*		30	98
Sweet gum	*Liquidambar*	*styraciflua*	45	148
Tree of heaven	*Ailanthus*	*altissima*	20	65
Tulip	*Liriodendron*	*tulipifera*	35	115
Tupelo	*Nyssa*	*sylvatica*	9	29
Walnut	*Juglans*		30	98
Willow	*Salix*	Golden; weeping; American; Kilmarnock; purple; corkscrew	3–9	10–29
Yew	*Taxus baccata*	Common; Irish	4–15	13–49

Plants as foodstuffs

Temperate fruits

Common name	Latin name	Family
Apple	*Malus pumila*	Rosaceae
Pear	*Pyrus communis*	Rosaceae
Quince	*Cydonia vulgaris*	Rosaceae
Peach; nectarine	*Prunus persica*	Rosaceae
Sweet cherry	*P. avium*	Rosaceae
Sour cherry; cooking cherry; morello	*P. cerasus*	Rosaceae
Plum	*P. domestica*	Rosaceae
Bullace; damson	*P. insititia*	Rosaceae
Gage; greengage; mirabelle	*P. insititia* var *italica*, var *syriaca*	Rosaceae Rosaceae
Cherry plum	*P. cerasifera*	Rosaceae
Japanese plum	*P. salicina*	Rosaceae
American plum	*P. americana*	Rosaceae
Apricot	*P. armeniaca*	Rosaceae
Medlar	*Mespilus germanica*	Rosaceae
Raspberry	*Rubus idaeus*	Rosaceae
American red raspberry	*R. ideaus* var *strigosus*	Rosaceae
Black raspberry	*R. occidentalis*	Rosaceae
Blackberry; bramble	*R. fruticosus*	Rosaceae
Evergreen blackberry	*R. laciniatus*	Rosaceae
Cloudberry	*R. chamaemorus*	Rosaceae
Pacific dewberry	*R. ursinus*	Rosaceae

Common name	Latin name	Family
Loganberry; boysenberry; veitchberry	*R. × loganbaccus*	Rosaceae
Wineberry	*R. phoenicolasius*	Rosaceae
Strawberry	*Fragaria × ananassa* (= *F. virginiana × F. chiloensis*)	Rosaceae
Gooseberry	*Ribes uva-crispa* (= *R. grossularia*)	Rosaceae
Blackcurrant	*R. nigrum*	Rosaceae
Redcurrant	*R. rubrum*	Rosaceae
Fig	*Ficus carica*	Moraceae
Olive	*Olea europaea*	Oleaceae
Mulberry; black mulberry	*Morus nigra*	Moraceae
Red mulberry	*M. rubra*	Moraceae
Grape	*Vitis vinifera*	Vitaceae
Frost grape	*V. riparia; V. vulpina*	Vitaceae
Bush or sand grape	*V. rupestris*	Vitaceae
Fox or skunk grape	*V. labrusca*	Vitaceae
Muscadine; bullace grape	*V. rotundifolia*	Vitaceae
Bilberry	*Vaccinium myrtillus*	Ericaceae
Cranberry	*V. oxycoccus; V. macrocarpon*	Ericaceae
Cowberry	*V. vitis-idaea*	Ericaceae
Lowbush blueberry	*V. angustifolium*	Ericaceae
Highbush blueberry	*V. corymbosum*	Ericaceae
Strawberry tree	*Arbutus unedo*	Ericaceae
Chinese gooseberry; kiwiberry	*Actinidia chinensis*	Actinidiaceae

Tropical and subtropical fruits

Common Name	Latin name	Family
Sweet orange	*Citrus sinensis*	Rutaceae
Sour, Seville or bitter orange	*C. aurantium*	Rutaceae
Lime	*C. aurantiifolia*	Rutaceae
Lemon	*C. limon*	Rutaceae
Rangpur lime; mandarin lime	*C.* × *limonia*	Rutaceae
Shaddock; pummelo	*C. maxima*	Rutaceae
Citron	*C. medica*	Rutaceae
King orange	*C.* × *nobilis*	Rutaceae
Grapefruit	*C.* × *paradisi*	Rutaceae
Mandarin; satsuma; tangerine; clementine	*C. reticulata*	Rutaceae
Kumquat	*Fortunella japonica*	Rutaceae
Loquat; Japanese medlar	*Eriobotrya japonica*	Rosaceae
Breadfruit	*Artocarpus altilis*	Moraceae
Jackfruit	*A. heterophyllus*	Moraceae
Cherimoya	*Annona cherimolia*	Annonaceae
Custard apple; bullock's heart	*A. reticulata*	Annonaceae
Soursop; guanabana	*A. muricata*	Annonaceae
Sugarapple; sweetsop	*A. squamosa*	Annonaceae
Banana; edible plantain	*Musa acuminata; M.* × *paradisiaca*	Musaceae
Fehi banana	*M. fehi*	Musaceae
Avocado; aguacate; alligator pear	*Persaea americana* (= *P. gratissima*)	Lauraceae
Coconut	*Cocos nucifera*	Palmae
Date	*Phoenix dactylifera*	Palmae
Pineapple	*Ananas comosus*	Bromeliaceae
Mango	*Mangifera indica*	Anacardiaceae
Cashew apple	*Anacardium occidentale*	Anacardiaceae
Granadilla; passion fruit	*Passiflora edulis*	Passifloraceae
Sweet granadilla	*P. ligularis*	Passifloraceae
Yellow granadilla	*P. laurifolia*	Passifloraceae
Sweet calabash	*P. maliformis*	Passifloraceae
Curuba	*P. mollissima*	Passifloraceae
Giant granadilla	*P. quadrangularis*	Passifloraceae
Papaw; pawpaw	*Carica papaya*	Caricaceae
Durian	*Durio zibethinus*	Bombacaceae
Mangosteen	*Garcinia mangostana*	Guttiferae
Rambutan	*Nephelium lappaceum*	Sapindaceae
Longan	*Euphoria longan*	Sapindaceae
Akee	*Blighia sapida*	Sapindaceae
Guava	*Psidium guajava*	Myrtaceae
Cape gooseberry	*Physalis peruviana*	Solanaceae
Tomatillo; jamberry	*P. ixocarpa*	Solanaceae
Mammey apple; mammee	*Mammea americana*	Guttiferae
Sapodilla	*Manilkara sapota*	Sapotaceae
Sapote	*Pouteria sapota* (= *Calocarpoum sapota*)	Sapotaceae
Tamarind	*Tamarindus indica*	Leguminosae

Common name	Latin name	Family
Carambola; caramba; blimbing; bilimbi	*Averrhoa carambola*	Oxalidaceae
Persimmon	*Diospyros kaki*	Ebenaceae
Pomegranate	*Punica granatum*	Punicaceae
Litchi; lychee	*Litchi chinensis*	Sapindaceae

Vegetables

Common name	Latin name	Family
BRASSICAS		
Cabbage, spring		Cruciferae
Cabbage, savoy		Cruciferae
Cauliflower		Cruciferae
Broccoli; calabrese	*Brassica oleracea*	Cruciferae
Kale		Cruciferae
Brussel sprouts		Cruciferae
Turnip; swede	*B. campestris*	Cruciferae
Pak-choi	*B. campestris,* subspecies *chinensis*	Cruciferae
Pe-tsai	*B. campestris,* subspecies *pekinensis*	Cruciferae
LEAF AND STEM VEGETABLES		
Asparagus	*Asparagus officinalis*	Liliaceae
Wild asparagus	*A. acutifolius*	Liliaceae
Chives	*Allium schoenoprasum*	Liliaceae
Celery	*Apium graveolens*	Umbelliferae
Fennel	*Foeniculum vulgare* var *vulgare*	Umbelliferae
Florence fennel; finocchio	*F. vulgare* var *azoricum*	Umbelliferae
Chicory; asparagus chicory; witloof; belgian endive	*Cichorium intybus*	Compositae
Radicchio; red verona chicory; treviso chicory; castelfranco chicory	*C. intybus*	Compositae
Grumolo; broad-leaved chicory	*C. intybus*	Compositae
Endive; escarolle; batavian endive	*C. endivia*	Compositae
Lettuce; cabbage lettuce; cos lettuce	*Lactuca sativa*	Compositae
Wild lettuce	*L. taraxaciflora*	Compositae
Spinach; summer or round-seeded, winter or prickly-seeded	*Spinacia oleracea*	Chenopodiaceae
Spinach beet	*Beta vulgaris* var *cicla*	Chenopodiaceae
Seakale beet; Swiss chard	*B. vulgaris* var *cicla*	Chenopodiaceae
Orache	*Atriplex hortensis*	Chenopodiaceae
New Zealand spinach	*Tetragonia expansa*	Aizoaceae

Plants

Plants as foodstuffs (continued)

Common name	Latin name	Family
Amaranth spinach	Amaranthus caudatus; A. hybridus; A. tricolor	Amaranthaceae
Sea kale	Crambe maritima	Cruciferae
Bamboo shoots	Bambusa arundinacea B. beecheyana; B. vulgaris; Phyllostachys dulcis; P. pubescens etc	Gramineae
Globe artichoke	Cynara scolymus	Compositae
Cardoon	C. cardunculus	Compositae
Okra; gumbo; lady's fingers	Hibiscus esculentus (= Abelmoschus esculentus)	Malvaceae
Jew's mallow	Corchorus olitorius	Tiliaceae
Jute	C. capsularis	Tiliaceae
Water spinach	Ipomoea aquatica	Convolvulaceae
Rhubarb, garden	Rheum rhabarbarum	Polygonaceae

ROOT VEGETABLES

Common name	Latin name	Family
Radish	Raphanus sativus	Cruciferae
Winter radish	R. sativus cv 'Longipinnatus'	Cruciferae
Black salsify	Scorzonera hispanica	Compositae
Salsify; oyster plant	Tragopogon porrifolius	Compositae
Carrot	Daucus carota subspecies sativus	Umbelliferae
Parsnip	Pastinaca sativa	Umbelliferae
Celeriac; turnip-rooted celery	Apium graveolens var rapaceum	Umbelliferae
Arracacha	Arracacia xanthorrhiza	Umbelliferae
Turnip-rooted parsley; hamburg parsley	Petroselinum crispum var tuberosum	Umbelliferae
Chervil, turnip-rooted	Chaerophyllum bulbosum	Umbelliferae
Jerusalem artichoke	Helianthus tuberosus	Compositae
Chinese artichoke	Stachys tuberifera	Labiatae
Oca	Oxalis tuberosa	Oxalidaceae
Ulluco; ullucu	Ullucus tuberosus	Basellaceae
Anu; anyu	Tropaeolum tuberosum	Tropaeolaceae
Yam bean	Pachyrhizus erosus	Leguminosae
Yam bean; potato bean	P. tuberosus	Leguminosae
Sacred or East Indian lotus	Nelumbo nucifera	Nymphaeaceae
Kaffir potato; Hausa potato	Plectranthus (Coleus) esculentus	Labiatae
Onion	Allium cepa	Liliaceae
Shallot	A. cepa var aggregatum (= A. ascalonicum)	Liliaceae
Welsh onion; Japanese onion	A. fistulosum	Liliaceae
Garlic	A. sativum	Liliaceae
Leek	A. porrum	Liliaceae

Fruit vegetables

Common name	Latin name	Family
Tomato	Lycopersicum esculentum	Solanaceae
Aubergine	Solanum melongena	Solanaceae
Cucumber	Cucumis sativa	Cucurbitaceae
Gherkin	C. anguria	Cucurbitaceae
Bitter gourd; bitter cucumber	Momordica charantia	Cucurbitaceae
Bottle gourd; calabash gourd; white gourd	Lagenaria siceraria	Cucurbitaceae
Snake gourd	Trichosanthes cucumerina	Cucurbitaceae
Wax, ash gourd	Benincasa hispida	Cucurbitaceae
Chayote; christophine	Sechium edule	Cucurbitaceae
pumpkins; marrows; squashes		
Breadfruit	Artocarpus altilis	Moraceae
Jackfruit	A. heterophyllus	Moraceae
Pepper; sweet pepper	Capsicum annuum	Solanaceae
Avocado; alligator pear	Persea americana	Lauraceae

Root crops

Common name	Latin name	Family
TEMPERATE		
Turnip	Brassica campestris ssp rapifera	Cruciferae
Swede; rutabaga	B. napus var napobrassica	Cruciferae
Mangel; mangel-wurzel; mangold	Beta vulgaris ssp vulgaris	Chenopodiaceae
Beet; sugarbeet; beetroot	B. vulgaris ssp vulgaris	Chenopodiaceae
Potato	Solanum tuberosum	Solanaceae
TROPICAL		
Sweet potato	Ipomoea batatas	Convolvulaceae
Topee-tambu	Calathea alloula	Marantaceae
Cassava; manihot	Manihot esculenta	Euphorbiaceae
Taro; tanier cocoyams; arrowroots		
Yam, white Guinea	Dioscorea rotundata	Dioscoreaceae
Yam, yellow Guinea	D. cayenensis	Dioscoreaceae
Yam, greater	D. alata	Dioscoreaceae
Yam, bitter	D. dumetorum	Dioscoreaceae
Yam, Asiatic	D. esculenta	Dioscoreaceae
Yam, American	D. trifida	Dioscoreaceae

Legumes and pulses

Common name	Latin name	Part consumed
COOL TEMPERATE AND WARM TEMPERATE		
Garden pea	Pisum sativum	Seeds; young pods
Field pea	P. arvense	Seeds
Asparagus pea; winged pea	Tetragonolobus purpureus	
French, kidney, haricot, green, runner, string, salad, wax bean	Phaseolus vulgaris	Young pods; seeds
Runner; scarlet runner	P. coccineus	Young pods
Butter, sieva, civet, Madagascar, Carolina sewee bean	P. lunatus	Seeds
Lima bean	P. limensis	Seeds
Soybean	Glycine max (G. soja)	Seeds; sprouts; oil
Lentil	Lens culinaris	Seeds
Broad bean	Vicia faba	Seeds
Lupin	Lupinus albus; L. pilosus; L. luteus; L. mutabilis	Seeds
Carob bean; locust bean; St John's bread	Ceratonia siliqua	Pods
TROPICAL		
Tepary bean	Phaseolus acutifolius var latifolius	Seeds
Cluster bean; guar	Cyamopsis tetragonolobus	Young pods; seeds
Goa bean; asparagus pea; winged pea	Psophocarpus tetragonolobus	Young pods
	P. palmettorum	Young pods
Yam bean; chopsui potato	Pachyrhizus erosus; P. tuberosus	Young pods; roots
Lablab; hyacinth	Dolichos lablab	Pods; seeds
Madras gram; horse gram	D. biflorus	Seeds
Chick pea	Cicer arietinum	Seeds
Bambara; groundnut; kaffir pea	Voandzeia subterranea	Seeds
Kersting's groundnut	Kerstingiella geocarpa	Seeds
Tamarind	Tamarindus indica	Pulp from pods; seeds
Moth bean	Vigna aconitifolia	Seeds
Adzuki bean	V. angularis	Seeds
Cowpea	V. unguiculata	Seeds
Black-eyed pea	V. unguiculata subspecies unguiculata	Seeds
Yard long bean	V. unguiculata subspecies sesquipedalis	Pods
Black gram	Vigna mungo (Phaseolus mungo)	Seeds; young pods
Green gram; mung bean	V. radiata (Phaseolus aureus)	Seeds; pods; sprouts

Common name	Latin name	Part consumed
Rice bean	V. umbellata	Seeds
Jack bean	Canavalia ensiformis	Young pods; seeds
Sword bean	C. gladiata	Young pods; seeds
Groundnut	Arachis hypogaea	Seeds; oil
Pigeon pea; Cajan congo pea; red gram	Cajanus cajan	Seeds
African locust bean	Parkia filicoidea; P. biglobosa	Seeds; pulp of pod
Yam bean	Sphenostylis stenocarpa	seeds

Main cereal crops

Common name	Latin name
Wheat	Triticum
wild emmer	T. diococcoides
cultivated emmer	T. diococcum
einkorns	T. monococcum var monococcum; var boeoticum
hard (durum)	T. durum
turgidum	T. turgidum
bread	T. aestivum var aestivum
spelt	T. spelta
club	T. compactum
Barley	Hordeum vulgare
two-rowed	H. distichum
six-rowed	H. hexastichum
Rye	Secale cereale
Maize	Zea mays
Rice	Oryza sativa
African rice	O. glaberrima
Oats	Avena
hexaploid	A. sativa; A. byzantina; A. nuda
tetraploid	A. abyssinica
diploid	A. strigosa; A. brevis
Sorghum	Sorghum bicolor
Millets	
finger or African	Eleusine coracana;
bulrush; pearl	Pennisetum americanum;
bajra; common; proso	Panicum miliaceum
Japanese barnyard; sanwa	Echinachloa frumentacea
Foxtail, German and Italian	Setaria italica
Teff	Eragrostis tef
Fonio; fundi	Digitaria spp
Koda; kodo	Paspalum scrobiculatum

Sugar and starch crops

Common name	Latin name	Family
SUGAR PLANTS		
Sugar cane	Saccharum officinarum	Gramineae
Sugar beet	Beta vulgaris	Chenopodiaceae
Sugar maple	Acer saccharum	Aceraceae

Natural history

Plants

Plants as foodstuffs (continued)

Common name	Latin name	Family
Black maple	A. nigrum	Aceraceae
Barley (germinating)	Hordeum vulgare	Gramineae
Sweet sorghum; sorgo	Sorghum bicolor	Gramineae
Wild date palm	Phoenix sylvestris	Palmae
Palmyra palm	Borassus flabellifer	Palmae
Toddy palm; sago palm; jaggery palm	Caryota urens	Palmae
Coconut palm	Cocos nucifera	Palmae
Gomuti palm; sugar palm	Arenga pinnata	Palmae
Honey palm; syrup palm	Jubaea chilensis	Oleaceae
Nypa palm	Nypa fruticans	Oleaceae
Manna ash	Fraxinus ornus	Oleaceae

STARCH PLANTS

Common name	Latin name	Family
Potato	Salanum tuberosum	Solanaceae
Cassava; manioc	Manihot esculenta	Euphorbiaceae
Arrowroot	Maranta arundinacea	Marantaceae
Queensland arrowroot	Canna edulis	Cannaceae
Taro	Colocasia esculenta	Araceae
Giant taro	Alocasia macrorrhiza	Araceae
Dasheen	Colocasia esculenta var globifera	Araceae
Giant swamp taro	Cyrtosperma chamissonis (C. edule)	Araceae
Tanier; cocoyam	Xanthosma atrovirens; X. sagittifolium; X. violaceum	Araceae
East Indian arrowroot	Curcuma angustifolia	Zingiberaceae
Fijian arrowroot; Tahitian arrowroot	Tacca leontopetaloides (T. pinnatifida)	Taccaceae
Greater Asiatic yam	Dioscorea alata	Dioscoreaceae
White Guinea yam	D. rotundata	Dioscoreaceae
Yellow Guinea yam	D. cayenensis	Dioscoreaceae
Air potato	D. bulbifera	Dioscoreaceae
Cush-cush; yampee	D. trifida	Dioscoreaceae
Sago palm	Metroxylon rumphii; M. sagu	Palmae
Sago palm; gomuti palm	Arenga pinnata	Palmae
American cabbage palm; caribe palm	Oreodoxa oleracea; Roystonea oleracea	Palmae

Common name	Latin name	Family
Kaffir bread	Encephalartos caffer	Zamiaceae
Bread tree	E. altensteinii	Zamiaceae
Sago palm; queen sago	Cycas circinalis	Cycadaceae
Japanese sago palm	C. revoluta	Cycadaceae
Maize	Zea mays	Gramineae
Wheat	Triticum spp	Gramineae
Rice	Oryza sativa	Gramineae

Edible nuts

Common name	Latin name	Main areas of cultivation
Hazelnut; cob; European filbert	Corylus avellana	Turkey; Italy; Spain; France; England; Oregon
Giant filbert	C. maxima (C. americana)	(As above)
Turkish cobnut	C. colurna	Turkey
Sweet chestnut	Castanea sativa	S Europe; N America
American chestnut	C. dentata	N America
Japanese chestnut	C. crenata	Japan; N America
Chinese chestnut	C. mollissima	China; Korea; N America
Almond	Prunus amygdalus (= P. dulcis)	Mediterranean; SW Asia; N America
Sweet almond	P. amygdalus var amygdalus	Americas
Bitter almond	P. amygdalus var amara	
Walnut	Juglans regia	Europe; Asia; N America
Black walnut; eastern walnut	J. nigra	N America
Butternut	J. cinerea	N America
Japanese walnut	J. ailanthifolia	Japan; N America
Chinese walnut	J. cathayensis	China; N America
Pecan	Carya illinoinensis	N America
Shagbark hickory	C. ovata	N America
Shellbark hickory	C. laciniosa	N America
Brazil nut; paranut	Bertholletia excelsa	Amazon region (wild)
Sapucaia; sapucaya	Lecythis sabucayo	S America (wild)
Monkey nut	L. usitata	S America (wild)
Cashew nut	Anacardium occidentale	Tropical S America; India; E Africa
Coconut	Cocos nucifera	India; Sri Lanka; Malaysia; Indonesia; Philippines

Natural history

Common name	Latin name	Main areas of cultivation	Common name	Latin name	Main areas of cultivation
Macadamia; Australia, or Queensland nut (smooth shell)	Macadamia integrifolia	Australia; California	Betel nut	Areca catechu	Old World tropics
			Kola	Cola nitida	W Africa; Caribbean
Macadamia nut (rough shell)	M. tetraphylla	Australia; California		C. acuminata	W Africa; Brazil
Moreton bay chestnut	Castanospermum australe	Australia (wild)	Water chestnut	Trapa natans; T. bicornis; T. maximowiczii	E Asia; Malaysia; India
Oysternut	Telfairia pedata	E Africa			
Peanut; ground nut	Arachis hypogaea	India; tropical Africa; China	Pine nut; pine kernel	Pinus pinea; P. pinaster	Mediterranean Mediterranean
			Swiss stone pine	P. cembra	Europe
Pilt nut	Canarium luzonicum; C. ovatum	Philippines	Mexican stone pine	P. cembroides	Mexico
Java almond	C. commune	Java			
Pistachio	Pistacia vera	E Mediterranean; India; S USA			

Herbs and spices

Common name	Latin name	Forms	Area of origin
Anise	Pimpinella anisum	Seeds; leaves	Middle East, now Southern Russia; Turkey; India; parts of Europe
Basil	Ocimum basilicum	Leaves	Europe
Bay	Laurus nobilis	Leaves	Mediterranean
Bergamot	Monarda didyma	Flowers; leaves	N America
Caraway	Carum carvi	Seeds (ground); leaves; tap roots	Temperate Asia; Europe; N America
Cardamom	Elettaria cardomomum	Pods; seeds (dried)	India; Middle East
Chervil	Anthriscus cerfolium	Leaves	S Russia, now Europe
Chilli	Capsicum annuum	Whole (fresh or dried)	N America; Europe
Chives	Allium schoenoprasum	Stems; flowers	Europe
Cinnamon	Cinnamomum zeylanicum	Bark (dried or ground)	Sri Lanka
Cloves	Eugenia aromatica	Buds (whole and ground)	SE Asia; Indonesia; Madagascar; Tanzania; Sri Lanka; Malaysia; Grenada
Coriander	Coriandrum sativum	Leaves; seeds (ground)	S Europe; Middle East
Cumin	Cuminum cyminum	Seeds (whole and ground)	The East; India; Egypt; Arabia
Dill	Anethum graveolens	Leaves; seeds	Scandinavia; Germany; C and E Europe
Fennel	Foeniculum vulgare	Leaves; stalks; seeds	S Europe
Ginger	Zingiber officinale	Root	Tropical Asia; Middle East; S Europe
Juniper	Juniperus communis	Berries	S Europe
Lovage	Levisticum officinale	Leaves; seeds; stems	Europe
Marjoram	Origanum majorana	Leaves	Mediterranean regions
Mint	Mentha	Leaves	Europe; Middle East
Mustard	Brassica nigra; B. juncea; B. alba	Seeds	Europe (white mustard – Mediterranean region)
Nutmeg	Myristica fragrans	Whole; ground	SE Asia
Oregano	Oregano vulgare	Leaves	Mediterranean regions
Paprika	Capsicum tetragonum	Fresh (whole); dried (ground)	Mexico; Spain; Morocco; Hungary
Parsley	Petroselinum crispum	Leaves	S Europe, now all the world's temperate regions
Poppy seeds	Papaver somniferum	Seeds	Middle East; India, N America; Europe
Rosemary	Rosmarinus officinalis	Leaves; flowers	Mediterranean region
Saffron	Crocus sativus	Flowers (dried and ground)	Mediterranean countries, particularly Spain

Herbs and spices (continued)

Common name	Latin name	Forms	Area of origin
Sage	*Salvia officinalis*	Leaves	N Mediterranean coast
Sassafras	*Sassafrass albidum, S. officinalis*	Leaves; bark (dried)	N America
Sesame seeds	*Sesamum indicum*	Seeds	Africa; India; China
Sorrel	*Rumex acetosa, R. scutatus*	Leaves	Europe; particularly France
Tamarind	*Tamarindus indica*	Pulp	E Africa; S Asia
Tansy	*Chrysanthemum vulgare*	Leaves	Europe
Tarragon	*Artemisia dracunculus*	Leaves	Siberia; now Europe
Thyme	*Thymus vulgaris*	Leaves	Mediterranean regions
Turmeric	*Curcuma longa*	Root (whole or ground)	India; China; Middle East
Vanilla	*Vanilla plainfolia*	Pods	S Mexico; Madagascar; C America; Puerto Rico; Réunion

FUNGI

Phylum	No. of species	Class	Examples	Characteristics of class
Zygomycota	600	Mucorales	Black bread mould *(Rhizopus stolonifer)*; Mucor	Many saprozoic on dung or organic debris. Others parasites of invertebrates, other fungi, and plants.
		Entomophthorales	*Basidiobolus*	Most parasites of animals, mainly insects.
		Zoopagales	*Cochlonema; Endocochlus*	Parasites of amoebas, nematodes, and other small animals.
Ascomycota	15 000	Hemiascomycetae	Yeasts, eg baker's yeast *(Sacchar-omyces cerevisiae)*	Morphologically simple. Short mycelia or none at all.
		Euascomycetae	Morels; truffles *(Tuber)*; most fungal partners in lichens; *Neurospora*	Largest and best known class of Ascomycota.
		Loculoascomycetae	*Mycosphaerella; Elsinoe*	Many are parasites of economically important food plants.
		Laboulbeniomycetae	*Rhizomyces; Amorphomyces*	Parasites of insects.
Basidiomycota	25 000	Heterobasidiomycetae	Jelly fungi; rusts; smuts	
		Homobasidiomycetae	Common mushrooms; shelf fungi; coral fungi; puffballs; earthstars; stinkhorns; bird's nest fungi	Contains most of the fungi known as mushrooms and toadstools.
Deuteromycota (Fungi Imperfecti)	25 000	Sphaeropsida	*Clypeoseptoria aparothospermi*	
		Melanconia	*Cryptosporium lunasporum*	
		Monilia	*Penicillium; Candida albicans*	Pathogenic yeasts; other yeasts that do not form asci or basidia.
		Mycelia Sterilia	*Rhizoctonia*	

HUMAN BEINGS

EARLY HUMANS

Evolution of early humans

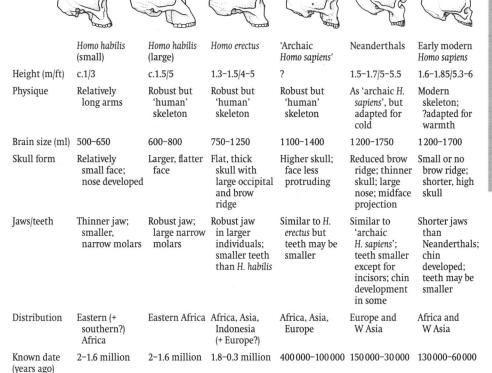

	Homo habilis (small)	Homo habilis (large)	Homo erectus	'Archaic Homo sapiens'	Neanderthals	Early modern Homo sapiens
Height (m/ft)	c.1/3	c.1.5/5	1.3–1.5/4–5	?	1.5–1.7/5–5.5	1.6–1.85/5.3–6
Physique	Relatively long arms	Robust but 'human' skeleton	Robust but 'human' skeleton	Robust but 'human' skeleton	As 'archaic H. sapiens', but adapted for cold	Modern skeleton; ?adapted for warmth
Brain size (ml)	500–650	600–800	750–1250	1100–1400	1200–1750	1200–1700
Skull form	Relatively small face; nose developed	Larger, flatter face	Flat, thick skull with large occipital and brow ridge	Higher skull; face less protruding	Reduced brow ridge; thinner skull; large nose; midface projection	Small or no brow ridge; shorter, high skull
Jaws/teeth	Thinner jaw; smaller, narrow molars	Robust jaw; large narrow molars	Robust jaw in larger individuals; smaller teeth than H. habilis	Similar to H. erectus but teeth may be smaller	Similar to 'archaic H. sapiens'; teeth smaller except for incisors; chin development in some	Shorter jaws than Neanderthals; chin developed; teeth may be smaller
Distribution	Eastern (+ southern?) Africa	Eastern Africa	Africa, Asia, Indonesia (+ Europe?)	Africa, Asia, Europe	Europe and W Asia	Africa and W Asia
Known date (years ago)	2–1.6 million	2–1.6 million	1.8–0.3 million	400 000–100 000	150 000–30 000	130 000–60 000

Homo habilis   Homo erectus   Homo sapiens

Human beings

Early human behaviour and ecology

Hominids and time periods (years ago)	Inference	Nature of the evidence
A Hominid ancestors ?8–5 million	Equatorial African origin.	Humans are genetically closest to African apes, which today are distributed across equatorial Africa; earliest hominid fossils are in eastern Africa.
B Earliest hominids 5–3 million	Habitually bipedal on the ground; occasionally arboreal.	Postcranial anatomy of fossils from Hadar in Ethiopia (but disagreements about similarity to modern human bipedalism and degree of arboreality).
	Inhabited a mosaic of grassland, woodland and thick shrub.	Faunas from Laetoli in Tanzania, Hadar and Makapansgat in South Africa.
3–2 million	Occupation of open savannas.	Fossil pollen and fauna.
	Emphasis on a fibrous plant diet in robust australopithecines.	Microwear on teeth; large teeth and jaws.
	First known manufacture of stone tools.	Tools from Ethiopia, Kenya, Malawi, and Zaire dated between 2.5 and 2.0 million years.
C Plio-Pleistocene hominids 2.0–1.5 million (Stone technology and changes in diet, brain size, etc. are usually associated with *Homo*)	Increased commitment to bipedalism on the ground.	Postcranial anatomy associated with archaic *Homo* established.
	Increased dexterity related to tool use and toolmaking, and possibly foraging.	Anatomy of hand bones and characteristics of stone tools and cores.
	Stones and animal bones carried repeatedly to specific sites.	Earliest known complex sites with many stone artifacts and fossils.
	Use of tools to procure and process food.	Bone and stone tools with distinctive traces of use.
	Dietary increase in protein and fat from large animals.	Cut marks made by stone tools on animal bones.
	Scavenging and possible hunting of large animals; processing of animals at specific spots.	Limb bones of animals concentrated at undisturbed archaeological sites.
	Increased cognitive capacities associated with making tools, foraging, social arrangements, and/or developing linguistic skills.	Increase in brain size from about a third to a half that of modern humans.
	Changes in maturation rate.	Implied by brain size increase and possible changes in tooth development.
	Increased mobility and predator defence.	Large stature evident in skeletal remains of early *Homo erectus* from West Turkana in Kenya.
D Early Pleistocene hominids 1.5–0.1 million	Occupation of new habitats and geographic zones.	Sites occur in previously unoccupied areas of eastern Africa; first appearance of hominids outside Africa.
	Definite preconception of tool form.	Biface handaxes of consistent shape made from rocks of varying original shape.
	Manipulation of fire.	Indications of fire differentially associated with archaeological sites.
	Increased levels of activity and stress on skeletons.	Massive development of postcranial and cranial bones.
E Late Pleistocene hominids 100 000–35 000 (Neanderthals)	Increased sophistication of toolkit and technology; still slow rate of change to tool assemblage.	Larger number of stone-tool types than before; complex preparation of cores.
	Intentional burial of dead and suggestions of ritual.	Preservation of skeletons, some with objects.
	Maintenance of high activity levels (locomotor endurance; powerful arms) and high levels of skeletal stress (eg teeth used as tools).	Robust skeletons, especially thick leg bones and large areas for muscle attachment on arm bones; prominent wear patterns on incisor teeth.
35 000–10 000 (fully modern *Homo sapiens*)	Decreased levels of activity and stress on skeleton.	Decrease in skeletal robusticity (also seen in early modern humans before 35 000 years ago).

Human beings

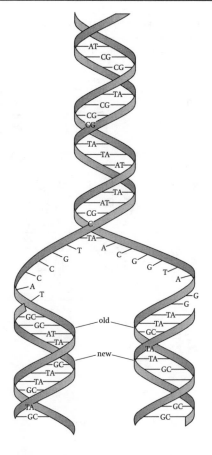

Hominids and time periods (years ago)	Inference	Nature of the evidence
	Enhanced technological efficiency.	Innovations in stone- and bone-tool production (eg blades and bone points).
	Innovations in hunting and other foraging activities, including systematic exploitation of particular animal species.	Evidence of spearthrower and harpoon, and trapping and netting of animals; animal remains in archaeological middens.
	Colonization of previously uninhabited zones.	For example, sites in tundra in Europe and Asia; colonization of the Americas (Australasia was probably first inhabited around 50 000 years ago).
	Elaboration of artistic symbolic expression and notation.	Engraving, sculpting and painting of walls and figurines; repetitive marks on bones; jewellery.
	Surge of technological and cultural differentiation and change.	Variation in toolkits over space and time.
	Harvesting and first cultivation of grains; first domestication of animals.	Evidence of seeds and fauna from sites dating to the end of the Pleistocene.

THE BODY

DNA

DNA or *deoxyribonucleic acid* contains the genetic information for most living organisms. Each human cell contains about 2 m/6.6 ft of DNA supercoiled on itself such that it fits within the cell nucleus (less than 10 μm (micrometres) in diameter).

DNA consists of four *bases* (adenine [A], guanine [G], thymine [T], and cytosine [C]), a sugar (2-deoxy-D-ribose), and phosphoric acid, arranged in the famous *double helical* structure discovered by geneticists James Watson and Francis Crick in 1953. In the helical structure, A pairs only with T, and G only with C.

DNA structure and replication, following Watson and Crick. The two strands of the double helix separate, and a new strand is assembled alongside each, the base sequence being determined by complementary pairing with the base sequence of the existing strand.

The genetic code

The four DNA bases A, G, T, and C, like the letters of the alphabet, can be used to store information. This genetic information is passed on via RNA or *ribonucleic acid* (consisting of the four bases adenine, guanine, cytosine, and uracil [U]), which provides a template for the assembly of amino acids in a particular sequence, thereby building a protein.

A group of three DNA or RNA bases is known as a *triplet* or *codon*, and codes for a particular amino acid. Information is passed from DNA to RNA by *complementary pairing*: A pairs only with U, and G only with C.

Genetic code in RNA triplets

1st base	2nd base				3rd base
	U	C	A	G	
U	Phenylalanine	Serine	Tyrosine	Cysteine	U
	Phenylalanine	Serine	Tyrosine	Cysteine	C
	Leucine	Serine	—[a]	—[a]	A
	Leucine	Serine	—[a]	Tryptophan	G
C	Leucine	Proline	Histidine	Arginine	U
	Leucine	Proline	Histidine	Arginine	C
	Leucine	Proline	Glutamine	Arginine	A
	Leucine	Proline	Glutamine	Arginine	G
A	Isoleucine	Threonine	Asparagine	Serine	U
	Isoleucine	Threonine	Asparagine	Serine	C
	Isoleucine	Threonine	Lysine	Arginine	A
	Methionine	Threonine	Lysine	Arginine	G
G	Valine	Alanine	Aspartic acid	Glycine	U
	Valine	Alanine	Aspartic acid	Glycine	C
	Valine	Alanine	Glutamic acid	Glycine	A
	Valine	Alanine	Glutamic acid	Glycine	G

[a] Chain termination.

The human chromosomes

The 46 human chromosomes, showing the banding patterns characteristic of each, grouped according to convention.

The human skeleton

The bones of the skeleton are often divided into two groups: the *axial skeleton* comprises the bones of the vertebral column, skull, ribs, and sternum; and the *appendicular skeleton* comprises the remainder.

1 Skull, displaying the frontal bone, and the front parts of the parietal and temporal bones. **2** Maxilla. **3** Mandible. **4** Clavicle. **5** Humerus. **6** Radius. **7** Ulna. **8** Sternum. **9** Scapula (obscured in this view by the upper ribs). **10** Ribs. **11** Vertebral column, displaying (from above to below) cervical, thoracic, lumbar, sacral, and coccygeal vertebrae. **12** Ilium. **13** Sacrum. **14** Coccyx. **15** Femur. **16** Fibula. **17** Tibia. **18** Bones of the hand, comprising the eight carpals, the five metacarpals, the three phalanges in each finger, and the two phalanges in the thumb. **19** Bones of the foot, comprising the seven tarsals, the five metatarsals, the two phalanges in the big toe, and the three phalanges in the other toes.

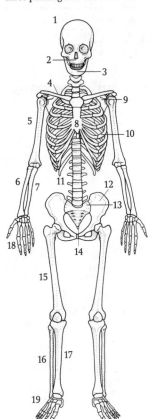

Bones of the human body

Skull
1	Occipital
2	Parietal – 1 pair
1	Sphenoid
1	Ethmoid
2	Inferior nasal conchae
1	Frontal – 1 pair, fused
2	Nasal – 1 pair
2	Lacrimal – 1 pair
2	Temporal – 1 pair
2	Maxilla – 1 pair
2	Zygomatic – 1 pair
1	Vomer
2	Palatine – 1 pair
1	Mandible – 1 pair, fused (jawbone)
$\overline{22}$	

The ears
2	Malleus (hammer)
2	Incus (anvil) } ossicles
2	Stapes (stirrups)
$\overline{6}$	

Vertebrae
7	Cervical
12	Thoracic
5	Lumbar
1	Sacral – 5, fused to form the sacrum
1	Coccyx – between 3 and 5, fused
$\overline{26}$	

Vertebral ribs
14	Ribs, 'true' – 7 pairs
10	Ribs, 'false' – 5 pairs of which 2 pairs are floating
$\overline{24}$	

Sternum (breastbone)
1	Manubrium
1	'The body' (sternebrae)
1	Xiphisternum
$\overline{3}$	
1	Hyoid (in the throat)

Pectoral girdle
2	Clavicle – 1 pair (collar bone)
2	Scapula (including coracoid) – 1 pair (shoulder blade)
$\overline{4}$	

Upper extremity (each arm)
1	Humerus
1	Radius
1	Ulna } forearm
	Carpus:
1	Scaphoid
1	Lunate
1	Triquetral
1	Pisiform
1	Trapezium } wrist
1	Trapezoid
1	Capitate
1	Hamate
5	Metacarpals
	Phalanges:
2	First digit
3	Second digit
3	Third digit } fingers
3	Fourth digit
3	Fifth digit
$\overline{30}$	

Pelvic girdle
	Ilium, ischium and pubis (combined) – 1 pair of hip
2	bones, innominate

Lower extremity (each leg)
1	Femur (thighbone)
1	Tibia
1	Fibula
1	Patella (kneebone)
	Tarsus:
1	Talus
1	Calcaneus
1	Navicular
1	Cuneiform medial
1	Cuneiform, inter- mediate
1	Cuneiform, lateral
1	Cuboid
5	Metatarsals
	Phalanges:
2	First digit
3	Second digit
3	Third digit } toes
3	Fourth digit
3	Fifth digit
$\overline{30}$	

Total
22	Skull
6	The ears
26	Vertebrae
24	Vertebral ribs
3	Sternum
1	Throat
4	Pectoral girdle
60	Upper extremity (arms) – 2 × 30
2	Hip bones
60	Lower extremity (legs) – 2 × 30
$\overline{208}$	

Human beings

Human beings

Muscles and internal organs

In human beings the musculature normally accounts for some 40% of the total body weight. There are 639 named muscles in the human anatomy.

1 Trapezius muscle
2 Deltoid muscles
3 Triceps muscles (the biceps, at the front of the arm, cannot be seen from this view)
4 Latissimus dorsi muscle
5 Gluteus maximus muscle (largest muscle in the body)
6 Kidney
7 Trachea
8 Lungs
9 Heart
10 Liver (only a small part of the liver can be seen in this illustration)
11 Stomach
12 Spleen
13 Colon
14 Small intestine
15 Appendix
16 Bladder

The heart

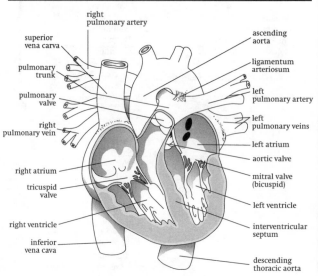

right pulmonary artery
superior vena carva
pulmonary trunk
pulmonary valve
right pulmonary vein
right atrium
tricuspid valve
right ventricle
inferior vena cava

ascending aorta
ligamentum arteriosum
left pulmonary artery
left pulmonary veins
left atrium
aortic valve
mitral valve (bicuspid)
left ventricle
interventricular septum
descending thoracic aorta

Human pulse rates

Normal restling pulse rates in healthy persons.

	Beats per minute
Foetus *in utero*	150
New born (full term)	140
First year	120
Second year	110
5 years	100
10 years	90
20 years	71
50 years	72
70 years	75
>80	78

The composition of blood

In an average human being blood accounts for 7–8% of body weight. Blood consists of:

Plasma: Water (90%), proteins (7%), nutrients, salts, nitrogen waste, carbon dioxide, hormones

Red blood cells (*erythrocytes*), 54% of which is haemoglobin. Normal count = 4–6 million per mm³

White blood cells (*leukocytes*). Normal count = 4 500–11 000 per mm³

Platelets (*thrombocytes*). Normal count = 150 000–300 000 per mm³

The brain in section

The ear

The eye

Normal eye

The image is in focus on the retina without a correcting lens in front.

Short-sighted or near-sighted eye (myopia)

(a) The eye is too long and the image is not in focus on the retina.
(b) The use of a concave lens brings the image into focus.

Long-sighted or far-sighted eye (hypermetropia)

(a) The eye is too short and the image is not in focus on the retina.
(b) The use of a convex lens brings the image into focus.

The teeth

The approximate times of eruption and shedding of teeth.

Milk			Permanent	
	Eruption	*Shed*		*Eruption*
Incisor 1	6–10 months	6–7 years	Incisor 1	7–8 years
Incisor 2	8–12 months	7–8 years	Incisor 2	8–9 years
Canine	16–22 months	10–12 years	Canine	10–12 years
Molar 1	13–19 months	9–11 years	Premolar 1	10–11 years
Molar 2	25–33 months	10–12 years	Premolar 2	11–12 years
			Molar 1	6–7 years
			Molar 2	12 years
			Molar 3	17–21 years

Note: The lower teeth usually appear before the equivalent upper teeth.

The reproductive organs

Females
Main female organs of reproduction
and surrounding structures

Males
Main male organs of reproduction
and surrounding structures

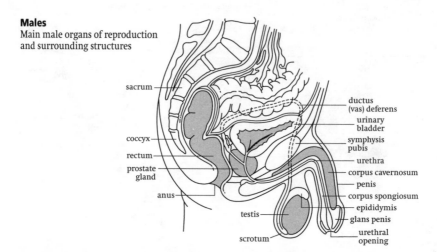

MEDICAL MATTERS

Communicable diseases

Name	Cause	Transmission	Incubation period
AIDS (Acquired Immune Deficiency Syndrome)	Human Immuno-deficiency Virus (HIV)	Sexual relations; sharing of syringes; blood transfusion	several years
Brucellosis	*Brucellus abortus* or *B meliteusis* bacteria	Cattle or goats	3–6 years
Chickenpox (varicella)	Varicella zoster virus (US) Herpes zoster virus (UK)	Infected persons; articles contaminated by discharge from mucous membranes	10–21 days
Cholera	*Vibrio cholerae* bacterium	Contaminated water and seafood	a few hours – 5 days
Common cold	Numerous viruses	Respiratory droplets of infected person	1–4 days
Diphtheria	*Corynebacterium diphtheriae* bacterium	Respiratory secretions and saliva of infected persons or carriers	2–6 days
Encephalitis	Viruses	Bite from infected mosquito	4–21 days
Gas gangrene	*Clostridium welchii* bacterium	Soil or soil-contaminated articles	1–4 days
Gonorrhoea	*Neisseria gonorrhoeae* bacterium	Urethral or vaginal secretions of infected persons	3–8 days
Hepatitis A (infectious)	Hepatitis A virus	Contaminated food and water	15–50 days
Hepatitis B (serum type B)	Hepatitis B virus	Infected blood; parenteral injection	6 weeks – 6 months
Infectious mononucleosis (US) Glandular fever (UK)	Epstein-Barr virus	Saliva; direct oral contact with infected person	2–6 weeks
Influenza	Numerous viruses (types A, B, C)	Direct contact; respiratory droplets, possibly airborne	1–4 days
Legionnaires' disease	*Legionella pneumophila* bacterium	Water droplets in infected humidifiers, cooling towers	1–3 days
Leprosy	*Mycobacterium leprae* bacillus	Droplet infection (minimally contagious)	variable
Malaria	*Plasmodium* protozoa	Bite from infected mosquito	6–37 days
Measles (rubeola)	Rubeola virus	Droplet infection	10–15 days
Meningitis	Various bacteria (bacterial meningitis) and viruses (viral meningitis)	Respiratory droplets	varies with causative agent
Mumps	Virus	Direct contact with infected persons; respiratory droplets and oral secretions	14–21 days
Paratyphoid fevers	*Salmonella* bacteria	Ingestion of contaminated food and water	1–14 days
Pneumonia	*Streptococcus pneumoniae* bacterium	Droplet infection	1–3 weeks
Poliomyelitis	Polio viruses	Direct contact with nasopharyngeal secretions of infected persons; vomit	7–21 days
Rabies	Virus	Bite from rabid animal	10 days – 6 months
Rubella (German measles)	Rubella virus	Direct contact or droplet spread of nasopharyngeal secretion	14–21 days
Scarlet fever	Group A haemolytic *Streptococcus* bacteria	Direct or indirect contact with infected persons, or droplet infection	1–5 days
Shingles	*see* chickenpox	*see* chickenpox	
Smallpox (variola)	Poxvirus variola	Direct contact; droplet	7–14 days
Syphilis	*Treponema pallidum* bacterium	Sexual relations; contact with open lesions; blood transfusion	10–90 days
Tetanus (lockjaw)	*Clostridium tetani* bacillus	Animal faeces and soil	3–21 days
Tuberculosis	*Mycobacterium tuberculosis* bacillus	Droplet spread; ingestion from contaminated milk	variable
Typhoid fever	*Salmonella typhi* bacillus	Contaminated food and water	7–21 days
Whooping cough (pertussis)	*Bordetella pertussis* bacterium	Droplet spread	10–21 days
Yellow fever	Arbovirus	Bite from infected mosquito	3–6 days

The geography of HIV infection

Although sub-Saharan Africa still has by far the most infections (some 6 million adults may be harbouring HIV), other regions are catching up fast. By the mid-1990s, the number of people infected in Asia could rise to 3 million, most of them in India and Thailand. (Early 1992 figures.)

WHO, 1993

25 000+

25 000+

50 000

1.5 million+

500 000

75 000+

8 million+

1.5 million

1 million +

Male and female
proportions

The occurrence of coronary heart disease

Age-standardized rates of mortality for men and women aged 40–49 in 1985.

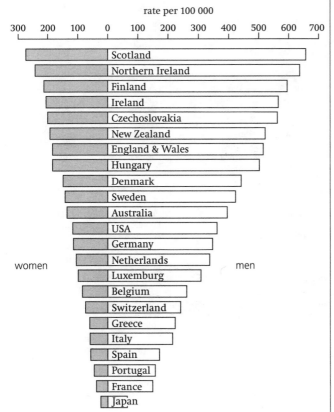

rate per 100 000

Estimates of most frequent cancers worldwide

Figures for 1980.

Males

		Number (thousands)	%
1	Lung	513.6	15.8
2	Stomach	408.8	12.6
3	Colon/rectum	286.2	8.8
4	Mouth/pharynx	257.3	7.9
5	Prostate	235.8	7.3
6	Oesophagus	202.1	6.2
7	Liver	171.7	5.3
8	Bladder	167.7	5.2
9	Lymphoma	139.9	4.3
10	Leukaemia	106.9	3.3

Females

		Number (thousands)	%
1	Breast	572.1	18.4
2	Cervix	465.6	15.0
3	Colon/rectum	285.9	9.2
4	Stomach	260.6	8.4
5	Corpus uteri	148.8	4.8
6	Lung	146.9	4.7
7	Ovary	137.6	4.4
8	Mouth/pharynx	121.2	3.9
9	Oesophagus	108.2	3.5
10	Lymphoma	98.0	3.2

Both sexes

		Number (thousands)	%
1	Stomach	669.4	10.5
2	Lung	660.5	10.4
3	Breast	572.1	9.0
4	Colon/rectum	572.1	9.0
5	Cervix	465.6	7.3
6	Mouth/pharynx	378.5	6.0
7	Oesophagus	310.4	4.9
8	Liver	251.2	4.0
9	Lymphoma	237.9	3.7
10	Prostate	235.8	3.7
11	Bladder	219.4	3.5
12	Leukaemia	188.2	3.0

Human beings

Phobias

An A to Z of phobias arranged by technical term

Technical term	Everyday name	Technical term	Everyday name	Technical term	Everyday name
Acero-	Sourness	Eoso-	Dawn	Nephelo-	Clouds
Achulo-	Darkness	Eremo-	Solitude	Noso- (patho-)	Disease
Acro-	Heights	Erete-	Pins	Ocho-	Vehicles
Aero-	Air	Ereuthro-	Blushing	Odonto-	Teeth
Agora-	Open spaces	Ergo-	Work	Oiko-	Home
Aichuro-	Points	Geno-	Sex	Olfacto-	Smell
Ailouro-	Cats	Geuma-	Taste	Omato-	Eyes
Akoustico-	Sound	Grapho-	Writing	Oneiro-	Dreams
Algo-	Pain	Gymnoto-	Nudity	Ophido-	Snakes
Amaka-	Carriages	Gyno-	Women	Ornitho-	Birds
Amatho-	Dust	Hade- (stygio-)	Hell	Ourano-	Heaven
Andro-	Men	Hamartio-	Sin	Pan- (panto-)	Everything
Anemo-	Wind	Hapto-	Touch	Partheno-	Girls
Angino-	Narrowness	Harpaxo-	Robbers	Patho- (noso-)	Disease
Anthropo-	Man	Hedono-	Pleasure	Patroio-	Heredity
Antlo-	Flood	Haemato-	Blood	Penia-	Poverty
Apeiro-	Infinity	Helmintho-	Worms	Phasmo-	Ghosts
Arachno-	Spiders	Hodo-	Travel	Phobo-	Fears
Astheno-	Weakness	Homichlo-	Fog	Photo-	Light
Astra-	Astral	Horme-	Shock	Pnigero-	Smothering
Ate-	Ruin	Hydro-	Water	Poine-	Punishment
Aulo-	Flute	Hypegia-	Responsibility	Poly-	Many things
Aurora-	Northern Lights	Hypno-	Sleep	Poto-	Drink
Bacilli-	Microbes	Ideo-	Ideas	Pterono-	Feathers
Baro-	Gravity	Kakorraphia-	Failure	Pyro-	Fire
Baso-	Walking	Karagalo-	Ridicule	Rypo-	Soiling
Batracho-	Reptiles	Keno-	Void	Satano-	Satan
Belone-	Needles	Kineso-	Motion	Sela-	Flashes
Bronto- (tonitro-)	Thunder	Klepto-	Stealing	Sidero-	Stars
Cheima-	Cold	Kopo-	Fatigue	Sito-	Food
Chiono-	Snow	Kristallo-	Ice	Sperma- (spermato-)	Germs
Chrometo-	Money	Lalio-	Stuttering	Stasi-	Standing
Chrono-	Duration	Linono-	String	Stygio- (hade-)	Hell
Chrystallo-	Crystals	Logo-	Words	Syphilo-	Syphilis
Claustro-	Closed spaces	Lysso- (mania-)	Insanity	Thalasso-	Sea
Cnido-	Stings	Mania- (lysso-)	Insanity	Thanato-	Death
Cometo-	Comets	Mastigo-	Flogging	Thasse-	Sitting
Cromo-	Colour	Mechano-	Machinery	Theo-	God
Cyno-	Dogs	Metallo-	Metals	Thermo-	Heat
Demo-	Crowds	Meteoro-	Meteors	Tonitro- (bronto-)	Thunder
Demono-	Demons	Miso-	Contamination	Toxi-	Poison
Dermato-	Skin	Mono-	One thing	Tremo-	Trembling
Dike-	Injustice	Musico-	Music	Triskaideka-	Thirteen
Dora-	Fur	Muso-	Mice	Xeno-	Strangers
Eisoptro-	Mirror	Necro-	Corpses	Zelo-	Jealousy
Elektro-	Electricity	Nelo-	Glass	Zoo-	Animals
Entomo-	Insects	Neo-	Newness		

An A to Z of phobias arranged by everyday name

Everyday name	Technical term	Everyday name	Technical term	Everyday name	Technical term
Air	Aero-	Glass	Nelo-	Robberies	Harpaxo-
Animals	Zoo-	God	Theo-	Ruin	Ate-
Astral	Astra-	Gravity	Baro-	Satan	Satano-
Birds	Orthino-	Heat	Thermo-	Sea	Thalasso-
Blood	Haemato-	Heaven	Ourano-	Sex	Geno-
Blushing	Ereuthro-	Heights	Acro-	Shock	Horme-
Carriages	Amaka-	Hell	Stygio- (hade-)	Sin	Hamartio-
Cats	Ailouro-	Heredity	Patroio-	Sitting	Thasso-
Closed spaces	Claustro-	Home	Oiko-	Skin	Dermato-
Clouds	Nephelo-	Ice	Kristallo-	Sleep	Hypno-
Cold	Cheima-	Ideas	Ideo-	Smell	Olfacto-
Colour	Cromo-	Infinity	Apeiro-	Smothering	Pnigero-
Comets	Cometo-	Injustice	Dike-	Snakes	Ophidio-
Contamination	Miso-	Insanity	Lysso- (mania-)	Snow	Chiono-
Corpses	Necro-	Insects	Entomo-	Soiling	Rypo-
Crowds	Demo-	Jealousy	Zelo-	Solitude	Eremo-
Crystals	Chrystallo-	Light	Photo-	Sound	Akoustico-
Darkness	Achluo-	Machinery	Mechano-	Sourness	Acero-
Dawn	Eoso-	Man	Anthropo-	Spiders	Arachno-
Death	Thanato-	Many things	Poly-	Standing	Stasi-
Demons	Demono-	Men	Andro-	Stars	Sidero-
Disease	Noso- (patho-)	Metals	Metallo-	Stealing	Klepto-
Dogs	Cyno-	Meteors	Meteoro-	Stings	Cnido-
Dreams	Oneiro-	Mice	Muso-	Strangers	Xeno-
Drinks	Poto-	Microbes	Bacilli-	String	Linono-
Duration	Chrono-	Mirrors	Eisoptro-	Stuttering	Lalio-
Dust	Amatho-	Money	Chrometo-	Syphilis	Syphilo-
Electricity	Elektro-	Motion	Kineso-	Taste	Geuma-
Everything	Pan- (panto-)	Music	Musico-	Teeth	Odonto-
Eyes	Omato-	Narrowness	Angino-	Thirteen	Triskaideka-
Failure	Kakorraphia-	Needles	Belone-	Thunder	Bronto- (tonitro-)
Fatigue	Kopo-	Newness	Neo-	Touch	Hapto-
Fears	Phobo-	Northern Lights	Aurora-	Travel	Hodo-
Feathers	Pterono-	Nudity	Gymnoto-	Trembling	Tremo-
Fire	Pyro-	One thing	Mono-	Vehicles	Ocho-
Flashes	Sela-	Open spaces	Agora-	Void	Keno-
Flogging	Mastigo-	Pain	Algo-	Walking	Baso-
Flood	Antlo-	Pins	Erete-	Water	Hydro-
Flute	Aulo-	Pleasure	Hedono-	Weakness	Astheno-
Fog	Homichlo-	Points	Aichuro-	Wind	Anemo-
Food	Sito-	Poison	Toxi-	Women	Gyno-
Fur	Dora-	Poverty	Penia-	Words	Logo-
Germs	Sperma-	Punishment	Poine-	Work	Ergo-
	(spermato-)	Reptiles	Batracho-	Worms	Helmintho-
Ghosts	Phasmo-	Responsibility	Hypegia-	Writing	Grapho-
Girls	Partheno-	Ridicule	Katagalo-		

Medical matters

Commonly used drugs

Human beings (side tab)

Common name	Drug type	Use	Comments
Adrenaline	Bronchodilator	Counteracts cardiac arrest; relieves severe allergic reactions; and controls symptoms of asthma.	Constricts blood vessels and is used to control bleeding in surgery.
Anabolic steroids	Male sex hormones	Increase muscle bulk and body growth. Help increase production of blood cells in some forms of anaemia.	Risk of serious side-effects. Abused by some athletes to improve performance.
Aspirin	Analgesic; anti-inflammatory; anti-platelet	Relieves pain; reduces fever; helps prevent blood clots from forming.	Introduced by Hermann Dresser, 1893. Can cause irritation to the stomach and even bleeding.
Beta blockers	Beta blockers	Treat angina, hypertension, and irregular heart rhythms. Can also prevent migraines.	Minor side-effects of reduced circulation and reduced capacity for strenuous exercise.
Chloral hydrate	Sleeping drug	Short-term treatment of insomnia.	Suitable for use by children.
Cimetidine	Anti-ulcer drug	Reduces level of acid and pepsin, and promotes healing of stomach and duodenal ulcers.	Also affects actions of certain enzymes in the liver. Prescribed only when possibility of stomach cancer has been ruled out.
Codeine	Narcotic analgesic	Relieves mild pain. Also effective as a cough suppressant.	Introduced at turn of century. Can be habit-forming, but addiction seldom occurs if drug used for limited period.
Cortisone	Corticosteroid	Treats rheumatoid arthritis. Anti-inflammatory drug.	Discovered by Edward Calvin Kendall, 1934, as adrenal cortisone extracts.
Co-trimoxazole	Antibacterial	Treats respiratory, constipating, and urinary tract infections.	Can have side-effects of nausea and vomiting.
Diazepam	Benzodiazepine anti-anxiety drug	Treats anxiety, insomnia. Also prescribed as muscle relaxant.	Can be habit-forming if taken over a long period.
Digoxin	Digitalis drug	Slows down rate of heart. Controls tiredness, breathlessness, and fluid retention.	Treatment must be monitored carefully.
Ethambutol	Antituberculosis	Used with other antituberculosis drugs it helps boost their effects.	Side-effect can be eye damage.
Frusemide	Loop diuretic	Treats fluid retention caused by heart failure and some liver and kidney disorders.	Discovered 1960.
Ibuprofen	Analgesic; anti-inflammatory	Treats symptoms of rheumatoid arthritis as well as headaches and menstrual pain.	Few-side effects and does not cause bleeding in the stomach.
Insulin	For diabetes	Supplements or replaces natural insulin in diabetes mellitus.	Isolated by Frederick Banting, C H Best, 1921. Only effective treatment for juvenile diabetes.
Magnesium hydroxide	Antacid	Neutralizes stomach acid. Also acts as laxative.	
Morphine	Narcotic analgesic	Relieves severe pain.	Discovered by Friedrich Serturner, 1805. Derives from opium and can be addictive.
Paracetamol/ acetaminophen	Analgesic	Relieves bouts of mild pain and fever. Does not cause damage to stomach.	First used by Joseph von Mering, 1893. Large doses can be toxic and an overdose can cause serious damage to liver and kidneys.
Penicillin	Antibiotic	Treats many common infections.	Discovered by Alexander Fleming, 1928. Can cause allergic reactions.
Pethidine	Narcotic analgesic	Used particularly to relieve pain in childbirth. Effect short-lasting.	Introduced by Hoechst, 1939. Habit-forming if taken over long period of time.
Phenylpropan- olamine	Decongestant	Relieves nasal congestion in colds and hay fever.	Can raise the heart rate and cause palpitations.
Quinidine	Anti-arrhythmic drug	Treats abnormal heart rhythms.	Can cause allergic reactions.

128

Common name	Drug type	Use	Comments
Quinine	Antimalarial drug	Treats malaria and leg cramps.	Discovered by P J Pelletier, J B Caventou, 1818. Now rarely prescribed due to side-effects of headaches, nausea, hearing loss and blurred vision.
Ranitidine	Anti-ulcer drug	Prevents gastric and duodenal ulcers. Reduces amount of acid produced by stomach.	Prescribed only when possibility of stomach cancer has been ruled out.
Salbutamol/ albuterol	Bronchodilator	Treats asthma, bronchitis, and emphysema.	Little stimulant effect on heart rate and blood pressure. Gives rapid relief and is more effective if inhaled rather than taken by mouth.
Sodium bicarbonate	Antacid	Relieves indigestion and discomfort caused by peptic ulcers. Relieves pain from urinary tract infections.	If given by injection, can also be effective in treatment of acidity of the blood.
Temazepam	Benzodiazepine sleeping drug	Short-term treatment of insomnia.	Can be habit-forming.
Terfenadine	Antihistamine	Treats allergic rhinitis, particularly hay fever.	Little or no sedative effect on the nervous system.
Testosterone	Male sex hormone	Increases fertility in men with testicular disorders. Also used to induce puberty in cases of hormone deficiency.	Can interfere with growth or cause over-rapid sexual development.
Tetracycline	Antibiotic	Treats pneumonia, bronchitis, and chest infections.	Common side-effects are nausea and vomiting.

Commonly abused drugs

Name	Common name	Effects	Comments
Alcohol	Booze, drink	Acts as central-nervous-system depressant, so reduces anxiety, impairs concentration, slows reactions.	Long-term effects include liver disease (cirrhosis, liver cancer, hepatitis), heart disease, and inflammation of stomach. Alcoholics have above-average chance of developing dementia.
Amphetamines	Uppers, speed, bennies	Promote feelings of alertness; increases speech and physical activity.	Can produce toxic effects, mood swings, circulatory and cardiac disturbances, feelings of paranoia, hallucinations, and convulsions.
Barbiturates (Nembutal, Seconal, Amytal)	Barbs, reds, downers	Calm the nerves; induce sleep; have hypnotic effect.	Highly addictive; overdose is lethal; can induce state of coma. Often fatal if taken with alcohol.
Benzodiazepines	Tranquillizers	Reduce mental activity and anxiety; slow body's reactions; reduce alertness.	Can cause dependency. Withdrawal symptoms occur on stopping the drug – anxiety, insomnia, panic attacks, head-aches, and palpitations.
Cocaine	Coke, crack, ice, snow (crack is a blend of cocaine, baking powder, and water)	Increases blood pressure, heart rate, breathing, and body temperature; gives feelings of euphoria, illusions of increased sensory awareness and mental and physical strength, decreased hunger, pain, and need for sleep.	Regular use can cause anxiety, insomnia, weight loss, increased paranoia, and psychosis. Crack is highly addictive and has more intense effects than cocaine. Increased risk of abnormal heart rhythms, high blood pressure, stroke, and death. Long-term consequences in clude mental deterioration, personality changes, paranoia, or violent behaviour.
Heroin	Junk, smack	Induces euphoria; relieves pain; often induces sleep.	Highly addictive; overdose can result in death; serum hepatitis is common; as are skin abscesses, inflammation of the veins, constipation, and respiratory depression.
Lysergic acid diethylamide	LSD, acid	Causes hallucinations, alters vision, raises temperature and heart-beat; evokes flashbacks.	Long-term use causes anxiety and depression, impaired memory and attention span, difficulty with abstract thinking.

Human beings

Commonly abused drugs (continued)

Name	Common name	Effects	Comments
Marijuana	Grass, pot, weed, dope	Increases heartbeat; heightens senses; gives feelings of euphoria and relaxation.	Reduces the ability to perform tasks requiring concentration; slows reactions; and impairs coordination.
MDMA	Ecstasy, E	Promotes mental relaxation, increased sensitivity to stimuli, and sometimes hallucinations.	High doses have amphetamine-like effects. Can produce severe or fatal reactions, sometimes after only one dose.
Mescaline	Peyote, cactus buttons	Induces hallucinations; affects sensations and perceptions.	Loss of control of normal thought processes; long-term depression and anxiety; can induce 'breaks from reality'.
Methadone		Induces sleep and feeling of relaxation.	Addictive; overdose can result in death.
Nicotine		Stimulates the nervous system; increases concentration; relieves tension and fatigue; increases heart rate and blood pressure.	Taken regularly, can cause increase in fatty acids in bloodstream, increased risk of heart disease, and circulatory problems; can also increase risk of peptic ulcers. Increased risk of lung, throat, and mouth cancers from tobacco smoke.
Nitrites	Poppers	Give the user a rapid high, felt as rush of energy. Heart rate increases; there are feelings of dizziness and nausea. High doses can cause fainting.	Lasting physical damage, in the form of cardiac problems, can occur.
Phencyclidine	PCP, angel dust	Gives feeling of euphoria; floating sensation; numbness; change in user's perception of the body; visual disturbances.	Can produce violent behaviour against the user or others; and schizophrenic-like psychosis which can last for days or weeks.
Solvents		Cause lightheadedness, dizziness, and drowsiness. Large doses can lead to loss of consciousness.	Some products can seriously disrupt heart rhythm or cause heart failure and sometimes death. Aerosols can cause suffocation by coating the lungs. Risk of death also from depression of the breathing mechanism. Long-term misuse leads to kidney and liver damage.

NUTRITION

Ideal weights for men and women over 25 years of age

Women				Men			
Height		Ideal weight		Height		Ideal weight	
(cm)	(in)	(kg)	(lb)	(cm)	(in)	(kg)	(lb)
153	60	46.3–53.9	102.0–118.8	155	61	53.5–63.9	117.9–140.9
155	61	47.6–55.3	104.9–121.9	157	62	54.8–65.3	120.8–143.9
157	62	48.9–57.1	107.8–125.9	160	63	56.2–67.1	143.7–147.9
160	63	50.3–58.9	110.9–129.8	162	64	57.6–68.9	127.0–151.9
162	64	51.7–61.2	114.0–134.9	165	65	58.9–70.8	129.9–156.1
165	65	53.5–63.0	117.9–138.9	168	66	60.8–73.0	134.0–160.9
168	66	55.3–64.8	121.9–142.8	170	67	62.6–75.3	138.0–166.0
170	67	57.1–66.7	125.9–147.0	173	68	65.4–77.1	144.2–170.0
173	68	58.9–68.5	129.9–151.0	175	69	66.2–78.9	145.9–173.9
175	69	60.8–70.3	134.0–155.0	178	70	68.0–81.2	149.9–179.0
178	70	62.6–72.1	138.0–158.9	180	71	69.8–83.5	153.9–184.1
180	71	64.4–73.9	142.0–162.9	183	72	71.6–86.7	157.8–191.1
183	72	66.2–75.7	145.9–166.9	185	73	73.5–87.9	162.0–193.8
185	73	68.0–77.6	149.9–171.0	188	74	75.7–90.2	166.9–198.8
188	74	69.8–79.3	153.9–174.8	190	75	78.0–92.5	171.9–203.9
				193	76	80.3–94.8	177.0–209.0

Composition of foods

Figures (approximate) per 100 g of food.

Food	Protein (g)	Carbohydrates (g)	Fat (g)	Fibre (g)	Energy value (calories[a])
Meat, poultry, fish					
Bacon, back, grilled	15	2	24	0	271
Bacon, streaky, grilled	16	2	27	0	308
Beef, minced	31	0	16	0	221
Beef, rump steak, grilled	30	0	12	0	218
Chicken, meat only, roast	19	0	4	0	142
Cod, cooked	19	0	1	0	94
Crab, cooked	18	1	5	0	129
Haddock, cooked	19	0	1	0	96
Ham, lean	22	0	5	0	168
Lamb chop, boned, grilled	24	0	29	0	353
Liver, cooked	20	6	13	0	254
Lobster, cooked	20	trace	3	0	119
Mackerel, cooked	25	0	11	0	188
Mussels, cooked	17	0	1	0	86
Pork chop, boned, grilled	28	0	24	0	328
Prawns, cooked	18	0	1	0	107
Salmon, cooked	20	0	13	0	196
Tuna, canned in brine	28	0	1	0	118
Turkey, meat only, roast	36	0	3	0	140
Vegetables					
Asparagus, cooked	2	4	trace	1	18
Aubergine/egg-plant, cooked	1	4	trace	2	14
Beans, broad, cooked	4	66	1	4	46
Beans, dried white, cooked	8	21	7	25	118
Beans, green, cooked	2	5	trace	4	25
Beetroot, cooked	1	7	trace	2	43
Broccoli, cooked	3	5	trace	4	26
Brussel sprouts, cooked	4	6	trace	3	18
Cabbage, cooked	2	trace	trace	2	11
Cabbage, raw	2	5	trace	3	25
Carrots, cooked	1	5	trace	3	20
Carrots, raw	1	6	trace	3	25
Cauliflower, cooked	2	4	trace	2	22
Celery, raw	1	2	trace	2	36
Chick peas, dry	20	50	6	15	320
Corn (on the cob)	3	21	1	5	91
Courgettes/zucchini, cooked	1	3	trace	1	14
Cucumber, raw	1	3	trace	trace	15
Leeks, cooked	1	7	0	4	25
Lentils, cooked	8	19	trace	4	106
Lettuce, raw	1	3	trace	1	12
Mushrooms, raw	3	4	trace	2	14
Onions, raw	2	9	trace	1	38
Parsnip, cooked	1	17	trace	4	50
Peas, fresh, cooked	5	4	trace	5	54
Pepper, green, raw	1	5	trace	1	14
Pepper, red, raw	1	7	trace	1	20
Potatoes, baked in skin	3	21	trace	2	86
Potatoes, boiled in skin	2	17	trace	2	75
Spinach, cooked	3	4	trace	6	23
Swede, cooked	1	4	trace	3	18
Turnip, cooked	1	5	trace	2	14
Fruit					
Apples	trace	15	trace	2	38
Apricots, dried	5	67	1	24	182
Apricots, raw	1	13	trace	2	25
Avocados	2	6	16	2	221
Bananas	1	22	trace	2	85

[a]Multiply calories by 4.187 to convert to kilojoules.

Nutrition

Composition of foods (continued)

Food	Protein (g)	Carbohydrates (g)	Fat (g)	Fibre (g)	Energy value (calories[a])
Blackberries	1	13	1	7	29
Blackcurrants	2	14	trace	9	29
Cherries	1	17	trace	1	70
Dates	2	73	1	7	214
Figs, dried	4	69	1	19	214
Grapefruit	1	11	trace	trace	41
Grapes	1	16	1	1	69
Melon, honeydew	1	5	trace	1	21
Melon, water	trace	5	trace	1	21
Nectarines	1	17	trace	2	64
Oranges, peeled	1	12	trace	2	49
Peaches	1	8	trace	1	38
Pears	1	15	trace	2	61
Pineapple	trace	14	trace	1	46
Prunes	1	77	trace	14	136
Raisins	3	77	trace	7	246
Raspberries	1	14	1	7	25
Strawberries	1	8	1	2	37
Tomatoes	1	5	trace	1	14

Dairy products
Butter, salted	1	trace	82	0	740
Cheese, Brie	19	2	23	0	314
Cheese, Cheddar	25	2	32	0	414
Cheese, cottage	17	2	4	0	96
Cheese, Edam	30	trace	23	0	314
Cream, double	2	3	48	0	446
Milk, cow's, skimmed	4	5	trace	0	36
Milk, cow's, whole	4	5	4	0	65
Yogurt, skimmed milk	3	5	2	0	50
Yogurt, whole milk	3	5	3	0	62

Grain products
Flour, white	9	80	1	4	350
Flour, wholemeal	13	56	2	10	318
Oatmeal, cooked	2	10	1	7	399
Oats, porridge	10	70	7	7	377
Pasta, dry	12	71	2	4	353
Rice, brown, cooked	3	26	1	1	129
Rice, white, cooked	3	33	trace	1	121

Legumes, nuts, and seeds
Almonds	19	20	54	15	564
Brazil nuts	14	11	67	9	618
Peanuts, fresh	26	19	48	8	571
Walnuts	15	16	64	5	525

Miscellaneous
Biscuit, chocolate digestive	6	64	25	4	506
Biscuit, digestive	7	62	23	5	486
Chocolate bar, plain	4	63	29	0	510
Crisps	6	40	37	11	517
Egg, boiled	13	1	12	0	163
Honey	trace	82	0	0	289
Jam	1	79	trace	1	261
Margarine	trace	1	80	0	730
Oil, vegetable	0	0	100	0	900
Orange juice	1	10	trace	0	45
Sugar	0	100	0	0	394

[a]Multiply calories by 4.187 to convert to kilojoules.

Main types of vitamin

Fat-soluble vitamins

Vitamin	Chemical name	Precursor	Main symptom of deficiency	Dietary source
A	Retinol	Beta-carotene	Xerophthalmia (eye disease)	Retinol: milk, butter, cheese; egg yolk; liver; fatty fish Carotene: green vegetables; yellow and red fruits and vegetables, especially carrots
D	Cholecalciferol	UV-activated 7-dehydro-cholesterol	Rickets; osteomalacia	Fatty fish; margarine; some fortified milks
K	Phytomenadione		Haemorrhagic problems	Green leafy vegetables; liver
E	Tocopherols		Multiple effects	Vegetable oils

Water-soluble vitamins

Vitamin	Chemical name	Main symptom of deficiency	Dietary source
C	Ascorbic acid	Scurvy	Citrus fruits; potatoes; green leafy vegetables
B-vitamins			
B_1	Thiamine	Beri-beri	Seeds and grains: widely distributed
B_2	Riboflavin	Failure to thrive	Liver; milk; cheese; yeast
—	Nicotinic acid	Pellagra	Meat; fish; cereals; pulses
B_6	Pyridoxine	Dermatitis; neurological disorders	Cereals; liver; meat; fruits; leafy vegetables
B_{12}	Cyanocobalamin	Anaemia	Meat; milk; liver
—	Folic acid	Anaemia	Liver; green vegetables
—	Pantothenic acid	Dermatitis	Widespread
—	Biotin	Dermatitis	Liver; kidney; yeast extracts

Main trace minerals

Mineral	Main symptom of deficiency	Dietary source	Proportion of total body weight (%)
Calcium	Rickets in children; osteoporosis in adults	Milk: butter; cheese; sardines; green leafy vegetables; citrus fruits	2.5
Chromium	Adult-onset diabetes	Brewer's yeast; black pepper; liver; wholemeal bread; beer	<0.01
Copper	Anaemia; Menkes' syndrome	Green vegetables; fish; oysters; liver	<0.01
Fluorine	Tooth decay; possibly osteoporosis	Fluoridated drinking water; seafood; tea	<0.01
Iodine	Goitre; cretinism in new-born children	Seafood; salt-water fish; seaweed; iodized salt; table salt	<0.01
Iron	Anaemia	Liver; kidney; green leafy vegetables; egg yolk; dried fruit; potatoes; molasses	0.01
Magnesium	Irregular heartbeat; muscular weakness; insomnia	Green leafy vegetables (eaten raw); nuts; whole grains	0.07
Manganese	Not known in humans	Legumes; cereals; green leafy vegetables; tea	<0.01
Molybdenum	Not known in humans	Legumes; cereals; liver; kidney; some dark-green vegetables	<0.01
Phosphorus	Muscular weakness; bone pain; loss of appetite	Meat; poultry; fish; eggs; dried beans and peas; milk products	1.1
Potassium	Irregular heartbeat; muscular weakness; fatigue; kidney and lung failure	Fresh vegetables; meat; orange juice; bananas; bran	0.10
Selenium	Not known in humans	Seafood; cereals; meat; egg yolk; garlic	<0.01
Sodium	Impaired acid-base balance in body fluids (very rare)	Table salt; other naturally occurring salts	0.10
Zinc	Impaired wound healing; loss of appetite; impaired sexual development	Meat; whole grains; legumes; oysters; milk	<0.01

Food additives

The prefix 'E' stands for European and indicates that an additive is accepted as safe throughout the European Community. It was introduced by the Food Labelling Regulations of 1984 and is used by food manufacturers in member states of the EC.
Any number without the prefix 'E' has been approved by the UK, but not yet by the European Community.
Also listed (without numbers) are additives with a long history of use in the food industry for which formal EC approval is either pending or deemed unnecessary.
In the United States, additives require approval by the US Food and Drug Administration (FDA).

Antioxidants

Stop fatty foods from going rancid and protect fat-soluble vitamins from the harmful effects of oxidation.

E300	L-ascorbic acid – *fruit drinks; also used to improve flour and bread dough*
E301	Sodium L–ascorbate
E302	Calcium L-ascorbate
E304	6-0-Palmitoyl-L-ascorbic acid (ascorbyl palmitate) – *Scotch eggs*
E306	Extracts of natural origin rich in tocopherols – *vegetable oils*
E307	Synthetic alpha-tocopherol – *cereal-based baby foods*
E308	Synthetic gamma-tocopherol
E309	Synthetic delta-tocopherol
E310	Propyl gallate – *vegetable oils; chewing gum*
E311	Octyl gallate
E312	Dodecyl gallate
E320	Butylated hydroxyanisole (BHA) – *soup mixes; cheese spread*
E321	Butylated hydroxytoluene (BHT) – *chewing gum*
E322	Lecithins – *low-fat spreads; also used as an emulsifier in chocolate*
	Diphenylamine
	Ethoxyquin – *used to prevent 'scald' (a discoloration) on apples and pears*

Preservatives

Protect against microbes which cause spoilage and food poisoning. They also increase storage life of foods.

E200	Sorbic acid – *soft drinks; fruit yoghurt; processed cheese slices*
E201	Sodium sorbate
E202	Potassium sorbate
E203	Calcium sorbate – *frozen pizza; flour confectionery*
E210	Benzoic acid
E211	Sodium benzoate
E212	Potassium benzoate
E213	Calcium benzoate
E214	Ethyl 4-hydroxybenzoate (ethyl para-hydroxybenzoate)
E215	Ethyl 4-hydroxybenzoate, sodium salt (sodium ethyl para-hydroxybenzoate)
E216	Propyl 4-hydroxybenzoate (propyl para-hydroxybenzoate).
E217	Propyl 4-hydroxybenzoate, sodium salt (sodium propyl para-hydroxybenzoate)
E218	Methyl 4-hydroxybenzoate (methyl para-hydroxybenzoate)
E219	Methyl 4-hydroxybenzoate, sodium salt (sodium methyl para-hydroxybenzoate) – *beer; jam; salad cream; soft drinks; fruit pulp; fruit-based pie fillings; marinated herring and mackerel*
E220	Sulphur dioxide
E221	Sodium sulphite
E222	Sodium hydrogen sulphite (sodium bisulphite)
E223	Sodium metabisulphite
E224	Potassium metabisulphite
E226	Calcium sulphite
E227	Calcium hydrogen sulphite (calcium bisulphite) – *dried fruit; dehydrated vegetables; fruit juices and syrups; sausages; fruit-based dairy desserts; cider, beer, and wine; also used to prevent browning of raw peeled potatoes and to condition biscuit doughs*
E228	Potassium bisulphite – *wines*
E230	Biphenyl (diphenyl)
E231	2-Hydroxybiphenyl (orthophenylphenol)
E232	Sodium biphenyl-2-yl oxide (sodium orthophenylphenate) – *surface treatment of citrus fruit*
E233	2-(Thiazol-4-yl) benzimidazole (thiabendazole) – *surface treatment of bananas*
234	Nisin – *cheese; clotted cream*
E239	Hexamine (hexamethylenetetramine) – *marinated herring and mackerel*
E249	Potassium nitrite
E250	Sodium nitrite
E251	Sodium nitrate
E252	Potassium nitrate – *bacon; ham; cured meats; corned beef; some cheeses*
E280	Propionic acid
E281	Sodium propionate
E282	Calcium propionate
E283	Potassium propionate – *bread and flour confectionery; Christmas pudding*

Colours

Make food more colourful, compensate for colour lost in processing.

E100	Curcumin – *flour confectionery; margarine*
E101	Riboflavin – *sauces*
101(a)	Riboflavin-5'-phosphate
E102	Tartrazine – *soft drinks*
E104	Quinoline yellow
E110	Sunset Yellow FCF – *biscuits*
E120	Cochineal – *alcoholic drinks*
E122	Carmoisine – *jams and preserves*
E123	Amaranth
E124	Ponceau 4R – *dessert mixes*
E127	Erythrosine BS – *glacé cherries*
128	Red 2G – *sausages*
E131	Patent Blue V
E132	Indigo Carmine
133	Brilliant Blue FCF – *canned vegetables*
E140	Chlorophyll
E141	Copper complexes of chlorophyll and chlorophyllins
E142	Green S – *pastilles*
E150	Caramel – *beer; soft drinks; sauces; gravy browning*
E151	Black PN

E153	Carbon Black (vegetable carbon) – *liquorice*
154	Brown FK – *kippers*
155	Brown HT – *chocolate cake*
E160(a)	*Alpha*-carotene; *beta*-carotene; *gamma*-carotene – *margarine; soft drinks*
E160(b)	Annatto; bixin; norbixin – *crisps/potato chips*
E160(c)	Capsanthin; capsorubin
E160(d)	Lycopene
E160(e)	*Beta*-apo-8'-carotenal
E160(f)	Ethyl ester of beta-apo-8'-carotenoic acid
E161(a)	Flavoxanthin
E161(b)	Lutein
E161(c)	Cryptoxanthin
E161(d)	Rubixanthin
E161(e)	Violaxanthin
E161(f)	Rhodoxanthin
E161(g)	Canthaxanthin
E162	Beetroot Red (betanin) – *ice-cream; liquorice*
E163	Anthocyanins – *yogurt*
E171	Titanium dioxide – *sweets*
E172	Iron oxides; iron hydroxides
E173	Aluminium
E174	Silver
E175	Gold – *cake decorations*
E180	Pigment Rubine (lithol rubine BK)
	Methyl violet – *used for the surface marking of raw or unprocessed meat*
	Paprika – *canned vegetables*
	Turmeric – *soup*

Sweeteners

There are two types of sweeteners; intense sweeteners and bulk sweeteners. Intense sweeteners have a sweetness many times that of sugar and are therefore used at very low levels. They are marked with * in the following list. Bulk sweeteners have about the same sweetness as sugar and are used at the same sort of levels as sugar.

	*Acesulfame potassium – *canned foods; soft drinks; table-top sweeteners*
	*Aspartame – *soft drinks; yogurts; dessert and drink mixes; sweetening tablets*
	Hydrogenated glucose syrup
	Isomalt
	Lactitol
E421	Mannitol – *sugar-free confectionery*
	*Saccharin
	*Sodium saccharin
	*Calcium saccharin – *soft drinks; cider; sweetening tablets; table-top sweeteners*
E420	Sorbitol; sorbitol syrup – *sugar-free confectionery; jams for diabetics*
	*Thaumatin – *table-top sweeteners; yogurt*
	Xylitol – *sugar-free chewing gum*

Emulsifiers and stabilizers

Enable oils and fats to mix with water in foods; add to smoothness and creaminess of texture; retard baked goods going stale.

E400	Alginic acid – *ice-cream; soft cheese*
E401	Sodium alginate – *cake mixes*
E402	Potassium alginate
E403	Ammonium alginate
E404	Calcium alginate
E405	Propane-1,2-diol alginate (propylene glycol alginate) – *salad dressings; cottage cheese*
E406	Agar – *ice-cream*

E407	Carrageenan – *quick-setting jelly mixes; milk shakes*
E410	Locust bean gum (carob gum) – *salad cream*
E412	Guar gum – *packet soups and meringue mixes*
E413	Tragacanth – *salad dressings; processed cheese*
E414	Gum arabic (acacia) – *confectionery*
E415	Xanthan gum – *sweet pickle; coleslaw*
416	Karaya gum – *soft cheese; brown sauce*
432	Polyoxyethylene (20) sorbitan monolaurate (Polysorbate 20)
433	Polyoxyethylene (20) sorbitan mono-oleate (Polysorbate 80)
434	Polyoxyethylene (20) sorbitan monopalmitate (Polysorbate 40)
435	Polyoxyethylene (20) sorbitan monostearate (Polysorbate 60)
436	Polyoxyethylene (20) sorbitan tristearate (Polysorbate 65) – *bakery products; confectionery creams*
E440	(i) Pectin
E440	(ii) Amidated pectin
	Pectin extract – *jams and preserves*
442	Ammonium phosphatides – *cocoa and chocolate products*
E460	Microcrystalline cellulose – *grated cheese*
	Alpha-cellulose (powdered cellulose) – *slimming bread*
E461	Methylcellulose – *low-fat spreads*
E463	Hydroxypropylcellulose
E464	Hydroxypropylmethylcellulose – *edible ices*
E465	Ethylmethylcellulose – *gateaux*
E466	Carboxymethylcellulose, sodium salt (CMC) – *jelly; gateaux*
E470	Sodium, potassium and calcium salts of fatty acids – *cake mixes*
E471	Mono- and di-glycerides of fatty acids – *frozen desserts*
E472(a)	Acetic acid esters of mono- and di-glycerides of fatty acids – *mousse mixes*
E472(b)	Lactic acid esters of mono- and di-glycerides of fatty acids – *dessert toppings*
E472(c)	Citric acid esters of mono- and di-glycerides of fatty acids – *continental sausages*
E472(d)	Tartaric acid esters of mono- and di-glycerides of fatty acids
E472(e)	Mono- and di-acetyltartaric acid esters of mono- and di-glycerides of fatty acids – *bread; frozen pizza*
E472(f)	Mixed acetic and tartaric acid esters of mono- and di-glycerides of fatty acids
E473	Sucrose esters of fatty acids
E474	Sucroglycerides – *edible ices*
E475	Polyglycerol esters of fatty acids – *cakes and gateaux*
E476	Polyglycerol esters of polycondensed fatty acids of castor oil (polyglycerol polyricinoleate) – *chocolate-flavour coatings for cakes*
E477	Propane-1,2-diol esters of fatty acids – *instant desserts*
E481	Sodium stearoyl-1-2-lactylate – *bread; cakes; biscuits*
E482	Calcium stearoyl-1-2-lactylate – *gravy granules*
E483	Stearyl tartrate
491	Sorbitan monostearate
492	Sorbitan tristearate
493	Sorbitan monolaurate
494	Sorbitan mono-oleate

Food additives (continued)

495   Sorbitan monopalmitate – *cake mixes*
Extract of quillaia – *used in soft drinks to promote foam*
Oxidatively polymerized soya-bean oil
Polyglycerol esters of dimerized fatty acids of soya-bean oil – *emulsions used to grease bakery tins*

Others

Acids, anti-caking agents, anti-foaming agents, bases, buffers, bulking agents, firming agents, flavour modifiers, flour improvers, glazing agents, humectants, liquid freezants, packaging gases, propellants, release agents, sequestrants, and solvents.

E170   Calcium carbonate – *base, firming agent, release agent, diluent; nutrient in flour*
E260   Acetic acid
E261   Potassium acetate
E262   Sodium hydrogen diacetate
262   Sodium acetate – *acid/acidity regulators (buffers) used in pickles, salad cream and bread; they contribute to flavour and provide protection against mould growth*
E263   Calcium acetate – *firming agent; also provides calcium which is useful in quick-set jelly mix*
E270   Lactic acid – *acid/flavouring protects against mould growth; salad dressings; soft margarines*
E290   Carbon dioxide – *carbonating agent/packaging gas and propellant; used in fizzy drinks*
296   DL-malic acid; L-malic acid
297   Fumaric acid – *acid/flavouring; used in soft drinks, sweets, biscuits, dessert mixes, and pie fillings*
E325   Sodium lactate – *buffer, humectant; used in jams, preserves, sweets, flour confectionery*
E326   Potassium lactate – *buffer; jams, preserves and jellies*
E327   Calcium lactate – *buffer, firming agent; canned fruit, pie filling*
E330   Citric acid
E331   Sodium dihydrogen citrate (monosodium citrate); disodium citrate; trisodium citrate
E332   Potassium dihydrogen citrate (monopotassium citrate); tripotassium citrate
E333   Monocalcium citrate; dicalcium citrate; tricalcium citrate – *acid/flavourings, buffers, sequestrants, emulsifying salts (calcium salts are firming agents); used in soft drinks, jams, preserves, sweets, UHT cream, processed cheese, canned fruit, dessert mixes, ice cream*
E334   L-(+)-tartaric acid
E335   Monosodium L-(+)-tartrate; disodium L-(+)-tartrate
E336   Monopotassium L-(+)-tartrate (cream of tartar); dipotassium L-(+)-tartrate
E337   Potassium sodium L-(+)-tartrate – *acid/flavourings, buffers, emulsifying salts, sequestrants; used in soft drinks, biscuit creams and fillings, sweets, jams, dessert mixes and processed cheese*
E338   Orthophosphoric acid (phosphoric acid) – *acid/flavourings; soft drinks, cocoa*
E339   Sodium dihydrogen orthophosphate; disodium hydrogen orthophosphate; trisodium orthophosphate

E340   Potassium dihydrogen orthophosphate; dipotassium hydrogen orthophosphate; tripotassium orthophosphate – *buffers, sequestrants, emulsifying salts; used in dessert mixes, non-dairy creamers, processed cheese*
E341   Calcium tetrahydrogen diorthophosphate; calcium hydrogen orthophosphate; tricalcium diorthophosphate – *firming agent, anti-caking agent, raising agent; cake mixes, baking powder, dessert mixes*
350   Sodium malate; sodium hydrogen malate
351   Potassium malate – *buffers, humectants; used in jams, sweets, cakes, biscuits*
352   Calcium malate; calcium hydrogen malate – *firming agent in processed fruit and vegetables*
353   Metatartaric acid – *sequestrant used in wine*
355   Adipic acid – *buffer/flavouring; sweets, synthetic cream desserts*
363   Succinic acid – *buffer/flavouring; dry foods and beverage mixes*
370   1,4-heptonolactone – *acid, sequestrant; dried soups, instant desserts*
375   Nicotinic acid – *colour stabilizer and nutrient; bread, flour, breakfast cereals*
380   Triammonium citrate – *buffer, emulsifying salt; processed cheese*
381   Ammonium ferric citrate – *dietary iron supplement; bread*
385   Calcium disodium ethylenediamine-NNN'N'-tetra-acetate (calcium disodium EDTA) – *sequestrant; canned shellfish*
E422   Glycerol – *humectant, solvent; cake icing, confectionery*
E450(a)   Disodium dihydrogen diphosphate; trisodium diphosphate; tetrasodium diphosphate; tetrapotassium diphosphate
E450(b)   Pentasodium triphosphate; pentapotassium triphosphate
E450(c)   Sodium polyphosphates, potassium polyphosphates – *buffers, sequestrants, emulsifying salts, stabilizers, texturizers, raising agents; used in whipping cream, fish and meat products, bread, processed cheese, canned vegetables*
500   Sodium carbonate; sodium hydrogen carbonate (bicarbonate of soda); sodium sesquicarbonate
501   Potassium carbonate; potassium hydrogen carbonate – *bases, aerating agents, diluents; used in jams, jellies, self-raising flour, wine, cocoa*
503   Ammonium carbonate; ammonium hydrogen carbonate – *buffer, aerating agent; cocoa, biscuits*
504   Magnesium carbonate – *base, anti-caking agent; wafer biscuits, icing sugar*
507   Hydrochloric acid
508   Potassium chloride – *gelling agent, salt substitute; table-salt replacement*
509   Calcium chloride – *firming agent in canned fruit and vegetables*
510   Ammonium chloride – *yeast food in bread*
513   Sulphuric acid
514   Sodium sulphate – *diluent for colours*
515   Potassium sulphate – *salt substitute*
516   Calcium sulphate – *firming agent and yeast food; bread*
518   Magnesium sulphate – *firming agent*
524   Sodium hydroxide – *base; cocoa, jams and sweets*

525	Potassium hydroxide – *base; sweets*
526	Calcium hydroxide – *firming agent, neutralizing agent; sweets*
527	Ammonium hydroxide – *diluent and solvent for food colours, base; cocoa*
528	Magnesium hydroxide – *base; sweets*
529	Calcium oxide – *base; sweets*
530	Magnesium oxide – *anti-caking agent; cocoa products*
535	Sodium ferrocyanide
536	Potassium ferrocyanide – *anti-caking agents in salt; crystallization aids in wine*
540	Dicalcium diphosphate – *buffer, neutralizing agent; cheese*
541	Sodium aluminium phosphate – *acid, raising agent; cake mixes, self-raising flour, biscuits*
542	Edible bone phosphate – *anti-caking agent*
544	Calcium polyphosphates – *emulsifying salt; processed cheese*
545	Ammonium polyphosphates – *emulsifier, texturizer; frozen chicken*
551	Silicon dioxide (silica) – *anti-caking agent; skimmed milk powder, sweeteners*
552	Calcium silicate – *anti-caking agent, release agent; icing sugar, sweets*
553(a)	Magnesium silicate, and synthetic magnesium trisilicate – *anti-caking agent; sugar confectionery*
553(b)	Talc – *release agent; tabletted confectionery*
554	Aluminium sodium silicate
556	Aluminium calcium silicate
558	Bentonite
559	Kaolin
570	Stearic acid – *anti-caking agents*
572	Magnesium stearate – *emulsifier, release agent; confectionery*
575	D-glucono-1,5-lactone (glucono delta-lactone) – *acid, sequestrant; cake mixes, continental sausages*
576	Sodium gluconate
577	Potassium gluconate – *sequestrants*
578	Calcium gluconate – *buffer, firming agent, sequestrant; jams, dessert mixes*
620	L-glutamic acid
621	Sodium hydrogen L-glutamate (monosodium glutamate; MSG)
622	Potassium hydrogen L-glutamate (monopotassium glutamate)
623	Calcium dihydrogen di-L-glutamate (calcium glutamate)
627	Guanosine 5'-disodium phosphate (sodium guanylate)
631	Inosine 5'-disodium phosphate (sodium inosinate)
635	Sodium 5'-ribonucleotide – *flavour enhancers used in savoury foods and snacks, soups, sauces and meat products*
636	Maltol
637	Ethyl maltol – *flavourings/flavour enhancers used in cakes and biscuits*
900	Dimethylpolysiloxane – *anti-foaming agent*
901	Beeswax
903	Carnauba wax – *glazing agents used in sugar and chocolate confectionery*
904	Shellac – *glazing agent used to wax apples*
905	Mineral hydrocarbons – *glazing/coating agent used to prevent dried fruit sticking together*
907	Refined microcrystalline wax – *release agent; chewing gum*
920	L-cysteine hydrochloride
925	Chlorine
926	Chlorine dioxide
927	Azodicarbonamide – *flour-treatment agents used to improve the texture of bread, cake, and biscuit doughs*
	Aluminium potassium sulphate – *firming agent; chocolate-coated cherries*
	2-Aminoethanol – *base; caustic lye used to peel vegetables*
	Ammonium dihydrogen orthophosphate; diammonium hydrogen othophosphate – *buffer, yeast food*
	Ammonium sulphate – *yeast food*
	Benzoyl peroxide – *bleaching agent in flour*
	Butyl stearate – *release agent*
	Calcium heptonate – *firming agent, sequestrant; prepared fruit and vegetables*
	Calcium phytate – *sequestrant; wine*
	Dichlorodifluoromethane – *propellant and liquid freezant used to freeze food by immersion*
	Diethyl ether – *solvent*
	Disodium dihydrogen ethylenediamine-NNN'N'-tetra-acetate (disodium dihydrogen EDTA) – *sequestrant; brandy*
	Ethanol (ethylalcohol)
	Ethyl acetate
	Glycerol mono-acetate (monoacetin)
	Glycerol di-acetate (diacetin)
	Glycerol tri-acetate (triacetin) – *solvents used to dilute and carry food colours and flavourings*
	Glycine – *sequestrant, buffer, nutrient*
	Hydrogen
	Nitrogen – *packaging gases*
	Nitrous oxide – *propellant used in aerosol packs of whipped cream*
	Octadecylammonium acetate – *anti-caking agent in yeast foods used in bread*
	Oxygen – *packaging gas*
	Oxystearin – *sequestrant, fat crystallization inhibitor; salad cream*
	Polydextrose – *bulking agent; reduced- and low-calorie foods*
	Propan-1,2-diol (propylene glycol)
	Propan-2-diol (isopropyl alcohol) – *solvents used to dilute colours and flavourings*
	Sodium heptonate – *sequestrant; edible oils*
	Spermaceti
	Sperm oil – *release agents*
	Tannic acid – *flavouring, clarifying agent; beer wine and cider*

Human beings

The world's top wine producers

Country	Proportion of total world wine production (%)	Quantity[a] (thousand tonnes)
Italy	20.6	5 980
France	20.3	5 891
Spain	10.4	3 030
Argentina	6.9	2 000
USSR	6.5	1 900
Germany	4	1 165
Romania	3.4	1 000
South Africa	3.2	944
Portugal	2.9	845

[a]Figures date from 1989.

Grape varieties

Although there are now over 4000 named varieties of grape, only a small number have a truly distinctive flavour and are capable of producing great wine. These *classic grapes* form the basis of an international category of wine. The *major varieties* are those grapes which are also fairly widespread across the international wine market but which are considered less distinctive than the classic grapes.

Australia

Classic grapes
RED
Cabernet Sauvignon
Pinot Noir
Syrah
WHITE
Riesling
Chardonnay
Sémillon

Major varieties
Muscat de Frontignan
Muscadelle

Areas
Adelaide Hills
Barossa Valley
Clare Valley
Coonawarra
Corowa-Rutherglen
Upper Hunter Valley
Lower Hunter Valley
Margaret River
Mount Barker
Mount Frankland
Padthaway
Yarra Valley

Central Europe

Classic grapes
RED
Cabernet Sauvignon
Pinot Noir
Merlot
WHITE
Riesling
Chardonnay
Sauvignon Blanc

Major varieties
Austria
Gewürztraminer

Müller-Thurgau
Muscat Ottonel
Pinot Gris
Pinot Blanc
Silvaner
Welschriesling

Bulgaria
Aligoté
Gewürztraminer

Czechoslovakia
Gewürztraminer
Pinot Blanc
Silvaner
Welschriesling

Hungary
Cabernet Franc
Gewürztraminer
Pinot Gris
Pinot Blanc
Silvaner
Welschriesling

Romania
Aligoté
Cabernet Franc
Gewürztraminer
Muscat Ottonel
Pinot Gris
Welschriesling

Russian Federation
Aligoté
Gewürztraminer
Muscat Ottonel

Yugoslavia (formerly)
Cabernet Franc
Gewürztraminer
Malvasia
Muscat Ottonel
Pinot Blanc
Pinot Gris
Welschriesling

France

Alsace
Classic grapes
RED
Pinot Noir
WHITE
Riesling

Major varieties
Gewürztraminer
Muscat
Pinot Gris

Areas
Brand
Eichberg
Geisberg
Gloeckelberg
Goldert Hatschbourg
Hengst
Kastelberg
Kessler
Kirchberg de Barr
Kirchberg de Ribeauville
Kitterle
Moenchberg
Saering
Schloss Rosacker
Sommerberg
Spiegel
Wiebelsberg

Bordeaux
Classic grapes
RED
Cabernet Sauvignon
Merlot
WHITE
Sémillon
Sauvignon Blanc

Major varieties
Cabernet Franc
Colombard

Merlot Blanc
Muscadelle
Trebbiano (Ugni Blanc)

Areas
Côtes de Blaye
Côtes de Bourg
Entre-deux-mers
Fronsac
Graves
Médoc
Pomerol
Sauternes
St-Emilion

Burgundy
Classic grapes
RED
Pinot Noir
WHITE
Chardonnay
Sauvignon Blanc

Major varieties
Gamay
Aligoté

Areas
Beaujolais
Chablis
Côte de Beaune
Côte Chalonnaise
Côte de Nuits
Hautes Côtes de Beaune
Hautes Côtes de Nuits
Maconnais

Champagne
Classic grapes
RED
Pinot Noir
WHITE
Chardonnay

Major varieties
Meunier

Areas
Ambonnay
Avize
Ay
Beaumont-sur-Vesle
Bisseuil
Bouzy
Champillon
Chigny-les-Roses
Chouilly
Cramant
Cuis
Cumieres
Dizy-Magenta
Grauves
Hautvillers
Le Mesnil-sur-Oger
Louvois
Mailly
Mareuil-sur-Ay
Montbre
Mutigny
Oger

Pierry
Puisieulx
Rilly-la-Montagne
Sillery
Tauxieres-Mutry
Tours-sur-Marne
Trepail
Vertus
Verzenay
Verzy
Villers-Marmery

Loire
Classic grapes
RED
Cabernet Sauvignon
Pinot Noir
WHITE
Chardonnay
Sauvignon Blanc
Chenin Blanc

Areas
Anjou
Anjou-Côteaux de la Loire
Anjou Gamay
Bonnezeaux
Bourgueil
Champigny
Côteaux de L'Aubance
Côteaux du Layon
Côteaux de Saumur
Jasnières
Menetou-Salon
Muscadet
Muscadet des Coteaux de la Loire
Muscadet de Sèvre-et-Maine
Pouilly Fumé
Pouilly-sur-Loire
Quarts de Chaume
Quincy
Reuilly
Rose d'Anjou
Sancerre
Saumur
Savennieres
Touraine
Vouvray-Montlouis

The Midi
Classic grapes
RED
Cabernet Sauvignon
Syrah
Merlot
WHITE
Chardonnay
Sauvignon Blanc
Chenin Blanc

Major varieties
Garnacha
Carignan
Cinsaut
Garnacha Blanca

Areas
Aude
Bouches-du-Rhone

Gard
Herault
Pyrenees-Orientales
Var
Vaucluse

Germany

Around 80 per cent of German vineyard produce is white wine. The predominant grape is the Riesling but listed below are also major local varieties which are significant in terms of both quantity and quality. They are listed in the order of the most widely planted variety per region.

Ahr
Pinot Noir
Blauer Portugieser
Riesling
Müller-Thurgau
Kerner

Baden
Pinot Noir
Pinot Gris
Chasselas
Riesling
Silvaner
Pinot Blanc
Blauer Portugieser

Franken
Müller-Thurgau
Silvaner
Riesling
Pinot Noir
Blauer Portugieser
Perle
Rieslaner

Hessische Bergstrasse
Riesling
Müller-Thurgau
Silvaner
Pinot Noir
Blauer Portugieser

Mittelrhein
Riesling
Müller-Thurgau
Kerner
Silvaner
Pinot Noir
Blauer Portugieser

Mosel-Saar-Ruwer
Riesling
Müller-Thurgau
Wiesser Elbling
Kerner

Nahe
Müller-Thurgau
Riesling
Silvaner
Kerner
Blauer Portugieser
Pinot Noir

Human beings

Nutrition

Grape varieties (continued)

Rheingau
Riesling
Müller-Thurgau
Pinot Noir
Silvaner
Blauer Portugieser

Rheinhessen
Müller-Thurgau
Silvaner
Scheurebe
Kerner
Riesling
Morio-Muscat
Blauer Portugieser
Pinot Noir

Rheinpfalz
Müller-Thurgau
Riesling
Kerner
Silvaner
Morio-Muscat
Blauer Portugieser
Scheurebe
Pinot Noir
Gewürztraminer

Württemberg
Riesling
Blauer Trollinger
Müller-Thurgau
Kerner
Silvaner
Blauer Portugieser
Schwarzriesling
Pinot Noir
Pinot Gris

Italy
Classic grapes
RED
Cabernet Sauvignon
Pinot Noir
Merlot
WHITE
Riesling
Chardonnay
Sauvignon Blanc

Major varieties
Barbera
Cabernet Franc
Carignan
Cinsaut
Garnacha
Muscat of Alexandria
Muscat Blanc
Muscat Blanc à Petits Grains
Nebbiolo
Pinot Blanc
Pinot Gris
Sangiovese
Trebbiano
Welschriesling

Areas
Friuli-Venezia Giulia
Lombardia
Piemonte
Trentino/Alto Adige
Veneto

New Zealand
Classic grapes
RED
Cabernet Sauvignon
Pinot Noir
WHITE
Riesling
Chardonnay
Sauvignon Blanc
Chenin Blanc

Major varieties
Gamay
Gewürztraminer
Müller-Thurgau
Palomino
Silvaner

Areas
Auckland
Canterbury
Hawke's Bay
Marlborough
Nelson
Northland
Poverty Bay
Waikato

South Africa
Classic grapes
RED
Cabernet Sauvignon
Pinot Noir
Syrah
Merlot
WHITE
Riesling
Chardonnay
Sémillon
Sauvignon Blanc
Chenin Blanc

Major varieties
Cinsaut
Colombard
Muscat of Alexandria
Muscat Blanc
Muscat Blanc à Petits Grains
Palomino
Trebbiano

Areas
Malmesbury
Montagu
Olifants River
Paarl
Robertson
Stellenbosch
Worcester

South America
Classic grapes
RED
Cabernet Sauvignon
Pinot Noir
Syrah
Merlot
WHITE
Riesling
Chardonnay
Sémillon
Sauvignon Blanc
Chenin Blanc

Major varieties
Argentina
Barbera
Cabernet Franc
Gewürztraminer
Muscat à Petits Grains
Tempranillo
Trebbiano

Brasil
Trebbiano

Chile
Cabernet Franc
Carignan
Gewürztraminer
Muscat of Alexandria
Muscat à Petits Grains
Pinot Blanc

Mexico
Carignan
Colombard
Gamay
Garnacha
Palomino
Pinot Gris
Tempranillo
Trebbiano

Uruguay
Barbera
Nebbiolo
Pinot Blanc

Spain and Portugal

Spain and Portugal grow few of the international classic grapes and are better known as exporters of their own locally grown grape varieties, such as the Palomino, Tempranillo, and Carignan.

Major varieties
Carignan
Garnacha
Malvasia
Palomino
Tempranillo

Areas
Algarve
Alicante

Bairrada
Bucelas
Carcavelos
Carineria
Colares
Dao
Douro
Jumilla
La Mancha
Malaga
Montilla-Moriles
Navarra
Penedes
Rioja (Alta, Alavesa, Baja)
Setubal
Tarragona
Valdepenas
Vinho Verde

USA

California
Major varieties grown in the region

Central Valley
Barbera
Carignan
Cinsaut
Emerald Riesling*
Flora
Garnacha

Muscat Blanc à Petits Grains
Palomino
Trebbiano
Zinfandel*

Mendocino, Lake
Carignan
Gamay Beaujolais
Garnacha
Gewürztraminer
Trousseau Gris
Zinfandel

Monterey, San Benito
Carignan
Colombard
Emerald Riesling
Folle Blanche
Gamay Beaujolais
Garnacha
Gewürztraminer
Melon de Bourgogne
Muscat Blanc à Petits Grains
Silvaner
Zinfandel

Napa
Cabernet Franc
Gamay Beaujolais
Gewürztraminer
Trousseau Gris
Zinfandel

San Luis Obispo, Santa Barbara
Gewürztraminer
Silvaner
Zinfandel

Sonoma
Carignan
Gamay Beaujolais
Gewürztraminer
Melon de Bourgogne
Muscadelle
Zinfandel

S California
Garnacha
Palomino
Zinfandel

*denotes quality grape varieties bred in California

Idaho
Major varieties
Gewürztraminer

Washington
Major varieties
Cabernet Franc
Garnacha
Gewürztraminer
Muscat Blanc à Petits Grains

Human beings

HISTORY

THE CALENDAR

Perpetual calendar 1801–2000

The calendar for each year is given under the corresponding letter below.

1801 I	1821 C	1841 K	1861 E	1881 M	1901 E	1921 M	1941 G	1961 A	1981 I
1802 K	1822 E	1842 M	1862 G	1882 A	1902 G	1922 A	1942 I	1962 C	1982 K
1803 M	1823 G	1843 A	1863 I	1883 C	1903 I	1923 C	1943 K	1963 E	1983 M
1804 B	1824 J	1844 D	1864 L	1884 F	1904 L	1924 F	1944 N	1964 H	1984 B
1805 E	1825 M	1845 G	1865 A	1885 I	1905 A	1925 I	1945 C	1965 K	1985 E
1806 G	1826 A	1846 I	1866 C	1886 K	1906 C	1926 K	1946 E	1966 M	1986 G
1807 I	1827 C	1847 K	1867 E	1887 M	1907 E	1927 M	1947 G	1967 A	1987 I
1808 L	1828 F	1848 N	1868 H	1888 B	1908 H	1928 B	1948 J	1968 D	1988 L
1809 A	1829 I	1849 C	1869 K	1889 E	1909 K	1929 E	1949 M	1969 G	1989 A
1810 C	1830 K	1850 E	1870 M	1890 G	1910 M	1930 G	1950 A	1970 I	1990 C
1811 E	1831 M	1851 G	1871 A	1891 I	1911 A	1931 I	1951 C	1971 K	1991 E
1812 H	1832 B	1852 J	1872 D	1892 L	1912 D	1932 L	1952 F	1972 N	1992 H
1813 K	1833 E	1853 M	1873 G	1893 A	1913 G	1933 A	1953 I	1973 C	1993 K
1814 M	1834 G	1854 A	1874 I	1894 C	1914 I	1934 C	1954 K	1974 E	1994 M
1815 A	1835 I	1855 C	1875 K	1895 E	1915 K	1935 E	1955 M	1975 G	1995 A
1816 D	1836 L	1856 F	1876 N	1896 H	1916 N	1936 H	1956 B	1976 J	1996 D
1817 G	1837 A	1857 I	1877 C	1897 K	1917 C	1937 K	1957 E	1977 M	1997 G
1818 I	1838 C	1858 K	1878 E	1898 M	1918 E	1938 M	1958 G	1978 A	1998 I
1819 K	1839 E	1859 M	1879 G	1899 A	1919 G	1939 A	1959 I	1979 C	1999 K
1820 N	1840 H	1860 B	1880 J	1900 C	1920 J	1940 D	1960 L	1980 F	2000 N

A

January
S	M	T	W	T	F	S
1	2	3	4	5	6	7
8	9	10	11	12	13	14
15	16	17	18	19	20	21
22	23	24	25	26	27	28
29	30	31				

February
S	M	T	W	T	F	S
				1	2	3	4
5	6	7	8	9	10	11
12	13	14	15	16	17	18
19	20	21	22	23	24	25
26	27	28				

March
S	M	T	W	T	F	S
				1	2	3	4
5	6	7	8	9	10	11
12	13	14	15	16	17	18
19	20	21	22	23	24	25
26	27	28	29	30	31	

April
S	M	T	W	T	F	S
						1
2	3	4	5	6	7	8
9	10	11	12	13	14	15
16	17	18	19	20	21	22
23	24	25	26	27	28	29
30						

May
S	M	T	W	T	F	S
	1	2	3	4	5	6
7	8	9	10	11	12	13
14	15	16	17	18	19	20
21	22	23	24	25	26	27
28	29	30	31			

June
S	M	T	W	T	F	S
					1	2	3
4	5	6	7	8	9	10
11	12	13	14	15	16	17
18	19	20	21	22	23	24
25	26	27	28	29	30	

July
S	M	T	W	T	F	S
						1
2	3	4	5	6	7	8
9	10	11	12	13	14	15
16	17	18	19	20	21	22
23	24	25	26	27	28	29
30	31					

August
S	M	T	W	T	F	S
		1	2	3	4	5
6	7	8	9	10	11	12
13	14	15	16	17	18	19
20	21	22	23	24	25	26
27	28	29	30	31		

September
S	M	T	W	T	F	S
					1	2
3	4	5	6	7	8	9
10	11	12	13	14	15	16
17	18	19	20	21	22	23
24	25	26	27	28	29	30

October
S	M	T	W	T	F	S
1	2	3	4	5	6	7
8	9	10	11	12	13	14
15	16	17	18	19	20	21
22	23	24	25	26	27	28
29	30	31				

November
S	M	T	W	T	F	S
			1	2	3	4
5	6	7	8	9	10	11
12	13	14	15	16	17	18
19	20	21	22	23	24	25
26	27	28	29	30		

December
S	M	T	W	T	F	S
					1	2
3	4	5	6	7	8	9
10	11	12	13	14	15	16
17	18	19	20	21	22	23
24	25	26	27	28	29	30
31						

B (leap year)

January
S	M	T	W	T	F	S
1	2	3	4	5	6	7
8	9	10	11	12	13	14
15	16	17	18	19	20	21
22	23	24	25	26	27	28
29	30	31				

February
S	M	T	W	T	F	S
				1	2	3	4
5	6	7	8	9	10	11
12	13	14	15	16	17	18
19	20	21	22	23	24	25
26	27	28	29			

March
S	M	T	W	T	F	S
					1	2	3
4	5	6	7	8	9	10
11	12	13	14	15	16	17
18	19	20	21	22	23	24
25	26	27	28	29	30	31

April
S	M	T	W	T	F	S
1	2	3	4	5	6	7
8	9	10	11	12	13	14
15	16	17	18	19	20	21
22	23	24	25	26	27	28
29	30					

May
S	M	T	W	T	F	S
		1	2	3	4	5
6	7	8	9	10	11	12
13	14	15	16	17	18	19
20	21	22	23	24	25	26
27	28	29	30	31		

June
S	M	T	W	T	F	S
					1	2
3	4	5	6	7	8	9
10	11	12	13	14	15	16
17	18	19	20	21	22	23
24	25	26	27	28	29	30

July
S	M	T	W	T	F	S
1	2	3	4	5	6	7
8	9	10	11	12	13	14
15	16	17	18	19	20	21
22	23	24	25	26	27	28
29	30	31				

August
S	M	T	W	T	F	S
			1	2	3	4
5	6	7	8	9	10	11
12	13	14	15	16	17	18
19	20	21	22	23	24	25
26	27	28	29	30	31	

September
S	M	T	W	T	F	S
						1
2	3	4	5	6	7	8
9	10	11	12	13	14	15
16	17	18	19	20	21	22
23	24	25	26	27	28	29
30						

October
S	M	T	W	T	F	S
	1	2	3	4	5	6
7	8	9	10	11	12	13
14	15	16	17	18	19	20
21	22	23	24	25	26	27
28	29	30	31			

November
S	M	T	W	T	F	S
				1	2	3
4	5	6	7	8	9	10
11	12	13	14	15	16	17
18	19	20	21	22	23	24
25	26	27	28	29	30	

December
S	M	T	W	T	F	S
						1
2	3	4	5	6	7	8
9	10	11	12	13	14	15
16	17	18	19	20	21	22
23	24	25	26	27	28	29
30	31					

History

Perpetual calendar 1801–2000 (continued)

C

January
S	M	T	W	T	F	S
		1	2	3	4	5
6	7	8	9	10	11	12
13	14	15	16	17	18	19
20	21	22	23	24	25	26
27	28	29	30	31		

January
S	M	T	W	T	F	S
	1	2	3	4	5	6
7	8	9	10	11	12	13
14	15	16	17	18	19	20
21	22	23	24	25	26	27
28	29	30	31			

February
S	M	T	W	T	F	S
					1	2
3	4	5	6	7	8	9
10	11	12	13	14	15	16
17	18	19	20	21	22	23
24	25	26	27	28		

February
S	M	T	W	T	F	S
					1	2
3	4	5	6	7	8	9
10	11	12	13	14	15	16
17	18	19	20	21	22	23
24	25	26	27	28		

March
S	M	T	W	T	F	S
					1	2
3	4	5	6	7	8	9
10	11	12	13	14	15	16
17	18	19	20	21	22	23
24	25	26	27	28	29	30
31						

March
S	M	T	W	T	F	S
					1	2
3	4	5	6	7	8	9
10	11	12	13	14	15	16
17	18	19	20	21	22	23
24	25	26	27	28	29	30
31						

E

January
S	M	T	W	T	F	S
		1	2	3	4	5
6	7	8	9	10	11	12
13	14	15	16	17	18	19
20	21	22	23	24	25	26
27	28	29	30	31		

February
S	M	T	W	T	F	S
					1	2
3	4	5	6	7	8	9
10	11	12	13	14	15	16
17	18	19	20	21	22	23
24	25	26	27	28		

March
S	M	T	W	T	F	S
					1	2
3	4	5	6	7	8	9
10	11	12	13	14	15	16
17	18	19	20	21	22	23
24	25	26	27	28	29	30
31						

April (C)
S	M	T	W	T	F	S
	1	2	3	4	5	6
7	8	9	10	11	12	13
14	15	16	17	18	19	20
21	22	23	24	25	26	27
28	29	30				

April (E)
S	M	T	W	T	F	S
	1	2	3	4	5	6
7	8	9	10	11	12	13
14	15	16	17	18	19	20
21	22	23	24	25	26	27
28	29	30				

May (C)
S	M	T	W	T	F	S
			1	2	3	4
5	6	7	8	9	10	11
12	13	14	15	16	17	18
19	20	21	22	23	24	25
26	27	28	29	30	31	

May (E)
S	M	T	W	T	F	S
			1	2	3	4
5	6	7	8	9	10	11
12	13	14	15	16	17	18
19	20	21	22	23	24	25
26	27	28	29	30	31	

June (C)
S	M	T	W	T	F	S
					1	2
3	4	5	6	7	8	9
10	11	12	13	14	15	16
17	18	19	20	21	22	23
24	25	26	27	28	29	30

June (E)
S	M	T	W	T	F	S
						1
2	3	4	5	6	7	8
9	10	11	12	13	14	15
16	17	18	19	20	21	22
23	24	25	26	27	28	29
30						

July (C)
S	M	T	W	T	F	S
	1	2	3	4	5	6
7	8	9	10	11	12	13
14	15	16	17	18	19	20
21	22	23	24	25	26	27
28	29	30	31			

July (E)
S	M	T	W	T	F	S
		1	2	3	4	5
6	7	8	9	10	11	12
13	14	15	16	17	18	19
20	21	22	23	24	25	26
27	28	29	30	31		

August (C)
S	M	T	W	T	F	S
				1	2	3
4	5	6	7	8	9	10
11	12	13	14	15	16	17
18	19	20	21	22	23	24
25	26	27	28	29	30	31

August (E)
S	M	T	W	T	F	S
					1	2
3	4	5	6	7	8	9
10	11	12	13	14	15	16
17	18	19	20	21	22	23
24	25	26	27	28	29	30

September (C)
S	M	T	W	T	F	S
1	2	3	4	5	6	7
8	9	10	11	12	13	14
15	16	17	18	19	20	21
22	23	24	25	26	27	28
29	30					

September (E)
S	M	T	W	T	F	S
1	2	3	4	5	6	7
8	9	10	11	12	13	14
15	16	17	18	19	20	21
22	23	24	25	26	27	28
29	30					

October (C)
S	M	T	W	T	F	S
		1	2	3	4	5
6	7	8	9	10	11	12
13	14	15	16	17	18	19
20	21	22	23	24	25	26
27	28	29	30	31		

October (E)
S	M	T	W	T	F	S
		1	2	3	4	5
6	7	8	9	10	11	12
13	14	15	16	17	18	19
20	21	22	23	24	25	26
27	28	29	30	31		

November (C)
S	M	T	W	T	F	S
					1	2
3	4	5	6	7	8	9
10	11	12	13	14	15	16
17	18	19	20	21	22	23
24	25	26	27	28	29	30

November (E)
S	M	T	W	T	F	S
					1	2
3	4	5	6	7	8	9
10	11	12	13	14	15	16
17	18	19	20	21	22	23
24	25	26	27	28	29	30

December (C)
S	M	T	W	T	F	S
1	2	3	4	5	6	7
8	9	10	11	12	13	14
15	16	17	18	19	20	21
22	23	24	25	26	27	28
29	30	31				

December (E)
S	M	T	W	T	F	S
1	2	3	4	5	6	7
8	9	10	11	12	13	14
15	16	17	18	19	20	21
22	23	24	25	26	27	28
29	30	31				

D (leap year)

January
S	M	T	W	T	F	S
	1	2	3	4	5	6
7	8	9	10	11	12	13
14	15	16	17	18	19	20
21	22	23	24	25	26	27
28	29	30	31			

February
S	M	T	W	T	F	S
					1	2
3	4	5	6	7	8	9
10	11	12	13	14	15	16
17	18	19	20	21	22	23
24	25	26	27	28	29	

March
S	M	T	W	T	F	S
					1	2
3	4	5	6	7	8	9
10	11	12	13	14	15	16
17	18	19	20	21	22	23
24	25	26	27	28	29	30
31						

F (leap year)

January
S	M	T	W	T	F	S
	1	2	3	4	5	
6	7	8	9	10	11	12
13	14	15	16	17	18	19
20	21	22	23	24	25	26
27	28	29	30	31		

February
S	M	T	W	T	F	S
					1	2
3	4	5	6	7	8	9
10	11	12	13	14	15	16
17	18	19	20	21	22	23
24	25	26	27	28	29	

March
S	M	T	W	T	F	S
						1
2	3	4	5	6	7	8
9	10	11	12	13	14	15
16	17	18	19	20	21	22
23	24	25	26	27	28	29
30	31					

April (D)
S	M	T	W	T	F	S
	1	2	3	4	5	6
7	8	9	10	11	12	13
14	15	16	17	18	19	20
21	22	23	24	25	26	27
28	29	30				

April (F)
S	M	T	W	T	F	S
		1	2	3	4	5
6	7	8	9	10	11	12
13	14	15	16	17	18	19
20	21	22	23	24	25	26
27	28	29	30			

May (D)
S	M	T	W	T	F	S
			1	2	3	4
5	6	7	8	9	10	11
12	13	14	15	16	17	18
19	20	21	22	23	24	25
26	27	28	29	30	31	

May (F)
S	M	T	W	T	F	S
				1	2	3
4	5	6	7	8	9	10
11	12	13	14	15	16	17
18	19	20	21	22	23	24
25	26	27	28	29	30	31

June (D)
S	M	T	W	T	F	S
						1
2	3	4	5	6	7	8
9	10	11	12	13	14	15
16	17	18	19	20	21	22
23	24	25	26	27	28	29
30						

June (F)
S	M	T	W	T	F	S
1	2	3	4	5	6	7
8	9	10	11	12	13	14
15	16	17	18	19	20	21
22	23	24	25	26	27	28
29	30					

July (D)
S	M	T	W	T	F	S
	1	2	3	4	5	6
7	8	9	10	11	12	13
14	15	16	17	18	19	20
21	22	23	24	25	26	27
28	29	30	31			

July (F)
S	M	T	W	T	F	S
	1	2	3	4	5	
6	7	8	9	10	11	12
13	14	15	16	17	18	19
20	21	22	23	24	25	26
27	28	29	30	31		

August (D)
S	M	T	W	T	F	S
				1	2	3
4	5	6	7	8	9	10
11	12	13	14	15	16	17
18	19	20	21	22	23	24
25	26	27	28	29	30	31

August (F)
S	M	T	W	T	F	S
					1	2
3	4	5	6	7	8	9
10	11	12	13	14	15	16
17	18	19	20	21	22	23
24	25	26	27	28	29	30
31						

September (D)
S	M	T	W	T	F	S
1	2	3	4	5	6	7
8	9	10	11	12	13	14
15	16	17	18	19	20	21
22	23	24	25	26	27	28
29	30					

September (F)
S	M	T	W	T	F	S
	1	2	3	4	5	6
7	8	9	10	11	12	13
14	15	16	17	18	19	20
21	22	23	24	25	26	27
28	29	30				

October (D)
S	M	T	W	T	F	S
		1	2	3	4	5
6	7	8	9	10	11	12
13	14	15	16	17	18	19
20	21	22	23	24	25	26
27	28	29	30	31		

October (F)
S	M	T	W	T	F	S
			1	2	3	4
5	6	7	8	9	10	11
12	13	14	15	16	17	18
19	20	21	22	23	24	25
26	27	28	29	30	31	

November (D)
S	M	T	W	T	F	S
					1	2
3	4	5	6	7	8	9
10	11	12	13	14	15	16
17	18	19	20	21	22	23
24	25	26	27	28	29	30

November (F)
S	M	T	W	T	F	S
						1
2	3	4	5	6	7	8
9	10	11	12	13	14	15
16	17	18	19	20	21	22
23	24	25	26	27	28	29
30						

December (D)
S	M	T	W	T	F	S
1	2	3	4	5	6	7
8	9	10	11	12	13	14
15	16	17	18	19	20	21
22	23	24	25	26	27	28
29	30	31				

December (F)
S	M	T	W	T	F	S
	1	2	3	4	5	6
7	8	9	10	11	12	13
14	15	16	17	18	19	20
21	22	23	24	25	26	27
28	29	30	31			

G

January
S	M	T	W	T	F	S
			1	2	3	4
5	6	7	8	9	10	11
12	13	14	15	16	17	18
19	20	21	22	23	24	25
26	27	28	29	30	31	

February
S	M	T	W	T	F	S
						1
2	3	4	5	6	7	8
9	10	11	12	13	14	15
16	17	18	19	20	21	22
23	24	25	26	27	28	

March
S	M	T	W	T	F	S
						1
2	3	4	5	6	7	8
9	10	11	12	13	14	15
16	17	18	19	20	21	22
23	24	25	26	27	28	29
30	31					

April
S	M	T	W	T	F	S
		1	2	3	4	5
6	7	8	9	10	11	12
13	14	15	16	17	18	19
20	21	22	23	24	25	26
27	28	29	30			

May
S	M	T	W	T	F	S
				1	2	3
4	5	6	7	8	9	10
11	12	13	14	15	16	17
18	19	20	21	22	23	24
25	26	27	28	29	30	31

June
S	M	T	W	T	F	S
1	2	3	4	5	6	7
8	9	10	11	12	13	14
15	16	17	18	19	20	21
22	23	24	25	26	27	28
29	30					

July
S	M	T	W	T	F	S
		1	2	3	4	5
6	7	8	9	10	11	12
13	14	15	16	17	18	19
20	21	22	23	24	25	26
27	28	29	30	31		

August
S	M	T	W	T	F	S
					1	2
3	4	5	6	7	8	9
10	11	12	13	14	15	16
17	18	19	20	21	22	23
24	25	26	27	28	29	30
31						

September
S	M	T	W	T	F	S
	1	2	3	4	5	6
7	8	9	10	11	12	13
14	15	16	17	18	19	20
21	22	23	24	25	26	27
28	29	30				

October
S	M	T	W	T	F	S
			1	2	3	4
5	6	7	8	9	10	11
12	13	14	15	16	17	18
19	20	21	22	23	24	25
26	27	28	29	30	31	

November
S	M	T	W	T	F	S
						1
2	3	4	5	6	7	8
9	10	11	12	13	14	15
16	17	18	19	20	21	22
23	24	25	26	27	28	29
30						

December
S	M	T	W	T	F	S
	1	2	3	4	5	6
7	8	9	10	11	12	13
14	15	16	17	18	19	20
21	22	23	24	25	26	27
28	29	30	31			

H (leap year)

January
S	M	T	W	T	F	S
			1	2	3	4
5	6	7	8	9	10	11
12	13	14	15	16	17	18
19	20	21	22	23	24	25
26	27	28	29	30	31	

February
S	M	T	W	T	F	S
						1
2	3	4	5	6	7	8
9	10	11	12	13	14	15
16	17	18	19	20	21	22
23	24	25	26	27	28	29

March
S	M	T	W	T	F	S
1	2	3	4	5	6	7
8	9	10	11	12	13	14
15	16	17	18	19	20	21
22	23	24	25	26	27	28
29	30	31				

April
S	M	T	W	T	F	S
		1	2	3	4	5
6	7	8	9	10	11	12
13	14	15	16	17	18	19
20	21	22	23	24	25	26
27	28	29	30			

May
S	M	T	W	T	F	S
				1	2	3
4	5	6	7	8	9	10
11	12	13	14	15	16	17
18	19	20	21	22	23	24
25	26	27	28	29	30	31

June
S	M	T	W	T	F	S
1	2	3	4	5	6	7
8	9	10	11	12	13	14
15	16	17	18	19	20	21
22	23	24	25	26	27	28
29	30					

July
S	M	T	W	T	F	S
		1	2	3	4	5
6	7	8	9	10	11	12
13	14	15	16	17	18	19
20	21	22	23	24	25	26
27	28	29	30	31		

August
S	M	T	W	T	F	S
						1
2	3	4	5	6	7	8
9	10	11	12	13	14	15
16	17	18	19	20	21	22
23	24	25	26	27	28	29
30	31					

September
S	M	T	W	T	F	S
	1	2	3	4	5	6
7	8	9	10	11	12	13
14	15	16	17	18	19	20
21	22	23	24	25	26	27
28	29	30				

October
S	M	T	W	T	F	S
			1	2	3	
4	5	6	7	8	9	10
11	12	13	14	15	16	17
18	19	20	21	22	23	24
25	26	27	28	29	30	31

November
S	M	T	W	T	F	S
1	2	3	4	5	6	7
8	9	10	11	12	13	14
15	16	17	18	19	20	21
22	23	24	25	26	27	28
29	30					

December
S	M	T	W	T	F	S
	1	2	3	4	5	
6	7	8	9	10	11	12
13	14	15	16	17	18	19
20	21	22	23	24	25	26
27	28	29	30	31		

I

January
S	M	T	W	T	F	S
				1	2	3
4	5	6	7	8	9	10
11	12	13	14	15	16	17
18	19	20	21	22	23	24
25	26	27	28	29	30	31

February
S	M	T	W	T	F	S
1	2	3	4	5	6	7
8	9	10	11	12	13	14
15	16	17	18	19	20	21
22	23	24	25	26	27	28

March
S	M	T	W	T	F	S
1	2	3	4	5	6	7
8	9	10	11	12	13	14
15	16	17	18	19	20	21
22	23	24	25	26	27	28
29	30	31				

April
S	M	T	W	T	F	S
			1	2	3	4
5	6	7	8	9	10	11
12	13	14	15	16	17	18
19	20	21	22	23	24	25
26	27	28	29	30		

May
S	M	T	W	T	F	S
					1	2
3	4	5	6	7	8	9
10	11	12	13	14	15	16
17	18	19	20	21	22	23
24	25	26	27	28	29	30
31						

June
S	M	T	W	T	F	S
	1	2	3	4	5	6
7	8	9	10	11	12	13
14	15	16	17	18	19	20
21	22	23	24	25	26	27
28	29	30				

July
S	M	T	W	T	F	S
			1	2	3	4
5	6	7	8	9	10	11
12	13	14	15	16	17	18
19	20	21	22	23	24	25
26	27	28	29	30	31	

August
S	M	T	W	T	F	S
						1
2	3	4	5	6	7	8
9	10	11	12	13	14	15
16	17	18	19	20	21	22
23	24	25	26	27	28	29
30	31					

September
S	M	T	W	T	F	S
		1	2	3	4	5
6	7	8	9	10	11	12
13	14	15	16	17	18	19
20	21	22	23	24	25	26
27	28	29	30			

October
S	M	T	W	T	F	S
				1	2	3
4	5	6	7	8	9	10
11	12	13	14	15	16	17
18	19	20	21	22	23	24
25	26	27	28	29	30	31

November
S	M	T	W	T	F	S
1	2	3	4	5	6	7
8	9	10	11	12	13	14
15	16	17	18	19	20	21
22	23	24	25	26	27	28
29	30					

December
S	M	T	W	T	F	S
		1	2	3	4	5
6	7	8	9	10	11	12
13	14	15	16	17	18	19
20	21	22	23	24	25	26
27	28	29	30	31		

J (leap year)

January
S	M	T	W	T	F	S
				1	2	3
4	5	6	7	8	9	10
11	12	13	14	15	16	17
18	19	20	21	22	23	24
25	26	27	28	29	30	31

February
S	M	T	W	T	F	S
1	2	3	4	5	6	7
8	9	10	11	12	13	14
15	16	17	18	19	20	21
22	23	24	25	26	27	28
29						

March
S	M	T	W	T	F	S
	1	2	3	4	5	6
7	8	9	10	11	12	13
14	15	16	17	18	19	20
21	22	23	24	25	26	27
28	29	30	31			

April
S	M	T	W	T	F	S
			1	2	3	
4	5	6	7	8	9	10
11	12	13	14	15	16	17
18	19	20	21	22	23	24
25	26	27	28	29	30	

May
S	M	T	W	T	F	S
					1	
2	3	4	5	6	7	8
9	10	11	12	13	14	15
16	17	18	19	20	21	22
23	24	25	26	27	28	29
30	31					

June
S	M	T	W	T	F	S
		1	2	3	4	5
6	7	8	9	10	11	12
13	14	15	16	17	18	19
20	21	22	23	24	25	26
27	28	29	30			

July
S	M	T	W	T	F	S
				1	2	3
4	5	6	7	8	9	10
11	12	13	14	15	16	17
18	19	20	21	22	23	24
25	26	27	28	29	30	31

August
S	M	T	W	T	F	S
1	2	3	4	5	6	7
8	9	10	11	12	13	14
15	16	17	18	19	20	21
22	23	24	25	26	27	28
29	30	31				

September
S	M	T	W	T	F	S
			1	2	3	4
5	6	7	8	9	10	11
12	13	14	15	16	17	18
19	20	21	22	23	24	25
26	27	28	29	30		

October
S	M	T	W	T	F	S
					1	2
3	4	5	6	7	8	9
10	11	12	13	14	15	16
17	18	19	20	21	22	23
24	25	26	27	28	29	30
31						

November
S	M	T	W	T	F	S
	1	2	3	4	5	6
7	8	9	10	11	12	13
14	15	16	17	18	19	20
21	22	23	24	25	26	27
28	29	30				

December
S	M	T	W	T	F	S
			1	2	3	4
5	6	7	8	9	10	11
12	13	14	15	16	17	18
19	20	21	22	23	24	25
26	27	28	29	30	31	

Perpetual calendar 1801–2000 (continued)

K

January

S	M	T	W	T	F	S
					1	2
3	4	5	6	7	8	9
10	11	12	13	14	15	16
17	18	19	20	21	22	23
24	25	26	27	28	29	30
31						

February

S	M	T	W	T	F	S
	1	2	3	4	5	6
7	8	9	10	11	12	13
14	15	16	17	18	19	20
21	22	23	24	25	26	27
28						

March

S	M	T	W	T	F	S
	1	2	3	4	5	6
7	8	9	10	11	12	13
14	15	16	17	18	19	20
21	22	23	24	25	26	27
28	29	30	31			

April

S	M	T	W	T	F	S
				1	2	3
4	5	6	7	8	9	10
11	12	13	14	15	16	17
18	19	20	21	22	23	24
25	26	27	28	29	30	

May

S	M	T	W	T	F	S
						1
2	3	4	5	6	7	8
9	10	11	12	13	14	15
16	17	18	19	20	21	22
23	24	25	26	27	28	29
30	31					

June

S	M	T	W	T	F	S
		1	2	3	4	5
6	7	8	9	10	11	12
13	14	15	16	17	18	19
20	21	22	23	24	25	26
27	28	29	30			

July

S	M	T	W	T	F	S
				1	2	3
4	5	6	7	8	9	10
11	12	13	14	15	16	17
18	19	20	21	22	23	24
25	26	27	28	29	30	31

August

S	M	T	W	T	F	S
1	2	3	4	5	6	7
8	9	10	11	12	13	14
15	16	17	18	19	20	21
22	23	24	25	26	27	28
29	30	31				

September

S	M	T	W	T	F	S
				1	2	3	4
5	6	7	8	9	10	11
12	13	14	15	16	17	18
19	20	21	22	23	24	25
26	27	28	29	30		

October

S	M	T	W	T	F	S
					1	2
3	4	5	6	7	8	9
10	11	12	13	14	15	16
17	18	19	20	21	22	23
24	25	26	27	28	29	30
31						

November

S	M	T	W	T	F	S
	1	2	3	4	5	6
7	8	9	10	11	12	13
14	15	16	17	18	19	20
21	22	23	24	25	26	27
28	29	30				

December

S	M	T	W	T	F	S
			1	2	3	4
5	6	7	8	9	10	11
12	13	14	15	16	17	18
19	20	21	22	23	24	25
26	27	28	29	30	31	

L (leap year)

January

S	M	T	W	T	F	S
					1	2
3	4	5	6	7	8	9
10	11	12	13	14	15	16
17	18	19	20	21	22	23
24	25	26	27	28	29	30
31						

February

S	M	T	W	T	F	S
	1	2	3	4	5	6
7	8	9	10	11	12	13
14	15	16	17	18	19	20
21	22	23	24	25	26	27
28	29					

March

S	M	T	W	T	F	S
		1	2	3	4	5
6	7	8	9	10	11	12
13	14	15	16	17	18	19
20	21	22	23	24	25	26
27	28	29	30	31		

April

S	M	T	W	T	F	S
					1	2
3	4	5	6	7	8	9
10	11	12	13	14	15	16
17	18	19	20	21	22	23
24	25	26	27	28	29	30

May

S	M	T	W	T	F	S
1	2	3	4	5	6	7
8	9	10	11	12	13	14
15	16	17	18	19	20	21
22	23	24	25	26	27	28
29	30	31				

June

S	M	T	W	T	F	S
			1	2	3	4
5	6	7	8	9	10	11
12	13	14	15	16	17	18
19	20	21	22	23	24	25
26	27	28	29	30		

July

S	M	T	W	T	F	S
				1	2
3	4	5	6	7	8	9
10	11	12	13	14	15	16
17	18	19	20	21	22	23
24	25	26	27	28	29	30
31						

August

S	M	T	W	T	F	S
	1	2	3	4	5	6
7	8	9	10	11	12	13
14	15	16	17	18	19	20
21	22	23	24	25	26	27
28	29	30	31			

September

S	M	T	W	T	F	S
				1	2	3
4	5	6	7	8	9	10
11	12	13	14	15	16	17
18	19	20	21	22	23	24
25	26	27	28	29	30	

October

S	M	T	W	T	F	S
						1
2	3	4	5	6	7	8
9	10	11	12	13	14	15
16	17	18	19	20	21	22
23	24	25	26	27	28	29
30	31					

November

S	M	T	W	T	F	S
		1	2	3	4	5
6	7	8	9	10	11	12
13	14	15	16	17	18	19
20	21	22	23	24	25	26
27	28	29	30			

December

S	M	T	W	T	F	S
				1	2	3
4	5	6	7	8	9	10
11	12	13	14	15	16	17
18	19	20	21	22	23	24
25	26	27	28	29	30	31

M

January

S	M	T	W	T	F	S
						1
2	3	4	5	6	7	8
9	10	11	12	13	14	15
16	17	18	19	20	21	22
23	24	25	26	27	28	29
30	31					

February

S	M	T	W	T	F	S
		1	2	3	4	5
6	7	8	9	10	11	12
13	14	15	16	17	18	19
20	21	22	23	24	25	26
27	28					

March

S	M	T	W	T	F	S
		1	2	3	4	5
6	7	8	9	10	11	12
13	14	15	16	17	18	19
20	21	22	23	24	25	26
27	28	29	30	31		

April

S	M	T	W	T	F	S
					1	2
3	4	5	6	7	8	9
10	11	12	13	14	15	16
17	18	19	20	21	22	23
24	25	26	27	28	29	30

May

S	M	T	W	T	F	S
1	2	3	4	5	6	7
8	9	10	11	12	13	14
15	16	17	18	19	20	21
22	23	24	25	26	27	28
29	30	31				

June

S	M	T	W	T	F	S
			1	2	3	4
5	6	7	8	9	10	11
12	13	14	15	16	17	18
19	20	21	22	23	24	25
26	27	28	29	30		

July

S	M	T	W	T	F	S
					1	2
3	4	5	6	7	8	9
10	11	12	13	14	15	16
17	18	19	20	21	22	23
24	25	26	27	28	29	30
31						

August

S	M	T	W	T	F	S
	1	2	3	4	5	6
7	8	9	10	11	12	13
14	15	16	17	18	19	20
21	22	23	24	25	26	27
28	29	30	31			

September

S	M	T	W	T	F	S
				1	2	3
4	5	6	7	8	9	10
11	12	13	14	15	16	17
18	19	20	21	22	23	24
25	26	27	28	29	30	

October

S	M	T	W	T	F	S
						1
2	3	4	5	6	7	8
9	10	11	12	13	14	15
16	17	18	19	20	21	22
23	24	25	26	27	28	29
30	31					

November

S	M	T	W	T	F	S
		1	2	3	4	5
6	7	8	9	10	11	12
13	14	15	16	17	18	19
20	21	22	23	24	25	26
27	28	29	30			

December

S	M	T	W	T	F	S
				1	2	3
4	5	6	7	8	9	10
11	12	13	14	15	16	17
18	19	20	21	22	23	24
25	26	27	28	29	30	31

N (leap year)

January

S	M	T	W	T	F	S
						1
2	3	4	5	6	7	8
9	10	11	12	13	14	15
16	17	18	19	20	21	22
23	24	25	26	27	28	29
30	31					

February

S	M	T	W	T	F	S
		1	2	3	4	5
6	7	8	9	10	11	12
13	14	15	16	17	18	19
20	21	22	23	24	25	26
27	28	29				

March

S	M	T	W	T	F	S
			1	2	3	4
5	6	7	8	9	10	11
12	13	14	15	16	17	18
19	20	21	22	23	24	25
26	27	28	29	30	31	

April

S	M	T	W	T	F	S
						1
2	3	4	5	6	7	8
9	10	11	12	13	14	15
16	17	18	19	20	21	22
23	24	25	26	27	28	29
30						

May

S	M	T	W	T	F	S
	1	2	3	4	5	6
7	8	9	10	11	12	13
14	15	16	17	18	19	20
21	22	23	24	25	26	27
28	29	30	31			

June

S	M	T	W	T	F	S
				1	2	3
4	5	6	7	8	9	10
11	12	13	14	15	16	17
18	19	20	21	22	23	24
25	26	27	28	29	30	

July

S	M	T	W	T	F	S
						1
2	3	4	5	6	7	8
9	10	11	12	13	14	15
16	17	18	19	20	21	22
23	24	25	26	27	28	29
30	31					

August

S	M	T	W	T	F	S
		1	2	3	4	5
6	7	8	9	10	11	12
13	14	15	16	17	18	19
20	21	22	23	24	25	26
27	28	29	30	31		

September

S	M	T	W	T	F	S
					1	2
3	4	5	6	7	8	9
10	11	12	13	14	15	16
17	18	19	20	21	22	23
24	25	26	27	28	29	30

October

S	M	T	W	T	F	S
1	2	3	4	5	6	7
8	9	10	11	12	13	14
15	16	17	18	19	20	21
22	23	24	25	26	27	28
29	30	31				

November

S	M	T	W	T	F	S
			1	2	3	4
5	6	7	8	9	10	11
12	13	14	15	16	17	18
19	20	21	22	23	24	25
26	27	28	29	30		

December

S	M	T	W	T	F	S
					1	2
3	4	5	6	7	8	9
10	11	12	13	14	15	16
17	18	19	20	21	22	23
24	25	26	27	28	29	30
31						

The seasons

N hemisphere	S hemisphere	Duration
Spring	Autumn	From vernal/autumnal equinox (c. 21 Mar) to summer/winter solstice (c. 21 Jun)
Summer	Winter	From summer/winter solstice (c. 21 Jun) to autumnal/spring equinox (c. 23 Sept)
Autumn	Spring	From autumnal/spring equinox (c. 23 Sept) to winter/summer solstice (c. 21 Dec)
Winter	Summer	From winter/summer solstice (c. 21 Dec) to vernal/autumnal equinox (c. 21 Mar)

Wedding anniversaries

In many Western countries, different wedding anniversaries have become associated with gifts of different materials. There is some variation between countries.

1st	Cotton	14th	Ivory
2nd	Paper	15th	Crystal
3rd	Leather	20th	China
4th	Fruit; flowers	25th	Silver
5th	Wood	30th	Pearl
6th	Sugar	35th	Coral
7th	Copper; wool	40th	Ruby
8th	Bronze; pottery	45th	Sapphire
9th	Pottery; willow	50th	Gold
10th	Tin	55th	Emerald
11th	Steel	60th	Diamond
12th	Silk; linen	70th	Platinum
13th	Lace		

Year equivalents

Jewish[a] (AM)	Islamic[b] (H)	Hindu[c] (SE)
5750 (30 Sep 1989–19 Sep 1990)	1410 (4 Aug 1989–23 Jul 1990)	1911 (22 Mar 1989–21 Mar 1990)
5751 (20 Sep 1990–8 Sep 1991)	1411 (24 Jul 1990–12 Jul 1991)	1912 (22 Mar 1990–21 Mar 1991)
5752 (9 Sep 1991–27 Sep 1992)	1412 (13 Jul 1991–1 Jul 1992)	1913 (22 Mar 1991–20 Mar 1992)
5753 (28 Sep 1992–15 Sep 1993)	1413 (2 Jul 1992–20 Jun 1993)	1914 (21 Mar 1992–21 Mar 1993)
5754 (16 Sep 1993–5 Sep 1994)	1414 (21 Jun 1993–9 Jun 1994)	1915 (22 Mar 1993–21 Mar 1994)
5755 (6 Sep 1994–24 Sep 1995)	1415 (10 Jun 1994–30 May 1995)	1916 (22 Mar 1994–21 Mar 1995)
5756 (25 Sep 1995–13 Sep 1996)	1416 (31 May 1995–18 May 1996)	1917 (22 Mar 1995–20 Mar 1996)
5757 (14 Sep 1996–1 Oct 1997)	1417 (19 May 1996–8 May 1997)	1918 (21 Mar 1996–21 Mar 1997)
5758 (2 Oct 1997–20 Sep 1998)	1418 (9 May 1997–27 Apr 1998)	1919 (22 Mar 1997–21 Mar 1998)
5759 (21 Sep 1998–10 Sep 1999)	1419 (28 Apr 1998–16 Apr 1999)	1920 (22 Mar 1998–21 Mar 1999)
5760 (11 Sep 1999–29 Sep 2000)	1420 (17 Apr 1999–5 Apr 2000)	1921 (22 Mar 1999–21 Mar 2000)

Gregorian equivalents are given in parentheses and are AD (= Anno Domini).
[a] Calculated from 3761 BC, said to be the year of the creation of the world. AM = Anno Mundi.
[b] Calculated from AD 622, the year in which the Prophet went from Mecca to Medina. H = Hegira.
[c] Calculated from AD 78, the beginning of the Saka era (SE), used alongside Gregorian dates in Government of India publications since 22 Mar 1957. Other important Hindu eras include: Vikrama era (58 BC), Kalacuri era (AD 248), Gupta era (AD 320), and Harsa era (AD 606).

Month equivalents

Gregorian equivalents to other calendars are given in parentheses; the figures refer to the number of solar days in each month.

Gregorian	Jewish	Islamic	Hindu
(Basis: Sun)	(Basis: Moon)	(Basis: Moon)	(Basis: Moon)
January (31)	Tishri (Sep–Oct) (30)	Muharram (Sep–Oct) (30)	Caitra (Mar–Apr) (29 or 30)
February (28 or 29)	Heshvan (Oct–Nov) (29 or 30)	Safar (Oct–Nov) (29)	Vaisakha (Apr–May) (29 or 30)
March (31)	Kislev (Nov–Dec) (29 or 30)	Rabi I (Nov–Dec) (30)	Jyaistha (May–Jun) (29 or 30)
April (30)	Tevet (Dec–Jan) (29)	Rabi II (Dec–Jan) (29)	Asadha (Jun–Jul) (29 or 30)
May (31)	Shevat (Jan–Feb) (30)	Jumada I (Jan–Feb) (30)	Dvitiya Asadha certain leap years
June (30)	Adar (Feb–Mar) (29 or 30)	Jumada II (Feb–Mar) (29)	Svrana (Jul–Aug) (29 or 30)
July (31)	Adar Sheni leap years only	Rajab (Mar–Apr) (30)	Dvitiya Sravana certain leap years
August (31)	Nisan (Mar–Apr) (30)	Shaban (Apr–May) (29)	Bhadrapada (Aug–Sep) (29 or 30)
September (30)	Iyar (Apr–May) (29)	Ramadan (May–Jun) (30)	Asvina (Sep–Oct) (29 or 30)
October (31)	Sivan (May–Jun) (30)	Shawwal (Jun–Jul) (29)	Karttika (Oct–Nov) (29 or 30)
November (30)	Tammuz (Jun–Jul) (29)	Dhu al-Qadah (Jul–Aug) (30)	Margasirsa (Nov–Dec) (29 or 30)
December (31)	Av (Jul–Aug) (30)	Dhu al-Hijjah (Aug–Sep) (29 or 30)	Pausa (Dec–Jan) (29 or 30)
	Elul (Aug–Sep) (29)		Magha (Jan–Feb) (29 or 30)
			Phalguna (Feb–Mar) (29 or 30)

Names of the months

Month	Name origin
January	Janus, the two-faced god of gates
February	Februa, day of purification (February 15)
March	Mars, god of War
April	Apru, Etruscan goddess of love
May	Maia, eldest daughter of Atlas
June	Juno, wife of Jupiter
July	Julius Caesar
August	Augustus, adopted son of Julius Caesar
September	The seventh month of the earlier Roman calendar
October	The eighth month of the earlier Roman calendar
November	The ninth month of the earlier Roman calendar
December	The tenth month of the earlier Roman calendar

Months: associations

In many Western countries, the months are traditionally associated with gemstones and flowers. There is considerable variation between countries. The following combinations are widely recognized in North America and the UK.

Month	Gemstone	Flower
January	Garnet	Carnation, snowdrop
February	Amethyst	Primrose, violet
March	Aquamarine, bloodstone	Jonquil, violet
April	Diamond	Daisy, sweet pea
May	Emerald	Hawthorn, lily of the valley
June	Alexandrite, moonstone, pearl	Honeysuckle, rose
July	Ruby	Larkspur, water lily
August	Peridot, sardonyx	Gladiolus, poppy
September	Sapphire	Aster, morning glory
October	Opal, tourmaline	Calendula, cosmos
November	Topaz	Chrysanthemum
December	Turquoise, zircon	Holly, narcissus, poinsettia

Names of the days

Day	Name origin
Sunday	Sun day
Monday	Moon day
Tuesday	Tiw's day (God of battle)
Wednesday	Woden's or Odin's day (God of poetry and the dead)
Thursday	Thor's day (God of thunder)
Friday	Frigg's day (Goddess of married love)
Saturday	Saturn's day (God of fertility and agriculture)

Chinese animal years and times 1984–2007

Chinese	English	Years		Time of day (hours)
Shu	Rat	1984	1996	2300–0100
Niu	Ox	1985	1997	0100–0300
Hu	Tiger	1986	1998	0300–0500
T'u	Hare	1987	1999	0500–0700
Lung	Dragon	1988	2000	0700–0900
She	Serpent	1989	2001	0900–1100
Ma	Horse	1990	2002	1100–1300
Yang	Sheep	1991	2003	1300–1500
Hou	Monkey	1992	2004	1500–1700
Chi	Cock	1993	2005	1700–1900
Kou	Dog	1994	2006	1900–2100
Chu	Boar	1995	2007	2100–2300

Chinese agricultural calendar

(Basis: Sun and Moon)

Fortnight

Li Chun ('Spring Begins')
Yu Shui ('Rain Water')
Jing Zhe ('Excited Insects')
Chun Fen ('Vernal Equinox')
Qing Ming ('Clear and Bright')
Gu Yu ('Grain Rains')
Li Xia ('Summer Begins')
Xiao Man ('Grain Fills')
Mang Zhong ('Grain in Ear')
Xia Zhi ('Summer Solstice')
Xiao Shu ('Slight Heat')
Da Shu ('Great Heat')
Li Qiu ('Autumn Begins')
Chu Shu ('Limit of Heat')
Bai Lu ('White Dew')
Qui Fen ('Autumn Equinox')
Han Lu ('Cold Dew')
Shuang Jiang ('Frost Descends')
Li Dong ('Winter Begins')
Xiao Xue ('Little Snow')
Da Xue ('Heavy Snow')
Dong Zhi ('Winter Solstice')
Xiao Han ('Little Cold')
Da Han ('Severe Cold')

Zodiac

Spring signs

Aries, the Ram
(Mar 21–Apr 19)

Taurus, the Bull
(Apr 20–May 20)

Gemini, the Twins
(May 21–Jun 20)

Summer signs

Cancer, the Crab
(Jun 21–Jul 22)

Leo, the Lion
(Jul 23–Aug 22)

Virgo, the Virgin
(Aug 23–Sep 22)

Autumn signs

Libra, the Balance
(Sep 23–Oct 22)

Scorpio, the Scorpion
(Oct 23–Nov 21)

Sagittarius, the Archer
(Nov 22–Dec 21)

Winter signs

Capricorn, the Goat
(Dec 22–Jan 29)

Aquarius, the
Water Bearer
(Jan 20–Feb 18)

Pisces, the Fishes
(Feb19–Mar 20)

History

WORLD CHRONOLOGY

World events

There are remarkably few events that have an obligatory place in any summary of world affairs. Judgements about the significance of an event are inevitably bound up with a country's cultural and social history, and are affected by a person's interests and tastes – all of which are inherent in any selection. The chief purpose of a chronological summary, however, is not to make authoritative decisions about significance (even if that were possible), but to present a series of events in such a way that interesting or informative relationships emerge. When a wide range of contexts is surveyed, including science and the arts alongside political history and world exploration, the (sometimes unexpected) contemporaneous juxtapositions can add a fresh dimension to our awareness of historical facts.

BC
c.9000 First walled city founded at Jericho.
c.6000 Çatal Hüyük flourishes in Anatolia.
c.3500 Sumerian civilization flourishes.
c.3500 Pictographic writing in Sumer.
c.3500 Earliest Chinese cities.
c.3500 Megalithic tombs in north-west Europe.
c.3500 Flax used for textiles in Middle East.
c.3100 Dynastic period begins in Egypt.
c.3000 Temple constructed at Uruk.
c.2680 Beginning of Old Kingdom in Egypt.
c.2590 Cheops begins Great Pyramid in Egypt.
c.2500 Beginning of Indus Valley civilization (to c.1500).
c.2500 Canaanite tribes settle in Palestine.
c.2500 Use of papyrus by Egyptians.
c.2300 Mesopotamian empire established.
c.2200 Beginning of Xia dynasty in China.
c.2100 Construction of ziggurat at Ur.
c.2000 Hittites invade Anatolia.
c.2000 Construction of Babylon.
c.2000 Beginning of Minoan civilization in Crete (to c.1450).
c.2000 Completion of Stonehenge.
1991 Beginning of Middle Kingdom in Egypt.
c.1860 Development of early Semitic alphabet.
c.1780 Hammurabi of Babylon promulgates legal code.
c.1650 Hyksos invasion of Egypt.
c.1600 Beginning of Mycenaean civilization in Greece.
1567 Beginning of New Kingdom in Egypt.
c.1500 Composition of the Vedas begun in India.
c.1360 Amenhotep IV (Akhenaton) establishes worship of Sun God.
c.1300 Construction of Temple of Abu Simbel for Rameses II.
c.1260 Archaeological dating of Trojan War.
c.1200 Olmec civilization begins to flourish in Mexico.
1175 Egypt divided into Upper and Lower Kingdoms.
c.1100 Phoenicians develop alphabetic script.
c.1066 Zhou dynasty in China.
c.1000 Israelite kingdoms established by David and Solomon.
c.1000 Building of the Temple in Jerusalem begins.
c.850 Homer writes *Iliad* and *Odyssey*.
814 Traditional year of the foundation of Carthage.
c.800 Beginning of period of composition of the Upanishads.
776 First Olympic Games in Greece.
753 Traditional year of the foundation of Rome.
671 Assyrian conquest of Egypt.
c.650 Iron technology in China.
c.650 Earliest Latin inscriptions.
621 Laws of Draco in Athens.
c.600 Age of Greek lyric poetry.

586 Babylonian captivity of the Jews.
581 First Phythian Games.
581 Building of Shwe Dagon Pagoda, Myanmar.
c.550 Cyrus the Great begins expansion of Persian Empire.
c.550 Abacus developed by Chinese.
c.530 Pythagoras founds school in Greece.
c.530 Temple of Apollo built at Corinth.
521 Darius the Great divides Persian Empire into satrapies.
c.520 Death of Lao Zi, founder of Taoism.
509 Foundation of Roman Republic.
490 Persians defeated by Athenians at Marathon.
c.483 Death of Siddhartha Gautama, founder of Buddhism.
480 Persians defeat Greeks at Thermopylae.
480 Greeks destroy Persian fleet at Salamis.
479 Death of Confucius.
462 Pericles' reforms in Athens.
c.460 Construction of Temple of Zeus at Olympia.
456 Death of Aeschylus.
450 Codification of Roman law (the Twelve Tables).
433 Completion of Parthenon at Athens.
431 Beginning of Peloponnesian War (until 404).
425 Death of Herodotus.
406 Death of Sophocles.
403 Overthrow of the Thirty Tyrants in Athens.
c.377 Death of Hippocrates.
c.370 Plato opens Academy in Athens.
359 Philip of Macedon becomes King of Macedonia.
c.350 Tomb of Mausolus completed.
c.350 Hill fort constructed at Maiden Castle, England.
347 Death of Plato.
336 Assassination of Philip of Macedon.
329 Alexander the Great reaches India.
322 Death of Aristotle.
310 Epicurus opens school of philosophy at Mitylene.
304 Foundation of Ptolemaic dynasty in Egypt.
c.300 Euclid teaching in Alexandria.
c.290 Foundation of library at Alexandria.
264 First Punic War begins (to 241).
c.250 Writing of the Septuagint.
238 Hamilcar begins conquest of Spain.
221 Qin dynasty unifies China.
221 Beginning of Great Wall of China.
218 Second Punic War begins (to 201).
218 Hannibal invades Italy from the north.
212 Death of Archimedes.
206 Han dynasty in China.
205 Scipio completes conquest of Spain.
168 Revolt of the Maccabees against Antiochus IV.
146 Romans destroy Corinth.
c.110 Opening of Silk Road across Central Asia.

c.100	Dionysius Thrax writes first Greek grammar.
51	Cleopatra becomes Queen of Egypt.
c.50	Julius Caesar writes account of Gallic Wars.
46	Adoption of Julian calendar.
44	Assassination of Julius Caesar.
43	Death of Cicero.
31	Beginning of Roman Empire.
30	Death of Antony and Cleopatra.
19	Death of Virgil.
6	Annexation of Judaea by Rome.
c.5	Birth of Jesus of Nazareth.

AD

5	Cunobelinus recognized by Romans as King of Britain.
14	Death of Augustus.
25	Han dynasty restored in China.
26	Pontius Pilate made procurator of Judaea.
27	Baptism of Jesus Christ.
c.30	Jesus of Nazareth crucified in Jerusalem.
c.34	Conversion of Saul of Tarsus.
43	Roman invasion of Britain.
46	St Paul begins missionary journeys.
54	Nero made emperor in Rome.
61	Defeat of British revolt under Boudicca.
64	Great Fire of Rome.
c.64	Saints Peter and Paul martyred at Rome.
c.65	Foundation of Glastonbury Abbey.
70	Jewish revolt, and destruction of Temple at Jerusalem.
79	Destruction of Pompeii by Vesuvius eruption.
80	Colosseum completed at Rome.
96	Persecution of Christians by Domitian.
c.100	Roman Empire at its peak.
c.105	Paper manufacture begins in China.
120	Earliest Chinese dictionary, by Hsu Shen.
122	Hadrian begins building of wall in Britain.
132	Jewish rebellion and dispersion.
c.150	Buddhism reaches China.
c.150	Ptolemy devises his theory of astronomy.
c.200	Compilation of Mahabharata.
c.200	Codification of Mishnah completed.
220	End of Han dynasty in China.
224	Beginning of Sassanid dynasty in Persia.
238	Gothic invasions of Roman Empire.
265	Six Dynasties in China (to 581).
286	Diocletian divides Empire into West and East.
285	Confucianism reaches Japan.
c.300	Rise of Mayan civilization in Mesoamerica.
312	Constantine unites Roman Empire.
313	Christianity recognized in Roman Empire.
319	Development of Arianism.
320	Chandragupta I founds Gupta Empire in N India.
325	Council of Nicaea formulates Nicene Creed.
330	Capital of Roman Empire moves to Constantinople.
c.350	Gothic Bible produced.
c.350	Fortification of London.
360	Picts and Scots attack Britain.
c.370	Hunnish invasions in Europe.
396	Last Olympic Games of classical times.
404	Latin translation of the Bible by St Jerome (Vulgate).
410	Visigoths sack Rome.
432	St Patrick begins mission to Ireland.
438	Theodosian Code of Roman law.
449	Angles, Saxons, and Jutes invade Britain.
455	Vandals sack Rome.
476	Last Western Roman emperor deposed.
480	End of Gupta Empire in N India.
481	Accession of Clovis I, founder of the Frankish kingdom.
c.515	St Benedict devises monastic rule.
534	Justinian introduces legal code.
552	Buddism introduced into Japan.
c.563	St Columba founds monastery at Iona.
597	St Augustine lands in Britain.
602	Foundation of Archbishopric of Canterbury.
618	Beginning of Tang dynasty in China.
622	Hegira of Mohammed.
625	Mohammed begins dictation of Koran.
632	Death of Mohammed.
641	Arabs begin conquest of North Africa.
664	Synod of Whitby decides date of Easter.
691	Dome of the Rock completed in Jerusalem.
710	Nara becomes capital of Japan.
711	Muslim invasion of Spain.
c.730	Printing begins in China.
732	Arab expansion in Europe stopped by Battle of Poitiers.
735	Death of St Bede.
749	Beginning of Abbasid caliphate.
762	Death of Li Bo, Chinese poet.
762	Foundation of Baghdad.
771	Accession of Charlemagne as King of the Franks.
774	Charlemagne conquers north Italy.
787	Beginning of Viking raids in Britain.
800	Charlemagne crowned Emperor in Rome.
828	Egbert of Wessex recognized as overlord of England.
c.860	Newspaper printed in China.
866	Danish kingdom established in England.
871	Accession of King Alfred the Great in England.
878	Alfred defeats Danes at Edington.
c.900	School of medicine founded at Salerno.
907	Five Dynasties era in China.
910	Foundation of Cluny Abbey.
960	Sung dynasty in China.
967	Fujiwara period begins in Japan.
987	Accession of Capetians in France.
990	Completion of Great Mosque at Córdoba.
c.1000	Inca Empire expands in Peru.
c.1000	Vikings reach America (Vinland).
c.1000	Iron Age settlement in Zimbabwe.
1014	Vikings defeated in Ireland at Clontarf.
1016	Canute made King of England.
1037	Death of Avicenna.
1040	Duncan, King of Scots, killed by Macbeth.
c.1050	Invention of movable type in China.
1054	Schism between Western and Eastern Christianity.
1065	Consecration of Westminster Abbey.
1066	Norman Conquest of England.
1086	Domesday Book completed.
1094	El Cid defeats the Moors at Valencia.
1096	First Crusade begins (to 1099).
1099	Church of Holy Sepulchre built in Jerusalem.
c.1100	Toltec capital built in Mexico.
1113	Foundation of the Knights Hospitallers of St John of Jerusalem.
1147	Second Crusade begins (to 1148)
c.1150	Angkor Wat temple built in Cambodia.
c.1150	Yoruba city states in Nigeria.
1154	Angevins rule in England and France.

World chronology

World events (continued)

c.1155 Beginnings of Paris University.
1156 Foundation of Moscow.
1163 Building of Notre Dame Cathedral, Paris, begins.
1170 Assassination of Thomas à Becket at Canterbury.
1175 Muslim Empire founded in India.
1187 Saladin captures Jerusalem.
1189 Third Crusade begins (to 1192).
1191 Crusaders capture Acre.
1195 Building of Chartres Cathedral begins.
c.1200 Rise of Mali Empire in West Africa.
1202 Fourth Crusade begins (to 1204)
1204 Crusaders capture Constantinople.
1206 Genghis Khan begins Mongol invasion of Asia.
1211 Delhi Sultanate begins under Iltutmish.
1212 The Children's Crusade.
1215 Magna Carta signed at Runnymede.
1215 Dominican Order of friars founded.
1217 Fifth Crusade begins (to 1221).
1228 Sixth Crusade begins (to 1229).
1236 Mongols conquer Russia.
1242 Alexander Nevsky defeats Teutonic Order.
1248 Seventh Crusade begins (to 1254).
1250 Beginning of Mamluk rule in Egypt.
1260 Ghibellines defeat Guelphs at Montaperti.
1261 Greek rule restored in Constantinople.
1264 Kublai Khan founds Yuan dynasty in China.
1270 Eighth Crusade begins (to 1272).
1271 Marco Polo first visits China.
1274 Death of St Thomas Aquinas.
1276 Edward I begins Welsh wars.
1280 Death of Albertus Magnus.
c.1290 Invention of spectacles.
1291 Knights of St John driven from Acre to Cyprus.
1291 Swiss Confederation begins.
1292 Death of Roger Bacon.
1294 Death of Kublai Khan.
c.1300 Foundation of Ottoman Empire.
1300 Rise of Benin Empire in Nigeria.
1302 First meeting of French estates general.
1306 Scots revolt under Robert Bruce.
1309 Papacy moves to Avignon (to 1377).
1311 Guild of Mastersingers founded at Mainz.
c.1313 Invention of cannon.
1314 Scots defeat English at Bannockburn.
1321 Death of Alighieri Dante.
1337 Hundred Years War begins between France and England.
1339 Building of Kremlin in Moscow.
c.1344 Aztecs build capital at Tenochtitlan.
1346 Edward III defeats French at Crécy.
1347 Black Death arrives in Europe (to 1351).
1353 Ottoman invasion of Europe begins.
1356 English defeat French at Poitiers.
1368 Ming dynasty in China.
1369 Timur (Tamerlane) begins conquest of Asia.
1371 House of Stewart ascends to Scottish throne.
1374 Death of Francesco Petrarch.
1377 Poll tax first introduced in England.
1378 Great Schism begins in West.
1380 John Wycliffe's translation of the Bible into English appears.
1381 Peasants' Revolt in England.
1397 Union of Denmark, Norway, and Sweden.
1399 Death of John of Gaunt.
1399 Henry IV deposes Richard II.

1400 Death of Geoffrey Chaucer.
1403 Henry IV defeats Percys at Shrewsbury.
1411 Foundation of the Guildhall in London.
1415 Defeat of French by Henry V at Agincourt.
1417 End of Great Schism.
1427 Defeat of Hussites in Bohemia.
1431 Joan of Arc burned at Rouen.
c.1445 Johannes Gutenberg introduces printing in Europe.
1450 Jack Cade's rebellion in England.
1453 End of Hundred Years War.
1453 Turks capture Constantinople.
1455 Wars of the Roses begin (to 1485).
1460 Death of Henry the Navigator.
1471 First European observatory at Nürnberg.
1475 William Caxton prints first book in English.
1479 Union of Aragon and Castile under Ferdinand and Isabella.
1485 Henry Tudor defeats Richard III at Bosworth.
1486 Portuguese reach Angola.
1487 Bartolomeu Diaz sails around Cape of Storms (Good Hope).
1492 Christopher Columbus reaches America.
1492 Jews expelled from Spain.
1492 Revolt of Perkin Warbeck in England (to 1499).
1497 John Cabot reaches Newfoundland.
1498 Christopher Columbus reaches South America.
1498 Vasco da Gama reaches India.
1499 Amerigo Vespucci reaches Venezuela.
1500 Pedro Álvarez Cabral reaches Brazil.
1506 Rebuilding of St Peter's, Rome, begins.
1508 Michelangelo Buonarroti begins painting of Sistine Chapel, Vatican (to 1512).
1509 Accession of Henry VIII.
1509 Watch invented in Nuremberg.
1513 Vasco Núñez de Balboa reaches Pacific Ocean.
1513 Juan Ponce de León reaches Florida.
1517 Martin Luther nails theses to church door at Wittenburg.
1517 Coffee introduced to Europe.
1519 Hernán Cortés begins conquest of Aztecs.
1519 Death of Leonardo da Vinci.
1520 Ferdinand Magellan reaches Pacific Ocean.
1520 Death of Raphael.
1521 Books begin to be printed at Cambridge.
1525 William Tyndale's English translation of New Testament published.
1526 Foundation of Mughal dynasty in India.
1531 Francisco Pizarro captures Inca capital.
1534 Henry VIII breaks with Rome.
1534 Ignatius Loyola founds Society of Jesus (Jesuits).
1535 Miles Coverdale publishes first complete Bible in English.
1536 Statute of Union between England and Wales.
1536 Suppression of monasteries begins in England.
1536 Jacques Cartier claims Canada for France.
1536 Akbar the Great defeats Hindus at Panipat.
1536 Death of Desiderius Erasmus.
1539 Death of Nanak, founder of Sikhism.
1539 Publication of the Great Bible in England.
1539 Word *encylopaedia* first used by Thomas Elyot.
1541 John Calvin founds church at Geneva.
1543 Nicolas Copernicus publishes *Of the Revolution of Celestial Bodies*.
1545 Council of Trent begins (to 1563), initiating the Counter-Reformation.
1546 Georgias Agricola makes first scientific

classification of minerals.
1549 Book of Common Prayer issued.
1558 England loses Calais to the French.
1558 Accession of Elizabeth I of England.
1559 Acts of Supremacy and Uniformity in England.
1560 Jacques Nicot brings tobacco into France.
1562 Netherlands revolt against Spain.
1562 Wars of Religion begin in France (to 1598).
1564 Death of Michelangelo Buonarroti.
1564 Birth of William Shakespeare.
1569 Union of Lublin unites Lithuania to Poland.
1569 James Fitzmaurice's rebellion in Ireland.
1569 Mercator Chart introduced.
1571 Turks defeated at Lepanto.
1571 Thirty-Nine Articles adopted in England.
1572 St Bartholomew's Day massacre in France.
1572 Beginning of Dutch rebellion against Spain.
1576 First theatre opens in England, at Shoreditch.
1577 Francis Drake leaves on world voyage.
1581 Independence of United Provinces (Netherlands).
1582 Introduction of Gregorian Calendar in Italy.
1584 Walter Raleigh sends first expedition to Virginia.
1587 Execution of Mary, Queen of Scots.
1587 First European Academy, in Italy.
1588 Defeat of Spanish Armada by England.
1589 Foundation of Bourbon dynasty in France.
1594 Death of Giovanni Aerluigi da Palestrina.
1600 British and Dutch East India companies founded.
1600 William Gilbert writes on electricity and magnetism.
1603 Accession of James VI of Scotland as James I of England.
1603 Tokugawa shogunate begins in Japan (to 1868).
1605 Discovery of Gunpowder Plot in London.
1607 Jamestown settlement in America.
1608 French found Quebec.
1610 Galileo Galilei records rings of Saturn and moons of Jupiter.
1610 Arrival of tea in Europe from China.
1611 Authorized Version of the Bible issued.
1614 Publication of John Napier's book on logarithms.
1615 Inigo Jones becomes surveyor-general in England.
1616 Death of William Shakespeare.
1616 Baffin discovers Baffin Bay.
1617 Ben Jonson made first poet laureate.
1618 Thirty Years War begins (to 1648).
1620 Puritans reach New England in *Mayflower*.
1622 Invention of the slide rule.
1624 Armand Jean du Plessis Richelieu becomes First Minister in France.
1625 Dutch found New Amsterdam.
1627 Maratha kingdom founded in India.
1628 William Harvey publishes treatise on circulation of the blood.
1629 Capture of Quebec by English from French.
1629 Colony of Massachusetts founded.
1632 Shah Jahan begins building of Taj Mahal (to 1654).
1635 Death of Lope de Vega.
1636 Foundation of Harvard University.
1638 Scottish Covenant drawn up.
1638 First printing press set up in America.
1640 English Long Parliament assembles.

1640 Stage-coaches introduced into England.
1641 Grand Remonstrance passed against Charles I.
1642 Abel Tasman sights Tasmania (Van Dieman's Land).
1642 Beginning of English Civil War.
1643 Death of Claudio Monteverdi.
1643 Evangelista Torricelli invents barometer.
1643 New England Confederation of colonies formed.
1644 Qing dynasty founded in China.
1645 Charles I defeated at Naseby.
1645 Abel Tasman circumnavigates Australia.
1647 Blaise Pascal constructs first calculating machine.
1648 Peace of Westphalia ends Thirty Years War.
1648 Wars of the Frondes begin in France (to 1653).
1649 Execution of Charles I of England.
1650 Otto von Guericke invents air pump.
1652 First Anglo-Dutch War.
1652 Dutch found Cape Colony.
1653 Oliver Cromwell appointed Lord Protector in England.
1660 Restoration of monarchy in England.
1660 Royal Society founded in London.
1660 Samuel Pepys begins his diary (1669).
1661 Louis XIV assumes absolute power in France.
1661 Bank of Sweden issues world's first banknotes.
1662 Robert Boyle states gas law.
1662 Death of Blaise Pascal.
1664 English rename New Amsterdam as New York.
1665 Great Plague of London at its height.
1666 Great Fire of London.
1669 Death of Rembrandt.
1670 Hudson's Bay Trading Company given Royal Charter.
1673 Death of Molière.
1674 Death of John Milton.
1675 Christopher Wren begins new St Paul's Cathedral (finished 1710).
1678 Popish Plot in England.
1679 Discovery of Niagara Falls.
1681 William Penn granted patent for land in North America.
1681 La Salle explores Mississippi.
1681 First (oil) street lamps in London.
1682 Edmund Halley observes 'his' comet.
1687 Isaac Newton publishes his *Principia*.
1688 William of Orange invited to England.
1688 Lloyd's coffee-house in London begins to be used as insurance centre.
1689 Grand Alliance against Louis XIV.
1690 James II defeated by William III at the Boyne.
1690 Foundation of Calcutta.
1694 Establishment of Bank of England.
1696 Accession of Peter I (the Great) as sole Tsar of Russia.
1699 Death of Jean Racine.
1700 Beginning of Great Northern War (to 1721).
1701 Tull invents horse-drawn seeding drill.
1701 Foundation of Yale University.
1702 War of Spanish Succession begins (to 1713).
1702 England's first daily newspaper issued, *The Daily Courant*.
1703 Foundation of St Petersburg.
1704 French defeated by Marlborough at Blenheim.
1705 Introduction of ship's wheel to replace tiller.
1707 Act of Union unites England and Scotland.
1707 Death of Aurungzebe.

World events (continued)

1709 Swedes defeated by Peter the Great at Poltava.
1714 Beginning of Hanoverian dynasty in England (George I).
1714 Gabriel Fahrenheit invents mercury thermometer.
1715 Jacobite rebellion in Britain.
1721 Rifle introduced into America.
1730 Founding of Methodism by John and Charles Wesley.
1735 Carolus Linnaeus publishes *Systema naturae*.
1738 Daniel Bernoulli states law of hydrodynamics.
1739 War of Jenkins's Ear between Britain and Spain.
1740 War of Austrian Succession (to 1748).
1741 Wrought iron first used in bridge construction.
1742 First performance of George Frideric Handel's *Messiah*.
1743 French explorers reach Rocky Mountains.
1745 Jacobite rebellion in Britain.
1746 Benjamin Franklin begins his research into electricity.
1747 Foundation of Afghanistan.
1750 Death of Johann Sabastian Bach.
1750 Nicolas Louis de Lacaille draws up star catalogue.
1751 Denis Diderot begins work on *Encyclopédie* (to 1776).
1752 Gregorian Calendar adopted in Britain.
1754 Black identifies carbon dioxide.
1755 Publication of Samuel Johnson's *Dictionary*.
1756 Beginning of Seven Years War (to 1763).
1756 Black Hole of Calcutta.
1757 British defeat French at Plassey.
1759 Quebec captured by James Wolfe.
1759 Death of George Frideric Handel.
1760 Identification of hydrogen by Henry Cavendish.
1762 Publication of Jean Jacques Rousseau's *Social Contract*.
1764 James Watt invents separate condenser for steam engine.
1767 Mason–Dixon line established.
1768 James Cook's first voyage to the Pacific.
1768 Richard Arkwright introduces spinning frame in England.
1769 Birth of Napoleon Bonaparte.
1770 James Bruce finds source of Blue Nile.
1770 James Cook arrives in Botany Bay.
1771 Karl Scheele discovers oxygen.
1772 First partition of Poland between Russian and Austria.
1772 Bridgewater Canal finished in England.
1773 Boston Tea Party.
1774 Accession of Louis XVI of France.
1774 Formulation of the rules of cricket.
1774 First commercial steam engine produced by James Watt and Matthew Boulton.
1775 US War of Independence begins (to 1783).
1776 American Declaration of Independence.
1776 Publication of Adam Smith's *Wealth of Nations*.
1778 Joseph Bramah invents water-closet.
1778 Death of Voltaire.
1779 Samuel Crompton produces spinning mule.
1781 British surrender to Washington at Yorktown.
1781 Publication of Emmanuel Kant's *Critique of Pure Reason*.
1781 William Herschel discovers Uranus.
1781 Charles Messier produces star catalogue.
1783 Britain recognizes independence of American colonies.

1783 United Empire Loyalists settle in Canada.
1783 Montgolfier brothers ascend in a balloon.
1784 Henry Cort introduces puddling process for iron.
1784 First official mail coach, Bristol–London.
1785 Edmund Cartwright patents power loom.
1786 Martin Klaproth discovers uranium.
1788 British found colony in Australia.
1788 Antoine Lavoisier shows air to be a mixture of oxygen and nitrogen.
1789 French Revolution begins.
1789 George Washington becomes first president of USA.
1789 Mutiny on the *Bounty*.
1789 US Post Office established.
1790 Luigi Galvani carries out electrical experiments.
1790 First table of chemical elements presented by Antoine Lavoisier.
1790 Foundation of Washington.
1790 Edmund Cartwright introduces steam-powered loom.
1791 Bill of Rights ratified by US Congress.
1791 Unsuccessful flight of Louis XVI.
1791 Death of Mozart.
1791 Publication of the first part of Thomas Paine's *The Rights of Man*.
1792 Foundation of French Republic.
1793 French Revolutionary Wars begin (to 1799).
1793 Execution of Louis XVI.
1793 Whitney patents cotton gin.
1794 End of 'Reign of Terror' in France.
1795 Park explores Niger River.
1795 Directory established in France.
1795 First settlements in New Zealand.
1796 Edward Jenner discovers smallpox vaccine.
1796 Aloys Senefelder invents lithography.
1797 MacArthur introduces merino sheep to Australia.
1798 Napoleon Bonaparte invades Egypt.
1798 Irish rebellion suppressed.
1798 Horatio Nelson defeats French at Aboukir Bay.
1798 Publication of William Wordsworth's and Samuel Taylor Coleridge's *Lyrical Ballads*.
1798 Publication of Thomas Malthus's *Essay on the Principle of Population*.
1799 Death of George Washington.
1799 Napoleon Bonaparte becomes First Consul.
1799 Ludwig van Beethoven writes first symphony.
1800 Act of Union between England and Ireland.
1800 Alessandro Volta makes first battery.
1801 Richard Trevithick builds steam carriage.
1801 First paddle steamer used in Scotland.
1802 Peace of Amiens between England and France.
1803 Beginning of Napoleonic Wars (to 1815).
1803 Louisiana Purchase in USA.
1804 Napoleon made Emperor.
1805 British defeat French and Spanish at Trafalgar.
1807 Abolition of slave trade in British Empire.
1808 Independence movements begin in South America.
1808 Peninsular War begins (to 1814).
1809 Death of Joseph Haydn.
1810 Chile and Mexico declare independence from Spain.
1810 John Dalton presents basis of atomic theory.

1811 Amedeo Avogrado formulates hypothesis on gas molecules.
1811 Alfred Krupp founds ironworks at Essen.
1812 Napoleon Bonaparte invades Russia.
1812 War between Britain and USA (to 1814).
1812 Luddite riots in England.
1812 Invention of cylinder printing press.
1815 Defeat of Napoleon Bonaparte at Battle of Waterloo.
1815 Congress of Vienna.
1816 Argentina declares independence from Spain.
1816 René-Théophile-Hyacinthe Laennec invents stethoscope.
1818 Defeat of Marathas by British in India.
1819 Florida Purchase in USA.
1819 Foundation of Singapore.
1819 Peterloo Massacre at Manchester.
1820 War of Greek Independence begins (to 1828).
1822 Foundation of Liberia for freed slaves.
1822 First photographic image made by Nicéphore Niépce.
1823 Monroe Doctrine formulated.
1823 First Ashanti War (to 1866).
1824 Death of Byron.
1825 First passenger steam railway in England.
1825 Opening of the Erie Canal.
1827 Michael Faraday becomes professor at Royal Institution.
1827 Death of Ludwig van Beethoven.
1828 Publication of Noah Webster's *Dictionary* in USA.
1829 Catholic Emancipation Act in Britain.
1829 Braille invents system of touch-reading for blind.
1829 Joseph Henry invents electromagnetic motor.
1829 First Oxford and Cambridge Boat Race.
1829 George Stephenson constructs the 'Rocket'.
1830 July Revolution in France.
1830 Independence of Belgium.
1831 Charles Darwin begins voyage on the *Beagle*.
1832 First Reform Act in Britain.
1832 First railway constructed in USA.
1832 Death of Johann Wolfgang von Goethe.
1833 First steam crossing of Atlantic by SS *Royal William*.
1834 German customs union (*Zollverein*) officially founded.
1834 Cyrus McCormick patents harvesting machine.
1835 Samuel Colt patents revolver.
1835 Beginning of construction of Great Western Railway in England.
1835 Foundation of Melbourne.
1835 Samuel Morse develops telegraph in USA.
1836 Boer Great Trek in South Africa.
1836 Siege of the Alamo in Texas.
1837 Isaac Pitman introduces his shorthand system.
1838 Anti-Corn Law League founded in Manchester.
1839 First Opium War between Britain and China (to 1842).
1839 First Grand National steeplechase in Liverpool.
1840 Marriage of Queen Victoria and Prince Albert.
1840 Introduction of penny postage stamps in Britain.
1840 Bicycle invented in Scotland.
1841 Act of Union joins Upper and Lower Canada.
1841 British annexation of New Zealand.
1842 British annexation of Hong Kong.
1842 Khyber Pass massacre.
1843 Opening of Isambard Kingdom Brunel's tunnel under the Thames.

1845 US annexation of Texas.
1846 Britain repeals Corn Laws.
1846 Mexican War begins (to 1848).
1846 Oregon Treaty defines US–Canadian boundary.
1846 Foundation of Smithsonian Institution in Washington, DC.
1846 Elias Howe invents sewing machine.
1847 Mormons emigrate to Utah.
1848 Revolutionary movements throughout Europe.
1848 Abdication of Louis Philippe in France.
1848 Communist Manifesto published.
1848 Linus Yale invents cylinder lock.
1848 Gold discovered in California.
1849 Death of Frédéric Chopin.
1849 Punjab annexed by Britain.
1849 David Livingstone begins explorations in Africa.
1851 Taiping rebellion in China (to 1865).
1851 Great Exhibition in London.
1851 First publication of *New York Times*.
1852 Louis Napoleon becomes Emperor of France.
1852 Elisha Otis invents lift with automatic brake.
1852 Wells Fargo & Co founded in USA.
1854 Beginning of Crimean War (to 1856).
1854 Georges Haussmann begins reconstruction of Paris.
1855 David Livingstone reaches Victoria Falls.
1856 Introduction of Bessemer process for steel.
1857 Indian Mutiny.
1858 Laying of first Atlantic cable.
1858 John Speke and Richard Burton reach Lake Tanganyika.
1859 Movement for unification of Italy begins (to 1870).
1859 Publication of Charles Darwin's *The Origin of Species*.
1859 Ferdinand de Lesseps begins work on Suez Canal.
1859 First American oil-wells drilled in Pennsylvania.
1860 Giuseppe Garibaldi's Expedition of the Thousand.
1861 American Civil War begins (to 1865).
1861 Emancipation of Russian serfs.
1861 Germ theory of disease proposed by Louis Pasteur.
1862 Otto von Bismarck appointed Prime Minister of Prussia.
1862 Gatling patents machine gun.
1863 Abraham Lincoln's Gettysburg Address.
1863 Beginning of underground railway in London.
1864 Paraguayan War begins (to 1870).
1864 Foundation of Red Cross in Geneva.
1865 American Civil War ends.
1865 Assassination of Abraham Lincoln.
1865 Publication of Lewis Carroll's *Alice in Wonderland*.
1866 Prussia defeats Austria in Seven-Weeks War.
1866 Winchester introduces repeating rifle.
1866 Mary Baker Eddy founds Christian Science movement.
1866 Gregor Mendel proposes laws of inheritance.
1867 US purchase of Alaska from Russia.
1867 Establishment of Dominion of Canada.
1867 Dual Monarchy established in Austria–Hungary.
1867 Publication of Karl Marx's *Das Kapital*.
1867 Nobel produces dynamite.
1867 South African diamond fields discovered.
1868 Meiji Restoration in Japan.
1869 Opening of Suez Canal.

World events (continued)

1869 Completion of first trans-continental railway in USA.
1869 Dmitri Mendeleyev draws up table of elements.
1870 Franco-Prussian War begins (to 1871).
1870 Papal infallibility declared.
1870 Death of Charles Dickens.
1871 German Empire proclaimed.
1871 Third Republic begins in France.
1872 Claude Monet's 'Impression: Sunrise' gives name to Impressionists.
1873 Christopher Sholes and Carlos Glidden design first commercial typewriter.
1873 James Clerk Maxwell publishes treatise on electricity and magnetism.
1875 William Gilbert and Arthur Sullivan produce their first operetta.
1876 George Custer defeated at Battle of Little Big Horn.
1876 Alexander Bell invents telephone.
1876 Nikolaus Otto devises four-stroke-cycle gas engine.
1877 Queen Victoria proclaimed Empress of India.
1877 Thomas Edison invents the phonograph.
1879 War of the Pacific begins (to 1883).
1879 Zulu War in South Africa.
1879 Woolworths opens first store.
1880 First Boer War (to 1881).
1881 Death of Fyodor Dostoevsky.
1881 Louis Pasteur develops immunization against anthrax.
1882 Phoenix Park murders in Dublin.
1882 Robert Koch discovers tuberculosis bacillus.
1882 Mahdi proclaimed as Messiah in Sudan.
1883 Opening of Brooklyn Bridge, New York.
1883 Death of Richard Wagner.
1883 Krakatoa volcanic explosion.
1884 Germany acquires South-West Africa.
1884 Discovery of gold in Transvaal.
1885 Belgium acquires Congo.
1885 Death of Charles Gordon at Khartoum.
1885 Foundation of Indian National Congress.
1885 Karl Benz builds his first motor cars in Germany.
1885 Completion of Canadian Pacific Railway.
1886 Partition of East Africa by Germany and Britain.
1886 Foundation of Johannesburg.
1886 Gottlieb Daimler produces motorcycle.
1886 Statue of Liberty erected in the USA.
1887 French establish Indo-Chinese Union.
1887 Michelson–Morley experiment on relative velocity of light.
1887 Goodwin invents celluloid film.
1887 Invention of pneumatic tyre by Dunlop.
1887 Heinrich Hertz discovers electromagnetic waves.
1887 First book on Esperanto published.
1888 Tesla makes alternating-current motor.
1888 Eastman produces Kodak camera.
1889 Foundation of British South Africa Company.
1889 Gustave Eiffel completes Tower in Paris.
1889 First skyscraper in America (in Chicago).
1890 Dismissal of Bismarck.
1890 Death of Vincent van Gogh.
1891 Beginning of Trans-Siberian Railway.
1893 Death of Piotr Ilyich Tchaikovsky.
1893 Lumière brothers invent cinematograph.
1894 Beginning of Sino-Japanese War (to 1895).

1894 Opening of Blackpool Tower.
1894 Opening of Manchester Ship Canal.
1894 Launch of first steam-turbine ship (*Turbinia*).
1895 Wilhelm Röntgen discovers X-rays.
1895 Guglielmo Marconi invents wireless telegraphy.
1895 Henry Wood begins Promenade Concerts in London.
1896 Italians defeated by Ethiopians at Battle of Adowa.
1896 Jameson Raid in South Africa.
1896 Establishment of Nobel Prizes.
1896 Henri Becquerel discovers radioactivity.
1897 Death of Johannes Brahms.
1897 First Women's Institute, in Canada.
1897 Joseph Thomson discovers the electron.
1897 Diesel demonstrates compression-ignition engine.
1898 The Curies isolate radium.
1898 Spanish–American War.
1898 Hundred Days of Reform in China.
1898 USA annexes Hawaii.
1898 Ebenezer Howard proposes 'garden city' concept.
1899 Second Boer War begins (to 1902).
1899 Permanent Court of Arbitration established in The Hague.
1900 Boxer uprising in China.
1900 Max Planck proposes quantum theory.
1900 Publication of Sigmund Freud's *The Interpretation of Dreams*.
1901 Establishment of Commonwealth of Australia.
1901 Guglielmo Marconi transmits wireless signals across the Atlantic.
1902 Enrico Caruso makes first gramophone record.
1903 Panama Canal Zone leased to USA.
1903 Wright brothers make their first flight.
1903 Henry Ford founds motor company.
1903 Publication of Bertrand Russell's *Principles of Mathematics*.
1904 Beginning of Russo–Japanese War (to 1905).
1904 Construction of first engine-powered lifeboat.
1905 Revolution in Russia against Tsar.
1905 Albert Einstein presents special theory of relativity.
1906 Major earthquake in San Francisco.
1906 Foundation of Rolls-Royce Ltd in England.
1906 Death of Henrik Ibsen.
1907 Dominion of New Zealand established.
1907 Cubist exhibition in Paris.
1907 Discovery of principal blood groups.
1908 Young Turks revolution.
1908 Robert Baden-Powell founds Boy Scout movement.
1908 First Model T Ford made.
1908 Great meteorite falls in Siberia.
1909 Sergei Diaghilev launches Ballets Russes.
1909 Robert Peary reaches North Pole.
1909 Louis Blériot makes first cross-Channel flight.
1910 Foundation of Union of South Africa.
1910 Beginning of Mexican revolution (to 1917).
1910 Annexation of Korea by Japan.
1910 Constitutional Crisis in Britain.
1910 Paul Ehrlich invents salvarsan as cure for syphilis.
1910 Death of Leo Tolstoy.
1911 Chinese Revolution.

1911 Ernest Rutherford propounds theory of atomic structure.
1911 Roald Amundsen first to reach South Pole.
1912 Beginning of Balkan Wars (to 1913).
1912 Sinking of SS *Titanic*.
1912 Republic of China established under Sun Yat-sen.
1912 Victor Hess discovers cosmic rays.
1914 First Charlie Chaplin films.
1914 Opening of Panama Canal.
1914 First World War begins (to 1918).
1916 Albert Einstein presents general theory of relativity.
1916 Battle of the Somme.
1916 Irish rebellion (to 1921).
1917 US Expeditionary Force in Europe.
1917 Russian Revolution.
1917 Civil war in Russia (to 1922).
1917 Balfour Declaration promises Jews a home in Palestine.
1918 End of First World War.
1918 Fourteen Points statement by President Wilson.
1918 Women over 30 given right to vote in Britain.
1919 May 4th movement in China.
1919 Foundation of Soviet Republic.
1919 Amritsar massacre in India.
1919 Bauhaus movement established in Germany.
1919 John Alcock and Arthur Brown make first Atlantic air crossing.
1919 First woman MP in House of Commons (Lady Astor).
1919 Adolf Hitler founds National Socialist German Workers' Party.
1919 Spartacist rising in Berlin crushed.
1920 League of Nations established.
1920 Radio broadcasting begins.
1921 Treaty partitions Ireland.
1922 USSR established.
1922 Benito Mussolini in power in Italy.
1922 Frederick Banting and Charles Best isolate insulin.
1922 BBC makes first regular broadcasts.
1922 Tomb of Tutankhamun discovered in Egypt.
1923 Munich putsch by Adolf Hitler.
1923 Republic proclaimed in Turkey.
1923 Major earthquake in Japan.
1924 Death of Vladimir Ilyich Lenin.
1925 Publication of Adolf Hitler's *Mein Kampf*.
1926 General Strike in Britain.
1926 Jiang Jieshi (Chiang Kai-shek) leads movement for reunification of China.
1926 John Logie Baird demonstrates television.
1927 Talking pictures begin.
1927 Charles Lindbergh's first solo flight across Atlantic.
1927 Duke Ellington begins playing at the Cotton Club.
1928 Alexander Fleming discovers penicillin.
1928 Walt Disney introduces Mickey Mouse.
1929 Wall Street crash.
1929 Lateran Treaty establishes Vatican as state.
1930 Amy Johnson's solo flight, England to Australia.
1931 Creation of republic in Spain.
1931 Japanese occupy Manchuria.
1931 Empire State Building built in New York.
1932 Foundation of Kingdom of Saudi Arabia.
1932 Chaco War between Paraguay and Bolivia (to 1935).

1933 Franklin Roosevelt introduces New Deal.
1933 Adolf Hitler becomes Chancellor of Germany.
1933 Reichstag Fire in Berlin.
1933 Prohibition repealed in the USA.
1933 Discovery of polythene.
1934 Long March of Chinese Communists begins (to 1935).
1934 Discovery of nuclear fission.
1935 Italian invasion of Abyssinia (Ethiopia).
1936 Beginning of Spanish Civil War (to 1939).
1936 Anti-Comintern Pact between Japan and Germany.
1936 Arab revolt in Palestine.
1936 British constitutional crisis over Edward VIII.
1936 John Maynard Keynes publishes his economic theory.
1936 First public television transmissions in Britain.
1936 *Queen Mary*'s maiden voyage.
1936 Crystal Palace destroyed by fire.
1937 War between Japan and China begins.
1937 Pablo Picasso paints 'Guernica'.
1937 Golden Gate Bridge completed in San Francisco.
1937 *Hindenburg* zeppelin destroyed by fire in USA.
1937 Jet engine tested.
1938 Germany occupies Austria.
1938 Munich Agreement.
1938 Discovery of nylon.
1938 Chester Carlson makes first xerographic print.
1939 Germany invades Czechoslovakia and Poland.
1939 Second World War begins.
1940 Evacuation of Dunkirk.
1940 Battle of Britain.
1940 Plutonium obtained by bombardment of uranium.
1941 Germany invades Russia.
1941 Japanese attack Pearl Harbor.
1941 Death of James Joyce.
1941 Orson Wells makes *Citizen Kane*.
1942 Construction of first nuclear reactor.
1942 Defeat of Germany at El Alamein.
1942 American defeat of Japan at Midway.
1942 Anglo-American landings in North Africa.
1943 Surrender of German army at Stalingrad.
1943 Capitulation of Italy.
1944 D-Day landing in Normandy.
1944 Perón in power in Argentina.
1944 Education Act in Britain.
1945 Atom bombs dropped on Japan.
1945 Second World War ends.
1945 Yalta Conference.
1945 Nuremberg War Crimes Tribunal opens.
1945 United Nations established.
1945 Republic of Yugoslavia established under Tito.
1946 Civil War in China (to 1949).
1946 Civil War in Indo-China (to 1954).
1946 Construction of first electronic digital computer.
1947 First supersonic flight.
1947 Independence of India and Pakistan.
1947 Greek Civil War (to 1949).
1947 Marshall Plan for European reconstruction.
1947 Dead Sea Scrolls found in Palestine.
1947 Christian Dior introduces 'New Look'.
1948 Creation of State of Israel.
1948 Communist rule established in Czechoslovakia.
1948 Berlin airlift.
1948 Formation of Organization of American States.
1948 First Arab–Israeli War.

World events (continued)

1948 Invention of the transistor.
1948 Creation of World Council of Churches.
1948 Assassination of Mohandas Gandhi.
1948 Apartheid policy begins in South Africa.
1948 Creation of World Health Organization.
1948 Kinsey report on sexual behaviour published.
1949 Formation of NATO.
1949 Communist victory in China.
1949 Creation of West and East Germany.
1949 Communist rule established in Hungary.
1950 Beginning of Korean War (to 1953).
1951 Nuclear power stations introduced.
1951 Festival of Britain.
1951 First turbo-jet airliner (*Comet*).
1952 Mau Mau rebellion begins in Kenya.
1952 Military revolt in Egypt.
1952 Contraceptive pill introduced.
1952 Accession of Elizabeth II of Britain.
1952 Detonation of first hydrogen bomb.
1953 Death of Josef Stalin.
1953 Edmund Hillary and Sherpa Tenzing conquer Everest.
1953 James Watson and Francis Crick show DNA molecule structure.
1954 Independence of Cambodia and Laos.
1954 Nationalist revolt in Algeria.
1954 Nasser in power in Egypt.
1954 Vietnam divided into North and South.
1954 Independent Television Authority set up in Britain.
1955 Formation of Warsaw Pact.
1955 Enosis (Greek unity) crisis in Cyprus (to 1959).
1956 Władysław Gomułka in power in Poland.
1956 Soviet forces crush Hungarian revolt.
1956 Second Arab–Israeli War.
1956 Suez Crisis.
1956 Neutrino experimentally observed.
1956 Rock-and-roll music era begins.
1957 Independence of Ghana.
1957 Treaty of Rome forms European Economic Community.
1957 Launch of first space satellite (*Sputnik 1*).
1957 Civil Rights violence at Little Rock, Arkansas.
1958 Fifth Republic formed in France under Charles de Gaulle.
1958 Introduction of stereo recordings.
1959 Formation of European Free Trade Association.
1959 Fidel Castro in power after Cuban revolution.
1959 First photograph of dark side of the Moon (*Luna 3*).
1959 First section of Britain's first motorway opened.
1960 Independence of many African states.
1960 Sharpeville massacre in South Africa.
1960 Development of the laser.
1961 John F Kennedy becomes US president.
1961 Berlin Wall built.
1961 South Africa becomes republic.
1961 Yuri Gagarin becomes first man in space (*Vostok 1*).
1962 Second Vatican Council begins (to 1965).
1962 Independence of Algeria.
1962 Cuban missile crisis.
1963 Assassination of John F Kennedy.
1963 Valentina Tereshkova becomes first woman in orbit.
1963 Beatles become internationally known.
1964 Publication of *Thoughts of Chairman Mao*.

1964 Civil Rights Bill in USA.
1964 Foundation of Palestine Liberation Organization.
1965 War between India and Pakistan.
1965 Unilateral declaration of independence by Rhodesia (Zimbabwe).
1966 Cultural Revolution in China.
1966 First lunar soft landing (*Luna 9*).
1966 Assassination of Hendrik Verwoerd in Cape Town, South Africa.
1967 Civil war in Nigeria, and secession of Biafra (to 1970).
1967 Third Arab–Israeli War ('Six-Day War').
1967 Oil tanker *Torrey Canyon* disaster.
1967 Christiaan Barnard carries out first heart transplant operation.
1968 Soviet invasion of Czechoslovakia.
1968 Student protest movement in many countries.
1968 Assassination of Martin Luther King, Jr.
1968 First manned lunar orbit (*Apollo 8*).
1968 Discovery of pulsars.
1969 First man on the moon (Neil Armstrong).
1969 Richard Nixon becomes US president.
1969 Outbreak of troubles in Northern Ireland.
1970 Boeing 747 'jumbo' jets introduced.
1971 East Pakistan becomes Bangladesh.
1971 Policy of détente introduced by USA with USSR and China.
1971 Decimal currency introduced into UK.
1972 Pocket calculators introduced.
1973 Fourth Arab–Israeli War.
1973 Britain joins European Economic Community.
1973 US forces withdraw from South Vietnam.
1973 Major famine in Ethiopia.
1973 Death of Pablo Picasso.
1974 Turkish invasion of Cyprus.
1974 Haile Selassie deposed in Ethiopia.
1974 Strategic Arms Limitation Treaty signed.
1974 Resignation of Richard Nixon after Watergate scandal.
1974 First 'test-tube babies'.
1975 End of Vietnam War.
1975 Civil war begins in Lebanon.
1975 Death of Francisco Franco.
1975 Dutch Elm disease widespread.
1975 *Apollo–Soyuz* space project.
1975 Domestic videorecorders introduced.
1975 Floppy disks introduced.
1976 Death of Mao Zedong.
1976 *Concorde* supersonic airliner begins transatlantic flights.
1976 First Bantustan established in South Africa (Transkei).
1977 Military coup in Pakistan.
1977 Jimmy Carter becomes US president.
1977 Death of Elvis Presley.
1977 Launch of *Voyager* missions to outer planets.
1978 Camp David Treaty between Egypt and Israel.
1978 John Paul II becomes Pope.
1979 Former President Bhutto executed in Pakistan.
1979 Idi Amin expelled from Uganda.
1979 Civil war in Nicaragua.
1979 Islamic Republic established in Iran under Ayatollah Khomeini.
1979 Invasion of Afghanistan by USSR.
1979 Vietnam invades Cambodia.
1979 Saddam Hussein becomes president of Iraq.

World chronology

1979 Margaret Thatcher becomes British prime minister.
1979 Walkman portable cassette player introduced.
1980 Death of Marshal Tito.
1980 Black majority rule in Zimbabwe.
1980 Major famine in East Africa.
1980 Creation of Solidarity union in Poland.
1980 Beginning of Iran–Iraq War (to 1988).
1980 Humber Bridge completed.
1980 Introduction of videodisk.
1980 Growth of Green movement in Europe.
1980 Assassination of John Lennon in New York.
1980 Björn Borg wins Wimbledon for fifth successive year.
1980 Eruption of Mt St Helens in USA.
1981 Ronald Reagan becomes US president.
1981 Martial law in Poland.
1981 Assassination of President Sadat of Egypt.
1981 Hunger strikers die in Northern Ireland.
1981 First re-usable space shuttle flight.
1981 Race riots in British cities.
1981 First reports of AIDS.
1981 IBM personal computer system introduced.
1982 War between Britain and Argentina over Falkland Islands.
1982 PLO expelled from Beirut.
1982 Israel withdraws from Sinai Peninsula.
1982 Draft treaty to control CFCs.
1982 Introduction of compact discs.
1983 Global warming effect demonstrated.
1983 US proposes 'star wars' missile programme.
1984 Assassination of Indira Gandhi.
1985 Mikhail Gorbachev in power in USSR.
1985 Halley's comet intercepted.
1986 Chernobyl nuclear power disaster.
1986 State of emergency in South Africa.
1986 US bombing of Libya.
1986 Kurt Waldheim becomes President of Austria.
1986 *Glasnost* and *perestroika* advocated by Gorbachev.
1986 *Challenger* space shuttle disaster.
1986 Hole in ozone layer reported.
1986 Iran–*Contra* scandal in USA.
1987 World population passes 5 thousand million.
1989 George Bush becomes US president.

1989 Soviet army completes withdrawal from Afghanistan.
1989 Solidarity prime minister elected in Poland (Tadeusz Mazowiecki).
1989 Tiananmen Square demonstration and massacre in Beijing.
1989 Death of Ayatollah Khomeini in Iran.
1989 Opening of Berlin Wall.
1989 End of Communist rule in Czechoslovakia.
1989 Invasion of Panama by USA.
1989 Execution of Nicolae Ceausescu in Romania.
1989 Death of Emperor Hirohito of Japan.
1989 F W de Klerk becomes President of South Africa.
1990 Reunification of Germany.
1990 Resignation of Margaret Thatcher in Britain.
1990 Independence of Armenia.
1990 Lech Walesa becomes President of Poland.
1990 Independence of Lithuania.
1990 Release of Nelson Mandela from prison in South Africa.
1990 Invasion of Kuwait by Iraq.
1990 F W de Klerk begins dismantling of South African apartheid system.
1991 Gulf War (Operation Desert Storm).
1991 Civil war begins in Yugoslavia.
1991 Nelson Mandela elected President of African National Congress.
1991 Independence of Baltic States recognized by USSR.
1991 Independence of Croatia, Macedonia, Slovenia.
1991 Independence of remaining republics of former Soviet Union.
1991 Formation of Commonwealth of Independent States.
1991 Resignation of Mikhail Gorbachev in Russia.
1991 Boris Yeltsin becomes Russian president.
1992 Independence of Bosnia and Herzegovina.
1992 Boutros Boutros-Ghali becomes UN secretary-general.
1993 Division of Czechoslovakia into Czech and Slovak Republics.
1993 Bill Clinton becomes US president.
1994 Nelson Mandela became South African president.

Seven wonders of the Ancient World

Name	Date built	History
Egyptian Pyramids	more than 4000 years ago	Oldest of the ancient wonders and the only one surviving today. Served as tombs for Egyptian pharoahs.
Colossus of Rhodes	c.305–292 BC	32 m (105 ft) high bronze statue of the sun god Helius. Destroyed by an earthquake in 224 BC.
Hanging Gardens of Babylon	6th century BC	Series of terraces of trees and flowers along the banks of the Euphrates. Built by Nebuchadnezzar II (also known in the Book of Daniel as Nebuchadrezzar).
Mausoleum at Halicarnassus, Asia Minor	4th century BC	Tomb of Mausolus built by his widow. Destroyed by an earthquake before the 15th century.
Pharos of Alexandria	c.270 BC	The world's first known lighthouse, at the entrance of Alexandria harbour in Egypt. 122 m/400 ft high. In ruins by 15th century.
Statue of Zeus at Olympia	5th century BC	9 m/30 ft high wooden statue of Greek god Zeus covered with gold and ivory. Designed by Athens sculptor Phidias. Destroyed by fire AD 475.
Temple of Artemis at Ephesus, Asia Minor	6th century BC	Marble temple in honour of goddess of hunting and the moon. Rebuilt in 4th century BC but destroyed by Goths in 3rd century AD.

Dynasties of China

Name	Date	History
Xia	c.2200–c.1523 BC	Emperor Yu Land reclaimed, bronze weapons made, grain cultivated, first use of written symbols
Shang or Yin	c.1480–1050 BC	First historic dynasty Agricultural society with class system First Chinese calendar Age of bronze casting
Zhou	c.1066–221 BC	Classical age Laws in place Money economy
Qin (Ch'in)	221–206 BC	Rule by Shi Huang-ti Unification of country begun Feudalism replaced by bureaucratic government Large part of Great Wall built
Han	206 BC–AD 220	Bureaucratic state based on Confucianism Buddhism introduced
Three Kingdoms (San-kuo)	AD 220–65	Divided into three states, Wei, Shu, and Wu Increased importance of Buddhism and Taoism
Tsin	265–420	Founded by Wei general N China ruled by series of barbarian dynasties
Sui	581–618	Country reunified and central government established Canal system constructed
Tang	618–907	Period of territorial expansion Buddhism suppressed Age of great poets, sculptors, and painters
Five Dynasties and Ten Kingdoms	907–60	Period of hardship with wars and official corruption First printing of paper money
Song (Sung)	960–1279	Great changes socially and intellectually Confucianism superceeds Taoism and Buddhism Central bureaucracy reformed Cultivation of tea and cotton on a large scale
Yuan	1279–1368	Founding of Mongol dynasty by Kublai Khan Confucianism out of favour End of dynasty in S China Riots in Mongolia
Ming	1368–1644	Mongols expelled Confucianism reinstated Porcelain production flourishes Great developments in architecture, the novel, and drama
Ch'ing (Manchu)	1644–1912	Decline of central authority Increase in European trade China divided into spheres of influence by foreign powers Last Chinese monarchy

Dynasties of Ancient Egypt

Period	Dynasty	Date	Major rulers	History
Early Dynastic Period	I	3110–2884 BC	Menes	Unification of Upper and Lower Egypt
	II	2884–2780 BC		Memphis founded
Old Kingdom	III	2780–2680 BC	Snefru	Step Pyramid built
	IV	2680–2565 BC	Khufu (Cheops); Khafre; Menkaure	Age of the great pyramids
	V	2565–2420 BC		
	VI	2420–2258 BC	Pepi I; Pepi II	

Period	Dynasty	Date	Major rulers	History
First Intermediate Period	VII, VIII	2258–2225 BC		Egypt divided politically Control by local monarchs
	IX, X	2225–2134 BC		Capital at Heracleopolis
	XI	2134–c.2000 BC	Mentuhotep II	Capital at Thebes Reunification
Middle Kingdom	XII	2000–1786 BC	Amenemhet I; Sesostris I; Amenemhet II; Sesostris II; Amenemhet III; Amenemhet IV	Conquest of Nubia
Second Intermediate Period	XIII–XVII	1786–1570 BC	Hyksos	Egypt liberated by Theban dynasty
New Kingdom	XVIII	1570–c.1342 BC	Amenhotep I; Thutmose I, II, Hatshepsut, Thutmose III, IV, Akhenaton; Tutankhamun	Period of empire building – extended from Syria to Southern Sudan Capital city Thebes Extensive building programme
	XIX	c.1342–1200 BC	Ramses I; Ramses II	
	XX	1200–1085 BC	Ramses III	New Kingdom declines
	XXI	1085–945 BC		Egypt divided – Amun rule in Thebes and pharaohs in Tanis
	XXII	945–745 BC	Sheshonk I	Libyan dynasty
	XXIII	745–718 BC		Nubian dynasty with invasion of Piankhi
	XXIV	718–712 BC		
	XXV	712–663 BC	Taharka	Invasion by Assyria – foreign domination follows
	XXVI	663–525 BC	Necho	
	XXVII	525–405 BC	Achaemenids of Persia; Darius II	Egypt revolts
	XXVIII, XXIX, XXX	405–332 BC	Nekhtnebf I	Last native dynasties, ending with conquest of Alexander the Great Capital at Sais, Mendes, then Sebennytos

Rulers of the Roman Empire

Name	Dates	History	Name	Dates	History
Augustus	27 BC–AD 14	Grandnephew of Julius Caesar	Didius Julianus	193	Bought office from the Praetorian guard
Tiberius	AD 14–37	Stepson of Augustus	Septimus Severus	193–211	Proclaimed emperor
Gaius Caesar (Caligula)	37–41	Grandnephew of Tiberius	Caracalla	211–17	Son of Severus
			Geta	211–12	Son of Severus and ruled together with Caracalla
Claudius I	41–54	Uncle of Caligula			
Nero	54–68	Stepson of Claudius	Macrinus	217–18	Proclaimed emperor by soldiers
Galba	68–9	Proclaimed emperor by soldiers	Heliogabalus (Elagabalus)	218–22	Cousin of Caracalla
Otho	69	Military commander			
Vespasian	69–79	Military commander	Alexander Severus	222–35	Cousin of Heliogabalus
Titus	79–81	Son of Vespasian			
Domitian	81–96	Son of Vespasian	Maximin	235–8	Proclaimed emperor by soldiers
Nerva	96–8	Elected interim ruler			
Trajan	98–117	Adopted son of Nerva	Gordian I and Gordian II, Balbinus, Pupienus	238	Proclaimed by senate and all ruled together
Hadrian	117–38	Ward of Trajan			
Antoninus Pius	138–61	Adopted by Hadrian			
Marcus Aurelius	161–80	Adopted by Antoninus Pius	Gordian III	238–44	Son of Gordian II
Lucius Verus	161–9	Adopted by Antoninus Pius and ruled together with Marcus Aurelius	Philip	244–9	Assassin of Gordian III
			Decius	249–51	Proclaimed emperor by soldiers
Commodus	180–92	Son of Marcus Aurelius	Hostilianus	251	Son of Decius
Pertinax	193	Proclaimed emperor by the Praetorian guard	Gallus	251–3	Military commander
			Aemilianus	253	Military commander

Rulers of the Roman Empire (continued)

Name	Dates	History
Valerian	253–60	Military commander
Gallienus	253–68	Son of Valerian; co-emperor with his father and later emperor in his own right
Claudius II	268–70	Military commander
Aurelian	270–5	Chosen by Claudius as successor
Tacitus	275–6	Chosen by senate
Florianus	276	Half-brother of Tacitus
Probus	276–82	Military commander
Carus	282–3	Proclaimed by the Praetorian guard
Carinus	283–5	Son of Carus
Numerianus	283–4	Son of Carus and ruled together with Carinus
Diocletian	284–305	Military commander; ruled together with Maximian and Constantius; Empire divided
Maximian	286–305	Appointed by Diocletian
Constantius I	305–6	Successor of Diocletian
Galerius	305–10	Emperor with Constantius
Maximin	308–13	Nephew of Galerius
Licinius	308–24	Appointed emperor in West by Galerius
Maxentius	306–12	Son of Maximin
Constantine I (the Great)	306–37	Son of Constantius
Constantine II	337–40	Son of Constantine I
Constans	337–50	Son of Constantine I
Constantius II	337–61	Son of Constantine I
Magnentius	350–3	Usurped Constans' throne
Julian	361–3	Nephew of Constantine I
Jovian	363–4	Elected by the army
Valentinian I	364–75	Proclaimed by the army; ruled in the West
Valens	364–78	Brother of Valentinian I; ruled in the East
Grantian	375–83	Son of Valentinian I; co-ruler in West with Valentinian II
Maximus	383–8	Usurper in the West
Valentinian II	375–92	Son of Valentinian I

Name	Dates	History
Eugenius	392–4	Usurper in West
Theodosius I (the Great)	375–95	Appointed ruler in the East by Gratian; last ruler of united empire
Arcadius	395–408	Son of Theodosius I; emperor in East
Theodosius II	408–50	Son of Arcadius; emperor in East
Marcian	450–7	Brother-in-law of Theodosius II; emperor in East
Leo I	457–74	Chosen by senate; emperor in East
Leo II	474	Grandson of Leo I; emperor in East
Honorius	395–423	Son of Theodosius I; emperor in West
Maximus	409–11	Usurper in Spain; emperor in West
Constantius III	421	Named joint emperor by Honorius; emperor in West
Valentinian III	425–55	Nephew of Honorius and son of Constantius III; emperor in West
Petronius Maximus	455	Bribed his way into office; emperor in West
Avitus	455–6	Placed in office by Goths; emperor in West
Majorian	457–61	Puppet emperor of Ricimer; emperor in West
Libius Severus	461–5	Puppet emperor of Ricimer; emperor in West
Anthemius	467–72	Appointed by Ricimer and Leo I; emperor in West
Olybrius	472	Appointed by Ricimer; emperor in West
Glycerius	473–4	Appointed by Leo I; emperor in West
Julius Nepos	474–5	Appointed by Leo I; emperor in West
Romulus Augustus	475–6	Placed in office by his father Orestes; emperor in West

The Roman Empire in the 1st century AD

Chief Roman roads in Britain

British royal family tree

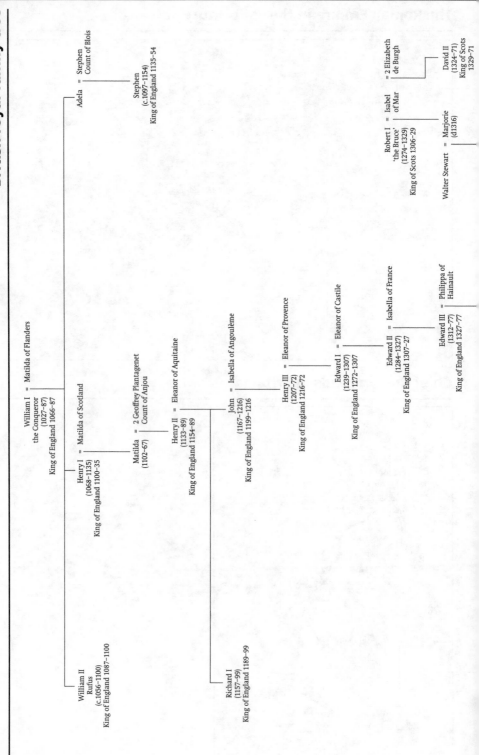

William I
the Conqueror
(1027–87)
King of England 1066–87
= Matilda of Flanders

William II
Rufus
(c.1056–1100)
King of England 1087–1100

Henry I
(1068–1135)
King of England 1100–35
= Matilda of Scotland

Adela = Stephen
Count of Blois

Stephen
(c.1097–1154)
King of England 1135–54

Matilda
(1102–67)
= 2 Geoffrey Plantagenet
Count of Anjou

Henry II
(1133–89)
King of England 1154–89
= Eleanor of Aquitaine

Richard I
(1157–99)
King of England 1189–99

John
(1167–1216)
King of England 1199–1216
= Isabella of Angoulême

Henry III
(1207–72)
King of England 1216–72
= Eleanor of Provence

Edward I
(1239–1307)
King of England 1272–1307
= Eleanor of Castile

Edward II
(1284–1327)
King of England 1307–27
= Isabella of France

Edward III
(1312–77)
King of England 1327–77
= Philippa of
Hainault

Robert I
'the Bruce'
(1274–1329)
King of Scots 1306–29
= Isabel
of Mar
= 2 Elizabeth
de Burgh

Walter Stewart = Marjorie
(d1316)

David II
(1324–71)
King of Scots
1329–71

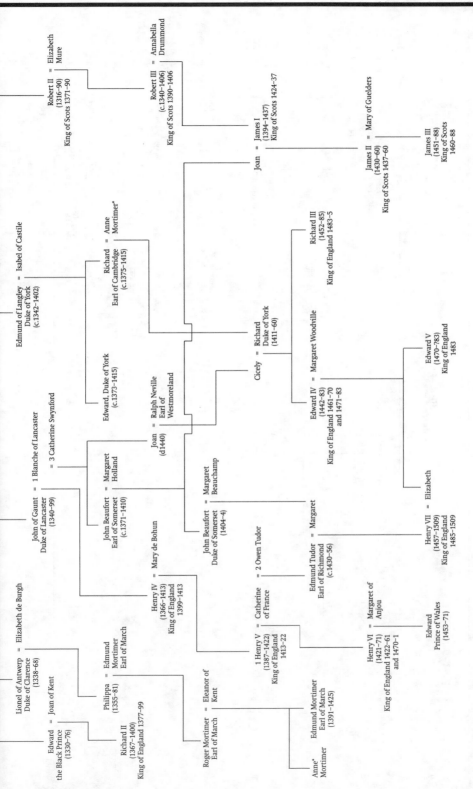

*denotes the same person occurring in a different part of the tree
1 denotes first marriage; 2, second marriage; 3, third marriage

British royal family tree (continued)

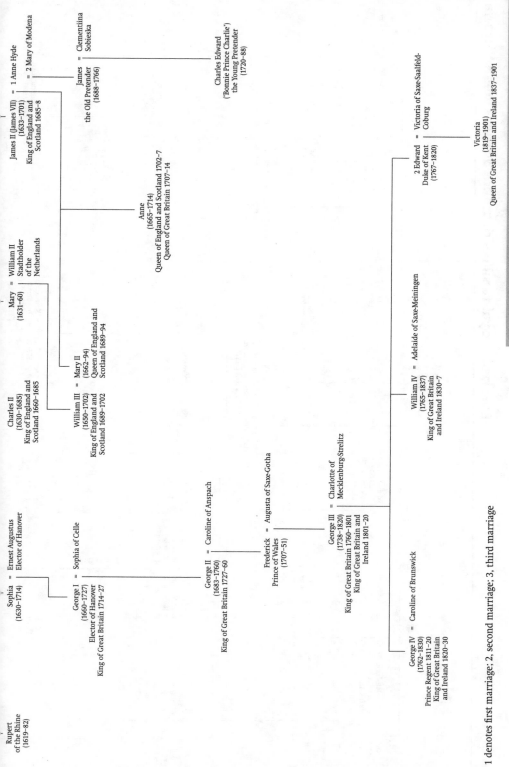

1 denotes first marriage; 2, second marriage; 3, third marriage

European royal families descended from Queen Victoria

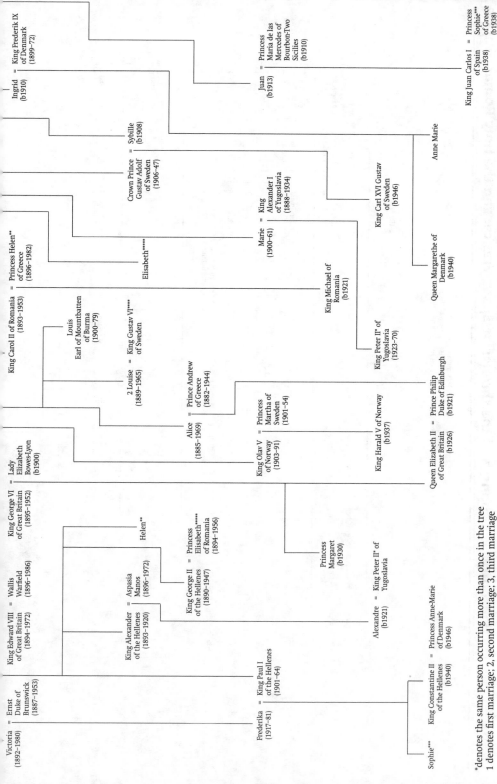

History

*denotes the same person occurring more than once in the tree
1 denotes first marriage; 2, second marriage; 3, third marriage

Habsburgs, Bourbons, and the thrones of Spain, France, and the Holy Roman Empire

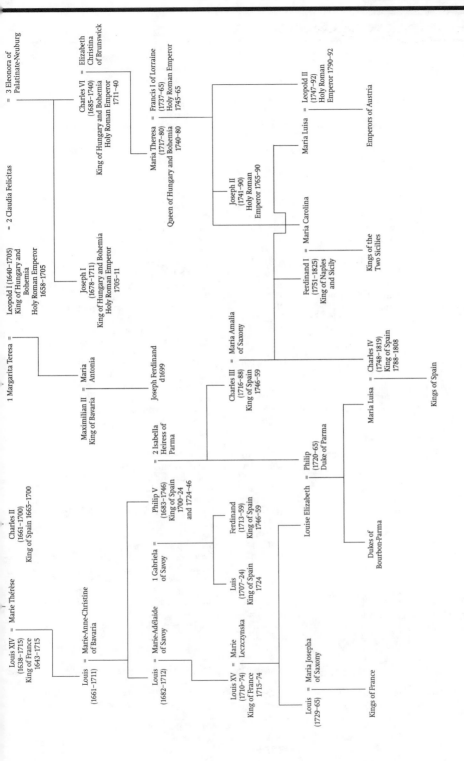

1 denotes first marriage; 2, second marriage; 3; third marriage

Rulers of England and Great Britain

Period	Name of ruler	Dates of rule	History
Saxons and Danes	Egbert	802–39	King of Essex.
	Ethelwulf	839–58	Son of Egbert. King of Wessex, Sussex, Kent, Essex.
	Ethelbald	858–60	Son of Ethelwulf. Displaced his father as King of Wessex.
	Ethelbert	860–5	Second son of Ethelwulf. United Kent and Wessex.
	Ethelred	865–71	Third son of Ethelwulf. King of Wessex.
	Alfred (the Great)	871–99	Fourth son of Ethelwulf. Defeated the Danes.
	Edward (the Elder)	899–924	Son of Alfred. United England and claimed Scotland.
	Athelstan (the Glorious)	924–39	Son of Edward. King of Mercia, Wessex.
	Edmund	939–46	Third son of Edward. King of Wessex, Mercia.
	Edred	946–55	Fourth son of Edward.
	Edwy (the Fair)	955–9	Eldest son of Edmund. King of Wessex.
	Edgar (the Peaceful)	959–75	Younger son of Edmund. Ruled all England.
	Edward (the Martyr)	975–8	Son of Edgar. Murdered by stepmother.
	Ethelred II (the Unready)	978–1016	Second son of Edgar.
	Edmund (Ironside)	1016	Son of Ethelred II. King of London.
	Canute	1016–35	The Dane. Became ruler by conquest.
	Harold I (Harefoot)	1037–40	Illegitimate son of Canute.
	Hardecanute	1040–2	Son of Canute by Emma. King of Denmark.
	Edward (the Confessor)	1042–66	Younger son of Ethelred II.
	Harold II	1066	Brother-in-law of Edward the Confessor. Last Saxon King.
House of Normandy	William I (the Conqueror)	1066–87	Became ruler by conquest.
	William II (Rufus)	1087–1100	Third son of William I.
	Henry I	1100–35	Youngest son of William I.
House of Blois	Stephen	1135–54	Grandson of William I.
House of Plantagenet	Henry II	1154–89	Grandson of Henry I.
	Richard I (Coeur de Lion)	1189–99	Third son of Henry II. Crusader.
	John	1199–1216	Youngest son of Henry II. Signed Magna Carta 1215.
	Henry III	1216–72	Son of John.
	Edward I (Longshanks)	1272–1307	Son of Henry III.
	Edward II	1307–27	Son of Edward I. Deposed by parliament.
	Edward III	1327–77	Son of Edward II.
	Richard II	1377–99	Grandson of Edward III. Deposed.
House of Lancaster	Henry IV	1399–1413	Grandson of Edward III.
	Henry V	1413–22	Son of Henry IV. Victor of Battle of Agincourt 1415.
	Henry VI	1422–61	Son of Henry V.
		1470–71	Second period of rule.
House of York	Edward IV	1461–70	Great-grandson of Edward III.
		1471–83	Second period of rule.
	Edward V	1483	Son of Edward IV. Murdered in Tower of London.
	Richard III (Crookback)	1483–5	Brother of Edward IV. Fell at Bosworth Field.
House of Tudor	Henry VII	1485–1509	Descendant of Edward III.
	Henry VIII	1509–47	Son of Henry VII. Created Church of England.
	Edward VI	1547–53	Son of Henry VIII (by Jane Seymour).
	Mary I	1553–8	Daughter of Henry VIII (by Catherine of Aragon).
	Elizabeth I	1558–1603	Younger daughter of Henry VIII (by Anne Boleyn).
House of Stuart	James I/James VI of Scotland	1603–25	Descendant of Henry VII. First King of Great Britain (official in 1607 with the Act of the Union).
	Charles I	1625–49	Son of James I. Beheaded.
Commonwealth	Oliver Cromwell	1653–8	Lord Protector.
	Richard Cromwell	1658–9	Lord Protector. Son of Oliver Cromwell.
House of Stuart	Charles II	1660–85	Son of Charles I.
	James II	1685–8	Younger son of Charles I. Deposed.
	William III	1689–1702	Son of Mary, daughter of Charles 1.

Period	Name of ruler	Dates of rule	History
	Mary II	1689–94	Daughter of James II. Ruled together with William III.
	Anne	1702–14	Younger daughter of James II.
House of Hanover	George I	1714–27	Great-grandson of James I.
	George II	1727–60	Only son of George I.
	George III	1760–1820	Grandson of George II.
	George IV	1820–30	Eldest son of George III.
	William IV	1830–7	Third son of George III.
	Victoria	1837–1901	Granddaughter of George III.
House of Saxe-Coburg	Edward VII	1901–10	Son of Victoria.
House of Windsor	George V	1910–36	Son of Edward VII.
	Edward VIII	1936	Eldest son of George V. Abdicated.
	George VI	1936–52	Second son of George V.
	Elizabeth II	1952–	Daughter of George VI.

MILITARY WARS AND CAMPAIGNS

Major wars of mediaeval and modern times

War	Dates	History
Norman Conquest of England	1066	France (William the Conqueror)–England (Harold II). Battle of Hastings (14 Oct 1066). Most decisive battle on English soil which led to the successful conquest by the Normans. Harold II died in battle. Began rule of a dynasty of Norman Kings and almost complete replacement of English nobility by Normans, Bretons, and Flemings.
The Crusades	1095–1272	Christians–Turks. Holy Wars authorized by the Pope; fought against infidels in the East, heretics who threatened Catholic unity, and against Christian lay powers who opposed the Papacy.
Conquests of Genghis Khan	1190–1227	Mongols–N China, Kara–Chitai Empire. Subjugation of hostile tribes – Naimans, Tanguts, and Turkish Uigurs.
War of the Sicilian Vespers	1282–1302	Sicily–France. Massacre of the French in Sicily marked the beginning of revolt of Sicilians against Charles of Anjou. War of Sicilian Vespers ensued. Angevins supported by papacy, Italian Guelphs, and Philip II of France, while Aragonese helped by Italian Ghibellines. James II ascended to throne, made peace with papacy, France, and Angevins (to whom he renounced Sicily) by Treaty of Anagni.
Hundred Years War	1337–1453	England–France. Edward III claimed French throne in 1340 and styled himself 'King of England and France'. Traditional rivalries exploded into a dynastic struggle. 1415 Battle of Agincourt – Henry V led overwhelming victory over French. 1417 English then began systematic conquest of Normandy, a task beyond their resources. Evicted from Guyenne (1453) which reduced England's French territories to Calais (lost in 1558) and the Channel Islands. However, the title of King of France was not relinquished until 1801.
Fall of Constantinople	1453	Turks–Byzantine Empire. Collapse of the Byzantine Empire. Since 1261, when Constantinople had been retaken from Latin rule by Michael VII Paleologus, the Byzantine Empire had been threatened by growing power of Ottoman Turks in Asia Minor. 1422 Ottoman Sultan of Turkey Murad II laid siege to the city. This failed but attempt thirty years later by Mehmed II succeeded. Constantinople fell 1453. Last Byzantine emperor Constantine XI Paleologus died in battle.
Wars of the Roses	1455–85	Civil wars in England. Between two rival factions of the House of Plantagenet – York (white rose) and Lancaster (red rose). Began when Richard, Duke of York, claimed protectorship of crown after King Henry VI's mental breakdown and ended with Henry Tudor's defeat of Richard III in Battle of Bosworth. Wars escalated by gentry and by aristocratic feuds.

History

Major wars of mediaeval and modern times (continued)

War	Dates	History
French Wars of Religion	1562–98	Catholics–Huguenots. Caused by growth of Calvinism, noble factionalism, and weak royal government. From 1550s Calvinist or Huguenot numbers increased, fostered by missionary activities of Geneva. Noble factions of Bourbons, Guise, and Montmorency were split by religion as well as by family interests. Civil wars were encouraged by Philip II's support of Catholic Guise faction and by Elizabeth I's aid to Huguenots. They ended when Henry of Navarre returned to Catholicism and crushed the Guise Catholic League.
Thirty Years' War	1618–48	France–Habsburg rulers. Power struggle between Kings of France and Habsburg rulers of Holy Roman Empire and Spain. War fuelled by conflict between Calvinism and Catholicism, and also by the underlying constitutional conflict between Holy Roman Emperor and the German Princes. With Frederick V's defeat (1620) and intervention by other powers (such as Sweden, Denmark, and France), the conflict intensified and spread. Spain collapsed and left the emperor isolated. Peace negotiations opened and ended German war at the Peace of Westphalia.
Bishops' Wars	1639–40	Scotland–England. Two wars between Charles I and Scotland caused by Charles I's unpopular policies towards the Scottish kirk. Resulted in English defeats and bankruptcy for Charles who was then forced to call the Short and Long Parliaments in 1640, bringing to an end his personal rule.
English Civil Wars	1642–51	Charles I–Parliamentarians. Parliamentary opposition to Royal policies. First battle at Edgehill (Oct 1642), but neither side victorious. Royalists then threatened London, the Parliamentarians' stronghold. By autumn the North and West were in their hands. Crucial event was 1643 alliance of Parliament with the Scots. This increased military strength helped the parliamentarians, led by Oliver Cromwell, defeat the Royalists at Marston Moor. 1646 saw end of first civil war with Charles' surrender to the Scots at Newark in May. 1646-8 negotiations between parliament and King began. Aug 1647 army presented King with Head of Proposals asking for religious tolerance and parliamentary control of the armed forces. Charles made secret pact with the Scots, promising to establish Presbyterianism in England. Scots invaded England and were only repulsed in Battle of Preston. Around 100 000 men died in the two wars (1 in 10 of the adult male population). Charles brought to trial by Cromwell (who was also signatory of his death warrant) and executed Jan 1649.
War of League of Augsburg	1688–97	Louis XIV–European Alliance. The third major war of Louis XIV of France in which his expansionist plans were blocked by the alliance led by England, United Provinces (of the Netherlands), and Austrian Habsburgs. The issue underlying the war was the balance of power between Bourbon and Habsburg dynasties. War began when French marched into the Palatinate while Austria was defeating Turks in the East. Grand alliance of United Provinces, England, Saxony, Bavaria, and Spain, all fearful of French annexations, joined together against France. The war was costly and lengthy. Louis XIV opened negotiations for peace 1696 and in 1697 Treaty of Rijswijk drawn up. This did not resolve conflict between Habsburgs and Bourbons, nor English and French, both of which erupted again only four years later in the War of Spanish Succession.
War of Spanish Succession	1701–14	Alliance–Louis XIV. Alliance of British, Dutch, and Habsburg Emperor against French, supported by Spanish. War arose out of conflict as to succession to throne of Spain following death of childless Charles II. Claimants were England, United Provinces, and France. When alliance collapsed the war was concluded by Treaties of Utrecht which divided inheritance among the powers. Britain's imperial power grew at the expense of France and Spain.
War of Jenkin's Ear	1739–43	Britain–Spain.

War	Dates	History
War of Austrian Succession	1740–8	Began in 1739 but then merged into the War of Austrian Succession. Anti-Spanish feeling in Britain provoked war as Captain Robert Jenkins claimed Spanish coastguards in the Caribbean cut off his ear. Prussia–Austria. Struggle for mastery of German states. Hostilities prompted by Frederick II of Prussia's seizure of Habsburg province of Silesia. French allied with Bavaria and Spain and later Saxony and Prussia. Austria was supported by Britain who feared France's hegemony in Europe which would threaten Britain's colonial and commercial empire. After 1744 this developed into a colonial conflict between Britain and the Franco-Spanish bloc. Peace concluded only by Treaty of Aix-la-Chapelle (1748) which preserved Austrian inheritance but also confirmed Prussian inheritance of Silesia.
Seven Years' War	1756–63	A major European conflict rooted in the rivalry between Austria and Prussia and the imminent colonial struggle between Britain and France in the New World and the Far East. Hostilities in N America (1754) pre-dated the Diplomatic Revolution in Europe (1756), which created two opposing power blocs: Austria, France, Russia, Sweden, and Saxony against Prussia, Britain, and Portugal. British maritime superiority countered Franco-Spanish naval power and prevented an invasion by the French. The European war, precipitated by Prussia's seizure of Saxony, was marked by many notable pitched land battles. Saved from total defeat when Russia switched sides, Frederick II of Prussia retained Silesia in 1763.
US War of Independence	1775–83	American settlers–Britain. Insurrection of thirteen of Britain's N American colonies. Began as civil war but America was later joined by France (1778), Spain (1779), and Netherlands (1780). America rejected Britain's offer of peace in the civil war conflicts and declared independence. Britain ultimately defeated.
French Revolutionary Wars	1792–1802	A series of campaigns between France and neighbouring European states hostile to the Revolution and to French hegemony, merging ultimately with the Napoleonic Wars.
Napoleonic Wars	1800–15	Fought to preserve French hegemony in Europe. Initially a guarantee for political, social, and economic changes of the Revolution, but increasingly became manifestation of Napoleon's territorial ambitions. War began with Napoleon's destruction of the Second Coalition (1800). Britain resumed hostilities (1803), prompting Napoleon to prepare for invasion and encouraging the formation of a Third Coalition. Britain retained naval superiority but Napoleon established territorial domination with the invasions of Spain (1808) and Russia (1812). French finally overwhelmed by the Fourth Coalition and war ended with the Battle of Waterloo (1815).
Peninsular War	1808–14	France–Britain. Struggle for the Iberian peninsula which began as Spanish revolt against imposition of Napoleon's brother, Joseph, as King of Spain, but developed into bitter conflict, with British forces under Wellington liberating Spain (1811). Following Napoleon's Moscow campaign (1812), French resources were overextended, enabling Wellington's army to invade SW France (1813–14).
Greek War of Independence	1821–8	Greece–Turkey. Greece fought alone until 1825 when her cause was seconded by Britain, Russia, and later France. Turks defeated and Greece's independence guaranteed by her allies.
Crimean War	1853–6	Britain and France – Russia. Fought in Crimean Peninsula by Britain and France against Russia. Origins lay in the Russian successes against the Turks in the Black Sea area, and the British and French desire to prevent further Russian expansion westward which threatened the Mediterranean and overland routes to India. Major battles were fought at the River Alma (Sep 1854), Balaclava (1854), and Inkermann (Nov 1854). Fall of Russian fortress at Sebastopol (Sep 1855) led to negotiations for peace. Finally agreed in Paris 1856 that Russia would cede South Bessarabia to Moldavia.
American Civil War	1861–5	Unionists – Confederates. Conflict between Unionists and Confederates. Dealt with two great

Major wars of mediaeval and modern times (continued)

War	Dates	History

issues: the nature of the Federal Union and the relative power of the states and central government; and the existence of Black slavery. When Lincoln and the Republican Party's election demonstrated that the South could no longer expect to control the high offices of state, eleven Southern states withdrew from the Union and established the Confederate States of America. War broke out (12 Apr 1861) when the Southern batteries opened fire on a Union emplacement in the harbour of Charlottesville. Lincoln at first defined the issue as preservation of the Union, without any reference to slavery, but he broadened the war aims (Jan 1861), proclaiming the emancipation of all slaves in areas then under arms against the government. The winning strategy began in 1863 when the Unionist General Grant won control of the whole Mississippi valley, isolating the western Confederate states from the rest. After several fierce battles (Gettysburg, Fredericksburg, and the Chattanooga campaign), the South's position became untenable and General Lee, leader of the Confederate forces, abandoned the Confederate capital in Apr 1865 and finally capitulated at Appomattox Court House. The last surrender took place on 26 May.

Franco-Prussian War — 1870 — France – Prussia.
Marked the end of French hegemony in Europe and the foundation of a German empire. In Napoleon III's ambition to conquer Prussia, Bismarck saw an opportunity to bring the S German states into unit with the Prussian-led N German states and build a strong German empire. Conflict was sparked off by disputed candidature for the French throne. The Ems Telegram, sent by Wilhelm I of Prussia refusing the French conditions, succeeded in provoking the French to declare war five days later. After only four weeks the French found themselves trapped at Metz. Main French army tried to relieve them but were surrounded and trapped by Germans at Sedan. French army, with Napoleon III and Macmahon, surrendered. French resistance continued with the new government, and the Germans then began to besiege Paris. Paris surrendered Jan 1871. Treaty of Frankfurt drawn up. Germany annexed Alsace and Lorraine, imposed a high war indemnity on France, and occupied northern territory until indemnity paid.

Boer Wars — 1880–1, 1899–1902 — Britain – Boers.
Wars fought by Britain for the mastery of South Africa. British had made several attempts to re-incorporate the Boers into a South African confederation. First war ended with defeat of British at Majuba Hill and the signing of the Pretoria and London conventions in 1881 and 1884. Second Boer War (1899–1902) can be divided into three phrases – series of Boer successes; counter-offensives by British which captured Pretoria; period of guerilla warfare. Boers effectively won the peace. Retained control of 'native affairs', won back representative government in 1907, and federated South Africa on their own terms (1910). Nevertheless, British interests in South Africa remained protected.

World War 1 — 1914–18 — Allies (Britain, France, Russia, Japan, and Italy) – Central Powers (Germany, Austria-Hungary, Turkey, and Bulgaria).
Origins lay in reaction of other great powers to ambitions of German Empire. The political tensions divided Europe into two camps – the Triple Alliance (Britain, France, and Russia) and the Triple Entente (Germany, Austria-Hungary, and Italy).
Catalyst to war was the assassination of heir to Habsburg throne, Franz Ferdinand, in Bosnia. Austria declared war on Serbia. Germany then declared war on Russia and France and invaded neutral Belgium. This brought the British into the war on the side of the French. Japan joined Britain, as did Italy in 1915. Germany was joined by Turkey (1914) and Bulgaria (1915). Military campaigns centre on France and Belgium in W Europe. First battle of Ypres prevented the Germans from reaching the ports. By end 1914 static line of defence had been established from Belgian coast to Switzerland. Position of stalemate reached. 1916 allies launched offensive for the W front but stopped by Germans who attacked

War	Dates	History
		French at Verdun. To relieve situation Battle of the Somme was launched but proved indecisive. Spring 1918 Germany launched major offensive on West but was driven back by the allies with help from USA. By November armistice was signed with allies having recaptured Belgium and nearly all French territory. Treaty of Versailles drawn up 1919 assigning responsibility for causing the war to Germany and establishing her liability for reparations payments. Germany lost all overseas territories and considerable territory in Poland. Rhineland demilitarized and occupied by allied forces. Germany called treaty a 'Diktat' and its harshness was bitterly resented throughout the interwar years.
Spanish Civil War	1936–9	Republicans–Nationalists (led by General Franco). Both sides attracted foreign assistance; Republic from the USSR and the International Brigades and the Nationalists from Fascist Italy and Nazi Germany. Nationalist victory due to balance of foreign aid, to nonintervention on part of the Western democracies and to greater internal unity in the Nationalist army under Franco.
World War 2	1939–45	Allies (Britain and British Commonwealth, China, France, USA, USSR)–Axis Powers (Germany, Italy, Japan). Origins lay in three different conflicts which merged after 1941: Germany's desire for expansion, Japan's struggle against China, conflict between Japanese and US interests in the Pacific. War in Europe caused by German unwillingness to accept Treaty of Versailles, which was systematically dismantled aided by the allied policy of appeasement. Increased German aggression finally resulted in the invasion of Czechoslovakia, after which Britain and France abandoned policy of appeasement and pledged support to Poland which was now threatened. Germany signed alliance with Russia and invaded Poland. Britain and France then declared war on Germany. Little fighting took place but Germany proceeded to occupy Norway and Denmark. German Blitzkrieg tactics (a combination of tank warfare and airpower) brought about the surrender of Holland in four days, Belgium in three weeks, and France in seven weeks. After failed attempt to gain air supremacy over Britain (Battle of Britain) the invasion of Britain was postponed. Germany then moved east into Greece and Yugoslavia. British military efforts were concentrated against Italy in Mediterranean and N Africa. Allied forces finally ejected German and Italian forces in mid-1943, invaded Sicily and Italy itself, and forced Italy to make a separate peace. June 1941 Germany invaded her ally Russia and advanced towards Moscow, Leningrad, and the Volga. After two years of occupation and the Battle of Stalingrad in winter 1942–3 (a major turning point in the allied campaign), they were driven out. Allies launched a second front through invasion of Normandy and Paris was liberated in August. Allies advanced into Germany and linked with the Russians on the River Elbe. Germans surrendered unconditionally at Rheims 7 May 1945. Japan's desire for expansion led to her attack on Pearl Harbor, Hawaii, and US declared war on Japan next day (8 Dec 1941). In reply, Germany and Italy declared war on US. Not until June 1942 did naval victories halt Japanese advance. Fighting continued until 1945 when US dropped two atomic bombs on Hiroshima and Nagasaki (6 and 9 Aug). Japan then surrendered.
First Indochinese War	1946–54	Vietnam–France. Vietnam controlled by France as colony 1883–1939 and then as a possession 1940–45. Ho Chi Minh proclaimed its independence on 2 Sep 1945 and French opposed the move. Ho Chi Minh led guerrilla warfare against French which ended in Vietnamese victory at Dien Bien Phu in May 1954. Agreement signed in Geneva providing temporary division of the country at the 17th parallel of latitude between the communist-dominated North and the US-supported South. Activities of procommunist rebels would lead to the second Vietnam War.
Korean War	1950–3	Communists and non-Communists. Communist North invaded South after series of border clashes. UN forces intervened driving the invaders back to Chinese frontier.

Major wars of mediaeval and modern times (continued)

War	Dates	History
		China entered conflict and with N Koreans occupied Seoul. UN forces counterattacked and retook territory south of 38th parallel.
Suez War	1956	Britain, France, Israel–Egypt. In July 1956 Egyptian President Abdel Nasser nationalized the Suez Canal following American and British decision not to finance construction of the Aswan Dam. When diplomacy failed France and Britain planned military action to regain control of the canal, allied with Israel. In Oct Israel invaded Egypt. Britain and France ordered Israel to leave and also landed at Port Said, apparently to enforce the UN ceasefire. Growing opposition at home, hostile position of USA, and the threatened intervention of the Soviets forced them to withdraw. The outcome of the incident was Israel regaining shipping rights to the canal, though France and Britain lost influence in the area.
Vietnam War	1956–75	The war between communist North Vietnam and non-communist South Vietnam, also known as the Second Indochinese War. The Geneva settlement had left North Vietnam under communist rule, and the South ruled first by the emperor Bas Dai (until 1955) and then by Ngo Dinh Diem's dictatorial regime. From 1961, US aid and numbers of 'military advisers' increased considerably. From 1964, US aircraft bombarded the North, and by 1968 over 500 000 troops were involved. These troops were withdrawn in 1973, and hostilities ceased in 1975 when the North's victory was completed with the capture of Saigon (renamed Ho Chi Minh City).
Six Day War	1967	Syrian bombings of Israeli villages intensified early 1967. Israeli air force shot down six Syrian planes. In retaliation Abdel Nasser mobilized Egyptian forces near Sinai border. Israel defeated Egyptian forces and established air superiority. War cost Arabs Old City of Jerusalem, Sinai and Gaza Strip, West Bank, and the Golan Heights.
Cambodian War	1970–5	Cambodia, S Vietnam, US–N Vietnam, Viet Cong, Khmer Rouge. Cambodia had achieved independence in 1953, under Prince Norodom Sihanouk. He assumed position of neutrality in Vietnam war and allowed Vietnamese communists sanctuary in Cambodia. In 1970 he was deposed by coup and US and S Vietnam forces invaded Cambodia to destroy communist sanctuaries. New Cambodian government faced growing threat from Cambodian communists (Khmer Rouge). US launched series of raids by which it hoped to halt Khmer activity but, after five years of civil war, Phnom Penh fell to Khmer Rouge. In 1979 Vietnamese forces invaded and installed a puppet government.
Iran–Iraq War	1980–8	Iran–Iraq. After the Islamic Revolution in Iran, the Iranians accused Baghdad of encouraging the Arabs of Iran's Khuzestan province to demand autonomy. Iraq also feared Iranian provocation of its own large Shi'ite population. Border fighting followed and Iraqi forces advanced into Iran (Sep 1980). Peace finally agreed in 1988 after deaths of around half a million on each side. Iraq accepted Iran's terms in 1990.
Falklands War	1982	Britain–Argentina. Argentinian invasion of the islands governed by Britain since 1933. War ended after three months in Argentinian surrender.
Gulf War	1991	Iraq–US led allies (29 member coalition). War caused by Iraqi invasion of Kuwait and failure to comply with UN resolution calling for withdrawal. Hostilities suspended after 43 days of fighting when Iraq accepted the UN resolution.
Yugoslavian Civil War	1991–	Declarations of independence by Slovenia, Macedonia, and Croatia considered illegal by central government. Confrontation between Croatia and Serb-dominated national army developed into civil war. Germany's recognition of the states of Croatia and Slovenia in the middle of December led to Serbian acceptance of peace plan at the end of that month. 10 000 UN peace-keeping soldiers deployed in Croatia. In Apr 1992 the UN then recognized independence of Bosnia-Herzegovina. Serbia still continued to battle the secessionists.

War	Dates	History
		May saw beginning of bombardment of Sarajevo, followed by bombardment of Dubrovnik at the end of that month. This brought about UN resolution to ban all exports to Yugoslavia. By July an estimated 700 000 people had been driven out of Bosnia since beginning of war, all due to Serbs' policy of 'ethnic cleansing' (aimed at driving Muslims out of areas shared with ethnic Serbs). In August the UN authorized use of military force to insure humanitarian aid getting through to Bosnia. In Sept Yugoslavia expelled from the UN.

The main crusades to the East

	Background	Leader(s)	Outcome
First Crusade (1096–9)	Proclaimed by Urban II to aid the Greeks against the Seljuk Turks in Asia Minor, liberate Jerusalem and the Holy Land from Seljuk domination, and safeguard pilgrim routes to the Holy Sepulchre.	Bohemond I Godfrey of Bouillon Raymond, Count of Toulouse Robert, Count of Flanders Robert Curthose, Duke of Normandy Stephen, Count of Blois	Capture of Nicaea in Anatolia (Jun 1097); Turks vanquished at Battle of Dorylaeum (Jul 1097); capture of Antioch in Syria (Jun 1098), Jerusalem (Jul 1099). Godfrey of Bouillon became ruler of the new Latin kingdom of Jerusalem, and defeated the Fatimids of Egypt near Ascalon in Palestine (Aug 1099). Three other crusader states were founded: Antioch, Edessa, Tripoli.
Second Crusade (1147–8)	Proclaimed by Eugenius III to aid the crusader states after the Muslim reconquest of Edessa (1144).	Conrad III of Germany Louis VII of France	German army heavily defeated by Turks near Dorylaeum (Oct 1147), and the French at Laodicea (Jan 1148); Damascus in Syria invested, but siege abandoned after four days (Jul 1148). The crusaders' military reputation was destroyed, and the Syrian Muslims united against the Latins.
Third Crusade (1189–92)	Proclaimed by Gregory VIII after Saladin's defeat of the Latins at the Battle of Hattin (Jul 1187) and his conquest of Jerusalem (Oct 1187). (By 1189 all that remained of the kingdom of Jerusalem was the port of Tyre.)	Frederick I Barbarossa Philip II Augustus of France Richard I of England	Cyprus conquered from Greeks (May 1191), and established as new crusader kingdom (survived until 1489); capture of Acre in Palestine (Jul 1191); Saladin defeated near Arsuf (Sep 1191); three-year truce guaranteeing safe conduct of Christian pilgrims to Jerusalem. Most cities and castles of the Holy Land remained in Muslim hands.
Fourth Crusade (1202–4)	Proclaimed by Innocent III to recover the Holy Places	Boniface of Montferrat	Despite papal objections, crusade diverted from Egypt or Palestine: (1) to Zara, a Christian town in Dalmatia, conquered for Venetians (Nov 1202); (2) to Byzantium, where embroilment in dynastic struggles led to sack of Constantinople (Apr 1204) and foundation of Latin Empire of Constantinople (survived until 1261). The crusading movement was discredited; the Latins in Palestine and Syria were hardly helped at all; the Byzantine empire never fully recovered; and the opportunity was lost of a united front between the Latins and Greeks against the Muslims.

History

The main crusades to the East (continued)

	Background	Leader(s)	Outcome
Fifth Crusade (1217–21)	Proclaimed by Innocent III when a six-year truce between the kingdom of Jerusalem and Egypt expired.	Andrew II of Hungary John of Brienne, King of Jerusalem Leopold, Duke of Austria	Three indecisive expeditions against Muslims in Palestine (1217); capture of Damietta in Egypt after protracted siege (May 1218–Nov 1219), further conquests attempted, but crusaders forced to relinquish Damietta (Aug 1221) and withdrew.
Sixth Crusade (1228–9)	Emperor Frederick II, who first took the Cross in 1215, married the heiress to the kingdom of Jerusalem in 1225. Excommunicated by Gregory IX for delaying his departure, he finally arrived at Acre in Sep 1228.	Frederick II	Negotiations with Egyptians secured Jerusalem and other places, including Bethlehem and Nazareth (Feb 1229); Frederick crowned King of Jerusalem in church of Holy Sepulchre (Mar 1229). Jerusalem was held until recaptured by the Khorezmian Turks in 1244.
Seventh Crusade (1248–54)	Proclaimed by Innocent IV after the fall of Jerusalem and defeat of the Latin army near Gaza by the Egyptians and Khorezmians (1244).	Louis IX of France	Capture of Damietta (June 1249); defeat at Mansurah (Feb 1250); surrender of crusaders during attempted withdrawal. Damietta relinquished and large ransoms paid (May 1250). Louis spent four years in Palestine, refortifying Acre, Caesarea, Joppa, and Sidon, and fruitlessly attempting to regain Jerusalem by alliances with the Mameluks and Mongols.
Eighth Crusade (1270–2)	Proclaimed after the Mameluk conquest of Arsuf, Caesarea, Haifa (1265). Antioch and Joppa (1268).	Charles of Anjou, King of Naples-Sicily Edward of England (later Edward I) Louis IX of France	Attacked Tunisia in N Africa (Jul 1270); Louis died in Aug; Charles concluded treaty with Tunis and withdrew; Edward negotiated 11 years' truce with Mameluks in Palestine. By 1291 the Latins had been driven from the Holy Land.

The American Civil War

1859
16 Oct John Brown's raid on Harper's Ferry

1860
6 Nov Abraham Lincoln elected President
20 Dec Secession of seven Southern states

1861
4 Feb Announcement of the Confederated States of America – Jefferson Davis named as President
4 Mar Inauguration of Lincoln as President
12 Apr Southern Bombardment of Fort Sumter
21 Jul First Battle of Bull Run

1862
6 Apr Battle of Shiloh
29–30 Aug Second Battle of Bull Run
17 Sep Battle of Antietam
22 Sep Preliminary Emancipation Proclamation
13 Dec Battle of Fredericksburg

1863
1 Jan Emancipation Proclamation
2 May Battle of Chancellorsville – death of Stonewall Jackson
3 Jul Battle of Gettysburg
4 Jul Fall of Vicksburg
19–20 Sep Battle of Chickamauga
24–25 Nov Battle of Chattanooga

1864
1 Sep Fall of Atlanta
15–16 Dec Battle of Nashville

1865
9 Apr Surrender of Confederate forces at Appomattox
14 Apr Assassination of Lincoln

EXPLORATION AND DISCOVERY

Journeys of exploration

Exploration and discovery

Great explorers

Name	Dates	Nationality	Major voyages of exploration
Amundsen, Roald	1872–1928	Norwegian	1911: Voyage to the South Pole.
Baffin, William	1584–1622	English	1616: Explores Baffin Bay.
Balboa, Vasco Núñez de	1475–1519	Spanish	1513: Reaches the Pacific Ocean.
Bougainville, Louis de	1729–1811	French	1766: Begins circumnavigation of the globe.
Cabral, Pedro Álvarez	c.1467–1520	Portuguese	1500: Reaches Brazil.
Cartier, Jacques	1491–1557	French	1534: Explores the coast of N America.
Cook, James	1728–79	English	1769: Maps coast of New Zealand and Australia. 1770: Lands at Botany Bay. 1775: Reaches S Georgia and the Sandwich Islands. 1778: Explores islands now known as Hawaii.
Davis, John	c.1550–1605	English	1585: Expedition to Greenland; discovers the Davis Strait.
Diaz, Bartolomeu	c.1450–1500	Portuguese	1488: Sails round Cape of Good Hope.
Diaz, Dinís	c.15th century	Portuguese	1446: Reaches Cape Verde and Senegal.
Drake, Francis	c.1540–96	English	1580: Completes circumnavigation of the globe.
Gama, Vasco da	c.1469–1525	Portuguese	1497: Sails round Cape of Good Hope. 1498: Explores coast of Madagascar and discovers sea route to India.
Gomes, Diogo	c.1440–84	Portuguese	1469: Crosses the equator.
Hillary, Edmund	1919–	New Zealander	1953: First ascent of Mount Everest, with Norgay Tenzing.
Hudson, Henry	c.1565–1611	English	1610: Discovers Hudson's Bay.
Livingstone, David	1813–73	English	1849: Reaches Lake Ngami. 1855: Reaches the Victoria Falls.
López de Cárdenas, García		Spanish	1540: Reaches the Grand Canyon.
Magellan, Ferdinand	c.1480–1521	Portuguese	1520: Discovers the Strait of Magellan. 1521: Explores the Philippines.
Mendoza, Pedro de	1487–1537	Spanish	1536: Founds Buenos Aires.
Nansen, Fridtjof	1861–1930	Norwegian	1888: Crosses Greenland.
Peary, Robert	1856–1920	American	1909: Successful voyage to reach North Pole.
Raleigh, Walter	1552–1618	English	1595: Explores Orinoco River. 1617: Explores Guiana.
Saussure, Horace	1740–99	Swiss	1787: First ascent of Mont Blanc.
Scott, Robert Falcon	1868–1912	English	1912: Reaches South Pole.
Shackleton, Ernest	1874–1922	English	1914: Leads expedition to Antarctica.
Stanley, Henry Morton	1841–1904	English	1874: Traces Congo to the Atlantic.
Tasman, Abel Janszoon	1603–c.1659	Dutch	1642: Reaches Tasmania and New Zealand.
Tenzing Norgay	1914–86	Nepalese	1953: First ascent of Mount Everest, with Edmund Hillary.
Verrazano, Giovanni da	1485–1528	Italian	1524: Reaches New York Bay and the Hudson River.
Vespucci, Amerigo	1454–1512	Italian	1499: Discovers mouth of River Amazon. 1501: Explores coast of S America.

Colonialism (imperialism)

The main era of imperialism was the period 1880–1914, when many European powers sought to gain territories in Africa and Asia. The motivation was, many suggest, economic, and territories were taken normally by force and subjected to rule by the imperial power. It is only in the twentieth century that colonialism has become generally regarded as illegitimate.

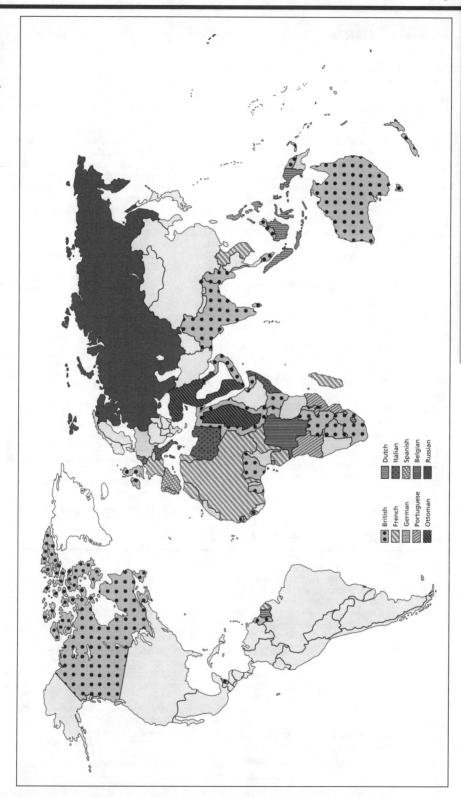

Legend:

British, French, German, Portuguese, Ottoman

Dutch, Italian, Spanish, Belgian, Russian

REVOLUTIONS

Events of the French Revolution

1789

Mar–May	Election of deputies to the Estates General.
5 May	Opening of the Estates General.
17 Jun	Title of National Assembly adopted by the Third Estate.
Jul	The 'Great Fear'.
14 Jul	Seizing of the Bastille in Paris.
4 Aug	Abolition of the feudal regime.
26 Aug	Declaration of the Rights of Man and Citizens.
Oct	Foundation of the Club des Jacobins.
5–6 Oct	Louis XVI brought to Paris from Versailles.
19 Oct	National Assembly installed in Paris.

1790

19–23 Jun	Abolition of hereditary nobility and titles.
July	Foundation of the Club des Cordeliers.

1791

20–21 Jun	Flight of the King to Varennes.
16 Jul	Foundation of the Club des Feuillants.
13 Sep	Acceptance of the Constitution by the King.
Oct	Formation of the Legislative Assembly.

1792

9–10 Aug	Attack of the Tuileries. Functions of the King suspended.
12 Aug	King and royal family imprisoned in the Temple.
2–6 Sep	Massacre of nobles and clergy in prisons.
21 Sep	Abolition of the monarchy.
22 Sep	Proclamation of the Republic.

1793

17 Jan	National Convention votes for the death of the King.
21 Jan	Execution of the King.
1 Feb	Declaration of war against England and Netherlands.
Mar	Tribunal created in Paris (later called the Revolutionary Tribunal).
6 Apr	Creation of the Committee of Public Safety.
27 Jul	Robespierre elected to the Committee of Public Safety.
5 Sep–27 Jul 1794	Reign of Terror.
11 Sep	Creation of the Revolutionary Army of Paris.
16 Oct	Trial and execution of Marie Antoinette.
24–31 Oct	Trial and execution of the Girondins.

1794

5 Apr	Execution of the Cordeliers, including Danton.
24 Mar	Execution of the Hébertists.
8 Jun	Inaugural Feast of the Supreme Being and of Nature.
27 Jul	(9 Thermidor) Fall of Robespierre.
19 Nov	Closure of the Club des Jacobins.

1795

21 Feb	Separation of Church and State.
31 May	Suppression of the Revolutionary Tribunal.
8 Jun	Death of Louis XVII in the Temple.
5 Oct	(13 Vendémiaire) Royalists crushed by Bonaparte.
27 Oct–4 Nov	Institution of the Directory.

1799

9 Nov	(18 Brumaire) Abolition of the Directory.

Events of the American Revolution

1765 Stamp Act crisis. Following the imposition of taxes on American colonists by the British Parliament (Stamp Acts), riots broke out. At the Stamp Act Congress, New York, 7–25 Oct, nine colonies adopted the Declaration of Rights opposing taxation without representation in Parliament. Acts withdrawn 17 Mar 1766.

1767 Townshend Acts imposed taxes on five categories of goods (glass, lead, paper, paint, and tea) imported into the American colonies. Repeal of all taxes, except that on tea, in 1770.

1770
5 Mar Boston massacre. First bloodshed of the American Revolution when British troops fired on rioting crowd at Boston customs house, killing five.

1773
16 Dec Boston Tea Party. Valuable cargo of tea thrown overboard by rebellious American colonists protesting British Parliament's 'Tea Act' (Apr 1773).

1774 The 'Intolerable Acts' are passed by the British Parliament in order to punish Massachusetts, considered the leader of rebels, for the Boston Tea Party. Involved the curtailing of self-rule and barred the use of Boston harbour until the destroyed cargo of tea had been paid for.

5 Sep–26 Oct First Continental Congress (a body of delegates from the thirteen colonies which assumed the duties of a national government), held in Philadelphia, protested British measures and called for civil disobedience.

1775

18 Apr Advance of British on Concord to destroy military stores of rebel American patriots.

19 Apr Beginning of fighting at Lexington and Concord.

17 Jun Battle of Bunker Hill, Massachusetts; technically an American defeat though British suffered high casualties.

1776

7 Jun Proposal in Continental Congress to declare independence from Britain.

2 Jul Resolution adopted.

4 Jul Approval of Declaration of Independence.

27 Aug British defeat of Washington in Battle of Long Island.

15 Sep British occupation of New York City.

1777

3 Jan Defeat of Lord Cornwallis by Washington at Battle of Princeton. Continental Congress adopted Stars and Stripes as flag of the United States.

11 Sep Battle of Brandywine. American retreat enabled British to occupy Philadelphia.

17 Oct Battle of Saratoga. British, under General John Burgoyne, forced to surrender.

15 Nov Articles of Confederation and Perpetual Union adopted by Continental Congress.

1778

6 Feb Assistance of the American patriots by French fleet after France and US sign treaty of aid.

18 Jun British evacuation from Philadelphia.

1781

26 Sep Arrival of joint American and French forces in Williamsburg near Yorktown where British forces, under Cornwallis, had retreated.

6–19 Oct Battle of Yorktown. Beginning of siege of Yorktown, Virginia. British troops heavily outnumbered by joint American and French forces. Eventual surrender of Cornwallis on 19 Oct.

1782

Mar Agreement by new British Cabinet to recognize independence of United States of America.

30 Nov Preliminary agreement signed in Paris.

Events of the Russian Revolution

1916

end Internal state of Russia precarious. Tsar politically isolated and universally unpopular.

1917

beginning Bolsheviks, under Lenin's leadership, cultivate feelings of discontent and organize strikes. February Revolution: On 8 March government of Tsar Nicholas II introduces bread and flour rationing in Petrograd. Mass strike begins. On third day of protest police begin firing on striking workers.

12 Mar The Petrograd Soviet of workers and the Duma form a 'Provisional Committee', later to become a 'Provisional Government'.

15 Mar Tsar Nicholas II abdicates.

Mar–May Conflict in the dual power begins to emerge. Disagreement on whether to continue the war (WWI) and war aims.

Apr Lenin returns from exile in Switzerland. Change of Bolshevik policy in supporting the provisional government. April Theses: Lenin advocates overthrow of provisional government and government by the soviets for the working class. Also advocates redistribution of land to peasants and signature of peace treaty with Germany. Policy of 'All Power to the Soviet'.

Jun Demonstrations called by the Petrograd Soviet to outmanoeuvre the Bolsheviks. Bolshevik support still strong. The July Days: Kronstadt sailors supporting Bolsheviks demonstrate in Petrograd. Demonstrators fired on and chaos follows. Prime Minister Lvov forced to resign and replaced by Kerensky (links to the Soviet). Bolsheviks held responsible for bloodshed and their newspapers closed and warrants for arrest of leaders issued. Lenin and Stalin flee. Trotsky and Kamenev imprisoned.

Sep Kornilov Affair: General Kornilov tries to move on Petrograd with his troops, under pretext of restoring order. Kerensky appeals to Bolsheviks for help in defeating Kornilov. Lenin recognizes the opportunity and forms a Red Guard of Bolshevik soldiers and workers, sets up Military Revolutionary Committee. Most of Kornilov's troops deserte, Kornilov arrested and Bolsheviks support increased further.

26 Oct October Revolution: Bolsheviks agree to make seizure of power 'the order of the day'. Kerensky mobilizes troops too late and they are defeated by troops loyal to the Bolsheviks. Insurrection, led by Trotsky, now begins. All main public buildings occupied. Kerensky flees. Bolsheviks assume power and effect series of radical reforms.

1989: Revolutionary year

15 Jan	Czechoslovakia: Pro-democracy demonstration in Prague attacked by police.
19 Jan	USSR: Defence cuts announced.
20 Jan	USSR: Nuclear cuts announced for Eastern Europe.
29 Jan	Hungary: Statement, by radical Communist Party member Imre Pozsgay, that the events of 1956 were not a counter-revolution, but a 'popular uprising'.
3 Feb	Paraguay: President Stroessner deposed by the army.
6 Feb	Poland: Solidarity begins official talks with the government.
15 Feb	Afghanistan: Withdrawal of Soviet army completed.
22 Feb	Czechoslovakia: Dissident author Vaclav Havel jailed for nine months.
14 Apr	USSR: Demonstrators shot in Tbilisi; Georgian leadership resigns.
17 Apr	Poland: Ban on Solidarity lifted.
20 Apr	China: Student demonstration broken up by police in Beijing (Peking).
25 Apr	USSR: Hardliners purged from Central Committee.
27 Apr	China: Major demonstration in Tiananmen Square, Beijing.
20–2 May	China: Army halted by large numbers of demonstrators.
26 May	China: Purge of moderates from government.
30 May	China: Statue of Democracy and Freedom erected in Tiananmen Square.
2 Jun	China: Army moves against demonstrators.
3 Jun	Iran: Death of Ayatollah Khomeini.
4 Jun	China: Army crushes student demonstrators, with undisclosed number of dead.
4 Jun	Poland: Free elections promised.
17 Jun	Hungary: Body of Imre Nagy disinterred and reburied in Bucharest.
21 Aug	Czechoslovakia: Demonstration to mark 21 years since crushing of the Prague Spring.
23 Aug	USSR: Human chain formed across Estonia, Latvia, and Lithuania, on 50th anniversary of Soviet annexation.
24 Aug	Poland: Solidarity prime minister elected, Tadeusz Mazowiecki.
10 Sep	Hungary: Border opened with Austria; thousands of East Germans travel across Hungary to the West.
19 Sep	Hungary: Free elections promised.
3 Oct	East Germany: Border closed as thousands more leave for the West.
9 Oct	East Germany: Large demonstrations in Leipzig.
15 Oct	South Africa: Release of Walter Sisulu and several other political prisoners.
18 Oct	East Germany: Resignation of Erich Honecker, replaced by Egon Krenz.
26 Oct	USSR: Gorbachev speech endorses developments in Eastern Europe.
31 Oct	East Germany: Half a million demonstrators in Leipzig.
1 Nov	East Germany: Border reopened to Czechoslovakia.
3 Nov	East Germany: East Germans permitted to travel across Czechoslovakia into West Germany without special formalities.
9 Nov	East Germany: Opening of the Berlin Wall.
10 Nov	Bulgaria: Todor Zhivkov deposed.
14 Nov	Namibia: Elections won by South West Africa People's Organization.
17 Nov	Czechoslovakia: Major demonstration in Prague, violently put down by police.
19 Nov	East Germany: Visit of West German Chancellor Kohl.
21 Nov	Czechoslovakia: Meeting between Prime Minister Ladislav Adamec and leaders of the demonstration.
24 Nov	Czechoslovakia: Resignation of Communist Party leadership.
30 Nov	Czechoslovakia: Communist Party gives up its leading role.
1 Dec	Vatican City: Meeting between the Pope and President Gorbachev (USSR).
3 Dec	Mediterranean: Meeting between Presidents Bush (USA) and Gorbachev; announcement of the end of the Cold War.
4 Dec	USSR: Formal condemnation of 1968 invasion of Czechoslovakia.
6 Dec	East Germany: Resignation of Egon Krenz.
7 Dec	Czechoslovakia: Resignation of Adamec.
10 Dec	Czechoslovakia: Noncommunist government appointed.
11 Dec	Bulgaria: Free elections promised.
14 Dec	South Africa: Talks between President de Klerk and Nelson Mandela (African National Congress).
14 Dec	Chile: Dictatorship ended with the election of Patricio Aylwin as President.
17 Dec	Romania: Many demonstrators killed in Timişoara.
17 Dec	Brazil: First President elected for nearly 30 years, Fernando Collor de Mello.
20 Dec	Panama: Invasion by USA; General Noriega deposed.
21 Dec	Romania: Major demonstration in Bucharest, with criticism of President Nicolae Ceausescu.
22 Dec	Romania: Ceausescu deposed.
25 Dec	Romania: Execution of Ceausescu and his wife, Elena.
28 Dec	Czechoslovakia: Election of Alexander Dubcek as Chairman of the Czech parliament.
29 Dec	Czechoslovakia: Election of Vaclav Havel as President.

POLITICAL LEADERS AND RULERS

Australia

Head of State: British monarch, represented by Governor-General.

Prime Minister

1901-3	Edmund Barton *Prot*
1903-4	Alfred Deakin *Prot*
1904	John Christian Watson *Lab*
1904-5	George Houstoun Reid *Free*
1905-8	Alfred Deakin *Prot*
1908-9	Andrew Fisher *Lab*
1909-10	Alfred Deakin *Fusion*
1910-13	Andrew Fisher *Lab*
1913-14	Joseph Cook *Lib*
1914-15	Andrew Fisher *Lab*
1915-17	William Morris Hughes *Nat Lab*
1917-23	William Morris Hughes *Nat*
1923-9	Stanley Melbourne Bruce *Nat*
1929-32	James Henry Scullin *Lab*
1932-9	Joseph Aloyslus Lyons *Un*
1939	Earle Christian Grafton Page *Co*
1939-41	Robert Gordon Menzies *Un*
1941	Arthur William Fadden *Co*
1941-5	John Joseph Curtin *Lab*
1945	Francis Michael Forde *Lab*
1945-9	Joseph Benedict Chifley *Lab*
1949-66	Robert Gordon Menzies *Lib*
1966-7	Harold Edward Holt *Lib*
1967-8	John McEwen *Co*
1968-71	John Grey Gorton *Lib*
1971-2	William McMahon *Lib*
1972-5	(Edward) Gough Whitlam *Lab*
1975-83	John Malcolm Fraser *Lib*
1983-91	Robert James Lee Hawke *Lab*
1991-	Paul Keating *Lab*

Co Country; *Free* Free Trade; *Lab* Labor; *Lib* Liberal; *Nat* Nationalist; *Nat Lab* National Labor; *Prot* Protectionist; *Un* United.

Canada

Head of State: British monarch, represented by Governor-General.

Prime Minister

1867-73	John Alexander MacDonald *Con*
1873-8	Alexander Mackenzie *Lib*
1878-91	John Alexander MacDonald *Con*
1891-2	John J C Abbot *Con*
1892-4	John Sparrow David Thompson *Con*
1894-6	Mackenzie Bowell *Con*
1896	Charles Tupper *Con*
1896-1911	Wilfrid Laurier *Lib*
1911-20	Robert Laird Borden *Con*
1920-1	Arthur Meighen *Con*
1921-6	William Lyon Mackenzie King *Lib*
1926	Arthur Meighen *Con*
1926-30	William Lyon Mackenzie King *Lib*
1930-5	Richard Bedford Bennett *Con*
1935-48	William Lyon Mackenzie King *Lib*
1948-57	Louis Stephen St Laurent *Lib*
1957-63	John George Diefenbaker *Con*
1963-8	Lester Bowles Pearson *Lib*
1968-79	Pierre Elliott Trudeau *Lib*
1979-80	Joseph Clark *Con*
1980-4	Pierre Elliott Trudeau *Lib*
1984	John Napier Turner *Lib*
1984-93	(Martin) Brian Mulroney *Con*
1993	Kim Campbell *Con*
1993-	Jean Chrétien *Lib*

Con Conservative; *Lib* Liberal.

France

Prime Minister

1815	Charles-Maruice, Prince de Talleyrand-Perigord
1815-18	Armand-Emmanuel Vignerot-Duplessis, Duc de Richelieu
1818-19	Jean Joseph, Marquis Dessolle
1819-20	Duc Élie Decazes
1820-1	Armand-Emmanuel Vignerot-Duplessis, Duc de Richelieu
1821-9	Guillaume-Aubin, Comte de Villèle
1829-30	Auguste, Prince de Polignac
1830-1	Jacques Lafitte
1831-2	Casimir Périer
1832-4	Nicolas Soult
1834	Etienne, Comte Gérard
1834	Napoléon Joseph Maret, Duc de Bassano
1834-5	Étienne Mortier, Duc de Trévise
1835-6	Achille, Duc de Broglie
1836	Adolphe Thiers
1836-9	Louis, Comte Molé
1839-40	Nicolas Soult
1840	Adolphe Thiers
1840-7	Nicolas Soult
1847-8	François Guyzot
1848	Jacques Charles Dupont de L'Eure
1848	Louis-Eugène Cavaignac
1848-9	Odilon Barrot
1849-70	*No Prime Minister*

Third Republic

1870-1	Jules Favre
1871-3	Jules Dufaure
1873-4	Albert, Duc de Broglie
1874-5	Ernest Louis Courtot de Cissey
1875-6	Louis Buffet
1876	Jules Dufaure
1876-7	Jules Simon
1877	Albert, Duc de Broglie
1877	Gaetan de Grimaudet de Rochebouét
1877-9	Jules Dufaure
1879	William H Waddington
1879-80	Louis de Freycinet
1880-1	Jules Ferry
1881-2	Léon Gambetta
1882	Louis de Freycinet
1882-3	Eugène Duclerc
1883	Armand Fallières
1883-5	Jules Ferry
1885-6	Henri Brisson
1886	Louis de Freycinet
1886-7	René Goblet
1887	Maurice Rouvier
1887-8	Pierre Tirard
1888-9	Charles Floquet
1889-90	Pierre Tirard
1890-2	Louis de Freycinet
1892	Émile Loubet
1892-3	Alexandre Ribot
1893	Charles Dupuy
1893-4	Jean Casimir-Périer
1894-5	Charles Dupuy
1895	Alexandre Ribot
1895-6	Léon Bourgeois
1896-8	Jules Méline
1898	Henri Brisson
1898-9	Charles Dupuy
1899-1902	Pierre Waldeck-Rousseau
1902-5	Emile Combes
1905-6	Maurice Rouvier
1906	Jean Sarrien
1906-9	Georges Clemenceau
1909-11	Aristide Briand
1911	Ernest Monis
1911-12	Joseph Caillaux
1912-13	Raymond Poincaré
1913	Aristide Briand
1913	Jean Louis Barthou
1913-14	Gaston Doumergue
1914	Alexandre Ribot
1914-15	René Viviani
1915-17	Aristide Briand
1917	Alexandre Ribot
1917	Paul Painlevé
1917-20	Georges Clemenceau

History

Political leaders and rulers (continued)

1920	Alexandre Millerand
1920–1	Georges Leygues
1921–2	Aristide Briand
1922–4	Raymond Poincaré
1924	Frédéric François-Marsal
1924–5	Édouard Herriot
1925	Paul Painlevé
1925–6	Aristide Briand
1926	Édouard Herriot
1926–9	Raymond Poincaré
1929	Aristide Briand
1929–30	André Tardieu
1930	Camille Chautemps
1930	André Tardieu
1930–1	Théodore Steeg
1931–2	Pierre Laval
1932	André Tardieu
1932	Édouard Herriot
1932–3	Joseph Paul-Boncour
1933	Édouard Daladier
1933	Albert Sarrault
1933–4	Camille Chautemps
1934	Édouard Daladier
1934	Gaston Doumergue
1934–5	Pierre Étienne Flandin
1935	Fernand Bouisson
1935–6	Pierre Laval
1936	Albert Sarrault
1936–7	Léon Blum
1937–8	Camille Chautemps
1938	Léon Blum
1938–40	Édouard Daladier
1940	Paul Reynaud
1940	Philippe Pétain

Vichy Government

1940–4	Philippe Pétain

Provisional Government of the French Republic

1944–6	Charles de Gaulle
1946	Félix Gouin
1946	Georges Bidault

Fourth Republic

1946–7	Léon Blum
1947	Paul Ramadier
1947–8	Robert Schuman
1948	André Marie
1948	Robert Schuman
1948–9	Henri Queuille
1949–50	Georges Bidault
1950	Henri Queuille
1950–1	René Pleven
1951	Henri Queuille
1951–2	René Pleven
1952	Edgar Faure
1952–3	Antoine Pinay
1953	René Mayer
1953–4	Joseph Laniel
1954–5	Pierre Mendès-France
1955–6	Edgar Faure
1956–7	Guy Alcide Mollet
1957	Maurice Bourgès-Maunoury
1957–8	Félix Gaillard
1958	Pierre Pflimin

1958–9	Charles de Gaulle

Fifth Republic

1959–62	Michel Debré
1962–8	Georges Pompidou
1968–9	Maurice Couve de Murville
1969–72	Jacques Chaban Delmas
1972–4	Pierre Mesmer
1974–6	Jacques René Chirac
1976–81	Raymond Barre
1981–4	Pierre Mauroy
1984–6	Laurent Fabius
1986–8	Jacques René Chirac
1988–91	Michael Rocard
1991–2	Edith Cresson
1992–3	Pierre Bérégovoy
1993–	Édouard Balladur

President

Third Republic

1870–1	*Commune*
1871–3	Louis Adolphe Thiers
1873–9	Marie Edmé de Mac-Mahon
1879–87	Jules Grévy
1887–94	Sadi Carnot
1894–5	Jean Paul Pierre Casimir-Périer
1895–9	François Félix Faure
1899–1906	Émile Loubet
1906–13	Armand Fallières
1913–20	Raymond Poincaré
1920	Paul Deschanel
1920–4	Alexandre Millerand
1924–31	Gaston Doumergue
1931–2	Paul Doumer
1932–40	Albert Lebrun
1940–5	*German occupation*
1945–7	*No President*

Fourth Republic

1947–54	Vincent Auriol
1954–8	René Coty

Fifth Republic

1958–69	Charles de Gaulle
1969–74	Georges Pompidou
1974–81	Valéry Giscard d'Estaing
1981–	François Mitterrand

Germany

Chancellor

1871–90	Otto von Bismarck
1890–4	Georg Leo, Graf von Caprivi
1894–1900	Chlodwic, Fürst zu Hohenlohe-Schillingfürst
1900–9	Bernard Heinrich, Prince von Bülow
1909–17	Theobald von Bethmann Hollweg
1917–18	Georg von Herfling
1918	Prince Max of Baden
1918	Friedrich Ebert
1919–20	Philipp Scheidemann

1920	Hermann Müller
1920–1	Konstantin Fehrenbach
1921–2	Karl Joseph Wirth
1922–3	Wilhelm Cuno
1923	Gustav Stresemann
1923–5	Wilhelm Marx
1925–6	Hans Luther
1926–8	Wilhelm Marx
1928–9	Hermann Müller
1929–32	Heinrich Brüning
1932–3	Franz von Papen
1933–45	Adolf Hitler (from 1934 *Führer*)

German Democratic Republic (East Germany)

President

1949–60	Wilhelm Pieck

Chairman of the Council of State

1960–73	Walter Ulbricht
1973–6	Willi Stoph
1976–89	Erich Honecker
1989	Egon Krenz
1989–90	Gregor Gysi *General Secretary as Chairman*

Premier

1949–64	Otto Grotewohl
1964–73	Willi Stoph
1973–6	Horst Sindermann
1976–89	Willi Stoph
1989–90	Hans Modrow
1990	Lothar de Maizière

The German Democratic Republic ceased to exist as a separate state and East Germany became part of the German Federal Republic in 1990.

German Federal Republic (until 1990 West Germany)

President

1949–59	Theodor Heuss
1959–69	Heinrich Lübke
1969–74	Gustav Heinemann
1974–9	Walter Scheel
1979–84	Karl Carstens
1984–	Richard, Baron von Weizsäcker

Chancellor

1949–63	Konrad Adenauer
1963–6	Ludwig Erhard
1966–9	Kurt Georg Kiesinger
1969–74	Willy Brandt
1974–82	Helmut Schmidt
1982–	Helmut Kohl

Russia and the Union of Soviet Socialist Republics

RUSSIA

Grand Duke of Moscow

House of Riurik

1283–1303	Daniel
1303–25	Yuri
1325–41	Ivan I Kalita

1341–53	Semeon
1353–9	Ivan II
1359–89	Dmitri I Donskoy
1389–1425	Vasily I
1425–62	Vasily II
1462–72	Ivan II 'the Great'

Ruler of all Russia
House of Riurik

1472–1505	Ivan III 'the Great'
1505–33	Vasily III
1533–47	Ivan IV 'the Terrible'

Tsar of Russia
House of Riurik

1547–84	Ivan IV 'the Terrible'
1584–98	Fedor I
1598–1605	Boris Godunov
1605	Fedor II
1605–6	Dmitri II (the 'false Dmitri')
1606–10	Vasily IV Shuisky
1610–13	*Civil war*

House of Romanov

1613–45	Mikhail (Michael Romanov)
1645–76	Alexei I Milhailovitch
1676–82	Fedor III
1682–1725	Peter I 'the Great' *Joint ruler to 1676*
1682–96	Ivan V *Joint ruler*
1725–7	Catherine I
1727–30	Peter II
1730–40	Anna Ivovna
1740–1	Ivan VI
1741–62	Elizabeth Petrovna
1762	Peter III
1762–96	Catherine II 'the Great'
1796–1801	Paul
1801–25	Alexander I
1825–55	Nicholas I
1855–81	Alexander II 'the Liberator'
1881–94	Alexander III
1894–1917	Nicholas II

SOVIET UNION
President

1917	Lev Borisovich Kamenev
1917–19	Yakov Mikhailovich Sverlov
1919–46	Mikhail Ivanovich Kalinin
1946–53	Nikolai Mikhailovich Shvernik
1953–60	Klimenti Efremovich Voroshilov
1960–4	Leonid Ilyich Brezhnev
1964–5	Anastas Ivanovich Mikoyan
1965–77	Nikolai Viktorovich Podgorny
1977–82	Leonid Ilyich Brezhnev
1982–3	Vasily Vasiliyevich Kuznetsov *Acting*

1983–4	Yuri Vladimirovich Andropov
1984	Vasily Vasiliyevich Kuznetsov *Acting*
1984–5	Konstantin Ustinovich Chernenko
1985	Vasily Vasiliyevich Kuznetsov *Acting*
1985–8	Andrei Andreevich Gromyko
1988–90	Mikhail Sergeevich Gorbachev

Executive President

1990–1	Mikhail Sergeevich Gorbachev

RUSSIAN FEDERATION
President

1991–	Boris Nikolayevich Yeltsin

United Kingdom

Prime Minister

1721–42	Robert Walpole, Earl of Oxford *Whig*
1742–3	Spencer Compton, Earl of Wilmington *Whig*
1743–54	Henry Pelham *Whig*
1754–6	Thomas Pelham (Pelham-Hollies), Duke of Newcastle *Whig*
1756–7	William Cavendish, 1st Duke of Devonshire *Whig*
1757–62	Thomas Pelham (Pelham-Hollies), Duke of Newcastle *Whig*
1762–3	John Stuart, 3rd Earl of Bute *Tory*
1763–5	George Grenville *Whig*
1765–6	Charles Watson Wentworth, 2nd Marquis of Rockingham *Whig*
1766–7	William Pitt, 1st Earl of Chatham *Whig*
1767–70	Augustus Henry Fitzroy, 3rd Duke of Grafton *Whig*
1770–82	Frederick, 8th Lord North *Tory*
1782	Charles Watson Wentworth, 2nd Marquis of Rockingham *Whig*
1782–3	William Petty, 2nd Earl of Shelburne *Whig*
1783	William Henry Cavendish, Duke of Portland *Coal*
1783–1801	William Pitt *Tory*
1801–4	Henry Addington *Tory*
1804–6	William Pitt *Tory*
1806–7	William Wyndham Grenville, 1st Baron Grenville *Whig*
1807–9	William Henry Cavendish, Duke of Portland *Coal*
1809–12	Spencer Perceval *Tory*
1812–27	Robert Banks Jenkinson, 2nd Earl of Liverpool *Tory*

1827	George Canning *Tory*
1827–8	Frederick John Robinson, 1st Earl of Ripon *Tory*
1828–30	Arthur Wellesley, 1st Duke of Wellington *Tory*
1830–4	Charles Grey, 2nd Earl Grey *Whig*
1834	William Lamb, 2nd Viscount Melbourne *Whig*
1834–5	Robert Peel *Con*
1835–41	William Lamb, 2nd Viscount Melbourne *Whig*
1841–6	Robert Peel *Con*
1846–52	Lord John Russell, 1st Earl Russell *Lib*
1852	Edward Geoffrey Smith Stanley, 14th Earl of Derby *Con*
1852–5	George Hamilton-Gordon, 4th Earl of Aberdeen *Peelite*
1855–8	Henry John Temple, 3rd Viscount Palmerston *Lib*
1858–9	Edward Geoffrey Smith Stanley, 14th Earl of Derby *Con*
1859–65	Henry John Temple, 3rd Viscount Palmerston *Lib*
1865–6	Lord John Russell, 1st Earl Russell *Lib*
1866–8	Edward Geoffrey Smith Stanley, 14th Earl of Derby *Con*
1868	Benjamin Disraeli *Con*
1868–74	William Ewart Gladstone *Lib*
1874–80	Benjamin Disraeli *Con*
1880–5	William Ewart Gladstone *Lib*
1885–6	Robert Arthur James Gascoyne-Cecil, 3rd Marquis of Salisbury *Con*
1886	William Ewart Gladstone *Lib*
1886–92	Robert Arthur James Gascoyne-Cecil, 3rd Marquis of Salisbury *Con*
1892–4	William Ewart Gladstone *Lib*
1894–5	Archibald Philip Primrose, 5th Earl of Rosebery *Lib*
1895–1902	Robert Arthur James Gascoyne-Cecil, 3rd Marquis of Salisbury *Con*
1902–5	Arthur James Balfour *Con*
1905–8	Henry Campbell-Bannerman *Lib*
1908–15	Herbert Henry Asquith *Lib*
1915–16	Herbert Henry Asquith *Coal*
1916–22	David Lloyd-George *Coal*
1922–3	Andrew Bonar Law *Con*
1923–4	Stanley Baldwin *Con*
1924	James Ramsay MacDonald *Lab*

History

Political leaders and rulers (continued)

1924–9	Stanley Baldwin *Con*
1929–31	James Ramsay MacDonald *Lab*
1931–5	James Ramsay MacDonald *Nat*
1935–7	Stanley Baldwin *Nat*
1937–40	(Arthur) Neville Chamberlain *Nat*
1940–5	Winston Leonard Spencer Churchill *Coal*
1945–51	Clement Richard Atlee *Lab*
1951–5	Winston Leonard Spencer Churchill *Con*
1955–7	(Robert) Anthony Eden, 1st Earl of Avon *Con*
1957–63	(Maurice) Harold Macmillan *Con*
1963–4	Alexander Frederick (Alec) Douglas-Home, Baron Home of the Hirsel *Con*
1964–70	(James) Harold Wilson *Lab*
1970–4	Edward Richard George Heath *Con*
1974–6	(James) Harold Wilson *Lab*
1976–9	(Leonard) James Callaghan *Lab*
1979–90	Margaret Hilda Thatcher *Con*
1990–	John Major *Con*

Coal Coalition; *Con* Conservative; *Lab* Labour; *Lib* Liberal; *Nat* Nationalist.

United States of America

President

Vice President in parentheses

1789–97	George Washington (1st) (John Adams)
1797–1801	John Adams (2nd) *Fed* (Thomas Jefferson)
1801–9	Thomas Jefferson (3rd) *Dem-Rep* (Aaron Burr, 1801–5) (George Clinton, 1805–9)
1809–17	James Madison (4th) *Dem-Rep* (George Clinton, 1809–12) *No Vice President 1812–13* (Elbridge Gerry, 1813–14) *No Vice President 1814–17*
1817–25	James Monroe (5th) *Dem-Rep* (Daniel D Tompkins)
1825–9	John Quincy Adams (6th) *Dem-Rep* (John Caldwell Calhoun)
1829–37	Andrew Jackson (7th) *Dem* (John Caldwell Calhoun, 1829–32) *No Vice President 1832–3* (Martin Van Buren, 1833–7)
1837–41	Martin Van Buren (8th) *Dem* (Richard Mentor Johnson)
1841	William Henry Harrison (9th) *Whig*
	(John Tyler)
1841–5	John Tyler (10th) *Whig* *No Vice President*
1845–9	James Knox Polk (11th) *Dem* (George Mifflin Dallas)
1849–50	Zachary Taylor (12th) *Whig* (Millard Fillmore)
1850–3	Milard Fillmore (13th) *Whig* *No Vice President*
1853–7	Franklin Pierce (14th) *Dem* (William Rufus King, 1853) *No Vice President 1853–7*
1857–61	James Buchanan (15th) *Dem* (John C Brechinridge)
1861–5	Abraham Lincoln (16th) *Rep* (Hannibal Hamlin, 1861–5) (Andrew Johnson, 1865)
1865–9	Andrew Johnson (17th) *Dem-Nat* *No Vice President*
1869–77	Ulysses Simpson Grant (18th) *Rep* (Schuyler Colfax, 1869–73) (Henury Wilson, 1873–5) *No Vice President 1875*
1877–81	Rutherford Birchard Hayes (19th) *Rep* (William A Wheeler)
1881	James Abram Garfield (20th) *Rep* (Chester Alan Arthur)
1881–5	Chester Alan Arthur (21st) *Rep* *No Vice President*
1885–9	Stephen Grover Cleveland (22nd) *Dem* (Thomas A Hendricks, 1885) *No Vice President 1885–9*
1889–93	Benjamin Harrison (23rd) *Rep* (Levi Parsons Morton)
1893–7	Stephen Grover Cleveland (24th) *Dem* (Adlai Ewing Stevenson)
1897–1901	William McKinley (25th) *Rep* (Garret A Hobart, 1897–9) *No Vice President 1899–1901* (Theodore Roosevelt, 1901)
1901–9	Theodore Roosevelt (26th) *Rep* *No Vice President 1901–5* (Charles W Fairbanks, 1905–9)
1909–13	William Howard Taft (27th) *Rep* (James S Sherman, 1909–12) *No Vice President 1912–13*
1913–21	Thomas Woodrow Wilson (28th) *Dem* (Thomas R Marshall)
1921–3	Warren G Harding (29th) *Rep* (Calvin Coolidge)
1923–9	Calvin Coolidge (30th) *Rep* *No Vice President 1923–5* (Charles Gates Dawes, 1925–9)
1929–33	Herbert Clark Hoover (31st) *Rep* (Charles Curtis)
1933–45	Franklin Delano Roosevelt (32nd) *Dem* (John N Garner, 1933–41) (Henry Agard Wallace, 1941–5) (Harry S Truman, 1945)
1945–53	Harry S Truman (33rd) *Dem* *No Vice President 1945–9* (Alben W Barkley, 1949–53)
1953–61	Dwight David Eisenhower (34th) *Rep* (Richard Milhous Nixon)
1961–3	John Fitzgerald Kennedy (35th) *Dem* (Lyndon Baines Johnson)
1963–9	Lyndon Baines Johnson (36th) *Dem* *No Vice President 1963–5* (Hubert Horatio Humphrey, 1965–9)
1969–74	Richard Milhous Nixon (37th) *Rep* (Spiro Theodore Agnew, 1969–73) *No Vice President Oct–Dec 1973* (Gerald Rudolph Ford, 1973–4)
1974–7	Gerald Rudolph Ford (38th) *Rep* *No Vice President Aug–Dec 1974* (Nelson Aldrich Rockefeller 1974–7)
1977–81	James Earl (Jimmy) Carter (39th) *Dem* (Walter Frederick Mondale)
1981–9	Ronald Wilson Reagan (40th) *Rep* (George Herbert Walker Bush)
1989–92	George Herbert Walker Bush (41st) *Rep* (J Danforth (Dan) Quayle)
1992–	William Jefferson (Bill) Clinton (42nd) *Dem* (Albert Arnold Gore, Jr)

Dem Democrat; *Dem-Rep* Democratic Republican; *Fed* Federalist; *Nat*; National Union; *Rep* Republican.

HUMAN GEOGRAPHY

The world political map

The world's largest nations by area

	Nation	Area km²	sq mi		Nation	Area km²	sq mi
1	Russian Federation	17 075 400	6 591 100	63	Finland	338 145	130 524
2	Canada	9 971 500	3 848 900	64	Malaysia	329 749	127 283
3	China, People's Republic of	9 597 000	3 704 000	65	Vietnam	329 566	127 212
4	United States	9 160 454	3 535 935	66	Norway	323 895	125 023
5	Brazil	8 511 965	3 285 618	67	Côte d'Ivoire	322 462	124 503
6	Australia	7 692 300	2 969 228	68	Poland	312 612	120 668
7	India	3 166 829	1 222 396	69	Italy	301 225	116 273
8	Argentina	2 780 092	1 073 115	70	Oman	300 000	115 800
9	Kazakhstan	2 717 300	1 048 878	71	Burkina Faso	274 540	105 972
10	Sudan, The	2 504 530	966 749	72	Ecuador	270 699	104 490
11	Algeria	2 460 500	949 753	73	New Zealand	270 534	104 426
12	Saudi Arabia	2 331 000	899 766	74	Gabon	267 667	103 319
13	Zaïre	2 234 585	905 365	75	Guinea	246 048	94 974
14	Mexico	1 978 800	763 817	76	United Kingdom	244 755	94 475
15	Indonesia	1 900 240	735 810	77	Ghana	238 686	92 133
16	Libya	1 758 610	678 823	78	Uganda	238 461	92 046
17	Iran	1 648 000	636 128	79	Romania	237 500	91 675
18	Mongolia	1 566 500	604 800	80	Laos	236 800	91 405
19	Peru	1 285 640	495 871	81	Philippines	229 679	115 676
20	Chad	1 284 640	495 871	82	Guyana	214 969	82 978
21	Ethiopia	1 251 282	483 123	83	Belarus	207 600	80 134
22	Angola	1 245 790	480 875	84	Kyrgyzstan	198 500	76 621
23	Mali	1 240 192	478 714	85	Senegal	196 840	75 980
24	South Africa	1 233 404	476 094	86	Syria	185 180	71 479
25	Niger	1 186 408	457 953	87	Cambodia	181 035	68 879
26	Colombia	1 140 105	440 080	88	Uruguay	176 215	68 018
27	Bolivia	1 098 580	424 052	89	Tunisia	164 150	63 362
28	Mauritania	1 029 920	397 549	90	Suriname	163 265	63 020
29	Egypt	1 001 449	386 559	91	Nicaragua	148 000	57 128
30	Tanzania	945 087	364 900	92	Nepal	145 391	56 121
31	Nigeria	923 768	356 574	93	Bangladesh	143 998	55 583
32	Venezuela	912 050	352 051	94	Tajikistan	143 100	55 200
33	Namibia	823 144	317 734	95	Greece	131 957	50 935
34	Pakistan	803 943	310 322	96	North Korea	122 098	47 130
35	Mozambique	789 800	304 863	97	Malawi	118 484	45 735
36	Turkey	779 452	300 868	98	Liberia	113 370	43 800
37	Chile	756 626	292 058	99	Benin	112 622	43 472
38	Zambia	752 613	290 509	100	Honduras	112 088	43 266
39	Myanmar (Burma)	678 576	261 930	101	Bulgaria	110 912	42 812
40	Afghanistan	647 497	249 934	102	Cuba	110 860	42 792
41	Somalia	637 357	246 201	103	Guatemala	108 889	42 031
42	Central African Republic	626 780	241 937	104	Iceland	103 000	40 000
43	Ukraine	603 700	233 028	105	Yugoslavia[a]	102 173	39 438
44	Madagascar	587 000	227 600	106	South Korea	98 913	38 180
45	Botswana	582 096	224 689	107	Jordan	96 188	37 129
46	Kenya	580 367	224 081	108	Hungary	93 036	35 912
47	France	551 000	212 686	109	Portugal	88 500	34 200
48	Yemen	531 570	205 186	110	Azerbaijan	86 600	33 428
49	Thailand	513 115	198 062	111	Austria	83 854	32 368
50	Spain	504 750	194 833	112	United Arab Emirates	83 600	32 300
51	Turkmenistan	488 100	188 400	113	Czech Republic	78 864	30 441
52	Cameroon	475 439	183 519	114	Panama	77 082	29 753
53	Papua New Guinea	462 840	178 656	115	Sierre Leone	72 325	27 917
54	Uzbekistan	447 400	172 696	116	Ireland	70 282	27 129
55	Iraq	434 925	167 881	117	Georgia	69 700	26 900
56	Sweden	411 479	158 830	118	Sri Lanka	65 610	25 325
57	Morocco	409 200	157 951	119	Lithuania	65 200	25 167
58	Paraguay	406 750	157 000	120	Latvia	64 600	24 900
59	Zimbabwe	391 090	150 961	121	Togo	56 600	21 848
60	Japan	381 945	147 431	122	Croatia	56 540	21 825
61	Germany	357 868	138 136	123	Bosnia-Herzegovina	51 129	19 736
62	Congo	341 945	132 000	124	Costa Rica	51 022	19 694
				125	Slovak Republic	49 035	18 927

Nation	Area km²	sq mi
126 Dominican Republic	48 442	18 699
127 Bhutan	46 600	18 000
128 Estonia	45 100	17 409
129 Denmark	43 076	16 627
130 Switzerland	41 228	15 914
131 Guinea-Bissau	36 260	13 996
132 Taiwan	36 000	13 896
133 Netherlands, The	33 929	13 097
134 Moldova	33 700	13 008
135 Belgium	30 540	11 788
136 Lesotho	30 460	11 758
137 Armenia	29 800	11 500
138 Albania	28 748	11 097
139 Equatorial Guinea	28 051	10 828
140 Burundi	27 834	10 744
141 Haiti	27 750	10 712
142 Solomon Islands	27 556	10 637
143 Rwanda	26 338	10 166
144 Macedonia, former Yugoslav Republic of	25 713	9 925
145 Djibouti	23 310	8 998
146 Belize	22 963	8 864
147 El Salvador	21 476	8 290
148 Israel	20 770	8 017
149 Slovenia	20 251	7 817
150 Fiji	18 333	7 076
151 Kuwait	17 818	6 878
152 Swaziland	17 363	6 702
153 Vanuatu	14 763	5 698
154 Bahamas, The	13 934	5 378
155 Qatar	11 437	4 415
156 Gambia, The	11 295	4 361
157 Jamaica	10 957	4 229
158 Lebanon	10 452	4 034

Nation	Area km²	sq mi
159 Cyprus	9 251	3 571
160 Brunei	5 765	2 225
161 Trinidad and Tobago	5 128	1 979
162 Cape Verde	4 033	1 557
163 Western Samoa	2 842	1 097
164 Luxembourg	2 586	998
165 Mauritius	1 865	720
166 Comoros	1 862	719
167 São Tomé and Príncipe	1 001	387
168 Dominica	751	290
169 Kiribati	717	277
170 Bahrain	678	262
171 Tonga	646	249
172 Singapore	618	238
173 St Lucia	616	238
174 Andorra	468	181
175 Antigua and Barbuda	442	171
176 Barbados	430	166
177 St Vincent and the Grenadines	390	150
178 Grenada	344	133
179 Malta	316	122
180 Maldives	300	116
181 St Kitts and Nevis	269	104
182 Liechtenstein	160	62
183 San Marino	61	23
184 Tuvalu	26	10
185 Nauru	21.3	8.2
186 Monaco	1.95	0.75

This list is not exhaustive, particularly among the smaller nations. Differences of status of many of the 'nations' listed also make direct comparisons difficult.

[a]Yugoslavia in this context consists of the states of Montenegro and Serbia only.

The world's largest nations by population

Nation	Population total (1990–2) estimates
1 China, People's Republic of	1 133 682 501
2 India	889 700 000
3 United States	248 709 837
4 Indonesia	184 796 000
5 Brazil	150 368 000
6 Russian Federation	148 800 000
7 Pakistan	130 130 000
8 Japan	123 156 678
9 Bangladesh	110 602 000
10 Nigeria	88 500 000
11 Mexico	84 400 000
12 Germany	80 293 000
13 Vietnam	69 200 000
14 Philippines	63 609 000
15 Iran	59 600 000
16 Turkey	56 473 035
17 United Kingdom	57 384 000
18 Italy	57 103 833
19 Thailand	56 814 000
20 France	56 614 493
21 Egypt	55 980 000
22 Ukraine	52 100 000
23 Ethiopia	49 240 000

Nation	Population total (1990–2) estimates
24 South Korea	43 633 000
25 Myanmar (Burma)	43 466 000
26 Spain	38 425 679
27 Poland	38 423 000
28 Zaïre	35 568 000
29 Colombia	33 392 000
30 Argentina	32 646 000
31 South Africa	32 000 000
32 Sudan, The	29 900 000
33 Tanzania	27 318 000
34 Canada	27 269 859
35 Algeria	26 400 000
36 Morocco	26 181 000
37 Kenya	24 031 000
38 Romania	23 397 000
39 Peru	22 361 000
40 North Korea	22 227 000
41 Taiwan	20 658 000
42 Uzbekistan	20 300 000
43 Venezuela	20 185 000
44 Nepal	19 611 000
45 Iraq	18 838 000
46 Uganda	18 794 000
47 Malaysia	18 630 000
48 Afghanistan	18 052 000

Nation	Population total (1990–2) estimates
49 Australia	17 807 000
50 Sri Lanka	17 464 000
51 Kazakhstan	16 700 000
52 Mozambique	16 142 000
53 Ghana	15 336 000
54 Saudi Arabia	15 267 000
55 Netherlands, The	15 231 000
56 Chile	13 173 000
57 Syria	12 965 000
58 Côte d'Ivoire	12 657 000
59 Cameroon	11 833 000
60 Madagascar	11 440 000
61 Ecuador	10 780 000
62 Cuba	10 603 000
63 Yemen	10 400 000
64 Yugoslavia[a]	10 400 000
65 Hungary	10 375 000
66 Czech Republic	10 362 000
67 Angola	10 301 000
68 Belarus	10 300 000
69 Greece	10 300 000
70 Zimbabwe	10 300 000
71 Belgium	9 968 000
72 Portugal	9 831 967
73 Guatemala	9 700 000

The world's largest nations by population (continued)

Nation	Population total (1990–2) estimates	Nation	Population total (1990–2) estimates	Nation	Population total (1990–2) estimates
74 Mali	9 214 000	117 Lithuania	3 700 000	157 Comoros	503 000
75 Burkina Faso	8 996 000	118 Togo	3 531 000	158 Suriname	402 000
76 Bulgaria	8 990 000	119 Ireland	3 525 719	159 Luxembourg	389 000
77 Cambodia	8 974 000	120 Armenia	3 500 000	160 Cape Verde	369 000
78 Malawi	8 754 000	121 New Zealand	3 434 000	161 Equatorial Guinea	360 000
79 Sweden	8 644 000	122 Albania	3 262 000	162 Malta	360 000
80 Zambia	8 452 000	123 Costa Rica	3 160 000	163 Solomon Islands	339 000
81 Tunisia	8 413 000	124 Uruguay	3 130 000	164 Brunei	268 000
82 Austria	7 812 000	125 Central African		165 Barbados	258 000
83 Niger	7 731 000	Republic	3 039 000	166 Bahamas, The	254 685
84 Somalia	7 497 000	126 Lebanon	2 800 000	167 Iceland	254 000
85 Bolivia	7 356 000	127 Singapore	2 792 000	168 Maldives	213 000
86 Senegal	7 277 000	128 Latvia	2 700 000	169 Belize	196 462
87 Rwanda	7 237 000	129 Liberia	2 575 000	170 Western Samoa	190 000
88 Azerbaijan	7 236 000	130 Panama	2 515 000	171 Vanuatu	154 000
89 Dominican		131 Jamaica	2 445 000	172 St Lucia	136 075
Republic	7 170 000	132 Congo	2 271 000	173 São Tomé and	
90 Switzerland	6 750 693	133 Mongolia	2 156 000	Príncipe	124 000
91 Haiti	5 862 000	134 Mauritania	2 100 000	174 St Vincent and the	
92 Guinea	5 755 000	135 Macedonia, former		Grenadines	115 000
93 Chad	5 678 000	Yugoslav		175 Tonga	102 000
94 Burundi	5 472 000	Republic of	2 033 964	176 Grenada	91 000
95 El Salvador	5 460 000	136 United Arab		177 Dominica	82 000
96 Georgia	5 400 000	Emirates	1 990 000	178 Kiribati	71 000
97 Slovak Republic	5 274 335	137 Slovenia	1 962 600	179 Antigua and Barbuda	63 880
98 Israel	5 240 000	138 Namibia	1 781 000	180 Andorra	54 507
99 Denmark	5 146 000	139 Lesotho	1 774 000	181 St Kitts and Nevis	43 100
100 Honduras	5 105 000	140 Oman	1 640 000	182 Monaco	29 712
101 Finland	5 029 000	141 Estonia	1 600 000	183 Liechtenstein	28 700
102 Tajikistan	4 969 000	142 Bhutan	1 511 000	184 San Marino	23 600
103 Croatia	4 760 000	143 Botswana	1 347 000	185 Nauru	9 333
104 Benin	4 630 000	144 Trinidad and		186 Tuvalu	9 317
105 Paraguay	4 520 000	Tobago	1 233 000		
106 Libya	4 450 000	145 Kuwait	1 200 000	This list is not exhaustive, particu-	
107 Laos	4 410 000	146 Gabon	1 170 000	larly among the smaller nations.	
108 Kyrgyzstan	4 400 000	147 Mauritius	1 080 000		
109 Bosnia-		148 Guinea-Bissau	964 000	All population figures provided are	
Herzegovina	4 364 574	149 Gambia, The	861 000	the last available authoritative	
110 Moldova	4 341 000	150 Swaziland	788 000	estimates for each country and	
111 Norway	4 259 000	151 Guyana	750 000	range from 1990 to 1992. For the	
112 Sierra Leone	4 151 000	152 Fiji	748 000	exact year for each figure, see indi-	
113 Nicaragua	4 130 000	153 Cyprus	568 000	vidual country entries.	
114 Jordan	3 943 000	154 Bahrain	531 000		
115 Papua New Guinea	3 834 000	155 Djibouti	530 000	aYugoslavia in this context consists	
116 Turkmenistan	3 809 000	156 Qatar	520 000	of the states of Montenegro and Serbia only.	

World population estimates

Date (AD)	Millions	Date (AD)	Millions	Date (AD)	Millions
1	200	1960	3 050	1992	5 480
1000	275	1970	3 700	2000	6 100
1250	375	1975	4 080	2050	11 000
1500	420	1980	4 450		
1700	615	1985	4 845	Estimates for 2000 and 2050 are	
1800	900	1986	4 936	United Nations 'medium' estimates.	
1900	1 625	1987	5 023	They should be compared with the	
1920	1 860	1988	5 111	'low' estimates for these years of	
1930	2 070	1989	5 201	5 400 and 8 500 and 'high' estimates	
1940	2 295	1990	5 246	of 7 000 and 13 000, respectively.	
1950	2 500	1991	5 385		

World population density

Tokyo
Osaka
Seoul
Shanghai
Guanzhou
Manila
Beijing
Tianyin
Chongqing
Calcutta
Bangkok
Jakarta
Bombay
Karachi
Moscow
Cairo
London
Paris
Rio de Janeiro
São Paulo
Buenos Aries
New York
San Francisco
Los Angeles
Mexico City

□ City with population greater than 5 million

• Dots indicate distribution of population

Notes

All population figures provided are the latest available authoritative figures. Estimates are indicated using the suffix 'e'.

Gross Domestic Product (GDP) and Gross National Product (GNP) figures are provided in US $ in millions (mn) or billions (bn = 1 000 mn).

In the majority of cases, the Heads of State/Heads of Government given are those in office since 1990. Unless stated, 'Head of State' refers to the president and 'Head of Government' to the prime minister.

AFGHANISTAN

Local name Afghānestān

Timezone GMT + 4.5

Area 647 497 km²/249 934 sq mi

Population total (1992) 18 052 000, plus an estimated 2.5 million members of nomadic tribes, and 3 million living in Pakistan and Iran as refugees

Status Democratic republic

Date of independence 1919

Capital Kabul

Languages Pushtu, Dari

Ethnic groups Pathans (50%), Tajik (20%), Uzbek (9%), Hazara (9%), Chahar Aimak (3%), Turkmen (2%), Baluchi (1%)

Religions Muslim (Sunni 84%, Shi'ite 15%)

Physical features Mountainous, landlocked country centred on and divided E–W by the Hindu Kush mountain range which reaches heights of over 7 000 m/24 000 ft. Three distinctive regions: fertile valley of Herat in NW; arid uplands in the S; and 129 495 km²/50 000 sq mi of desert in the SW plateau (including the Rigestan Desert). Amu Darya (Oxus) R forms N border.

Climate Continental climate. Summers warm everywhere except on highest peaks. Rain mostly during spring and autumn; average annual rainfall 338 mm/13.25 in. Winters generally cold, with much snow at higher altitudes (central highlands have a sub-polar climate); at lower levels desert or semi-arid climate.

Currency 1 Afghani (Af) = 100 puls

Economy Traditionally based on agriculture, especially wheat, fruit, vegetables, maize, barley, cotton, sugar-beet, sugar cane, sheep, cattle, goats. Natural-gas production in the N, largely for export. Most sectors have been affected by civil war, especially sugar, carpets, textiles. Natural resources also include oil, coal, copper, sulphur, lead, zinc, iron, salt, precious and semi-precious stones. Many of these resources remain untapped owing to inaccessibility. Main trading partners: Eastern European and CIS countries, Japan, China.

GDP (1989) $3 bn, per capita $200

History Nation first formed in 1747, under Ahmed Shah Durrani; seen as a bridge between India and the Middle East. Britain tried but failed to gain control during a series of Afghan Wars (the last in 1919); independence declared in 1919 after World War 1. Feudal monarchy survived until after World War 2, when the constitution became more liberal under several Soviet-influenced five-

year economic plans. King deposed in 1973, and a republic formed; new constitution, 1977. Coup (1979) brought to power Hafizullah Amin, which led to invasion by USSR forces and establishment of Babrak Karmal as Head of State. New constitution in 1987 provided for an executive President, bicameral National Assembly, and Council of Ministers. Soviet withdrawal implemented 1988–9; new regime met with heavy guerrilla resistance from the Mujahadeen (Islamic fighters). Resignation of President Najibullah in April 1992; Islamic State of Afghanistan declared, 1992. Continuing unrest and disunity among Mujahadeen groups, hindering implementation of UN-backed peace plans. In Dec 1992 a recently created constituent assembly elected Burhanuddin Rabbani as President for two years and also appointed a Parliament.

Head of State

1987–92	Mohammad Najibullah
1992–	Burhanuddin Rabbani

Head of Government

1989–90	Sultan Ali Keshtmand
1990–2	Fazl Haq Khaleqiar
1992–3	Abdul Sabur Fareed
1993–	Gulbardin Hekmatyar

ALBANIA

Local name Shqïpëri

Timezone GMT + 1

Area 28 748 km²/11 097 sq mi

Population total (1991e) 3 303 000

Status Republic

Date of independence 1912

Capital Tiranë

Languages Albanian (official) (Gheg and Tosk, the main dialects), Greek

Ethnic groups Albanian (96%), Greek (2%), Macedonian, Vlach, Gypsy, Bulgarian

Religions Muslim (Sunni 70%), Roman Catholic (5%), Greek Orthodox (2%) (before April 1991, Albania was constitutionally atheist)

Physical features Mountainous country, relatively inaccessible and untravelled. Geologically active – earthquakes severe and relatively frequent. N Albanian Alps rise to 2 692 m/8 832 ft; mountainous highlands (N, S, and E) account for c.70% of the land. Coastal lowland in the W is agricultural. Rivers include the Drin i zi, Shkumbin, Seman, Vijosë. 45% of land is forested; 25% is arable, mostly grain-producing; c.20% is permanent pasture land.

Climate Mediterranean climate, hot and dry on the plains in summer. Average annual temperatures, 8–9°C (Jan), 24–5°C (Jul). Thunderstorms frequent. Mild, damp, cyclonic winters.

Currency 1 Lek (L) = 100 qintars

Economy Seventh five-year plan (1981–5) focused on industrial expansion, especially in oil (new sources were located), mining, chemicals, natural gas; hydroelectric power plans for several rivers (eg the Koman hydroelectric complex on the Drin i zi R); agricultural product processing, textiles, oil products, cement. Main crops are wheat, sugar-beet, maize, potatoes, fruit, grapes, oats. All industry is nationalized; progressive transformation of farm cooperatives into state farms. Chromate, low-grade iron ore, and soft coal are exported. Other natural resources: crude petroleum, asphalt, lignite (brown coal), phosphorus, bauxite, precious metals.

GNP (1991) $4.0 bn, (1987) per capita $1 300

History Albanians descended from Illyrians, who occupied W Balkan peninsula c.1000 BC. King Argon and, after him, his wife Teuta conquered many territories, provoking the military might of Rome. Despite Roman occupation and invasions by Visigoths, Slavs, and Huns, the Albanians were one of the few peoples to retain their Illyrian language and customs. Turkish invasions began in 14th-c; independence followed the end of Turkish rule in 1912. Italian forces occupied the country in 1914–20. Albania became a republic in 1925, and a monarchy in

1928, under King Zog I. Occupied by Germany and Italy during World War 2. A new republic was instigated in 1946, headed by Enver Hoxha (until 1985). Dispute with the Soviet Union in 1961 led to withdrawal from Warsaw Pact in 1968, but close links with China maintained. People's Socialist Republic instituted in 1976; renamed Republic of Albania in 1991; first free elections in 1991, gave a decisive majority to the Communists, however general strike and demonstrations forced government to resign. Communist party renamed itself the Socialist Party, however the Democratic Party was elected in 1992 elections. People's Assembly (supreme legislative body) elects the President and Council of Ministers.

Head of State

1991–2 Fatos Nano *Provisional*
1992–   Sali Berisha

Head of Government

(People's Socialist Republic)
1981–91 Adil Carcani
(Republic of Albania)
1991   Ylli Bufi
1991–2 Vilson Ahmeti
1992–   Alexander Meksi

ALGERIA

Local name(s) Al-Jazā'ir (Arabic), Algérie (French)

Timezone GMT + 1

Area 2 460 500 km²/949 753 sq mi

Population total (1992) 26 400 000

Status Democratic republic

Date of independence 1962

Capital Algiers (Alger)

Languages Arabic (official), Berber, French

Ethnic groups Arab (75%), Berber (25%)

Religions Muslim (Sunni 99%), Roman Catholic (0.5%)

Physical features Mountainous area in N Africa: mountains rise in a series of ridges and plateaux to the Atlas Saharien; Ahaggar Mts in the far S, rising to 2918 m/ 9 573 ft at Mt Tahat. 85% of land is Saharan desert.

Climate Mediterranean in N, with cool, rainy winters and hot dry summers. Average annual temperatures 12°C (Jan), 25°C (Jul). Average annual rainfall 400–800 mm/15.8–31.5 in (mostly Nov–Mar); essentially rainless Saharan climate in S.

Currency 1 Algerian Dinar (AD, DA) = 100 centimes

Economy Petroleum products account for about 30% of national income. Natural-gas liquification. Jointly built with Italy first trans-Mediterranean gas pipeline. Agriculture mainly on N coast: wheat, barley, oats, grapes, citrus fruits, vegetables. Also food processing, textiles, clothing.

GNP (1989) $53.1 bn, per capita $2 170

History Islamic Berber empires followed collapse of Numidian, Roman, Vandal, and Byzantine rule. Turkish invasion in 16th-c. French colonial campaign in 19th-c led to French control from 1902. Guerrilla war (1954–62) with French forces by the National Liberation Front (FLN) led to independence in 1962. First President of the republic, Ahmed Ben Bella, replaced after coup in 1965. New constitution in 1976; military took control of government in 1992, and a state of emergency was declared. Leg-

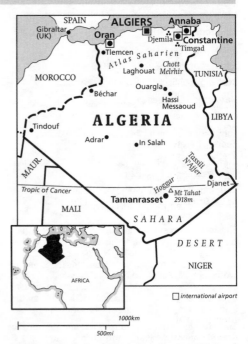

☐ *international airport*

1000km
500mi

islative power is shared by the President and National Assembly.

Head of State

1978–92	Chadli Benjedid
1992	Mohamed Boudiaf
1992–4	Ali Kafi
1994–	Lamine Zeroual

Head of Government

1984–91	Mouloud Hamrouche
1991–2	Sid Ahmed Ghozali
1992–3	Belaid Abdesselam
1993–	Redha Melek

AMERICAN SAMOA >> UNITED STATES OF AMERICA

ANDORRA

Local name Vallée d'Andorre (French), Valls d'Andorra (Spanish)

Timezone GMT + 1

Area 468 km²/181 sq mi

Population total (1991e) 51 000

Status Independent State

Capital Andorra la Vella

Languages Catalan (official), French, Spanish

Ethnic groups Catalan (50%), Andorran (29%), French (8%), Portuguese (7%)

Religion Roman Catholic (94%)

Physical features Mountainous country, located on the S slopes of the C Pyrénées between France and Spain, peaks reaching 2 946 m/9 665 ft at Coma Pedrosa. Two valleys (del Norte and del Orient) of the R Valira.

Climate Alpine climate: heavy snow in winter, warm summers. Average annual temperature 2°C (Jan), 19°C (Jul); lowest average monthly rainfall, 34 mm/1.34 in (Jan).

Currency 1 French Franc (Fr) = 100 centimes, 1 Peseta (Pta, Pa) = 100 céntimos

Economy

No restriction on currency exchange, and no direct value-added taxes, therefore a marketing centre for goods imported from Europe and Asia. Commerce, agriculture; skiing at five mountain resorts; in recent years, textiles, publishing, leather, mineral water, tourism.

GDP (1990e) $727 mn, per capita $14 000

History

One of the oldest states in Europe, under the joint protection of France and Spain since 1278; Co-Princes of Principality are the President of France and the Bishop of Urgel. General Council of the Valley appoints the head of the government. Independent state since 5 May 1993.

Heads of State (Co-Princes)
(President of France)
1981– François Mitterand
(Bishop of Urgel, Spain)
1971– Joan Martí Alanís

Head of Government (Chief Executive)
1989– Óscar Ribas Reig

ANGOLA

Local name Angola

Timezone GMT + 1

Area 1 245 790 km²/480 875 sq mi

Population total (1991e) 10 301 000

Status Republic

Date of independence 1975

Capital Luanda

Languages Portuguese (official), Bantu languages, including: Ovimbundu, Kimbundu, Bakongo, Chokwe

Ethnic groups Ovimbundu (37%), Mbundu (22%), Bakongo (13%), Lunda-Tchokwe (5%); also Nganguela, Nyaneka-Humbe, Herero, Ambo, Portuguese

Religions Traditional religions (12%), Roman Catholic (68%), Protestant (20%)

Physical features Located in SW Africa. Narrow coastal plain. In S and E the planalto central (central plateau, continuation of great SW African plateau), covers c.60% of the country. In N, highland plateau, mean elevation 1200 m/4 000 ft; highest point, Serro Môco 2619 m/8 592 ft. Coastal desert in W; in the E, upland escarpments. C.40% of land forested.

Climate Tropical plateau climate. At Huambo, on the plateau, average annual rainfall 1 450 mm/57 in; rainfall varies greatly from SW to NE (negligible rainfall on SW coastal desert caused by Benguela current). Average daily temperatures 24–9°C; temperature much reduced on the coast, which is semi-desert as far N as Luanda.

Currency 1 New Kwanza (kw, kz) = 100 Iweis

Economy Reserves of several minerals; extraction and refining of oil (mainly off the coast of Cabinda Province) provides over 90% of current export earnings. Diamond exporter; large producer of honey. Principal livestock are

cattle, goats, pigs, sheep; agriculture and fishing (mackerel and sardines) industries small; several airfields and railways.

GDP (1990e) $4 700 mn, per capita $600

Angola (continued)

History Became a Portuguese colony in 1482 after exploration. Slave trade flourished, causing friction and war (in early 17th-c, c.10 000 slaves were exported from Luanda annually). Boundaries formally defined during the Berlin West Africa Congress (1884–5). Became an overseas province of Portugal in 1951; Portuguese finally withdrew in 1975, and the People's Republic of Angola achieved full independence. Civil war followed independence, involving three internal factions – the Marxist MPLA (Popular Movement for the Liberation of Angola), UNITA (the National Union for the Total Independence of Angola), and the FNLA (National Front for the Liberation of Angola). Cuban combat troops arrived in 1976, at request of MPLA. At the end of 1988, Geneva agreement linked arrangements for independence of Namibia with withdrawal of Cuban troops, and the cessation of South African attacks and support for UNITA. Peace agreement in 1991 established a one-party state, governed by a President, Council of Ministers, and National People's Assembly. Adopted the name Republic of Angola; first multi-party legislative elections held in Sep 1992. MPLA victory rejected by UNITA led to resumption of conflict in 1993.

Head of State
1975–9   Antonio Agostinho Neto
1979–   José Eduardo dos Santos

Head of Government
1991–2   Fernando José Frana Van Dúnem
1992–   Marcolino José Carlos Moco

ANGUILLA >> UNITED KINGDOM

ANTIGUA AND BARBUDA

Local name Antigua and Barbuda

Timezone GMT – 4

Area 442 km²/171 sq mi; (Antigua: 280 km²/108 sq mi; Barbuda: 161 km²/62 sq mi; Redonda: 1 km²/0.4 sq mi)

Population total (1991) 63 880

Status Independent republic within the Commonwealth

Date of independence 1981

Capital St John's (on Antigua)

Language English (official)

Ethnic groups African descent (92%), Portuguese, Lebanese, British (4%)

Religions Anglican (80%), Roman Catholic (10%)

Physical features Group of three islands in the Leeward group of the Lesser Antilles, E Caribbean. W part of Antigua rises to 470 m/1 542 ft at Boggy Peak. Barbuda is a flat coral island reaching only 44 m/144 ft at its highest point, with a large lagoon on its W side. Redonda is an uninhabited, volcanic island, rising to 305 m/1 000 ft at its highest point.

Climate Tropical. Temperatures range from 24°C (Jan) to 27°C (Aug–Sep); mean annual rainfall 1 000 mm/40 in.

Currency 1 East Caribbean Dollar (EC$) = 100 cents

Economy Tourism; sugar (40% of national income, marked decline in 1960s, now recovering); cotton.

GDP (1989e) $353.5 mn, per capita $5 500

History Antigua claimed for Spain by Columbus in 1493; colonized by British in 1632; ceded to Britain in 1667. Barbuda colonized from Antigua in 1661; administered as part of the Leeward Is Federation, 1871–1956; an associated state of the UK in 1967. Independence achieved in 1981. Legislative power is vested in a bicameral parliament; Governor-General appoints the Prime Minister and Cabinet.

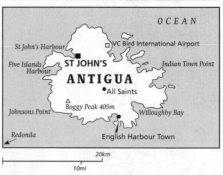

Head of State
(British monarch represented by Governor-General)
1981–   Sir Wilfred E Jacobs

Head of Government
1981–94   Vere Cornwall Bird
1994–   Lester Bird

ANTILLES, NETHERLANDS >> NETHERLANDS

ARGENTINA

Local name Argentina

Timezone GMT – 3

Area American continent: 2 780 092 km²/1 073 115 sq mi on Antarctic continent: 964 250 km²/372 200 sq mi

Population total (1991e) 32 646 000

Status Republic

Date of independence 1816

Capital Buenos Aires

Language Spanish (official)

Ethnic groups European origin (c.85%), Mestizo European/Indian origin (15%)

Religions Roman Catholic (90%), Protestant (2%)

Physical features Argentina can be divided into four regions: sub-tropical NE plains, the Pampa, Patagonia, and the Andes. The Andes stretch the entire length of Argentina (N–S), forming the boundary with Chile; Highest peak, Aconcagua 6 960 m/22 831 ft. Uneven, semi-desert, arid steppes in the S (Patagonia); grassy, treeless Pampa to E. N Argentina is drained by the Paraguay, Paraná, and Uruguay rivers, which join in the R Plate estuary. Island of Tierra del Fuego off the S tip.

Climate Moderately humid sub-tropical climate in the NE. Average annual temperature 16°C; average annual rainfall 500–1 000 mm/20–40 in. Semi-arid in interior S lowlands; Pampa temperate, dry in W and humid in E, with temperatures ranging from tropical to moderately cool; S directly influenced by strong prevailing westerlies.

Currency 1 Peso = 100 centavos (formerly the austral)

Economy Major contribution to economy from agricultural produce and meat processing. Deposits of oil and natural gas, chiefly off the coast of Patagonia; important reserves of iron ore, coal, copper, lead, zinc, gold, silver, uranium, manganese.

GDP (1990) $70.1 bn, per capita $2 162

History Pre-colonially, nomadic Indian hunters lived in S and Inca farmers in NW; after a long battle the country was settled in the 16th-c by the Spanish. Declared independence as the federal Republic of Argentina in 1816, and United Provinces of the Río de la Plata established. Dictatorship of Juan Manuel de Rosas during

1000km / 500mi

□ international airport

1829–52; federal constitution in 1853. Ranchers' oligarchy of 1916 was ended by military coup in 1930. Acquisition of the Gran Chaco after war with Paraguay, 1865–70; considerable European settlement since the opening up of the Pampas in the 19th-c. Juan Perón elected president (1946 and 1973); eventually succeeded by his wife Isabel (Martínez de Perón) who was deposed in 1976. Attempt to control the Falkland Is (1982) failed following war with the UK; successive military governments, until federal constitution re-established in 1983, with election of Raúl Alfonsín. Governed by a President and a bicameral National Congress, with a Chamber of Deputies and a Senate.

Head of State/Government
1983–8   Raúl Alfonsín
1989–   Carlos Saúl Menem

ARMENIA

Local name Armenia

Timezone GMT + 3

Area 29 800 km²/11 500 sq mi

Population total (1992e) 3 500 00

Status Republic

Date of independence 1991

Capital Yerevan

Language Armenian (official)

Ethnic groups (1991) Armenian (90%), Azer (3%), Kurd (2%), Russian (2%) (ethnic conflict since 1990 makes accurate statistical analysis impossible)

Religions Christian (Armenian Church), Russian Orthodox

Physical features Mountainous region in S Transcaucasia, rising to 4 090 m/13 418 ft at Mt Aragats (W). Rivers include Razdan and Vorotan; largest mountain lake is the Sevan, 1 401 km²/541 sq mi – this is the main source of irrigation system and hydroelectric power.

Armenia (continued)

Climate Varies with elevation; chiefly dry and continental with considerable regional variation.

Currency 1 Rouble (R) = 100 kopecks

Economy Large mineral resources, chiefly copper; also molybdenum, gold, silver. Electrical equipment and machinery, chemicals, textiles, cognac. Agriculture based on fruits, wheat, wine grapes, cotton, tobacco.

GDP Not available

History Proclaimed a Soviet Socialist Republic in 1920; constituent republic of the USSR from 1936; civil war over Nagorno-Karabakh began in 1989. Declaration of independence in 1990; independence recognized and joined CIS in 1991. Ongoing conflict with Azerbaijan over disputed enclave of Nagorno-Karabakh.

Head of State
1991–   Levon Ter-Petrosian

Head of Government
1991–2   Gagik Arutynian
1992–3   Khasrov Haroutunian
1993–   Hrand Bagratian

ARUBA >> NETHER-   LANDS, THE

AUSTRALIA

Local name Australia

Timezone GMT + 8 (Western Australia); GMT + 10 (New South Wales, Queensland, Tasmania, Victoria, Australian Capital Territory); GMT + 9.5 (South Australia, Northern Territory)

Area 7 692 300 km²/2 969 228 sq mi

Population total (1991) 16 850 540

Status Independent state within the Commonwealth

Date of independence 1901

Capital Canberra

Language English (official)

Ethnic groups European descent (95%), Aboriginal (1.5%)

Religions Anglican (30%), Roman Catholic (25%)

Physical features Smallest continent; consists largely of plains and plateaux, most of which average 600 m/ 2 000 ft above sea level. Four main regions: Western Craton (or Western Shield), the Great Artesian Basin, the Great Dividing Range (or Eastern Uplands), and the Flinders-Mt Lofty ranges. W Australian Plateau occupies nearly half of the country; MacDonnell Ranges lie in the centre, highest point Mt Liebig, 1 525 m/5 000 ft. Most of the plateau is dry, barren desert; Nullarbor Plain in the S is crossed by the Trans-Australian Railway; Great Dividing Range parallel to the Great Barrier Reef, rising to 2 228 m/ 7 310 ft at Mt Kosciusko, Australia's highest point. Great Barrier Reef off NE coast stretches for over 1 900 km/ 1 200 mi. Island of Tasmania rises to 1 617 m/5 305 ft at Mt Ossa; it is separated from the mainland by the Bass Strait. The longest river is the Murray; its chief tributaries are the Darling, Murrumbidgee, Lachlan; Lake Eyre occupies 8 800 km²/3 400 sq mi. C.18% of area is forested; c.6% is arable.

Climate More than a third of Australia receives under 260 mm/10 in mean annual rainfall; less than a third receives over 500 mm/20 in. Prolonged drought and frequent heatwaves in many areas. Average daily temperature 26–34°C (Nov) and 19–31°C (Jul) in N; rainfall varies from 286 mm/15.2 in (Jan) to zero (Jul). Fertile land with a temperate climate and reliable rainfall only in the lowlands and valleys near the E and SE coast, and a small part of the SW corner; Tasmania and Mt Kosciusko have snowfields in winter.

Currency 1 Australian Dollar ($A) = 100 cents

Economy Free-enterprise economy. World's largest wool producer, and a top exporter of veal and beef; most important crop is wheat. Major mineral producer; discoveries of petroleum reserves, bauxite, nickel, lead, zinc, copper, tin, uranium, iron ore, and other minerals in early 1960s. Manufacturing industry has expanded rapidly since 1945, especially engineering, shipbuilding, car manufacture, metals, textiles, clothing, chemicals, food processing, wine. Self-sufficient in lumber; marine fishing (especially tuna) is important, as are tourism and winter sports.

GDP (1990) $311 bn, per capita $18 054

History Aboriginal people thought to have arrived in Australia from SE Asia c.40 000 years ago. First European visitors were the Dutch, who explored the Gulf of Carpentaria in 1606 and settled in 1616; became known as New Holland in 1644. Captain James Cook arrived in Botany Bay in 1770, and claimed the E coast for Britain; New South Wales was established as a penal colony in 1788. Gold discovered in New South Wales and Victoria in 1851, and in Western Australia in 1892. Transportation of convicts to E Australia ended in 1840, but continued until 1853 in Tasmania and 1868 in Western Australia; during this period the colonies drafted their own constitutions and set up governments: New South Wales (1855), Tasmania and Victoria (1856), South Australia (1857), Queensland (1860), and Western Australia (1890). Commonwealth of Australia established in 1901, with Canberra subsequently chosen as capital, (1901). Policy of preventing immigration by non-Whites remained in force from the end of the 19th-c until 1974. Northern Territory self-governing since 1978. Divided into six states and two territories: each state has its own legislature, government, and constitution; legislature comprises a bicameral Federal Parliament with a Prime Minister and Cabinet; British monarch is Head of State, represented by a Governor-General.

Head of State
(British monarch represented by Governor-General)
1952–   Bill Hayden

Head of Government
1983–91   Robert Hawke
1991–   Paul Keating

>> Political leaders and rulers

Australian States

Name	Area		State capital
	km²	sq mi	
Australian Capital Territory	2 400	930	Canberra
New South Wales	801 400	309 400	Sydney
Northern Territory	1 346 200	519 800	Darwin
Queensland	1 727 200	666 900	Brisbane
South Australia	984 000	379 900	Adelaide
Tasmania	67 800	26 200	Hobart
Victoria	227 600	87 900	Melbourne
Western Australia	2 525 500	975 000	Perth

External territories

Name	Area		Population total	Date under Australian administration
	km²	sq mi		
The Ashmore and Cartier Islands	3.0	2.0	Uninhabited	1931
Australian Antarctic Territory	6 043 852.0	2 332 927.0	Uninhabited	1936
Christmas Island	155.0	60.0	(1990e) 1 300	1958
Cocos (Keeling) Islands	14.2	5.5	(1990) 613	1955
Coral Sea Island	2.0*	0.8*	Uninhabited	1969
Heard Island and McDonald Islands	412.0	159.0	Uninhabited	1947
Norfolk Island	35.0	13.0	(1991) 1 912	1913

* Land figure only. Islands cover 1 000 000 km²/286 000 sq mi of ocean.

AUSTRIA

Local name Österreich

Timezone GMT + 1

Area 83 854 km²/32 368 sq mi

Population total (1991e) 7 812 000

Status Republic

Date of independence 1955

Capital Vienna (Wien)

Languages German (official), Croatian, Slovene

Ethnic groups Austrian (99%), Croatian, Slovakian, Turkish, German

Religions Roman Catholic (85%), Protestant (12%), Muslim (1%), Jewish (1%)

Physical features One of most mountainous countries in Europe; lies at E end of the Alps. Highest point, Grossglockner, 3 797 m/12 457 ft; largest lake, Neusiedler See. Divided into three regions: Alpine; the highland Bohemian Massif; and the hilly lowland region, including the Vienna basin. R Danube drains whole country; most densely forested country in central Europe (40% of land is forested).

Climate Three climatic regions: the Alps (often sunny in winter, but cloudy in summer); the Danube valley and Vienna basin (driest region); and the SE, a region of often severe winters but warmer summers. Average annual temperature: 2°C (Jan), 20°C (Jul) in Vienna. Most rain in summer months; average annual rainfall 868 mm/ 34 in. Winters cold, especially with winds from the E or NE; humid, continental climate in NE.

Currency 1 Schilling (S, Sch) = 100 Groschen

Economy Mixed free market. Principal agricultural areas to the N of the Alps, and along both sides of the Danube. Principal crops: cereals. Dairy cattle and pigs; wine industry; wide range of metal and mineral resources; tourism (summer and winter). Well-developed transportation networks; river ports at Linz and Vienna; airports at Vienna, Graz, Linz, Klagenfurt, Salzburg, Innsbruck. Much of Austria's power produced hydro-electrically.

GDP (1991e) $163 bn, per capita $21 087

☐ *international airport*

History Early Iron-Age settlement at Hallstatt; later Illyrian settlers driven out by the Celts. Part of Roman Empire until 5th-c, then occupied by Germanic tribes, most significantly Bavarians. Charlemagne drove out the Slavic Avars who also settled in the region. The area became a duchy and passed to the Habsburg family in 1282, who made it the foundation of their Empire. Hungarian nationalism and Habsburg defeats in 19th-c led to the dual monarchy of Austria–Hungary from 1867. Nationalist protest resulted in assassination of Archduke Ferdinand in 1914 and World War 1, which ended the Austrian Empire; republic established in 1918. Annexed by the German Reich in 1938 (the *Anschluss*) and named Ostmark; occupied by British, American, French, and Russian troops from 1945. Obtained independence in 1955; neutrality declared, since when Austria has been a haven for many refugees. Governed by a Federal Assembly; the Federal President appoints a Federal Chancellor.

Head of State (Federal President)
1986–92   Kurt Waldheim
1992–   Thomas Klestil

Head of Government (Federal Chancellor)
1986–   Franz Vranitzky

AZERBAIJAN

Local name Azerbaijan

Timezone GMT + 3

Area 86 600 km²/33 428 sq mi

Population total (1992e) 7 236 000

Status Republic

Date of independence 1991

Capital Baku

Languages Azeri (official), Russian

Ethnic groups Azeri (83%), Russian (6%), Armenian (6%)

(ethnic conflict since 1990 makes accurate statistical analysis impossible)

Religion Shi'ite Muslim

Physical features Mountainous country in E Transcaucasia: 10% of country is above 1 494 m/4 900 ft; 40% of land is lowland, 396–1 494 m/1 300–4 900 ft; Bazar-Dyuzi rises to 4 480 m/14 698 ft. Rivers include the Kara and Araks.

Climate Central and eastern Azerbaijan is dry and subtropical with mild winters and long, hot summers (often as hot as 43°C). SE is humid with annual rainfall of 1 193–1 396 mm/47–55 in.

Currency 1 Manat = 100 gopik

Economy Once the former Soviet Union's most important oil-producing region, but now in decline. Manufacturing industries include building materials, chemicals, textiles; mineral resources include natural gas, iron, copper, lead, zinc; exports include cotton, wheat, tobacco.

GDP Not available

History Proclaimed a Soviet Socialist Republic in 1920; constituent republic of the USSR in 1936. Declaration of independence in 1991; became a member of UN in 1992. Ongoing conflict with Armenia over disputed enclave of Nagorno-Karabakh.

Head of State
1991–2   Ayaz Mutalibov
1992   Yagub Mamedov *Interim*
1992–3   Abulfaz Elchibey
1993–   Geidar Aliyev

Head of Government
1991–2   Gasan Gasanov
1992–3   Feirus Mustafayev
1993   Rakhim Guseinov
1993–   Panakh Guseinov

AZORES >> PORTUGAL

BAHAMAS

Local name Bahamas

Timezone GMT – 5

Area 13 934 km²/5 378 sq mi

Population total (1991) 254 685

Status Independent state within the Commonwealth

Date of independence 1973

Capital Nassau

Language English (official)

Ethnic groups African (85%), European/N American descent (15%)

Religions Baptist (29%), Anglican (29%), Roman Catholic (23%)

Physical features Coral archipelago of 700 islands and 2 400 uninhabited cays, forming a chain extending c.800 km/500 mi SE from the coast of Florida. Population centres on the two oceanic banks of Little and Great Bahama. Highest point, Mt Alvernia, 120 m/394 ft.

Climate Sub-tropical. Average temperatures 21°C (Jan) and 27°C (Jul); mean annual rainfall 750–1 500 mm/30–60 in. Hurricanes frequent (Jun–Nov).

Currency 1 Bahamian Dollar (BA$, B$) = 100 cents

Economy Market economy based on tourism; important financial centre (no income tax); oil refining, fishing, rum and liqueur distilling; cement; pharmaceuticals.

GDP (1990e) $2.8 bn, per capita $11 055

History Visited by Columbus in 1492, but first permanent European settlement not until 1647 by British and Bermudan religious refugees. British Crown Colony from

1717; independence in 1973. Governed by a bicameral Parliament.

Head of State
(British monarch represented by Governor-General)
1988–92   Sir Henry Taylor
1992–   Clifford Darling

Head of Government
1973–92   Sir Lynden O Pindling
1992–   Hubert Alexander Ingraham

Human geography

BAHRAIN

Local name Al-Bahrayn

Timezone GMT + 3

Area 678 km²/262 sq mi

Population total (1992e) 531 000

Status Independent state

Date of independence 1971

Capital Manama

Languages Arabic (official), Farsi, Urdu and English

Ethnic groups Bahraini Arab (63%), Asian (13%), Arab (10%), Iranian (9%)

Religions Muslim (Shi'ite 60%), Sunni 40%)

Physical features Island of Bahrain c.48 km/30 mi long, 13–16 km/8–10 mi wide, area 562 km²/217 sq mi. Highest point Jabal Du Khan, 135 m/443 ft. Largely bare and infertile.

Climate Temperate (Dec–Mar); hot and humid (particularly Jun–Sep); cool N/NE winds with a little rain (Dec–Mar). Average annual rainfall 35 mm/1.4 in; average annual temperature 19°C (Jan), 36°C (Jul).

Currency 1 Bahrain Dinar (BD) = 1 000 fils

Economy Major centre for oil trading, banking, commerce.

GDP (1989e) $3.4 bn, per capita $7 300

History Flourishing centre of trade during 2000–1800 BC. Treaty of protection with the UK in 1861; independence in 1971, with a constitutional monarchy governed by an Emir. National Assembly dissolved in 1975 and has not yet been revived. Historic territorial dispute with

Qatar over the Hawar Is began with the brief occupation of Fasht al-Dibal by Qatari troops in 1986. Bahrain joined UN coalition during the Iraqi invasion of Kuwait in 1990.

Head of State (Emir)
1971–   Shaikh Isa bin Sulman al-Khalifa

Head of Government
1971–   Shaikh Khalifa bin Sulman al-Khalifa

BALEARIC ISLANDS >> SPAIN

BANGLADESH

Local name Bangladesh

Timezone GMT + 6

Area 143 998 km²/55 583 sq mi

Population total (1992e) 110 602 000

Status Republic

Date of independence 1971

Capital Dhaka

Languages Bengali (official), also local dialects and English are widely spoken

Ethnic groups Bengali (98%), Bihari (1%), tribal: Garo, Khasi, Santal (1%)

Religions Muslim (86%), Hindu (12%), Buddhist (1%), small Christian majority

Physical features Mainly a vast, low-lying alluvial plain, cut by a network of rivers, canals, swamps, marshes. Main rivers the Ganges (Padma), Brahmaputra (Jamuna), Meghna; joining in the S to form the largest

delta in the world, subject to frequent flooding. Chittagong Hill Tracts in the E rise to 1 200 m/3 900 ft.

Climate Tropical climate; monsoon season (Jun–Oct).

Currency 1 Taka (TK) = 100 paisa

Economy Agriculture, especially rice (employs 86% of population); and supplies 80% of the world's jute. Also paper, aluminium, textiles, glass, shipbuilding, fishing, natural gas.

GDP (1990e) $20.2 bn, per capita $180

History Part of the State of Bengal until Muslim East Bengal created in 1905, separate from Hindu West Bengal. Reunited in 1911; partitioned again in 1947, with West Bengal remaining in India and East Bengal forming East Pakistan. Rebellion in 1971 led to independence as the People's Republic of Bangladesh. Political unrest led to suspension of constitution, and assassination of first President, Sheikh Mujib, in 1975; further coups in 1975, 1977, and 1982; constitution restored in 1986; last military dictator, Hossain Mohammad Ershad, overthrown in

1990; constitutional amendments in 1991 restricted powers of President to ceremonial and restored full powers to unicameral legislature, *Jatiya Sangsad*.

Head of State
1983–90   Hossain Mohammad Ershad
1990–1   Shehabuddin Ahmed *Acting*
1991–   Abdur Rahman Biswas

Head of Government
1989–91   Kazi Zafar Ahmed
1991–   Begum Khaleda Zia

BARBADOS

Local name Barbados

Timezone GMT – 4

Area 430 km²/166 sq mi

Population total (1991e) 258 000

Status Independent state within the Commonwealth

Date of independence 1966

Capital Bridgetown

Language English (official)

Ethnic groups African (80%), mixed race (16%)

Religions Anglican (40%), Protestant (15%), Roman Catholic (4%)

Physical features Small, triangular island in the Atlantic Ocean; length 32 km/20 mi (NW–SE); rising to 340 m/1 115 ft at Mt Hillaby. Ringed by a coral reef.

Climate Tropical climate, with average annual temperature 27°C; mean annual rainfall 1 420 mm/56 in.

Currency 1 Barbados Dollar (Bds$) = 100 cents

Economy Market economy based on tourism and sugar cane; cotton, bananas; natural gas; textiles.

GDP (1990e) $1400 mn, per capita $5 405

History Colonized by the British in 1627; self-government in 1961; independent within the Commonwealth in 1966. Executive power rests with the Prime Minister, appointed by a Governor-General, the Senate, and the House of Assembly.

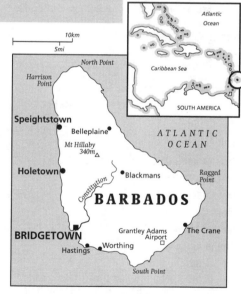

Head of State
(British monarch represented by Governor-General)
1984–90   Hugh Springer
1990–   Dame Nita Barrow

Head of Government
1987–   L Erskine Sandiford

BELARUS (BELORUSSIA)

Local name Belarus

Timezone GMT + 3

Area 207 600 km²/80 134 sq mi

Population total (1992e) 10 300 000

Status Republic

Date of independence 1991

Capital Minsk (Mensk)

Languages Belorussian (official), Russian

Ethnic groups (1989) Belorussian (78%), Russian (13%), Polish (4%), Ukrainian (3%), Jewish (1%)

Religions Roman Catholic, Orthodox

Physical features Hilly lowlands with marshes, swamps. Dzyarzhynskaya Mt rises to 346 m/1 135 ft. Largest lake, Narach. Belaruskaya Hrada, largest glacial ridge, runs NW into Minsk Upland. Rivers include the Pripyat and Dnepr; Pripyat marshes in E.

Climate Varies from maritime, near Baltic, to continental and humid. Average annual temperatures, 18°C (Jul), – 6°C (Jan); average annual rainfall 550–700 mm/22–8 in.

Currency Belorussian Rouble = 100 kopec (in parallel with the Russian Rouble); currency coupons for food, alcohol, tobacco

Economy Main exports include textiles, timber, chemical products, fertilizers, electrical goods. Valuable resource: peat marshes.

GDP Not available

History Neolithic remains widespread. Colonized by E Slavic tribes in the 5th-c; Mongols conquered Slavs in the 13th-c. Catherine the Great of Russia acquired E Belorussia (White Russia) in the first Polish partition in 1772;

gained Minsk in 1793 and the remainder in 1795. W Belorussia ceded to Poland in 1921 as part of the Treaty of Riga which ended Soviet–Polish War; regained by Soviet Union as part of Nazi–Soviet Non-aggression Pact of 1939, and Belorussia became Belorussian Soviet Socialist Republic; admitted to UN 1945. Declared independence in 1991; co-founder of Commonwealth of Independent States (CIS) in 1991.

Head of State
1991–4   Stanislav Shushkevich
1994–   Mechislav Grib

Head of Government
1991–   Vyacheslav Kebich

BELAU >> UNITED STATES OF AMERICA

BELGIUM

Local names Belgique (French), België (Flemish)

Timezone GMT + 1

Area 30 540 km²/11 788 sq mi

Population total (1991) 9 978 681

Status Kingdom

Date of independence 1830

Capital Brussels

Languages Flemish/Dutch (56%), French (32%), German (1%); (Brussels officially bilingual Flemish/French)

Ethnic groups Flemish (Teutonic origin) (55%), Walloon (French Latin) (33%)

Religions Roman Catholic (75%), Muslim (1%), Protestant (0.4%)

Physical features Mostly low-lying, with some hills in the SE region (Ardennes), average elevation 300–500 m/ 1 000–1 600 ft. Large areas of fertile soil, intensively cultivated for many centuries; main river systems linked by complex network of canals. Low-lying, dune-fringed coastline.

Climate Cool and temperate with strong maritime influences. Average annual temperatures 2°C (Jan), 18°C (Jul) in Brussels; average annual rainfall 825 mm/ 35 in.

Currency 1 Belgian Franc (BFr) = 100 centimes

Economy One of the earliest countries in Europe to industrialize, using rich coalfields of the Ardennes; Flanders textile industry; long-standing centre for European trade; major iron and steel industry, with wide range of metallurgical and engineering products; agriculture mainly livestock. Full economic union (Benelux Economic Union) between Belgium, Netherlands, and Luxembourg in 1948. Brussels is the headquarters of several major international organizations, including the Commission of the EC.

GDP (1990) $144.8 bn, per capita $14 600

History Part of the Roman Empire until 2nd-c; then became part of the Frankish Empire following Celt and Germanic invasions. Ruled by the Habsburgs from 1477 until the Peace of Utrecht in 1713, when sovereignty passed to Austria. Conquered by the French in 1794; part of the French Republic and Empire until 1815, then united with the Netherlands. Belgian rebellion against Dutch rule in 1830, led to recognition as an independent kingdom under Leopold of Saxe-Coburg. Occupied by Germany in both World Wars. Became a constitutional monarchy with bicameral Parliament. Political tension between Walloons in S and Flemings in N in 1980; federal constitution divided Belgium into the autonomous regions of Flanders, Wallonia, and Brussels in 1989. Constitutional Monarch has limited powers; a Chamber of Deputies and a Senate.

Head of State (Monarch)
1950–93   Baudouin I
1993–   Albert II

Head of Government
1981–92   Wilfried Martens
1992–   Jean-Luc Dehaene

☐ international airport

BELIZE

Local name Belice (Spanish)

Timezone GMT – 6

Area 22 963 km²/8 864 sq mi

Population total (1992e) 196 000

Status Independent state within the Commonwealth

Date of independence 1981

Capital Belmopan

Languages English (official), Spanish, Garifuna, Maya

Ethnic groups Creole (40%), mestizo (33%), Mayan (9.5%), Carib (8%)

Religions Roman Catholic (62%), Protestant (30%)

Physical features Located in C America. Extensive coastal plain; swampy in the N, fertile in the S; Maya Mts extend almost to the E coast, rising to 1 120 m/ 3 674 ft at Victoria Peak; Belize R flows W–E. Inner coastal waters protected by world's second longest barrier reef.

Climate Generally sub-tropical, but tempered by trade winds. Average annual temperature 24°C (Jan), 27°C (Jul); variable rainfall; average annual rainfall 1 295 mm/51 in (N), 4 445 mm/175 in (S). Hurricanes frequent.

Currency 1 Belize Dollar (Bz$) = 100 cents

Economy Developing free-market economy based on timber and forest products, more recently on agriculture.

GDP (1990) $290 mn, per capita $1 320

History Evidence of early Mayan settlement. Colonized in the 17th-c by shipwrecked British sailors and disbanded soldiers from Jamaica; created a British colony in 1862; administered from Jamaica until 1884. Internal self-government in 1964; changed name from British Honduras to Belize in 1973; full independence in 1981. Guatemalan claims over Belize territory have led to a

☐ international airport

continuing British military presence. Bicameral National Assembly, comprising a House of Representatives and a Senate.

Head of State
(British Monarch represented by Governor-General)
1981–   Dame Minita Elvira Gordon

Head of Government
1989–93   George Cadle Price
1993–   Manuel Esquivel

BENIN

Local name Bénin

Timezone GMT + 1

Area 112 622 km²/43 472 sq mi

Population total (1991e) 4 883 000

Status Republic

Date of independence 1960

Capital Porto Novo (nominal), Cotonou (political and economic)

Languages French (official), Fon (47%), Adja (12%), Bariba (10%), Yoruba (9%), Fulani (6%), Somba (5%), Aizo (5%)

Ethnic groups Fon (40%), Yoruba (10%), Bariba (20%), minority of Fulani nomads

Religions Traditional beliefs (c.70%), Christian (15%), Muslim (13%)

Physical features Located in N Africa. Rises from a 100 km/62 mi-long, sandy coast with lagoons to low-lying plains; savannah plateau, c. 400 m/1 300 ft, in N; descend to forested lowlands in S fringing the Bight of Benin. Atakora Mts rise to over 500 m/1 600 ft in NW. Rivers included Ouémé, Alibori, Mekrou. Pendjari National Park in NW.

Climate Tropical climate divided into three zones: in the S, rain throughout the year, especially during the Guinea Monsoon (May–Oct); in C, two rainy seasons (peaks in May–Jun and Oct); in the N, one rainy season (Jul–Sep). Dry season in N (Oct–Apr): hot, with low humidity, subject to the dry harmattan wind from the NE.

Currency 1 CFA Franc (CFAFr) = 100 centimes

Economy Agriculture, especially palm-oil products, cashew nuts, maize, cassava, rice, cotton, coffee; no known natural resources in commercial quantity; small offshore oilfield.

GDP (1991) $1.7 bn, per capita $400

History Pre-colonially a collection of small, warring principalities, including the Fon Kingdom of Dahomey (founded 17th-c). Portuguese colonial activities centred on slave trade; subjugated by French, becoming the

French Protectorate of Dahomey in 1892. Territory within French West Africa from 1904; independent from 1960. Marxist-Leninist regime gained power in 1972; name changed from Dahomey to the People's Republic of Benin in 1975. Marxism-Leninism abandoned in 1989, and a new multi-party constitution approved in 1990; changed name to Republic of Benin in 1990; multi-party elections held in 1991. President elected for five-year term, and a National Assembly.

Head of State
1990–1   Ahmed Kerekou
1991–   Nicéphore Soglo

Head of Government
1990–1   Nicéphore Soglo

BERMUDA >> UNITED KINGDOM

BHUTAN

Local name Druk-yul

Timezone GMT + 5.5

Area 46 600 km²/18 000 sq mi

Population total (1992e) 1 511 000

Status Kingdom

Capital Thimphu

Languages Dzongkha (official) (60%), Nepalese (25%), English

Ethnic groups Bhote (60%), Gurung (15%), Assamese (13%)

Religions Lamaistic Buddhist (75%), Hindu (20%), Muslim (5%)

Physical features High peaks of E Himalayas in the N, over 7 000m/23 000 ft; forested mountain ridges with fertile valleys descend to low foothills in the S; rivers include Wong Chu, Manas. Permanent snowfields in the mountains; sub-tropical forest in S.

Climate Affected by altitude. Snowcapped in glaciated N. Average monthly temperatures 4°C (Jan), 17°C (Jul); torrential rain common, average 1 000 mm/40 in (C valleys) and 5 000 mm/200 in (S).

Currency 1 Ngultrum (Nu) = 100 chetrum

Economy Largely based on agriculture, mainly rice, wheat, maize, mountain barley, potatoes, vegetables, fruit (especially oranges); also timber (large area of plantation forest).

GDP (1989) $273 mn, per capita $199

History British involvement since treaty of 1774 with the East India Company; S part of the country annexed in 1865; Anglo-Bhutanese Treaty signed, in which Britain agreed not to interfere in internal affairs of Bhutan in 1910; similar treaty (Indo-Bhutan Treaty of Friendship) signed with India in 1949. Governed by a maharajah from 1907; he is now addressed as King of Bhutan. National Assembly (*Tsogdu*) established in 1953; constitutional monarchy with power shared between the King, the Council of Ministers, the National Assembly, and the monastic head of the kingdom's Buddhist priesthood.

Head of State/Government (Monarch)
1972–   Jigme Singye Wangchuk

BOLIVIA

Local name Bolivia

Timezone GMT – 4

Area 1 098 580 km²/424 052 sq mi

Population total (1991e) 7 356 000

Status Republic

Date of independence 1825

Capital La Paz (administrative), Sucre (legal)

Languages Spanish, Quechua, Aymará (all used officially)

Ethnic groups Mestizo (30%), Quechua (30%), Aymará (25%)

Religions Roman Catholic (95%), Baha'i (3%)

Physical features Landlocked country, bounded W by the Cordillera Occidental of the Andes, rising to 6 542 m/21 463 ft at Sajama. Separated from the Cordillera Real to the E by the flat, 400 km/250 mi-long Altiplano plateau, 3 600 m/11 800 ft. Major lakes, Titicaca and Poopó.

Climate Varies with altitude, ranging from consistently warm (26°C) and damp conditions (1 800 mm/71 in of rainfall per year) in NE rainforests of Amazon Basin, to drought conditions in S; over 500 m/16 000 ft conditions become sub-polar.

Currency 1 Boliviano (Bs) = 100 centavos

Economy Dependent on minerals for foreign exchange; silver largely exhausted, but replaced by tin (a fifth of world supply); oil- and natural-gas pipelines to Argentina and Chile; illegally-produced cocaine.

GDP (1990) $4.8 bn, per capita $690

History Part of Inca Empire, conquered by Spanish in 16th-c. Independence after war of liberation in 1825;

much territory lost after wars with neighbouring countries. Several changes of government and military coups during 1964–82; returned to civilian rule in 1982. Governed by a bicameral Congress and an elected President and a Cabinet.

Head of State/Government
1982–5	Hernán Siles Suazo
1985–9	Victor Paz Estenssoro
1989–93	Jaime Paz Zamora
1993–	Gonzalo Sanchez de Lozada

Human geography

BOSNIA–HERZEGOVINA

Local name Bosnia i Hercegovina

Timezone GMT + 2

Area 51 129 km²/19 736 sq mi

Population total (1991) 4 364 574

Status Republic

Date of independence 1992

Capital Sarajevo

Language Serbo-Croatian

Ethnic groups (Pre-civil war) Slav (44%), Serbian (31%), Croatian (17%)

Religions Muslim (Sunni), Serbian Orthodox, Roman Catholic

Physical features Mountainous region in the Balkan peninsula, noted for its stone gorges, lakes, rivers, mineral springs; reaches heights of 1 800 m/6 000 ft above sea level. Principal rivers are Bosna, Una, Drina, Neretva, Sava. In the SW lies the dry, limestone plateau (karst).

Climate Ranges from Mediterranean to mildly continental; sirocco wind brings rain from SW; strong NE wind (*bora*) affects coastal area in winter.

Currency 1 Dinar (D, Dn) = 100 paras

Economy Highly industrialized, particularly iron and steel; large cellulose factory at Banja Luka; forestry strong in Bosnia. Inflation rate high; war (1992–3) disrupted all economic activity.

GDP Not available

History Annexed by Austria in 1908; Serbian opposition to the annexation led to the murder of Archduke Francis Ferdinand and World War 1. Ceded to Yugoslavia in 1918. Declaration of sovereignty in 1991; Bosnian Serbs proclaimed three autonomous regions (Bosanska Krajina, Romanija, and Northern Bosnia) in 1991. Declaration of

independence in 1992 led to ongoing military conflict between formerly integrated communities of Bosnians, Croats, and Serbs; UN peace-keeping forces deployed, and air-exclusion ('no-fly') zone imposed in 1992.

Head of State
1992– Alija Izetbegovic

Head of Government
1992 Jure Pelivan
1992–3 Mile Akmadzic
1993– Haris Silajdzic

BOTSWANA

Local name Botswana

Timezone GMT + 2

Area 581 730 km²/224 711 sq mi

Population total (1991e) 1 347 000

Status Independent republic within the Commonwealth

Date of independence 1966

Capital Gaborone

Languages English (official), Tswana

Ethnic groups Tswana (75%), Shona (12%), San (Bushmen) (3%), Khoikhoin (Hottentot) (3%), Ndebele (1%)

Religions Traditional beliefs (49%), Protestant (29%), African Christian (12%), Roman Catholic (9%)

Physical features Landlocked S African republic. Undulating, sand-filled plateau, part of the S African

Plateau; mean elevation c.1 000 m/3 300 ft. The N–S plateau divides country into two regions: hilly grasslands (velt) to E, and Okavango Swamps to W. Most of the population lives in fertile, hilly E. SE terrain hilly, 1 402 m/ 4 600 ft; dry scrubland, savannah, and the Kalahari Desert in W; salt lakes in N.

Climate Largely sub-tropical; rainfall in N and E almost totally in summer (Oct–Apr). Average annual temperature 26°C (Jan), 13°C (Jul) in Gaborone; average annual rainfall 450 mm/17.7 in.

Currency 1 Pula (P, Pu) = 100 thebes

Economy Mainly subsistence farming, especially livestock; continual problems of drought and disease. Some crops, especially sorghum. Main minerals, nickel, diamonds (jointly mined by the government and De Beers Consolidated Mines of South Africa), cobalt. Tourism, especially wildlife observation. Central Kalahari Game

Reserve (54 388 km²/21 000 sq mi) attracts tourists. Principal trading partners, members of South African Customs Union.

GDP (1990) $3.1 bn, per capita $2 500

History San (Bushmen) were the earliest inhabitants, followed by Sotho peoples who migrated to Botswana c.1600. Explored by Europeans in 1801; visited by missionaries during 19th-c; London Missionary Society established a mission on the Kuruman R in 1813; Ndebele raided Botswana; Boers arrived in 1835; gold was discovered in 1867. Under British protection from 1885; S became a Crown Colony, then part of Cape Colony in 1895; N became the Bechuanaland Protectorate. Self-government from 1964; independence and change of name to Botswana in 1966. Governed by a legislative National Assembly, a President, and a Cabinet; House of Chiefs considers chieftaincy matters but has no right of veto.

Head of State/Government
1980–   Quett K J Masire

BRAZIL

Local name Brasil

Timezone GMT −2 (Atlantic Islands); GMT −3 (E); GMT −4 (mid-W); GMT −5 (extreme W)

Area 8 511 965 km²/3 285 618 sq mi

Population total (1992e) 151 381 000

Status Republic

Date of independence 1822

Capital Brasília

Language Portuguese (official)

Ethnic groups White (55%), mixed (38%), Black (6%)

Religions Roman Catholic (89%), Protestant, Spiritualist

Physical features Located in E and C South America. Low-lying Amazon basin in the N; where forest canopy cleared, soils susceptible to erosion. Brazilian plateau in the C and S, average height 600–900 m/2 000–3 000 ft; Guiana Highlands (S) contain Brazil's highest peak, Pico da Neblina, 3 014 m/9 888 ft. Eight river systems, notably Amazon (N), São Francisco (C), Paraguay, Paraná, and Uruguay (S). 30% of population concentrated on a thin coastal strip on the Atlantic, c.100 km/325 mi wide.

Climate Almost entirely tropical, equator passing through the N region, and Tropic of Capricorn through the SE. Amazon basin, annual rainfall 1 500–2 000 mm/60–80 in; no dry season; average midday temperatures 27–32°C. Dry region in the NE, susceptible to long droughts. Hot, tropical climate on narrow coastal strip,

with rainfall varying greatly N–S. S states have a seasonal temperate climate.

Currency 1 Cruzeiro (Cr$) = 100 centavos

Economy One of the world's largest farming countries, agriculture employing 35% of population; world's largest exporter of coffee, second largest exporter of

Brazil (continued)

cocoa and soya beans. Iron-ore reserves (possibly world's largest). Timber reserves, the third largest in the world; but continuing destruction of the Amazon rainforest is causing much concern; road network being extended through the Amazon rainforest.

GDP (1990) $388 bn, per capita $2540

History Claimed for the Portuguese by Pedro Alvares Cabral in 1500, first settlement at Salvador da Bahia. King of Portugal moved seat of government to Brazil in 1808; his son, Dom Pedro, declared himself emperor in 1818; independence established in 1822; Dom Pedro forced to abdicate in 1831 and was succeeded by his 14-year-old son, Dom Pedro II in 1840. Abolition of slavery in 1888, persuaded former slave-owners in declining sugar-plantation areas to join Republican opposition to the king, who was overthrown in the coup of 1889. Ruled by dictator, Getúlio Vargas, 1930–45; Vargas deposed by military, and liberal republic restored in 1946; he was returned to office in 1950, but committed suicide in 1954. Capital moved from Rio de Janeiro to Brasília in 1960; another coup in 1964 led to a military-backed presidential regime. President da Costa e Silva resigned and military junta took control in 1969. New elections in 1985. new constitution approved, transferring power from the President to the Congress in 1988; bicameral National Congress.

Head of State/Government
1985–90   José Sarney
1990–2   Fernando Collor de Mello
1992–   Itamar Franco *Interim*

BRITISH ANTARCTIC TERRITORY >> UNITED KINGDOM

BRITISH INDIAN OCEAN TERRITORY >> UNITED KINGDOM

BRITISH VIRGIN ISLANDS >> UNITED KINGDOM

BRUNEI

Local name Negara Brunei Darussalam

Timezone GMT + 8

Area 5765 km²/2225 sq mi

Population total (1992e) 268000

Status Independent state

Date of independece 1984

Capital Bandar Seri Begawan

Languages Malay (official), English

Ethnic groups Malay (65%), Chinese (20%)

Religions Muslim (Sunni 65%), Buddhist (12%), Christian (9%)

Physical features Swampy coastal plain; equatorial rainforest covers 75% of land area. Rivers include Belait, Tutong Brunei. Mountainous tract on Sarawak border, average height 500 m/1640 ft.

Climate Tropical; high temperatures and humidity and no marked seasons. Average daily temperature 24–30°C; average annual rainfall 2540 mm/100 in on coast, doubling in the interior.

Currency 1 Brunei Dollar (Br$) = 100 sen

Economy Largely dependent on oil (discovered 1929) and gas resources.

GDP (1989) $3.1 bn, per capita $9600

History Formerly a powerful Muslim sultanate, with dominion over all of Borneo, its neighbouring islands, and parts of the Philippines by early 16th-c. Under British protection from 1888. Occupied by Japanese in 1941; liberated and reverted to former status as a British residency in 1945; internal self-government in 1971 and full independence in 1984. A constitutional monarchy with the Sultan as Head of State, who presides over a Council of Cabinet Ministers, a Religious Council, and a Privy Council.

□ *international airport*

Head of State/Government (Sultan)
1967–   Muda Hassanal Bolkiah Mu'izzadin Waddaulah

Human geography

BULGARIA

Local name Bǎlgarija

Timezone GMT + 2

Area 110 912 km²/42 812 sq mi

Population total (1992e) 8 990 000

Status Republic

Date of independence 1908

Capital Sofia

Languages Bulgarian (official), Turkish

Ethnic groups Bulgarian (85%), Turkish (9%)

Religions Bulgarian Orthodox (85%), Muslim (13%)

Physical features Traversed W–E by the Balkan Mts, averaging 2000 m/6 500 ft; in the SW, Rhodope Mts, rising to 3000 m/9 600 ft. Rivers include Maritsa, Iskur, Danube.

Climate Continental climate, with hot summers, cold winters. Average annual temperatures −2°C (Jan), 21°C (Jul); average annual rainfall 635 mm/25 in.

Currency 1 Lev (Lv) = 100 stotinki

Economy Mainly agricultural produce; coal, iron ore; offshore oil (Black Sea), natural gas; tourism; tobacco, wine exports.

GNP (1990) $47.3 bn, per capita $5 300

History Bulgars crossed the Danube in the 7th-c. Their empire continually at war with Byzantines until destroyed by Turks in the 14th-c; remained under Turkish rule during 1396–1878. Full independence in 1908; became a kingdom, 1908–46. Aligned with Germany in both World Wars. Occupied by USSR in 1944; Socialist People's Republic founded in 1946. Unicameral National Assembly established in 1971. Proclaimed Republic of Bulgaria in 1990; new constitution in 1991, with a directly elected President, and a 250-member National Assembly.

200km / 100mi · international airport

Head of State
1989–90	Petar Mladenov
1990–	Zhelyu Zhelev

Head of Government
1990–1	Dimitar Popov
1991–2	Filip Dimitrov
1992–	Lyuben Berov

BURKINA FASO

Local name Burkina Faso

Timezone GMT

Area 274 200 km²/105 870 sq mi

Population total (1992e) 8 776 000

Status Republic

Date of independence 1960

Capital Ouagadougou

Languages French (official), with Moré, Mossi, Mande, Fulani, Lobi, and Bobo also spoken

Ethnic groups Mossi (48%), over 50 other groups

Religions Traditional beliefs (45%), Muslim (43%), Christian (12%)

Physical features Landlocked republic in W Africa. Low-lying plateau, falling away to the S; tributaries of the

□ international airport

Human geography (side tab)

Burundi

Burkina Faso (continued)

Volta and Niger unnavigable in dry season; wooded savannahs in S; semi-desert in N.

Climate Tropical. Average annual rainfall 894 mm/35 in; dry season (Dec–May), rainy season (Jun–Oct); average annual temperature 24°C (Jan), 28°C (Jul) in Ouagadougou. Violent storms (Aug); subject to drought conditions.

Currency 1 CFA Franc (CFAFr) = 100 centimes

Economy Based on agriculture, largely at subsistence level; millet, corn, rice, livestock, peanuts, sugar cane, cotton.

GDP (1989) $1.7 bn, per capita $205

History Mossi empire in 18th–19th-c; Upper Volta created by French in 1919; abolished in 1932, with most land joined to Ivory Coast. Original borders reconstituted in 1947; autonomy within French community in 1958; independence in 1960, with several military coups since. Changed name from Upper Volta to Burkina Faso ('land of upright men') in 1984. End of military rule in 1991, after a draft constitution was adopted by national referendum; governed by a President elected on a seven-year mandate, and a 107-member National Assembly.

Head of State
1984–7   Thomas Sankara *Chairman*
1987–   Blaise Compaoré

Head of Government
1992–   Youssouf Ouedraogo

BURMA >> MYANMAR

BURUNDI

Local name Burundi

Timezone GMT + 2

Area 27 834 km²/10 744 sq mi

Population total (1990e) 5 472 000

Status Republic

Date of independence 1962

Capital Bujumbura

Languages French and Kirundi (official), Swahili

Ethnic groups Hutu (82%), Tutsi (14%), Twa Pygmy (1%)

Religions Roman Catholic (62%), traditional beliefs (32%)

Physical features Located in C Africa. Lies across Nile–Congo watershed; interior plateau, c.1 500 m/5 000 ft; highest point, Mt Karonje 2 685 m/8 809 ft. River Ruzizi forms part of NW frontier with Zaïre and links Lake Kiki in Rwanda, with Lake Tanganyika in S and E; river Maragarazi valley in E.

Climate Equatorial. Moderately wet; dry season (Jun–Sep). Average annual temperature 23°C; average annual rainfall at Bujumbura, 850 mm/33.5 in.

Currency 1 Burundi Franc (BuFr, FBu) = 100 centimes

Economy Mainly agriculture; cash crops include coffee, cotton, tea; light consumer goods, shoes, blankets; reserves of rare-earth metals.

GDP (1989) $1.2 bn, per capita $220

History Ruled by the Tutsi kingdom, 16th-c. Occupied by Germany in 1890, and included in German East Africa, 1890. League of Nations mandated territory, administered by Belgians in 1919. Joined with Rwanda to become the UN Trust Territory of Ruanda-Urundi in 1946. Independent from 1962; full republic following the overthrow of the monarchy from 1966. Civil war, 1972; military coup, 1976. New constitution provided a National Assembly, 1981; Assembly dissolved and constitution suspended after 1987 coup; Military Council for National Salvation disbanded in 1990; new constitution in 1992.

☐ *international airport*

Head of State
1987–93   Pierre Buyoya *Military Junta*
1993   Melchior Ndadye
1994   Cyprien Ntaryamina
1994–   Sylvestre Ntibantunganya *Interim*

Head of Government
1988–93   Adrien Sibomana
1993–94   Sylvie Kinigi
1994–   Anatole Kanyerkiko *Acting*

Human geography

CAMBODIA

Local name Cambodia

Timezone GMT + 7

Area 181 035 km²/69 879 sq mi

Population total (1992e) 8 974 000

Status Republic

Date of independence 1953

Capital Phnom Penh

Languages Khmer (official), French

Ethnic groups Khmer (93%), Chinese (3%), Cham (2%)

Religions Theravada Buddhist (88%), Muslim (2%)

Physical features Republic of S Indo-China, SE Asia. Crossed E by floodplain of Mekong R; Cardamom mountain range 160 km/100 mi across Thailand border, rising to 1 813 m/5 948 ft at Phnom Aural; Tonle Sap (Greek Lake) in NW.

Climate Tropical monsoon climate, with a wet season (May–Sep). High temperatures in lowland region throughout the year; average annual temperature 21°C (Jan), 29°C (Jul); average annual rainfall 5 000 mm/71 in (SW), 1 300 mm/51 in (interior lowlands).

Currency 1 Riel (CRl) = 100 sen

Economy Most of population employed in subsistence agriculture, rice and corn; industrial development disrupted by the civil war.

GDP (1989) $890 mn, per capita $130

History Originally part of Fou-Nan Kingdom, then part of the Khmer Empire, 7th-c. In dispute with Vietnamese and Thais from 15th-c. French Protectorate, 1863; part of Indo-China, 1887. Independence in 1953. Prince Sihanouk deposed and Khmer Republic formed in 1970; fighting throughout the country involved troops from N and S Vietnam and the USA. Surrender of Phnom Penh to the Khmer Rouge, and country renamed Kampuchea, 1975; attempt to reform economy on cooperative lines by Pol Pot (1975–8) caused the deaths of an estimated 3 million people. Further fighting 1977–8; Phnom Penh captured by the Vietnamese, causing Khmer Rouge to flee, in 1979. 1981 constitution established a Council of State and a Council of Ministers; name of Cambodia restored, 1989; Vietnamese troops completed withdrawal, 1989. UN peace plan agreed, with ceasefire and return of Sihanouk as Head of State in 1991; administrative power currently held by State of Cambodia (SOC) government; free elections held in September 1993.

Head of State

1975–6	Prince Norodom Sihanouk
1976–81	Khieu Samphan
1981–91	Heng Samrin
1991–	Prince Norodom Sihanouk

Head of Government

1976–9	Pol Pot
1979–81	Khieu Samphan
1981–5	Chan Si
1985–	Hun Sen

CAMEROON

Local name Cameroun

Timezone GMT + 1

Area 475 439 km²/183 519 sq mi

Population total (1992e) 12 700 000

Status Republic

Date of independence 1960

Capital Yaoundé

Languages French and English (official); 24 major African languages including Fang, Bamileke, Luanda, Fulani, Tika, Maka

Ethnic groups Highlanders (31%), Equatorial Bantu (19%), Kirdi (11%), Fulani (10%)

Religions Christian (40%), traditional beliefs (39%), Muslim (21%)

Physical features Located in W Africa. Equatorial forest, with low coastal plain. C plateau 1 300 m/4 200 ft.

Human geography

Canada

Cameroon (continued)

W forested and mountainous; Mt Cameroon, 4 070 m/ 13 353 ft (active volcano and the highest peak in W Africa). Low savannah, semi-desert towards L Chad; rivers include Sanaga and Dja.

Climate Rain all year in equatorial S; daily temperature in Yaoundé 27–30°C; average annual rainfall 4 030 mm/159 in.

Currency 1 CFA Franc (CFAFr) = 100 centimes

Economy Agriculture (employs c.80% of workforce); world's fifth largest producer of cocoa; tourism, especially to national parks.

GDP (1991) $11.6 bn, per capita $1 010

History First explored by Portuguese navigator Fernando Po; later by traders from Spain, Netherlands, Britain. German protectorate of Kamerun from 1884. Divided into French and British Cameroon in 1919; confirmed by League of Nations mandate in 1922; UN trusteeships, 1946. French Cameroon independent as Republic of Cameroon in 1960: N sector of British Cameroon voted to become part of Nigeria, S sector part of Cameroon; became Federal Republic of Cameroon, with separate parliaments, 1961. Federal system abolished in 1972, and name changed to United Republic of Cameroon. Changed name to the Republic of Cameroon in 1984. Legislation adopted for a multi-party system in 1990; governed by a President, an executive Prime Minister, a Cabinet, and a National Assembly.

Head of State
1982–   Paul Biya

Head of Government
1991–2   Sadou Hayatou
1992–   Simon Achidi Achu

CANADA

Local name Canada

Timezone GMT W – 9, to E – 3

Area 9 971 500 km²/3 848 900 sq mi

Population total (1992e) 27 400 000

Status Independent nation within the Commonwealth

Date of independence 1867 (Dominion of Canada)

Capital Ottawa

Languages English and French (official)

Ethnic groups British origin (45%), French origin (29%), other European, Indian, and Inuit (23%)

Religions Roman Catholic (49%), United Church (18%), Anglican (12%)

Physical features Dominated in the NE by the Canadian Shield. Flat prairie country S and W of the Shield, stretching to the Western Cordillera, which includes the Rocky, Cassiar, and Mackenzie Mts. Coast Mts flank a rugged, heavily indented coastline; Mt Logan in the Yukon, 5 950 m/19 521 ft, is the highest peak in Canada. Major rivers; the Mackenzie (W), and St Lawrence (E).

Great Bear, 31 330 km²/11 030 sq mi, and Great Slave, 28 570 km²/11 030 sq mi, are lakes in NW Territories.

Climate N coast permanently ice-bound or obstructed by ice floes, but for Hudson Bay (frozen c.9 months each year). Mild winters and warm summers on Pacific coast and around Vancouver Island. Average annual rainfall 145 mm/57 in.

Currency 1 Canadian Dollar (C$, Can$) = 100 cents

Economy Traditionally based on natural resources and agriculture: world's second largest exporter of wheat; world's largest producer of asbestos, zinc, silver, nickel; second largest producer of potash, gypsum, molybdenum, sulphur. Hydroelectricity, oil (especially Alberta), natural gas; major industrial development in recent decades.

GDP (1990) $516 bn, per capita $19 500

History Evidence of Viking settlement c.1000. Newfoundland claimed for England in 1583; Champlain founded Québec in 1608. Hudson's Bay Company founded in 1670; conflict between British and French in late 17th-c; Britain gained large areas from Treaty of

Province and territory capitals shown in bold type ☐ international airport

2000km

1000mi

Utrecht, 1713. After Seven Years' War, during which British General James Wolfe captured Québec from Louis Montcalm's forces in 1759, Treaty of Paris gave Britain almost all France's possessions in N America. Province of Québec created in 1774; migration of loyalists from USA after War of Independence led to division of Québec into Upper and Lower Canada. Reunited as Canada in 1841; Dominion of Canada created (1867) by confederation of Québec, Ontario, Nova Scotia, and New Brunswick; Rupert's Land and Northwest Territories bought from Hudson's Bay Company, 1869–70; joined by Manitoba (1870), British Columbia (1871), Prince Edward I (1873), Alberta and Saskatchewan (1905), and Newfoundland (1949). Recurring political tension in recent decades arising from French-Canadian separatist movement in Québec. Canada Act in 1982, gave Canada full responsibility for constitution; bicameral Federal Parliament includes Senate and a House of Commons; British monarch is Head of State, represented by a Governor-General.

Head of State

(British monarch represented by Governor-General)
1990–   Ramon John Hnatyshyn

CANARY ISLANDS >> SPAIN

Head of Government

1984–93	Brian Mulroney
1993	Kim Campbell
1993–	Jean Chrétien

>> Political leaders and rulers

Canadian provinces and territories

Name	Area		Capital
	km²	sq mi	
Alberta	661190	255285	Edmonton
British Columbia	947800	365945	Victoria
Manitoba	649950	250945	Winnipeg
New Brunswick	73440	28355	Fredericton
Newfoundland	405720	156648	St John's
Northwest Territories	3426320	1322902	Yellowknife
Nova Scotia	55490	21424	Halifax
Ontario	1068580	412578	Toronto
Prince Edward Island	5660	2185	Charlottetown
Québec	1540680	594856	Québec City
Saskatchewan	652380	251883	Regina
Yukon Territory	483450	186660	Whitehorse

CAPE VERDE

Local name Cabo Verde

Timezone GMT − 1

Area 4 033 km²/1 557 sq mi

Population total (1991e) 386 000

Status Island group

Date of independence 1975

Capital Praia (on São Tiago Island)

Languages Portuguese (official), Crioulo (Portuguese-based creole)

Ethnic groups Creole (mulatto) (60%), African (28%), European (2%)

Religion Roman Catholic (80%), others (20%)

Physical features Island group in the Atlantic Ocean off W Coast of Africa, c.500 km/310 mi W of Dakar, Senegal; Barlavento (windward) group in N, Sotaven to (leeward) group in S. Mostly mountainous islands of volcanic origin. Highest peak, Pico do Cano, 2 829 m/9 281 ft; active volcano on Fogo I. Fine sandy beaches on most islands.

Climate Arid climate; located at N limit of tropical rain belt, low and unreliable rainfall (Aug–Sep). Small temperature range throughout year; average annual temperature 23°C; average annual rainfall 250 mm/10 in.

Currency 1 Escudo (CVEsc) = 100 centavos

Economy Suffering because of drought; substantial emigration in early 1970s. C.70% of workforce are farmers occupying irrigated inland valleys; increase in fishing since 1975.

GDP (1989) $281 mn, per capita $760

CAYMAN ISLANDS >> UNITED KINGDOM

CENTRAL AFRICAN REPUBLIC

Local name République Centrafricaine

Timezone GMT + 1

Area 622 984 km²/240 535 sq mi

Population total (1990e) 3 039 000

Status Republic

Date of independence 1960

Capital Bangui

Languages French (official), Sangho

Ethnic groups Baya (34%), Banda (28%), Sara (10%), over 80 other groups

Religions Christian (50%), (Protestant 25%, Roman Catholic 25%), also Muslim and traditional beliefs

Physical features Located in C Africa. Plateau forming a watershed between Chad and Congo river basins. Massif des Bongos rises 1 400 m/4 593 ft in NW; granite

□ *international airport*

History Colonized by Portuguese in 15th-c, also used as a penal colony. Administered with Portuguese Guinea until 1879; overseas province of Portugal from 1951. Independence in 1975. Governed by a President, Council of Ministers, and People's National Assembly; multi-party elections held, 1991.

Head of State
1975–91   Aristides Pereira
1991–   Antonio Mascarenhas Monteiro

Head of Government
1975–91   Pedro Pires
1991–   Carlos Veiga

□ *international airport*

ranges of Mont Karre, 1 220 m/4 003 ft in W.

Climate Tropical; single rainy season in N (May–Sep); average annual rainfall 875–1 000 mm/34–9 in. More equatorial climate in S; rainfall 1 500–2 000 mm/60–80 in.

Currency 1 CFA Franc (CFAFr) = 100 centimes

Economy Agriculture employs c.85% of working population; also sawmilling, brewing, diamond splitting, leather and tobacco processing.

GDP (1990e) $1.3 bn, per capita $440

History Part of French Equatorial Africa (Ubangi Shari). Autonomous republic within the French community, 1958; independence in 1960. Coup deposed country's first President, David Dacko, in 1965; Jean-Bédel Bokassa declared himself emperor for life, and country's name changed to the Central African Empire, 1976. Bokassa

deposed and country reverted to a republic in 1979; military coup established Committee for National Recovery, 1981–5; Committee dissolved and National Assembly established, 1987. Movement toward multi-party democracy, 1991; elections scheduled for 1993.

Head of State

1960–6	David Dacko
1966–79	Jean-Bédel Bokassa (from 1977, Emperor Bokassa I)
1979–81	David Dacko
1981–93	André Kolingba
1993–	Ange-Felix Patasse

Head of Government

1991–2	Edouard Frank
1992–3	Thimothée Malendoma
1993	Enoch Derant Lakoue
1993	Jean-Luc Mandaba

CHAD

Local name Tchad

Timezone GMT + 1

Area 1 284 640 km²/495 871 sq mi

Population total (1990e) 5 678 000

Status Republic

Date of independence 1960

Capital N'Djamena

Languages Arabic and French (official), many local languages spoken

Ethnic groups Sara, Bagirmi, and Kreish (30%); Sudanic Arab (26%), Teda (17%), Masalit, Maba, Mimi (6%), over 200 groups

Religions Muslim (50%), Christian (Roman Catholic 21%, Protestant 12%), and local religions

Physical features Landlocked in C Africa; mostly arid, semi-desert plateau at edge of Sahara Desert; average altitude of 200–500 m/650–1 650 ft; Tibesti Mts (N) rise to 3 415 m/11 204 ft at Emi Koussi; rivers in S (Chari and Logne) flow NW to Lake Chad.

Climate Tropical, moderately wet in S (May–Oct); hot, arid N, almost rainless; C plain hot, dry, with brief rainy season (Jun–Sep).

Currency 1 CFA Franc (CFAFr) = 100 centimes

Economy Severely damaged in recent years by drought, locusts, and civil war. Export of cotton, kaolin, animal products. Salt mined around L Chad.

GDP (1989e) $1.1 bn, per capita $205

History Part of French Equatorial Africa, 1908; colonial status, 1920; independence in 1960. Libyan troops occupied the Aozou Strip in extreme N, 1973; fighting between Libyan-supported rebels and French-supported government until cease-fire agreed in 1987. New constitution established a National Assembly, 1989; replaced by a Provisional Council of the Republics, 1991. Chad and Libya presented their individual territorial claims to Aozou Strip, 1990; president Habré ousted by coup and

□ international airport

new constitution adopted, 1991. Progress towards a multi-party system and future presidential and general elections, 1992.

Head of State

| 1982–90 | Hissne Habré |
| 1990– | Idriss Déby Interim |

Head of Government

1991–2	Jean Alingue Bawoyeu
1992–3	Joseph Yodemane
1993	Fidèle Moungar
1993–	Delwa Kassire Koumakoye

CHANNEL ISLANDS >> UNITED KINGDOM

Chile

CHILE

Local name Chile

Timezone GMT −4

Area 756 626 km²/292 058 sq mi (excluding territory claimed in Antarctica)

Population total (1992e) 13 600 000

Status Republic

Date of independence 1818

Capital Santiago

Language Spanish (official)

Ethnic groups Mestizo (92%), Indian (6%), European (2%)

Religions Roman Catholic (89%), Protestant (10%), small Jewish and Muslim minority

Physical features Coastal Cordillera, Pampa Central, and the Chilean Andes are parallel regions running almost the entire length of the country; narrow coastal belt, backed by Andean mountain ridges rising in the NW to 6 880 m/22 572 ft at Ojos del Salado. Atacama Desert in far NW which is rich in minerals; arable land and forest in the S; S Andes still experiences volcanic activity. Main river, the Bío-Bío. Punta Arenas is located on the southern tip of Chile's mainland. Chilean possessions include a rock measuring 424 m/1 390 ft on Horn Island in the Wollaston group, and 1 250 000 km²/482 628 sq mi of Antarctic territory.

Climate Varied climate (spans 37° of latitude, with altitudes from Andean peaks to coastal plain). Extreme aridity in N Atacama Desert, temperatures averaging 20°C; cold, wet, and windy in far S; Mediterranean climate in C Chile, with warm wet winters and dry summers. Average temperature at Santiago 19°C (Jan), 8°C (Jul); average annual rainfall 375 mm/14.8 in.

Currency 1 Chilean Peso (Ch$) = 100 centavos

Economy Based on agriculture and mining. Wheat, corn, potatoes, sugar beet, fruit, livestock; fishing in N, timber in S. Copper, iron ore, nitrates, silver, gold, coal, molybdenum; oil and gas discovered in far S (1945); steel, wood pulp, cellulose, mineral processing.

GDP (1991) $32 bn, per capita $2 500

History Originally occupied by South American Indians. Arrival of Spanish in 16th-c; part of Viceroyalty of Peru; independence from Spain declared in 1810, with a provisional government set up in Santiago. Spain reasserted its authority in 1814; the patriot leader, Bernardo O'Higgins, escaped and returned, with the mil-

itary help of José de San Martín, to defeat the Spanish at Chacabuco, 1817; O'Higgins became the first president and independence was declared in 1818. Border disputes with Bolivia, Peru, and Argentina brought Chilean victory in War of the Pacific, 1879–84. Economic unrest in late 1920s led to military dictatorship under Carlos Ibáñez until 1931. Marxist coalition government of Salvador Allende Gossens ousted in 1973, and replaced by military junta under Augusto Pinochet Ugarte, which banned all political activity. Constitution providing for eventual return to democracy came into effect in 1981; plebiscite held in 1988 resulted in a defeat for Pinochet's candidacy as President beyond 1990, and limited political reforms. National Congress restored, comprising a Senate and a Chamber of Deputies in 1990.

Head of State/Government
1973–90 Augusto Pinochet Ugarte
1990–4 Patricio Aylwin Azócar
1994– Eduardo Frei Ruíz-Tagle

Human geography

1000km / 500mi □ international airport

CHINA

Local name Zhongguo

Timezone GMT + 8

Area 9 597 000 km²/3 704 000 sq mi (also claims island of Taiwan)

Population total (1990) 1 133 682 501

Status People's republic

Capital Beijing (Peking)

Languages Standard Chinese (Putonghua) or Mandarin, also Yue (Cantonese), Wu, Minbei, Minnan, Xiang, Gan and Hakka

Ethnic groups Han Chinese (93%), over 50 minorities, including Chuang, Manchu, Hui, Miao, Uighur, Hani, Kazakh, Tai and Yao

Religions Officially atheist; widespread Confucianism and Taoism (20%), Buddhism (6%)

Physical features Over two-thirds of country are upland hills, mountains, and plateaux. Highest mountains in the W, where the Tibetan plateau rises to average altitude of 4 000 m/13 000 ft; Mt Everest rises to 8 848 m/29 028 ft on the Nepal–Tibet border. Land descends to desert/semidesert of Sinkiang and Inner Mongolia (NE); broad and fertile plains of Manchuria (NE); further E and S, Sichuan basin, drained by Yangtze R (5 980 km/3 720 mi in length); Huang He (Yellow) R runs for 4 840 km/3 010 mi. Heavily populated S plains and E coast, with rich, fertile soils.

Climate Varied, with seven zones. (1) NE China: cold winters, with strong N winds, warm and humid summers, unreliable rainfall. (2) C China: warm and humid summers, sometimes typhoons or tropical cyclones on coast. (3) S China: partly within tropics; wettest area in summer, frequent typhoons. (4) SW China: summer temperatures moderated by altitude, winters mild with little rain. (5) Xizang autonomous region: high plateau surrounded by mountains; winters severe with frequent light snow and hard frost. (6) Xinjiang and W interior: arid desert climate, cold winters; rainfall well distributed throughout year. (7) Inner Mongolia: extreme continental climate; cold winters, warm summers.

Currency 1 Renminbi Yuan (RMBY, $, Y) = 10 jiao = 100 fen

Economy Since 1949, economy largely based on heavy industry; more recently, light industries. Special economic zones set up to attract foreign investment. Rich mineral deposits; largest oil-producing country in Far East. Major subsistence crops include rice, grain, beans, potatoes, tea, sugar, cotton.

China (continued)

GDP (1989e) $413 bn, per capita $370

History Chinese civilization believed to date from the Xia dynasty (2200–1799 BC); Qin dynasty (221–207 BC) unified warring states and provided system of centralized control. Expansion W during Western and Eastern Han dynasties (206 BC–AD 220), and Buddhism introduced from India. Split into Three Kingdoms (Wei, Shu, Wu, 220–65). From 4th-c, series of N dynasties set up by invaders, with several dynasties in S; gradually reunited during the Sui (581–618) and Tang (618–907) dynasties. Partition into the Five Dynasties (907–60). Song (Sung) dynasty (960–1279), remembered for literature, philosophy, inventions. Kublai Khan established Mongol Yuan dynasty which ruled China 1279–1368; visits by Europeans, such as Marco Polo, 13th–14th-c. Ming dynasty (1368–1644) increased contacts with West. Overthrown by Manchus, who ruled China during 1644–1911 under the Qing dynasty, and enlarged empire to include Manchuria, Mongolia, Tibet, Taiwan. Opposition to foreign imports led to Opium Wars 1839–42, 1858–60; Sino-Japanese War, 1895; Boxer Rising, 1900. Republic of China founded by Sun Yatsen in 1912. Unification under Jiang Jieshi (Chiang Kai-shek), who made Nanjing capital in 1928. Conflict between Nationalists and Communists led to the Long March, 1934–5, with Communists moving to NW China under Mao Zedong (Mao Tse-tung). Nationalist defeat by Mao and withdrawal to Taiwan in 1949; People's Republic of China proclaimed, 1949, with capital at Beijing. First Five-Year Plan (1953–7) period of nationalization and collectivization. Great Leap Forward, 1958–9, emphasized local authority and establishment of rural communes; Cultural Revolution initiated by Mao Zedong, 1966. Many policies reversed after Mao's death in 1976, and drive towards rapid industrialization and wider trade relations with West. After 1980, Deng Xiaoping became the dominant figure within the ruling Chinese Communist Party; he retired from his last official post in 1990, but still remains the most influential figure in Chinese politics. Governed by elected National People's Congress who elect a State Council.

Head of State
1988–93   Yang Shangkun
1993–   Jiang Zeuin

Head of Government
1987–   Li Peng

COLOMBIA

Local name Colombia

Timezone GMT – 5

Area 1 140 105 km²/440 080 sq mi

Population total (1992e) 33 392 000

Status Republic

Date of independence 1819

Capital Bogotá

Language Spanish (official)

Ethnic groups Mestizo (58%), Amerindian (10%), European descent (20%)

Religion Roman Catholic (95%), other (5%)

Physical features Located in NW South America, includes several island possessions (Providencia, San Andrés and Mapelo). Andes run N–S, dividing narrow coastal plains from forested lowlands of Amazon basin; Cordillera Central rises 5000 m/16 000 ft to the high peak of Nev. de Huila, 5 750 m/18 865 ft. Rivers include Vaupés, Magdalena, Cauca and Guaviare.

Climate Hot, humid coastal plains (NW and W); annual rainfall over 2 500 mm/100 in; drier period on Caribbean coast (Dec–Apr); hot, humid tropical lowlands in E.

Currency 1 Colombian Peso (Col$) = 100 centavos

Economy Virtually self-sufficient in food; major crops include coffee, bananas, cotton. Leather; gold, silver, emeralds, coal, oil. Widespread illegal cocaine trafficking.

GDP (1990e) $43 bn, per capita $1 300

History Spanish occupation from early 16th-c, displacing Amerindian peoples. Governed by Spain within Viceroyalty of Peru, later Viceroyalty of New Granada. Independence in 1819, after the campaigns of Simón Bolívar. Union with Ecuador, Venezuela, and Panama as

Gran Colombia, 1821–30. Civil war in 1950s; considerable political unrest in 1980s. New constitution in 1991; governed by a President, bicameral Congress and Cabinet.

Head of State/Government
1978–82   Julio César Turbay Ayala
1982–6   Belisario Betancur
1986–90   Virgilio Barco Vargas
1990–   César Gaviria Trujillo

COMMONWEALTH OF INDEPENDENT STATES, THE (CIS)

A multilateral group of independent states which were once members of the USSR. The CIS was formed in Dec 1991; membership included all the states that once comprised the USSR, with the exceptions of the Baltic States (Latvia, Lithuania and Estonia), and Georgia; and the partial exceptions of Azerbaijan and Moldova which have observer status only. Georgia joined in December 1993.

CIS >> ARMENIA, BELARUS, KAZAKHSTAN, KYRGYZSTAN, RUSSIA, TAJIKISTAN, TURKMENISTAN, UKRAINE, UZBEKISTAN

3000km
1500mi

Human geography

COMOROS

Local name Comores

Timezone GMT + 3

Area 1 862 km²/719 sq mi

Population total (1990) 503 000

Status Federal republic

Date of independence 1975

Capital Moroni (on Njazidja Island)

Languages Arabic, French (official), Kiswahili

Ethnic groups Comorian (97%), Makua (2%)

Religions Sunni Muslim (86%), Roman Catholic (14%)

Physical features Located in the Mozambique Channel between mainland Africa and Madagascar. A group of three volcanic islands: Njazidja (Grande Comore), Nzwani (Anjouan), and Mwali (Mohéli). Largest island, Njazidja, with an active volcano, Mt Kartala, 2 361 m/7 746 ft.

Climate Tropical; dry season (May–Oct), hot, humid season (Nov–Apr). Average temperatures, 20°C (Jul), 28°C (Nov).

Currency 1 Comorian Franc (CFr) = 100 centimes

Economy Largely agricultural economy: vanilla, copra, cacao, sisal, coffee, cloves, vegetable oils; perfume.

GDP (1990e) $245 mn, per capita $530

History Under French control, 1843–1912; French overseas territory, 1947. Internal political autonomy from 1961; unilateral independence declared in 1975. Mayotte, island in the archipelago, has remained under French rule. Established as a Federal Islamic Republic in 1978; a one-party state, governed by a President, a Council of Ministers, and a unicameral Federal Assembly.

Head of State/Government
1976–8   Ali Soilih
1978–89   Ahmed Abdallah Abderemane
1989–   Said Mohammed Djohar

Map >> MADAGASCAR

CONGO

Local name Congo

Timezone GMT + 1

Area 341 945 km²/132 000 sq mi

Population total (1990e) 2 271 000

Status Republic

Date of independence 1960

Capital Brazzaville

Language French (official), with local languages, including Kongo and Téké

Ethnic groups Kongo (45%), Sangha (15%), Téké (20%)

Religions Roman Catholic (54%), Protestant (25%), local traditional beliefs

Physical features Niari valley rises to 1 040 m/3 412 ft at Mont de la Lékéti. Mainly covered by dense grassland, mangrove, and tropical rainforest. Rivers include Sangha and Alima in N.

Climate Hot, humid equatorial climate; annual rainfall 1 250–1 750 mm/50–70 in, annual daily temperature 28–33°C in Brazzaville. Dry season (Jun–Sep).

Currency 1 CFA Franc (CFAFr) = 100 centimes

Economy Mainly agriculture and forestry; sugar cane, coffee, cocoa, palm oil, tobacco; oil, timber, diamonds; sugar-refining.

GDP (1989e) $2.26 bn, per capita $1 050

History Visited by Portuguese, 14th-c. Part of French Equatorial Africa, known as 'Middle Congo', 1908–58; independence as Republic of Congo in 1960. Military coup created first Marxist state in Africa, renamed People's Republic of the Congo in 1968. Congolese Labour Party (PCT), the single ruling party in Congo, renounced Marxism in 1990; transitional government formed in 1991, and country renamed the Republic of Congo. New constitution in 1992, recognized a multi-party system. Executive authority vested in the President who elects a Prime Minister and a Cabinet.

Head of State
1979–92   Denis Sassou-Nguesso
1992–   Pascal Lissouba

Head of Government
1991–2   André Milongo
1992   Stephane Bongho-Nouarra
1992–3   Claude Antoine Dacosta
1993–   Jacques-Joachim Yhombi-Opango

COOK ISLANDS >> NEW ZEALAND

CORSICA >> FRANCE

COSTA RICA

Local name Costa Rica

Timezone GMT – 6

Area 51 022 km²/19 694 sq mi

Population total (1992e) 3 160 000

Status Republic

Date of independence 1821

Capital San José

Language Spanish (official)

Ethnic groups European (87%), mestizo (7%), black/mulatto (3%), E Asian (mostly Chinese) (2%), Amerindian (1%)

Religions Roman Catholic (85%), Protestant (15%)

Physical features Second smallest republic in C America. Formed by series of volcanic ridges: Cordillera de Guanacaste (NW), Cordillera Central, and Cordillera de Talamanca; highest peak, Chirripó Grande, 3 819 m/12 529 ft. C plateau; swampy land near coast, rising to tropical forest.

Human geography

Climate Tropical. Small temperature range; abundant rainfall; dry season (Dec–May). Average annual temperature 26–8°C.

Currency 1 Costa Rican Colón (CR¢) = 100 céntimos

Economy Primarily agriculture, mainly coffee (especially in Meseta Central), bananas, sugar, cattle. Silver, bauxite; exploration for oil in collaboration with Mexico.

GDP (1990e) $5.5 bn, per capita $1 810

History Visited by Columbus, 1502; named Costa Rica ('rich coast') in the belief that vast gold treasures existed. Independence from Spain in 1821; member of Federation of Central America, 1824–39. New constitution in 1949, established Costa Rica as a democratic state. Governed by an executive President, a Legislative Assembly, and a Cabinet.

Head of State/Government

1986–90	Oscar Arias Sánchez
1990–4	Rafael Angel Calderón Fournier
1994–	José María Figueres

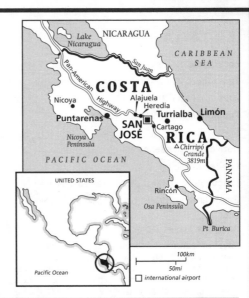

CÔTE D'IVOIRE

Local name Côte d'Ivoire

Timezone GMT

Area 322 462 km²/124 503 sq mi

Population total (1990e) 12 100 000

Status Republic

Date of independence 1960

Capital Yamoussoukro (formerly Abidjan)

Languages French (official), Akan, Kru

Ethnic groups Akan (41%), Kru (17%), Voltaic (16%), Malinke (15%), Southern Mande (10%)

Religions Traditional beliefs (65%), Muslim (23%), Christian (12%)

Physical features Sandy beaches and lagoons backed by broad forest-covered coastal plain; Mt Nimba massif in NW, 1 752 m /5 748 ft. Rivers include Comoé, Sassandra, Bandama.

Climate Tropical, varying with distance from coast. Average annual rainfall at Yamoussoukro 2 100 mm/ 83 in; average annual temperatures 25–7°C.

Currency 1 CFA Franc (CFAFr) = 100 centimes

Economy Largely based on agriculture (employs c.82% of the population): palm oil, rice, maize, ground nuts, bananas; world's largest cocoa producer, third largest coffee producer.

GDP (1989) $9.5 bn, per capita $820

History Explored by Portuguese, 15th-c. Declared a French protectorate in 1889; colony, 1893; territory within French West Africa, 1904. Independence in 1960. Constitution provides for a multi-party system, however opposition parties only allowed to function since 1990. Post of Prime Minister created in 1990; governed

by a National Assembly, an executive President, and a Council of Ministers.

Head of State

1960–93	Félix Houphouët-Boigny
1993–	Henri Bédié

Head of Government

1990–93	Alassane D Ouattara
1993–	Daniel Kablan Duncan

CROATIA

Local name Hrvatska

Timezone GMT + 2

Area 56 540 km²/21 825 sq mi

Population total (1992e) 4 600 000

Status Republic

Date of independence 1991

Capital Zagreb

Language Serbo-Croatian (with Roman alphabet)

Ethnic groups (1990) Croat (75%), Serb (12%), Slovenes (1%)

Religions Roman Catholic, Eastern Orthodox

Physical features Fertile Pannonian Plain in C and E ; mountainous, barren coastal region near Dinaric Alps; Adriatic coast to W. One third of country is forested. Main rivers: Drava, Danube, Sava. Coastal Velebit and Velika Kapela ranges reach heights of 2 200 m/7 200 ft; islands include Korčula, Lõsinj, Dugt Otok, Cres.

Climate Continental in Pannonian Basin: average temperatures 19°C (Jul), −1°C (Jan); average annual rainfall 750 mm/30 in. Mediterranean climate on Adriatic coast: average temperatures 24°C (Jul), 6°C (Jan).

Currency 1 Dinar = 100 paras

Economy Agriculture. Corn, oats, sugar-beet, potatoes, meat and dairy products. Tourism on Adriatic coast. Electrical engineering; metal-working; machinery manufacture; lumber; aluminium, textiles, petroleum refining, chemicals rubber. Natural resources include bauxite, coal, copper, iron. All economic activity adversely affected by war of independence.

GDP Not available

History Slavic Croat tribes (Chrobati, Hrvati) migrated to White Russia (now Ukraine) during 6th-c; converted to Christianity between 7th and 9th-c and adopted Roman alphabet. Frankish and Byzantine invaders were repelled, and Croat kingdom reached its peak during 11th-c; Lázló I of Hungary claimed Croatian throne in 1091. Turkish defeat of Hungary in 1526 placed Pannonian Croatia under Ottoman rule; the rest of Croatia elected Ferdinand of Austria as their king and fought Turkey. Croatia and Slovenia became part of Hungary until collapse of Austria-Hungary in 1918; formed the Kingdom of Serbs, Croats and Slovenes with Montenegro

□ international airport

and Serbia in 1918. Changed name to Yugoslavia in 1929; proclaimed an independent state during occupation by the Axis Powers, 1941–5; became a republic of Yugoslavia again in 1945. Nationalist upsurges during 1950s against Communist rule culminated in a bloody war with Serbian-dominated Yugoslav army in 1991; declaration of independence, 1991. Autonomy claimed by Serb-dominated Krajina area; UN peacekeeping forces deployed in 1992. Continued fighting between Croatian forces and Bosnian Serbs in the civil war in Bosnia-Herzegovina.

Head of State
1991–   Franjo Tudjman

Head of Government
1991–2   Franjo Greguric
1992–3   Hrvoje Sarinic
1993–   Nikica Valentic

CUBA

Local name Cuba

Timezone GMT − 5

Area 110 860 km²/42 792 sq mi

Population total (1990e) 10 603 000

Status Republic

Date of independence 1902

Capital Havana

Language Spanish (official)

Ethnic groups Mulatto (50%), Spanish (37%), African origin (11%)

Religions Roman Catholic (40%), Protestant (3%), Afro-Cuban syncretist (2%), non-religious (55%): Castro regime discourages religious practice

Human geography

Physical features Archipelago in the Caribbean Sea, comprising the island of Cuba, Isla de la Juventud, and c.1600 islets and cays. Main island of Cuba, 1250 km/ 777 mi. Three mountainous regions range E–W, the Oriental, including Cuba's highest peak, Pico Turquino, 2005 m/6578 ft, Central, and Occidental ranges. Longest river is Rio Cauto in E.

Climate Subtropical climate, warm and humid. Average annual temperature 25°C; dry season (Nov–Apr); mean annual rainfall, 1375 mm/54 in; hurricanes (Jun–Nov).

Currency 1 Cuban Peso (Cub$) = 100 centavos

Economy World's second largest sugar producer (accounting for 75% of export earnings); world's fifth largest producer of nickel; fish, coffee, tobacco, citrus fruits, rice.

GNP (1990e) $20.9 bn, per capita $2000

History Visited by Columbus in 1492; Spanish colony until 1898, following revolution under José Martí with support of USA. Independence in 1902. Struggle against dictatorship of General Batista led by Fidel Castro Ruz was finally successful in 1959, and a Communist state was established; invasion of Cuban exiles with US support was defeated at Bay of Pigs in 1961. US naval blockade, after Soviet installation of missile bases discovered in Cuba (Cuban Missile Crisis), 1962. Communist Party of Cuba established as the sole legal party in 1965. President of

the State Council is Head of State; State Council, appointed by National Assembly of People's Power.

Head of State/Government
1956–76   Osvaldo Dorticós Torrado
1976–   Fidel Castro Ruz

CYPRUS

Local names Kipros (Greek), Kibris (Turkish)

Timezone GMT + 3

Area 9251 km²/3571 sq mi

Population total (1990e) 568000

Status Republic

Date of independence 1960

Capital Nicosia

Languages Greek and Turkish (official), English

Ethnic groups Greek (78%), Turkish (18%), other (4%)

Religions Greek Orthodox (78%), Sunni Muslim (18%), other Christian (4%)

Physical features Third largest island in Mediterranean. Kyrenia Mts extend 150 km/90 mi along N coast, Mt Kyparissovouno, 1024 m/3360 ft. Forest-covered Troödos Mts in SW, rising to 1951 m/6401 ft at Mt Olympus. Fertile alluvial Mesaoria plain extends across island centre; SE plateau region slopes towards indented coastline, with several long, sandy beaches. Major rivers include the Pedios, Karyota, Kouris.

Climate Mediterranean, with hot, dry summers and warm, wet winters. Average annual rainfall ranges from 300–400 mm/12–16 in on the Mesaoria Plain to 1200 mm/ 47 in in the Troödos Mts. Mean daily temperatures in Nicosia 10°C (Jan), 28°C (Jul); temperatures range from 22°C on Troödos Mts, to 29°C on Central plain (Jul–Aug). Snow on higher land in winter.

Currency 1 Cyprus Pound (£C) = 100 cents

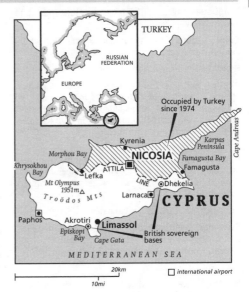

Economy Main exports include cement, clothing, footwear, citrus, potatoes, grapes, wine. Tourism also recovering (now accounting for c.15% of national income). Famagusta (chief port prior to 1974 Turkish invasion) now under Turkish occupation, and declared closed by Cyprus government. Turkish Cypriot economy heavily dependent on agriculture.

Cyprus (continued)

GDP (1990) $5.3 bn, per capita $7 585

History Recorded history of 4 000 years. Rulers included Greeks, Ptolemies, Persians, Romans, Byzantines, Arabs, Franks, Venetians, Turks (1571–1878), and British. British Crown Colony from 1925. Greek Cypriot demands for union with Greece (*enosis*) led to guerrilla warfare, under Grivas and Makarios, and four-year state of emergency, 1955–9. Independence in 1960, with Britain retaining sovereignty over bases at Akrotiri and Dhekelia. Greek–Turkish fighting throughout 1960s, with UN peacekeeping force sent in 1964; Greek Junta engineered coup d'état in 1972; Turkish invasion in 1974 led to occupation of over a third of the island. Island divided into two parts by the Attila Line, cutting through Nicosia where it is called the Green Line. Almost all Turks now live in N sector (37% of island); governed by a President (head of state), elected by the Greek community, and House of Representatives; Turkish members ceased to attend in 1983, when the Turkish community declared itself independent (as 'Turkish Republic of Northern Cyprus', with Rauf Denktas as president, recognized only by Turkey). UN peace proposals rejected in 1984; summit meeting between Kyprianou (Greek president of Cyprus) and Denktas failed, 1985. President Georgios Vassiliou renewed talks with Denktas in 1988; peace talks abandoned in 1989; new President, Glafkos Clirides in 1993.

Head of State/Government
1988–93   Georgios Vassiliou
1993–   Glafkos Clirides

CZECHOSLOVAKIA >> CZECH REPUBLIC; SLOVAK REPUBLIC

CZECH REPUBLIC

Local name Českà republika

Timezone GMT + 1

Area 78 864 km²/30 441 sq mi

Population total (1990e) 10 362 000

Status Republic

Date of independence 1993

Capital Prague

Languages Czech (official), with Hungarian and Slovak widely spoken

Ethnic groups Czech (94%), Slovak (4%), Hungarian, Polish, German, and Ukrainian minorities

Religions Roman Catholic, Protestant

Physical features Landlocked in C Europe. Bohemian Massif, average height, 900 m/2 953 ft, surrounds the Bohemian basin in W; Elbe-Moldau river system flows N into E Germany; fertile Danube plain in S Vltava valley of Moravia divides Czech from Slovak Republic. C.40% land is arable.

Climate Continental, with warm, humid summers and cold, dry winters. Average annual temperatures 2°C (Jan), 19°C (Jul) in Prague; average annual rainfall, 483 mm/19 in.

Currency 1 Koruna (Kcs) = 100 halér̆

Economy Steel production around Ostrava coalfields; machinery, iron, glass, chemicals, motor vehicles, cement; wheat, sugar beet, potatoes, rye, corn, barley.

GDP Not yet available

History Originally ruled by Austrian Habsburgs; Czech lands united with Slovakia to form separate state of Czechoslovakia in 1918. Occupied by Germany in 1938; government in exile in London during World War 2.

□ *international airport*

200km
100mi

EUROPE

GERMANY   Elbe   Snezka 1603m
Erzgebirge   Liberec   SILESIA   POLAND   Odra
Cheb   PRAGUE   Pardubice   Ostrava
Plzeň   CZECH   Olomouc
BOHEMIA   REPUBLIC   Brno   MORAVIA
Danube   Vltava   České Budějovice   Morava
SLOVAK REPUBLIC
VIENNA
AUSTRIA

Czechoslovakian independence, with loss of some territory to USSR in 1946; communist rule imposed by Russia following 1948 coup. Attempt at liberalization by Dubček terminated by intervention of Warsaw Pact troops in 1968. Fall from power of the Communist Party in 1989; 1992 agreement to divide Czechoslovakia into its constituent republics, Czech and Slovak, by Jan 1993. Czech Republic now comprises former provinces of Bohemia, Silesia, Moravia.

Head of State
1993–   Václav Havel

Head of Government
1993–   Václav Klaus

DENMARK

Local name Danmark

Timezone GMT + 1

Area 43 076 km²/16 627 sq mi (excluding Greenland and Faroe Islands)

Population total (1991e) 5 146 469

Status Kingdom

Capital Copenhagen

Language Danish (official)

Ethnic groups Danish (97%), Turkish (0.5%), other Scandinavian (0.4%)

Religions Evangelical Lutheran (97%), Roman Catholic (0.5%), Jewish (0.1%)

Physical features Consists of most of the Jutland peninsula, several islands in the Baltic Sea, and some of the N Frisian Is in the North Sea. Coastline 3 400 km/ 2 100 mi. Uniformly low-lying; no large rivers and few lakes. Shoreline indented by many lagoons and fjords, largest is Lim Fjord.

Climate Modified by Gulf Stream; cold and cloudy winters, warm and sunny summers. Average annual temperatures range from 0.5°C (Jan) to 17°C (Jul); average annual rainfall 800 mm/32 in.

Currency 1 Danish Krone (Dkr) = 100 øre

Economy Lack of raw materials has resulted in development of processing industries; intensive agriculture; wide range of food processing; machinery, textiles, furniture, electronics; dairy products. Joined European Economic Community in 1973.

GDP (1990) $78 bn, per capita $15 200

History Part of Viking kingdoms, 8th–10th-c; Danish Empire under Canute, 11th-c. Joined with Sweden and Norway under Queen Margrethe of Denmark, 1389; Sweden separated from union in 16th-c, followed by

□ international airport

Norway in 1814; Schleswig-Holstein lost to Germany in 1864; N Schleswig returned after plebiscite in 1920. Occupied by Germany during World War 2. Iceland independent from 1944; Greenland and Faroe Is remain dependencies. Constitutional monarchy since 1849; unicameral system adopted in 1953; legislative power lies with the Monarch and the Diet jointly.

Head of State (Monarch)
1972–   Margrethe II

Head of Government
1982–93   Poul Schlüter
1993–   Poul Nyrop Rasmussen

Faroe Islands (Faeroe)

Local name Faerøerne (Danish)

Timezone GMT

Area 1 400 km²/540 sq mi

Population total (1990e) 47 449

Status Self-governing region of Denmark

Capital Tórshavn

Languages Faroese (official, derived from Old Norse), Danish

Religion Evangelical Lutheran

Physical features Group of 22 sparsely vegetated volcanic islands in the N Atlantic between Iceland and the Shetland Is; 17 inhabited. Largest islands: Strømø, Østerø, Vagø, Suderø, Sandø, Bordø.

Climate Mild winters, overcast cool summers.

Currency 1 Danish Krone (Dkr) = 100 øre

Economy Main produce: fish, crafts, potatoes. Denmark provides an annual economic subsidy.

GNP (1986) per capita $16 800

History Settled by Norse in 8th-c; part of Norway from 11th-c; passed to Denmark in 1380. Self-governing region of Denmark since 1948. Parliament restored in 1852; unicameral Parliament (*Lagting*) consists of 34 members.

Head of State (Monarch)
1972–   Margrethe II

Head of Government
1988–   Atli Dam

Human geography

Human geography

Denmark (continued)

Greenland (Kalaalit Nunaat)

Local names Kalaalit Nunaat (Greenlandic), Grønland (Danish), Kalâtdlit-Nunât (Inuit)

Timezone GMT – 3

Area 2 175 600 km²/839 781 sq mi

Population total (1991e) 55 533

Status Self-governing province of Denmark

Capital Nuuk (Godthåb)

Languages Danish (official), Inuit

Ethnic groups Largely Inuit (Eskimo), with Danish admixtures

Religions Lutheran, Shamanist

Physical features Located in N Atlantic and Arctic Oceans. Largely covered by an ice-cap (up to 4 300 m/ 14 000 ft thick). Coastal mountains rise to 3 702 m/ 12 145 ft at Gunnbjørn Fjeld (SE). Less than 5% of island is habitable.

Climate Arctic to subarctic.

Currency 1 Danish Krone (Dkr) = 100 øre

Economy Largely dependent on fishing from ice-free SW ports; hunting for seal and fox furs in N and E. Reserves of lead, zinc, molybdenum, uranium, coal, cryolite.

GDP Not available

History Settled by seal-hunting Eskimos from N America c.2500 BC. Norse settlers in SW, 12th–15th-c AD; explored by Frobisher and Davis, 16th-c; Danish colony from 1721. Self-governing province of Denmark, 1979; elected Provincial Council sends two members to the Danish Parliament.

Head of State (Monarch)
1972–   Margrethe II

Head of Government
1987–   Jonathan Motzfeldt

DJIBOUTI

Local name Jumhouriyya Djibouti

Timezone GMT + 3

Area 23 200 km²/8 958 sq mi

Population total (1991e) 541 000

Status Republic

Date of independence 1977

Capital Djibouti

Language Arabic (official)

Ethnic groups Somali (47%), Afar (20%), Arab (mostly Yemeni) (6%), European (4%), other refugees (10%)

Religions Muslim (94%), Christian (Roman Catholic 4%, Protestant 1%, Orthodox 1%)

Physical features Located in NE Africa. Series of plateaux dropping down from mountains to flat, low-lying, rocky desert; fertile coastal strip around the Gulf of Tadjoura. Highest point, Moussa Ali, rising to 2 020 m/ 6 627 ft in the N.

Climate Semi-arid climate, with hot season (May–Sep). Very high temperatures on coastal plain all year round; average temperatures 26°C (Jan), 36°C (Jul); slightly lower humidity and temperatures in interior highlands. Low rainfall; average annual rainfall 130 mm/5 in.

Currency 1 Djibouti Franc (DF, DjFr) = 100 centimes

Economy Crop-based agriculture possible only with irrigation; livestock-raising among nomadic population; some fishing on coast. Port of Djibouti provides an important transit point for Red Sea trade, particularly for Ethiopia. Small industrial sector.

GDP (1989e) $344 mn, per capita $1 030

History French colonial interest in mid-19th-c; annexed by France as French Somaliland, 1896. French Overseas Territory, following World War 2; French Territory of the

Afars and the Issas, 1967; independence, 1977. Political parties combined in 1979 to form People's Progress Assembly (RPP) as single ruling party; overwhelming majority voted in favour of a multi-party constitution, 1992. Governed by a President, a Legislative Chamber, an executive Prime Minister, and a Council.

Head of State
1977–   Hassan Gouled Aptidon

Head of Government
1978–   Barkat Gourad Hamadou

international airport

DOMINICA

Local name Dominica

Timezone GMT – 4

Area 751 km²/290 sq mi

Population total (1991e) 86 000

Status Independent republic within the Commonwealth

Date of independence 1978

Capital Roseau

Languages English (official), with French widely spoken

Ethnic groups African or mixed African-European descent (97%), Amerindian (2%)

Religions Christian (Roman Catholic 77%, Protestant 16%)

Physical features Island in the Windward group of the West Indies; c.50 km/30 mi long and 26 km/16 mi wide. Rises to 1 447 m/4 747 ft at Morne Diablotin; volcanic origin; central ridge, with several rivers. 67% of land area forested.

Climate Warm and humid tropical climate; temperatures ranging 26–32°C. Rainy season (Jun–Oct); heavy rainfall, varies from 1 750 mm/69 in average on the coast, to 6 250 mm/246 in inland.

Currency 1 East Caribbean Dollar (EC$) = 100 cents

Economy Agriculture; tourism; coconut-based products, cigars, citrus fruits (notably limes), bananas, coconuts, bay oil.

GDP (1989) $153 mn, (1985) per capita $1 090

History Visited by Columbus in 1493; colonization attempts by French and British in 18th-c; British Crown Colony from 1805; part of Federation of the West Indies, 1958–62. Independent republic within the Commonwealth, 1978; governed by a House of Assembly, a President, a Prime Minister, and a Cabinet.

Head of State
1984–93   Clarence Augustus Seignoret
1993–   Crispin Sorhaindo

Head of Government
1980–   Mary Eugenia Charles

DOMINICAN REPUBLIC

Local name República Dominicana

Timezone GMT – 4

Area 48 442 km²/18 699 sq mi

Population total (1991) 7 384 000

Status Republic

Date of independence 1844

Capital Santo Domingo

Language Spanish (official)

Ethnic groups Spanish, or mixed Spanish and African descent

Religions Roman Catholic (92%), other (mostly Evangelical Protestant and followers of voodoo) (8%)

Physical features Crossed NW–SE by Cordillera Central, with many peaks over 3 000 m/10 000 ft; Pico Duarte, 3 175 m/10 416 ft is highest peak in the Caribbean. Wide coastal plain in E. Main rivers include Yaque del Sur, Yaque del Norte, Yuna (E).

Climate Tropical maritime climate with rainy season (May–Nov). Santo Domingo, average temperature 24°C (Jan), 27°C (Jul). Annual rainfall 1 400 mm/55 in. Hurricanes (Jul–Nov).

Currency 1 Dominican Peso (RD$, DR$) = 100 centavos

Economy Mainly agriculture, especially sugar, cocoa; tourism expanding with new resort complexes on N coast.

GDP (1990) $7.1 bn, (1991) per capita $998

History Visited by Columbus in 1492; Spanish colony, 16th–17th-c; E province of Santo Domingo remained Spanish after partition of Hispaniola in 1697. Taken over by Haiti on several occasions; independence from Haiti in 1844, as Dominican Republic. Occupied by USA, 1916–24, 1965. Comprises of 26 provinces and a National District which contains the capital; governed by a President and a National Congress (Senate and Chamber of Deputies).

Head of State/Government
1982–6 Salvador Jorge Blanco
1986– Joaquín Videla Balaguer

ECUADOR

Local name Ecuador

Timezone GMT – 5

Area 270 699 km²/104 490 sq mi (including the Galápagos Islands, 7 812 km²/3 015 sq mi)

Population total (1992e) 10 607 000

Status Republic

Date of independence 1830

Capital Quito

Languages Spanish (official), with Quechua also spoken

Ethnic groups Indian (25%), Mestizo (55%), Spanish (10%), African (10%)

Religions Roman Catholic (94%), other (6%)

Physical features Located in NW S America; includes the Galápagos Is, Ecuadorian island group on the equator 970 km/600 mi W of S American mainland. Coastal plain in the W, descending from rolling hills (N) to broad lowland basin; Andean uplands in C rising to snow-capped peaks which include Cotopaxi, 5 896 m/19 343 ft.

Forested alluvial plains in the E, dissected by rivers flowing from the Andes towards the Amazon (source of the Amazon located in Peru).

Climate Hot and humid, wet equatorial climate. Rain throughout year (especially Dec–Apr); average annual rainfall 1 115 mm/44 in. Average annual temperatures, 15°C (Jan), 14°C (Jul).

Currency 1 Sucre (Su, S/.) = 100 centavos

Economy Agriculture (employs c.50% of population); beans, cereals, livestock; bananas, coffee, fishing (especially shrimps); petrochemicals, steel, cement, pharmaceuticals; oil piped from the Oriente basin in E to refineries at Esmeraldas.

GDP (1990) $10.9 bn, (1989) per capita $1 040

History Formerly part of Inca Empire; taken by Spanish, 1534; within Viceroyalty of New Granada. Independent, 1822; joined with Panama, Colombia, and Venezuela to form Gran Colombia; left union, to become independent republic, 1830. Highly unstable political history. Comprises 21 provinces, including the Galápagos Is, each administered by a governor; governed by a President and a unicameral National Congress.

Head of State/Government
1988–92   Rodrigo Borja Cevallos
1992–   Sixto Durán Ballén

EGYPT

Local name Misr

Timezone GMT + 2

Area 1 001 449 km²/386 559 sq mi

Population total (1992e) 55 980 000

Status Republic

Date of independence 1922

Capital Cairo

Language Arabic (official)

Ethnic group Population mainly of E Hamitic origin (90%)

Religions Sunni Muslim (c.90%), minority largely Coptic Christian (c.10%)

Physical features R Nile flows N from Sudan, dammed S of Aswan, creating L Nasser; huge delta N of Cairo, 250 km/150 mi across and 160 km/100 mi N–S. Narrow Eastern Desert, sparsely inhabited, between Nile and Red Sea; broad Western Desert, covering over two-thirds of the country. Sinai Peninsula (S), desert region with mountains rising to 2 637 m/8 651 ft at Gebel Katherîna, Egypt's highest point. 90% of population lives on Nile floodplain (c.3% of country's area).

Climate Mainly desert climate, except for 80 km/50 mi wide Mediterranean coastal fringe; very hot on coast where dust-laden khamsin wind blows N from Sahara (Mar–Jun). Alexandria, average maximum daily temperatures 18–30°C; elsewhere rainfall less than 50 mm/12 in.

Currency 1 Egyptian Pound (E£, LE) = 100 piastres

Economy Agriculture on floodplain of R Nile accounts for about a third of national income; building of Aswan High Dam extended irrigated cultivation. A major tourist area.

GDP (1990e) $37 bn, per capita $700

History Neolithic cultures on R Nile from c.6000 BC; Pharaoh dynasties from c.3100 BC; Egyptian power greatest during the New Empire period, 1576–1085 BC. Became Persian province, 6th-c BC; conquered by Alexander the Great, 4th-c BC; Ptolemaic Pharaohs ruled Egypt until 30 BC. Conquered by Arabs, AD 672. Suez Canal constructed in 1869; revolt in 1879 put down by British

in 1882; British protectorate from 1914. Declared independence in 1922. King Farouk deposed by Nasser, 1952; Egypt declared a republic, 1953. Attack on Israel followed by Israeli invasion in 1967; Suez Canal remained blocked 1967–75. Changed name to Arab Republic of Egypt, 1971. Yom Kippur War, 1973, against Israel; Israel returned disputed Taba Strip, 1989. Participated in Gulf War with US-led coalition, 1991. Governed by a People's National Assembly, a President, a Prime Minister, and a Council of Ministers.

Head of State
1981–   Mohammed Hosni Mubarak

Head of Government
1986–   Atef Sidqi

Human geography

EL SALVADOR

Local name El Salvador

Timezone GMT – 6

Area 21 476 km²/8 290 sq mi

Population total (1991e) 5 418 000

Status Republic

Date of independence 1841

Capital San Salvador

Language Spanish (official)

Ethnic groups Spanish-Indian (89%), Indian (mostly Pipil) (5%)

Religions Roman Catholic (93%), other (mostly Evangelical Protestant) (7%)

Physical features Smallest of C America republics. Two volcanic ranges run E-W; narrow coastal belt in S, rises to mountains in N; highest point, Santa Ana, 2381 m/ 7 812 ft. Many volcanic lakes; earthquakes common.

Climate Varies greatly with altitude; hot tropical on coastal lowlands; single rainy season (May–Oct); temperate uplands. Average annual temperature at San Salvador 24°C (Jul), 22°C (Jan); average annual rainfall 1 775 mm/170 in.

Currency 1 Colón (ES$) = 100 centavos

Economy Largely based on agriculture; main crops coffee and cotton; sugar, maize, balsam (world's main source); chemicals, rubber, rubber goods, oil products.

GDP (1990) $5.1 bn, per capita $940

History Originally part of the Aztec kingdom. Conquest by Spanish in 1526; independence from Spain in 1821;

member of the Central American Federation until its dissolution in 1839; independent republic in 1841. War with Honduras, 1965, 1969; considerable political unrest in 1970s and 80s, with guerrilla activity directed against the US-supported government; civil war, 1979–91. Peace plan agreed, 1991. Governed by a President, and a Council of Ministers; unicameral Legislative Assembly.

Head of State/Government

1984–9   José Napoleón Duarte
1989–   Alfredo Cristiani Burkard

ENGLAND >> UNITED KINGDOM

EQUATORIAL GUINEA

Local name Guinea Ecuatorial

Timezone GMT + 1

Area 26 016 km²/10 042 sq mi (mainland area) 28 051 km²/10 828 sq mi (total area)

Population total (1991e) 360 000

Status Republic

Date of independence 1968

Capital Malabo

Language Spanish (official)

Ethnic groups Mainland population, mainly Fang (83%), Bubi (10%), Ndowe (4%), Annobonés (2%), Bujeba (1%)

Religions Roman Catholic (80%), traditional beliefs (5%)

Physical features Located in WC Africa. Comprises the mainland area (Río Muni) and several islands in the Gulf of Guinea. Mainland rises sharply from a narrow coast of mangrove swamps towards the heavily forested African plateau. Bioko, fertile volcanic island in NW, contains Guinea's highest point, Pico de Basilé, 3 007 m/ 9 865 ft.

Climate Hot and humid equatorial climate. Average maximum daily temperature, 29–32°C; average annual rainfall c.2 000 mm/80 in.

Currency 1 CFA Franc (CFA Fr) = 100 centimes

Economy Largely based on agriculture; cocoa, coffee, timber, bananas, cassava, palm oil, sweet potatoes.

GDP (1989e) $149 mn, (1989) per capita $430

History First visited by Europeans in 15th-c; island of Fernando Po claimed by Portugal, 1494–1788; occupied by Britain, 1781–1843; rights to the area acquired by Spain, 1844. Independence, 1968. Military coup, 1975; governed by Supreme Military Council headed by a President. New constitution, 1991.

Head of State
1968–79   Francisco Macias Nguema
1979–   Teodoro Obiang Nguema Mbasogo

Head of Government
1993–   Silvestre Siale Bileka

ESTONIA

Local name Eesti

Timezone GMT + 2

Area 45 100 km²/17 409 sq mi

Population total (1990e) 1 600 000

Status Republic

Date of independence 1991

Capital Tallinn

Languages Estonian (official), also Russian

Ethnic groups Estonian (65%), Russian (28%), Ukrainian (3%), Belorussian (2%)

Religions Evangelical Lutheran, with Orthodox minority

Physical features Consists of mainland area and c.800 islands (including the Baltic island of Saaremaa). S covered with morainal hills, C with elongated glacial hills usually arrayed in the direction of glacial movement. Most lakes and rivers drain either E into Lake Peipus, N into the Gulf of Finland; a few W into Gulf of Riga.

Climate Mild climate. Average annual temperatures 23–5°C (Feb) and 17°C (Jul); average annual rainfall 650 mm/26 in.

Currency 1 Kroon = 100 centts

Economy Major industries: agricultural machinery, electric motors; agricultural produce of grain, vegetables; livestock.

GDP (1991e) $10.8 bn, per capita not available

History Ceded to Russia, 1721; independence, 1918; proclaimed a Soviet Socialist Republic, 1940. Occupied by Germany in World War 2. Resurgence of nationalist movement in the 1980s; declared independence, 1991. 105-member Parliament; 495-member Congress of Estonia.

☐ *international airport*

Head of State
1991–2   Arnold Rüütel
1992–   Lennart Meri

Head of Government
1991–2   Edgar Savisaar
1992   Tiit Vahi
1992–   Mart Laar

ETHIOPIA

Local name Ityopiya

Timezone GMT + 3

Area 1 251 282 km²/483 123 sq mi

Population total (1991e) 53 131 000

Status Republic

Capital Addis Ababa

Language Amharic (official)

Ethnic groups Galla (40%), Amhara and Tigray (32%)

Religions Muslim (45%), Ethiopian Orthodox (37%), traditional beliefs (11%)

Physical features Located in NE Africa. Dominated by mountainous C plateau, mean elevation 1 800–2 400 m/6–8 000 ft; split diagonally by the Great Rift Valley. Highest point, Ras Dashan Mt, 4 620 m/15 157 ft. Crossed E–W by Blue Nile. Danakil Depression (NE) dips to 116 m/381 ft below sea level.

Climate Tropical climate, moderated by higher altitudes; distinct wet season (Apr–Sep). Hot, semi-arid NE and SE lowlands receive less than 500 mm/20 in of rainfall annually. Severe droughts in 1980s caused widespread famine, deaths, and resettlement.

Currency 1 Ethiopian Birr (Br) = 100 cents

Economy One of the world's poorest countries; over 80% of population employed in agriculture, especially subsistence farming. Production severely affected by drought. Distribution of foreign aid hindered by internal civil war and poor local organization.

GDP (1991) $6.6 bn, per capita $130

History Oldest independent country in sub-Saharan Africa; first Christian country in Africa. Eritrea occupied by Italy, 1882. Independence of Abyssinia (former name of Ethiopia) recognized by League of Nations, 1923. Haile Selassie became Emperor in 1930, and began programme of modernization and reform. Italian invasion in 1935; annexation as Italian East Africa, 1936–41. Italians forced from Ethiopia by the Allies, and Haile Selassie returned to power in 1941. Military coup in 1974. Ongoing conflict with Somalia over Ogaden region; internal conflict with regional separatist Eritrean and Tigrean forces. Transfer of power to People's Democratic Republic in 1987; government overthrown by separatist forces in 1991. Council of Representatives formed; movement towards independence for Eritrea, which has functioned as an autonomous region since the fall of the government in 1991; Eritrea formally recognized as an independent state in May 1993.

Head of State
1987–91   Mengistu Haile Mariam
1991–   Meles Zenawi

Head of Government
1991–   Tamirat Layne

FAROE ISLANDS >> DENMARK

FALKLAND ISLANDS >> UNITED KINGDOM

FIJI

Local name Viti

Timezone GMT + 11

Area 18 333 km²/7 076 sq mi

Population total (1992e) 748 000

Status Republic

Date of independence 1970

Capital Suva (on Viti Levu Island)

Language English (official)

Ethnic groups Indigenous Fijians (44%), Indian (51%)

Religions Native Fijians, mainly Christian (Methodist c.85%, Roman Catholic 12%); Indo-Fijians, mainly Hindu (c.70%) and Muslim (25%)

Physical features Melanesian group of 844 islands and islets in the SW Pacific Ocean. Highest peak, Tomaniivi (Mt Victoria) on Viti Levu, 1 324 m/4 344 ft. Most smaller islands consist of limestone, little vegetation. Great Sea Reef stretches 500 km/300 mi along W fringe. Dense tropical forest on wet, windward side (SE); mainly treeless on dry, leeward side.

Climate Tropical oceanic climate, high humidity. Average annual temperature 27°C, ranging from 35°C (Dec–Apr) to 16°C (Jun–Sep). Heavy rainfall; occasional hurricanes.

Currency 1 Fiji Dollar (F$) = 100 cents

Economy Agriculture; sugar cane (accounts for over two-thirds of export earnings); bananas, ginger; Gold, silver, limestone, timber. Major tourist area.

GDP (1990) $1.3 bn, per capita $1 840

History Visited by Tasman in 1643, and by Cook in 1774; British colony from 1874; independence within the Commonwealth, 1970. 1987 election brought to power an Indian-dominated coalition, which led to military coups (May and Sep), and proclamation of a republic outside the Commonwealth. Civilian government restored, Dec 1987. New constitution, 1990; bicameral Parliament of a nominated Senate and an elected House of Representatives.

Head of State
1987–93   Penaia Ganilau
1993–   Kamisese Mara *Acting*

Head of Government
1987–92   Kamisese Mara
1992–   Sitiveni Rabuka

FINLAND

Local name Suomi (Finnish)

Timezone GMT + 2

Area 338 145 km²/130 524 sq mi

Population total (1991) 5 029 002

Status Republic

Date of independence 1917

Capital Helsinki

Languages Finnish and Swedish (official), also Saame (Lappish)

Ethnic groups Finnish (94%), Swedish, Lappish, Russian minorities

Religions Lutheran (90%), Finnish/Greek Orthodox

Physical features Low-lying, glaciated plateau, average height 150 m/500 ft. Highest peak Haltiatunturi, 1 328 m/ 4 357 ft, on NW border. Over 60 000 shallow lakes in SE, providing a system of inland navigation. Over a third of the country is located N of the Arctic Circle. Archipelago of Saaristomeri (SW), with over 17 000 islands; including Åland Is (Ahvenanmaa) (SW). Forest covers 65% of the country, water covers 10%.

Climate Extreme, N of the Arctic Circle: average annual temperatures –30°C (Jan), 27°C (Jul); half annual precipitation falls as snow; sun does not go down beyond the horizon for over 70 days during summer. Average temperatures –6°C (Jan), 17°C (Jul) at Helsinki; average annual rainfall 618 mm/24 in.

Currency 1 Markka (FMk) = 100 penni

Economy Traditional focus on forestry, farming. Rapid economic growth since 1950s; metals, clothing, chemicals; copper, iron-ore mining; wide use of hydroelectric power.

GDP (1990) $77 bn, per capita $15 500

History Ruled by Sweden from 1157 until ceded to Russia in 1809; Grand Duchy of the Russian Czar, 19th-c. Independent republic, 1917; parliamentary system

Finland (continued)

created, 1928. Invaded by Soviets, 1939–40 (Winter War); lost territory to USSR, including Petsamo and Porkkala peninsula, 1944. Signed a friendship treaty with Soviet Union in 1948 (renewed 1955, 1970, 1983), undertaking to resist any attack made on the Soviet Union launched through Finnish territory. Harri Holkeri became Finland's first post-war conservative Prime Minister, 1987. Governed by a single-chamber House of Representatives and President assisted by a Council of State.

Head of State

1982–94	Mauno Koivisto
1994–	Martti Ahtisaarsi

Head of Government

1987–91	Harri Holkeri
1991–	Esko Aho

FRANCE

Local name France

Timezone GMT + 1

Area 551 000 km²/212 686 sq mi

Population total (1991e) 56 681 000

Status Republic

Capital Paris

Languages French (official), Breton, Occitan and Alsatian are also spoken

Ethnic groups Celtic and Latin origin (91%), Breton, Catalan, and large immigrant population (including Portuguese, Algerian, Moroccan, and Arab minorities)

Religions Roman Catholic (90%), Protestant (4%), Muslim (3%), Jewish (1%)

Physical features Bounded S and E by large mountain ranges, notably (interior) the Massif Central, Jura, and Alps (E), rising to 4 807 m/15 771 ft at Mont Blanc, and the Pyrénées (S). Chief rivers include Loire (longest at 1 020 km/633 mi), Rhône, Seine, Garonne. 60% of land is arable.

Climate Mediterranean climate in S, with warm, moist winters and hot, dry summers. Average temperatures, 3°C (Jan), 18°C (Jul). Continental climate in E. Average annual rainfall 786 mm/31 in.

Currency 1 French Franc (Fr) = 100 centimes

Economy Main industries include wine, fruit, cheese; perfume, textiles, clothing; steel, chemicals, machinery, cars, aircraft. Natural resources of coal, iron ore, bauxite, timber. Tourism important.

GDP (1990) $873 bn, per capita $15 500

History Celtic-speaking Gauls dominant by 5th-c BC; part of Roman Empire, 125 BC to 5th-c AD. Feudal monarchy founded by Hugh Capet in 987. Plantagenets of England acquired several territories, 12th-c; lands gradually recovered in Hundred Years' War, 1337–1453, apart from Calais (regained in 1558). Capetian dynasty followed by the Valois, from 1328, and the Bourbons, from 1589. Wars of Religion, 1562–95. Monarchy overthrown by the French Revolution, 1789; First Republic declared, 1792; First Empire, ruled by Napoleon, 1804–14; monarchy restored, 1814–48. Second Republic, 1848–52, and Second Empire, 1852–70, ruled by Louis Napoleon. Third Republic, 1870–1940; great political instability between World Wars, with several governments holding office for short periods. Occupied by Germany 1940–4, with pro-German government at Vichy, and Free French

□ *international airport*

in London under de Gaulle. Fourth Republic, 1946; war with Indo-China, 1946–54; conflict in Algeria, 1954–62. Fifth Republic, 1958. Governed by a President, an appointed Prime Minster, a Council of Ministers; a bicameral National Assembly and a Senate.

Head of State

Fifth Republic

1969–74	Georges Pompidou
1974–81	Valéry Giscard d'Estaing
1981–	François Mitterrand

Head of Government

Fifth Republic

1991–2	Edith Cresson
1992–3	Pierre Bérégovoy
1993–	Edouard Balladur

>> Political leaders and rulers

Internal Collective Territory

Island of Corsica in the Mediterranean Sea: area 8 680 km²/3 350 sq mi; capital, Ajaccio; GMT + 1

Regions of France

400km
200mi

Overseas departments

Name	Area		Capital	GMT
	km²	sq mi		
Guadeloupe	1779	687	Basse-Terre	– 4
Guiana	90909	35091	Cayenne	– 3.5
Martinique	1079	416	Fort-de-France	– 4
Mayotte	374	144	Dzaoudzi	+ 3
Réunion	2512	970	St Denis	+ 4
St Pierre et Miquelon	240	93	St Pierre	– 3

Overseas territories

Name	Area		Capital/ chief centre	GMT
	km²	sq mi		
French Polynesia	3941	1521	Papeete	– 6
New Caledonia	18575	7170	Nouméa	+ 11
Southern and Antarctic Territories	10100	3900	Port-aux-Français	
Wallis and Futuna	274	106	Matu Utu	+ 12

GABON

Local name Gabon

Timezone GMT + 1

Area 267667 km²/103319 sq mi

Population total (1991e) 1079000

Status Republic

Date of independence 1960

Capital Libreville

Languages French (official), Fang, Myene, Bateke, and other Bantu dialects spoken

Ethnic groups c.40 Bantu tribes (Fang 30%, Eshira 25%, Bateke and Bapounou 10%) and c.10% expatriate Africans and Europeans

Religions Christian (96%) (Roman Catholic 65%, Protestant 19%, other 12%), traditional beliefs

Physical features Located in W Africa, lies on the equator for 880 km/550 mi W–E. Land rises towards the African central plateau, cut by several rivers, notably the Ogooué and N'Gounié. Highest point, Mont Ibounoji, 980 m/3 215 ft.

Climate Typical equatorial climate: hot, wet, and humid. Mean annual temperature 27°C; annual average rainfall 1 250–2 000 mm/50–80 in inland.

Currency 1 CFA Franc (CFAFr) = 100 centimes

Economy Small area of land under cultivation, but employing 65% of population; coffee, cocoa, palm oil, rubber; timber extraction. Rapid economic growth since independence, largely because of offshore oil, natural gas, and minerals; manganese, uranium, iron ore.

GDP (1991) $5.3 bn, per capita $4 400

History Visited by Portuguese, 15th-c. Under French control from mid-19th-c; a slave ship was captured by the French in 1849, the liberated slaves forming the settlement of Libreville. Occupied by France in 1885; one of four territories of French West Africa, 1910. Indepen-

dence, 1960; multi-party elections held, 1990. New constitution, 1991; governed by a President, an appointed Council of Ministers, and a legislative National Assembly.

Head of State
1960–7 Léon M'ba
1967– Omar (Albert-Bernard, to 1973) Bongo

Head of Government
1975–90 Léon Mébiame (Mébiane)
1990– Casimir Oyé M'ba

GAMBIA, THE

Local name Gambia

Timezone GMT

Area 11 295 km²/4 361 sq mi

Population total (1991e) 860 000

Status Independent republic within the Commonwealth

Date of independence 1965

Capital Banjul

Languages English (official), also Madinka, Wolof and Fula

Ethnic groups Madinka (40%), Fula (19%), Wolof (15%), Dyola (10%), Sonike (8%)

Religions Muslim (85%), Christian (14%), traditional local beliefs (1%)

Physical features Located in W Africa; surrounded, except for coastline, by Senegal. Strip of land 322 km/200 mi E–W along the R Gambia. Flat country, not rising above 90 m/295 ft; c.25% of land is arable.

Climate Tropical climate; average temperatures 23°C (Jan), 27°C (Jul), rising upland to over 40°C. Rainy season (Jun–Sep) with high humidity and high night temperatures; rainfall decreasing inland.

Currency 1 Dalasi (D, Di) = 100 butut

Economy Agriculture, especially groundnuts; cotton, rice, millet, sorghum, fruit, vegetables, livestock; ground-

nut processing, brewing, soft drinks, agricultural machinery assembly, metal working, clothing, tourism.

GDP (1990) $196 mn, per capita $230

History Visited by Portuguese in 1455; settled by English in 17th-c; independent British Crown Colony from 1843. Independent member of Commonwealth, 1965; republic, 1970. Joined Confederation of Senegambia, 1982–9; signed treaty of friendship with Senegal, 1991. Governed by a House of Representatives, a President and a Cabinet.

Head of State/Government
1965–   Dawda Kairaba Jawara

GEORGIA

Local name Georgia

Timezone GMT + 3

Area 69 700 km²/26 900 sq mi

Population total (1990e) 5 400 000

Status Republic

Date of independence 1991

Capital Tbilisi

Languages Georgian (official), also Russian

Ethnic groups Georgian (69%), Armenian (9%), Russian (7%), Azerbaijani (5%), Ossetian (3%), Abkhazian (2%)

Religion Georgian Church, independent of the Russian Orthodox Church since 1917

Physical features Mountainous country in C and W Transcaucasia; contains the Greater Caucasus (N) and Lesser Caucasus (S); highest point in the republic, Mt Shkhara, 5 203 m/17 070 ft. Chief rivers, Kura and Rioni. C.39% of land is forested.

Climate Great Caucasus in N borders temperate and subtropical climatic zones; average temperatures 1–3°C (Jan), 25°C (Jul) in E Transcaucasia. Humid, subtropical climate with mild winters in W. Mediterranean climate with humid winters, dry summers in N Black Sea region.

Currency (1992) 1 Rouble (R) = 100 kopecks

Economy Kakhetia region famed for its orchards and wines; holiday resorts, spas on the Black Sea; manganese, coal, iron and steel, oil refining; tea, fruits, tung oil, tobacco, vines, silk, textiles, food processing.

GDP Not available

History Proclaimed a Soviet Socialist Republic in 1921; linked with Armenia and Azerbaijan as Transcaucasian Republic, 1922–36; made a constituent republic within the Soviet Union, 1936. Declaration of independence, 1991; quest for regional autonomy led to declaration of secession by S Ossetia, 1991, and declaration of independence by Abkhazia, 1992. Failed to join new Commonwealth of Independent States (CIS), 1991. President Gamsakhurdia overthrown in civil war, Jan 1992, brought military council to power; Parliament dismissed and powers transferred to a State Council headed by Shevardnadze, 1992; new interim constitution, 1992; Head of State holds executive power, advised by Cabinet of Ministers.

Head of State
1991–2   Zviad Gamsakhurdia
1992   Military Council
1992–   Eduard Shevardnadze (Chairman of State Council) *Interim*

Head of Government
1992–3   Tengiz Sigua
1993–   Otar Patatsia

GERMANY

Local name Bundesrepublik Deutschland

Timezone GMT + 1

Area 357 868 km²/138 136 sq mi

Population total (1992e) 80 293 000

Status Federal republic

Capital Berlin

Languages German (official)

Ethnic groups German (93%), Turkish (2%), Yugoslav (1%), Italian (1%), other European Community (3%)

Religions Lutheran (55%), Roman Catholic (38%), Muslim (3%)

Physical features Lowland plains rise SW through C uplands and Alpine foothills to the Bavarian Alps; highest peak, the Zugspitze, 2 962 m/9 718 ft. C uplands include the Rhenish Slate Mts, Black Forest, and Harz Mts. Rhine crosses the country S–N; complex canal system links chief rivers, Elbe, Weser, Danube, Rhine, Main.

Climate Oceanic influences strongest in NW, where winters are mild, stormy; elsewhere continental climate. Lower winter temperatures in E and S, with considerable snowfall; average annual temperatures −0.5°C (Jan) to 19°C (Jul); average annual rainfall 600–700 mm/ 23–7 in.

Currency 1 Deutsche Mark (DM) = 100 Pfennige

Economy Economically powerful member of EC (accounts for 30% of European Community output): substantial heavy industry in NW, wine in Rhine and Moselle valleys; increasing tourism, especially in the S; leading manufacturer of vehicles, electrical and electronic goods. Much less development in the E, after the period of socialist economy; following unification, a major socio-economic division emerged between W and E, leading to demonstrations in the E provinces in 1991.

GDP (1991) $1 157 bn, per capita $14 600

History Ancient Germanic tribes united in 8th-c within the Frankish Empire of Charlemagne; elective monarchy after 918 under Otto I, with Holy Roman Empire divided into several hundred states. After Congress of Vienna, 1814–15, a confederation of 39 states under Austria. Under Bismarck, Prussia succeeded Austria as the leading German power. Union of Germany and foundation of the second Reich in 1871, with King of Prussia as hereditary German Emperor; aggressive foreign policy, eventually leading to World War 1. After German defeat, second Reich replaced by democratic Weimar Republic. World economic crisis led to collapse of Weimar Republic and rise of National Socialist movement in 1929; Adolph Hitler became dictator of the totalitarian Third Reich in 1933; acts of aggression led to World War 2 and a second defeat for Germany, with collapse of the German political regime. Partition of Germany in 1945, with occupation zones given to UK, USA, France, and USSR, who formed a Control Council. USSR withdrew from the Control Council in 1948, dividing Germany into W and E: W Germany controlled by the three remaining powers, UK, USA and France; E administered by USSR.

West Germany (former Federal Republic of Germany) Area 249 535 km²/96 320 sq mi; population total (1990) 62 679 035; including West Berlin. Established in 1949; gained full sovereignty, 1954. Entered NATO, 1955; founder member of the European Economic

☐ *international airport*

Germany (continued)

Community, 1957. Federal system of government, built around 10 provinces (*Länder*) with considerable powers; two-chamber legislature, consisting of Federal Diet (*Bundestag*) and Federal Council (*Bundesrat*).

East Germany (former German Democratic Republic) Area 108 333 km²/41 816 sq mi; population total (1990) 16 433 796. Administered by USSR after 1945 partition, and Soviet model of government established, 1949. Anti-Soviet demonstrations put down, 1953; recognized by USSR as an independent republic, 1954. Flow of refugees to West Germany continued until 1961, largely stopped by the Berlin Wall built along zonal boundary, dividing western sectors of Berlin from eastern, 1961. Governed by the People's Chamber, a single-chamber parliament (*Volkskammer*) which elected a Council of State, a Council of Ministers, and a National Defence Council. Movement for democratic reform culminated in Nov 1989 in the opening and removal of the Wall and other border crossings to the West, and a more open government policy. First free all-German elections since 1932, held in Mar 1990, paved the way for a currency union with West Germany in Jul 1990, and full political unification in Oct 1990.

United Germany The 10 provinces of West Germany joined by the 5 former East German provinces abolished after World War 2 (Brandenburg, Mecklenburg-West, Pomerania, Saxony, Saxony-Anhalt, Thuringia), along with unified Berlin. West German electoral system adopted in East Germany; first national elections, Dec 1990.

Länder of Germany

Head of State
1990–   Richard von Weizsäcker

Head of Government (Federal Chancellor)
1990–   Helmut Kohl

>> Political leaders and rulers

GHANA

Local name Ghana

Timezone GMT

Area 238 537 km²/92 100 sq mi

Population total (1991e) 15 616 000

Status Republic

Date of independence 1957

Capital Accra

Languages English (official), Akan, Ewe, Ga, several minority languages

Ethnic groups c.75 tribal groups, including Akan (44%), Mole-Dagbani (16%), Ewe (13%), and Ga (8%)

Religions Christian (43%), traditional local beliefs (38%), Muslim (12%)

Physical features Located in W Africa. Low-lying plains inland, leading to the Ashanti plateau (W) and R Volta basin (E), dammed to form L Volta. Mountains (E) rise to 885 m/2 903 ft at Mt Afadjado. Ashanti plateau in W and Akwapin Toto Mts in E.

Climate Tropical climate, including a warm dry coastal belt (SE); a hot, humid SW corner; and a hot, dry savannah (N). Average temperatures 27°C (Jan), 25°C (Jul) in Accra.

Currency 1 Cedi (¢) = 100 pesewas

Economy Agriculture; cocoa (world's leading producer) provides two-thirds of export revenue; tourism; commercial reserves of oil, diamonds, gold, manganese, bauxite, timber.

GDP (1990e) $5 080 mn, per capita $410

History Visited by Europeans in 15th-c. Centre of slave trade, 18th-c. Modern state created by union of two former British territories, British Gold Coast (Crown Colony, 1874) and British Togoland, merged to form Ghana and declared independence, 1957. Independent republic within the Commonwealth, 1960; first British colony in Africa to achieve independence, 1979. Constitution provides for a Parliament, an executive President, a Cabinet, and a Council of State. Series of military coups (1966, 1972, 1979, 1982) led to the creation of a Provisional National Defence Council, which rules by decree. New multi-party constitution, 1992, allowing for a directly elected executive President and legislature.

Head of State/Government
(Chairman of the Provisional National Defence Council)
1981–   Jerry John Rawlings

GIBRALTAR >> UNITED KINGDOM

Human geography

GREECE

Local name Ellás

Timezone GMT + 2

Area 131 957 km²/50 935 sq mi

Population total (1992e) 10 300 000

Status Republic

Date of independence 1830

Capital Athens (Athínai)

Languages Greek (official), English and French widely spoken

Ethnic groups Greek (98%), Albanian, Slav, Turkish minorities, and others (2%)

Religions Christian (98%) (Greek Orthodox 97.5%, Roman Catholic 0.4%, Protestant 0.1%), Muslim, Judaism, and others (2%)

Physical features Located in SE Europe, occupying the S part of the Balkan peninsula and numerous islands in the Aegean and Ionian seas; mainland includes the Peloponnese (S), connected via the narrow Isthmus of Corinth. Over 1 400 islands (only 169 inhabited), including Crete, the largest, 8 336 km²/3 218 sq mi, Rhodes, Milos, Corfu, Lesbos, Kos. Nearly 80% of Greece is moun-tainous or hilly. Pindus Mts run N to S; highest point, Mt Olympus, 2 917 m/9 570 ft. Principal rivers include the Nés-tos, Strimón, Arakhthos. C.30% of land is arable or under permanent cultivation; c.20% is forested.

Climate Mediterranean climate for coast and islands, with mild, rainy winters and hot, dry summers. Rainfall almost entirely in winter; island of Corfu receives maxi-mum rainfall 1 320 mm/52 in. Severe winters in moun-tains. Average annual temperatures 9°C (Jan), 28°C (Jul) in Athens.

Currency 1 Drachma (Dr) = 100 lepta

Economy Strong service sector accounts for c.60% of national income. Agriculture based on cereals, cotton, tobacco, fruit, figs, raisins, wine, olive oil, vegetables; major tourist area, especially on islands; world's largest shipping fleet (under own and other flags). Member of the EC from 1981.

GDP (1990) $76 bn, per capita $7 650

History Prehistoric civilization culminated in the Minoan-Mycenean culture of Crete. Dorians invaded from the N, 12th-c BC; Greek colonies established along N and S Mediterranean and on the Black Sea; many city-states on mainland, notably Sparta and Athens. Persian inva-

Greece (continued)

sions, 5th-c BC, repelled at Marathon, Salamis, Plataea, Mycale. Greek literature and art flourished in 5th-c BC. Conflict between Sparta and Athens (Peloponnesian War) weakened both and hegemony passed to Thebes, and then Macedon under Philip II, 4th-c BC; his son, Alexander the Great, conquered the Persian Empire. Macedonian power was broken by the Romans in 197 BC; part of the Eastern Roman and Byzantine empires. Ruled by the Ottoman Turks from 15th-c until 19th-c; national reawakening led to independence as kingdom in 1830. Territorial gains after Balkan War and World War 1. Absorbed over 1 000 000 refugees after defeat in Asia Minor in 1922; republic established, 1924-35. German occupation, 1941-4; civil war, 1944-9; military coup, 1967; abolition of monarchy, 1969. Democracy restored, 1974; governed by a Prime Minister; a Cabinet, a unicameral Parliament, and a President.

Head of State
1985-90   Christos Sartzetakis
1990-   Konstantinos Karamanlis

Head of Government
1989-90   Xenofon Zolotas
1990-3   Konstantinos Mitsotakis
1993-   Andreas Papandreou

☐ international airport

GREENLAND >> DENMARK

GRENADA

Local name Grenada

Timezone GMT - 4

Area 344 km²/133 sq mi

Population total (1992e) 100 000

Status Independent state within the Commonwealth

Date of independence 1974

Capital St George's

Languages English (official), French patois

Ethnic groups African descent (84%), mixed (12%), E Indian (3%) European (1%)

Religions Roman Catholic (64%), Protestant (21%)

Physical features Most southerly of the Windward Is, E Caribbean. Comprises the main island of Grenada, 34 km/21 mi long, 19 km/12 mi wide; and the S Grenadines. Grenada is volcanic in origin, with a ridge of mountains along its entire length, the highest point, Mt St Catherine, rising to 840 m/2 756 ft. Many rivers and lakes, including Grand Étang.

Climate Sub-tropical climate; average annual temperature 23°C. Wet season (Jun-Dec); annual rainfall varies from 1 270 mm/150 in (coast) to 5 000 mm/200 in (interior). Lies within Caribbean hurricane zone.

Currency 1 East Caribbean Dollar (EC$) = 100 cents

Economy Economy based on agriculture, notably fruit, vegetables, cocoa, nutmegs, bananas, mace. Processing of agricultural products and their derivatives.

GDP (1990e) $119 mn, per capita $1 400

History Visited by Columbus and named Concepción, 1498. Settled by French, mid-17th-c; ceded to Britain, 1763; retaken by France, 1779; ceded again to Britain, 1783; British Crown Colony, 1877. Independence, 1974. Popular people's revolution, 1979; Prime Minister Maurice Bishop killed during further uprising, 1983; a group of Caribbean countries requested US involvement, and

GUADELOUPE >> FRANCE

GUAM >> UNITED STATES OF AMERICA

troops invaded the island in Oct 1983, to restore stable government. Governed by a Senate, a House of Representatives, a Prime Minister, and a Cabinet.

Head of State
(British monarch represented by Governor-General)
1978–93   Sir Paul Scoon
1993–   Sir Reginald O Palmer

Head of Government
1989–90   Ben Jones *Acting*
1990–   Nicholas Braithwaite

GUATEMALA

Local name Guatemala

Timezone GMT – 6

Area 108 889 km²/42 031 sq mi

Population total (1992e) 9 718 000

Status Republic

Date of independence 1838

Capital Guatemala City

Languages Spanish (official), c.40% speak Indian dialects, including Quiche, Cakchiquel, Kekchi

Ethnic groups Amerindian (45%), Ladino (45%)

Religions Roman Catholic (75%), Protestant (25%)

Physical features Northernmost of the C American republics. Over two-thirds mountainous, with large forested areas; narrow Pacific coastal plain, rising steeply to highlands of 2 500–3 000 m/8 000–10 000 ft. Many volcanoes on S edge of highlands; low undulating tableland of El Petén to the N.

Climate Humid tropical climate on lowlands and coast; average annual temperatures 17°C (Jan), 21°C (Jul) in Guatemala City. Rainy season (May–Oct); average annual rainfall 1 316 mm /51.8 in. Area subject to hurricanes and earthquakes.

Currency 1 Quetzal (Q) = 100 centavos

Economy Agricultural products account for c.65% of exports, chiefly coffee, bananas, cotton, sugar. On higher ground, wheat, maize, beans; on the Pacific coastal plain, cotton, sugar cane, rice, beans.

GDP (1990) $11.1 bn, per capita $1 180

History Mayan and Aztec civilizations before Spanish conquest, 1523–4; independence as part of the Federation of Central America, 1821; independence as the Republic of Guatemala, 1838; 1985 constitution provides for the

GUIANA >> FRANCE

☐ *international airport*

election of a President (who appoints a Cabinet), and a National Assembly. A claim is still made over Belize to the East.

Head of State/Government
1986–91   Marco Vinicio Cerezo Arévalo
1991–3   Jorge Serrano Elias
1993–   Ramiro de León Carpio

GUINEA

Local name Guinée

Timezone GMT

Area 246 048 km²/94 974 sq mi

Population total (1992e) 7 800 000

Status Republic

Date of independence 1958

Capital Conakry

Languages French (official), Fulani, Malinké, Susu, Kissi, Kpelle

Ethnic groups Fulani (40%), Malinké (25%), Susu (11%), Kissi (6%), Kpelle (5%)

Religions Muslim (85%), Christian (10%), traditional beliefs (5%)

Physical features Located in W Africa. Coast characterized by mangrove forests, rising to a forested and widely cultivated narrow coastal plain; Fouta Djallon massif beyond, c.900 m/3 000 ft; higher peaks near Senegal frontier include Mt Tangue, 1 537 m/5 043 ft. Savannah plains in E; forested Guinea Highlands in S.

Climate Tropical climate; wet season (May–Oct). Annual rainfall 4 923 mm/194 in at Conakry; average temperature 32°C (dry season) on coast, 23°C (wet season).

Currency 1 Guinean Franc (GFr) = 100 cauris

Economy Agriculture (employs 75% of population); rich in minerals, with a third of the world's bauxite reserves; gold, diamonds. Independence brought a fall in production as a result of withdrawal of French expertise and investment.

GDP (1989) $2.7 bn, per capita $380

☐ international airport

History Part of Mali empire, 16th-c. French protectorate, 1849; governed with Senegal as Rivières du Sud. Separate colony, 1893; constituent territory within French West Africa, 1904; overseas territory, 1946. Independent republic, 1958. Death of Sékou Touré, Guinea's first President (1961–84); coup in 1984 established a Military Committee for National Recovery (CMRN); CMRN replaced by a mixed military and civilian Transitional Committee of National Recovery (CTRN) in 1991. Governed by a President and a Council of Ministers; new constitution approved in 1990.

Head of State/Government
1961–84   Ahmed Sékou Touré
1984–   Lansana Conté

GUINEA-BISSAU

Local name Guiné-Bissau

Timezone GMT

Area 36 125 km²/13 948 sq mi

Population total (1992e) 1 000 000

Status Republic

Date of independence 1973

Capital Bissau

Languages Portuguese (official), Criolo, Balante

Ethnic groups Balante (30%), Fulani (20%), Manjaca (14%), Mandingo (13%), Pepel (10%)

Religions Traditional beliefs (54%), Muslim (38%), Christian (5%)

Physical features Located in W Africa. Indented coast backed by forested coastal plains; main rivers, Geba and Cacheu. Low-lying, with savannah-covered plateaux (S, E), rising to 310 m/1 017 ft on the Guinea border. Includes the heavily-forested Bijagos archipelago located in the Atlantic Ocean off the shores of the mainland.

☐ international airport

pendence in 1973. Military coup, 1980; governed by a President and Council of Ministers. New constitution, 1984. National Assembly elects Council of State; President of the Council of State is also the Head of Government. Introduction of a multi-party system, 1991.

Head of State
1980–4   João Bernardo Vieira (President of the Military Council)
1984–   João Bernardo Vieira (President of the State Council)

Head of Government
1992–   Carlos Correia

Climate Tropical climate, hot and humid. Wet season (Jun–Oct); average annual rainfall at Bissau, 1 950 mm/76.8 in. Average annual temperature 24°C (Jan), 27°C (Jul) in Bissau.

Currency 1 Guinea-Bissau Peso (GBP, PG) = 100 centavos

Economy Based on agriculture, especially rice, maize, beans, peanuts, coconuts, palm oil, groundnuts, shrimps, fish, timber. Reserves of petroleum, bauxite, phosphate.

GDP (1989) $154 mn, (1991) per capita $160

History Visited by the Portuguese in 1446; Portuguese colony, 1879; overseas territory of Portugal, 1952; inde-

GUYANA

Local name Guyana

Timezone GMT – 3.5

Area 214 969 km²/82 978 sq mi

Population total (1992e) 800 000

Status Co-operative republic

Date of independence 1966

Capital Georgetown

Languages English (official), Hindi, Urdu, Amerindian dialects

Ethnic groups E Indian (51%), mixed African (31%), Amerindian (5%) (Carib 4%, Arawak 1%)

Religions Christian (42%), Hindu (37%), Muslim (9%)

Physical features Located on N coast of S America. Inland forest covers c.85% of land area. Highest peak: Mt Roraima, rising to 2 875 m/9 432 ft in the Pakaraima Mts (W). Main rivers, Essequibo, Rupununi, and Corantijn, with many rapids and waterfalls in upper courses.

Climate Equatorial climate in the lowlands; hot, wet, with constant high humidity. Average annual temperature 26°C (Jan), 27°C (Jul) in Georgetown. Two seasons of high rainfall (May–Jul, Nov–Jan); average annual rainfall 2 175 mm/87 in.

Currency 1 Guyana Dollar (G$) = 100 cents

Economy High unemployment, influenced by labour unrest, low productivity, and high foreign debt. Economy largely based on sugar, rice, bauxite, shrimps, livestock, cotton, molasses, timber.

GDP (1989) $248 mn, (1987) per capita $380

History Sighted by Columbus, 1498. Settled by the Dutch, late 16th-c. Several areas ceded to Britain, 1814; consolidated as British Guiana, 1831. Independence, 1966; Cooperative republic within the Commonwealth, 1970; governed by a President who holds executive power and appoints a Prime Minister, and a National Assembly, elected every five years.

Head of State/Government
1985–92   Hugh Desmond Hoyte
1992–   Cheddi Jagan

Prime Minister and First Vice-President
1985–92   Hamilton Green
1992–   Samuel Hinds

Human geography

HAITI

Local name Haïti

Timezone GMT – 5

Area 27 750 km²/10 712 sq mi

Population total (1991e) 6 286 000

Status Republic

Date of independence 1804

Capital Port-au-Prince

Languages French (official), with Creole French widely spoken

Ethnic groups African descent (95%), European (mulatto) (5%)

Religions Roman Catholic (80%), Protestant (10%)

Physical features Consists of two mountainous peninsulas, (Massif du Nord (N) and Massif de la Hotte (S), separated by a deep structural depression, the Plaine du Cul-de-Sac. Highest peak, La Selle, 2 680 m/8 793 ft. Includes islands of Gonâve (W) and Tortue (N).

Climate Tropical climate. Average annual temperatures 25°C (Jan) 29°C (Jul) in Port-au-Prince. Wet season (May–Sep); average annual rainfall for N coast and mountains 1 475–1 950 mm/58–77 in, but only 500 mm/20 in on W side. Hurricanes common.

Currency 1 Gourde (G, Gde) = 100 centimes

Economy Based on agriculture; large plantations grow coffee, sugar, sisal, rice, bananas, corn, sorghum, cocoa; sugar refining, textiles, flour milling; cement, bauxite; tourism; light assembly industries.

GDP (1990e) $2.7 bn, per capita $440

History Visited by Columbus, 1492. Created when W third of island ceded to France as Saint-Domingue, 1697. Slave rebellion followed by independence as Haiti, 1804. United with Santo Domingo (Dominican Republic), 1822–44. Under US occupation, 1915–34. Duvalier family had absolute power, 1957–86; after 1986 coup, new constitution provided for a bicameral National Congress con-

sisting of a Senate and a National Assembly. Military coup in 1992 forced Jean-Bertrand Aristide to flee the country, and a provisional government was created. Marc Bazin resigned as head of an army-backed coalition government, 1993; talks between deposed President, Aristide and coup leader Cédras reached deadlock, Jun 1993.

Head of State

1990	Ertha Pascal-Trouillot *Interim*
1990–1	Jean-Bertrand Aristide
1991	Raoul Cédras *Military Junta*
1991–2	Joseph Nerette *Interim*

Head of Government

1992–3	Marc Bazin
1993–	Robert Malval

HONDURAS

Local name Honduras

Timezone GMT – 6

Area 112 088 km²/43 266 sq mi

Population total (1992e) 5 105 500

Status Republic

Date of independence 1821

Capital Tegucigalpa

Languages Spanish (official), a number of Indian dialects are also spoken by aboriginal population

Ethnic groups Spanish–Indian origin (90%), Indian (7%)

Religions Roman Catholic (85%), Protestant (mainly Fundamentalist, Moravian, and Methodist) (10%)

Physical features Coastal lands (S) separated from Caribbean coastlands by mountains running NW–SE. S plateau rises to 2 849 m/9 347 ft at Cerro de las Minas. Also includes Bay Is in the Caribbean Sea and nearly 300 islands in the Gulf of Fonseca.

Climate Tropical climate in coastal areas, temperate in C and W. Average annual temperatures 19°C (Jan), 23°C (Jul) in Tegucigalpa. Two wet seasons in upland areas (May–Jul, Sep–Oct).

Currency 1 Lempira (L, La) = 100 centavos

Economy Agriculture (provides a third of national income), forestry, mining, cattle raising; bananas, coffee, beef, cotton, tobacco, sugar; exports of silver, lead and zinc; offshore oil exploration in the Caribbean.

GDP (1990e) $4.9 bn, (1989) per capita $960

History Centre of Mayan culture, 4th–9th-c. Settled by the Spanish in early 16th-c, and became province of Guatemala. Independence from Spain, 1821; joined Federation of C America; independence, 1838. Several military coups in 1970s. A democratic constitutional republic, governed by a President and a National Assembly.

Head of State/Government
1982–6   Roberto Suazo Córdova
1986–90   José Azcona Hoyo
1990–4   Rafael Callejas
1994–   Carlos Roberto Reina

HONG KONG >> UNITED KINGDOM

HUNGARY

Local name Magyarország

Timezone GMT + 1

Area 93 036 km²/35 912 sq mi

Population total (1991e) 10 588 000

Status Republic

Date of independence 1918

Capital Budapest

Language Hungarian (Magyar) (official)

Ethnic groups Magyar (96%), German (2%), Slovak (1%), Romanian and Yugoslav minorities

Religions Roman Catholic (67%), Calvinist (20%), Lutheran (5%)

Physical features Drained by the R Danube (flows N–S) and its tributaries. Crossed (W) by a low spur of the Alps; highest peak, Kékestetö, 1 014 m/3 327 ft. Frequent flooding, especially in the Great Plains (E). 54% of land is arable; 18% forested.

Climate Fairly extreme continental climate, due to landlocked position. Average annual temperature 0°C (Jan), 21°C (Jul) in Budapest. Wettest in spring and early summer; average annual rainfall 600 mm/23.6 in. Cold winters; R Danube sometimes frozen over for long periods. Frequent fogs.

Currency 1 Forint (Ft) = 100 fillér

Economy Large-scale nationalization as part of centralized planning strategy of the new republic, 1946–9. Greater independence to individual factories and farms, from 1968. Grain, potatoes, sugar beet, fruit, wine; coal, bauxite, lignite; metallurgy, engineering, chemicals, textiles, food processing.

GNP (1990e) $60.9 bn, per capita $5 800

History Kingdom formed under St Stephen I, 11th-c. Conquered by Turks, 1526; part of Habsburg Empire,

17th-c. Austria and Hungary reconstituted as a dual monarchy, 1867; republic, 1918; communist revolt led by Béla Kun, 1919; monarchical constitution restored in 1920. New republic with communist government, 1949; uprising crushed by Soviet forces, 1956. During 1989, pressure for political change towards a multi-party system; multi-party elections in 1990 saw an end to communist rule. Governed by a National Assembly which elects a Presidential Council and Council of Ministers.

Head of State
1989–90   Mátyás Szúrös
1990–   Árpád Göncz

Head of Government
1988–90   Miklós Németh
1990–3   József Antall
1993–   Peter Boross

ICELAND

Local name Ísland

Timezone GMT

Area 103 000 km²/40 000 sq mi

Population total (1991e) 259 000

Status Republic

Date of independence 1944

Capital Reykjavík

Language Icelandic (official)

Ethnic groups Homogeneous (96%), with European minorities

Religions Protestant (95%) (Evangelical Lutheran 93%, other Lutheran 2%), Roman Catholic (1%), non-religious (1%)

Physical features Several active volcanoes, including Hekla, 1 491 m/4 920 ft; Helgafell, 215 m/706 ft; and Surtsey, 174 m/570 ft. Famous for its geysers; many towns are heated by subterranean hot water. Heavily indented coastline with many long fjords. High ridges rise to 2 119 m/6 952 ft at Hvannadalshnjúkur (SE). Several large snowfields and glaciers.

Climate Changeable; summers cool and cloudy, mild winters. Average annual temperature 1°C (Jan), 11°C (Jul); Reykjavík generally ice-free throughout year. Average monthly rainfall reaches 94 mm/3.7 in (Oct).

Currency 1 Króna (1Kr, 1SK) = 100 aurar

Economy Based on inshore and deep-water fishing (75% of national income); stock and dairy farming, potatoes, greenhouse vegetables; aluminium, diatomite; tourism.

GDP (1990) $4.2 bn, per capita $16 300

History Settled by the Norse, 9th-c; world's oldest Parliament (*Althing*), 10th-c. Union with Norway, 1262;

union with Denmark, 1380. Independent kingdom in personal union with Denmark, 1918; independent republic, 1944. Extension of the fishing limit around Iceland in 1958 and 1975 precipitated the 'Cod War' disputes with the UK. Governed by a bicameral Parliament (*Althing*), a President, a Prime Minister, and a Cabinet.

Head of State
1980–   Vigdís Finnbogadóttir

Head of Government
1988–91   Steingrímur Hermannsson
1991–   Davíd Oddsson

INDIA

Local name Bhārat (Hindi)

Timezone GMT + 5.5

Area 3 166 829 km²/1 222 396 sq mi

Population total (1992e) 889 700 000

Status Republic

Date of independence 1947

Capital New Delhi

Languages Hindi and English (official); others include Urdu, Panjabi, Gujarati, Marathi, Bengali, Oriya, Kashmiri, Assamese, Kannada, Malayalam, Sindhi, Tamil and Telugu

Ethnic groups Indo-Aryan (72%), Dravidian (25%), with Mongoloid and other minorities

Religions Hindu (83%), Muslim (11%), Christian (2%), Sikh (2%), Buddhist (1%)

Physical features Seventh largest country in the world, located in S Asia; includes Andaman and Nicobar Is in the Bay of Bengal, and Laccadive Is in the Indian Ocean. Folded mountain ridges and valleys in N, highest peaks over 7 000 m/23 000 ft; C river plains of the Ganges, Yamuna, Ghaghari, and Brahmaputra to the S – control measures needed to prevent flooding. Thar Desert in NW bordered by semi-desert areas; Deccan Plateau in the S peninsula, with hills and wide valleys, bounded by the Western and Eastern Ghats; the coastal plains are important areas of rice cultivation.

Climate Dominated by the Asiatic monsoon. Rains come from the SW (Jun–Oct); rainfall decreases E–W on the N plains, with desert conditions in extreme W; tropical in S even in cool season. Average annual temperature 14°C (Jan), 31°C (Jul) in New Delhi; average annual rainfall 640 mm/25.2 in. Cyclones and storms on SE coast (especially Oct–Dec).

Currency 1 Indian Rupee (Re, Rs) = 100 paisa

Economy Agriculture employs over two-thirds of the labour force; tea, rice, wheat, coffee, sugar cane, cotton, jute, oil seed, maize, pulses, milk. Floods and drought cause major problems. Considerable increase in industrial production since independence; iron, steel, oil products, chemicals, fertilizers, chromite, barytes, oil, natural gas; tourism.

GDP (1990e) $220 830 mn, per capita $290

History Indus civilization emerged c.2500 BC, destroyed in 1500 BC by the Aryans, who developed the Brahmanic caste system. Mauryan Emperor Asoka unified most of India, and established Buddhism as the state religion in the 3rd-c BC; spread of Hinduism in the 2nd-c BC. Muslim influences during 7th-8th-c AD, with sultanate established at Delhi. Mughal Empire established by Babur in 1526 and extended by Akbar and Aurangzeb. Portuguese, French, Dutch, and British footholds in India in the 18th-c; conflict between France and Britain, 1746–63. Development of British interests represented by the East India Company. British power established after the Indian Mutiny crushed in 1857; movement for independence from the late 19th-c. Government of India Act of 1919 allowed election of Indian ministers to share power with appointed British governors; a further Act in 1935 allowed election of independent provincial governments. Passive-resistance campaigns of Mohandas Gandhi from 1920s; independence granted in 1947, on condition that a Muslim state be established (Pakistan). Indian states later reorganized on a linguistic basis. Pakistan–India war over disputed territory in Kashmir and Jammu, 1948. Federal democratic republic within the Commonwealth in 1950. Hindu–Muslim hostility, notably in 1978, and further India–Pakistan conflict in 1965 and 1971. Separatist movements continue, especially relating to Sikh interests in the Punjab; suppression of militant Sikh movement in 1984 led to assassination of Indira Gandhi; Rajiv Gandhi assassinated, 1991. Each of the 25 states administered by a governor appointed by the President; each

state has an Assembly. The President, advised by a Council of Ministers, appoints a Prime Minister; Parliament comprises the President, an Upper House, and a House of the People.

Head of State

1987–92	Ramaswami Venkataraman
1992–	Shankar Dayal Sharma

Head of Government

1989–90	Vishwanath Pratap Singh
1990–1	Chandra Shekhar
1991–	P V Narasimha Rao

INDONESIA

Local name Indonesia

Timezone GMT + 7 to + 9

Area 1 906 240 km²/735 809 sq mi

Population total (1992e) 184 796 000

Status Republic

Date of independence 1945

Capital Jakarta

Languages Bahasa Indonesia (official), English, Dutch, and Javanese widely spoken

Ethnic groups Madurese (40%), Javanese (33%), Sudanese (15%), Bahasa Indonesian (12%)

Religions Muslim (88%), Christian (9%) (Roman Catholic 6%, Protestant 2%), Hindu (2%), Buddhist (1%)

Physical features World's largest island group of 13 677 islands and islets, of which c.6 000 are inhabited. Five main islands: Sumatra, Java, Kalimantan (two-thirds of Borneo I), Sulawesi, Irian Jaya (W half of New

Guinea I). Characterized by mountainous volcanic landscape and equatorial rainforest. Over 100 volcanic peaks on Java, 15 active.

Climate Hot and humid equatorial climate; dry season (Jun–Sep), rainy season (Dec–Mar). Average annual temperature 26°C (Jan), 27°C (Jul) in Jakarta; average annual rainfall 1 775 mm/69 in.

Currency 1 Indonesian Rupiah (Rp) = 100 sen

Economy Mainly agrarian, notably rice. Oil, natural gas, and petroleum products from Borneo and Sumatra account for nearly 60% of national income. Small manufacturing industry.

GDP (1990e) $94 bn, per capita $490

History Settled in early times by Hindus and Buddhists, whose power lasted until the 14th-c; Islam introduced in the 14th–15th-c. Portuguese settlers in the early 16th-c. Dutch East India Company established, 1602. Japanese occupation in World War 2. Independence proclaimed with Sukarno as President in 1945; changed name from

Indonesia (continued)

☐ *international airport*

Netherlands East Indies to the Republic of the United States of Indonesia in 1949. Federal system replaced by unified control in 1950, and the unitary Republic of Indonesia proclaimed (W New Guinea remained under Dutch control until 1963 and is now called Irian Jaya). Military coup, 1966. Governed by a President elected by a People's Consultative Assembly, and advised by a Cabinet and several advisory agencies. Separatist movements in Irian Jaya and East Timor; United Nations refuses to recognize Indonesian sovereignty in East Timor.

Head of State/Government

1968–   T N J Suharto

IRAN

Local name Īrān

Timezone GMT + 3.5

Area 1 648 000 km²/636 128 sq mi

Population total (1992e) 59 600 000

Status Islamic Republic

Date of independence 1925

Capital Teheran

Languages Farsi (Persian) (official), several minority languages including Kurdish, Baluchi, Luri, and Turkic (including Afshari, Shahsavani, and Turkish)

Ethnic groups Persian (63%), Turkic (18%), other Iranian (13%), Kurdish (3%), Arab, and other Semitic (3%)

Religions Muslim (Shi'ite 92%, Sunni 5%), Zoroastrian (2%), Jewish, Baha'i, and Christian (1%)

Physical features Largely composed of a vast arid C plateau, average elevation 1 200 m/4 000 ft. Bounded N by the Elburz Mts, rising to 5 670 m/18 602 ft at Mt Damavand; Zagros Mts in W and S.

Climate Mainly a desert climate, hot and humid on Arabian Gulf. Average annual temperatures 2°C (Jan), 30°C (Jul) in Teheran; average annual rainfall 246 mm/9.7 in. Frequent earthquakes.

Currency 1 Iranian Rial (RIs, RI) = 100 dinars

Economy World's fourth largest oil producer, but production severely disrupted by 1978 revolution, and Iran–Iraq War and Gulf War, 1991. Agriculture and

☐ *international airport*

forestry (employs a third of population); natural gas, iron ore, copper, coal, salt; textiles, sugar refining, petrochemicals; traditional handicrafts (especially carpets).

GDP (1990) $80 bn, per capita $1 400

History Early centre of civilization, dynasties including the Achaemenids and Sassanids; ruled by Arabs, Turks, and Mongols until the Sasavid dynasty in the 16th–18th-c, and the Qajar dynasty in the 19th–20th-c. Military coup in 1921, with independence under Reza Shah Pahlavi, 1925; changed name from Persia to Iran, 1935. Protests against Shah's regime in 1970s led to revolution in 1978. Exile of Shah, and proclamation of Islamic Republic under Ayatollah Khomeini, 1979; Islamic Cultural Revolution under Khomeini saw a return to strict observance of Muslim principles and traditions. Occupation of US Embassy in Teheran, 1979–81; Iran–Iraq War following invasion of Iraq, 1980–8. Overall authority exercised by appointed spiritual leader: post of Prime Minister abolished in 1989; governed by a President and a Consultative Assembly (*Majlis*).

Leader of the Islamic Republic

1979–89	Ayatollah Khomeini
1989–	Ayatollah Sayed Ali Khamenei

Head of State/Government

1981–9	Seyed Ali Khamenei
1989–	Ali Akbar Hashemi Rafsanjani

IRAQ

Local name Al-'Irāq

Timezone GMT + 3

Area 434 925 km²/167 881 sq mi

Population total (1992e) 18 838 000

Status Republic

Date of independence 1932

Capital Baghdad

Languages Arabic (official), also English, Kurdish, Persian, Turkish, and Assyrian spoken

Ethnic groups Arab (79%), Kurd (largely in NE) (16%), Persian (3%), Turkish (2%)

Religions Muslim (95%) (Shi'ite 63%, Sunni 32%), Christian (3%)

Physical features Comprises the vast alluvial tract of the Tigris–Euphrates lowland (ancient Mesopotamia); Tharthar and Euphrates rivers, divided by Al Jazirah plain, flow over dense swampland and join to form the navigable Shatt al-Arab. Mountains (NE) rise to over 3 000 m/ 9 800 ft; desert in other areas.

Climate Mainly arid climate; summers very hot and dry; winters often cold. Average annual temperature 10°C (Jan), 35°C (Jul) in Baghdad; average annual rainfall 140 mm/15.5 in.

Currency 1 Iraqi Dinar (ID) = 1 000 fils

Economy World's second largest producer of oil, but production severely disrupted during both Gulf Wars (several oil installations destroyed); natural gas, oil refining, petrochemicals, cement, textiles; dates, cotton, winter wheat, rice, sheep, cattle.

GDP (1989) $35 bn, per capita $1 950

History Part of the Ottoman Empire from 16th-c until World War I. Captured by British forces, 1916; British-mandated territory, 1921; independence under Hashemite dynasty, 1932; monarchy replaced by military rule, and Iraq declared a republic, 1958. Since 1960s, Kurdish nationalists in NE have been fighting to establish a separate state. Invasion of Iran in 1980, led to the Iran–Iraq War, lasting until a ceasefire in 1988. Invasion and annexation of Kuwait in Aug 1990 led to the 1991 Gulf

□ *international airport*

War (Jan–Feb): UN sanctions imposed on Iraq in 1991, and a successful land, sea, and air offensive by UN ended the war. Rebellions against the government by Kurds (N Iraq) and Shi'ites (S Iraq) were quelled, however, and in 1992 the UN was forced to impose a no-fly zone over S Iraq to protect the Shi'ites, and a security zone in N Iraq to protect Kurdish refugees. Governed by Revolutionary Command Council, which elects a President and shares legislative authority with the National Assembly. Kurdish regional assembly has limited powers of legislation.

Head of State/Government

1968–79	Said Ahmad Hassan al Bakr
1979–	Sadam Hussein at-Takriti

IRELAND, REPUBLIC OF

Local name Éire (Gaelic)

Timezone GMT

Area 70 282 km²/27 129 sq mi

Population total (1991) 3 525 719

Status Republic (occupying S, C, and NW Ireland; bounded NE by Northern Ireland, part of the UK)

Capital Dublin

Languages Irish Gaelic and English (official)

Ethnic groups Celtic (94%), small English minority

Religions Roman Catholic (95%), Anglican (Church of Ireland) (3%), Presbyterian (1%)

Physical features Mountainous landscapes in W, part of Caledonian system of Scandinavia and Scotland with quartzite peaks weathered into conical mountains such as Croagh Patrick, 765 m/2510 ft; landscape of ridges and valleys in SW, rising towards Macgillycuddy's Reek Mts. Lowlands in E drained by slow-moving rivers such as the Shannon (S), Liffey (E), and Slaney (SE).

Climate Mild and equable climate. Average annual temperature 5°C (Jan), 15°C (Jul); rainfall heaviest in W, often over 3000 mm/120 in.

Currency 1 Irish Pound/Punt (1£, IR£) = 100 new pence

Economy Primarily agriculture (two-thirds of country covered by improved agricultural land); forestry developed since 1950s; fishing; food, drink, tobacco, textiles; recent growth in light engineering; synthetic fibres, electronics, pharmaceuticals; several peat-fired power stations; Kinsale natural-gas field near Cork; major tourist area. Member of the EC, 1973.

GDP (1990) $33.9 bn, per capita $9 690

History Occupied by Goidelic-speaking Celts during the Iron Age; conversion to Christianity by St Patrick, 5th-c; SE attacked by Vikings, c.800. Henry II of England declared himself lord of Ireland in 1171, but English influence restricted to area round Dublin (the Pale); Henry VIII took the title 'King of Ireland' in 1542. Catholic rebellion during English Civil War suppressed by Oliver Cromwell, 1649–50; supporters of deposed Catholic King James II were defeated by William III at Battle of the Boyne in 1690; struggle for Irish freedom developed in 18th–19th-c, including such revolutionary movements as Wolfe Tone's United Irishmen, 1796–8, and later Young Ireland, 1848, and the Fenians, 1866–7. Act of Union in 1801. Catholic Relief Act enabling Catholics to sit in Parliament, 1829. Population reduced by half during famine, 1846; Land Acts, 1870–1903, attacking Irish poverty. Home Rule Bills introduced by Gladstone, 1886, 1893; third Home Rule Bill passed in 1914, but never came into effect because of World War I. Armed rebellion, 1916; republic proclaimed by Sinn Fein, 1919. Partition proposed by Britain, 1920; treaty signed, giving dominion status, 1921; right of Northern Ireland to opt out was exercised, and frontier agreed, 1925. Renamed Éire in 1937. Left Commonwealth, 1949; Anglo-Irish Agreement signed, 1985. A President (*Uachtarán na h'Éireann*) is elected for seven years; there is a Prime Minister (*Taoiseach*); the National Parliament (*Oireachtas*) includes

a House of Representatives (*Dail Éireann*) and a Senate (*Seanad Eireann*).

Head of State

1976–90	Patrick J Hillery
1990–	Mary Robinson

Head of Government

1987–92	Charles Haughey
1992–	Albert Reynolds

Counties of Ireland

County	Area		Population	Admin. centre
	sq km	sq mi	(1991)	
Carlow	896	346	40 942	Carlow
Cavan	1 891	730	52 796	Cavan
Clare	3 188	1 231	90 918	Ennis
Cork	7 459	2 880	410 369	Cork
Donegal	4 830	1 865	128 117	Lifford
Dublin	922	356	1 025 304	Dublin
Galway	5 939	2 293	180 364	Galway
Kerry	4 701	1 815	121 894	Tralee
Kildare	1 694	654	122 656	Naas
Kilkenny	2 062	796	73 365	Kilkenny
Laoighis (Leix)	1 720	664	52 314	Portlaoise
Leitrim	1 526	589	25 301	Carrick
Limerick	2 686	1 037	161 956	Limerick
Longford	1 044	403	30 296	Longford
Louth	821	317	90 724	Dundalk
Mayo	5 398	2 084	110 713	Castlebar
Meath	2 339	903	105 370	Trim
Monaghan	1 290	498	51 293	Monaghan
Offaly	1 997	771	58 494	Tullamore
Roscommon	2 463	951	51 897	Roscommon
Sligo	1 795	693	54 756	Sligo
Tipperary	4 254	1 642	132 772	Clonmel
Waterford	1 869	710	91 624	Waterford
Westmeath	1 764	681	61 880	Mullingar
Wexford	2 352	908	102 869	Wexford
Wicklow	2 025	782	97 265	Wicklow

Human geography

ISRAEL

Local names Yisra'el (Hebrew), Isrā'īl (Arabic)

Timezone GMT + 2

Area 20770 km²/8017 sq mi (within boundaries defined by 1949 armistice agreements)

Population total (1992e) 5240000 (excluding E Jerusalem and Israeli settlers in occupied territories)

Status Republic

Date of independence 1948

Capital Jerusalem

Languages Hebrew and Arabic (official), also European languages spoken

Ethnic groups Jewish (83%), Arab (11%)

Religions Jewish (85%), Muslim (11%), Christian and others (4%)

Physical features Extends 420 km/261 mi N–S; width varies from 20 km/12 mi to 116 km/72 mi. Mountainous interior, rising to 1 208 m/3 963 ft at Mt Meron; mountains near Galilee (Lake Tiberius) and Samaria in the West Bank, dropping E to below sea-level in the Jordan–Red Sea rift valley; R Jordan forms part of E border. Dead Sea, between Israel and Jordan, 400 m/ 1 286 ft below sea level, is the largest lake and has no outlet. Negev desert (S) occupies c.60% of the country's area.

Climate Mediterranean climate in N and C, with hot, dry summers and warm, wet winters. Average annual temperature 9°C (Jan), 23°C (Jul) in Jerusalem; rainfall 528 mm/21 in.

Currency 1 New Israeli Shekel (NIS) = 100 agorot

Economy Over 90% of exports are industrial products; major tourist area, primarily to the religious centres; copper, potash, phosphates, citrus fruits, cotton, sugar beet, bananas, beef and dairy products; a world leader in agrotechnology, with areas of intensive cultivation. The *kibbutz* system produces c.40% of food output, but in recent years has turned increasingly towards industry.

GNP (1990) $46.5 bn, per capita $10 500

History Zionist movement founded by Theodor Herzl, end of 19th-c; thousands of Jews returned to Palestine, then part of the Ottoman Empire; Britain given League of Nations mandate to govern Palestine and establish Jewish national home there, 1922. British evacuated Palestine, and Israel proclaimed independence in 1948; invasion by Arab nations, resulting in armistice, 1949. Israel gained control of the Gaza Strip, Sinai Peninsula (as far as the Suez Canal), West Bank of the R Jordan

Israel and the PLO signed an agreement in September 1993, allowing Palestine self-government in the Gaza Strip and Jerico, and a lesser degree of self-rule in the West Bank

(including E sector of Jerusalem), and the Golan Heights in Syria, during the Six-Day War in 1967. Camp David conference between Egypt and Israel, 1978; Israeli withdrawal from Sinai, 1979. Invasion of Lebanon, forcing the PLO to leave Beirut, 1982–5; renewed tension with uprising of Arabs in occupied territories (the *intifada*) since 1988. Missile attacks by Iraq in Gulf War, 1991. A parliamentary democracy, with a Prime Minister and a Cabinet, and a unicameral Parliament (*Knesset*); President elected for a maximum of two five-year terms.

Head of State
1978–83	Yitzhak Navon
1983–93	Chaim Herzog
1993–	Ezer Weizmann

Head of Government
1988–92	Yitzhak Shamir
1992–	Yitzhak Rabin

Human geography

ITALY

Local name Italia

Timezone GMT + 1

Area 301 225 km²/116 273 sq mi

Population total (1991) 57 103 833

Status Republic

Capital Rome

Languages Italian (official), with German spoken in the Trentino-Alto Adige, French in Valle d'Aosta, and Slovene in Trieste-Gorizia

Ethnic groups Homogeneous (98%), with German–Italian, French–Italian, and Slovene–Italian minorities

Religions Roman Catholic (83%), non-religious (14%)

Physical features Comprises the boot-shaped peninsula extending south into the Mediterranean Sea, as well as Sicily, Sardinia, and some smaller islands. Italian peninsula extends c.960 km/600 mi SE from the Lombardy plains; Apennines rise to peaks above 2 000 m/ 6 500 ft; Alps form a border in N. Broad, fertile Lombardo-Venetian plain in basin of R Po; several lakes at foot of the Alps, including Maggiore, Como, Garda; flat and marshy on Adriatic coast (N); coastal mountains descend steeply to the Ligurian Sea on the Riviera (W). Mt Vesuvius, 1 289 m/4 230 ft, and Vulcano, 502 m/1 650 ft, are also active volcanoes. Island of Sicily separated from the mainland by the 4 km/2.5 mi wide Strait of Messina; the island includes the volcanic cone of Mt Etna, 3 390 m/11 122 ft.

Climate Warm and temperate in S; hot and sunny summers, short cold winters. Average annual temperatures 7°C (Jan), 25°C (Jul); average annual rainfall 657 mm/ 26 in. Cold, wet, often snowy in higher peninsular areas; Mediterranean climate in coastal regions; Adriatic coast colder than the W coast, and receives less rainfall.

Currency 1 Italian Lira (L, Lit) = 100 centesimi

Economy Industry largely concentrated in N; machinery, iron and steel. Tourism. Poorer agricultural region in S; Po valley a major agricultural region, with wheat, maize, sugar, potatoes, rice, beef, dairy farming; foothills of the Alps produce apples, peaches, walnuts, wine; further S, citrus fruits, vines, olives, tobacco.

GDP (1990) $844 bn, per capita $14 600

History Inhabited by the Etruscans (N), Latins (C), and Greeks (S) in pre-Roman times. Most regions part of the Roman Empire by 3rd-c BC; invaded by barbarian tribes in 4th-c AD; last Roman emperor deposed, 476. Ruled by the Lombards and by the Franks under Charlemagne, who was crowned Emperor of the Romans in 800; part of the Holy Roman Empire under Otto, 962. Conflict between popes and emperors throughout Middle Ages; dispute between Guelphs and Ghibellines, 12th-c; divided among five powers, 14th–15th-c (Kingdom of Naples, Duchy of Milan, republics of Florence and Venice, the papacy). Major contribution to European culture through the Renaissance. Numerous republics set up after the French Revolution; Napoleon crowned King of Italy in 1805. Upsurge of liberalism and nationalism (*Risorgimento*) in 19th-c; unification achieved under Vic-

□ *international airport*

Regions of Italy

tor Emmanuel II of Sardinia, aided by Cavour and Garibaldi, by 1870. Fought alongside Allies in World War I. Fascist movement brought Mussolini to power, 1922; conquest of Abyssinia, 1935–6, and Albania, 1939; alliance with Hitler in World War 2 led to the end of the

Italian Empire. Monarchy abolished and became a democratic republic in 1946. Parliament consists of a Chamber of Deputies and a Senate; the President of the Republic is Head of State and appoints a Prime Minister. Continued political instability, with over 45 governments in power since the formation of the republic.

Head of State
1985–92   Francesco Cossiga
1992–   Oscar Luigi Scalfaro

Head of Government
1989–92   Giulio Andreotti
1992–3   Giuliano Amato
1993–4   Carlo Azeglio Ciampi
1994–   Sylvio Berlusconi

JAMAICA

Local name Jamaica

Timezone GMT – 5

Area 10 957 km²/4 229 sq mi

Population total (1992e) 2 445 000

Status Independent state within the Commonwealth

Date of independence 1962

Capital Kingston

Languages English (official), with Jamaican Creole widely spoken

Ethnic groups African (76%), Afro-European (15%), East Indian and Afro-Indian (3%), White (3%), Chinese and Afro-Chinese (1%)

Religions Christian (Protestant 56%, Roman Catholic 5%), non-religious (17%)

Physical features Third largest island in the Caribbean; maximum length, 234 km/145 mi; width, 35–82 km/22–51 mi. Mountainous and rugged, particularly in the E, where the Blue Mt Peak rises to 2 256 m/7 401 ft. Over 100 small rivers, several used for hydroelectric power.

Climate Humid, tropical climate at sea-level; more temperate at higher altitudes. Average annual temperature 24°C (Jan), 27°C (Jul); mean annual rainfall 1 980 mm/70 in; virtually no rainfall on S and SW plain. Lies within the hurricane belt.

Currency 1 Jamaican Dollar (J$) = 100 cents

Economy Plantation agriculture (still employs about a third of workforce); sugar, bananas, citrus fruits, coffee, cocoa, ginger, coconuts; bauxite (world's second largest producer); cement, fertilizer, textiles, rum, chemical products; tourism.

GDP (1990) $3.9 bn, per capita $150

History Visited by Columbus in 1494; settled by Spanish in 1509. West African slave labour imported for work on sugar plantations from 1640. British occupation from 1655. Self-government, 1944; independence, 1962. Governor-General appoints Prime Minister and Cabinet; bicameral Parliament consists of House of Representatives and a Senate.

Head of State
(British monarch represented by Governor-General)
1991–   Howard Cooke

Head of Government
1989–1992 Michael Norman Manley
1992–   Percival Patterson

JAPAN

Local name Nihon (Nippon)

Timezone GMT + 9

Area 377 728 km²/145 803 sq mi

Population total (1991) 123 156 678

Status Monarchy

Capital Tokyo

Language Japanese (official)

Ethnic groups Japanese (99%), with Korean minorities

Religions Shintoist (40%), Buddhist (39%), Christian (4%)

Physical features Island state comprising four large islands (Hokkaido, Honshu, Kyushu, Shikoku) and several small islands. Consists mainly of steep mountains with many volcanoes; Hokkaido (N) central range runs N–S, rising to over 2 000 m/6 500 ft, falling to coastal uplands and plains. Honshu, the largest island, comprises parallel arcs of mountains bounded by narrow coastal plains, and includes Mt Fuji, 3 776 m/12 388 ft; heavily populated Kanto plain in E. Shikoku and Kyushu (SW) consist of clusters of low cones and rolling hills,

Jordan

Japan (continued)

mostly 1 000–2 000 m/3 000–6 000 ft. Ryukyu chain of volcanic islands to the S, largest Okinawa.

Climate Oceanic climate, influenced by the Asian monsoon. Heavy winter rainfall on W coasts of Honshu and in Hokkaido; short, warm summers in N, and severe winters, with heavy snow; variable winter weather throughout Japan, especially in N and W; typhoons in summer and early autumn; mild and almost subtropical winters in S Honshu, Shikoku, and Kyushu. Average annual temperatures 5°C (Jan), 25°C (Jul) in Tokyo.

Currency 1 Yen (¥, Y) = 100 sen

Economy Limited natural resources (less than 20% of land under cultivation); intensive crop production (principally of rice); timber, fishing, engineering, ship-building, textiles, chemicals; major industrial developments since 1960s, especially in computing, electronics, and vehicles.

GNP (1990) $2.1 trillion, per capita $17 100

History Originally occupied by the Ainu; developed into small states, 4th-c. Culture strongly influenced by China, 7th–9th-c; ruled by feudal shoguns until power passed to the emperor, 1867; limited contact with the West until the Meiji Restoration, 1868. In a successful war with China, 1894–5; gained Formosa (Taiwan) and S Manchuria. Formed alliance with Britain in 1902. War with Russia, 1904–5; Russia ceded southern half of Sakhalin. Korea annexed in 1910. Joined allies in World War 1, 1914; received German Pacific islands as mandates, 1919. War with China; occupied Manchuria, 1931–2; renewed fighting, 1937. Entered World War 2 with surprise attack on the US fleet at Pearl Harbour, Hawaii, 1941; occupied British and Dutch possessions in SE Asia, 1941–2; pushed back during 1943–5. Atomic bombs dropped on Hiroshima and Nagasaki by allied forces in 1945, ending World War 2 with Japanese surrender; allied control commission took power, and Formosa and Manchuria returned to China. Emperor Hirohito became figurehead ruler, 1946; full sovereignty regained, 1952; joined United Nations, 1958. Strong economic growth in 1960s. Regained Bonin,

Okinawa, and Volcano Islands, 1972. A constitutional monarchy with an Emperor as Head of State; a Prime Minister, and a Cabinet; bicameral Diet (*Kokkai*), with a House of Representatives and a House of Councillors.

Head of State (Emperor)
1989–   Akihito

Head of Government (Prime Minister)
1989–91   Toshiki Kaifu
1991–3   Kiichi Miyazawa
1993–   Morihiro Hosokawa

JORDAN

Local name Al'Urdun

Timezone GMT + 2

Area 96 188 km²/37 129 sq mi
(including 6 644 km²/2 565 sq mi in the West Bank)

Population total (1992e) 3 943 000

Status Hashemite kingdom

Date of independence 1946

Capital Amman

Language Arabic (official)

Ethnic groups Arab (99%), Circassian, Armenian, Turkish, Kurd minorities

Religions Muslim (Sunni 95%), Christian (including Roman Catholic, Anglican, Coptic, Greek Orthodox, and Evangelical Lutheran) (5%)

Physical features Located in Middle East. Divided N–S by Red Sea–Jordan rift valley, much lying below sea level; lowest point, –400 m/–1 312 ft at the Dead Sea. Highest point, Jebel Ram, 1 754 m/5 754 ft; land levels out to the Syrian desert (E). C.90% of Jordan is desert.

Climate Mediterranean; hot, dry summers, cool, wet winters; desert area uniformly hot, sunny; rainfall below 200 mm/8 in; average annual temperatures 8°C (Jan), 25°C (Jul) in Amman.

Currency 1 Jordan Dinar = 1 000 fils

Economy Oil, cement, potash, phosphate (world's third largest exporter), light manufacturing; cereals, vegetables, citrus fruits, olives.

GDP (1987) $4.3 bn, (1988) per capita $1 127

History Part of Roman Empire; Arab control, 7th-c; part of Turkish Empire, 16th-c until World War 1. Area divided into Palestine (W of R Jordan) and Transjordan (E of R Jordan), administered by Britain; independence as Transjordan in 1946; British mandate over Palestine ended in 1948; renamed Jordan in 1949; Israeli control of West Bank after Six-Day War in 1967; civil war, following attempts by Jordanian army to expel Palestinian guerrillas from West Bank, 1970–1. Claims to the West Bank ceded to the Palestine Liberation Organization in 1974; links with the West Bank cut, PLO established a government in exile in 1988. Martial law formally abolished by King Hussein in 1992, and ban on political parties lifted. Monarch is Head of State and appoints a Prime Minister, who selects a Council of Ministers; Parliament consists of a Senate and a House of Representatives.

Head of State (Monarch)
1952 –   Hussein II

Head of Government
1991   Taher al-Masri
1991–3   Sharif Zaid bin Shaker
1993–   Abdul Salam Majali

Golan Heights and West Bank
occupied by Israel since 1967

KAZAKHSTAN

international airport

Local name Kazakhstan

Timezone GMT + 5

Area 2 717 300 km²/1 048 878 sq mi

Population total (1992e) 16 700 000

Status Republic

Date of independence 1991

Capital Almaty (Alma-Ata)

Languages Kazakh (official), Russian, German

Ethnic groups Kazakh (40%), Russian (37%), German (6%), Ukrainian (5%)

Religions Muslim (Sunni), Christian (Russian Orthodox, Protestant)

Human geography

Human geography

Kazakhstan (continued)

Physical features Bounded E by China and W by Caspian Sea. Second largest republic in former USSR. Mountain ranges in E and SE; steppeland (N) gives way to desert (S); lowest elevation near the E shore of the Caspian Sea, 132 m/1 433 ft below sea-level. Main rivers, Irtysh, Syr Darya, Ural, Ili. Largest lake, L Balkhash. Space launch centre at Tyuratam, near Baikonur.

Climate Continental; hot summers, extreme winters. Wide range of temperatures, from −17°C in N and C ranges, to −3°C in S (Jan), 20°C in N, 29°C in S (Jul). Strong, dry winds common in NW.

Currency (1992) 1 Rouble (R) = 100 kopecks

Economy Coal, iron ore, bauxite, copper, nickel, oil; oil refining, metallurgy, heavy engineering, chemicals, leatherwork, footwear, food processing; cotton, fruit, grain, sheep.

GNP (1992e) $41.7 bn, per capita $2470

History Under the control of the Mongols, 13th-c; gradually under Russian rule, 1730–1853. Became constituent republic of USSR in 1936. Independence movement, 1990–1; independence declared in 1991, and joined new Commonwealth of Independent States (CIS). Joined the CSCE (Conference on Security and Cooperation in Europe) in 1992.

Head of State
1991–   Nursultan A Nazarbayev

Head of Government
1991–   Sergei Tereshchenko

KENYA

Local name Kenya

Timezone GMT + 3

Area 564 162 km²/217 766 sq mi

Population total (1991e) 25 241 000

Status Republic

Date of independence 1963

Capital Nairobi

Languages English and Swahili (official), with many local languages spoken

Ethnic groups Kikuyu (21%), Luhya (14%), Luo (13%), Kalenjin (11%), Kamba (11%), Kisii (6%), Meru (6%)

Religions Christian (66%) (Roman Catholic 28%, Protestant 38%), local beliefs (26%), Muslim (6%)

Physical features Crossed by the Equator; SW plateau rises to 600–3 000 m/2 000–10 000 ft, includes Mt Kenya, 5 200 m/17 058 ft; Great Rift Valley (W) runs N–S; dry, arid semi-desert in the N, generally under 600 m/2 000 ft; rivers include Tana and Athi; L Turkana in NW.

Climate Tropical climate on coast, with high temperatures and humidity. Average annual temperature 18°C (Jan), 16°C (Jul) in Nairobi; average annual rainfall 958 mm/38 in.

Currency 1 Kenyan shilling (KSh) = 100 cents

Economy Agriculture (accounts for c.35% of national income); coffee, tea, cashew nuts, rice, wheat, maize, sugar cane; textiles, chemicals, cement, oil refining, tobacco, rubber. Reserves of soda ash, salt, limestone, lead, gemstones, silver, gold. 14 national parks attract large numbers of tourists.

GDP (1990) $8.5 bn, per capita $380

History Very early fossil hominids found in the region by anthropologists. Coast settled by Arabs, 7th-c. Portuguese control, 16th–17th-c; British control as East African Protectorate from 1895; British colony in 1920. Independence movement led to Mau Mau rebellion, 1952–60; independence within the Commonwealth in 1963. Declared Republic of Kenya in 1964; first leader, Jomo Kenyatta. Anti-government riots for the approval of multi-party politics, 1990; constitutional amendments passed, 1992. Governed by a President with a unicameral National Assembly.

Head of State/Government
1978 –   Daniel Arap Moi

KIRIBATI

Local name Kiribati

Timezone GMT – 12

Area 717 km²/277 sq mi

Population total (1990e) 71 100

Status Republic

Date of independence 1979

Capital Bairiki (on Tarawa Atoll)

Languages English (official) and Gilbertese

Ethnic groups Micronesian, small Polynesian and non-Pacific minorities

Religions Roman Catholic (54%), Kiribati Protestant (39%), Baha'i (2%), Seventh-day Adventist (2%), Mormon (2%)

Physical features Group of 33 low-lying islands scattered over c.3 000 000 km²/1 200 000 sq mi of the C Pacific Ocean. Comprises the Gilbert Is Group, Phoenix Is, and 8 of the 11 Line Islands, including Christmas I. Islands seldom rise to more than 4 m/13 ft and usually consist of a reef enclosing a lagoon.

Climate Maritime equatorial climate in central islands, tropical further N and S; periodic drought in some islands. Wet season (Nov–Apr); subject to typhoons. Average annual temperatures 28°C (Jan), 27°C (July) in Tarawa; average annual rainfall 1 977 mm/78 in.

Currency 1 Australian Dollar ($A) = 100 cents

Economy 50% of land under permanent cultivation. Main exports include fish, particularly tuna. Phosphates; copra, coconuts, bananas, pandanus, breadfruit, papaya. Sea fishing.

GDP (1990) $36 mn, (1988) per capita $430

History Gilbert and Ellice Is proclaimed a British protectorate in 1892; became a Crown Colony, 1916. Occupied by Japan during World War II, but driven out by US forces. Ellice Is severed links with Gilbert Is to form separate dependency of Tuvalu in 1975; Gilbert Is independence as Kiribati in 1979. A sovereign and democratic republic, with a President and an elected House of Assembly.

Head of State/Government
1979–91 Ieremia T Tabai
1991– Teatao Teannaki

KOREA, NORTH

Local name Chōson Minjujuüi In'min Konghwaguk

Timezone GMT + 9

Area 122 098 km²/47 130 sq mi

Population total (1992e) 22 227 000

Status Democratic people's republic

Date of independence 1948

Capital Pyongyang

Language Korean (official)

Ethnic groups Korean (99.8%), Chinese (0.2%)

Religions Atheist or non-religious (68%), Buddhist (2%), Christian (1%)

Physical features Located in E Asia, in the N half of the Korean peninsula. Separated from South Korea to the S by a demilitarized zone of 1 262 km²/487 sq mi. Volcanic peak of Mount Paek-tu rises 2 744 m/9 003 ft in NE. Yalu river valley marks Korean–Chinese border in NW; fertile Chaeryong and Pyongyang plains in SW. 74% of land is forested, 18% is arable.

Climate Temperate; warm summers, severely cold winters; often rivers freeze for up to 3–4 months in winter. Average annual temperatures –8°C (Jan), 24°C (Jul); average annual rainfall 916 mm/26 in.

Currency 1 Won (NKW) = 100 chon

Economy Agriculture (employs c.48% of workforce, generally on large-scale collective farms); rice, maize, vegetables, livestock, wheat, barley, beans, tobacco. Timber, fishing. Severely affected during the Korean War, but rapid recovery with Soviet and Chinese aid. Machine building, mining, chemicals, textiles.

GNP (1988) $20 bn, per capita $2 180

History (>> KOREA, SOUTH history); formally annexed by Japan, 1910. N area occupied by Soviet troops following invasion by US and Russian troops and the dividing of the country into N and S in 1945. Democratic People's Republic of Korea declared in 1948; Korean War, 1950–3; demilitarized zone established, 1953. Friendship and mutual-assistance treaty signed with China in 1961. Unsuccessful reunification talks in 1980; became a member of UN, 1991; non-aggression agreement signed

Korea, North (continued)

with S Korea in 1991. Governed by a President and a Supreme People's Assembly.

Head of State
1972– Kim Il-sung

Head of Government
1988–92 Yon Hyong-muk
1992– Kang Song San

KOREA, SOUTH

Local name Taehan-Min'guk

Timezone GMT + 9

Area 98 913 km²/38 180 sq mi

Population total (1992e) 43 663 000

Status Republic

Date of independence 1948

Capital Seoul

Language Korean (official)

Ethnic groups Korean (99.9%), Chinese (0.1%)

Religions Buddhist (18%), Christian (Protestant 41%, Roman Catholic 3%), Confucianist (1%)

Physical features Occupies the S half of the Korean peninsula. Bordered N by North Korea, from which it is separated by a demilitarized zone at 38°N. Taebaek Sanmaek Mt range runs N–S along the E coast; descends to broad, undulating coastal lowlands. Rivers include Naktong and Han. C.3 000 islands off the W and S coasts; largest island is Cheju do, which contains Korea's highest peak, Hallasan, 1 950 m/6 398 ft.

Climate Extreme continental climate, cold winters, hot summers. Average annual temperatures –5°C (Jan), 25°C (Jul); average annual rainfall 1 250 mm/49 in.

Currency 1 Won (W) = 100 chon

Economy Light consumer goods, with a shift towards heavy industries; petrochemicals, textiles, electrical machinery, steel, ships, fish. One of the world's largest deposits of tungsten. Only a fifth of land suitable for cultivation; rice, wheat, barley, grain, pulses, tobacco.

GNP (1990) $238 bn, per capita $5 600

History Originally split into three rival kingdoms,

united in 668 AD by the Silla dynasty; succeeded by the Koryo dynasty in 935 AD. Yi dynasty, 1392–1910. Independence recognized by China, 1895; annexation by Japan, 1910. Entered by Russia (from N) and USA (from S) to enforce the Japanese surrender, dividing the country in N and S at the 38th parallel, 1945. Declared Republic of Korea in 1948; North Korean forces invaded in 1950; UN forces assisted South Korea in stopping the advance, 1950–3. Military coup, 1961; assassination of Park Chung Hee, 1979. Became a member of UN in 1991; non-aggression pact signed with N Korea in 1991. Governed by a President, a State Council, and a National Assembly.

Head of State

| 1988–93 | Roh Tae-woo |
| 1993– | Kim Young Sam |

Head of Government

1988–90	Kang Young-hoon
1990–1	Ro Jai-bong
1991–2	Chung Won-shik
1992–3	Hyun Soong Jong
1993	Hwang In Sung
1993–	Lee Hoi Chang

KUWAIT

Local name Dowlat al Kuwait (Arabic)

Timezone GMT + 3

Area 17 818 km²/6 878 sq mi

Population total (1992e) 1 200 000

Status Independent state

Date of independence 1961

Capital Kuwait City

Language Arabic (official)

Ethnic groups Kuwaiti (52%), non-Kuwaiti Arab (45%), Asian (3%)

Religions Muslim (90%), Christian (8%), Hindu (2%)

Physical features Consists of mainland and nine offshore islands. Terrain flat or gently undulating, rising SW to 271 m/889 ft; Wadi al Batin on W border with Iraq; low ridges in NE generally stony with sparse vegetation.

Climate Hot and dry climate; summer temperatures very high, often above 45°C (Jul–Aug); humidity often over 90%. Sandstorms common all year. Average annual temperature 14°C (Jan) to 37°C (Jul) in Kuwait City; average annual rainfall 111 mm/4 in.

Currency 1 Kuwaiti Dinar (KD) = 1 000 fils

Economy Oil discovered, 1938, and before the Gulf War provided 95% of government revenue. Active programme of economic diversification; petrochemicals, fertilizers, construction materials, asbestos, batteries. Agriculture gradually expanding; dates, citrus fruits, timber, livestock.

GDP (1989) $19.9 bn, per capita $19 700

History Port founded in 18th-c. British protectorate, 1914; full independence from Britain in 1961. Invasion and annexation by Iraq (Aug 1990), leading to Gulf War (Jan–Feb 1991), with severe damage to Kuwait City, Kuwaiti government-in-exile in Saudi Arabia. Kuwait liberated with the aid of UN forces in 1991, and govern-

ment returned from exile; new Cabinet formed headed by Crown Prince as Prime Minister; large refugee emigration; major post-war problems, including burning of Kuwaiti oil wells by Iraq and pollution of Gulf waters by oil. Emir is Head of State, governing through an appointed Prime Minister and a Council of Ministers.

Head of State (Emir)

| 1978– | Jabir al-Ahmad al-Jabir |

Head of Government (Prime Minister)

| 1978– | Saad al-Abdallah al-Salim |

Human geography

KYRGYZSTAN

Local name Kyrgyzstan

Timezone GMT + 5

Area 198 500 km²/76 621 sq mi

Population total (1990e) 4 400 000

Status Republic

Date of independence 1991

Capital Bishkek (formerly Frunze)

Language Kyrgyz (official)

Ethnic groups Kyrgyz (52%), Russian (21%), other (27%)

Religion Sunni Muslim (chief religion)

Physical features Located in C Asia, bounded SE and E by China. Largely occupied by the Tien Shan Mts; highest point within the republic at Pik Pobedy, 7 439 m/24 406 ft. Chief river, the Naryn. Largest lake, L Issyk-Kul.

Climate Typical desert climate in N, W, and SE; hot, dry summers in valleys. Mean annual temperature −18°C (Jan), 28°C (Jul).

Currency (1992) 1 Rouble (R) = 100 kopecks

Economy Metallurgy; machines; coal; natural gas; textiles, food processing, gold. Wheat, cotton, tobacco, animal husbandry.

GNP (1992e) $6.9 bn, per capita $1 550

History Part of an independent Turkestan republic,

□ international airport

1917–24; proclaimed a constituent republic of the USSR, 1936. State of emergency declared in Bishkek, and Askar Akayev chosen by Supreme Soviet as state President in 1990; declaration of independence, 1991, and joined new Commonwealth of Independent States (CIS); joined the CSCE (Conference on Security and Cooperation in Europe) in 1992.

Head of State
1990–   Askar Akayev

Head of Government
1991–3   Tursunbek Chyngyshev
1993–   Apas Jumagulov

LAOS

Local name Lao

Timezone GMT + 7

Area 236 800 km²/91 405 sq mi

Population total (1992e) 4 410 000

Status Republic

Date of independence 1949

Capital Vientiane

Languages Lao (official), French, and tribal languages

Ethnic groups Laotian (60%), hill tribes (35%)

Religions Buddhist (58%), animist (largely the Lao-Theung) (34%), Christian (2%)

Physical features Landlocked country on the Indo-Chinese peninsula. Dense jungle and rugged mountains (E), rising to 2 751 m/9 025 ft on Vietnamese border, and 2 820 m/9 252 ft at Phou Bia on the Xieng Khouang plateau. Mekong R flows NW–SE, fertile Mekong floodplains in W. 4% of land is arable, 58% forested.

Climate Monsoonal climate; average annual rainfall 1 715 mm/67.5 in; (heaviest, May–Sep). Average annual temperature 21°C (Jan), 27°C (Jul) in Vientiane.

Currency (1992) 1 Kip (Kp) = 100 at

Economy Agricultural economy suffered severely in

□ international airport

the civil war; rice, coffee, tobacco, cotton, spices, opium. Tin, iron ore, potash; forestry, rubber, cigarettes, matches; textiles.

GDP (1990) $600 mn, per capita $150

History Visited by Europeans, 17th-c; French protectorate, 1893. Occupied by Japanese in World War 2. Independence from France in 1949; civil war, 1953–75, between the Lao government, supported by the USA, and the communist-led Patriotic Front *(Pathet Lao)*, supported by North Vietnam. Monarchy abolished and communist republic established in 1975. Headed by a President and governed by a Prime Minister.

Head of State
1987–91	Phoumi Vongvichit
1991–2	Kaysone Phomvihane
1992–	Nouhak Phoumsavan

Head of Government
1975–91	Kaysone Phomvihane
1991–	Khamtay Siphandone

LATVIA

Local name Latvija (Latvian)

Timezone GMT + 2

Area 64 600 km²/24 900 sq mi

Population total (1990e) 2 700 000

Status Republic

Date of independence 1991

Capital Riga

Language Latvian (official)

Ethnic groups Latvian (52%), Russian (34%), Belorussian (5%), Ukrainian (4%), Polish (2%), Lithuanian (1%)

Religions Predominantly Evangelical Lutheran, with Orthodox and Roman Catholic minorities

Physical features Flat, glaciated region. Highest point, central Vidzeme (Livonia) elevation, 312 m/1 024 ft. Over 40% forested. Coastline ranges over 472 km/293 mi; wooded lowland, marshes, lakes; NW coast indented by the Gulf of Riga. Chief river, Daugava.

Climate Mild climate, with high humidity; only c.30–40 days of sunshine annually; summers cool and rainy. Average mean temperature –2°C (Jan), 17°C (Jul); average annual rainfall 700–800 mm/28–31 in.

Currency (1991) 1 Latvian Rouble (R) = 100 kopecks (new currency planned: lat)

Economy Machine-building, metalworking, electrical engineering, electronics, chemicals, furniture, food processing, fishing, timber, paper and woollen goods, meat and dairy products.

GDP Not available

History Incorporated into USSR, 1721; independent state, 1918–40; proclaimed a Soviet Socialist Republic in

☐ *international airport*

1940. Occupied by Germany in World War 2; USSR regained control in 1944; nationalism overt from 1988. Coalition government elected in 1989; declared independence in 1991. Congress of Latvia instituted and granted United Nations membership, 1991.

Head of State
1991–3	Anatolijs Gorbunovs
1993–	Guntis Ulmanis

Head of Government
1991–3	Ivars Godmanis
1993–	Valdis Birkas

LEBANON

Local names Al-Lubnān (Arab), Liban (French)

Timezone GMT + 2

Area 10 452 km²/4 034 sq mi

Population total (1992e) 2 800 000

Status Republic

Date of independence 1943

Capital Beirut

Languages Arabic (official), French, English, and Armenian also spoken

Ethnic groups Arab (83%), Palestinian (9%), Armenian (5%), Syrian, Kurdish, Turkish, and Greek (3%)

Religions Muslim (c.75%), Christian (c.25%), also c.17 religious sects including Armenian, Greek, Roman Catholic, Alawite, Druze, and Jewish

Lesotho

Lebanon (continued)

Physical features Narrow coastal plain rises gradually E to the Lebanon Mts (Jebel Liban) rising to 3 087 m/10 128 ft at Qornet es Saouda. Arid E slopes fall abruptly to the fertile El Beqaa plateau, average elevation 1 000 m/3 300 ft. Anti-Lebanon range (Jebel esh Sharqi) in the E. R Litani flows S between the two ranges.

Climate Mediterranean climate, varying with altitude; hot, dry summers, warm, moist winters; average annual temperatures 13°C (Jan), 27°C (Jul). Average annual rainfall 920 mm/36 in; much drier and cooler in the Bekaa valley.

Currency 1 Lebanese Pound/Livre (LL, £L) = 100 piastres

Economy Commercial and financial centre of the Middle East until the civil war, which severely damaged economic infrastructure and reduced industrial and agricultural production; oil refining, textiles, chemicals, food processing. Citrus fruits, apples, grapes, bananas, sugar beet, olives, wheat. Tourism has virtually collapsed.

GDP (1990) $3.3 bn, per capita $1 000

History Part of the Ottoman Empire from 16th-c. After the massacre of (Catholic) Maronites by (Muslim) Druzes in 1860, Maronite area around Jabal Lubnan granted special autonomous status; Greater Lebanon, based on this area, created in 1920 under French mandate; Muslim coastal regions incorporated, despite great opposition. Constitutional republic in 1926; independence, 1943. Palestinian resistance units established in Lebanon by late 1960s despite government opposition, including the Palestine Liberation Organization (PLO); several militia groups developed in the mid-1970s. Following terrorist attacks, Israel invaded S Lebanon, 1978 and 1982; heavy Israeli bombardment of Beirut forced the withdrawal of Palestinian forces in 1982; unilateral withdrawal of Israeli and Syrian forces from Lebanon brought clashes between the Druze eg (backed by Syria) and Christian Lebanese militia; ceasefire announced in late 1982, broken many times since. Syrian troops entered Beirut in 1988 in an attempt to restore order; release of Western hostages taken by militant groups began in 1990; timetable for militia disarmament introduced,

1991. Constitution (in semi-suspension since 1988) provides for a Council of Ministers, a President (a Maronite Christian), Prime Minister (a Sunni Muslim), a Cabinet, and a Parliament, equally divided between Christians and Muslims.

Head of State
1989–   Elias Hrawi

Head of Government
1990   Selim al-Hoss
1990–2   Umar Karami
1992   Rashid al-Solh
1992–   Rafiq al-Hariri

LESOTHO

Local name Lesotho

Timezone GMT + 3

Area 30 355 km²/11 720 sq mi

Population total (1991e) 1 801 000

Status Independent kingdom within the Commonwealth

Date of independence 1960

Capital Maseru

Languages Lesotho (Sesotho) and English (official), Zulu, Afrikaans, French, Xhosa also spoken

Ethnic groups Sotho (99%), Zulu, Tembu, and Fingo tribes, European and Asian minorities

Religions Roman Catholic (44%), Protestant (mostly Lesotho Evangelical) (30%), Anglican (12%), other Christian (8%), traditional beliefs (6%)

Physical features S African kingdom completely bounded by South Africa. Drakensberg Mts in NE and E, highest peak Thabana-Ntlenyana, 3 482 m/11 424 ft. Serious soil erosion, especially in W. Main rivers, the Orange and the Caledon. Mountainous land, particularly in SW with the Maloti Mountain range.

Climate Mild, dry winters; warm summer season (Oct–Apr). Average annual temperatures 15°C (Jan), 25°C (Jul); average annual rainfall 725 mm/28.5 in (Oct–Apr).

Currency 1 Loti (*plural* Maloti) (M, LSM) = 100 lisente

Economy Economy based on intensive agriculture and contract labour working in South Africa; wheat, peas,

Human geography

beans, barley, cattle. Diamonds, textiles, pharmaceuticals; jewellery, crafts, wool, mohair.

GDP (1990) $420 mn, per capita $240

History Originally inhabited by hunting and gathering bushmen; Bantu arrived 16th-c, and Basotho nation established. Incorporated in Orange Free State in 1854; under British protection as Basutoland, 1869. Independence, 1960; declared Kingdom of Lesotho in 1966, as a hereditary monarchy within the Commonwealth; constitution suspended and country ruled by Council of Ministers, 1970–86; Prime Minister deposed by coup and political activity banned, 1986, with Military Council as effective ruling body. King Moshoeshoe dethroned by military council in 1990, and replaced by eldest son. Ramaema took over as Chairman of the Military Council following bloodless coup in 1991. Civilian government introduced and role of Prime Minister recreated to replace Chairman of Military Council, Jun 1993.

Head of State (Monarch)
1966–90   Moshoeshoe II
1990–   Letsie III

Head of Government (Chairman of Military Council until 1993, now Prime Minister)
1986–91   Justin Metsing Lekhanya
1991–3   Elias Tutsoane Ramaema
1993–   Ntsu Mokhehle

LIBERIA

Local name Liberia

Timezone GMT

Area 111 370 km²/42 989 sq mi

Population total (1991e) 2 730 000

Status Republic

Date of independence 1847

Capital Monrovia

Languages English (official) with 20 dialects/languages of Niger-Congo spoken

Ethnic groups Indigenous tribes (including Kpelle, Bassa, Gio, Kru, Gola, Kissi, Vai, and Bella) (95%), Americo-Liberians (repatriated slaves from the USA) (5%)

Religions Traditional animist beliefs (70%), Muslim (20%), Christian (10%)

Physical features Low coastal belt with lagoons, beaches, and mangrove marshes. Land rises inland to mountains, reaching 1 752 m/5 748 ft at Mt Nimba. Rivers include Mano, Moro, St Paul, St John, Cess, Duoubé, Cavalla.

Climate Equatorial climate; high temperatures, abundant rainfall; high humidity during rainy season (Apr–Sep), especially on coast. Average annual temperatures 26°C (Jan), 24°C (Jul); average annual rainfall 5 138 mm/202 in.

Currency 1 Liberian Dollar (L$) = 100 cents

Economy Based on minerals, especially iron ore. Two-thirds of the population rely on subsistence agriculture;

rubber, timber, palm oil, rice, cassava, coffee, cocoa, coconuts. Large merchant fleet, including the registration of many foreign ships.

GNP (1989) $1.0 bn, per capita $440

Liberia (continued)

History Mapped by the Portuguese in 15th-c. Created as a result of the activities of several US philanthropic societies, wishing to establish a homeland for former slaves; founded in 1822; constituted as the Free and Independent Republic of Liberia in 1847. Military coup and assassination of President, 1980, established a People's Redemption Council, with a chairman and a Cabinet. New constitution in 1986, with an elected Senate and a House of Representatives. Civil war, followed by arrival of West African peacekeeping force in 1990; interim Government of National Unity installed.

Head of State/Government
1986–90   Samuel K Doe
1990–   Amos Sawyer *Acting*

LIBYA

Local name Lībiyā

Timezone GMT + 1

Area 1758 610 km²/678 823 sq mi

Population total (1992e) 4 450 000

Status Republic

Date of independence 1951

Capital Tripoli

Languages Arabic (official), with English and French widely spoken

Ethnic groups Berber and Arab (96%), Greek, Maltese, Italian, Egyptian, Pakistani, Turk, Indian, and Tunisian minorities (3%)

Religions Sunni Muslim (96%), Christian (Roman Catholic, Anglican, Coptic Orthodox) (3%), Jewish (1%)

Physical features Mainly low-lying Saharan desert or semi-desert; 93% of land is contained in the arid Saharan plateau. Land rises (S) to over 2000 m/6 500 ft in the Tibesti massif; highest point, Pic Bette, 2 286 m/7 500 ft. Comparatively fertile region in Gefara plain and Jabal Nafusah plateau in Tripolitania region.

Climate Mediterranean climate on coast; rainy season (Oct–Mar) in NW and NE upland regions. Average annual temperature 11°C (Jan), 27°C (Jul) in Tripoli; average annual rainfall 400 mm/15.7 in.

Currency 1 Libyan Dinar (LD) = 1000 millemes

Economy Former agricultural economy; barley, olives, fruit, dates, almonds, tobacco. Relatively poor until economy transformed by discovery of oil and natural gas, 1959; petroleum processing; iron, steel, aluminium; textiles. Nomadic farming in S.

GNP (1989) $24 bn, (1986) per capita $5 500

History Controlled by Phoenicians, Carthaginians, Greeks, Vandals, and Byzantines; Arab domination during 7th-c; Turkish rule from 16th-c. Italians gained control in 1911; named Libya by the Italians in 1934. Heavy fighting during World War 2, followed by British and French control; independent Kingdom of Libya, 1951. Military coup established a republic under Muammar al-Gaddafi, 1969; governed by a Revolutionary Command Council; foreign military installations closed down in early 1970s. Libyan troops occupied Aozou Strip, 1973. Strained relations with other countries due to controversial activities, including alleged organization of international terrorism; diplomatic relations severed by UK after the murder of a policewoman in London, 1984; Tripoli and Benghazi bombed by US Air Force in response to alleged terrorist activity, 1986. Libya and Chad presented their individual territorial claims to Aozou Strip in 1990.

Head of State/Government
1969–   Muammar al-Gaddafi

LIECHTENSTEIN

Local name Liechtenstein

Timezone GMT + 1

Area 160 km²/62 sq mi

Population total (1990e) 28 700

Status Independent principality

Date of independence 1719

Capital Vaduz

Language German (official)

Ethnic groups Liechtensteiner (64%), Swiss (16%), Austrian (8%), German (4%)

Religions Roman Catholic (87%), Protestant (9%)

Physical features Alpine principality, located in C Europe. Fourth smallest country in the world; land boundary 76 km/47 mi; bounded W by the R Rhine. Mean altitude, 450 m/1 475 ft; forested mountains rise to 2 599 m/8 527 ft in the Grauspitz. Samina River flows N.

Climate Mild, equable climate; temperatures range from −15°C (Jan), 20–8°C (Jul). Average annual rainfall 1 050–1 200 mm/41–47 in.

Currency 1 Swiss Franc (SFr, SwF) = 100 centimes

Economy Industrial sector developing since 1950s; export-based, centred on specialized and high-tech production; metal-working, engineering, chemicals, pharmaceuticals. International banking and finance. Tourism.

GDP (1987) $1 bn, per capita $32 000

History Became a sovereign state in 1342. Independent principality within Holy Roman Empire, 1719; part of Holy Roman Empire until 1806. Became a sovereign state in 1342. Adopted Swiss currency, 1921; united with Switzerland in a customs union in 1923. Became a member of UN in 1990; joined European Free Trade Association (EFTA) in 1991. Constitutional monarchy ruled by hereditary princes of the House of Liechtenstein; governed by a Prime Minister, four Councillors, and a unicameral Parliament.

Head of State (Monarch)
1989–   Hans Adam II

Head of Government
1978–93   Hans Brunhart
1993   Markus Büchel
1993–   Mario Frick

LITHUANIA

Local name Lietuva

Timezone GMT + 2

Area 65 200 km²/25 167 sq mi

Population total (1990e) 3 700 000

Status Republic

Date of independence 1991

Capital Vilnius

Language Lithuanian (official)

Ethnic groups Lithuanian (80%), Russian (9%), Polish (7%), Belorussian (2%)

Religions Roman Catholic, small minority of Evangelical Lutherans and Evangelical Reformists

Physical features Glaciated plains cover much of the area; central lowlands with gentle hills in W and higher terrain in SE. Highest point, Jouzapine in the Asmenos Hills, 294 m/964 ft. 25% forested; some 3 000 small lakes mostly in E and SE; complex sandy dunes on Kursiu Marios lagoon. Chief river, the Nemunas.

Climate Continental climate, affected by maritime weather of W Europe and continental E. Baltic Sea influences a narrow coastal zone. Average annual temperatures −5°C (Jan), 16°C (Jul); average annual rainfall 630 mm/25 in.

Currency (1991) 1 Rouble (R) = 100 kopecks (new currency planned: litas)

Economy Electrical engineering, computer hardware, instruments, machine tools, ship building. Synthetic fibres, fertilizers, plastics, food processing, oil refining. Cattle, pigs, poultry, grain, potatoes, vegetables.

GDP Not available

international airport

History United with Poland, 1385–1795; intensive russification led to revolts in 1905 and 1917. Occupied by Germany in both World Wars; proclaimed a republic in 1918; annexed by the USSR, 1940; growth of nationalist movement in the late 1980s; declared independence in 1990, but not recognized until 1991.

Head of State
1991–3   Vytautas Landsbergis
1993–   Algirdas Brazauskas

Head of Government
1991–2   Gediminas Vagnorius
1992   Aleksandras Abisala
1992–3   Bronislovas Lubys
1993–   Adolfas Šleževičius

LUXEMBOURG

Local names Lëtzebuerg (Letz), Luxembourg (French), Luxemburg (German)

Timezone GMT + 1

Area 2 586 km²/998 sq mi

Population total (1992e) 389 800

Status Grand Duchy

Date of independence 1867

Capital Luxembourg

Languages French, German, Letzeburgesch

Ethnic groups Luxemburger (73%), Portuguese (9%), Italian (5%), French (3%), Belgian (3%), German (2%)

Religions Roman Catholic (97%), Protestant (2%), Jewish (1%)

Physical features Divided into the two natural regions of Ardennes (Ösling) (N); forest in N, and Gutland in S, flatter, average height 250 m/820 ft. Principal rivers include the Sûre, Our, Moselle.

Climate Mild climate, influenced by warm S wind (*Fröhn*). Average annual temperatures 0.7°C (Jan), 18°C (Jul) in Luxembourg; average annual rainfall, 1 050–1 200 mm/41–7 in.

Currency 1 Luxembourg Franc (LFr) = 100 centimes

Economy Important international centre based in city of Luxembourg; iron and steel, food processing; chemicals, tyres, metal products. Mixed farming, dairy farming; wine; forestry; tourism.

GDP (1990) $6.9 bn, per capita $18 000

History Made a Grand Duchy by the Congress of Vienna in 1815; granted political autonomy, 1838; recognized as a neutral independent state, 1867. Occupied by Germany in both World Wars; joined Benelux economic union, 1948; neutrality abandoned on joining NATO, 1949. A hereditary monarchy with the Grand

□ *international airport*

Duke as Head of State; Parliament consists of Chamber of Deputies and State Council; Head of Government is the Minister of State.

Head of State (Grand Dukes and Duchesses)
1919–64   Charlotte (*in exile, 1940–4*)
1964–   Jean

Head of Government
1984–   Jacques Santer

MACAO >> PORTUGAL

MACEDONIA, FORMER YUGOSLAV REPUBLIC OF

Local name Makedonija

Timezone GMT + 2

Area 25 713 km²/9 925 sq mi

Population total (1991) 2 033 964

Status Republic

Date of independence 1991

Capital Skopje

Language Macedonian (Slavic language belonging to the Indo-European family)

Ethnic groups (1981) Macedonian Slav (67%), Albanian (21%), Turk (4%), Serbian (3%), Bulgarian and Greek minorities

Religions Macedonian Orthodox Christian, Muslim

Physical features Landlocked, mountainous region, bordered by Serbia, Bulgaria, Greece, Albania; divided from Greek Macedonia by the Kožuf and Nidže ranges, highest point, Korab, 2 764 m/9 068 ft. Main rivers, Struma and Vardar.

Climate Continental; average annual temperatures 0°C (Jan), 24°C (Jul); often heavy winter snowfalls; average annual rainfall 500 mm/20 in.

Currency (1992) Dinar

Economy Agriculture; wheat, barley, corn, rice, tobacco; sheep, cattle. Mining of minerals, iron ore, lead, zinc, nickel. Steel, chemicals, textiles.

GDP Not available

History Part of Macedonian, Roman, and Byzantine Empires; settled by Slavs in 6th-c; conquered by Bulgars

Human geography

in 7th-c; and by Serbia, 14th-c; incorporated into Serbia after the Balkan Wars; united in 1918, in what later became Yugoslavia, but continuous demands for autonomy persisted. Occupied by Bulgaria during World War 2, 1941–44. Declaration of independence, 1991; international discussions continue over the name under which the country will be accorded international recognition (the adjacent province of Greece bears the name Macedonia).

Head of State
1991–   Kiro Gligorov

Head of Government
1991–   Branko Crvenkovski

□ international airport

EUROPE

MADAGASCAR

Local name Madagasikara

Timezone GMT + 3

Area 592 800 km²/228 821 sq mi

Population total (1991e) 12 185 000

Status Republic

Date of independence 1960

Capital Antananarivo

Languages Malagasy (official), with French widely spoken

Ethnic groups Malagasy (99%) (including Merina 26%, Betsimisaraka 15%, Betsileo 12%)

Religions Traditional animist beliefs (47%), Christian (48%) (Roman Catholic 26%, Protestant 23%), Muslim (5%)

Physical features World's fifth largest island, length (N–S) 1 580 km/982 mi. Dissected N–S by a ridge of mountains (Tsaratananan Range), rising to 2 876 m/9 436 ft at Maromokotra. Cliffs (E) drop down to a coastal plain through tropical forest; terraced descent (W) through savannah to coast, heavily indented in N.

Climate Tropical, variable rainfall; average annual rainfall 1 000–1 500 mm/40–60 in, higher in tropical coastal region; average annual temperatures 21°C (Jan), 15°C (Jul).

Currency 1 Madagascar Franc (FMG, MgFr) = 100 centimes

Economy Chiefly agricultural economy; rice, manioc, coffee, sugar, vanilla, cotton, peanuts, tobacco, livestock. Food processing, tanning, cement, soap, paper, textiles, oil products. Graphite, chrome, coal, ilmenite.

GDP (1990) $2.5 bn, per capita $200

History Settled by Indonesians in 1st-c AD and by

□ international airport

Malawi

Madagascar (continued)

African traders in 8th-c; visited by Portuguese, 16th-c. French established trading posts in late 18th-c; claimed as a protectorate by the French in 1895; autonomous overseas French territory (Malagasy Republic), 1958; independence, 1960; became Madagascar, 1977. Governed by a President, who appoints a Council of Ministers and is guided by a Supreme Revolutionary Council; National People's Assembly is elected every five years.

Head of State
1975–93   Didier Ratsiraka
1993–   Albert Zafy

Head of Government
1991-3   Guy Willy Razanamasy
1993–   Francisque Ravony

MADEIRA (ISLANDS) >> PORTUGAL

MALAWI

Local name Malawi (Malaêi)

Timezone GMT + 2

Area 118 484 km²/45 735 sq mi

Population total (1991e) 9 438 000

Status Republic

Date of independence 1964

Capital Lilongwe

Languages English and Chichewa (official)

Ethnic groups Maravi (including Nyanja, Chewa, Tonga, Tumbuka) (60%), Lomwe (18%), Yao (13%), Ngoni (7%), also Asian and European minorities

Religions Protestant (55%), Roman Catholic (20%), Muslim (20%), traditional animist beliefs (3%)

Physical features Crossed N–S by the Great Rift Valley; contains Africa's third largest lake, L Malawi; main river, Shire. Shire highlands (S) rise to nearly 3 000 m/10 000 ft at Mt Mulanje.

Climate Tropical climate in S; high year-round temperatures, 28–37°C; average annual temperatures 23°C (Jan), 16°C (Jul) in Lilongwe. Average annual rainfall, 740 mm/30 in. More moderate temperatures in central areas.

Currency 1 Kwacha (MK) = 100 tambala

Economy Based on agriculture (employs 90% of population); tobacco, sugar, tea, cotton, groundnuts, maize. Textiles, matches, cigarettes, beer, spirits, shoes, cement.

GDP (1990) $1.6 bn, per capita $175

History Visited by the Portuguese in 17th-c. European contact established by David Livingstone, 1859; Scottish church missions in the area; claimed as the British

Protectorate of Nyasaland, 1891; British colony, 1907; in the 1950s joined with N and S Rhodesia to form the Federation of Rhodesia and Nyasaland; independence, 1964; republic, 1966. Governed by a President, a Cabinet and a National Assembly.

Head of State/Government
1966–   Hastings Kamuzu Banda

MALAYSIA

Local name Malaysia

Timezone GMT + 8

Area 329 749 km²/127 283 sq mi

Population total (1992e) 18 630 000

Status Republic

Date of independence 1957

Capital Kuala Lumpur

Languages Bahasa Malaysia (Malay) (official), also Chinese, English, and Tamil widely spoken

Ethnic groups Malay (59%), Chinese (32%), Indian (9%)

Religions Muslim (53%), Buddhist (17%), Chinese folk-religionist (12%), Hindu (7%), Christian (6%)

Physical features Independent federation of states located in SE Asia, comprising 11 states and a federal territory in Peninsular Malaysia, and the E States of Sabah and Sarawak on the island of Borneo. Mountain chain of granite and limestone running N–S, rising to Mt Tahan, 2 189 m/7 182 ft; peninsula length 700 km/435 mi, width up to 320 km/200 mi. Mostly tropical rainforest and mangrove swamp. Mt Kinabalu on Sabah, Malaysia's highest peak, 4 094 m/13 432 ft.

Climate Tropical climate strongly influenced by monsoon winds; high humidity. Average annual rainfall in the peninsula, 260 mm/10 in (S), 800 mm/32 in (N). Average daily temperatures, 21–32°C in coastal areas, 12–25°C in mountains.

Currency 1 Malaysian Dollar/Ringgit (M$) = 100 cents

Economy Discovery of tin in the late 19th-c brought European investment. Rubber trees introduced from Brazil. Minerals including iron ore, bauxite. Oil, natural gas; electronic components, electrical goods; tourism.

GDP (1990) $43 bn, per capita $2 460

History Part of Srivijaya Empire from 9th–14th-c; Hindu and Muslim influences, 14th–15th-c; Portugal, the Netherlands, and Britain vied for control from the 16th-c. Singapore, Malacca, and Penang formally incorporated into the British Colony of the Straits Settlements in 1826; British protection extended over Perak, Selangor, Negeri Sembilan, and Pahang, constituted into the Federated Malay States, 1895; protection treaties with several other states (Unfederated Malay States), 1885–1930. Occupied by Japanese in World War 2; Federation of Malaya, 1948; independence in 1957; constitutional

1	Langkawi
2	Penang
3	Cameron Highlands
4	Mt Tahan 2189m
5	Kuala Terengganu
6	Melaka (Malacca)
7	**Johor Baharu**
8	Kuching
9	Bintulu
10	Labuan
11	Kota Kinabalu
12	Sandakan
13	Petaling Jaya
14	George Town

monarchy of Malaysia, 1963; Singapore withdrew from the Federation in 1965. Governed by a bicameral Federal Parliament; Head of State is a Monarch elected for five years by his fellow sultans; advised by a Prime Minister and a Cabinet.

Head of State (Sultan)
1989–94   Azlan Muhibuddin Shah
1994–   Ja'afar ibni Abdul Rahman

Head of Government
1981–   Mahathir bin Mohamad

MALDIVES

Local name Dhivehi Jumhuriya

Timezone GMT + 5.5

Area 300 km²/116 sq mi

Population total (1991e) 226 000

Status Independent republic within the Commonwealth

Date of independence 1968

Capital Malé

Languages Dhivehi (official), Arabic, Hindi, and English widely spoken

Ethnic groups Sinhalese (Dravidian extraction mainly), also Arab, Negrito, African influences

Religion Almost 100% Sunni Muslim

Physical features Island archipelago in the Indian Ocean; comprises c.1 190 islands (202 inhabited) in a chain of 20 coral atolls; many small and low-lying with sandy beaches fringed with coconut palms; none of the islands rising above 1.8 m/5 ft. 10% of land is arable, 3% forested.

Climate Generally warm and humid; wet season created by SW monsoons (Apr–Oct), dry season by NE monsoon (Dec–Mar). Average annual rainfall, 2 100 mm /83 in; average daily temperature 22°C.

Currency 1 Rufiyaa (MRf, Rf) = 100 laaris

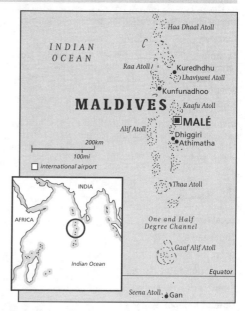

Economy Agriculture; breadfruit, banana, mango, cassava, sweet potato, millet. Fishing, shipping, tourism.

Maldives (continued)

GDP (1989) $136 m, per capita $670

History Former dependency of Ceylon (Sri Lanka); British protectorate, 1887–1965; became a Republic within the Commonwealth in 1953; Sultan restored in 1954; independence outside the Commonwealth, 1965; rejoined Commonwealth, 1982. Governed by a president, a ministers' *Majlis* (cabinet), and a citizens' *Majlis* of 48 members elected for five years.

Head of State/Government

1978–   Maumoon Abdul Gayoom

MALI

Local name Mali

Timezone GMT

Area 1 240 192 km²/478 714 sq mi

Population total (1991e) 8 338 000

Status Republic

Date of independence 1960

Capital Bamako

Languages French (official), local languages (including Bambara) widely spoken

Ethnic groups Mande (Bambara, Malinke, Sarakole) (50%), Peul (Fulani nomads) (17%), Voltaic (including Senufo, Bura, Senouto, Minianka) (12%), Songhai (6%), Tuareg and Moor (5%)

Religions Muslim (90%), traditional animist beliefs (9%), Christian (1%) (Roman Catholic 0.5%, Protestant 0.5%)

Physical features Landlocked country on the fringe of the Sahara; lower part of the Hoggar massif (N); arid plains 300–500 m/1 000–1 600 ft; mainly savannah land in the S. Main rivers, Niger and Bani. Featureless desert land (N).

Climate Subtropical in S and SW, with rainy season (Jun–Oct). Average rainfall c.1 000 mm/140 in; average annual temperatures 24°C (Jan), 27°C (Jul) in Bamako.

Currency 1 CFA Franc (CFAFr) = 100 centimes

Economy Mainly subsistence agriculture; crops severely affected by drought conditions; fishing, livestock, food processing, textiles, leather, cement. Some tourism.

GDP (1989) $2 bn, per capital $250

History Mediaeval state controlling the trade routes between savannah and Sahara, reaching its peak in the 14th-c. Governed by France, 1881–95; territory of French Sudan (part of French West Africa) until 1959; partner-

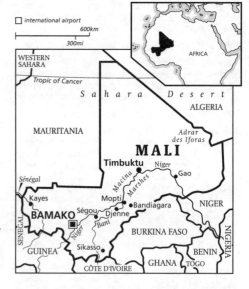

ship with Senegal as the Federation of Mali, 1959; separate independence, 1960. Under 1979 constitution (suspended, 1991) governed by a President elected every six years, and a National Assembly.

Head of State

1969–91	Moussa Traoré
1991–2	*Military Junta* (Amadou Toumani Touré)
1992–	Alpha Oumar Konaré

Head of Government

1988–91	*No Prime Minister*
1991–2	Soumana Sacko
1992–3	Younoussi Touré
1993–4	Abdoulaye Sekou Sow
1994–	Ibrahim Boubakar Keita

MALTA

Local name Malta

Timezone GMT + 2

Area 316 km²/122 sq mi

Population total (1992e) 360 000

Status Independent republic within the Commonwealth

Date of independence 1964

Capital Valletta

Languages English and Maltese (official)

Ethnic groups Maltese (mixed Arabic, Sicilian, Norman, Spanish, English, Italian racial origin) (95%), English (2%)

Religions Roman Catholic Apostolic (97%), Anglican Communion (2%)

Physical features Archipelago, comprising the islands of Malta (246 km²/95 sq mi), Gozo (67 km²/26 sq mi), and Comino (2.7 km²/1 sq mi), with the uninhabited islets of

Cominotto, Filfla, and St Paul. Highest point, 252 m/830 ft, on island of Malta. Well-indented coastline with natural harbours, rocky coves; no rivers.

Climate Mediterranean, hot, dry summers, cool, rainy winters; rainy season (Oct–Mar); average annual rainfall 578 mm/22.7 in. Average annual temperatures 13°C (Jan), 26°C (Jul) in Valletta.

Currency 1 Maltese pound (LM) = 100 cents

Economy Tourism; ship repair (naval dockyards now converted to commercial use). Developing as a trans-shipment centre for the Mediterranean; tobacco, plastic and steel goods, paints, detergents. Potatoes, tomatoes, oranges, grapes.

GDP (1989) $2.3 bn, per capita $6 564

History Controlled at various times by Phoenicia, Greece, Carthage, and Rome; conquered by Arabs in 9th-c. Given to the Knights Hospitallers in 1530; British Crown Colony, 1815. Important strategic base in both World Wars; for its resistance to heavy air attacks, the island was awarded the George Cross, 1942. Achieved independence in 1964; republic, 1974; British military base closed in 1979. Governed by a President, a Prime Minister, a Cabinet and a House of Representatives.

Head of State
1989–   Vincent Tabone

Head of Government
1987–   Edward Fenech-Adami

MARIANA ISLANDS, NORTHERN >> UNITED STATES OF AMERICA

MARSHALL ISLANDS

Timezone GMT + 12

Area c.180 km²/70 sq mi

Population total (1992e) 50 000

Status Republic

Date of independence 1986

Capital Dalap-Uliga-Darrit (municipality on Majuro Atoll)

Languages Marshallese (Kajin-Majol) (official), English and Japanese also spoken

Ethnic group Micronesian (99%)

Religions Christian (Protestant 90%, Roman Catholic 8%)

Physical features Archipelago in C Pacific Ocean; comprising 34 islands, including Kwajalein and Jaluit, and 870 reefs; two parallel chains of coral atolls, Ratik (E) and Ralik (W), extending c.925 km/800 mi in length; volcanic islands, rise no more than a few metres above sea level.

Climate Hot and humid; wet season (May–Nov); typhoon season (Dec–Mar); average annual temperature 27°C.

Currency 1 US Dollar ($, US$) = 100 cents

Economy Farming; fishing; tropical agriculture; coconuts, tomatoes, melons, breadfruit.

GDP (1989) $63 m, per capita $1 500

History Explored by the Spanish, 1529. Part of UN Trust Territory of the Pacific, 1949–78, administered by the USA. US nuclear weapon tests held on Bikini and Eniwetak atolls, 1946–62. Self-governing republic, 1979; compact of free association with the USA in 1986 with US recognizing independence of Marshall Islands; trusteeship ended, 1990. Governed by a President elected by a Parliament.

Head of State/Government
1979–   Amata Kabua

MARTINIQUE >> FRANCE

MAURITANIA

Local names Mūritāniyā (Arabic), Mauritanie (French)

Timezone GMT

Area 1 029 920 km²/397 549 sq mi

Population total (1992e) 2 100 000

Status Islamic republic

Date of independence 1960

Capital Nouakchott

Mauritania (continued)

Languages Arabic (official), French and local languages also spoken

Ethnic groups Moor (30%), Black (30%), mixed (40%)

Religions Sunni Muslim (99%), Roman Catholic (1%)

Physical features Saharan zone in N comprises two-thirds of the country; coastal zone has minimal rainfall; Sahelian zone, with savannah grasslands; Sénégal R zone, the chief agricultural region. Highest point, Kediet Ijill, 915 m/3 002 ft in the NW.

Climate Dry, tropical climate, with sparse rainfall. Average annual temperatures 22°C (Jan), 28°C (Jul) in Nouakchott. Rainy season (May–Sep) in S, with occasional tornadoes; average annual rainfall 158 mm/6.2 in.

Currency 1 Ouguiyja (U, UM) = 5 khoums

Economy Subsistence agriculture (employs 80% of population); crop success constantly under threat from drought; livestock, cereals, vegetables, dates. Mining of iron ore, copper, gypsum.

GDP (1989) $953 m, per capita $490

History Visited by Portuguese in 15th-c. French protectorate within French West Africa, 1903; French colony, 1920; independence in 1960; military coup in 1979; new constitution in 1991; became a republic, 1992. Governed by an executive President (6-year term), who appoints a Prime Minister, a National Assembly, and a Senate.

Head of State
1984– Moaouia Ould Sidi Mohammed Taya

Head of Government
1991– Sidi Mohammed Ould Boubaker

MAURITIUS

Local name Mauritius

Timeone GMT + 4

Area 1 865 km²/720 sq mi

Population total (1991e) 1 083 000

Status Republic within the Commonwealth

Date of independence 1968

Capital Port Louis

Languages English (creole-English) (official), French, Hindi, Urdu, Bojpoori, and Hakka also spoken

Ethnic groups Indo-Mauritian (68%), Creole (27%), Sino-Mauritian (3%), Franco-Mauritian (2%)

Religions Hindu (53%), Roman Catholic (26%), Muslim (13%), Protestant (4%)

Physical features Comprises the main island, 20 adjacent islets and the dependencies of Rodrigues I, Agalega I, and Cargados Carajos Is (St Brandon Is). Volcanic main island; highest peak, 826 m/2 710 ft, Piton de la Petite Rivière Noire. Dry, lowland coast with wooded savannah, mangrove swamp, and (E) bamboo. Surrounded by coral reefs enclosing lagoons and sandy beaches.

Climate Humid tropical-maritime climate; average annual temperatures 23°C (Jan), 27°C (Jul) in Port Louis;

average annual rainfall 1 000 mm/39 in. Lies within Indian cyclone belt.

Currency 1 Mauritian Rupee (MR, MauRe) = 100 cents

Economy Sugar-cane (employs over 25% of the workforce); clothing; diamond-cutting, watches, rum, fertilizer; tea, tobacco, vegetables; fishing; tourism.

GDP (1989) $2 bn, per capita $1 950

History Visited by the Portuguese and Dutch in 16th-c; settled by the French in 1715; ceded to Britain, 1814; governed jointly with Seychelles as a single colony until

1903; independent sovereign state within the Commonwealth, 1968; links with British monarchy broken, 1992, became a republic, remaining within the Commonwealth. President (ceremonial post) is elected by the National Assembly; Prime Minister appoints the Council of Ministers; a unicameral National Assembly.

Head of State
1992   Veerasamy Ringadoo
1992–   Cassam Uteem

Head of Government
1982–   Aneerood Jugnauth

MAYOTTE >> FRANCE

MEXICO

Local name México

Timezone GMT – 8 to – 6

Area 1 978 800 km²/763 817 sq mi

Population total (1992e) 84 440 000

Status Republic

Date of independence 1821

Capital Mexico City

Languages Spanish (official), indigenous languages

Ethnic groups Indian-Spanish (mestizo) (60%), Amerindian (30%), White (9%)

Religions Roman Catholic (80%), Protestant (3%)

Physical features Narrow coastal plains. Land rises steeply to C plateau, c.2 400 m/7 800 ft; volcanic peaks to S, notably Citlaltépetl, 5 699 m/18 697 ft. Limestone lowlands of the Yucatán peninsula stretch into the Gulf of Mexico (SE). Region subject to earthquakes.

Climate Tropical climate in S; severe, arid conditions N and W. Average annual temperatures 13°C (Jan), 16°C (Jul) in Mexico City; average annual rainfall 747 mm /29.4 in.

Currency 1 Mexican Peso (Mex$) = 100 centavos

Economy Wide range of mineral exports; major discoveries of oil and natural gas in the 1970s (now world's fourth largest producer). Fluorite and graphite (world's leading producer). Large petrochemical industry.

GDP (1990) $236 bn, per capita $2 680

History Centre of Indian civilizations for over 2 500 years; Gulf Coast Olmecs based at La Venta, Zapotecs at Monte Albán near Oaxaca, Mixtecs at Mitla, Toltecs at Tula, Maya in the Yucatán, Aztecs at Tenochtitlán;

Spanish arrival in 1516; Vice-royalty of New Spain established; struggle for independence from 1810; federal republic, 1824; lost territory to the USA, 1836, and after the Mexican War, 1846–8; civil war, 1858–61. Occupation of Mexico City by French forces in 1863–7. Revolution, 1910–7. Financial crisis, 1982–4, foreign debt estimated c.$800 000 m. Major earthquake in Mexico City, 1985, killed c.7 000. Governed by a President, a Cabinet, and a bicameral Congress with a Senate and a Chamber of Deputies.

Head of State/Government
1988–   Carlos Salinas de Gortari

MICRONESIA >> UNITED STATES OF AMERICA

MOLDOVA

Local name Moldova

Timezone GMT + 2

Area 33 700 km²/13 008 sq mi

Population total (1992e) 4 341 000

Status Republic

Date of independence 1991

Capital Kishinev

Languages Moldovan (official), Ukrainian also spoken

Ethnic groups Moldovan (64%), Ukrainian (14%), Russian (13%), Gagauzi (4%), Jewish (2%)

Religions Christian (mainly Russian Orthodox, also Baptist and Roman Catholic)

Physical features Landlocked area consisting of hilly plains, average elevation of 147 m/482 ft, cut by river valleys, ravines, and gullies; uplands in C, Kodry Hills, reach highest point, Mt Balaneshty, 429 m/1 409 ft. Chief rivers, the Dnestr and Prut. Level plain of Bel'tsy Steppe and uplands (N); eroded Medobory-Toltry limestone ridges border R Prut (N).

Climate Warm, moderately continental; long dry periods in S. Average annual temperatures –5°C (N), –3°C (S) (Jan), 20°C (N), 23°C (S) (Jul); average annual rainfall 450–550 mm/18–22 in.

Currency (1992) 1 Rouble (R) = 100 kopecks (new currency planned: leu)

Economy Main exports include wine, tobacco, food-canning, machinery, electrical engineering, knitwear, textiles, fruit.

GDP Not available

History Formerly part of Romania (the region known as Bessarabia); W part remained in Romania, Bessarabia in E became the Moldavian Soviet Socialist Republic in 1940. Occupied by Romania, who allied with Germany in World War 2; recaptured by USSR in 1944. Moldavian language granted official status, 1989, leading to tension between ethnic Russians and Moldovans. Declaration of independence, 1991, joined new Commonwealth of Independent States (CIS); tension due to separatist pressure from Gagauz and Dnestr Russian minorities, 1990–1; admitted to Conference on Security and Cooperation in Europe (CSCE), 1992. Governed by a President, a Prime Minister and a Supreme Soviet (380-seat legislative body).

Head of State
1991– Mircea Snegur

Head of Government
1991–2 Valeriu Muravschi
1992– Andrei Sangeli

MONACO

Local name Monaco

Timezone GMT + 1

Area 1.95 km²/0.75 sq mi

Population total (1991e) 29 712

Status Principality

Capital Monaco-Ville

Languages French (official), English, Italian, and Monegasque also spoken

Ethnic groups French (58%), Italian (16%), Monegasque (16%)

Religion Roman Catholic (95%)

Physical features Located on Mediterranean Riviera, close to the Italian frontier with France; surrounded landward by the French department of Alpes-Maritimes; steep and rugged landscape. Area available for commercial development has been extended by land reclaimed from sea.

Climate Mediterranean; warm, dry summers, mild, wet winters. Average annual temperatures 10°C (Jan), 23°C (Jul); average annual rainfall 758 mm/30 in.

Currency 1 French Franc (Fr) = 100 centimes

Economy Tourism; chemicals, printing, textiles, plastics.

GDP Not available

History Under the protection of France since the 17th-c, apart from a period under Sardinia, 1815–61; 1911 constitution ended power of the Prince as an absolute ruler. Constitution of 1911 suspended in 1959; new constitution adopted, 1962. Governed by a Prince as Head of State, a Minister of State, heading a Council of Government, and a National Council.

Head of State (Prince)
1949–   Rainier III

Head of Government (Minister of State)
1986–91   Jean Ausseil
1991–   Jacques Dupont

Map >> FRANCE

MONGOLIA

Local name Mongol Ard Uls

Timezone GMT + 7 (W), + 8 (C), + 9 (E)

Area 1 566 500 km²/604 800 sq mi

Population total (1992e) 2 156 300

Status State

Date of independence 1911

Capital Ulan Bator

Languages Khalka (official), Russian and Chinese spoken by respective minorities

Ethnic groups Mongol (Khalka, Dorbed, Buryat, Dariganga) (90%), Kazakh (4%), Russian (2%), other (4%)

Religions Formerly Tibetan Buddhist (now only a single monastery remains in Ulan Bator); unreliable data on current situation as a result of religious suppression in 20th-c

Physical features Landlocked mountainous country. Highest point, Tavan-Bogdo-Uli, 4 373 m/14 347 ft. High ground mainly in W, with mountains lying NW–SE to form Mongolian Altai chain; lower SE area runs into the Gobi Desert; lowland plains; mainly arid grasslands.

Climate Extreme continental climate, with hard and long-lasting frosts in winter; arid desert conditions prevail in the S. Average annual temperatures –26°C (Jan), 16°C (Jul); average annual rainfall 208 mm/18.2 in.

Currency 1 Tugrik (Tug) = 100 möngö

Economy Traditionally a pastoral nomadic economy; series of 5-year plans aiming for an agricultural-industrial economy; 70% of agricultural production derived from cattle raising; foodstuffs, animal products. Coal, gold, uranium, lead.

GDP (1990) $2.2 bn, per capita $1 000

History Originally the homeland of nomadic tribes,

□ international airport

which united under Genghis Khan in the 13th-c to become part of the great Mongol Empire; assimilated into China, and divided into Inner and Outer Mongolia. Outer Mongolia declared itself an independent monarchy, 1911. Changed name to Mongolian People's Republic, 1924, not recognized by China until 1946. Governed by a Great People's Khural (parliament), a Council of Ministers, and a Presidium; chairman of Presidium is Head of State. Changed name to State of Mongolia, 1992, and new constitution established.

Head of State
1990–   Punsalmaagiyn Ochirbat

Head of Government
1990–2   Dashiyn Byambasuren
1992–   Puntsagiyn Jasray

MOROCCO

Local name Al-Magrib

Timezone GMT

Area 409 200 km²/157 951 sq mi

Population total (1992e) 26 240 000

Status Kingdom

Date of independence 1956

Capital Rabat

Languages Arabic (official), Berber, Spanish, and French also widely spoken

Ethnic groups Arab-Berber (99%), non-Moroccan (0.7%), Jewish (0.2%)

Religions Sunni Muslim (98%), Christian (1%), Jewish (0.2%)

Physical features Dominated by a series of mountain ranges, rising in the Atlas Mts (S) to 4 165 m/13 664 ft at Jebel Toubkal. Broad coastal plain. Main rivers, Drâ'ar (S and SW) and Moulouya (N) draining into the Mediterranean.

Climate Mediterranean climate on N coast; semi-arid in S; Sahara virtually rainless. Average annual temperatures 13°C (Jan), 22°C (Jul) in Rabat; average annual rainfall 564 mm/22.2 in.

Currency 1 Moroccan Dirham (DH) = 100 Moroccan francs

Economy Agriculture (employs over 50% of population). Largest known reserves of phosphate in world. Fishing, textiles, cement, soap, tobacco, chemicals, paper, timber products. Tourism centred on the four imperial cities and the warm Atlantic resorts.

GDP (1990) $25.4 bn, per capita $990

History N coast occupied by Phoenicians, Carthaginians, and Romans since 12th-c BC; invasion by Arabs in 7th-c AD. Conflicting French and Spanish interest in the region in 19th-c; Treaty of Fez in 1912, established Spanish Morocco (capital, Tétouan) and French Morocco (capital, Rabat); Tangier became an international zone, 1923–56;

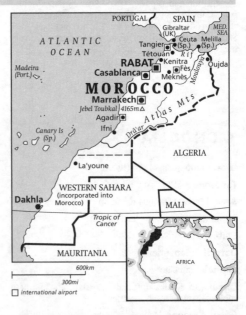

international airport

protectorates gained independence, 1956; became Kingdom of Morocco, 1957. Spanish withdrew from former Spanish Sahara (Western Sahara) in 1975; Morocco laid claim to this area using the 'Green March' as a gesture of peaceful occupation; Mauritania withdrew from southern third of territory in 1979, leaving Morocco fighting with the Polisario for the whole of Western Sahara; ceasefire agreement signed in 1990. A 'constitutional' monarchy, but the King presides over his appointed Cabinet, which is led by a Prime Minister; a unicameral Chamber of Representatives. >> WESTERN SAHARA

Head of State (Monarch)
1961–   King Hassan II

Head of Government
1985–92   Azzedine Laraka
1992–   Mohammed Karim Lamrani

MOZAMBIQUE

Local name Moçambique

Timezone GMT + 2

Area 799 380 km²/308 641 sq mi

Population total (1991e) 16 142 000

Status Republic

Date of independence 1975

Capital Maputo

Languages Portuguese (official), Swahili and Bantu dialects widely spoken

Ethnic groups Makua/Lomwe (52%), Thonga (23%), Malawi (12%), Shona (6%), Yao (3%)

Religions Local animist beliefs (60%), Christian (majority Roman Catholic) (30%), Muslim (10%)

Physical features Located in SE Africa. Main rivers, the Zambezi and Limpopo provide irrigation and hydroelectricity. Savannah plateau inland, mean elevation 800–1 000 m/2 699–4 000 ft; highest peak, Mt Binga, 2 436 m/7 992 ft. S of Zambezi is low-lying coast with sandy beaches and mangroves; low hills of volcanic origin inland, Zimbabwe plateau further N.

Climate Tropical with high humidity; rainy season

(Dec–Mar); drought conditions in S. Average annual temperatures 26°C (Jan), 18°C (Jul) in Maputo; average annual rainfall 560 mm/30 in.

Currency 1 Metical (Mt, MZM) = 100 centavos

Economy Badly affected by drought (1981–4), internal strife, and lack of foreign exchange; agriculture (employs c.85% of population); cashew nuts, tea, cotton, sugar cane, copra, sisal, groundnuts, fruit, rice, cereals, tobacco. Forestry; livestock. Reserves of gemstones and minerals.

GDP (1989) $1.6 bn, per capita $110

History Originally inhabited by Bantu peoples from the N, 1st–4th-c AD; coast settled by Arab traders; visited by Portuguese explorers by late 15th-c; part of Portuguese Africa since 1751; Mozambique Portuguese East Africa in late 19th-c. Overseas province of Portugal, 1951; independence movement formed in 1962, the Frente de Libertação de Moçambique (FRELIMO), with armed resistance to colonial rule; independence as the People's Republic of Mozambique, 1975; continuing civil war, with first peace talks in 1990; socialist one-party state, 1975–90. New constitution and change of name to Republic of Mozambique in 1990; peace accord signed between Chissanó (President of Mozambique) and Dhlakama (leader of the Renamo-Mozambique National Resistance), 1992. President (term of 5 years) rules with an Assembly of the Republic.

Head of State
1986– Joaquim Alberto Chissanó

Head of Government
1986– Mario de Graça Machungo

MYANMAR (BURMA)

Local name Pyidaungsu Myanma Naingngandaw

Timezone GMT + 6.5

Area 678 576 km²/261 930 sq mi

Population total (1992e) 43 466 000

Status Union

Date of independence 1948

Capital Yangon (Rangoon)

Languages Burmese (official), also tribal languages spoken

Ethnic groups Burman (Tibeto-Chinese) (72%), Shan (9%), Karen (7%), Chinese (3%), Indian (2%)

Religions Theravada Buddhist (85%), animist, Muslim, Hindu, Christian minorities (15%)

Physical features Bordered in the N, E, and W by mountains rising (N) to Hkakabo Razi, 5 881 m/19 294 ft. Located on Chinese frontier, forming part of Kumon Range; Chin Hills (W) descend into upland forests of the Arakan-Yoma range (S). Principal rivers, Irrawaddy, Salween, and Sittang.

Climate Tropical monsoon climate; equatorial on coast; humid temperate in extreme N; SW monsoon season (Jun–Sep); cool, dry season (Nov–Apr); hot, dry

Myanmar (Burma) (continued)

season (May–Sep). Average annual temperatures 23°C (Jan), 27°C (Jul) in Yangon; average annual rainfall 2616 mm/103 in.

Currency 1 Kyat (K) = 100 pyas

Economy Largely dependent on agriculture; rice, pulses, sugar cane; forestry (hardwoods). Textiles, pharmaceuticals, petroleum refining, and mining of minerals.

GDP (1990) $16.8 bn, per capita $408

History First unified in the 11th-c by King Anawrahta; invasion by Kubla Khan, 1287; second dynasty established under King Tabinshweti in 1486, but plagued by internal disunity and wars with Siam from 16th-c; new

dynasty under King Alaungpaya, 1752; annexed to British India following Anglo-Burmese wars (1824–86); separated from India, 1937; occupied by Japanese in World War 2. Independence as Union of Burma under Prime Minister U Nu in 1948; military coup under U Ne Win, 1962; single-party socialist republic, 1974. Army coup in 1988, leading to formation of a State Law and Order Restoration Council, headed by a Chairman. Name changed to Union of Myanmar in 1989 and renamed capital Yangon.

Head of State/Government

1988–92	Saw Maung
1992–	General Than Shwe *Military Junta*

NAMIBIA

Local name Namibia

Timezone GMT – 2

Area 824 292 km²/318 261 sq mi

Population total (1991e) 1 520 000

Status Republic

Date of independence 1990

Capital Windhoek

Languages English (official), Afrikaans, German, local languages

Ethnic groups African (chiefly Ovambo) (85%), White (7%), mixed (8%)

Religions Christian (Lutheran, Roman Catholic, Dutch Reformed, and Anglican) (90%), traditional animist beliefs (10%)

Physical features Located in SW Africa; Namib Desert runs parallel along the Atlantic Ocean coast; inland plateau, mean elevation 1 500 m/5 000 ft. Highest point, Brandberg, 2 606 m/8 550 ft. Kalahari Desert to the E and S. Orange R forms S frontier with South Africa.

□ international airport

Climate Arid, continental tropical climate. Average maximum daily temperature, 20–30°C; 49°C (Nov–Apr) in coastal desert (Namib); average annual rainfall 360 mm/14 in at Windhoek.

Currency 1 South African Rand (R) = 100 cents

Economy Agriculture (employs c.60% of population); indigenous subsistence farming in N. Major world producer of diamonds and uranium. Fishing; brewing; textiles; plastics.

GNP (1990) $1.8 bn, per capita $1 240

History Visited by British and Dutch missionaries from late 18th-c; German protectorate, 1884; mandated to South Africa by the League of Nations in 1920; UN assumed direct responsibility in 1966, changing name to

Namibia, 1968, and recognizing the Southwest Africa People's Organization (SWAPO) as representative of the Namibian people in 1973; South Africa continued to administer the area as Southwest Africa. SWAPO commenced guerrilla activities, 1966; bases established in S Angola, involving Cuban troops in 1970s; interim administration installed by South Africa in 1985; full independence, 1990. Governed by a President, a Prime Minister and a Cabinet, and an elected National Assembly.

Head of State

1990–	Sam Daniel Nujoma

Head of Government

1990–	Hage Geingob

NAURU

Local name Naeoro (Nauruan)

Timezone GMT + 11.5

Area 21.3 km²/8.2 sq mi

Population total (1991e) 9 333

Status Republic

Date of independence 1968

Capital Yaren District (No official capital)

Languages Nauruan (official), English

Ethnic groups Nauruans (62%), Pacific islanders (26%), Asian (9%), Caucasian (3%)

Religions Christian (Nauruan Protestant, Roman Catholic)

Physical features Small isolated island in WC Pacific Ocean, 4 000 km/2 500 mi NE of Sydney, Australia. Ground rises from sandy beaches to give fertile coastal belt, c.100–300 m/300–1 000 ft wide, the only cultivable soil. Central plateau inland, highest point 65 m/213 ft. Mainly phosphate-bearing rocks.

Climate Tropical, hot, and humid. Average annual temperatures 27°C (Jan), 28°C (Jul); average annual rainfall 1 524 mm/60 in; monsoon season (Nov–Feb).

Currency 1 Australian Dollar ($A) = 100 cents

Economy Based on phosphate mining, now limited reserves; coconuts, some vegetables; tourism; tax haven.

GNP (1989) $60 m, per capita not available

History Under German administration from 1880s to 1914; after 1919, League of Nations mandate, administered by Australia; occupied by Japan, 1942–5; independence movement, 1960s; self-government, 1966; full independence, 1968. 18-member unicameral Parliament, elected every 3 years. Parliament elects a President, who appoints a Cabinet.

Head of State/Government
1989–   Bernard Dowiyogo

NEPAL

Local name Nepāl

Timezone GMT + 5.5

Area 145 391 km²/56 121 sq mi

Population total (1992e) 19 800 000

Status Kingdom

Capital Kathmandu

Languages Nepali (official), Maithir, Bhojpuri

Ethnic groups Nepalese (58%), Bihari (19%), Tamang (4%), Tharu (3%), Newar (3%)

Religions Only official Hindu state in the world: Hindu (90%), Buddhist (5%), Muslim (3%), Christian (0.2%)

Physical features Landlocked, rises steeply from the Ganges basin in India. High fertile valleys in the 'hill country' at 1 300 m/4 300 ft, notably the Vale of Kathmandu (a world heritage site). Dominated by the Himalayas (glaciated), highest peak, Mt Everest, 8 848 m/ 29 028 ft.

Climate Varies from subtropical lowland with hot, humid summers and mild winters, to an alpine climate over 3 300 m/10 800 ft, with permanently snow-covered peaks. Average annual temperatures 0°C (Jan), 24°C (Jul) in Kathmandu; monsoon season (Jun–Sep); average annual rainfall 1 428 mm/56 in.

Currency 1 Nepalese Rupee (NRp, NRs) = 100 paise/pice

Economy Agriculture (employs 90% of population); rice, jute, cereals, sugar cane; agricultural and forest-based goods. Carpets; garments, handicrafts; hydroelectric power developing. Tourism increasingly important.

GDP (1990) $3.1 bn, per capita $160

History Originally a group of independent hill states,

united in 18th-c; parliamentary system introduced, 1959; replaced by village councils (*panchayats*), 1960; a constitutional monarchy ruled by hereditary King. Period of unrest in 1990, followed by reduction of King's powers, a new constitution and fresh elections, 1991. King now rules with a Council of Ministers, a bicameral Parliament consisting of an elected House of Representatives and a National Council.

Head of State (Monarch)
1972–   Birendra Bir Bikram Shah Deva

Head of Government
1990   Lokendra Bahadur Chand
1990–1   Krishna Prasad Bhattarai
1991–   Girija Prasad Koirala

NETHERLANDS, THE

Local name Nederland

Timezone GMT + 1

Area 33 929 km²/13 097 sq mi

Population total (1992e) 15 129 150

Status Kingdom

Date of independence 1830

Capital Amsterdam

Language Dutch (official)

Ethnic groups Dutch (Germanic/Gallo-Celtic descent) (99%), Indonesian/Surinamese (1%)

Religions Roman Catholic (40%), Protestant (Dutch Reformed Church and other Protestant churches) (31%)

Physical features Generally low and flat, except SE where hills rise to 321 m/1 053 ft. Much of coastal area below sea-level, reaching lowest point –6.7 m/–19.7 ft N of Rotterdam; protected by coastal dunes and artificial dykes; highest point, Vaalserberg, in SE. 27% of land area is below sea level, an area inhabited by c.60% of population.

Climate Cool, temperate maritime climate, with continental influences. Average annual temperatures 2°C (Jan), 17°C (Jul); average annual rainfall exceeds 700 mm/27 in, evenly distributed throughout the year.

Currency 1 Guilder (Gld)/ Florin (f) = 100 cents

Economy Rotterdam and newly-constructed Europort are the major European ports of transshipment, handling goods for EC member countries. Amsterdam is a world diamond centre. World's largest exporter of dairy produce; highly intensive agriculture; horticulture. Engineering, chemicals, oil products, natural gas, high technology and electrical goods; fishing; tourism.

GDP (1990) $218 bn, per capita $14 600

History Part of Roman Empire to 4th-c AD; part of Frankish Empire by 8th-c. Incorporated into the Holy Roman Empire; lands passed to Philip II, who succeeded to Spain and the Netherlands in 1555; attempts to stamp out Protestantism led to rebellion, 1572; seven N provinces united against Spain in 1579; United Provinces independence, 1581. Overrun by the French, 1795–1813, who established the Batavian Republic; united with Belgium as the Kingdom of the United Netherlands until 1830, when Belgium withdrew. Neutral in World

international airport

100km
50mi

War 1; occupied by Germany, World War 2, with strong Dutch resistance; joined with Belgium and Luxembourg to form the Benelux economic union, 1948; conflict over independence of Dutch colonies in SE Asia in late 1940s; joined NATO, 1949; independence granted to former colonies, Indonesia, 1949, with the addition of W New Guinea, 1963, and Suriname, 1975. A parliamentary democracy under a constitutional monarchy; government led by a Prime Minister; States General (*Staten-Generaal*) consists of a 75-member First Chamber, and a 150-member Second Chamber.

Head of State (Monarch)
1980– Beatrix

Head of Government
1982– Ruud F M Lubbers

Aruba

Timezone GMT

Area 193 km²/74.5 sq mi

Population total (1992e) 69 000

Status Self-governing region of the Netherlands

Date of independence Planned for 1996

Capital Oranjestad

Languages Dutch (official) with Papiamento, English, and Spanish widely spoken

Ethnic groups Large majority of mixed European/Caribbean Indian descent

Religions Christian (Roman Catholic and Protestant), small Hindu, Muslim, Confucian, and Jewish minorities

Physical features Island in the Caribbean, the westernmost of the Lesser Antilles, N of Venezuela; flat, rocky terrain, dry, with little vegetation.

Climate Dry, tropical, with little seasonal temperature variation. Average annual temperature 27°C; annual rainfall often falls to below 488 mm/19 in; lies just outside the Caribbean hurricane belt.

Currency 1 Aruban Guilder/Florin = 100 cents

Economy Lack of natural resources limits agriculture and manufacturing. Depends heavily on thriving tourist industry.

GDP (1989) $1 168 m, per capita not available

History Claimed by Dutch in 1634, but remained undeveloped. Construction of an oil refinery brought employment and prosperity in 1929. Acquired full internal self-government within kingdom of the Netherlands, 1954, as part of the Netherlands Antilles; growing resentment led to a campaign for Aruba's independence; closure of oil refinery, 1985; obtained separate status from the Netherlands Antilles with full internal autonomy in 1986, pending full independence in 1996. Sovereign of the Netherlands is Head of State, represented by a Governor-General, a Council of Ministers and a unicameral legislature.

Head of State
(Dutch monarch represented by Governor-General)
1986–   Felipe B Tromp

Head of Government
1986–89   Henry Eman
1989–   Nelson Oduber

Map >> VENEZUELA

Netherlands Antilles

Local name Nederlandse Antillen

Timezone GMT – 4

Area 993 km²/383 sq mi

Population total (1990e) 190 556

Status Self-governing region of the Netherlands

Capital Willemstad (on Curaçao Island)

Languages Dutch (official), Papiamento, English, and Spanish widely spoken

Ethnic groups Large majority of mixed European/Caribbean Indian descent

Religions Christian (mainly Roman Catholic)

Physical features Islands in the Caribbean Sea, comprising the Southern group (Leeward Is) of Curaçao and Bonaire, 60–110 km/37–68 mi N of the Venezuelan coast, and the Northern group (Windward Is) of St Maarten, St Eustatius, and Saba. Terrain generally hilly, with volcanic interiors.

Climate Tropical maritime climate; average annual temperature 28°C. Average annual rainfall varies from 500 mm/20 in (S) to 1 000 mm/39.4 in (N); Northern group subject to hurricanes (Jul–Oct).

Currency 1 Netherland Antilles Guilder/Florin = 100 cents

Economy Based on refining of crude oil imported from Venezuela. Aim of industrial diversification; ship repairing; tourism.

History Visited by Columbus, initially claimed for Spain; small-scale Spanish colonization in Curaçao, 1511; occupied by Dutch settlers in 17th-c. Acquired full internal self-government within Kingdom of the Netherlands, 1954. Aruba separated from the other islands, 1986. Sovereign of the Netherlands is Head of State, represented by a Governor, a Council of Ministers and a unicameral legislature.

Head of State
(Dutch monarch represented by Governor-General)
1983–90   Rene Romer
1990–   Jaime Saleh

Head of Government
1988–   Maria Liberia Peters

NEW CALEDONIA >> FRANCE

NEW ZEALAND

Local name Aotearoa (Maori)

Timezone GMT + 12

Area 268 812 km²/103 761 sq mi

Population total (1991) 3 434 950

Status Independent member of the Commonwealth

Date of independence 1947

Capital Wellington

Languages English and Maori (official)

Ethnic groups European (mainly British, Australian and Dutch) (87%), Maori (9%)

Religions Christian (59%) (Anglican 25%, Presbyterian 18%, Roman Catholic 16%)

Physical features Consists of two principal islands (North and South) separated by the Cook Strait, and several minor islands. North Island mountainous in the centre with many hot springs; peaks rise to 2 797 m/ 9 176 ft at Mt Ruapehu. South Island mountainous for its whole length, rising in the Southern Alps to 3 764 m/ 12 349 ft at Mt Cook, New Zealand's highest point (however, in 1991, Mt Cook transformed by a massive landslide that lowered its summit by 11 m to 3 753 m/12 313 ft). Many glaciers and mountain lakes. Largest area of level lowland is the Canterbury Plain, E side of South Island. L Taupo, largest natural lake, occupies an ancient volcanic crate; major lakes include Te Anau and Wakatipu.

Climate Cool, temperate climate, almost subtropical in extreme N. Mean temperature range, 18°C in N, 9°C in S; lower temperatures in South Island; highly changeable weather, all months moderately wet. Average annual temperature 16–23°C (Jan), 8–13°C (Jul) in Auckland; average annual rainfall 1 053 mm/41 in; subject to periodic subtropical cyclones.

Currency 1 New Zealand Dollar ($NZ) = 100 cents

Economy Farming, especially sheep and cattle; one of the world's major exporters of dairy produce; third largest exporter of wool. Kiwi fruit, venison. Textiles; timber, food processing. Substantial coal and natural gas reserves; hydroelectric power. Tourism.

GDP (1991) $40 bn, per capita $12 200

History Settled by Maoris from E Polynesia by c.1000 AD. First European sighting by Abel Tasman in 1642, named Staten Landt; later known as Nieuw Zeeland, after the Dutch Province. Visited by Captain Cook in 1769; first European settlement in 1792; dependency of New South

□ *international airport*

Wales until 1840. Outbreaks of war between immigrants and Maoris, 1860–70. Dominion of New Zealand, 1907; independent within the Commonwealth, 1947. Governed by a Prime Minister, a Cabinet and a unicameral, 97-member House of Representatives; elections every 3 years.

Head of State
(British monarch represented by Governor-General)
1990– Dame Catherine Tizard

Head of Government
1984–9 David Russell Lange
1989–90 Geoffrey Palmer
1990– James Brendan Bolger

Overseas territories

Name	Area		Capital	Population total
	km²	sq mi		
Cook Islands	238	92	Avarua	(1992e) 17 900
Niue	263	101	Alofi	(1991e) 2 000
Ross Dependency	3 540	159 626	—	uninhabited
Tokelau	10	4	Nukunonu	(1991) 1 578

NICARAGUA

Local name Nicaragua

Timezone GMT – 6

Area 148 000 km²/57 128 sq mi

Population total (1992e) 4 130 000

Status Republic

Date of independence 1821

Capital Managua

Languages Spanish (official), indigenous Indian languages and English (creole-English)

Ethnic groups Mestizo (69%), White (17%), Black (9%), Indian (Sumu, Mikito, Ramaguie peoples) (5%)

Religions Roman Catholic (95%), Protestant (5%)

Physical features Mountainous W half, with volcanic

ranges rising to over 2 000 m/6 500 ft (NW). Two large lakes, L Nicaragua and L Managua, behind the coastal mountain range. Rolling uplands and forested plains to the E. Many short rivers flow into the Pacific Ocean and the lakes.

Climate Tropical climate; average annual temperatures, 26°C (Jan), 30°C (Jul) at Managua. Rainy season (May–Nov), high humidity; average annual rainfall 1 140 mm/45 in.

Currency 1 New Córdoba (C$) = 100 centavos

Economy Agriculture (accounts for over two-thirds of total exports); cotton, coffee, sugar cane, rice, corn, tobacco. Oil, natural gas. Gold, silver, chemicals, textiles.

GDP (1990) $1.7 bn, per capita $470

History Colonized by Spaniards, early 16th-c; independence from Spain in 1821; left the Federation of Central America in 1838. Dictatorship under Anastasio Somoza, 1938; Sandinista National Liberation Front seized power in 1979, and established a socialist junta of national reconstruction. Under the 1987 constitution, a President and a 96-member Constituent Assembly are elected for 6-year terms. Former supporters of the Somoza government (the Contras), based in Honduras and supported by the USA, carried out guerrilla activities against the junta from 1979; ceasefire and disarmament agreed in 1990.

Head of State/Government
1984–90   Daniel Ortega Saavedra
1990–   Violeta Barrios de Chamorro

□ international airport

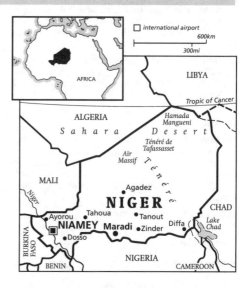

□ international airport

NIGER

Local name Niger

Timezone GMT + 1

Area 1 267 000 km²/489 191 sq mi

Population total (1991e) 8 154 000

Status Republic

Date of independence 1960

Capital Niamey

Languages French (official) with Hausa, Songhai, Fulfulde, Tamashek, and Arabic widely spoken

Ethnic groups Hausa (54%), Djerma and Songhai (22%), Fulani (9%), Tuareg (8%), Beriberi (4%), Arab (2%)

Religions Muslim (80%), traditional beliefs and small Christian minority (primarily Roman Catholic) (20%)

Physical features Occupies S fringe of Sahara Desert, on a high plateau; Hamada Mangueni plateau (far N); Aïr Massif (C); Ténéré du Tafassasset desert (E); W Talk desert (C and N). Water in quantity found only in the SW (R Niger) and SE (L Chad).

Climate One of the hottest countries in the world. Average annual temperature 16°C (Jun–Oct), 41°C (Feb–May). Rainy season in S (Jun–Oct); rainfall decreases N to almost negligible levels in desert areas; average annual rainfall at Niamey, 554 mm/22 in.

Currency 1 CFA Franc (CFAFr) = 100 cents

Economy Dominated by agriculture and mining; production badly affected by severe drought conditions in 1970s. Uranium, tin, phosphates, coal, salt, natron. Building materials, textiles, food processing.

GDP (1989) $2.1 bn, per capita $290

Niger (continued)

History Occupied by the French, 1883–99; territory within French West Africa, 1904; independence in 1960; military coup, 1974. Governed by a Higher Council for National Orientation led by a President who appoints a Council of Ministers. Elected National Assembly in 1989; constitution suspended in 1991; multi-party constitution adopted, 1992.

Head of State

1987–93	Ali Saibou
1993–	Mahamane Ousmane

Head of Government

1990–1	Aliou Mahamidou
1991–3	Amadou Cheiffou *Interim*
1993–	Mahamoudou Issoufou

NIGERIA

Local name Nigeria

Timezone GMT + 1

Area 923 768 km²/356 574 sq mi

Population total (1991) 88 500 000

Status Republic

Date of independence 1960

Capital Abuja

Languages English (official), Hausa, Yoruba, Ibo, and other Niger-Congo dialects widely used

Ethnic groups Over 250 tribal groups, notably Hausa and Fulani, Yoruba and Ibo (65%); Kanuri, Tiv, Edo, Nupe, and Ibidio (25%)

Religions Muslim (50%), Christian (34%), indigenous animist beliefs (10%)

Physical features Long, sandy shoreline with mangrove swamp, dominated by R Niger delta. Undulating area of tropical rainforest and oil palm bush behind a coastal strip; open woodland and savannah further N. Numerous rivers, notably the Niger and the Benue. Gotel Mts on SE frontier, highest point, Mt Vogel, 2024 m/6 640 ft.

Climate Tropical; uniformly high temperatures. Average annual temperatures 21–7°C (Jan), 25–6°C (Jul); dry season in the N (Oct–Apr); average annual rainfall 1 836–2 497 mm/54–98 in. Subject to influence of the Saharan Harmattan in N.

Currency 1 Naira (N) = 100 kobo

Economy Oil (provides c.90% of exports); agriculture (employs 50% of population); palm oil, groundnuts, cotton, cassava, rice, sugar cane, tobacco. Fishing, livestock, forestry. Natural gas, tin, iron ore, columbite (world's largest supplier), tantalite, limestone. Pulp, paper, textiles, rubber.

GDP (1990) $28 bn, per capita $230

History Centre of the Nok culture, 500 BC–AD 200; Muslim immigrants, 15th–16th-c. British colony at Lagos, 1861; protectorates of N and S Nigeria, 1900; amalgamated as the Colony and Protectorate of Nigeria in 1914; federation, 1954; independence, 1960; federal republic, 1963; military coup, 1966; E area formed Republic of Biafra in 1967; civil war, and surrender of Biafra in 1970; military coups 1983 and 1985. A President rules with an Armed Forces Ruling Council, which appoints a Council of Ministers.

Head of State/Government

1983–4	Mohammadu Buhari
1985–93	Ibrahim B Babangida
1993	Ernest Shonekan *Interim*
1993–	Sanni Abacha

NIUE >> NEW ZEALAND

NORTHERN IRELAND >> UNITED KINGDOM

NORTH KOREA >> KOREA, NORTH

NORTHERN MARIANA ISLANDS >> UNITED STATES OF AMERICA

NORWAY

Local name Norge

Timezone GMT + 1

Area 323 895 km²/125 023 sq mi

Population total (1991e) 4 259 000

Status Kingdom

Date of independence 1905

Capital Oslo

Languages Norwegian (official) (in the varieties of Bokmål and Nynorsk), Lappish- and Finnish-speaking minorities

Ethnic groups Germanic (Nordic, Alpine, Baltic descent) (97%), Sami/Lapp minority in far N

Religions Evangelical Lutheran (94%), Baptist, Pentecostalist, Methodist, and Roman Catholic (6%)

Physical features Mountainous country; Kjölen Mts form the N part of the boundary with Sweden; Jotunheimen range in SC Norway; much of the interior over 1 500 m/5 000 ft. Numerous lakes, the largest being L Mjøsa, 368 km²/142 sq mi. Irregular coastline with many small islands and long deep fjords.

Climate Arctic winter climate in interior highlands, snow, strong winds and severe frosts; comparatively mild conditions on coast. Average annual temperatures −4°C (Jan), 17°C (Jul) in Oslo; average annual rainfall 683 mm /27 in; rainfall heavy on W coast.

Currency 1 Norwegian Krone (NKr) = 100 øre

Economy Based on extraction and processing of raw materials, using plentiful hydroelectric power. Oil and natural gas from North Sea fields. Land under cultivation, less than 3%; productive forests covered 21% of land area in 1985.

GDP (1990) $74 bn, per capita $17 400

History A united kingdom achieved by St Olaf in the 11th-c, whose successor, Cnut, brought Norway under Danish rule; united with Sweden and Denmark, 1389. Annexed by Sweden as a reward for assistance against Napoleon, 1814; growing nationalism resulted in independence, 1905. Declared neutrality in both World Wars, but occupied by Germany, 1940–4; joined NATO, 1949; joined European Free Trade Association, 1960. A limited, hereditary monarchy; government led by a Prime Minister; Parliament (*Storting*) comprises upper (*Lagting*) and lower (*Odelsting*) chambers.

Head of State (Monarch)
1957–91   Olav V
1991–   Harald V

Head of Government
1989–90   Jan P Syse
1990–   Gro Harlem Brundtland

□ international airport

400km
200mi

Human geography

OMAN

Local name 'Umān

Timezone GMT + 4

Area 300 000 km²/115 800 sq mi

Population total (1992e) 1 640 000

Status Sultanate

Date of independence 1951

Capital Muscat

Languages Arabic (official), English, Baluchi (and other Mahri languages), Urdu and Indian dialects also spoken

Ethnic groups Arab, with small Baluchi, Iranian, Indian, Pakistani, and W European minorities

Religions Ibadhi Muslim (75%), Sunni Muslim, Shi'a Muslim and Hindu (25%)

Physical features Located on the SE corner of the Arabian peninsula; the tip of the Musandam peninsula in the Strait of Hormuz is separated from the rest of the country by an 80 km/50 mi strip belonging to the United Arab Emirates. Several peaks in the Hajjar Mt range, Jabal Akhdar ridge rises to 3 000 m/10 000 ft. Vast sand desert in NE; Dhofar uplands in SW.

Oman (continued)

Climate Desert climate, hot and arid; hot, humid on coast (Apr–Oct). Average annual temperature 22°C (Jan), 33°C (Jul); light monsoon rains in S (Jun–Sep); average annual rainfall 99 mm/3.9 in.

Currency 1 Rial Omani (RO) = 1 000 baizas

Economy Oil discovered, 1964, now provides over 90% of government revenue; natural gas an important source of industrial power. C.70% of the population relies on agriculture; alfalfa, wheat, tobacco, fruit, vegetables, fishing.

GDP (1989) $7.7 bn, per capita not available

History Dominant maritime power of the W Indian Ocean in 16th-c. Independent from UK, 1951; separatist tribal revolt, 1964, led to a police coup that installed the present Sultan in 1970. Opened airbases to Western forces, following Iraqi invasion of Kuwait, 1990. Independent state ruled by a Sultan who is both Head of State and Premier, and who appoints a Cabinet and a Consultative Council, which replaced the Consultative Assembly, 1992.

Head of State/Government (Sultan)
1932–70   Said bin Taimur
1970–   Qaboos bin Said

international airport

PAKISTAN

Local name Pākistān

Timezone GMT + 5

Area 803 943 km²/310 322 sq mi

Population total (1992e) 117 430 130

Status Republic

Date of independence 1947

Capital Islamabad

Languages Urdu and English (official), Punjabi, Sindhi, Pashto, Urdu, Baluchi, and Brahvi mainly spoken

Ethnic groups Punjabi (66%), Sindhi (13%), Baluchi (3%), Pathan and Muhajir minorities, also Afghan refugees in W Pakistan

Religions Muslim (97%) (Sunni 77%, Shi'a 20%), Christian, Hindu, Parsee, Buddhist minorities

Physical features R Indus flows from Himalayas to Karachi, forming a vast, fertile, densly populated alluvial floodplain in E. Bounded N and W by mountains rising to 8 611 m/28 250 ft at K2, and 8 126 m/26 660 ft at Nanga Parbat. Mostly flat plateau, low-lying plains and arid desert to the S. Major rivers include Jhelum, Chenab, Indus, Sutlej.

Climate Continental, with many temperature variations; dominated by the Asiatic monsoon; severe winters in mountainous regions. Average annual temperatures 10°C (Jan), 32°C (Jul) in Islamabad; average annual rainfall 900 mm/35 in; rainy season (Jun–Oct).

Currency 1 Pakistan Rupee (PRs, Rp) = 100 paisa

1 ISLAMABAD
2 Rawalpindi
3 Peshawar
4 Chenab
5 Ravi
6 Sutlej

international airport

Economy Agriculture (employs 55% of labour force). Cotton production important, supporting major spinning, weaving, and processing industries. Sugar cane; textiles; natural gas; tobacco; salt; uranium.

GDP (1990) $43 bn, per capita $380

History Remains of Indus Valley civilization over 4000 years ago; Muslim rule under the Mughal Empire, 1526–1761. British rule over most areas, 1840s; separated from India to form a state for the Muslim minority, 1947; consisted of West Pakistan (Baluchistan, North-West Frontier, West Punjab, Sind) and East Pakistan (East Bengal), physically separated by 1610 km/1000 mi. Occupied Jammu and Kashmir, 1949 (disputed territory with India, and the cause of wars in 1965 and 1971). Proclaimed an Islamic republic, 1956; differences between E and W Pakistan developed into civil war in 1971; E Pakistan became an independent state (Bangladesh). Military coup in 1977; Benazir Bhutto became first woman premier of a modern Islamic state, 1988. Governed by an elected President and a bicameral Federal Parliament.

Head of State
1988–93   Ghulam Ishaq Khan
1993–   Farooq Ahmed Leghan

Head of Government
1988–90   Benazir Bhutto
1990   Ghulam Mustafa Jatoi
1990–93   Mian Mohammad Nawaz Sharif
1993–   Benazir Bhutto

PALAU >> UNITED STATES OF AMERICA

PANAMA

Local name Panamá

Timezone GMT – 5

Area 77082 km²/29753 sq mi

Population total (1992e) 2515000

Status Republic

Date of independence 1903

Capital Panama City

Languages Spanish (official), English and indigenous languages (including Cuna, Chibchan, Choco)

Ethnic groups Mestizo (mixed Spanish-Indian) (70%), West Indian (14%), White (10%), Indian (6%)

Religions Christian (Roman Catholic 93%, Protestant 6%), Jewish, Muslim, and Baha'i minorities

Physical features Mostly mountainous; Serranía de Tabasará (W) rises to 3475 m/11401 ft at Volcán Baru. Azuero peninsula (Península de Azuero) in the S; lake-studded lowland cuts across the isthmus. Dense tropical forests on the Caribbean coast. Panama Canal, 82 km/ 51 mi long, connects Pacific and Atlantic oceans.

Climate Tropical, with uniformly high temperatures. Average annual temperature 26°C (Jan), 27°C (Jul) in Panama City; dry season (Jan–Apr) only; average annual rainfall 1770 mm/69.7 in.

Currency 1 Balboa (B, Ba) = 100 cents

Economy Canal revenue (accounts for 80% of country's wealth); great increase in banking sector since 1970; attempts to diversify include oil refining, cigarettes, paper products; tourism; copper, gold, silver; bananas, coffee, cacao, sugar cane.

GDP (1990) $4.8 bn, per capita $1980

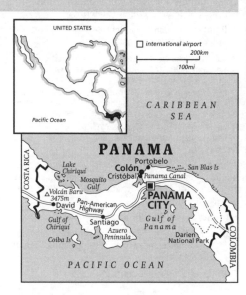

History Visited by Columbus in 1502; under Spanish colonial rule until 1821; joined the Republic of Greater Colombia; separation from Colombia after a US-inspired revolution, 1903. Assumed sovereignty of the 8 km/ 5 mi-wide Canal zone, previously administered by the USA in 1979. Military were the ruling force led by Manuel Noriega, 1983–9; US invasion in 1989, deposed Noriega and installed Guillermo Endara Galimany as President. Governed by a President, a Cabinet, and a unicameral Legislative Assembly.

Head of State/Government
1989–   Guillermo Endara

PAPUA NEW GUINEA

Local name Papua New Guinea

Timezone GMT + 10

Area 462 840 km²/178 656 sq mi

Population total (1992e) 3 834 000

Status Independent state within the Commonwealth

Date of independence 1975

Capital Port Moresby

Languages Pidgin English and Motu (official parliamentary languages), Tok Pisin, and c.750 indigenous languages spoken

Ethnic groups Papuan (80%), Melanesian (15%), Polynesian, Chinese, and European minorities

Religions Christian (Protestant 64%, Roman Catholic 33%), local beliefs

Physical features Island group in SW Pacific Ocean, comprising E half of the island of New Guinea, the Bismarck and Louisiade archipelagos, the Trobriand and D'Entrecasteaux Is, and other off-lying groups. Complex system of mountains, highest point, Mt Wilhelm, 4 509 m /14 793 ft. Mainly covered with tropical rainforest; vast mangrove swamps along coast. Archipelago islands are mountainous, mostly volcanic and fringed with coral reefs.

Climate Typical monsoon, with temperatures and humidity constantly high. Average annual temperature 28°C (Jan), 26°C (Jul); average annual rainfall 2 000–2 500 mm /80–100 in.

Currency 1 Kina (K) = 100 toea

Economy Farming, fishing, and forestry (engages c.75% of workforce); vegetables, sugar, peanuts. Natural gas; brewing; tourism.

GDP (1989) $2.7 bn, per capita $725

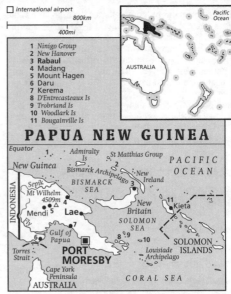

□ international airport

1 Ninigo Group
2 New Hanover
3 **Rabaul**
4 Madang
5 Mount Hagen
6 Daru
7 Kerema
8 D'Entrecasteaux Is
9 Trobriand Is
10 Woodlark Is
11 Bougainville Is

History British protectorate in SE New Guinea, 1884; some of the islands under German protectorate, 1884; German New Guinea in NE in 1899. German colony annexed by Australia in World War 1; Australia mandated to govern both British and German areas, 1920. Combined as the United Nations Trust Territory of Papua and New Guinea in 1949; independence within the Commonwealth, 1975. A Governor-General represents the British Crown; governed by a Prime Minister and a Cabinet, with a unicameral National Parliament.

Head of State
(British monarch represented by Governor-General)
1991–   Wiwa Korowi

Head of Government
1988–92   Rabbie Namiliu
1992–   Paias Wingti

PARAGUAY

Local name Paraguay

Timezone GMT – 3

Area 406 750 km²/157 000 sq mi

Population total (1992e) 4 520 000

Status Republic

Date of independence 1811

Capital Asunción

Languages Spanish (official), but Guaraní also spoken

Ethnic groups Mestizo (mixed Spanish-Guaraní Indian) (95%), Amerindian, Black, European, and Asian minorities

Religions Roman Catholic (97%), Mennonite, Baptist/ Anglican minorities

Physical features Landlocked, in C South America; divided into two regions by the R Paraguay. Gran Chaco in the W, mostly cattle country or scrub forest. More

□ international airport

fertile land in the E; Paraná plateau at 300–600 m/ 1 000–2 000 ft, mainly wet, treeless savannah.

Climate Tropical NW, with hot summers, warm winters; temperate in SE. Average annual temperatures 27°C (Jan), 18°C (Jul) in Asunción; average annual rainfall 1 316 mm/52 in.

Currency 1 Guaraní (G) = 100 céntimos

Economy Agriculture (employs 40% of the labour force); oilseed, cotton, wheat, tobacco, corn, rice, sugar cane. Pulp, timber, textiles, cement, glass.

GDP (1990) $4.7 bn, per capita $1 100

History Originally inhabited by Guaraní Indians; arrival of the Spanish in 1537; arrival of Jesuit missionaries, 1609; independence from Spain in 1811; War of the Triple Alliance against Brazil, Argentina, and Uruguay, 1865–70; Chaco War with Bolivia, 1932–5; civil war in 1947. General Alfredo Stroessner seized power, 1954, forced to stand down following a coup in 1989; new constitution, creating post of Vice-President, 1992. Governed by a President, an appointed Council of Ministers, and a bicameral National Congress.

Head of State/Government
1989–93   Andres Rodriguez
1993–   Juan Carlos Wasmosy

PERU

Local name Perú

Timezone GMT – 5

Area 1 285 640 km²/495 871 sq mi

Population total (1992e) 22 454 000

Status Republic

Date of independence 1821

Capital Lima

Languages Spanish and Quechua (official), Aymará also spoken

Ethnic groups South American Indian (45%), Mestizo (mixed Indian and European) (37%), White (15%), Black, Japanese, and Chinese (3%)

Religions Roman Catholic (90%), Anglican, Methodist, Peruvian Baha'i minorities

Physical features Arid plains and foothills on the coast, with areas of desert and fertile river valleys. Central Sierra, average altitude 3 000 m/10 000 ft, contains 50% of the population. Highest peak, Mt Huascarán, 6 768 m/22 204 ft, in W. Forested Andes and Amazon basin (E), with major rivers flowing to the Amazon.

Climate Mild temperatures all year on coast; dry, arid desert in the S; typically wet, tropical climate in Amazon basin. Average annual temperatures 23°C (Jan), 17°C (Jul) in Lima; average annual rainfall 48 mm/1.9 in.

Currency 1 New Sol = 100 centavos

Economy One of the world's leading producers of silver, zinc, lead, copper, gold, iron ore. 80% of Peru's oil extracted from the Amazon forest. Cotton, potatoes, sugar, olives. Tourism, especially to ancient sites.

GDP (1989) $19.3 bn, (1990) per capita $898

History Highly developed Inca civilization; arrival of Spanish in 1531; Vice-royalty of Peru established. Independence declared in 1821; frequent border disputes in 19th-c (eg War of the Pacific, 1879–83). Several military coups; terrorist activities by Maoist guerrillas. Bicameral

600km
300mi
☐ international airport

Congress consists of a Senate and a National Chamber of Deputies; an elected President appoints a Council of Ministers.

Head of State
1985–90   Alan García Pérez
1990–   Alberto Keinya Fujimori

Head of Government
1991–2   Alfonso de los Heros
1992–   Oscar de la Puente Raygada
1993–   Alfonso Bustamente y Bustamente

PHILIPPINES

Local name Filipinas

Timezone GMT + 8

Area 299 679 km²/115 676 sq mi

Population total (1992e) 63 609 000

Status Republic

Date of independence 1946

Capital Manila

Languages Tagalog (Filipino), and English (official), over 87 local languages, including Cebuano, Ilocano, Bicol, and Samar-Leyte

Ethnic groups Tagalog (Filipino) with Chinese, Spanish, and American minorities

Religions Roman Catholic (83%), Protestant (9%), Muslim (5%), Buddhist (3%)

Physical features An archipelago of more than 7 100 islands and islets, NE of Borneo. Largest island, Luzon 108 172 km²/41 754 sq mi. Mindanao, 94 227 km²/36 372 sq mi, has active volcano Apo, 2 954 m/9 690 ft, and mountainous rainforest. Mount Pinatubo volcano, 1 758 m/5 770 ft, situated 90 km/56 mi NW of Manila. Largely mountainous islands.

Climate Tropical, maritime; warm and humid throughout year. Average annual temperature 25°C (Jan), 28°C (Jul) in Manila; average annual rainfall 2 083 mm/82 in. Frequent typhoons and occasional earth tremors and tsunamis (tidal waves).

Currency 1 Philippine Peso (PP, ₱) = 100 centavos

Economy Farming (employs c.50% of workforce); rice, pineapples, mangos, vegetables, livestock, sugar, tobacco, rubber, coffee. Oil, copper, gold. Textiles; vehicles; tourism.

GNP (1990) $45.2 bn, per capita $700

History Claimed for Spain by Magellan in 1521. Ceded to the USA after the Spanish-American War, 1898; became a self-governing Commonwealth, 1935. Occupied by the Japanese in World War 2; independence, 1946. Communist guerrilla activity in N; Muslim sepa-

The Visayas:
1 Panay
2 Masbate
3 Samar
4 Negros
5 Cebu
6 Bohol
7 Leyte

□ international airport

ratist movement in S; martial law following political unrest, 1972–81; exiled political leader Benigno Aquino assassinated on returning to Manila, 1983. Coup in 1986 ended the 20-year rule of President Ferdinand Marcos; new constitution, 1987; attempted coup, 1989, with continuing political unrest. Eruption of Mount Pinatubo, 1991. Governed by a President and a bicameral legislature, comprising a Senate and a House of Representatives.

Head of State/Government
1986–92   Maria Corazon Aquino
1992–   Fidel Ramos

PITCAIRN ISLANDS >> UNITED KINGDOM

POLAND

Local name Polska

Timezone GMT + 1

Area 312 683 km²/120 695 sq mi

Population total (1991e) 37 799 000

Status Republic

Date of independence 1918

Capital Warsaw

Language Polish (official)

Ethnic groups Polish (99%), Ukrainian, Belorussian, and Jewish minorities

Religions Roman Catholic (94%), small Jewish and Muslim minorities

Physical features Part of the great European plain, with the Carpathian and Sudetes Mts (S) rising in the High Tatra to 2 499 m/8 199 ft at Mt Rysy. Polish plateau in N, cut by the Bug, San, and Wisła (Vistula) rivers. Richest coal basin in Europe in the W (Silesia). Flat Baltic coastal area. Forests cover 20% of land.

Climate Continental climate, with severe winters, hot summers. Average annual temperatures –4°C (Jan), 19°C (Jul) in Warsaw; average annual rainfall 550 mm/22 in.

Currency 1 Złoty (ZI) = 100 groszy

Human geography (side tab)

Economy Nearly 50% of the land under cultivation; major producer of coal; zinc, lead, sulphur; shipbuilding, machinery, vehicles, electrical equipment; textiles.

GDP (1990) $158 bn, per capita $4 200

History Emergence as a powerful Slavic group in 11th-c. United with Lithuania, 1569; divided between Prussia, Russia, and Austria, 1772, 1793, 1795; semi-independent state after Congress of Vienna, 1815. Incorporated into the Russian Empire; after World War 1, declared an independent Polish state, 1918; partition between Germany and the USSR, 1939; invasion by Germany, 1939; major resistance movement, and a government in exile during World War 2. People's Democracy established under Soviet influence, 1944; rise of independent trade union, Solidarity, 1980; state of martial law imposed, 1981–3; loss of support for communist government and major success for Solidarity in 1989 elections. Proclaimed Polish Republic, 1989, and constitution amended to provide for a bicameral National Assembly.

Head of State
1989–9   Wojciech Jaruzelski
1990–   Lech Walesa

Head of Government
1989–91   Tadeusz Mazowiecki
1991   Jan Krzysztof Bielecki
1991–2   Jan Olszewski
1992   Waldemar Pawlak
1992–3   Hanna Suchocka
1993–   Waldemar Pawlak

POLYNESIA, FRENCH >> FRANCE

international airport

PORTUGAL

Local name Portugal

Timezone GMT + 1

Area 91 630 km²/35 370 sq mi

Population total (1991) 9 831 967

Status Republic

Capital Lisbon

Languages Portuguese (official), with many dialectal variations

Ethnic groups Homogeneous (Mediterranean stock), with small African minority

Religions Roman Catholic (97%), Protestant (1%), Muslim minority

Physical features Located on W side of Iberian peninsula; includes semi-autonomous Azores and Madeira Is. Chief mountain range, the Serra da Estrêla (N), rising to 1991 m/6 532 ft. Main rivers, Douro, Tagus, Guadiana, are the lower courses of rivers beginning in Spain.

Climate Cool, maritime climate in N; warmer Mediterranean type in S; most rainfall in winter. Average annual temperature 11°C (Jan), 22°C (Jul) in Lisbon; average annual rainfall 686 mm/27 in.

Currency 1 Escudo (Esc) = 100 centavos

Economy Several labour-intensive areas, including textiles, leather, wood products, cork, ceramics; timber;

international airport

Portugal (continued)

wine, fish; chemicals, electrical machinery, steel, ship-building; minerals, cereals, pulses, fruit, olive oil; c.20% of land is forested.

GDP (1990) $57 bn, per capita $5 580

History Became a kingdom under Alfonso Henriques in 1140; major period of world exploration and beginning of Portuguese Empire in 15th-c. Under Spanish domination, 1580–1640; invaded by the French, 1807; island of Azores granted semi-autonomy in 1895; monarchy overthrown and republic established in 1910. Dictatorship of Dr Salazar, 1928–68; military coup in 1974, followed by 10 years of political unrest under 15 governments; island of Madeira gained partial autonomy in 1980; Macao is still administered by Portugal; joined EC in 1985. Governed by a President, elected for five years, a Prime Minister and Council of Ministers, and a 230-member unicameral Assembly of the Republic, elected every four years.

Head of State
1986–   Mário Alberto Nobre Lopez Soares

Head of Government
1986–   Aníbal Cavaço Silva

Azores

Local name Ilhas dos Açôres

Timezone GMT – 1

Area 2 300 km²/900 sq mi

Population total (1991) 241 794

Status Semi-autonomous region of Portugal

Capital Ponta Delgada (on São Miguel Island)

Physical features Island archipelago of volcanic origin, 1 400–1 800 km/870–1 100 mi W of mainland Portugal. Three widely separated groups of nine islands; Flores and Corvo (NW), Terceira, Graciosa, São Jorge, Faial (Fayal), Pico (C), and Santa Maria with the Formigas Islands and São Miguel, the principal island (E). Highest point, Pico, 2 351 m/7 713 ft. Volcanic terrain.

Economy Agriculture; grain, fruit, tea, tobacco, wine.

History Settled by the Portugese in 1439; under Spanish rule, 1580–1640. New constitution established in 1832, when islands were grouped into three administrative districts. Given limited autonomous administration in 1895. Has no central government, but a General Council.

Madeira (islands)

Local name Ilha de Madeira

Timezone GMT

Area 796 km²/307 sq mi

Population total (1991) 263 306

Status Semi-autonomous region of Portugal

Capital Funchal (on Madeira Island)

Physical features Main island in an archipelago off the coast of N Africa, 990 km/615 mi SW of Lisbon; consists of Madeira, Porto Santo and three uninhabited islands. Highest point, Pico Ruivo de Santana, 1 861 m/6 106 ft on Madeira.

Economy Agriculture; sugar cane, fruit, fishing, Madeira (a fortified wine). Embroidery, crafts; tourism.

History
Occupied by the Portuguese in 15th-c; occupied by Britain, 1801, and 1807–14. Gained partial autonomy, 1980, but remains a Portuguese overseas territory. Locally-elected government, and Assembly.

Macao

Local name Macáu

Timezone GMT + 8

Area 16 km²/6 sq mi

Population total (1991) 401 873

Status Territory under Portguese administration

Capital Nome de Deus de Macau

Languages Portuguese and Cantonese (official), with English generally spoken

Ethnic group Chinese (99%)

Religions Roman Catholic, Buddhist

Physical features Flat, maritime tropical peninsula in SE China; also includes the nearby islands of Taipa and Colôane; on the Pearl R delta, 64 km/40 mi W of Hong Kong. Ferry links with Hong Kong.

Climate Subtropical; cool winters, warm summers.

Currency 1 Pataca = 100 avos

Economy Textiles, electronics, toys, tourism, fishing.

History Portuguese trade with China began in 16th-c; Macao became a Portuguese colony, 1557. Right of permanent occupation granted to Portugal by the Sino-Portuguese treaty, 1887. Portugal changed Macao's status from overseas province to a 'territory under Portuguese administration' in 1979. Sino-Portuguese negotiations on the transfer of administration began in 1986; in 1987 Portugal and China agreed that Macao would revert to China in 1999, when it will become a 'special administrative region' of China. Governor appointed by Portugal; Legislative Assembly.

Head of State/Government (Governor)
1987–   Carlos Melancia

Map >> CHINA

PUERTO RICO >> UNITED STATES OF AMERICA

QATAR

Local name Qatar

Timezone GMT + 3

Area 11 437 km²/4 415 sq mi

Population total (1992e) 520 000

Status Independent state

Date of independence 1971

Capital Doha

Languages Arabic (official), English

Ethnic groups Arab (40%), Pakistani (18%), Indian (18%), Iranian (10%)

Religion Sunni Muslim (95%)

Physical features Low-lying state on the E coast of the Arabian Peninsula, comprising the Qatar Peninsula and numerous small offshore islands. The peninsula, 160 km/100 mi long and 50–80 km/34–50 mi wide, slopes gently from the Dukhan Heights 98 m/321 ft, to the E shore. Barren terrain, mainly sand and gravel. Coral reefs offshore.

Climate Desert climate; average temperatures 23°C (Jan), 35°C (Jul); high humidity; sparse rainfall; average annual rainfall 62 mm/2.4 in.

Currency 1 Qatar Riyal (QR) = 100 dirhams

Economy Based on oil. Offshore gas reserves thought to be an eighth of known world reserves; oil refineries, petrochemicals, liquefied natural gas, fertilizers, steel, cement, ship repairing, engineering; fishing.

GDP (1988) $6.6 bn, (1990) per capita $12 500

History British protectorate after Turkish withdrawal in 1916; independence, 1971; palace coup brought Khalifah bin Hamad to power, 1972; historic territorial dispute with Bahrain over Hawar Is following brief occupation of Fasht-al Dibal (a coral reef being reclaimed from sea by Bahrain) by Qatari troops. A hereditary monarchy, with an Emir who is both Head of State and Prime Minister; Council of Ministers is assisted by a 30-member nominated Consultative Council.

Head of State/Government (Emir)
Family name: al-Thani
1960–72   Ahmad bin Ali
1972–   Khalifa bin Hamad

RÉUNION >> FRANCE

ROMANIA

Local name Romănia

Timezone GMT + 2

Area 237 500 km²/91 675 sq mi

Population total (1991e) 23 397 000

Status Republic

Date of independence 1918

Capital Bucharest

Languages Romanian (official), with French, Hungarian, and German widely spoken

Ethnic groups Romanian (89%), Hungarian (7%), German (2%), Ukrainian, Serb, Croat, Russian, Turk, and Gypsy (2%)

Religions Eastern Orthodox Christian (80%), Roman Catholic (6%), Calvinist, Lutheran, Baptist (4%)

Physical features Carpathian Mts form the heart of the country; highest peak, Negoiu, 2 548 m/8 359 ft. Crossed by many rivers; c.3 500 glacial ponds, lakes, and coastal lagoons. Over 25% of land is forested.

Climate Continental, with cold, snowy winters and warm summers; winters can be severe; mildest along the Black Sea coast. Average annual temperatures range from 7°C (N), to 11°C (S), −3°C (Jan), 24°C (Jul); average annual rainfall 579 mm/22.8 in.

Currency 1 Leu (plural lei) = 100 bani

Economy Gradual change from agricultural to industrial economy (since World War 2). State owns nearly 37% of farm land, mainly organized as collectives and state farms; wheat, maize, sugar beet, fruit, potatoes; livestock. Oil, natural gas. Iron and steel, metallurgy, engineering, chemicals, textiles, electronics, timber; tourism.

GDP (1990) $69 bn, per capita $3 000

History Formed from the unification of Moldavia and Wallachia in 1862; monarchy created in 1866; Transylvania, Bessarabia, and Bucovina united with Romania, 1918. Support given to Germany in World War 2; occupied by Soviet forces, 1944; monarchy abolished and People's Republic declared, 1947. Socialist Republic declared, 1965; increasingly independent from the USSR from the 1960s; leading political force was the Romanian Communist Party, led by dictator Nicolae Ceaucescu; popular uprising due to violent repression of protest led to the overthrow of the Ceaucescu regime, 1989. New constitution, 1991, gave executive power to a directly elected President, who elects a Prime Minister and a Cabinet; a Chamber of Deputies and a Senate.

Head of State
1989–   Ion Iliescu

Head of Government
1989–91   Petre Roman
1991–2   Theodor Stolojan
1992–   Nicolae Vacaroiu

ROSS DEPENDENCY >> NEW ZEALAND

RUSSIA (RUSSIAN FEDERATION)

Local name Rossiyskaya (Rossiyskaya Federatsiya)

Timezone GMT ranges from + 3 to + 13

Area 17 075 400 km²/6 591 100 sq mi

Population total (1992e) 148 800 000

Status Republic

Date of independence 1991

Capital Moscow

Languages Russian (official), and c.100 different languages

Ethnic groups Russian (82%), Tatars (3%), Ukrainian (3%)

Religions Christian (Russian Orthodox 25%), non-religious (60%), Muslim

Physical features Occupying much of E Europe and N Asia; consists of c.75% of the area of the former USSR and contains over 50% of its population. Vast plains dominate the W half; Ural Mts separate the E European Plain (W) from the W Siberian Lowlands (E); E of the R Yenisey lies the C Siberian Plateau; N Siberian Plain further E; Caucasus on S frontier. Lena, Ob, Severnaya Dvina, Pechora, Yenisey, Indigirka, and Kolyma rivers flow to the Arctic Ocean; Amur, Argun, and rivers of the Kamchatka

Peninsula flow to the Pacific Ocean; Caspian Sea basin includes the Volga and Ural rivers. Over 20 000 lakes, the largest being the Caspian Sea, L Taymyr, L Baikal.

Climate Half of country covered by snow for 6 months of year; coldest region, NE Siberia, average annual temperature −46°C (Jan), 16°C (Jul). Summers in rest of country generally short and hot; average annual temperature −18−9°C (Jan), 16−24°C (Jul) in Moscow; average annual rainfall 500−750 mm/ 20−30 in.

Currency Rouble (R)

Economy Oil fields in W Siberia (provide 50% of country's petroleum). Series of 5-year plans since 1928 promoted industry; heavy-industry products include chemicals, construction materials, machine tool, and steel-making. Mining, major producer of iron ore, manganese, natural gas, nickel, and platinum, also coal, copper, gold, zinc, tin, lead. Agriculture, primarily wheat, fruit, vegetables, tobacco, cotton, sugar beet. Textiles; timber.

GDP Not available
Former USSR GNP (1989) 1 064 000 m, per capita $3 800

History Conquered by Mongols in 13th-c; Ivan IV (the Terrible) became first ruler to be crowned Tsar, 1547; Time of Trouble, 1604−13; under Peter the Great, territory expanded to the Baltic Sea and St Petersburg founded as capital, 1703. Napoleon invasion failed in 1812; Crimean War, 1853−6; emancipation of the serfs, 1861; assassination of Alexander II, 1881; Balkan War with Turkey, 1877−8; Russo-Japanese War, 1904−5; establishment of a parliament (*Duma*) with limited powers in 1906. Russia allied with Britain and France, World War I; revolution overthrew Nicholas II, Bolsheviks (Communists) seized power under the dictatorship of Lenin in 1917; Russia forced to withdraw from War; renamed the Russian Soviet Federated Socialist Republic, 1918, and Moscow

was reinstated as the capital; Russia became part of the Union of Soviet Socialist Republics (USSR), established in 1922. Death of Lenin, 1924; Trotsky deported in 1928 by which time Stalin acquiring dictatorial power. USSR fought with the Allies against Germany in World War II; from 1946 development of the Cold War between East and West; troops intervened in Afghanistan in 1979. Radical reform of the system under the leadership of Gorbachev, 1985−91; first contested elections in Soviet history held, and the end of the Cold War announced, 1989; troops withdrawn from Afghanistan, 1989. During war over Nagorno Karabakh troops sent to Azerbaijan to defuse situation, 1990; declarations of sovereignty made by Baltic republics, recognized by Russian leadership, but not by USSR. Yeltsin first elected president of Russian Republic in 1991; coup attempt to remove Gorbachev (president of USSR) from power failed in Aug 1991; his position was, however, undermined by Yeltsin who encouraged the rapid dissolution of the Soviet Union and banished communist structures; Yeltsin began negotiations for the formation of a new confederal Commonwealth of Independent States (CIS); Gorbachev resigned and USSR was dissolved at end Dec 1991. Russian Republic became independent and a founder member of the CIS in 1991. Legislative power exercised by Congress of People's Deputies and the bicameral Supreme Soviet; as a preliminary to a new Russian constitution, a Federal Treaty was signed by the 21 republics which are constituent parts of the Russian Federation in Mar 1992.

Head of State
1991−   Boris Yeltsin

Head of Government
1991−2   Yegor Gaidar *Acting*
1992−   Victor Chernomyrdin *Interim*

>> Political leaders and rulers

RWANDA

Local name Rwanda

Timezone GMT + 2

Area 26338 km²/10166 sq mi

Population total (1991e) 7902000

Status Republic

Date of independence 1962

Capital Kigali

Languages French and Kinyarwanda (official), with Kiswahili widely used in commerce

Ethnic groups Hutu (84%), Tutsi (14%), Pygmoid Twa (1%)

Religions Roman Catholic (65%), local indigenous beliefs (17%), Protestant (9%), Muslim (9%)

Physical features Landlocked in C Africa; mountainous, with many of the highest mountains formed by volcanoes. Highest point Karisimbi, 4507 m/14787 ft, in the Virunga range. W third drains into L Kivu and then the R Congo, remainder drains towards the R Nile. L Kivu and R Ruzizi form W border as part of Africa's Great Rift Valley.

Climate Tropical climate, influenced by high altitude. Average annual temperature 19°C (Jan), 21°C (Jul) in Kigali. Average annual rainfall 1000 mm/40 in in Kigali; two wet seasons (Oct–Dec, Mar–May); highest rainfall in the W, decreasing in the C uplands and to the N and E.

Currency 1 Rwanda Franc (RF) = 100 centimes

Economy Based largely on agriculture; coffee, tea, pyrethrum, maize, beans, livestock. Minerals. Plastic goods, textiles.

GDP (1989) $2.1 bn, per capita $310

History In the 16th-c the Tutsi tribe moved into the country and took over from the Hutu, forming a monarchy. German protectorate, 1899; mandated with Burundi to Belgium as the Territory of Ruanda-Urundi in 1919. United Nations Trust Territory administered by Belgium, after World War 2; unrest in 1959 led to a Hutu revolt and the overthrow of Tutsi rule; independence, 1962. Military coup, 1973; return to civilian rule, 1980; further fighting, 1990, 1994. Governed by a National Development Council of 70 members, a President, and a Council of Ministers. New constitution providing for a multi-party democracy in 1991, and introduced the post of Prime Minister.

Head of State
1973–94   Juvenal Habyarimana
1994–   Théodore Sindikubwabo *Interim*

Head of Government
1991–2   Sylvestre Nsanzimana
1992–3   Dismas Nsengiyaremye
1993   Agathe Uwilingiymana
1994–   Jean Kambanda *Acting*

SAINT HELENA AND DEPENDENCIES >> UNITED KINGDOM

SAINT KITTS AND NEVIS

Local name Saint Christopher (Kitts) and Nevis

Timezone GMT – 4

Area 269 km²/104 sq mi

Population total (1992e) 43100

Status Independent state within the Commonwealth

Date of independence 1983

Capital Basseterre

Languages English (official), with creole-English widely spoken

Ethnic groups Black African descent (94%), mulatto (3%), White (1%)

Religions Christian (Anglican 36%, Methodist 32%, other Protestant 8%, Roman Catholic 11%)

Physical features Located in the N Leeward Is, E Caribbean; comprises the islands of St Christopher (St Kitts), Nevis, and Sombrero. Volcanic origin with mountain ranges rising to 1156 m/3793 ft at Mt Misery. Nevis dominated by a central peak rising to 985 m/3232 ft.

Climate Tropical, warm climate. Average annual temperature 26°C; average annual rainfall 1375 mm/54 in. Low humidity, modified by sea winds; hurricanes possible (Jul–Oct).

Currency 1 East Caribbean Dollar (EC$) = 100 cents

Economy Sugar and its products (supply 60% of total exports); copra, cotton, electrical appliances, footwear, garments, tourism.

GDP (1988) $97 m, per capita not available

History St Kitts was the first British colony in the W

Indies, 1623. Control disputed between France and Britain, 17th–18th-c; ceded to Britain in 1783. St Kitts and Nevis united in 1882. Area gained full internal self-government, 1967; Anguilla declared itself independent from the control of St Kitts, which led to British troops intervention, 1969; island reverted to being a British dependent territory, 1971 and was formally separated from St Kitts-Nevis, 1980; independence of St Kitts-Nevis, 1983; British monarch is represented by a Governor-General. Governed by a Prime Minister and two legisla-

tive chambers; island of Nevis has its own legislature (the Nevis Island Assembly), and executive, which has exclusive responsibility for the island's internal administration.

Head of State
(British monarch represented by Governor-General)
1983–   Sir Clement Athelston Arrindell

Head of Government
1983–   Kennedy Alphonse Simmonds

SAINT LUCIA

Local name Saint Lucia

Timezone GMT – 4

Area 616 km²/238 sq mi

Population total (1991) 136 041

Status Independent state within the Commonwealth

Date of independence 1979

Capital Castries

Languages English (official), with French patois widely spoken

Ethnic groups African descent (90%), mixed (6%), East Indian (3%), Caucasian (1%)

Religions Christian (Roman Catholic 90%, Protestant 7%, Anglican 3%)

Physical features Second largest of the Windward Is, E Caribbean. Volcanic island. Forested mountainous centre rising to 950 m/3 117 ft at Mt Gimie. Sulphurous springs of Qualibou and twin peaks of Gros and Petit Pitons (SW).

Climate Tropical climate; average temperature 26°C;

wet season (Jun–Dec), dry season (Jan–Apr); average annual rainfall 1 500 mm/59 in (lowlands), 3 500 mm/138 in (mountainous zone).

Currency 1 East Caribbean Dollar (EC$) = 100 cents

Economy Tourism (fastest-growing sector of the economy); bananas, cocoa, copra, citrus fruits, coconut oil; garments, textiles, electronic components; oil refining and transshipment.

GDP (1989) $267 m, per capita $1 810

History Reputedly visited by Columbus in 1502; disputed ownership between England and France, 17th–18th-c; British Crown Colony, 1814. Full internal autonomy, 1967; independence, 1979. British monarch represented by a Governor-General; House of Assembly, elected every five years, and a Senate.

Head of State
(British monarch represented by Governor-General)
1988–   Stanislaus A James

Head of Government
1982–   John George Melvin Compton

Map >> VENEZUELA

SAINT PIERRE AND MIQUELON >> FRANCE

SAINT VINCENT AND THE GRENADINES

Local name Saint Vincent and the Grenadines

Timezone GMT – 4

Area 390 km²/150 sq mi

Population total (1991e) 114 000

Status Independent state within the Commonwealth

Date of independence 1979

Capital Kingstown

Languages English (official), with French patois widely spoken

Ethnic groups Black African descent (82%), mixed (14%), White, Asian, and Amerindian minorities

Religions Christian (Anglican 42%, Methodist 21%, Roman Catholic 12%)

Physical features Island group of the Windward Is, E Caribbean, comprising the island of St Vincent and the N Grenadine Is. St Vincent volcanic in origin; highest peak, Soufrière, active volcano 1 234 m/4 048 ft (N), most recent eruption, 1979.

Climate Tropical climate, average annual temperature, 25°C; average annual rainfall 1 500 mm/60 in (coast), 3 800 mm/150 in (interior).

Currency 1 East Caribbean Dollar (EC$) = 100 cents

Economy Based on agriculture; bananas, arrowroot (world's largest producer), coconuts, spices, sugar cane. Food processing, textiles; tourism.

GDP (1989) $146 m, per capita $1 315

History Visited by Columbus in 1498; British control in 1763. Part of West Indies Federation, 1958–62; achieved internal self-govenment in 1969; independence, 1979. British sovereign represented by a Governor-General. A Prime Minister leads a unicameral National Assembly.

Head of State
(British monarch represented by Governor-General)
1989–   David Jack

Head of Government
1984–   James FitzAllen Mitchell

Map >> VENEZUELA

SALVADOR >> EL SALVADOR
SAMOA, AMERICAN >> UNITED STATES OF AMERICA
SAMOA, WESTERN >> WESTERN SAMOA

SAN MARINO

Local name San Marino

Timezone GMT + 1

Area 61 km²/23 sq mi

Population total (1992e) 23 600

Status Republic

Capital San Marino

Language Italian (official)

Ethnic groups Sanmarinesi (San Marino citizens) (87%), Italian (12%)

Religion Roman Catholic (95%)

Physical features Landlocked in C Italy; smallest republic in the world, land boundaries, 34 km/21 mi. Ruggedly mountainous, centred on the limestone ridges of Monte Titano, 793 m/2 602 ft, and the valley of the R Ausa.

Climate Temperate climate, with cool winters, warm summers. Average annual temperatures –6°C (Jan), 26°C (Jul); moderate rainfall; average annual rainfall 880 mm /35 in.

Currency 1 Italian Lira (L, Lit)/1 San Marino Lira = 100 centesimi

Economy Wheat, grapes, cheese, livestock; postage stamps, tourism, textiles, pottery; chemicals, paints, wine.

GDP (1990) $393 m, per capita not available

History Founded by a 4th-c Christian saint as a refuge against religious persecution. Treaty of friendship with the Kingdom of Italy, preserving independence, 1862. In World War 2, followed Italy and declared war on Britain in 1940; declared neutrality shortly before Italian surrender in 1943. Governed by an elected 60-member unicameral Parliament (the Grand and General Council) and an 11-member Congress of State. Parliament elects two of its members every six months to act as Captains-Regent (*Capitani Reggenti*), with the functions of Head of State.

Head of State/Government (Captains-Regent)
Oct 1992–Mar 1993 Romeo Morri/Marino Zanotti
Apr 1993–Sep 1993 Patricia Busignani/Salvatore Tonelli

Map >> ITALY

SÃO TOMÉ AND PRÍNCIPE

Local name São Tomé e Príncipe

Timezone GMT + 1

Area 1001 km²/387 sq mi

Population total (1991e) 124 000

Status Democratic republic

Date of independence 1975

Capital São Tomé

Languages Portuguese (official), with a number of creoles spoken

Ethnic groups Portuguese-African descent, African minority

Religions Roman Catholic (80%), Seventh Day Adventist, and Evangelical Protestant

Physical features Equatorial volcanic islands in the Gulf of Guinea, off the coast of Equatorial Guinea, W Africa; comprise São Tomé, Príncipe, and several smaller islands. São Tomé (area 845 km²/ 326 sq mi), greatest height, 2 024 m/6 640 ft, Pico de São Tomé in central volcanic uplands. Heavily forested.

Climate Tropical climate. Average annual temperature 27°C (coast), 20°C (mountains); rainy season (Oct–May); annual average rainfall 500–1 000 mm/20–40 in.

Currency 1 Dobra (Db) = 100 centimos

Economy Based on agriculture (employs c.70% of population); cocoa, copra, palm kernels, coffee, wine, fishing. Restructured economy since 1985, with greater involvement in commerce, banking, and tourism.

GDP (1989) $46 m, per capita $384

History Visited by the Portuguese, 1469–72. Portuguese colony in 1522. Resistance to Portuguese rule led to riots in 1953, and the formation of an overseas liberation movement based in Gabon. Independence, 1975; sole legal party was the Movement for the Liberation of São Tomé and Príncipe, until new constitution in 1990, approved multi-party democratic system and created a National Assembly. Criticism of economic reforms forced Trovoada to dismiss the government, Apr 1992, and appoint a new Prime Minister.

Head of State
1975–91 Manuel Pinto da Costa
1991–   Miguel Trovoada

Head of Government
1991–2 Daniel Daio
1992–   Norberto José d'Alva Costa Alegre

SAUDI ARABIA

Local name Al-'Arabīyah as-Sa'ūdīyah (Arabic)

Timezone GMT + 3

Area 2 331 000 km²/899 766 sq mi

Population total (1992e) 15 267 000

Status Kingdom

Capital Riyadh (Ar-Riyād)

Language Arabic (official)

Ethnic groups Arab (90%), Afro-Asian (10%)

Religions Muslim (Sunni 85%, Shi'ite 15%), small Christian minority

Physical features Comprises four-fifths of the Arabian peninsula. Red Sea coastal plain bounded E by mountains; highlands in SW contain Jebel Abha, Saudi Arabia's highest peak, 3 133m/10 279 ft; Arabian peninsula slopes gently N and E towards oil-rich Al Hasa plain on the Arabian Gulf; interior comprises two extensive areas of sand desert, the An Nafud (N) and Rub' al-Khali (the Great Sandy Desert) (S); salt flats numerous in E lowlands. Large network of wadis drains NE. 95% of land is arid or semi-arid desert.

Climate Hot, dry climate; average temperatures 21°C (N), 26°C (S), rise to 50°C in the interior; night frosts common in N and highlands. Red Sea coast hot and humid; average annual temperatures 14°C (Jan), 33°C (Jul) in Riyadh; average annual rainfall 100 mm/4 in.

Currency 1 Saudi Arabian Riyal (SAR, SRls) = 100 halalah

Economy Oil discovered in 1930s; now the world's leading oil exporter (reserves account for c.25% of world's known supply). Rapidly-developing construction industry. Large areas opened up for cultivation in 1980s; agriculture; wheat, dates, livestock. Pilgrimage trade.

GDP (1989) $79 bn, per capita $4 800

History Famed as the birthplace of Islam, a centre of pilgrimage to the holy cities of Mecca, Medina, and Jedda.

Modern state founded by Ibn Saud who by 1932 united the four tribal provinces of Hejaz (NW), Asir (SW), Najd (C), and Al Hasa (E); governed as an absolute monarchy based on Islamic law and Arab Bedouin tradition. King (official title: Custodian of the Two Holy Mosques (Mecca and Medina)) is Head of State and Prime Minister, assisted by a Council of Ministers; there is no parliament. Royal decree, 1992, provided for the creation of a 60-member Consultative Council to be appointed every 4 years.

Head of State/Government (Monarch)
Family name: Al-Saud
1982–   Fahd ibn Abdul Aziz

SCOTLAND >> UNITED KINGDOM

SENEGAL

Local name Sénégal (French)

Timezone GMT

Area 196 790 km²/75 729 sq mi

Population total (1991e) 7 952 000

Status Republic

Date of independence 1960

Capital Dakar

Languages French (official), with various ethnic languages spoken

Ethnic groups Wolof (36%), Fulani (13%), Serer (19%), Toucouleur (9%), Diola (9%), Mandingo (9%), European and Lebanese (1%)

Religions Sunni Muslim (91%), Roman Catholic (5%), local beliefs (3%)

Physical features Located in W Africa. Extensive low-lying basin of savannah and semi-desert vegetation to the N; sand dunes along coastline. Dunes and mangrove forests in S, where land rises to around 500 m/1 640 ft. Lowland savannah and semi-desert regions of N drain into R Sénégal, which forms the N and NE boundary with Mauritania and Mali.

Climate Tropical climate; rainy season (Jun–Sep); high humidity levels and high night-time temperatures, especially on the coast. Average temperature, 22–8°C; average annual rainfall 541 mm/21 in at Dakar.

Currency 1 CFA Franc (CFAFr) = 100 centimes

Senegal (continued)

Economy Agriculture (employs c.75% of workforce); groundnuts, cotton, sugar, millet, sorghum, maize, livestock. Minerals, iron ore, gold. Oil, natural gas. Fishing, timber; textiles, chemicals. Shipbuilding and repairing. Tourism.

GDP (1989) $4.7 bn, per capita $615

History Part of the Mali Empire, 14th-15th-c; French established a fort at Saint-Louis in 1658. Incorporated as a territory within French West Africa, 1902. Autonomous state within the French community, 1958; joined with French Sudan as independent Federation of Mali, 1959; withdrew in 1960 to become a separate independent republic. Joined with The Gambia to form the Confederation of Senegambia, 1982-9; Confederation collapsed, 1989, following violent clashes between Senegalese and Mauritanians. Governed by a President (elected for a 5-year term), a Prime Minister, a Cabinet and an 120-member National Assembly.

Head of State
1981– Abdou Diouf

Head of Government
1991– Habib Thiam

SEYCHELLES

Local name Seychelles

Timezone GMT + 4

Area 453 km²/175 sq mi

Population total (1992e) 68 700

Status Republic

Date of independence 1976

Capital Victoria (on Mahé Island)

Languages Creole (official since 1981), French, and English

Ethnic groups Seychellois (Asian, African, and European admixtures), Malagasy (3%), Chinese (2%), English (1%)

Religions Roman Catholic (90%), Anglican (8%), other (2%)

Physical features Island group in SW Indian Ocean, N of Madagascar, comprising 115 islands. Main islands include Mahé (largest), Praslin, and La Digue. Islands fall into two main groups, a compact group of 41 mountainous islands rising steeply from the sea, highest point 906 m/2 972 ft on Mahé; and a group of low-lying coralline islands and atolls to the SW, flat, waterless and mostly uninhabited.

Climate Tropical climate. Average annual temperature 27°C (Jan), 26°C (Jul); wet humid season (Dec–May); average annual rainfall 2375 mm/93.5 in.

Currency 1 Seychelles Rupee (SR) = 100 cents

Economy Agriculture; fruit, vegetables, livestock, cinnamon, copra. Brewing, plastics, steel fabricated goods, fishing; tourism.

GDP (1989) $285 m, per capita $4 170

History Colonized by the French in 1768; captured by Britain, 1794; incorporated as a dependency of Mauritius, 1814; separate Crown Colony, 1903. Independent republic within the Commonwealth, 1976; constitution, 1979, established a one-party state. Governed by a President, elected for a 5-year term, a Council of Ministers, and a unicameral National Assembly. Legislation legalizing the activity of opposition parties adopted, 1991.

Head of State/Government
1977– France-Albert René

SIERRA LEONE

Local name Sierra Leone

Timezone GMT

Area 71 740 km²/27 692 sq mi

Population total (1991e) 4 274 000

Status Republic

Date of independence 1961

Capital Freetown

Languages English (official), with Krio widely spoken

Ethnic groups African origin (99%) (including Mendes, Temnes, Limbas, Korankos, and Lokos)

Religions Local beliefs (70%), Sunni Muslim (25%), Christian (Protestant 6%, Roman Catholic 2%)

Physical features Low narrow coastal plain in W Africa. Rises to an average height of 500 m/1 600 ft in the Loma Mts (E), highest point, Loma Mansa, 1 948 m/6 391 ft; Tingi Mts rise to 1 853 m/6 079 ft (SE). Principal rivers include the Great Scarcies, Rokel, Gbangbaia, Jong, and Sewa.

Climate Equatorial climate; temperatures uniformly high throughout the year. Average annual temperature 27°C. Rainy season (May–Oct). Highest rainfall on coast; average annual rainfall 3 436 mm/135 in at Freetown.

Currency 1 Leone (Le) = 100 cents

Economy Mining (most important sector of the economy); diamonds (represent c.60% of exports); bauxite, gold, titanium, iron ore, and other mineral and metal ores. Subsistence agriculture (employs over 70% of population); rice, coffee, cocoa, citrus fruits. Timber; food processing.

GDP (1989) $1.3 bn, per capita $325

History First visited by Portuguese navigators and British slave traders; land bought from local chiefs by English philanthropists who established settlements for freed slaves, 1780s; British Crown Colony, 1808; hinterland declared a British protectorate, 1896. Independence

☐ international airport

declared within the Commonwealth as a constitutional monarchy in 1961; period of military rule, 1967–8; became a republic, 1971; established as a one-party state in 1978. New constitution, 1991, allowing for multi-party politics, and interim government formed until general elections. Interrupted by military coup in 1992, government overthrown, House of Representatives dissolved, and Supreme Council of State (SCS) and Civilian Council of State Secretaries (Cabinet) established.

Head of State/Government
1985–92   Joseph Saidu Momoh
1992–   Valentine Strasser

SINGAPORE

Local name Singapore

Timezone GMT + 8

Area 618 km²/238 sq mi

Population total (1992e) 2 792 000

Status Republic

Date of independence 1965

Capital Singapore City

Languages English, Malay, Chinese, and Tamil (official)

Ethnic groups Chinese (77%), Malay (15%), Indian (6%)

Religions Chinese population mainly Buddhists, Malay mainly Muslim, also Taoist, Christian, and Hindu minorities

Physical features Located at the S tip of the Malay Peninsula, SE Asia; consists of the island of Singapore and c.50 adjacent islets; linked to Malaysia by a causeway across the Johor Strait. Singapore Island is low-lying, rising to 177 m/581 ft at Bukit Timah. Seletar River drains N–E. Deep-water harbour (SE).

Climate Equatorial climate; high humidity; no clearly defined seasons. Average annual temperature range, 21–34°C; average annual rainfall, 2 438 mm/96 in.

Currency 1 Singapore Dollar/Ringgit (S$) = 100 cents

Economy Major transshipment centre (one of world's largest ports); oil refining; rubber, food processing, chemicals, electronics; ship repair; financial services; fishing.

GDP (1990) $34.6 bn, (1988) per capita $12 700

Human geography

Singapore (continued)

History Originally part of the Sumatran Sri Vijaya kingdom; leased by the British East India Company, on the advice of Sir Stamford Raffles, from the Sultan of Johore, 1819; Singapore, Malacca, and Penang incorporated as the Straits Settlements in 1826; British Crown Colony, 1867. Occupied by the Japanese, 1942–5; self-government, 1959; part of the Federation of Malaya from 1963 until its establishment as an independent state in 1965. A Prime Minister, elected every four years, leads a unicameral Parliament of 81 members, elected for four years.

Head of State
1985–93   Wee Kim Wee
1993–   Ong Teng Cheong

Head of Government
1959–90   Lee Kuan Yew
1990–   Goh Chok Tong

SLOVAK REPUBLIC

Local name Slovenska republiká

Timezone GMT + 1

Area 49 035 km²/18 927 sq mi

Population total (1991) 5 274 335

Status Republic

Date of independence 1993

Capital Bratislava

Languages Slovak (official), with Czech and Hungarian widely spoken

Ethnic groups Slovak (87%), Hungarian (11%), Czech (1%), with German, Polish, and Ukrainian minorities

Religions Roman Catholic (70%), Protestant (6%)

Physical features Dominated by the Carpathian Mountains, consisting of a system of E–W ranges separated by valleys and basins. Ranges include the Low Tatras of the Inner Carpathians, 1 829 m/6 000 ft, and the highest point, Gerlachovsky Peak, 2655 m/8 710 ft in the Tatra Mts (N). Main rivers include the Danube, Vah, Hron. National parks at Pieniny, Low and High Tatra.

Climate Continental climate; warm humid summers, cold dry winters; snow remains on the mountains for 130 days of the year. Average annual temperature –4°C (Jan), 18°C (Jul) in Bratislava; average annual rainfall 500–650 mm/20–30 in.

Currency 1 Slovak Crown = 100 halers

Economy Agricultural region, especially cereals, wine, fruit. Steel production in Košice. Heavy industry suffering since previously dependent on state subsidies.

GDP Not available

History Settled in 5th–6th-c by Slavs; part of Great Moravia in 9th-c; part of Magyar Empire from 10th-c; became part of Kingdom of Hungary, 11th-c. United with Czech lands to form the separate state of Czecho-

☐ international airport

slovakia in 1918. Under German control, 1938–9; Slovakia became a separate republic under German influence, 1939; Czechoslovakia regained its independence, 1945; under Communist rule following 1948 coup. Attempt at liberalization by Dubček terminated by intervention of Warsaw Pact troops in 1968; from 1960s, Slovaks revived efforts to gain recognition for Slovak rights; fall from power of Communist party in 1989. 1992 agreement to divide Czechoslovakia into its constituent republics, led to declaration of independence of Slovak Republic, 1993.

Head of State
1993–   Michal Kovac

Head of Government
1993–   Vladimir Meciar

SLOVENIA

Local name Slovenija

Timezone GMT + 2

Area 20 251 km²/7 817 sq mi

Population total (1991e) 1 974 000

Status Republic

Date of independence 1991

Capital Ljubljana

Languages Slovene, Serbo-Croat

Ethnic group Slovene (90%)

Religions Roman Catholic, Protestant, some Eastern Orthodox

Physical features Mountainous republic between Austria and Croatia. Slovenian Alps (NW) rise to 2 863 m/9 393 ft at Triglav in the Julian Alps (Julijske Alpe). Rivers include Sava, Savinja, and Drava. Chief port, Koper.

Climate Continental climate; more Mediterranean in W. Average annual temperature –1°C (Jan), 19°C (Jul) in Ljubljana; average annual rainfall 1 600 mm/63 in.

Currency (1991) 1 Slovene Tolar = 100 paras

Economy Agriculture; maize, wheat, sugar beet, potatoes, livestock, wine, timber, lignite. Textiles; large iron and steel plants; vehicles. Coal, lead, mercury mining in W.

GDP Not available

History Settled by Slovenes, 6th–8th-c; later controlled by Slavs and Franks; part of the Austro-Hungarian Empire until 1918; people's republic within Yugoslavia, 1946. Declaration of full sovereignty in 1990; declaration of independence from Yugoslavia as the Republic of Slovenia, 1991; opposed by central government, brief period of fighting upon the intervention of the federal army who withdrew in Aug 1991. Tricameral legislature

100km
50mi
□ international airport

replaced by a bicameral National Assembly, consisting of a 90-seat Chamber of Deputies and a 40-member State Council. Chamber of Associated Labour abolished and a new constitution reduced the role of the President in Dec 1991.

Head of State
1991–   Milan Kučan

Head of Government
1991–2   Lojze Peterle
1992–   Janez Drnovšek

SOLOMON ISLANDS

Local name Solomon Islands

Timezone GMT + 11

Land area 27 556 km²/10 637 sq mi

Population total (1992e) 329 000

Status Independent state within the Commonwealth

Date of independence 1978

Capital Honiara

Languages English (official), with pidgin English and c.80 local languages also spoken

Ethnic groups Melanesian (93%), Polynesian (4%), Micronesian (1.5%), European (1%), Chinese (0.5%)

Religions Christian (95%) (Protestant 41%, Anglican 34%, Roman Catholic 19%)

Physical features Archipelago of several hundred islands in the SW Pacific Ocean, stretching c.1 400 km/870 mi, between Papua New Guinea (NW) and Vanuatu

□ international airport
600km
300mi

Solomon Islands (continued)

(SE). Six main islands, Choiseul, Guadalcanal, Malaita, New Georgia, San Cristobal (now Makira), Santa Isabel. Highest point, Mt Makarakomburu, 2 477 m/8 126 ft, on Guadalcanal (largest island). Large islands have forested mountain ranges and coastal belts. Anuta, Fataka, and Tikopia islands are volcanic.

Climate Equatorial climate; high humidity. Average annual temperature 27°C. Maximum rainfall Nov–Apr; average annual rainfall, c.3500 mm/138 in; periodic cyclones.

Currency 1 Solomon Islands Dollar (SI$) = 100 cents

Economy Based on agriculture; forestry, livestock, fisheries, taro, rice, bananas, yams, copra, oil palm, rice. Milling, fish processing; crafts.

GDP (1989) $156 m, per capita $570

History Visited by the Spanish in 1568. S Solomon Is placed under British protection, 1893; outer islands (Santa Cruz group) added to the protectorate, 1899. Scene of fierce fighting in World War 2. Achieved internal self-government in 1976; independence, 1978. British monarch is represented by a Governor-General; Prime Minister leads a unicameral National Parliament of 38 members elected for four years.

Head of State
(British monarch represented by Governor-General)
1988–   Sir George Lepping

Head of Government
1989–93   Solomon Mamaloni
1993–   Frances Billy Hilly

SOMALIA

Local name Somaliya

Timezone GMT + 3

Area 637 357 km²/246 201 sq mi

Population total (1991e) 6 709 000

Status Republic

Date of independence 1960

Capital Mogadishu

Languages Somali, Arabic (official)

Ethnic groups Somali (85%), Bantu (15%), with Arab, European, and Asian minorities

Religions Sunni Muslim (99%), small Christian minority

Physical features Occupies the E Horn of Africa, where dry coastal plain broadens to the S, and rises inland to a plateau c.1000 m/3300 ft. Forested mountains on the Gulf of Aden coast rise to 2 416 m/7 926 ft at Mt Shimbiris. Main rivers, Jubba and Webi Shabeelle.

Climate Predominantly arid; average daily maximum temperatures 28–32°C in Mogadishu. Average annual rainfall 490 mm/19.3 in; heavier rainfall (Apr–Sep) on E coast. Serious, persistent threat of drought.

Currency 1 Somali Shilling (SoSh) = 100 cents

Economy Agriculture (c.50% nomadic people raising cattle, sheep, goats, camels); bananas, sugar, spices, cotton, rice, citrus fruits, tobacco, iron ore; textiles; fishing.

GDP (1989) $1.7 bn, per capita $170

History Settled by Muslims in 7th-c; Italian, French, and British interests after the opening of the Suez Canal, 1869. After World War 2, Somalia formed by the amalgamation of Italian and British protectorates. Independence, 1960; from the 1960s, territorial conflict with Ethiopia over Ogaden which has a large Somali population; military coup, 1969; peace agreement with Ethiopia, 1989. Governed by a President, a Council of Ministers, and a People's Assembly; new constitution

approved, 1990. NE region seceded as Somaliland Republic, 1991; civil war, 1991–2, forced UN troops to intervene to safeguard food supplies for starving population, 1992.

Head of State
1980–91   Mohammed Siad Barre
1991–   Ali Mahdi Muhammed *Interim*

Head of Government
1987–90   Mohammed Ali Samater
1990–1   Mohammed Hawadie Madar
1991–   Umar Arteh Ghalib

SOUTH AFRICA

Local name Suid-Afrika (Afrikaans)

Timezone GMT + 2

Area 1 233 404 km²/476 094 sq mi

Population total (1992e) 32 000 000

Status Republic

Date of independence 1961

Capitals Cape Town (legislative); Pretoria (administrative); Bloemfontein (judicial)

Languages English and Afrikaans (official), many African languages spoken, including Xhosa, Zulu, and Sesotho

Ethnic groups Black African (70%), White (18%), Asian (3%), Coloured (9%)

Religions Christian (most Whites and Coloureds and c.60% Africans), traditional beliefs, Hindu, Muslim, and Judaist minorities

Physical features Occupies the S extremity of the African plateau, comprising the four provinces of Cape, Natal, Orange Free State and Transvaal; also includes six non-independent national states of Gazankulu, Lebowa, QwaQwa, KwaZulu, KaNgwane, and KwaNdebele. Fringed by fold mountains and a lowland coastal margin to the W, E, and S; N interior comprises the Kalahari Basin, scrub grassland, and arid desert; Great Escarpment rises E to 3 482 m/11 424 ft at Thabana-Ntlenyana. Orange R flows W to meet the Atlantic; chief tributaries, Vaal and Caledon rivers.

Climate Subtropical in E; average annual temperature 4°C (Jan), 17°C (Jul) in Cape Town; average annual rainfall 1 008 mm/39.7 in Durban. Dry moistureless climate on W coast. Desert region further N, annual average rainfall less than 30 mm/1.2 in.

Currency 1 Rand (R) = 100 cents

Economy Industrial growth as a result of 19th-c gold (c.50% of export income) and diamond discoveries. Grain, wool, sugar, tobacco, cotton, citrus fruit, dairy products, livestock, fishing. Motor vehicles, machinery, chemicals, fertilizers, textiles, clothes, metal products, electronics, computers, tourism.

GDP (1990) $101 bn, per capita $2 600

History Originally inhabited by Khoisan tribes; Portuguese reached the Cape of Good Hope in late 15th-c; settled by Dutch, 1652; arrival of British, 1795; British annexation of the Cape, 1806; Great Trek by Boers NE across the Orange R to Natal, 1806; first Boer republic founded, 1839; Natal annexed by the British in 1842, but the Boer republics of Transvaal (founded 1852) and Orange Free State (1854) were recognized; South African Wars, 1880–1, 1899–1902; Transvaal, Natal, Orange Free State, and Cape Province joined as the Union of South Africa, a dominion of the British Empire, 1910. Sovereign state within the Commonwealth from 1931–61. Independent republic, 1961; independence granted by South Africa to Transkei (1976), Bophuthatswana (1977), Venda (1979) and Ciskei (1981), not recognized internationally. Politics dominated by treatment of non-White majority following the apartheid (racial segregation) policy after

1948; continuing racial violence and strikes led to a state of emergency in 1986, and several countries imposed economic and cultural sanctions. Progressive dismantling of apartheid system by F W de Klerk from 1990; Black Nationalist leader Nelson Mandela was freed after more than 27 years in prison, and the African National Congress was unbanned, 1990. Readmitted into international sport, USA lifted trade and investment sanctions in 1991; most remaining apartheid legislation abolished, 1991. New constitution, 1993. Governed by a 400-seat National Assembly and a 90-seat Senate. Elections in May 1994 brought victory to the ANC.

Head of State/Government

1989–	Frederick Willem de Klerk
1994–	Nelson Rolihlahla Mandela

South African States

Name	Area		State capital
	km²	sq mi	
Cape Province (Kaapprovinsie)	641 379	247 636	Cape Town
Natal	91 785	36 073	Pietermaritzburg
Orange Free State (Oranje Vrystaat)	127 993	49 418	Bloemfontein
Transvaal	262 499	101 331	Pretoria
Independent Black Homelands			
Bophuthatswana	44 000	17 000	Mmabatho
Ciskei	7 700	3 000	Bisho
Transkei	43 800	16 900	Umtata
Venda	6 500	2 500	Thohoyandou
Non-independent Black Homelands (National States)			
Gazankulu	6 561	2 533	Giyani
KaNgwane	3 823	1 476	Nyamasane
KwaNdebele	2 860	1 100	Siyabuswa
KwaZulu	30 151	11 642	Ulundi
Lebowa	22 503	8 688	Lebowakgom
QwaQwa	502	194	Phuthaditjhaba

Spain

SOUTH GEORGIA >> UNITED KINGDOM

SOUTH KOREA >> KOREA, SOUTH

SOUTH SANDWICH ISLANDS >> UNITED KINGDOM

SPAIN

Local name España (Spanish)

Timezone GMT + 1

Area 504 750 km²/194 833 sq mi

Population total (1991e) 39 384 000

Status Kingdom

Capital Madrid

Languages Spanish (official) with Catalan, Galician, and Basque also spoken in their respective regions

Ethnic groups Spanish (Castilian, Valencian, Andalusian, Asturian) (73%), Catalan (16%), Galician (8%), Basque (2%)

Religions Roman Catholic (99%), other Christian (including Anglican, Baptist, Evangelical, Mormon, Jehovah's Witnesses) and Muslim minorities

Physical features Located in SW Europe, occupying four-fifths of the Iberian peninsula. Includes the Canary Is, Balearic Is, several islands off the coast of N Africa, as well as the Presidios of Ceuta and Melilla in N Morocco. Mostly a furrowed C plateau (the Meseta, average height 700 m/2 300 ft) crossed by mountains; Andalusian or Baetic Mts (SE) rise to 3 478 m/11 411 ft at Mulhacén; Pyrénées (N) rise to 3 404 m/11 168 ft at Pico de Aneto. Rivers run E–W, notably the Tagus, Ebro, Guadiana, Miño, Duero, Guadalquivir, Segura, Júcar.

Climate Continental climate in the Meseta and Ebro Basin, with hot summers, cold winters, low rainfall; highest rainfall in the mountains. S Mediterranean coast has warmest winter temperatures on European mainland. Average annual temperatures 5°C (Jan), 25°C (Jul) in Madrid; average annual rainfall 419 mm/16.5 in.

Currency 1 Peseta (Pta, Pa) = 100 céntimos

Economy Traditional agricultural economy gradually being supplemented by varied industries; textiles, iron, steel, shipbuilding, electrical appliances, cars, wine; forestry; fishing; tourism; zinc and other mineral ores; cereals, olives, almonds, pomegranates. Member of EC, 1986.

GDP (1990) $435 bn, per capita $11 100

History Early inhabitants included Iberians, Celts, Phoenicians, Greeks, and Romans; Muslim domination from the 8th-c. Christian reconquest completed by 1492; a monarchy since the unification of the Kingdoms of Castile, León, Aragón, and Navarre, largely achieved by 1572; 16th-c exploration of the New World, and the growth of the Spanish Empire; period of decline after the Revolt of the Netherlands, 1581, and the defeat of the Spanish Armada in 1588; War of the Spanish Succession, 1701–14; Peninsular War against Napoleon, 1808–14; war with the USA in 1898 led to the loss of Cuba, Puerto Rico, and remaining Pacific possessions. Dictatorship under Primo de Rivera (1923–30), followed by exile of the King and establishment of the Second Republic in 1931;

major international airport

1 PRINCIPADO DE ASTURIAS 4 COMUNIDAD FORAL DE NAVARRA
2 CANTABRIA 5 LA RIOJA
3 PAÍS VASCO 6 COMUNIDAD DE MADRID

military revolt headed by Franco in 1936 led to civil war and a Fascist dictatorship. Prince Juan Carlos of Bourbon nominated to succeed Franco in 1969; acceded, 1975. Under 1978 constitution, the Kingdom of Spain is a constitutional monarchy; Monarch appoints the Prime Minister. Governed by a bicameral Parliament (Cortes Generales) comprising a Congress of Deputies and a Senate. There has been a move towards local government autonomy with the creation of 17 self-governing regions.

Head of State (Monarch)
1975–   Juan Carlos I

Head of Government
1982–   Felipe González Márquez

Balearic islands

Local name Islas Baleares

Area 5014 km²/1935 sq mi

Population total (1991) 702 770

Status Province of Spain

Capital Palma de Mallorca

Physical features Archipelago of five major islands and 11 islets in the Mediterranean, near the E coast of Spain. E group of islands consists of Mallorca (Majorca), Menorca, Cabrera; Ibiza and Formentera (W group). Popular tourist resorts.

Climate Continental; average annual temperatures 11°C (Jan), 25°C (Jul); average annual rainfall 347 mm/14 in.

Currency 1 Peseta (Pta, Pa) = 100 céntimos

Economy Tourism; fruit, wine, grain, cattle, fishing, textiles, chemicals, cork, timber.

Canary islands

Local name Islas Canarias

Area 7273 km²/2807 sq mi

Population total (1991) 456 474

Status Forms two provinces of Spain

Chief town Las Palmas

Physical features Island archipelago, located in the Atlantic, 100 km/60 mi off the NW coast of Africa. Includes the islands of Tenerife, La Palma, Gomera, Hierro, Grand Canary (Gran Canaria), Fuerteventura, Lanzarote, and several uninhabited islands. Major ports, Las Palmas, Santa Cruz. Volcanic and mountainous, the Pico de Teide rises to 3718 m/12198 ft on Tenerife. Tourist resorts on main islands.

Climate Continental; average annual temperature 18°C (Jan), 24°C (Jul); average annual rainfall 196 mm/8 in.

Currency 1 Peseta (Pta, Pa) = 100 céntimos

Economy Tourism; agriculture, fishing, canning, textiles, leatherwork, footwear, cork, timber, chemical and metal products.

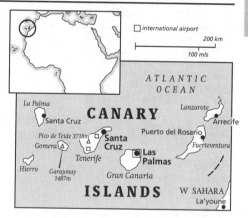

SRI LANKA

Local name Sri Lanka

Timezone GMT + 5.5

Area 65610 km²/25325 sq mi

Population total (1992e) 17464000

Status Republic

Date of independence 1972

Capital Sri-Jayawardenapura (since 1983); (former capital, Colombo)

Languages Sinhala, Tamil (official), English also spoken

Ethnic groups Sinhalese (74%), Tamil (18%), Muslim (7%), Burgher, Malay, and Veddha (1%)

Religions Buddhist (69%), Hindu (15%), Christian (8%), Muslim (8%)

Sri Lanka (continued)

Physical features Island state in the Indian Ocean; separated from the Indian sub-continent by the Palk Strait, linked by a series of coral islands known as Adam's Bridge. Low-lying areas in N and S, surrounding SC uplands. Highest peak, Pidurutalagala, 2524 m/8281 ft. Coastal plain fringed by sandy beaches and lagoons. C.50% of land is tropical monsoon forest or open woodland.

Climate Equatorial, tropical climate; modified temperatures in interior according to altitude. Average annual temperature 27°C in Sri-Jayawardenapura; average annual rainfall 2527 mm/99.5 in; greatest rainfall on SW coast and in the mountains. Monsoon season (Dec–Feb) in NE, dry, semi-arid for rest of year.

Currency 1 Sri Lanka Rupee (SLR, SLRs) = 100 cents

Economy Agriculture (employs 51% of labour force); rice, rubber, tea, coconuts, spices, sugar cane; timber, fishing. Graphite, coal, precious and semi-precious stones. Electricity produced largely by water power. Textiles, chemicals, paper.

GDP (1990) $6.6 bn, per capita $380

History Visited by the Portuguese in 1505; taken by the Dutch, 1658; British occupation in 1796; British colony, 1802; Tamil labourers brought in from S India during colonial rule, to work on coffee and tea plantations. Dominion status, 1948; changed former name of Ceylon and became the independent republic of Sri Lanka in 1972. Governed by a President and a National State Assembly. Acute political tension exists between the Buddhist Sinhalese majority and the Hindu Tamil minority, who wish to establish an independent state in the N and E. Considerable increase in racial violence in the area during the 1980s; state of emergency declared, 1983.

Head of State	
1989–93	Ranasinghe Premadasa
1993–	Dingiri Banda Wijedunga

Head of Government	
1989–93	Dingiri Banda Wijedunga
1993–	Ranil Wickremasinghe

SUDAN, THE

Local name As-Sūdān (Arabic)

Timezone GMT + 2

Area 2 505 870 km²/967 243 sq mi

Population total (1992e) 29 900 000

Status Republic

Date of independence 1956

Capital Khartoum

Languages Arabic (official), local languages, including Darfurian, Nilotic, and Nilo-Hamitic, are also spoken

Ethnic groups Black (52%), Arab (39%), Beja (6%)

Religions Muslim (Sunni 70%), traditional animist beliefs (20%), Christian (5%)

Physical features Largest country on the African continent, astride the middle reaches of the R Nile. E edge formed by Nubian Highlands and an escarpment rising c.2 000 m/6 500 ft on the Red Sea. Imatong Mts (S) rise to 3 187 m/10 456 ft at Kinyeti, highest point in Sudan.

Human geography

Darfur Massif in the W. White Nile flows N to meet the Blue Nile at Khartoum.

Climate Tropical, continental; desert conditions in NW, with temperatures rarely falling below 24°C; hottest months (Jul–Aug); sandstorms common. Average annual temperature 23°C (Jan), 32°C (Jul) in Khartoum; average annual rainfall 157 mm/6.2 in.

Currency 1 Sudanese pound (LSd, £S) = 100 piastres

Economy Dominated by agriculture (employs c.75% of population). Commercial farming (N) and livestock farming (S). Large-scale irrigation schemes, fed by dams. Major famines, especially 1984–5, 1990–1. Gum arabic (80% of world supply). Reserves of copper, lead, iron ore, chromite, manganese, gold. Development hindered by poor transport system.

GDP (1990) $8.5 bn, per capita $330

History Christianized in 6th-c; Muslim conversion from 13th-c; Egyptian control of N Sudan, early 19th-c; Mahdi unified W and C tribes in a revolution, 1881; fall of
Khartoum, 1885; combined British-Egyptian offensive, 1898, leading to a jointly administered condominium. Independence in 1956. Period of military rule following coup in 1985. Drought and N–S rivalry have contributed to years of instability and several coups. A transitional constitution of 1987 provided for a President, a Prime Minister, a Council of Ministers, and a Legislative Assembly. Military coup, 1989, suspended constitution and dissolved National Assembly which was replaced by a Revolutionary Command Council. Continuing civil war between N and S, 1990; peace talks began, April 1993, and unilateral ceasefire was agreed.

Head of State/Government
1989–   Omar Hassan Ahmad al-Bashir

SURINAME

Local name Suriname

Timezone GMT – 3.5

Area 163 265 km²/63 020 sq mi

Population total (1992e) 410 000

Status Republic

Date of independence 1975

Capital Paramaribo

Languages Dutch (official), Hindu and Javanese (native languages), Sranan Tongo, Chinese and Spanish also spoken

Ethnic groups Hindustani (East Indian) (37%), Creole (31%), Javanese (15%), Amerindian (3%), Chinese (2%), European (1%)

Religions Hindu (27%), Protestant (25%), Roman Catholic (23%), Muslim (20%), indigenous beliefs (5%)

Physical features Located in NE South America. N natural regions, range from coastal lowland through savannah to mountainous upland; coastal strip covered by swamp; highland interior (S) overgrown with dense tropical forest. Highest point, Juliana Top, 1 230 m/4 035 ft, in SC. Seven major rivers including Marowijne (E), Corantijn (W), Suriname.

Climate Equatorial tropical, uniformly hot and humid; two rainy seasons (May–Jul, Nov–Jan). Average annual temperatures 22–33°C in Paramaribo. Average monthly rainfall 310 mm/12.2 in (N), 67 mm/2.6 in (S).

Currency 1 Suriname Guilder/Florin (SGld, F) = 100 cents

Economy Based on agriculture and mining, but hindered by lack of foreign exchange. Bauxite mining (provides c.80% of export income). Sugar cane, rice, citrus fruits, coffee, bananas, oil palms, cacao, fishing. Vast timber resources.

GDP (1989) $1.3 bn, per capita $3 400

History Sighted by Columbus in 1498. First settled by the British, 1651; taken by the states of Zeeland, 1667; captured by the British, 1799; restored to the Netherlands, 1818 and remained part of Netherland West Indies

as Dutch Guiana. Independence as the Republic of Suriname, 1975; emigration of c.40% of population to the Netherlands, following independence. Military coup, 1980; ban on political activities lifted in 1985. 1987 constitution provides for a National Assembly, and a President elected by the Assembly.

Head of State (President)
1990–1   Johan Kraag
1991–   Runaldo Venetiaan

Head of Government (Vice-President)
1988–90   Henck Arron
1990–1   Jules Wijdenbosch
1991–   Jules Adjodhia

SWAZILAND

Local name Swaziland

Timezone GMT + 2

Area 17 363 km²/6 702 sq mi

Population total (1991e) 859 000

Status Kingdom

Date of independence 1968

Capital Mbabane

Languages English and Siswati (official)

Ethnic groups African (97%), European (3%)

Religions Christian (Roman Catholic, Anglican, Methodist, and Evangelical Lutheran) (57%), traditional animist beliefs (40%)

Physical features Landlocked, in SE Africa. Divided into four topographical regions, mountainous Highveld (W), highest point Emblembe, 1 862 m/6 109 ft; heavily populated Middleveld (C), descending to 600–700 m/2 000–2 300 ft; rolling, bush-covered Lowveld (E), irrigated by river systems. Lubombo escarpment, covering 90% of the territory. Main rivers, Komati, Usutu, Mbuluzi, flow W–E.

Climate Temperate; tropical in W, with relatively little rain, 500–890 mm/20–35 in; susceptible to drought; subtropical and drier in C. Average annual temperature 15°C (Jul), 22°C (Jan) in Mbabane; average annual rainfall 1 402 mm/55 in; rainy season (Nov–Mar).

Currency 1 Lilangeni (plural Emalangeni) (Li, E) = 100 cents

Economy Agriculture (employs 70% of population); maize, groundnuts, beans, sorghum, cotton, tobacco, pineapples, citrus. Sugar refining, several hydroelectric schemes; asbestos, iron ore, coal, textiles, cement, paper, chemicals.

GNP (1990) $563 m, (1989) per capita $900

History Arrival of Swazi in the area, early 19th-c; boundaries with the Transvaal decided, and indepen-

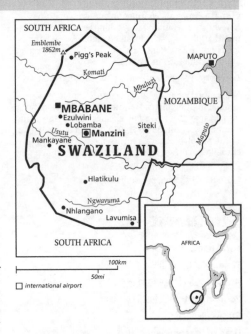

dence guaranteed in 1881; British agreed to Transvaal administration in 1894; British High Commission territory, 1903. Independence as a constitutional monarchy within the Commonwealth in 1968. All political parties are banned under 1978 constitution. Governed by a bicameral Parliament consisting of a National Assembly and a Senate. The King has considerable executive power, appoints a Cabinet and Prime Minister.

Head of State (Monarch)
1986– Mswati III

Head of Government
1989–93 Obed Dlamini *Acting*
1993– Jameson Mbilini Dlamini

SWEDEN

Local name Sverige (Swedish)

Timezone GMT + 1

Area 411 479 km²/158 830 sq mi

Population total (1991) 8 644 119

Status Kingdom

Capital Stockholm

Languages Swedish (official), Finnish and Lapp in N

Ethnic groups Swedish (91%), Finns, with Polish, Turkish, W German, Chilean, Iranian, and other minorities

Religions Lutheran Protestant (93%), Roman Catholic (2%), Scandinavian Jewish minorities

Physical features Occupies the E side of the Scandinavian peninsula. 15% of country lies N of the Arctic

Circle. Large amount of inland water (9%); chief lakes being Vänern, Vättern, and Mälaren. Many coastal islands, notably Gotland and Öland. C.57% forested. Kjölen Mts (W) form much of the boundary with Norway; highest peak, Kebnekaise, 2 111 m/6 926 ft. Several rivers flow SE towards the Gulf of Bothnia.

Climate Continental, with cold winters and mild summers; rainfall lowest in NE; winters warmer in SW. Enclosed parts of Baltic Sea often freeze in winter and can remain frozen for up to 6 months. Continuous daylight in N during Arctic summer produces mean temperatures of –10°C (Jan), 15°C (Jul).

Currency 1 Swedish Krona (Skr) = 100 øre

Economy Gradual shift in the economy from the traditional emphasis on raw materials (timber and iron ore) to advanced technology; transportation equipment, electronics, electrical equipment, chemicals, engineering, steelmaking, non-ferrous metals. Hydroelectricity provides 70% of power. Wheat, barley, oats, sugar beet, cattle, fishing. Tourism.

GDP (1990) $137 bn, per capita $16 200

History Formed from the union of the kingdoms of the Goths and Svears in 7th-c; Danes continued to rule in the extreme S (Skåne) until 1658; united with Denmark and Norway under Danish leadership, 1389; union ended in 1527, following revolt led by Gustavus Vasa; Sweden acquired Norway from Denmark, 1814; union with Norway dissolved, 1905; a neutral country since 1814. Social Democratic Party controlled government, 1932–76 and returned to power, 1982. Applied for European Community membership, 1990. A representative and parliamentary democracy, with a Monarch as Head of State. Governed by a Prime Minister and a unicameral Parliament (*Riksdag*) elected every three years.

Head of State (Monarch)
1973– Carl XVI Gustaf

Head of Government
1986–91 Ingvar Carlsson
1991– Carl Bildt

SWITZERLAND

Local names Schweiz (German), La Suisse (French), Svizzera (Italian)

Timezone GMT + 1

Area 41 228 km²/15 914 sq mi

Population total (1991e) 6 783 000

Status Confederation

Date of independence 1291

Capital Bern (Berne)

Languages German, French, Italian, Romansch (official), Spanish and Turkish also spoken

Ethnic groups (of Swiss nationals) German (74%), French (20%), Italian (4%), Romansch (1%)

Religions Christian (Roman Catholic 49%, Protestant 48%), Jewish minority

Physical features Landlocked, with Alps running roughly E–W in the S. Highest peak, Dufourspitze, 4 634 m/15 203 ft; Pre-Alps (NW) average 2 000 m/6 500 ft; sparsely-forested Jura Mts run SW–NW; mean altitude of C plateau, 580 m/1 900 ft, fringed with great lakes. Chief

rivers, Rhine, Rhône, Inn, and tributaries of the Po. C.3 000 sq km/1 160 sq mi of glaciers, notably the Aletsch.

Climate Temperate climate, subject to Atlantic, Mediterranean and E and C European influences; warm summers, with considerable rainfall; perennial snow cover above 3 00m/9 842 ft. Average annual temperature 0°C (Jan), 19°C (Jul) in Bern; average annual rainfall 986 mm/39 in. The Föhn (warm wind) noticeable late winter and spring in the Alps.

Currency 1 Swiss Franc (SFr, SwF) = 100 centimes

Economy Increased specialization and development in high-technology products; machinery, precision instruments, watches, drugs, chemicals, textiles. A major financial centre; headquarters of many international organizations. All-year tourist area. Dairy farming, wheat, potatoes, sugar beet, grapes, apples.

GDP (1990) $126 bn, per capita $18 700

History Part of the Holy Roman Empire in 10th-c; Swiss Confederation created, 1291; expanded during 14th-c; centre of the Reformation, 16th-c; Swiss independence and neutrality recognized under the Treaty of Westphalia, 1648. Conquered by Napoleon, who instituted the

Switzerland (continued)

Helvetian Republic in 1798; organized as a confederation of cantons in 1815; federal constitution, 1848; Red Cross founded in 1863. Neutral in both World Wars; helped form European Free Trade Association in 1960; Jura became 23rd canton of Switzerland, 1979. Bicameral Federal Association comprising of a Council of States (*Ständerat*) and a National Council (*Nationalrat*). President elected yearly by Federal Council.

Head of State/Government
1990   Arnold Koller
1991   Flavio Cotti
1992   Réné Felber
1993   Adolf Ogi
1994   Otto Stich

SYRIA

Local name As-Sūrīyah (Arabic)

Timezone GMT + 2

Area 185 180 km²/71 479 sq mi

Population total (1992e) 12 958 000

Status Republic

Date of independence 1946

Capital Damascus

Languages Arabic (official), Kurdish, Armenian, Aramaic, and Circassian also spoken

Ethnic groups Arab (90%), Kurd, Armenian, Turkish, Circassian, and Assyrian

Religions Muslim (Sunni Muslim 74%, Alawite, Druse, and other sects 16%), Christian (10%)

Physical features Narrow Mediterranean coastal plain; Jabal al Nusayriyah mountain range rises to c.1 500 m/5 000 ft; steep drop (E) to Orontes R valley; Anti-Lebanon range (SW) rises to 2 814 m/9 232 ft at Mt Hermon; open steppe and desert to the E.

Climate Coastal Mediterranean, hot, dry summers, mild, wet winters. Desert or semi-desert climate in 60% of country; annual rainfall below 200 mm/8 in. Khamsin wind causes temperatures to rise to 43–9°C; average annual temperatures 7°C (Jan), 27°C (Jul) in Damascus.

Currency 1 Syrian pound (LS, Syr £)= 100 piastres

Economy Oil (most important source of export revenue since 1974). Euphrates dam project (begun 1978) presently supplies 97% of domestic electricity. Intended to increase arable land by 6 400 km²/2 500 sq mi. Food processing; textiles; tobacco; cement.

Golan Heights and West Bank occupied by Israel since 1967

GDP (1990) $20 bn, per capita $1 600

History Part of Phoenician Empire; Islam introduced in 7th-c; conquered by Turks, 11th-c; part of Ottoman Empire in 1517. Brief period of independence in 1920, then made a French mandate; independence in 1946. Merged with Egypt and Yemen to form United Arab Republic, 1958; re-established itself as independent state under present name in 1961. Golan Heights region seized by Israel, 1967; after outbreak of civil war in Lebanon (1975),

Syrian troops sent to restore order, have remained as part of the Arab peace-keeping force. From mid-1970s have been increasingly involved in Lebanon; breaking of diplomatic relations with Great Britain in 1986. Condemned Iraqi invasion of Kuwait and sent allied forces troops in Gulf War in 1990, restoring relations. Accepted US proposals for terms of an Arab–Israeli peace conference, 1991.

Head of State
1971–   Hafez al-Assad

Head of Government
1987–   Mahmoud Zuabi

TAIWAN

Local name T'aiwan

Timezone GMT + 8

Area 36 000 km²/13 896 sq mi

Population total (1992e) 20 727 000

Status Republic

Date of independence 1949

Capital Taipei

Languages Mandarin Chinese (official), various dialects including Taiwanese and Hakka also spoken

Ethnic groups Han Chinese (98%), small (Polynesian) aboriginal minority

Religions Taoist, Buddhist, Christian (Protestant and Roman Catholic)

Physical features Consists of Taiwan I and several smaller islands c.130 km/80 mi off the SE coast of mainland China. Mountain range runs N–S, covering two-thirds of the island; highest peak, Yu Shan 3 997 m/13 113 ft. Low-lying land mainly in the W. Crossed by the Tropic of Cancer.

Climate Tropical monsoon-type climate; hot, humid summers, mild, short winters. Wet season (May–Sep); typhoons common (Jul–Sep). Average daily temperature 12–19°C (Jan), 24–33°C (Jul) in Taipei; average annual rainfall 2 500 mm/98 in.

Currency 1 New Taiwan Dollar (NT$) = 100 cents

Economy Progressed from agriculture to industry since 1950s. High technology, textiles, electronics, plastics, petrochemicals, machinery. Natural gas, limestone, marble, asbestos. Sugar, bananas, pineapples, citrus fruits, vegetables, tea, fish.

GNP (1990) $150.2 bn, per capita $7 380

History Taiwan (Formosa) visited by the Portuguese in 1590. Conquered by Manchus, 17th-c; ceded to Japan following Sino-Japanese War in 1895. Returned to China, 1945. Nationalist government moved to Taiwan by Jiang Jieshi (Chang Kai-shek); government still maintains claim to legal jurisdiction over mainland China and continues to designate itself as the Republic of China. Pro-

tected by US naval forces during Korean War, 1950–3; signed mutual defence pact with USA, 1954–79. End of state of civil war with People's Republic of China declared by President Lee Teng-hui in 1991. Governed by a President, who appoints a premier; elections held for a reformed National Assembly in 1991. Plans for a new 161-member Parliament (Yuan) and a 52-member Control Yuan before end of 1993.

Head of State (President)
1987–   Lee Jeng-hui

Head of Government (Premier)
1989–90   Lee Huan
1990–3   Hau Pei-tsun
1993–   Lien Chan

TAJIKISTAN (TADZHIKISTAN)

Local name Tojikiston

Timezone GMT + 5

Area 143 100 km²/55 200 sq mi

Population total (1992e) 4 969 000

Status Republic

Date of independence 1991

Capital Dushanbe

Languages Tajik (official), Russian

Ethnic groups Tajik (59%), Uzbek (23%), Russian (13%)

Religion Sunni Muslim

Physical features Republic in SE Middle Asia. Tien Shan, Gissar-Alai, and Pamir ranges cover over 90% of the area; highest peaks, Communism Peak, 7 495 m/ 24 590 ft, and Lenin Peak, 7 134 m/23 405 ft, located in N part of Pamirs. R Pyandzh flows E–W along the S border till it is joined by R Valksh to form R Amu Darya. Lakes include L Kara-Kul (largest) and L Sarez.

Climate Continental. Subtropical valley areas, hot, dry summers; annual mean temperature –0.9°C (Jan), 27°C (Jul); average annual rainfall 150–250 mm/6–10 in. In highlands, average mean temperature –3°C (Jan); average annual rainfall 60–80 mm/2–3 in.

Currency Rouble (R)

Economy Oil, natural gas, coal, lead, zinc, machinery, metalworking, chemicals, food processing; cotton, wheat, maize, vegetables, fruit; hot mineral springs and health resorts.

GDP Not available

History Conquered by Persia, and Alexander the Great; invaded by Arabs in 8th-c; Turkish invasion, 10th-c. Until mid 18th-c, part of the emirate of Bukhara, which in effect became a protectorate of Russia, 1868. Following the Russian Revolution (1917), became part of Turkestan Soviet Socialist Autonomous Republic in 1918; scene of

the Basmachi revolt, 1922–3; Tajik Autonomous Soviet Socialist Republic created as part of the Uzbek SSR, 1924; became a Soviet Socialist Republic in 1929. Declaration of independence from the Soviet Union, 1991; joined new Commonwealth of Independent States (CIS), 1991. Republican Communist Party remained in power until civil war began in Dushanbe, 1992.

Head of State

1991–2	Rakhman Nabiyev
1992	Akbarsho Iskandrov *Chair of the Supreme Soviet*
1992–	Imomali Rakhmanov *Acting*

Head of Government

1991–3	Abdumalik Abdullojanov *Acting*
1993–	Abduljalil Samadov *Acting*

TANZANIA

Local name Tanzania

Timezone GMT + 3

Area 945 087 km²/364 900 sq mi

Population total (1991e) 26 869 000

Status Republic

Date of independence 1961

Capital Dodoma

Languages Swahili and English (official), various tribal languages

Ethnic groups Bantu (99%) (including Nyamwezi and Sukuma 21%, Swahili 9%, Hehet and Bena 6%, Makonde 6%, Haya 6%), Arab, Asian, and European minorities

Religions Mainland: Christian (34%), Muslim (33%), traditional animist beliefs (33%); Zanzibar: Muslim (96%), Hindu (4%)

Physical features Largest E African country, just S of the Equator; includes the islands of Zanzibar, Pemba, and Mafia. Coast fringed by long sandy beaches protected by coral reefs; rises towards a C plateau, average elevation 1 000 m/3 300 ft. Rift Valley branches round L Victoria (N), several high volcanic peaks, notably Mt Kilimanjaro, 5 895 m/ 19 340 ft. Extensive Serengeti Plain to the NW. Other main lakes, L Tanganyika and L Rukwa.

Climate Tropical. Hot, humid climate on coast and off-shore islands; average temperatures 27°C (Jan), 23°C (Jul); average annual rainfall 1 000 mm/40 in. Hot and dry on C plateau, average annual rainfall 250 mm/10 in; semi-temperate conditions above 1 500 mm/5 000 ft.

Currency 1 Tanzanian Shilling (TSh) = 100 cents

Economy Agriculture; rice, sorghum, coffee, sugar, cloves (most of world's market), coconuts, tobacco, cotton. Reserves of iron, coal, tin, gypsum, salt, phosphate, gold, diamonds, oil. Tourism.

GDP (1989) $5.9 bn, per capita $240

History Swahili culture developed, 10th–15th-c. Zanzibar became the capital of the Omani empire in 1840s; became a British protectorate, 1890; German East Africa established in 1891. British mandate to administer Tanganyika in 1919. First E African country to gain independence and become a member of the Commonwealth, 1961; republic, 1962; Zanzibar given independence as a constitutional monarchy with Sultan as Head of State; Sultan overthrown, 1964, and Act of Union between Zanzibar and Tanganyika led to the United Republic of Tanzania; a one-party state following 1965 constitution. Legislation was passed allowing for opposition parties in 1991, following a unanimous vote for a multi-party system. Governed by a President, a Cabinet, and a National Assembly.

Head of State
1985–   Ndugu Ali Hassan Mwinyi

Head of Government
1985–90   Joseph S Warioba
1990–   John Malecela

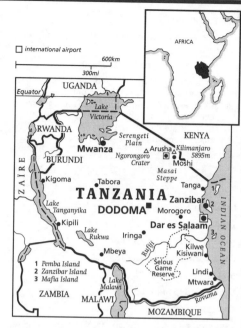

THAILAND

Local name Muang Thai

Timezone GMT + 7

Area 513 115 km²/198 062 sq mi

Population total (1992e) 56 800 000

Status Kingdom

Capital Bangkok (Krung Thep)

Languages Thai (official), Malay and English also spoken

Ethnic groups Thai (75%), Chinese (14%), Khmer and Mon minorities

Religions Theravada Buddhist (95%), Muslim, Hindu, Sikh and Christian (4%)

Physical features Agricultural region dominated by the floodplain of the Chao Phraya R. NE plateau rises above 300 m/1 000 ft and covers a third of the country. Mountainous N region rising to 2 595 m/8 514 ft at Doi Inthanon. Narrow, low-lying S region separates the Andaman Sea from the Gulf of Thailand. Covered in tropical rainforest, except sparsely vegetated Khorat plateau (NE).

Climate Equatorial climate in the S; tropical monsoon climate in the N and C; high temperatures and humidity; wet season (Jun–Oct). Average annual temperature 26°C (Jan), 28°C (Jul) in Bangkok; average annual rainfall 1 400 mm/55 in.

Currency 1 Baht (B) = 100 satang

Economy Agriculture; rice, maize, bananas, pineapple, sugar cane, rubber, teak; textiles, electronics, cement, chemicals, food processing, tourism. Tin (world's third largest supplier), tungsten (world's second

Human geography

Thailand (continued)

largest supplier), manganese, antimony, lead, zinc, copper, natural gas.

GNP (1989) $64.4 bn, per capita $1170

History Evidence of Bronze Age communities, 4000 BC. Thai nation founded, 13th-c. Only country in S and SE Asia to have escaped colonization by a European power; occupied by the Japanese in World War 2. 'Revolution' brought end to absolute monarchial rule, 1932; followed by periods of military rule interspersed with brief periods of democratic government. 1991 constitution

(with amendments) provides for a National Legislative Assembly comprising a House of Representatives, an appointed Senate, and a cabinet headed by a Prime Minister; King is Head of State.

Head of State (Monarch)
1946–   Bhumibol Adulyadej (Rama IX)

Head of Government
1991–2   Anand Panyarachun *Military Junta*
1992   Suchinda Kraprayoon
1992–   Chuan Leekpai

TOGO

Local name République Togolaise (French)

Timezone GMT

Area 56790 km²/21941 sq mi

Population total (1991e) 3810000

Status Republic

Date of independence 1960

Capital Lomé

Languages French (official), local languages (Ewe, mostly in S, 47%), Hamitic people in N, mostly Voltaic speaking)

Ethnic groups Ewe (35%), Kabyè (22%), Mina (6%), with c.34 other ethnic groups, European and Syrian-Lebanese minorities

Religions Traditional animist beliefs (50%), Christian (35%), Muslim (10%)

Physical features Located in W Africa. Land rises from the lagoon coast of the Gulf of Guinea, past low-lying plains to the Atakora Mts running NE–SW in the N. Highest peak, Pic Baumann, 986 m/3 235 ft; flat plains in NW. Main rivers, Oti, Mono.

Climate Tropical, high temperatures and humidity; wet seasons (Mar–Jul, Oct–Nov); single rainy season in N (Jul–Sep). Average annual temperature 27°C (Jan), 24°C (Jul) in Lomé; average annual rainfall 875 mm/34 in. Dry Saharan Harmattan blows from NE (Oct–Apr).

Currency 1 CFA Franc (CFAFr) = 100 centimes.

Economy Largely agricultural economy; coffee, cocoa, cotton, cassava, maize, rice, timber. Phosphates, bauxite, limestone, iron ore, marble. Cement, steel, oil refining, food processing, crafts, textiles, beverages.

GDP (1989) $1.3 bn, per capita $390

History Formerly part of the Kingdom of Togoland; German protectorate, 1884–1914; mandate of the League of Nations in 1922, divided between France (French Togo) and Britain (part of British Gold Coast). Trusteeships of the United Nations, 1946; French Togo became an autonomous republic within the French Union in 1956; British Togoland voted to join the Gold Coast (Ghana) in

1957; independence, 1960. Military coups in 1963, 1967; return to civilian rule in 1980. Riots in protest at slow rate of reform, 1991; at the National Conference in Aug 1991, President Eyadema was stripped of all powers, National Assembly was dissolved, and a transitional legislature, the High Council of the Republic, was established in its place. Political situation remains unstable.

Head of State
1967–91   Gnassingbé Eyadéma

Head of Government
1991–   Joseph Kokou Koffigoh *Interim*

TOKELAU >> NEW ZEALAND

TONGA

Local name Tonga

Timezone GMT + 13

Area 646 km²/249 sq mi

Population total (1992e) 102900

Status Independent kingdom within the Commonwealth

Date of independence 1970

Capital Nuku'alofa

Languages Tongan and English (official)

Ethnic groups Tongan (98%), other Polynesian, European minorities

Religions Christian (Free Wesleyan Methodists 47%, Roman Catholic 14%, Mormon 9%, Anglican minorities)

Physical features Island group in the SW Pacific Ocean, 2250 km/1400 mi NE of New Zealand. Consists of 169 islands, 36 inhabited, divided into three main groups, Ha'apai, Tongatapu, and Vava'u. Tongatapu, largest island, inhabited by two-thirds of the population. W islands mainly volcanic, some still active. Highest point, extinct volcano of Kao, 1014 m/3327 ft.

Climate Semi-tropical. Average annual temperature 26°C (Jan), 21°C (Jul) in Nuku'alofa; average annual rainfall 1750 mm/69 in. Occasional hurricanes in summer months.

Currency 1 Pa'anga/Tongan Dollar (T$) = 100 seniti

Economy Largely based on agriculture; copra, coconuts, bananas, watermelons, yams, taro, cassava, groundnuts, rice, maize, tobacco, sugar cane. Tourism and cottage handicrafts are small, but growing, industries.

GDP (1989) $89 m, per capita $910

History Early settlers were Polynesians. Visited by Dutch in early 17th-c; visited by the British explorer, James Cook in 1773; Methodist missionaries converted most of population to Christianity during early 19th-c; Chief Taufa'ahau united the islands and declared himself the first Monarch of Tonga in 1845; became a British protectorate, 1900, under its own monarchy. Independence, 1970. Governed by a Sovereign, a Privy Council, and a unicameral Legislative Assembly of Cabinet members, nobles, and elected people's representatives.

Head of State (Monarch)
1965–   Taufa'ahau Tupou IV

Head of Government (Prime Minister)
1970–91   Fatafehi Tu'ipelehake
1991–   Baron Vaea

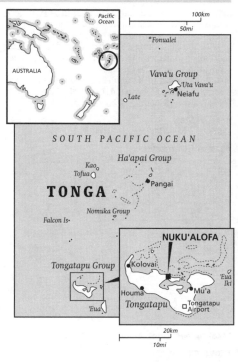

TRINIDAD AND TOBAGO

Local name Trinidad and Tobago

Timezone GMT – 4

Area 5128 km²/1979 sq mi

Population total (1992e) 1300000

Status Independent republic within the Commonwealth

Date of independence 1962

Capital Port of Spain

Languages English (official), Hindi, French, Spanish

Ethnic groups African (43%), East Indian (40%), mixed (14%), Chinese (1%)

Religions Christian (Roman Catholic 34%, Protestant 29%), Hindu (25%), Muslim (6%)

Physical features Southernmost islands of the Lesser Antilles, SE Caribbean. Trinidad, area 4828 km²/1864 sq mi, traversed by three mountain ranges (N, C and S), rising to 940 m/3084 ft at El Cerro del Aripo. Drained by Caroni, Ortoire and Oropuche rivers. Tobago, area 300 km²/116 sq mi, Main Ridge extends along most of island, rising to 576 m/1890 ft.

Climate Tropical, hot and humid. Average annual temperature 29°C; dry season (Jan–May); wet season (Jun–Dec); average annual rainfall 1270 mm/50 in (SW Trinidad), 2540 mm/100 in (Tobago mountains).

Currency 1 Trinidad and Tobago Dollar (TT$) = 100 cents

Economy Oil and gas (main industries). Industrial complex, W coast of Trinidad; cement, oil refining, petrochemicals; cocoa, coffee, fruit; tourism.

Trinidad and Tobago (continued)

GDP (1989) $4 bn, per capita $3 363

History Trinidad visited by Columbus in 1498; settled by Spain in 16th-c, and acquired by Britain in 1797. Tobago captured by French, 1781 and acquired by Britain in 1802; Tobago became a British colony, 1814. Trinidad and Tobago united as British Crown Colony, 1899. Independent member of the Commonwealth, 1962; republic in 1976. Governed by a President and bicameral Parliament, comprising a Senate and House of Representatives. There is also a 15-member Tobago House of Assembly.

Head of State
1987–   Noor Mohammed Hassanali

Head of Government
1986–91   Arthur Napoleon Raymond Robinson
1991–   Patrick Manning

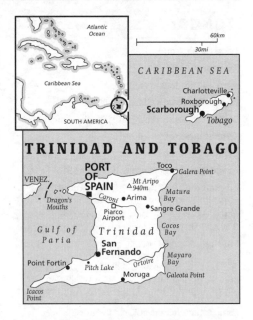

TUNISIA

Local names Tunis (Arabic), Tunisie (French)

Timezone GMT + 1

Area 164 150 km²/63 362 sq mi

Population total (1992e) 8 413 000

Status Republic

Date of independence 1956

Capital Tunis

Languages Arabic (official), French and Berber widely spoken

Ethnic groups Arab (98%), European (1%), small Jewish minority

Religions Sunni Muslim (98%), Christian (1%), small Jewish minority

Physical features Located in N Africa, on Mediterranean coast. Atlas Mts (NW) rise to 1 544 m/5 065 ft at Jebel Chambi. Majardah river valley is the most fertile area (N). From Tabussah range, land descends across a plateau to the Saharan desert (S) and a coastal plain (E).

Climate Mediterranean in N, with hot, dry summers, mild, rainy winters; extreme desert-continental conditions in S, with little rainfall. Average annual temperature 9°C (Jan), 26°C (Jul); average annual rainfall 400 mm/15.7 in.

Currency 1 Tunisian Dinar (TD,D) = 1 000 millèmes

Economy Agriculture (employs c.50% of population, but of declining importance); wheat, barley, grapes. Olive oil (world's fourth largest producer). Phosphates (fifth largest producer).

GDP (1990e) $10 bn, per capita $1 235

History Ruled by Phoenicians, Carthaginians, Romans, Byzantines, Arabs, Spanish, and Turks. Under the control of the Ottoman Empire in 1574; French protectorate, 1883. Gained internal self-government in 1955; independence, 1956; monarchy abolished and republic declared in 1957. Executive power held by President, who appoints the Prime Minister and Council of Ministers. Unicameral legislature, National Assembly, elected every five years.

Head of State
1987–   Zine al-Abidine bin Ali

Head of Government
1989–   Hamed Karoui

TURKEY

Local name Türkiye Cumhuriyeti

Timezone GMT + 3

Area 779 452 km²/300 868 sq mi

Population total (1992e) 59 200 000

Status Republic

Capital Ankara

Languages Turkish (Türkçe) (official), Kurdish and Arabic; Greek, Armenian, and Yiddish minorities

Ethnic groups Turkish (85%), Kurd (12%)

Religions Sunni Muslim (98%), Greek Orthodox, Armenian, and Jewish minorities

Physical features Lying partly in Europe and partly in Asia, W area (Thrace), E area (Anatolia). Turkish Straits (Dardanelles, Sea of Marmara, Bosporus) connect the Black Sea (NE) and Mediterranean Sea (SW). Mountainous area, Taurus Mts, cover the entire S part of Anatolia; highest peak Mt Ararat, 5 165 m/16 945 ft. Sources of rivers Euphrates and Tigris in E.

Climate Mediterranean climate on Aegean and Mediterranean coasts, with hot, dry summers, warm, wet winters; mean temperature 19°C (Jul). Average annual temperatures 0.3°C (Jan), 23°C (Jul) in Ankara; average annual rainfall 723 mm/28 in.

Currency 1 Turkish Lira (TL) = 100 kurus

Economy Agriculture (employs c.50% of workforce); cotton, tobacco, fruits, nuts, livestock. Minerals, textiles, glass, and cement. Many Turks find work elsewhere in Europe, especially Germany.

GDP (1991) $119 bn, per capita $1 905

History Seljuk sultanate replaced by the Ottoman in NW Asia Minor in 13th-c. Turkish invasion of Europe, first in Balkans in 1375; fall of Constantinople, 1453; empire at its peak under Sulaiman the Magnificent in 16th-c. Young Turks seized power in 1908; Balkan War, 1912–13. Allied with Germany during World War 1.

| □ international airport | 1 Antakya (Antioch) | 3 Ataturk Dam |
| | 2 Iskenderun (Alexandretta) | 4 Keban Dam |

Republic followed Young Turk revolution, led by Kemal Atatürk, 1923; policy of westernization and economic development. Neutral throughout most of World War 2, then sided with Allies. Military coups in 1960 and 1980. Strained relations with Greece, and invasion of Cyprus, 1974. Aided the allied forces during the Gulf War in 1991. Constitution provides for a single-chamber National Assembly; a President appoints a Prime Minister and a Council of Ministers.

Head of State
1989–93 Turgut Özal
1993–   Süleyman Demirel

Head of Government
1989–91 Yıldırım Akbulut
1991   Mesut Yılmaz
1991–3   Süleyman Demirel
1993–   Tansu Çiller

TURKMENISTAN

Local name Turkmenostan

Timezone GMT + 4

Area 488 100 km²/188 400 sq mi

Population total (1992) 3 809 000

Status Republic

Date of independence 1991

Capital Ashkhabad (Ashgabad)

Languages Turkmenian (official), other Turkic languages, Russian

Ethnic groups Turkmen (72%), Russian (10%), Uzbek, Kazakh, Ukrainian minorities

Religion Sunni Muslim

Physical features Kara Kum (Black Sands) desert, area 310 800 km²/120 000 sq mi, covers c.80% of the country. Turan Plain covers four-fifths of Turkmenistan. Foothills in the S; Kopet Dag mountain range is volcanic. Other foothills are spurs of the Kugitangtau and Pamir-Alay ranges. Rivers Amu Darya and Murghab.

Climate Continental, great variation of temperatures. Temperatures range from 50°C (Jul) in Kara Kum, to −33°C (Jan) in the Kushka; in the mountains. Average annual rainfall 120–250 mm/5–10 in.

Currency Rouble (R) (1993 New currency: Manat)

Economy Mineral resources of oil, natural gas, sulphur, potassium, and salt. Oil, gas extraction (main industries). Textiles. Cotton production. Agriculture; raising of Karakul sheep, Turkoman horses, and camels.

Turkmenistan (continued)

GDP Not available

History Part of the ancient Persian empire; ruled by Seljuk Turks during 11th-c; conquered by Genghis Khan and the Mongols during 13th-c; Uzbeks invaded in 15th-c; divided into two: one part belonged to the Khanate of Khiva (which became part of the Russian empire), and the other to the Khanate of Bukhara. Turkistan Autonomous Soviet Socialist Republic formed in 1922; full Soviet Socialist Republic in 1924. Declared sovereignty in 1990; independence and membership of Commonwealth of Independent States, 1991; UN membership, 1992. Republic consists of five provinces: Ashgabad, Chardjou, Drasnovodsk, Mary, Tashauz.

Head of State
1990–   Saparmurad Niyazov

Head of Government
1991–   Khan Akhmedov

TURKS AND CAICOS ISLANDS >> UNITED KINGDOM

TUVALU

Local name Tuvalu

Timezone GMT + 12

Area 26 km²/10 sq mi

Population total (1992e) 9 500

Status Independent state within the Commonwealth

Date of independence 1978

Capital Funafuti (Fongafale)

Languages Tuvaluan, English

Ethnic group Polynesian (96%)

Religions Christian (Protestant Church of Tuvalu, Roman Catholic, Baha'i) (97%), small Muslim minority

Physical features Island group in the SW Pacific, 1 050 km/650 mi off Fiji; comprises nine low-lying coral atolls, running NW–SE in a chain 580 km/360 mi long. Consists of the islands of Funafuti, Nukufetau, Nukulailai, Nanumea, Niutao, Nanumanga, Nui, Vaitupu, and Niulakita. All low-lying, highest point, 4.6 m/15 ft, on Niulakita.

Climate Hot, humid climate. Average annual temperatures 29°C (Jan), 27°C (Jul) in Funafuti; average annual rainfall 3 535 mm/139 in.

Currency 1 Australian Dollar ($A) = 100 cents

Economy Subsistence economy; agriculture, coconuts, copra, tropical fruit; fish. Handcrafted products, postage stamps.

GDP (1989e) $4.6 m, per capita $530

History Invaded by Samoans in 16th-c. British protectorate, as the Ellice Is, 1892. Administered as a colony jointly with Gilbert Is (now Kiribati), 1915. American soldiers occupied the Ellice Islands during World War 2, to counter the advance of the Japanese in 1942. Separate constitution, following 1974 referendum; independence as a constitutional monarchy within the Commonwealth, 1978. Tuvalu Trust Fund set up by Britain, Australia, New Zealand, and South Korea, 1987. British monarch represented by a Governor-General. Governed by a Prime Minister, a Cabinet, and a unicameral Parliament.

Head of State
(British monarch represented by Governor-General)
1978–   Toaripi Lauti

Head of Government
1989–93   Bikenibeu Paeniu
1993–   Kamuta Laatasi

Map >> KIRIBATI

UGANDA

Local name Uganda (Swahili)

Timezone GMT + 3

Area 241 038 km²/150 645 sq mi

Population total (1992e) 17 500 000

Status Republic

Date of independence 1962

Capital Kampala

Languages English (official), Swahili, Luganda (Ganda), Ateso, and Luo are also spoken

Ethnic groups Ganda, with Bantu, Nilotic and Hamitic minorities

Religions Christian (66%) (Roman Catholic 33%, Protestant 33%), traditional animist beliefs (18%), Muslim (16%)

Physical features Landlocked country in E Africa, mainly plateau, height 900–1 000 m/3 000–3 250 ft. Dry savannah or semi-desert in the N; fertile L Victoria basin; highest point in Uganda and Zaïre, Margherita Peak, 5 110 m/16 765 ft. Main lakes, Victoria (SE), George and Edward (SW), Albert (W), Kwania and Kyoga (C), Bisina (formerly L Salisbury) (E). Main rivers are the upper reaches of R Nile, the Victoria Nile, and the Albert Nile.

Climate Tropical climate; temperatures rarely rise above 29°C, or fall below 15°C (S). Average annual temperature 23°C (Jan), 21°C (Jul); average annual rainfall 1 150 mm/45 in.

Currency 1 Uganda Shilling = 100 cents

Economy Agriculture; coffee (over 90% of exports), tea, sugar, cotton; bananas, plantains, cassavas, potatoes, sweet potatoes, maize, sorghum.

GDP (1989) $4.9 bn, per capita $290

History Visited by Arab traders in 1830s; explored by Speke, 1860s; granted to the British East Africa Company, 1888; Kingdom of Buganda became a British protectorate in 1893; other territory included by 1903. Independence, 1962; Dr Milton Obote assumed all powers, 1966. Coup led by General Idi Amin Dada in 1971; Amin's regime overthrown, 1979. Further coup in 1985, overthrew Milton Obote, General Tito Okello became President; National Resistance Movement (NRM) captured Kampala, 1986, and Museveni became President. Governed by a President, a Cabinet, a Prime Minister, and a National Resistance Council; awaiting drafting of a new constitution.

Head of State
1986– Yoweri Kaguta Museveni

Head of Government
1986–91 Samson B Kisekka
1991– George Cosmas Adyebo

□ *international airport*
1 *Lake Kwania*
2 *Lake George*

UKRAINE

Local name Ukraina

Timezone GMT + 2

Area 603 700 km²/233 028 sq mi

Population total (1992e) 52 100 000

Status Republic

Date of independence 1991

Capital Kiev

Languages Ukrainian (official), Russian

Ethnic groups Ukrainian (73%), Russian (22%), Moldovan, Bulgarian, and Polish minorities

Religions Orthodox (Autocephalous and Russian) (76%), Roman Catholic (14%), Jewish (2%), Baptist, Mennonite, Protestant, and Muslim (8%)

Physical features Most fertile area of former USSR, consisting largely of black soil steppes, forming a substantial part of the East European Plain. Borders the Black Sea and Sea of Azov (S); Carpathian Mts, 2 061 m/ 6 762 ft at Mt Goverla (SW); Crimean Mts (S). Main rivers, Dnepr, Yuzhny, Bug. Donets coalfield, area 25 900 km²/10 000 sq mi.

Climate Moderate, mild winters, hot summers (SW); average annual temperatures –3°C (Jan), 23°C (Jul); average annual rainfall in Crimea 400–610 mm/16–24 in.

Currency (1992) Roubles replaced with karbovanet coupons, pending introduction of the new Ukrainian currency (the hryvna)

Economy Important industrial bases for iron and steel manufacture, chemical and engineering bases. Shipbuilding on Black Sea. Agriculture (was the USSR's major wheat producer); wheat, corn, rye, potatoes, cotton, flax, sugar beet. Coal and salt deposits in Donets basin.

GNP (1990) $47.6 bn, (1989) per capita $4 700

History Conquered by Mongols in 1240; dominated by Poland, 13–16th-c; applied to Moscow for help fighting Poland in return for sovereignty, 1654. Declared independence from Russia in 1918, after Russian Revolution; became a member of the USSR, 1922; suffered

Human geography

Ukraine (continued)

devastation during World War 2. Chernobyl was the site of the world's worst nuclear accident, 1986. Declared independence which was recognized by UN and US, 1991. Ongoing disputes with Russia over control of the Black Sea Fleet and status of the Crimea; introduction of border controls and new currency, 1993, in contravention of CIS agreements. Governed by a President and 450-seat Supreme Council.

Head of State
1991–   Leonid M Kravchuk

Head of Government
1990–2   Vitold P Fokin
1992–3   Leonid Kuchma
1993–   Yukhim Zvyagilsky

UNITED ARAB EMIRATES

Local name Ittihād al-Imārat al-'Arabīyah

Timezone GMT + 4

Area 83 600 km²/32 300 sq mi

Population total (1992e) 1 990 000

Status Federation of autonomous emirates

Date of independence 1971

Capital Abu Dhabi

Languages Arabic (official), English, Farsi, Urdu, and Hindi also spoken

Ethnic groups Emirian (19%), other Arab (23%), S Asian (50%)

Religions Muslim (Sunni 80%, Shi'ite 16%), Christian (4%), small Hindu minority

Physical features Seven states in EC Arabian peninsula on S shore (Trucial Coast) of the Arabian Gulf. Al Fujairah has a coastline along the Gulf of Oman. Salt marshes predominate on coast. Barren desert and gravel plain inland. Hajar Mts in Al Fujairah rise to over 1 000 m/3 000 ft in E.

Climate Hot, dry desert climate, extreme summer temperatures exceeding 40°C and limited rainfall; frequent sandstorms. Average annual temperatures 23°C (Jan), 42°C (Jul) in Dubai; average annual rainfall 60 mm/2.4 in.

Currency 1 United Arab Emirates Dirham (DH) = 100 fils

Economy Based on oil and gas (main producers, Abu Dhabi, Dubai). Important commercial and trading centre. Saline water supplies have restricted agriculture to oases and irrigated valleys of Hajar Mts. Vegetables, fruits, dates, dairy farming. Tourism.

GDP (1989) $27.3 bn, per capita $12 100

History Originally peopled by sea-faring tribes, converted to Islam in 7th-c; Mecca conquered by powerful sheikdom of Carmathians; upon its collapse piracy common, area known as the Pirate Coast. Portuguese explorers arrived in 16th-c; British East India Company arrived in 17th-c; British attacked the coastal ports, 1819–20 and exacted a pledge to renounce piracy in the General Treaty, 1820; became known as Trucial Coast after signing of Treaty of Maritime Peace in Perpetuity, 1853; administered by British India, 1873–1947, and thereafter by London Foreign Office. Trucial States Council formed in 1960. Federated and became United Arab Emirates in 1971, comprising seven emirates: Abu Dhabi, Ajman, Dubai, Al Fujairah, Ras al Khaimah, Sharjah, and Umm al Qaiwain. Ras al Khaimah joined federation, 1972. Governed by Supreme Council of the seven emirate rulers (each of whom is an absolute Monarch in own state). BCCI scandal, 1992, adversely affected the federation, which was a major shareholder.

Head of State

1971–   Zayed bin Sultan al-Nahyan

Head of Government

1979–90   Rashid bin Said al-Maktoum
1990–   Maktoum bin Rashid al-Maktoum

UNITED KINGDOM (UK)

Local names United Kingdom of Great Britain and Northern Ireland, Great Britain, Britain

Timezone GMT

Area 244 755 km²/94 475 sq mi

Population total (1992e) 57 384 000

Status Kingdom

Capital London

Languages English (official), Irish Gaelic, Scots Gaelic (Gallic), Welsh

Ethnic groups English (82%), Scottish (10%), Irish (2%), Welsh (2%), West Indian, Asian, and African (2%), Arabic, Turkish, and Greek minorities

Religions Christian (90%) (Anglican 63%, Roman Catholic 14%, Presbyterian 4%, Methodist 3%, Baptist 1%, Orthodox 1%, other 6%), Muslim (3%), Sikh (1%), Hindu (1%), Jewish (1%), other (1%)

Physical features Varied landscape, comprising the mountainous Lake District in NW, rocky moors in SW, hilly downs of S and SE, and the low, marshy fenlands of C and E. The Cheviot Hills separate Scotland and England. Highest point, Ben Nevis in Scotland, 1 342 m/4 406 ft. The Pennines form a ridge down the middle of England, from Lake District to C. Highest point in England and Wales, Mt Snowdon in Wales, 1 085 m/3 560 ft. In N Ireland, the Sperrin Mts and the granite Mourne Mts rise to heights over 610 m/2 000 ft.

Climate Temperate maritime climate. SW airstream determines weather, bringing depressions (causing wet weather) or N winds (bringing drier and colder); some regional diversity, but no world climate systems' boundaries pass through the islands. On average, wetter and slightly warmer in W. Rainfall evenly distributed throughout the year; average annual rainfall 1 600 mm/ 60 in (W), 800 mm/30 in (C and E).

Currency 1 Pound Sterling (£) = 100 pence

Economy Service industries. Agriculture, potatoes, wheat, barley, and sugar beets. Livestock. Large fishing industry. Deposits of iron ore; oil and gas from N Sea; coal industry declining. Highly developed financial systems; London the commercial and financial centre of Western world. UK one of the world's largest trading nations, relying heavily on imports. Exports include machinery, transport equipment, petroleum, chemicals, textiles.

GDP (1990) $858.3 bn, per capita $15 000

History Migrations and settlements resulted in the insular Celtic nation; invaded by Rome in 1 AD; Romans withdrew in the 5th-c; constantly attacked by Scandinavian tribes; defeated by Alfred in 878; united under the kings of Wessex in 10th-c; Edward the Confessor died, 1066, leaving a disputed succession; Norman invasion under William, Duke of Normandy, 1066. Edward I conquered Wales in 1301; Hundred Years' War with France, 1337–1453. Recurring plagues of Black Death, 1347–1400, wiped out one-third of population. Wars of the Roses, 1455–85, resulted in victory for House of Lancaster. Establishment of Church of England and split from Church of Rome in 1533; union with Wales in 1536; coronation of Elizabeth I, 1558; execution of Mary Queen of Scots, 1587; defeat of the Spanish Armada, 1588; English Civil War, 1642–6 and 1648–9; execution of Charles I, 1649. England and Scotland joined by the Act of Union in 1707; 1714–60, development of parliamentary government under Hanoverian kings; revolt of the American colonies, 1775–81. Ireland officially joined to Great Britain, 1801. World War 1, 1914–18; became the United

□ major international airport

Human geography

United Kingdom (continued)

Kingdom of Great Britain and Northern Ireland following the establishment of the Irish Free State, 1922. General Strike in 1926; abdication of Edward VIII, 1936. World War 2, 1939–45. National Health system implemented in 1948; Indian independence, 1947. Joined EC, 1973. Falklands War with Argentina, 1982. Involvement in Gulf War, 1991. A kingdom with the Monarch as Head of State. Governed by a bicameral Parliament, comprising an elected 650-member House of Commons and a House of Lords; a Cabinet is appointed by the Prime Minister.

Head of State (Monarch)
1952–   Elizabeth II

Head of Government
1979–90   Margaret Hilda Thatcher
1990–   John Major

>> **Political leaders and rulers**

England

Area 130357 km²/50318 sq mi

Population total (1992e) 48378300

Status Constituent part of the United Kingdom

Capital London

Languages English (official), with c.100 minority languages

Ethnic groups & Religions (>> UNITED KINGDOM)

Physical features Largest area within the United Kingdom, forming the S part of the island of Great Britain. Since 1974 divided into 46 counties; includes the Isles of Scilly, Lundy, and the Isle of Wight. Largely undulating lowland, rising (S) to the Mendips, Cotswolds, Chilterns, and North Downs, (N) to the N–S ridge of the Pennines, and (NW) to the Cumbria Mts. Drained E by the Tyne, Tees, Humber, Ouse, and Thames Rivers, and W by the Eden, Ribble, Mersey, and Severn Rivers. Lake District (NW) includes Derwent Water, Ullswater, Windermere and Bassenthwaite. Linked to Europe by ferry and hovercraft, and (from 1994) the Channel Tunnel.

Economy North Sea oil and gas, coal, tin, china clay, salt, potash, lead ore, iron ore. Vehicles, heavy engineering, petrochemicals, pharmaceuticals, textiles, food processing, electronics, telecommunications, publishing, brewing, fishing, livestock, agriculture, horticulture, pottery and tourism.

History (>> UNITED KINGDOM)

Counties of England

County	Area		Population	Admin Centre
	km²	sq mi	(1992e)	
Avon[a]	1345	520	968400	Bristol
Bedfordshire	1235	477	536600	Bedford
Berkshire	1259	486	758000	Reading
Buckinghamshire	1883	727	645700	Aylesbury
Cambridgeshire	3409	1316	677700	Cambridge
Cheshire	2328	899	966900	Chester
Cleveland[a]	583	225	560000	Middlesbrough
Cornwall	3564	1376	475400	Truro
Cumbria[a]	6810	2629	490200	Carlisle
Derbyshire	2631	1016	947300	Matlock
Devon	6711	2591	1045100	Exeter
Dorset	2654	1025	664200	Dorchester
Durham	2436	941	607100	Durham
Essex	3672	1418	1555800	Chelmsford
Gloucestershire	2643	1020	541300	Gloucester
Greater London[a]	1579	610	6904600	no central authority
Greater Manchester[a]	1287	497	2573500	no central authority
Hampshire	3777	1458	1587500	Winchester
Hereford and Worcester[a]	39261	516	690400	Worcester
Hertfordshire	1634	631	994300	Hertford
Humberside[a]	3512	1356	881400	Beverley
Isle of Wight	381	147	125600	Newport
Kent	3731	1441	1538300	Maidstone
Lancashire	3063	1183	1413500	Preston
Leicestershire	2553	986	902300	Leicester
Lincolnshire	5915	2284	596800	Lincoln
Merseyside[a] [b]	652	252	1445700	Liverpool
Norfolk	5368	2073	762900	Norwich
Northamptonshire	2367	914	590200	Northampton
Northumberland	5032	1943	307200	Morpeth
Nottinghamshire	2164	836	1025300	Nottingham
Oxfordshire	2608	1007	587100	Oxford
Shropshire	3490	1347	412800	Shrewsbury
Somerset	3451	1332	472500	Taunton
Staffordshire	2716	1049	1051800	Stafford
Suffolk	3797	1466	648000	Ipswich
Surrey	1679	648	1036700	Kingston upon Thames
Sussex, East	1795	693	720600	Lewes

Sussex, West	1989	768	712600	Chichester
Tyne and Wear[a][b]	540	208	1134400	Newcastle upon Tyne
Warwickshire	1981	765	491900	Warwick
West Midlands[a][b]	899	347	2630500	Birmingham
Wiltshire	3481	1344	579400	Trowbridge
Yorkshire, North	8309	3208	723100	Northallerton
Yorkshire, South	1560	602	1304300	Barnsley
Yorkshire, West[b]	2039	787	2093500	Wakefield

[a] New counties in 1974 were formed as follows:

Avon: parts of Somerset and Gloucestershire

Cleveland: parts of Durham and Yorkshire

Cumbria: Cumberland, Westmoreland, parts of Lancashire and Yorkshire

Greater London: London and most of Middlesex

Greater Manchester: parts of Lancashire, Cheshire, and Yorkshire

Hereford and Worcester: Hereford, most of Worcestershire

Humberside: parts of Yorkshire and Lincolnshire

Merseyside: parts of Lancashire and Cheshire

West Midlands: parts of Staffordshire, Warwickshire, and Worcestershire

Tyne and Wear: parts of Northumberland and Durham

[b] The councils of these metropolitan councils were abolished in 1986

1	NORTHUMBERLAND	16	DERBYSHIRE
2	TYNE & WEAR	17	LEICESTERSHIRE
3	DURHAM	18	NORTHAMPTONSHIRE
4	CLEVELAND	19	CAMBRIDGESHIRE
5	CUMBRIA	20	NORFOLK
6	LANCASHIRE	21	SUFFOLK
7	MERSEYSIDE	22	STAFFORDSHIRE
8	GREATER MANCHESTER	23	SHROPSHIRE
9	CHESHIRE	24	WEST MIDLANDS
10	NORTH YORKSHIRE	25	WARWICKSHIRE
11	WEST YORKSHIRE	26	HEREFORD & WORCESTER
12	SOUTH YORKSHIRE	27	OXFORDSHIRE
13	HUMBERSIDE	28	BUCKINGHAMSHIRE
14	LINCOLNSHIRE	29	BEDFORDSHIRE
15	NOTTINGHAMSHIRE	30	HERTFORDSHIRE

31	GREATER LONDON
32	ESSEX
33	KENT
34	EAST SUSSEX
35	WEST SUSSEX
36	SURREY
37	BERKSHIRE
38	HAMPSHIRE
39	ISLE OF WIGHT
40	GLOUCESTERSHIRE
41	AVON
42	WILTSHIRE
43	DORSET
44	SOMERSET
45	DEVON
46	CORNWALL & ISLES OF SCILLY

Scotland

Area 78742 km²/30394 sq mi

Population total (1992e) 5111200

Status Constituent part of the United Kingdom

Capital Edinburgh

Languages English, Scots Gaelic (Gallic) (known or used by c.80000 residents)

Physical features Comprises the N part of the UK, and includes the island groups of Outer and Inner Hebrides, Orkney and Shetland. Divided into Southern Uplands, rising to 843 m/2766 ft at Merrick; Central Lowlands (most densely populated area); and Northern Highlands, divided by the fault line following the Great Glen, and rising to 1342 m/4406 ft at Ben Nevis. W coast heavily indented; several wide estuaries on E coast, primarily Firths of Forth, Tay and Moray. Many freshwater lochs in the interior, largest being Loch Lomond, 70 km²/27 sq mi, and deepest Loch Morar, 310 m/1020 ft.

Economy Based on coal, but all heavy industry declined through the 1980s, with closure of many pits. Oil services on E coast. Tourism, especially in Highlands. Shipbuilding, steel, whisky, textiles, agriculture, forestry.

History Roman attempts to limit incursions of N tribes marked by Antonine Wall and Hadrian's Wall. Beginnings of unification in 9th-c. Wars between England and Scotland in Middle Ages; Scottish independence

declared by Robert Bruce, recognized 1328; Stuart succession in 14th-c; crowns of Scotland and England united in 1603; parliaments united under Act of Union, 1707;

Scotland (continued)

unsuccessful Jacobite rebellions in 1715 and 1745. Devolution proposal rejected, 1979. Since 1974, divided into 12 regions and 53 districts.

Regions of Scotland

Name	Area		Population total (1992e)	Admin centre
	km²	sq mi		
Borders	4672	1804	104800	Newton St Boswells
Central	2631	1016	272700	Stirling
Dumfries and Galloway	6370	2459	147900	Dumfries
Fife	1307	505	349900	Glenrothes
Grampian	8704	3361	522400	Aberdeen
Highland	25391	9804	205900	Inverness
Lothian	1755	678	750600	Edinburgh
Strathclyde	13537	5225	2290700	Glasgow
Tayside	7493	2893	394600	Dundee
Orkney Is	976	377	19710	Kirkwall
Shetland Is	1433	553	22640	Lerwick
Western Is	2898	1119	29350	Stornoway

Wales

□ international airport

Local name Cymru (Welsh)

Area 20761 km²/8014 sq mi

Population total (1992e) 2898500

Status Principality (Constituent part of the United Kingdom)

Capital Cardiff

Languages English, Welsh

Physical features Situated on the W coast of the UK, divided into 8 counties since 1974; includes the island of Anglesey off the NW coast. Land rises to 1085 m/3560 ft at Snowdon (NW), also Cambrian Mts (C); Brecon Beacons (S). Drained by the Severn, Clwyd, Dee, Conwy, Dovey, Taff, Towy, and Wye rivers.

Economy Coal; slate, lead, steel. Industrialized S valleys and coastal plain. Tourism in N and NW. Ferries to Ireland at Holyhead, Fishguard. Important source of water for England.

History Rhodri Mawr united Wales against Saxons, Norse, and Danes in 9th-c. Edward I of England established authority over Wales, building several castles, 12th–

13th-c. Edward I's son created first Prince of Wales in 1301; 14th-c revolt under Owen Glendower. Politically united with England by Act of Union in 1535. Centre of Nonconformist religion since 18th-c; University of Wales, 1893, with constituent colleges. Political nationalist movement (Plaid Cymru) returned first MP in 1966; Welsh television channel; 1979 referendum opposed devolution.

Counties of Wales

Name	Area km²	Area sq mi	Population total (1992)	Admin centre
Clwyd	2426	937	414600	Mold
Dyfed	5768	2227	351100	Carmarthen
Gwent	1376	531	449400	Cwmbran
Gwynedd	3869	1494	239700	Caernarvon
Powys	5077	1960	119200	Llandrindod Wells
Glamorgan, Mid	1018	393	542800	Cardiff
Glamorgan, South	416	161	410400	Cardiff
Glamorgan, West	817	315	371200	Swansea

Northern Ireland (Ulster)

Area 14120 km²/5450 sq mi

Population total (1991) 1594000

Status Constituent division of the United Kingdom

Capital Belfast

Languages English, Irish Gaelic

Religions Christian (Roman Catholic 28%, Presbyterian 23%, Church of Ireland 19%)

Physical features Occupies the NE part of Ireland, centred on Lough Neagh. Mourne Mts in SE; highest point, Slieve Donard, 847 m/2 786 ft, in the former Co. Down. R Mourne, 82 km/51 mi in length.

Economy Agriculture. Service industries, shipbuilding, engineering, chemicals. Linen, textiles. Economy badly affected by the sectarian troubles since 1969.

History Separate Parliament established in 1920, with a 52-member House of Commons and a 26-member Senate; Protestant majority in the population, generally supporting political union with Great Britain; many of the Roman Catholic minority look for union with the Republic of Ireland. Violent conflict between the communities broke out in 1969, leading to the establishment of a British army peace-keeping force. Sectarian murders and bombings continued both within and outside the province; as a result of the disturbances, Parliament was abolished in 1973. Powers are now vested in the UK Secretary of State for Northern Ireland; formation of a 78-member Assembly, 1973; replaced by a Constitutional Convention in 1975. Assembly re-formed in 1982, but Nationalist members did not take their seats. Under the 1985 Anglo-Irish agreement, the Republic of Ireland was given a consultative role in the government of Northern Ireland; all Northern Ireland MPs in the British Parliament resigned in protest in 1986. Continuing controversy in the late 1980s; fresh talks between all main parties and the Irish government, 1992; breakthrough in December 1993 with the Downing Street Declaration; however, still no agreement as IRA and Sinn Fein continue to demand 'clarification' of the Declaration.

Districts of Northern Ireland

Name	Area km²	Area sq mi	Population total (1991)	Admin centre
Antrim	563	217	44516	Antrim
Ards	369	142	64764	Newtownards
Armagh	672	259	51817	Armagh
Ballymena	638	246	55641	Ballymena
Ballymoney	419	162	24198	Ballymoney
Banbridge	444	171	33482	Banbridge
Belfast	140	54	279237	Belfast
Carrickfergus	87	34	32750	Carrickfergus
Castlereagh	85	33	50799	Belfast
Coleraine	485	187	50438	Coleraine
Cookstown	623	240	31082	Cookstown
Craigavon	383	147	74986	Craigavon
Down	646	249	58008	Downpatrick
Dungannon	779	301	45428	Dungannon
Fermanagh	1876	715	54033	Enniskillen
Larne	338	131	29419	Larne
Limavady	587	227	22567	Limavady

cont.

United Kingdom (UK)

Northern Ireland (Ulster) (continued)

Name	Area km²	Area sq mi	Population total (1991)	Admin centre	Name	Area km²	Area sq mi	Population total (1991)	Admin centre
Lisburn	444	171	99 458	Lisburn	Newry and Mourne	895	346	82 943	Newry
Londonderry/ Derry	382	147	95 371	Londonderry/ Derry	Newtownabbey	152	59	74 005	Newtownabbey
					North Down	73	28	71 832	Bangor
Magherafelt	573	221	36 293	Magherafelt	Omagh	1 129	436	45 809	Omagh
Moyle	495	191	14 789	Ballycastle	Strabane	870	336	36 141	Strabane

BRITISH ISLANDS
Channel Islands

Timezone GMT

Area 194 km²/75 sq mi

Population total (1992) 145 000

Status Crown dependency of the United Kingdom

Capital St Helier (on Jersey), St Peter Port (on Guernsey)

Languages English and Norman-French

Physical features Island group of the British Isles in the English Channel, W of Normandy. Comprises the islands of Guernsey, Jersey, Alderney, Sark, Herm, Jethou, Brechou, and Lihou.

Economy Tourism, fruit, vegetables, flowers, dairy produce, Jersey and Guernsey cattle. Used as a tax haven. Not part of the European Community.

History Granted to the Dukes of Normandy in 10th-c. Only British possession to have been occupied by Germany during World War 2. A dependent territory of the British Crown, with individual legislative assemblies and legal system; divided into the Bailiwick of Guernsey and the Bailiwick of Jersey. Bailiff presides over the Royal Court and the Representative Assembly (the States).

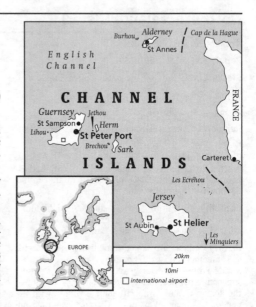

Isle of Man

Timezone GMT

Area 572 km²/221 sq mi

Population total (1991) 69 788

Status Crown dependency of the United Kingdom

Capital Douglas

Languages English (Manx survived as an everyday language until 19th-c)

Physical features Island in the Irish Sea; rises to 620 m/ 2 034 ft at Snaefell.

Economy Tourism, agriculture, fishing, light engineering. Used as a tax haven. Not part of European Community. Annual Tourist Trophy motorcycle races held here.

History Ruled by the Welsh, 6th–9th-c; then by the Scandinavians, Scots, and English. Purchased by the British Government between 1765 and 1828. The island has its own Parliament, the bicameral Court of Tynwald, which consists of the elected House of Keys and the Legislative Council. Acts of the British Parliament do not generally apply to Man.

BRITISH DEPENDENT TERRITORIES
Anguilla

Timezone GMT – 4

Area 155 km²/60 sq mi

Population total (1992) 8 800

Capital The Valley

Physical features Most northerly of the Leeward Is, E Caribbean; also includes Sombrero I and several other offshore islets and cays. Low-lying coral island, covered in low scrub and fringed with white coral-sand beaches.

Climate Tropical climate. Average annual temperature ranges from 24–30°C; low and erratic annual rainfall, 550–1 250 mm/22–50 in; hurricane season (Jul–Oct).

Currency 1 East Caribbean Dollar (EC$) = 100 cents

Economy Tourism, fishing, peas, corn, sweet potatoes, salt, boatbuilding.

History Colonized by English settlers from St Kitts in 1650; ultimately incorporated in the colony of St Kitts-Nevis-Anguilla. Separated, 1980. Governor appointed by the British sovereign; Legislative Assembly.

Bermuda

Timezone GMT – 4

Area 53 km²/20 sq mi

Population total (1990) 59 588

Capital Hamilton

Physical features Archipelago in W Atlantic, c.900 km/560 mi E of Cape Hatteras, N Carolina. C.150 low-lying coral islands and islets, 20 inhabited, 7 linked by causeways and bridges; largest island, (Great) Bermuda. Highest point, Gibb's Hill, 78 m/256 ft.

Climate Subtropical climate; generally humid; rain throughout year; warm summers, mild winters.

Currency 1 Bermuda Dollar = 100 cents

Economy Mainly year-round tourism; increasingly an international company business centre. Petroleum products, pharmaceuticals, aircraft supplies, boatbuilding, ship repair, vegetables, citrus fruits. Fish-processing centre.

History Formerly called Somers Is, discovered by Spanish mariner, Juan Bermudez, in early 16th-c; colonized by English settlers, 1612. Important naval station, and (to 1862) penal settlement. Internal self-government in 1968; movement for independence caused tension in the 1970s, including assassination of the Governor-General. Bicameral legislature.

British Antarctic Territory

British colonial territory, designated 1962; 20°–80°W and S of 60°S; includes South Orkney Is, South Shetland Is, Antarctic Graham Land Peninsula, and the land mass extending to the South Pole. Area, 5 700 000 km²/2 200 000 sq mi. Land area covered by ice and fringed by floating ice shelves. Population solely of scientists of the British Antarctic Survey. Territory administered by a High Commissioner in the Falkland Is.

British Indian Ocean Territory

British territory, 1 900 km/1 180 mi NE of Mauritius, c.2 300 islands, comprising the Chagos Archipelago. Area, 60 km²/23 sq mi; covering c.54 400 km²/21 000 sq mi of Indian Ocean. Tropical maritime climate, hot and humid; acquired by France, 18th-c; annexed by Britain, 1814. Bought by the Crown in 1967; population working on copra plantations were resettled in Mauritius or the Seychelles, 1967–73. Construction of a naval and air base by Britain and US started on Diego Garcia, the largest island. Population total (1991) 2900. No permanent civilian population.

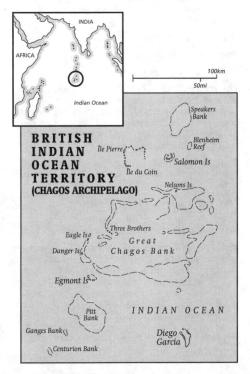

British Virgin Islands

Timezone GMT – 4

Area 153 km²/59 sq mi

Population total (1991) 16 644

Capital Road Town (on Tortola Island)

Physical features Island group at the NW end of the Lesser Antilles chain, E Caribbean, NE of Puerto Rico. Comprises 4 large islands (Tortola, Virgin Gorda, Anegada, Jost Van Dyke) and over 30 islets and cays; only 16 inhabited.Hilly terrain, except for flat coral island of Anegada. Highest point, Sage Mt, 540 m/1 772 ft, on Tortola I.

Climate Subtropical climate; average annual temperatures 17–28°C (Jan), 26–31°C (Jul); average annual rainfall 1 270 mm/50 in.

Currency 1 US Dollar (US$) = 100 cents

Economy Tourism (accounts for 50% of national income). Construction and stone extraction. Rum, paint, gravel, livestock, coconuts, sugar cane, fruit and vegetables, fish.

History Tortola colonized by British planters in 1666; constitutional government in 1774; part of the Leeward Is, 1872. Separate Crown Colony in 1956. Governor represents the British sovereign. Executive Council and Legislative Council.

Cayman Islands

Timezone GMT – 5

Area 260 km²/100 sq mi

Population total (1991e) 27 000

Capital George Town

Physical features Located in W Caribbean, comprising the islands of Grand Cayman, Cayman Brac, and Little Cayman, c.240 km/150 mi S of Cuba. Low-lying, rising to 42 m/138 ft on Cayman Brac plateau. Ringed by coral reefs.

Climate Tropical climate. Average temperatures 24–32°C (May–Oct), 16–24°C (Nov–Apr); average annual rainfall 1 420 mm/56 in; hurricane season (Jul–Nov).

Currency 1 Cayman Island Dollar (CI$) = 100 cents

Economy Tourism. International finance, property development; over 450 banks and trust companies established on the islands. Oil transshipment. Crafts, jewellery, vegetables, tropical fish.

History Visited by Colombus in 1503; ceded to Britain, 1670; colonized by British settlers from Jamaica. British Crown Colony in 1962. A Governor represents the British sovereign, and presides over a Legislative Assembly.

Falkland Islands

Timezone GMT – 4

Area c.12 200 km²/4 700 sq mi

Population total (1991) 2 121

Capital Stanley (on East Falkland)

Physical features Located in the S Atlantic, c.650 km/ 400 mi NE of the Magellan Strait. Consists of East Falkland and West Falkland, separated by the Falkland Sound, with over 200 small islands. Hilly terrain, rising to 705 m/2 313 ft at Mt Usborne (East Falkland) and 700 m/ 2 297 ft at Mt Adam (West Falkland).

Climate Cold, strong westerly winds; low rainfall. Narrow temperature range 19°C (Jan), 2°C (Jul); average annual rainfall 635 mm/25 in.

Currency 1 Falkland Pound = 100 pence

Economy Agriculture; oats, sheep. Service industries to the continuing military presence in the islands.

History Seen by several early navigators, including Capt John Strong in 1689–90, who named the islands. French settlement, 1764; British base established in 1765; French yielded their settlement to the Spanish in 1767. Occupied in the name of the Republic of Buenos Aires in 1820; Britain asserted possession, became a British Crown Colony, 1833; formal annexation in 1908 and 1917. The whole island claimed since independence by Argentina. Falklands War, precipitated by the Argentine invasion of

the islands in Apr 1982, led to the dispatch of the British Task Force and the return of the islands to British rule in Jun 1982. External affairs and defence are the responsibility of the British government, which appoints civil and military commissioners. Internal affairs are governed by executive and legislative councils.

Human geography

South Georgia

British Dependent Territory, located in the S Atlantic, c.500 km/300 mi E of the Falkland Islands. Area, c.3 750 km²/1 450 sq mi. Barren, mountainous, snow-covered island, length, 160 km/100 mi; discovered by the London merchant De la Roche in 1675. Landing by Captain Cook in 1775; British annexation, 1908 and 1917. Burial place of Ernest Shackleton, the British explorer, who died at S Georgia in 1922. Sealing and whaling centre until 1965. Invaded by Argentina and recaptured by Britain in April 1982. Territory administered from the Falkland Islands.

South Sandwich Islands

British Dependent Territory; group of small, uninhabited islands in the S Atlantic, c.720 km²/450 sq mi SE of South Georgia; 56° 18-59° 25S 26° 15W. Discovered by Captain Cook, 1775; annexed by Britain, 1908 and 1917; administered from the Falkland Islands.

Gibraltar

Timezone GMT + 1

Area 6.5 sq km/2.5 sq mi

Population total (1991) 29 613

Capital Gibraltar

Physical features Narrow rocky peninsula rising steeply from the low-lying coast of SW Spain at the E end of the Strait of Gibraltar, 8 km/5 mi from Algeciras. Narrows to limestone massif, 'The Rock', height 426 m/ 1 398 ft, connected to the Spanish mainland by a sandy plain. Home of the Barbary apes, the only native monkeys in Europe.

Climate Mediterranean climate, with mild winters, warm summers. Average annual temperature range 13–29°C.

Currency 1 Gibraltar Pound = 100 pence

Economy Largely dependent on the presence of British forces. Royal Naval Dockyard converted to a commercial yard, 1985. Transshipment trade; fuel supplies to shipping; tourism.

History Settled by Moors in 711. Taken by Spain, 1462; ceded to Britain in 1713; Crown Colony, 1830. Played a key role in Allied naval operations during both World Wars. Proposal to end British rule defeated by referendum, 1967; Spanish closure of frontier, 1969–85; Spain continues to claim sovereignty. British Monarch represented by a Governor and House of Assembly. Military base; important strategic point of control for the W Mediterranean.

Hong Kong

Timezone GMT + 8

Area 1 066.5 km²/411.7 sq mi

Population total (1992e) 5 700 00

Capital Hong Kong

Languages English and Cantonese (official), with Mandarin widely spoken

Ethnic groups Chinese (98%), including many illegal immigrants from China and refugees from Vietnam; 59% of population born in Hong Kong, 37% in China

Religions Buddhist, Taoist and Confuncianist majorities, Christian, Muslim, Hindu, Sikh, and Jewish minorities

Physical features Located off the coast of SE China, on the South China Sea. Divided into Hong Kong Island, Kowloon, and New Territories (includes most of the colony's 235 islands). Highest point, Tai Mo Shan, 957 m/ 3 140 ft. Hilly terrain, sharply indented coastline. Natural harbour between Kowloon and Hong Kong Island. Built-up areas on artificially levelled or reclaimed land.

Climate Subtropical climate, with hot, humid summers

1 *Cheung Chau*	4 *Tsing Yi*	7 Kai Tak Airport
2 *Hei Ling Chau*	5 *Stonecutters Island*	8 *Kau Sai Chau*
3 *Peng Chau*	6 *Tai Mo Shan 957m*	9 *High Island*

Hong Kong (continued)

and cool, dry winters. Average annual temperatures 16°C (Jan), 29°C (Jul); average annual rainfall 2225 mm/ 88 in.

Currency 1 Hong Kong Dollar (HK$) = 100 cents

Economy Based on banking, import–export trade, tourism, shipbuilding, and a diverse range of light industry. An important freeport acting as a gateway to China for the West.

History Ceded to Britain in 1842; New Territories leased to Britain, 1898. Occupied by the Japanese in World War 2. British Crown Colony, Governor represents the British Crown, advised by an Executive Council. In 1997, Britain's 99-year lease of the New Territories will expire, whereupon Hong Kong will be restored to China; China has designated Hong Kong a special administrative region from 1997; it will remain a freeport, foreign markets will be retained, and the Hong Kong dollar will remain as official currency; however, anxiety over the colony's political future remains.

Montserrat (Emerald Isle)

Timezone GMT – 4

Area 106 km²/41 sq mi

Population total (1992e) 12 500

Capital Plymouth

Physical features Volcanic island in the Leeward Is, E Caribbean. Mountainous, heavily forested. Highest point, Chance's Peak, 914 m/2 999 ft; seven active volcanoes.

Climate Tropical climate, with low humidity. Average annual rainfall 1 500 mm/60 in; hurricanes occur (Jun–Nov).

Currency 1 East Caribbean Dollar (EC$) = 100 cents

Economy Tourism (accounts for 25% of national income). Cotton, peppers, livestock, electronic assembly, crafts, rum distilling, postage stamps.

History Visited by Colombus in 1493. Colonized by English and Irish settlers, 1632. Plantation economy based on slave labour; British Crown Colony, 1871. Joined Federation of the West Indies, 1958–62. Island severely damaged by hurricane Hugo, 1989. British sovereign represented by a Governor, with an Executive Council and a Legislative Council.

Pitcairn Islands

Timezone GMT – 9

Area 27 km²/10 sq mi

Population total (1992) 56

Capital Adamstown

Physical features Volcanic island group in the SE Pacific Ocean, E of French Polynesia. Comprises Pitcairn Island, 4.5 km²/1.7 sq mi, and the uninhabited islands of Ducie, Henderson, and Oeno; Pitcairn Island rises to 335 m/1 099 ft.

Climate Equable climate. Average annual temperatures 24°C (Jan), 19°C (Jul); average annual rainfall 2 000 mm/ 80 in.

Currency 1 New Zealand Dollar ($NZ) = 100 cents

Economy Postage stamps; tropical and subtropical crops; crafts, forestry.

History Visited by the British in 1767; occupied by nine mutineers from HMS *Bounty* in 1790. Overpopulation led to emigration to Norfolk I, 1856; some returning in 1864; transferred to Fiji, 1952; now a UK Dependent Territory, governed by the High Commissioner in New Zealand.

Saint Helena and Dependencies

Timezone GMT

Area 122 km²/47 sq mi

Population total (1991) 6 695

Capital Jamestown (on St Helena Island)

Physical features Volcanic group of islands in the S Atlantic, 1 920 km/1 200 mi from the SW coast of Africa. Includes St Helena, Ascension, Gough I, Inaccessible I, Nightingale I, and Tristan da Cunha. Rugged, volcanic terrain. Highest point, Diana's Peak, 823 m/2 700 ft.

Climate Tropical marine; mild, tempered by SE 'trade' winds.

Currency 1 St Helena Pound (£) = 100 pence

Economy Fish (mostly tuna); agriculture, coffee; postage stamps; heavily subsidized by the UK.

History Discovered by the Portuguese on St Helena's feast day in 1502; annexed by the Dutch, 1633; annexed by the East India Company, 1659. Napolean exiled here, 1815–21. Ascension and Tristan da Cunha made dependencies in 1922; evacuated between 1961–3, following volcanic eruption. Governed by an executive council and 12-member elected Legislative Council.

Turks and Caicos islands

Timezone GMT – 5

Area 500 km²/200 sq mi

Population total (1991) 9983

Capital Cockburn Town

Physical features Two island groups comprising c.30 islands and cays, forming the SE archipelago of the Bahamas chain, W Atlantic Ocean. Turk I and Caicos I are separated by 35 km/22 mi. Only 6 of the other islands are inhabited.

Climate Subtropical climate. Average annual tempera-tures 24–7°C (Jan), 29–32°C (Jul); average annual rainfall 525 mm/21 in; occasional hurricanes.

Currency 1 US Dollar ($, US$) = 100 cents

Economy Tourism is a rapidly expanding industry. Corn, beans, fishing, fish processing.

History Visited by the Spanish in 1512. Linked formally to the Bahamas, 1765. Transferred to Jamaica in 1848; British Crown Colony, 1972; internal self-government, 1976. British sovereign represented by a Governor, who presides over a Council.

UNITED STATES OF AMERICA (USA)

Local names United States, America

Timezone GMT – 5 (E coast) to – 8 (W coast)

Area 9160454 km²/3535935 sq mi

Population total (1992e) 255600000

Status Federal republic

Date of independence 1776

Capital Washington, DC.

Languages English, large Spanish-speaking minority

Ethnic groups European origin (including 6.2% Hispanic) (86.2%), African American (11%), Asian and Pacific (1.6%), Native American, Aleut, and Inuit (0.7%)

Religions Christian (86%) (Protestant 61%, Roman Catholic 25%), atheist (7%), other (5%), Jewish (2%)

Physical features Includes the separate states of Alaska (GMT – 9) and Hawaii (GMT – 10). E Atlantic coastal plain is backed by the Appalachian Mts from the Great Lakes to Alabama, a series of parallel ranges including the Allegheny, Blue Ridge, and Catskill Mts; plain broadens out (S) towards the Gulf of Mexico and into the Florida peninsula; Gulf Plains stretch N to meet the Great Plains from which they are separated by the Ozark Mts; further W, Rocky Mts rise to over 4300 m/14400 ft. Highest point in US, Mt McKinley, Alaska, 6194 m/20321 ft. Death Valley, –86 m/–282 ft, is the lowest point. Drainage N is into the St Lawrence R or the Great Lakes; in the E, the Hudson, Delaware, Potomac, and other rivers flow E to the Atlantic Ocean; central plains drained by the great Red River–Missouri–Mississippi system and by other rivers flowing into the Gulf of Mexico. Main rivers in W, Columbia and Colorado. Deserts cover much of Texas, New Mexico, Arizona, Utah, Nevada.

Climate Climate varies from conditions found in hot, tropical deserts (SW), to those typical of Arctic continental regions on the northern Pacific Coast. Continental climate on High Plains, with summer dust storms and winter blizzards; temperate continental on Central Plains; continental Mid West and the Great Lakes, with very cold winters; cool temperate in N Appalachians, warm temperate in S; subtropical to warm temperate on the Gulf Coast, with plentiful rainfall and frequent hurricanes and tornadoes; temperate maritime on the Atlantic coast, with heavy snowfall in N; cool temperate in New England, with warm summers and severe winters. Mean annual temperatures range from 29°C in Florida, to –13°C in Alaska; average annual temperatures in Chicago, –3°C (Jan), 24°C (Jul); in Arizona, 11°C (Jan), 32°C (Jul); average annual rainfall in Alabama, 1640 mm/65 in, in Arizona, 180 mm/7 in. Hot and humid in Hawaii, with average annual rainfall 1524–5080 mm/ 60–200 in.

Currency 1 US Dollar ($, US$) = 100 cents

Economy One of the world's most productive industrial nations. Highly diversified economy. Vast mineral and agricultural resources. Major exporter of grains, cereals, potatoes, sugar, fruit; livestock farming of beef, veal pork. Chief exports include aircraft, cars, machinery, chemicals, military equipment, non-fuel minerals. Advanced system of communications and transportation. Leader in space-exploration programme of the 1970s.

GDP (1991) $5677.5 bn, per capita $19082

History First settled by groups who migrated from Asia across the Bering Straits over 25000 years ago. Explored by the Norse in 9th-c; and by the Spanish in 16th-c, who settled in Florida and Mexico. In the 17th-c, settlements by the British, French, Dutch, Germans, and Swedes; many Black Africans introduced as slaves to work on the plantations; British control during 18th-c after defeat of French in Seven Years' war. Revolt of the English-speaking colonies in the War of Independence, 1775–83, resulted in the creation of the United States of America. Louisiana sold to the USA by France in 1803 (the Louisiana Purchase) and the westward movement of settlers began; Florida ceded by Spain in 1819, and further Spanish states joined the Union between 1821–53. 11

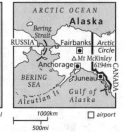

Hawaii
Niihua Kauai
Kaula
Oahu
Honolulu Molokai
Lanai Maui
Kahoolawe
Mauna Kea 4205m
Hawaii
PACIFIC OCEAN

ARCTIC OCEAN
Alaska
Bering Strait
RUSSIA Fairbanks Arctic Circle
Mt McKinley 6194m
Anchorage CANADA
BERING SEA Juneau
Aleutian Is Gulf of Alaska

200km | international airport
100mi

1000km | airport
500mi

United States of America (USA)

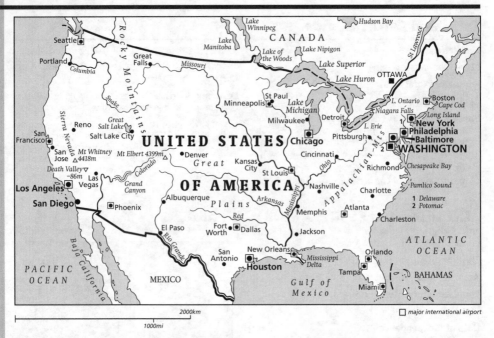

☐ major international airport

2000km
1000mi

Southern states left the Union over the slavery issue and formed the Confederacy, 1860–1. Civil War, 1861–5, ended in victory for the North, and the Southern states later rejoined the Union. Alaska purchased from Russia in 1867; Hawaiian islands annexed in 1898. Several other islands formally associated with the USA, such as Puerto Rico, American Samoa, and Guam. In the 19th-c, arrival of millions of immigrants from Europe and the Far East; more recent arrival of large numbers of Spanish-speaking people, mainly from Mexico and the West Indies. Entered World War 1 on the side of the Allies, 1917, and again in World War 2 in 1941. Became the chief world power opposed to communism, a policy which led to involvement in the Korean War (1950–3) and Vietnam (1956–75). Campaign for Black civil rights developed, 1960s, and eventually led to Civil Rights Act (1964). Invasion of Grenada, 1983; mid 1980s rapprochement of US and USSR; invasion of Panama, 1989; involvement in Gulf War, 1991; military intervention in Somalia, 1993. Congress consists of 435-member House of Representatives, and a 100-member Senate. A President elected every 4 years by a college of state representatives,

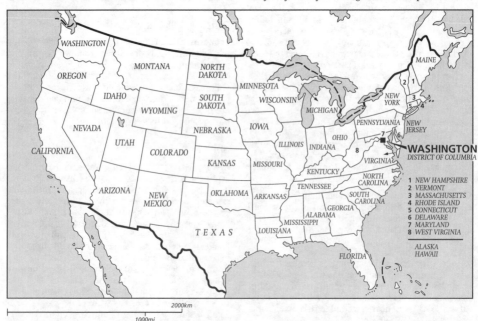

2000km
1000mi

appoints an executive Cabinet responsible to Congress. Divided into 50 federal states and the District of Columbia; each state having its own two-body legislature and governor.

Head of State/Government (President)
1989–93   George Herbert Walker Bush
1993–   William Jefferson Clinton

>> **Political leaders and rulers**

American States

(Timezones: two sets of figures indicate that different zones operate in a state. The second figure refers to Summer Time (Apr–Oct, approximately)
2 Aleutian/Hawaii Standard Time : 3 Alaska Standard Time : 4 Pacific Standard Time : 5 Mountain Standard Time : 6 Central Standard Time : 7 Eastern Standard Time

Name	Area km²	sq mi	Capital	Time zone	Population figures (1992)	Nickname(s)
Alabama (AL)	133 911	51 705	Montgomery	7/8	4 040 587	Camellia State, Heart of Dixie
Alaska (AK)	1 518 748	586 412	Juneau	3/4	550 043	Mainland State, The Last Frontier
Arizona (AZ)	295 249	114 000	Phoenix	5	3 665 288	Apache State, Grand Canyon State
Arkansas (AR)	137 403	53 187	Little Rock	6/7	2 350 725	Bear State, Land of Opportunity
California (CA)	411 033	158 706	Sacramento	4/5	29 760 021	Golden State
Colorado (CO)	269 585	104 091	Denver	5/6	3 294 394	Centennial State
Connecticut (CT)	12 996	5 018	Hartford	7/8	3 287 116	Nutmeg State, Constitution State
Delaware (DE)	5 296	2 045	Dover	7/8	666 168	Diamond State, First State
District of Columbia (DC)	173.5	67.0	Washington	7/8	606 900	
Florida (FL)	151 934	58 664	Tallahassee	6/7, 7/8	12 937 926	Everglade State, Sunshine State
Georgia (GA)	152 571	58 910	Atlanta	7/8	6 478 216	Empire State of the South, Peach State
Hawaii (HI)	16 759	6 471	Honolulu	2	1 108 229	Aloha State
Idaho (ID)	216 422	83 564	Boise	4/5, 5/6	1 006 749	Gem State
Illinois (IL)	145 928	56 345	Springfield	6/7	11 430 602	Prairie State, Land of Lincoln
Indiana (IN)	93 715.5	36 185	Indianapolis	6/7, 7/8	5 544 159	Hoosier State
Iowa (IA)	145 747	56 275	Des Moines	6/7	2 776 755	Hawkeye State, Corn State
Kansas (KS)	213 089	82 277	Topeka	5/6, 6/7	2 477 574	Sunflower State, Jayhawker State
Kentucky (KY)	104 658	40 410	Frankfort	6/7, 7/8	3 685 296	Bluegrass State
Louisiana (LA)	123 673	47 752	Baton Rouge	6/7	4 219 973	Pelican State, Sugar State, Creole State
Maine (ME)	86 153	33 265	Augusta	7/8	1 227 928	Pine Tree State
Maryland (MD)	27 090	10 460	Annapolis	7/8	4 781 468	Old Line State, Free State
Massachusetts (MA)	21 455	8 284	Boston	7/8	6 016 425	Bay State, Old Colony
Michigan (MI)	151 579	58 527	Lansing	6/7, 7/8	9 295 297	Wolverine State, Great Lake State
Minnesota (MN)	218 593	84 402	St Paul	6/7	4 375 099	Gopher State, North Star State
Mississippi (MS)	123 510	47 689	Jackson	6/7	2 573 216	Magnolia State
Missouri (MO)	180 508	69 697	Jefferson City	6/7	5 117 073	Bullion State, Show Me State
Montana (MT)	380 834	147 046	Helena	5/6	799 065	Treasure State, Big Sky Country
Nebraska (NE)	200 342	77 355	Lincoln	5/6, 6/7	1 578 385	Cornhusker State, Beef State

Human geography

American States (continued)

Name	Area km²	Area sq mi	Capital	Time zone	Population figures (1992)	Nickname(s)
Nevada (NV)	286 341	110 561	Carson City	4/5	1 201 833	Silver State, Sagebrush State
New Hampshire (NH)	24 032	9 279	Concord	7/8	1 109 252	Granite State
New Jersey (NJ)	20 167	7 787	Trenton	7/8	7 730 188	Garden State
New Mexico (NM)	314 914	121 593	Santa Fe	5/6	1 515 069	Sunshine State, Land of Enchantment
New York (NY)	127 185	49 108	Albany	7/8	17 990 455	Empire State
North Carolina (NC)	136 407	52 699	Raleigh	7/8	6 628 637	Old North State, Tar Heel State
North Dakota (ND)	180 180	69 567	Bismarck	5/6, 6/7	638 800	Flickertail State, Sioux State
Ohio (OH)	107 040	41 330	Columbus	7/8	10 847 115	Buckeye State
Oklahoma (OK)	181 083	69 919	Oklahoma City	6/7	3 145 585	Sooner State
Oregon(OR)	251 409	97 073	Salem	4/5	2 842 321	Sunset State, Beaver State
Pennsylvania (PA)	117 343	45 308	Harrisburg	7/8	11 881 643	Keystone State
Rhode Island (RI)	3 139	1 212	Providence	7/8	1 003 464	Little Rhody, Plantation State
South Carolina (SC)	80 579	31 113	Columbia	7/8	3 486 703	Palmetto State
South Dakota (SD)	199 723	77 116	Pierre	5/6, 6/7	696 004	Sunshine State, Coyote State
Tennessee (TN)	109 149	42 144	Nashville	6/7, 7/8	4 887 185	Volunteer State
Texas (TX)	691 003	266 807	Austin	5/6, 6/7	16 936 510	Lone Star State
Utah (UT)	219 880	84 899	Salt Lake City	5/6	1 722 850	Mormon State, Beehive State
Vermont (VT)	24 899	9 614	Montpelier	7/8	562 758	Green Mountain State
Virginia (VA)	105 582	40 767	Richmond	7/8	6 187 358	Old Dominion State, Mother of Presidents
Washington (WA)	176 473	68 139	Olympia	4/5	5 486 692	Evergreen State, Chinook State
West Virginia (WV)	62 758	24 232	Charleston	7/8	1 793 477	Panhandle State, Mountain State
Wisconsin (WI)	145 431	56 153	Madison	6/7	4 891 769	Badger State, America's Dairyland
Wyoming (WY)	253 315	97 809	Cheyenne	5/6	453 588	Equality State

UNITED STATES FORMAL DEPENDENCIES
American Samoa

Local name São Paulo de Loanda (Portuguese)

Timezone GMT − 11

Area 197 km²/76 sq mi

Population total (1990) 46 773

Capital Fagatogo

Languages English (official), Samoan

Physical features Located in the US Pacific Ocean, some 3 500 km/2 175 mi N of New Zealand. Five principal volcanic islands (including Tutuila, Aunu'u, Ofu, Olosega, Ta'u, Rose, Swains I) and two coral atolls. Main island, Tutuila, 109 km²/42 sq mi, rises to 653 m/ 2 142 ft. Islands mostly hilly, with large areas covered by thick bush and forest.

Climate Tropical maritime climate; average annual temperatures 28°C (Jan), 27°C (Jul) in Fagatogo; plentiful rainfall; rainy season (Nov–Apr); dry season (May–Oct); average annual rainfall 5 000 mm/200 in.

Economy Principal crops, taro, breadfruit, yams, bananas, coconuts. Tuna fishing; local inshore fishing, handicrafts.

History US acquired rights to American Samoa in 1899 and the islands were ceded by their chiefs, 1900–25. Now an unincorporated territory of the USA, administered by the Department of the Interior. Bicameral legislature established, 1948, comprising the Senate and the House of Representatives.

Human geography

Guam

Local name Guam

Timezone GMT + 10

Area 541 km²/209 sq mi

Population total (1990e) 138 000

Status Unincorporated territory of the United States of America

Capital Agaña

Languages Chamorro and English (official), Japanese is also spoken

Ethnic groups Chamorro (47%), Caucasian (18%), Filipino (29%), Micronesian (13%)

Religion Roman Catholic

Physical features Largest and southernmost of the Mariana Islands, covering c.48 km/30 mi in the Pacific Ocean; volcanic island fringed by a coral reef. Relatively flat limestone plateau, with narrow coastal plains in N, low rising hills in C and mountains in S. Highest point, 406 m/1 332 ft at Mt Lamlam.

Climate Tropical maritime climate; average annual temperature 24–30°C; average annual rainfall 2 125 mm/ 84 in; wet season (Jul–Dec).

Currency 1 US Dollar (US$) = 100 cents

Economy Economy highly dependent on government activities. Military installations cover 35% of the island. Diversifying industrial and commercial projects. Oil refining, dairy products, furniture, watches, copra, processed fish. Rapidly growing tourist industry.

History Originally settled by Malay-Filipino peoples; Ferdinand Magellan landed on the island in 1521. Claimed for Spain in 1565; rebellion against Spanish missionaries, 1670–95. US consulate established, 1855; ceded to US by Spain after defeat in Spanish-American War in 1898. Occupied by Japan, 1941–4. Unincorporated territory of the US, Organic Act, 1950. Elected Governor and a unicameral legislature.

Puerto Rico, The Commonwealth of

Local name Puerto Rico

Timezone GMT – 4

Area 8 897 km²/3 434 sq mi

Population total (1990) 3 522 037

Status Commonwealth

Capital San Juan

Languages Spanish (official), with English widely spoken

Religion Roman Catholic

Physical features Easternmost island of the Greater Antilles. Almost rectangular in shape; crossed W–E by mountains, rising to 1 338 m/4 389 ft at Cerro de Punta. Coastal plain belt in N. Islands of Vieques and Culebra also belong to Puerto Rico.

Climate Tropical maritime climate; average annnual temperature 25°C; high humidity.

Currency 1 US Dollar (US$) = 100 cents

Economy Manufacturing is the most important sector of the economy. Food processing, petrochemicals, electrical equipment, pharmaceuticals. Textiles, clothing. Livestock, tobacco, sugar, pineapples, coconuts. Tourism.

History Originally occupied by Carib and Arawak Indi-

ans; visited by Columbus in 1493; remained a Spanish colony until ceded to the US, 1898. High levels of emigration to the US from 1940s–50s; became a semi-autonomous Commonwealth in association with US, 1952. Executive power is exercised by a Governor; a bicameral Legislative Assembly consists of a Senate and House of Representatives.

Virgin Islands, United States

Local name US Virgin Islands

Timezone GMT – 4

Area 342 km²/132 sq mi

Population total (1990) 101 809 (St Croix 50 139, St Thomas 48 166, St John 3 504)

Status Territory

Capital Charlotte Amalie (on St Thomas Island)

Languages English (official), with Spanish and Creole widely spoken

Ethnic groups West Indian, French, Hispanic

Physical features Nine islands and 75 islets in the Lesser Antilles, Caribbean Sea. Three main inhabited islands, St Croix, St Thomas, and St John. Volcanic origin,

Human geography

Virgin Islands, United States (continued)

mostly hilly or rugged and mountainous. Highest peak, Crown Mt, 474 m/1 555 ft on St Thomas.

Climate Subtropical climate. Average annual temperatures 21–9°C (Dec–Mar), 24–31°C (Jun–Sep); low humidity; rainy season (May–Nov). Subject to severe droughts, floods and earthquakes.

Currency 1 US Dollar (US$) = 100 cents

Economy Tourism (chief industry). St Croix industries include oil and alumina products, clocks and watches, textiles, rum, fragrances, petrochemicals. Vegetables, fruit, sorghum.

History Originally inhabited by Ciboney Indians, followed by Arawak Indians, then Caribs; discovered by Columbus in 1493. Denmark colonized St Thomas and St John, 1665 and 1718, and bought St Croix from France, 1733. Purchased by US in 1917; now an unincorporated territory of the US. A Governor heads a unicameral legislature.

Micronesia, Federated States of

Timezone GMT + 11

Area 700 km²/270 sq mi

Population total (1992e) 114 000

Status Republic

Date of independence 1991

Capital Palikir (on Pohnpei Island)

Languages English (official), with several indigenous languages also spoken

Ethnic groups Trukese (41%), Pohnpeian (26%)

Religions Roman Catholic, Protestant

Physical features Group of four states in the W Pacific Ocean (Yap, Truk, Ponape, Kosrae). Comprises all the Caroline I except Belau. Islands vary from high mountainous terrain to low coral atolls.

Climate Tropical climate, with occasional typhoons; heavy rainfall all year.

Currency 1 US Dollar (US$) = 100 cents

Economy Agriculture; farming and fishing; tropical fruits, coconuts, vegetables. Few mineral resources.

GDP Not available

History Settled by Spanish seafarers in 1565. Formally annexed by Spain in 1874; sold to Germany, 1899; control mandated to Japan by League of Nations, 1920. American Navy took control following Japan's defeat in World War 2, 1945; part of UN Trust Territory of the Pacific, 1947. Compact of free association with the US in 1982; trusteeship ended in 1990. Independent state, 1991, under Compact of Free Association, the US continues to control its defence and foreign relations. Governed by a President and a National Congress.

Head of State/Government
1991–   Bailey Olter

Mariana Islands, Northern

Located in N Pacific Ocean, area 471 km²/182 sq mi. Limestone southern islands, volcanic northern islands. Capital Saipan. Population total (1990) 43 345. Tropical marine climate. Part of UN Trust Territory of the Pacific, 1947–78. Became a self-governing US Commonwealth Territory, 1978–90; trusteeship ended 1990.

Belau (Palau)

Consists of c. 350 Pacific Ocean islands; 8 inhabited. Area, 494 km²/191 sq mi. Population total (1990) 15 122; capital Koror. Part of US Trust Territory of the Pacific, 1947; proclaimed a republic, 1981; Compact of Free Association signed with US, 1982, needs to gain the required 75% support of the voters of Belau before it can be recognized as self-governing. Remains the only surviving part of Trust Territory which has not formally achieved independence.

OTHER AMERICAN ISLANDS

BAKER, HOWLAND, AND JARVIS ISLANDS
1 500–1 650 mi SW of the Hawaiian group, Pacific Ocean; uninhabited since World War 2; under Interior Department.

Uruguay

Human geography

JOHNSTON ATOLL
Consists of four small islands, SW of Hawaii: Johnston, Sand, Hikina, and Akau; used for military purposes, otherwise uninhabited.

KINGMAN REEF
Uninhabited reef S of Hawaii, under Navy control.

MIDWAY ISLANDS
Atoll and two islands, Eastern and Sand, lying NW of Hawaii, in N Pacific; unpopulated apart from US naval personnel.

PALMYRA
Atoll 1 000 mi S of Hawaii; privately owned; under Interior Department.

WAKE ISLAND
Uninhabited but for US naval personnel, Wake I lies between Guam and Midway I; sister islands, Wilkes and Peale.

NAVASSA
Caribbean island between Jamaica and Haiti, 100 mi S of Guatanámo Bay, Cuba; covers c.3 sq mi and is reserved by US for a lighthouse, administered by US Coast Guard; uninhabited.

URUGUAY

Local name Uruguay

Timezone GMT – 3

Area 176 215 km²/68 018 sq mi

Population total (1992e) 3 130 000

Status Republic

Date of independence 1828

Capital Montevideo

Language Spanish (official)

Ethnic groups European (mainly Spanish, Italian) (90%), mestizo (8%)

Religions Roman Catholic (66%), Protestant (2%), Jewish (2%), unaffiliated (30%)

Physical features Located in E South America. Grass covered plains (S) rise to a high, sandy plateau, traversed SE and NW by the Cuchilla Grande and Cuchilla de Haedo, rising to 501 m/1 644 ft at Cerro Mirados. R Negro flows SW to meet the R Uruguay on the Argentine frontier.

Climate Temperate, with warm summers, mild winters. Average annual temperature 10°C (Jul), 22°C (Jan) in Montevideo; average annual rainfall 978 mm/38 in; rainy season (Apr–May), occasional droughts.

Currency 1 New Uruguayan Peso (NUr$, UrugN$) = 100 centésimos

Economy Traditionally based on livestock and agriculture; meat, wool, fish, wheat, barley, maize, rice. Naturally-occurring minerals include granite and marble. Hydroelectric power, food processing and packing, light engineering, cement, textiles, leather, steel.

GDP (1990e) $9.2 bn, per capita $2 970

History Originally occupied by Charrúas Indians. Visited by the Spanish in 1516; part of the Spanish Viceroyalty of Río de la Plata in 1726; province of Brazil, 1814–25; independence as the Eastern Republic of Uruguay, 1828. Unrest caused by Tupamaro guerrillas in late 1960s and early 1970s; military rule until 1985. A President is advised by a Council of Ministers. Bicameral legislature consists of a Senate and Chamber of Deputies.

Head of State/Government
1984–90   Julio María Sanguinetti Cairolo
1990–   Luis Alberto Lacalle Herrera

Uzbekistan

USSR (FORMER) >> CIS, LATVIA, LITHUANIA, ESTONIA, GEORGIA

UZBEKISTAN

Local name Ozbekiston Republikasy

Timezone GMT + 5

Area 447 400 km²/172 696 sq mi

Population total (1992e) 20 300 000

Status Republic

Date of independence 1991

Capital Tashkent

Language Uzbek

Ethnic groups Uzbek (71%), Russian (8%), Tajik (5%), Kazakh (4%)

Religion Sunni Muslim

Physical features Located in C and N Middle Asia. Four-fifths of area is flat, sandy plain/desert (W); Turan Plain (NW) rises near the Aral Sea to 90 m/ 300 ft above sea level; delta of major river R Amu Darya forms alluvial plain over C Kara-Kalpak. Sultan-Uizdag Mts rise to 500 m/1 600 ft; Kyzyl Kum broken by hills in SE; lowest point, Mynbulak, −12 m/−39 ft; Pskem Mts in E rise to 4 299 m/14 104 ft at Beshtor Peak.

Climate Dry and continental. Average annual temperatures in S, −12°C (Jan), 32–40°C (Jul); low rainfall.

Currency Rouble (R)

Economy Deposits of coal, natural gas, oil, gold, lead, copper, and zinc. Third largest cotton-growing area in the world; silk, wool. Agriculture dependent on irrigated land; abundant orchards and vineyards. Industry powered hydroelectrically.

GDP Not available

History Conquered by Alexander the Great in 4th-c BC; invaded by Mongols under Genghis Khan, 13th-c; Genghis Khan's grandson, Shibaqan, inherited the area.

Converted to Islam in 14th-c, under the ruler of Kipchak, Uzbek; became part of Tamerlane the Great's empire, 16th-c. Conquered by Russia, mid-19th-c; became the Uzbek Republic in 1924, and Uzbekistan Soviet Socialist Republic in 1925. Declared independence, 1991, and President Karimov resigned after supporting coup against Gorbachev; Communist party outlawed; joined CIS in 1991; Karimov elected President, with restricted opposition. Highest legislative body, 500-seat Supreme Soviet. New constitution adopted in 1992.

Head of State
1991–   Islam A Karimov

Head of Government
1991–   Abdulhashim Mutalov

VANUATU

Local name Ripablik Blong Vanuatu

Timezone GMT + 11

Area 14 763 km²/5 698 sq mi

Population total (1992e) 154 000

Status Independent republic within the Commonwealth

Date of independence 1980

Capital Port Vila (on Efate Island)

Languages Bislama, English, and French (official)

Ethnic groups Melanesian (95%), Micronesian, Polynesian, and European minorities

Religions Christian (70%) (Presbyterian 40%, Roman Catholic 15%, Anglican 15%), indigenous beliefs (8%), other (15%)

Physical features Mountainous, volcanic Y-shaped island chain in SW Pacific Ocean, 400 km/250 mi NE of New Caledonia. Consisting of 12 islands and 60 islets; two-thirds of population occupy the 4 main islands of Efate, Espiritu Santo, Malekula, and Tanna. Highest peak, rises to 1 888 m/6 194 ft, on Espiritu Santo. Islands comprise raised coral beaches fringed by reefs. Several active volcanoes.

Climate Tropical, high temperatures; hot and rainy season (Nov–Apr) when cyclones may occur. Average annual temperatures, 27°C (Jan), 22°C (Jul) in Vila; average annual rainfall 2 103 mm/83 in.

Currency 1 Vatu (VT) = 100 centimes

Economy Agriculture; subsistence farming and plantations. Yams, breadfruit, taro, copra, beef, cocoa, coffee, timber; manganese, fish processing, foodstuffs, crafts. Tourism rapidly increasing, especially from cruise ships.

GDP (1989e) $137 m, per capita $860

Human geography

History Visited by the Spanish in 1606; charted and named the New Hebrides by British explorer James Cook, 1774; under Anglo-French administration as the condominium of the New Hebrides, 1906. Escaped Japanese occupation during World War 2. Independence as the Republic of Vanuatu, 1980. Governed by a President, Prime Minister, and a Cabinet, and a representative Assembly.

Head of State

1989– Frederick Karlomuana Timakata

Head of Government

1980–91 Walter Lini
1991 Donald Kalpokas
1991– Maxime Carlot

Map >> SOLOMON ISLANDS

VATICAN CITY STATE

Local name Stato della Città del Vaticano

Timezone GMT + 1

Area 0.44 km²/0.17 sq mi

Population total (1991e) 1000

Status Papal sovereign state

Date of independence 1929

Capital The Holy See, Vatican City

Languages Latin and Italian

Ethnic groups Italian, European, and various minorities

Religion Roman Catholic

Physical features The world's smallest state, situated on the Vatican hill in Rome, on W bank of R Tiber. Architectural features include the Vatican Palace and Museum, St Peter's, the Pope's summer villa at Castel Gandolfo, and the Sistine Chapel. Three entrances to the city in the care of the Pontifical Swiss Guard, 'The Bronze Doors', the Arch of Charlemagne, or the 'Arch of Bells', and the Via di Porta Angelica.

Climate Mediterranean; average annual temperature 7°C (Jan), 25°C (Jul); average annual rainfall 657 mm/26 in.

Currency 1 Vatican Lira (L, Lit) = 100 centesimi

Economy The state is supported by special collections and donations from Catholic congregations around the world; issues its own stamps and coinage, and has own communications and banking systems; tourism; pilgrimages.

Income (1991) income $109 m, expenses $196 m

History Papacy's temporal authority exercised from a palace built on Rome's Vatican hill in 1377; extended to much of central Italy by 16th-c; incorporated into the emerging Italian state during the fight to unite Italy, 1860–70. The Lateran Treaty of 1929 recognized the Holy See's sovereignty in the Vatican City State and Catholicism became Italy's state religion. Karol Wojtyla became the first non-Italian pontiff since the 16th-c in 1978; in 1985, a concordat, replacing the Lateran Treaty, affirmed independence of the Vatican, but ended some of its privileges, Roman Catholicism ceased to be the state religion, and Rome lost its status as a 'sacred city'. Sovereignty exercised by Pope, who is elected for life by a conclave of the College of Cardinals.

Head of State (Sovereign Pontiff/Pope)
1978– Pope John Paul II (Karol Wojtyla)

Head of Government (Secretary of State)
1990– Cardinal Angelo Sodano

Map >> ITALY

VENEZUELA

Local name República de Venezuela

Timezone GMT – 4

Area 912 050 km²/352 051 sq mi

Population total (1992e) 20 185 000

Status Republic

Date of independence 1830

Capital Caracas

Languages Spanish (official), Italian, c.25 Indian languages also spoken in the interior

Ethnic groups Mestizo (69%), European (20%), African origin (9%), Indian (2%)

Religions Roman Catholic (96%), Protestant (2%)

Physical features Occupies most of the N coast of S America. Guiana Highlands (SE) cover almost half the country; Venezuelan Highlands in the W and along the coast, highest point, Pico Bolívar 5 007 m/16 411 ft. Vast grasslands (*Llanos*) in the Orinoco basin. Chief river, Orinoco; largest lake in S America, L Maracaibo, 21 486 km²/

Venezuela (continued)

8 296 sq mi. Highest waterfall in the world, Angel Falls 979 m/3 212 ft.

Climate Tropical, generally hot and humid. Average annual temperatures 18°C (Jan), 21°C (Jul) in Caracas; one rainy season (Apr–Oct); average annual rainfall 833 mm/33 in.

Currency 1 Bolívar (B) = 100 céntimos

Economy Since 1920s, based on oil from Maracaibo (now provides over 90% of export revenue). Aluminium (second-highest source of revenue). Iron ore, gold, diamonds. Only 4% of the land is under permanent cultivation; beef and dairy farming; coffee, cocoa, cotton, rice, tobacco, sugar.

GDP (1990e) $42.4 bn, per capita $2 150

History Originally inhabited by Caribs and Arawaks. Seen by Columbus in 1498. Spanish settlers, 1520; frequent revolts against Spanish colonial rule. Independence movement under Simón Bolívar, leading to the establishment of the State of Gran Colombia (Colombia, Ecuador, Venezuela), 1821; independent republic in 1830. Governed by an elected bicameral National Congress, comprising a Senate and a Chamber of Deputies; a President is advised by a Council of Ministers.

Head of State/Government
1989–93   Carlos Andrés Pérez
1993   Ramon José Velásquez *Iterim*
1993–   Rafael Caldera Rodríguez

VIETNAM

Local name Công Hòa Xã Hôi Chu Nghĩa Viêt Nam (Vietnamese)

Timezone GMT + 7

Area 329 566 km²/127 212 sq mi

Population total (1992e) 69 200 000

Status Socialist republic

Date of independence 1976

Capital Hanoi

Languages Vietnamese (official), French, Chinese, English, Khmer

Ethnic groups Vietnamese (85–90%), Chinese (3%), various minorities include Khmer, Cham, Hmong, Nung, and Tay, local dialects

Religions Buddhist (principal), Taoist, Confucian, Muslim, Roman Catholic, Hoa Hoa, Cao Dai, Protestant, and animist beliefs

Physical features Occupies a narrow strip along the coast of the Gulf of Tongking and the S China Sea on Indochinese peninsula in SE Asia. Highest peak Fan-si-Pan, 3 143 m/10 312 ft; Mekong R delta (S) and Red R delta (N) linked by narrow coastal plain. Heavily forested mountains and plateaux.

Climate Tropical, monsoon climate; sub-tropical in N. Average annual temperatures 17°C (Jan), 29°C (Jul) in Hanoi; average annual rainfall 1 830 mm/72 in; typhoons and flooding frequent in N and SW.

Currency 1 Dông = 10 hao = 100 xu

Economy Agriculture (employs over 70% of the workforce); however, natural disasters, war, and political unrest have adversely affected economy. Vietnam War brought depopulation of the countryside and considerable destruction of forest and farmland. Exports include coal, minerals, rice, rubber, sugar cane.

GNP (1990e) $15.2 bn, per capita $230

History Under the influence of China for many centuries. Regions of Tongking (N), Annam (C), and Cochin-China (S) united as Vietnamese Empire in 1802; French protectorates established in Cochin-China, 1867, and in

Annam and Tongking in 1884; formed the French Indo-Chinese Union with Cambodia and Laos in 1887. Occupied by the Japanese in World War 2; communist Viet-Minh League under Ho Chi Minh formed after the War, not recognized by France; Indo-Chinese war, resulting in French withdrawal, 1946–54; 1954 armistice divided the country between the communist 'Democratic Republic' in the N, and the 'State' of Vietnam in the S. Civil war led to US intervention on the side of S Vietnam in 1965. Fall of Saigon, 1975; reunification as the Socialist Republic of Vietnam, 1976; large numbers of refugees tried to find homes in the W in the late 1970s; Hanoi invaded neighbouring Cambodia, overthrowing hostile Khmer Rouge government, 1978; Chinese responded with invasion of Vietnam in 1979 - greatly increased the number trying to leave the country by sea (Vietnamese boat people). In 1984, Hanoi agreed to talks with US about whereabouts of missing US servicemen. Limited troop withdrawals from Laos and Cambodia, 1989; Vietnam supported Cambodian peace agreement, 1991. New constitution, 1992, replaced Council of Ministers with a Prime Minister and a Cabinet.

Head of State

1986–91	Nguyen Van Linh
1991–2	Do Muoi
1992–	Le Duc Anh

Head of Government

1988–91	Do Muoi
1991–	Vo Van Kiet

VIRGIN ISLANDS, BRITISH >> UNITED KINGDOM

VIRGIN ISLANDS, US >> UNITED STATES OF AMERICA

WALLIS AND FUTUNA >> FRANCE

WESTERN SAHARA >> MOROCCO

WESTERN SAHARA

Timezone GMT

Area 252 126 km²/97 321 sq mi

Population total (1992e) 200 000

Status Under dispute, still officially part of Morocco

Capital Ad Dakhla

Languages Arabic (Hassaniya and Moroccan), French, Berber dialects, Spanish

Ethnic groups Mainly of Arab and Berber descent

Religion Sunni Muslim

Physical features Located in NW Africa, between Morocco (N), Mauritania (S), and Atlantic Ocean (E); low, flat terrain rising to small mountains in S and NE.

Climate Hot, dry desert; limited rainfall; fog and heavy dew produced by cold offshore currents.

Currency 1 Moroccan Dirham (DH) = 100 Moroccan francs

Economy Limited by low rainfall and few natural resources. Fishing and phosphate mining are main sources of income.

GDP Not available

History Spanish province known as Spanish Sahara (Western Sahara) since 1884. Partitioned by Morocco and Mauritania after its Spanish status ended in 1975; independence proclaimed in 1976, as Saharan Arab Democratic Republic (SADR); Morocco refused to withdraw its claim to the region, resulting in fighting between Morocco and Polisario guerrillas; Mauritania withdrew its claim after signing a peace treaty with the Polisario Front in 1979; SADR admitted to the Organization of African Unity, 1982. UN-supervised talks to decide the region's future began in 1990; Polisario guerrilla warfare stopped under UN ceasefire, Sep 1991. Renewed fighting in Feb 1993; UN Security Council approved referendum to determine the country's political future, scheduled end 1993. UN Secretary-General visited for self-determination talks during May-Jun 1993.

Main SADR government leaders [a]

Head of State
Mohammed Abdelazziz

Head of Government
Mahfoud Ali Beiba

[a]Officially administered by Morocco and the Moroccan government.

Map >> MOROCCO

WESTERN SAMOA

Local name Samoa i Sisifo (Samoan)

Timezone GMT – 11

Area 2 842 km²/1 097 sq mi

Population total (1992e) 190 000

Status Independent state within the Commonwealth

Date of independence 1962

Capital Apia

Languages Samoan and English (official)

Ethnic groups Polynesian, with Pacific Islanders, Euronesian, Chinese, and European minorities

Religions Christian (99%) (Protestant 70%, Roman Catholic 20%, other 9%)

Physical features Two large (Upolu, Savai'i) and seven small islands in the South Pacific Ocean, 2 600 km/ 1 600 mi NE of Auckland, New Zealand. Formed from ranges of extinct volcanoes, rising to 1 829 m/6 001 ft on Savai'i; last volcanic activity, 1905–11. Thick tropical vegetation; several coral reefs along coast.

Climate Tropical climate; cool, dry season (May–Nov), average temperature 22°C; rainy season (Dec–Apr) with temperatures reaching 36°C; average annual rainfall, 2 775 mm/109 in; frequent hurricanes.

Currency 1 Tala (WS$) = 100 sene

Human geography

Western Samoa (continued)

Economy Largely agricultural subsistence economy; taro, yams, breadfruit, pawpaws, coconuts, cocoa, bananas. Tourism increasing. Internal transportation system depends largely on roads and ferries. Charter air service operates between the two main islands.

GDP (1990e) $115 m, per capita $620

History Visited by the Dutch in 1772; 1889 commission divided Samoa between Germany (which acquired Western Samoa) and the US (which acquired Tutuila and adjacent small islands, now known as American Samoa); New Zealand granted a League of Nations mandate for Samoa, 1919. UN Trust Territory under New Zealand, 1946. Independence in 1962. Became a member of the Commonwealth in 1970. Governed by a Monarch as Head of State for life, a Prime Minister, and a 47-member Legislative Assembly (Fono).

Head of State (O le Ao O le Malo)
1963–   Malietoa Tanumafili II

Head of Government
1988–   Tofilau Eti Alesana

YEMEN

Local name Al-Yaman (Arabic)

Timezone GMT + 3

Area 531 570 km²/205 186 sq mi

Population total (1992e) 12 150 000

Status Republic

Date of independence 1967

Capitals Sana (political), Aden (commercial)

Languages Arabic (official), English

Ethnic groups Arab (96%), with Indo-Pakistani, Somali, Amhara and Swahili, Persian, Jewish, and European minorities

Religions Muslim (Sunni 53%, Shiite 47%), small Christian, Hindu, and Yemeni Jew minorities

Physical features Occupies the SW corner of the Arabian peninsula. Narrow coastal plain, backed by mountains rising to 3 000–3 500 m/10 000–11 500 ft; highlands, central plateau and maritime range of former South Yemen form the most fertile part of the country. Former North Yemen is largely desert and mountainous.

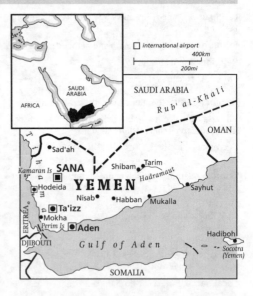

Climate Hot and humid climate; lowland and desert regions in NE receive an average annual rainfall of 100 mm/ 4 in; hot and humid on Tihamat coastal strip with mean temperature of 29°C; mild and temperate in interior highlands, with cool winters. Average annual temperatures 25°C (Jan), 32°C (Jul) in Aden; average annual rainfall, 46 mm/1.8 in.

Currency 1 Yemeni Riyal (YR, YRI) = 100 fils (former N Yemen)
1 Yemeni Dinar (YD) = 1 000 fils (1 Dinar = 26 Riyals) (former S Yemen)

Economy Based on agriculture (largely subsistence) and light industry; cotton has overtaken coffee as chief cash crop. Irrigation schemes likely to increase area under cultivation. Qat, a narcotic leaf, now a major enterprise. Hides, vegetables, dried fish. Crude- and refined-oil industry. Textiles, cement, aluminium, salt.

GDP (1990e) $5.3 bn, per capita $545

History Part of the Minaean kingdom from 1200–650 BC; converted to Islam in 7th-c; Turkish occupation, 1538–1630 and 1872–1918; between and after Turkish rule, Yemen under the rule of the Hamid al-Din dynasty. Sovereignty of Yemen acknowledged by Saudi Arabia and Britain in 1934. Joined Arab League in 1945. Egypt-backed revolution in 1962, resulting in civil war; Yemen Arab Republic (North Yemen) declared, 1962; royalists defeated, 1969. Neighbouring People's Republic of South Yemen established, 1967, when Britain ended 129 years of rule in Aden and the Marxist National Liberation Front took over; the People's Republic comprised Aden and 16 of the 20 protectorate states once under British control; renamed People's Democratic Republic of Yemen in 1970. Negotiations to merge the two Yemens began in 1979; unification was proclaimed and ratified in 1990; new state called Republic of Yemen. Former President of North Yemen was declared President of the unified state, and the former President of South Yemen became Prime Minister. Supported Iraq during Gulf War of 1991. Elections scheduled for Nov 1992 postponed until Apr 1993. Coalition government formed in May 1993. Governed by a president, a Prime Minister, a House of Representatives and an Advisory Council.

Head of State

1990–   Ali Abdullah Saleh

Head of Government

1990–   Haider Abu Bakr al-Attas

YUGOSLAVIA

Local name Jugoslavija

Timezone GMT + 2

Area Prior to 1991: 256 409 km²/98 974 sq mi
Since 1991: 102 173 km²/39 438 sq mi (comprising the states of Montenegro and Serbia)

Population total Prior to 1991: 23 860 000
Since 1991: (1992e) 10 400 000 (comprising the states of Montenegro and Serbia)

Status Federal Republic

Date of independence Now comprises the republics of Serbia and Montenegro. Formerly (to 1991) a federation of six republics (additionally, Bosnia and Herzegovina, Croatia, Macedonia, Slovenia) formerly united in 1918 as an independent Federal Republic

Capital Belgrade (Serbia)

Languages Serbo-Croat, with Albanian and Hungarian also spoken

Ethnic groups Prior to 1991: Serbian (36%), Croatian (20%), Bosnian (10%), Slovene (8%), Albanian (8%), Macedonian (6%), Montenegrin (3%), other (9%)
Since 1991: continuing civil war prevents accurate recording of ethnic group data

Religions Prior to 1991: Serbian Orthodox (41%), Roman Catholic (32%), other Christian (11%), Muslim (10%)
Since 1991: continuing civil war prevents accurate recording of religious groups

Physical features Mountainous country with fertile valleys. Julian and Karawanken Alps rise (N) to 2 863 m/ 9 393 ft at Triglav; Adriatic fringed by the Dinaric Alps; fertile Danubian plain in NE Serbia. Chief river, R Danube, also the Tisza, Drava, Sava, and Morava. Limestone karst plateaux in W along coast.

Climate Moderate, continental climate. Average annual temperatures 0°C (Jan), 22°C (Jul) in Belgrade; average annual rainfall 610 mm/24 in.

Currency 1 Yugoslav Dinar (D, Din) = 100 paras

Economy Ongoing conflict and escalating violence has crippled the economy of the countries involved. Formerly agriculture; corn, wheat, tobacco, sugar beets. Mining and manufacturing industries. Exports of textiles, leather goods, machinery. Natural resources of copper, coal, timber, iron, lead, zinc, bauxite.

GNP Prior to 1991: (1990e) $120.1 bn, per capita $5 040
Since 1991: not available

History Serbs, Croats, and Slovenes united under one monarch in 1918; formation of new state did not quell long-held nationalist feelings; in an attempt to create a sense of common patriotism King Alexander changed the kingdom's name to Yugoslavia in 1929. Civil war between Serbian royalists (Chetniks), Croatian nationalists, and Communists. Occupied by Germany in World War 2; Federal People's Republic established under Tito, 1945. Revised constitution in 1974, instituted a rotating leadership, with the Prime Minister elected annually. Governed by a bicameral Federal Assembly, comprising a Federal Chamber and a Chamber of Republics and Provinces. Following a break with the USSR in 1948, the country followed an independent form of communism and a general policy of non-alignment. At the end of the 1980s political disagreement between the federal republics increased; ethnic unrest in Serbia (Kosovo); Slovenian unilateral declaration of independence, 1990, followed by Macedonian and Croatian declarations, 1991, considered illegal by central government; inter-republic talks on Yugoslavia's future, but confrontation between Croatia and Serb-dominated National Army developed into civil war, 1991. Serbian support of Serb guerrillas in Bosnia resulted in UN sanctions, mid-1992;

Human geography

Yugoslavia (continued)

arrival of UN Protection Force in 1992; Federal Republic of Yugoslavia declared in 1992, consisting of only two of the six republics that made up former Yugoslavia, Montenegro and Serbia. The new state remains unrecognized due to continuing fighting; failure of the Vance-Owen Peace Plan, 1993, leading to increasing uncertainty about the future of a residual Yugoslavia. >> BOSNIA AND HERZEGOVINA, CROATIA, MACEDONIA, SLOVENIA

Head of State

1989–90	Janez Drnovsek
1990–1	Borisav Jovic
1991–2	Stipe Mesic
1992–3	Dobrica Cosic
1993	Milos Radulovic (*Acting*)
1993–	Zoran Lilic

Head of Government

1989–91	Ante Markovic
1991–3	Milan Panic
1993–	Radoje Kontic

ZAÏRE

Local name République du Zaïre

Timezone GMT + 1 (W) to + 2 (E)

Area 2 234 585 km²/905 365 sq mi

Population total (1992e) 37 900 000

Status Republic

Date of independence 1960

Capital Kinshasa

Languages French (official), English, with various Bantu dialects (including Swahili, Lingala, Ishiluba, and Kikongo) spoken

Ethnic groups Bantu, with Sudanese, Nilotes, Pygmies, Hamite and Angolan minorities

Religions Christian (70%) (Roman Catholic 50%, Protestant 20%), Kimbanguist (10%), Muslim (10%), traditional beliefs (10%)

Physical features Located in C Africa, land rises E from a low-lying basin to a densely forested plateau. Ruwenzori Mts (NE) rise to 5 110 m/16 765 ft in the Mt Stanley massif; Mitumba Mts further S. Rift Valley chain of lakes, Albert, Edward, Kivu, and Tanganyika; Zaïre R.

Climate Equatorial, hot and humid. Average annual temperature, 26°C (Jan), 23°C (Jul) in Kinshasa; average annual rainfall 1 125 mm/44 in; dry coastal region; dry season (May–Sep) S of the Equator, (Dec–Feb) N of the Equator.

Currency 1 Zaïre (Z) = 100 makuta (singular likuta)

Economy Subsistence farming employs c.80% of population; palm oil, rubber, quinine, fruit, vegetables, tea, cocoa. Extensive mineral reserves. World's biggest producer of cobalt. Industrial diamonds, copper; coffee, petroleum, cotton, tobacco processing, chemicals, cement.

GDP (1990e) $6.6 bn, per capita $180

History Visited by the Portuguese in 1482. Expeditions of Henry Morton Stanley, 1874–7; claimed by King Leopold of Belgium, recognized, 1885; Congo Free State ceded to the state, 1907 and renamed Belgian Congo. Independence as the Democratic Republic of the Congo in 1960; shortly after, mineral-rich Katanga (later, Shaba) province claimed independence, leading to civil war; UN peace-keeping force present until 1964. Renamed the

1 Lake Albert
2 Lake Edward
3 Lake Kivu

Republic of Zaïre in 1971. Further conflict, 1977–8, as Katangese rebels invaded Shaba province from Angola. President Mobutu announced proposals for the introduction of a new constitution in 1990, including the adoption of a three-party system; dissatisfaction with proposals resulted in boycotting of elections scheduled for 1992. Controversial changes to constitution in Apr 1993 gave president power to appoint the Prime Minister. Birindwa appointed in Mar 1993; ensuing conflict; EC refused to acknowledge Birindwa's premiership, Apr 1993. UN intervention requested; UN mission sent in May 1993; continuing unrest.

Head of State

1965–	Mobutu Sese Seko (formerly Joseph Mobutu)

Head of Government

1989–91	Lunda Bululu
1991	Mulumba Lukeji
1991	Etienne Tshisekedi
1991	Bernardin Mungul Diaka
1991–2	Jean Nguza Karl-I-Bond
1992–3	Etienne Tshisekedi
1993–	Fouistin Birindwa (*Acting*)

ZAMBIA

Local name Zambia

Timezone GMT + 2

Area 752 613 km²/290 586 sq mi

Population total (1992e) 8 400 000

Status Independent republic within the Commonwealth

Date of independence 1964

Capital Lusaka

Languages English (official), with c.70 local languages (including Tonga, Kaonde, Lunda, and Luvale) also spoken

Ethnic groups Bantu (99%), including Bemba Nyanja, Barotse, Mambwe, and Swahili peoples

Religions Christian (75%), local beliefs (23%), Muslim and Hindu (1%)

Physical features High plateau in SC Africa, altitude 1 000–1 400 m/3 300–4 600 ft; highest point, 2 067 m/6 781 ft, SE of Mbala. A number of rivers drain southwards to join Zambezi R in N, including R Luangwa. Highest waterfall, Kalambo Falls, 221 m/726 ft. Man-made L Kariba in S, 440 km²/170 sq mi.

Climate Warm temperate climate on plateau; tropical in lower valleys; although in C Africa and subequatorial, protected from very high temperatures by altitude. Three distinct seasons, hot, dry (Aug–Oct), warm, wet (Nov–Apr), dry, cool (May–Jul). Average annual temperatures, 21°C (Jan), 16°C (Jul) in Lusaka. Average annual rainfall 836 mm/33 in.

Currency 1 Kwacha (K) = 100 ngwee

Economy Based on copper and cobalt, (provide over 50% of national income); lead, zinc, tobacco, coal, copper, cobalt. Corn, tobacco, rice, sugar cane, groundnuts, cotton. Sugar refining, glassware, tyres, brewing, oil refining.

GDP (1990) $4.7 bn, per capita $580

History European influence followed Livingstone's discovery of the Victoria Falls in 1855. Administered by the British South Africa Company under Rhodes; Northern and Southern Rhodesia declared a British sphere of influence, 1889–90; became Northern Rhodesia, 1911. British protectorate in 1924. Joined with Southern Rhodesia and Nyasaland as the Federation of Rhodesia and Nyasaland, 1953; Federation dissolved, 1963. Independence as the Republic of Zambia in 1964. President has executive power and legislative power is held by 125-member National Assembly. New multi-party constitution adopted in 1991.

Head of State (President)
1964–91   Kenneth Kaunda
1991–   Frederick Chiluba

Head of Government (Vice-President)
1989–91   Malimba Masheke
1991–   Levy Mwanawasa

ZIMBABWE

Local name Zimbabwe

Timezone GMT + 2

Area 390 759 km²/150 873 sq mi

Population total (1992e) 10 300 000

Status Independent republic within the Commonwealth

Date of independence 1980

Capital Harare

Languages English (official), Ndebele and Shona widely spoken

Ethnic groups Bantu (97%) (including Shona 71%, Ndebele 16%), European (2%)

Religions Syncretic Christian/local beliefs (50%), Christian (25%), traditional animist beliefs (24%), small Muslim minority

Physical features Landlocked country in SC Africa; mostly savannah (tropical grassland). Highveld ridge crosses SW to NE to join the Inyanga Mts on Mozambique border, highest point, Mt Inyangani, 2 592 m/8 504 ft; Highveld flanked by lower plateau, Middleveld; Lowveld, altitude, 300 m/1 000 ft, lies NE. Tropical hardwood forests (SE). Chief rivers, Zambezi, Limpopo, and Sabi.

Climate Subtropical climate, strongly influenced by altitude. Average annual temperature 21°C (Jan), 14°C (Jul) in Harare; average annual rainfall 828 mm/33 in; rainfall increases from SW to NE; wet season (Nov–Mar).

Currency 1 Zimbabwe Dollar (Z$) = 100 cents

Human geography

Zimbabwe (continued)

Economy Agriculture (involves 70% of population), manufacturing and mining; sugar, cotton, livestock. Natural resources, gold, copper, chrome, nickel, tin, asbestos. Tourism to national parks. Major industries in steel, textiles, vehicles, and chemicals.

GDP (1990e) $5.6 bn, per capita $540

History Mediaeval Bantu kingdom during 12–16th-c, with capital at Great Zimbabwe. Visited by Livingstone in the 1850s; Southern Rhodesia under British influence in the 1880s as the British South Africa Company under Cecil Rhodes. Divided into Northern and Southern Rhodesia in 1911. Southern Rhodesia became a self-governing British colony, 1923. Northern and Southern Rhodesia and Nyasaland formed a multi-racial federation, 1953. Independence of Nyasaland and Northern Rhodesia in 1963; opposition to the independence of Southern Rhodesia under African rule resulted in a Unilateral Declaration of Independence (UDI) by the White-dominated government, 1965. Economic sanctions and internal guerrilla activity forced the government to negotiate with the main African groups: the Zimbabwe African People's Union (ZAPU), led by Joshua Nkomo, the Zimbabwe African National Union (ZANU), led by Robert Mugabe, and the United African National Council (UANC), led by Bishop Abel Muzorewa. Independence as the Republic of Zimbabwe in 1980. Since 1987, the post of executive President has combined the posts of Head of State and Head of Government. Bicameral legislature replaced, 1990, by new single-chamber Parliament, the House of Assembly.

Head of State/Government
1987–   Robert Gabriel Mugabe

SOCIETY

ANTHROPOLOGY

Nations of the world: general data

In the case of countries that do not use the Roman alphabet (such as the Arabic countries), there is variation in the spelling of names and currencies, depending on the system of transliteration used.

Where more than one language is shown with a country, the status of the languages may not be equal. Some languages have a 'semi-official' status, or are used for a restricted set of purposes, such as trade or tourism.

Population census estimates are for 1990 or later.

English name	Local name	Official name (in English)	Capital (English name in parentheses)	Language(s)	Currency	Population
Afghanistan	Afghānestān	Republic of Afghanistan	Kabul	Dari, Pushtu	1 Afghani (Af) = 100 puls	18 052 000
Albania	Shqipëri	Republic of Albania	Tiranë (Tirana)	Albanian	1 Lek (L) = 100 qintars	3 262 000
Algeria	Al-Jazā'ir (Arabic); Algérie (French)	Democratic and Popular Republic of Algeria	El Djazaïr (Algiers)	Arabic	1 Algerian Dinar (AD DA) = 100 centimes	26 400 000
Andorra	Andorra	Principality of Andorra; the Valleys of Andorra	Andorra La Vella	Catalan	1 French Franc (Fr) = 100 centimes; 1 Peseta (Pta) = 100 céntimos	54 507
Angola	Angola	People's Republic of Angola	Luanda	Portuguese	1 New Kwanza (kw, kz) = 100 lwei	10 301 000
Antigua and Barbuda	Antigua and Barbuda	Antigua and Barbuda	St John's	English	1 East Caribbean Dollar (EC$) = 100 cents	63 880
Argentina	Argentina	Argentine Republic	Buenos Aires	Spanish	1 Peso (A) = 100 centavos	32 646 000
Armenia	Armenia	Republic of Armenia	Yerevan	Armenian	1 Rouble (R) = 100 kopecks	3 500 000
Australia	Australia	Commonwealth of Australia	Canberra	English	1 Australian Dollar ($A) = 100 cents	17 807 000
Austria	Österreich	Republic of Austria	Vienna	German	1 Schilling (S, Sch) = 100 Groschen	7 812 000
Azerbaijan	Azerbaijan	Republic of Azerbaijan	Baku	Azerbaijani	1 Dram (Drm) = 100 louma	7 236 000
Bahamas	Bahamas	Commonwealth of the Bahamas	Nassau	English	1 Bahamian Dollar (BA$, B$) = 100 cents	254 685
Bahrain	Al-Bahrayn	State of Bahrain	Al-Manāmah (Manama)	Arabic	1 Bahrain Dinar (BD) = 1000 fils	531 000
Bangladesh	Bangladesh	People's Republic of Bangladesh	Dhaka (Dacca)	Bengali	1 Taka (TK) = 100 paisa	110 602 000
Barbados	Barbados	Barbados	Bridgetown	English	1 Barbados Dollar (Bds$) = 100 cents	258 000
Belarus	Belarus	Republic of Belarus	Mensk (Minsk)	Belorussian, Russian	1 Belorus rouble = 100 kopecks	10 300 000
Belgium	Belgique (French); België (Flemish)	Kingdom of Belgium	Bruxelles (Brussels)	Flemish, French, German	1 Belgian Franc (BFr) = 100 centimes	9 978 681
Belize	Belize	Belize	Belmopan	English	1 Belize Dollar (Bz$) = 100 cents	196 000
Benin	Bénin	Republic of Benin	Porto-Novo	French	1 CFA Franc (CFAFr) = 100 centimes	4 630 000
Bhutan	Druk-Yul	Kingdom of Bhutan	Thimphu/Thimpu	Dzongkha	1 Ngultrum (Nu) = 100 chetrum	1 511 000
Bolivia	Bolivia	Republic of Bolivia	La Paz/Sucre	Spanish, Aymara, Quechua	1 Boliviano (Bs) = 100 centavos	7 356 000
Bosnia-Herzegovina	Bosnia i Hercegovina	Republic of Bosnia-Herzegovina	Sarajevo	Serbo-Croat	1 Dinar (D, din) = 100 paras	4 364 574
Botswana	Botswana	Republic of Botswana	Gaborone	English, Setswana	1 Pula (P, Pu) = 100 thebes	1 347 000

	Brazil	State of Brunei, Abode of Peace			1 Cruzeiro (US$) = 100 centavos	268 000
Brunei	Brunei Darussalam	State of Brunei, Abode of Peace	Bandar Seri Begawan	Malay, English	1 Brunei Dollar (Br$) = 100 cents	268 000
Bulgaria	Bălgarija	Republic of Bulgaria	Sofija (Sofia)	Bulgarian	1 Lev (Lv) = 100 stotinki	8 990 000
Burkina Faso	Burkina Faso	Burkina Faso	Ouagadougou	French	1 CFA Franc (CFAFr) = 100 centimes	8 776 000
Burma see Myanmar						
Burundi	Burundi	Republic of Burundi	Bujumbura	French, (Ki) Rundi	1 Burundi Franc (BuFr, FBu) = 100 centimes	5 472 000
Cambodia	Cambodia	State of Cambodia	Phnum Pénh (Phnom Penh)	Khmer	1 Riel (CRl) = 100 sen	8 974 000
Cameroon	Cameroun	Republic of Cameroon	Yaoundé	English, French	1 CFA Franc (CFAFr) = 100 centimes	11 933 000
Canada	Canada	Canada	Ottawa	English, French	1 Canadian Dollar (C$, Can$) = 100 cents	27 296 859
Cape Verde	Cabo Verde	Republic of Cape Verde	Praia	Portuguese	1 Escudo (CVEsc) = 100 centavos	369 000
Central African Republic	République Centrafricaine	Central African Republic	Bangui	French	1 CFA Franc (CFAFr) = 100 centimes	3 039 000
Chad	Tchad	Republic of Chad	N'djamena	Arabic, French	1 CFA Franc (CFAFr) = 100 centimes	5 678 000
Chile	Chile	Republic of Chile	Santiago	Spanish	1 Chilean Peso (Ch$) = 100 centavos	13 600 000
China	Zhongguo	People's Republic of China	Beijing/Peking	Mandarin Chinese	1 Renminbi Yuan (RMBY, $, Y) = 10 jiao = 100 fen	1 133 682 501
Colombia	Colombia	Republic of Colombia	Bogotá	Spanish	1 Colombian Peso (Col$) = 100 centavos	33 392 000
Comoros	Comores	Federal Islamic Republic of the Comoros	Moroni	Arabic, French	1 Comorian Franc (CFr) = 100 centimes	503 000
Congo	Congo	Republic of Congo	Brazzaville	French	1 CFA Franc (CFAFr) = 100 centimes	2 271 000
Costa Rica	Costa Rica	Republic of Costa Rica	San José	Spanish	1 Costa Rican Colón (CR¢) = 100 céntimos	3 160 000
Côte d'Ivoire (Ivory Coast)	Côte d'Ivoire	Republic of Côte d'Ivoire	Abidjan/Yamoussoukro	French	1 CFA Franc (CFAFr) = 100 centimes	12 100 000
Croatia	Croatia	Republic of Croatia	Zagreb	Serbo-Croat	1 Dinar (D, din) = 100 paras	4 600 000
Cuba	Cuba	Republic of Cuba	La Habana (Havana)	Spanish	1 Cuban Peso (Cub$) = 100 centavos	10 603 000
Cyprus	Kypros (Greek); Kibris (Turkish)	Republic of Cyprus	Lavkosia (Nicosia)	Greek, Turkish	1 Cyprus Pound (£C) = 100 cents	568 000
Czech Republic	Česká Republika	Czech Republic	Praha (Prague)	Czech	1 Koruna (Kčs) = 100 halér̆	15 605 000
Denmark	Danmark	Kingdom of Denmark	Kobenhavn (Copenhagen)	Danish	1 Danish Krone (Dkr) = 100 øre	5 146 469
Djibouti	Djibouti	Republic of Djibouti	Djibouti	Arabic, French	1 Djibouti Franc (DF, DjFr) = 100 centimes	541 000
Dominica	Dominica	Commonwealth of Dominica	Roseau	English	1 East Caribbean Dollar (EC$) = 100 cents	86 000
Dominican Republic	República Dominicana	Dominican Republic	Santo Domingo	Spanish	1 Dominican Peso (RD$, DR$) = 100 centavos	7 384 000

Society

Nations of the world: general data (continued)

English name	Local name	Official name (in English)	Capital (English name in parentheses)	Official language(s)	Currency	Population
Ecuador	Ecuador	Republic of Ecuador	Quito	Spanish	1 Sucre (Su, S/.) = 100 centavos	10 607 000
Egypt	Misr	Arab Republic of Egypt	Al-Qāhirah (Cairo)	Arabic	1 Egyptian Pound (E£, LE) = 100 piastres	55 980 000
El Salvador	El Salvador	Republic of El Salvador	San Salvador	Spanish	1 Colón (ES₵) = 100 centavos	5 460 000
Equatorial Guinea	Guinea Ecuatorial	Republic of Equatorial Guinea	Malabo	Spanish	1 CFA Franc (CFAFr) = 100 centimes	417 000
Eritrea	Eritrea	Eritrea	Asmara	Arabic, English	1 Ethiopian birr (Br) = 100 cents	3 500 000
Estonia	Eesti; Estonskaya (Russian)	Republic of Estonia	Tallinn	Estonian, Russian	1 Kroon (EEK) = 100 centts	1 600 000
Ethiopia	Ityopiya	People's Democratic Republic of Ethiopia	Adis Abeba (Addis Ababa)	Amharic	1 Ethiopian Birr (Br) = 100 cents	49 240 000
Federated states of Micronesia	Federated States of Micronesia	Federated States of Micronesia	Palikir, on Ponape	English	1 US Dollar (US $) = 100 cents	102 000
Fiji	Fiji	Sovereign Democratic Republic of Fiji	Suva	English	1 Fijiau Dollar (F$) = 100 cents	742 000
Finland	Suomi (Finnish); Finland (Swedish)	Republic of Finland	Helsingfors (Helsinki)	Finnish, Swedish	1 Markka (FMk) = 100 penni	5 029 002
France	France	Republic of France	Paris	French	1 French Franc (Fr) = 100 centimes	56 614 493
Gabon	Gabon	Gabonese Republic	Libreville	French	1 CFA Franc (CFAFr) = 100 centimes	1 172 000
Gambia, The	Gambia	Republic of the Gambia	Banjul	English	1 Dalasi (D, Di) = 100 butut	861 000
Georgia	Sakartvelos	Republic of Georgia	Tbilisi	Georgian, Armenian, Russian	1 Rouble (R) = 100 kopecks	5 400 000
Germany	Bundesrepublik Deutschland	Federal Republic of Germany	Berlin	German	1 Deutsche Mark (DM) = 100 pfennig	80 293 000
Ghana	Ghana	Republic of Ghana	Accra	English	1 Cedi (¢) = 100 pesewas	15 028 000
Greece	Ellás	Hellenic Republic	Athínai (Athens)	Greek	1 Drachma (Dr) = 100 lepta	10 264 156
Greenland	Kalâtdlit-Nunât Grønland (Danish)	Greenland	Nuuk	Greenlandic, Danish	1 Danish Krona (DKr) = 100 øre	55 533
Grenada	Grenada	Grenada	St George's	English	1 East Caribbean Dollar (EC$) = 100 cents	91 000
Guatemala	Guatemala	Republic of Guatemala	Guatemala City	Spanish	1 Quetzal (Q) = 100 centavos	9 718 000
Guinea	Guinée	Republic of Guinea	Conakry	French	1 Guinea Franc (GFr) = 100 cauris	5 755 000
Guinea-Bissau	Guiné-Bissau	Republic of Guinea-Bissau	Bissau	Portuguese	1 Guinea-Bissau Peso (GBP, PG) = 100 centavos	964 125
Guyana	Guyana	Co-operative Republic of Guyana	Georgetown	English	1 Guyana Dollar (G$) = 100 cents	750 000
Haiti	Haiti	Republic of Haiti	Port-au-Prince	Hatian Creole, French	1 Gourde (G, Gde) = 100 centimes	6 286 000
Holland see Netherlands, The						
Honduras	Honduras	Republic of Honduras	Tegucigalpa	Spanish	1 Lempira (L, La) = 100 centavos	5 105 000

Hong Kong	Xiang Kang (Cantonese); Hong Kong (English)	Hong Kong	none	English, Cantonese	1 Hong Kong Dollar (HK$) = 100 cents	5822000
Hungary	Magyarország	Republic of Hungary	Budapest	Magyar	1 Forint (Ft) = 100 fillér	10375000
Iceland	Ísland	Republic of Iceland	Reykjavík	Icelandic	1 Krónur (IKr, ISK) = 100 aurar	259000
India	Bhārat (Hindi)	Republic of India	New Delhi	Hindi, English	1 Indian Rupee (Re, Rs) = 100 paise	889700000
Indonesia	Indonesia	Republic of Indonesia	Jakarta	Bahasa Indonesia	1 Rupiah (Rp) = 100 sen	184796000
Iran	Īrān	Islamic Republic of Iran	Tehrān (Tehran)	Farsi	1 Iranian Rial (RIs, RI) = 100 dinars	59600000
Iraq	Al-'Irāq	Republic of Iraq	Baghdād (Baghdad)	Arabic	1 Iraqi Dinar (ID) = 1000 fils	18838000
Ireland	Éire (Gaelic); Ireland (English)	Republic of Ireland	Baile Átha Cliath (Dublin)	Irish, English	1 Irish Pound/Punt (I£, IR£) = 100 pence	3525719
Israel	Yisra'el (Hebrew); Isrā'īl (Arabic)	State of Israel	Yerushalayim (Jerusalem)	Hebrew, Arabic	1 New Israeli Shekel (NIS) = 100 agorot	5240000
Italy	Italia	Italian Republic	Roma (Rome)	Italian	1 Italian Lira (L, Lit) = 100 centesimi	57103833
Ivory Coast see Côte d'Ivoire						
Jamaica	Jamaica	Jamaica	Kingston	English	1 Jamaican Dollar (J$) = 100 cents	2445000
Japan	Nippon	Japan	Tōkyō (Tokyo)	Japanese	1 Yen (¥, Y) = 100 sen	123156678
Jordan	Al'Urdunn	Hashemite Kingdom of Jordan	'Ammān (Amman)	Arabic	1 Jordan Dinar = 1000 fils	3943000
Kampuchea see Cambodia						
Kazakhstan	Kazakhstan	Republic of Kazakhstan	Almaty (Alma-Ata)	Kazakh, Russian	Tenge	16700000
Kenya	Kenya	Republic of Kenya	Nairobi	Swahili, English	1 Kenyan shilling (KSh) = 100 cents	24031000
Kiribati	Kiribati	Republic of Kiribati	Tarawa	English, Gilbertese	1 Australian Dollar ($A) = 100 cents	71100
Korea, North	Choson Minjujuui In'min Konghwaguk	Democratic People's Republic of Korea	P'yongyang (Pyongyang)	Korean	1 Won (NKW) = 100 chon	22227000
Korea, South	Taehan-Min'guk	Republic of Korea	Soul (Seoul)	Korean	1 Won (W) = 100 chon	43663000
Kuwait	al-Kuwayt	State of Kuwait	al-Kuwayt (Kuwait City)	Arabic	1 Kuwaiti Dinar (KD) = 1000 fils	1200000
Kyrgyzstan	Kirgizstan	Republic of Kyrgyzstan	Bishek	Kyrgyz, Russian	1 Som (R) = 100 kopecks	4400000
Laos	Lao	Lao People's Deomocratic Republic	Viangchan (Vientiane)	Lao	1 Kip (Kp) = 100 at	4410000
Latvia	Latvija; Latviskaya (Russian)	Republic of Latvia	Riga	Latvian, Russian	1 Lat (Ls) = 100 santims	2700000
Lebanon	al-Lubnān	Republic of Lebanon	Bayrūt (Beirut)	Arabic	1 Lebanese Pound/Livre (LL, £L) = 100 piastres	2800000
Lesotho	Lesoto	Kingdom of Lesotho	Maseru	Sesotho, English	1 Loti (pl Maloti) (M, LSM) = 100 lisente	1774000
Liberia	Liberia	Republic of Liberia	Monrovia	English	1 Liberian Dollar (L$) = 100 cents	2575000
Libya	Lībiyā	Socialist People's Libyan Arab Jamahiriya	Tarābulus (Tripoli)	Arabic	1 Libyan Dinar (LD) = 1000 millemes	4450000
Liechtenstein	Liechtenstein	Principality of Liechtenstein	Vaduz	German	1 Swiss Franc (SFr, SwF) = 100 centimes	28777
Lithuania	Lietuva	Republic of Lithuania	Vilnius	Lithuanian, Russian	1 Litas (Lt) = 100 centas	3700000

Nations of the world: general data (continued)

English name	Local name	Official name (in English)	Capital (English name in parentheses)	Official language(s)	Currency	Population
Luxembourg	Lëtzebuerg; Luxemburg (French); Luxemburg (German)	Grand Duchy of Luxembourg	Luxembourg	French, German, Luxembourgish	1 Luxembourg Franc (FL, flux) = 100 centimes	389800
Macedonia, Former Yugoslav Republic of	Makedonija	Former Yugoslav Republic of Macedonia	Skopje	Macedonian	1 Dinar (D, Dn) = 100 paras	2 033 964
Madagascar	Madagasikara	Democratic Republic of Madagascar	Antananarivo	Malagasy, French	1 Malagasy Franc (FMG, MgFr) = 100 centimes	11440000
Malawi	Malaŵi	Republic of Malawi	Lilongwe	Chichewa, English	1 Kwacha (MK) = 100 tambala	8754000
Malaysia	Malaysia	Malaysia	Kuala Lumpur	Malay	1 Malaysian Dollar/Ringgit (M$) = 100 cents	18630000
Maldives	Maldive; Divehi Jumhuriya	Republic of Maldives	Malé	Dhivehi	1 Rufiyaa (MRf, Rf) = 100 laari	213000
Mali	Mali	Republic of Mali	Bamako	French	1 CFA Franc (CFAFr) = 100 centimes	9214000
Malta	Malta	Republic of Malta	Valletta	Maltese, English	1 Maltese pound (LM) = 100 cents	360000
Marshall Islands		Republic of the Marshall Islands	Dalap-Uliga-Darrit, on Majuro	Marshallese, (Kahjn-Majol)	1 US Dollar (US $) = 100 cents	49000
Mauritania	Mauritanie (French); Muritaniya (Arabic)	Islamic Republic of Mauritania	Nouakchott	Arabic	1 Ouguiya (U, UM) = 5 khoums	2100000
Mauritius	Mauritius	Mauritius	Port Louis	English	1 Mauritian Rupee (MR, MauRe) = 100 cents	1083000
Mexico	México	United Mexican States	Ciudad de México (Mexico City)	Spanish	1 Mexican Peso (Mex$) = 100 centavos	84 440 000
Moldova	Moldova	Republic of Moldova	Kishinev	Romanian, Moldovan	Leu	4341000
Monaco	Monaco	Principality of Monaco	Monaco	French	1 French Franc (F) = 100 centimes	29712
Mongolia	Mongol Ard Uls	Mongolian People's Republic	Ulaanbaatar (Ulan Bator)	Khalkha	1 Tugrik (Tug) = 100 möngös	2156300
Morocco	Al-Magrib	Kingdom of Morocco	Rabat	Arabic	1 Dirham (DH) = 100 centimes	26340000
Mozambique	Moçambique	Republic of Mozambique	Maputo	Portuguese	1 Metical (Mr, MZM) = 100 centavos	16110000
Myanmar	Pyidaungsu; Myanma Naingngandaw	Union of Myanmar	Yangón (Rangoon)	Burmese	1 Kyat (K) = 100 pyas	43466000
Namibia	Namibia	Republic of Namibia	Windhoek	English	1 South African Rand (R) = 100 cents	1781000
Nauru	Naeoro (Nauruan); Nauru (English)	Republic of Nauru	Yaren District	Nauruan, English	1 Australian Dollar ($A) = 100 cents	9333
Nepal	Nepāl	Kingdom of Nepal	Kathmandu	Nepali	1 Nepalese Rupee (NRp, NRs) = 100 paise/pice	19800000

The		Netherlands	's-Gravenhage (The Hague)			
New Zealand	New Zealand (English); Aotearoa (Maori)	New Zealand	Wellington	English, Maori	1 New Zealand Dollar ($NZ) = 100 cents	3 434 950
Nicaragua	Nicaragua	Republic of Nicaragua	Managua	Spanish	1 Córdoba Oro (C$) = 100 centavos	4 130 000
Niger	Niger	Republic of Niger	Niamey	French	1 CFA Franc (CFAFr) = 100 centimes	7 731 000
Nigeria	Nigeria	Federal Republic of Nigeria	Abuja	English	1 Naira (N, ₦) = 100 kobo	88 500 000
Norway	Norge	Kingdom of Norway	Oslo	Norwegian	1 Norwegian Krone (NKr) = 100 øre	4 259 000
Oman	'Umān	Sultanate of Oman	Masqat (Muscat)	Arabic	1 Omani Rial (RO) = 1000 baizas	1 640 000
Pakistan	Pākistān	Islamic Republic of Pakistan	Islāmābād (Islamabad)	Urdu	1 Pakistan Rupee (PRs, Rp) = 100 paisas	130 130 000
Panama	Panamá	Republic of Panama	Panamá (Panama City)	Spanish	1 Balboa (B, Ba) = 100 cents	2 515 000
Papua New Guinea	Papua New Guinea	Independent State of Papua New Guinea	Port Moresby	English, Tok Pisin	1 Kina (K) = 100 toea	3 834 000
Paraguay	Paraguay	Republic of Paraguay	Asunción	Spanish	1 Guaraní (₲) = 100 céntimos	4 520 000
Peru	Perú	Republic of Peru	Lima	Spanish, Quechua	1 New Sol = 100 centavos	22 454 000
Philippines	Filipinas	Republic of the Philippines	Manila	English, Pilipino	1 Philippine peso (PP, ₱) = 100 centavos	63 609 000
Poland	Polska	Republic of Poland	Warszawa (Warsaw)	Polish	1 Złoty (Zł) = 100 groszy	38 423 000
Portugal	Portugal	Republic of Portugal	Lisboa (Lisbon)	Portuguese	1 Escudo (Esc) = 100 centavos	9 831 967
Puerto Rico	Puerto Rico	Commonwealth of Puerto Rico	San Juan	Spanish, English	1 US Dollar (US$) = 100 cents	3 522 039
Qatar	Qatar	State of Qatar	Ad-Dawhah (Doha)	Arabic	1 Qatar Riyal (QR) = 100 dirhams	520 000
Romania	România	Republic of Romania	București (Bucharest)	Romanian	1 Leu (pl lei) = 100 bani	23 397 000
Russia	Rossiyskaya	Russian Federation	Moskva (Moscow)	Russian	1 Rouble (R) = 100 kopecks	148 800 000
Rwanda	Rwanda	Republic of Rwanda	Kigali	Kinyarwanda, French	1 Rwanda Franc (RF) = 100 centimes	7 237 000
Saint Kitts and Nevis	Saint Christopher/Kitts and Nevis	Federation of Saint Kitts and Nevis	Basseterre	English	1 East Caribbean Dollar (EC$) = 100 cents	43 100
Saint Lucia	Saint Lucia	Saint Lucia	Castries	English	1 East Caribbean Dollar (EC$) = 100 cents	136 041
Saint Vincent and the Grenadines	Saint Vincent and the Grenadines	Saint Vincent and the Grenadines	Kingstown	English	1 East Caribbean Dollar (EC$) = 100 cents	115 000
San Marino	San Marino	Most Serene Republic of San Marino	San Marino	Italian	1 Italian Lira (L, Lit) = 100 centesimi	23 000
São Tomé and Príncipe	São Tomé e Príncipe	Democratic Republic of São Tomé and Príncipe	São Tomé	Portuguese	1 Dobra (Db) = 100 centimos	124 000
Saudi Arabia	al-'Arabīyah as-Sa'ūdīyah	Kingdom of Saudi Arabia	Ar-Riyād (Riyādh)	Arabic	1 Saudi Arabian Riyal (SAR, SRls) = 100 halalah	15 267 000
Senegal	Sénégal	Republic of Senegal	Dakar	French	1 CFA Franc (CFAFr) = 100 centimes	7 952 000
Seychelles	Seychelles	Republic of Seychelles	Victoria	Creole French, English, French	1 Seychelles Rupee (SR) = 100 cents	68 700

Nations of the world: general data (continued)

English name	Local name	Official name (in English)	Capital (English name in parentheses)	Official language(s)	Currency	Population
Sierra Leone	Sierra Leone	Republic of Sierra Leone	Freetown	English	1 Leone (Le) = 100 cents	4 274 000
Singapore	Singapore	Republic of Singapore	Singapore City	Chinese, English, Malay, Tamil	1 Singapore Dollar/Ringgit (S$) = 100 cents	2 792 000
Slovak Republic	Slovenská republika	Slovak Republic	Bratislava	Slovak	1 Slovak Koruna (SK) = 100 hal	5 274 335
Slovenia	Slovenija	Republic of Slovenia	Ljubljana	Slovene, Serbo Croat	1 Slovene Tolar = 100 paras	1 974 600
Solomon Islands	Solomon Islands	Solomon Islands	Honiara	English	1 Solomon Islands Dollar (SI$) = 100 cents	339 000
Somalia	Somaliya	Somali Democratic Republic	Muqdisho (Mogadishu)	Arabic, Somali	1 Somali Shilling (SoSh) = 100 cents	7 497 000
South Africa	South Africa (English); Suid-Afrika (Afrikaans)	Republic of South Africa	Pretoria/Cape Town	Afrikaans, English	1 Rand (R) = 100 cents	32 000 000
Spain	España	Kingdom of Spain	Madrid	Spanish	1 Peseta (Pta, Pa) = 100 céntimos	38 425 679
Sri Lanka	Sri Lanka	Democratic Socialist Republic of Sri Lanka	Colombo/Sri Jaya-wardenapura	Sinhala, Tamil	1 Sri Lanka Rupee (SLR, SLRs) = 100 cents	17 464 000
Sudan	As-Súdán	Republic of the Sudan	Al-Khar tum (Khartoum)	Arabic	1 Sudanese pound (LSd, £S) = 100 piastres	29 900 000
Suriname	Suriname	Republic of Suriname	Paramaribo	Dutch	1 Suriname Guilder/Florin (SGld, F) = 100 cents	410 000
Swaziland	Swatini	Kingdom of Swaziland	Mbabane	English, Siswati	1 Lilangeni (pl Emalangeni) (Li, E) = 100 cents	788 000
Sweden	Sverige	Kingdom of Sweden	Stockholm	Swedish	1 Swedish Krona (Skr) = 100 øre	8 644 119
Switzerland	Schweiz (German); Suisse (French); Svizzera (Italian)	Swiss Confederation	Bern (Berne)	French, German, Italian, Romansch	1 Swiss Franc (SFr, SwF) = 100 centimes	6 750 693
Syria	As-Súriyah	Syrian Arab Republic	Dimashq (Damascus)	Arabic	1 Syrian pound (LS, Syr) = 100 piastres	12 958 000
Tajikistan	Tojikiston	Republic of Tajikistan	Dushanbe	Tajik, Uzbek, Russian	1 Rouble (R) = 100 kopecks	4 969 000
Taiwan	T'aiWan	Republic of China	Taibei (T'aipei, Taipei)	Mandarin Chinese	1 New Taiwan Dollar (NT$) = 100 cents	20 727 000
Tanzania	Tanzania	United Republic of Tanzania	Dodoma	Swahili, English	1 Tanzanian Shilling (TSh) = 100 cents	27 318 000
Thailand	Muang Thai	Kingdom of Thailand	Krung Thep (Bangkok)	Thai	1 Baht (B) = 100 satang	56 800 000
Togo	Togo	Republic of Togo	Lomé	French	1 CFA Franc (CFAFr) = 100 centimes	3 531 000
Tonga	Tonga	Kingdom of Tonga	Nuku'alofa	English, Tongan	1 Pa'anga/Tongan Dollar (T$) = 100 seniti	102 900
Trinidad and Tobago	Trinidad and Tobago	Republic of Trinidad and Tobago	Port of Spain	English	1 Trinidad and Tobago Dollar (TT$) = 100 cents	1 233 000
Tunisia	Tunis (Arabic); Tunisie (French)	Republic of Tunisia	Tunis	Arabic	1 Tunisian Dinar (TD, D) = 1000 milimes	8 413 000
Turkey	Türkiye	Republic of Turkey	Ankara	Turkish	1 Turkish Lira (TL) = 100 kurus	56 473 035

			Capital	Languages	Currency	Population
Turkmenistan	Turkmenostan	Republic of Turkmenistan	Ashkhabad	Turkmenian, Russian	1 Rouble (R) = 100 kopecks	3 809 000
Tuvalu	Tuvalu	Tuvalu	Funafuti	English	1 Australian Dollar = 100 cents	9500
Uganda	Uganda	Republic of Uganda	Kampala	English, Swahili	1 Uganda Shilling = 100 cents	18 794 000
Ukraine	Ukraine	Republic of Ukraine	Kiev	Ukranian, Russian	1 Rouble (R) = 100 kopecks	52 100 000
United Arab Emirates	Ittiḥād al-Imārāt al-'Arabiyah	United Arab Emirates	Abū Zabi (Abu Dhabi)	Arabic	1 Dirham (DH) = 100 fils	1 990 000
United Kingdom	United Kingdom/ (Great) Britain	United Kingdom of Great Britain and Northern Ireland	London	English	1 Pound Sterling (£) = 100 new pence	57 384 000
United States of America	United States of America (USA)	United States of America	Washington, DC	English	1 US Dollar ($, US$) = 100 cents	248 709 873
Uruguay	Uruguay	Oriental Republic of Uruguay	Montevideo	Spanish	1 Uruguayan New Peso (NUr$, UrugN$) = 100 centimos	3 130 000
Uzbekistan	Ozbekiston	Republic of Uzbekistan	Tashkent	Uzbek, Russian	Som	21 300 000
Vanuatu	Vanuatu	Republic of Vanuatu	Port Vila	English, French, Bislama	1 Vatu (VT) = 100 centimes	154 000
Venezuela	Venezuela	Republic of Venezuela	Caracas	Spanish	1 Bolívar (B) = 100 céntimos	20 185 000
Vietnam	Viêt-nam	Socialist Republic of Vietnam	Ha-noi (Hanoi)	Vietnamese	1 Dông = 10 hao = 100 xu	69 000 000
Western Samoa	Western Samoa (English); Samoa i Sisifo (Samoan)	Independent State of Western Samoa	Apia	English, Samoan	1 Tala (WS$) = 100 sene	190 000
Yemen	Al-Yaman	Republic of Yemen	Sana/Aden	Arabic	1 Yemeni Riyal (YR, YRl) = 100 fils; 1 Yemeni Dinar (YD) = 1000 fils	12 150 000

Yugoslavia see Croatia, Bosnia and Herzegovina, Macedonia, Slovenia

Zaire	Zaire	Republic of Zaire	Kinshasa	French	1 Zaire (Z) = 100 makuta (sing. likuta)	35 568 000
Zambia	Zambia	Republic of Zambia	Lusaka	English	1 Kwacha (K) = 100 ngwee	8 452 000
Zimbabwe	Zimbabwe	Republic of Zimbabwe	Harare	English	1 Zimbabwe Dollar (Z$) = 100 cents	9 709 000

Anthropology

Tribal peoples and their ways of life

The population figures here must be taken as a very rough guide. An exact enumeration is impossible, because of the difficulty of census-taking in many areas, the problem of defining who is and is not 'tribal', and the fact that available figures have been collected at different dates with different biases.

Inuit: 98 500. Hunting and fishing; paid employment; state support.

North American Indians: 2.6 million. Farming, hunting, fishing and trapping; paid employment; state support.

Central American Indians: 13 million. Farming; paid employment.

Arabian Noma 5 million. Here and farming; employment.

African Nomadic Pastorali 14 million. Herding and s farming; paid employmen

'Pygmies': 170 000. Gathering and huntin client labour for farm

Andean Indians: 17.5 million. Farming; paid employment.

South American Lowland Indians: 1 million. Farming, fishing and hunting; a few nomadic gatherer hunters; now some paid employn

Endangered tribes

Peoples who face the worst threats in today's world include:

Yanomami (Brazil): The Yanomami of the Brazilian and Venezuelan rain forest were one of the last major Amazonian peoples to keep their land and way of life intact. But since 1987 their land has become the scene of a gold rush as tens of thousands of prospectors have invaded it. In 1987–9, 1 500 of the 9 000 or so Yanomami in Brazil died of diseases caught from the miners. In 1991, the Yanomami's land was given legal protection, but this will be difficult to enforce.

Tribes of the Chittagong Hills (Bangladesh): The lands of these ten tribes – subsistence farmers and Buddhists by religion – have, since the 1970s, been invaded by Bengali Muslim settlers. A movement demanding more local autonomy for the tribes has led to repression by the Bangladesh military and the area has been sealed off. There have been reports of the torture and killing of thousands of villagers and the burning of villages.

San ('Bushmen') of the Kalahari (Namibia, South Africa, Botswana, and Angola): The group of peoples known as Bushmen, San, and other names has been hunted and exploited for centuries by both blacks and whites. Farms, ranches, and game parks now occupy most of their former hunting grounds. Today, in spite of romantic images perpetuated by the media, almost none follow the old hunter-gatherer way of life. Most are now farm labourers for little or no pay, or depend on government handouts. Some are attempting to remain independent by taking up subsistence farming and herding.

0. Herding, farming and employment.

Arctic peoples: 1 million. Herding and fishing; paid employment.

Central Asian Pastoral Nomads (Russia, Mongolia, Afghanistan)**:** 7.2 million. Herding; paid employment.

Chinese minority peoples: 86 million. Farming, herding, gathering and hunting; paid employment.

Ainu: 50 000. Farming; paid employment.

Tribal peoples of Taiwan: 310 000. Farming; paid employment.

Tribal peoples of the Philippines: 6.5 million. Farming, gathering and hunting; paid employment.

Tribal peoples of the Indian subcontinent: 78 million. Farming, gathering and hunting; paid employment.

Tribal peoples of Southeast Asia: 16.6 million. Farming, gathering and hunting; paid employment.

Pacific peoples: 1.5 million. Farming and fishing; paid employment; state support.

Australian Aborigines: 250 000. Formerly nomadic gathering and hunting, now mainly settled; paid employment; state support.

Maori: 404 000. Farming, hunting and fishing; paid employment.

San ('Bushmen'): 87 000. Formerly nomadic gathering and hunting; now mainly paid employment; state support.

Society

Population

Growth of world population
by billion and year.

World population	Year	Elapsed years
1 billion	1805	indefinite
2 billion	1926	121
3 billion	1960	34
4 billion	1974	14
5 billion	1987	13
6 billion	1998	11
7 billion	2010	12
8 billion	2023	13
9 billion	2040	17
10 billion	2070	30

The projected slowing down of world population growth to a peak of 10 billion in 2070 is based on the following assumptions: increased use of contraception in developing countries, and an ageing of the global population (with fertile adults making up a smaller percentage of the whole).

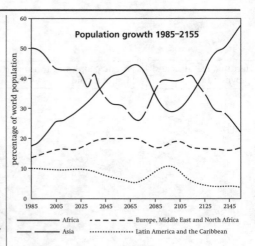

Population growth 1985–2155

Africa — — — Europe, Middle East and North Africa
Asia .... Latin America and the Caribbean

Projected population growth, by geographic region

Region	Population (millions)		Growth rate (%)		Birth rate (per 1000)		Death rate (per 1000)	
	1985	2025	1985–90	2020–5	1985–90	2020–5	1985–90	2020–5
World	4840	8188	1.71	0.94	26.9	17.6	9.8	8.2
Africa	560	1495	3.05	1.74	45.0	24.1	14.5	6.7
Asia	2819	4758	1.80	0.89	27.4	17.0	9.2	8.1
America	666	1035	1.58	0.72	23.4	15.3	7.9	8.2
Europe	770	863	0.45	0.15	14.7	13.0	10.3	11.5
Oceania	25	36	1.37	0.59	19.6	15.0	8.2	9.1

UK population summary

	United Kingdom			England and Wales			Wales	Scotland			Northern Ireland		
	Persons	Males	Females	Persons	Males	Females	Persons	Persons	Males	Females	Persons	Males	Females
	Enumerated population: census figures (thousands)												
1801	–	–	–	8893	4255	4638	587	1608	739	869	–	–	–
1851	22259	10855	11404	17928	8781	9146	1163	2889	1376	1513	1442	698	745
1901	38237	18492	19745	32528	15729	16799	2013	4472	2174	2298	1237	590	647
1911	42082	20357	21725	36070	17446	18625	2421	4761	2309	2452	1251	603	648
1921[a]	44027	21033	22994	37887	18075	19811	2656	4882	2348	2535	1258	610	648
1931[a]	46038	22060	23978	39952	19133	20819	2593	4843	2326	2517	1243	601	642
1951	50225	24118	26107	43758	21016	22742	2599	5096	2434	2662	1371	668	703
1961	52709	25481	27228	46105	22304	23801	2644	5179	2483	2697	1425	694	731
1966[b]	53788	26044	27745	47136	22841	24295	2663	5168	2479	2689	1485	724	761
1971	55515	26952	28562	48750	23683	25067	2731	5229	2515	2714	1536	755	781
1981	55848	27104	28742	49155	23873	25281	2792	5131	2466	2664	1533	750	783
	Usually resident												
1981	55089	26803	28286	48522	23625	24897	2750	5035	2428	2607	1532	749	783
	Resident population: mid-year estimates (thousands)												
1958	51652	24887	26765	45109	21744	23365	2615	5141	2460	2682	1402	684	719
1959	51956	25043	26913	45386	21885	23501	2623	5163	2472	2690	1408	686	722
1960	52372	25271	27102	45775	22097	23678	2629	5178	2482	2696	1420	692	728
1961	52807	25528	27279	46196	22347	23849	2635	5184	2485	2698	1427	696	732
1962	53292	25826	27465	46657	22631	24026	2652	5198	2495	2703	1437	700	737
1963	53625	25992	27633	46973	22787	24186	2664	5205	2500	2705	1447	705	741
1964	53991	26191	27800	47324	22978	24346	2677	5208	2501	2707	1458	711	747
1965	54350	26368	27982	47671	23151	24521	2693	5210	2501	2709	1468	716	752
1966	54643	26511	28132	47966	23296	24671	2702	5201	2496	2704	1476	719	757
1967	54959	26673	28286	48272	23451	24821	2710	5198	2496	2702	1489	726	763
1968	55214	26784	28429	48511	23554	24957	2715	5200	2498	2702	1503	733	770

Society

	United Kingdom			England and Wales			Wales	Scotland			Northern Ireland		
	Persons	Males	Females	Persons	Males	Females	Persons	Persons	Males	Females	Persons	Males	Females
1969	55461	26908	28553	48738	23666	25072	2722	5208	2503	2706	1514	739	776
1970	55632	26992	28641	48891	23738	25153	2729	5214	2507	2707	1527	747	781
1971	55928	27167	28761	49152	23897	25255	2740	5236	2516	2720	1540	755	786
1972	56097	27259	28837	49327	23989	25339	2755	5231	2513	2717	1539	758	782
1973	56223	27332	28891	49459	24061	25399	2773	5234	2515	2719	1530	756	774
1974	56236	27349	28887	49468	24075	25393	2785	5241	2519	2722	1527	755	772
1975	56226	27361	28865	49470	24091	25378	2795	5232	2516	2716	1524	753	770
1976	56,216	27360	28856	49459	24089	25370	2799	5233	2517	2716	1524	754	770
1977	56190	27345	28845	49440	24076	25364	2801	5226	2515	2711	1523	754	769
1978	56178	27330	28849	49443	24067	25375	2804	5212	2509	2704	1523	754	770
1979	56240	27373	28867	49508	24113	25395	2810	5204	2505	2699	1530	755	773
1980	56330	27411	28919	49603	24156	25448	2816	5194	2501	2693	1533	755	778
1981	56352	27049	28943	49634	24160	25474	2814	5180	2495	2685	1538	754	784
1982	56306	27386	28920	49601	24143	25459	2807	5167	2490	2677	1538	754	784
1983	56347	27417	28931	49654	24176	25478	2808	5150	2485	2665	1543	756	788
1984	56460	27487	28973	49764	24244	25519	2807	5146	2484	2662	1551	760	791
1985	56618	27574	29044	49924	24330	25594	2812	5137	2481	2656	1558	763	795
1986	56763	27647	29116	50075	24403	25672	2821	5121	2475	2646	1567	768	798
1987	56930	27737	29193	50243	24493	25750	2836	5112	2471	2641	1575	773	802
1988	57065	27813	29253	50393	24576	25817	2857	5094	2462	2632	1578	774	804
1989	57236	27907	29330	50562	24669	25893	2873	5091	2460	2630	1583	777	806
1990	57411	28013	29398	50719	24766	25953	2881	5102	2467	2636	1589	780	809

[a] Figures for Northern Ireland are estimated. The population at the census of 1926 was 1257000 (608000 males and 649000 females).   [b] Except for Northern Ireland, where a full census was taken, figures are based on the 10 per cent samples census.

Marriage and divorce rates: EC comparison

	Marriages per 1000 eligible population		Divorces per 1000 existing marriages			Marriages per 1000 eligible population		Divorces per 1000 existing marriages	
	1981	1989	1981	1989		1981	1989	1981	1989
United Kingdom	7.1	6.8	11.9	12.6	Irish Republic	6.0	5.0	0.0	0.0
Belgium	6.5	6.4	6.1	8.6	Italy	5.6	5.4	0.9	2.1
Denmark	5.0	6.0	12.1	13.6	Luxembourg	5.5	5.8	5.9	10.0
France	5.8	5.0	6.8	8.4	Netherlands	6.0	6.1	8.3	8.1
Germany (former West)	5.8	6.4	7.2	8.7	Portugal	7.7	7.1	2.8	–
Greece	7.3	6.1	2.5	–	Spain	5.4	5.6	1.1	–

SOCIAL INSTITUTIONS

Aristocratic ranks

England	France	Holy Roman Empire (Germany)	Italy	Spain
king	roi	Kaiser	re	rey
prince	duc	Herzog	duca	duque
duke	prince	Pfalzgraf	principe	principe
marquess	marquis	Markgraf	marchese	marques
earl	comte	Landgraf	conde	conde
viscount	vicomte		visconte	vizconde
baronet				

Society

Honours

Country	Name of honour	Date instituted	History
Denmark	Order of the Dannebrog	1219	One of the most ancient orders in existence and awarded for general merit.
France	Croix de Guerre	1915	Military decoration created in 1915 and 1939 to reward bravery in the two world wars.
	Légion d'Honneur	1802	First order of the French Republic created by Napoleon I as a reward for distinguished civil and military service. Open to all citizens regardless of birth or religion.
Germany	Iron Cross	1813	Instituted first by Prussia and then reinstated by Hitler in 1939. Military decoration awarded for bravery in war time.
	Pour le Mérite	1740	Established by Frederick II the Great. There was a class for military achievement and one for scientific and artistic achievement.
Japan	Chrysanthemum, Order of the	1877	Japan's highest order. Instituted by Emperor Meiji and awarded mainly to members of the Japanese Royal Family, foreign royals, and heads of state. Award exclusive to males.
	Paulownia Sun, Order of the	1888	Founded by Emperor Meiji to reward outstanding military and civil merit. Only awarded to men.
	Rising Sun, Order of the	1875	This was originally the Order of Merit awarded for exceptional civil or military merit.
Netherlands	Order of the House of Orange	1905	The equivalent of the Royal Victorian Order and rewards services to the Royal House.
	Military Order of William	1815	The highest military decoration to military of all ranks and civilians for courageous acts and devotion to duty. Founded by William I.
	Netherlands Lion	1815	An award for patriotism and outstanding devotion to duty, also for scientific and artistic achievements.
United Kingdom	Bath, The Most Honourable Order of the	1725	Order of chivalry formally created by George I in 1725, but traditionally instituted by Henry IV in 1399. The motto of the order is *Tria juncta in uno* (Three joined in one).
	British Empire, The Most Noble Order of the Knight/Dame of the Grand Cross (GBE) Knight/Dame Commander (K/DBE) Commander (CBE) Officer (OBE) Member (MBE)	1917	Founded by George V and the first order of knighthood to be presented to members of both sexes. Appointments made on the recommendations of Government ministers. There are five orders.
	Companions of Honour, Order of the (CH)	1917	Founded by George V to reward men and women for national services. Motto *In action faithful and in honour clear*.
	Distinguished Service Order (DSO)	1886	Military service order in recognition of special services by army and navy officers.
	Garter, The Most Noble Order of the	c.1344–51	The most ancient order of chivalry, founded by Edward III. Motto *Honi soit qui mal y pense* (Shamed be he who thinks badly of it).
	George Cross (GC)	1940	Named after George VI and awarded 'For Gallantry' (acts of great heroism).
	Merit, Order of (OM)	1902	Founded by Edward VII for eminent service in the military or for distinguished performances in science, the arts, and the promotion of culture.
	Royal Victorian Order (RVO) Knight/Dame Grand Cross (GCVO) Knight/Dame Commander (K/DCVO) Commander (CVO) Lieutenant (LVO) Member (MVO)	1896	Knighthood instituted by Queen Victoria to reward distinguished service to the sovereign. There are five orders.
	Thistle, The Most Ancient and Noble Order of the	c.1460–88	Scottish order of chivalry, probably instituted by James III. Motto *Nemo me impune lacessit* (No-one provokes me with impunity).

Society

Country	Name of honour	Date instituted	History
	Victoria Cross (VC)	1856	Instituted by Queen Victoria. The highest military award in honour of great bravery.
United States	Congressional Medal of Honor	1862	Established by the US Congress and awarded in its name. The country's highest military decoration. Awarded to members of the armed services who, during a military action, risk their lives in acts of bravery beyond the call of duty.
	Legion of Merit, The	1942	Awarded to native American officers and foreigners for exceptional service in peace and war.
	Medal for Merit	1942	Awarded to civilians who have performed an outstanding service in peace or wartime.
	Presidential Medal of Freedom	1963	The highest decoration awarded to civilians in peacetime. The medal is presented in recognition of outstanding achievement in any of a variety of fields, including the arts.
	Purple Heart, The	1782	Originally an award for gallantry. Revived in 1932 and awarded in recognition of wounds received in action.

Forms of address

In the formulae given below, F stands for forename and S for surname.

Very formal ceremonial styles for closing letters are now seldom used: 'Yours faithfully' is assumed below, unless otherwise indicated.

Forms of spoken address are given only where a special style is followed.

Holders of courtesy titles are addressed according to their rank, but without 'The', 'The Right Hon.' or 'The Most Hon.'

Ranks in the armed forces, and ecclesiastical and ambassadorial ranks, precede titles in the peerage, eg 'Colonel the Earl of –' or 'The Rev the Marquess of –'.

Although the correct forms of address are given below for members of the British Royal Family, it is more normal practice for letters to be addressed to their private secretary, equerry, or lady-in-waiting.

More detailed information about forms of address is to be found in Debrett's *Correct Form* and Black's *Titles and Forms of Address*.

Ambassadors (foreign)
Address on envelope: 'His/Her Excellency the Ambassador of –' or 'His/Her Excellency the – Ambassador'. (The wife of an ambassador is not entitled to the style 'Her Excellency'.) *Begin*: 'Your Excellency'. (Within the letter, refer to 'Your Excellency' once, thereafter as 'you'.) *Close*: 'I have the honour to be, Sir/Madam (or according to rank), Your Excellency's obedient servant'. *Spoken address*: 'Your Excellency' at least once, and then 'Sir' or 'Madam', or by name.

Archbishop (Anglican communion)
Address on envelope: 'The Most Reverend Lord Archbishop of –'. (The Archbishops of Canterbury and York are Privy Counsellors, and should be addressed as 'The Most Reverend and Right Hon, the Lord Archbishop of –'.) *Begin*: 'Dear Archbishop' or 'My Lord Archbishop'. *Spoken address*: 'Your Grace'. *Begin an official speech*: 'My Lord Archbishop.'

Archbishop (any, US form)
Address on envelope: 'The Most Reverend [F– S–], Archbishop of–'. *Begin*: 'Your Excellency'.

Archbishop (Roman Catholic)
Address on envelope: 'His Grace the Archbishop of –'. *Begin*: 'My Lord Archbishop'. *Close*: 'I remain, Your Grace, Yours faithfully' or 'Yours faithfully'. *Spoken address*: 'Your Grace'.

Archdeacon
Address on envelope: 'The Venerable the Archdeacon of –'. *Begin*: 'Dear Archdeacon' or 'Venerable Sir'. *Spoken address*: 'Archdeacon'. *Begin an official speech*: 'Venerable Sir'.

Baron
Address on envelope: 'The Right Hon. the Lord–'. *Begin*: 'My Lord'. *Spoken address*: 'My Lord'.

Baron's wife (Baroness)
Address on envelope: 'The Right Hon. the Lady [S–]'. *Begin*: 'Dear Madam'. *Spoken address*: 'Madam'.

Baroness (in her own right)
Address on envelope: either as for Baron's wife, or 'The Right Hon. the Baroness [S–]'. Otherwise, as for Baron's wife.

Baronet
Address on envelope: 'Sir [F– S–], Bt'. *Begin*: 'Dear Sir'. *Spoken address*: 'Sir [F–]'.

Baronet's wife
Address on envelope: 'Lady [S–]'. If she has the title 'Lady' by courtesy, 'Lady [F– S–]'. If she has the courtesy style 'The Hon.', this precedes 'Lady'. *Begin*: 'Dear Madam'. *Spoken address*: 'Madam'.

Bishop (Anglican communion)
Address on envelope: 'The Right Reverend the Lord Bishop of –'. (The Bishop of London is a Privy Counsellor, so is addressed as 'The Right Rev. and Right Hon. the Lord Bishop of London'. The Bishop of Meath is styled 'The Most Reverend'.) *Begin*: 'Dear Bishop' or 'My Lord'. *Spoken address*: 'Bishop'. *Begin an official speech*: 'My Lord'.

Bishop (Episcopal Church in Scotland)
Address on envelope: 'The Right Reverend [F– S–], Bishop of –'. Otherwise as for a bishop of the Anglican communion. The bishop who holds the position of Primus is addressed as 'The Most Reverend the Primus'. *Begin*: 'Dear Primus'. *Spoken address*: 'Primus'.

Society

Social institutions

Forms of address (continued)

Bishop (Episcopal, US form)
Address on envelope: 'The Right Reverend [F– S–], Bishop of –'. *Begin*: 'Right Reverend Sir'.

Bishop (Roman Catholic)
Address on envelope: 'His Lordship the Bishop of –' or 'The Right Reverend [F– S–] Bishop of –'. In Ireland, 'The Most Reverend' is used instead of 'The Right Reverend'. If an auxiliary bishop, address as 'The Right Reverend [F– S–], Auxiliary Bishop of –'. *Begin*: 'My Lord' or (more rarely) 'My Lord Bishop'. *Close*: 'I remain, my Lord' or (more rarely), 'my Lord Bishop', Yours faithfully', or simply 'Yours faithfully'. *Spoken address*: 'My Lord' or (more rarely) 'My Lord Bishop'.

Bishop (Roman Catholic, US form)
Address on envelope: 'The Most Reverend [F– S–], Bishop of –'. *Begin*: 'Most Reverend Sir' or 'Your Excellency'.

Bishop (Other churches, US form)
Address on envelope: 'The Reverend [F– S–]'. *Begin*: 'Reverend Sir'.

Cabinet Minister *see* Secretary of State

Canon (Anglican communion)
Address on envelope: 'The Reverend Canon [F– S–]'. *Begin*: 'Dear Canon' or 'Dear Canon [S–]'. *Spoken address*: 'Canon' or 'Canon [S–]'.

Canon (Roman Catholic)
Address on envelope: 'The Very Reverend Canon [F– S–]'. *Begin*: 'Very Reverend Sir'. *Spoken address*: 'Canon [S–]'.

Cardinal
Address on envelope: 'His Eminence Cardinal [S–]'. If an archbishop, 'His Eminence the Cardinal Archbishop of –'. *Begin*: 'Your Eminence' or (more rarely) 'My Lord Cardinal'. *Close*: 'I remain, Your Eminence' (or 'My Lord Cardinal'), Yours faithfully'. *Spoken address*: 'Your Eminence'.

Cardinal (US form)
Address on envelope: 'His Eminence [F–] Cardinal [S–]'. *Begin*: 'Your Eminence'.

Clergy (Anglican communion)
Address on envelope: 'The Reverend [F– S–]'. *Begin*: 'Dear Sir' or 'Dear Mr [S–]'.

Clergy (Roman Catholic)
Address on envelope: 'The Reverend [F– S–]'. If a member of a religious order, the initials of the order should be added after the name. *Begin*: 'Dear Reverend Father'.

Clergy (Other churches)
Address on envelope: 'The Reverend [F– S–]'. *Begin*: 'Dear Sir/Madam' or 'Dear Mr/Mrs/etc. [S–]'.

Countess
Address on envelope: 'The Right Hon. the Countess of –'. *Begin*: 'Dear Madam'. *Spoken address*: 'Madam'.

Dean (Anglican)
Address on envelope: 'The Very Reverend the Dean of –'. *Begin*: 'Dear Dean' or 'Very Reverend Sir'. *Spoken address*: 'Dean'. *Begin an official speech*: 'Very Reverend Sir'.

Doctor
Physicians, anaesthetists, pathologists, and radiologists are addressed as 'Doctor'. In the UK, surgeons, whether they hold the degree of Doctor of Medicine or not, are known as 'Mr/Mrs'. In England and Wales, obstetricians

and gynaecologists are addressed as 'Mr/Mrs', but in Scotland, Ireland, and elsewhere as 'Doctor'. In addressing a letter to the holder of a doctorate, the initials DD, MD, etc. are placed after the ordinary form of address, eg 'The Rev John Smith, DD'. The 'Rev Dr Smith' and 'Dr John Brown' are also used.

Dowager
Address on envelope: On the marriage of a peer or baronet, the widow of the previous holder of the title becomes 'Dowager' and is addressed 'The Right Hon. the Dowager Countess of –', 'The Right Hon. the Dowager Lady –', etc. If there is already a Dowager still living, she retains this title, the later widow being addressed 'The Most Hon. [F–]. Marchioness of –', 'The Right Hon. [F–], Lady –', etc. However, many Dowagers prefer the style which includes their Christian names to that including the title Dowager. *Begin*: as for a peer's wife.

Duchess
Address on envelope: 'Her Grace the Duchess of –'. *Begin*: 'Dear Madam'. *Spoken address*: 'Your Grace'. (For Royal Duchess, *see* Princess.)

Duke
Address on envelope: 'His Grace the Duke of –'. *Begin*: 'My Lord Duke'. *Spoken address*: 'Your Grace'. (For Royal Duke, *see* Prince.)

Earl
Address on envelope: 'The Right Hon. the Earl of –'. *Begin*: 'My Lord'. *Spoken address*: 'My Lord'. (For Earl's wife, *see* Countess.)

Governor of a colony or **Governor-General**
Address on envelope: 'His Excellency (ordinary designation), Governor(-General) of –'. (The Governor-General of Canada has the rank of 'Right Honourable', which he retains for life.) The wife of a Governor-General is styled 'Her Excellency' within the country her husband administers. *Begin*: according to rank. *Close*: 'I have the honour to be, Sir (or 'My Lord', if a peer), Your Excellency's obedient servant'. *Spoken address*: 'Your Excellency'.

Governor (US, state)
Address on envelope: 'The Honorable [F– S–], Governor of –'. *Begin*: 'Sir/Madam'. *Spoken address*: 'Governor [S–]'.

Judge, High Court
Address on envelope: 'The Hon. Mr/Mrs Justice [S–]. *Begin*: 'Dear Sir/Madam'; if on judicial matters, 'My Lord/Lady'. *Spoken address*: 'Sir/Madam'; only on the bench or when dealing with judicial matters should a High Court Judge be addressed as 'My Lord/Lady' or referred to as 'Your Lordship/Ladyship'.

Judge, Circuit
Address on envelope: 'His/Her Honour Judge [S–]'. If a Knight, 'His Honour Judge Sir [F– S–]'. *Begin*: 'Dear Sir/Madam'. *Spoken address*: 'Sir/Madam'; address as 'Your Honour' only when on the bench or dealing with judicial matters.

Judge (US, federal)
Address on envelope: 'The Honorable [F– S–], Judge of the United States District Court of the – District of –'. *Begin*: 'Sir/Madam'. *Spoken address*: 'Judge [S–]'.

Justice of the Peace (England and Wales)
When on the bench, refer to and address as 'Your Worship'; otherwise according to rank. The letters 'JP' may

be added after the person's name in addressing a letter, if desired.

Knight Bachelor
As Baronet, except that 'Bt' is omitted. Knight of the Bath, of St Michael and St George, etc. *Address on envelope*: 'Sir [F– S–], with the initials 'GCB', 'KCB', etc. added. *Begin*: 'Dear Sir'.

Knight's wife
As Baronet's wife, or according to rank.

Lady Mayoress
Address on envelope: 'The Lady Mayoress of –'. *Begin*: 'My Lady Mayoress'. *Spoken address*: '(My) Lady Mayoress'.

Lord Mayor
Address on envelope: The Lord Mayors of London, York, Belfast, Cardiff, and Dublin, and also Melbourne, Sydney, Adelaide, Perth, Brisbane, and Hobart, are styled 'The Right Hon. the Lord Mayor of –'. Other Lord Mayors are styled 'The Right Worshipful the Lord Mayor of –'. *Begin*: 'My Lord Mayor', even if the holder of the office is a woman. *Spoken address*: '(My) Lord Mayor'.

Marchioness
Address on envelope: 'The Most Hon. the Marchioness of –'. *Begin*: 'Dear Madam'. *Spoken address*: 'Madam'.

Marquess
Address on envelope: 'The Most Hon. the Marquess of –'. *Begin*: 'My Lord'. *Spoken address*: 'My Lord'.

Mayor
Address on envelope: 'The Worshipful the Mayor of –'; in the case of cities and certain towns, 'The Right Worshipful'. *Begin*: 'Mr Mayor'. *Spoken address*: 'Mr Mayor'.

Mayoress
Address on envelope: 'The Mayoress of –'. *Begin*: 'Madam Mayoress' is traditional, but some now prefer 'Madam Mayor'. *Spoken address*: 'Mayoress' (or 'Madam Mayor').

Member of Parliament
Address on envelope: Add 'MP' to the usual form of address. *Begin*: according to rank.

Monsignor
Address on envelope: 'The Reverend Monsignor [F– S–]'. If a canon, 'The Very Reverend Monsignor (Canon) [F– S–]'. *Begin*: 'Reverend Sir'. *Spoken address*: 'Monsignor [S–]'.

Officers in the Armed Forces
Address on envelope: The professional rank is prefixed to any other rank, eg 'Admiral the Right Hon. the Earl of –', 'Lieut.-Col. Sir [F– S–], KCB'. Officers below the rank of Rear-Admiral, and Marshal of the Royal Air Force, are entitled to 'RN' (or 'Royal Navy') and 'RAF' respectively after their name. Army officers of the rank of Colonel or below may follow their name with the name of their regiment or corps (which may be abbreviated). Officers in the women's services add 'WRNS', 'WRAF', 'WRAC'. *Begin*: according to social rank.

Officers (retired and former)
Address on envelope: Officers above the rank of Lieutenant (in the Royal Navy), Captain (in the Army), and Flight Lieutenant may continue to use and be addressed by their armed forces rank after being placed on the retired list. The word 'retired' (or in an abbreviated form) should not normally be placed after the person's name. Former officers in the women's services do not normally continue to use their ranks.

Pope
Address on envelope: 'His Holiness, the Pope'. *Begin*: 'Your Holiness' or 'Most Holy Father'. *Close*: if a Roman Catholic, 'I have the honour to be your Holiness's most devoted and obedient child' (or 'most humble child'); if not Roman Catholic, 'I have the honour to be (or 'remain') Your Holiness's obedient servant'. *Spoken address*: 'Your Holiness'.

Prime Minister, UK
Address on envelope: according to rank. The Prime Minister is a Privy Counsellor (see separate entry) and the letter should be addressed accordingly. *Begin*: according to rank.

Prince
Address on envelope: If a Duke, 'His Royal Highness the Duke of –'; if not a Duke, 'His Royal Highness the Prince [F–]', if a child of the sovereign; otherwise 'His Royal Highness Prince [F–] of [Kent or Gloucester]'. *Begin*: 'Sir'. Refer to as 'Your Royal Highness'. *Close*: 'I have the honour to remain (or be) Sir, Your Royal Highness's most humble and obedient servant'. *Spoken address*: 'Your Royal Highness' once, thereafter 'Sir'.

Princess
Address on envelope: If a Duchess, 'Her Royal Highness the Duchess of –'; if not a Duchess, the daughter of a sovereign is addressed as 'Her Royal Highness the Princess [F–]', followed by any title she holds by marriage. 'The' is omitted in addressing a princess who is not the daughter of a sovereign. A Princess by marriage is addressed 'HRH Princess [husband's F–] of –'. *Begin*: 'Madam'. Refer to as 'Your Royal Highness'. *Close*: as for Prince, substituting 'Madam' for 'Sir'. *Spoken address*: 'Your Royal Highness' once, thereafter 'Ma'am'.

Privy Counsellor
Address on envelope: If a peer, 'The Right Hon. the Earl of –, PC'; if not a peer, 'The Right Hon. [F– S–]', without the 'PC'. *Begin*: according to rank.

Professor
Address on envelope: 'Professor [F– S–]'; the styles 'Professor Lord [S–]' and 'Professor Sir [F– S–]' are often used, but are deprecated by some people. If the professor is in holy orders, 'The Reverend Professor'. *Begin*: 'Dear Sir/Madam', or according to rank. *Spoken address*: according to rank.

Queen
Address on envelope: 'Her Majesty the Queen'. *Begin*: 'Madam, with my humble duty'. Refer to as 'Your Majesty'. *Close*: 'I have the honour to remain (or 'be'). Madam, Your Majesty's most humble and obedient servant'. *Spoken address*: 'Your Majesty' once, thereafter 'Ma'am'. *Begin an official speech*: 'May it please Your Majesty'.

Rabbi
Address on envelope: 'Rabbi [initial and S–]' or, if a doctor, 'Rabbi Doctor [initial and S–]'. *Begin*: 'Dear Sir'. *Spoken address*: 'Rabbi [S–]' or '[Doctor S–]'.

Secretary of State
Address on envelope: 'The Right Hon. [F– S–], MP. Secretary of State for –', or 'The Secretary of State for –'. Otherwise according to rank.

Viscount
Address on envelope: 'The Right Hon. the Viscount –'. *Begin*: 'My Lord'. *Spoken address*: 'My Lord'.

Viscountess
Address on envelope: 'The Right Hon. the Viscountess –'. *Begin*: 'Dear Madam'. *Spoken address*: 'Madam'.

Heraldry

Heraldry is the granting and devising of pictorial devices (arms) used originally on the shields of knights in armour to distinguish different sides in battle. In the early 12th-c these devices became hereditary in Europe through the male line of descent.

A glossary of terms

Armorial bearings	Hereditary symbols used to distinguish individuals, institutions and corporations.
Billet	Oblong figure.
Billette	Field with ten or more billets irregularly arranged.
Blazonry	The science of describing pictorial signs used in heraldry.
Charges	Heraldic signs or symbols.
Chevron	Inverted v-shaped stripe.
Chief	Top third of the shield.
Compartment	Ground or foundation on which supporters stand.
Crest	Object placed on top of helmet and bound to it by the wreath of colours (which shows the two main colours used in the shield).
Dexter side	Right-hand side.
Escutcheon	The shield on which a coat of arms is represented.
Field	Basic colour (tincture) or background of the shield.
Helmet	Placed on top of the shield.
Inescutcheon	Small figure shaped like shield in the middle of the shield.
Lozenge	Parallelogram.
Lozengy	Field divided transversely by diagonal lines.
Mascle	Lozenge voided.
Mantling or lambrequin	This is hung from the helmet and is designed to act as a shield for the wearer. It is painted with the principle colour of the shield.
Ordinaries	Basic charges.
Orle	Inner border not touching the edge of the shield.
Pile	Inverted pyramid.
Roundel	Circular symbol.
Shield	Coat of arms.
Sinister side	Left-hand side.
Supporters	Animals or human figures on either side of the shield.
Tressure	Smaller version of orle.

Metals

Argent	Silver.
Or	Gold.

Furs

Ermine	White field with black spots.
Ermines	Black field with white spots.
Erminois	Gold field with black spots.
Pean	Black field with gold spots.
Vair	Blue and white.

Colours

Azure	Blue.
Gules	Red.
Murrey	Tint between gules and purpure.
Purpure	Purple.
Sable	Black.
Tenne	Orange-tawny.
Vert	Green.

Partition lines

Impalement or dimidation – shield divided by straight line (top to bottom) into two parts.
Party per pale – division of field into two equal parts by perpendicular line.
Party per fess – field divided by horizontal line into two equal parts.
Party per bend.
Party per chevron.
Party per saltire.
Gyronny of eight.

Pale   Bend   Fess   Chief

Chevron   Saltire   Gyronny of eight

Heraldic descriptions of animals and their posture

Addorsed	Creatures placed back to back.
Combattant	Two animals fighting on hindlegs.
Couchant	Lying down.
Displayed	Birds with wings extended.
Dormant	Sleeping.
At gaze	Looking full face.
Passant	Walking.
Rampant	On hind legs.
Rampant guardant	On hind legs but full-faced.
Reguardant	Looking back.
Statant	Standing.
Trippant	At a trot (one foot raised).

Law and crime

Courts

England and Wales		Scotland
CRIMINAL		CRIMINAL

England and Wales

CRIMINAL

House of Lords	Judges (5) known as Law Lords or Lords of Appeal in Ordinary. Head is the Lord Chancellor (the only judge who is also a member of the government).
Court of Appeal	Established 1966 to replace Court of Criminal appeal. Head is known as the Lord Chief Justice.
Crown Court	Established 1971 to replace Court of Quarter Sessions. 92 places in England and Wales where crown court sessions held. Organized in six circuits – Midlands and Oxford, N Eastern, Northern, S Eastern, Wales and Chester, Western.
Magistrates Court	Tries around 97% of all criminal cases. c.24 500 lay magistrates.

CIVIL

House of Lords	See above.
Court of Appeal	Judges (3) known as Lord Justices of Appeal. Head of Civil Division known as Master of the Rolls.
High Court	Established by the Judicature Acts 173–5. Chancery (11 judges) – deals with trusts and probate matters. Queen's Bench (54 judges) – deals with the Judicial Review. Family (16 judges) – deals with divorce and ward proceedings.
County Court	Established 1846. Deals with cases of contract and tort where amount does not exceed £5000, landlord and tenant disputes, and matrimonial cases (including divorce).

SPECIALIZED CIVIL COURTS

Small Claims Court	Deals with low-value debt enforcement.
Bankruptcy Court	Deals with bankruptcy, but only in London.
Restrictive Practices Court	Deals with commercial disputes.

Scotland

CRIMINAL

High Court of Justiciary in Edinburgh
High Court of Justice
Sheriff Court
District Court

CIVIL

House of Lords
Court of Session (Inner House)
Court of Session (Outer House)
Sheriff Principal Court
Sheriff Court

Northern Ireland

CRIMINAL

House of Lords
N Ireland Court of Appeal
Crown Court

CIVIL

House of Lords
N Ireland Court of Appeal
High Court of Justice
County Court
Magistrates Court

The judiciary and legal representatives

	1972	1981	1990
England & Wales			
The Judiciary			
Judges[a,b]			
Lord Justice	14	18	27
High Court Judges	70	74	83
Circuit Judges	233	334	427
Recorders	325	446	752
Assistant Recorders			421
District Judges[b]	134	150	223
Magistrates[c]	20 539	25 435	27 011[i]
Legal representatives			
Barristers[d]	2 919	4 685	6 645
Solicitors[e]	26 327	39 795	55 685
Scotland[b]			
The Judiciary			
Judges	19	21	24
Sheriffs[f]		78	101
Stipendiary Magistrates	3	3	4
Justices of the Peace[g]			904
Legal representatives[g]			
Advocates	48	134	276
Solicitors	3 374	5 065	7 087

	1972	1981	1990
Northern Ireland[h]			
The Judiciary			
Judges			
High Court Judges		8	10
County Court	5	10	13
Circuit Registrars	0	4	4
Resident Magistrates	17	15	17
Legal representatives			
Barristers	88	203	308
Solicitors		888	1 295

[a]Excludes deputy judges and, for 1972 and 1981, assistant recorders. [b]Figures relate to 31 Dec each year. [c]Figures relate to 1 Jan each year. [d]Figures relate to 1 Oct each year. [e]Number who applied for a practising certificate in year ending 31 Oct. [f]Numbers not available before local government reorganization in 1975. [g]On rota for court duty, 31 March 1990. [g]Practising. [h]Figures are at 1971, 1981 and 1990. [i]Figures are for 1989.
Source: CSO.

Social institutions

Law and crime (continued)
Members of the Supreme Court of the United States[a]

Name: State apptd. from	Term of service	Date of birth	Date of death
CHIEF JUSTICES			
John Jay, NY	1789–95	1745	1829
John Rutledge, SC	1795	1739	1800
Oliver Ellsworth, CT	1796–1800	1745	1807
John Marshall, VA	1801–35	1755	1835
Roger B. Taney, MD	1836–64	1777	1864
Salmon P. Chase, OH	1864–73	1808	1873
Morrison R. Waite, OH	1874–88	1816	1888
Melville W. Fuller, IL	1888–1910	1833	1910
Edward D. White, LA	1910–21	1845	1921
William H. Taft, CT	1921–30	1857	1930
Charles E. Hughes, NY	1930–41	1862	1948
Harlan F. Stone, NY	1941–46	1872	1946
Frederick M. Vinson, KY	1946–53	1890	1953
Earl Warren, CA	1953–69	1891	1974
Warren E. Burger, VA	1969–86	1907	–
William H. Rehnquist, AZ	1986–	1924	–
ASSOCIATE JUSTICES			
James Wilson, PA	1789–98	1742	1798
John Rutledge, SC	1789–91	1739	1800
William Cushing, MA	1789–1810	1732	1810
John Blair, VA	1789–96	1732	1800
James Iredell, NC	1790–9	1751	1799
Thomas Johnson, MD	1791–3	1732	1819
William Paterson, NJ	1793–1806	1745	1806
Samuel Chase, MD	1796–1811	1741	1811
Bushrod Washington, VA	1798–1829	1762	1829
Alfred Moore, NC	1799–1804	1755	1810
William Johnson, SC	1804–34	1771	1834
Henry B. Livingston, NY	1806–23	1757	1823
Thomas Todd, KY	1807–26	1765	1826
Gabriel Duval, MD	1811–35	1752	1844
Joseph Story, MA	1811–45	1779	1845
Smith Thompson, NY	1823–43	1768	1843
Robert Trimble, KY	1826–28	1777	1828
John McLean, OH	1830–61	1785	1861
Henry Baldwin, PA	1830–44	1780	1844
James M. Wayne, GA	1835–67	1790	1867
Philip P. Barbour, VA	1836–41	1783	1841
John Catron, TN	1837–65	1786	1865
John McKinley, AL	1837–52	1780	1852
Peter V. Daniel, VA	1841–60	1784	1860
Samuel Nelson, NY	1845–72	1792	1873
Levi Woodbury, NH	1845–51	1789	1851
Robert C. Grier, PA	1846–70	1794	1870
Benjamin R. Curtis, MA	1851–57	1809	1874
John A. Campbell, AL	1853–61	1811	1889
Nathan Clifford, ME	1858–81	1803	1881
Noah H. Swayne, OH	1862–81	1804	1884
Samuel F. Miller, IA	1862–90	1816	1890
David Davis, IL	1862–77	1815	1886
Stephen J. Field, CA	1863–97	1816	1899
William Strong, PA	1870–80	1808	1895
Joseph P. Bradley, NJ	1870–92	1813	1892
Ward Hunt, NY	1873–82	1810	1886
John M. Harlan, KY	1877–1911	1833	1911
William B. Woods, GA	1880–87	1824	1887
Stanley Matthews, OH	1881–9	1824	1889
Horace Gray, MA	1882–1902	1828	1902
Samuel Blatchford, NY	1882–93	1820	1893
Lucius Q. C. Lamar, MS	1888–93	1825	1893
David J. Brewer, KS	1889–1910	1837	1910
Henry B. Brown, MI	1890–1906	1836	1913
George Shiras, Jr., PA	1892–1903	1832	1924
Howell E. Jackson, TN	1893–5	1832	1895
Edward D. White, LA	1894–1910	1845	1921
Rufus W. Peckham, NY	1896–1909	1838	1909
Joseph McKenna, CA	1898–1925	1843	1926
Oliver W. Holmes, MA	1902–32	1841	1935
William R. Day, OH	1903–22	1849	1923
William H. Moody, MA	1906–10	1853	1917
Horace H. Lurton, TN	1910–14	1844	1914
Charles E. Hughes, NY	1910–16	1862	1948
Willis Van Devanter, WY	1910–37	1859	1941
Joseph R. Lamar, GA	1910–16	1857	1916
Mahlon Pitney, NJ	1912–22	1858	1924
James C. McReynolds, TN	1914–41	1862	1946
Louis D. Brandeis, MA	1916–39	1856	1941
John H. Clarke, OH	1916–22	1857	1945
George Sutherland, UT	1922–38	1862	1942
Pierce Butler, MN	1923–39	1866	1939
Edward T. Sanford, TN	1923–30	1865	1930
Harlan F. Stone, NY	1925–41	1872	1946
Owen J. Roberts, PA	1930–45	1875	1955
Benjamin N. Cardozo, NY	1932–38	1870	1938
Hugo L. Black, AL	1937–71	1886	1971
Stanley F. Reed, KY	1938–57	1884	1980
Felix Frankfurter, MA	1939–62	1882	1965
William O. Douglas, CT	1939–75	1898	1980
Frank Murphy, MI	1940–9	1890	1949
James F. Byrnes, SC	1941–2	1879	1972
Robert H. Jackson, PA	1941–54	1892	1954
Wiley B. Rutledge, IA	1943–9	1894	1949
Harold H. Burton, OH	1945–58	1888	1964
Tom C. Clark, TX	1949–67	1899	1977
Sherman Minton, IN	1949–56	1890	1965
John M. Harlan, NY	1955–71	1899	1971
William J. Brennan, Jr, NJ	1956–90	1906	–
Charles E. Whittaker, MO	1957–62	1901	1973
Potter Stewart, OH	1958–81	1915	1985
Byron R. White, CO	1962–	1917	–
Arthur J. Goldberg, IL	1962–5	1908	–
Abe Fortas, TN	1965–9	1910	1982
Thurgood Marshall, NY	1967–91	1908	–
Harry A. Blackmun, MN	1970–	1908	–
Lewis F. Powell, Jr, VA	1972–87	1907	–
William H. Rehnquist, AZ	1972–86	1924	–
John Paul Stevens, IL	1975–	1920	–
Sandra Day O'Connor, AZ	1981–	1930	–
Antonin Scalia, DC	1986–	1936	–
Anthony M. Kennedy, CA	1988–	1936	–
David H. Souter, NH	1990–	1939	–
Clarence Thomas, DC	1991–	1948	–

[a]The Supreme Court has nine members – a chief justice and eight associate justices – appointed by the President with the advice and consent of the Senate. It is the highest federal court and, in addition to its jurisdiction relating to appeals, it exercises oversight of the constitution through the power of judicial review of the acts of state and federal legislatures, and the executive.

ARMED FORCES

Defence forces and expenditure

Country	Total active duty personnel (1991)[a]	Military expenditure as percentage of GDP[b] (1988)	Country	Total active duty personnel (1991)[a]	Military expenditure as percentage of GDP[b] (1988)
Australia	68 300	2.7	New Zealand	11 300	2.2
Austria	44 000	1.2	Nicaragua	30 500	17.2
Canada	86 600	2.1	Norway	32 700	3.2
China	3 030 000	3.9	Oman	25 500	19.1
CIS (Former USSR)	3 400 000	11.9	Pakistan	565 000	6.9
Denmark	31 700	2.2	Peru	120 000	4.9
Egypt	420 000	7.8	Philippines	108 500	1.7
France	453 100	3.9	Poland	305 000	8.7
Germany	476 300	2.9	Portugal	61 800	3.3
Greece	158 500	6.5	Romania	200 800	6.5
Hungary	86 500	6.3	Saudi Arabia	76 500	16.5
India	1 265 000	3.5	Singapore	55 500	5.3
Iran	528 000	7.9	South Africa	72 400	4.3
Iraq	382 500	32.0	Spain	257 400	2.2
Israel	141 000	13.8	Sri Lanka	22 000	4.6
Italy	389 600	2.6	Sudan	71 500	2.4
Japan	246 400	1.0	Sweden	63 000	2.8
Jordan	101 300	21.0	Switzerland	3 500	2.1
Kenya	23 600	3.6	Syria	404 000	10.9
Korea, N	1 111 000	20.0	Taiwan	370 000	5.2
Korea, S	750 000	4.3	Thailand	283 000	3.1
Kuwait	8 200	5.1	Turkey	647 400	3.9
Libya	85 000	11.1	USSR see CIS		
Luxembourg	800	1.0	United Arab		
Malaysia	12 900	2.8	Emirates	44 000	6.8
Mexico	175 000	0.6	United Kingdom	300 100	4.3
Morocco	195 500	6.0	United States	2 029 600	6.3
Mozambique	58 000	8.4	Vietnam	1 041 000	19.4
Netherlands	101 400	3.0			

[a]Figures are approximate. [b]Gross Domestic Product.

Ranks in the UK armed forces

Army	Royal Air Force	Navy
1 Field Marshal	1 Marshal of the RAF	1 Admiral of the Fleet
2 General (Gen.)	2 Air Chief Marshal	2 Admiral (Adm.)
3 Lieutenant-General (Lt.-Gen.)	3 Air Marshal	3 Vice-Admiral (Vice-Adm.)
4 Major-General (Maj.-Gen.)	4 Air Vice-Marshal	4 Rear-Admiral (Rear-Adm.)
5 Brigadier (Brig.)	5 Air Commodore (Air Cdre)	5 Commodore (1st & 2nd Class) (Cdre)
6 Colonel (Col.)	6 Group Captain (Gp Capt.)	6 Captain (Capt.)
7 Lieutenant-Colonel (Lt.-Col.)	7 Wing Commander (Wg Cdr.)	7 Commander (Cdr.)
8 Major (Maj.)	8 Squadron Leader (Sqn. Ldr.)	8 Lieutenant-Commander (Lt.-Cdr.)
9 Captain (Capt.)	9 Flight Lieutenant (Flt. Lt.)	9 Lieutenant (Lt.)
10 Lieutenant (Lt.)	10 Flying Officer (FO)	10 Sub-Lieutenant (Sub-Lt.)
11 Second Lieutenant (2nd Lt.)	11 Pilot Officer (PO)	11 Acting Sub-Lieutenant (Acting Sub-Lt.)

Society

POLITICS

United Nations membership

Grouped according to year of entry.

1945	Argentina, Australia, Belgium, Belorussian SSR (Belarus, 1991), Bolivia, Brazil, Canada, Chile, China (Taiwan to 1971), Colombia, Costa Rica, Cuba, Czechoslovakia (to 1993), Denmark, Dominican Republic, Ecuador, Egypt, El Salvador, Ethiopia, France, Greece, Guatemala, Haiti, Honduras, India, Iran, Iraq, Lebanon, Liberia, Luxembourg, Mexico, Netherlands, New Zealand, Nicaragua, Norway, Panama, Paraguay, Peru, Philippines, Poland, Saudi Arabia, South Africa, Syria, Turkey, Ukranian SSR (Ukraine, 1991), USSR (Russia, 1991), UK, USA, Uruguay, Venezuela, Yugoslavia[a] (to 1992)
1946	Afghanistan, Iceland, Sweden, Thailand
1947	Pakistan, Yemen (N, to 1990)
1948	Burma (Myanmar, 1989)
1949	Israel
1950	Indonesia
1955	Albania, Austria, Bulgaria, Cambodia, Ceylon (Sri Lanka, 1970), Finland, Hungary, Ireland, Italy, Jordan, Laos, Libya, Nepal, Portugal, Romania, Spain
1956	Japan, Morocco, Sudan, Tunisia
1957	Ghana, Malaya (Malaysia, 1963)
1958	Guinea
1960	Cameroon, Central African Republic, Chad, Congo, Côte d'Ivoire, Cyprus, Dahomey (Benin, 1975), Gabon, Madagascar, Mali, Niger, Nigeria, Senegal, Somalia, Togo, Upper Volta (Burkina Faso, 1984), Zaïre
1961	Mauritania, Mongolia, Sierra Leone, Tanganyika (within Tanzania, 1964)
1962	Algeria, Burundi, Jamaica, Rwanda, Trinidad and Tobago, Uganda
1963	Kenya, Kuwait, Zanzibar (within Tanzania, 1964)
1964	Malawi, Malta, Tanzania, Zambia
1965	Maldives, Singapore, The Gambia
1966	Barbados, Botswana, Guyana, Lesotho
1967	Yemen (S, to 1990)
1968	Equatorial Guinea, Mauritius, Swaziland
1970	Fiji
1971	Bahrain, Bhutan, China (People's Republic), Oman, Qatar, United Arab Emirates
1973	Bahamas, German Democratic Republic (within GFR, 1990), German Federal Republic
1974	Bangladesh, Grenada, Guinea-Bissau
1975	Cape Verde, Comoros, Mozambique, Papua New Guinea, São Tomé and Principe, Suriname
1976	Angola, Seychelles, Western Samoa
1977	Djibouti, Vietnam
1978	Dominica, Solomon Islands
1979	St Lucia
1980	St Vincent and the Grenadines, Zimbabwe
1981	Antigua and Barbuda, Belize, Vanuatu
1983	St Christopher and Nevis
1984	Brunei
1990	Liechenstein, Namibia, Yemen (formerly N Yemen and S Yemen)
1991	Estonia, Federated States of Micronesia, Latvia, Lithuania, Marshall Islands, N Korea, S Korea
1992	Armenia, Azerbaijan, Bosnia-Herzegovina, Croatia, Georgia, Kazakhstan, Kyrgysztan, Moldova, San Marino, Slovenia, Tajikistan, Turkmenistan, Uzbekistan
1993	Andorra, Czech Republic, Eritrea, Former Yugoslav Republic of Macedonia, Monaco, Slovak Republic

[a] Yugoslavia was excluded from UN membership in 1992 and asked to reapply.

Main bodies of the United Nations

General Assembly	Plenary body which controls much of the UN's work, supervises the subsidiary organs, sets priorities, and debates major issues of international affairs.
Security Council	Has fifteen members, but is dominated by five permanent members (China, France, Russia, UK, USA). Primary role is to maintain international peace and security. Empowered to order mandatory sanctions, call for ceasefires, and establish peace-keeping forces.
Secretariat	Headed by Secretary General. Staff of 66 000 worldwide answerable to UN only and are engaged in considerable diplomatic work.
International Court of Justice	Consists of fifteen judges appointed by the Council and the Assembly. Jurisdiction depends on consent of the states who are parties to a dispute. Also offers advisory opinions to various organs of UN.
Economic and Social Council	Elected by the General Assembly. It supervises the work of various committees, commissions and expert bodies in the economic and social area, and coordinates the work of UN specialized agencies.
Trusteeship Council	Oversees the transition of Trust territories to self-government.

Specialized agencies of the United Nations

Abbreviated form	Full title and location	Area of concern
ILO	International Labour Organization, Geneva	Social justice.
FAO	Food and Agriculture, Rome	Improvement of the production and distribution of agricultural products.
UNESCO	United Nations Educational, Scientific and Cultural Organization, Paris	Stimulation of popular education and the spread of culture.
ICAO	International Civil Aviation Organization, Montreal	Encouragement of safety measures in international flight.
IBRD	International Bank for Reconstruction and Development, Washington	Aid of development through investment.
IMF	International Monetary Fund, Washington	Promotion of international monetary cooperation.
UPU	Universal Postal Union, Berne	Uniting members within a single postal territory.
WHO	World Health Organization, Geneva	Promotion of the highest standards of health for all people.
ITU	International Telecommunication Union, Geneva	Allocation of frequencies and regulation of procedures.
WMO	World Meteorological Organization, Geneva	Standardization and utilization of meteorological observations.
IFC	International Finance Corporation, Washington	Promotion of the international flow of private capital.
IMCO	Inter-governmental Maritime Consultative Organization, London	The coordination of safety at sea.
IDA	International Development Association, Washington	Credit on special terms to provide assistance for less-developed countries.
WIPO	World Intellectual Property Organization, Geneva	Protection of copyright, designs, inventions, etc.
IFAD	International Fund for Agricultural Development, Rome	Increase of food production in developing countries by the generation of grants or loans.
UNIDO	United Nations Industrial Development Organization, Vienna	Promotion of industrialization of developing countries, with special emphasis on manufacturing sector. Provides technical assistance and advice, as well as help with planning.
IAEA[a]	International Atomic Energy Association, Vienna	Promotes research and development into peaceful uses of nuclear energy, and oversees system of safeguards and controls governing misuse of nuclear materials for military purposes.
UNICEF[b]	United Nations Children's Fund, New York	Provides primary healthcare and education in developing countries.
UNHCR[b]	United Nations High Commissioner for Refugees, Geneva	Protects rights and interests of refugees; organizes emergency relief and longer-term solutions, eg local integration, resettlement, or voluntary repatriation

[a]Linked to UN but not specialized agency.   [b]Specialized bodies established by the General Assembly and supervised jointly with the Economic and Social Council.

United Nations Secretaries General

1946–53	Trygve Lie *Norway*
1953–61	Dag Hammarskjöld *Sweden*
1962–71	U Thant *Burma*
1971–81	Kurt Waldheim *Austria*
1982–92	Javier Pérez de Cuéllar *Peru*
1992–	Boutros Boutros Ghali *Egypt*

Commonwealth Secretaries General

1965–75	Arnold Smith *Canada*
1975–90	Shridath S Ramphal *Guyana*
1990–	Emeka Anyaoku *Nigeria*

Commonwealth members

The 'Commonwealth' is a free association of independent nations formerly subject to British imperial government, and maintaining friendly and practical links with the UK. In 1931 the Statute of Westminster established the British Commonwealth of Nations; the adjective 'British' was deleted after World War 2. Most of the states granted independence, beginning with India in 1947, chose to be members of the Commonwealth.

Name of country	Year of joining	Name of country	Year of joining	Name of country	Year of joining
Antigua and Barbuda[a]	1981	Kiribati	1979	Seychelles	1976
Australia[a]	1931	Lesotho	1966	Sierra Leone	1961
Bahamas[a]	1973	Malawi	1964	Singapore	1965
Bangladesh[a]	1972	Malaysia	1957	Solomon Islands[a]	1978
Barbados[a]	1966	Maldives	1982	Sri Lanka	1948
Belize[a]	1981	Malta	1964	Swaziland	1968
Botswana	1966	Mauritius[a]	1968	Tanzania	1961
Brunei	1984	Nauru	1968	Tonga	1970
Canada[a]	1931	New Zealand[a]	1931	Trinidad and Tobago	1962
Cyprus	1961	Nigeria	1960	Tuvalu[a]	1978
Dominica	1978	Pakistan	1947	Uganda	1962
Gambia, The	1965		left 1962,	United Kingdom	1931
Ghana	1957		rejoined 1989	Vanuatu	1980
Grenada[a]	1974	Papua New Guinea[a]	1975	Western Samoa	1970
Guyana	1966	St Kitts and Nevis[a]	1983	Zambia	1964
India	1947	St Lucia[a]	1979	Zimbabwe	1980
Jamaica[a]	1962	St Vincent and the	1979		
Kenya	1963	Grenadines[a]			

[a]Member states recognizing the Queen, represented by a Governor-General, as their Head of State.

Ireland resigned from the association in 1948, and South Africa in 1961.

The European Union

The European Union (previously the European Community) is a community of twelve states in Western Europe created for the purpose of achieving economic and political integration. While the Union has grown in the 1970s and 1980s and continues to progress towards economic union, political integration still seems a distant possibility.

Name of country	Year of joining	No. of seats in European Parliament
Belgium	1958	24
Denmark	1973	16
France	1958	81
Germany	1958	81
Greece	1981	24
Ireland	1973	15
Italy	1958	81
Luxembourg	1958	6
Netherlands	1958	25
Portugal	1986	24
Spain	1986	60
United Kingdom	1973	81

Representation of political parties in the European Parliament[a]

Party	No. of seats
Socialists	179
European People's Party	162
Liberal Democratic Reformists	45
European United Left	29
Greens	27
European Democratic Alliance	21
Rainbow Alliance	15
European Right	14
Coalition Left	13
Independents	13

[a]The figures represent the political groupings in the parliament since 1989.

European Union policies and policy makers

	Date established	Role
Common Agricultural Policy (CAP)	1962	Basic principles are free trade within the community for agricultural goods; preference for domestic production; control of imports from the rest of the world. Objectives are increased agricultural productivity; reasonable prices for consumers; stability of markets and food supplies.

	Date established	Role
Council of Ministers, Brussels	1974	Composed of foreign ministers from each member state, representing national interests within the context of the Union. It is the main body within the Union influencing legislation. Decisions are now taken on the basis of unanimity rather than majority voting.
European Atomic Energy Commission (EURATOM)	1957	Objective is to promote peaceful ways of using atomic energy.
European Coal and Steel Community (ECSC)	1952	Created common framework of laws and institutions to regulate coal and steel industries. Has powers to set quotas and minimum prices. Has abolished currency restrictions, border charges, and discrimination in transport rates.
European Commission, Brussels	1967	This is the bureaucracy of the EU, conducting both administrative and political business. Its functions are to uphold the European ideal, propose new policy initiatives, and ensure that existing policies are implemented. Comprises seventeen members elected by the member countries. The Commission makes decisions by a majority vote and is directly responsible to the European parliament.
European Court of Justice, Luxembourg	1958	Judges cases involving member states; interprets Union treaties and legislation; decides on whether Union law has been breached by any member states.
European Investment Bank, Luxembourg	1958	Finances capital investment projects to help development of the Union. Each member country appoints a minister to the Board of Governors. Bank's capital is made up from the member states' subscriptions. It is a non-profit-making organization.
European Monetary System (EMS)	1979	Financial system set up by EU members with the aim of stabilizing and harmonizing currencies. Member states use a special currency – the European Currency Unit (ECU). A percentage of the members' foreign exchange reserve is deposited with the European Monetary Cooperation Fund, and ECUs are received in exchange.
European Parliament, Brussels	1979 (start of direct elections)	The representative assembly of the EU. It has no legislative power but is able to dismiss the Commission if deemed necessary and to reject or amend the Union budget. It has been directly elected since 1979 and elections are held every five years.

International alliances

Name of organization	Function
Arab League	Founded in 1945 with the aim of encouraging Arab unity. League today has twenty-one member states.
Association of South-East Asian Nations (ASEAN)	Formed in 1967 to promote economic cooperation between Indonesia, Malaysia, the Philippines, Thailand, and Singapore. Brunei joined 1984.
Caribbean Community and Common Market (CARICOM)	Established in 1973 with three objectives: coordination of foreign policy among member states; provision of common services; cooperation in matters of health, education, culture, and industrial relations. There are thirteen member states.
Commonwealth, The	Free association of independent states formerly subject to British imperial rule and maintaining friendly and practical links with the UK.
Council for Mutual Economic Assistance (COMECON)	A body founded by Stalin in 1949 and dominated by the Soviet Union. Its purpose was ostensibly economic integration of the Eastern Bloc as a counterbalance to the economic powers of the EC and EFTA. The ten member states were the USSR, Bulgaria, Cuba, Czechoslovakia, East Germany, Hungary, Mongolia, Poland, Romania, and Vietnam. Disbanded in 1991 and replaced by the Organization for International Economic Cooperation.

Politics

International alliances (continued)

Name of organization	Function
Council of Europe	Established in 1949, an association of European states which has a Committee of Foreign Ministers and a representative Parlimentary Assembly meeting at Strasbourg to discuss matters of concern.
Economic Community of West African States (ECOWAS)	Founded in Lagos in 1975 to promote cultural, economic, and social development of West Africa through mutual cooperation. Measures include gradual elimination of trade barriers and improvement of communication and transportation. Supreme authority is invested in the annual summit of all member states' (sixteen) heads of government.
European Economic Community (often commonly referred to as EC)	An association, established in 1958, which is essentially a customs union, with a common external tariff and common market with the removal of barriers to trade among the members. From 1994, it became known as the European Union.
European Free Trade Association (EFTA)	Established in 1960 with the aim of securing free trade of industrial goods between members. Also aimed to create single market in N Europe. Relations expanded with non-EC states in recent years, particularly E Europe. Free trade agreements already signed with Czechoslovakia and Turkey. Economic cooperation declarations signed with Bulgaria, Estonia, Latvia, Lithuania, Romania, Slovenia.
League of Nations	An international organization formed in 1919. Main aims were to preserve international peace and security by speedy settlement of disputes and promotion of disarmament. After World War 2 it transferred its functions to the United Nations.
Nordic Council	Established in 1952 as advisory body on economic and social cooperation, comprising parliamentary delegates from Denmark, Iceland, Norway, Sweden, Finland, Greenland, and Faroe and Åland Islands.
North Atlantic Treaty Organization (NATO)	Established in 1949, it is a permanent military alliance established originally to defend W Europe against Soviet aggression. Treaty commits members to regard an armed attack on one of them as an attack on all of them, and for all to assist the country attacked by such actions as are deemed necessary.
Organization for Economic Cooperation and Development (OECD)	Set up in 1961 to assist member states to develop economic and social policies aimed at high sustained economic growth with financial stability. It has twenty-four members.
Organization for European Economic Cooperation (OEEC)	Established in 1948 by sixteen European countries and by the occupying forces on behalf of W Germany. Formal aims were to promote trade, stability, and expansion. Replaced in 1961 by the OECD.
Organization of African Unity (OAU)	Founded in 1963 by representatives of thirty-two African governments and dedicated to the eradication of all forms of colonialism in Africa. It had fifty-one members in 1990.
Organization of Arab Petroleum Exporting Countries (OAPEC)	Founded in 1968, under the umbrella of OPEC, by Saudi Arabia, Kuwait, and Libya. By 1972 all Arab oil producers had joined.
Organization of Central American States	Established in 1951 by Costa Rica, El Salvador, Guatemala, Honduras, and Nicaragua to promote economic, social, and cultural cooperation. In 1965 this was extended to include political and educational cooperation.
Organization of the Petroleum Exporting Countries (OPEC)	Created in 1960 as a permanent inter-governmental organization which aimed to unify and coordinate the policies of members and to determine the best means of protecting their interests.
Warsaw Pact	Consisted of the countries which signed the East European Mutual Assistance Treaty in Warsaw in 1955 – Albania, Bulgaria, Czechoslovakia, East Germany, Hungary, Poland, Romania, and the USSR. Established a unified military command of the armed forces of all the signatories. All members were committed to giving immediate assistance to any other party attacked in Europe. Formally dissolved in 1991.
Western European Union (WEU)	Founded in 1955 to coordinate defence and other policies, replacing the European Defence Community. Members include Belgium, France, Germany, Italy, Luxembourg, Netherlands, and the UK. Consists of a Council of Ministers, a representative assembly in the Consultative Assembly of the Council of Europe, and a Standing Armaments Committee which works in cooperation with NATO.

Some political systems

Country	Form of government	System of voting
Argentina	Federal republic Two chambers – Senate and Chamber of Deputies	Simple plurality
Australia	Federal commonwealth Two chambers – Senate and House of Representatives	Alternative vote
Austria	Federal republic Two chambers – Federal Council and National Council	Proportional representation (party list)
Belgium	Parliamentary state and constitutional monarchy Two chambers – Senate and House of Representatives	Proportional representation (party list)
Botswana	Unitary republic One chamber – National Assembly	Simple plurality
Brazil	Federal republic Two chambers – Senate and Chamber of Deputies	Proportional representation (party list)
Canada	Federal commonwealth Two chambers – Senate and House of Commons	Simple plurality
China	People's republic One chamber – National People's Congress	–
Cyprus	Unitary republic One chamber – House of Representatives	Proportional representation (second ballot)
Denmark	Parliamentary state and constitutional monarchy One chamber – Folketing	Proportional representation (party list)
Egypt	Unitary republic One chamber – People's Assembly	Proportional representation (second ballot)
Ethiopia	Unitary republic One chamber – National Assembly	Simple plurality
Finland	Constitutional republic One chamber – Eduskunta	Proportional representation (party list)
France	Constitutional republic Two chambers – Senate and National Assembly	Proportional representation (second ballot)
Germany	Federal republic Two chambers – Bundestag and Bundesrat	Proportional representation (additional member)
Greece	Unitary republic One chamber – Greek Chamber of Deputies	Proportional representation (party list)
India	Federal republic Two chambers – Council of States and House of the People	Simple plurality
Indonesia	Unitary republic One chamber – People's Consultative Assembly	Proportional representation (party list)
Iran	Islamic republic One chamber – Islamic Consultative Assembly	Proportional representation (second ballot)
Iraq	Republic One chamber – National Assembly	Simple plurality
Ireland	Republic Two chambers – Senate and House of Representatives	Proportional representation (single transferable vote)
Israel	Republic One chamber – Knesset	Proportional representation (party list)
Italy	Republic Two chambers – Senate and Chamber of Deputies	Proportional representation (party list)
Jamaica	Parliamentary State Two chambers – Senate and House of Representatives	Simple plurality
Japan	Parliamentary state and monarchy Two chambers – House of Councillors and House of Representatives	Limited vote
Luxembourg	Parliamentary state and constitutional monarchy One chamber – Chamber of Deputies	Proportional representation (party list)
Malaysia	Federation Two chambers – Senate and House of Representatives	Simple plurality
Malta	Unitary republic One chamber – House of Representatives	Proportional representation (single transferable vote)
Mexico	Federal state Two chambers – Senate and Chamber of Deputies	Proportional representation (additional member)
Netherlands	Parliamentary state and constitutional monarchy Two chambers – First Chamber and Second Chamber	Proportional representation (party list)

Proportional representation Any system of voting designed to ensure that the representation of voters is in proportion to their numbers.

Alternative vote Uses single-member constituencies, each voter choosing a candidate by marking 1 against his/her name. First-preference votes are counted and if one candidate obtains more than 50 per cent of all votes, he/she is elected.

Second ballot Simple majority election is held and if no one gets more than 50 per cent of total vote, the candidate with the fewest votes is eliminated and a second election is held.

Party list Political parties fighting the election produce a list of candidates, presented in descending order of preference. In many cases, the elector votes for the party of his/her choice and seats are then allocated to each party according to the total number of votes received. Names are taken from the lists to fill the seats.

Additional member This system also uses party lists but allows the voter to cast two votes, one for the party and one for the candidate. Half the assembly is elected on simple plurality basis; the other half, using party lists, is chosen so that chamber membership accurately reflects the national vote.

Single transferable vote Uses multi-member constituencies. All candidates are listed on the ballot paper and the voter states his/her order of preference. All votes cast are counted and the 'electoral quota' (the minimum number of votes needed to be elected) is calculated. Any candidates with this quota or more is automatically elected.

Limited vote Multi-member constituencies each return members, but voters are allowed only one non-transferable vote. The three, four or five candidates winning most votes in each constituency are then returned on a simple plurality basis.

Simple plurality Also known as the 'first-past-the-post' system. The party that gains the majority of votes cast secures all the available assembly seats.

ECONOMY

Selected indices of world agricultural and food production (1979–81 = 100)

Region or country	Total agricultural production						Total food production						Per capita food production					
	1986	1987	1988	1989	1990	1991[a]	1986	1987	1988	1989	1990	1991[a]	1986	1987	1988	1989	1990	1991[a]
Developed countries	109	108	105	109	111	107	109	108	105	110	111	107	105	103	100	104	104	100
United States	100	100	94	102	105	104	102	100	94	103	105	103	96	94	89	95	96	94
Canada	124	116	103	114	127	125	125	116	104	115	128	126	118	109	96	105	116	113
Europe	109	109	108	110	109	108	109	109	108	110	109	108	107	106	105	107	105	104
Japan	106	102	97	99	99	100	108	106	104	102	102	104	104	99	95	97	97	98
Oceania	109	108	113	112	116	115	107	102	110	109	111	109	99	96	95	97	97	94
South Africa	97	101	105	111	103	105	97	102	105	112	104	109	85	87	88	92	83	82
Former USSR	118	117	117	120	120	107	119	119	119	123	122	108	113	112	110	114	114	98
Less-developed countries	122	125	132	136	140	141	123	125	132	136	140	141	109	108	112	113	114	112
South and East Asia[b]	127	130	137	144	150	150	127	130	138	143	149	149	114	114	118	121	124	121
China	135	142	144	149	162	159	135	140	142	148	159	156	125	128	128	131	140	135
India	123	122	138	147	148	150	124	124	139	148	149	151	109	106	117	122	120	120
Indonesia	138	138	144	149	160	163	138	140	147	152	163	166	122	121	125	127	133	133
Korea, South	114	104	111	109	113	105	116	106	113	111	114	107	106	96	103	99	102	94
Malaysia	144	151	162	169	173	178	161	170	183	199	204	209	138	141	148	157	157	157
Pakistan	133	136	141	150	155	162	129	130	136	146	150	156	103	100	101	105	104	105
Philippines	104	103	105	110	114	115	102	102	104	109	114	115	88	85	85	86	88	87
Thailand	114	114	127	132	124	134	112	111	126	130	118	129	100	98	107	110	99	106
Vietnam	130	135	138	149	158	165	128	133	135	147	132	161	113	115	115	121	125	127
Western Asia	123	121	128	118	130	127	126	123	130	119	155	129	104	99	102	91	98	94
Iran	145	142	137	133	153	157	145	143	138	134	132	158	115	110	103	98	110	110
Turkey	114	115	121	113	121	119	115	116	121	112	121	120	99	98	100	91	96	94
Africa[c]	120	119	126	130	130	134	120	119	126	129	130	134	100	96	98	98	96	95
Egypt	133	137	137	140	148	143	140	146	148	153	161	156	120	122	121	122	126	119
Ethiopia	106	102	103	107	110	108	108	102	105	108	110	110	95	88	87	87	87	84
Morocco	160	139	173	176	162	189	160	138	173	175	161	188	137	116	140	139	124	142
Nigeria	126	128	138	149	151	155	126	128	139	149	151	155	104	102	106	111	109	108
Sudan, The	103	93	117	91	90	109	102	90	117	89	90	110	85	73	92	68	87	80
Zaire	119	122	125	128	129	130	119	121	125	127	129	130	99	99	96	97	95	93
Latin America	110	115	121	123	123	113	113	116	123	126	129	128	99	100	104	104	102	102
Argentina	96	98	109	107	105	103	96	99	108	109	105	103	89	89	97	96	92	88
Brazil	110	128	130	138	128	131	115	126	135	142	132	136	101	108	113	117	107	108
Colombia	110	111	118	125	132	134	114	116	123	133	136	137	100	100	105	111	111	110
Mexico	111	111	118	117	119	124	112	111	118	119	121	126	97	95	98	96	96	98
Peru	109	114	124	123	109	112	109	116	126	123	111	115	95	99	105	101	89	90
Venezuela	124	118	121	129	135	135	124	118	121	129	137	138	104	97	97	101	104	101
World	116	116	119	123	125	124	116	116	118	123	125	124	104	103	103	105	105	102

[a]Preliminary. [b]Excludes Japan. [c]Excludes South Africa. *Source:* Food and Agriculture Organization of the United Nations, *FAO Quarterly Bulletin of Statistics.*

	Number (thousands)	Proportion of labour force[b] (%)					Number (millions)				
	1990	1981–9	1990	1991	1992	1993	1981–89	1990	1991	1992	1993
North America	8000.2	7.5	5.8	7.1	7.4	6.8	9.6	8.0	9.9	10.4	9.8
Canada	1110.3	9.5	8.1	10.3	10.4	10.0	1.2	1.1	1.4	1.4	1.4
United States	6889.9	7.3	5.5	6.7	7.1	6.5	8.4	6.9	8.4	9.0	8.4
Japan	1325.3	2.6	2.1	2.1	2.2	2.3	1.5	1.3	1.4	1.4	1.5
Central and Western Europe	6340.7	8.2	6.3	7.0	7.7	7.7	8.0	6.3	7.1	7.9	7.9
Austria	114.8	3.3	3.3	3.7	4.0	4.2	0.1	0.1	0.1	0.1	0.2
Belgium	364.9	11.5	8.7	9.3	9.7	9.6	0.5	0.4	0.4	0.4	0.4
France	2170.5	9.4	8.9	9.4	9.8	9.8	2.2	2.2	2.3	2.4	2.4
Germany	1454.7	6.0	4.9	4.3	4.7	4.8	1.7	1.5	1.3	1.4	1.5
Ireland	179.0	15.0	13.7	15.8	16.9	16.6	0.2	0.2	0.2	0.2	0.2
Luxembourg	2.4	1.4	1.3	1.4	1.4	1.3	0	0	0	0	0
Netherlands	345.0	9.0	6.4	5.9	6.5	6.9	0.5	0.3	0.3	0.4	0.4
Switzerland	22.0	0.6	0.6	1.3	2.5	2.5	0	0	0	0.1	0.1
United Kingdom	1687.5	10.0	5.9	8.3	9.8	9.7	2.8	1.7	2.4	2.8	2.7
Southern Europe	7505.2	12.1	11.3	11.7	11.9	12.1	7.6	7.5	7.9	8.1	8.3
Greece	280.9	7.0	7.0	8.2	9.4	10.3	0.3	0.3	0.3	0.4	0.4
Italy	2654.4	10.6	11.1	11.0	11.2	11.5	2.4	2.7	2.7	2.7	2.8
Portugal	220.0	7.4	4.7	4.1	5.0	5.4	0.3	0.2	0.2	0.2	0.3
Spain	2441.0	18.8	16.3	16.3	16.1	15.5	2.6	2.4	2.5	2.4	2.3
Turkey	1909.0	11.0	10.0	11.5	11.8	12.2	1.9	1.9	2.2	2.3	2.5
Nordic countries	543.1	4.5	4.4	6.0	7.6	7.5	0.5	0.5	0.7	0.9	0.9
Denmark	271.7	9.1	9.5	10.4	10.7	10.2	0.3	0.3	0.3	0.3	0.3
Finland	88.2	4.9	3.5	7.6	11.3	10.9	0.1	0.1	0.2	0.3	0.3
Iceland	2.3	0.8	1.8	1.7	2.6	2.4	0	0	0	0	0
Norway	111.8	2.9	5.2	5.5	5.8	5.3	0.1	0.1	0.1	0.1	0.1
Sweden	69.2	2.2	1.5	2.7	4.5	5.2	0.1	0.1	0.1	0.2	0.2
Oceania	713.9	7.1	7.1	9.7	10.6	10.2	0.6	0.7	1.0	1.1	1.1
Australia	589.9	7.7	6.9	9.6	10.4	9.9	0.6	0.6	0.8	0.9	0.9
New Zealand	124.0	4.6	7.8	10.3	11.8	12.0	0.1	0.1·	0.2	0.2	0.2
OECD Europe	14389.1	9.3	8.0	8.7	9.3	9.3	16.1	14.4	15.7	16.9	17.0
EC	12071.8	9.9	8.4	8.8	9.4	9.4	13.8	12.1	12.8	13.7	13.7
Total OECD	24428.5	7.5	6.2	7.1	7.5	7.3	27.8	24.4	27.9	29.9	29.4

[a] For sources and definitions, see *OECD Economic Outlook*, No. 51, June 1992. [b] The rates are not necessarily comparable between countries. Figures relate to unemployment in the Organization for Economic Cooperation and Development (OECD) area.

Inflation and unemployment

	GNP/GDP deflator (% change from preceding year)			Unemployment rate[a] (%)		
	1990	1991	1992	1990	1991	1992
North America						
Canada	3.0	2.7	1.9	8.1	10.3	10.4
United States	4.1	3.6	2.8	5.5	6.7	7.1
Japan	2.1	1.9	1.7	2.1	2.1	2.2
Central and Western Europe						
Austria	2.9	3.8	4.2	3.3	3.7	4.0
Belgium	3.0	3.1	3.1	8.7	9.3	9.7
France	3.1	3.0	3.1	8.9	9.4	9.8
Germany	3.4	4.6	4.5	4.9	4.3	4.7
Ireland[b]	-0.5	2.7	3.5	13.7	15.8	16.9
Luxembourg	2.1	1.6	3.8	1.3	1.4	1.4
Netherlands	2.9	3.3	3.1	6.4	5.9	6.5
Switzerland	5.3	5.2	4.5	0.6	1.3	2.5
United Kingdom	6.4	6.9	5.1	5.9	8.3	9.8
Southern Europe						
Greece	20.5	19.5	14.8	7.0	8.2	9.4
Italy	7.6	7.3	5.3	11.1	11.0	11.2
Portugal	14.3	13.6	11.3	4.7	4.1	5.0
Spain	7.3	6.9	6.0	16.3	16.3	16.1
Turkey	54.4	56.0	59.0	10.0	11.5	11.8
Nordic countries						
Denmark	2.1	3.0	2.3	9.5	10.4	10.7
Finland	5.2	3.5	2.7	3.5	7.6	11.3
Iceland	13.6	8.2	3.7	1.8	1.7	2.6
Norway	4.5	1.5	0.0	5.2	5.5	5.8
Sweden	9.4	7.5	2.3	1.5	2.7	4.5
Oceania						
Australia	4.2	1.3	2.6	6.9	9.6	10.4
New Zealand	5.0	1.3	1.8	7.8	10.3	11.8
Total OECD	4.4	4.1	3.5	6.2	7.1	7.5

[a] Figures for 1991 onwards are estimated and projections. [b] GNP. *Source*: OECD, *Economic Outlook No. 51*.

Interest rates

Short-term: Three-month money market rates

Long-term

Energy production and consumption

Production of crude oil
Production of crude oil + NGL (1000 tonnes).

	1982	1983	1984	1985	1986	1987	1988	1989	1990
Australia	19766	19226	23138	26764	27436	27236	27171	24581	27998
Austria	1306	1281	1216	1161	1133	1082	1217	1198	1190
Canada	66467	68215	75885	75767	75662	80320	84038	81708	81554
Denmark	1686	2152	2314	2892	3621	4602	4734	5531	5994
France	2338	2317	2699	3243	3446	3645	3728	3627	3377
Germany	4234	4094	4030	4073	4031	3727	3946	3791	3594
Greece	1032	1241	1320	1322	1333	1221	1118	916	830
Italy	1789	2265	2295	2408	2558	3943	4841	4604	4668
Japan	420	441	426	553	647	621	607	560	553
Netherlands	1894	2900	3433	4069	4995	4663	4271	3814	3976
New Zealand	681	672	864	1282	1427	1370	1634	1829	1891
Norway	24411	30611	35050	38431	42375	49541	56351	74872	82058
Spain	1757	3185	2512	2383	2094	1852	1718	1333	1144
Sweden	14	23	13	8	4	4	3	3	3
Turkey	2333	2203	2087	2110	2394	2627	2569	2876	3712
United Kingdom	103218	114921	125924	127642	127053	123306	114459	91811	91616
United States	477469	479038	490624	493323	477001	462070	453910	424141	411848
OECD total	710815	734785	773830	787431	777210	771830	766315	727195	726006
IEA	708477	732468	771131	784188	773764	768185	762587	723568	722629
EU	117948	133075	144527	148032	149131	146959	138815	115427	115199
OECD Europe	146012	167193	182893	189742	195037	200213	198955	194376	202162
North America	543936	547253	566509	569090	552663	542390	537948	505849	493402
Pacific	20867	20339	24428	28599	29510	29227	29412	26970	30442

Consumption of oil
Final consumption of oil (1000 tonnes).

	1982	1983	1984	1985	1986	1987	1988	1989	1990
Australia	25575	24041	25146	25373	25769	25927	27469	28635	28893
Austria	8564	8801	8643	8641	9034	9290	9029	8955	9383
Belgium	15358	14431	14393	15280	17362	16977	17446	16851	16781
Canada	65539	62494	62894	62632	63215	65003	67608	69330	66448
Denmark	9190	8851	9012	9351	9287	8870	8329	7867	7789
Finland	9276	8845	8624	8241	9153	9461	9603	9589	9399
France	77343	77444	75186	74864	75072	75362	76008	76355	76618
Germany	96765	97320	99902	100896	106854	103487	104430	97348	102405
Greece	8671	8557	8661	8804	8585	9264	9643	10271	10421
Iceland	498	502	523	519	527	568	597	647	701
Ireland	3586	3432	3474	3486	3561	3636	3524	3702	4013
Italy	59730	60367	60790	59686	59723	61293	62465	63050	62151
Japan	137609	141074	147816	146503	149854	154206	163289	166433	170399
Luxembourg	992	956	964	1027	1105	1275	1297	1439	1580
Netherlands	16640	17983	18329	17676	19196	19097	19284	18895	19396
New Zealand	3509	3390	3508	3460	3559	3800	3885	4138	4334
Norway	7330	7239	7616	7886	8254	8974	8097	7902	7733
Portugal	6625	6210	6439	6401	6662	7004	7806	8164	8629
Spain	32947	33647	33411	32960	33052	33937	38258	37925	38941
Sweden	17252	15640	14615	15249	15919	14832	14802	14100	13702
Switzerland	10921	11970	11529	12572	12615	12516	12571	12676	12597
Turkey	13487	14301	14121	14744	16010	18329	18389	18744	20170
United Kingdom	58700	58080	58826	58439	61759	62140	65795	65951	65592
United States	620754	606367	632277	632551	647028	665395	684258	678899	667372
OECD total	1306861	1291942	1326699	1327241	1363155	1390643	1433882	1427866	1425847
IEA	1229020	1213996	1250990	1251858	1287556	1314713	1357277	1350864	1348528
EU	386547	387278	389387	388870	402218	402342	414285	407818	414316
OECD Europe	453875	454576	455058	456722	473730	476312	487373	480431	488001
North America	686293	668861	695171	695183	710243	730398	751866	748229	734220
Pacific	166693	168505	176470	175336	179182	183933	194643	199206	203626

Society

Production of natural gas
Production of natural gas (terajoules = 10^{12}J).

	1982	1983	1984	1985	1986	1987	1988	1989	1990
Australia	448025	468474	490073	522852	571092	588928	610477	627770	797666
Austria	48196	43925	46059	42249	40351	42024	45524	47644	46376
Belgium	1218	720	1478	1591	1043	1105	664	523	450
Canada	2861188	2687109	2930295	3191627	3007437	3253860	3836221	4062975	4157425
Denmark	–	–	9450	44841	77967	99244	98310	124992	127277
France	257074	259824	246820	209382	164608	152642	125478	121284	117403
Germany	555584	592478	620149	562459	515366	595606	554826	546308	545985
Greece	3375	3215	3538	3324	4555	5200	6237	6290	6404
Ireland	76966	82296	87282	92491	62923	62815	75676	85365	87127
Italy	549363	492598	521357	536769	601505	616473	626563	640451	652664
Japan	83991	85549	87517	91293	86369	88953	86025	82415	83851
Netherlands	2533357	2691648	2716794	2838839	2603758	2611144	2307408	2522206	2540607
New Zealand	80617	87270	115150	144851	168521	162678	178157	182770	181937
Norway	1028772	1041391	1097348	1088677	1129393	1193171	1202853	1242770	1130703
Spain	–	2931	9295	10681	15491	29630	37724	66069	59228
Switzerland	567	567	544	1356	1244	1011	933	633	511
Turkey	1482	2575	1608	2026	17518	11384	3792	6665	8120
United Kingdom	1477735	1523736	1491242	1661741	1738971	1829288	1761317	1724074	1903539
United States	19400350	17567532	19020959	17959454	17486128	18062977	18594050	18872910	19250285
OECD total	29407860	27633838	29496958	29006503	28294240	29408133	30152235	30964114	31697558
IEA	29150786	27374014	29250138	28797121	28129632	29255491	30026757	30842830	31580155
EU	5454672	5649446	5707405	5962118	5786187	6003147	5594203	5837562	6040684
OECD Europe	6533689	6737904	6852964	7096426	6974693	7250737	6847305	7135274	7226394
North America	22261538	20254641	21951254	21151081	20493565	21316837	22430271	22935885	23407710
Pacific	612633	641293	692740	758996	825982	840559	874659	892955	1063454

Consumption of natural gas
Final consumption of natural gas (terajoules = 10^{12}J).

	1982	1983	1984	1985	1986	1987	1988	1989	1990
Australia	268071	279458	288868	325855	351019	373259	379194	392113	416329
Austria	109788	108049	117167	124053	119026	119319	117497	121946	128446
Belgium	282278	281516	298715	307960	289182	307094	300492	309632	317260
Canada	1547409	1556272	1672882	1762068	1694642	1676577	1857560	1922112	1875250
Denmark	–	611	2290	11663	24842	33007	41867	45319	50990
Finland	19004	20553	22893	22650	24665	34672	34199	46846	60230
France	916941	967941	1043320	1082051	1100111	1118938	1080565	1096430	1124470
Germany	1278578	1335635	1417736	1476059	1475980	1593526	1570262	1598672	1644549
Greece	1176	1231	1876	2458	2734	3362	4515	4300	4289
Iceland	–	–	–	–	–	–	–	40	40
Ireland	21298	18154	23363	23928	34194	39084	39678	43480	46721
Italy	861496	878446	958043	1001102	1064683	1175210	1256430	1359584	1414339
Japan	62241	59696	64162	63104	59687	57711	59851	60060	60393
Luxembourg	12636	11883	12824	14059	14043	15181	16256	18261	19533
Netherlands	992189	1005050	1044629	1122029	1087448	1143382	1044693	1043171	1070082
New Zealand	26399	37268	62395	61726	62353	62585	64463	66475	66170
Spain	39833	46302	55448	63793	75300	95509	129498	180381	201194
Sweden	–	–	–	2997	7009	9010	10747	12729	15532
Switzerland	44233	49289	56066	58845	60466	65223	66421	72621	78310
Turkey	1482	2575	1608	1336	1766	2043	7926	19176	33062
United Kingdom	1749094	1769156	1800516	1912911	1937863	2010528	1934484	1904382	1958159
United States	13540099	12913405	13850620	13255530	12626853	13074037	14196865	14886865	14757447
OECD total	21774245	21342490	22795421	22696177	22113866	23009266	24213463	25204595	25342795
IEA	20857304	20374549	21752101	21614126	21013755	21890328	23132898	24108125	24218285
EU	6155519	6315925	6658760	7018013	7106380	7534821	7418740	7603612	7851586
OECD Europe	6330026	6496391	6856494	7227894	7319312	7765097	7655530	7876970	8167206
North America	15087508	14469677	15523502	15017598	14321495	14750614	16054425	16808977	16632697
Pacific	356711	376422	415425	450685	473059	493555	503508	518648	542892

Energy production and consumption (continued)

Production of coal
Production of hard coal (1000 tonnes).

	1982	1983	1984	1985	1986	1987	1988	1989	1990
Australia	89 453	98 267	104 583	117 504	133 383	147 718	134 807	147 804	159 417
Belgium	6 576	6 119	6 342	6 237	5 625	4 370	2 487	1 893	1 036
Canada	22 379	22 583	32 063	34 310	30 542	32 651	38 585	38 794	37 672
France	16 895	17 021	16 594	15 124	14 394	13 743	12 142	11 471	10 487
Germany	96 318	89 620	84 868	88 849	87 125	82 380	79 319	77 451	76 553
Ireland	62	75	70	57	54	45	45	43	35
Italy	–	–	–	–	29	14	40	74	58
Japan	17 606	17 062	16 644	16 382	16 012	13 049	11 223	10 187	8 262
New Zealand	2 107	2 255	2 307	2 279	2 176	2 327	2 227	2 554	2 427
Norway	440	502	451	507	437	399	264	339	311
Portugal	178	185	194	237	236	261	230	258	281
Spain	15 423	15 419	15 289	16 091	15 895	14 101	14 205	14 525	14 743
Sweden	13	13	13	12	12	25	30	–	11
Turkey	4 008	3 539	3 632	3 605	3 526	3 461	3 256	3 038	2 745
United Kingdom	121 427	116 448	49 549	90 793	104 645	101 645	101 661	98 285	89 303
United States	712 381	656 568	755 550	738 844	738 413	762 341	784 864	811 296	853 647
OECD total	1 105 266	1 045 676	1 088 149	1 130 831	1 152 494	1 178 530	1 185 385	1 218 012	1 256 988
IEA	1 088 371	1 028 655	1 071 555	1 115 707	1 138 100	1 164 787	1 173 243	1 206 541	1 246 501
EU	256 879	244 887	172 906	217 388	227 993	216 559	210 129	204 000	192 496
OECD Europe	261 340	248 941	177 002	221 512	231 968	2 200 444	213 679	207 377	195 563
North America	734 760	679 151	787 613	773 154	768 955	794 992	823 449	850 090	891 319
Pacific	109 166	117 584	123 534	136 165	151 571	163 094	148 257	160 545	170 106

Consumption of coal
Final consumption of hard coal (1000 tonnes).

	1982	1983	1984	1985	1986	1987	1988	1989	1990
Australia	3 648	3 613	4 020	4 678	4 791	4 806	4 815	5 013	5 098
Austria	404	592	835	661	633	538	447	397	405
Belgium	2 608	2 138	2 420	2 559	2 168	2 095	2 057	2 567	2 485
Canada	1 510	1 382	1 495	1 723	1 675	1 708	1 797	1 729	1 671
Denmark	444	296	543	684	599	632	662	639	574
Finland	1 093	1 088	1 145	1 256	1 096	1 264	1 108	1 377	1 379
France	6 468	5 763	6 114	7 068	6 978	7 065	7 182	7 154	7 411
Germany	7 211	7 495	7 825	7 481	6 950	6 923	7 105	6 809	7 057
Greece	491	1 054	1 333	1 443	1 408	1 364	1 396	1 276	1 380
Iceland	25	37	55	69	74	60	67	71	65
Ireland	1 267	1 446	1 444	1 507	1 700	1 574	1 474	1 391	1 271
Italy	2 170	1 731	2 223	2 783	1 455	1 935	1 202	1 302	1 912
Japan	11 745	9 468	10 419	10 859	9 777	11 009	12 942	14 245	18 961
Luxembourg	259	144	166	176	181	197	161	195	197
Netherlands	290	323	721	770	759	1 040	1 070	1 109	1 170
New Zealand	1 393	1 294	1 317	1 276	1 280	1 488	1 739	1 725	1 786
Norway	591	640	682	682	623	660	773	770	734
Portugal	63	144	193	320	575	704	809	839	820
Spain	3 773	3 740	3 715	3 585	3 452	3 247	3 379	3 306	2 762
Sweden	510	570	696	713	704	729	798	930	949
Switzerland	468	427	605	594	516	505	440	439	462
Turkey	1 152	1 051	1 498	1 655	1 616	1 948	2 409	2 380	2 736
United Kingdom	15 398	14 526	12 762	16 120	16 448	15 054	14 567	12 520	11 176
United States	62 299	64 605	70 717	68 386	67 682	66 224	67 549	66 063	67 381
OECD total	125 280	123 567	132 943	137 048	133 140	132 769	135 948	134 246	139 842
IEA	118 787	117 767	126 774	129 911	126 088	125 644	128 699	127 021	132 366
EU	40 442	38 800	39 459	44 496	42 673	41 830	41 064	39 107	38 215
OECD Europe	44 685	43 205	44 975	50 126	47 935	47 534	47 106	45 471	44 945
North America	63 809	65 987	72 212	70 109	69 357	67 932	69 346	67 792	69 052
Pacific	16 786	14 375	15 756	16 813	15 848	17 303	19 496	20 983	25 845

Production of electricity
Total production of electricity (gigawatt hours = thousand million watts).

	1982	1983	1984	1985	1986	1987	1988	1989	1990
Australia	105387	106298	112308	120962	126383	132670	138959	147788	154571
Austria	42891	42625	42382	44534	44653	50517	49025	50174	50414
Belgium	50696	52707	54657	57322	58676	63367	65349	67482	70846
Canada	387482	407981	437098	459045	468593	496335	505966	499538	482025
Denmark	23707	22186	22620	29064	30739	29449	27965	22312	25745
Finland	41175	42197	45287	49716	49266	53402	53878	53817	54563
France	279209	296812	324509	344301	362784	378309	391926	406891	420155
Germany	366877	373813	394884	408706	408266	418262	431164	440896	449497
Greece	23272	23983	24804	27740	28237	30272	33394	34456	35002
Iceland	3633	3828	3977	3900	4114	4210	4478	4537	4510
Ireland	10931	11178	11593	12088	12652	13064	13228	13833	14515
Italy	184445	182880	182669	185740	192330	201372	203561	210750	216891
Japan	581358	618377	648671	671952	676360	719067	753728	798757	857273
Luxembourg	941	830	896	942	1022	1019	1331	1372	1377
Netherlands	60312	59650	62778	62947	67158	68419	69611	73050	71866
New Zealand	24598	26138	27064	27334	28169	28686	29471	30578	31251
Norway	93156	106370	106666	103292	97284	104283	110019	119197	121601
Portugal	15418	18161	19247	18900	20355	20135	22489	25808	28500
Spain	114569	117196	120042	127363	129150	133390	139571	147842	150622
Sweden	100050	109391	123843	137140	138651	146571	146230	143091	146536
Switzerland	53580	53137	50566	56492	57564	59890	60690	54767	55787
Turkey	26552	27347	30613	34219	39695	44353	48049	52043	57543
United Kingdom	272783	277474	282469	297555	301590	302455	308136	313825	318977
United States	2376635	2449040	2562773	2621929	2639724	2732532	2874797	2957915	2980908
OECD total	5239657	5429599	5692416	5903183	5983415	6232029	6483015	6670719	6800975
IEA	4956815	5128959	5363930	5554982	5616517	5849510	6086611	6259291	6376310
EU	1403160	1436870	1501168	1572668	1612959	1659513	1707725	1758517	1803993
OECD Europe	1764197	1821765	1904502	2001961	2044186	2122739	2180094	2236143	2294947
North America	2764117	2857021	2999871	3080974	3108317	3228867	3380763	3457453	3462933
Pacific	711343	750813	788043	820248	830912	880423	922158	977123	1043095

Consumption of electricity
Final consumption of electricity (gigawatt hours = thousand million watts).

	1982	1983	1984	1985	1986	1987	1988	1989	1990
Australia	86894	87645	93457	98070	104238	109068	115783	122658	128034
Austria	33447	33987	35602	37018	37380	38770	40156	41453	43160
Belgium	43202	44418	46555	48303	49328	51822	54083	55988	57984
Canada	309508	324015	348708	364550	381490	388648	407379	416235	413671
Denmark	22441	22724	23846	25358	26717	27691	28051	28769	29290
Finland	38959	41985	45352	48519	49516	52986	55150	56635	58835
France	214812	226761	236827	249392	264299	276089	281721	293092	301912
Germany	317246	325337	340388	349634	354238	363477	369075	376501	380810
Greece	20146	21551	22991	23833	24115	25035	26898	28009	28471
Iceland	3239	3364	3537	3441	3602	3694	4023	4092	4053
Ireland	8564	8852	9254	9762	10201	10590	10724	11279	11868
Italy	161159	160460	169490	173609	178993	188411	198048	206837	214084
Japan	514960	546630	574161	592713	595377	631556	665669	707171	758438
Luxembourg	3403	3512	3745	3793	3812	3893	3983	4068	4127
Netherlands	56259	57459	59485	61449	62268	65136	68317	70597	73506
New Zealand	21340	22991	23955	24233	25304	25767	26666	27280	27791
Norway	77803	82812	88738	91415	90109	93187	94194	94421	93833
Portugal	15332	16167	16666	17644	18558	19438	20783	22041	23544
Spain	91290	95601	100093	102828	105036	109215	114160	122434	124932
Sweden	89423	94863	103267	113076	114424	119773	119846	119799	120477
Switzerland	36731	37970	39665	41321	42348	43591	44327	45502	46578
Turkey	22657	23581	26630	28462	30812	35107	38009	41259	44951
United Kingdom	224756	227536	232177	242564	250163	258447	265231	270398	274834
United States	2010450	2073145	2205571	2253015	2274601	2376361	2492363	2565134	2626165
OECD total	4424021	4583366	4850160	5004002	5096929	5317752	5544639	5731652	5891348
IEA	4205970	4353241	4609796	4751169	4829028	5037969	5258895	5434468	5585383
EU	1178610	1210378	1261517	1308169	1347728	1399244	1441074	1490013	1525362
OECD Europe	1480869	1528940	1604308	1671421	1715919	1786352	1836779	1893174	1937249
North America	2319958	2397160	2554279	2617565	2656091	2765009	2899742	2981369	3039836
Pacific	623194	657266	691573	715016	724919	766391	808118	857109	914263

Energy production and consumption (continued)

Production of nuclear energy
Production of nuclear energy (gigawatt hours).

	1982	1983	1984	1985	1986	1987	1988	1989	1990
Belgium	15664	24106	27743	34601	39394	41967	43102	41217	42722
Canada	38337	48610	52210	60521	71267	77261	82867	79872	72886
Finland	16776	17720	18867	19059	19059	19646	19554	19090	19215
France	108919	144261	191234	224100	254155	265520	275521	303931	314081
Germany	63577	65833	92577	125902	119580	130515	145082	149390	147159
Italy	6804	5783	6887	7024	8758	174	–	–	–
Japan	102430	114291	134264	159578	168305	187758	178659	182869	202272
Netherlands	3897	3589	3711	3899	4216	3556	3675	4019	3502
Spain	8771	10661	23086	28044	37458	41271	50466	56126	54273
Sweden	39045	41004	50926	58561	69951	67385	69424	65603	68185
Switzerland	15133	15710	18440	22558	22581	23003	22792	22836	23636
United Kingdom	43972	49928	53979	61095	59079	55238	63456	71734	65747
United States	299739	311298	347292	406712	438880	482586	558591	561116	611473
OECD total	763064	852794	1021216	1211654	1312683	1395880	1513189	1557803	1625151
IEA	654145	708533	829982	987554	1058528	1130360	1237668	1253872	1311070
EU	251604	304161	399217	484665	522640	538241	581302	626417	627484
OECD Europe	322558	378595	487450	584843	634231	648275	693072	733946	738520
North America	338076	359908	399502	467233	510147	559847	641458	640988	684359
Pacific	102430	114291	134264	159578	168305	187758	178659	182869	202272

Production of hydro energy
Production of hydro energy (gigawatt hours).

	1982	1983	1984	1985	1986	1987	1988	1989	1990
Australia	14570	12913	12890	14964	15511	14744	14963	15161	14785
Austria	30880	30589	29469	31603	31680	36725	36541	36146	32492
Belgium	1051	1174	1318	1350	1398	1469	1167	975	897
Canada	257865	266024	286196	303720	310697	316288	307553	291448	296919
Denmark	31	39	34	33	29	29	32	27	32
Finland	13088	13579	13246	12333	12389	13795	13361	13029	10931
France	71298	70888	67537	63663	64694	72365	78216	50602	57350
Germany	19646	18933	18470	17613	18544	20587	20714	19145	18366
Greece	3561	2340	2862	2805	3348	2964	2593	2147	1997
Iceland	3445	3628	3779	3704	3884	3957	4211	4259	4204
Ireland	1203	1178	1045	1180	1264	1116	1205	991	983
Italy	44081	44216	45434	44595	44531	42585	43547	37484	35079
Japan	84039	87995	76723	87946	86074	80846	95884	97825	95835
Luxembourg	494	452	450	510	534	552	825	825	823
Netherlands	–	–	–	3	3	1	2	37	120
New Zealand	17987	20198	20107	19707	21788	22078	23162	21999	23167
Norway	92888	106049	106339	102946	96819	103753	109544	118698	121137
Portugal	6982	8134	9817	10783	8542	9185	12302	6079	9303
Spain	27394	28865	33420	33033	27416	28167	36233	20047	26165
Sweden	55604	64066	68481	71589	61494	72442	70467	71921	73105
Switzerland	37405	36362	31180	33004	33925	35766	36803	30790	30982
Turkey	14167	11343	13426	12045	11872	18618	28949	17939	23148
United Kingdom	5637	6459	6060	6926	7001	6243	6964	6569	7062
United States	312305	335451	324361	283960	293752	252192	225169	267714	282638
OECD total	1115621	1170875	1172644	1160015	1157189	1156467	1170407	1131857	1167520
IEA	1040878	1096359	1101328	1092648	1088611	1080145	1087980	1076996	1105966
EU	181378	182678	186447	182494	177304	185263	203800	144928	158177
OECD Europe	428855	448294	452367	449718	429367	470319	503676	437710	454176
North America	570170	601475	610557	587680	604449	568480	532722	559162	579557
Pacific	116596	121106	109720	122617	123373	117668	134009	134985	133787

OECD Organization for Economic Cooperation and Development
IEA International Energy Agency
EU European Union

Growth industries: the ten highest by output

	Australia 1974–86	Canada 1981–6	France 1972–85	Germany 1978–86	Japan 1970–85	United Kingdom 1968–84	United States 1972–85
1	Real estate *DFD*	Computers *Exports*	Computers *DFD*	Computers *Exports*	Computers *DFD*	Computers *Exports*	Computers *DFD*
2	Communications *DFD*	Motor vehicles *Exports*	Communications *DFD*	Aerospace *Exports*	Pharmaceuticals *Tech.*	Real estate *Tech.*	Electronics *DFD*
3	Utilities *DFD*	Electronics *Exports*	Electronics *Exports/DFD*	Communications *DFD*	Electronics *Exports/DFD*	Electronics *Exports*	Communications *DFD*
4	Nonferrous *Exports*	Real estate *DFD*	Pharmaceuticals *DFD*	Real estate *Tech.*	Motor vehicles *Exports*	Finance and insurance *DFD*	Instruments *DFD*
5	Instruments *DFD*	Pharmaceuticals *DFD*	Aerospace *Exports*	Finance and insurance *DFD*	Communications *DFD*	Mining *Exports*	Social services *DFD*
6	Pharmaceuticals *DFD*	Plastics *DFD*	Finance and insurance *DFD*	Plastics *Exports*	Instruments *DFD*	Government *DFD*	Finance and insurance *DFD*
7	Transport services *DFD*	Finance and insurance *DFD*	Social services *DFD*	Electrical machinery *Exports*	Aerospace *Tech.*	Pharmaceuticals *DFD*	Trade *DFD*
8	Mining *Exports*	Communications *DFD*	Utilities *DFD*	Motor vehicles *Exports*	Real estate *DFD*	Communications *DFD*	Real estate *DFD*
9	Agriculture *DFD/Exports*	Trade *DFD*	Instruments *Exports*	Transport services *Exports*	Government *DFD*	Utilities *DFD*	Plastics *DFD*
10	Electronics *DFD*	Wood *Exports*	Government *DFD*	Social services *DFD*	Plastics *DFD*	Plastics *DFD*	Aerospace *DFD*

Tech. (technical change), *DFD* (domestic final demand), and *Exports* refer to the primary factor promoting growth in a particular industry.
Source: OECD, STAN input-output database.

GODS OF MYTHOLOGY

Principal Greek gods

Greek gods of mythology

Aeolus God of the winds
Aphrodite Goddess of love, beauty, and procreation
Apollo God of prophecy, poetry, music, archery, and healing
Ares God of war
Artemis Goddess of the moon, hunting, and fertility
Athene Goddess of wisdom; protectress of Athens
Boreas God of the north wind
Cronus Father of Zeus
Cybele Goddess of fertility and the mountains
Demeter Goddess of fruit, crops, and vegetation
Dionysus God of wine
Eros God of love
Gaea Goddess of the earth
Hades God of the underworld
Hebe Goddess of youth
Hecate Goddess of magic, ghosts, and witchcraft
Helios God of the sun
Hephaestus God of fire

Hera Goddess of marriage and women; queen of heaven
Hermes God of science and commerce; messenger of the gods
Hestia Goddess of the hearth
Iris Goddess of the rainbow; messenger of the gods
Morpheus God of dreams
Nemesis Goddess of vengeance
Nereus Sea god
Nike Goddess of victory
Oceanus Sea god
Pan God of pastures, forests, flocks, and herds
Persephone Goddess of the underworld
Poseidon God of the sea
Rhea Mother of the gods
Selene Moon goddess
Uranus God of the sky
Zeus Overlord of the Olympian gods and goddesses; lord of heaven

Principal Roman gods

The twelve major gods of Olympus are shown in **bold** type. Bacchus in some accounts supplants Vesta. Pluto and Proserpine are gods of the Underworld.

Religion and mythology

Roman gods of mythology

Apollo God of the sun, music, poetry, prophecy, and healing
Bacchus God of wine
Bellona Goddess of war
Ceres Corn goddess
Cupid God of love
Diana Goddess of fertility, hunting, and the moon
Faunus God of prophecy
Flora Goddess of flowers
Janus God of gates and doors
Juno Goddess of marriage and women
Jupiter Supreme god; lord of heaven
Lares Gods of the household and state
Libitina Goddess of funerals
Maia Goddess of growth and increase

Mars God of war
Mercury Messenger god; also god of commerce
Minerva Goddess of wisdom, the arts, and trades
Mithras The sun god; god of light
Neptune God of the sea
Ops Goddess of fertility
Pales Goddess of flocks and shepherds
Pluto God of the underworld
Pomona Goddess of fruit trees and fruit
Proserpine Goddess of the underworld
Saturn God of seed time and harvest
Venus Goddess of beauty and love
Vertumnus God of the seasons
Vesta Goddess of the hearth
Vulcan God of fire

Norse gods of mythology

Aegir God of the sea
Aesir Race of warlike gods, including Odin, Thor, Tyr
Alcis Twin gods of the sky
Balder Son of Odin and favourite of the gods
Bor Father of Odin
Bragi God of poetry
Eir Goddess of medicine
Fafnir Dragon god
Fjorgynn Mother of Thor
Freya Goddess of love and fertility
Frey God of fertility, sun, and rain
Frigg Goddess of married love; wife of Odin
Gefion Goddess who received virgins after death
Heimdall Warden of the gods
Hel Goddess of death; Queen of Niflheim, the land of mists
Hermod Son of Odin
Hoenir Companion to Odin and Loki
Hoder Blind god who killed Balder
Idunn Guardian goddess of the golden apples of youth; wife of Bragi
Kvasir God of wise utterances
Logi Fire god

Loki God of mischief
Mimir God of wisdom
Nanna Goddess wife of Balder
Nehallenia Goddess of plenty
Nerthus Goddess of earth
Njord God of ships and the sea
Norns Goddesses of destiny
Odin (Woden, Wotan) Chief of the Aesir family of gods, the 'father' god; the god of war, learning, and poetry
Otr Otter god
Ran Goddess of the sea
Sif Goddess wife of Thor
Sigyn Goddess wife of Loki
Thor (Donar) God of thunder and sky, and good crops
Tyr God of battle, and victory
Ull God of the hunt
Valkyries Female helpers of the gods of war
Vanir Race of benevolent gods, including Njord, Frey, and Freya
Vidar Slayer of the wolf, Fenvir
Vor Goddess of truth
Weland (Volundr, Weiland, Wayland) Craftsman god

Egyptian gods

	Alternative names	
Amun	Ammon, Amen, Amon	King of the gods
Anubis	Anpu	God of the dead
Aton	Aten	Sun god, later made chief and only god (for a short time)
Atum	Tem, Tum	Creator of the gods and men
Bast	Bastet, Ubasti	Goddess of music and dance
Bes	Bisu	Originally protector of the royal house, later god of recreation
Buto	Edjo, Udjo, Wadjet, Wadjit	Goddess of Lower Egypt and defender of the King
Geb	Keb, Seb	God of the earth
Hapi	Hap, Hep, Apis	God of the Nile
Hathor	Athyr	Originally a personification of the sky, also goddess of love and festivity
Horus	Hor	Originally the god of Lower Egypt, later identified with the reigning King
Isis	Aset, Eset	Queen of the gods
Khenty-Imentiu	Khenti-Amentiu	Warrior god, god of the underworld before Osiris
Khnum	Khnemu	God of the cataract region, earlier associated with the underworld
Khons	Khensu, Khonsu, Chons	Moon god

Religion and mythology

	Alternative names	
Ma'at	Mayet	Goddess of law, truth, and justice
Min		God of fertility and harvest
Mont	Mentu, Month	War god of Upper Egypt, also lord of the sky with Re
Nefertum	Nefertem, Nefertemu	God of the lotus
Neith	Neit	Goddess of the loom and war
Nekhbet	Nekhebet	Protectress of childbirth
Nut	Neuth, Nuit	Goddess of the sky
Osiris	Usire	Originally fertility god, later supreme god, king of the underworld
Ptah	Phtah	God of fertility, creator of the universe
Re	Phra, Ra	King of the gods, chief state god
Sati	Satet, Satis	Goddess of the inundation and of fertility
Seker	Sokar, Sokaris	God of darkness and decay
Seshat	Sesheta	Goddess of writing and history
Shu		God of light and supporter of the sky
Taurt	Apet, Opet, Tawaret, Thoueris	Goddess of maternity
Thoth	Djhowtey	Moon god

MODERN RELIGIONS

Religion	Branch/ denomination	Sacred texts	State religion in	Estimated no. of adherents (worldwide)
Baha'ism		Kitabal-Aqdas, Haft Wadi, Bayan, al-Kalimat al-Maknnah		5 402 000
Buddhism	Therevada Mahayana Tantrism	Tripitaka	Bhutan, Cambodia, Thailand	309 000 000
Christianity	Anglican	Bible	UK (England)	1 783 660 000
	Baptist			
	Church of Christ			
	Lutheran		Denmark, Iceland, Norway, Sweden	
	Methodist			
	Mormon	Book of Mormon		
	Orthodox		Greece	
	Pentecostal			
	Presbyterian		UK (Scotland)	
	Roman Catholic		Argentina, Bolivia, Costa Rica, Dominican Republic, Malta, Paraguay, Peru	
Confucianism	Unitarian	The Analects, Su Ching, Shi Ching, Li Chi, I Ching, Lu		5 750 000
Hinduism	Vishnu Shiva Shakti	Rigveda, Yajurveda, Samaveda, Atharveda	Nepal	719 269 000
Islam (Muslim)	Sunni Shi'a Sufi Ismaili	Koran, Hadith	Afghanistan, Algeria, Bahrain, Bangladesh, Comoros, Egypt, Iran, Iraq, Jordan, Kuwait, Libya, Malaysia, Maldives, Mauritania, Morocco, Oman, Pakistan, Qatar, Saudi Arabia, Somalia, Sudan, Tunisia, United Arab Emirates, Yemen	950 726 000
Jainism	Digambara Swetabara	Siddhanta, Pakrit texts		3 724 000
Judaism		Torah, Talmud		17 615 000
Sikhism		Guru Granth Sahib (Adi Granth)		18 460 500
Shintoism		Kojiki, Nohon Shoki		3 162 800
Taoism	Tao Te Ching			190 000 000

Books of the Bible

Old Testament
Law (Pentateuch)
Genesis
Exodus
Leviticus
Numbers
Deuteronomy

Prophets
(FORMER)
Joshua
Judges
Samuel 1 & 2
Kings 1& 2

(LATTER)
Isaiah
Jeremiah
Ezekiel
Book of twelve prophets (Hosea, Joel, Amos, Obadiah, Jonah, Micah, Nahum, Habakkuk, Zephaniah, Haggai, Zechariah, Malachi)

Writings
Psalms
Proverbs
Job
Song of Songs
Ruth
Lamentations
Ecclesiastes
Esther
Daniel
Ezra
Nehemiah
Chronicles 1 & 2

New Testament
Gospels (Matthew, Mark, Luke, John)
Acts of the Apostles
13 Letters attributed to Paul (Romans, Corinthians 1 & 2, Galatians, Ephesians, Philippians, Colossians, Thessalonians 1 & 2, Timothy 1 & 2, Titus, Philemon)
Letter to the Hebrews
7 General or 'Catholic' letters (James, Peter 1 & 2, John 1, 2 & 3, Jude)
Book of Revelation

Apocrypha
Baruch
Additions to the Book of Daniel
Book of Ecclesiasticus
Additions to the Book of Esther
Books of Esdras
Letter of Jeremiah
Book of Judith
Books of the Maccabees
Book of Tobit (Tobias)
Wisdom of Solomon

The Old Testament Apocrypha are a collection of Jewish writings found in the Greek version of the Hebrew Bible, but not found in the Hebrew Bible itself. Roman Catholics consider them as inspired and authoritative, and deuterocanonical, while Protestants attribute less authority to them.

New Testament Apocrypha are Christian documents similar in title, form, or content to many New Testament works, being called Gospels, Acts, Epistles, or Apocalypses, but are not widely accepted as canonical.

Christian religious vestments

chimere Worn by bishops over the rochet; of black or scarlet, open at the front.

cope In the pre-Christian era, a long cloak; now a costly embroidered vestment, semi-circular in shape, worn by bishops and priests on special occasions.

cotta Similar to the surplice, but shorter, especially in the sleeves; sometimes used by clergy and servers in place of the surplice.

girdle Cord worn about the waist.

hood Worn by clergy at choir offices, a mediaeval headdress, now worn hanging down the back; it denotes a university degree.

maniple Worn over the left arm by bishops, priests, and deacons at the Eucharist; originally a napkin.

orphreys The embroidered strips, customarily cross-shaped, on a chasuble.

rochet Worn by bishops, similar to an alb, but used without girdle or apparels.

stole Once a napkin or towel carried by servants on the left shoulder; now folded and narrow, worn over both shoulders.

surplice Of white linen, reaching to the knees; worn by choir and servers as well as clergy.

alb A long white garment reaching to the ankles; derived from an ancient tunic.

amice A linen square worn round the back to protect the other vestments; formerly a neckcloth.

apparels Ornamental panels at the foot of the alb, front and back, and on the amice.

cassock The long black gown worn under other vestments; formerly, the daily working costume of the clergy.

chasuble The outer sleeveless vestment worn by a priest or bishop when celebrating Holy Communion; derived from the commonest outdoor garment of classical times.

Movable Christian feasts

Dates for the years 1990–2000.

Year	Ash Wednesday	Easter	Ascension	Whit Sunday[a]	Sundays after Trinity	First Sunday in Advent	Trinity Sunday	Corpus Christi
1990	28 Feb	15 Apr	24 May	3 Jun	24	2 Dec	10 Jun	14 Jun
1991	13 Feb	31 Mar	9 May	19 May	26	1 Dec	26 May	30 May
1992	4 Mar	19 Apr	28 May	7 Jun	23	29 Nov	14 Jun	18 Jun
1993	24 Feb	11 Apr	20 May	30 May	24	28 Nov	6 Jun	10 Jun
1994	16 Feb	3 Apr	12 May	22 May	25	27 Nov	29 May	2 Jun
1995	1 Mar	16 Apr	25 May	4 Jun	24	3 Dec	11 Jun	15 Jun
1996	21 Feb	7 Apr	16 May	26 May	25	1 Dec	2 Jun	6 Jun
1997	12 Feb	30 Mar	8 May	18 May	26	30 Nov	25 May	29 May
1998	25 Feb	12 Apr	21 May	31 May	24	29 Nov	7 Jun	11 Jun
1999	17 Feb	4 Apr	13 May	23 May	25	28 Nov	30 May	3 Jun
2000	8 Mar	23 Apr	1 Jun	11 Jun	23	3 Dec	18 Jun	22 Jun

Ash Wednesday, the first day of Lent, can fall at the earliest on 4 Feb and at the latest on 10 Mar.

Palm (Passion) Sunday is the Sunday before Easter; Good Friday is the Friday before Easter; Holy Saturday (often referred to as Easter Saturday) is the Saturday before Easter; Easter Saturday, in traditional usage, is the Saturday following Easter.

Easter Day can fall at the earliest on 22 Mar and at the latest on 25 Apr. Ascension Day can fall at the earliest on 30 Apr and at the latest on 3 Jun. Whit Sunday can fall at the earliest on 10 May and at the latest on 13 Jun. There are no fewer than 22 and not more than 27 Sundays after Trinity. The first Sunday of Advent is the Sunday nearest to 30 Nov.

[a]Whit Sunday commemorates the day of Pentecost.

Major immovable Christian feasts

Jan 1	Solemenity of Mary, Mother of God	Aug 22	Queenship of Mary
Jan 6	Epiphany	Sep 8	Birthday of the Virgin Mary
Jan 7	Christmas Day (Eastern Orthodox)[a]	Sep 14	Exaltation of the Holy Cross
Jan 11	Baptism of Jesus	Oct 2	Guardian Angels
Jan 25	Conversion of Apostle Paul	Nov 1	All Saints
Feb 2	Presentation of Jesus (Candlemas Day)	Nov 2	All Souls
Feb 22	The Chair of Peter, Apostle	Nov 9	Dedication of the Lateran Basilica
Mar 25	Annunciation to the Virgin Mary	Nov 21	Presentation of the Virgin Mary
Jun 24	Birth of John the Baptist	Dec 8	Immaculate Conception
Aug 6	Transfiguration	Dec 25	Christmas Day
Aug 15	Assumption of the Virgin Mary	Dec 28	Holy Innocents

[a]Fixed feasts in the Julian Calendar fall 13 days later than the Gregorian Calendar date.

The dates of Easter

Dates for the years 1900–2099.

	0	---1	---2	---3	---4	---5	---6	---7	---8	---9
1900	15 Apr	7 Apr	30 Mar	12 Apr	3 Apr	23 Apr	15 Apr	31 Mar	19 Apr	11 Apr
1910	27 Mar	16 Apr	7 Apr	23 Mar	12 Apr	4 Apr	23 Apr	8 Apr	31 Mar	20 Apr
1920	4 Apr	27 Mar	16 Apr	1 Apr	20 Apr	12 Apr	4 Apr	17 Apr	8 Apr	31 Mar
1930	20 Apr	5 Apr	27 Mar	16 Apr	1 Apr	21 Apr	12 Apr	28 Mar	17 Apr	9 Apr
1940	24 Mar	13 Apr	5 Apr	25 Apr	9 Apr	1 Apr	21 Apr	6 Apr	28 Mar	17 Apr
1950	9 Apr	25 Mar	13 Apr	5 Apr	18 Apr	10 Apr	1 Apr	21 Apr	6 Apr	29 Mar
1960	17 Apr	2 Apr	22 Apr	14 Apr	29 Mar	18 Apr	10 Apr	26 Mar	14 Apr	6 Apr
1970	29 Mar	11 Apr	2 Apr	22 Apr	14 Apr	30 Mar	18 Apr	10 Apr	26 Mar	15 Apr
1980	6 Apr	19 Apr	11 Apr	3 Apr	22 Apr	7 Apr	30 Mar	19 Apr	3 Apr	26 Mar
1990	15 Apr	31 Mar	19 Apr	11 Apr	3 Apr	16 Apr	7 Apr	30 Mar	12 Apr	4 Apr
2000	23 Apr	15 Apr	31 Mar	20 Apr	11 Apr	27 Mar	16 Apr	8 Apr	23 Mar	12 Apr
2010	4 Apr	24 Apr	8 Apr	31 Mar	20 Apr	5 Apr	27 Mar	16 Apr	1 Apr	21 Apr
2020	12 Apr	4 Apr	17 Apr	9 Apr	31 Mar	20 Apr	5 Apr	28 Mar	16 Apr	1 Apr
2030	2 Apr	13 Apr	28 Mar	17 Apr	9 Apr	25 Mar	13 Apr	5 Apr	25 Apr	10 Apr
2040	1 Apr	21 Apr	6 Apr	29 Mar	17 Apr	9 Apr	25 Mar	14 Apr	5 Apr	18 Apr
2050	10 Apr	2 Apr	21 Apr	6 Apr	29 Mar	18 Apr	2 Apr	22 Apr	14 Apr	30 Mar
2060	18 Apr	10 Apr	26 Mar	15 Apr	6 Apr	29 Mar	11 Apr	3 Apr	22 Apr	14 Apr
2070	30 Mar	19 Apr	10 Apr	26 Mar	15 Mar	7 Apr	19 Apr	11 Apr	3 Apr	23 Apr
2080	7 Apr	30 Mar	19 Apr	4 Apr	26 Mar	15 Apr	31 Mar	20 Apr	11 Apr	3 Apr
2090	16 Apr	8 Apr	30 Mar	12 Apr	4 Apr	24 Apr	15 Apr	31 Mar	20 Apr	12 Apr

Popes

Antipope refers to a pontiff set up in opposition to one asserted to be canonically chosen.

until c.64	Peter
c.64–c.76	Linus
c.76–c.90	Anacletus
c.90–c.99	Clement I
c.99–c.105	Evaristus
c.105–c.117	Alexander I
c.117–c.127	Sixtus I
c.127–c.137	Telesphorus
c.137–c.140	Hyginus
c.140–c.154	Pius I
c.154–c.166	Anicetus
c.166–c.175	Soter
175–89	Eleutherius
189–98	Victor I
198–217	Zephyrinus
217–22	Callistus I
217–c.235	Hippolytus *Antipope*
222–30	Urban I
230–5	Pontian
235–6	Anterus
236–50	Fabian
251–3	Cornelius
251–c.258	Novatian *Antipope*
253–4	Lucius I
254–7	Stephen I
257–8	Sixtus II
259–68	Dionysius
269–74	Felix I
275–83	Eutychianus
283–96	Caius
296–304	Marcellinus
308–9	Marcellus I
310	Eusebius
311–14	Miltiades
314–35	Sylvester I
336	Mark
337–52	Julius I
352–66	Liberius
355–65	Felix II *Antipope*
366–84	Damasus I
366–7	Ursinus *Antipope*
384–99	Siricius
399–401	Anastasius I
402–17	Innocent I
417–18	Zosimus
418–22	Boniface I
418–19	Eulalius *Antipope*
422–32	Celestine I
432–40	Sixtus III
440–61	Leo I 'the Great'
461–8	Hilarus
468–83	Simplicius
483–92	Felix III (II)
492–6	Gelasius I
496–8	Anastasius II
498–514	Symmachus
498	Laurentius *Antipope*
501–5	Laurentius *Antipope*
514–23	Hormisdas
523–6	John I
526–30	Felix IV (III)
530–2	Boniface II
530	Dioscorus *Antipope*

533–5	John II
535–6	Agapetus I
536–7	Silverius
537–55	Vigilius
556–61	Pelagius I
561–74	John III
575–9	Benedict I
579–90	Pelagius II
590–604	Gregory I 'the Great'
604–6	Sabinianus
607	Boniface III
608–15	Boniface IV
615–18	Deusdedit (Adeodatus I)
619–25	Boniface V
625–38	Honorius I
640	Severinus
640–2	John IV
642–9	Theodore I
649–55	Martin I
654–7	Eugenius I[a]
657–72	Vitalian
672–6	Adeodatus II
676–8	Donus
678–81	Agatho
682–3	Leo II
684–5	Benedict II
685–6	John V
686–7	Cono
687	Theodore *Antipope*
687–92	Paschal *Antipope*
687–701	Sergius I
701–5	John VI
705–7	John VII
708	Sisinnius
708–15	Constantine
715–31	Gregory II
731–41	Gregory III
741–52	Zacharias
752	Stephen II (not consecrated)
752–7	Stephen II (III)
757–67	Paul I
767–9	Constantine II *Antipope*
768	Philip *Antipope*
768–72	Stephen III (IV)
772–95	Adrian I
795–816	Leo III
816–17	Stephen IV (V)
817–24	Paschal I
824–7	Eugenius II
827	Valentine
827–44	Gregory IV
844	John *Antipope*
844–7	Sergius II
847–55	Leo IV
855–8	Benedict III
855	Anastasius Bibliothecarius *Antipope*
858–67	Nicholas I 'the Great'
867–72	Adrian II
872–82	John VIII
882–4	Marinus I
884–5	Adrian III

885–91	Stephen V (VI)
891–6	Formosus
896	Boniface VI
896–7	Stephen VI (VII)
897	Romanus
897	Theodore II
898–900	John IX
900–3	Benedict IV
903	Leo V
903–4	Christopher *Antipope*
904–11	Sergius III
911–13	Anastasius III
913–14	Lando
914–28	John X
928	Leo VI
928–31	Stephen VII (VIII)
931–5	John XI
936–9	Leo VII
939–42	Stephen IX
942–6	Marinus II
946–55	Agapetus II
955–64	John XII
963–5	Leo VIII
964–6	Benedict V
965–72	John XIII
973–4	Benedict VI
974	Boniface VII *Antipope*
984–5	Boniface VII *Antipope*
974–83	Benedict VII
983–4	John XIV
985–96	John XV
996–9	Gregory V
997–8	John XVI *Antipope*
999–1003	Sylvester II
1003	John XVII
1004–9	John XVIII
1009–12	Sergius IV
1012–24	Benedict VIII
1012	Gregory *Antipope*
1024–32	John XIX
1032–44	Benedict IX
1045	Sylvester III
1045	Benedict IX (second reign)
1045–6	Gregory VI
1046–7	Clement II
1047–8	Benedict IX (third reign)
1048	Damasus II (Poppo)
1048–54	Leo IX (Bruno of Toul)
1055–7	Victor II (Gebhard of Hirschberg)
1057–8	Stephen IX (X) (Frederick of Lorraine)
1058–9	Benedict X (John of Tusculum) *Antipope*
1059–61	Nicholas II (Gerard of Burgundy)
1061–73	Alexander II (Anselm of Lucca)
1061–72	Honorius II (Peter Cadalus) *Antipope*
1073–85	Gregory VII (St Hilderbrand)

Religion and mythology

1080, 1084–1100	Clement III (Guibert of Ravenna) *Antipope*	1265–8	Clement IV (Guy le Gros Foulques)	1447–55	Nicholas V (Tommaso Parentuce III)
1086–7	Victor III (Desidenus)	1271–6	Gregory X (Tebaldo Visconti)	1455–8	Callistus III (Alfonso de Borja)
1088–99	Urban II (Odo of Chatillon)	1276	Innocent V (Pierre de Champagni)	1458–64	Pius II (Enea Silvio de Piccolomini)
1099–1118	Paschal II (Raneiro da Bieda)	1276	Adrian V (Ottobono Fieschi)	1464–71	Paul II (Pietro Barbo)
1100–2	Theodoric *Antipope*	1276–7	John XXI^c (Pietro Rebuli-Giuliani)	1471–84	Sixtus IV (Francesco della Rovere)
1102	Albert *Antipope*			1484–92	Innocent VIII (Giovanni Battista Cibo)
1105–11	Sylvester IV *Antipope*	1277–80	Nicholas III (Giovanni Gaetano Orsini)	1492–1503	Alexander VI (Rodrigo Borgia)
1118–19	Gelasius II (John of Gaeta)	1281–5	Martin IV (Simon de Brie)	1503	Pius III (Francesco Todoeschini-Piccolomini)
1118–21	Gregory VIII (Maurice of Braga) *Antipope*	1285–7	Honorius IV (Giacomo Savelli)	1503–13	Julius II (Giuliano della Rovere)
1119–24	Callistus II (Guy of Burgundy)	1288–92	Nicholas IV (Girolamo Masci)	1513–21	Leo X (Giovanni de' Medici)
1124–30	Honorius II (Lamberto dei Fagnani)	1294	Celestine V (Pietro di Morrone)	1522–3	Adrian VI (Adrian Dedel)
1124	Celestine II *Antipope*	1294–1303	Boniface VIII (Benedetto Castani)	1523–34	Clement VII (Giulio de' Medici)
1130–43	Innocent II (Gregory Parareschi)	1303–4	Benedict XI (Niccolo Boccasini)	1534–49	Paul III (Allessandro Farnese)
1130–8	Anacletus II *Antipope*	1305–14	Clement V (Raymond Bertrand de Got)	1550–5	Julius III (Gianmaria del Monte)
1138	Victor IV^b *Antipope*	1316–34	John XXII (Jacques Duèse)	1555	Marcellus II (Marcello Cervini)
1143–4	Celestine II (Guido di Castello)	1328–30	Nicholas V (Pietro Rainalducci) *Antipope*	1555–9	Paul IV (Giovanni Pietro Caraffa)
1144–5	Lucius II (Gherardo Caccianemici)	1334–42	Benedict XII (Jacques Fournier)	1559–65	Pius IV (Giovanni Angelo Medici)
1145–53	Eugenius III (Bernardo Paganelli)	1342–52	Clement VI (Pierre Roger de Beaufort)	1566–72	Pius V (Michele Ghislieri)
1153–4	Anastasius IV (Corrado della Subarra)	1352–62	Innocent VI (Étienne Aubert)	1572–85	Gregory XIII (Ugo Buoncompagni)
1154–9	Adrian IV (Nicholas Breakspear)	1362–70	Urban V (Guillaume de Grimoard)	1585–90	Sixtus V (Felice Peretti)
1159–81	Alexander III (Orlando Bandinelli)	1370–8	Gregory XI (Pierre Roger de Beaufort)	1590	Urban VII (Giambattista Castagna)
1159–64	Victor IV^b (Ottaviano di Monticelli) *Antipope*	1378–89	Urban VI (Bartolomeo Prignano)	1590–1	Gregory XIV (Niccolo Sfondrati)
1164–8	Paschal III (Guido of Crema) *Antipope*	1378–94	Clement VII (Robert of Geneva) *Antipope*	1591	Innocent IX (Gian Antonio Facchinetti)
1168–78	Callistus III (John of Struma) *Antipope*	1389–1404	Boniface IX (Pietro Tomacelli)	1592–1605	Clement VIII (Ippolito Aldobrandini)
1179–80	Innocent III (Lando da Sessa)	1394–1423	Benedict XIII (Pedro de Luna) *Antipope*	1605	Leo XI (Alessandro de' Medici-Ottaiano)
1181–5	Lucius III (Ubaldo Allucingoli)	1404–6	Innocent VII (Cosmato de' Migliorati)	1605–21	Paul V (Camillo Borghese)
1185–7	Urban III (Uberto Crivelli)	1406–15	Gregory XII (Angelo Correr)	1621–3	Gregory XV (Alessandro Ludovisi)
1187	Gregory VIII (Alberto di Morra)	1409–10	Alexander V (Petros Philargi) *Antipope*	1623–44	Urban VIII (Maffeo Barberini)
1187–91	Clement III (Paolo Scolari)	1410–15	John XXIII (Baldassare Cossa) *Antipope*	1644–55	Innocent X (Giambattista Pamfili)
1191–8	Celestine III (Giacinto Boboni-Orsini)	1417–31	Martin V (Oddone Colonna)	1655–67	Alexander VII (Fabio Chigi)
1198–1216	Innocent III (Lotario de'Conti)	1423–9	Clement VIII (Gil Sanchez Muñoz) *Antipope*	1667–9	Clement IX (Guilio Rospigliosi)
1216–27	Honorius III (Cancio Savelli)	1425–30	Benedict XIV (Bernard Garnier) *Antipope*	1670–6	Clement X (Emilio Altieri)
1227–41	Gregory IX (Ugolino di Segni)	1431–47	Eugenius IV (Gabriele Condulmer)	1676–89	Innocent XI (Benedetto Odescalchi)
1241	Celestine IV (Goffredo Castiglione)	1439–49	Felix V (Amadeus VIII of Savoy) *Antipope*	1689–91	Alexander VIII (Pietro Vito Ottoboni)
1243–54	Innocent IV (Sinibaldo de' Fieschi)			1691–1700	Innocent XII (Antonio Pignatelli)
1254–61	Alexander IV (Rinaldo di Segni)			1700–21	Clement XI (Gian
1261–4	Urban IV (Jacques Pantaléon)				

Modern religions

Popes (continued)

	Francesco Albani)	1775–99	Pius VI (Giovanni Angelo Braschi)	1903–14	Pius X (Giuseppe Sarto)
1721–4	Innocent XIII (Michelangelo dei Conti)	1800–23	Pius VII (Luigi Barnaba Chiaramonti)	1914–22	Benedict XV (Giacomo della Chiesa)
1724–30	Benedict XIII (Pietro Francesco Orsini)	1823–9	Leo XII (Annibale della Genga)	1922–39	Pius XI (Achille Ratti)
1730–40	Clement XII (Lorenzo Corsini)	1829–30	Pius VIII (Francesco Saveno Castiglioni)	1939–58	Pius XII (Eugenio Pacelli)
1740–58	Benedict XIV (Prospero Lambertini)	1831–46	Gregory XVI (Bartolomeo Alberto Cappellari)	1958–63	John XXIII (Angelo Giuseppe Roncalli)
1758–69	Clement XIII (Carlo Rezzonico)	1846–78	Pius IX (Giovanni Maria Mastai Ferretti)	1963–78	Paul VI (Giovanni Battista Montini)
1769–74	Clement XIV (Lorenzo Ganganelli)	1878–1903	Leo XIII (Vincenzo Gioacchino Pecci)	1978	John Paul I (Albino Luciani)
				1978–	John Paul II (Karol Jozef Wojtyla)

[a]Elected during the banishment of Martin I. [b]Different individuals. [c]There was no John XX.

Holy orders

Major orders Bishop, Priest, Deacon, (Sub-deacon)
Minor orders Porter, Lector, Exorcist, Acolyte

In the Roman Catholic church there are now only the orders of Bishop, Priest, Deacon and the ministries of acolyte and lector, following the *motu proprio* of Pope Paul VI, 1973.

Saints' days

The official recognition of Saints, and the choice of a Saint's Day, varies greatly between different branches of Christianity, calendars, and localities. Only major variations are included below, using the following abbreviations:

C Coptic   G Greek
E Eastern   W Western

January
1   Basil (E); Fulgentius; Telemachus
2   Basil and Gregory of Nazianzus (W); Macarius of Alexandria; Seraphim of Sarov
3   Geneviève
4   Angela of Foligno
5   Simeon Stylites (W)
7   Cedda; Lucian of Antioch (W); Raymond of Penyafort
8   Atticus (E); Gudule; Severinus
9   Hadrian the African
10 Agatho; Marcian
12 Ailred; Benedict Biscop
13 Hilary of Poitiers
14 Kentigern
15 Macarius of Egypt; Maurus; Paul of Thebes
16 Honoratus
17 Antony of Egypt
19 Wulfstan
20 Euthymius; Fabian; Sebastian
21 Agnes; Fructuosus; Maximus (E); Meinrad
22 Timothy (G); Vincent

23 Ildefonsus
24 Babylas (W); Francis de Sales
25 Gregory of Nazianzus (E)
26 Paula; Timothy and Titus; Xenophon (E)
27 Angela Merici
28 Ephraem Syrus (E); Paulinus of Nola; Thomas Aquinas
29 Gildas
31 John Bosco; Marcella

February
1   Bride; Pionius
3   Anskar; Blaise (W); Werburga; Simeon (E)
4   Gilbert of Sempringham; Isidore of Pelusium; Phileas
5   Agatha; Avitus
6   Dorothy; Paul Miki and companions; Vedast
8   Theodore (G); Jerome Emiliani
9   Teilo
10 Scholastica
11 Benedict of Aniane; Blaise (E); Caedmon; Gregory II
12 Meletius
13 Agabus (W); Catherine dei Ricci; Priscilla (E)
14 Cyril and Methodius (W); Valentine (W)
16 Flavian (E); Pamphilus (E); Valentine (G)
18 Bernadette (France); Colman; Flavian (W); Leo I (E)
20 Wulfric
21 Peter Damian
23 Polycarp

25 Ethelbert; Tarasius; Walburga
26 Alexander (W); Porphyrius
27 Leander
28 Oswald of York

March
1   David
2   Chad; Simplicius
3   Ailred
4   Casimir
6   Chrodegang
7   Perpetua and Felicity
8   Felix; John of God; Pontius
9   Frances of Rome; Gregory of Nyssa; Pacian
10 John Ogilvie; Macarius of Jerusalem; Simplicius
11 Constantine; Oengus; Sophronius
12 Gregory (the Great)
13 Nicephorus
14 Benedict (E)
15 Clement Hofbauer
17 Gertrude; Joseph of Arimathea (W); Patrick
18 Anselm of Lucca; Cyril of Jerusalem; Edward
19 Joseph
20 Cuthbert; John of Parma; Martin of Braga
21 Serapion of Thmuis
22 Catherine of Sweden; Nicholas of Flüe
23 Turibius de Mongrovejo
30 John Climacus

April

1 Hugh of Grenoble; Mary of Egypt (*E*); Melito
2 Francis of Paola; Mary of Egypt (*W*)
3 Richard of Chichester
4 Isidore of Seville
5 Juliana of Liège; Vincent Ferrer
7 Hegesippus; John Baptist de la Salle
8 Agabus (*E*)
10 Fulbert
11 Gemma Galgani; Guthlac; Stanislaus
12 Julius I; Zeno
13 Martin I
15 Aristarchus; Pudus (*E*); Trophimus of Ephesus
17 Agapetus (*E*); Stephen Harding
18 Mme Acarie
19 Alphege; Leo IX
21 Anastasius (*E*); Anselm; Beuno; Januarius (*E*)
22 Alexander (*C*)
23 George
24 Egbert; Fidelis of Sigmaringen; Mellitus
25 Mark; Phaebadius
27 Zita
28 Peter Chanel; Vitalis and Valeria
29 Catherine of Siena; Hugh of Cluny; Peter Martyr; Robert
30 James (the Great) (*E*); Pius V

May

1 Asaph; Joseph the Worker; Walburga
2 Athanasius
3 Phillip and James (the Less) (*W*)
4 Gotthard
5 Hilary of Arles
7 John of Beverley
8 John (*E*); Peter of Tarantaise
10 Antoninus; Comgall; John of Avila; Simon (*E*)
11 Cyril and Methodius (*E*); Mamertus
12 Epiphanius; Nereus and Achilleus; Pancras
14 Matthias (*W*)
16 Brendan; John of Nepomuk; Simon Stock
17 Robert Bellarmine; Paschal Baylon
18 John I
19 Dunstan; Ivo; Pudens (*W*); Pudentiana (*W*)
20 Bernardino of Siena
21 Helena (*E*)
22 Rita of Cascia
23 Ivo of Chartres
24 Vincent of Lérins
25 Aldhelm; Bede; Gregory VII; Mary Magdalene de Pazzi

26 Philip Neri; Quadratus
27 Augustine of Canterbury
30 Joan of Arc

June

1 Justin Martyr; Pamphilus
2 Erasmus; Marcellinus and Peter; Nicephorus (*G*); Pothinus
3 Charles Lwanga and companions; Clotilde; Kevin
4 Optatus; Petrock
5 Boniface
6 Martha (*E*); Norbert
7 Paul of Constantinople (*W*); Willibald
8 William of York
9 Columba; Cyril of Alexandria (*E*); Ephraem (*W*)
11 Barnabas; Bartholomew (*E*)
12 Leo III
13 Anthony of Padua
15 Orsisius; Vitus
17 Alban; Botulph
19 Gervasius and Protasius; Jude (*E*); Romuald
20 Alban
21 Alban of Mainz; Aloysius Gonzaga
22 John Fisher and Thomas More; Niceta; Pantaenus (*C*); Paulinus of Nola
23 Etheldreda
24 Birth of John the Baptist
25 Prosper of Aquitaine
27 Cyril of Alexandria (*W*); Ladislaus
28 Irenaeus
29 Peter and Paul
30 First Martyrs of the Church of Rome

July

1 Cosmas and Damian (*E*); Oliver Plunket
3 Anatolius; Thomas
4 Andrew of Crete (*E*); Elizabeth of Portugal; Ulrich
5 Anthony Zaccaria
6 Maria Goretti
7 Palladius; Pantaenus
8 Kilian; Aquila and Prisca (*W*)
11 Benedict (*W*); Pius II
12 John Gualbert; Veronica
13 Henry II; Mildred; Silas
14 Camillus of Lellis; Deusdedit; Nicholas of the Holy Mountain (*E*)
15 Bonaventure; Jacob of Nisibis; Swithin; Vladimir
16 Eustathius; Our Lady of Mt Carmel
17 Ennodius; Leo IV; Marcellina; Margaret (*E*); Scillitan Martyrs
18 Arnulf; Philastrius
19 Marcrina; Symmachus

20 Aurelius; Margaret (*W*)
21 Lawrence of Brindisi; Praxedes
22 Mary Magdalene
23 Apollinaris; Bridget of Sweden
25 Anne and Joachim (*E*); Christopher; James (the Great) (*W*)
26 Anne and Joachim (*W*)
27 Pantaleon
28 Innocent I; Samson; Victor I
29 Lupus; Martha (*W*); Olave
30 Peter Chrysologus; Silas (*G*)
31 Giovanni Colombini; Germanus; Joseph of Arimathea (*E*); Ignatius of Loyola

August

1 Alphonsus Liguori; Ethelwold
2 Eusebius of Vercelli; Stephen I
4 Jean-Baptise Vianney
6 Hormisdas
7 Cajetan; Sixtus II and companions
8 Dominic
9 Matthias (*G*)
10 Laurence; Oswald of Northumbria
11 Clare; Susanna
13 Maximus (*W*); Pontian and Hippolytus; Radegunde
14 Maximilian Kolbe
15 Arnulf; Tarsicius
16 Roch; Simplicianus; Stephen of Hungary
17 Hyacinth
19 John Eudes; Sebaldus
20 Bernard; Oswin; Philibert
21 Jane Frances de Chantal; Pius X
23 Rose of Lima; Sidonius Apollinaris
24 Bartholomew (*W*); Ouen
25 Joseph Calasanctius; Louis IX; Menas of Constantinople
26 Blessed Dominic of the Mother of God; Zephyrinus
27 Caesarius; Monica
28 Augustine of Hippo
29 Beheading of John the Baptist; Sabina
30 Pammachius
31 Aidan; Paulinus of Trier

September

1 Giles; Simeon Stylites (*E*)
2 John the Faster (*E*)
3 Gregory (the Great)
4 Babylas (*E*); Boniface I
5 Zacharias (*E*)
9 Peter Claver; Sergius of Antioch
10 Finnian; Nicholas of Tolentino; Pulcheria
11 Deiniol; Ethelburga; Paphnutius
13 John Chrysostom (*W*)

Saints' days (continued)

15 Catherine of Genoa; Our Lady of Sorrows
16 Cornelius; Cyprian of Carthage; Euphemia; Ninian
17 Robert Bellarmine; Hildegard; Lambert; Satyrus
19 Januarius (W); Theodore of Tarsus
20 Agapetus or Eustace (W)
21 Matthew (W)
23 Adamnan; Linus
25 Sergius of Rostov
26 Cosmas and Damian (W); Cyprian of Carthage; John (E)
27 Frumentius (W); Vincent de Paul
28 Exuperius; Wenceslaus
29 Michael (Michaelmas Day); Gabriel and Raphael
30 Jerome; Otto

October

1 Remigius; Romanos; Teresa of the Child Jesus
2 Leodegar (Leger)
3 Thérèse de Lisieux; Thomas de Cantilupe
4 Ammon; Francis of Assisi; Petronius
6 Bruno; Thomas (G)
9 Demetrius (W); Denis and companions; Dionysius of Paris; James (the Less) (E); John Leonardi
10 Francis Borgia; Paulinus of York
11 Atticus (E); Bruno; Nectarius
12 Wilfrid
13 Edward the Confessor
14 Callistus I; Cosmas Melodus (E)
15 Lucian of Antioch (E); Teresa of Avila
16 Gall; Hedwig; Lullus; Margaret Mary Alacoque
17 Ignatius of Antioch; Victor
18 Luke
19 John de Brébeuf and Isaac Jogues and companions; Paul of the Cross; Peter of Alcántara
21 Hilarion; Ursula
22 Abercius
23 John of Capistrano; James
24 Anthony Claret
25 Crispin and Crispinian; Forty Martyrs of England and Wales; Gaudentius
26 Demetrius (E)
28 Firmilian (E); Simon and Jude
30 Serapion of Antioch
31 Wolfgang

November

1 All Saints; Cosmas and Damian (E)
2 Eustace (E); Victorinus
3 Hubert; Malachy; Martin de Porres; Pirminius; Winifred
4 Charles Borromeo; Vitalis and Agricola
5 Elizabeth (W)
6 Illtyd; Leonard; Paul of Constantinople (E)
7 Willibrord
8 Elizabeth (E); Willehad
9 Simeon Metaphrastes (E)
10 Justus; Leo I (W)
11 Martin of Tours (W); Menas of Egypt; Theodore of Studios
12 Josaphat; Martin of Tours (E); Nilus the Ascetic
13 Abbo; John Chrysostom (E); Nicholas I
14 Dubricius; Gregory Palamas (E)
15 Albert the Great; Machutus
16 Edmund of Abingdon; Eucherius; Gertrude (the Great); Margaret of Scotland; Matthew (E)
17 Elizabeth of Hungary; Gregory Thaumaturgus; Gregory of Tours; Hugh of Lincoln
18 Odo; Romanus
19 Mechthild; Nerses
20 Edmund the Martyr
21 Gelasius
22 Cecilia
23 Amphilochius; Clement I (W); Columban; Felicity; Gregory of Agrigentum
25 Clement I (E); Mercurius; Mesrob
26 Siricius
27 Barlam and Josaphat
28 Simeon Metaphrastes
29 Cuthbert Mayne
30 Andrew; Frumentius (G)

December

1 Eligius
2 Chromatius
3 Francis Xavier
4 Barbara; John Damascene; Osmund
5 Clement of Alexandria; Sabas
6 Nicholas
7 Ambrose
10 Miltiades
11 Damasus; Daniel
12 Jane Frances de Chantal; Spyridon (E); Vicelin
13 Lucy; Odilia
14 John of the Cross; Spyridon (W)
16 Eusebius
18 Frumentius (C)
20 Ignatius of Antioch (G)
21 Peter Canisius; Thomas
22 Anastasia (E); Chrysogonus (E)
23 John of Kanty
26 Stephen (W)
27 John (W); Fabiola; Stephen (E)
29 Thomas à Becket; Trophimus of Arles
31 Sylvester

Buddhism

Founder
Prince Siddhartha Gautama (Buddha), c.563–483 BC

Date founded
c.500 BC, India

Beliefs
'Four Noble Truths':
All life is permeated by suffering
Source of suffering is desire for existence
This cause can be eliminated
Way of doing this is by treading 'The Eightfold Path'
'The Eightfold Path' leads to 'nirvana' – ultimate state of peace

Major festivals[a]
Buddha's birth
Buddha's enlightenment
Buddha's first sermon
Buddha's death

[a]These take place on different dates in the countries in which Buddhism is practised.

Christianity

Founder
Jesus of Nazareth (Jesus Christ), c.4 BC–AD 30

Date founded
1st-c AD

Beliefs
Trinity – God as three in one (Father, Son, Holy Spirit)
God as creator of universe
Original sin
God as judge
Incarnation
Redemption/Salvation
Resurrection

Confucianism

Founder
K'ung Fu-tzu, 551–479 BC

Date founded
6th-c BC, China

Beliefs
Human beings are teachable, improvable, and perfectible
Person can shape his/her own destiny
Self-knowledge and self-realization are attainable through learning
Sense of humanity should infuse society and politics (social participation)
Ritual and tradition

Major Chinese festivals

January/February	Chinese New Year
February/March	Lantern Festival
March/April	Festival of Pure Brightness
May/June	Dragon Boat Festival
July/August	Herd Boy and Weaving Maid
August	All Souls' Festival
September	Mid-Autumn Festival
September/October	Double Ninth Festival
November/December	Winter Solstice

Hinduism

Founder
Aryan invaders of India of Vedic religion

Date founded
c.1500 BC, India

Beliefs
Sacred power (Brahman) is sole reality, the creator, transformer, and preserver of everything
Hindu Trinity of Brahma, Visnu, and Shiva
Authority of the Veda
Respect for life
Rebirth
Soul emancipated by the Three Margas – duty, knowledge, devotion

Major festivals
S = Sukla, 'waxing fortnight'.
K = Krishna 'waning fortnight'.

Caitra	S9	Ramanavami (Birthday of Lord Rama)
Asadha	S2	Rathayatra (Pilgrimage of the Chariot at Jagannath)
Sravana	S11–15	Jhulanayatra ('Swinging the Lord Krishna')
Sravana	S15	Rakshabandhana ('Tying on lucky threads')
Bhadrapada	K8	Janamashtami (Birthday of Lord Krishna)
Asvina	S7–10	Durga-puja (Homage to Goddess Durga) (Bengal)
Asvina	S1–10	Navaratri (Festival of 'Nine Nights')
Asvina	S15	Lakshmi-puja (Homage to Goddess Lakshmi)
Asvina	K15	Diwali, Dipavali ('String of Lights')
Kartikka	S15	Guru Nanak Jananti (Birthday of Guru Nanak)
Magha	K5	Sarasvati-puja (Homage to Goddess Sarasvati)
Magha	K13	Maha-sivaratri (Great Night of Lord Shiva)
Phalguna	S14	Holi (Festival of Fire)
Phalguna	S15	Dolayatra (Swing Festival) (Bengal)

Islam

Founder
Mohammed, AD c.570–632

Date founded
7th-c AD, Arabian peninsula

Beliefs
Unity of God
God as creator and sustainer of the universe
Man superior to nature but still servant of God
Pride is cardinal sin
God always ready to pardon – repentance and redemption possible
Prophets are recipients of revelations from God – they, with God, show a person the 'right way'

Religion and mythology

Islam (continued)

Major festivals

1	Muharram	New Year's Day; starts on the day which celebrates Mohammed's departure from Mecca to Medina in AD 622
12	Rabi I	Birthday of Mohammed (Mawlid al-Nabi) AD 572; celebrated throughout month of Rabi I
27	Rajab	'Night of Ascent' (Laylat al-Mi'raj) of Mohammed to Heaven
1	Ramadan	Beginning of month of fasting during daylight hours
27	Ramadan	'Night of Power' (Laylat al-Qadr); sending down of the Koran to Mohammed
1	Shawwal	'Feast of breaking the Fast' ('Id al-Fitr); marks the end of Ramadan
8–13	Dhu-I-Hijja	Annual pilgrimage ceremonies at and around Mecca; month during which the great pilgrimage (Hajj) should be made
10	Dhu-I-Hijja	Feast of the Sacrifice ('Id al-Adha)

Jainism

Founder
Vardhamana Mahavira, 599–527 BC

Date founded
c.600 BC, India

Beliefs
World eternal and uncreated
All phenomena linked by chain of cause and effect
Nonviolence to other living creatures (Ahimsa)
Perfection and purification of soul leads to its emancipation and the ultimate attribute of omniscience
Soul has to pass through various stages of spiritual development before freeing itself of karmic bondages
Right conduct, right knowledge, right belief

Judaism

Founders
Abraham, c.2000 BC, and Moses, c.1200 BC

Date founded
c.2000 BC

Beliefs
Unity of God
God as teacher through instruction of Torah
God as redeemer
Resurrection
Coming of the 'Mashiah' who will establish new age in Israel

Major festivals

1–2	Tishri	Rosh Hashanah (New Year)
3	Tishri	Tzom Gedaliahu (Fast of Gedaliah)
10	Tishri	Yom Kippur (Day of Atonement)
15–21	Tishri	Sukkoth (Feast of Tabernacles)
22	Tishri	Shemini Atzeret (8th Day of the Solemn Assembly)
23	Tishri	Simhat Torah (Rejoicing of the Law)
25	Kislev–2–3 Tevet	Hanukkah (Feast of Dedication)
10	Tevet	Asara be-Tevet (Fast of 10th Tevet)
13	Adar	Taanit Esther (Fast of Esther)
14–15	Adar	Purim (Feast of Lots)
15–22	Nisan	Pesach (Passover)
5	Iyar	Israel Independence Day
6–7	Sivan	Shavuoth (Feast of Weeks)
17	Tammuz	Shiva Asar be-Tammuz (Fast of 17th Tammuz)
9	Av	Tisha be-Av (Fast of 9th Av)

The ancient tribes of Israel

Asher Descended from Jacob's eighth son (Z).
Benjamin Descended from Jacob's twelfth and youngest son (R).
Dan Descended from Jacob's fifth son (B).
Issachar Descended from Jacob's ninth or tenth son (L).
Joseph Descended from Jacob's eleventh son (R).
Ephraim Descended from Joseph's younger son.
Manasseh Descended from Joseph's elder son.
Judah Descended from Jacob's fourth son (L).
Levi Descended from Jacob's third son (L). (No territory, as it was a priestly caste.)
Naphtali Descended from Jacob's ninth or tenth son (B).
Reuben Descended from Jacob's first son (L).
Simeon Descended from Jacob's second son (L).
Zebulun Descended from Jacob's sixth son (L).

B = borne by Bilhah
L = borne by Leah
R = borne by Rachel
Z = borne by Zilpal

Israel during the period of the Judges – approximate tribal areas

Shintoism

Founder
No founder

Date originated
6th-c AD, Japan

Beliefs
Polytheistic – belief in 'kami' (deities)
Sincerity arising from awareness of the divine
Spiritual and physical purification
Continuity/communion with ancestry

Major Japanese festivals

1–3	Jan	Oshogatsu (New Year)
3	Feb	Setsubun
3	Mar	Ohinamatsuri (Doll *or* Girls' Festival)
5	May	Tango no Sekku (Boys' Festival)
7	Jul	Hoshi matsuri *or* Tanabata (Star Festival)
13–15	Jul	Obon (Buddhist All Souls)
15	Nov	Shichi-go-San (Seven-five-three age celebrations for 7-year-old girls, 5-year-old boys, and 3-year-old girls)

Sikhism

Founder
Guru Nanak, AD 1469–1539

Date founded
c.15th-c AD, India

Beliefs
Unity of God
Birth, death, and rebirth
Guidance of the Guru to 'moksa' (release) and the way of God
Worship of the Adi Granth

Taoism

Founder
Lao Zi, 6th-c BC

Date founded
600 BC, China

Beliefs
Interaction of human society and the universe
Divine nature of sovereign
Cult of Heaven
Law of return
State of original purity
Worship of ancestors

Religious symbols

The Trinity

Equilateral triangle | Triangle in circle | Circle within triangle | Trefoil | Triquetra | Triquetra and circle | Interwoven circles

God the Father

All-seeing eye | Hand of God | Hand of God | Lamb of God | Fish | Dove descending | Sevenfold flame

Old Testament

Menorah (seven branch candlestick) | Abraham | The Ten Commandments | Pentateuch (The Law) | Marked doorposts and lintel (Passover) | Twelve tribes of Israel | Star of David

Crosses

Aiguisée | Avellane | Barbée | Trefly | Canterbury | Celtic | Cercelée | Cross crosslet

Crux ansata | Entrailed | Fleurée | Globical | Graded (Calvary) | Greek | Iona | Jerusalem

Latin | Maltese | Millvine | Papal | Patée | Patée formée | Patonce | Patriarchal (or Lorraine) | Pommel or Pommée

Potent | Raguly or Ragulée | Russian Orthodox | St Andrew's (Saltire) | St Peter's | Tau (St Anthony's)

Monograms
IHC (Latin form) (from Gk IHCOYC 'Jesus') | Chi Rho (from Gk XPICTOC 'Christ')

The Christian Church Year

Advent | Christmas | Epiphany | Lent | Maundy Thursday | Good Friday | Easter Day | Ascension | Pentecost

Other symbols

Ankh (Egyptian) | Yin-yang Tao symbol of harmony | Torii (Shinto) | Om (Hinduism, Buddhism, Jainism; sacred syllable) | Ik-onkar (Sikhism; symbol of God) | Swastika (originally symbol of the Sun) | Yantra: Sri Cakra (wheel of fortune)

COMMUNICATIONS

TRANSPORTATION

Road

Main USA Interstate highways

Odd-number Interstates run South–North; even-number, West–East.

I5	San Diego–Los Angeles–Sacramento–Seattle–Vancouver, Can
I8	San Diego–Tucson
I10	Los Angeles–Phoenix–San Antonio–Houston–New Orleans–Jacksonville
I15	San Diego–Las Vegas–Salt Lake City–Great Falls
I20	Fort Worth–Dallas–Jackson–Birmingham–Atlanta–Columbia
I25	Albuquerque–Colorado Springs–Denver–Buffalo
I30	Dallas–Little Rock
I35	San Antonio–Austin–Fort Worth–Oklahoma City–Wichita–Kansas City–Des Moines–Minneapolis/St Paul–Duluth
I40	Flagstaff–Albuquerque–Oklahoma City–Little Rock–Memphis–Nashville–Greensboro
I45	Dallas–Houston
I55	New Orleans–Jackson–Memphis–St Louis–Chicago
I59	New Orleans–Birmingham–Chattanooga
I64	St Louis–Louisville–Lexington–Charleston
I65	Mobile–Birmingham–Nashville–Louisville–Indianapolis–Chicago
I70	Denver–Kansas City–St Louis–Indianapolis–Columbus–Philadelphia–Baltimore
I71	Louisville–Cincinatti–Columbus
I74	Davenport–Indianapolis–Cincinatti
I75	Tampa–Atlanta–Cincinatti–Toledo–Detroit
I78	Harrisburg–New York
I80	San Francisco–Salt Lake City–Des Moines–Cleveland–New York
I81	Knoxville–Roanoake–Syracuse
I85	Montgomery–Atlanta–Greensboro–Petersburg
I90	Seattle–Billings–Sioux Falls–Chicago–Cleveland–Boston
I94	Billings–Bismarck–Minneapolis/St Paul–Madison–Milwaukee–Chicago–Detroit
I95	Miami–Jacksonville–Richmond–Washington, DC–Baltimore–New York–Boston–Augusta

British motorways

M1	Belfast–Dungannon (N Ireland)
M1	London–Northampton–Leicester–Nottingham–Sheffield–Leeds
M2	Belfast–Randalstown (N Ireland)
M2	Strood–Faversham (Medway)
M3	London–Basingstoke–Winchester
M4	London–Reading–Newport–Cardiff–Swansea
M5	Birmingham–Bristol–Exeter
M6	Birmingham–Wolverhampton–Stoke-on-Trent–Preston–Lancaster–Carlisle
M8	Edinburgh–Glasgow–Longbank
M9	Edinburgh–Stirling
M10	M1–St Albans spur
M11	London–Cambridge
M18	Rotherham–M62 junction 35 (Goole)
M20	Swanley (London)–Folkestone
M23	Redhill–Crawley
M25	London orbital motorway
M26	Chipstead–M20 junction 3
M27	Portsmouth–Southampton–Cadnam
M32	M4–Bristol spur
M40	London–Oxford–Birmingham
M42	Birmingham–Solihull–Tamworth–Appleby Magna
M45	Watford–Dunchurch
M50	Ross-on-Wye–M5 junction 8
M53	Chester–Wallasey
M54	Telford–M6 junction 10a
M55	Fulwood–Blackpool
M56	Chester–Altringham (N Cheshire)
M57	Liverpool–Aintree
M58	Aintree–Wigan
M61	Manchester–Preston
M62	Liverpool–Manchester–Leeds–North Cave (N Humberside)
M63	Salford–Stockport
M65	Blackburn–Burnley–Colne
M66	Middleton–Ramsbottom
M67	Denton–Mottram in Langendale (Manchester ring)
M69	Leicester–Coventry
M73	M74–Glasgow spur (Maryville–Mollisburn)
M74	Millbank–Maryville
M74	Carlisle–Gretna Green
M80	Longcroft–M9 junction 9 (Haggs)
M85	M90–Perth spur (Perth–Friarton Bridge)
M90	Perth–Inverkeithing
M180	Stainforth–Elsham (S Humberside)
M181	M180–Scunthorpe spur
M271	M27–Totton spur
M275	M27–Portsmouth spur
M606	M62–Bradford spur
M621	M62–Leeds spur
M876	M80–Kincardine Bridge (Banknock–Stenhousemuir)

International E-routes (Euroroutes)

Reference and intermediate roads (class A roads) have two-digit numbers; branch, link, and connecting roads (class B roads, not listed here), have three-digit numbers.

North–South orientated reference roads have two-digit odd numbers ending in the figure 5, and increasing from west to east. East–West orientated roads have two-digit even numbers ending in the figure 0, and increasing from north to south.

Intermediate roads have two-digit odd numbers (for N–S roads) or two-digit even numbers (for E–W roads) falling within the numbers of the reference roads between which they are located.

Only a selection of the towns and cities linked by E-roads given.

[···] indicates a sea crossing.

West–East orientation

Reference roads

E10	Narvik–Kiruna–Luleå
E20	Shannon–Dublin ··· Liverpool–Hull ··· Esbjerg–Nyborg ··· Korsør-Køge–Copenhagen ··· Malmö–Stockholm ··· Tallin–St Petersburg

Transportation

Road (continued)

E30 Cork–Rosslare ··· Fishguard–London–Felixstowe
··· Hook of Holland–Utrecht–Hanover–
Berlin–Warsaw–Smolensk–Moscow

E40 Calais–Brussels–Aachen–Cologne–Dresden–
Krakow–Kiev–Rostov na Donu

E50 Brest–Paris–Metz–Nurenberg–Prague–
Mukačevo

E60 Brest–Tours–Besançon–Basle–Innsbruck–
Vienna–Budapest–Bucharest–Constanţa

E70 La Coruña–Bilbao–Bordeaux–Lyon–Torino–
Verona–Trieste–Zagreb–Belgrade–
Bucharest–Varna

E80 Lisbon–Coimbra–Salamanca–Pau–Toulouse–
Nice–Genoa–Rome–Pescara ··· Dubrovnik–
Sofia–Istanbul–Erzincan–Iran

E90 Lisbon–Madrid–Barcelona ··· Mazara del
Vallo–Messina ··· Reggio di Calabria–Brindisi
··· Igoumenitsa–Thessaloniki–Gelibolu ···
Lapseki–Ankara–Iraq

Intermediate roads

E06 Olderfjord–Kirkenes

E12 Mo i Rana–Umeå ··· Vaasa–Helsinki

E14 Trondheim–Sundsvall

E16 Londonderry–Belfast ··· Glasgow–Edinburgh

E18 Craigavon–Larne ··· Stranraer–Newcastle ···
Stavanger–Oslo–Stockholm–Kappelskär ···
Mariehamn ··· Turku–Helsinki–Leningrad

E22 Holyhead–Manchester–Immingham ···
Amsterdam–Hamburg–Sassnitz ···
Trelleborg–Norrköping

E24 Birmingham–Ipswich

E26 Hamburg–Berlin

E28 Berlin–Gdańsk

E32 Colchester–Harwich

E34 Antwerp–Bad Oeynhausen

E36 Berlin–Legnica

E42 Dunkirk–Aschaffenburg

E44 Le Havre–Luxembourg–Giessen

E46 Cherbourg–Liège

E48 Schweinfurt–Prague

E52 Strasbourg–Salzburg

E54 Paris–Basle–Munich

E56 Nuremberg–Sattledt

E58 Vienna–Bratislava

E62 Nantes–Geneva–Tortona

E64 Turin–Brescia

E66 Fortezza–Székesfehérvár

E68 Szeged–Braşov

E72 Bordeaux–Toulouse

E74 Nice–Alessandria

E76 Migliarino–Florence

E78 Grosseto–Fano

E82 Porto–Tordesillas

E84 Keşan–Silivri

E86 Krystalopigi–Yefira

E88 Ankara–Refahiye

E92 Igoumenitsa–Volos

E94 Corinth–Athens

E96 Izmir–Sivrihisar

E98 Topbogazi–Syria

North–South orientation

Reference roads

E05 Greenock–Birmingham–Southampton ···
Le Havre–Paris–Bordeaux–Madrid–Algeciras

E15 Inverness–Edinburgh–London–Dover ···
Calais–Paris–Lyon–Barcelona–Algeciras

E25 Hook of Holland–Luxembourg–Strasbourg–
Basle–Geneva–Turin–Genoa

E35 Amsterdam–Cologne–Basle–Milan–Rome

E45 Gothenburg ··· Frederikshavn–Hamburg–
Munich–Innsbruck–Bologna–Rome–Naples–
Villa S Giovanni ··· Messina–Gela

E55 Kemi-Tornio–Stockholm–Helsingborg ···
Helsinger–Copenhagen–Gedser ··· Rostock–
Berlin–Prague–Salzburg–Rimini–Brindisi ···
Igoumenitsa–Kalamata

E65 Malmö–Ystrad–Świnoujście–Prague–Zagreb–
Dubrovnik–Bitolj–Antirrion ··· Rion–
Kalamata – Kissamos–Chania

E75 Karasjok–Helsinki ··· Gdańsk–Budapest–
Belgrade–Athens ··· Chania–Sitia

E85 Černovcy–Bucharest–Alexandropouli

E95 St Petersburg–Moscow–Yalta

Intermediate roads

E01 Larne–Dublin–Rosslare ··· La Coruña–Lisbon–
Seville

E03 Cherbourg–La Rochelle

E07 Pau–Zaragoza

E09 Orléans–Barcelona

E11 Vierzon–Montpellier

E13 Doncaster–London

E17 Antwerp–Beaune

E19 Amsterdam–Brussels–Paris

E21 Metz–Geneva

E23 Metz–Lausanne

E27 Belfort–Aosta

E29 Cologne–Sarreguemines

E31 Rotterdam–Ludwigshafen

E33 Parma–La Spezie

E37 Bremen–Cologne

E39 Kristiansand–Aalborg

E41 Dortmund–Altdorf

E43 Würzburg–Bellinzona

E47 Nordkap–Oslo–Copenhagen–Rødby ···
Puttgarden–Lübeck

E49 Magdeburg–Vienna

E51 Berlin–Nurenberg

E53 Plzeň–Munich

E57 Sattledt–Ljubljana

E59 Prague–Zagreb

E61 Klagenfurt–Rijeka

E63 Sodankylä–Naantali ··· Stockholm–Gothenburg

E67 Warsaw–Prague

E69 Tromsø–Tornio

E71 Košice–Budapest–Split

E73 Budapest–Metkovič

E77 Gdańsk–Budapest

E79 Oradea–Calafat ··· Vidin–Thessaloniki

E81 Halmeu–Piteśti

E83 Bjala–Sofia

E87 Tulcea–Eceabat ··· Çanakkale–Antalya

E89 Gerede–Ankara

E91 Toprakkale–Syria

E93 Orel–Odessa

E97 Trabzon–Aşkale

E99 Doğubeyazit–Ş Urfa

European road distances

Road distances between some cities, given in kilometres. To convert to statute miles, multiply number given by 0.6214.

	Athens	Barcelona	Brussels	Calais	Cherbourg	Cologne	Copenhagen	Geneva	Gibraltar	Hamburg	Hook of Holland	Lisbon	Lyons	Madrid	Marseilles	Milan	Munich	Paris	Rome	Stockholm
Barcelona	3313																			
Brussels	2963	1318																		
Calais	3175	1326	204																	
Cherbourg	3339	1294	583	460																
Cologne	2762	1498	206	409	785															
Copenhagen	3276	2218	966	1136	1545	760														
Geneva	2610	803	677	747	853	1662	1418													
Gibraltar	4485	1172	2256	2224	2047	2436	3196	1975												
Hamburg	2977	2018	597	714	1115	460	460	1118	2897											
Hook of Holland	3030	1490	172	330	731	269	269	895	2428	550										
Lisbon	4532	1304	2084	2052	1827	2290	2971	1936	676	2671	2280									
Lyons	2753	645	690	739	789	714	1458	158	1817	1159	863	1778								
Madrid	3949	636	1558	1550	1347	1764	2498	1439	698	2198	1730	668	1281							
Marseilles	2865	521	1011	1059	1101	1035	1778	425	1693	1479	1183	1762	320	1157						
Milan	2282	1014	925	1077	1209	911	1537	328	2185	1238	1098	2250	328	1724	618					
Munich	2179	1365	747	977	1160	583	1104	591	2565	3805	851	2507	724	2010	1109	331				
Paris	3000	1033	285	280	340	465	1176	513	1971	877	457	1799	471	1273	792	856	821			
Rome	817	1460	1511	1662	1794	1497	2050	995	2631	1751	1683	2700	1048	2097	1011	586	946	1476		
Stockholm	3927	2868	1616	1786	2196	1403	650	2068	3886	949	1500	3231	2108	3188	2428	2187	1754	1827	2707	
Vienna	1991	1802	1175	1381	1588	937	1455	1019	2974	1155	1205	2935	1157	2409	1363	898	428	1249	1209	2105

UK road distances

Road distances between British centres are given in statute miles, using routes recommended by the Automobile Association based on the quickest travelling time. To convert to kilometres, multiply number given by 1.6093.

	Aberdeen	Birmingham	Bristol	Cambridge	Cardiff	Dover	Edinburgh	Exeter	Glasgow	Holyhead	Hull	Leeds	Liverpool	Manchester	Newcastle	Norwich	Nottingham	Oxford	Penzance	Plymouth	Shrewsbury	Southampton	Stranraer	York
Birmingham	430																							
Bristol	511	85																						
Cambridge	468	101	156																					
Cardiff	532	107	45	191																				
Dover	591	202	198	121	234																			
Edinburgh	130	293	373	337	395	457																		
Exeter	584	157	81	233	119	248	446																	
Glasgow	149	291	372	349	393	490	45	444																
Holyhead	457	151	232	246	209	347	325	305	319															
Hull	361	136	227	157	246	278	229	297	245	215														
Leeds	336	115	216	143	236	265	205	288	215	163	59													
Liverpool	361	98	178	195	200	295	222	250	220	104	126	72												
Manchester	354	88	167	153	188	283	218	239	214	123	97	43	34											
Newcastle	239	198	291	224	311	348	107	361	150	260	121	91	170	141										
Norwich	501	161	217	62	252	167	365	295	379	309	153	173	232	183	258									
Nottingham	402	59	151	82	170	202	268	222	281	174	92	73	107	71	156	123								
Oxford	497	63	74	82	109	148	361	152	354	218	188	171	164	153	253	144	104							
Penzance	696	272	195	346	232	362	561	112	559	419	411	401	366	355	477	407	265	265						
Plymouth	624	199	125	275	164	290	488	45	486	347	341	328	294	281	410	336	328	193	78					
Shrewsbury	412	48	128	142	110	243	276	201	272	104	164	116	64	69	216	205	724	113	315	242				
Southampton	571	128	75	133	123	155	437	114	436	296	253	235	241	227	319	192	471	67	227	155	190			
Stranraer	241	307	386	361	406	503	130	457	88	332	259	232	234	226	164	393	1048	371	572	502	287	447		
York	325	128	221	153	241	274	191	291	208	190	38	24	100	71	83	185	2108	185	406	340	144	252	228	
London	543	118	119	60	155	77	405	170	402	263	215	196	210	199	280	115	1157	56	283	215	162	76	419	209

Communications

Transportation

Road (continued)
International car index marks

A	Austria	ET	Egypt	MEX	Mexico	SF	Finland
ADN	former Yemen PDR	ETH	Ethiopia	MS	Mauritius[a]	SGP	Singapore[a]
AFG	Afghanistan	F	France	MW	Malawi[a]	SME	Suriname[a]
AL	Albania	FJI	Fiji[a]	N	Norway	SN	Senegal
AND	Andorra	FL	Liechtenstein	NA	Netherlands	SU	former USSR
AUS	Australia[a]	FR	Faroe Is		Antilles	SWA	Namibia[a]
B	Belgium	GB	UK[a]	NIC	Nicaragua	SY	Seychelles[a]
BD	Bangladesh[a]	GBA	Alderney[a]	NL	Netherlands	SYR	Syria
BDS	Barbados[a]	GBG	Guernsey[a]	NZ	New Zealand[a]	T	Thailand[a]
BG	Bulgaria	GBJ	Jersey[a]	P	Portugal	TG	Togo
BH	Belize	GBM	Isle of Man[a]	PA	Panama	TN	Tunisia
BR	Brazil	GBZ	Gibraltar	PAK	Pakistan[a]	TR	Turkey
BRN	Bahrain	GCA	Guatemala	PE	Peru	TT	Trinidad and
BRU	Brunei[a]	GH	Ghana	PL	Poland		Tobago[a]
BS	Bahamas[a]	GR	Greece	PNG	Papua New Guinea[a]	USA	USA
BUR	Myanmar (Burma)	GUY	Guyana[a]	PY	Paraguay	V	Vatican City
C	Cuba	H	Hungary	RA	Argentina	VN	Vietnam
CDN	Canada	HK	Hong Kong[a]	RB	Botswana[a]	WAG	Gambia
CH	Switzerland	HKJ	Jordan	RC	Taiwan	WAL	Sierra Leone
CI	Côte d'Ivoire	I	Italy	RCA	Central African	WAN	Nigeria
CL	Sri Lanka[a]	IL	Israel		Republic	WD	Dominica[a]
CO	Colombia	IND	India[a]	RCB	Congo	WG	Grenada[a]
CR	Costa Rica	IR	Iran	RCH	Chile	WL	St Lucia[a]
CS	Czechoslovakia	IRL	Ireland[a]	RH	Haiti	WS	W Samoa
CY	Cyprus[a]	IRQ	Iraq	RI	Indonesia[a]	WV	St Vincent and the
D	Germany	IS	Iceland	RIM	Mauritania		Grenadines[a]
DDR	former E Germany	J	Japan[a]	RL	Lebanon	YU	Yugoslavia
DK	Denmark	JA	Jamaica[a]	RM	Madagascar	YV	Venezuela
DOM	Dominican	KWT	Kuwait	RMM	Mali	Z	Zambia[a]
	Republic	L	Luxembourg	RN	Niger	ZA	South Africa[a]
DY	Benin	LAO	Laos PDR	RO	Romania	ZRE	Zaïre
DZ	Algeria	LAR	Libya	ROK	Korea, Republic of	ZW	Zimbabwe[a]
E	Spain	LB	Liberia	ROU	Uruguay		
EAK	Kenya[a]	LR	Latvia	RP	Philippines		
EAT	Tanzania[a]	LS	Lesotho[a]	RSM	San Marino		
EAU	Uganda[a]	M	Malta[a]	RU	Burundi		
EAZ	Tanzania[a]	MA	Morocco	RWA	Rwanda		
EC	Ecuador	MAL	Malaysia[a]	S	Sweden		
ES	El Salvador	MC	Monaco	SD	Swaziland[a]		

[a]Countries in which the rule of the road is drive on the left; in other countries, drive on the right.

British car index marks

AA	Bournemouth	BA	Manchester	BX	Haverfordwest	CU	Newcastle upon
AB	Worcester	BB	Newcastle upon	BY	London NW		Tyne
AC	Coventry		Tyne			CV	Truro
AD	Gloucester	BC	Leicester	CA	Chester	CW	Preston
AE	Bristol	BD	Northampton	CB	Manchester	CX	Huddersfield
AF	Truro	BE	Lincoln	CC	Bangor	CY	Swansea
AG	Hull	BF	Stoke-on-Trent	CD	Brighton		
AH	Norwich	BG	Liverpool	CE	Peterborough	DA	Birmingham
AJ	Middlesbrough	BH	Luton	CF	Reading	DB	Manchester
AK	Sheffield	BJ	Ipswich	CG	Bournemouth	DC	Middlesbrough
AL	Nottingham	BK	Portsmouth	CH	Nottingham	DD	Gloucester
AM	Swindon	BL	Reading	CJ	Gloucester	DE	Haverfordwest
AN	Reading	BM	Luton	CK	Preston	DF	Gloucester
AO	Carlisle	BN	Manchester	CL	Norwich	DG	Gloucester
AP	Brighton	BO	Cardiff	CM	Liverpool	DH	Dudley
AR	Chelmsford	BP	Portsmouth	CN	Newcastle upon	DJ	Liverpool
AS	Inverness	BR	Newcastle upon		Tyne	DK	Manchester
AT	Hull		Tyne	CO	Exeter	DL	Portsmouth
AU	Nottingham	BS	Inverness	CP	Huddersfield	DM	Chester
AV	Peterborough	BT	Leeds	CR	Portsmouth	DN	Leeds
AW	Shrewsbury	BU	Manchester	CS	Glasgow	DO	Lincoln
AX	Cardiff	BV	Preston	CT	Lincoln	DP	Reading
AY	Leicester	BW	Oxford			DR	Exeter

418

Code	Location	Code	Location	Code	Location	Code	Location
DS	Glasgow	GL	Truro	KD	Liverpool	MY	London SE
DT	Sheffield	GM	Reading	KE	Maidstone		
DU	Coventry	GN	London SW	KF	Liverpool	NA	Manchester
DV	Exeter	GO	London SW	KG	Cardiff	NB	Manchester
DW	Cardiff	GP	London SW	KH	Hull	NC	Manchester
DX	Ipswich	GR	Newcastle upon Tyne	KJ	Maidstone	ND	Manchester
DY	Brighton			KK	Maidstone	NE	Manchester
		GS	Luton	KL	Maidstone	NF	Manchester
EA	Dudley	GT	London SW	KM	Maidstone	NG	Norwich
EB	Peterborough	GU	London SE	KN	Maidstone	NH	Northampton
EC	Preston	GV	Ipswich	KO	Maidstone	NJ	Brighton
ED	Liverpool	GW	London SE	KP	Maidstone	NK	Luton
EE	Lincoln	GX	London SE	KR	Maidstone	NL	Newcastle upon Tyne
EF	Middlesbrough	GY	London SE	KS	Edinburgh		
EG	Peterborough			KT	Maidstone	NM	Luton
EH	Stoke-on-Trent	HA	Dudley	KU	Sheffield	NN	Nottingham
EJ	Haverfordwest	HB	Cardiff	KV	Coventry	NO	Chelmsford
EK	Liverpool	HC	Brighton	KW	Sheffield	NP	Worcester
EL	Bournemouth	HD	Huddersfield	KX	Luton	NR	Leicester
EM	Liverpool	HE	Sheffield	KY	Sheffield	NS	Glasgow
EN	Manchester	HF	Liverpool			NT	Shrewsbury
EO	Preston	HG	Preston	LA	London NW	NU	Nottingham
EP	Swansea	HH	Carlisle	LB	London NW	NV	Northampton
ER	Peterborough	HJ	Chelmsford	LC	London NW	NW	Leeds
ES	Dundee	HK	Chelmsford	LD	London NW	NX	Dudley
ET	Sheffield	HL	Sheffield	LE	London NW	NY	Cardiff
EU	Bristol	HM	London C	LF	London NW		
EV	Chelmsford	HN	Middlesbrough	LG	Chester	OA	Birmingham
EW	Peterborough	HO	Bournemouth	LH	London NW	OB	Birmingham
EX	Norwich	HP	Coventry	LJ	Bournemouth	OC	Birmingham
EY	Bangor	HR	Swindon	LK	London NW	OD	Exeter
		HS	Glasgow	LL	London NW	OE	Birmingham
FA	Stoke-on-Trent	HT	Bristol	LM	London NW	OF	Birmingham
FB	Bristol	HU	Bristol	LN	London NW	OG	Birmingham
FC	Oxford	HV	London C	LO	London NW	OH	Birmingham
FD	Dudley	HW	Bristol	LP	London NW	OJ	Birmingham
FE	Lincoln	HX	London C	LR	London NW	OK	Birmingham
FF	Bangor	HY	Bristol	LS	Edinburgh	OL	Birmingham
FG	Brighton			LT	London NW	OM	Birmingham
FH	Gloucester	JA	Manchester	LU	London NW	ON	Birmingham
FJ	Exeter	JB	Reading	LV	Liverpool	OO	Chelmsford
FK	Dudley	JC	Bangor	LW	London NW	OP	Birmingham
FL	Peterborough	JD	London C	LX	London NW	OR	Portsmouth
FM	Chester	JE	Peterborough	LY	London NW	OS	Glasgow
FN	Maidstone	JF	Leicester			OT	Portsmouth
FO	Gloucester	JG	Maidstone	MA	Chester	OU	Bristol
FP	Leicester	JH	Reading	MB	Chester	OV	Birmingham
FR	Preston	JJ	Maidstone	MC	London NE	OW	Portsmouth
FS	Edinburgh	JK	Brighton	MD	London NE	OX	Birmingham
FT	Newcastle upon Tyne	JL	Lincoln	ME	London NE	OY	London NW
FU	Lincoln	JM	Reading	MF	London NE		
FV	Preston	JN	Chelmsford	MG	London NE	PA	Guildford
FW	Lincoln	JO	Oxford	MH	London NE	PB	Guildford
FX	Bournemouth	JP	Liverpool	MJ	Luton	PC	Guildford
FY	Liverpool	JR	Newcastle upon Tyne	MK	London NE	PD	Guildford
		JS	Inverness	ML	London NE	PE	Guildford
GA	Glasgow	JT	Bournemouth	MM	London NE	PF	Guildford
GB	Glasgow	JU	Leicester	MN	not used	PG	Guildford
GC	London SW	JV	Lincoln	MO	Reading	PH	Guildford
GD	Glasgow	JW	Birmingham	MP	London NE	PJ	Guildford
GE	Glasgow	JX	Huddersfield	MR	Swindon	PK	Guildford
GF	London SW	JY	Exeter	MS	Edinburgh	PL	Guildford
GG	Glasgow			MT	London NE	PM	Guildford
GH	London SW	KA	Liverpool	MU	London NE	PN	Brighton
GJ	London SW	KB	Liverpool	MV	London SE	PO	Portsmouth
GK	London SW	KC	Liverpool	MW	Swindon	PP	Luton
				MX	London SE	PR	Bournemouth

Road (continued)

PS	Aberdeen	SL	Dundee	UG	Leeds	WC	Chelmsford
PT	Newcastle upon Tyne	SM	Glasgow	UH	Cardiff	WD	Dudley
		SN	Dundee	UJ	Shrewsbury	WE	Sheffield
PU	Chelmsford	SO	Aberdeen	UK	Birmingham	WF	Sheffield
PV	Ipswich	SP	Dundee	UL	London C	WG	Sheffield
PW	Norwich	SR	Dundee	UM	Leeds	WH	Manchester
PX	Portsmouth	SS	Aberdeen	UN	Exeter	WJ	Sheffield
PY	Middlesbrough	ST	Inverness	UO	Exeter	WK	Coventry
		SU	Glasgow	UP	Newcastle upon Tyne	WL	Oxford
RA	Nottingham	SV	spare			WM	Liverpool
RB	Nottingham	SW	Glasgow	UR	Luton	WN	Swansea
RC	Nottingham	SX	Edinburgh	US	Glasgow	WO	Cardiff
RD	Reading	SY	spare	UT	Leicester	WP	Worcester
RE	Stoke-on-Trent			UU	London C	WR	Leeds
RF	Stoke-on-Trent	TA	Exeter	UV	London C	WS	Bristol
RG	Newcastle upon Tyne	TB	Liverpool	UW	London C	WT	Leeds
		TC	Bristol	UX	Shrewsbury	WU	Leeds
RH	Hull	TD	Manchester	UY	Worcester	WV	Brighton
RJ	Manchester	TE	Manchester			WW	Leeds
RK	London NW	TF	Reading	VA	Peterborough	WX	Leeds
RL	Truro	TG	Cardiff	VB	Maidstone	WY	Leeds
RM	Carlisle	TH	Swansea	VC	Coventry		
RN	Preston	TJ	Liverpool	VD	series withdrawn	YA	Taunton
RO	Luton	TK	Exeter	VE	Peterborough	YB	Taunton
RP	Northampton	TL	Lincoln	VF	Norwich	YC	Taunton
RR	Nottingham	TM	Luton	VG	Norwich	YD	Taunton
RS	Aberdeen	TN	Newcastle upon Tyne	VH	Huddersfield	YE	London C
RT	Ipswich			VJ	Gloucester	YF	London C
RU	Bournemouth	TO	Nottingham	VK	Newcastle upon Tyne	YG	Leeds
RV	Portsmouth	TP	Portsmouth			YH	London C
RW	Coventry	TR	Portsmouth	VL	Lincoln	YJ	Brighton
RX	Reading	TS	Dundee	VM	Manchester	YK	London C
RY	Leicester	TT	Exeter	VN	Middlesbrough	YL	London C
		TU	Chester	VO	Nottingham	YM	London C
SA	Aberdeen	TV	Nottingham	VP	Birmingham	YN	London C
SB	Glasgow	TW	Chelmsford	VR	Manchester	YO	London C
SC	Edinburgh	TX	Cardiff	VS	Luton	YP	London C
SCY	Truro (Isles of Scilly)	TY	Newcastle upon Tyne	VT	Stoke-on-Trent	YR	London C
				VU	Manchester	YS	Glasgow
SD	Glasgow			VV	Northampton	YT	London C
SE	Aberdeen	UA	Leeds	VW	Chelmsford	YU	London C
SF	Edinburgh	UB	Leeds	VX	Chelmsford	YV	London C
SG	Edinburgh	UC	London C	VY	Leeds	YW	London C
SH	Edinburgh	UD	Oxford			YX	London C
SJ	Glasgow	UE	Dudley	WA	Sheffield	YY	London C
SK	Inverness	UF	Brighton	WB	Sheffield		

Fastest cars

Name of car	Speed		Date	Type
	(km/h)	(mph)		
Thrust 2 (Rolls-Royce Avon 302)	1019.467	633.468	1983	Jet-powered
Speed-O-Motive/Spirit 76	696.331	432.692	1991	Single-piston engine
Bluebird	690.909	429.054	1964	Gas-turbine engine
Jaguar XJ 220	341	212.3	1991	Piston-engined
Mercedes C III/3	327.3	203.3	1978	Diesel-engined
No. 744 Steamin' Demon	234.33	145.607	1985	Steam-powered
Electric car	111.40	69.21	1991	Electricity-powered

Communications

British road signs

Instruction signs

Generally circular. A red border circle indicates a prohibition; blue signs indicate permitted activities.

Entry to
20 mph zone

End of
20 mph zone

School crossing
patrol

Maximum speed

National speed
limit applies

Stop and
give way

Give way to traffic
on major road

No vehicles

No entry for
vehicular traffic

No right turn

No left turn

No U-turns

No
overtaking

Give priority to
vehicles from
opposite direction

No motor
vehicles

No motor
vehicles except
solo motorcycles,
scooters or mopeds

Manually
operated
temporary
'STOP' sign

No vehicles with
over 12 seats
except regular
scheduled, school
and work buses

No cycling

No pedestrians

No goods vehicles
over maximum
gross weight
shown (in tonnes)

No vehicle or
combination of
vehicles over
length shown

No vehicles over
height shown

No vehicles over
width shown

No vehicles over
maximum gross
weight shown
(in tonnes)

Axle weight limit
in tonnes

No stopping
(clearway)

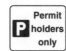
Parking restricted to use
by people named on sign

No stopping during
times shown except
for as long as
necessary to set down
or pick up passengers

Qualifications

End of
restriction

Exception for
loading/unloading goods

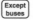
Exception for regular
scheduled, school and
work buses

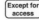
Exception for access to
premises and land adjacent
to the road where there is
no alternative route

Transportation

Road (continued)

Warning signs

Generally triangular.

Distance to
'STOP' line ahead

Crossroads

Junction on
bend ahead

T-junction

Staggered
junction

Distance to
'Give Way' line ahead

Sharp deviation
of route to left
(or right if
chevrons
reversed)

Double bend first
to left (symbol
may be reversed)

Bend to right
(or left if symbol
reversed)

Roundabout

Uneven road

Plate below
some signs

Dual carriageway
ends

Road narrows on right
(left if symbol reversed)

Road narrows
on both sides

Two-way traffic
crosses one-way road

Two-way traffic
straight ahead

Traffic signals   Failure of traffic light signals   Slippery road   Steep hill downwards   Steep hill upwards

Gradients may be shown as a rate
eg 20° = 1.5

Communications

European road signs

Austria

Diversion / Umleitung

Tram turns at yellow or red

Federal road with priority

Federal road without priority

U-turn compulsory

Street lights not on all night

Buses only

Belgium

You may pass right or left

No parking from 1st to 15th of month

No parking from 16th to end of month

Bulgaria

Difficult section of road

Recommended maximum speed

U-turn allowed

Denmark

Sight-seeing

Pass either side

Beginning of 1 hr parking zone

End of parking zone

Finland

Traffic merges

Compulsory slow lane

Recommended speed in a bend

Diversion due to road works

8-18

Prohibition applies between 08.00 and 18.00 hours Mon-Fri

(8-14)

Prohibition applies between 08.00 and 14.00 hours (Saturday)

10-14

Prohibition applies between 10.00 and 14.00 hours (Sunday)

France

Keep well over to the right

"Priority road" sign

Germany

"End of priority" sign

Diversion or relief route

Give way to traffic

Traffic on the roundabout has priority

Itineraire Bis (Bison Futé) - Alternative (Holiday) routes

Diversion / Umleitung

Recommended speed limit

Emergency diversion for motorway traffic

Hungary

Tram or bus stop

Autobann number

Road number

Parking 2 hours (disc required)

Route for heavy vehicles

Lane reserved for buses from 07.00 to 19.00 hrs

Italy

Track for motorcycles

Road for motor vehicles

Restricted parking

Netherlands

Overtaking by vehicles with trailers prohibited

No entry for pedestrians

Stop when meeting public transport bus on mountain road

Easily inflammable forest

Traffic in parallel lanes

Lane reserved for slow vehicles

Cycle track

Danger–trams crossing

Built-up area

End of built-up area

Norway

End of (B) road

2 hours maximum (disc obligatory)

Parking prohibited (see panel)

Stopping prohibited (see panel)

Tunnel

Passing place (on narrow roads)

Parking prohibited (upper panel) Allowed (lower)

Parking 2 hrs from 08.00-17.00 hrs

Portugal

Parking 2 hrs from 08.00-18.00 hrs (16.00 hrs Sat)

End of parking prohibition

Spain

Recommended maximum speed

Turning permitted

Tourist Accommodation

Sight-seeing

Conpulsory lane for motorcycles

Conpulsory lane for lorries

Tunnel

Sweden

Meeting point (narrow roads)

Slow lane

Width of carriageway

Switzerland

Caution – blind person

Caution – deaf/handicapped person

e.g. at pedestrian crossing

Postal vehicles have priority

Parking disc compulsory

Slow lane

Motorway

Semi-motorway

Tunnel (lights compusory)

Flashing red light (level crossing)

Alternately flashing lights (level crossing)

Road (continued)

USA road signs

Instruction signs

Stop   4-way stop   Do not enter   Yield   Wrong way   No right turn   No U-turn   One way

Speed limit   Speed zone ahead   Slower traffic keep right   Speed limit with minimum limit posted   School speed limit   Divided highway   Two-way left-turn lanes   No turn on red

Warning signs

Crossroads   Side road   Divided highway   Two-way traffic   Merge   Railroad crossing   No passing zone   Narrow bridge

Road curves   Right reverse turn   Winding road   Stop ahead   Yield ahead   School crossing   School zone   Pedestrian crossing

Steep downgrade   Slippery when wet   Low clearance   Truck crossing   Deer crossing   Cattle crossing   Farm machinery   No bicycles

Road construction   Flagperson ahead   Freeway exit ramp speed limit

Services signs

Rest area   Telephone   Hospital   Campground   Trailer sites

Communications

Rail

UK rail travel times

Intercity routes on British Rail; times are given in hours and minutes for the shortest available weekday services.

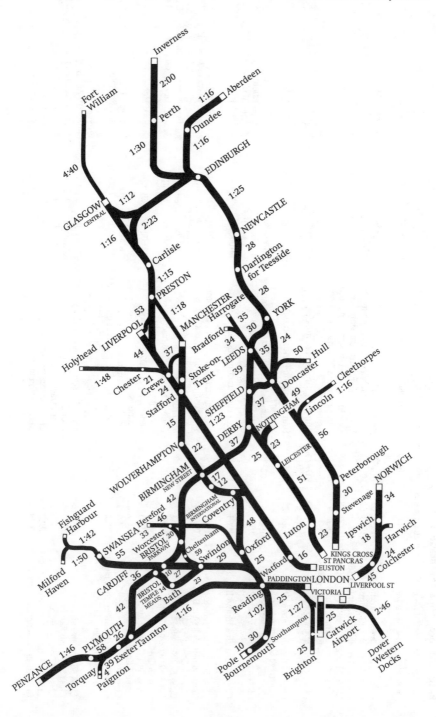

Rail (continued)

British Rail locomotive classifications

This list gives the details of diesel and electric locomotives operating on BR.

Locomotive	Built	Weight (tonnes)	Transmission	Maximum tractive effort (lb)	Maximum speed (mph)	Engine	Wheel diameter
Class 03 British Rail shunter 0-6-0	1958-62	31	Mechanical	15300 lb	28 mph	Gardner 204 hp	3'7"
Class 08 British Rail shunter 0-6-0	1953-62	50	Two English Electric traction motors	35000 lb	15-20 mph	English Electric 400 hp	4'6"
Class 09 British Rail shunter 0-6-0	1959-62	50	Two English Electric traction motors	25000 lb	27 mph	English Electric 350 hp	4'6"
Class 20 English Electric type 1 Bo-Bo	1957-68	73-4	Four English Electric traction motors	42000 lb	60 mph	English Electric 1000 hp	3'7"
Class 26 Birmingham Railway Carriage & Wagon type 2 Bo-Bo	1958-9	75	Four Crompton-Parkinson traction motors	42000 lb	60 mph	Sulzer 1160 hp	3'7"
Class 31 Brush type 2 AlA-AlA	1957-62	107-13	Four Brush traction motors	42800 lb	80-90 mph	English Electric 1470 hp	3'7" (driven) 3'3" (centre)
Class 33 Birmingham Railway Carriage & Wagon type 3 Bo-Bo	1960-2	78-9	Four Crompton-Parkinson traction motors	45000 lb	60-85 mph	Sulzer 1550 hp	3'7"
Class 37 English Electric type 3 Co-Co	1960-5	102-20	Six English Electric traction motors	56000 lb	80 mph	English Electric 1750 hp	3'7"
Class 43 HST Power Cars Bo-Bo	1974-82	70	Four Brush traction motors	17980 lb	125 mph	Paxman Valenta Mirrlees Blackstone	3'4"
Class 47 British Rail and Brush type 4 Co-Co	1963-7	117-25	Six Brush traction motors	60000 lb	75-95 mph	Sulzer 2580 hp	3'9"
Class 50 English Electric type 4 Co-Co	1967-8	117	Six English Electric traction motors	48500 lb	100 mph	English Electric 2700 hp	3'7"
Class 56 British Rail & Brush type 5 Co-Co	1976-84	125	Six Brush traction motors	61800 lb	80 mph	Rushton-Paxman 3250 hp	3'9"
Class 58 BREL type 5 Co-Co	1983-7	129	Six Brush traction motors	61800 lb	80 mph	Rushton-Paxman 3300 hp	3'8"
Class 59 General Motors type 5 Co-Co	1985-9 (USA)	126	General Motors D77B traction motors	113500 lb	60 mph	General Motors 3300 hp	3'4"
Class 59/1 General Motors type 5 Co-Co	1990 (Canada)	126	General Motors D77B traction motors	113500 lb	60 mph	General Motors 3300 hp	3'4"
Class 60 Brush type 5 Co-Co	1989-92	126	Brush traction motors	106500 lb	60 mph	Mirrlees 3100 hp	3'8"
Class 73 British Rail/English Electric electro-diesel Bo-Bo	1962-7	76-7	Four English Electric traction motors	34000-42000 lb	60-90 mph	English Electric 600 hp	3'4"
						Voltage	
Class 86 British Rail Bo-Bo	1965-6	83-7	Four AEI traction motors	46500-58000 lb	75-110 mph	660-750V DC third rail	3'9 1/2"
Class 87 British Rail Bo-Bo	1973-5	83	Four GEC traction motors	58000 lb	110 mph	25 kV AC overhead	3'9 1/2"
Class 89 Brush Co-Co	1986	105	Brush traction motor	46000 lb	125 mph	25 kV AC overhead	3'9 1/4"
Class 90 BREL General Electric Bo-Bo	1987-90	85	GEC traction motors	43100 lb	110 mph	25 kV AC overhead	3'9 1/4"
Class 91 BREL General Electric Bo-Bo	1988-91	82	GEC traction motors		140 mph	25 kV AC overhead	3'3 1/4"

Wheel configuration

Basic configurations for steam locomotives operative on British railways 1825–1992.

Tank	Tender	
0–4–0	0–4–0	
0–4–2	0–4–2	
0–4–4	0–6–0	
0–6–0	2–4–0	
0–6–2	2–6–0	'Mogul'
0–6–4	2–6–2	'Prairie'
0–8–0	2–8–0	'Consolidation'
2–4–0	2–8–2	'Mikado'
2–4–2	2–10–0	
2–6–2	4–2–2	'Single'
2–6–4	4–4–0	
4–4–2	4–4–2	'Atlantic'
	4–6–0	
	4–6–2	'Pacific'
	4–6–4	

Fastest trains

	Speed		
	(km/h)	(mph)	
British Rail scheduled train			
Edinburgh–London *Scottish Pullman*	158.9	98.7 (average)	
Fastest British locomotive			
Class 91 25kV Electric	260	162	1989
Fastest train on a national rail system			
TGV (Train à Grande Vitesse), France	515	320	1990
Fastest steam locomotive			
LNER 4-6-2 No. 4468, *Mallard*, England	201.16	126	1938
Fastest railed vehicle			
Mach 8 unmanned rocket sled, USA	9851	6121	1982

Air

Aeroplane classification

Executive/Business jets

Type	Range	Capacity (max. seats)	Origin	Engines (turbofans)	Span/length (m)
BAe 125	Medium	14	UK	2 Viper or 2 TFE731	14.33/15.46 (Series 700)
BAe 1000	Medium/long	15	UK	2 PW305	15.66/16.42
Sabreliner	Short	10	US	2 JT12A or 2 CF700 or 2 TFE731	15.37/14.30 (Series 65)
Swearingen SJ30	Short	6	US	2 FJ44	11/12.9
Beechcraft Model 400 Beechjet/Diamond	Medium	8	US Japan	2 JT15D	13.25/13.15 (Beechjet)
Dassault-Breguet Mystère-Falcon 10/100	Medium		France	2 TFE731	13.08/13.85
IAI 1125 Astra	Medium	6	Israel	2 TFE731	16.05/16.94
Dassault-Breguet Mystère-Falcon 20/200	Medium	10	France	2 CF700 or 2 ATF3-6	16.30/17.15
Dassault-Breguet Falcon-50	Medium/long	9	France	3 TFE731	18.86/18.5
Dassault-Breguet Mystère-Falcon 900	Medium/long	19	France	3 TFE731	19.33/19
Dassault Mystère-Falcon 2000	Medium/long	12	France	2 CFE738	19.3/19.23

Passenger jet airliners

Type	Range	Capacity (max. seats)	Origin	Engines (turbofans)	Span/length (m)
Swept-wing, underwing engines					
Boeing 737-100/200	Short/medium	115 (100) 130 (200)	US	2 JT8D	28.35/30.48
Boeing 737-300/400	Short	149 (300) 170 (400)	US	2 CFM56	28.88/33.4 (300) 28.88/36.45 (400)
Boeing 737-500	Medium	108	US	2 CFM56	28.88/36.45
Airbus A320[a]	Short/medium	179	European consortium	2 CFM56 or V2500	33.91/35.75
Tu-204	Medium	214	Russia	2 PS-90 or RB211	42/46.22
Airbus A300[a]	Medium	330	European consortium	2 CF6 or JT9D	44.84/53.62
Airbus A310[a]	Medium	240	European consortium	2 CF6 or JT9D	43.9/46.6

Communications

Air (continued)

Type	Range	Capacity (max. seats)	Origin	Engines (turbofans)	Span/length (m)
Boeing 767	Medium	255	US	2 RB211, GE CF6-80 PW JTD9-7R4, or PW4050	47.57/48.51 or 54.94
Boeing 757	Medium	204	US	2 RB 211 or PW2037	37.95/47.32
Airbus A330[a]	Medium/long	335	European consortium	2 CF6 Trent, or PW4000	60.3/63.5
McDonnell Douglas DC-10	Medium/long	380	US	3 CF6 or JT9D	50.41/55.5
McDonnell Douglas MD-11	Medium/long	405	US	3 PW4360, Trent, or CF6	51.66/61.21
Boeing 777	Long	400	US	2 PW4073, GE 90, or Trent	60.25/63.72
McDonnell Douglas DC8	Medium/long	173	US	4 JT3D	43.41/45.87
DC-8 Super 60		259			45.23/57.12 (Super 63)
Boeing 707	Medium/long	195	US	4 JT3D	44.2/46.61
Ilyushin Il-86 'Camber'	Short	350	Russia	4 Kuznetsov	48.06/59.54
Ilyushin Il-96-300	Medium/long	300	Russia	4 PS-90A	57.66/55.35
Airbus A340[a]	Medium/long	335	European consortium	4 CFM56	60.3/63.65
Boeing 747	Medium/long	490	US	4 JT9D, CF6 or RB211	59.64/70.51
Boeing 747-400	Long	630	US	4 CF6, RB211, or PW4256	64.92/70.66
BAe 146	Short	93	UK	4 ALF502	26.34/26.16 (Series 100)

[a]The Airbus is built jointly by Aérospatiale in France, MBB (Deutsche Airbus) in Germany, and British Aerospace PLC in UK.

Swept-wing, rear engines

Type	Range	Capacity (max. seats)	Origin	Engines (turbofans)	Span/length (m)
Aérospatiale Caravelle	Short	139	France	2 Avon or JT8D	34.30/36.24 (Series 12)
BAe One-Eleven	Short	119	UK	2 Spey	28.5/32.61 (Series 500)
Fokker F28 Fellowship	Short	85	Netherlands	2 Spey	25.07/26.76 (Mk 6000)
Fokker 100	Short	110	Netherlands	2 Tay	28.08/35.53
McDonnell Douglas DC-9	Short	125	US	2 JT8D	28.47/38.28 (Series 40)
McDonnell Douglas MD-80	Short/medium	172	US	2 JT8D	32.85/41.3
Tupolev Tu-134 'Crusty'	Short	72	Russia	2 Soloviev	29/34.35
Tupolev Tu-154 'Careless'	Medium	180	Russia	3 Kuznetsov or Soloviev	37.55/47.9
Boeing 727	Medium	189	US	3 JT8D	32.92/46.69 (200)
Ilyushin Il-62 'Classic'	Long	186	Russia	4 Kuznetsov or Soloviev	43.2/53.12
Yakovlev Yak-42 'Clobber'	Short	120	Russia	3 D-36	34.90/36.38

Delta wing

Type	Range	Capacity (max. seats)	Origin	Engines (turbofans)	Span/length (m)
Aérospatiale/BAe Concorde[a]	Long	128	France/UK	4 Olympus 593	25.56/61.66

[a]World's only fully operational supersonic airliner

Regional/Commuter Aircraft (20 passengers or more)

Type	Range	Seats	Origin	Engines	Span/length (m)
Jets					
Canadair Challenger	Medium	28	Canada	2 ALF502 or CF34	18.83/20.82
Canadair Regional Jet	Short	50	Canada	2 CF34	21.44/26.95
Yakovlev Yak-40 'Codling'	Short	32	Russia	3 Ivchenko	25/20.36
Propeller planes					
Fairchild Metro	Short	20	US	2 TPE331 turboprop	17.37/18.09
Convair CV-240/340/440 Metropolitan	Short	40/44/52	US	2 R-2800 piston	32.12/24.14
Convair 540/580/600/640	Short	56	US	2 Allison 501 or Dart turboprop	32.12/24.14
Martin 4-0-4	Short	40	US	2 R2800 piston	28.44/22.75
Ilyushin Il-14 'Crate'	Short	28	Russia	2 Ash-82 piston	31.69/22.3
Douglas DC-3/Dakota	Short	36	US	2 R-1830 piston	28.96/19.63
Curtiss C-46 Commando	Short	62	US	2 R-2800 piston	32.92/23.26
BAe Jetstream 41	Short	29	UK	2 TPE331 turboprop	18.29/19.25
Gulfstream Aerospace Gulfstream I/I-C	Long	24	US	2 Dart turboprop	23.92/19.43
NAMC YS-11A	Short/medium	60	Japan	2 Dart turboprop	32/26.3
Ilyushin Il-114	Short	60	Russia	2 TV7 turboprop	30/26.31
BAe ATP	Short/medium	64	UK	2 PW126 turboprop	30.63/26
Saab 304A	Short	34	Sweden	2 CT7 turboprop	21.44/19.72
Saab 2000	Short/medium	50	Sweden	2 GMA 2 100A turboprop	24.76/27.93
EMBRAER EMB-110 Bandeirante	Short	21	Brazil	2 PT6A turboprop	15.32/15.08
EMBRAER EMB-120 Brasilia	Short	30	Brazil	2 PW115 turboprop	19.78/20
Aérospatiale N 262/Frégate	Short	26	France	2 Bastan turboprop	21.9/19.28
Fokker F27 Friendship	Short/medium	52	Netherlands	2 Dart turboprop	29/25.06 (Mk 500)
Fokker 50	Short	58	Netherlands	2 PW125 turboprop	29/25.24
Antonov An-24 'Coke'/An-26 'Curl'	Short	50	Ukraine	2 Ivchenko turboprop	29.2/23.53
DH DHC-4A Caribou	Short (STOL[a])	30	Canada	2 R-2000 piston	29.15/22.13
DH DHC-5E Transporter	Short	44	Canada	2 CT64 turboprops	29.26/24.08
DH DHC-8 Dash 8	Short	40	Canada	2 PW120 turboprop	25.89/22.25
Airtech CN-235	Short	44	Spain/Indonesia	2 CT7 turboprop	25.81/21.35
Avions de Transport Régional ATR42/72	Short	50/74	France/Italy	2 PW120 turboprop	24.57/22.67 (ATR42)
LET L-610	Short	40	Czecho-slovakia	2 M602 or CT-7 turboprop	25.6/21.4
Dornier Do 328	Short	33	Germany	2 PW119 turboprop	20.98/21.22
CASA C-212 Aviocar	Short (STOL[a])	26	Spain	2 TPE331 turboprop	19/15.16
DH DHC-6 Twin Otter	Short	20	Canada	2 PT6 turboprop	19.81/15.77
Shorts 330-200	Short	30	UK	2 PT6A turboprop	22.76/17.69
Shorts 360	Short	36	UK	2 PT6A turboprop	22.75/21.49

Communications

Air (continued)

Type	Range	Seats	Origin	Engines	Span/length (m)
Vickers Viscount	Short	65	UK	4 Dart turboprop	28.56/25.04
Ilyushin Il-18/Il-20 'Coot'	Medium	122	Russia	4 Ivchenko turboprop	37.4/35.9
Lockheed L-188 Electra	Medium	98	US	4 Allison 501 turboprop	30.18/31.81
Douglas DC-4	Short	44	US	4 R-2000 piston	35.8/28.6
DH DHC Dash 7 (STOL[a])	Short	50	Canada	4 PT6 turboprop	28.35/24.58

[a]STOL = short take-off and landing.

World air distances

Air distances between some major cities, given in statute miles. To convert to kilometres, multiply number given by 1.6093.

[a]Shortest route.

	Amsterdam	Anchorage	Beijing	Buenos Aires	Cairo	Chicago	Delhi	Hong Kong	Honolulu	Istanbul	Johannesburg	Lagos	London	Los Angeles	Mexico City	Montreal	Moscow	Nairobi	Paris	Perth	Rome	Santiago	Sydney	Tokyo
Anchorage	4475																							
Beijing	6566	4756																						
Buenos Aires	7153	8329	12000																					
Cairo	2042	6059	6685	7468																				
Chicago	4109	28	7599	5587	6135																			
Delhi	3985	8925	2368	8340	2753	8119																		
Hong Kong	5926	5063	1235	3124	5098	7827	2345																	
Honolulu	8368	2780	6778	8693	9439	4246	7888	5543																
Istanbul	1373	6024	4763	7783	764	5502	2833	5998	9547															
Johannesburg	5606	1042	10108	5725	4012	8705	6765	6728	12892	4776														
Lagos	3161	7587	8030	4832	2443	7065	5196	7541	10367	3207	2854													
London	217	4472	5054	6985	2187	3956	4169	5979	7252	1552	5640	3115												
Los Angeles	5559	2333	6349	6140	7589	1746	8717	7231	2553	6994	10443	7716	5442											
Mexico City	5724	3751	7912	4592	7730	1687	9806	8794	4116	7255	10070	7343	5703	1563										
Montreal	3422	3100	7557	5640	5431	737	7421	8564	4923	4795	8322	5595	3252	2482	2307									
Moscow	1338	4291	3604	8382	1790	5500	2698	4839	8802	1089	6280	4462	1550	6992	6700	4393								
Nairobi	4148	8714	8888	7427	2203	8177	4956	7301	11498	2967	1809	2377	4246	9688	9949	7498	3951							
Paris	261	4683	5108	6892	1995	4140	4089	5987	7463	1394	5422	2922	220	5633	5714	3434	1540	4031						
Perth	9118	8368	4987	9734	7766	11281	5013	3752	7115	7846	5564	10209	9246	9535	11098	12402	8355	7373	12587					
Rome	809	5258	5306	6931	1329	4828	3679	5773	8150	852	4802	2497	898	6340	6601	5431	1478	3349	688	8309				
Santiago	7714	7919	13622	710	8029	5328	12715	3733	8147	10109	5738	6042	8568	5594	4168	5551	10118	7547	461	15129	7548			
Sydney	1039	8522	5689	7760	9196	9324	6495	4586	5078	9883	7601	11700	10565	7498	9061	9980	9425	9410	10150	2037	10149	13092		
Tokyo	6006[a]	3443	1313	13100	6362	6286	3656	1807	3831	5757	8535	9130[a]	6218	5451	7014	6913	4668	8565	6208[a]	4925	6146	11049	4640	
Washington	3854	3430	7930	6097	5859	590	7841	8385	4822	5347	8199	5472	3672	2294	1871	493	4884	7918	3843	11829	4495	5061	9792	6763

Communications

World flying times

Approximate flying times between some major cities. Times quoted (in hours and minutes) are flying time only. In many cases, in order to travel between two points, it is necessary to change aircraft one or more times. Time between flights has not been included.

	Amsterdam	Anchorage	Beijing	Buenos Aires	Cairo	Chicago	Delhi	Hong Kong	Honolulu	Istanbul	Johannesburg	Lagos	London	Los Angeles	Mexico City	Montreal	Moscow	Nairobi	Paris	Perth	Rome	Santiago	Sydney	Tokyo
Anchorage	9.00																							
Beijing	16.50	11.45																						
Buenos Aires	17.45	10.48	28.31																					
Cairo	4.20	13.20	13.15	20.40																				
Chicago	8.35	5.44	15.15	15.40	18.40																			
Delhi	8.15	16.50	6.40	26.20	7.00	20.05																		
Hong Kong	15.15	11.40	3.00	29.35	10.55	17.05	6.05																	
Honolulu	16.42	5.44	10.55	19.00	22.50	9.25	16.50	13.05																
Istanbul	3.15	12.15	15.40	18.45	2.00	12.20	7.35	17.35	21.05															
Johannesburg	13.15	19.50	20.10	12.30	8.55	21.40	23.45	14.55	30.25	16.30														
Lagos	6.40	14.55	22.35	9.55	8.20	14.55	14.55	22.30	23.40	8.05	6.55													
London	1.05	8.30	18.05	16.35	5.35	8.30	10.35	16.05	17.15	3.50	13.10	6.25												
Los Angeles	11.15	6.13	15.25	13.45	21.00	5.00	19.30	15.50	5.15	14.50	24.10	17.25	11.00											
Mexico City	12.27	10.49	18.45	10.25	16.47	5.15	20.42	19.10	8.35	15.42	25.42	19.07	14.35	3.20										
Montreal	7.40	7.91	27.30	16.00	12.35	2.20	17.35	23.05	12.50	10.15	20.10	13.25	7.00	6.40	4.45									
Moscow	3.15	12.15	8.40	22.05	5.25	12.15	7.35	18.00	21.00	4.40	13.30	10.10	3.45	14.45	18.10	10.45								
Nairobi	8.15	17.00	16.00	24.55	4.55	17.00	10.45	12.45	25.45	7.15	3.45	6.20	8.30	19.30	20.42	15.30	12.50							
Paris	1.10	9.00	16.35	15.35	5.05	9.00	10.45	16.40	18.05	3.10	15.50	7.45	1.05	12.50	13.25	6.25	4.00	9.20						
Perth	20.35	17.25	11.15	25.20	17.10	23.00	9.30	8.15	17.25	15.25	14.20	25.55	19.30	19.30	22.50	26.30	19.40	23.00	21.40					
Rome	2.20	12.00	16.10	14.40	3.25	11.35	8.50	15.10	19.13	2.35	12.25	6.55	2.25	14.35	5.35	8.10	4.10	7.20	1.55	20.00				
Santiago	20.50	19.13	22.34	2.10	25.10	17.15	29.05	19.15	8.35	21.00	19.55	24.25	21.55	16.00	12.00	14.50	24.05	29.05	19.45	26.00	18.50			
Sydney	23.05	16.35	16.15	20.45	17.20	21.10	13.50	10.35	11.50	18.40	31.50	28.35	21.55	18.10	18.05	24.50	19.40	31.35	25.05	4.35	23.50	24.30		
Tokyo	11.40	7.20	3.50	28.30	19.40	12.55	9.45	4.20	7.05	14.05	25.00	18.40	11.50	11.55	16.25	18.55	9.25	19.55	16.45	10.05	17.40	27.55	9.15	
Washington	8.55	7.25	25.50	11.00	14.20	1.45	20.10	24.15	10.55	11.25	21.20	14.45	8.10	5.25	7.50	2.50	12.30	17.10	9.25	22.45	12.40	17.40	23.35	12.40

US air distances

Air distances between US cities, given in statute miles. To convert to kilometres, multiply number given by 1.6093.

	Atlanta	Boston	Chicago	Dallas	Denver	Detroit	Houston	Kansas City	Los Angeles	Miami	Minneapolis	New Orleans	New York	Oklahoma City	Omaha	Philadelphia	Phoenix	Pittsburgh	Portland	St Louis	Salt Lake City	San Antonio	San Francisco	Seattle
Boston	946																							
Chicago	606	867																						
Dallas	721	1555	796																					
Denver	1208	1767	901	654																				
Detroit	595	632	235	982	1135																			
Houston	689	1603	925	217	864	1095																		
Kansas City	681	1254	403	450	543	630	643																	
Los Angeles	1946	2611	1745	1246	849	1979	1379	1363																
Miami	595	1258	1197	1110	1716	1146	964	1239	2342															
Minneapolis	906	1124	334	853	693	528	1046	394	1536	1501														
New Orleans	425	1367	837	437	1067	936	305	690	1671	674	1040													
New York	760	187	740	1383	1638	509	1417	1113	2475	1090	1028	1182												
Oklahoma City	761	1505	693	181	500	911	395	312	1187	1223	694	567	1345											
Omaha	821	1282	416	585	485	651	793	152	1330	1393	282	841	1155	418										
Philadelphia	665	281	678	1294	1569	453	1324	1013	2401	1013	980	94	1268	1094										
Phoenix	1587	2300	1440	879	589	1681	1015	1043	370	1972	1270	1301	2143	833	1037	2082								
Pittsburgh	526	496	412	1061	1302	201	1124	769	2136	1013	726	918	340	1010	821	267	1814							
Portland	2172	2537	1739	1637	985	1959	1834	1492	834	2700	1426	2050	2454	1484	1368	2411	1009	2148						
St Louis	484	1046	258	546	781	440	667	229	1592	1068	448	604	892	462	342	813	1262	553	1708					
Salt Lake City	1589	2105	1249	1010	381	1489	1204	919	590	2088	991	1428	1989	865	839	1932	507	1659	630	1156				
San Antonio	875	1764	1041	247	793	1215	191	697	1210	1143	1097	495	1587	407	824	1502	843	1277	1714	786	1086			
San Francisco	2139	2704	1846	1476	956	2079	1636	1498	337	2585	1589	1911	2586	1383	1433	2521	651	2253	550	1735	599	1482		
Seattle	2182	2496	1720	1670	1019	1932	1874	1489	954	2725	1399	2087	2421	1520	1368	2383	1109	2124	132	1709	689	1775	678	
Washington, DC	532	414	590	1163	1464	385	1189	927	2288	919	909	969	229	1158	1000	136	1956	184	2339	696	1839	1361	2419	2307

Communications

Communications

Air (continued)
International time zones

Some countries have adopted half-hour time zones which are indicated on the map as a combination of two coded zones.

Fastest aeroplanes

A Mach number (Ma) denotes the ratio of the speed of an aircraft to the speed of sound under the same conditions of pressure and density. Mach 1.0 = 1 226 kph/762 mph. Mach 0.5 = 613 kph/381mph. Mach numbers less than 1 indicate subsonic speed, those greater than 1 indicate supersonic speed.

Type	Aircraft	Speed		Mach
		(km/h)	(mph)	
Airliner	Aérospatiale/BAe Concorde	2 333	1450	2
Autogyro/gyroplane	WA-116F	193.9	120.3	0.2
Biplane	Italian Fiat CR42B	520	323	0.4
Bomber	Dassault Mirage IV	2 333	1450	2
	General Dynamics FB-111A (swing-wing)	3 065	1 905	2.5
	Tupolev Tu-22M (swing-wing), *Backfire*	3 065	1 905	2.5
Flying boat	Martin XP6M-1 Seamaster	911.98	566.69	0.8
Helicopter	Westland Lynx	400.87	249.09	0.3
Combat jet	USSR Mikoyan MiG-25 Foxbat-B	3 395	2 110	3
Reconnaisance jet	USAF Lockheed SR-71A, *Blackbird*	3 529.5	2 193.17	3
Piston-engine	Grumman F8F Bearcat (modified), *Rare Bear*	850.24	528.33	0.7
Propeller-driven	USSR Tu-95/142, *Bear*	925	575	0.8
Ultralight	Gypsy Skycycle	104.6	65	0.1

Aircraft registration codes

These codes are painted on all aircraft, showing their country of registration.

AP	Pakistan	HB	Switzerland &	PZ	Suriname
A2	Botswana		Lichtenstein	P2	Papua New Guinea
A3	Tonga	HC	Ecuador	P4	Aruba
A40	Oman	HH	Haiti	RA	Russia
A5	Bhutan	HI	Dominican Republic	RDPL	Laos, People's Democratic
A6	United Arab Emirates	HK	Colombia		Republic
A7	Qatar	HL	Republic of Korea	RP	Philippines
A9C	Bahrain	HP	Panama	SE	Sweden
B	China (People's Republic)	HR	Honduras	SP	Poland
B	China/Taiwan (R o C)	HS	Thailand	ST	Sudan
C, CF	Canada	HV	The Vatican	SU	Egypt
CC	Chile	HZ	Saudi Arabia	SX	Greece
CCCP	former USSR	H4	Solomon Islands	S2	Bangladesh
CN	Morocco	I	Italy	S5	Slovenia
CP	Bolivia	JA	Japan	S7	Seychelles
CS	Portugal	JY	Jordan	S9	São Tomé
CU	Cuba	J2	Djibouti	TC	Turkey
CX	Uruguay	J3	Grenada	TF	Iceland
C2	Nauru	J5	Guinea Bissau	TG	Guatemala
C3	Andorra	J6	St Lucia	TI	Costa Rica
C5	The Gambia	J7	Dominica	TJ	Cameroon
C6	The Bahamas	J8	St Vincent and the	TL	Central African Republic
C9	Mozambique		Grenadines	TN	Congo Brazzaville
D	Germany	LN	Norway	TR	Gabon
DQ	Fiji	LV	Argentina	TS	Tunisia
D2	Angola	LX	Luxembourg	TT	Chad
D4	Cape Verde Islands	LY	Lithuania	TU	Côte d'Ivoire
D6	Comoros Islands	LZ	Bulgaria	TY	Benin
EC	Spain	MT	Mongolia	TZ	Mali
EI	Eire	N	US	T2	Tuvalu
EL	Liberia	OB	Peru	T3	Kiribati
EP	Iran	OD	Lebanon	T7	San Marino
ER	Moldova	OE	Austria	UK	Uzbekistan
ES	Estonia	OH	Finland	UR	Ukraine
ET	Ethiopia	OK	Czech Republic	VH	Australia
EW	Belarus	OO	Belgium	VN	Vietnam
EY	Tajikistan	OY	Denmark	VP-F	Falkland Islands
EZ	Turkmenistan	P	Korea (PDR)	VP-LA	Anguilla
F	France	PH	Netherlands	VP-LM	Montserrat
G	Great Britain	PJ	Netherland Antilles	VP-LV	British Virgin Islands
HA	Hungary	PK	Indonesia	VQ-T	Turks and Caicos Islands
		PP, PT	Brazil	VR-B	Bermuda

Communications

Transportation

Air (continued)

VR-C	Cayman Islands	Z	Zimbabwe	5Y	Kenya
VR-G	Gibraltar	ZA	Albania	6O	Somalia
VR-H	Hong Kong	ZK	New Zealand	6V	Senegal
VT	India	ZP	Paraguay	6Y	Jamaica
V2	Antigua and Barbuda	ZS	South Africa	7O	Yemen
V3	Belize	3A	Monaco	7P	Lesotho
V4	St Kitts and Nevis	3B	Mauritius	7Q	Malawi
V5	Namibia	3C	Equatorial Guinea	7T	Algeria
V7	Marshall Islands	3D	Swaziland	8P	Barbados
V8	Brunei	3X	Guinea	8Q	Maldives
XA, XB,	Mexico	4K	Azerbaijan	8R	Guyana
XC		4R	Sri Lanka	9A	Croatia
XT	Burkina Faso	4U	United Nations	9G	Ghana
XU	Cambodia		Organization	9H	Malta
XV	Vietnam	4X	Israel	9J	Zambia
XY	Myanmar (Burma)	5A	Libya	9K	Kuwait
YA	Afghanistan	5B	Cyprus	9L	Sierra Leone
YJ	Vanuatu	5H	Tanzania	9M	Malaysia
YK	Syria	5N	Nigeria	9N	Nepal
YL	Latvia	5R	Madagascar	9Q , 9T	Zaïre
YN	Nicaragua	5T	Mauritania	9U	Burundi
YR	Romania	5U	Niger	9V	Singapore
YS	El Salvador	5V	Togo	9XR	Rwanda
YU	Yugoslavia	5W	Western Samoa	9Y	Trinidad and Tobago
YV	Venezuela	5X	Uganda		

Airline designators

Code	Airline	Country	Code	Airline	Country
AA	American Airlines	US	CM	COPA (Compania Panamena de Aviación)	Panama
AC	Air Canada	Canada	CO	Continental Airlines	US
AF	Air France	France	CP	Canadian Airlines International	Canada
AH	Air Algerie	Algeria	CS	Continental Micronesia	Mariana Islands
AI	Air India	India			
AJ	Air Belgium	Belgium	CU	Cubana	Cuba
AM	AEROMEXICO	Mexico	CX	Cathay Pacific Airways	Hong Kong
AN	Ansett Australia	Australia	CY	Cyprus Airways	Cyprus
AQ	Aloha Airlines	US	CZ	China Southern Airways	China
AR	Aerolineas Argentinas	Argentina	DL	Delta Airlines	US
AS	Alaska Airlines	US	DO	Dominicana de Aviación	Dominican Republic
AT	Royal Air Maroc	Morocco			
AY	Finnair	Finland	DS	Air Senegal	Senegal
AZ	Al Italia	Italy	DT	TAAG Angola Airlines	Angola
BA	British Airways	UK	DU	Hemus Air	Bulgaria
BB	Sansa	Costa Rica	DX	Danair	Denmark
BD	British Midland	UK	DY	Alyemda-Democratic Yemen Airlines	Yemen Republic
BG	Biman Bangladesh Airlines	Bangladesh			
BH	Augusta Airways	Australia	EI	Air Lingus	Ireland
BI	Royal Brunei Airways	Brunei	EK	Emirates	United Arab Emirates
BJ	Safe Air	New Zealand			
BL	Pacific Airways	Vietnam	ET	Ethiopian Airlines	Ethiopia
BM	Belize Air International	Belize	EW	Eastwest Airlines	Australia
BO	Bouraq Indonesia Airlines	Indonesia	FC	Berliner Speziel Flug	Germany
BP	Air Botswana	Botswana	FG	Ariana Afghan Airlines	Afghanistan
BU	Braathens SAFE	Norway	FI	Icelandair	Iceland
BW	BWIA International Trinidad and Tobago Airways	Trinidad and Tobago	FJ	Air Pacific	Fiji
			FO	Western New South Wales Airlines	Australia
BY	Britannia Airways	UK			
CA	Air China	China	FQ	Air Aruba	Aruba
CB	Suckling Airways	UK	FR	Ryanair (Dublin)	Ireland
CI	China Airlines	Taiwan	GA	Garuda Indonesia	Indonesia
CJ	China Northern Airlines	China	GC	Lina Congo	Congo
CK	Gambia Airways	Gambia	GF	Gulf Air Company	Bahrain

Code	Airline	Country
GH	Ghana Airlines	Ghana
GI	Air Guinée	Guinea
GL	Gronlandsfly	Greenland
GN	Air Gabon	Gabon
GR	Aurigny Air Services	Channel Islands
GT	GB Airways	UK
GY	Guyana Airways Corporation	Guyana
HA	Hawaiian Airlines	US
HM	Air Seychelles	Seychelles
HP	America West Airlines	US
HV	Transavia Airlines	Netherlands
HY	Uzbekistan Airways	Uzbekistan
IB	Iberia	Spain
IC	Indian Airlines	India
IE	Solomon Airlines	Solomon Islands
IF	Great China Airlines	China
IL	Istanbul Airways	Turkey
IP	Airlines of Tasmania	Australia
IR	Iranair	Islamic Republic of Iran
IV	Air Gambia	Gambia
IY	Yemenia-Yemen Airways	Yemen
JE	Manx Airlines	Isle of Man
JG	Swedair	Sweden
JL	Japan Airlines	Japan
JM	Air Jamaica	Jamaica
JQ	Trans Jamaica Airlines	Jamaica
JU	JAT Jugoslovenski Aerotransport	Yugoslavia
JY	Jersey European Airways	Channel Islands
KE	Korean Air	Republic of Korea
KL	KLM Royal Dutch Airlines	Netherlands
KM	Air Malta	Malta
KP	Kiwi International Airlines	US
KQ	Kenya Airways	Kenya
KU	Kuwait Airways	Kuwait
KV	Transkei Airways	South Africa
KX	Cayman Airways	Grand Cayman
KY	Waterwings Airways	New Zealand
LA	Lan-Chile	Chile
LC	Loganair	UK
LF	Linjeflyg	Sweden
LG	Luxair	Luxembourg
LH	Lufthansa	Germany
LN	Jamahiriya Libyan Arab Airlines	Libya
LO	LOT Polish Airlines	Poland
LU	Theron Airways	South Africa
LY	El Al Israel Airlines	Israel
LZ	Balkan-Bulgarian Airlines	Bulgaria
MA	Malev Hungarian Airlines	Hungary
MD	Air Madagascar	Madagascar
MH	Malaysia Airlines	Malaysia
MK	Air Mauritius	Mauritius
MN	Commercial Airways	South Africa
MR	Air Mauritania	Mauritania
MS	Egyptair	Egypt
MV	Ansett WA	Australia
NF	Air Vanuatu	Vanuatu
NG	Lauda Air	Austria
NH	All Nippon Airways	Japan
NM	Mount Cook Airlines	New Zealand
NN	Air Martinique	Martinique

Code	Airline	Country
NO	Aus-Air	Australia
NQ	Orbi Georgian Airways	Georgia
NR	Norontair	Canada
NU	Southwest Airlines	Japan
NV	Northwest Territorial Airways	Canada
NW	Northwest Airlines	US
NZ	Air New Zealand	New Zealand
OA	Olympic Airways	Greece
OB	Monarch Air	Australia
OG	Air Guadeloupe	Guadeloupe
OK	Czechoslovak Airlines	Czech Republic
OM	Air Mongol	Mongolian People's Republic
ON	Air Nauru	Republic of Nauru
OO	Sky West Airlines	US
OR	Air Comores	Comoros
OS	Austrian Airlines	Austria
OU	Croatia Airlines	Republic of Croatia
OV	Estonian Air	Estonia
PB	Air Burundi	Burundi
PC	Fiji Air	Fiji
PH	Polynesian Airlines	Samoa
PK	Pakistan International Airlines	Pakistan
PL	Aeroperu	Peru
PR	Philippine Airlines	Philippines
PS	Ukraine International Airlines	Ukraine
PU	PLUNA (Primeras Lineas Uruguayas de Navigación Aerea)	Uruguay
PV	Latvian Airlines	Latvia
PX	Air Niugini	Papua New Guinea
PY	Surinam Airways	Suriname
PZ	LAP (Lineas Aereas Paraguayas)	Paraguay
QC	Air Zaïre	Zaïre
QF	Qantas Airways	Australia
QL	Lesotho Airways	Lesotho
QM	Air Malawi	Malawi
QU	Uganda Airlines	Uganda
QV	Lao Aviation	Laos PDR
QX	Horizon Airlines	US
QZ	Zambia Airways	Zambia
RA	Royal Nepal Airlines	Nepal
RB	Syrian Arab Airlines	Syria
RG	Varig Brazilian Airlines	Brazil
RJ	Royal Jordanian	Jordan
RK	Air Afrique	Côte d'Ivoire
RO	Tarom	Romania
RY	Air Rwanda	Rwanda
SA	South African Airways	South Africa
SD	Sudan Airways	Sudan
SH	SAHSA (Servicio Aero de Honduras)	Honduras
SJ	Southern Air	New Zealand
SK	SAS (Scandinavian Air)	Sweden
SN	Sabena	Belgium
SQ	Singapore Airlines	Singapore
SR	Swissair	Switzerland
SU	Aeroflot	Russia
SV	Saudia	Saudi Arabia
SW	Air Namibia	Namibia
TC	Air Tanzania	Tanzania
TE	Lithuanian Airlines	Lithuania
TG	Thai Airways International	Thailand

Communications

Air (continued)

Code	Airline	Country
TK	Turkish Airlines	Turkey
TM	LAM Linhas Aereas de Moçambique	Mozambique
TN	Australian Airlines	Australia
TP	TAP Air Portugal	Portugal
TU	Tunis Air	Tunisia
TW	TWA (Trans World Airlines)	US
UA	United Airlines	US
UB	Myanma Airlines	Myanmar (Burma)
UI	Norlandair	Iceland
UK	Air UK	UK
UL	Air Lanka	Sri Lanka
UM	Air Zimbabwe	Zimbabwe
UP	Bahamasair	Bahamas
US	US Air	US
UY	Cameroon Airlines	Cameroon
VA	VIASA (Venezolana Internacional de Aviación)	Venezuela
VE	Avensa	Australia
VH	Air Burkina	Burkina Faso
VJ	Cambodia Airlines	Cambodia
VN	Vietnam Airlines	Vietnam
VO	Tyrolean Airlines	Austria
VR	Transportes Aereos de Cabo Verde	Cape Verde
VS	Virgin Atlantic Airways	UK
VU	Air Ivoire	Côte d'Ivoire
VX	ACES (Aerlineas Centrales de Colombia)	Colombia
WG	Taiwan Airlines	Taiwan
WI	Rottnest Airbus	Australia
WJ	Labrador Airways	Canada
WN	Southwest Airlines	US
WR	Royal Tongan Airlines	Tonga
WT	Nigeria Airways	Nigeria
WY	Oman Air	Oman
XX	Aeronaves del Peru	Peru
YJ	National Airlines	South Africa
YK	Cyprus Turkish Airlines	Cyprus
YN	Air Creebec	Canada
YU	Dominair	Dominican Republic
YZ	Transportes Aereos da Guiné Bissau	Guinea Bissau
ZB	Monarch Airlines	UK
ZC	Royal Swazi National Airways	Swaziland
ZP	Virgin Air	Virgin Islands
ZQ	Ansett New Zealand	New Zealand
ZX	Air BC	Canada
2J	Azerbaijan Hava Yollari	Azerbaijan
7E	Nepal Airways	Nepal
7Y	Albanian Airlines	Albania
8Y	Ecuato Guineana de Aviación	Equatorial Guinea
9U	Air Moldova	Republic of Moldova

US local airports

Aberdeen, SD
Abilene, TX
Abingdon, VA
Aiken, SC
Air Park–Dallas
Akron Canton, OH
Akron-Fulton Intl, OH
Akron-Washington County, CO
Alabaster, AL
Alamogordo, NM
Alamosa, CO
Albany County, NY
Albuquerque-Coronado, NM
Albuquerque Intl, NM
Alexandria, MN
Alexandria, IN
Allentown, PA
Allentown–Queen City, PA
Alliance, NE
Alma, GA
Alpine, TX
Alton–St Louis, IL
Altoona, PA
Amarillo Intl, TX
Anchorage Intl, AK
Anchorage–Merrill Field, AK
Anderson, IN
Anderson, SC

Appleton, WI
Ardmore Downtown, OK
Ardmore Municipal, OK
Arlington, TX
Asheboro, NC
Asheville, NC
Ashland, OR
Ashland, WI
Aspen, CO
Astoria, OR
Athens, GA
Atlanta Dekalb-Peachtree, GA
Atlanta Fulton-Brown, GA
Atlantic, IA
Atlantic City, NJ
Atlantic City-Bader, NJ
Auburn, AL
Auburn, ME
Augusta Bush, GA
Augusta Daniel, GA
Augusta State, ME
Aurora, IL
Aurora, CO
Aurora State, OR
Austin, MN
Austin Executive, TX
Austin Mueller, TX
Austin Straubel Intl, WI
Avon Park, FL
Bainbridge, GA

Bakersfield, CA
Ballston Spa, NY
Baltimore-Martin State, MD
Baltimore-Washington Intl, MD
Bangor Intl, ME
Banning, CA
Bardstown, KY
Barre-Montpelier, VT
Barrow, AK
Bartow, FL
Baton Rouge, LA
Battle Creek, MI
Baudette Intl, MN
Beach, ND
Beaufort-Morehead City, NC
Beaumont, TX
Beaumont–Port Arthur, TX
Beaver Falls, PA
Bedford, MA
Bedford, PA
Belfast, ME
Bellingham, WA
Bend Sunriver, OR
Benton Harbor, MI
Bentonville, AR
Berlin, NJ
Bermuda Dunes, CA

Beulah, ND
Beverly, MA
Big Bear City, CA
Big Spring, TX
Big Timber, MT
Billings, MT
Binghamton, NY
Birmingham, AL
Bismarck, ND
Blacksburg, VA
Blanding, UT
Bloomington, IL
Bloomington, IN
Bluefield-Mercer Co, WV
Bluffton, OH
Blytheville Municipal, AR
Boca Raton, FL
Boeing Field/King Co Intl, WA
Boise, ID
Boston–Logan Intl, MA
Bozeman, MT
Bradford, PA
Brainerd, MN
Brandywine, PA
Breckenridge, TX
Bremerton, WA
Bridgeport, CT
Bridgeport, TX
Brooksville, FL
Brownfield, TX

Brownsville, TX
Brunswick, GA
Brunswick McKinnon, GA
Bryan, TX
Buena Vista, CO
Buffalo, NY
Burbank, CA
Burlington, CO
Burlington Intl, VT
Burnet, TX
Butler, PA
Cahokia/St Louis, IL
Calexico Intl, CA
California City, CA
Camden, SC
Canadian, TX
Carbondale
 Murphysboro, IL
Caribou, ME
Carlsbad, CA
Carlsbad, NM
Carrollton, GA
Cartersville, GA
Carthage, MO
Casa Grande, AZ
Casper, WY
Castroville, TX
Cave Junction, OR
Cedar City, UT
Cedar Rapids, IA
Centennial, CO
Central Nebraska
 Regional, NE
Centralia, IL
Challis, ID
Chambersburg, PA
Champaign, IL
Chanute, KS
Charles City, IA
Charleston, WV
Charleston Intl, SC
Charleston-Executive, SC
Charlotte Douglas Intl, NC
Charlottesville, VA
Chattanooga-Lovell, TN
Cherokee, IA
Chesapeake, VA
Cheyenne, WY
Chicago Dupage, IL
Chicago Meigs, IL
Chicago Midway, IL
Chicago O'Hare Intl, IL
Chicago Wheeling, IL
Chickasha, OK
Chicopee, MA
Childress, TX
Chino, CA
Chisholm-Hibbing, MN
Cincinatti Blue Ash, OH
Cincinatti Lunken, OH
Circleville, OH
Clarksburg, WV
Clarksdale, MS
Clarksville, TN
Cleburne, TX
Cleveland, MS
Cleveland, OH

Cleveland Cuyahoga, OH
Cleveland Hopkins Intl, OH
Clinton, IA
Cloverdale, CA
Coatsville, PA
Coeur d'Alene, ID
College Park, MD
Colorado City, TX
Colorado Springs, CO
Columbia, CA
Columbia Metro, SC
Columbia Mt Pleasant, TN
Columbia Owens
 Downtown, SC
Columbia Regional, MO
Columbus, IN
Columbus, NE
Columbus Bolton Fld, OH
Columbus Metro, GA
**Columbus-Port
 Columbus**, OH
Concord, CA
Connersville, IN
Conroe-Montgomery Co,
 TX
Conway, SC
Corpus Christi Intl, TX
Corvallis, OR
Covelo, CA
Covington/Cincinatti, KY
Craig, CO
Crescent City, CA
Crestview, FL
Crete, NE
Cumberland Regional, MD
Cushing, OK
Dalhart, TX
Dallas Addison, TX
Dallas-Fort Worth, TX
Dallas Love, TX
Dallas Redbird, TX
Danbury, CT
Danville, IL
Danville, VA
Davenport, IA
Dayton Cox Intl, OH
Dayton General, OH
Daytona Beach, FL
Decatur, AL
Decatur, IL
Del Rio Intl, TX
Deland, FL
Delano, CA
Delavan, WI
Delaware, OH
Denison, IA
Denton, TX
Denver, CO
Denver Jeffco, CO
Des Moines Intl, IA
Destin, FL
Detroit, MI
Detroit City, MI
Detroit-Grosse Ile, MI
Detroit-Willow Run, MI
Diamond Head, MS
Dickinson, ND

Dodge City, KS
Doersom, PA
Dothan, AL
Douglas, GA
Douglas, WY
Douglas Bisbee, AZ
Downtown Airpark
 Oklahoma City, OK
Driggs, ID
Dublin, GA
Du Bois, PA
Dubuque, IA
Duluth Intl, MN
Duncan Halliburton Fld,
 OK
Durango La Plata, CO
Durhamville, NY
Dyersburg, TN
Eagle, CO
Eagle Pass, TX
El Dorado Downtown, AR
El Monte, CA
El Paso Intl, TX
El Paso-W Texas, TX
Elk, OK
Elkin, NC
Elmira, NY
Ely, MN
Ely, NV
Emporia, KS
Erie, PA
Escanaba, MI
Estherville, IA
Eugene Mahlon Sweet, OR
Eureka Murray Field, CA
Evansville, IN
Everett, WA
Fairbanks Intl, AK
Fairhope Point Clear, AL
Fargo, ND
Farmingdale, NY
Farmington, MO
Fayetteville, AR
Fayetteville, NC
Fergus Falls, MN
Findlay, OH
Fitchburg, MA
Flagstaff Pulliam, AZ
Flora, IL
Fort Collins Loveland, CO
Fort Dodge, IA
Fort Lauderdale, FL
Fort Lauderdale
 Executive, FL
Fort Morgan, CO
Fort Myers, FL
Fort Pierce, FL
Fort Smith, AR
Fort Wayne, IN
Fort Wayne Smith Field, IN
Fort Worth Meacham, TX
Fortuna, CA
Frederick, MD
Frederick, OK
Frenchville, ME
Fresno Air Terminal, CA
Fullerton, CA

Gainesville, FL
Gaithersburg, MD
Galesburg, IL
Gallatin, TN
Galveston, TX
Gary, IN
Gastonia, NC
Georgetown, DE
Gillette, WY
Glendale Municipal, AZ
Glens Falls, NY
Golden Triangle
 Regional, MS
Goodland, KS
Graham, TX
Grand Canyon, AZ
Grand Junction, CO
Grand Prairie, TX
Grand Rapids, MI
Grand Rapids, MN
Grandview, MO
Grayson County, TX
Great Barrington, MA
Great Falls Intl, MT
Green River, UT
Greeneville, TN
Greensboro, NC
Greenville, KY
Greenville, MS
Greenville Donaldson, SC
Greenville Downtown, SC
Greenwood, MS
Greenwood, SC
Greer, SC
Groton, CT
Grove City, PA
Gulfport, MS
Hagerstown, MD
Hailey, ID
Half Moon Bay, CA
Hammond, LA
Hammonton, NJ
Hancock, MI
Hanover, VA
Harbor Springs, MI
Harlingen, TX
Harrison, AR
Hartford, CT
Hartford, KY
Hartford Springfield, CT
Hartsfield-Atlanta Intl, GA
Hastings, NE
Hawesville, KY
Hawthorne, CA
Hawthorne, NV
Hayden Yampa Valley, CO
Hayward, CA
Hebbronville, TX
Helena, MT
Hendersonville, NC
Hickory, NC
Hilo Intl, HI
Hilton Head, SC
Hobbs, NM
Holbrook, AZ
Holland Tulip City, MI
Hollister, CA

Communications

Transportation

Air (continued)

Honolulu Intl, HI
Hornell, NY
Horseshoe Bay, TX
Houma, LA
Houston Clover Field, TX
Houston Ellington Field, TX
Houston Gulf, TX
Houston Hobby, TX
Houston Hooks Memorial, TX
Houston Intercontinental, TX
Houston–W Houston, TX
Huntingburg, IN
Huntington Beach, CA
Huntsville, AL
Huron, SD
Hutchinson, KS
Hutchinson County, TX
Hyannis, MA
Immokalee, FL
Indianapolis Brookside, IN
Indianapolis Greenwood, IN
Indianapolis Intl, IN
Indianapolis–Mt Comfort, IN
Indianapolis Terry, IN
Iowa City, IA
Islip, NY
Ithaca Tompkins County, NY
Jackson, MS
Jackson, WY
Jackson Thompson, MS
Jacksonville, IL
Jacksonville, TX
Jacksonville Craig, FL
Jacksonville Intl, FL
Jamestown, ND
Janesville, WI
Jeffersonville, IN
Johnson City, KS
Johnson County Executive, KS
Johnson County Industrial, KS
Joliet, IL
Jonesboro, AR
Joplin, MO
Josephine County, OR
Juneau, AK
Juneau, WI
Kahului, HI
Kailua-Kona, HI
Kalamazoo, MI
Kalispell, MT
Kalispell City, MT
Kankakee, IL
Kansas City Downtown, MO
Kauai, HI
Kearney, NE
Kelso, WA
Kenai, AK

Kendall Tamiami Executive, FL
Kenosha, WI
Keokuk, IA
Kerrville, TX
Ketchikan Intl, AK
Key West Intl, FL
Killeen, TX
Kingston, NY
Kingsville, TX
Kinston, NC
Kirksville, MO
Kissimmee, FL
Klamath Falls, OR
Knoxville, TN
Knoxville Downtown, TN
Kosciusko, MS
La Crosse, WI
La Grange Callaway, GA
La Porte, TX
La Verne, CA
Laconia, NH
Lafayette, IN
Lafayette, LA
Lafayette, TN
Lake Placid, NY
Lake Tahoe, CA
Lake Wales, FL
Lakeland, FL
Lakeport, CA
Lamar, CO
Lambertville, MI
Lampasas, TX
Lancaster, CA
Lancaster, PA
Lancaster, TX
Lansing, IL
Lansing, MI
Laramie, WY
Laredo Intl, TX
Las Cruces, NM
Las Vegas, NM
Las Vegas, NV
Lawrence, MA
Lawrenceville, IL
Lebanon, NH
Lebanon, TN
Leesburg, VA
Lewisburg, WV
Lewistown, MT
Lexington Blue Grass, KY
Lima, OH
Lincoln, CA
Lincoln, NE
Little Falls, MN
Little Rock, AR
Livermore, CA
Lock Haven, PA
Lompoc, CA
Lone Rock, WI
Long Beach, CA
Longview, TX
Lorain-Elyria, OH
Los Angeles Intl, CA
Los Banos, CA

Louisville, KY
Louisville Standiford, KY
Lubbock Intl, TX
Lubbock Town and Country, TX
Lufkin, TX
Lynchburg, VA
Macon, GA
Madera, CA
Madison, WI
Madisonville, KY
Magnolia, AR
Mammoth June Lakes, CA
Manassas, VA
Manchester, NH
Manhattan, KS
Mankato, MN
Mansfield, LA
Mansfield, OH
Manville, NJ
Marathon, FL
Marianna, FL
Marion, OH
Mariposa-Yosemite, CA
Marquette, MI
Marshall, MN
Marshfield, WI
Mason City, IA
Massena Intl, NY
Mattoon Charleston, IL
Maxton, NC
McAlester, OK
McAllen, TX
McCall, ID
McCook, NE
McGregor, TX
McPherson, KS
Medford, OR
Medina, OH
Melbourne, FL
Melfa, VA
Memphis Intl, TN
Meridian, MS
Mesa Falcon Field, AZ
Miami Intl, FL
Miami Opa Locka, FL
Middle Georgia Regional, GA
Midland Intl, TX
Millersburg, OH
Millinocket, ME
Milwaukee Timmerman, WI
Milwaukee–Gen Mitchell, WI
Mineola, TX
Minneapolis, MN
Minneapolis Anoka-Blaine, MN
Minneapolis–Flying Cloud, MN
Minocqua-Woodruff, WI
Minot Intl, ND
Missoula, MT
Mobile, AL

Mobile-Brookley, AL
Modesto City County, CA
Moline, IL
Monahans, TX
Moncks Corner, SC
Monroe, LA
Monroe, NC
Monroeville, AL
Monterey, CA
Montgomery, AL
Montgomery, NY
Montrose, CO
Morganton, NC
Morrilton Municipal, AR
Morristown, NJ
Morristown, TN
Moses Lake, WA
Moultrie, GA
Moundsville, WV
Mount Pleasant, MI
Mount Pleasant, TX
Mount Pocono, PA
Mount Sterling, KY
Mount Vernon, IL
Mountain Home, AR
Muncie, IN
Murfreesboro, TN
Muscatine, IA
Muscle Shoals, AL
Muskegon, MI
Nantucket, MA
Napa, CA
Nashville, TN
Natchez, MS
Nenana, AK
Neosho, MO
New Braunfels, TX
New Castle, IN
New Castle, PA
New Castle County, DE
New Hanover Intl, NC
New Haven, CT
New Iberia, LA
New Kent County, VA
New Orleans Intl, LA
New Orleans Lakefront, LA
New Roads, LA
New York Kennedy Intl, NY
New York La Guardia, NY
Newark, OH
Newark Intl, NJ
Newnan Coweta, GA
Newport News, VA
Newton, KS
Niagara Falls, NY
Nogales Intl, AZ
Norfolk, NE
Norfolk Intl, VA
Norman, OK
North Las Vegas Air Terminal, NV
North Myrtle Beach, SC
North Platte, NE
Norwood, MA

Novato, CA
Oakdale, CA
Oakland, CA
Ogden, UT
Oklahoma City, OK
Oklahoma City
 Expressway, OK
Oklahoma
 City–Sundance, OK
Oklahoma City–Wiley
 Post, OK
Olive Branch, MS
Olney, TX
Olympia, WA
Omaha Eppley, NE
Omaha Millard, NE
Ontario, CA
Ontario, OR
Orangeburg, SC
Orlando Executive, FL
Orlando Intl, FL
Oroville, CA
Oshkosh, WI
Ottumwa, IA
Owatonna, MN
Owensboro, KY
Owosso, MI
Oxford, CT
Oxford, MS
Oxnard, CA
Paducah, KY
Pahokee, FL
Palacios, TX
Palm Beach Intl, FL
Palm Springs, CA
Pampa, TX
Panama City, FL
Paris, TX
Parkersburg Wood
 County, WV
Parsons, KS
Pascagoula, MS
Pasco, WA
Paso Robles, CA
Patterson, LA
Pecos, TX
Pendleton, OR
Pensacola, FL
Peoria, IL
Perkasie, PA
Perry, GA
Perryton, TX
Philadelphia, PA
Philadelphia Intl, PA
Phoenix, AZ
Phoenix–Deer Valley, AZ
Phoenix–Goodyear, AZ
Pierre, SD
Pittsburg, KS
Pittsburgh Allegheny Co,
 PA
Pittsburgh Intl, PA
Pittsburgh Metro, PA
Plainfield, IL
Plainview, TX
Plattsburgh, NY
Plymouth, IN

Plymouth, MA
Pocahontas, IA
Point Lookout, MS
Pompano Beach, FL
Ponca City, OK
Pontiac, MI
Port Angeles, WA
Port Huron, MI
Portland, ME
Portland Hillsboro, OR
Portland Intl, OR
Portland Troutdale, OR
Portsmouth, VA
Prattville, AL
Prescott, AZ
Presque Isle, ME
Price, UT
Princeton, ME
Providence, RI
Provo, UT
Pueblo, CO
Quakertown, PA
Racine, WI
Raleigh County, WV
Raleigh-Durham, NC
Rapid City, SD
Rawlins, WY
Reading, PA
Redding, CA
Redlands, CA
Redmond, OR
Redwood Falls, MN
Reedley, CA
Reidsville, NC
Reno, NV
Reno-Stead, NV
Renton, WA
Rexburg, ID
Rhinelander, WI
Rialto, CA
Richmond Intl, VA
Riverside, CA
Roanoke, VA
Robinson, IL
Rochester, MN
Rochester, NY
Rockford, IL
Rocky Mount, NC
Rolla, ND
Romeoville, IL
Roswell, NM
Roundup, MT
Russell, KS
Russellville, AR
Rutland, VT
Sacramento, CA
Sacramento
 Metropolitan, CA
Saginaw, MI
Saginaw-Browne, MI
Salina, KS
Salinas, CA
Salisbury, MD
Salisbury, NC
Salt Lake City Intl, UT
San Angelo, TX
San Antonio, TX

San Antonio Intl, TX
San Diego, CA
San Diego Brown Field, CA
San Diego Montgomery, CA
San Francisco Intl, CA
San José, CA
San Luis Obispo, CA
Sandusky, OH
Sanford, FL
Sanford, NC
Santa Ana, CA
Santa Barbara, CA
Santa Fe, NM
Santa Maria, CA
Santa Monica, CA
Saranac Lake, NY
Sarasota, FL
Saratoga, WY
Savannah, GA
Scottsbluff, NE
Scottsdale, AZ
Seattle-Tacoma Intl, WA
Sedalia, MO
Selinsgrove, PA
Selma, AL
Selmer, TN
Shamokin, PA
Shawnee, OK
Sheboygan Falls, WI
Sheridan, WY
Shirley, NY
Shreveport, LA
Sidney, MT
Sikeston, MO
Sioux City, IA
Sioux Falls, SD
Slidell, LA
Smyrna, TN
Snyder, TX
Somerset, KY
Somerset, PA
Sonoma County, CA
South Bend, IN
Southern Pines, NC
Southwest Georgia
 Regional, GA
Sparta, MI
Sparta, TN
Spencer, IA
Spokane Felts Field, WA
Spokane Intl, WA
Springfield, IL
Springfield, KY
Springfield, MO
Springhill, LA
St Anthony, GA
St Cloud, MN
St Francis, KS
St John, NB
St Joseph, MO
St Louis, MO
St Paul, MN
St Petersburg, FL
Stanton, TX
Statesboro, GA
Statesville, NC
Stephenville, TX

Stevens Point, WI
Stewart Intl, NY
Stillwater, OK
Stockton, CA
Stuart, FL
Sugar Land Municipal, TX
Sweetwater, TX
Syracuse, NY
Tacoma, WA
Tallahassee, FL
Tampa, FL
Tampa Intl, FL
Taos, NM
Taylorville, IL
Teterboro, NJ
Texarkana, AR
Tifton, GA
Tillamook, OR
Titusville, FL
Toccoa, GA
Toledo, OH
Tonopah, NV
Topeka, KS
Trenton, NJ
Tri-City Regional, TN
Truckee, CA
Tucson, AZ
Tulsa, OK
Tupelo, MS
Tuscaloosa, AL
Tuskegee, AL
Twentynine Palms, CA
Twin Falls, ID
Tyler, TX
Ukiah, CA
Union City, TN
Valdosta, GA
Van Nuys, CA
Vancouver, WA
Vernal, UT
Vero Beach, FL
Victoria, TX
Waco, TX
Wadsworth, OH
Walla Walla, WA
Walnut Ridge, AR
Walterboro, SC
Wapakoneta, OH
Warsaw, IN
Waseca, MN
Washington, DC
Washington Dulles Intl, DC
Waterloo, IA
Watertown, SD
Watertown, WI
Watertown Intl, NY
Waukegan, IL
Waukesha, WI
Wausau, WI
Wasau–Stevens Point, WI
Wellsville, NY
Wenatchee-Pangborn
 Memorial, WA
West Bend, WI
West Dover, VT
West Memphis, AR
West Palm Beach, FL

Air (continued)

West Plains, MO
Westchester Co White
  Plains, NY
Westfield, MA
Westhampton Beach, NY
Wichita, KS
Wichita Falls, TX
Wichita Falls Valley, TX

Wildwood, NJ
Wilkes-Barre, PA
Willcox Cochise, AZ
Willimantic, CT
Williston, ND
Willmar, MN
Willoughby, OH

Wilson Industrial Air
  Center, NC
Winchester, VA
Winslow, AZ
Winston-Salem, NC
Woodward, OK
Worcester, MA
Worland, WY

Xenia, OH
Yakima, WA
Yankton, SD
York, PA
Youngstown, OH
Yuma, AZ
Zanesville, OH

UK local airports

This list comprises only the airports in Britain which offer passenger services. Major international airports are highlighted in **bold**.

Airport	Other name	Location	Type of traffic
England			
Bembridge		Isle of Wight	Charter, IT services
Birmingham	Elmdon	NE of Birmingham	Scheduled, charter, IT, freight services
Blackpool	Squires Gate	S of Blackpool	Scheduled, charter, IT services
Bournemouth	Hurn	NE of Bournemouth	Scheduled, freight services
Bristol	Lulsgate	SW of Bristol	Scheduled, charter, IT services
Cambridge	Teversham	E of Cambridge	Scheduled, charter, IT services
Carlisle	Crosby	NE of Carlisle	Scheduled services; light aircraft
Coventry	Baginton	S of Coventry	Scheduled, charter, IT services; club and private aircraft
East Midlands	Castle Donington	SW of Kegworth	Scheduled, charter, IT, freight services; club and private aircraft
Exeter	Clyst Honiton	E of Exeter	Scheduled, charter, IT services
Gatwick		S of London	Scheduled, charter, IT services
Gloucestershire	Staverton	W of Cheltenham	Charter, IT services
Heathrow		W of London	Scheduled services
Humberside	Kirmington	E of Scunthorpe	Scheduled, charter, IT services
Kent International	Manston	NW of Ramsgate	Non-scheduled, charter, IT, freight services
Land's End	St Just	W of Penzance	Scheduled services; club and private aircraft
Leeds/Bradford	Yeadon	W of Leeds	Scheduled, charter, IT services
Liverpool	Speke	SE of Liverpool	Scheduled, charter, IT, mail services; club and private aircraft
London City	STOLport	London	Scheduled services, occasional charter, IT services
Luton		SE of Luton	Scheduled, charter, IT, freight services; club aircraft
Lydd		SW of New Romney	Scheduled, charter, IT services; club and private aircraft
Manchester	Ringway	S of Manchester	Scheduled, charter, IT services; club and private aircraft
Newcastle	Woolsington	NW of Newcastle	Scheduled, charter, IT services
Newquay	St Mawgan	NE of Newquay	Scheduled services; occasional company charter flights
Norwich	Horsham St Faith	N of Norwich	Scheduled, charter, IT services
Penzance		E of Penzance	Scheduled helicopter services
Plymouth City		N of Plymouth	Scheduled services; private and club aircraft
Sheffield		NE of Sheffield	Scheduled services
Shoreham		W of Shoreham	Air taxi, private, club, school flights
Southampton	Eastleigh	NE of Southampton	Scheduled, freight services; private and club aircraft
Southend	Rochford	N of Southend	Scheduled, charter, IT, freight services; private and club aircraft
Stansted		E of Bishop's Stortford	Scheduled, charter, IT, freight services
Teesside	Middleton St George	E of Darlington	Scheduled, charter, IT services; school; air taxi; light aircraft
Alderney		SW Alderney	Passenger services
Guernsey		SW of St Peter Port	Scheduled, charter, freight services

Airport	Other name	Location	Type of traffic
Isle of Man	Ronaldsway	SW of Douglas	Scheduled services, occasional charter, IT services
Jersey		NW of St Helier	Scheduled services, occasional charter, IT services
Scilly Isles	St Mary's	E of Hugh Town	Scheduled, helicopter, skybus services
Northern Ireland			
Belfast City	Harbour/Sydenham	Belfast	Scheduled services
Belfast International	Aldergrove	NW of Belfast	Scheduled, charter, IT, freight services
Eglinton		N of Londonderry	Scheduled services; light aircraft
Scotland			
Aberdeen	Dyce	NW of Aberdeen	Scheduled, charter, IT, helicopter services
Barra	North Bay	Barra	Scheduled services; air taxi
Benbecula		NW Benbecula	Scheduled services
Colonsay		Colonsay	Scheduled services
Dundee	Riverside	W of Dundee	Business charter service
Eday		W Orkney	Scheduled services
Edinburgh	Turnhouse	W of Edinburgh	Scheduled, charter, IT, freight services; club and private aircraft
Fair Isle		Shetland	Scheduled services
Fetlar		Shetland	Scheduled services
Glasgow	Abbotsinch	W of Glasgow	Scheduled, charter, IT services
Hoy	Longhope	Orkney	Scheduled services
Inverness	Dalcross	NE of Inverness	Scheduled and non-scheduled helicopter services
Islay/Port Ellen	Glenegedale	S Islay	Scheduled services
Kirkwall		Orkney	Scheduled services; oil-industry traffic
Machrihanish	Campbeltown	Kintyre	Scheduled services
North Ronaldsay		SW Orkney	Scheduled services
Oronsay		Oronsay	Scheduled services
Papa Stour		S Shetland	Scheduled services
Papa Westray		W Orkney	Scheduled services
Prestwick		S of Kilmarnock	Charter, IT services
Sanday		C Orkney	Scheduled services
Stornoway		E of Stornoway	Scheduled services; transit stop
Stronsay		NW Orkney	Scheduled services
Sumburgh		Shetland	Scheduled helicopter services; oil-industry traffic
Tingwall	Lerwick	Shetland	Scheduled services
Unst	Baltasound	Shetland	Scheduled services
Westray		N Orkney	Scheduled services
Whalsay		NE Shetland	Scheduled services
Wick		Wick	Scheduled services
Wales			
Cardiff-Wales	Rhoose	SW of Cardiff	Scheduled, charter, IT, freight services

International airports

Abadan	Iran
Abu Dhabi	United Arab Emirates
Adana	Turkey
Adelaide	Australia
Agno	Lugano, Switzerland
Ain el Bay	Constantine, Algeria
Albany County	New York, USA
Ålborg Roedslet	Nørresundby, Denmark
Albuquerque	New Mexico, USA
Alexandria	Egypt
Alfonso Bonilla Aragon	Cali, Columbia
Alicante	Spain
Almería	Spain
Amarillo	Texas, USA
Amborovy	Majunga, Madagascar
Amilcar Cabral International	Sal Island, Cape Verde
Aminu	Kano, Nigeria
Anchorage	Alaska, USA
Archangel	Russia
Arlanda	Stockholm, Sweden
Arnos Vale	St Vincent
Arrecife	Lanzarote, Canary Islands
Arturo Marino Benitez	Santiago, Chile
Asturias	Spain
Ataturk	Istanbul, Turkey
Auckland	New Zealand
Augusto C Sandino	Managua, Nicaragua
Baghdad	Iraq
Bahrain	Bahrain
Bali/Ngurah Rai	Denpasar, Indonesia
Balice	Cracow, Poland
Bandar Seri Begawan	Brunei
Baneasa	Bucharest, Romania

Air (continued)

Bangkok	Thailand	Costa Smeralda	Olbia, Sardinia
Barajas	Madrid, Spain	Côte d'Azure	Nice, France
Barcelona	Spain	Cotonou	Benin
Basle-Mulhouse	Basle, Switzerland	Cristoforo Colombo	Genoa, Italy
Beijing	China	Crown Point	Scarborough, Tobago
Beira	Mozambique	Cuscatlán	El Salvador
Beirut	Khaldeh, Lebanon	D F Malan	Cape Town, South Africa
Belfast	UK	Dalaman	Turkey
Belgrade	Serbia	Dallas/Fort Worth	Texas, USA
Belize City	Belize	Damascus	Syria
Ben Gurion	Tel Aviv, Israel	Dar-es-Salaam	Tanzania
Benina	Benghazi, Libya	Darwin	Australia
Benito Juarez	Mexico City, Mexico	Des Moines	Iowa, USA
Berlin-Schonefeld	Berlin, Germany	Detroit-Wayne County	Detroit, MI, USA
Berlin-Tegel	Berlin, Germany	Deurne	Antwerp, Belgium
Berne	Switzerland	Dhahran	Al Khobar, Saudi Arabia
Billund	Denmark	Djibouti	Djibouti
Birmingham	Alabama, USA	Doha	Qatar
Blackburne/Plymouth	Montserrat	Dois de Julho	Salvador, Brazil
Blagnac	Toulouse, France	Domodedovo	Moscow, Russia
Bole	Addis Ababa, Ethiopia	Don Miguel Hidalgo	Guadalajara, Mexico
Bombay	India	y Castilla	
Borispol	Kiev, Ukraine	Dorval	Montreal, Canada
Boukhalef	Tangier, Morocco	Douala	Cameroon
Boulogne	France	Dresden	Germany
Bourgas	Bulgaria	Dubai	United Arab Emirates
Bradley	Hartford, CT, USA	Dublin	Ireland
Brasília	Brazil	Dubrovnik	Croatia
Bremen	Germany	Dulles	Washington, DC, USA
Brisbane	Australia	Düsseldorf	Germany
Brnik	Ljubljana, Slovenia	Ecterdingen	Stuttgart, Germany
Bromma	Stockholm, Sweden	Edmonton	Canada
Brussels National	Belgium	Eduardo Gomes	Manaus, Brazil
Buffalo	New York, USA	Eindhoven	Netherlands
Bujumbura	Burundi	El Alto	La Paz, Bolivia
Bulawayo	Zimbabwe	El Dorado	Bogotá, Colombia
Butmir	Sarajevo, Bosnia-Herzegovina	El Paso	Texas, USA
Cairns	Queensland, Australia	Elat	Israel
Cairo	Egypt	Elmas	Cagliari, Italy
Calabar	Nigeria	Entebbe	Uganda
Calcutta	India	Entzheim	Strasbourg, France
Calgary	Canada	Eppley Airfield	Omaha, Nebraska, USA
Cancún	Mexico	Erie	Pennsylvania, USA
Cannon	Reno, NV, USA	Ernestso Cortissoz	Barranquilla, Colombia
Canton	Akron, OH, USA	Esbjerg	Denmark
Capodichino	Naples, Italy	Esenboga	Ankara, Turkey
Carrasco	Montevideo, Uruguay	Faleolo	Apia, Samoa
Carthage	Tunis, Tunisia	Faro	Portugal
Cebu	Philippines	Ferihegy	Budapest, Hungary
Chang Kai-shek	Taipei, Taiwan	Findel	Luxembourg
(Jiang Tieshi)		Fiumicino	Rome, Italy
Changi	Singapore	(Leonardo da Vinci)	
Charleroi (Gossilies)	Belgium	Flesland	Bergen, Norway
Charles de Gaulle	Paris, France	Fontanarossa	Catania, Sicily
Charleston	South Carolina, USA	Fornebu	Oslo, Norway
Charleston	West Virginia, USA	Fort de France	Lamentin, Martinique
Charlotte	North Carolina, USA	Fort Lauderdale	Florida, USA
Château Bougon	Nantes, France	Fort Myers	Florida, USA
Christchurch	New Zealand	Frankfurt am Main	Germany
Ciampino	Rome, Italy	Freeport	Bahamas
Cologne-Bonn	Cologne, Germany	Frejorgues	Montpellier, France
Columbus	Ohio, USA	Fuenterrabía	San Sebastián, Spain
Congonhas	São Paulo, Brazil	Fuerteventura	Canary Islands
Copenhagen	Kastrup, Denmark	Fuhlsbuttel	Hamburg, Germany
Cork	Ireland	G Marconi	Bologna, Italy

Communications

Galileo Galilei	Pisa, Italy
Gatwick	London, UK
G'Bessia	Conakry, Guinea Republic
Gen Abelard L Rodriguez	Tijuana, Mexico
Gen Juan N Alvarez	Acapulco, Mexico
Gen Manuel Marquez de Leon	La Paz, Mexico
Gen Mariano Escobedo	Monterrey, Mexico
Gen Mitchell	Milwaukee, WI, USA
Gen Rafael Buelna	Mazatlán, Mexico
Geneva	Switzerland
Gerona/Costa Brava	Gerona, Spain
Gillot	St Denis de la Reunion
Golden Rock	St Kitts
Goleniów	Szczecin, Poland
Glasgow	UK
Granada	Spain
Grantley Adams	Bridgetown, Barbados
Greater Cincinatti	Ohio, USA
Greater Pittsburgh	Pennsylvania, USA
Guam	Guam
Guararapes	Recife, Brazil
Guarulhos	São Paulo, Brazil
Halifax	Canada
Halim Perdanakusama	Jakarta, Indonesia
Hamilton Kindley Field	Hamilton, Bermuda
Hancock Field	Syracuse, NY, USA
Hannover-Langenhagen	Hanover, Germany
Hanoi	Vietnam
Harare	Zimbabwe
Harrisburg	Pennsylvania, USA
Hartsfield	Atlanta, Georgia, USA
Hassan	Laayoune, Morocco
Hato	Curaçao, Netherlands Antilles
Hahaya	Moroni, Comoros
Hanedi	Tokyo, Japan
Heathrow	London, UK
Hellenikon	Athens, Greece
Henderson Field	Honiari, Solomon Islands
Heraklion	Crete, Greece
Hewanorra	St Lucia
Ho Chi Minh City	Vietnam
Hong Kong	Hong Kong
Hongqiao	Shanghai, China
Honolulu	Hawaii, US
Hopkins	Cleveland, OH, USA
Houari Boumedienne	Dar-el-Beida, Algeria
Houston	Texas, USA
Ibiza	Balearics, Spain
Indianapolis	Indiana, USA
Indira Ghandi	Delhi, India
Inezgane	Agadir, Morocco
Islamabad	Pakistan
Isle Verde	San Juan, Puerto Rico
Izmir	Turkey
Itazuke	Fukuoka, Japan
Ivanka	Bratislava, Slovak Republic
Ivato	Antananarivo, Madagascar
J F Kennedy	New York, USA
Jackson Field	Port Moresby, Papua New Guinea
Jacksonville	Florida, USA
James M Cox	Dayton, OH, USA
Jan Smuts	Johannesburg, South Africa
Jomo Kenyatta	Nairobi, Kenya
Jorge Chavez	Lima, Peru
Jose Marti	Havana, Cuba
Juan Santa Maria	Alajuela, Costa Rica
Kagoshima	Japan
Kalmar	Sweden
Kamazu	Lilongwe, Malawi
Kansas City	Missouri, USA
Kaohsiung	Taiwan
Karachi	Pakistan
Karpathos	Karpathos, Greece
Katunayake	Colombo, Sri Lanka
Keflavík	Reykjavík, Iceland
Kent County	Grand Rapids, MI, USA
Kerkyra	Corfu, Greece
Key West	Florida, USA
Khartoum	Sudan
Khoramaksar	Aden, Yemen
Khwaja Rawash	Kabul, Afghanistan
Kigali	Rwanda
Kimpo	Seoul, South Korea
King Abdul Aziz	Jeddah, Saudi Arabia
King Khaled	Riyadh, Saudi Arabia
Kingsford Smith	Sydney, Australia
Kjevik	Kristiansand, Norway
Klagenfurt	Austria
Komaki	Nagoya, Japan
Kos	Greece
Kota Kinabalu	Sabah, Malaysia
Kotoka	Accra, Ghana
Kranebitten	Innsbruck, Austria
Kuching	Sarawak, Malaysia
Kungsangen	Norrköping, Sweden
Kuwait International	Kuwait
La Aurora	Guatemala City, Guatemala
La Coruña	Spain
La Guardia	New York, USA
La Mesa	San Pedro Sula, Honduras
La Parra	Jerez de la Frontera, Spain
Lahore	Pakistan
Landvetter	Gothenburg, Sweden
Larnaca	Cyprus
Las Americas	Santo Domingo, Dominican Republic
Las Palmas	Gran Canaria, Canary Islands
Le Raizet	Point-à-Pitre, Guadeloupe
Leipzig	Germany
Les Angades	Oujda, Morocco
Lesquin	Lille, France
Lester B Pearson	Toronto, Canada
Libreville	Gabon
Lic Gustavo Diaz Ordaz	Puerto Vallarta
Lic Manuel Crecencio Rejon	Mérida, Mexico
Liège (Bierset)	Belgium
Linate	Milan, Italy
Lincoln	Nebraska, USA
Lindbergh	San Diego, USA
Linz	Austria
Lisbon	Portugal
Little Rock	Arkansas, USA
Llabanère	Perpignan, France
Logan	Boston, MA, USA
Lomé	Togo
London City	UK
Long Beach	California, USA
Los Angeles	California, USA
Loshitsa	Minsk, Belarus
Louis Botha	Durban, South Africa

Transportation

Air (continued)

Louisville	Kentucky, USA
Lourdes/Tarbes	Juillan, France
Luanda	Angola
Luano	Lubumashi, Zaïre
Lubbock	Texas, USA
Luis Munoz Marin	San Juan, Puerto Rica
Lungi	Freetown, Sierra Leone
Luqa	Malta
Lusaka	Zambia
Luxor	Egypt
Maastricht	Netherlands
McCarran	Las Vegas, NV, USA
McCoy	Orlando, FL, USA
Mactan	Cebu, Philippines
Mahon	Menorca
Mais Gate	Port au Prince, Haiti
Málaga	Spain
Male	Maldives
Malpensa	Milan, Italy
Managua	Nicaragua
Manchester	New Hampshire, USA
Manchester	UK
Maputo	Mozambique
Marco Polo	Venice, Italy
Mariscal Sucre	Quito, Ecuador
Maseru	Lesotho
Matsapha	Manzini, Swaziland
Maupertus	Cherbourg, France
Maxglan	Salzburg, Austria
Maya Maya	Brazzaville, Congo
Medina	Saudi Arabia
Meenambakkam	Madras, India
Mehrabad	Teheran, Iran
Melita	Djerba, Tunisia
Memphis	Tennessee, USA
Menara	Marrakech, Morocco
Merignac	Bordeaux, France
Miami	Florida, USA
Midway	Chicago, IL, USA
Mingaladon Yangon	Myanmar, (Burma)
Ministro Pistarini	Buenos Aires, Argentina
Minneapolis/St Paul	Minneapolis, USA
Mirabel	Montreal, Canada
Mogadishu	Somalia
Mohamed V	Casablanca, Morocco
Moi	Mombasa, Kenya
Monroe County	Rochester, NY, USA
Morelos	Mexico City, Mexico
Münster/Osnabrück	Germany
Murmansk	Russia
Murtala Muhammed	Lagos, Nigeria
Nadi	Fiji
Nagasaki	Japan
Narita	Tokyo, Japan
Narssarsuaq	Greenland
Nashville	Tennessee, USA
Nassau	Bahamas
Nauru	Nauru
N'djamena	Chad
N'Djili	Kinshasa, Zaïre
Nejrab	Aleppo, Syria
Newcastle	UK
New Orleans	Louisiana, USA
Newark	New Jersey, USA
Niamey	Niger
Ninoy Aquino	Manila, Philippines
Niš	Yugoslavia
Norfolk	Virginia, USA
Norman Manley	Kingston, Jamaica
North Front	Gibraltar
Nouadhibou	Mauritania
Nouakchott	Mauritania
Novo-Alexeyevka	Tblisi, Georgia
Nuremburg	Germany
Oakland	California, USA
Octeville	Le Havrets, France
Odense	Denmark
O'Hare	Chicago, IL, USA
Okecie	Warsaw, Poland
Okinawa	Naha, Japan
Oran	Algeria
Orebro	Sweden
Orlando	Florida, USA
Orly	Paris, France
Osaka	Japan
Osvaldo Veira	Bissau, Guinea Bissau
Otopeni	Bucharest, Romania
Ougadougou	Burkina Faso
Owen Roberts	Grand Cayman
Pago Pago	Samoa
Palese	Bari, Italy
Palma	Majorca
Pamplona	Spain
Panama City	Panama
Paphos	Cyprus
Papola Casale	Brindisi, Italy
Paradisi	Rhodes, Greece
Patenga	Chittagong, Bangladesh
Penang	Malaysia
Peninsula	Monterey, CA, USA
Peretola	Florence, Italy
Perth	Australia
Peshawar	Pakistan
Peterson Field	Colorado Springs, CO, USA
Philadelphia	Pennsylvania, USA
Piarco	Port of Spain, Trinidad
Pleso	Zagreb, Croatia
Pochentong	Phnom Penh, Cambodia
Point Salines	Grenada
Pointe Noire	Congo
Polonia	Medan, Indonesia
Ponta Delgado	São Miguel, Azores
Port Bouet	Abidjan, Côte d'Ivoire
Port Harcourt	Nigeria
Portland	Maine, USA
Portland	Oregon, USA
Port Sudan	Sudan
Porto Pedra Rubras	Oporto, Portugal
Praia	Cape Verde
Prestwick	UK
Princess Beatriz	Aruba
Provence	Marseille, France
Pula	Croatia
Pulkovo	St Petersburg, Russia
Punta Arenas	Chile
Punta Raisi	Palermo, Italy
Queen Alia	Amman, Jordan
Raleigh/Durham	North Carolina, USA
Ras al Khaimah	United Arab Emirates
Rebiechowo	Gdańsk, Poland
Regina	Canada
Reina Sofia	Tenerife

Communications

15
123

Rejon	Merida, Mexico	Subang	Kuala Lumpur, Malaysia
Richmond	Virginia, USA	Sunan	Pyongyang, North Korea
Riem	Munich, Germany	Tacoma	Washington, USA
Rio de Janeiro	Brazil	Tallahassee	Florida, USA
Riyadh	Saudi Arabia	Tamatve	Madagascar
Roberts	Monrovia, Liberia	Tampa	Florida, USA
Rochambau	Cayenne, French Guiana	Tegucigalpa	Toncontin, Honduras
Robert Mueller	Austin, TX, USA	Thalerhof	Graz, Austria
Municipal		Theodore Francis	Providence, RI, USA
Ronchi dei Legionari	Trieste, Italy	Thessalonika	Greece
Rotterdam	Netherlands	Timehri	Georgetown, Guyana
Ruzyne	Prague, Czech Republic	Timişoara	Romania
Saab	Linköping, Sweden	Tirana	Albania
St Eufemia	Lamezia Terma, Italy	Tito Menniti	Reggio Calabria, Italy
St Louis	Missouri, USA	Tontouta	Noumea, New Caledonia
St Thomas	Virgin Islands	Townsville	Australia
Sainte Foy	Quebec, Canada	Tribhuyan	Kathmandu, Nepal
Sale	Rabat, Morocco	Tripoli	Libya
Salgado Filho	Porto Alegre, Brazil	Trivandrum	India
Salt Lake City	Utah, USA	Truax Field	Madison, WI, USA
San Antonio	Texas, USA	Tucson	Arizona, USA
San Diego	California, USA	Tullamarine	Melbourne, Australia
San Francisco	California, USA	Turin	Italy
San Giusto	Pisa, Italy	Turku	Finland
San Javier	Murcia, Spain	Turnhouse	Edinburgh, UK
San José	California, USA	Ulemiste	Tallinn, Estonia
San Pablo	Seville, Spain	Unokovo	Moscow, Russia
San Salvador	El Salvador	Uplands	Ottowa, Canada
Sanaa	Yemen	V C Bird	Antigua
Sangster	Montego Bay, Jamaica	Vaasa	Finland
Santa Caterina	Funchal, Madeira	Vagar	Faeroe Islands
Santa Cruz	La Palma, Canary Islands	Valencia	Spain
Santa Isabel	Malabo, Guinea	Vancouver	Canada
Santander	Spain	Vantaa	Helsinki, Finland
Santiago	Spain	Varna	Bulgaria
Santos Dumont	Rio de Janeiro, Brazil	Verona	Italy
São Tomé	São Tomé	Victoria	British Columbia, Canada
Satolas	Lyon, France	Vigie	St Lucia
Schiphol	Amsterdam, Netherlands	Vigo	Spain
Schwechat	Vienna, Austria	Vilnius	Lithuania
Seeb	Muscat, Oman	Vilo de Porto	Santa Maria, Azores
Senou	Bamako, Mali	Viracopos	São Paulo, Brazil
Seychelles	Mahe, Seychelles	Vitoria	Spain
Sfax	Tunisia	Washington	Baltimore, MD, USA
Shannon	Ireland	Wattay	Vientiane, Laos
Sharjah	United Arab Emirates	Wellington	New Zealand
Sheremetyevo	Moscow, Russia	Wichita	Kansas, USA
Silvio Pettirossi	Asuncion, Paraguay	Will Rogers	Oklahoma City, OK, USA
Simon Bolivar	Caracas, Venezuela	Winnipeg	Manitoba, Canada
Simon Bolivar	Guayaquil, Ecuador	Yoff	Dakar, Senegal
Sir Seewoosagur	Plaisance, Mauritius	Yundam	Banjul, Gambia
Ramgoolam		Zakynthos	Greece
Sir Seretse Khama	Gaborone, Botswana	Zia	Dhaka, Bangladesh
Skanes	Monastir, Morocco	Zürich	Switzerland
Skopje	Macedonia		
Sky Harbour	Phoenix, AZ, USA		
Snilow	Lwow, Ukraine		
Sofia	Bulgaria		
Sola	Stavanger, Norway		
Sondica	Bilbao, Spain		
Søndre Strømfjord	Greenland		
Spilve	Riga, Latvia		
Split	Croatia		
Spokane	Washington, USA		
Stansted	UK		
Stapleton	Denver, CO, USA		
Sturup	Malmö, Sweden		

TELECOMMUNICATIONS

International direct-dialling codes

This table gives the international telephone direct-dialling codes for most countries.

It is not always possible to dial internationally from every country to every other country, and there are sometimes restrictions and special numbers within a country, for which it is necessary to consult the local telephone directory.

Dialling procedure is as follows:

(a) Dial out, using the access code of the country from which you are making the call; you may need to wait for a dialling tone or announcement (shown by + in the table below).

(b) Then dial the code of the country you are calling, followed by any area or city code, and the subscriber number. (When making an international call, it is usually necessary to omit any initial 0 or 9 of an area/city code.)

Country	Dialling-out code	Dialling-in code	Country	Dialling-out code	Dialling-in code
Albania	none	355	Dominican	1 800 751 2701[a]	1 809
Algeria	00+	213	Republic		
Andorra	00	33 628	Ecuador	none	593
Angola	none	244	Egypt	00	20
Anguilla	00	1 809	El Salvador	0	503
Antigua and Barbuda	011	1 809	Equatorial Guinea	00	240
Antilles (Netherlands)	00	599	Ethiopia	none	251
Argentina	00	54	Falkland Islands	00	500
Aruba	00	2978	Faroe Islands	00	298
Ascension Island	00	247	Fiji	none	679
Australia	0011	61	Finland	990	358
Austria	00	43	France	19+	33
Azores	00	351	French Guiana	00	594
Bahamas	011	1 809	French Polynesia	00	689
Bahrain	0	973	Gabon	00	241
Bangladesh	00	880	Gambia	000[a]	220
Barbados	011	1 809	Germany	00	49
Belgium	00+	32	Ghana	0194[a]	233
Belize	none	501	Gibraltar	00	350
Benin	none	229	Greece	00	30
Bermuda	011	1 809	Greenland	none	299
Bhutan	00	975	Grenada	none	1 809
Bolivia	0800 0044[a]	591	Guadeloupe	00	590
Botswana	none	267	Guam	00	671
Brazil	00	55	Guatemala	00	502
Brunei Darussalam	00	673	Guinea	00	224
Bulgaria	00	359	Guinea-Bissau	00	245
Burkina Faso	00	226	Guyana	169[a]	592
Cameroon	00	237	Haiti	none	509
Canada	011	1	Honduras	00	504
Canary Islands	00	34	Hong Kong	001	852
Cape Verde	00	238	Hungary	00+	36
Cayman Islands	00	1 809	Iceland	90	354
Central African Republic	00	236	India	00	91
Chad	00	235	Indonesia	00	62
Chile	00	56	Iran	00	98
China	00	86	Iraq	00	964
Christmas Island	00	672	Ireland, Republic of	00	353
Cocos Island	00	672	Israel	00	972
Colombia	90	57	Italy	00	39
Congo	00	242	Jamaica	none	1 809
Cook Islands	00	682	Japan	001	81
Costa Rica	00	506	Jordan	0	962
Côte d'Ivoire	00	225	Kenya	000	254
Cuba	none	53	Kiribati	00	686
Cyprus	00	357	Korea, PDR (North)	00	850
Czech Republic	00	42	Korea, South	001	82
Denmark	009	45	Latvia	0107	0132
Djibouti	none	253	Kuwait	00	965
Dominica	none	1 809	Lebanon	00	961

International dialling codes (continued)

Country	Dialling-out code	Dialling-in code	Country	Dialling-out code	Dialling-in code
Lesotho	00	266	St Kitts and Nevis	00+	1 809
Liberia	00	231	St Lucia	none	1 809
Libya	00	218	St Pierre and Miquelon	00	508
Liechtenstein	00	41 75	St Vincent and	none	1 809
Luxembourg	00	352	the Grenadines		
Macao	00	853	Samoa, American	none	684
Madagascar	none	261	Samoa, Western	none	685
Madeira	00	35191	San Marino	00	39
Malawi	101	265	São Tomé and Principe	00	239
Malaysia	00	60	Saudi Arabia	00	966
Maldives	none	960	Senegal	00	221
Mali	00	223	Seychelles	0	248
Malta	00	356	Sierra Leone	none	232
Marshall Islands	00	692	Singapore	005	65
Martinique	00	596	Slovakia	00	42
Mauritania	00	222	Solomon Islands	00	677
Mauritius	none	230	Somalia	none	252
Mayotte	00	269	South Africa	09	27
Mexico	98	52	Spain	07+	34
Micronesia	00	691	Sri Lanka	00	94
Monaco	19+	33 93	Suriname	001	597
Montserrat	00	1 809	Swaziland	0992	268
Morocco	00	212	Sweden	009	46
Mozambique	none	258	Switzerland	00	41
Myanmar (Burma)	none	95	Syria	00	963
Namibia	091	264	Taiwan	002	886
Nauru	none	674	Tanzania	none	255
Nepal	none	977	Thailand	001	66
Netherlands	09+	31	Togo	none	228
New Caledonia	00	687	Tonga	none	676
New Zealand	00	64	Trinidad and Tobago	01	1 809
Nicaragua	none	505	Tunisia	00	216
Niger	none	227	Turkey	9+9	90
Nigeria	009	234	Turks and Caicos Islands	00	1 809
Niue	00	683	Tuvalu	00	688
Norfolk Island	00	672	Uganda	none	256
Northern Mariana Islands	00	670	United Arab Emirates	00	971
Norway	095	47	UK	010	44
Oman	00	968	Uruguay	00	598
Pakistan	00	92	USA	011	1
Palau	00	680	Vanuatu	none	678
Panama	00	507	Venezuela	00	58
Papua New Guinea	31	675	Vietnam	00	84
Paraguay	none	595	Virgin Islands (UK)	00	1 809 49
Peru	00	51	Virgin Islands (US)	00	1 809
Philippines	00	63	Yemen - north, south	00	967, 969
Poland	0+0	48	Yugoslavia	99	38
Portugal	00	351	Zaïre	none	243
Puerto Rico	135	1 809	Zambia	00	260
Qatar	0	974	Zimbabwe	110	263
Réunion	00	262			
Romania	none	40			
Russia	810	7			
Rwanda	none	250			
St Helena	00	290			

Afghanistan, Laos, and Sudan can be reached only through the international operator.

[a]Denotes 'UK Direct' numbers.

LANGUAGES

Indo-European languages

The Indo-European family, reflecting geographical distribution

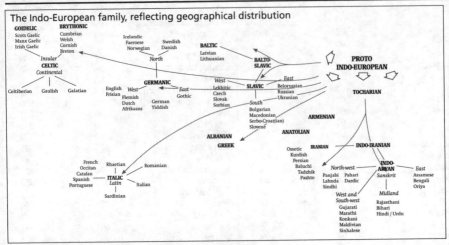

Language families: numbers of speakers

Estimates of the numbers of speakers in the main language families of the world in the 1980s. The list includes Japanese and Korean, which are not clearly related to any other languages.

Main language families	Speakers
Indo-European	2 000 000 000
Sino-Tibetan	1 040 000 000
Niger-Congo	260 000 000
Afro-Asiatic	230 000 000
Austronesian	200 000 000
Dravidian	140 000 000
Japanese	120 000 000
Altaic	90 000 000

Main language families	Speakers
Austro-Asiatic	60 000 000
Korean	60 000 000
Tai	50 000 000
Nilo-Saharan	30 000 000
Amerindian (North, Central, South America)	25 000 000
Uralic	23 000 000
Miao-Yao	7 000 000
Caucasian	6 000 000
Indo-Pacific	3 000 000
Khoisan	50 000
Australian aborigine	50 000
Palaeosiberian	25 000

The top twenty languages

Speaker estimates for the world's top 20 languages. The first column lists the languages on the basis of the number of mother-tongue (first-language) speakers they have. The second column gives population estimates for those countries where the language has official status. Note that the totals do not always coincide, since some major languages (such as Javanese and Telugu) are not official languages of whole countries, and some languages (such as Malay and Tagalog) are official languages of multilingual countries. The second-column figures are often over-estimates, as by no means everyone in the countries where a second language is recognized (eg India) will be fluent in it; on the other hand, the figures are of some interest as indicators of the way languages are moving.

Mother-tongue speakers (millions)	Official language populations (millions)	Mother-tongue speakers (millions)	Official language populations (millions)
1 Chinese (1 000)	1 English (1 400)	11 French (70)	11 Japanese (120)
2 English (350)	2 Chinese (1 000)	12 Panjabi (70)	12 German (100)
3 Spanish (250)	3 Hindi (700)	13 Javanese (65)	13 Urdu (85)
4 Hindi (200)	4 Spanish (280)	14 Bihari (65)	14 Italian (60)
5 Arabic (150)	5 Russian (270)	15 Italian (60)	15 Korean (60)
6 Bengali (150)	6 French (220)	16 Korean (60)	16 Vietnamese (60)
7 Russia (150)	7 Arabic (170)	17 Telugu (55)	17 Persian (55)
8 Portuguese (135)	8 Portuguese (160)	18 Tamil (55)	18 Tagalog (50)
9 Japanese (120)	9 Malay (160)	19 Marathi (50)	19 Thai (50)
10 German (100)	10 Bengali (150)	20 Vietnamese (50)	20 Turkish (50)

World language families

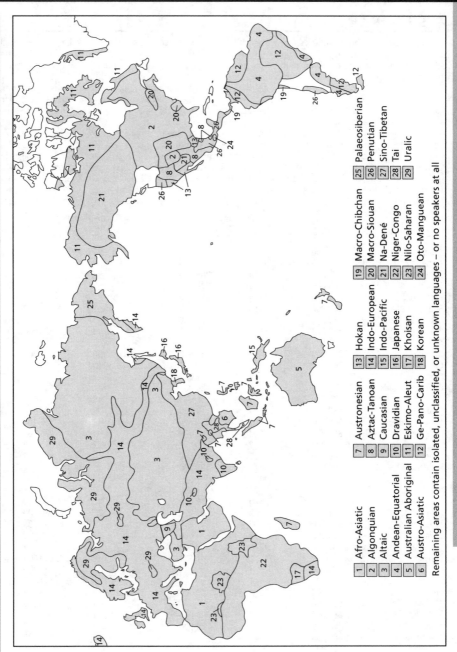

1	Afro-Asiatic
2	Algonquian
3	Altaic
4	Andean-Equatorial
5	Australian Aboriginal
6	Austro-Asiatic

7	Austronesian
8	Aztac-Tanoan
9	Caucasian
10	Dravidian
11	Eskimo-Aleut
12	Ge-Pano-Carib

13	Hokan
14	Indo-European
15	Indo-Pacific
16	Japanese
17	Khoisan
18	Korean

19	Macro-Chibchan
20	Macro-Siouan
21	Na-Dené
22	Niger-Congo
23	Nilo-Saharan
24	Oto-Manguean

25	Palaeosiberian
26	Penutian
27	Sino-Tibetan
28	Tai
29	Uralic

Remaining areas contain isolated, unclassified, or unknown languages – or no speakers at all

English speakers

This table lists only those countries where English has official or special status. Those who have learned English as a foreign language in countries (eg China, Germany) where it has no such status are not included in the listing.

Areas where English is a creole or creolized pidgin are identified by (c) (eg Sierra Leone). Most of these varieties have been placed in the 'First language' column, increasing the grand total there by 57 million.

Figures for English as a second language are often unknown (?) or uncertain. Where a total is preceded by ? (eg Botswana) it has been derived from the numbers of people in the country who have completed their secondary education, and who are thus likely to have achieved a reasonable standard of use. This total excludes any first-language speakers listed for that country.

In first-language countries (eg Canada), no totals are given for second-language use when agreed estimates do not exist; as a result, the world total of second-language speakers is probably a considerable underestimate. If we assume (conservatively) that 50% of the remaining population in these countries have English as a second language, the total increases to 145 million. If we also assume (again, conservatively) that in second-language countries (eg Pakistan) 15% of the remaining population might have some command of English, the total reaches 300 million—a commonly quoted figure for world use of English as a second language.

Populations are given for 1990. The world population has been increasing at about 1.7% per annum since this time.

Country	Population	First language		Second language	
		%	Total	%	Total
American Samoa	39 700	?	?	99	39 300
Antigua and Barbuda	80 600	95 (c)	76 600	?	?
Australia	17 073 000	90	15 365 000	95	1 622 000
Bahamas	253 000	90	228 000	?	?
Barbados	257 000	100 (c)	257 000		
Belize	189 000	65 (c)	123 000	?	?
Bermuda	59 300	95	56 300	?	?
Botswana	1 295 000	?	?	?	?26 000
British Virgin I	12 200	95 (c)	11 600	?	?
Brunei[a]	259 000	4	10 000	?36	?93 200
Cameroon	11 900 000	?	?	50 (c)	5 950 000
Canada	26 620 000	60	15 972 000	?	?
Cayman Islands	26 000	100	26 000		
Cook Islands	19 300	?	?	?13	?2 500
Dominica	82 200	4	3 300	?9	?7 400
Fiji	740 000	?	?	?8	?59 200
Gambia	860 000	? (c)	?	?3	?25 800
Ghana	15 020 000	?	?	7	1 000 000
Gibraltar	300 800	35	10 800	?	?
Grenada	101 000	100 (c)	101 000		
Grenada	101 000	100 (c)	101 000		
Guam	132 000	21	28 000	?	?
Guyana	756 000	75 (c)	567 000	?	?
Hong Kong	5 841 000	2	117 000	25	1 460 000
India[a]	844 000 000	?	?	4	33 760 000
Ireland	3 509 000	95	3 334 000	?	?
Jamaica	2 391 000	97 (c)	2 319 000	?	?
Kenya	2 487 200	?	?	?9	2 239 000
Kiribati	71 100	?	?	?41	?29 200
Lesotho	1 760 000	?	?	?23	?404 800
Liberia	2 595 000	96 (c)	2 500 000	?	?
Malawi	8 830 000	?	?	5	470 000
Malaysia	17 886 000	2	300 000	30	5 366 000
Malta	353 000	20	70 500	?	?
Mauritius	1 080 000	?	?	?11	?119 000
Montserrat	12 000	100 (c)	12 000		
Namibia	1 300 000	10	130 000	?	?
Nauru	9 000	7	600	?	?
New Zealand	3 389	93	3 152 000	?	?
Nigeria	88 500 000	50 (c)	44 250 000	?	?
N Marianas	45 000	90 (c)	40 500	?	?
Pakistan[a]	122 600 000	?	?	2	2 450 00
Palau	14 300	?	?	98	14 000
Papua New Guinea	3 671 000	66 (c)	2 460 000	?	?
Philippines	61 480 000	?	?	50	30 740 000
Puerto Rico	3 336 000	?	?	45	1 500 000

Country	Population	First language		Second language	
		%	Total	%	Total
St Kitts	44 100	100	44 100	?	?
St Lucia	151 000	18	28 000	?	?
St Vincent and the Grenadines	115 000	100 (c)	115 000		
Seychelles[a]	68 700	3	2 000	?	?
Sierra Leone	4 151 000	?95 (c)	3 943 000	?	?
Singapore	2 718 000	?	?	40	1 087 00
Solomon Islands	319 000	?	?	35 (c)	111 600
South Africa	30 797 000	10	3 080 000	15	4 620 000
Suriname[a]	411 000	?	?	80	328 800
Swaziland	770 000	?	?	?4	30 800
Tanzania	24 403 000	?	?	15	3 660 000
Tonga	96 300	?	?	1	1 000
Trinidad and Tobago	1 233 000	50 (c)	616 500	?	?
Tuvalu	9 100	?	?	6	550
Uganda	16 928 000	?	?	?3	507 800
United Kingdom	57 384 000	98	56 236 000	?	?
UK Islands	201 500	100	201 500		
United States[a]	251 394 000	88	221 227 000	?	?
US Virgin Islands	107 000	80 (c)	86 000	?	?
Vanuatu	147 000	?	?	88	129 000
Western Samoa	186 000	?	?	?57	?106 000
Zambia	8 456 000	?	?	?11	?930 000
Zimbabwe	9 370 000	?	?	?32	?2 998 000
Other dependencies	33 000	60	19 80040	13 200	
Totals	1 660 457 400		377 120 100		101 901 150
	(1 661 000 000)		(377 000 000)		(102 000 000)

[a]Countries in which English has a special status. English is an official language in all other countries listed in the table.

English letter frequencies

Here is a selection of frequency orders found in one comparative study of different styles of American English (after A. Zettersten, 1969):

(a) press reporting

(b) religious writing

(c) scientific writing

(d) general fiction

(e) average rank order, based on a description of 15 categories of text totalling over a million words

(f) order used by Samuel Morse (1791–1872) in compiling the Morse Code

(g) quantities of type found in a printer's office, on which Samuel Morse's frequency ordering was based

Rank order by frequency of use (overleaf)

English sound frequencies

In southern British English (Received Pronunciation) an analysis of the frequency of vowels and consonants in conversation produced the following totals (after D B Fry, 1947).

Consonants	(%)		(%)	Vowels	(%)		(%)
n	7.58	b	1.97	ə	10.74	ʊ	0.86
t	6.42	f	1.79	ɪ	8.33	ɑː	0.79
d	5.14	p	1.78	e	2.97	aʊ	0.61
s	4.81	h	1.46	aɪ	1.83	ɜ	0.52
l	3.66	ŋ	1.15	ʌ	1.75	ɛə	0.34
ð	3.56	g	1.05	eɪ	1.71	ɪə	0.21
r	3.51	ʃ	0.96	iː	1.65	ɔɪ	0.14
m	3.22	j	0.88	əʊ	1.51	ʊə	0.06
k	3.09	ʤ	0.60	a	1.45		
w	2.81	ʧ	0.41	ɒ	1.37		
z	2.46	θ	0.37	ɔː	1.24		
v	2.00	ʒ	0.10	uː	1.13		

Communications

English letter frequencies (continued)

(a)	(b)	(c)	(d)	(e)	(f)	(g)
e	e	e	e	e	e	12000
t	t	t	t	t	t	9000
a	i	a	a	a	a	8000
o	a	i	o	o	i	8000
n	o	o	h	i	n	8000
i	n	n	n	n	o	8000
s	s	s	i	s	s	8000
r	r	r	s	r	h	6400
h	h	h	r	h	r	6200
l	l	l	d	l	d	4400
d	d	c	l	d	l	4000
c	c	d	u	c	u	3400
m	u	u	w	u	c	3000
u	m	m	m	m	m	3000
f	f	f	c	f	f	2500
p	p	p	g	p	w	2000
g	y	g	f	g	y	2000
w	w	y	y	w	g	1700
y	g	b	p	y	p	1700
b	b	w	b	b	b	1600
v	v	v	k	v	v	1200
k	k	k	v	k	k	800
j	x	x	j	x	q	500
x	j	q	x	j	j	400
q	q	j	z	q	x	400
z	z	z	q	z	z	200

English sound frequencies (continued)

The vowel system of Received Pronunciation

/iː/	as in sea	/eɪ/	as in ape
/ɪ/	as in him	/aɪ/	as in time
/e/	as in get	/ɔɪ/	as in boy
/æ/	as in sat	/əʊ/	as in so
/ʌ/	as in sun	/aʊ/	as in out
/ɑː/	as in father	/ɪə/	as in deer
/ɒ/	as in dog	/ɛə/	as in care
/ɔː/	as in saw	/ʊə/	as in poor
/ʊ/	as in put		
/uː/	as in soon		
/ɜː/	as in bird		
/ə/	as in about		

The consonant system of Received Pronunciation

/p/	as in pie	/z/	as in zoo
/b/	as in by	/ʃ/	as in shoe
/t/	as in tie	/ʒ/	as in beige
/d/	as in die	/h/	as in hi
/k/	as in coo	/m/	as in my
/g/	as in go	/n/	as in no
/tʃ/	as in chew	/ŋ/	as in sing
/dʒ/	as in jaw	/l/	as in lie
/f/	as in fee	/r/	as in row
/v/	as in view	/w/	as in way
/θ/	as in thin	/j/	as in you
/ð/	as in the		
/s/	as in so		

The trancription is the one used by A C Gimson in *An Introduction to the Pronunciation of English* (London, 1980).

Comparative word frequencies

Rank	French	German	Written English	Spoken English	Rank	French	German	Written English	Spoken English
1	de	der	the	the	11	que (p)	auf	on	is
2	le (a)	die	of	and	12	dans	mit	at	yes
3	la (a)	und	to	I	13	il	sich	he	was
4	et	in	in	to	14	à	daß	with	this
5	les	des	and	of	15	en	dem	by	but
6	des	den	a	a	16	ne	sie	be	on
7	est	zu	for	you	17	on	ist	it	well
8	un (a)	das	was	that	18	qui	im	an	he
9	une (a)	von	is	in	19	au	eine	as	have
10	du	für	that	it	20	se	DDR	his	for

a = article   *p* = pronoun

Alphabets

The development of the early alphabet

Phoenician	Old Hebrew	Early Greek	Classical Greek	Etruscan	Early Latin	Modern Roman
						Aa
						Bb
						Cc
						Dd
						Ee
						Ff
						Gg
						Hh
						Ii
						Jj
						Kk
						Ll
						Mm
						Nn
						Oo
						Pp
						Qq
						Rr
						Ss
						Tt
						Uu
						Vv
						Ww
						Xx
						Yy
						Zz

A version of the runic alphabet found in Britain

Rune	Value	Rune	Value
	f		ï
	u		p
	p		x
	o		s
	r		t
	k		b
	g		c
	w		m
	h		l
	n		ng
	i		œ
	j		d

Alphabetic codes

Columns: Semaphore, Letters, Morse, Braille

Letter	Morse
A	.-
B	-...
C	-.-.
D	-..
E	.
F	..-.
G	--.
H	....
I	..
J	.---
K	-.-
L	.-..
M	--
N	-.
O	---
P	.--.
Q	--.-
R	.-.
S	...
T	-
U	..-
V	...-
W	.--
X	-..-
Y	-.--
Z	--..

Nato alphabet

Letter	Code name	Pronunciation	Letter	Code name	Pronunciation
A	Alpha	AL-FAH	N	November	NO-VEM-BER
B	Bravo	BRAH-VOH	O	Oscar	OSS-CAH
C	Charlie	CHAR-LEE	P	Papa	PAH-PAH
D	Delta	DELL-TAH	Q	Quebec	KEY-BECK
E	Echo	ECK-OH	R	Romeo	ROW-ME-OH
F	Foxtrot	FOKS-TROT	S	Sierra	SEE-AIR-RAH
G	Golf	GOLF	T	Tango	TAN-GO
H	Hotel	HOH-TELL	U	Uniform	YOU-NEE-FORM
I	India	IN-DEE-AH	V	Victor	VIK-TAH
J	Juliet	JEW-LEE-ETT	W	Whiskey	WISS-KEY
K	Kilo	KEY-LOH	X	Xray	ECKS-RAY
L	Lima	LEE-MAH	Y	Yankee	YANG-KEY
M	Mike	MIKE	Z	Zulu	ZOO-LOO

Language

Transliteration to the Latin alphabet

Arabic

Letter	Name	Trans[a]
ا	'alif	'
ـب	ba	b
ـت	ta	t
ـث	tha	th
ج	jim	j
ح	ha	h
خ	kha	kh
ﺀ	dal	d
ذ	dha	th
ر	ra	r
ز	za	z
سـ	sin	s
شـ	shin	sh
ص	sad	s
ض	dad	d
ط	ta	t
ظ	za	z
ع	'ain	'
غ	ghain	gh
ف	fa	f
ق	qaf	q
ك	kaf	k
ل	lam	l
م	mim	m
ن	nun	n
ﻫ	ha	h
و	waw	w
ﺉ	ya	y

Russian

Letter	Name	Trans[a]
F f		a
< ,		b
D d		v
U u		g
L l		d
T t		e
: ;		ž, zh
P p		z
B b		i
Q q		j
R r		k
K k		l
V v		m
Y y		n
J j		o
G g		p
H h		r
C c		s
N n		t
E e		u
A a		f
{ [		h, kh, ch
W w		c, ts
X x		č, ch
I i		š, sh
O o		šč, shch
) (		"
S s		y
M m		'
" ,		è
? /		ju, yu
Z z		ja, ya

German

Letter	Name	Trans[a]
A a		a
Ä ä		ae
B b		b
C c		c
D d		d
E e		e
F f		f
G g		g
H h		h
I i		i
J j		j
K k		k
L l		l
M m		m
N n		n
O o		o
Ö ö		oe
P p		p
Q q		q
R r		r
S s		s
T t		t
U u		u
Ü ü		ue
V v		v
W w		w
X x		x
Y y		y
Z z		z

Hebrew

Letter	Name	Trans[a]
א	'aleph	'
ב	beth	b
ג	gimel	g
ד	daleth	d
ה	he	h
ו	waw	w
ז	zayin	z
ח	heth	h
ט	teth	t
י	yodh	y, j
כ ך	kaph	k
ל	lamedh	l
מ ם	mem	m
נ ן	nun	n
ס	samekh	s
ע	'ayin	'
פ ף	pe	p, f
צ ץ	saddhe	s
ק	qoph	q
ר	resh	r
שׁ	shin	sh, s
שׂ	śin	s
ת	t aw	t

Greek

Letter		Name	Trans[a]
A	α	alpha	a
B	β	beta	b
Γ	γ	gamma	g
Δ	δ	delta	d
E	ε	epsilon	e
Z	ζ	zeta	z
H	η	eta	e, e
Θ	θ	theta	th
I	ι	iota	i
K	κ	kappa	k
Λ	λ	lambda	l
M	μ	mu	m
N	ν	nu	n
Ξ	ξ	xi	x
O	o	omicron	o
Π	π	pi	p
P	ρ	rho	r
Σ	σ	sigma	s
T	τ	tau	t
Y	υ	upsilon	y
Φ	φ	phi	ph
X	χ	chi	ch, kh
Ψ	ψ	psi	ps
Ω	ω	omega	o, o

[a]Transliteration.

There is no agreement over the use of a single transliteration system in the case of Arabic, Hebrew, and Russian. The equivalents given here are widely used, but several other possibilities can be found.

Typefaces

The typefaces shown are modern versions of the main groups under which most typefaces may be classified. The dates indicating the introduction of each group are approximate. The roman numbers and names refer to categories in the most recent British Standard for the classification of typefaces, BS 2961 : 1967.

𝔅𝔩𝔞𝔠𝔨𝔩𝔢𝔱𔱱𝔢𝔯 c.1450 (IX, Graphic)

𝔄𝔅ℭ𝔇𝔈𝔉𝔊ℌ𝔍𝔍𝔎𝔏𝔐𝔑𝔒𝔓𝔔ℜ𝔖𝔗𝔘𝔙𝔚𝔛𝔜𝔷
abcdefghijklmnopqrstuvwxyz

14 and 8 pt London

Venetian c.1470 (I, Humanist)

ABCDEFGHIJKLMNOPQRSTUVWXYZ
abcdefghijklmnopqrstuvwxyz

14 and 8 pt Garamond

Old Face c.1495 (II, Garalde)

ABCDEFGHIJKLMNOPQRSTUVWXYZ
abcdefghijklmnopqrstuvwxyz

14 and 8 pt Goudy old style

Transitional c.1757 (III, Transitional)

ABCDEFGHIJKLMNOPQRSTUVWXYZ
abcdefghijklmnopqrstuvwxyz

14 and 8 pt Baskerville

Modern c.1785 (IV, Didone)

ABCDEFGHIJKLMNOPQRSTUVWXYZ
abcdefghijklmnopqrstuvwxyz

14 and 8 pt Bodoni

Grotesque c.1816 (VI, Lineale a, b)

ABCDEFGHIJKLMNOPQRSTUVWXYZ
abcdefghijklmnopqrstuvwxyz

14 and 8 pt Helvetica

Slab-serif c.1830 (V, Slab-serif)

ABCDEFGHIJKLMNOPQRSTUVWXYZ
abcdefghijklmnopqrstuvwxyz

14 and 8 pt Rockwell

Sans-serif c.1918 (VI, Lineale c, d)

ABCDEFGHIJKLMNOPQRSTUVWXYZ
abcdefghijklmnopqrstuvwxyz

14 and 8 pt Gill Sans

Script c.1557 (VIII, Script)

ABCDEFGHIJKLMNOPQRSTUVWXYZ
abcdefghijklmnopqrstuvwxyz

14 and 8 pt

International phonetic alphabet

Consonants

	Bilabial	Labiodental	Dental	Alveolar	Postalveolar	Retroflex	Palatal	Velar	Uvular	Pharyngeal	Glottal
Plosive	p b			t d		ʈ ɖ	c ɟ	k g	q ɢ		ʔ
Nasal	m	ɱ		n		ɳ	ɲ	ŋ	N		
Trill	B			r					R		
Tap or Flap				ɾ		ɽ					
Fricative	ɸ β	f v	θ ð	s z	ʃ ʒ	ʂ ʐ	ç ʝ	x ɣ	χ ʁ	ħ ʕ	h ɦ
Lateral fricative				ɬ ɮ							
Approximant		ʋ		ɹ		ɻ	j	ɰ			
Lateral approximant				l		ɭ	ʎ	L			
Ejective stop	p'			t'		ʈ'	c'	k'	q'		
Implosive	ɓ ɓ			ɗ ɗ			ʄ ʄ	ƙ ɠ	ʠ ʛ		

Where symbols appear in pairs, the one to the right represents a voiced consonant. Shaded areas denote articulations judged impossible.

Vowels

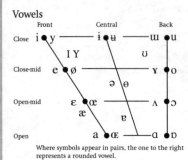

Where symbols appear in pairs, the one to the right represents a rounded vowel.

Suprasegmentals

ˈ	Primary stress	ˌfoʊnəˈtɪʃən
ˌ	Secondary stress	
ː	Long	eː
ˑ	Half-long	eˑ
̆	Extra-short	ĕ
.	Syllable break	ɹi.ækt
|	Minor (foot) group	
‖	Major (intonation group)	
‿	Linking (absence of break)	
↗	Global rise	
↘	Global fall	

Tones & word accents

Level		Contour	
é̋ or ˥	Extra high	ě ˩˥	Rising
é ˦	High	ê ˥˩	Falling
ē ˧	Mid	é̌ ˦˥	High rising
è ˨	Low	è̌ ˩˨	Low rising
è̏ ˩	Extra low	ê̌ ˧˦˧	Rising-falling etc.
↓	Downstep		
↑	Upstep		

Other symbols

ʍ	Voiceless labial-velar fricative
w	Voiced labial-velar approximant
ɥ	Voiced labial-palatal approximant
ʜ	Voiceless epiglottal fricative
ʢ	Voiced epiglottal fricative
ʡ	Epiglottal plosive
ɕ ʑ	Alveolo-palatal fricatives
ɺ	Additional mid central vowel
ʘ	Bilabial click
ǀ	Dental click
ǃ	(Post)alveolar click
ǂ	Palatoalveolar click
ǁ	Alveolar lateral click
ɺ	Alveolar lateral flap
ɧ	Simultaneous ʃ and x

k͡p
t͡s Affricates and double articulations can be represented by two symbols joined by a tie if necessary.

Diacritics

̥	Voiceless	n̥ d̥	̹	More rounded	ɔ̹	ʷ	Labialized	tʷ dʷ	̃	Nasalized	ẽ
̬	Voiced	s̬ t̬	̜	Less rounded	ɔ̜	ʲ	Palatalized	tʲ dʲ	ⁿ	Nasal release	dⁿ
ʰ	Aspirated	tʰ dʰ	̟	Advanced	u̟	ˠ	Velarized	tˠ dˠ	ˡ	Lateral release	dˡ
̈	Breathy voiced	b̤ a̤	̠	Retracted	i̠	ˤ	Pharyngealized	tˤ dˤ	̚	No audible release	d̚
̰	Creaky voiced	b̰ a̰	̈	Centralized	ë	̴	Velarized or pharyngealized	ɫ			
̼	Linguolabial	t̼ d̼	̽	Mid-centralized	e̽	̝	Raised	e̝ (ɹ̝ = voiced alveolar fricative)			
̪	Dental	t̪ d̪	̩	Syllabic	ɹ̩	̞	Lowered	e̞ (β̞ = voiced bilabial approximant)			
̺	Apical	t̺ d̺	̯	Non-syllabic	e̯	̘	Advanced Tongue Root	e̘			
̻	Laminal	t̻ d̻	˞	Rhoticity	ɚ	̙	Retracted Tongue Root	e̙			

Communications

Deaf fingerspelling

British

A   B   C   D

E   F   G   H

I   J   K   L

M   N   O   P

Q   R   S   T

U   V   W   X

Y   Z

American

A   B   C   D

E   F   G   H

I   J   K   L

M   N   O   P

Q   R   S   T

U   V   W   X

Y   Z

Communications

Communications

Proof-correction symbols

Instruction	Textual mark	Marginal mark
Leave unchanged	- - - under characters	
Remove extraneous marks	Encircle marks to be removed	✗
Delete	/ through character(s) or ⊢ through words	
Delete and close up	through character(s) or	
Insert in text the matter indicated in the margin	⅄	New matter followed by ⅄
Substitute character or substitute part of one or more words	/ through character or ⊢ through word(s)	New character or new word(s)
Substitute ligature eg æ for separate letters	through characters affected	eg æ
Substitute or insert full stop or decimal point	/ through character or ⅄	⊙
Substitute or insert comma, semicolon, colon, etc	/ through character or ⅄	, / ; / ⊙ / ( )	
Substitute or insert character in 'superior' position	/ through character or ⅄	under character eg ²
Substitute or insert character in 'inferior' position	/ through character or ⅄	over character eg ₂
Substitute or insert single or double quotation marks or apostrophe	/ through character or ⅄	ʼʼ and/or ʻʼ
Substitute or insert ellipsis	/ through character or ⅄	...
Substitute or insert hyphen	/ through character or ⅄	
Substitute or insert rule	/ through character or ⅄	Give the size of the rule in the marginal mark 1 em | 4 mm |

Instruction	Textual mark	Marginal mark
Substitute or insert oblique	/ through character or ⅄	⊘
Wrong fount. Replace by character(s) of correct fount	Encircle character(s)	⊗
Change damaged character(s)	Encircle character(s)	✗
Set in or change to italic	— under character(s) Where space does not permit textual marks, encircle the affected area instead	
Change italic to upright type	Encircle character(s)	
Set in or change to capital letters	☰ under character(s)	☰
Set in or change to small capital letters	☰ under character(s)	☰
Set in or change to bold type	∿ under character(s)	∿
Set in or change to bold italic type	∿ under character(s)	
Change capital letters to lower-case letters	Encircle character(s)	
Change small capital letters to lower-case letters	Encircle character(s)	
Close up. Delete space between characters or words	(linking characters eg a_scribe	
Insert space between characters	| between characters	
Insert space between words	between words	Give the size of the space when necessary
Reduce space between characters	| between characters	Give the amount by which the space is to be reduced, when necessary

458

Instruction	Textual mark	Marginal mark
Reduce space between words	⌢ between words	Give the amount by which the space is to be reduced, when necessary
Make space appear equal between characters or words	I between characters or words	
Close up to normal interline spacing	(each side of column) linking lines	
Insert space between lines or paragraphs	or	Give the size of the space when necessary
Reduce space between lines or paragraphs	or	Give amount by which the space is to be reduced, when necessary
Start new paragraph		
Run on (no new paragraph)		
Transpose characters or words	between characters or words, numbered when necessary	
Transpose lines		Rules extend from the margin into the text with each line to be transposed numbered in the correct sequence
Transpose a number of lines	3 / 2 / 1	
Centre	[enclosing matter to be centred]	
Indent		Give the amount of the indent
Cancel indent		
Move matter specified distance to the right*	enclosing matter to be moved to the right	

Instruction	Textual mark	Marginal mark
Move matter specified distance to the left*	enclosing matter to be moved to the left	
Set line to specified measure*	and/or	
Set column to specified measure*		
Take over character(s), word(s) or line to next line, column or page		The textual mark surrounds the matter to be taken over and extends into the margin
Take back character(s), word(s) or line to previous line, column or page		The textual mark surrounds the matter to be taken back and extends into the margin
Raise matter*	over matter to be raised / under matter to be raised	
Lower matter*	over matter to be lowered / under matter to be lowered	
Move matter to position indicated*	Enclose matter to be moved and indicate new position	
Correct vertical alignment		
Correct horizontal alignment	Single line above and below misaligned matter	placed level with the head and foot of the relevant line

* Give the exact dimensions when necessary.

Symbols in general use

&	Ampersand (and)	*	Born (in genealogy)	○	Full moon
&c	Et cetera	†	Died	☾	Moon, last quarter
@	At; per (in costs)	*	Hypothetical or		
×	By (measuring dimensions,		unacceptable form (in	**In meteorology**	
	eg 3 × 4)		linguistics)	▲▲▲	Cold front
£	Pound	☠	Poison; danger	▬▬▬	Warm front
$	Dollar (also peso, escudo,	♂, □	Male	▬▼▬▼	Stationary front
	etc, in certain countries)	♀, ○	Female	▲▲▲▲	Occluded front
¢	Cent (also centavo, etc, in	⌗	Bishop's name follows		
	certain countries)	☎	Telephone number follows	**In cards**	
©	Copyright	☞ ☞	This way	♥	Hearts
®	Registered trademark	✂ ✂	Cut here	♦	Diamonds
¶	New paragraph			♠	Spades
§	New section	**In astronomy**		♣	Clubs
ˮ	Ditto	●	New moon		
		☽	Moon, first quarter		

First-name preferences

Boys, England and Wales

	1920s		1950s		1960s		1970s		1980s
1	John	1	David	1	Paul	1	Stephen	1	Andrew
2	William	2	John	2	David	2	Mark	2	David
3	George	3	Peter	3	Andrew	3	Paul	3	Daniel
4	James	4	Michael	4	Stephen	4	Andrew	4	Christopher
5	Ronald	5	Alan	5	Mark	5	David	5	Stephen
6	Robert	6	Robert	6	Michael	6	Richard	6	Matthew
7	Kenneth	7	Stephen	7	Ian	7	Matthew	7	Paul
8	Frederick	8	Paul	8	Gary	8	Daniel	8	James
9	Thomas	9	Brian	9	Robert	9	Christopher	9	Mark
10	Albert	10	Graham	10	Richard	10	Darren	10	Michael
11	Eric	11	Philip	11	Peter	11	Michael	11	Adam
12	Edward	12	Anthony	12	John	12	James	12	Richard
13	Arthur	13	Colin	13	Anthony	13	Robert	13	Darren
14	Charles	14	Christopher	14	Christopher	14	Simon	14	Robert
15	Leslie	15	Geoffrey	15	Darren	15	Jason	15	Lee

Girls, England and Wales

	1920s		1950s		1960s		1970s		1980s
1	Joan	1	Susan	1	Trac(e)y	1	Claire	1	Sarah
2	Mary	2	Linda	2	Deborah	2	Sarah	2	Emma
3	Joyce	3	Christine	3	Julie	3	Nicola	3	Claire
4	Margaret	4	Margaret	4	Karen	4	Emma	4	Kelly
5	Dorothy	5	Carol	5	Susan	5	Joanne	5	Rebecca
6	Doris	6	Jennifer	6	Alison	6	Helen	6	Gemma
7	Kathleen	7	Janet	7	Jacqueline	7	Rachel	7	Rachel
8	Irene	8	Patricia	8	Helen	8	Lisa	8	Lisa
9	Betty	9	Barbara	9	Amanda	9	Rebecca	9	Victoria
10	Eileen	10	Ann	10	Sharon	10	Karen	10	Laura
11	Doreen	11	Sandra	11	Sarah	11	Michelle	11	Catherine
12	Lilian	12	Pamela	12	Joanne	12	Victoria	12	Nicola
13	Vera	13	Pauline	13	Jane	13	Catherine	13	Michelle
14	Jean	14	Jean	14	Catherine	14	Amanda	14	Joanne
15	Marjorie	15	Jacqueline	15	Angela	15	Trac(e)y	15	Lindsay

Boys, USA

	1920s		1950s		1970s		1980s (white)		1980s (non-white)
1	Robert	1	Robert	1	Michael	1	Michael	1	Michael
2	John	2	Michael	2	Robert	2	Christopher	2	Christopher
3	William	3	James	3	David	3	Matthew	3	James

4	James	4	John	4	James	4	David	4	Jason
5	Charles	5	David	5	John	5	Jason	5	Robert
6	Richard	6	William	6	Jeffrey	6	Daniel	6	Anthony
7	George	7	Thomas	7	Steven	7	Robert	7	Brandon
8	Donald	8	Richard	8	Christopher	8	Eric	8	Kevin
9	Joseph	9	Gary	9	Brian	9	Brian	9	David
10	Edward	10	Charles	10	Mark	10	Joseph	10	Charles
11	Thomas	11	Ronald	11	William	11	Ryan	11	Aaron
12	David	12	Dennis	12	Eric	12	James	12	Brian
13	Frank	13	Steven	13	Kevin	13	Steven	13	Eric
14	Harold	14	Kenneth	14	Scott	14	John	14	John
15	Arthur	15	Joseph	15	Joseph	15	Jeffrey	15	Darryl

Girls, USA

	1920s		1950s		1970s		1980s (white)		1980s (non-white)
1	Mary	1	Linda	1	Michelle	1	Jennifer	1	Tiffany
2	Barbara	2	Mary	2	Jennifer	2	Sarah	2	Crystal
3	Dorothy	3	Patricia	3	Kimberly	3	Nicole	3	Ebony
4	Betty	4	Susan	4	Lisa	4	Jessica	4	Erica
5	Ruth	5	Deborah	5	Tracy	5	Katherine	5	Lakisha
6	Margaret	6	Kathleen	6	Kelly	6	Stephanie	6	Latoya
7	Helen	7	Barbara	7	Nicole	7	Elizabeth	7	Nicole
8	Elizabeth	8	Nancy	8	Angela	8	Amanda	8	Candice
9	Jean	9	Sharon	9	Pamela	9	Melissa	9	Danielle
10	Ann(e)	10	Karen	10	Christine	10	Lindsay	10	Brandi
11	Patricia	11	Carol(e)	11	Dawn	11	Rebecca	11	Jennifer
12	Shirley	12	Sandra	12	Amy	12	Lisa	12	Angela
13	Virginia	13	Diane	13	Deborah	13	Rachel	13	April
14	Nancy	14	Catherine	14	Karen	14	Lauren	14	Kimberly
15	Joan	15	Christine	15	Julie	15	Andrea	15	Stephanie

First-name meanings

The meanings of the most popular first names listed above are given here along with a few other well-known names.

Name	Original meaning
Aaron	High mountain (Hebrew)
Adam	Redness (Hebrew)
Alan	?Rock, noble (Celtic)
Albert	Noble bright (Germanic)
Alexander	Defender of men (Greek)
Alison	French diminutive of Alice; of noble kind
Amanda	Fit to be loved (Latin)
Amy	Loved (French)
Andrea	Female form of Andrew
Andrew	Manly (Greek)
Angela	Messenger, angel (Greek)
Ann(e)	English form of Hannah
Anthony	Roman family name
April	Name of the month
Arthur	?Bear, stone (Celtic)
Barbara	Strange, foreign (Greek)
Barry	Spear, javelin (Celtic)
Beatrice	Bringer of joy (Latin)
Benjamin	Son of my right hand (Hebrew)
Bernard	Bear + brave (Germanic)
Beth	Pet form of Elizabeth
Betty	Pet form of Elizabeth
Bill/Billy	Pet form of William
Bob	Pet for of Robert
Brandi	Variant of Brandy, from the common noun

Name	Original meaning
Brandon	Place name; broom-covered hill (Germanic)
Brian	?Hill (?Celtic)
Candice	Meaning unknown
Carl	Man, husbandman (Germanic)
Carol(e)	Form of Caroline, Italian female form of Charles
Catherine	?Pure (Greek)
Charles	Man, husbandman (Germanic)
Christine	French form of Christina ultimately from Christian; anointed
Christopher	Carrier of Christ (Greek)
Claire	Bright, shining (Latin)
Colin	Form of Nicholas
Craig	Rock (Celtic)
Crystal	Female use of the common noun
Daniel	God is my judge (Hebrew)
Danielle	Female form of Daniel
Darren	Irish surname
Darryl	Surname; uncertain origin
David	?Beloved, friend (Hebrew)
Dawn	Female use of the common noun
Dean	Surname; valley or leader
Deborah	Bee (Hebrew)
Dennis	Of Dionysus (Greek), the god of wine
Derek	Form of Theodoric; ruler of the people (Germanic)

First-name meanings (continued)

Name	Original meaning
Diane	French form of Diana; divine (Latin)
Donald	World mighty (Gaelic)
Donna	Lady (Latin)
Doreen	From Dora, a short form of Dorothy; gift of God
Doris	Woman from Doris (Greek)
Dorothy	Gift of God (Greek)
Ebony	Female use of the common noun
Edward	Property guardian (Germanic)
Eileen	Irish form of ?Helen
Elizabeth	Oath/perfection of God (Hebrew)
Emily	Roman family name
Emma	All-embracing (Germanic)
Eric	Ruler of all (Norse)
Erica	Female form of Eric
Eugenie	French form of Eugene; well-born (Greek)
Frank	Pet form of Francis; Frenchman
Frederick	Peaceful ruler (Germanic)
Gail	Pet form of Abigail; father rejoices (Hebrew)
Gareth	Gentle (Welsh)
Gary	?Surname; US place name
Gavin	Scottish form of Gawain; hawk + white (Welsh)
Gemma	Gem (Italian)
Geoffrey	?Peace (Germanic)
George	Husbandman, farmer (Greek)
Graham	Germanic place name
Hannah	Grace, favour (Hebrew)
Harold	Army power/ruler (Germanic)
Harry	Pet form of Henry; home ruler (Germanic)
Hayley	English place name; hay-meadow
Heather	Plant name
Helen	Bright/shining one (Greek)
Ian	Modern Scottish form of John
Irene	Peace (Greek)
Jacqueline	French female form of Jacques (James)
James	Latin form of Jacob; one who takes by the heel (Hebrew)
Jane	From Latin Johanna, female form of John
Janet	Diminutive form of Jane
Jason	Form of Joshua; Jehovah is salvation (Hebrew)
Jeffrey	US spelling of Geoffrey
Jean	French form of Johanna, from John
Jennifer	Fair/white + yielding/smooth (Celtic)
Jeremy	English form of Jeremiah; Jehova exalts (Hebrew)
Jessica	He beholds (Hebrew)
Joan	Contracted form of Johanna, from John
Joanne	French form of Johanna, from John
John	Jehovah has been gracious (Hebrew)
Jonathan	Jehovah's gift (Hebrew)
Joseph	Jehovah adds (Hebrew)
Joyce	?Joyful (?Latin)
Julie	French female form of Latin Julius; descended from Jove
Karen	Danish form of Katarina (Catherine)
Katherine	US spelling of Catherine
Kathleen	English form of Irish Caitlin (from Catherine)
Kelly	Irish surname; warlike one
Kenneth	English form of Gaelic; fair one or fire-sprung
Kerry	Irish place name
Kevin	Handsome at birth (Irish)
Kimberly	South African place name
Lakisha	La + ?Aisha; woman (Arabic)
Latoya	La + form of Tonya (Antonia)
Laura	Bay, laurel (Latin)
Lauren	Diminutive of Laura
Lee	Germanic place name; wood, clearing
Leslie	Scottish place name
Lilian	Lily (Italian)
Linda	Serpent (symbol of wisdom) (Germanic)
Lindsay	Scottish place name
Lisa	Pet form of Elizabeth
Margaret	Pearl (Greek)
Marjorie	From Marguerite, French form of Margaret
Mark	English form of Marcus, from Mars, god of war
Martin	From Mars, god of war (Latin)
Mary	Greek form of Miriam (Hebrew); unknown meaning
Matthew	Gift of the Lord (Hebrew)
Melissa	Bee (Greek)
Michael	Like the Lord (Hebrew)
Michelle	English spelling of French, Michèle from Michael
Nancy	Pet form of Ann
Natalie	Birthday of the Lord (Latin)
Neil	Champion (Irish)
Nicholas	Victory people (Greek)
Nicola	Italian female form of Nicholas
Nicole	French female form of Nicholas
Pamela	?All honey (Greek)
Patricia	Noble (Latin)
Paul	Small (Latin)
Pauline	French female form of Paul
Peter	Stone, rock (Greek)
Philip	Fond of horses (Greek)
Rachel	Ewe (Hebrew)
Rebecca	?Noose (Hebrew)
Richard	Strong ruler (Germanic)
Robert	Fame bright (Germanic)
Ronald	Counsel + power (Germanic)
Ruth	?Companion (Hebrew)
Ryan	Irish surname
Sally	Pet form of Sarah
Samantha	Female form of Samuel; heard/name of God (Hebrew)
Sandra	Pet form from Alexandra
Sarah	Princess (Hebrew)
Scott	Surname from Scotland
Sharon	The plain (Hebrew)
Shaun	English spelling of Irish Sean, from John
Shirley	Bright clearing (Germanic)
Simon	Form of Simeon; listening attentively (Hebrew)
Stephanie	French female form of Stephen
Stephen	Crown (Greek)
Stuart	Steward (Germanic)
Susan	Short form of Susannah; lily (Hebrew)
Teresa	Woman of Theresia (Greek)
Thomas	Twin (Hebrew)

Communications

Name	Original meaning		Name	Original meaning
Tiffany	Manifestation of God (Greek)		Vincent	Conquer (Latin)
Timothy	Honouring God (Greek)		Virginia	Maiden (Latin)
Trac(e)y	?Pet form of Teresa		Walter	Ruling people (Germanic)
Vera	Faith (Slavic)		Wayne	Surname; wagon-maker
Victoria	Victory (Latin)		William	Will + helmet (Germanic)
			Zoë	Life (Greek)

Common abbreviations

AA	Alcoholics Anonymous
AA	Automobile Association
AA(A)	anti-aircraft (artillery)
AAA	Amateur Athletics Association
AAA	American Automobile Association
ABA	Amateur Boxing Association
ABA	American Broadcasting Association
ABC	Australian Broadcasting Corporation
ABM	antiballistic missile
ABTA	Association of British Travel Agents
AC	alternating current
ACAS	Advisory, Conciliation, and Arbitration Service
ACLU	American Civil Liberties Union
ACT	Australian Capital Territory
ACTH	adrenocorticotrophic hormone
ACTU	Australian Council of Trade Unions
AD	anno Domini (in the year of Our Lord)
A-D	analog-to-digital (in computing)
ADH	antidiuretic hormone
ADP	adenosine diphosphate
AEA	Atomic Energy Authority (UK)
AEC	Atomic Energy Commission (USA)
AFC	American Football Conference
AFL/CIO	American Federation of Labor/Congress of Industrial Organizations
AFP	Agence France Presse
AFV	armoured fighting vehicle
AGM	annual general meeting
AGR	advanced gas-cooled reactor
AH	anno Hegirae (in the year of Hegira)
AHF	anti-haemophilic factor
AI	artificial intelligence
AID	artificial insemination by donor
AIDS	Acquired Immune Deficiency Syndrome
AIF	Australian Imperial Force
AIH	artificial insemination by husband
ALCM	air-launched cruise missile
ALGOL	algorithmic language
ALP	Australian Labor Party
ALU	arithmetic and logic unit
AM	amplitude modulation
AMA	American Medical Association
AMU	atomic mass unit
ANC	African National Congress
ANS	autonomic nervous system
ANSI	American National Standards Institute
ANZAC	Australian and New Zealand Army Corps
ANZUS	Australia, New Zealand and the United States
AOB	any other business
AONB	Area of Outstanding Natural Beauty
AP	Associated Press
APEX	Association of Professional, Executive, Clerical, and Computer Staff
APL	A Programming Language
APR	annual percentage rate
APRA	Alianza Popular Revolutionaria Americana (American Popular Revolutionary Alliance)
AR	aspect ratio
ARCIC	Anglican–Roman Catholic International Commission
A/S	Advanced/Supplementary
ASA	American Standards Association
ASCII	American Standards Code for Information Interchange
ASDIC	Admiralty Submarine Detection Investigation Committee
ASEAN	Association of South-East Asian Nations
ASL	American Sign Language
ASLEF	Associated Society of Locomotive Engineers and Firemen
ASLIB	Association of Special Libraries and Information Bureaux
ASM	air-to-surface missile
ASPCA	American Society for the Prevention of Cruelty to Animals
ASSR	Autonomous Soviet Socialist Republic
ASTMS	Association of Scientific, Technical, and Managerial Staffs
ATP	adenosine triphosphate
ATS	Auxiliary Territorial Service
ATV	Associated Television
AU	astronomical unit
AV	audio-visual
AWACS	Airborne Warning and Control System
AWU	Australian Workers' Union
B&W	black and white
BAFTA	British Academy of Film and Television Arts
BALPA	British Airline Pilots' Association
BASIC	Beginners All-purpose Symbolic Instruction Code
BASIC	British American Scientific International Commercial (English)
BBC	British Broadcasting Corporation
BC	before Christ
BCD	binary coded decimal
BCG	bacille (bacillus) Calmette Guérin
BCS	Bardeen, Cooper & Schrieffer (theory)
BEF	British Expeditionary Force
BEV	Black English Vernacular
BHP	Broken Hill Proprietary Company
BIA	Bureau of Indian Affairs
BIS	Bank for International Settlements
BLAISE	British Library Automated Information Service
BMA	British Medical Association

Common abbreviations (continued)

BOSS	Bureau of State Security (South Africa)
BP	blood pressure
BSE	bovine spongiform encephalopathy
BSI	British Standards Institution
BST	British Summer Time
btu	British thermal unit
BUF	British Union of Fascists
BUPA	British United Provident Association
CAB	Citizen's Advice Bureau
CACM	Central American Common Market
CAD	computer-aided design
CAI	computer-aided instruction
CAL	computer-aided learning
CAM	computer-aided manufacture
CAP	Common Agricultural Policy
CARICOM	Caribbean Community
CARIFTA	Caribbean Free Trade Area
CATV	cable television
CB	citizen's band (radio)
CBE	Commander of the (Order of the) British Empire
CBI	Confederation of British Industry
CBS	Columbia Broadcasting System
CCD	charge-coupled device
CCK	cholecystokinin-pancreozymin
CCR	camera cassette recorder
CCTV	closed-circuit television
CD	Civil Defence
CD	compact disc
CDC	Centers for Disease Control
CDROM	compact disc read-only memory
CDU	Christian Democratic Union
CENTO	Central Treaty Organization
CERN	Organisation Européene pour la Recherche Nucléaire (formerly, Conseil Européen pour la Recherche Nucléaire)
CGS	centimetre-gram-second
CGT	capital gains tax
CGT	Confédération Générale du Travail
CH	Companion of Honour
CHAPS	Clearing House Automated Clearing System
CHIPS	Clearing House Interbank Payments System
CIA	Central Intelligence Agency
CID	Criminal Investigation Department
CIO	Congress of Industrial Organizations
CM	Congregation of the Mission
CMG	Companion of (the Order of) St Michael & St George
CNAA	Council for National Academic Awards
CND	Campaign for Nuclear Disarmament
CNES	Centre National d'Espace
CNS	central nervous system
COBOL	Common Business Oriented Language
COMAL	Common Algorithmic Language
COMECON	Council for Mutual Economic Assistance
CORE	Congress of Racial Equality
CP	Congregation of the Passion
CPI	Consumer Price Index
CP/M	control program monitor
CPR	cardio-pulmonary resuscitation
CPU	central processing unit
CRO	cathode-ray oscilloscope
CRT	cathode-ray tube

CSE	Certificate of Secondary Education
CSF	cerebrospinal fluid
CSIRO	Commonwealth Scientific and Industrial Research Organization
CSO	colour separation overlay
CTT	capital transfer tax
CV	cultivar
CVO	Commander of the Royal Victorian Order
CVS	chorionic villus sampling
CWA	County Women's Association
CWS	Cooperative Wholesale Society
D-A	digital-to-analog (in computing)
DALR	dry adiabatic lapse rate
D&C	dilation and curettage
DBE	Dame Commander of the (Order of the) British Empire
DBMS	database management system
DBS	direct broadcasting from satellite
DC	direct current
DCF	discounted cash flow
DCMG	Dame Commander Grand Cross of (the Order of) St Michael and St George
DCVO	Dame Commander of the Royal Victorian Order
DDT	dichloro-diphenyl-trichloroethane
DES	Department of Education and Science
DES	diethylstilboestrol
DFC	Distinguished Flying Cross
DHA	District Health Authority
DIA	Defence Intelligence Agency
DLP	Democratic Labor Party (Australia)
DMSO	dimethyl sulphoxide
DNA	deoxyribonucleic acid
DOS	disk-operating system
DSN	Deep Space Network
DSO	Distinguished Service Order
DST	daylight-saving time
DTP	desk-top publishing
EAC	European Atomic Commission
EARM	electrically alterable read-only memory
EBCDIC	extended binary-coded decimal interchange code
EBU	European Boxing Union
EBU	European Broadcasting Union
EC	European Community
ECA	European Commission on Agriculture
ECF	extracellular fluid
ECG	electrocardiograph
ECM	European Common Market
ECO	European Coal Organization
ECOSOC	Economic and Social Council (of the United Nations)
ECOWAS	Economic Community of West African States
ECSC	European Coal and Steel Community
ECT	electroconvulsive therapy
ECTG	European Channel Tunnel Group
ECU	European currency unit
EDC	European Defence Community
EDVAC	Electronic Discrete Variable Automatic Computer
EEG	electroencephalograph
EEOC	Equal Employment Opportunity Commission

Communications

EFA	European Fighter Aircraft
EFC	European Forestry Commission
EFTA	European Free Trade Association
EGF	epidermal growth factor
EI	Exposure Index
ELDO	European Launcher Development Organization
ELF	Eritrea Liberation Front
EMF	electromotive force
EMS	European Monetary System
EMU	electromagnetic units
ENIAC	Electronic Numeral Indicator and Calculator
EOKA	Ethniki Organosis Kipriakou Agonos (National Organization of Cypriot Struggle)
EP	European Parliament
EPA	Environmental Protection Agency
EPR	Einstein-Podolsky-Rosen (paradox)
EPR	electron paramagnetic resonance
EPROM	electronically programmable read-only memory
ERNIE	Electronic Random Number Indicator Equipment
ERW	enhanced radiation weapon
ESA	Environmentally Sensitive Area
ESA	European Space Agency
ESC	electronic stills camera
ESCU	European Space Operations Centre
ESO	European Southern Observatory
ESP	extra-sensory perception
ESRO	European Space Research Organization
ESTEC	European Space Research and Technology Centre
ETU	Electricians Trade Union
EUFA	European Union Football Associations
EURATOM	European Atomic Energy Community
FA	Football Association
FAA	Federal Aviation Administration
FAO	Food and Agriculture Organization
FBI	Federal Bureau of Investigation
FCA	Farm Credit Administration
FCC	Federal Communications Commission
FDIC	Federal Deposit Insurance Corporation
FIFA	Fédération Internationale de Football Association (International Association Football Federation)
FIMBRA	Financial Intermediaries, Managers and Brokers Regulatory Association
FLN	Front de Libération Nationale (National Liberation Front)
FM	frequency modulation
FORTRAN	formula translation
FPS	foot-pound-second
FRELIMO	Frente de Libertação de Moçambique (liberation Front of Mozambique)
FSH	follicle-stimulating hormone
FTC	Federal Trade Commission
GAR	Grand Army of the Republic
GATT	General Agreement on Tariffs and Trade
GBE	Knight/Dame Grand Cross of (the Order of the) British Empire
GC	George Cross
GCC	Gulf Co-operation Council
GCE	General Certificate of Education

GCHQ	Government Communications Headquarters
GCMG	Knight/Dame Grand Cross of (the Order of) St Michael and St George
GCSE	General Certificate of Secondary Education
GCVO	Knight/Dame Grand Cross of the Royal Victorian Order
GDI	gross domestic income
GDP	gross domestic product
GEO	geosynchronous Earth orbit
GESP	generalized extra-sensory perception
GH	growth hormone
GLC	gas-liquid chromatography
GLCM	ground-launched cruise missile
GM	George Medal
GMC	General Medical Council
GMT	Greenwich Mean Time
GNP	gross national product
GnRH	gonadotrophin-releasing hormone
GP	General Practitioner
GPSS	General Purpose System Simulator
GUT	grand unified theory
HCG	human chorionic gonadotrophin
HE	His/Her Excellency
HEP	hydro-electric power
HF	high frequency
HGV	heavy goods vehicle
HIH	His/Her Imperial Highness
HIM	His/Her Imperial Majesty
HLA	human leucocyte antigen
HM	His/Her Majesty
HMG	His/Her Majesty's Government
HMI	His/Her Majesty's Inspectorate
HMO	health maintenance organization
HMS	His/Her Majesty's Ship/Service
HMSO	His/Her Majesty's Stationery Office
HNC	Higher National Certificate
HND	Higher National Diploma
HP	horsepower
HR	House of Representatives
HRH	His/Her Royal Highness
IAEA	International Atomic Energy Agency
IBRD	International Bank for Reconstruction and Development
ICAO	International Civil Aviation Organization
ICFTU	International Confederation of Free Trade Unions
ICI	Imperial Chemical Industries
IDA	International Development Agency
IFAD	International Fund for Agricultural Development
IFC	International Finance Corporation
ILO	International Labour Organization
IMCO	Intergovernmental Maritime Consultative Organization
IMF	International Monetary Fund
INLA	Irish National Liberation Army
INRI	Iesus Nazarenus Rex Iudeorum (Jesus of Nazareth, King of the Jews)
IPA	International Phonetic Alphabet
IQ	intelligence quotient
IR	infrared
IRA	Irish Republican Army
IRB	Irish Republican Brotherhood
IRBM	intermediate-range ballistic missile

Communications

Common abbreviations (continued)

ISBN	International Standard Book Number		MATV	Master Antenna Television
ISO	International Organization for Standardization		MBE	Member of the Order of the British Empire
ISSN	International Standard Serial Number		MCA	monetary compensation amount
ITA	Initial Teaching Alphabet		MCC	Marylebone Cricket Club
ITCZ	intertropical convergence zone		MDMA	methylenedioxymethamphetamine
ITN	Independent Television News		ME	myalgic encephalomyelitis
ITT	International Telephone and Telegraph Corporation		MH	Medal of Honor
			MHD	magnetohydrodynamics
ITU	International Telecommunication Union		MICR	magnetic ink character recognition
ITV	Independent Television		MIRED	micro reciprocal degrees
IUCN	International Union for the Conservation of Nature and Natural Resources		MIRV	multiple independently targetted re-entry vehicle
IUD	intra-uterine device		MKSA	metre-kilogram-second-ampere
IUPAC	International Union of Pure and Applied Chemistry		MLR	minimum lending rate
			MMF	magnetomotive force
IUPAP	International Union of Pure and Applied Physics		MMI	man-machine interaction
			MOH	Medal of Honor
IVF	in vitro fertilization		MPC	megaparsec
IVR	International Vehicle Registration		MPS	marginal propensity to save
IWW	Industrial Workers of the World		MPTP	methylphenyltetrahydropyridine
			MRA	Moral Rearmament
JET	Joint European Torus		MSC	Manpower Services Commission
JP	Justice of the Peace		MSG	monosodium glutamate
JPL	Jet Propulsion Laboratory		MSH	melanocyte-stimulating hormone
			MVD	Ministerstvo Vnutrennykh Del (Ministry for Internal Affairs)
KADU	Kenya African Democratic Union			
KANU	Kenya African National Union		MVO	Member of the Royal Victorian Order
KB	Knight Bachelor; Knight of the Bath			
KBE	Knight Commander of the (Order of the) British Empire		NAACP	National Association for the Advancement of Coloured People
KC	King's Counsel		NANC	non-adrenergic non-cholinergic
KCB	Knight Commander of the Bath		NASA	National Aeronautics and Space Administration
KCMG	Knight Commander Grand Cross of (the Order of) St Michael and St George		NASDA	National Space Development Agency
KCVO	Knight Commander of The Royal Victorian Order		NATO	North Atlantic Treaty Organization
			NBC	National Broadcasting Corporation
KG	Knight of the Order of the Garter		NDE	near-death experience
KGB	Komitet Gosudarstvennoye Bezhopaznosti (Committee of State Security)		NEDO	National Economic Development Office
			NEP	new economic policy
KKK	Ku Klux Klan		NF	National Front
KMT	Kuomintang		NFC	National Football Conference
kPC	kiloparsec		NGC	new general catalogue
KT	Knight of the Thistle		NGF	nerve growth factor
			NHL	National Hockey League
LAFTA	Latin American Free Trade Association		NHS	National Health Service
LAN	local area network		NIH	National Institutes of Health
LAUTRO	Life Assurance and Unit Trust Companies		NKVD	Narodnyi Komissariat Vnutrennikh Del (People's Commissariat of Internal Affairs)
LCD	liquid-crystal display			
LDC	less-developed country			
LEA	Local Education Authority		NLRB	National Labor Relations Board
LED	light-emitting diode		NMR	nuclear magnetic resonance
LEO	low Earth orbit		NOW	National Organization for Women
LFA	less favoured area		NPT	Non-Proliferation Treaty
LH	luteinizing hormone		NRA	National Recovery Administration
LHRH	luteinizing-hormone-releasing hormone		NRAO	National Radio Astronomy Observatory
LIFFE	London International Financial Futures Exchange		NSF	National Science Foundation
			NSPCC	National Society for the Prevention of Cruelty to Children
LISP	list processing			
LMS	London Missionary Society		NTSC	National Television System Commission
LPG	liquefied petroleum gas		NUM	National Union of Mineworkers
LSD	lysergic acid diethylamide		NUT	National Union of Teachers
LSI	large-scale integration		NVC	non-verbal communication
LVO	Lieutenant of the Royal Victorian Order			
			OAPEC	Organization of Arab Petroleum Exporting Countries
MAC	multiplexed analogue component			
MAO	monoamine oxidase			

Communications

OAS	Organisation de l'Armée Secrète (Secret Army Organization)	PLA	People's Liberation Army
OAS	Organization of American States	PLC	public limited company
OAU	Organization of African Unity	PLO	Palestine Liberation Organization
OB	Order of the Bath	PM of F	Presidential Medal of Freedom
OB	outside broadcast	PNLM	Palestine National Liberation Movement
OBE	Officer of the (Order of the) British Empire	POW	prisoner of war
OCARM	Order of the Brothers of the Blessed Virgin Mary of Mount Carmel	PPI	plan position indicator
		PR	proportional representation
		PRO	Public Record Office
OCART	Order of Carthusians	PRO	public relations officer
OCR	optical character recognition/reader	PROM	programmable read-only memory
OCSO	Order of the Reformed Cistercians of the Strict Observance	PSBR	public sector borrowing requirement
		PTA	parent-teacher association
OD	ordnance datum	PTFE	polytetrafluoroethylene
ODC	Order of Discalced Carmelites	PVA	polyvinyl acetate
ODECA	Organizacion de Estados Centro Americanos (Organization of Central American States)	PVC	polyvinyl chloride
		PWA	Public Works Administration
		PWR	pressurized-water reactor
OECD	Organization for Economic Co-operation and Development	PYO	pick-your-own
		QC	Queen's Counsel
OEEC	Organization for European Economic Co-operation	QCD	quantum chromodynamics
		QED	quantum electrodynamics
OEM	Original Equipment Manufacturer	RA	Royal Academy
OFM	Order of Friars Minor	R&A	Royal & Ancient Golf Club of St Andrews
OFMCap	Order of Friars Minor Capuchin	RAAF	Royal Australian Air Force
OFMConv	Order of Friars Minor Conventual	RADA	Royal Academy of Dramatic Art
OGPU	Otdelenie Gosudarstvenni Politcheskoi Upravi (Special Government Political Administration)	RAF	Royal Air Force
		RAM	random access memory
		RAM	Royal Academy of Music
OM	Order of Merit	RAN	Royal Australian Navy
OMCap	Order of Friars Minor of St Francis Capuccinorum	RDA	recommended daily allowance
		REM	rapid eye movement
OOBE	out-of-body experience	RGB	red, green and blue (colour television)
OP	Order of Preachers	RHA	Regional Health Authority
OPEC	Organization of Petroleum Exporting Countries	RISC	Reduced Instruction Set Computer
		RKKA	Rabochekrest'yanshi Krasny (Red Army of Workers and Peasants)
OSA	Order of the Hermit Friars of St Augustine		
OSB	Order of St Benedict	RM	Royal Marines
OSFC	Order of Friars Minor of St Francis Capuccinorum	RMS	root mean square
		RN	Royal Navy
OTC	over-the-counter (stocks and shares, drugs)	RNA	ribonucleic acid
		RNLI	Royal National Lifeboat Institution
OTEC	ocean thermal energy conversion	ROM	read-only memory
OU	Open University	RP	received pronunciation
OXFAM	Oxford Committee for Famine Relief	RPI	retail price index
		RPM	resale price maintenance
PAC	Pan-African Congress	RPM	revolutions per minute
PAC	political action committee	RS	Royal Society
PAL	phase alternation line	RSPB	Royal Society for the Protection of Birds
PAYE	pay as you earn	RSPCA	Royal Society for the Prevention of Cruelty to Animals
PC	parsec		
PC	personal computer	RTG	radio-isotope thermo-electric generator
PC	Poor Clares	RVO	Royal Victorian Order
PCP	phenylcyclohexylpiperidine	SA	Sturm Abteilung (Storm Troopers)
PDGF	platelet-derived growth factor	SALR	saturated adiabatic lapse rate
PDR	precision depth recorder	SALT	Strategic Arms Limitation Talks
PEN	International Association of Poets, Playwrights, Editors, Essayists, and Novelists	SAS	Special Air Service
		SBR	styrene butadiene rubber
		SCID	severe combined immuno-deficiency
PEP	Political and Economic Planning	SCLC	Southern Christian Leadership Conference
PF	Patriotic Front		
PGA	Professional Golfers' Association	SDI	selective dissemination of information
PH	Purple Heart	SDI	strategic defence initiative
PIN	personal identification number	SDP	Social Democratic Party
PK	psychokinesis	SDR	special drawing rights
PKU	phenylketonuria		

Common abbreviations (continued)

SDS	Students for a Democratic Society
SDU	Social Democratic Union
SEAQ	Stock Exchange Automated Quotations
SEATO	South-East Asia Treaty Organization
SEC	Securities and Exchange Commission
SECAM	Séquence Electronique Couleur avec Mémoire (Electronic Colour Sequence with Memory)
SERPS	State earnings-related pension scheme
SHAEF	Supreme Headquarters Allied Expeditionary Force
SHAPE	Supreme Headquarters Allied Powers, Europe
SHF	super-high frequency
SI	Système International (International System)
SIB	Securities and Investments Board
SIOP	single integrated operation plan
SJ	Society of Jesus
SLBM	submarine-launched ballistic missile
SLCM	sea-launched cruise missile
SLDP	Social and Liberal Democratic Party
SLE	systemic lupus erythematosus
SLR	single-lens reflex
SNCC	Student Non-Violent Co-ordinating Committee
SNOBOL	String-Oriented Symbolic Language
SNP	Scottish National Party
SOCist	Cistercians of Common Observance
SOE	Special Operations Executive
SONAR	sound navigation and ranging
SQUID	superconducting quantum interference device
SRO	self-regulatory organization
SRO	single room occupancy
SS	Schutzstaffel (Protective Squad)
SSR	Soviet Socialist Republic
SSSI	Site of Special Scientific Interest
START	Strategic Arms Reduction Talks
STOL	short take-off and landing
SWAPO	South-West Africa People's Organization
SWS	slow-wave sleep
TAB	Totalizator Agency Board
TARDIS	time and relative dimensions in space
TASS	Telegrafnoe Agentsvo Sovetskovo Soyuza (Telegraph Agency of the Soviet Union)
TCDD	tetrachlorodibenzo-p-dioxin
TEFL	Teaching English as a Foreign Language
TESL	Teaching English as a Second Language
TGWU	Transport and General Workers Union
TNT	trinitrotoluene
TT	Tourist Trophy
TTL	through the lens
TUC	Trades Union Congress
TV	television
TVA	Tennessee Valley Authority
UAE	United Arab Emirates
UAP	United Australia Party
UCAR	Union of Central African Republics
UCCA	University Central Council on Admissions
UDA	Ulster Defence Association
UDI	Unilateral Declaration of Independence
UEFA	Union of European Football Associations
UFO	unidentified flying object
UHF	ultra-high frequency
UHT	ultra-high temperature
UK	United Kingdom
UN	United Nations
UNCTAD	United Nations Conference on Trade and Development
UNDC	United Nations Disarmament Commission
UNDP	United Nations Development Programme
UNEP	United Nations Environment Programme
UNESCO	United Nations Economic, Scientific and Cultural Organization
UNFAO	United Nations Food and Agriculture Organization
UNGA	United Nations General Assembly
UNHCR	United Nations High Commission for Refugees
UNHRC	United Nations Human Rights Commissioner
UNICEF	United Nations Children's Fund (formerly UN International Children's Emergency Fund)
UNIDO	United Nations Industrial Development Organization
UNO	United Nations Organization
UNRWA	United Nations Relief and Works Agency for Palestine Refugees in the Near East
UNSC	United Nations Security Council
UNSG	United Nations Secretary General
UNTT	United Nations Trust Territory
UPU	Universal Postal Union
USA	United States of America
USAF	United States Air Force
USCG	United States Coast Guard
USIS	United States Information Service
USSR	Union of Soviet Socialist Republics
VA	Veterans Administration
VAT	value-added tax
VC	Victoria Cross
VCR	video cassette recorder
VD	venereal disease
VDU	visual display unit
VHF	very high frequency
VHS	video home system
VIP	vasoactive intestinal polypeptide
VLF	very low frequency
VLSI	very large scale interpretation
VOA	Voice of America
VSEPR	valence-shell electron pair repulsion
VSO	Voluntary Service Overseas
VTOL	vertical take-off and landing
VTR	video tape recorder
WAAC	Women's Auxiliary Army Corps
WAAF	Women's Auxiliary Air Force
WAC	Women's Army Corps
WASP	White Anglo-Saxon Protestant
WBA	World Boxing Association
WBC	World Boxing Council
WCC	World Council of Churches
WEA	Workers' Educational Association
WFTU	World Federation of Trade Unions
WHO	World Health Organization
WI	(National Federation of) Women's Institutes

WIPO	World Intellectual Property Organization		WVS	Women's Voluntary Service	
WMO	World Meteorological Organization		WWF	World Wildlife Fund	
WPA	Work Projects Administration		YHA	Youth Hostels Association	
WRAC	Women's Royal Army Corps		YMCA	Young Men's Christian Association	
WRAF	Women's Royal Air Force		YMHA	Young Men's Hebrew Association	
WRNS	Women's Royal Naval Service		YWCA	Young Women's Christian Association	
WRVS	Women's Royal Voluntary Service		YWHA	Young Women's Hebrew Association	

MEDIA

News agencies

Agency		Headquartered	Agency		Headquartered
AA	Anadol Ajansi	Ankara	CNS	China News Service	Beijing
AAP	Australian Associated Press	Sydney	COLPRENSA	Colprensa	Bogota
AASA	Agence Arabe Syrienne d'Information	Damascus	CP	Canadian Press	Toronto
ADN	Allgemeiner Deutscher Nachrichtendienst	Berlin	CSTK	Ceskoslovenska Tiskova Kancelar	Prague
AE	Agence Europe	Brussels	DPA	Deutsche Presse Agentur	Hamburg
AFP	Agence France Presse	Paris	EFE	Agencia EFE	Madrid
AIO	Agencia Informativa Orbe de Chile	Santiago	ENA	Eastern News Agency	Dhaka
			ETA	Eesti Teadate Agentuur	Tallinn
AIP	Agence Ivoirienne de Presse	Abidjan	EXTEL	Exchange and Telegraph Company	London
ALD	Agence Los Diarios	Buenos Aires			
ALI	Agencia Lusa de Informacao	Lisbon	FIDES	Agenzia Internazionale Fides	Vatican City
AM	Agencia Meridional	Rio de Janeiro			
AN	Agencia Nacional	Brasilia	GNA	Agence Guinéenne de Presse	Conakry
ANA	Athenagence	Athens			
ANGOP	Angola Agêcia Naticiosa N'gola Press	Luanda	GNA	Ghana News Agency	Accra
			GNA	Guyana News Agency	Georgetown
ANP	Algemeen Nederlands Persbureau	The Hague	HHA	Hurriyet Haber Ajasi	Istanbul
			HINA	Hrvatska Izvjestajna Novinska Agencija	Zagreb
ANSA	Agenzia Nazionale Stampa Associate	Rome	IC	Inforpress Centroamericana	Guatemala
ANTARA	Indonesian National News Agency	Jakarta	INA	Iraqi News Agency	Baghdad
			IPS	Inter Press Service	Rome
AP	Associated Press	New York	IRNA	Islamic Republic News Agency	Tehran
APA	Austria Presse Agentur	Vienna			
APP	Agence Parisienne de Presse	Paris	ITIM	Associated Israel Press	Tel Aviv
APP	Associated Press of Pakistan	Islamabad	JAMPRESS	Jampress	Kingston
APS	Agence de Presse Senegalaise	Dakar	JANA	Jamahiriya News Agency	Tripoli
			JIJI	Jiji Tsushin-Sha	Tokyo
APS	Algeria Presse Service	Algiers	JTA	Jewish Telegraphic Agency	Jerusalem
ATA	Albanian Telegraphic Agency	Tirana	KCNA	Korean Central News Agency	Pyongyang
AUP	Australian United Press	Melbourne	KNA	Kenya News Agency	Nairobi
BATRA	Jordan News Agency	Amman	KPL	Khao San Pathet Lao	Vientiane
BELGA	Agence Belga	Brussels	KUNA	Kuwait News Agency	Kuwait City
BERNAMA	Malaysian National News Agency	Kuala Lumpur	KYODO	Kyodo Tsushin	Tokyo
			LAI	Logos Agencia de Informacion	Madrid
BOPA	Botswana Press Agency	Gaborone	LETA	Latvijas Telegrafa Agentura	Riga
BSS	Bangladesh Sangbad Sangstha	Dhaka	MENA	Middle East News Agency	Cairo
			MTI	Magyar Tavariti Iroda	Budapest
BTA	Bulgarska Telegrafitscheka Agentzia	Sofia	NA	Noticias Argentinas	Buenos Aires
			NAEWOE	Naewoe Press	Seoul
CANA	Caribbean News Agency	Bridgetown	NAN	News Agency of Nigeria	Lagos
CIP	Centre d'Information de Presse	Brussels	NOTIMEX	Noticias Mexicanas	Mexico City
			NOVOSTI	Agentstvo Pechati Novosti	Moscow
CNA	Central News Agency	Taipei	NPS	Norsk Presse Service	Oslo
CNA	Cyprus News Agency	Nicosia	NTB	Norsk Telegrambyra	Oslo

Communications

Media

News agencies (continued)

Agency		Headquartered	Agency		Headquartered
NZPA	New Zealand Press Agency	Wellington	SLENA	Sierra Leone News Agency	Freetown
OPA	Orbis Press Agency	Prague	SOFIAPRES	Sofia Press Agency	Sofia
OTTFNB	Oy Suomen Tietoimisto Notisbyran Ab	Helsinki	SOPAC-NEWS	South Pacific News Service	Wellington
PA	Press Association	London	SPA	Saudi Press Agency	Riyadh
PANA	Pan-African News Agency	Dakar	SPK	Saporamean Kampuchea	Phnom Penh
PAP	Polska Agencija Prasowa	Warsaw	STA	Slovenska Tiskovna Agencija	Ljubljana
PNA	Philippines News Agency	Manila	TANJUG	Novinska Agencija Tanjug	Belgrade
PPI	Pakistan Press International	Karachi	TAP	Tunis Afrique Presse	Tunis
PRELA	Prensa Latina	Havana	TASS	Telegraph Agency of the Sovereign States	Moscow
PS	Presse Services	Paris			
PTI	Press Trust of India	Bombay	TT	Tidningarnes Telegrambyra	Stockholm
RB	Ritzaus Bureau	Copenhagen	UNI	United News of India	New Delhi
REUTERS	Reuters	London	UPI	United Press International	New York
ROMPRESS	Romanian News Agency	Bucharest	UPP	United Press of Pakistan	Karachi
SAPA	South African Press Association	Johannesburg	VNA	Vietnam News Agency	Hanoi
			XINHUA	Xinhua	Beijing
SDA	Schweizerische Depeschenagentur	Berne	YONHAP	Yonhap (United) Press Agency	Seoul
SIP	Svensk Internationella Pressbyran	Stockholm	ZIANA	Zimbabwe Inter-Africa News Agency	Harare

Government information departments

Country	Department	Country	Department
Afghanistan	Ministry of Information and Culture	Cameroon	Ministry of Information and Culture
American Samoa	Public Information Office	Cape Verde	Ministry of Information, Culture, and Sport
Andorra	Ministry of Tourism and Sport	Central African Republic	Ministry of Communication
Angola	Ministry of Information		
Antigua & Barbuda	Public Information Division	Chad	Ministry of Information, Culture, and Civic Orientation
Argentina	Secretaria de Información Publica (SIP)	Chile	Communications Secretariat; Office of the Minister Secretary-General of the Government
Bahamas	Office of the Prime Minister		
Bahrain	Ministry of Information		
Bangladesh	Press Information Department		
Barbados	Barbados Government Information Service (BGIS)	Colombia	Ministry of Communications
Belau	Public Information Division	Comoros	Ministry of Information and Broadcasting
Belize	Government Information Service	Congo	Ministry of Information
Benin	Ministry of Culture and Communications	Costa Rica	General Directorate of Information and the Press
Bermuda	Department of Information Services	Côte d'Ivoire	Ministry of Communications
		Cuba	Publications Office
Bhutan	Department of Information and Broadcasting	Cyprus	Press and Information Office
		Cyprus, north	Public Information Office
Bolivia	Ministry of Information	Denmark	Statens Informationstjeneste
Botswana	Department of Information and Broadcasting	Djibouti	Ministry of the Interior
		Dominica	Office of the Prime Minister
Brazil	Serviço Nacional das Informaçaos	Ecuador	Secretariat for Public Information
Brunei	Department of Broadcasting and Information	Egypt	Ministry of Information
		El Salvador	Centro de Información Nacional
Burkina Faso	Ministry of Information and Culture	Ethiopia	Ministry of Information and National Guidance
Burundi	Ministry of Communication	Faroe Islands	Faroes Government
Cambodia	Ministry of Information and Culture	Fiji	Ministry of Information

France	Service d'Information et de Diffusion	Namibia	Ministry of Information and Broadcasting
Gabon	Ministry of Information, Posts, and Telecommunications	Nauru	Office of the President
		Nepal	Department of Information
Gambia	Ministry of Information and Tourism	Netherlands	Foreign Information Service
		Nicaragua	Communications Media Bureau
Germany	Press and Information Office of the Federal Government	Niger	Ministry of Information
		Nigeria	Ministry of Information
Ghana	Castle Information Bureau; Secretariat for Information	Northern Marianas	Governor's Office
		Oman	Ministry of Information
Gibraltar	General Division	Pakistan	Ministry of Information and Broadcasting
Greece	General Secretariat for Press and Information	Palestine	Information Department (of the Palestine Liberation Organization)
Greenland	Greenland Home Government; Ministry for Greenland		
Grenada	Ministry of Information	Papua New Guinea	Office of Information
Guam	Governor's Office	Paraguay	Ministry of the Interior
Guinea	Department for Information, Culture, and Tourism	Peru	Instituto Nacional de Comunicación Social
Guinea-Bissau	Ministry of Information and Telecommunications	Philippines	Office of the Press Secretary; Philippine Information Agency
Haiti	Ministry of Information	Qatar	Ministry of Information and Culture
Hong Kong	Government Information Service		
Iceland	Prime Minister's Office	Rwanda	L'Office Rwandais d'Information
India	Press Information Bureau	St Kitts & Nevis	Government Headquarters
Indonesia	Ministry of Information	St Lucia	Ministry of Information and Broadcasting
Iran	Ministry of Information		
Iraq	Ministry of Information and Culture	St Vincent & the Grenadines	Ministry of Information
Israel	Government Press Office	San Marino	Secretariat of State for Foreign and Political Affairs
Jamaica	Ministry of Information and Culture		
		São Tomé & Príncipe	Ministry of Information; Directorate of Information
Jordan	Ministry of Information	Saudi Arabia	Ministry of Information
Kenya	Ministry of Information and Broadcasting	Senegal	Ministry of Culture and Communications
Kiribati	Department of Information	Seychelles	Department of Information and Telecommunications
Korea, South	Ministry of Public Information		
Kuwait	Ministry of Information	Sierra Leone	Ministry of Information and Broadcasting
Laos	Committee for Information, Press, Radio, and Television and Broadcasting	Singapore	Ministry of Communications and Information
Latvia	Department of Information	Solomon Islands	Government Information Service
Lebanon	Ministry of Information		
Lesotho	Ministry of Information and Broadcasting	Somalia	Ministry of Information and National Guidance
Liberia	Ministry of Information	South Africa	Bureau of Information
Liechtenstein	Press and Information Office	Spain	Ministry of the Government Spokesperson
Lithuania	Information Department		
Luxembourg	Ministry of State	Sri Lanka	Department for Broadcasting and Information
Madagascar	Ministry of Information		
Malawi	Department of Information	Sudan	Ministry and Culture and Information
Malaysia	Ministry of Information		
Maldives	Department of Information and Broadcasting	Swaziland	Broadcasting and Information Service
Mali	Ministry of Information and Telecommunications	Syria	Ministry of Information
		Taiwan	Government Information Office
Malta	Department of Information	Tanzanian	Ministry of Information and Broadcasting
Marshall Islands	Office of the Chief Secretary		
Mauritania	Ministry of Information	Thailand	Public Relations Department
Mauritius	Ministry of Communications and Information	Togo	Ministry of Information
		Tonga	Government Information Unit
Monaco	Directorate of Tourism	Trinidad & Tobago	Government Information Service
Morocco	Ministry of Information		
Mozambique	Ministry of Information	Turkey	General Directorate of Press and Information
Myanmar	Ministry of Information		

Government information departments (continued)

Tuvalu	Broadcasting and Information Division	United Arab Emirates	Ministry of Information and Culture
Uganda	Ministry of Information and Broadcasting	United Kingdom	Central Office of Information

Publishing

Newspaper publishers' associations

Argentina	Asociación de Editores de Diarios de Buenos Aires
Australia	Australian Newspapers Council; Country Press Australia; Regional Dailies of Australia
Austria	Verband Österreichischer Zeitungsherausgeber und Zeitungsverleger (VÖZZ)
Bangladesh	Bangladesh Council of Newspapers and News Agencies
Belgium	Belgische Vereniging van de Dagbladuitgevers
Brazil	Asociaçio Brasileira de Imprensa
Canada	Canadian Daily Newspaper Publishers' Association
Chile	Asociación Nacional de la Prensa
Colombia	Asociación Nacional de Medios de Communicación
Denmark	Danske Dagblades Forening (DDF)
El Salvador	Asociación Salvadoreña de Empresarios de Radiodifusión (ASDER)
Finland	Sanomalehtien Liitto/Tindningamas Förbund
France	Fédération Nationale de la Presse Française
Germany	Bundesverband Deutscher Zeitungsverleger
Guinea	Guinean Association of Independent Press Publishers (AGEPI)
Hong Kong	Hsiangkang Hua Wenpaoyeh Hsieh-hui; Newspaper Society of Hong Kong/ Hsiangkang Paoyeh Kunghui
India	Indian Languages Newspapers' Association; Indian Newspaper Society
Indonesia	Serikat Penerbit Suratkabar
Israel	Igud Ha'itonim Hayomiyim Beyisra'el
Italy	Federazione Italiana Editori Giornali; Federazione Nazionale della Stampa Italiana
Japan	Nihon Shimbun Kyokai; Nihon Zasshi Kyokai
Korea, South	Han'guk Shinmun Hypuhoe
Lebanon	Niqabat al-Mukhbirun al-Lubnaniyun
Luxembourg	Association Luxembourgeoise des Editeurs de Journaux
Malaysia	Persatuan Penerbit-Penerbit Akhbar Malaysia
Mexico	Asociación de Diarios Independentes; Asociación de Editores de Periódicos Diarios de la República Mexicana
Netherlands	Vereniging De Nederlandse Dagbladpers
New Zealand	Community Newspapers' Association; Newspaper Publishers' Association of New Zealand
Nigeria	Newspaper Proprietors' Organization of Nigeria
Norway	Norsk Presseforbund; Norsk Avisers Landsforbund
Pakistan	All Pakistan Newspapers Society
Philippines	National Press Club of the Philippines
Portugal	Associaçio da Imprensa Diária
South Africa	Newspaper Press Union
Spain	Asociación de Editores de Diarios Españoles (AEDE); Federación de Asociaciones de la Prensa de España (FAPE)
Sri Lanka	Sri Lanka Press Association
Sweden	Svenska Tidningsutgivareföreningen
Switzerland	Schweizerischer Verband der Zeitungs und Zeitschriftenverleger/ Association Suisse des Editeurs de Journaux et Periodiques
Thailand	Samakom Nangsupim Hang Prathet Thai
Uganda	Uganda News Editors' and Proprietors' Association
United Kingdom	Newspaper Society; Newspaper Publishers' Association; Scottish Daily Newspaper Society
USA	American Newspaper Publishers' Association (ANPA); American Society of Newspaper Editors (ASNE); National Newspaper Association (NNA)
Uruguay	Asociación de Diarios del Uruguay
Venezuela	Bloque de Prensa Venezolano

Major British newspapers

Paper	Location	Circulation	Issue
Daily Express	London	1 562 829	Daily
Daily Mail	London	1 701 661	Daily
Daily Mirror	London	2 911 098	Daily
Daily Sport	Manchester	210 000	Daily
Daily Star	London	859 474	Daily
Daily Telegraph	London	1 058 676	Daily
European	London	167 457	Daily
Financial Times	London	286 179	Daily
Glasgow Herald	Glasgow	122 101	Daily
Guardian	London	412 654	Daily
Independent	London	376 923	Daily
Independent on Sunday	London	372 187	Weekly
Mail on Sunday	London	1 907 537	Weekly
Morning Star	London	8 500	Daily
News of the World	London	4 845 016[a]	Weekly
Observer	London	554 900	Weekly

Paper	Location	Circulation	Issue
People	London	2 278 983	Weekly
Racing Post	London	47 221	Daily
Scotland on Sunday	Edinburgh	72 941	Weekly
Scotsman	Edinburgh	85 903	Daily
Sporting Life	London	79 169	Daily
Sun	London	3 689 931	Daily
Sunday Mirror	London	2 809 637	Weekly
Sunday Post	Dundee	1 198 041	Weekly
Sunday Sport	London	370 559	Weekly
Sunday Telegraph	London	569 039	Weekly
Sunday Times	London	1 147 708	Weekly
Times	London	390 475	Daily
Today	London	470 620	Daily

[a]Largest circulation of any paper in Western world.

Daily Monday through Saturday.

Best-selling European newspapers

Included are newspapers with circulations of 250 000 and over.

Paper	Location	Circulation	Issue
Austria			
Kleine Zeitung	Graz	275 000	Weekly
Die Ganze Woche	Vienna	850 000	2-weekly
Kurier	Vienna	620 000	Daily & Sun
Neue Kronenzeitung	Vienna	1 000 000	Daily
Belgium			
Antwerpse Post (Dutch/nederlands)	Antwerp	313 327	Weekly
Die Nieuwe Gazet Antwerp (Dutch/nederlands)	Antwerp	298 882	Daily
Visite (Dutch/nederlands)	Berchem	574 355	Monthly
Belgique No 1 (French)	Brussels	530 000	Weekly
L'Echo (French)	Brussels	380 000	Weekly
Groupe AZ (French)	Brussels	1 625 000	Weekly
Groep AZ (Dutch/nederlands)	Brussels	2 800 000	Weekly
Vlan (French)	Brussels	425 000	Weekly
De Gentenaar (Dutch/nederlands)	Ghent	326 000	Daily
Het Nieuwsblad (Dutch/nederlands)	Groot-Bijgaarden	382 397	Daily
De Standaard (Dutch/nederlands)	Groot-Bijgaarden	382 397	Daily
Hier Groep (Dutch/nederlands)	Hasselt	350 000	Weekly
Publi-Hebdo	Liege	382 000	Weekly
Deze Week in (Dutch/nederlands)	Roeselare	840 000	Weekly
Bulgaria			
Duma	Sofia	300 000	Daily
Otechestven Front (Fatherland Front)	Sofia	280 000	Daily

Paper	Location	Circulation	Issue
Czech Republic			
Práce (Labour)	Prague	350 000	Daily
Rudé Právo (Red Light)	Prague	340 000	Daily
Éire			
Sunday World	Dublin	263 088	Weekly
France			
Sud-Ouest	Bordeaux	367 860	Daily
La Montagne	Clermont Ferrand	250 288	Daily
L'Est Républicain	Heillecourt	251 236	Daily
Le Progrès	Lyons	353 608	Daily
Nice Matin	Nice	258 205	Daily
Le Figaro	Paris	428 700	Daily
France-Dimanche	Paris	706 338	Weekly
France-Soir	Paris	334 035	Daily
Ici Paris	Paris	422 796	Weekly
Le Journal Dimanche	Paris	360 029	Weekly
Le Monde	Paris	381 549	Daily
Le Parisien	Paris	365 661	Daily
VSD (Vendredi, Samedi, Dimanche)	Paris	261 612	Weekly
Ouest-France	Rennes	739 047	Daily
La Nouvelle République du Centre-Ouest	Tours	271 504	Daily
Le Dauphiné Libéré	Veurey-Voroize	813 209	Daily
Germany			
Augsburger Allgemeine	Augsburg	362 000	Daily
BZ-Berlin	Berlin	279 269	Daily
Berliner Zeitung	Berlin	425 000	Daily
Bild Berlin	Berlin	250 000	Daily
Junge Welt	Berlin	330 000	Daily
Express Köln	Cologne	437 104	Daily
Lausitzer Rundschau	Cottbus	291 000	Daily
Sächsische Zeitung	Dresden	513 000	Daily
Rheinische Post	Düsseldorf	391 489	Daily
Das Volk	Erfurt	401 000	Daily
Westdeutsche Allgemeine Zeitung (WAZ)	Essen	1 236 304	Daily
Frankfurter Allgemeine Zeitung (FAZ)	Frankfurt/Main	366 703	Daily
Bild	Hamburg	4 416 240	Daily
Die Zeit	Hamburg	488 212	Weekly
Hannoversche Allgemeine Zeitung (HAZ)	Hannover	511 027	Daily
HNA Hessische/Niedersäch Allgemeine	Kassel	272 249	Daily
Leipziger Volkszeitung	Leipzig	484 000	Daily
Volksstimme	Magdeburg	379 407	Daily
Süddeutsche Zeitung (SZ)	Magdeburg	386 287	Daily
Super Zeitung	Munich	600 000	Daily
Nürnberger Nachrichten	Nuremburg	325 000	Daily
Nordwest Zeitung	Oldenburg	317 077	Daily

Media

Publishing (continued)

Paper	Location	Circulation	Issue
Neue Osnabrücker Zeitung	Osnabruck	299572	Daily
Ostee Zeitung	Rostock	293000	Daily
Sonntag Aktuell	Stuttgart	877140	Weekly
Stuttgarter Zeitung	Stuttgart	509710	Daily
Südwest Presse	Ulm	367129	Daily
Hungary			
Népsport (People's Sport)	Budapest	250000	Daily
Népszabadsag (People's Freedom)	Budapest	450000	Daily
Reform	Budapest	385000	Weekly
Vasárnapi Hirek	Budapest	270595	Weekly
Italy			
Corriere Della Sera	Milan	644856	Daily
La Gazzetta Dello Sport	Milan	814889	Daily
Il Sole 24 Ore	Milan	258771	Daily
Corriere Dello Sport-Stadio	Rome	542275	Daily
Il Messaggero	Rome	400000	Daily
La Repubblica	Rome	826224	Daily
La Stampa	Turin	406951	Daily
Netherlands			
De Telegraaf	Amsterdam	725700	Daily
De Volkskrant	Amsterdam	340038	Daily
Algemeen Dagblad	Rotterdam	417000	Daily
Norway			
Aftenposten	Oslo	262892	Daily
Poland			
Gazeta Wyborcza	Warsaw	550000	Daily
Zycie Warszawy (Warsaw Life)	Warsaw	250000	Daily
Romania			
Ardevarul	Bucharest	250000	Daily
România Liberia	Bucharest	400000	Daily
Slovakia			
Práca	Bratislava	260300	Daily
Pravda	Bratislava	260000	Daily
Spain			
ABC	Madrid	280356	Daily
El Pais	Madrid	377528	Daily
Sweden			
Göteborg-Posten	Gothenburg	281000	Daily
Aftonbladet	Stockholm	480000	Daily
Dagens Nyheter	Stockholm	519000	Daily
Expressen	Stockholm	575000	Daily
Turkey			
Milliyet (Nationalism)	Istanbul	250000	Daily
Sabah (Morning)	Istanbul	506671	Daily
Russia			
Izvestiya	Moscow	10130000	Daily
Komsomolskaya Pravda (Youth Truth)	Moscow	20354000	Daily

Paper	Location	Circulation	Issue
Moskovskaya Pravda	Moscow	725000	Daily
Pravda	Moscow	7700000	Daily
Rabochaya Tribuna (Worker's Tribune)	Moscow	1405000	Daily
Selskaya Zhizn (Country Life)	Moscow	5772000	Daily
Sotsialisticheskaya Industriya	Moscow	1500000	Daily
Sovetski Sport	Moscow	4863000	Daily
Trud (Labour)	Moscow	21429000	Daily
Vechernyaya Moskva (Evening News)	Moscow	650000	Daily

Daily = Monday through Saturday

US newspapers

The highest circulation figures are quoted, whether they be for a paper's Sunday or weekday issue. All papers listed have circulation figures of over 100000. No free papers are listed.

Paper	Location	Circulation	Issue
Alabama			
News	Birmingham	207138	Daily
Arizona			
New Times	Phoenix	135000	Weekly
Republic	Phoenix	517212	Daily
Star	Tucson	159698	Daily
Arkansas			
Arkansas Democrat	Little Rock	223663	Daily
Arkansas Gazette	Little Rock	165880	Daily
California			
Bee	Fresno	179731	Daily
Press-Telegram	Long Beach	128750	Daily
Central News	Los Angeles	210000	Weekly
Daily News (Japanese)	Los Angeles	215586	Daily
Daily News	Los Angeles	214205	Daily & Sun
Herald-Examiner	Los Angeles	303320	Daily & Sun
Investors Daily	Los Angeles	100503	Daily
L.A. Times	Los Angeles	1196323	Daily & Sun
La Opinion (Spanish)	Los Angeles	105918	Daily & Sun
Tribune	Oakland	121537	Daily & Sun
Press-Enterprise	Riverside	163246	Daily & Sun
Sacramento Bee	Sacramento	328018	Daily & Sun
Sun	San Bernadino	100688	Daily & Sun
Tribune	San Diego	115673	Daily
Union	San Diego	436225	Daily & Sun
San Francisco Chronicle	San Francisco	562887	Daily
San Francisco Examiner	San Francisco	136346	Daily
Sun Examiner/ Chronicle	San Francisco	716339	Weekly

Paper	Location	Circulation	Issue
Wall Street Journal, western edition	San Francisco	388 013	Daily
Mercury News	San Jose	330 791	Daily & Sun
Register	Santa Ana	406 696	Daily & Sun
Daily Breeze	Torrance	100 000	Daily & Sun
Colorado			
Gazette Telegraph	Colorado Springs	115 883	Daily
Post	Denver	407 561	Daily & Sun
Rocky Mountain News	Denver	407 889	Daily & Sun
Connecticut			
Hartford Courant	Hartford	314 846	Daily & Sun
Register	New Haven	135 569	Daily & Sun
Delaware			
News Journal	Wilmington	139 833	Daily
District of Columbia			
Washington Post	Washington	1 137 034	Daily & Sun
Washington Times	Washington	100 000	Weekly
Florida			
News Journal	Daytona Beach	106 169	Daily & Sun
Sun-Sentinel	Fort Lauderdale	305 804	Daily
News Press	Fort Myers	102 016	Daily & Sun
Florida Times-Union	Jacksonville	245 414	Daily & Sun
Florida Today	Melbourne	106 878	Daily
Miami Herald	Miami	520 075	Daily & Sun
State Paper	Miami	140 000	Daily
Suncoast News	New Port Richey	172 000	2-weekly
Sentinel	Orlando	376 003	Daily
Herald-Tribune	Sarasota	130 872	Daily
Times	St Petersburg	424 432	Daily & Sun
Tribune & Times	Tampa	364 269	Daily & Sun
Palm Beach Post	West Palm Beach	212 129	Daily
Georgia			
Atlanta Constitution	Atlanta	316 793	Mon–Fri
Dekalb News/Sun	Decatur	104 000	Weekly
Macon Telegraph & News	Macon	100 488	Daily & Sun
Illinois			
Chicago Sun Times	Chicago	548 091	Daily
Chicago Tribune	Chicago	1 101 966	Daily & Sun
Wall Street Journal, midwest edition	Chicago	513 653	Daily
Journal Star	Peoria	110 115	Daily & Sun
Indiana			
Courier	Evansville	116 962	Daily & Sun
Journal-Gazette	Fort Wayne	139 275	Daily & Sun
News	Indianapolis	101 091	Daily
Star	Indianapolis	411 044	Daily & Sun
Iowa			
Register	Des Moines	346 275	Daily & Sun
Kansas			
Wichita Eagle	Wichita	198 906	Daily & Sun
Kentucky			
Herald Leader	Lexington	157 908	Daily & Sun
Courier Journal	Louisville	325 443	Daily & Sun
Louisiana			
Times Picayune	New Orleans	278 990	Daily & Sun
Maryland			
Sun	Baltimore	494 112	Daily
Massachusetts			
The Boston Globe	Boston	791 605	Daily & Sun
Boston Herald	Boston	358 925	Daily & Sun
Christian Science Monitor	Boston	104 314	Mon–Fri
Phoenix	Boston	134 000	Weekly
Patriot Ledger	Quincy	101 639	Daily
Union	Springfield	156 880	Daily
Telegram & Gazette	Worcester	135 891	Daily
Michigan			
Free Press	Detroit	636 182	Daily & Sun
News	Detroit	500 980	Daily & Sun
Journal	Flint	107 940	Daily
Press	Grand Rapids	191 095	Daily & Sun
Minnesota			
Star Tribune	Minneapolis	666 840	Daily & Sun
Pioneer Press Dispatch	St Paul	261 557	Daily
Mississippi			
Clarion Ledger	Jackson	123 052	Daily
Missouri			
Star	Kansas City	322 400	Mon–Fri
Post Dispatch	St Louis	561 630	Daily & Sun
Nebraska			
World Herald	Omaha	284 223	Daily & Sun
Nevada			
Las Vegas Review Journal	Las Vegas	165 078	Daily & Sun
New Jersey			
Asbury Park Press	Asbury Park	228 140	Daily
Courier-Post	Camden-Cherry Hill	101 803	Mon–Fri & Sun
Record	Hackensack	228 158	Daily & Sun
Star-Ledger	Newark	693 183	Daily & Sun
North Jersey Herald News	Passaic	140 260	Daily & Sun
Press	Pleasantville	102 241	Daily & Sun
New Mexico			
Journal	Albuquerque	158 078	Daily & Sun
New York			
Times-Union	Albany	173 944	Daily & Sun
News	Buffalo	378 574	Daily & Sun
Newsday	Long Island	714 128	Daily & Sun
Times-Herald Record	Middletown	101 097	Daily & Sun
Daily News	New York	1 401 403	Daily & Sun
New York Post	New York	510 219	Daily
The New York Times	New York	1 686 974	Daily & Sun
Village Voice	New York	147 000	Weekly
Wall Street Journal	New York	1 857 131	Mon–Fri
Suffolk Life	Riverhead	468 000	Weekly

Media

Publishing (continued)

Paper	Location	Circulation	Issue
Democrat & Chronicle	Rochester	260 322	Daily & Sun
North Carolina			
Observer	Charlotte	298 749	Daily & Sun
News & Record	Greensboro	130 977	Daily & Sun
News & Observer	Raleigh	184 226	Daily & Sun
Journal	Winston-Salem	107 331	Daily & Sun
Ohio			
Beacon Journal	Akron	222 899	Daily & Sun
The Cincinnati Post	Cincinnati	104 264	Daily
Enquirer	Cincinnati	342 076	Daily & Sun
Plain Dealer	Cleveland	560 871	Daily
Dispatch	Columbus	389 319	Daily & Sun
News	Dayton	230 918	Daily
Blade	Toledo	215 463	Daily & Sun
Vindicator	Youngstown	134 931	Daily & Sun
Oklahoma			
Oklahoman	Oklahoma City	326 284	Daily & Sun
Oregon			
Oregonian	Portland	431 989	Daily & Sun
This Week	Portland	442 000	Weekly
Pennsylvania			
Morning Call	Allentown	181 784	Daily & Sun
Daily News	Philadelphia	225 063	Daily
News Gleaner	Philadelphia	109 000	Weekly
Philadelphia Enquirer[a]	Philadelphia	978 300	Daily & Sun
Times-Northeast	Philadelphia	137 000	Weekly
The Pittsburgh Press	Pittsburgh	554 402	Daily
Post-Gazette	Pittsburgh	162 520	Daily
Rhode Island			
Bulletin	Providence	265 210	Mon–Fri
South Carolina			
News & Courier	Charleston	125 714	Daily
State	Columbia	172 936	Daily & Sun
Tennessee			
News-Free Press	Chattanooga	107 373	Daily & Sun
Commercial Appeal	Memphis	288 866	Daily & Sun
Tennessean	Nashville	264 790	Daily & Sun
Texas			
American Statesman	Dallas	219 857	Daily & Sun
Dallas Morning News	Dallas	585 950	Daily & Sun
Dallas Times Herald	Dallas	340 297	Daily & Sun
Wall Street Journal, southwest edition	Dallas	187 177	Daily
Star-Telegram	Fort Worth	267 558	Daily & Sun
Houston Chronicle	Houston	620 779	Daily & Sun
Houston Post	Houston	370 449	Daily & Sun
Express-News	San Antonio	273 227	Daily & Sun
Light	San Antonio	234 011	Daily & Sun

Paper	Location	Circulation	Issue
Utah			
Tribune	Salt Lake City	140 977	Daily & Sun
Virginia			
U.S.A. Today	Arlington	1 748 218	Mon–Fri
News Leader	Richmond	259 093	Daily
Times & World News	Roanoke	126 795	Daily & Sun
Washington			
Post-Intelligencer	Seattle	205 357	Daily
Times	Seattle	233 995	Daily
Chronicle	Spokane	145 507	Daily
News-Tribune	Tacoma	134 866	Daily & Sun
Wisconsin			
Journal	Milwaukee	505 074	Daily & Sun
Sentinel	Milwaukee	176 549	Daily

Daily = Monday through Saturday

[a]The oldest daily in USA

Canadian newspapers

All papers listed have circulations of 10 000 or over. In each case the highest circulation figure is given, whether it be for the paper's Sunday or weekly issue.

Paper	Location	Circulation	Issue
Alberta			
Calgary Herald	Calgary	163 206	Daily
Calgary Sun	Calgary	100 466	Daily
Edmonton Journal	Edmonton	190 875	Daily & Sun
Edmonton Sun	Edmonton	125 058	Daily
Daily Herald Tribune	Grand Prairie	11 674	Daily
Lethbridge Herald	Lethbridge	24 720	Daily
News	Medicine Hat	13 942	Daily
Advocate	Red Deer	22 028	Daily
St Albert Gazette	St Albert	10 000	Weekly
British Columbia			
Abbotsford News	Abbotsford	40 700	2-weekly
Chilliwack	Chilliwack	12 700	Weekly
Delta Optimist	Delta	34 500	Weekly
Kamloops Daily News	Kamloops	19 083	Daily
Daily Courier	Kelowna	18 833	Daily
Advance	Langley	10 000	Daily
Daily Free Press	Nanaimo	10 600	Daily
Citizen	Prince George	21 649	Daily
Richmond Review	Richmond	40 000	2-weekly
North Shore News	Vancouver	58 500	3-weekly
Province	Vancouver	227 432	Mon–Fri & Sun
Vancouver Sun	Vancouver	267 290	Daily
Times-Colonist	Victoria	78 796	Daily
Manitoba			
Sun	Brandon	17 748	Daily & Sun
Carillon	Steinbach	13 000	Weekly
Winnipeg Free Press	Winnipeg	227 290	Daily

Paper	Location	Circulation	Issue
New Brunswick			
L'Acadie Nouvelle (French)	Caraquet	14 442	Daily
Le Madawaska (French)	Madawaska	10 000	Weekly
Gleaner	Fredericton	29 775	Daily
Times-Transcript	Moncton	53 344	Daily
Telegraph-Journal	Moncton	61 562	Daily
Newfoundland			
Western Star	Corner Brook	11 240	Daily
Evening Telegram	St John's	57 740	Daily
Nova Scotia			
Chronicle-Herald	Halifax	87 250	Daily
Daily News	Halifax	37 000	Daily & Sun
Mail-Star	Halifax	55 230	Daily
Advertiser	Kentville	10 258	Weekly
Evening News	New Glasgow	11 735	Daily
Cape Breton Post	Sydney	31 741	Daily
Ontario			
Examiner	Barrie	14 742	Daily
Intelligencer	Belleville	19 021	Daily
Expositor	Brantford	32 319	Daily
Recorder & Times	Brockville	16 711	Daily
Burlington Weekend Post	Burlington	40 000	Weekly
Daily Reporter	Cambridge	14 728	Daily
Chatham Daily News	Chatham	16 553	Daily
Standard-Freeholder	Cornwall	18 430	Daily
Daily Mercury	Guelph	19 547	Daily
Hamilton Recorder	Hamilton	20 000	Weekly
Spectator	Hamilton	114 877	Daily
Spectator	Burlington	22 282	Daily
Whig Standard	Kingston	42 007	Daily
Kitchener-Waterloo Record	Kitchener	80 917	Daily
Lindsay Daily Post	Lindsay	10 011	Mon–Fri
London Free Press	London	124 879	Daily
Mississauga News	Mississauga	105 000	Weekly
Review	Niagara Falls	23 000	Daily
Nugget	North Bay	24 109	Daily
Packet	Orillia	11 219	Daily
Oshawa Times	Oshawa	20 905	Daily
This Week	Oshawa	60 000	Weekly
Citizen	Ottawa	234 455	Daily
Le Droit (French)	Ottawa	39 762	Daily
Ottawa Sun	Ottawa	40 790	Mon–Fri & Sun
Sun Times	Owen Sound	24 198	Daily
Examiner	Peterborough	27 089	Mon–Fri
Sarnia Observer	Sarnia	23 979	Daily
Star	Saute Ste Marie	26 757	Daily
Reformer	Simcoe	10 577	Mon–Fri
Standard	St Catharines	43 134	Daily
Times-Journal	St Thomas	10 145	Daily
Beacon Herald	Stratford	13 788	Daily
Sudbury Star	Sudbury	29 483	Daily
Chronicle-Journal	Thunder Bay	38 141	Mon–Fri
Daily Press	Timmins	13 283	Daily
Canadian Jewish News	Toronto	50 587	Weekly
Corriere Canadese (Italian)	Toronto	22 500	Daily
Daily Racing Form	Toronto	10 357	Daily & Sun
Etobicoke Guardian	Etobicoke	66 000	2-weekly
Financial Post	Toronto	186 358	Tues–Sat
Globe & Mail	Toronto	320 000	Daily
Toronto Star	Toronto	767 799	Daily
Toronto Sun	Toronto	500 000	Daily
Welland-Port Colborne Tribune	Welland	17 937	Daily
Windsor Star	Windsor	85 632	Daily
Woodstock-Ingersoll Sentinel Review	Woodstock	10 170	Daily
Québec			
Progrès-Dimanche	Chicoutimi	50 963	Weekly
Le Quotidien	Chicoutimi	31 140	Daily
La Parole	Drummond-ville	29 000	Weekly
La Voix de l'Est	Granby	15 520	Daily
Le Devoir	Montreal	29 508	Daily
Gazette (English)	Montreal	246 698	Daily
Le Guide de Montréal Nord	Montreal	16 800	Weekly
Le Journal de Montréal	Montreal	345 098	Daily
La Presse	Montreal	310 587	Daily
Le Journal de Québec	Québec	109 353	Daily
Le Soleil	Québec	141 797	Daily
L'Etoile du Lac	Roberval	11 300	Weekly
La Frontière	Rouyn	12 500	Weekly
La Tribune	Sherbrooke	44 590	Daily
L'Eclaireur Progrès -Beauce Nouvelle	St Georges	25 200	Weekly
Le Courrier	St Hyancinthe	13 063	Weekly
Le Canada Français	St Jean	15 417	Weekly
Le Nouvelliste	Trois Rivieres	49 722	Daily
L'Union des Cantons de l'Est	Victoriaville	12 538	Weekly
Saskatchewan			
Leader-Post	Regina	68 944	Daily
Star-Phoenix	Saskatoon	63 587	Daily
Prince Edward Island			
Guardian	Charlottetown	19 699	Daily
Journal Pioneer	Summerside	11 256	Daily

Daily = Monday through Saturday

Australian newspapers

All papers listed have circulations of over 10 000. Free papers are not listed.

Paper	Location	Circulation	Issue
Australian Capital Territory			
Canberra Times	Canberra	44 000	Daily
New South Wales			
Border Morning Mail	Albury	25 196	Daily
Richmond River Express Examiner	Casino	13 400	Weekly

Communications

Publishing (continued)

Paper	Location	Circulation	Issue
Newcastle & Lake Macquarie Post	Newcastle	104 510	Weekly
Newcastle Herald	Newcastle	52 225	Daily
Australian	Sydney	138 497	Daily
Australian Financial Review	Sydney	76 637	Daily
Daily Telegraph Mirror	Sydney	480 000	Daily
Sun-Herald	Sydney	550 354	Weekly
Sunday Telegraph	Sydney	562 000	Weekly
Sydney Morning Herald	Sydney	378 313	Daily
Weekend Australian	Sydney	280 000	Weekly
Advertiser	Parramatta	102 918	Weekly
Bankstown-Canterbury Express	Bankstown	75 000	Weekly
Blacktown Advocate	Blacktown	41 371	Weekly
Farm & Garden	Castle Hill	20 746	Weekly
Hawkesbury Courier	North Richmond	14 700	Weekly
Hornsby & Upper North Shore Advocate	Hornsby	46 547	Weekly
Liverpool-Fairfield Champion	Liverpool	67 450	Weekly
Macarthur Advertiser	Campbell-town	28 369	Weekly
Manly Daily	Manly	80 784	Daily
Mosman & Lower North Shore Daily	Spit Junction	21 179	Daily
North Shore Times	Parramatta	103 980	2-weekly
Northern District Times	Eastwood	51 915	Weekly
Penrith Press	Parramatta	56 542	Weekly
St George & Sutherland Shire Leader	Hurstville	118 383	Weekly
Western Standard	Druitt	25 690	Weekly
Western Suburbs Courier	Waterloo	62 624	Weekly
Northern Daily Leader	Tamworth	11 600	Daily
Daily Advertiser	Wagga Wagga	16 413	Daily
Illawarra Mercury	Wollongong	36 680	Daily

Northern Territory

Paper	Location	Circulation	Issue
Northern Territory News	Darwin	19 500	Daily

Queensland

Paper	Location	Circulation	Issue
Courier-Mail	Brisbane	250 918	Daily
Sun	Brisbane	362 319	Daily
Sunday Mail	Brisbane	348 000	Weekly
Drum	Bundaberg	20 000	Weekly
Cairns Post	Cairns	20 665	Daily
Queensland Times	Ipswich	17 100	Daily
Daily Mercury	Mackay	16 670	Daily
Sunshine Coast Daily	Maroochy-dore	20 787	Daily
Rockhampton Morning Bulletin	Rockhampton	24 000	Daily
Toowoomba Chronicle	Toowoomba	30 644	Daily

Paper	Location	Circulation	Issue
Townsville Bulletin	Townsville	25 750	Daily

South Australia

Paper	Location	Circulation	Issue
Adelaide Advertiser	Adelaide	213 341	Daily
News	Adelaide	129 819	Daily
Sunday Mail	Adelaide	268 029	Weekly
City Messenger	Adelaide	24 573	Weekly
Community Courier	Adelaide	33 770	Weekly
Eastern Suburbs Messenger	Adelaide	23 170	Weekly
Elizabeth Salisbury News Review	Adelaide	61 286	Weekly
Guardian	Adelaide	45 640	Weekly
Hills & Valley Gazette	Adelaide	20 582	Weekly
North East Leader	Adelaide	32 882	Weekly
Payneham Messenger	Adelaide	29 570	Weekly
Parkside Messenger	Adelaide	28 932	Weekly
Southern Times	Adelaide	48 415	Weekly
Standard	Adelaide	29 931	Weekly
Weekly Times	Adelaide	41 190	Weekly
Westside	Adelaide	23 315	Weekly
Mount Barker Courier	Adelaide	13 000	Weekly

Tasmania

Paper	Location	Circulation	Issue
Advocate	Burnie	27 293	Daily
Mercury	Hobart	53 864	Daily
Sunday Tasmanian	Hobart	54 753	Weekly
Examiner	Launceton	38 500	Daily

Victoria

Paper	Location	Circulation	Issue
Ballarat Courier	Ballarat	23 595	Daily
Ballarat News	Ballarat	31 000	Weekly
Bendigo Advertiser	Bendigo	16 500	Daily
Geelong Advertiser	Geelong	31 991	Daily
Geelong News	Geelong	46 261	2-weekly
Wimmera Mail-Times	Horsham	10 046	3-weekly
Midland Express	Kyneton	19 907	Weekly
Age	Melbourne	339 905	Daily
Herald-Sun	Melbourne	680 000	Daily
Sunday Age	Melbourne	119 756	Weekly
Sunday Herald Sun	Melbourne	600 000	Weekly
Sunday Observer	Melbourne	90 844	Weekly
Truth	Melbourne	240 433	2-weekly
Weekly Times	Melbourne	118 000	Weekly
Broadmeadows Observer	Glenroy	27 767	Weekly
Brunswick Sentinel	Northcote	19 487	Weekly
Chadstone Progress	Northcote	93 863	Weekly
Coburg Courier	Northcote	28 078	Weekly
Dandenong Journal	Dandenong	34 160	Weekly
Diamond Valley News	Northcote	28 065	Weekly
Doncaster Mirror	Cheltenham	26 297	Weekly

Paper	Location	Circulation	Issue
Doncaster & Templestowe News	Northcote	25 974	Weekly
Essendon Gazette	Glenroy	26 598	Weekly
Footsaray & Western Suburbs Advertiser	Dandenong	44 108	Weekly
Frankston Peninsula News	Dandenong	11 801	Weekly
Frankston Standard	Cheltenham	42 273	Weekly
Heidelberger	Northcote	24 831	Weekly
Keilor Messenger	Glenroy	27 022	Weekly
Knox Sherbrooke News	Boronia	39 446	Weekly
Northcote Leader	Northcote	22 789	Weekly
Nunawading Gazette	Blackburn	32 975	Weekly
Progress Press	Blackburn	79 329	Weekly
Ringwood & Croydon Mail	Blackburn	36 315	Weekly
Sandringham & Brighton Advertiser	Cheltenham	23 098	Weekly
Standard Times	Cheltenham	22 836	Weekly
Sunshine Advocate	Dandenong	33 004	Weekly
Waverley Gazette	Glenwaverley	42 048	Weekly
Whittlesea Post	Northcote	19 516	Weekly
Malvern Caulfield Progress	Oakleigh	59 355	Weekly
Berwick City News	Packenham	25 100	Weekly
Warrnambool Standard	Warrnambool	12 900	Daily

Western Australia

Paper	Location	Circulation	Issue
Sunday Times	Perth	324 700	Weekly
West Australia	Perth	252 503	Daily

Daily = Monday through Saturday

New Zealand newspapers

All papers listed have circulation figures of over 10 000.

Paper	Location	Circulation	Issue
National Business Review	Auckland	19 900	Weekly
New Zealand Herald	Auckland	246 458	Daily

Paper	Location	Circulation	Issue
North Shore Times Advertiser	Auckland	56 000	3-weekly
Sunday News	Auckland	154 000	Weekly
Sunday Star	Auckland	120 000	Weekly
Marlborough Express	Blenheim	10 400	Daily
Press	Christchurch	95 933	Daily
Star	Christchurch	57 957	Daily
Weekend Star	Christchurch	23 502	Weekly
Otago Daily Times	Dunedin	52 000	Daily
Gisborne Herald	Gisborne	10 582	Daily
Waikato Times	Hamilton	41 090	Daily
Hawke's Bay Herald Tribune	Hastings	20 349	Daily
Southland Times	Invertargill	34 504	Daily
News Gazette	Kawerau	11 000	Weekly
Daily Telegraph	Napier	16 500	Daily
Nelson Evening Mail	Nelson	19 549	Daily
Daily News	New Plymouth	30 454	Daily
Taranaki Herald	New Plymouth	10 410	Daily
Evening Standard	Palmerston North	25 911	Daily
Daily Post	Rotorua	13 992	Daily
Bay of Plenty Times	Tauranga	21 061	Daily
Timaru Herald	Timaru	16 339	Daily
South Waikato News	Tokoroa	10 441	2-weekly
Wanganui Chronicle	Wanganui	16 549	Daily
Contact	Wellington	130 377	Weekly
Dominion	Wellington	87 466	Weekly
Eastern News	Wellington	13 550	Weekly
Evening Post	Wellington	76 770	Daily
Hutt News	Wellington	38 550	Weekly
Independent Herald	Wellington	18 823	Weekly
New Zealand Times	Wellington	89 247	Weekly
Northern Advocate	Whangarei	16 654	Daily

Daily = Monday through Saturday

South African newspapers

All papers listed have circulations of over 10 000.

Paper	Location	Circulation	Issue
Bophuthatswana			
Mafikeng Mail (English)	Mafikeng	10 000	Daily
Mafikeng Mail & Botswana Guardian (English)	Mafikeng	17 000	Weekly
Cape Province			
Argus (English)	Cape Town	102 060	Daily
Die Burger (Afrikaans)	Cape Town	79 113	Daily
Cape Times (English)	Cape Town	60 316	Daily
Weekend Argus (English)	Cape Town	113 614	Weekly
Daily Dispatch (English)	East London	33 505	Daily

Media

Publishing (continued)

Paper	Location	Circulation	Issue
Indaba (black community) (English)	East London	37 108	Weekly
Paarl Post (English & Afrikaans)	Paarl	10 000	Weekly
Eastern Province Herald (English)	Port Elizabeth	28 336	Daily
Evening Post (English)	Port Elizabeth	22 596	Daily
Weekend Post (English)	Port Elizabeth	39 141	Weekly
Gemsbok Kourier (English & Afrikaans)	Roosevelt Park	10 000	Weekly
South (English)	Woodstock	25 000	Weekly

Natal
Daily News (English)	Durban	100 570	Daily
Ilanga (Zulu)	Durban	142 277	2-weekly
Leader (Indian community) (English)	Durban	15 000	Weekly
Natal Mercury (English)	Durban	62 549	Daily
Post (Natal) (English)	Durban	47 500	Weekly
Sunday Tribune (English)	Durban	124 547	Weekly
Newcastle Advertiser (English & Afrikaans)	Newcastle	18 000	Weekly
Natal Witness (English)	Pietermaritzburg	26 927	Daily
Highway Mail (English)	Pinetown	28 920	Weekly
Northglen News (English)	Pinetown	14 136	Weekly

Orange Free State
Die Volksblad (Afrikaans)	Bloemfontein	27 268	Daily
Vista (English)	Welkom	26 375	2-weekly

Transvaal
Benoni City Times en Oosrandse Nuus (English & Afrikaans)	Benoni	23 500	Weekly
Brakpan Herald (English & Afrikaans)	Benoni	12 885	Weekly
Germiston City News (English)	Benoni	28 296	Weekly
Highveld Herald/Die Hoevelder (English & Afrikaans)	Ermelo	15 000	Weekly
Beeld (Afrikaans)	Johannesburg	103 887	Daily
Boksburg Advertiser/ (English & Afrikaans) *Boksburg Volksblad*	Johannesburg	24 150	Weekly
Business Day (English)	Johannesburg	32 871	Mon–Fri
Citizen (English)	Johannesburg	138 512	Daily
City Press (English)	Johannesburg	144 416	Weekly
New Nation (English)	Johannesburg	49 538	Weekly
Randfontein Herald (English & Afrikaans)	Johannesburg	12 016	Weekly
Rapport (English)	Johannesburg	370 565	Weekly
Sowetan (English)	Johannesburg	174 043	Daily
Star (English)	Johannesburg	218 405	Daily
Sunday Star (English)	Johannesburg	97 142	Weekly
Sunday Times (English)	Johannesburg	509 888	Weekly
Die Transvaler (Afrikaans)	Johannesburg	49 580	Daily
Vaderland (Afrikaans)	Johannesburg	150 000	Daily
Vrye Weekblad (Afrikaans)	Johannesburg	14 000	Weekly
Weekly Mail (English)	Johannesburg	31 000	Weekly
Heidelberg Nigel Heraut (English & Afrikaans)	Kempton Park	27 500	Weekly
Western Transvaal Record (English & Afrikaans)	Klerksdrop	11 040	Weekly
Lebowa, Gazankulu & Venda Times (English & N Sesotho)	Pietersburg	16 500	Weekly
Die Noord Transvaaler (Afrikaans)	Pietersburg	18 000	Weekly
Hoofstadv (Afrikaans)	Pretoria	11 855	Daily
Pretoria News (English)	Pretoria	26 880	Daily
De Echo (English & Afrikaans)	Secunda	12 300	Weekly
Springs & Brakpan Advertiser (English & Afrikaans)	Springs	12 994	Weekly
Vanderbijlpark Vaal Weekblad (English & Afrikaans)	Vanderbijlpark	13 268	Weekly

Venda
Thohoyuandou (English, Afrikaans, & Venda)	Venda	33 000	Weekly

Daily = Monday through Saturday

Broadcasting stations and networks

Main terrestrial television broadcasters and stations

Country	Public service broadcaster	Commercial broadcaster	Military
Albania	Radiotelevisione Shqiptar		
Australia	Australian Broadcasting Corporation (ABC) (satellite) Special Broadcasting Service (SBS) (satellite) Imparja Television Pty Ltd (satellite)	6th Metropolitan TV Channel Seven Network (satellite) Nine Network (satellite) Network Ten Australia (satellite)	
Austria	Österreichischer Rundfunk (ORF): ORF FS 1 & ORF FS 2	3 Sat SAT1, RTL, RTL2	
Azores	Radiotelevisão Portuguesa (RTO)		AFRTS (US Air Force)
Belarus	Belaruskaje Telebačanne Ostankino Kanal 1 (OK-1) Rossijskoje Televidenije (RTV)	TV Peterburg (TV-P)	
Belgium	Belgische Radio En Televisie (BRTN): TV1 & TV2 (Dutch) Radio Télévision Belge de la Communaute (French) Culturelle Française (RTBF-TV) Tele-21 (French)	Canal Plus RTL-TVi	
Bosnia & Herzegovina	Televizija Sarajevo		
Bulgaria	Bâlgarska Televizija Russian television relay		
Canada	Canadian Broadcasting Corporation/ Société Radio Canada (satellite) Société de Radio-Télévision du Québec TV Ontario (satellite)	City TV (satellite) Canwest Global System (satellite) CTV Television Network Ltd Le Reseau de Télévision (TVA) Télévision Quatre Saisons	
Croatia	Hrvatska Televisija (HTV)		
Czech & Slovak Republics	Československá Televize Cesk Televize (CTV) Slovenska Televize (ST)	CT3 (Czech) Channel 3 (Slovavia)	
Denmark	Danmarks Radio (8 channels)	TV-2	
Estonia	Estonian TV Ostankino TV (Moscow) Russian TV	TV-Petersburg (TV-P)	
Faroe Islands	Sjónvarp Føroya		
Finland	Oy Yleisradio AB: YLE TV1 & YLE TV 2	MTV Oy Channel 3 Finland (MTV 3)	
France	France 2 France 3 (FR3) La Sept Arte Tele Monte Carlo	Télévision Française 1 (TF1) Canal Plus M6 Metropole TV Tele Toulouse Tele Bleue Tele Lyon Metropole 8 Mont Blanc Aqui TV RTL TV	

Broadcasting stations and networks (continued)

Country	Public service broadcaster	Commercial broadcaster	Military
Germany	ARD (Programmdirektion Deutsches Fernsehen) Russian television relays Zweites Deutsches Fernsehen (ZDF)	Vox (Westschienenkanal) CFN/RFC-TV (Canada) Deutsches Sportfernsehen (DSF)	US Forces Television Germany SSVC Television (UK) Belgium Forces Television French Forces Television
Gibraltar	GBC Television		
Greece	Elliniki Tileorassi-1 (ET-1) Elliniki Tileorassi-2 (ET-2) Elliniki Tileorassi-3 (ET-3) AFN TV	Antenna TV Mega Channel New Channel Kanali 29 7X TeleCity New Television Sky TV	
Hungary	Magyar Televísió		
Iceland	Ríkisútvarpid - Sjónvarp Stöd 2		
Ireland	Radio Telefis Eireann (RTE) Network 2	Ulster TV (overspill) Channel 4 (overspill)	
Italy	Radiotelevisione Italiana: RAI Uno, RAI Due, & TV 3 Rundfunkanstalt SüdTirol (RAS)	Canale 5 Circuito 5 Stelle Italia 1 Italia 7 Italia 9 Junior TV Odeon Rete A Rete Quattro Tele Monte Carlo Tele Più 2 Sport Video Music	
Latvia	Latvijas Televizija (LTV)		
Lithuania	Lietuvos Televisija LRT Kauno Direkcija RYTU Lietuvos Televizija Russian television relays	Panevezio Telestudija Kauno Telestukija Plius	
Luxembourg		Tele Luxembourg (RTL) Hei Elei	
Macedonia	Televizija Makedonije: TV Makedonije, & TV Skopje		
Malta	Xandir Television		
Monaco		Tele Monte Carlo	
Montenegro	TV Crne Gore		
Netherlands	Nederlandse Omroepprogrammia Stichting (NOS): NOS 1, 2 & 3		American Forces Network
New Zealand	Television New Zealand Canterbury Television (CTV)	TV3	
Norway	Norsk Rikskringkasting	TV 2 Norway Philips Petroleum 66: TV 1 & 2	

Communications

Country	Public service broadcaster	Commercial broadcaster	Military
Poland	Telewizja Polska: TP 1 & 2 Tele-9	Top Kanal Independent TV Echo TV	
Portugal	Radiotelevisão Portuguesa (RTP): RTP 1 & 2	SIC Televisão Independente	
Romania	Radioteleviziumea Româna: TV 1 & 2	SOTI Antenna Independenta	
Russia	Rossijskaja Gosudarstvennaja Teleradiokompanija: 'Ostankino' (OK), Ostankino Kanal 1 (OK-1), & Ostankino Kanal 4 (OK-4) Vserossijskaja Gosudarstvennaja Teleradiokompanija (VGTRK) Rossijskoje Televidenije (RTV)	TV-Peterburg (TV-P)	
Serbia	TV Srbije–TV Beograd TV Srbije–TV Novi Sad TV Srbile-TV Pristina TV Politika NTV Studio B		
Slovenia	Televizija Slovenia		
South Africa	South African Broadcasting Corporation (SABC-TV) Contemporary Community Value TV Transkei TV	M-Net Television Bophuthatswana Television Trinity Broadcasting – Ciskei MNET Transkei Trinity Broadcasting – Transkei	
Spain	Radiotelevision Española (RTVE) La2 Televisio Valenciana - Canal 9 TV Vasca-Euskal Telebista	Televisio de Catalunya TV3 Canal 33 Television Murciana ETB1 7 ETB2 Tele Madrid TV de Galicia (TVG)	(US Air Force): AFRTS
Sweden	Sveriges Television AB STV 2 Kanal 1 Finnish television relay	TV4 Nordisk Television Co	
Switzerland	Swiss Broadcasting Company (SBC) DRS (German) TSR (French) TSI (Italian)	Telecine Teleclub	
Ukraine	Ukrajinska Telebačennja (UT-1 + 2) Ostankino Kanal 1 (OK-1)		
United Kingdom	British Broadcasting Company (BBC) Independent Television Commission Anglia Television Border Television Carlton Television Ltd Central Independent Telelvision Channel 4 Channel Television Data Broadcasting International Ltd GMTV Ltd Grampian Television Granada Television HTV Wales HTV West	British Sky Broadcasting Independent Television News (ITN) Independent Television Association (ITVA)	

Broadcasting stations and networks (continued)

Country	Public service broadcaster	Commercial broadcaster	Military
	London Weekend Television		
	Meridian Broadcasting Ltd		
	Scottish Television		
	Teletext UK Ltd		
	Tyne Tees Television		
	Ulster Television		
	Westcountry Television Ltd		
	Yorkshire Television		
US	Public Broadcasting Service (PBS)	ABC Television Division	
	TV Marti	CBS Inc.	
		Fox Television Network	
		National Broadcasting Company	
Yugoslavia (former)	Udruzenje Jugoslovenskih Radiotelevizija		

Major European television broadcasts by satellite

Satellite	Program/Programme	Owner	Satellite	Program/Programme	Owner

63° E Intelsat 602	M-Net (Johannesburg)
	SABC-TV (Johannesburg)
	Channel 3 (Bangkok
	  Entertainment Co)
	Channel 9 (Mass Comms.
	  Org. of Thailand)
	IRIB TV 2
	IRIB TV 1
	AFRTS-E2
	Rete 4 (Italy)
	Italia 1
	Canale 5 (Italy
		Inter-
		national
				West-3
				Deutschlandfunk
				DSF (Deutsches Sport-
				  fernsehen)
				Bayerisches Fernsehen
				  (regional German TV)	

60° E Intelsat 604	Wir in Bayern
	  (Germany)
	Bayern Journal
	AFN-Television
	interSTAR
	TRT TV4 (Turkey)
	TRT TV3
	TRT TV1
	TRT TV2
	TV Gap
		Inter-
		national
			19.2° E Astra 1A	Screen Sports
				RTL Plus (German &
				  English)
				Scansat TV3 (Swedish)
				Eurosport
				Lifestyle TV
				Sat-1 (German)
				TV 1000 Succekanalen
				  (Scandinavian)
				SKY One (English)
				Teleclub
				3-Sat
				FilmNet (Scandinavian)
				SKY News (English)
				RTL-4 (Dutch)
				Pro 7 (German)
				MTV
				SKY Movies Plus
					Luxem-
					bourg

53° E Gorizont 11	Ostanko TV1 MIR-Station	CIS			

40° E Gorizont 12	Rossia TV 2
	TV 5 Europe (French)
	RTP International
	  (Portuguese)
		CIS	19.2° E Astra 1B	Premiere
				The Movie Channel
				Eins Plus
				Sky Sports
				DSF (Deutsches
				  Sportfernsehen)
				MTV
				UK Gold
				JSTV
				NHK (Japanese)
				TCC (The Children's
				  Channel)
				N3
				Sky Movies Gold
				Home Video
				  Channel
				TV Asia	

28.5° E Kopernikus (DFS-2)	Wir in Niedersachsen RTL Nord	Germany			
23.5° E Kopernikus (DFS-1)	SAT 1 3 Sat ARTE (French/German) VOX Eins Plus RTL Plus n-tv PRO 7 Premiere DSR (16 channels)	Germany			

Communications

Satellite	Program	Owner
	Scansat TV 3 (Denmark)	
	CNN International	
	BSkyB	
	Scansat TV3 (Norway)	
16° E Eutelsat II f3	Eurostep (Dutch)	European
	Antenna Tres (Spanish)	
	RTV Zagreb	
	Tele 5 (Spanish)	
	Canal Plus Español (Spanish)	
	Polish Television's Third Program	
	Hungaria TV	
	RTP International	
	HBB-TV/HAS-TV (Turkish)	
	TV 7 Tunisia	
	TV PLUS (Dutch)	
13° E Eutelsat II f1	Eurosport	European
	Super Channel/Channel e	
	Der Kabelkanal	
	TV 5 Europe	
	RTL-2 (German)	
	Deutsche Welle Fernsehen	
	WorldNet	
	TRT (Turkish)	
	Red Hot Dutch (Adult)	
	Middle East Broadcasting Centre	
	ARD Eins (German)	
	FilmNet Plus (Belgium)	
	FilmNet (Dutch)	
	VisEurope	
	BrightStar	
	WTN/ITN	
	EuroPace	
	TV Sport (France)	
10° E Eutelsat II f1	RAI Uno (Italy)	European
	RAI Due	
	TVE-Internaçional (Spain)	
	Show TV (Turkey)	
	Teleon (Turkey)	
	interSTAR (Turkey)	
	SIP Canal Courses	
	TV Campus	
7° E Eutelsat II f4	ET 1 (Greece)	European
	Kanal 6 (Turkish)	
	CYBC (Cyprus)	
	RTV Beograd (Serbia)	
5° E Tele-X	TV4 (Swedish)	Scandinavian
	NRK (Norwegian TV)	
	TV5 Nordic	
	Kompetenskanalen	
	SSC Tele-X/1	

Satellite	Program	Owner
1° W Intelsat 512	TVN (Norwegian)	International
	Nordisk TV4 (Norway)	
	SVT-2 (Sweden)	
	SVT-1 (Sweden)	
	IBA TV 1 & 2 & 3	
5° W Télécom 2B	RFO/France 2	France
	Métropole 6	
	ARTE	
	Canal Plus	
	TF 1	
	Canal J(eunesse)	
	Canal Jimmy	
	Cine Cinema	
8° W Télécom 2A	Canal Plus	France
	France 2	
	Cine Cinefil	
	Canal J	
	Canal Jimmy	
	MCM Euromusique	
	Planette	
	TV Sport	
11° W Gorizont 7	EBU Moscow	CIS
14° W Gorizont 15	Ostankino TV 1/Brightside TV	CIS
	Moscow Visnews	
18.5° W Intelsat 515	STV 1	International
	TV Norge	
	TV-4 Norway	
	STV 2	
	TV 2 (Norway)	
19° W TDF 1A/B	Monte Carlo Music	France
	Canal Plus (French)	
	ARTE (French & German)	
	France 2	
19.2° W TV-Sat 1/2	RTL Plus	Germany
	Sat-1	
	3 Sat	
	DSR (16 channels)	
	Eins Plus	
21.5° W Intelsat K	BrightStar	International
27.5° W Intelsat 601	BBC World Service TV	International
	WorldNet	
	Canal France Internationale	
	CNN International	
	TVE (Spain)	
	Bravo	
	The Parliamentary Channel	
	The Children's Channel	
	Discovery Channel	
	KinderNet	
	The Learning Channel	
	Ladbroke Horse Racing	
	Country Music TV Europe	
	Kanal Market (Turkish)	

Communications

Broadcasting stations and networks (continued)
Major radio broadcasters

Country	Public service	Commercial	Military
Albania	Radiotelevisione Shqiptar Trans World Radio	Radio Valira	
Andorra	Servei de Telecomunicacions d'Andorra (STA) Radio Andorra		
Australia	Australian Broadcasting Corporation (ABC) Domestic Shortwave Service Northern Territory Shortwave Service Public Broadcasting Association of Australia Special Broadcasting Service (SBS)	Federation of Australian Radio Broadcasters	
Austria	Österreichischer Rundfunk (ORF)		
Belarus	Belaruskaje Radyjo		
Belgium	Belgische Radio en Televisie (BRTN) (Dutch) Radio-Télévision Belge de la Communaute Française (RTBF) (French) Belgisches Rundfunk & Fernsehzentrum der Deutschsprachigen Gemeinschaft (BRF)	Radio Contact Radio Nostalgie Network (Dutch) Radio Nostalgie Network (French)	US Forces Network, SHAPE British Forces Broadcasting
Bosnia & Herzegovina	Radiotelevizija Sarajevo		
Bulgaria	Bulgarian National Radio Horizont Christo Botev Orphei Znanie	Radio Express Radio Larik Radio Tanra Radio FM Channel Kom Radio Vesselina Channel TNN Radio Galatea	
Canada	Canadian Broadcasting Corporation/ Société Radio-Canada Radio Canada International CBC Northern Quebec Shortwave Service Sackville Relay Facility		
Croatia	Hrvatska Radio Televizija (HRT)		
Czech & Slovak Republics	Československý Rozhlas Czech & Slovak Radios International	Radio Free Europe	
Denmark	Danmarks Radio		
Estonia	Eesti Raadio		
Faroe Islands	Útvarp Føroya (Danish)		
Finland	Oy Yleisradio AB		
France	Télédiffusion de France (TDF) Radio Télévision Française d'Outre-Mer (RFO) Radio France Internationale France Internationale Radio France Radio Monte Carlo	Sud Radio Europe 1 Radio Monte Carlo NRJ	
Germany	ARD Deutsche Welle Deutschlandsender Kultur	Antenne Bayern Radio Hamburg Radio FFH	Voice of America (VOA) Radio Volga (Russian Armed Forces) American Forces Network Europe (AFN)

Country	Public service	Commercial	Military
	Rias Berlin Radio Moscow relay BBC Berlin relay	OK Radio Europe 1	British Forces Broadcasting Service Canadian Forces Network Radio Forces Françaises de Berlin
Gibraltar	Gibraltar Broadcasting Corporation British Forces Broadcasting Service Gibraltar		Armed Forces Radio Service (US Air Force)
Greece	Elliniki Radiophonia (ERA) Voice of America	Antenna Sky Athina 98.4 Radio Athens	
Hungary	Magyar Radio	Radio Danubius Calypso 873 Radio Bridge	
Iceland	Icelandic National Broadcasting Service Ríkisútvarpid		Navy Broadcasting Service (US Navy)
Ireland	Radio Telefís Éireann Radió Na Gaeltachta	Atlantic 252	
Italy	RAI-Radiotelevisione Italiana	Rundfunk Anstalt SüdTirol (RAS) Radio Tirol Adventist World Radio Europe Nexus International Broadcasting Association	S European Broadcasting (US Armed Forces)
Latvia	Latvijas Radio Liepajas Radio	Radio AA Radio Dejas Radio Sigulda	
Lithuania	Lietuvos Radijas Radio Vilnius LRT Kauno Programų Direkcija Majak relay	Radiocentras M-1 Vilniaus Varpas Znad Wilii Titanika	
Luxembourg		Radio-Télé-Luxembourg	
Macedonia	Radiotelevizija Makedonije		
Malta	Malta Broadcasting Authority Voice of the Mediterranean Deutsche Welle Relay Maltă		
Moldova	Radioteleviziunea Naţională Radio Moldova International Radio Moscow relay		
Monaco		Radio Monte Carlo Riviera Radio Trans World Radio	
Montenegro	Radio Podgorica		
Netherlands	NOS Stichting Ether Reclame Ster Nozema RNW		US Forces Network (SHAPE) British Forces Broadcasting Service Canadian Forces Network–Brunssum
New Zealand	Radio New Zealand Radio New Zealand International	RNZ Community Net National Radio Net Independent Broadcasters Association	

Communications

Broadcasting stations and networks (continued)

Country	Public service	Commercial	Military
Norway	Teledirektoratet Norsk Rikskringkasting Foreign Service Svalbard (Spitsbergen)		
Poland	Polskie Radio I Telewizja Rozglosina Harcerska Radio Mazury		

Portugal	Radiodifusão Portuguesa (RDP)
	RDP International–Radio Portugal
	Rádio Renascença Lda Emissora
	  Católica Portuguesa
	Sociedade de Radioretransmissao Ld
	Radio Trans Europe
	Voice of America relay
		Radio Altitude	American Forces
			  Radio & TV Service

Romania	Radio Romania Radio Romania International RM6	Radio Contact Romania	

Russia	Rossiyskaya Gosudarstvennaya
	  Teleradiokompaniya 'Ostankino'
	Vserossiyskaya Gosudarsdtvennaya
	  Teleradiokompniya
	Radio Moscow International
	Radio Aum Shinrikyo		

Serbia	Radiotelevizija Srbije Radio Beograd Music Radio Youth Radio Radio Politika Radio 'Pingvin' Radio Novi Sad		
Slovenia	Radiotelevizija Slovenia		
South Africa	South African Broadcasting Corporation (SABC) Channel Africa Ciskeian Broadcasting Corporation Transkei Broadcasting Corporation Radio Thohoyandou (Venda Radio)	Home Services Bophuthatswana Broadcasting Radio 702 Capital Radio (Transkei)	
Spain	Ente Publico Radiotelvision Española Radio Nacional de España Radio Exterior de España Sociedad Española de Radiodifusion (SER)	Cadena de Ondas Populares Españolas (COPE) Onda Cero Radio Antena 3 de Radio Cadena Dial Radio Minuto Eusko Irrati Telebista (Basque) Radiotelevision Galicia Radiotelevision de Andalucia Radiotelevision Valencia Canal Sur Radio	
Sweden	Svensk Rundradio AB Sveriges Radio AB Sveriges Utbildningsradio AB		

Country	Public service	Commercial	Military
Switzerland	Swiss Broadcasting Corporation Swiss Radio International United Nations Broadcasting from Geneva Broadcasts from the International Committee of the Red Cross, Geneva		
Ukraine	Derzhavna Teleradiomovna Kompaniya Ukrayiny Radio Ukraine International Radio Moscow relay		

United
  Kingdom
	British Broadcasting Corporation
	BBC Radio Scotland
	BBC Radio Wales/Radio Cymru
	BBC Radio Ulster
	BBC World Service
	Voice of America
		Classic FM
		Virgin Radio
			British Forces
			  Broadcasting Services

US	National Public Radio
	Voice of America
	VOA Europe
	Radio Marti
	United Nations Radio
	BBC relays
		ABC Radio Networks
		CBS Radio Division
		NBC Radio
		Mutual Radio Network
		National Black Network
		Sheridan Broadcasting
		  Network
		C-Span Audio Networks
		KCBI International
		International Broadcast
		  Station KGEI
		Radio Station KJES
		KTBN
		KVOH
		Radio Earth International,
		  Inc
		Radio Miami International
		WEWN Catholic Radio
		  Service
		WHRI World Harvest Radio
		WMLK
		World International
		  Broadcasters, Inc
		Worldwide Christian Radio
		WRNO Worldwide
		World Service of the
		  Christian Science Monitor
		World Wide Gospel Radio,
		  Inc
		WYFR-Family Radio
		Organization of the
		  American States
			US Armed Forces
			  Radio & Television
			  Service

Vatican City State	Vatican Radio		

Yugoslavia
  (former)
	Udruženje Jugoslovenskih Radiotelevizija
	  (JRT)
	Radiotelevizija Srbije
	Radiotelevizija Crne Gore
	Foreign Service–Radio Jugoslavija		

Communications

Communications

British national radio stations

BBC Radio
Radio 1	Pop and rock music
Radio 2	Popular music, comedy, arts, entertainment
Radio 3	Classical music, documentaries, arts, cricket (seasonal)
Radio 4	News, documentaries, drama, entertainment
Radio 5	Sport, education, children's programmes, World Service

BBC World Service
World Service in English
African Service: Swahili, Somali, Hausa
Arabic Service
Central European Service: Czech, Slovak, Hungarian, Polish, Finnish
Eastern Service: Bengali, Burmese, Hindi, Nepali, Pahto, Persian, Sinhalese,
  Tamil, Urdu
Far Eastern Service: Cantonese, Mandarin, Indonesian, Thai, Vietnamese
French & Portuguese Service
German Service
Latin American Service: Spanish, Portuguese
Russian & Ukrainian Service
Southeast European Service: Bulgarian, Romanian, Serbian, Croatian, Slovene,
  Greek, Turkish
BBC English (broadcasts series of English-language teaching courses worldwide)
BBC Monitoring (overseas and regional radio and television news)
Topical Tapes — provides tapes of programmes for use by overseas radio stations &
  produces 'Calling the Falklands'
BBC Transcription — produces and sells recorded BBC programmes to overseas radio
  stations

National regional radio
Radio Scotland
  Radios Aberdeen, Highland & Orkney
Radio Ulster
Radio Wales
Radio Cymru (Welsh)

Independent national radio stations
Classic FM
Virgin Radio

SCIENCE AND TECHNOLOGY

MATHEMATICS

Signs and symbols

+	plus; positive; underestimate	∞	infinity
−	minus; negative; overestimate	→	approaches the limit
±	plus or minus; positive or negative; degree of accuracy	√	square root
∓	minus or plus; negative or positive	³√, ⁴√	cube root, fourth root, etc
×	multiplies (colloq. 'times') (6×4)	%	per cent
·	multiplies (colloq. 'times') (6·4); scalar product of two vectors (**A·B**)	′	prime; minute(s) of arc; foot/feet
		″	double prime; second(s) of arc; inch(es)
÷	divided by (6÷4)	⌒	arc of circle
/	divided by; ratio of (6/4)	°	degree of arc
—	divided by; ratio of (⁶/₄)	∠, ∠ˢ	angle(s)
!	factorial (4!=4×3×2×1)	⩝	equiangular
=	equals	⊥	perpendicular
∔,≠	not equal to	‖	parallel
≡	identical with	○, Ⓢ	circle(s)
≢,≇	not identical with	△, ⚠	triangle(s)
≙	corresponds to	□	square
:	ratio of (6:4)	▭	rectangle
::	proportionately equals (1:2::2:4)	▱	parallelogram
≈	approximately equal to; equivalent to; similar to	≅	congruent to
>	greater than	∴	therefore
≫	much greater than	∵	because
≯	not greater than	⁼ᵐ	measured by
<	less than	Δ	increment
≪	much less than	Σ	summation
≮	not less than	Π	product
⩾,≥, ≧	equal to or greater than	∫	integral sign
⩽,≤, ≦	equal to or less than	∇	del: differential operator
∝	directly proportional to	∪	union
( )	parentheses	∩	intersection
[ ]	brackets	∈	is an element of
{ }	braces	⊂	strict inclusion
—	vinculum: division (a̅−b̅); chord of circle or length of line (AB); arithmetic mean (X)	⊃	contains
		⇒	implies
		⇐	implied by
		⇔	implies and is implied by

Important formulae

Circumference, area, and volume

The value of π is approximately $3 \cdot 1416$.

Circle

Circumference $= 2\pi r = \pi d$.
Area $= \pi r^2 = \frac{1}{4}\pi d^2$.

Sphere

Surface area $= 4\pi r^2 = \pi d^2$.
Volume $= \frac{4}{3}\pi r^3 = \frac{1}{6}\pi d^3$.
Surface area of zone
  bounded by parallel
  planes $= 2\pi rh$.

Prism, including **cylinder**

p = perimeter of base

Surface area (exclud-
  ing ends) $= ph$.
Volume $= Ah$.

For the **circular cylinder**:
Surface area (excluding ends) $= 2\pi rh$.
Volume $= \pi r^2 h$.

Pyramid, including **cone**

Volume $= \frac{1}{3}Ah$.

For the **circular cone**:
Surface area (excluding base) $= \pi rl$.
Volume $= \frac{1}{3}\pi r^2 h$.

Parallelogram
Area $= bh$.

Triangle
Area $= \frac{1}{2}bh$.

Trapezium
Area $= \frac{1}{2}(a+b)h$.

Algebra

Series

$$\sum_{i=1}^{n} i = \frac{1}{2}n(n+1) \text{ (an \textbf{arithmetic progression})}; \quad \sum_{i=1}^{n} i^2 = \frac{1}{6}n(n+1)(2n+1); \quad \sum_{i=1}^{n} i^3 = \frac{1}{4}n^2(n+1)^2.$$

Logarithms

$\log_b x = \log_c x / \log_c b$; in particular, $\log_b x = \ln x / \ln b$.
To any base, $\log 1 = 0$; $\log(xy) = \log x + \log y$; $\log(x/y) = \log x - \log y$; $\log x^k = k \log x$.

Factorials

$0! = 1$, $(i+1)! = (i+1) \times i!$ for $i = 0, 1, 2, \ldots$

For large values of n, **Stirling's approximation** is $\ln(n!) \approx \frac{1}{2}\ln(2\pi) + (n + \frac{1}{2})\ln n - n + \frac{1}{12n}$

Binomial coefficients (i denotes a natural number)

For any real n, $\binom{n}{i} = \dfrac{n(n-1)\ldots(n-i+1)}{i!}$.

This may be calculated from the inductive definition $\binom{n}{0} = 1$, $\binom{n}{i+1} = \dfrac{n-i}{i+1}\binom{n}{i}$ for $i = 0, 1, 2, \ldots$

Science and technology

The 'Pascal triangle' rule: $\binom{n+1}{i} = \binom{n}{i-1} + \binom{n}{i}$.

If n is also a natural number, and if $_nC_i$ denotes the number of subsets of i elements contained in a set of n elements, then $_nC_i = \binom{n}{i} = \dfrac{n!}{i!(n-i)!}$

The binomial theorem: If n is a natural number, $(b+a)^n = \sum_{i=0}^{n} \binom{n}{i} b^{n-i} a^i$.

Quadratic functions and equations

Completing the square: If $a \neq 0$, $ax^2 + bx + c = a\left(x + \dfrac{b}{2a}\right)^2 + \dfrac{4ac - b^2}{4a}$,

so that

$$ax^2 + bx + c = 0 \Leftrightarrow x = \dfrac{-b \pm \sqrt{(b^2 - 4ac)}}{2a}.$$

Cubic equations

If $a \neq 0$, and the roots of $ax^3 + bx^2 + cx + d = 0$ are α, β, γ, then

$$\alpha + \beta + \gamma = -b/a, \ \beta\gamma + \gamma\alpha + \alpha\beta = c/a, \ \alpha\beta\gamma = -d/a.$$

Complex numbers

The **modulus-argument form** of z is $z = [r,\theta] = r(\cos\theta + j\sin\theta) = r\exp(\theta j)$, where r, θ are real.

The **product rule** $[r, \theta] \times [s, \phi] = [rs, \theta + \phi]$.

De Moivre's theorem for integral index: $[1,\theta]^n = [1,n\theta]$, or $(\cos\theta + j\sin\theta)^n = \cos n\theta + j\sin n\theta$.

The roots of $z^n = 1$ are $z = [1, 2\pi k/n] = \exp\{2\pi(k/n)j\}$ for $k = 0, 1, 2, ..., n-1$. In particular,

the roots of $z^3 = 1$ are ω, ω^2, where $\omega = \cos 2/3\pi + j\sin 2/3\pi = -1/2 + (1/2\sqrt{3})j$, so that $\omega^3 = 1$ and $1 + \omega + \omega^2 = 0$.

Vectors

Products

If the vectors $\mathbf{a}$, $\mathbf{b}$ are represented by column matrices $\begin{bmatrix} a_1 \\ a_2 \\ a_3 \end{bmatrix}$, $\begin{bmatrix} b_1 \\ b_2 \\ b_3 \end{bmatrix}$ of their components with respect to a rectangular

system of right-handed axes, or as $a_1\mathbf{i} + a_2\mathbf{j} + a_3\mathbf{k}$, $b_1\mathbf{i} + b_2\mathbf{j} + b_3\mathbf{k}$, then $\mathbf{a} \cdot \mathbf{b} = a_1b_1 + a_2b_2 + a_3b_3$;

$$\mathbf{a} \times \mathbf{b} = \begin{bmatrix} a_2b_3 - a_3b_2 \\ a_3b_1 - a_1b_3 \\ a_1b_2 - a_2b_1 \end{bmatrix} = (a_2b_3 - a_3b_2)\mathbf{i} + (a_3b_1 - a_1b_3)\mathbf{j} + (a_1b_2 - a_2b_1)\mathbf{k}.$$

Scalar triple product: $[\mathbf{a} \cdot \mathbf{b} \cdot \mathbf{c}] = \mathbf{a} \cdot (\mathbf{b} \times \mathbf{c}) = \mathbf{b} \cdot (\mathbf{c} \times \mathbf{a}) = \mathbf{c} \cdot (\mathbf{a} \times \mathbf{b}) = \det \begin{bmatrix} a_1 & b_1 & c_1 \\ a_2 & b_2 & c_2 \\ a_3 & b_3 & c_3 \end{bmatrix}$.

Vector triple product: $\mathbf{a} \times (\mathbf{b} \times \mathbf{c}) = (\mathbf{a} \cdot \mathbf{c})\mathbf{b} - (\mathbf{a} \cdot \mathbf{b})\mathbf{c}$; $(\mathbf{a} \times \mathbf{b}) \times \mathbf{c} = (\mathbf{a} \cdot \mathbf{c})\mathbf{b} - (\mathbf{b} \cdot \mathbf{c})\mathbf{a}$.

Mathematics

Trigonometry

Formulae involving sines

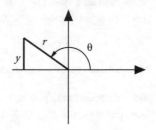

Coordinates: $\qquad y = r \sin\ \theta.$

For any angle θ: $\qquad \sin(90° - \theta) = \cos\ \theta,$

$$\sin(180° - \theta) = \sin\ \theta,$$

$$\sin(360° - \theta) = -\sin\ \theta.$$

In a right-angled triangle: $\qquad \text{sine (angle)} = \dfrac{\text{opposite side}}{\text{hypotenuse}}.$

Formulae involving cosines

Coordinates: $\qquad x\ = r \cos\theta.$

For any angle θ: $\qquad \cos(90° - \theta) = \sin\theta,$

$$\cos(180° - \theta) = -\cos\ \theta,$$

$$\cos(360° - \theta) = \cos\ \theta.$$

In a right-angled triangle: $\qquad \text{cosine (angle)} = \dfrac{\text{adjacent side}}{\text{hypotenuse}}.$

Formulae involving tangents

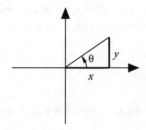

Coordinates: $\qquad y = x \tan\ \theta.$

For any angle θ: $\qquad \tan\theta = \dfrac{\sin\ \theta}{\cos\ \theta}$

$$\tan(90° - \theta) = \dfrac{1}{\tan\ \theta}.$$

$$\tan(180° - \theta) = -\tan\ \theta,$$

$$\tan(360° - \theta) = -\tan\ \theta.$$

In a right-angled triangle: $\qquad \text{tangent (angle)} = \dfrac{\text{opposite side}}{\text{adjacent side}}.$

$\sec\theta = \dfrac{1}{\cos\theta},\ \tan\theta = \dfrac{\sin\ \theta}{\cos\ \theta}\quad [\theta \neq (k + {}^1/_2)\,\pi\,];$

$\operatorname{cosec}\theta\ (\text{or } \csc\theta) = \dfrac{1}{\sin\theta},\ \cot\theta = \dfrac{1}{\tan\theta} = \dfrac{\cos\theta}{\sin\theta}\quad [\theta \neq k\,\pi].$

Pythagorean formulae: $\cos^2\theta + \sin^2\theta = 1;\quad 1 + \tan^2\theta = \sec^2\theta;\quad \cot^2\theta + 1 = \operatorname{cosec}^2\theta.$

Additional formulae: $\sin(\theta \pm \phi) = \sin\theta \cos\phi \pm \cos\theta \sin\phi;\quad \cos(\theta \pm \phi) = \cos\theta \cos\phi \mp \sin\theta \sin\phi;$

$\tan(\theta \pm \phi) = \dfrac{\tan\theta \pm \tan\phi}{1 \mp \tan\theta \tan\phi}.$

Triangle formulae: In the triangle ABC,

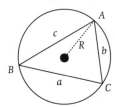

$$\frac{a}{\sin A} = \frac{b}{\sin B} = \frac{c}{\sin C} = 2R \text{ (the \textbf{sine rule})};$$

$$a^2 = b^2 + c^2 - 2bc \cos A, \text{ or } \cos A = \frac{b^2 + c^2 - a^2}{2bc} \text{ (the \textbf{cosine rule})}.$$

Calculus

Chain rule: If $y = f(u)$ and $u = g(x)$, then $\dfrac{dy}{dx} = \dfrac{dy}{du} \times \dfrac{du}{dx}$.

Taylor's polynomial approximation

For small h, $\quad f(a + h) \approx f(a) + f'(a) \cdot h + \dfrac{1}{2!} f''(a) \cdot h^2 + \dots + \dfrac{1}{n!} f^{(n)}(a) \cdot h^n$.

The remainder (error) can be expressed as $\dfrac{1}{(n+1)!} f^{(n+1)}(\xi) \cdot h^{n+1}$, where ξ is some number between a and $a + h$.

Power series with intervals of validity

$$(1 + x)^m = \sum_{i=0}^{\infty} \binom{m}{i} x^i \quad \text{for } |x| < 1. \text{ and sometimes also for } x = 1 \text{ and/or } x = -1.$$

$$\ln(1 + x) = \sum_{i=0}^{\infty} (-1)^{i+1} \frac{x^i}{i} \quad \text{for } -1 < x \leq 1.$$

$$e^x = \sum_{i=0}^{\infty} \frac{x^i}{i!} \quad \text{for all } x.$$

Indefinite integrals: In the following we take $a > 0$ and omit the additive constant.

$f(x)$	$\int f(x)\,dx$	$f(x)$	$\int f(x)\,dx$
$x^n \ (n \neq -1)$	$x^{n+1}/(n+1)$	$\sin x$	$-\cos x$
$1/x$	$\ln|x|, x \neq 0$	$\cos x$	$\sin x$
$\dfrac{1}{x^2 + a^2}$	$\dfrac{1}{a}\tan^{-1}\dfrac{x}{a}$	$\tan x$	$\ln |\sec x|$

Integration by parts: $\displaystyle\int u \frac{dv}{dx}\,dx = uv - \int \frac{du}{dx}\,v\,dx.$

Curvature: $\kappa = \dfrac{d\psi}{ds} = \dfrac{x'y'' - x''y'}{[(x')^2 + (y')^2]^{3/2}}.$

Important formulae (continued)

NUMERICAL METHODS

Simpson's rule, in which n must be *even*, giving an *odd* number of ordinates:

$$\int_{x_0}^{x_n} f(x)\,dx \approx \tfrac{1}{3}h\left[(y_0 + y_n) + 4\,(y_1 + y_3 + \ldots + y_{n-1}) + 2\,(y_2 + y_4 + \ldots + y_{n-2})\right].$$

Newton–Raphson method: If p_n is an approximation to a root of $f(x) = 0$, then

$$p_{n+1} = p_n - \frac{f(p_n)}{f'(p_n)}$$

is generally a better one. The error is approximately

$$\frac{[f(p_n)]^2 f''(p_n)}{2\,[f'(p_n)]^3}$$

Conics

Name of curve	Standard form of equation	Standard parametric forms	Eccentricity e	Foci F and F'	Directrices d and d'	Asymptotes
Parabola	$y^2 = 4ax$	$(ap^2, 2ap)$	1	$(a, 0)$	$x = -a$	none
Ellipse	$\dfrac{x^2}{a^2} + \dfrac{y^2}{b^2} = 1$	$(a\cos\theta, b\sin\theta)$	$\dfrac{\sqrt{(a^2 - b^2)}}{a} < 1$	$(\pm ae, 0)$	$x = \pm\dfrac{a}{e}$	none
Circle	$x^2 + y^2 = a^2$	$(a\cos\theta, a\sin\theta)$	0	$(0, 0)$	none	none
Hyperbola	$\dfrac{x^2}{a^2} - \dfrac{y^2}{b^2} = 1$	$(a\sec\phi, b\tan\phi)$ or $(\pm a\cosh u, b\sinh u)$	$\dfrac{\sqrt{(a^2 + b^2)}}{a} > 1$	$(\pm ae, 0)$	$x = \pm\dfrac{a}{e}$	$\dfrac{x}{a} \pm \dfrac{y}{b} = 0$

Probability

$P\,(A \text{ and } B) + P\,(A \text{ and } \sim B) = P\,(A); \quad P\,(A \text{ or } B) = P\,(A) + P\,(B) - P\,(A \text{ and } B).$

Conditional probability: $P\,(A\,|\,B) = P\,(A \text{ and } B)\,/P\,(B).$

Bayes' theorem: $P\,(A\,|\,B) = \dfrac{P\,(B\,|\,A) \times P\,(A)}{P\,(B\,|\,A) \times P\,(A) + P\,(B\,|\sim A) \times P\,(\sim A)}.$

Parameters

Mean $\mu = E\,(X) = \Sigma x_i p(x_i)$ or $\int x\phi(x)\,dx$ (evaluated over the possibility space).

Variance $\sigma^2 = V\,(X) = E\,((X-\mu)^2) = E\,(X^2) - \mu^2 = \Sigma x_i^2 p(x_i) - \mu^2$ or $\int x^2\phi\,(x)\,dx - \mu^2.$

Expectation

For a single random variable, $E\,(aX + b) = aE\,(X) + b, V\,(aX+b) = a^2 V\,(X).$

For two random variables, $E\,(X \pm Y) = E\,(X) \pm E\,(Y), V\,(X \pm Y) = V\,(X) + V\,(Y) \pm 2\mathrm{cov}\,(X, Y),$

where the covariance $\mathrm{cov}\,(X,Y) = E\,((X-\mu_X)\,(Y-\mu_Y)) = E\,(XY) - \mu_X\mu_Y.$

If X, Y are independent, $\mathrm{cov}\,(X, Y) = 0$ so that $V\,(X \pm Y) = V\,(X) + V\,(Y).$

Particular probability models

Discrete

	Parameter	Probability $p(i)$	Probability generator	Mean	Variance	Meaning of $p(i)$
Binomial $B\,(n, a)$	P (success) $= a$ P (failure) $= b$	$\dfrac{n!\,a^i b^i}{i!\,j!}$ $[i + j = n]$	$(b + at)^n$	na	nab	probability of i successes in n independent trials
Geometric	$[a + b = 1]$	ab^{i-1} $[i \geqslant 1]$	$at/(1 - bt)$	$1/a$	b/a^2	probability that the first success occurs at the ith trial
Poisson	Mean λ in unit interval	$\dfrac{\lambda^i e^{-\lambda}}{i!}$ $[i \geqslant 0]$	$e^{\lambda(t-1)}$	λ	λ	probability of i occurrences in unit interval

Statistics

Statistical measures

If n is the sample size and $f\,(x_i)$ the frequency of occurrence of the value x_i in the sample (so that $n = \Sigma f\,(x_i)$), then:

sample mean m (or $\bar{x}$) $= \dfrac{1}{n}\sum_i x_i f\,(x_i).$

Conic sections

Cone (sometimes double) cut by a plane in (a) a single point; (b) a pair of straight lines; (c) a hyperbola; (d) a parabola; (e) a circle; (f) an ellipse.

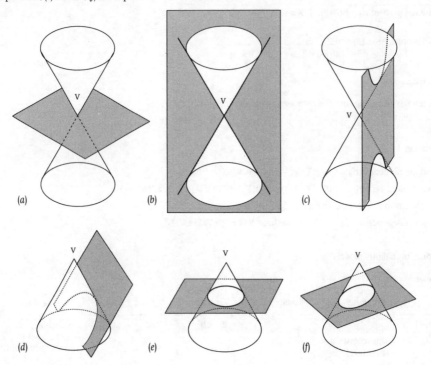

(a)   (b)   (c)

(d)   (e)   (f)

Pythagoras' theorem

A mathematical proposition advanced by Pythagoras, that in any right-angled triangle, the square on the hypotenuse is equal to the sum of the squares on the other two sides. The converse of the theorem is also true: in any triangle in which the square on the longest side is equal to the sum of the squares on the other two sides, the angle opposite the longest side is a right angle. Although known to the Babylonians, tradition ascribes to Pythagoras himself the first proof, probably based on the first diagram. The commoner proof (the second diagram), proving first that the area of square *ABXY* is equal to that of the rectangle *APRS*, was given by Euclid.

Pythagoras' theorem: $c^2 = a^2 + b^2$

Pythagoras' theorem: $AC^2 = AB^2 + BC^2$

MEASUREMENT

Basic SI units

The SI (Système International d'Unitiés) system of units has seven basic units from which all derived units are obtained. Multiples and submultiples of the basic units may be used with approved prefixes.

1 metre *(unit of length) symbol:* m
The metre is the length equal to 1 650 763.73 wavelengths in vacuum corresponding to the quantized electron transition between energy levels $2p^{10}$ and $5d^5$ of the krypton-86 atom.

2 kilogram *(unit of mass) symbol:* kg
The kilogram is the unit of mass equal to the mass of the international prototype kilogram kept at Sèvres, France.

3 second *(unit of time) symbol:* s
The second is the duration of 9 192 631 770 periods of the radiation corresponding to the quantized electron transition between two hyperfine levels of the ground state of the caesium-133 atom.

4 ampere *(unit of electric current) symbol:* A
The ampere is that constant electric current which, if maintained in two straight parallel conductors of infinite length, of negligible cross-section and placed 1 metre apart in vacuum, would produce between these conductors a force equal to 2×10^{-7} newton/ metre.

5 kelvin *(unit of temperature) symbol:* K
The kelvin, unit of thermodynamic temperature is the fraction 1/273.16 of the thermodynamic temperature of the triple point of water.

6 candela *(unit of luminous intensity) symbol:* cd
The candela is the luminous intensity, in a perpendicular direction, of a surface 1/600 000 metre^2 of a black body at the freezing point of platinum at a pressure of 101 325 newton/metre^2.

7 mole *(unit of amount of substance) symbol:* mol
The mole is the amount of substance containing as many elementary units as there are carbon atoms in 0.012 kilogram of carbon-12. The elementary unit may be an atom, a molecule, an ion or an electron.

Two supplementary units are also used:
radian *(unit of plane angle) symbol:* rad
The radian is the unit of measurement of angle and is the angle subtended at the centre of a circle by an arc equal in length to the circle radius.

steradian *(unit of solid angle) symbol:* sr
The steradian is the unit of measurement of solid angle and is the solid angle subtended at the centre of a circle by a spherical cap equal in area to the square of the circle radius.

SI conversion factors

This table gives the conversion factors for many British and other units which are still in common use, showing their equivalents in terms of the International System of Units (SI). The column labelled 'SI equivalent' gives the SI value of 1 unit of the type named in the first column, e.g. 1 calorie is 4.187 joules. The column labelled 'Reciprocal' allows conversion the other way, eg 1 joule is 0.239 calories. (All values are to three decimal places.) As a second example, 1 dyne is 10 μN = 10×10^{-6} N = 10^{-5} N; so 1 newton is $0.1 \times 10^{+6} = 10^5$ dyne. Finally, 1 torr is 0.133 kPa = 0.133 $\times 10^3$ Pa; so 1 Pa is 7.501×10^{-3} torr.

Unit name	Symbol	Quantity	SI equivalent	Unit	Reciprocal
acre		area	0.405	hm^2	2.471
ångström[a]	Å	length	0.1	nm	10
astronomical unit	AU	length	0.150	Tm	6.684
atomic mass unit	amu	mass	1.661×10^{-27}	kg	6.022×10^{26}
bar	bar	pressure	0.1	MPa	10
barn	b	area	100	fm^2	0.01
barrel (US) = 42 US gal	bbl	volume	0.159	m^3	6.290
British thermal unit	btu	energy	1.055	kJ	0.948
calorie	cal	energy	4.187	J	0.239
cubic foot	cu ft	volume	0.028	m^3	35.315
cubic inch	cu in	volume	16.387	cm^3	0.061
cubic yard	cu yd	volume	0.765	m^3	1.308
curie[a]	Ci	activity of radionuclide	37	GBq	0.027
degree = 1/90 rt angle	°	plane angle	$\pi/180$	rad	57.296
degree Celsius	°C	temperature	1	K	1
degree Centigrade	°C	temperature	1	K	1
degree Fahrenheit	°F	temperature	5/9	K	1.8
degree Rankine	°R	temperature	5/9	K	1.8
dyne	dyn	force	10	μN	0.1
electronvolt	eV	energy	0.160	aJ	6.241
erg	erg	energy	0.1	μJ	10
fathom (6ft)		length	1.829	m	0.547
fermi	fm	length	1	fm	1
foot	ft	length	30.48	cm	0.033
foot per second	ft s^{-1}	velocity	0.305	m s^{-1}	3.281
			1.097	km h^{-1}	0.911
gallon (UK)[a]	gal	volume	4.546	dm^3	0.220

SI Conversion factors (continued)

Unit name	Symbol	Quantity	SI equivalent	Unit	Reciprocal
gallon (US)[a] = 231cu in	gal	volume	3.785	dm^3	0.264
gallon (UK) per mile		consumption	2.825	$dm^3\,km^{-1}$	0.354
gauss	Gs, G	magnetic flux density	100	μT	0.01
grade = 0.01 rt angle	rt angle	plane angle	$\pi/200$	rad	63.662
grain	gr	mass	0.065	g	15.432
hectare[a]	ha	area	1	hm^2	1
horsepower	hp	power	0.746	kW	1.341
inch	in	length	2.54	cm	0.394
kilogram-force	kgf	force	9.807	N	0.102
knot[a]		velocity	1.852	$km\,h^{-1}$	0.540
light year	ly	length	9.461×10^{15}	m	1.057×10^{-16}
litre	l	volume	1	dm^3	1
Mach number	Ma	velocity	1193.3	$km\,h^{-1}$	8.380×10^{-4}
maxwell	Mx	magnetic flux	10	nWb	0.1
metric carat		mass	0.2	g	5
micron	μ	length	1	μm	1
mile (nautical)[a]		length	1.852	km	0.540
mile (statute)		length	1.609	km	0.621
miles per hour (mph)	mile h^{-1}	velocity	1.609	$km\,h^{-1}$	0.621
minute = $(1/60)°$	′	plane angle	$\pi/10\,800$	rad	3437.75
oersted	Oe	magnetic field strength	$1/(4\pi)$	$kA\,m^{-1}$	4π
ounce (avoirdupois)	oz	mass	28.349	g	0.035
ounce (troy) = 480 gr		mass	31.103	g	0.032
parsec	pc	length	30857	Tm	0.0000324
phot	ph	illuminance	10	klx	0.1
pint (UK)	pt	volume	0.568	dm^3	1.760
poise	P	viscosity	0.1	Pa s	10
pound	lb	mass	0.454	kg	2.205
pound force	lbf	force	4.448	N	0.225
pound force/in		pressure	6.895	kPa	0.145
poundal	pdl	force	0.138	N	7.233
pounds per square inch	psi	pressure	6.895×10^3	kPa	0.145
rad[a]	rad	absorbed dose	0.01	Gy	100
rem[a]	rem	dose equivalent	0.01	Sv	100
right angle = $\pi/2$ rad		plane angle	1.571	rad	0.637
röntgen[a]	R	exposure	0.258	$mC\,kg^{-1}$	3.876
second = $(1/60)′$	″	plane angle	$\pi/648$	mrad	206.265
slug		mass	14.594	kg	0.068
solar mass	M	mass	1.989×10^{30}	kg	5.028×10^{-31}
square foot	sq ft	area	9.290	dm^2	0.108
square inch	sq in	area	6.452	cm^2	0.155
square mile (statute)	sq mi	area	2.590	km^2	0.386
square yard	sq yd	area	0.836	m^2	1.196
standard atmosphere	atm	pressure	0.101	MPa	9.869
stere	st	volume	1	m^3	1
stilb	sb	luminance	10	$kcd\,m^{-2}$	0.1
stokes	St	viscosity	1	$cm^2\,s^{-1}$	1
therm = 10^5 btu		energy	0.105	GJ	9.478
ton = 2240 lb		mass	1.016	Mg	0.984
ton-force	tonf	force	9.964	kN	0.100
ton-force/sq in		pressure	15.444	MPa	0.065
tonne	t	mass	1	Mg	1
torr, or mmHg	torr	pressure	0.133	kPa	7.501
X unit		length	0.100	pm	10
yard	yd	length	0.914	m	1.093

[a]In temporary use with SI.

SI prefixes

Factor	Prefix	Symbol	Factor	Prefix	Symbol	Factor	Prefix	Symbol
10^{18}	exa-	E	10^2	hecto-	h	10^{-9}	nano-	n
10^{15}	peta-	P	10^1	deca-	da	10^{-12}	pico-	p
10^{12}	tera-	T	10^{-1}	deci-	d	10^{-15}	femto-	f
10^9	giga-	G	10^{-2}	centi-	c	10^{-18}	atto-	a
10^6	mega-	M	10^{-3}	milli-	m			
10^3	kilo-	k	10^{-6}	micro-	μ			

Common measures

Metric units		Imperial equivalent	Imperial units		Metric equivalent
Length			*Length*		
	1 millimetre (mm)	0.03937 in		1 inch	2.54 cm
10 mm	1 centimetre (cm)	0.39 in	12 in	1 foot	30.48 cm
10 cm	1 decimetre (dm)	3.94 in	3 ft	1 yard	0.9144 m
100 cm	1 metre (m)	39.37 in	1 760 yd	1 mile	1.6093 km
1000 m	1 kilometre (km)	0.62 mi			
			Area		
Area				1 square inch	6.45 cm^2
	1 square millimetre	0.0016 sq in	144 sq in	1 square foot	0.0929 m^2
	1 square centimetre	0.155 sq in	9 sq ft	1 square yard	0.836 m^2
100 cm^2	1 square decimetre	15.5 sq in	4 840 sq yd	1 acre	0.405 ha
10 000 cm^2	1 square metre	10.76 sq ft	640 acres	1 square mile	259 ha
10 000 m^2	1 hectare	2.47 acres			
			Volume		
Volume				1 cubic inch	16.3871 cm^2
	1 cubic centimetre	0.016 cu in	1 728 cu in	1 cubic foot	0.028 m^2
1 000 cm^3	1 cubic decimetre	61.024 cu in	27 cu ft	1 cubic yard	0.765 m^2
1 000 dm^3	1 cubic metre	35.31 cu ft			
		1.308 cu yd	*Liquid volume*		
				1 pint	0.57 l
Liquid volume			2 pt	1 quart	1.14 l
	1 litre	1.76 pt	4 qt	1 gallon	4.55 l
100 l	1 hectolitre	22 gal			
			Weight		
Weight				1 ounce	28.3495 g
	1 gram	0.035 oz	16 oz	1 pound	0.4536 kg
1 000 g	1 kilogram	2.2046 lb	14 lb	1 stone	6.35 kg
1 000 kg	1 tonne	0.0842 ton	8 st	1 hundredweight	50.8 kg
			20 cwt	1 ton	1.016 t

Conversion factors

Imperial to metric			Multiply by
Length			
inches	→	millimetres	25.4
inches	→	centimetres	2.54
feet	→	metres	0.3048
yards	→	metres	0.9144
statute miles	→	kilometres	1.6093
nautical miles	→	kilometres	1.852
Area			
square inches	→	square centimetres	6.4516
square feet	→	square metres	0.0929
square yards	→	square metres	0.8361
acres	→	hectares	0.4047
square miles	→	square kilometres	2.5899
Volume			
cubic inches	→	cubic centimetres	16.3871
cubic feet	→	cubic metres	0.0283
cubic yards	→	cubic metres	0.7646
Capacity			
UK fluid ounces	→	litres	0.0284
US fluid ounces	→	litres	0.0296
UK pints	→	litres	0.5682

US pints	→	litres	0.4732
UK gallons	→	litres	4.546
US gallons	→	litres	3.7854
Weight			
ounces (avoirdupois)	→	grams	28.3495
ounces (troy)	→	grams	31.1035
pounds	→	kilograms	0.4536
tons (long)	→	tonnes	1.016

Metric to imperial			Multiply by
Length			
millimetres	→	inches	0.0394
centimetres	→	inches	0.3937
metres	→	feet	3.2806
metres	→	yards	1.9036
kilometres	→	statute miles	0.6214
kilometres	→	nautical miles	0.54
Area			
square centimetres	→	square inches	0.155
square metres	→	square feet	10.764
square metres	→	square yards	1.196
hectares	→	acres	2.471
square kilometres	→	square miles	0.386

Science and technology

Conversion factors (continued)

Volume			Multiply by
cubic centimetres	→	cubic inches	0.061
cubic metres	→	cubic feet	35.315
cubic metres	→	cubic yards	1.308

Capacity			
litres	→	UK fluid ounces	35.1961
litres	→	US fluid ounces	33.8150
litres	→	UK pints	1.7598
litres	→	US pints	2.1134
litres	→	UK gallons	0.2199
litres	→	US gallons	0.2642

Weight			
grams	→	ounces (avoirdupois)	0.0353
grams	→	ounces (troy)	0.0322
kilograms	→	pounds	2.2046
tonnes	→	tons (long)	0.9842

Conversion tables: length

in	cm
1/8	0.3
1/4	0.6
3/8	1
1/2	1.3
5/8	1.6
3/4	1.9
7/8	2.2
1	2.5
2	5.1
3	7.6
4	10.2
5	12.7
6	15.2
7	17.8
8	20.3
9	22.9
10	25.4
11	27.9
12	30.5
13	33
14	35.6
15	38.1
16	40.6
17	43.2
18	45.7
19	48.3
20	50.8
21	53.3
22	55.9
23	58.4
24	61
25	63.5
26	66
27	68.6
28	71.1
29	73.7
30	76.2
40	101.6
50	127
60	152.4
70	177.8
80	203.2
90	228.6
100	254

Exact conversion: 1 in = 2.540 cm

cm	in
1	0.39
2	0.79
3	1.18
4	1.57
5	1.97
6	2.36
7	2.76
8	3.15
9	3.54
10	3.94
11	4.33
12	4.72
13	5.12
14	5.51
15	5.91
16	6.3
17	6.69
18	7.09
19	7.48
20	7.87
21	8.27
22	8.66
23	9.06
24	9.45
25	9.84
26	10.24
27	10.63
28	11.02
29	11.42
30	11.81
31	12.2
32	12.6
33	12.99
34	13.39
35	13.78
36	14.17
37	14.57
38	14.96
39	15.35
40	15.75
50	19.69
60	23.62
70	27.56
80	31.5
90	35.43
100	39.37

Exact conversion: 1 cm = 0.3937 in

in	mm
1/8	3.2
1/4	6.4
3/8	9.5
1/2	12.7
5/8	15.9
3/4	19
7/8	22.2
1	25.4
2	50.8
3	76.2
4	101.6
5	127
6	152.4
7	177.8
8	203.2
9	228.6
10	254
11	279.4
12	304.8
13	330.2
14	355.6
15	381

Exact conversion: 1 mm = 0.0394 in

mm	in
1	0.04
2	0.08
3	0.12
4	0.16
5	0.2
6	0.24
7	0.28
8	0.31
9	0.35
10	0.39
11	0.43
12	0.47
13	0.51
14	0.55
15	0.59
16	0.63
17	0.67
18	0.71
19	0.75
20	0.79
25	0.98
50	1.97
100	3.94

Exact conversion: 1 in = 25.40 cm

ft	m
1	0.3
2	0.6
3	0.9
4	1.2
5	1.5
6	1.8
7	2.1
8	2.4
9	2.7
10	3.0
15	4.6
20	6.1
25	7.6
30	9.1
35	10.7
40	12.2
45	13.7
50	15.2
75	22.9
100	30.5
200	61.0
300	91.4
400	121.9
500	152.4
600	182.9
700	213.4
800	243.8
900	274.3
1000	304.8
1500	457.2
2000	609.6
2500	762.0
3000	914.4
3500	1066.8
4000	1219.2
5000	1524.0
10000	3048.0

Exact conversion: 1 ft = 0.3048 m

m	ft
1	3.3
2	6.6
3	9.8
4	13.1
5	16.4
6	19.7
7	23.0
8	26.2
9	29.5

m	ft
10	32.8
15	49.2
20	65.5
25	82.0
30	98.4
35	114.8
40	131.2
45	147.6
50	164.0
75	246.1
100	328.1
200	656.2
300	984.3
400	1312.3
500	1640.4
600	1968.5
700	2296.6
800	2624.7
900	2952.8
1000	3280.8
1500	4921.3
2000	6561.7
2500	8202.1
3000	9842.5
3500	11482.9
4000	13123.4
5000	16404.2
10000	32808.4

Exact conversion: 1 m = 3.2808 ft

yd	m
1	0.9
2	1.8
3	2.7
4	3.7
5	4.6
6	5.5
7	6.4
8	7.3
9	8.2
10	9.1
15	13.7
20	18.3
25	22.9
30	27.4
35	32.0
40	36.6
45	41.1
50	45.7
75	68.6

yd	m
100	91.4
200	182.9
220	201.2
300	274.3
400	365.8
440	402.3
500	457.2
600	548.6
700	640.1
800	731.5
880	804.7
900	823.0
1000	914.4
1500	1371.6
2000	1828.8
2500	2286.0
5000	4572.0
10000	9144.0

Exact conversion: 1 yd = 0.9144 m

m	yd
1	1.1
2	2.2
3	3.3
4	4.4
5	5.5
6	6.6
7	7.7
8	8.7
9	9.8
10	10.9
15	16.4
20	21.9
25	27.3
30	32.8
35	38.3
40	43.7
45	49.2
50	54.7
75	82.0
100	109.4
200	218.7
220	240.6
300	328.1
400	437.4
440	481.2
500	546.8
600	656.2
700	765.5
800	874.9

		mi*	km	mi*	km	km	mi	km	mi	km	mi
880	962.4										
900	984.2	7	11.3	80	128.7	1	0.6	50	31.1	2500	1553.4
1000	1093.6	8	12.9	85	136.8	2	1.2	55	34.2	5000	3106.9
1500	1640.4	9	14.5	90	144.8	3	1.9	60	37.3		
2000	2187.2	10	16.1	95	152.9	4	2.5	65	40.4		
2500	2734.0	15	24.1	100	160.9	5	3.1	70	43.5		
5000	5468.1	20	32.2	200	321.9	6	3.7	75	46.6		
10000	10936.1	25	40.2	300	482.8	7	4.3	80	49.7		
		30	48.3	400	643.7	8	5.0	85	52.8		
		35	56.3	500	804.7	9	5.6	90	55.9		
		40	64.4	750	1207.0	10	6.2	95	59.0		
		45	72.4	1000	1609.3	15	9.3	100	62.1		
		50	80.5	2500	4023.4	20	12.4	200	124.3		
		55	88.5	5000	8046.7	25	15.5	300	186.4		
		60	96.6			30	18.6	400	248.5		
		65	104.6			35	21.7	500	310.7		
		70	112.7			40	24.9	750	466.0		
		75	120.7			45	28.0	1000	621.4		

Exact conversion: 1 m = 1.0936 yd

mi*	km
1	1.6
2	3.2
3	4.8
4	6.4
5	8.0
6	9.7

*Statute miles
Exact conversion: 1 mi = 1.6093 km

Exact conversion: 1 km = 0.6214 mi

Conversion tables: area

sq in	cm²	cm²	sq in	sq ft	m²	acre	hectares	hectares	acre	sq mi	km²
1	6.45	13	2.02	250	23.23	1	0.40	9	22.2	17	44.0
2	12.90	14	2.17	500	46.45	2	0.81	10	24.7	18	46.6
3	19.35	15	2.33	750	69.68	3	1.21	11	27.2	19	49.2
4	25.81	16	2.48	1000	92.90	4	1.62	12	29.7	20	51.8
5	32.26	17	2.64			5	2.02	13	32.1	21	54.4
6	38.71	18	2.79			6	2.43	14	34.6	22	57.0
7	45.16	19	2.95			7	2.83	15	37.1	23	59.6
8	51.61	20	3.10			8	3.24	16	39.5	24	62.2
9	58.06	25	3.88			9	3.64	17	42	25	64.7
10	64.52	50	7.75			10	4.05	18	44.5	30	77.7
11	70.97	75	11.63			11	4.45	19	46.9	40	103.6
12	77.42	100	15.50			12	4.86	20	49.4	50	129.5
13	83.87	125	19.38			13	5.26	25	61.8	60	155.4
14	90.32	150	23.25			14	5.67	50	123.6	70	181.3
15	96.77					15	6.07	75	185.3	80	207.2
16	103.23					16	6.47	100	247.1	90	233.1
17	109.68					17	6.88	250	617.8	100	259.0
18	116.13					18	7.28	500	1235.5	200	518.0
19	122.58					19	7.69	750	1853.3	300	777.0
20	129.03					20	8.09	1000	2471.1	400	1036.0
25	161.29					25	10.12	1500	3706.6	500	1295.0
50	322.58					50	20.23			600	1554.0
75	483.87					75	30.35			700	1813.0
100	645.16					100	40.47			800	2072.0
125	806.45					250	101.17			900	2331.0
150	967.74					500	202.34			1000	2590.0

Exact conversion: 1 cm² = 0.155 sq in
Exact conversion: 1 sq in = 6.4516 cm²
Exact conversion: 1 hectare = 2.471 acres

cm²	sq in	sq ft	m²	m²	sq ft	acre	hectares	sq mi	km²	sq mi	km²
1	0.16	1	0.09	1	10.8	750	303.51	1	2.6		
2	0.31	2	0.19	2	21.5	1000	404.69	2	5.2	1500	3885.0
3	0.47	3	0.28	3	32.3	1500	607.03	3	7.8	2000	5180.0
4	0.62	4	0.37	4	43.1			4	10.4	2500	6475.0
5	0.78	5	0.46	5	53.8			5	12.9	3000	7770.0
6	0.93	6	0.56	6	64.6			6	15.5	3500	9065.0
7	1.09	7	0.65	7	75.3			7	18.1	4000	10360.0
8	1.24	8	0.74	8	86.1			8	20.7	5000	12950.0
9	1.40	9	0.84	9	96.9			9	23.3	7500	19424.9
10	1.55	10	0.93	10	107.6			10	25.9	10000	25899.9
11	1.71	11	1.02	11	118.4			11	28.5		
12	1.86	12	1.11	12	129.2			12	31.1	km²	sq mi
		13	1.21	13	139.9			13	33.7	1	0.39
		14	1.30	14	150.7			14	36.3	2	0.77
		15	1.39	15	161.5			15	38.8	3	1.16
		16	1.49	16	172.2			16	41.4	4	1.54
		17	1.58	17	183					5	1.93
		18	1.67	18	193.8					6	2.32
		19	1.77	19	204.5						
		20	1.86	20	215.3						
		25	2.32	25	269.1						
		50	4.65	50	538.2						
		75	6.97	75	807.3						
		100	9.29	100	1076.4						
				250	2691						
				500	5382						
				750	8072.9						
				1000	10763.9						

Exact conversion: 1 sq ft = 0.0929 m²
Exact conversion: 1 m² = 10.7639 sq ft
Exact conversion: 1 acre = 0.4047 hectare

hectares	acre
1	2.5
2	4.9
3	7.4
4	9.9
5	12.4
6	14.8
7	17.3
8	19.8

Science and technology

Conversion tables: area (continued)

km²	sq mi	km²	sq mi	km²	sq mi	km²	sq mi	km²	sq mi	km²	sq mi
7	2.70	15	5.79	23	8.88	80	30.89	700	270.27	3 500	1 351.4
8	3.09	16	6.18	24	9.27	90	34.75	800	308.88	4 000	1 544.4
9	3.47	17	6.56	25	9.65	100	38.61	900	347.49	5 000	1 930.5
10	3.86	18	6.95	30	11.58	200	77.22	1 000	386.1	7 500	2 895.8
11	4.25	19	7.34	40	15.44	300	115.83	1 500	579.2	10 000	3 861.0
12	4.63	20	7.72	50	19.31	400	154.44	2 000	772.2		
13	5.02	21	8.11	60	23.17	500	193.05	2 500	965.3		
14	5.41	22	8.49	70	27.03	600	231.66	3 000	1 158.3		

Exact conversions:
1 sq mi = 2.589999 km²
1 km² = 0.3861 sq mi

Conversion tables: volume

cu in	cm³	cm³	cu in	cu ft	m³	m³	cu ft	cu yd	m³	m³	cu yd
1	16.39	1	0.61	1	0.03	1	35.3	1	0.76	1	1.31
2	32.77	2	1.22	2	0.06	2	70.6	2	1.53	2	2.62
3	49.16	3	1.83	3	0.08	3	105.9	3	2.29	3	3.92
4	65.55	4	2.44	4	0.11	4	141.3	4	3.06	4	5.23
5	81.93	5	3.05	5	0.14	5	176.6	5	3.82	5	6.54
6	93.32	6	3.66	6	0.17	6	211.9	6	4.59	6	7.85
7	114.71	7	4.27	7	0.20	7	247.2	7	5.35	7	9.16
8	131.10	8	4.88	8	0.23	8	282.5	8	6.12	8	10.46
9	147.48	9	5.49	9	0.25	9	317.8	9	6.88	9	11.77
10	163.87	10	6.10	10	0.28	10	353.1	10	7.65	10	13.08
11	180.26	11	6.71	11	0.31	11	388.5	11	8.41	11	14.39
12	196.64	12	7.32	12	0.34	12	423.8	12	9.17	12	15.70
13	213.03	13	7.93	13	0.37	13	459.1	13	9.94	13	17.00
14	229.42	14	8.54	14	0.40	14	494.4	14	10.70	14	18.31
15	245.81	15	9.15	15	0.42	15	529.7	15	11.47	15	19.62
20	327.74	20	12.20	20	0.57	20	706.3	20	15.29	20	26.16
50	819.35	50	30.50	50	1.41	50	1 765.7	50	38.23	50	65.40
100	1 638.71	100	61.00	100	2.83	100	3 531.5	100	76.46	100	130.80

Exact conversions:
1 cu in = 16.3871 cm³ | 1 cm³ = 0.0610 cu in | 1 cu ft = 0.0283 m³ | 1 m³ = 35.3147 cu ft | 1 cu yd = 0.7646 m³ | 1 m³ = 1.3080 cu yd

Conversion tables: capacity

Liquid measure

UK fl oz	l	US fl oz	l	l	UK fl oz	US fl oz	UK pt	l	US pt	l	l	UK pt	US pt
1	0.0284	1	0.0296	1	35.2	33.8	1	0.57	1	0.47	1	1.76	2.11
2	0.0568	2	0.0592	2	70.4	67.6	2	1.14	2	0.95	2	3.52	4.23
3	0.0852	3	0.0888	3	105.6	101.4	3	1.70	3	1.42	3	5.28	6.34
4	0.114	4	0.118	4	140.8	135.3	4	2.27	4	1.89	4	7.04	8.45
5	0.142	5	0.148	5	176.0	169.1	5	2.84	5	2.37	5	8.80	10.57
6	0.170	6	0.178	6	211.2	202.9	6	3.41	6	2.84	6	10.56	12.68
7	0.199	7	0.207	7	246.4	236.7	7	3.98	7	3.31	7	12.32	14.79
8	0.227	8	0.237	8	281.6	270.5	8	4.55	8	3.78	8	14.08	16.91
9	0.256	9	0.266	9	316.8	304.3	9	5.11	9	4.26	9	15.84	19.02
10	0.284	10	0.296	10	352.0	338.1	10	5.68	10	4.73	10	17.60	21.13
11	0.312	11	0.326	11	387.2	372.0	11	6.25	11	5.20	11	19.36	23.25
12	0.341	12	0.355	12	422.4	405.8	12	6.82	12	5.68	12	21.12	25.36
13	0.369	13	0.385	13	457.5	439.6	13	7.38	13	6.15	13	22.88	27.47
14	0.397	14	0.414	14	492.7	473.4	14	7.95	14	6.62	14	24.64	29.59
15	0.426	15	0.444	15	527.9	507.2	15	8.52	15	7.10	15	26.40	31.70
20	0.568	20	0.592	20	703.9	676.3	20	11.36	20	9.46	20	35.20	105.67
50	1.42	50	1.48	50	1 759.8	1 690.7	50	28.41	50	23.66	50	87.99	211.34
100	2.84	100	2.96	100	3 519.6	3 381.5	100	56.82	100	47.32	100	175.98	422.68

Exact conversions:
1 fl oz = 0.0284 l | 1 fl oz = 0.0296 l | 1 l = 35.1961 UK fl oz
1 l = 33.8140 US fl oz | 1 UK pt = 0.5682 l
1 UK pt = 1.20 US pt | 1 US pt = 0.4732 l
1 US pt = 0.83 UK pt | 1 l = 1.7598 UK pt, 2.1134 US pt
1 US cup = 8 US fl oz

Conversion tables: capacity (continued)

UK gal	l		l	UK gal	US gal
1	4.55		1	0.22	0.26
2	9.09		2	0.44	0.53
3	13.64		3	0.66	0.79
4	18.18		4	0.88	1.06
5	22.73		5	1.10	1.32
6	27.28		6	1.32	1.58
7	31.82		7	1.54	1.85
8	36.37		8	1.76	2.11
9	40.91		9	1.98	2.38
10	45.46		10	2.20	2.64
11	50.01		11	2.42	2.91
12	54.55		12	2.64	3.17
13	59.10		13	2.86	3.43
14	63.64		14	3.08	3.70
15	68.19		15	3.30	3.96
16	72.74		16	3.52	4.23
17	77.28		17	3.74	4.49
18	81.83		18	3.96	4.76
19	86.37		19	4.18	5.02
20	90.92		20	4.40	5.28
21	95.47		21	4.62	5.55
22	100.01		22	4.84	5.81
23	104.56		23	5.06	6.08
24	109.10		24	5.28	6.34
25	113.65		25	5.50	6.60
50	227.30		50	11.00	13.20
75	340.96		75	16.50	19.81
100	454.61		100	22.00	26.42

Exact conversion:
1 UK gal = 4.546 l

Exact conversion: 1 l = 0.220 UK gal
1 l = 0.2642 US gal

US gal	l		UK gal	US gal		US gal	UK gal
1	3.78		1	1.2		1	0.8
2	7.57		2	2.4		2	1.7
3	11.36		3	3.6		3	2.5
4	15.14		4	4.8		4	3.3
5	18.93		5	6		5	4.2
6	22.71		6	7.2		6	5
7	26.50		7	8.4		7	5.8
8	30.28		8	9.6		8	6.7
9	34.07		9	10.8		9	7.5
10	37.85		10	12		10	8.3
11	41.64		11	13.2		11	9.2
12	45.42		12	14.4		12	10
13	49.21		13	15.6		13	10.8
14	52.99		14	16.8		14	11.7
15	56.78		15	18		15	12.5
16	60.57		20	24		16	13.3
17	64.35		25	30		17	14.1
18	68.14		50	60		18	15
19	71.92					19	15.8
20	75.71					20	16.6
21	79.49					25	20.8
22	83.28					50	41.6
23	87.06					75	62.4
24	90.85					100	83.3
25	94.63						
50	189.27						
75	283.90						
100	378.54						

Exact conversion:
1 US gal = 3.7854 l

Exact conversion:
1 UK gal =
1.200929 US gal

Exact conversion:
1 US gal =
0.832688 UK gal

Other liquid-capacity measures

UK qt	l		US qt	l
1	1.14		1	0.95
2	2.27		2	1.89
3	3.41		3	2.84
4	4.55		4	3.78
5	5.68		5	4.73
10	11.36		10	9.46

Exact conversion:
1 UK qt = 1.1365 l

Exact conversion:
1 US qt = 0.9463 l

l	US qt	UK qt
1	0.88	1.06
2	1.76	2.11
3	2.64	3.17
4	3.52	4.23
5	4.40	5.28
10	8.80	10.57

Exact conversions: 1 l = 0.220 UK gal
1 l = 1.0567 US qts

cu in	l		cu ft	l
1	0.016		1	28.3
2	0.033		2	56.6
3	0.049		3	84.9
4	0.066		4	4.23
5	0.082		5	5.28
10	0.164		10	283.1

Exact conversion:
1 cu in = 0.0164 l

Exact conversion:
1 cu ft = 28.3161 l

l	cu in	cu ft
1	61	0.03
2	122	0.07
3	183	0.11
4	244	0.14
5	305	0.18
10	610	0.35

Exact conversions: 1 l = 61.0255 cu in
1 l = 0.0353 cu ft

Conversion tables: capacity (continued)

Petrol consumption
Use UK table and US table independently.

per UK gal		per l	
mi	km	mi	km
30	48	6.6	10.61
35	56	7.7	12.38
40	64	8.8	14.15
45	72	9.9	15.92
50	80	11	17.69

per US gal		per l	
mi	km	mi	km
30	48	7.9	12.78
35	56	9.3	14.91
40	64	10.6	17.04
45	72	11.9	19.17
50	80	13.2	21.30

Dry capacity measures

UK bu	m^3	l
1	0.037	36.4
2	0.074	72.7
3	0.111	109.1
4	0.148	145.5
5	0.184	181.8
10	0.369	363.7

Exact conversions:
1 UK bu = 0.0369 m^3
1 UK bu = 36.3677 l

US bu	m^3	l
1	0.035	35.2
2	0.071	70.5
3	0.106	105.7
4	0.141	140.9
5	0.175	176.2
10	0.353	352.4

Exact conversions:
1 US bu = 0.9353 m^3
1 US bu = 35.2381 l

m^3	UK bu	US bu
1	27.5	28.4
2	55.0	56.7
3	82.5	85.1
4	110	113
5	137	142
10	275	284

Exact conversions:
1 m^3 = 27.4962 UK bu
1 m^3 = 28.3776 US bu

l	UK bu	US bu
1	0.027	0.028
2	0.055	0.057
3	0.082	0.085
4	0.110	0.114
5	0.137	0.142
10	0.275	0.284

Exact conversions:
1 l = 0.0275 UK bu
1 l = 0.0284 US bu

UK pecks	l	US pecks	l
1	9.1	1	8.8
2	18.2	2	17.6
3	27.3	3	26.4
4	36.4	4	35.2
5	45.5	5	44
10	90.9	10	88.1

Exact conversion: Exact conversion:
1 UK peck =   1 US peck =
9.0919 l   8.8095 l

l	UK pecks	US pecks
1	0.110	0.113
2	0.220	0.226
3	0.330	0.339
4	0.440	0.454
5	0.550	0.567
10	1.100	1.135

Exact conversions:
1 l = 0.1100 UK pecks
1 l = 0.1135 US pecks

US qt	m^3	l
1	1 101	1.1
2	2 202	2.2
3	3 304	3.3
4	4 405	4.4
5	5 506	5.5
10	11 012	11

Exact conversions:
1 US qt = 1101.2209 cm^3
1 US qt = 1.1012 l

US pt	m^3	l
1	551	0.55
2	1 101	1.10
3	1 652	1.65
4	2 202	2.20
5	2 753	2.75
10	5 506	5.51

Exact conversions:
1 US pt = 550.6105 cm^3
1 US pt = 0.55061 l

Science and technology

Conversion tables: weight

oz^a	g
1	28.3
2	56.7
3	85
4	113.4
5	141.7
6	170.1
7	198.4
8	226.8
9	255.1
10	283.5
11	311.7
12	340.2
13	368.5
14	396.9
15	425.2
16	453.6

[a] Avoirdupois.
Exact conversion:
1 oz (avdp) = 28.3495 g

g	oz
1	0.04
2	0.07
3	0.11
4	0.14
5	0.18
6	0.21
7	0.25
8	0.28
9	0.32
10	0.35
20	0.71
30	1.06
40	1.41
50	1.76
60	2.12
70	2.47
80	2.82
90	3.18
100	3.53

Exact conversion:
1 g = 0.0353 oz (avdp)

lb	kg
1	0.45
2	0.91
3	1.36
4	1.81
5	2.27
6	2.72
7	3.18
8	3.63
9	4.08
10	4.54
11	4.99
12	5.44
13	5.90
14	6.35
15	6.80
16	7.26
17	7.71
18	8.16
19	8.62
20	9.07
25	11.34
30	13.61
35	15.88
40	18.14
45	20.41
50	22.68
60	27.24
70	31.78
80	36.32
90	40.86
100	45.36
200	90.72
250	113.40
500	226.80
750	340.19
1000	453.59

Exact conversion:
1 lb = 0.454 kg

kg	lb
1	2.2
2	4.4
3	6.6
4	8.8
5	11
6	13.2
7	15.4
8	17.6
9	19.8
10	22
11	24.3
12	26.5
13	28.7
14	30.9
15	33.1
16	35.3
17	37.5
18	39.7
19	41.9
20	44.1
25	55.1
30	66.1
35	77.2
40	88.2
45	99.2
50	110.2
60	132.3
70	154.4
80	176.4
90	198.5
100	220.5
200	440.9
250	551.2
500	1102.3
750	1653.5
1000	2204.6

Exact conversion:
1 kg = 2.205 lb

st	lb	st	lb
1	14	13	182
2	28	14	196
3	42	15	210
4	56	16	224
5	70	17	238
6	84	18	252
7	98	19	266
8	112	20	280
9	126		
10	140		
11	154		
12	168		

Exact conversions:
1 st = 14 lb
1 lb = 0.07 st

st	kg
1	6.35
2	12.70
3	19.05
4	25.40
5	31.75
6	38.10
7	44.45
8	50.80
9	57.15
10	63.50

Exact conversions:
1 st = 6.350 kg
1 kg = 0.1575 st

$UK\ cwt^b$	kg
1	50.8
2	102
3	152
4	203
5	254
10	508
15	762
20	1016
50	2540
75	3810
100	5080

Exact conversion:
1 UK cwt = 50.8023 kg

$UK\ cwt^b$	$US\ cwt^b$
1	1.12
2	2.24
3	3.36
4	4.48
5	5.6
10	11.2
15	16.8
20	22.4
50	56
75	84
100	102

Exact conversion:
1 UK cwt = 1.1199 US cwt

US tons	t
1	0.91
2	1.81
3	2.72
4	3.63
5	4.54
10	9.07
15	13.61
20	18.14
50	45.36
75	68.04
100	90.72

Exact conversion:
1 US ton = 0.9072 t

[b] Hundredweights: long, UK 112 lb; short, US 100 lb

US cwt	kg
1	45.4
2	90.7
3	136
4	181
5	227
10	454
15	680
20	907
50	2268
75	3402
100	4536

Exact conversion:
1 US cwt = 45.3592 kg

UK tons	t
1	1.02
2	2.03
3	3.05
4	4.06
5	5.08
10	10.16
15	15.24
20	20.32
50	50.80
75	76.20
100	101.61

Exact conversion:
1 UK ton = 1.0160 t

UK tons	US tons
1	1.12
2	2.24
3	3.36
4	4.48
5	5.6
10	11.2
15	16.8
20	22.4
50	56
75	84
100	102

Exact conversion:
1 UK ton = 1.1199 US tons

Conversion tables: weight (continued)

kg	UK cwt	US cwt		US cwt	UK cwt		t	UK tons[a]	US tons[a]		US tons[a]	UK tons[a]
1	0.0197	0.022		1	0.89		1	0.98	1.10		1	0.89
2	0.039	0.044		2	1.79		2	1.97	2.20		2	1.79
3	0.059	0.066		3	2.68		3	2.95	3.30		3	2.68
4	0.079	0.088		4	3.57		4	3.94	4.40		4	3.57
5	0.098	0.11		5	4.46		5	4.92	5.50		5	4.46
10	0.197	0.22		10	8.93		10	9.84	11.02		10	8.93
15	0.295	0.33		15	13.39		15	14.76	16.53		15	13.39
20	0.394	1.44		20	17.86		20	19.68	22.05		20	17.86
50	0.985	1.10		50	44.64		50	49.21	55.11		50	44.64
75	1.477	1.65		75	66.96		75	73.82	82.67		75	66.96
100	1.970	2.20		100	89.29		100		98.42 110.23		100	89.29

Exact conversions:
1 kg = 0.0197 UK cwt
 = 0.0220 US cwt

Exact conversion:
1 US cwt =
 0.8929 UK cwt

Exact conversions:
1 t = 0.9842 UK ton
 = 1.1023 US ton

Exact conversion:
1 US ton =
 0.8929 UK ton

[a]Tons: long, UK 2240 lb; short, US 2000 lb

Conversion table: tyre pressures

lb per sq in	kg/cm²
10	0.7
15	1.1
20	1.4
24	1.7
26	1.8
28	2
30	2.1
40	2.8

Conversion table: oven temperatures

Gas Mark	Electricity		Rating
	°C	°F	
1/2	120	250	Slow
1	140	275	
2	150	300	
3	170	325	
4	180	350	Moderate
5	190	375	
6	200	400	Hot
7	220	425	
8	230	450	Very hot
9	260	500	

Temperature conversion

To convert	To	Operations
°Fahrenheit	°Celsius	$-32, \times 5, \div 9$
°Fahrenheit	°Rankine	$+ 459.67$
°Fahrenheit	°Réaumur	$-32, \times 4, \div 9$
°Celsius	°Fahrenheit	$\times 9, \div 5, + 32$
°Celsius	Kelvin	$+ 273.16$
°Celsius	°Réaumur	$\times 4, \div 5$
Kelvin	°Celsius	$- 273.16$
°Rankine	°Fahrenheit	-459.67
°Réaumur	°Fahrenheit	$\times 9, \div 4, + 32$
°Réaumur	°Celsius	$\times 5, \div 4$

Carry out operations in sequence.

Temperature scales

	Kelvin	Celsius (centigrade)	Fahrenheit	Rankine	Réaumur
steam point	373	100°	212°	672°	80°
ice point	27	0°	32°	492°	0°
absolute zero	0	−273°	−460°	0°	−218°

Conversion tables: temperature

Degrees Fahrenheit (°F) → degrees Celsius (centigrade) (°C)

°F	°C	°F	°C	°F	°C	°F	°C	°F	°C	°F	°C
1	−17.2	37	2.8	73	22.8	109	42.8	145	62.8	181	82.8
2	−16.7	38	3.3	74	23.3	110	43.3	146	63.3	182	83.3
3	−16.1	39	3.9	75	23.9	111	43.9	147	63.9	183	83.9
4	−15.5	40	4.4	76	24.4	112	44.4	148	64.4	184	84.4
5	−15.0	41	5.0	77	25.0	113	45.0	149	65.0	185	85.0
6	−14.4	42	5.5	78	25.5	114	45.5	150	65.5	186	85.5
7	−13.9	43	6.1	79	26.1	115	46.1	151	66.1	187	86.1
8	−13.3	44	6.7	80	26.7	116	46.7	152	66.7	188	86.7
9	−12.8	45	7.2	81	27.2	117	47.2	153	67.2	189	87.2
10	−12.2	46	7.8	82	27.8	118	47.8	154	67.8	190	87.8
11	−11.6	47	8.3	83	28.3	119	48.3	155	68.3	191	88.3
12	−11.1	48	8.9	84	28.9	120	48.9	156	68.9	192	88.8
13	−10.5	49	9.4	85	29.4	121	49.4	157	69.4	193	89.4
14	−10.0	50	10.0	86	30.0	122	50.0	158	70.0	194	90.0
15	−9.4	51	10.5	87	30.5	123	50.5	159	70.5	195	90.5
16	−8.9	52	11.1	88	31.1	124	51.1	160	71.1	196	91.1
17	−8.3	53	11.7	89	31.7	125	51.7	161	71.7	197	91.7
18	−7.8	54	12.2	90	32.2	126	52.2	162	72.2	198	92.2
19	−7.2	55	12.8	91	32.8	127	52.8	163	72.8	199	92.8
20	−6.7	56	13.3	92	33.3	128	53.3	164	73.3	200	93.3
21	−6.1	57	13.9	93	33.9	129	53.9	165	73.9	201	93.9
22	−5.5	58	14.4	94	34.4	130	54.4	166	74.4	202	94.4
23	−5.0	59	15.0	95	35.0	131	55.0	167	75.0	203	95.0
24	−4.4	60	15.5	96	35.5	132	55.5	168	75.5	204	95.5
25	−3.9	61	16.1	97	36.1	133	56.1	169	76.1	205	96.1
26	−3.3	62	16.7	98	36.7	134	56.7	170	76.7	206	96.7
27	−2.8	63	17.2	99	37.2	135	57.2	171	77.2	207	97.2
28	−2.2	64	17.8	100	37.8	136	57.8	172	77.8	208	97.8
29	−1.7	65	18.3	101	38.3	137	58.3	173	78.3	209	98.3
30	−1.1	66	18.9	102	38.9	138	58.9	174	78.9	210	98.9
31	−0.5	67	19.4	103	39.4	139	59.4	175	79.4	211	99.4
32	0	68	20.0	104	40.0	140	60.0	176	80.0	212	100.0
33	0.5	69	20.5	105	40.5	141	60.5	177	80.5		
34	1.1	70	21.1	106	41.1	142	61.1	178	81.1		
35	1.7	71	21.7	107	41.7	143	61.7	179	81.7		
36	2.2	72	22.2	108	42.2	144	62.2	180	82.2		

Degrees Celsius (centigrade) (°C) → degrees Fahrenheit (°F)

°C	°F	°C	°F	°C	°F	°C	°F	°C	°F	°C	°F
1	33.8	18	64.4	35	95.0	52	125.6	69	156.2	86	186.8
2	35.6	19	66.2	36	96.8	53	127.4	70	158.0	87	188.6
3	37.4	20	68.0	37	98.6	54	129.2	71	159.8	88	190.4
4	39.2	21	69.8	38	100.4	55	131.0	72	161.6	89	192.2
5	41.0	22	71.6	39	102.2	56	132.8	73	163.4	90	194.0
6	42.8	23	73.4	40	104.0	57	134.6	74	165.2	91	195.8
7	44.6	24	75.2	41	105.8	58	136.4	75	167.0	92	197.6
8	46.4	25	77.0	42	107.6	59	138.2	76	168.8	93	199.4
9	48.2	26	78.8	43	109.4	60	140.0	77	170.6	94	201.2
10	50.0	27	80.6	44	111.2	61	141.8	78	172.4	95	203.0
11	51.8	28	82.4	45	113.0	62	143.6	79	174.2	96	204.8
12	53.6	29	84.2	46	114.8	63	145.4	80	176.0	97	206.6
13	55.4	30	86.0	47	116.6	64	147.2	81	177.8	98	208.4
14	57.2	31	87.8	48	118.4	65	149.0	82	179.6	99	210.2
15	59.0	32	89.6	49	120.2	66	150.8	83	181.4	100	212.0
16	60.8	33	91.4	50	122.0	67	152.6	84	183.2		
17	62.6	34	93.2	51	123.8	68	154.4	85	185.0		

Science and technology

Numerical equivalents

Arabic	Roman	Greek	Binary numbers
1	I	α′	1
2	II	β′	10
3	III	γ′	11
4	IV	δ′	100
5	V	ε′	101
6	VI	ζ′	110
7	VII	ξ′	111
8	VIII	η′	1000
9	IX	θ′	1001
10	X	ι′	1010
11	XI	ια′	1011
12	XII	ιβ′	1100
13	XIII	ιγ′	1101
14	XIV	ιδ′	1110
15	XV	ιε′	1111
16	XVI	ιζ′	10000
17	XVII	ιξ′	10001
18	XVIII	ιη′	10010
19	XIX	ιθ′	10011
20	XX	κ′	10100
30	XXX	λ′	11110
40	XL	μ′	10100
50	L	ν′	110010
60	LX	ξ′	111100
70	LXX	ο′	1000110
80	LXXX	π′	1010000
90	XC	‚ο′	1011010
100	C	ρ′	1100100
200	CC	σ′	11001000
300	CCC	τ′	100101100
400	CD	υ′	110010000
500	D	φ′	111110100
1000	M	‚α	1111101000
5000	‾V	‚ε	1001110001000
10000	‾X	‚ι	10011100010000
100000	‾C	‚ρ	11000011010100000

Fraction	Decimal
$1/2$	0.5000
$1/3$	0.3333
$2/3$	0.6667
$1/4$	0.2500
$3/4$	0.7500
$1/5$	0.2000
$2/5$	0.4000
$3/5$	0.6000
$4/5$	0.8000
$1/6$	0.1667
$5/6$	0.8333
$1/7$	0.1429
$2/7$	0.2857
$3/7$	0.4286
$4/7$	0.5714
$5/7$	0.7143
$6/7$	0.8571
$1/8$	0.1250
$3/8$	0.3750
$5/8$	0.6250
$7/8$	0.8750
$1/9$	0.1111
$2/9$	0.2222
$4/9$	0.4444
$5/9$	0.5555
$7/9$	0.7778
$8/9$	0.8889
$1/10$	0.1000
$3/10$	0.3000
$7/10$	0.7000
$9/10$	0.9000
$1/11$	0.0909
$2/11$	0.1818
$3/11$	0.2727
$4/11$	0.3636
$5/11$	0.4545
$6/11$	0.5454
$7/11$	0.6363

Fraction	Decimal
$8/11$	0.7272
$9/11$	0.8181
$10/11$	0.9090
$1/12$	0.0833
$5/12$	0.4167
$7/12$	0.5833
$11/12$	0.9167
$1/16$	0.0625
$3/16$	0.1875
$5/16$	0.3125
$7/16$	0.4375
$9/16$	0.5625
$11/16$	0.6875
$13/16$	0.8125
$15/16$	0.9375
$1/20$	0.0500
$3/20$	0.1500
$7/20$	0.3500
$9/20$	0.4500
$11/20$	0.5500
$13/20$	0.6500
$17/20$	0.8500
$19/20$	0.9500
$1/32$	0.0312
$3/32$	0.0938
$5/32$	0.1562
$7/32$	0.2187
$9/32$	0.2812
$11/32$	0.3437
$13/32$	0.4062
$15/32$	0.4687
$17/32$	0.5312
$19/32$	0.5937
$21/32$	0.6562
$23/32$	0.7187
$25/32$	0.7812
$27/32$	0.8437
$29/32$	0.9062
$31/32$	0.9687

%	Decimal	Fraction
1	0.01	$1/100$
2	0.02	$1/50$
3	0.03	$3/100$
4	0.04	$1/25$
5	0.05	$1/20$
6	0.06	$3/50$
7	0.07	$7/100$
8	0.08	$2/25$
$8 1/3$	0.089	$1/12$
9	0.09	$9/100$
10	0.1	$1/10$
11	0.11	$11/100$
12	0.12	$3/25$
$12 1/2$	0.125	$1/8$
13	0.13	$13/100$
14	0.14	$7/50$
15	0.15	$3/20$
16	0.16	$4/25$
$16 2/3$	0.167	$1/6$
17	0.17	$17/100$
18	0.18	$9/50$
19	0.19	$19/100$
20	0.20	$1/5$
21	0.21	$21/100$
22	0.22	$11/50$
23	0.23	$23/100$
24	0.24	$6/25$
25	0.25	$1/4$
26	0.26	$13/50$
27	0.27	$27/100$
28	0.28	$7/25$
29	0.29	$29/100$
30	0.30	$3/10$
31	0.31	$31/100$
32	0.32	$8/25$
33	0.33	$33/100$
$33 1/3$	0.333	$1/3$
34	0.34	$17/50$
35	0.35	$7/20$
36	0.36	$9/25$
37	0.37	$37/100$
38	0.38	$19/50$
39	0.39	$39/100$
40	0.40	$2/5$
41	0.41	$41/100$
42	0.42	$21/50$
43	0.43	$43/100$
44	0.44	$11/25$
45	0.45	$9/20$
46	0.46	$23/50$
47	0.47	$47/100$
48	0.48	$12/25$
49	0.49	$49/100$
50	0.50	$1/2$
55	0.55	$11/20$
60	0.60	$3/5$
65	0.65	$13/20$
70	0.70	$7/10$
75	0.75	$3/4$
80	0.80	$4/5$
85	0.85	$17/20$
90	0.90	$9/10$
95	0.95	$19/20$
100	1.00	1

Multiplication table

	2	3	4	5	6	7	8	9	10	11	12	13	14	15	16	17	18	19	20	21	22	23	24	25
2	4	6	8	10	12	14	16	18	20	22	24	26	28	30	32	34	36	38	40	42	44	46	48	50
3	6	9	12	15	18	21	24	27	30	33	36	39	42	45	48	51	54	57	60	63	66	69	72	75
4	8	12	16	20	24	28	32	36	40	44	48	52	56	60	64	68	72	76	80	84	88	92	96	100
5	10	15	20	25	30	35	40	45	50	55	60	65	70	75	80	85	90	95	100	105	110	115	120	125
6	12	18	24	30	36	42	48	54	60	66	72	78	84	90	96	102	108	114	120	126	132	138	144	150
7	14	21	28	35	42	49	56	63	70	77	84	91	98	105	112	119	126	133	140	147	154	161	168	175
8	16	24	32	40	48	56	64	72	80	88	96	104	112	120	128	136	144	152	160	168	176	184	192	200
9	18	27	36	45	54	63	72	81	90	99	108	117	126	135	144	153	162	171	180	189	198	207	216	225
10	20	30	40	50	60	70	80	90	100	110	120	130	140	150	160	170	180	190	200	210	220	230	240	250
11	22	33	44	55	66	77	88	99	110	121	132	143	154	165	176	187	198	209	220	231	242	253	264	275
12	24	36	48	60	72	84	96	108	120	132	144	156	168	180	192	204	216	228	240	252	264	276	288	300
13	26	39	52	65	78	91	104	117	130	143	156	169	182	195	208	221	234	247	260	273	286	299	312	325
14	28	42	56	70	84	98	112	126	140	154	168	182	196	210	224	238	252	266	280	294	308	322	336	350
15	30	45	60	75	90	105	120	135	150	165	180	195	210	225	240	255	270	285	300	315	330	345	360	375
16	32	48	64	80	96	112	128	144	160	176	192	208	224	240	256	272	288	304	320	336	352	368	384	400
17	34	51	68	85	102	119	136	153	170	187	204	221	238	255	272	289	306	323	340	357	374	391	408	425
18	36	54	72	90	108	126	144	162	180	198	216	234	252	270	288	306	324	342	360	378	396	414	432	450
19	38	57	76	95	114	133	152	171	190	209	228	247	266	285	304	323	342	361	380	399	418	437	456	475
20	40	60	80	100	120	140	160	180	200	220	240	260	280	300	320	340	360	380	400	420	440	460	480	500
21	42	63	84	105	126	147	168	189	210	231	252	273	294	315	336	357	378	399	420	441	462	483	504	525
22	44	66	88	110	132	154	176	198	220	242	264	286	308	330	352	374	396	418	440	462	484	506	528	550
23	46	69	92	115	138	161	184	207	230	253	276	299	322	345	368	391	414	437	460	483	506	529	552	575
24	48	72	96	120	144	168	192	216	240	264	288	312	336	360	384	408	432	456	480	501	528	552	576	600
25	50	75	100	125	150	175	200	225	250	275	300	325	350	375	400	425	450	475	500	525	550	575	600	625

Squares, cubes, and roots

No.	Square	Cube	Square root	Cube root	No.	Square	Cube	Square root	Cube root
1	1	1	1.000	1.000	13	169	2 197	3.606	2.351
2	4	8	1.414	1.260	14	196	2 744	3.742	2.410
3	9	27	1.732	1.442	15	225	3 375	3.873	2.466
4	16	64	2.000	1.587	16	256	4 096	4.000	2.520
5	25	125	2.236	1.710	17	289	4 913	4.123	2.571
6	36	216	2.449	1.817	18	324	5 832	4.243	2.621
7	49	343	2.646	1.913	19	361	6 859	4.359	2.668
8	64	512	2.828	2.000	20	400	8 000	4.472	2.714
9	81	729	3.000	2.080	25	625	15 625	5.000	2.924
10	100	1 000	3.162	2.154	30	900	27 000	5.477	3.107
11	121	1 331	3.317	2.224	40	1 600	64 000	6.325	3.420
12	144	1 728	3.464	2.289	50	2 500	125 000	7.071	3.684

Science and technology

International paper sizes

A series

	mm	in		mm	in
A0	841 × 1189	33.11 × 46.81	B5	176 × 250	6.93 × 9.84
A1	594 × 841	23.39 × 33.1	B6	125 × 176	4.92 × 6.93
A2	420 × 594	16.54 × 23.29	B7	88 × 125	3.46 × 4.92
A3	297 × 420	11.69 × 16.54	B8	62 × 88	2.44 × 3.46
A4	210 × 297	8.27 × 11.69	B9	44 × 62	1.73 × 2.44
A5	148 × 210	5.83 × 8.27	B10	31 × 44	1.22 × 1.73
A6	105 × 148	4.13 × 5.83			
A7	74 × 105	2.91 × 4.13	**C series**		
A8	52 × 74	2.05 × 2.91		mm	in
A9	37 × 52	1.46 × 2.05	C0	917 × 1 297	36.00 × 51.20
A10	26 × 37	1.02 × 1.46	C1	648 × 917	25.60 × 36.00
			C2	458 × 648	18.00 × 25.60
B series			C3	324 × 458	12.80 × 18.00
	mm	in	C4	229 × 324	9.00 × 12.80
B0	1 000 × 1414	39.37 × 55.67	C5	162 × 229	6.40 × 9.00
B1	707 × 1000	27.83 × 39.37	C6	114 × 162	4.50 × 6.40
B2	500 × 707	19.68 × 27.83	C7	81 × 114	3.20 × 4.50
B3	353 × 500	13.90 × 19.68	DL	110 × 220	4.33 × 8.66
B4	250 × 353	9.84 × 13.90	C7/6	81 × 162	3.19 × 6.38

All sizes in these series have sides in the proportion of 1 : √2.
A series is used for writing paper, books and magazines; **B** series for posters; **C** series for envelopes.

PHYSICS

Basic equations

Density

$$\text{density} = \frac{\text{mass}}{\text{volume}} \qquad \text{volume} = \frac{\text{mass}}{\text{density}}$$

mass = volume × density

Velocity

$v = u + at$

where v is the final velocity, u the original velocity, a the acceleration, and t the time taken

Pressure

$$\text{pressure} = \frac{\text{force}}{\text{area}} \qquad P = \frac{F}{A}$$

Energy

potential energy = weight × height above ground
kinetic energy = $\frac{1}{2} mv^2$
where m is the mass and v is the velocity

Waves

speed = frequency × wavelength $\quad v = f\lambda$

Electricity

charge = current × time
(coulombs) (amperes) (seconds)

$$\frac{\text{resistance}}{\text{(ohms)}} = \frac{\text{voltage (volts)}}{\text{current (amperes)}} \qquad R = \frac{V}{I}$$

$V = I \times R$

Electrical power

power = voltage × current $\quad P = V \times I$
(watts) (volts) (amperes)

$V = \dfrac{P}{I}$ and $I = \dfrac{P}{V}$

Forces of nature

	Gravity	Electro-magnetism	Weak nuclear force	Strong nuclear force
Range m	Infinite	Infinite	10^{-18} (sub-atomic)	10^{-15} (sub-atomic)
Relative strength	6×10^{-39}	1/137	10^{-5}	1
Examples of application	Orbit of Earth around Sun	Force between electrical charges	Radio-active β-decay	Binds atomic nucleus together

Elementary particles

Fundamental particles (matter particles)
Electrons
Muons
Neutrinos
Quarks
Taus

Force particles
Gluons
Gravitons
Photons
W and Z bosons

Some common physical qualities and their units

Physical quantity	Symbol	SI unit	SI symbol	Physical quantity	Symbol	SI unit	SI symbol
Acceleration, deceleration	a	metre/second² kilometre/hour/ second	m s⁻² km h⁻¹ s⁻¹	Inductance	L	henry (volt second/ ampere) (weber/ampere)	H (V s A⁻¹) (Wb A⁻¹)
Angular velocity	ω	radian/second	rad s⁻¹; s⁻¹	Induced emf	e	volt (weber/second)	V (Wb s⁻¹)
Capacitance	C	farad (coulomb/volt)	F (CV⁻¹)	Magnetic field strength	H	ampere/metre	A m⁻¹
Coefficient of viscosity	η	poise, decapoise (newton second/ metre²) (kilogram/metre/ second)	N s m⁻² kg m⁻¹ s⁻¹	Magnetic flux	ϕ	weber	Wb
				Magnetic flux density	B	tesla (weber/metre²)	T (Wb m⁻²)
Density	ρ	kilogram/metre³ kilogram/millilitre	kg m⁻³ kg ml⁻¹	Magnetic permeability	μ	henry/metre	H m⁻¹
Displacement, distance	S	metre	m	Mass	m	kilogram	kg
Electric charge	Q, q	coulomb	C	Mechanical power	–	watt (joule/second)	W (J s⁻¹)
Electric current	I, i	ampere (coulomb/second)	A C s⁻¹	Moment of inertia	I	kilogram metre²	kg m²
Electrical energy	–	megajoule, kilowatt-hour	MJ kWh	Momentum	mv	kilogram metre/ second	kg m s⁻¹
Electric intensity, field strength	E $(= -dV/dr)$	newton/coulomb volt/metre	N C⁻¹ V m⁻¹	Pressure	P	pascal (newton/metre²)	Pa (N m⁻²)
Electric pd	V	volt (joule/coulomb)	V (J C⁻¹)	Quantity of substance	–	mole	mol
Electrical power	–	watt (joule/second)	W (J s⁻¹)	Specific heat capacity	s	joule/kilogram/ kelvin	J kg⁻¹ K⁻¹
Electromotive force (emf)	E	volt (watt/ampere)	V (W A⁻¹)	Specific latent heats of fusion, vaporization	L	joule/kilogram	J kg⁻¹
Electrical conductance	S	siemen (ohm ⁻¹)	A V⁻¹	Surface tension	T, γ	newton/metre	N m⁻¹
Electrical resistance	R	ohm (volt/ampere)	Ω (V A⁻¹)	Torque, moment of force, moment of couple	–	newton metre	N m
Electric permittivity	ε	farad/metre	F m⁻¹	Velocity gradient	dv/dr	metre/second/metre	(m s⁻¹ m⁻¹)
Frequency	f	hertz (cycles/second)	Hz (s⁻¹)	Velocity, speed	u, v	metre/second kilometre/hour	m s⁻¹ km h⁻¹
Force	F	newton (kilogram metre/ second²)	N (kg m s⁻²)	Volume	V	metre³ millilitre	m³ ml
				Wavelength	λ	metre	m
Gravitational intensity, field strength	–	newton/kilogram	N kg⁻¹	Weight	W	newton, kilogram-force	N kgf
Heat capacity of a body	ms	joule/kelvin	J K⁻¹	Work, energy	–	joule (newton metre)	J (N m)

Newton's laws

First law: The velocity of an object does not change unless a force acts on the object.

Second law: A force F applied to an object of mass m causes an acceleration a according to $F = ma$.

Third law: Every action has an equal and opposite reaction.

Newton's law of gravitation

$F = Gm_1m_2/r^2$ where F is the force between objects of mass m_1 and m_2 separated by distance r, and G is the gravitational constant.

Einstein's principle of relativity

All physical laws are the same in all frames of reference in uniform motion with respect to one another.

If the energy of a body changes by amount E then its mass must change by E/c^2 where c is the velocity of light (or, expressed in its better-known form, $E=mc^2$).

Physics

Magnetism

A magnetic field is a region of magnetic influence around a magnet, moving charge, or current-carrying wire; denoted by B (unit: tesla), the magnetic flux density, and by H (unit: ampere/metre), the magnetic field strength.

Lines of magnetic field circulate around current-carrying wire.

Circuit symbols

Optics

Reflection at a mirror

The law of reflection says that angles A and B are the same.

Double-convex converging lens

Double-concave diverging lens

Basic telescope

A long-focal-length objective lens and a short-focal-length eyepiece are required.

Science and technology

516

Basic compound microscope.

The object lens forms an enlarged real image of the object, which is then viewed via the eyepiece. A short-focal-length objective lens and eyepiece are required. A 'virtual image' is an image which cannot be projected onto a screen.

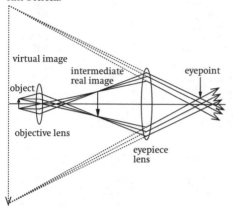

Prism

A beam of white light falling onto a prism splits into constituent colours (wavelengths), since the bending of light at an air–glass surface depends on the light wavelength, and white light comprises a mixture of colours. The white light is *dispersed* into a spectrum: the spectrum is really a continuous range of colours, not simply six as shown. With lenses, the actual bending of light occurs only at air–glass interfaces.

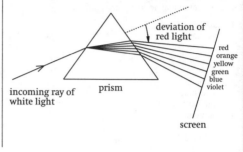

Physical constants

1986 recommended values of the main fundamental physical constants of physics and chemistry, based on a least-squares adjustment with 17 degrees of freedom. The digits in parentheses are the one-standard-deviation uncertainty in the last digits of the given value. (After Cohen and Taylor, 1987)

Quantity	Symbol	Value	Units	Relative uncertainty
Universal constants				
Speed of light in vacuum	c	299 792 458	m s^{-1}	(exact)
Permeability of vacuum	μ_0	$4\pi \times 10^{-7}$	N A^{-2}	
		$= 12.566370614\dots$	10^{-7} N A^{-2}	(exact)
Permittivity of vacuum $1/\mu_0 c^2$	ε_0	$8.854187187\dots$	10^{-12} F m^{-1}	(exact)
Newtonian constant of gravitation	G	6.67259(85)	10^{-11} m^3 kg^{-}1 s^{-2}	128
Planck constant	h	6.6260755(40)	10^{-34} J s	0.60
	$h/2\pi$	1.05457266(63)	10^{-34} J s	0.60
Electromagnetic constants				
Elementary charge	e	1.60217733(49)	10^{-19} C	0.30
	e/h	2.41798836(72)	10^{14} A J^{-1}	0.30
Magnetic flux quantum, $h/2e$	Φ_0	2.06783461(61)	10^{-15} Wb	0.30
Josephson frequency–voltage quotient	$2e/h$	4.8359767(14)	10^{-14} Hz V^{-1}	0.30
Bohr magneton, $eh/2m_e$	μ_B	9.2740154(31)	10^{-24} J T^{-1}	0.34
Nuclear magneton, $eh/2m_p$	μ_N	5.0507866(17)	10^{-27} J T^{-1}	0.34
Atomic constants				
Fine-structure constant, $\mu_0 ce^2/2h$	α	7.29735308(33)	10^{-3}	0.045
	α^{-1}	137.0359895(61)		0.045
Rydberg constant, $m_e c\alpha^2/2h$	R_∞	10 973 731.534(13)	m^{-1}	0.0012
Bohr radius, $\alpha/4\pi R_\infty$	a_0	0.529177249(24)	10^{-10} m	0.045
Quantum of circulation	$h/2m_e$	3.63694807(33)	10^{-4} m^2 s^{-1}	0.089
	h/m_e	7.27389614(65)	10^{-4} m^2 s^{-1}	0.089
Electron				
Electron mass	m_e	9.1093897(54)	10^{-31} kg	0.59
		5.48579903(13)	10^{-4} u	0.023
Electron–muon mass ratio	m_e/m_μ	4.83633218(71)	10^{-3}	0.15
Electron–proton mass ratio	m_e/m_p	5.44617013(11)	10^{-4}	0.020
Electron specific charge	$-e/m_e$	$-1.75881962(53)$	10^{11} C kg^{-1}	0.30
Compton wavelength, $h/m_e c$	λ_c	2.42631058(22)	10^{-12} m	0.089
$\lambda_c/2\pi = \alpha a_0 = \alpha^2/4\pi R_\infty$	λ_c	3.86159323(35)	10^{-13} m	0.089
Classical electron radius, $\alpha^2 a_0$	r_e	2.81794092(38)	10^{-15} m	0.13
Electron magnetic moment	μ_e	928.47701(31)	10^{-26} J T^{-1}	0.34
Electron g factor, $2(1+a_e)$	g_e	2.002319304386(20)		1×10^{-5}
Electron–proton magnetic moment ratio	μ_e/μ_p	658.2106881(66)		0.010

Physical constants (continued)

Quantity	Symbol	Value	Units	Relative uncertainty (ppm)
Muon				
Muon mass	m_μ	1.8835327(11)	10^{-28} kg	0.61
		0.113428913(17)	u	0.15
Muon magnetic moment	μ_μ	4.4904514(15)	10^{-26} J T^{-1}	0.33
Muon g factor, $2(1+a_\mu)$	g_μ	2.002331846(17)		0.0084
Muon–proton magnetic moment ratio	μ_μ/μ_p	3.18334547(47)		0.15
Proton				
Proton mass	m_p	1.6726231(10)	10^{-27} kg	0.59
		1.007276470(12)	u	0.012
Proton Compton wavelength, $h/m_p c$	$\lambda_{C,p}$	1.32141002(12)	10^{-15} m	0.089
$\lambda_{C,p}/2\pi$	$\lambda_{C,p}$	2.10308937(19)	10^{-16} m	0.089
Proton magnetic moment	μ_p	1.41060761(47)	10^{-26} J T^{-1}	0.34
in Bohr magnetons	μ_p/μ_B	1.521032202(15)	10^{-3}	0.010
in nuclear magnetons	μ_p/μ_N	2.792847386(63)		0.023
Proton gyromagnetic ratio	γ_p	26 752.2128(81)	10^4 s^{-1} T^{-1}	0.30
	$\gamma_p/2\pi$	42.577469(13)	MHz T^{-1}	0.30
Uncorrected (H$_2$0, sph., 25°C)	γ'_p	26 751.525581)	10^4 s^{-1} T^{-1}	0.30
	$\gamma'_p/2\pi$	42.576375(13)	MHz T^{-1}	0.30
Neutron				
Neutron mass	m_n	1.6749286(10)	10^{-27} kg	0.59
		1.008664904(14)	u	0.014
Neutron Compton wavelength, $h/m_n c$	$\lambda_{C,n}$	1.31959110(12)	10^{-15} m	0.089
$\lambda_{C,n}/2\pi$	$\lambda_{C,n}$	2.10019445(19)	10^{-16} m	0.089
Physico-chemical constants				
Avogadro constant	N_A, L	6.0221367(36)	10^{23} mol^{-1}	0.59
Atomic mass constant, $m_u = {}^1/_{12}m\,({}^{12}C)$	m_u	1.6605402(10)	10^{-27} kg	0.59
Faraday constant, $N_A e$	F	96 485.309(29)	C mol^{-1}	0.30
Molar gas constant	R	8.314510(70)	J mol^{-1} K^{-1}	8.4
Boltzmann constant, R/N_A	k	1.380658(12)	10^{-23} J K^{-1}	8.5
Molar volume (ideal gas), RT/p				
$T = 273.15$ K, $p = 101\,325$ Pa	V_m	0.02241410(19)	m^3 mol^{-1}	8.4
Stefan–Boltzmann constant, $(\pi^2/60)\,k^4/\hbar^3 c^2$	σ	5.67051(19)	10^{-8} W m^{-2} K^{-4}	34
First radiation constant, $2\pi h c^2$	C_1	3.7417749(22)	10^{-16} W m^2	0.60
Second radiation constant, hc/k	C_2	0.01438769(12)	m K	8.4

The electromagnetic spectrum

Radioactivity units

The activity of a radioactive source is expressed in *becquerels*, Bq, where 1 Bq is one decay per second. Particles from different substances may be produced in similar numbers but with very different energies. This is taken into account using a second unit, the *gray*, Gy, which measures the energy deposited in some object by the radiation: the *absorbed dose*. Different types of radiation cause different degrees of biological damage, even if the total energy deposited is the same; for example, 1 Gy of alpha radiation causes 20 times as much damage as 1 Gy of beta radiation. This potential for causing harm is expressed as the *dose equivalent* (unit: sievert, Sv), which is the product of the absorbed dose in Gy and a *relative biological effectiveness* (RBE) factor. Radiation limits for working places and the environment are expressed in Sv. Names, definitions, and units are summarized in the table.

Name	Definition	Unit	Old unit
Activity	Rate of disintegrations	Bq	Ci (curie)
Absorbed dose	Energy deposited in object, divided by mass of object	Gy	rad
Dose equivalent	Absorbed dose $\times$ RBE	Sv	rem

RBE	Radiation
20	Alpha
10	Neutron
1	Beta, gamma, X-ray

Sound-intensity level

Source	Sound-intensity level (dB)[a]
Jet aircraft	120
Heavy machinery	90
Busy street	70
Conversation	50
Whisper	20

[a]dB = decibels.

Science and technology

CHEMISTRY

Table of elements

Atomic weights are taken from the 1983 list of the International Union of Pure and Applied Chemistry. For radioactive elements, the mass number of the most stable isotope is given in square brackets.

Symbol	Element	Atomic no.	Weight
Ac	Actinium	89	[227]
Ag	Silver	47	107.8682
Al	Aluminium	13	26.98154
Am	Americium	95	[243]
Ar	Argon	18	39.948
As	Arsenic	33	74.9216
At	Astatine	85	[210]
Au	Gold	79	196.9665
B	Boron	5	10.811
Ba	Barium	56	137.33
Be	Beryllium	4	9.01218
Bi	Bismuth	83	208.9804
Bk	Berkelium	97	[247]
Br	Bromine	35	79.904
C	Carbon	6	12.011
Ca	Calcium	20	40.078
Cd	Cadmium	48	112.41
Ce	Cerium	58	140.12
Cf	Californium	98	[251]
Cl	Chlorine	17	35.453
Cm	Curium	96	[249]
Co	Cobalt	27	58.9332
Cr	Chromium	24	51.9961
Cs	Caesium/Cesium	55	132.9054
Cu	Copper	29	63.546
Dy	Dysprosium	66	162.50
Er	Erbium	68	167.26
Es	Einsteinium	99	[252]
Eu	Europium	63	151.96
F	Fluorine	9	18.998403
Fe	Iron	26	55.847
Fm	Fermium	100	[257]
Fr	Francium	87	[223]
Ga	Gallium	31	69.723
Gd	Gadolinium	64	157.25
Ge	Germanium	32	72.59
H	Hydrogen	1	1.00794
He	Helium	2	4.002602
Hf	Hafnium	72	178.49
Hg	Mercury	80	200.59
Ho	Holmium	67	164.9304
I	Iodine	53	126.9045
In	Indium	49	114.82
Ir	Iridium	77	192.22
K	Potassium	19	39.0983
Kr	Krypton	36	83.80
La	Lanthanum	57	138.9055
Li	Lithium	3	6.941
Lr	Lutetium	71	174.967
Lw	Lawrencium	103	[260]
Md	Mendelevium	101	[258]
Mg	Magnesium	12	24.305
Mn	Manganese	25	54.9380
Mo	Molybdenum	42	95.94
N	Nitrogen	7	14.0067
Na	Sodium	11	22.98977
Nb	Niobium	41	92.9064
Nd	Neodymium	60	144.24
Ne	Neon	10	20.179
Ni	Nickel	28	58.69
No	Nobelium	102	[259]
Np	Neptunium	93	[237]
O	Oxygen	8	15.9994
Os	Osmium	76	190.2
P	Phosphorus	15	30.97376
Pa	Protactinium	91	[231]
Pb	Lead	82	207.2
Pd	Palladium	46	106.42
Pm	Promethium	61	[145]
Po	Polonium	84	[209]
Pr	Praseodymium	59	140.9077
Pt	Platinum	78	195.08
Pu	Plutonium	94	[244]
Ra	Radium	88	[226]
Rb	Rubidium	37	85.4678
Re	Rhenium	75	186.207
Rh	Rhodium	45	102.9055
Rn	Radon	86	[222]
Ru	Ruthenium	44	101.77
S	Sulphur/sulfur	16	32.066
Sb	Antimony	51	121.75
Sc	Scandium	21	44.95591
Se	Selenium	34	78.96
Si	Silicon	14	28.0855
Sm	Samarium	62	150.36
Sn	Tin	50	118.710
Sr	Strontium	38	87.62
Ta	Tantalum	73	180.9479
Tb	Terbium	65	158.9254
Tc	Technetium	43	[99]
Te	Tellurium	52	127.60
Th	Thorium	90	232.0381
Ti	Titanium	22	47.88
Tl	Thallium	81	204.383
Tm	Thulium	69	168.9342
U	Uranium	92	238.0289
Une	Unnilennium	109	[266]
Unh	Unnilhexium	106	[263]
Unp	Unnilpexium	105	[262]
Unq	Unnilquadium	104	[261]
Uns	Unnilseptium	107	[262]
V	Vanadium	23	50.9415
W	Tungsten	74	183.85
Xe	Xenon	54	131.29
Y	Yttrium	39	88.9059
Yb	Ytterbium	70	173.04
Zn	Zinc	30	65.39
Zr	Zirconium	40	91.224

Periodic table of elements

1	2							3	4	5	6	7	8
1 **H** Hydrogen 1.00794												1 **H** Hydrogen 1.00794	2 **He** Helium 4.00260
3 **Li** Lithium 6.941	4 **Be** Beryllium 9.01218							5 **B** Boron 10.81	6 **C** Carbon 12.011	7 **N** Nitrogen 14.0067	8 **O** Oxygen 15.9994	9 **F** Fluorine 18.998403	10 **Ne** Neon 20.179
11 **Na** Sodium 22.98977	12 **Mg** Magnesium 24.305				*Transition series*			13 **Al** Aluminium 26.98154	14 **Si** Silicon 28.0855	15 **P** Phosphorus 30.97376	16 **S** Sulphur 32.06	17 **Cl** Chlorine 35.453	18 **Ar** Argon 39.948

Transition series

1	2	21	22	23	24	25	26	27	28	29	30	3	4	5	6	7	8
19 **K** Potassium 39.0983	20 **Ca** Calcium 40.08	21 **Sc** Scandium 44.9559	22 **Ti** Titanium 47.88	23 **V** Vanadium 50.9415	24 **Cr** Chromium 51.996	25 **Mn** Manganese 54.9380	26 **Fe** Iron 55.847	27 **Co** Cobalt 58.9332	28 **Ni** Nickel 58.69	29 **Cu** Copper 63.546	30 **Zn** Zinc 65.38	31 **Ga** Gallium 69.72	32 **Ge** Germanium 72.59	33 **As** Arsenic 74.9216	34 **Se** Selenium 78.96	35 **Br** Bromine 79.904	36 **Kr** Krypton 83.80
37 **Rb** Rubidium 85.4678	38 **Sr** Strontium 87.62	39 **Y** Yttrium 88.9059	40 **Zr** Zirconium 91.22	41 **Nb** Niobium 92.9064	42 **Mo** Molybdenum 95.94	43 **Tc** Technetium (98)	44 **Ru** Ruthenium 101.07	45 **Rh** Rhodium 102.9055	46 **Pd** Palladium 106.42	47 **Ag** Silver 107.8682	48 **Cd** Cadmium 112.41	49 **In** Indium 114.82	50 **Sn** Tin 118.69	51 **Sb** Antimony 121.75	52 **Te** Tellurium 127.60	53 **I** Iodine 126.9045	54 **Xe** Xenon 131.29
55 **Cs** Caesium 132.9054	56 **Ba** Barium 137.33	57–71 Lanthanide series (rare earth elements) ★	72 **Hf** Hafnium 178.49	73 **Ta** Tantalum 180.7479	74 **W** Tungsten 180.7479	75 **Re** Rhenium 186.207	76 **Os** Osmium 190.2	77 **Ir** Iridium 192.2	78 **Pt** Platinum 195.08	79 **Au** Gold 196.9665	80 **Hg** Mercury 200.59	81 **Tl** Thallium 204.383	82 **Pb** Lead 207.2	83 **Bi** Bismuth 208.9804	84 **Po** Polonium (209)	85 **At** Astatine (210)	86 **Rn** Radon (222)
87 **Fr** Francium (223)	88 **Ra** Radium 226.0254	89–103 Actinide series (radioactive rare earth elements) ☆	104 **Unq** Unnilquadium (261)	105 **Unp** Unnilpentium (262)	106 **Unh** Unnilhexium (263)	107 **Uns** Unnilseptium (262)	108 **Une** Unnilennium (266)										

★

57 **La** Lanthanum 138.9055	58 **Ce** Cerium 140.12	59 **Pr** Praseodymium 140.9077	60 **Nd** Neodymium 144.24	61 **Pm** Promethium (145)	62 **Sm** Samarium 150.36	63 **Eu** Europium 151.96	64 **Gd** Gadolinium 157.25	65 **Tb** Terbium 158.9254	66 **Dy** Dysprosium 162.50	67 **Ho** Holmium 164.9304	68 **Er** Erbium 167.26	69 **Tm** Thulium 168.9342	70 **Yb** Ytterbium 173.04	71 **Lu** Lutetium 174.967

☆

89 **Ac** Actinium 227.0278	90 **Th** Thorium 232.0381	91 **Pa** Protactinium 231.0359	92 **U** Uranium 238.0289	93 **Np** Neptunium 237.0482	94 **Pu** Plutonium (244)	95 **Am** Americium (243)	96 **Cm** Curium (247)	97 **Bk** Berkelium (247)	98 **Cf** Californium (252)	99 **Es** Einsteinium (254)	100 **Fm** Fermium (257)	101 **Md** Mendelevium (258)	102 **No** Nobelium (259)	103 **Lr** Lawrencium (260)

Atomic number — 86

Rn — Symbol

Radon — Element name

(222) — Atomic weight (most stable isotope of radioactive elements in parentheses)

Science and technology

Physical properties of metals

Metal	Electron structure	Electronegativity	Atomic number	Melting point (°C)	Boiling point (°C)
Aluminium (Al)	$(Ne)3s^23p^1$	1.5	13	659	2447
Barium (Ba)	$(Xe)6s^2$	0.9	56	710	1637
Beryllium (Be)	$(He)2s^2$	1.5	4	1283	2477
Caesium (Cs)	$(Xe)6s'$	0.7	55	29	685
Calcium (Ca)	$(Ar)4s^2$	1.0	20	850	1492
Chromium (Cr)	$(Ar)3d^54s'$	1.6	24	2176	2915
Cobalt (Co)	$(Ar)3d^74s^2$	1.8	27	1768	3150
Copper (Cu)	$(Ar)3d^{10}4s'$	1.9	29	1356	2855
Iron (Fe)	$(Ar)3d^64s^2$	1.8	26	1812	3160
Lead (Pb)	$(Xe)5d^{10}6s^26p^2$	1.8	82	328	1751
Lithium (Li)	$(He)2s^1$	1.0	3	181	1331
Magnesium (Mg)	$(Ne)3s^2$	1.2	12	650	117
Manganese (Mn)	$(Ar)3d^54s^2$	1.5	25	1517	2314
Nickel (Ni)	$(Ar)3d^84s^2$	1.8	28	1728	3110
Potassium (K)	$(Ar)4s^1$	0.8	19	63	766
Rubidium (Rb)	$(Kr)5s^1$	0.8	37	39	701
Sodium (Na)	$(Ne)3s^1$	0.9	11	98	890
Strontium (Sr)	$(Kr)5s^2$	1.0	38	770	1367
Tin (Sn)	$(Kr)4d^{10}5s^25p^2$	1.8	50	232	2690
Titanium (Ti)	$(Ar)3d^24s^2$	1.5	22	1673	2750
Vanadium (V)	$(Ar)3d^34s^2$	1.6	23	2190	3650
Zinc (Zn)	$(Ar)3d^{10}4s^2$	1.6	30	693	1181

Symbols used in chemistry

Polymers

Polymer	Repeat unit	Properties and uses
Polyamides		
Nylon-6,6		Textile fibre, threads, ropes. Moulded gears and electrical insulation
Nylon-6,10		Sports equipment. Bristles for brushes
Nomex		Heat-resistant polymer in space suits. Also for parachute cords
Polyesters and polycarbonates		
Terylene, Dacron		Textile fibre. Basis for magnetic tape and photographic film

Polymer	Repeat unit	Properties and uses
Lexan		Tough and transparent Bullet-proof windows, safety glass Food containers Car components

Polyethers

Polyglycol 166		Making urethanes and speciality elastomers, eg for oil and fuel hoses, oil-well equipment
Delrin, Celcon		Tough plastic for gears, pipes, pens

Phenol-based

Bakelite		Hard thermosetting polymer Telephones, buttons, electrical insulators
Poly(melamine formaldehyde)		Laminated surfaces, eg table tops, cupboards

Polyurethanes

Polyurethane		Foam rubber, synthetic leather
Lycra		Expanded foam rubber, carpet underlays, clothing

Alkenes

ABS[a] polymers contain these four types of repeat unit		Tough structural plastic or rubber Telephones, pipes, many moulded articles
Polybutadiene (butadiene rubber)		Alternative to natural rubber Footwear, tyres, toys

[a]ABS = acrylonitrile–butadiene–styrene

Polymer	Repeat unit	Properties and uses
Neoprene		Adhesive golf-ball covers, liquid seals
Polythene [a](polyethene)		Tough plastic Fibres, thin films, extrusion-moulded objects, toys, bottles
Butyl rubber		Tyre inner tubes, raincoats, seals
Natural rubber (poly (*cis*-1,4-isoprene))		After vulcanization, used in car, and other, tyres
PTFE (poly(tetra-fluoroethene), Teflon)		Highly water-repellent Nonstick cooking ware Industrial uses where very low friction needed
Polystyrene		Transparent, glass-like Wide variety of moulded and expanded objects Packing and insulation
Perspex (poly(methyl methacrylate))		Transparent, glass-like Windows, fibre optics, illuminated signs
PVC (polyvinyl chloride)		Hard inflexible polymer With plasticizer, used in tubing, thin films, car-seat covers, floor tile

Alkynes

Polyethyne (polyacetylene)	delocalized electrons	With iodine, an electrically conducting polymer

Inorganic

Silicone rubber		Seals, hoses, waterproofing, 'silicone grease'
Carbon fibres	Carbon layers with layers parallel to axis of fibre	Very high-strength fibres, eg in aeroplane and boat building
Polythiazyl	$-S{=}N-$	An electrically conducting polymer Semiconductor at very low temperatures

[a]There are two main types of polyethene; low-density polyethene (LDPE) has considerable branching; high-density polyethene (HDPE) has no branching.

Hazardous substances symbols

| Harmful/ irritant | Toxic | Radioactive | Flammable | Corrosive | Oxidizing/ supports fire | Explosive |

TECHNOLOGY

Major technological inventions

Date	Invention	Inventor/discoverer
1752	Lightning conductor	Benjamin Franklin
1764	Spinning jenny	James Hargreaves
1768	Spinning frame	Richard Arkwright
1769	Condenser (steam engine)	James Watt
1774	Telegraph (electric)	Georges Louis Lesage
1775	Steam ship	Jacques Perrier
1776	Submarine	David Bushnell
1779	Spinning mule	Samuel Crompton
1780	Circular saw	Gervinus
1783	Hot-air balloon	Jacques and Joseph Montgolfier
1784	Safety lock	Joseph Bramah
1785	Chemical bleaching	Claude Berthollet
1792	Cotton gin	Eli Whitney
1792	Gas lighting	William Murdoch
1795	Preserving jar (foods)	Francois Appert
1798	Lithography	Aloys Senefelder
1799	Sheet paper-making machine	Louis Robert
1800	Electric battery	Alessandro Volta
1802	Wood-planing machine	Joseph Bramah
1804	Locomotive	Richard Trevithick
1807	Conveyor belt	Oliver Evans
1810	Canning	Nicholas Appert
1812	Photographic lens	William H Wollaston
1813	Power loom	William Horrocks
1823	Waterproof material	Charles Macintosh
1824	Cement	Joseph Aspdin
1829	Typewriter	William Burt
1831	Electric generator	Michael Faraday
1834	Harvesting machine	Cyril McCormick
1835	Revolver	Samuel Colt
1835	Computer	Charles Babbage
1838	Photography (on paper)	William Henry Fox Talbot
1839	Bicycle	Kirkpatrick Macmillan
1843	Underground railway	Charles Pearson
1845	Hydraulic crane	W G Armstrong
1846	Sewing machine	Elias Howe
1846	Rotary printing press	Richard Hoe
1850	Synthetic oil	James Young
1850	Refrigerator	James Harrison and Alexander Twining
1851	Mechanical lift	Elisha Otis
1854	Hydraulic lift	Elisha Otis
1855	Celluloid	Alexander Parks
1855	Steel production	Henry Bessemer

Date	Invention	Inventor/discoverer
1856	Synthetic dye	William Henry Perkin
1876	Microphone	Alexander Graham Bell
1861	Colour photography	James Clerk Maxwell
1866	Telegraph (transatlantic)	Willliam Thompson (Lord Kelvin)
1867	Pasteurization	Louis Pasteur
1868	Tungsten steel	Robert Mushet
1868	Traffic lights	J P Knight
1871	Pneumatic drill	Samuel Ingersoll
1872	Electric typewriter	Thomas Edison
1873	Barbed wire	Joseph Glidden
1876	Telephone	Alexander Graham Bell
1877	Electric welding	Elisha Thomson
1877	Gramophone	Thomas Edison
1878	Electric railway	Ernst Werner von Siemens
1879	Electric lamp	Thomas Edison
1880	Pendulum seismograph	James Ewing, Thomas Gray, and Sir John Milne
1882	Electric flat iron	Harry W Seeley
1883	Automatic machine gun	Sir Hiram (Stevens) Maxim
1884	Fountain pen	Lewis Waterman
1884	Car (internal combustion engine)	Gottlieb Daimler
1885	Adding machine	William Burroughs
1885	Petrol engine	Gottlieb Daimler
1885	Motorcycle	Gottlieb Daimler
1886	Car (petrol engine)	Karl Benz
1887	Celluloid film	Goodwin
1888	Pneumatic tyre	John Boyd Dunlop
1888	Alternating-current motor	Nikola Tesla
1888	Gramophone record	Emil Berliner
1889	Photographic film	George Eastman
1892	Escalator	Jesse Reno
1894	Automatic loom	J H Northrop
1894	Cinematograph	Auguste and Louis Lumière
1894	Turbine ship	Charles Parsons
1895	X-ray	Wilhelm Röntgen
1895	Safety razor	King C Gillette
1898	Diesel engine	Rudolf Diesel
1900	Cellophane	J E Brandenburger
1900	Airship	Graf Ferdinand von Zeppelin
1901	Radio	Guglielmo Marconi
1901	Vacuum cleaner (electric)	Hubert Cecil Booth

Major technological inventions (continued)

Date	Invention	Inventor/discoverer	Date	Invention	Inventor/discoverer
1902	Windscreen wipers	Mary Anderson	1948	Transistor	William Shockley,
1903	Electrocardiagraph	Wilhelm Einthoven			John Bardeen, and
1903	Aeroplane	Orville and			Walter Brattain
		Wilbur Wright	1950	Gas-turbine powered	Rover Motor Co.
1906	Freeze-drying	Arsene D'Arsonval and		car	
		Georges Bordas	1954	Solar battery	Bell Telephone Co.
1907	Electric washing	Hurley Machine Co.	1956	Video recorder	Ampex Co.
	machine		1959	Hovercraft	Christopher Cockerell
1907	Facsimile machine	Arthur Korn	1959	Microchip	Kilby and Robert
	(fax)				Noyce
1907	Bakelite	Leo Bakeland	1960	Laser	Charles Townes
1911	Neon light	Georges Claude	1967	Laser-surgery	Cincinatti, US
1913	Stainless steel	Harry Brearley		operating theatre	
1924	Loudspeaker	Rice-Kellogg	1969	Concorde supersonic	Britain–France
1926	Television	John Logie Baird	1969	Test-tube baby	Robert Edwards,
1926	Liquid-fuel rocket	Robert Goddard			Patrick Steptoe
1933	Electron microscope	Max Knoll and	1969	V/STOL Harrier	Hawker Siddeley
		Ernst Ruska	1970	747 Jumbo jet	Boeing
1934	Cat's eyes	Percy Shaw	1971	Microprocessor	Marcian Hoff
1935	Parking meter	Carlton C Magee	1972	Pocket calculator	
1937	Turbo jet	Frank Whittle	1976	Industrial robot	
1938	Ball-point pen	Laszlo and Georg Biró	1976	Space shuttle	NASA
1938	Nylon	Wallace Carrothers	1978	TGV high-speed train	France
1938	Xerography	Charles Carson	1979	Walkman	Sony
1939	Helicopter	Igor Sikorsky	1979	Compact disc	Philips and Sony
1939	Atom bomb	Otto Frisch, Niels Bohr,	1981	Personal computer	IBM
		and Rudolf Peierls	1985	Battery-powered	Clive Sinclair
1941	Terylene	J R Whinfield and		vehicle (C5)	
		J T Dickson	1986	Laser instruments for	
1942	Turbo-prop engine	Max Mueller		heart and eye surgery	
1944	Digital computer	Harvard University	1986	Pocket telephone	
1945	Microwave oven	Percy Le Baron Spencer	1987	Digital audio tape	
			1988	Video walkman	Sony

The world's tallest structures

Name of structure	Location	Year	Height m	Height ft
Warszawa Radio Mast	Konstantynow, Poland	1974	646	2 120
KTHI-TV	North Dakota, US	1963	629	2 063
CN Tower	Toronto, Canada	1975	553	1 815
Ostankino TV Tower	Nr Moscow, Russia	1967	537	1 762
WRBL-TV & WTVM	Georgia, US	1963	533	1 749
WBIR-TV	Tennessee, US	1963	533	1 749
Moscow TV Tower	Moscow, Russia		528	1 732
KFVS-TV	Missouri, US	1960	510	1 672
WSPD-TV	Kentucky, US		499	1 638
WGAN-TV	Maine, US	1959	493	1 619
KSWS-TV	New Mexico, US	1956	490	1 610
WKY-TV	Oklahoma, US		487	1 600
KW-TV	Oklahoma, US	1954	479	1 572
Bren Tower	Nevada, US	1962	465	1 527
Sears Tower	Chicago, Illinois, US	1974	443	1 454
World Trade Centre	New York City, US	1973	412	1 350
Empire State Building	New York City, US	1930	381	1 200
Empire State Building	New York City, US	1988	368	1 250
Bank of China	Hong Kong	1973	346	1 136
John Hancock Centre	Chicago, Illinois, US	1968	343	1 127
Chrysler Building	New York City, US	1930	319	1 046
Library Tower	Los Angeles, US	1989	310	1 017
Texas Commercial Plaza	Houston, Texas, US	1981	305	1 000
Allied Bank Plaza	Houston, Texas, US	1983	302	991

The world's highest dams

Name	Date completed	Place	Height m	Height ft
Bhakra	1963	India	226	741
Chicoasen	1981	Mexico	265	869
Chirkey	1977	Ukraine	233	764
Chivor	1975	Columbia	237	778
Contra	1965	Switzerland	220	722
Dabaklamm	uncompleted	Austria	220	722
El Cajon	1984	Honduras	226	741
Grande Dixence	1962	Switzerland	285	935
Guavio	1989	Columbia	250	820
Hoover	1936	Arizona/ Nevada, US	221	726
Inguri	1984	Georgia, US	272	892
Kinshau	1985	India	253	830
Mauvoisin	1957	Switzerland	237	777
Mica	1972	Canada	242	794
Mihoesti	1983	Romania	242	794
Nurek	1980	Tadzhikistan	300	984
Oroville	1968	California	235	770
Rogun	1985	Tadzhikistan	325	1066
Sayano-Shushenk	1980	Russia	242	794
Tehri	uncompleted	India	261	856
Vaiont	1961	Italy	265	869

The world's longest tunnels

Name	Date completed	Place	Length km	Length mi
Aki	1975	Japan	12.8	8
Apennine	1934	Italy	17.7	11
Cascade	1929	US	14.5	9
Channel	1994 (scheduled)	UK/France	49.9	31
Chesapeake Bay	1964	US	28	17.65
Dai-shimizu	1979	Japan	22.5	14
Flathead	1970	US	12.8	8
Frejus (Mont Cenis)	1871	France/Italy	12.8	8
Hokuriku	1962	Japan	14.5	9
Kammon	1975	Japan	19.3	12
Lotschberg	1913	Switzerland	14.5	9.03
Mersey	1934	UK	4	2.5
Mont Blanc	1965	France/Italy		
Moscow subway	1990	Russia	37.9	23.5
Mount MacDonald	1989	Canada	14.6	9.1
Rokko (rail)	1972	Japan	16	10
Rove	1927	France	7.12	4.42
San Fransisco Subway	1971	US	5.8	3.6
Seikan	1985	Japan	53.9	33.49
Shin Shimizu	1961	Japan	12.8	8
Simplon I and II	1906, 1922	Switzerland/ Italy	19.3	12
St Gotthard (rail)	1882	Switzerland	14.9	9.26

The world's longest bridges

Name	Date completed	Place	Length m	Length ft
Akashi-Kaikyo	uncompleted	Japan	83910	12828
Ambassador	1929	Detroit, US	564	1850
Angostura	1967	Venezuela	1678	5507
Bendorf	1965	Koblenz, Germany	1030	3378
Bosporus	1973	Istanbul, Turkey	1074	3524
Commodore John Bay	1974	Pennsylvania, US	501	1644
Forth Road Bridge	1964	Scotland, UK	900	3000
George Washington Bridge	1931	New York City, US	1067	3500
Golden Gate	1937	San Francisco, US	1280	4200
Humber	1981	UK	1410	4626
Kincardine	1936	Scotland, UK	822	2696
Little Belt	1970	Denmark	600	1968
Luzhniki	1959	Russia	2027	6650
Mackinac	1957	Michigan, US	1158	3800
Minami-Bisan-Seto	1988	Japan	1100	3609
New Gorge	1977	Virginia, US	3839	12596
Oakland Bay (Transbay)	1936	San Francisco, US	426.7	1400
Osland Island	1972	Sweden	6060	19882
Philadelphia-Camden	1926	US	533	1750
Quebec rail	1917	Canada	549	1850
Rio Nileroi	1972	Brazil	1025	3363
Salazar	1966	Lisbon, Portugal	1013	3323
Save Bridge	1970	Mozambique	872	2860
Second Lake Washington	1963	Seattle, US	3839	12596
Seto-Ohashi	1988	Japan	13220	43374
Skarnsundet	1991	Norway	530	1739
Sydney Harbour	1932	Sydney, Australia	503	1650
Tatara	1997 (scheduled)	Japan	890	2920
Tay II	1887	Scotland, UK	3552	11653
Tete	1971	Mozambique	872	2360
Verrazano-Narrows	1964	New York Harbor, US	1298	4260
Yokohama Bay	1989	Japan	855	2805

Science and technology

COMPUTERS

Programming languages

Language	Derivation of name	Applications
Ada		A high-level procedural language designed for programming computers for real-time applications – more specifically, where the computer is controlling the behaviour of military devices.
ALGOL	(ALGOrithmic Language)	One of the first languages developed for mathematical and scientific use. It introduced a number of new concepts and has been very influential in the design of other languages.
Assembly language		A low-level language which is a notation for representing machine code in human-readable form.
BASIC	(Beginners' All-purpose Symbolic Instruction Code)	A simple high-level language that can be used for general-purpose computing, especially on microcomputers. Designed for beginners.
C		Provides all the structure of a high-level language with certain low-level features that do not require the programmer to use assembly language. It is fast and portable and is the language in which the UNIX operating system was developed.
C++		An object-orientated language that is a descendent of C but in the tradition of ALGOL.
COBOL	(COmmon Business Oriented Language)	A high-level language that is the standard for all business data processing.
FORTRAN	(FORmula TRANslation)	A high-level language widely used for scientific computing; current standard is FORTRAN 77, but dates from 1956.
Hypertalk		A scripting language that is the basis of Hypercard.
LISP	(LISt Processing)	A high-level functional language with the imperative features designed for the processing of non-numeric data. Used for symbolic manipulation and in Artificial Intelligence.
LOGO		A graphics language used mainly for teaching small children.
Machine code		A low-level language into which all high-level languages must be translated before they can run. Machine codes are specific to machines and are in fact a series of machine-readable instructions.
ML	(Meta Language)	A high-level functional language used mainly for research purposes.
Modula 2		A high-level imperative language, derived from Pascal, in which programs may be written in modular form, ie built up from independently-written modules.
Pascal		A high-level imperative language descended from ALGOL, and originally designed for teaching purposes.
PROLOG	(PROgramming in LOGic)	A high-level declarative language, designed for use in Artificial Intelligence.
Smalltalk		One of the first object-orientated languages, developed at Xerox Palo Alto Research Center.

The development of computers

Name of instrument	Inventor	Date developed	Comments
Abacus		Middle Ages	Calculations performed with sliding counters.
Mechanical adding machine	Blaise Pascal, France	1642	
Stepped reckoner	Gottfried Leibniz, Germany	1673	Mechanical instrument able to multiply, divide and extract square roots as well as add.
Analytical engine	Charles Babbage, Britain	1830	First automatic computer. Able to combine arithmetic processes with decisions based on own computations.
Boolean algebra	George Boole, Britain	mid 19th century	Boole discovered analogy of algebraic symbols and those of logic. Binary logic operations brought about electronic computer switching theory and procedures.
Data-processing cards	Hermann Hollerith, US	1890	Introduction of perforated cards with pattern of holes which could be read by machine designed to sort and manipulate the data represented by the holes.
Prototype of electromechanical digital computer	John Atanasoff, US	1939	
Calculator	Howard Aiken, US	1939	
Automatic Sequence Controlled calculator (Harvard Mark I)	Howard Aiken, US	1944	Series of instructions coded on punched paper tape entered and output recorded on cards or by electric typewriter.
Colossus	Alan Turing, Britain	1943	Special-purpose electronic computer designed to decipher codes.
ENIAC (Electronic Numerical integrator and Calculator)	J Presper Eckert and John W Mauchly	1946	Marked the beginning of the first generation of modern computers. This was the first all-purpose electronic digital computer.
Transistor	Shockley, Bardeen and Brattain	1948	Reliable with low power consumption.
EDSAC	Cambridge University	1949	First working version of a stored-program computer, ie instructions stored in computer's memory.
EDVAC (Electronic Discrete Variable Automatic Computer)	John Neumann	1950	Stored-program computer.
UNIVAC (Universal Automatic Computer)	Eckert and Mauchly	1951	Used memory system made of mercury delay lines which gave access time of 500 microseconds. First computer able to handle numerical and alphabetical data with equal ease.
Harvard Mark III		mid 1950s	Magnetic drum memory provided large storage capacity.
Integrated circuit (IC)		1960s/70s	IC allowed construction of large-scale (mainframe) computers with high operating speeds.
LSI (Large-scale Integration)		1960s/70s	Thousands of transistors and related devices could be packed onto a single integrated circuit.
RAM (Random Access Memory)		1960s/70s	RAM chip used in constructing semiconductor memory units.

The development of computers (continued)

Name of instrument	Inventor	Date developed	Comments
PDP-8	DEC (Digital Equipment)	1963	First minicomputer.
IBM System/360	IBM	1964	First family of compatible computers launched.
Control Data CD6000		1965	First supercomputer developed.
Intel 4004	Marian Hoff, US	1971	First microprocessor. (An integrated circuit with all arithmetic, logic and control circuitry necessary to serve the central processing unit (CPU).)
Altair 8800		1975	First personal computer.
Xerox Start System		1981	First windows, icons, menus, and pointing devices system developed.
Optical microchip		1988	Used light instead of electricity.
Water-scale silicon memory chip		1989	Able to store 200 million characters.
Windows	Microsoft	1990	Windows 3 released, a windowing environment for computers.

ARTS AND CULTURE

LITERATURE

Novelists

Name	Dates	Place of birth	Selected works
Achebe, Chinua (Albert Chinualumogu)	1930–	Ogidi, Nigeria	*Things Fall Apart* (1958); *Anthills of the Savannah* (1987)
Ackroyd, Peter	1949–	London	*The Last Testament of Oscar Wilde* (1983); *Chatterton* (1988)
Adams, Douglas (Noel)	1952–	Essex	*The Hitch Hiker's Guide to the Galaxy* (1979)
Adams, Richard (George)	1920–	Newbury, Berkshire	*Watership Down* (1972); *Shardik* (1974); *The Girl in a Swing* (1980)
Alcott, Louisa M(ay)	1832–88	Germantown, Pennsylvania	*Little Women* (1868)
Amis, Kingsley (William)	1922–	London	*Lucky Jim* (1954); *That Uncertain Feeling* (1956); *Jake's Thing* (1978); *The Old Devils* (1986)
Amis, Martin	1949–	Oxford	*The Rachel Papers* (1973); *London Fields* (1990); *Time's Arrow* (1991)
Angelou, Maya (Marguerita Johnson)	1928–	St Louis, Missouri	*I Know Why The Caged Bird Sings* (1970); *All God's Children Need Travelling Shoes* (1986)
Archer, Jeffrey (Howard)	1940–	Somerset	*Not a Penny More, Not a Penny Less* (1975); *Kane and Abel* (1979); *First Among Equals* (1984); *A Twist in the Tale* (1989)
Asimov, Isaac	1920–92	Petrovichi, USSR	*Foundation* (1951), *The Disappearing Man and other stories* (1985); *Nightfall* (1990)
Atwood, Margaret (Eleanor)	1939–	Ottawa, Canada	*The Handmaid's Tale* (1985); *Cat's Eye* (1989)
Austen, Jane	1775–1817	Steventon, Hampshire	*Sense and Sensibility* (1811); *Pride and Prejudice* (1813); *Mansfield Park* (1814); *Emma* (1815); *Persuasion* (1818)
Auster, Paul	1947–	Newark, New Jersey	*The New York Trilogy* (1985–6); *Moon Palace* (1989); *The Music of Chance* (1990)
Bainbridge, Beryl	1934–	Liverpool	*The Dressmaker* (1973); *Injury Time* (1977); *Forever England* (1986)
Baldwin, James (Arthur)	1924–87	Harlem, New York City	*Go Tell It On the Mountain* (1954); *Another Country* (1962)
Ballard, J(ames) G(raham)	1930–	Shanghai, China	*The Drowned World* (1962); *The Terminal Beach* (1964); *Empire of the Sun* (1984)
Balzac, Honoré de	1799–1850	Tours	*La Comédie humaine* (1827–47); *Illusions perdues* (1837–43)
Banks, Iain	1954–	Fife, Scotland	*The Wasp Factory* (1984); *The Bridge* (1986)
Barnes, Djuna	1892–1982	New York	*Nightwood* (1936)
Barnes, Julian	1946–	Leicester	*Flaubert's Parrot* (1984); *Staring at the Sun* (1986); *A History of the World in $10^1/_2$ Chapters* (1989); *The Porcupine* (1992)
Barstow, Stan(ley)	1928–	Horbury, Yorkshire	*A Kind of Loving* (1960)
Bates, H(erbert) E(rnest)	1905–74	Northamptonshire	*The Two Sisters* (1926); *The Jacaranda Tree* (1949); *The Darling Buds of May* (1958); *Oh, To Be in England* (1963)
Bawden, Nina	1925–	London	*The Birds on the Trees* (1970); *Walking Naked* (1981); *The Ice House* (1983)
Beckett, Samuel (Barclay)	1906–89	Dublin	*Murphy* (1938); *Malone Dies* (1951); *The Unnameable* (1953)
Bedford, Sybille (née Schoenebach)	1911–	Charlottenburg, Germany	*A Legacy* (1956); *Jigsaw: An Unsentimental Education* (1989)
Bellow, Saul	1915–	Quebec, Canada	*Herzog* (1964); *Humboldt's Gift* (1975); *The Dean's December* (1982)
Bennett, Arnold	1867–1931	Hanley, Staffordshire	*Anna of the Five Towns* (1902); *Clayhanger* series (1910–18)
Binchy, Maeve	1940–	Dublin	*Light a Penny Candle* (1982); *Echoes* (1985); *Firefly Summer* (1987); *Circle of Friends* (1990)
Blackmore, R(ichard) D(oddridge)	1825–1900	Longworth, Oxfordshire	*Lorna Doone* (1869)
Böll, Heinrich	1917–85	Cologne	*And Never Said a Solitary Word* (1953); *The Unguarded House* (1954); *The Bread of Our Early Years* (1955)
Borges, Jorge Luis	1899–1986	Buenos Aires	*Fictions* (1945); *El Aleph* (1949); *Labyrinths* (1953)
Bowen, Elizabeth (Dorothea Cole)	1899–1973	Dublin	*The Death of the Heart* (1938); *The Heat of the Day* (1949)
Bowles, Paul	1910–	New York City	*The Sheltering Sky* (1949)

Literature

Novelists (continued)

Name	Dates	Place of birth	Selected works
Boyd, William	1952–	Accra, Ghana	*A Good Man in Africa* (1982); *An Ice Cream War* (1983); *Brazzaville Beach* (1990)
Bradbury, Malcolm (Stanley)	1932–	Sheffield	*Eating People Is Wrong* (1959); *The History Man* (1975)
Bradbury, Ray(mond)	1920–	Waukegan, Illinois	*Fahrenheit 451* (1953); *Something Wicked This Way Comes* (1962)
Bradford, Barbara Taylor	1933–	Leeds	*A Woman of Substance* (1979); *Hold the Dream* (1985)
Bragg, Melvyn	1939–	Carlisle	*The Hired Man* (1969); *The Maid of Buttermere* (1987); *A Time to Dance* (1990)
Brittain, Vera	1893–1970	Stoke-on-Trent	*Testament of Youth* (1933); *Testament of Friendship* (1940)
Brontë, Anne	1820–49	Thornton, Yorkshire	*Agnes Grey* (1845); *The Tenant of Wildfell Hall* (1848)
Brontë, Charlotte	1816–55	Thornton, Yorkshire	*Jane Eyre* (1847); *Shirley* (1849); *Villette* (1853)
Brontë, Emily	1818–48	Thornton, Yorkshire	*Wuthering Heights* (1847)
Brookner, Anita	1928–	London	*Hotel du Lac* (1984); *Family and Friends* (1985); *Brief Lives* (1991)
Buchan, John	1875–1940	Perth, Scotland	*The Thirty-Nine Steps* (1915)
Buck, Pearl (née Sydenstricker)	1892–1973	Hillsborough, Virginia	*The Good Earth* (1931); *Pavilion of Women* (1946)
Bulgakov, Mikhail	1891–1940	Kiev	*The Master and Margarita* (1928–40); *The White Guard* (1925); *Heart of a Dog* (1925)
Bunyan, John	1628–88	Elstow, nr Bedford	*The Pilgrim's Progress* (1678, 1684)
Burgess, Anthony (John Anthony Burgess Wilson)	1917–	Manchester	*A Clockwork Orange* (1962); *Earthly Powers* (1980); *Kingdom of the Wicked* (1985); *Any Old Iron* (1989)
Burroughs, William S(eward)	1914–	St Louis, Missouri	*The Naked Lunch* (1959); *The Soft Machine* (1961); *The Wild Boys* (1971); *Exterminator!* (1974); *Cities of the Red Night* (1981)
Butler, Samuel	1835–1902	Langar Rectory, Nottinghamshire	*Erewhon* (1872); *The Way of All Flesh* (1903)
Byatt, A(ntonia) S(usan)	1936–	Sheffield	*The Shadow of a Sun* (1964); *The Virgin in the Garden* (1978); *Possession* (1989)
Caldwell, Erskine	1903–87	Georgia	*Tobacco Road* (1932); *God's Little Acre* (1933); *Journeyman* (1935)
Calvino, Italo	1923–87	Santiago de Las Vegas, Cuba	*Invisible Cities* (1972); *The Castle of Crossed Destinies* (1969); *If on a Winter's Night a Traveller* (1979)
Camus, Albert	1913–60	Mondovi, Algeria	*The Outsider* (1942); *The Plague* (1947); *The Fall* (1956)
Canetti, Elias	1905–	Russe, Bulgaria	*Auto da Fé* (1936); *Crowds and Power* (1960); *A Torch in my Ear* (1980)
Capote, Truman	1924–84	New Orleans	*Other Voices; Other Rooms* (1948); *Breakfast at Tiffany's* (1958); *In Cold Blood* (1966)
Carey, Peter	1943–	Bacchus Marsh, Victoria	*Bliss* (1981); *Illywhacker* (1985); *Oscar and Lucinda* (1988); *The Tax Inspector* (1991)
Carroll, Lewis (Charles Lutwidge Dodgson)	1832–98	Daresbury, Cheshire	*Alice's Adventures in Wonderland* (1865); *Through the Looking Glass and What Alice Found There* (1872); *The Hunting of the Snark* (1876)
Carter, Angela	1940–92	London	*The Magic Toyshop* (1967); *The Infernal Desire Machines of Dr Hoffman;* (1972); *Nights at the Circus* (1984); *Wise Children* (1991)
Cartland, (Mary) Barbara (Hamilton)	1901–	Birmingham	*The Husband Hunters* (1976); *Wings on My Heart* (1954); *The Castle Made for Love* (1985)
Cary, (Arthur) Joyce (Lunel)	1888–1957	Londonderry	*The Horse's Mouth* (1944)
Cather, Willa (Sibert)	1876–1947	Winchester, Virginia	*O Pioneers!* (1913); *My Antonia* (1918); *One of Ours* (1922); *The Professor's House* (1925); *My Mortal Enemy* (1926); *Death Comes for the Archbishop* (1927); *Sapphira and the Slave Girl* (1940)
Chandler, Raymond	1888–1959	Chicago	*The Big Sleep* (1939); *Farewell, My Lovely* (1940); *The High Window* (1942); *The Lady in the Lake* (1943); *The Long Goodbye* (1953)
Chatwin, Bruce	1940–89		*In Patagonia* (1977); *On the Black Hill* (1982); *Utz* (1988)
Chesterton, G(ilbert) K(eith)	1874–1936	London	*The Innocence of Father Brown* (1911)

Name	Dates	Place of birth	Selected works
Christie, Dame Agatha (Mary Clarissa)	1890–1976	Torquay, Devon	*Murder on the Orient Express* (1934); *Death on the Nile* (1937); *Ten Little Niggers* (1939); *Curtain* (1975)
Clarke, Arthur C(harles)	1917–	Minehead, Somerset	*Childhood's End* (1953); *The Fountains of Paradise* (1979); *The Garden of Rama* (1991)
Cleland, John	1709–89	London	*Fanny Hill* (1750)
Coetzee, J(ohn) M(ichael)	1940–	Cape Town	*Life and Times of Michael K* (1983)
Collins, Wilkie	1824–89	London	*The Woman in White* (1860); *No Name* (1862); *Armadale* (1866); *The Moonstone* (1868)
Compton-Burnett, Ivy	1892–1969	Pinner, Middlesex	*A House and its Head* (1935); *A Family and a Fortune* (1939); *Manservant and Maidservant* (1947)
Conrad, Joseph (originally Jozef Teodor Konrad Nalecz Korzeniowski)	1857–1924	Berdichev, Ukraine	*Lord Jim* (1900); *Heart of Darkness* (1902); *Nostromo* (1904); *The Secret Agent* (1907); *Chance* (1914)
Cookson, Dame Catherine (Ann)	1906–	East Jarrow, Tyne and Wear	*The Glass Virgin* (1969); *Tilly Trotter* (1981)
Cooper, James Fenimore	1789–1851	Burlington, New Jersey	*The Pioneers* (1823); *The Last of the Mohicans* (1826)
Cooper, Jilly	1937–	Yorkshire	*Men and Supermen* (1972); *Riders* (1978); *Class* (1979); *Rivals* (1988); *Polo* (1991)
Crane, Stephen	1871–1900	Newark, New Jersey	*The Red Badge of Courage* (1895)
Davies, Robertson	1913–	Thamesville, Ontario	*Tempest Tost* (1951); *Leaven of Malice* (1952); *A Mixture of Frailties* (1958); *What's Bred In the Bone* (1985)
De Beauvoir, Simone	1908–86	Paris	*The Second Sex* ((1949); *Les Mandarins* (1954); *Memoirs of a Dutiful Daughter* (1959)
Defoe, Daniel	1660–1731	Stoke Newington, London	*Robinson Crusoe* (1719); *Moll Flanders* (1722); *A Journal of the Plague Year* (1722)
Deighton, Len (Leonard Cyril)	1929–	London	*The Ipcress File* (1962); *Funeral in Berlin* (1965); *Spy Hook* (1988); *Spy Line* (1989); *Spy Sinker* (1990)
DeLillo, Don	1936–	New York City	*End Zone* (1972); *Ratner's Star* (1976); *The Names* (1982); *White Noise* (1985)
De Quincey, Thomas	1785–1859	Manchester	*Confessions of an English Opium Eater* (1821)
Dibdin, Michael	1947–		*Dirty Tricks* (1991); *Cabal* (1992); *The Dying of the Light* (1993)
Dickens, Charles	1812–70	Landport, Portsmouth	*Oliver Twist* (1837–9); *David Copperfield* (1849–50); *Bleak House* (1852–3); *Great Expectations* (1860–1)
Dinesen, Isak (Karen Blixen)	1885–1962	Rungsted, Denmark	*Seven Gothic Tales* (1934); *Out of Africa* (1937)
Doctorow, E(dgar) L(awrence)	1931–	New York City	*Ragtime* (1975)
Dos Passos, John (Roderigo)	1896–1970	Chicago	*Manhattan Transfer* (1925); *USA* (1930–6)
Dostoevsky, Fyodor Mikhailovich	1821–81	Moscow	*Crime and Punishment* (1866); *The Idiot* (1868–9) *The Brothers Karamazov* (1880)
Doyle, Sir Arthur Conan	1859–1930	Edinburgh	*The Memoirs of Sherlock Holmes* (1894); *The Hound of the Baskervilles* (1902); *The Lost World* (1912)
Drabble, Margaret	1939–	Sheffield	*The Millstone* (1965); *Jerusalem the Golden* (1967); *The Ice Age* (1977); *A Natural Curiosity* (1989)
Dreiser, Theodore	1871–1945	Terre Haute, Indiana	*Sister Carrie* (1900); *Jennie Gerhardt* (1911)
Du Maurier, Dame Daphne	1907–89	London	*Rebecca* (1938); *My Cousin Rachel* (1951)
Durrell, Gerald Malcolm	1925–	Jamshedpur, India	*The Overloaded Ark* (1953); *My Family and Other Animals* (1956)
Durrell, Lawrence (George)	1912–90	Darjeeling, India	*Prospero's Cell* (1945); *'Alexandria Quartet'* (1957–60)
Eco, Umberto	1929–	Alessandria, Piedmont	*The Name of the Rose* (1981); *Foucault's Pendulum* (1989)
Eliot, George (originally Mary Ann, later Marian Evans)	1819–80	Arbury, Warwickshire	*Adam Bede* (1859); *The Mill on the Floss* (1860); *Silas Marner* (1861); *Middlemarch* (1871-2); *Daniel Deronda* (1874-6)
Ellis, Alice Thomas (Anna Margaret Haycraft, née Lindholm)	1932–	Liverpool	*The Sin Eater* (1977); *The 27th Kingdom* (1982); *The Inn at the Edge of the World* (1990)
Faulkner, William Harrison	1897–1962	New Albany, Mississippi	*Sartoris* (1929); *The Sound and the Fury* (1929); *Absalom, Absalom!* (1936)

Novelists (continued)

Name	Dates	Place of birth	Selected works
Fielding, Henry	1707–54	Sharpham Park, nr Glastonbury	*Joseph Andrews* (1742); *Tom Jones* (1749)
Fitzgerald, F(rancis) Scott (Key)	1896–1940	St Paul, Minnesota	*The Great Gatsby* (1925); *Tender is the Night* (1934)
Fitzgerald, Penelope (Mary) (née Knox)	1916–	Lincoln	*The Bookshop* (1978); *Offshore* (1979); *The Gate of Angels* (1990)
Flaubert, Gustave	1821–80	Rouen	*Madame Bovary* (1857); *Salammbo* (1862); *Sentimental Education* (1869); *Bouvard et Pécuchet* (1881)
Fleming, Ian	1908–64	Lancaster	*Casino Royale* (1953); *From Russia with Love* (1957); *Dr No* (1958); *Goldfinger* (1959); *The Man with the Golden Gun* (1965)
Ford, Ford Madox (Ford Hermann Hueffer)	1873–1939	Merton, Surrey	*The Fifth Queen* (1906); *The Good Soldier* (1915); *Parade's End* (1924–8)
Forester, C(ecil) S(cott)	1899–1966	Cairo	*The Happy Return* (1937); *The African Queen* (1935)
Forster, E(dward) M(organ)	1879–1970	London	*A Room with a View* (1908), *Howards End* (1910); *A Passage to India* (1922–4); *Maurice* (1913, published 1971)
Forsyth, Frederick	1938–	Ashford, Kent	*The Day of the Jackal* (1971); *The Odessa File* (1972); *The Fourth Protocol* (1984)
Fowles, John (Robert)	1926–	Leigh-on-Sea	*The Collector* (1963); *The Magus* (1966, revised 1977); *The French Lieutenant's Woman* (1969)
France, Anatole (Jacques-Anatole-François Thibault)	1844–1924	Paris	*Le Crime de Sylvestre Bonnard* (1881); *Les Dieux ont soif* (1912)
Fraser, Antonia (Lady Antonia Pinter)	1932–	London	*Mary Queen of Scots* (1969); *Quiet as a Nun* (1977); *A Splash of Red* (1981)
French, Marilyn	1929–	New York City	*The Women's Room* (1977); *The Bleeding Heart* (1980); *Her Mother's Daughter* (1987)
Gaddis, William	1922–	New York City	*JR* (1976); *Carpenter's Gothic* (1985)
Galsworthy, John	1867-1933	Coombe, Surrey	*The Forsyte Saga* (1906–28)
García Márquez, Gabriel	1928–	Aracataca, Colombia	*One Hundred Years of Solitude* (1967); *Chronicle of a Death Foretold* (1982); *Love in the Time of Cholera* (1985); *The General in his Labyrinth* (1989)
Gaskell, Mrs Elizabeth	1810–65	London	*Cranford* (1853); *North and South* (1855)
Genet, Jean	1910–86	Paris	*Our Lady of the Flowers* (1944); *The Miracle of the Rose* (1946)
Gibbons, Stella (Dorothea)	1902–89	London	*Cold Comfort Farm* (1933)
Gide, André (Paul Guillaume)	1869–1951	Paris	*The Immoralist* (1902); *Strait is the Gate* (1909); *The Vatican Cellars* (1914); *The Pastoral Symphony* (1919); *The Counterfeiters* (1926)
Gilchrist, Ellen	1935–		*The Annunciation* (1983); *I Cannot Get You Close Enough* (1990); *Net of Jewels* (1993)
Goethe, Johann Wolfgang von	1749–1832	Frankfurt-am-Main	*The Sorrows of Young Werther* (1774); *Wilhelm Meister's Apprenticeship* (1796); *Elective Affinities* (1809)
Gogol, Nikolai Vasilievich	1809–52	Sorochintsi, Poltava	*The Overcoat* (1835); *Diary of a Madman* (1835); *Dead Souls* (1842); *The Odd Women* (1893)
Golding, William (Gerald)	1911–93	St Columb Minor, Cornwall	*Lord of the Flies* (1954); *The Spire* (1964); *Rites of Passage* (1980); *The Paper Men* (1984); *Close Quarters* (1987); *Fire Down Below* (1989)
Goldsmith, Oliver	1728–74	Kilkenny West, County Kilkenny	*The Vicar of Wakefield* (1766)
Gordimer, Nadine	1923–	Springs, Transvaal	*Occasion for Loving* (1963); *A Guest of Honour* (1970); *The Conservationist* (1974); *A Sport of Nature* (1987)
Gorky, Maxim (Aleksei Maksimovich Peshkov)	1868–1936	Nizhny Novgorod (New Gorky)	*The Mother* (1906–7); *Childhood* (1913); *The Life of Klim Samgin* (1925–36)
Grahame, Kenneth	1859–1932	Edinburgh	*The Wind in the Willows* (1908)
Grass, Günter (Wilhelm)	1927–	Gdánsk (Formerly Danzig)	*The Tin Drum* (1959); *Cat and Mouse* (1961); *The Meeting at Telgte* (1979)
Graves, Robert (von Ranke)	1895–1985	Wimbledon	*No Decency Left* (1932); *The Real David Copperfield* (1933); *I, Claudius* (1934)
Greene, (Henry) Graham	1904–91	Berkhamstead, Hertfordshire	*Brighton Rock* (1938); *The Power and the Glory* (1940); *The Third Man* (1950); *The Honorary Consul* (1973)
Haggard, Sir Henry Rider	1856–1925	Buckinghamshire	*King Solomon's Mines* (1885); *She: A History of Adventure* (1887)

Name	Dates	Place of birth	Selected works
Hammett, (Samuel) Dashiell	1894–1961	Maryland	*The Maltese Falcon* (1930); *The Thin Man* (1932)
Hamsun, Knut	1859–1952	Oudsrandsdal, Valley, Norway	*Hunger* (1890); *Mysteries* (1892); *Pan* (1894); *Victoria* (1898); *Growth of the Soil* (1917)
Hardy, Thomas	1840–1928	Higher Bockhampton, Dorset	*Far from the Madding Crowd* (1874); *The Mayor of Casterbridge* (1886); *Tess of the D'Urbervilles* (1891); *Jude the Obscure* (1896)
Hartley, L(eslie) P(oles)	1895–1972	Whittlesey, Cambridgeshire	*The Go-Between* (1953)
Heller, Joseph	1923–	Brooklyn, New York	*Catch 22* (1961); *Something Happened* (1974); *Picture This* (1988)
Hemingway Ernest (Miller)	1899–1961	Chicago, Illinois	*A Farewell to Arms* (1929); *For Whom the Bell Tolls* (1940); *The Old Man and the Sea* (1952)
Hesse, Herman	1877–1962	Calw, Württemberg	*Siddhartha* (1922); *Steppenwolf* (1927); *The Glass Bead Game* (1945)
Highsmith, Patricia	1921–	Fort Worth	*Strangers on a Train* (1949); *The Talented Mr Ripley* (1956); *Ripley Under Ground* (1971); *Ripley Under Water* (1991)
Hoban, Russell (Conwell)	1925–	Lansdale, Pennsylvania	*Turtle Diary* (1975); *Riddley Walker* (1980); *Pilgermann* (1983)
Holt, Victoria (Eleanor Alice Burford Hibbert) also writes as Philippa Carr, Jean Plaidy	1906–93	London	*Catherine de 'Medici* (1969 – as JP); *Will You Love Me in September* (1981 – as PC); *The Captive* (1989 – as VH)
Hugo,Victor (Marie)	1802–85	Besançon	*Notre Dame de Paris* (1831); *Les Misérables* (1862)
Hulme, Keri	1947–	Christchurch, New Zealand	*The Bone People* (1983); *Lost Possessions* (1984)
Hurston, Zora Neale	1903–60	Eatonville, Florida	*Their Eyes Were Watching God* (1937); *Moses: Man of the Mountain* (1939)
Huxley, Aldous (Leonard)	1894–1963	Godalming, Surrey	*Brave New World* (1932); *Eyeless in Gaza* (1936); *Island* (1962)
Irving, John	1942–	Exeter, New Hampshire	*The World According to Garp* (1978); *The Hotel New Hampshire* (1981); *A Prayer for Owen Meany* (1989)
Isherwood, Christopher (William Bradshaw)	1904–	Disley, Cheshire	*Mr Norris Changes Trains* (1935); *Goodbye to Berlin* (1939); *Down There on a Visit* (1962)
Ishiguro, Kazuo	1954–	Japan	*An Artist of the Floating World* (1986); *The Remains of the Day* (1989)
Jacobson, Dan	1929–	Johannesburg	*A Dance in the Sun* (1950); *Evidence of Love* (1960); *The Rape of Tamar* (1970)
James, Henry	1843–1916	New York	*The Portrait of a Lady* (1881); *The Bostonians* (1886); *The Turn of the Screw* (1898); *The Awkward Age* (1899); *The Ambassadors* (1903); *The Golden Bowl* (1904)
Jerome, Jerome K(lapka)	1859–1927	Walsall, Staffordshire	*Three Men in a Boat* (1889)
Jhabvala, Ruth Prawer	1927–	Cologne, Germany	*Heat and Dust* (1975); *In Search of Love and Beauty* (1983)
Johnston, Jennifer	1930–	Dublin	*The Captains and the Kings* (1972); *How Many Miles to Babylon* (1974); *The Invisible Worm* (1991)
Joyce, James (Augustine Aloysius)	1882–1941	Dublin	*Dubliners* (1914); *A Portrait of the Artist as a Young Man* (1914–15); *Ulysses* (1922); *Finnegan's Wake* (1939)
Kafka, Franz	1883–1924	Prague	*The Metamorphosis* (1916); *The Trial* (1925); *The Castle* (1926); *America* (1927)
Kazantzakis, Nikos	1883–1957	Heraklion, Crete	*Zorba The Greek* (1946)
Keillor, Garrison	1942–	Anoka, Minnesota	*Lake Wobegone Days* (1985); *Leaving Home* (1987); *WLT: A Radio Romance* (1992)
Kelman, James	1946–	Glasgow	*The Busconductor Hines* (1984); *A Chancer* (1985), *Greyhound for Breakfast* (1987); *A Disaffection* (1989)
Keneally, Thomas	1935–	Sydney	*A Dutiful Daughter* (1971); *Schindler's Ark* (1982)
Kerouac, Jack	1922–69	Lowell, Massachusetts	*On The Road* (1957)
Kesey, Ken	1935–	La Junta, Colorado	*One Flew Over The Cuckoo's Nest* (1962)
King, Stephen	1947–	Portland, Maine	*Carrie* (1974); *The Shining* (1977); *Christine* (1983); *Misery* (1987)
Kingsley, Charles	1819–75	Holne, Decon	*Westward Ho!* (1855); *The Heroes* (1856); *The Water Babies* (1863)
Kipling, Rudyard	1865–1936	Bombay	*The Jungle Book* (1894); *Kim* (1901); *Just So Stories* (1902)
Koestler, Arthur	1905–83	Budapest	*Darkness at Noon* (1940); *Arrival and Departure* (1943)
Kundera, Milan	1929–	Brno	*Life is Elsewhere* (1973); *The Book of Laughter and Forgetting* (1979); *The Unbearable Lightness of Being* (1984); *Immortality* (1991)

Novelists (continued)

Name	Dates	Place of birth	Selected works
Laclos, Pierre Choderlos de	1741–1803	Amiens	*Les Liaisons Dangereuses* (1782)
La Fayette, Marie Madeleine Pioche de Lavergne, Comtesse de	1634–93	Paris	*Zaïde* (1670); *La Princesse de Clèves* (1678)
Lampedusa, Giuseppe Tomasi di	1896–1957	Palermo, Sicily	*The Leopard* (1958)
Lawrence, D(avid) H(erbert)	1885–1930	Eastwood, Nottinghamshire	*Sons and Lovers* (1913); *The Rainbow* (1915); *Women in Love* (1920); *Lady Chatterley's Lover* (1928)
Le Carré, John (David John Moore Cornwell)	1931–	Poole, Dorset	*Tinker, Tailor, Soldier, Spy* (1974); *Smiley's People* (1980); *The Little Drummer Girl* (1983); *The Russia House* (1989)
Lee, Harper	1926–	Monroeville, Alabama	*To Kill A Mockingbird* (1960)
Lee, Laurie	1914–90	Slad, Gloucestershire	*Cider With Rosie* (1959); *As I Walked Out One Midsummer Morning* (1969)
Lehmann, Rosamond (Nina)	1901–90	Bourne End, Buckinghamshire	*Dusty Answer* (1927); *An Invitation to the Waltz* (1932); *The Ballad and the Source* (1944); *The Echoing Grove* (1953)
Leroux, Gaston	1868–1927	France	*The Phantom of the Opera* (1911)
Lessing, Doris	1919–	Kermanshah, Iran	*The Grass is Singing* (1950); *The Golden Notebook* (1962); *Canopus in Argus Archives* (1979-83); *The Fifth Child* (1988)
Levi, Primo	1919–87	Turin	*If This is a Man* (1947); *The Periodic Table* (1985)
Lewis, (Harry) Sinclair	1885–1951	Sauk Center, Minnesota	*Main Street* (1920); *Babbitt* (1922); *Martin Arrowsmith* (1925); *Elmer Gantry* (1927)
Lively, Penelope (Margaret)	1933–	Cairo, Egypt	*The Road to Lichfield* (1977); *Moon Tiger* (1987); *City of the Mind* (1991)
Llosa, Mario Vargas	1936–	Arequipa, Peru	*The City of Dogs* (1964); *Aunt Julia and the Scriptwriter* (1977)
Lodge, David	1935–	London	*Changing Places* (1975); *Small World* (1984); *Nice Work* (1988)
London, Jack (Griffith)	1876–1916	San Francisco	*The Call of the Wild* (1903); *White Fang* (1907); *Martin Eden* (1909)
Lurie, Alison	1926–	Chicago	*Love and Friendship* (1962); *The War Between the Tates* (1974); *The Truth About Lorin Jones* (1988)
Macauley, Rose	1881–1958	Rugby, Warwickshire	*Dangerous Ages* (1921); *The Towers of Trebizond* (1956)
Mailer, Norman	1923–	Long Branch, New Jersey	*The Naked and the Dead* (1948); *Barbary Shore* (1951); *An American Dream* (1965); *The Executioner's Song* (1979)
Malraux, André	1901–76	Paris	*La Condition Humaine* (1933)
Mann, Thomas	1875–1955	Lübeck	*Death in Venice* (1913); *The Magic Mountain* (1924); *Dr Faustus* (1947)
Mansfield, Katherine (Katherine Mansfield Beauchamp)	1888–1923	Wellington, New Zealand	*Prelude* (1918); *Bliss* (1920); *The Garden Party* (1922)
Mars-Jones, Adam	1954–	London	*Lantern Lecture* (1981); *The Darker Proof* (1987)
Maugham, Somerset	1874–1965	Paris	*Of Human Bondage* (1915); *The Moon and Sixpence* (1919); *The Razor's Edge* (1945)
Maupassant, Guy de	1850–93	Miromesnil	*Bel-ami* (1885)
Maupin, Armistead	1944–	Washington D.C.	*Tales of the City* (1978); *More Tales of the City* (1980); *Further Tales of the City* (1982); *Significant Others* (1988); *Sure of You* (1990); *Maybe The Moon* (1992)
Mauriac, François	1885–1970	Bordeaux	*Le Baiser au Lepreux* (1922); *Thérèse Desqueyroux* (1927)
McCullers, Carson	1917–67	Columbus, Georgia	*The Heart is a Lonely Hunter* (1940); *The Member of the Wedding* (1940); *The Ballad of the Sad Café* (1951)
McEwan, Ian (Russell)	1948–	Aldershot, Hampshire	*First Love, Last Rites* (1975); *The Cement Garden* (1978); *The Child in Time* (1987); *The Innocent* (1990); *Black Dogs* (1992)
McGahern, John	1934–	Dublin	*The Leavetaking* (1975); *The Pornographer* (1979); *Amongst Women* (1990)
Melville, Herman	1819–91	New York	*Typee* (1846); *Omoo* (1847); *Moby Dick* (1851)
Meredith, George	1828–1909	Portsmouth	*The Egoist* (1879); *Diana of the Crossways* (1885)
Miller, Henry Valentine	1891–1980	New York	*Tropic of Cancer* (1934); *Tropic of Capricorn* (1938)
Mishima, Yukio (Hiraoka Kimitake)	1925–70	Tokyo	*Confessions of a Mask* (1949); *The Temple of the Golden Pavilion* (1959); *The Sea of Fertility* (1965–70)

Name	Dates	Place of birth	Selected works
Mitchell, Margaret	1900–49	Atlanta, Georgia	*Gone with the Wind* (1936)
Mitford, Nancy	1904–73	London	*Love in a Cold Climate* (1949); *Don't Tell Alfred* (1960)
Mo, Timothy	1950–	Hong Kong	*The Monkey King* (1978); *Sour Sweet* (1982); *An Insular Possession* (1986)
Moore, Brian	1921–	Belfast	*Judith Hearne* (1955; later retitled *The Lonely Passion of Judith Hearne*)
Mosley, Nicholas	1923–	London	*Spaces of the Dark* (1951); *Accident* (1965); *Hopeful Monsters* (1991)
Murdoch, Dame Iris	1919–	Dublin	*The Bell* (1958); *The Sea,The Sea* (1978); *The Philosopher's Pupil* (1983); *The Book and the Brotherhood* (1987)
Nabokov, Vladimir	1899–1977	St Petersburg	*Lolita* (1958)
Naipaul, V(idiadhar) S(urajprasad)	1932–	Trinidad	*A House for Mr Biswas* (1961); *In a Free State* (1971); *A Bend in the River* (1979)
Nesbit, E(dith)	1858–1924	London	*Five Children and It* (1902); *The Railway Children* (1906)
Oates, Joyce Carol	1938–	New York	*A Garden of Earthly Delights* (1967); *Them* (1969); *Wonderland* (1971)
O'Brien, Edna	1932–	Tuamgranay, County Clare	*The Country Girls* (1960); *August is a Wicked Month* (1964); *A Pagan Place* (1971)
Okri, Ben	1959–	Minna, Nigeria	*The Famished Road* (1991); *Songs of Enchantment* (1993)
Orczy, Baroness (Mrs Montague Barstow)	1865–1947	Tarnaörs, Hungary	*The Scarlet Pimpernel* (1905)
Orwell, George (Eric Arthur Blair)	1903–50	Bengal	*Down and Out in Paris and London* (1933); *Animal Farm* (1945); *Nineteen Eighty-Four* (1949)
Pasternak, Boris	1890–1960	Moscow	*Doctor Zhivago* (1957)
Paton, Alan	1903–88	Pietermaritzburg, Natal	*Cry, the Beloved Country* (1948)
Peacock, Thomas Love	1785–1866	Weymouth, Dorset	*Headlong Hall* (1816); *Nightmare Abbey* (1818); *Crotchet Castle* (1883)
Peake, Mervyn (Laurence)	1911–68	Kuling, China	*Titus Groan* (1946); *Gormenghast* (1950); *Titus Alone* (1959)
Plath, Sylvia	1932–63	Boston	*The Bell Jar* (1963)
Powell, Anthony	1905–	London	*A Dance to the Music of Time* (1951–75); *The Fisher King* (1986)
Priestley, J(ohn) B(oynton)	1894–1984	Bradford	*The Good Companions* (1929); *Angel Pavement* (1930)
Proust, Marcel	1871–1922	Paris	*Remembrance of Things Past* (1912–27)
Pushkin, Alexander (Sergeyevich)	1799–1837	Moscow	*The Prisoner of the Caucasus* (1821); *Eugene Onegin* (1828); *Boris Godunov* (1831)
Pynchon, Thomas	1937–	Glen Cove, New York	*V* (1963); *The Crying of Lot 49* (1966); *Gravity's Rainbow* (1973); *Vineland* (1992)
Radcliffe, Ann	1764–1823	London	*The Mysteries of Udolpho* (1794); *The Italian* (1797)
Rendell, Ruth	1930–	London	*A Judgement in Stone* (1977); *The Killing Doll* (1980); *Heartstones* (1987)
Rhys, Jean (Ella Gwendoline Rhys Williams)	1894–1979	Dominica, West Indies	*Wide Sargasso Sea* (1966); *Tigers Are Better Looking* (1968)
Richardson, Samuel	1689–1761	Macworth, Derbyshire	*Pamela* (1740); *Clarissa* (1747-8); *Sir Charles Grandison* (1753–4)
Richler, Mordecai	1931–	Montreal	*The Apprenticeship of Duddy Kravitz* (1959); *Solomon Gursky Was Here* (1989)
Roth, Philip	1933–	Newark, New Jersey	*Portnoy's Complaint* (1969); *My Life As a Man* (1974); *The Counterlife* (1986)
Rubens, Bernice	1928–	Cardiff	*The Elected Member* (1970); *Our Father* (1987); *Kingdom Come* (1990)
Rushdie, Salman	1947–	Bombay	*Midnight's Children* (1981); *Shame* (1983); *The Satanic Verses* (1988), *Haroun and the Sea of Stories* (1990)
Sackville-West, Vita	1892–1962	Knole, Kent	*The Edwardians* (1930); *All Passion Spent* (1931); *Signposts in the Sea* (1961)
Sade, Donatien Alphonse François, Comte de (known as Marquis)	1740–1814	Paris	*Justine* (1791); *La Philosphie dans le Boudoir* (1795); *Juliette* (1797); *Les Crimes de L'Amour* (1800)
Salinger, J(erome) D(avid)	1919–	New York	*Catcher in the Rye* (1951); *Franny and Zooey* (1961)

Literature

Novelists (continued)

Name	Dates	Place of birth	Selected works
Sand, George (Amandine Aurore Lucile Dupin)	1804–76	Paris	*Lelia* (1833); *La Petite Fadette* (1849)
Sartre, Jean-Paul	1905–80	Paris	*Nausea* (1949); *The Roads to Freedom* (1945–9)
Scott, Paul (Mark)	1920–78	London	*The Jewel in the Crown* (1965); *Staying On* (1977)
Scott, Sir Walter	1771–1832	Edinburgh	*The Lady of the Lake* (1810); *Waverley* (1814); *Rob Roy* (1817); *The Bride of Lammermoor* (1819)
Seth, Vikram	1952–	Calcutta	*From Heaven Lake* (1983); *The Golden Gate* (1986); *A Suitable Boy* (1993)
Sharpe, Tom (Thomas Ridley)	1928–	London	*Blott on the Landscape* (1975); *Porterhouse Blue* (1978); *Wilt* (1976)
Shelley, Mary (Wollstonecraft)	1797–1851	London	*Frankenstein* (1818)
Schreiner, Olive	1855–1920	Wittebergen, S Africa	*The Story of an African Farm* (1883)
Shute, Nevil (Nevil Shute Norway)	1899–1960	Ealing	*A Town Like Alice* (1949)
Sillitoe, Alan	1928–	Nottingham	*Saturday Night and Sunday Morning* (1958); *The Loneliness of the Long Distance Runner* (1959)
Sinclair, Upton	1878–1968	Baltimore	*The Jungle* (1906); *Dragon's Teeth* (1942)
Singer, Isaac Bashevis	1904–91	Radzymin, Poland	*The Family Moskat* (1950); *Satan in Goray* (1955); *The Slave* (1962)
Smollett, Tobias	1721–71	Cardross, Dunbartonshire	*The Adventures of Roderick Random* (1748); *The Adventures of Peregrine Pickle* (1751)
Solzhenitsyn, Alexander Isayevich	1918–	Kislovodsk, Caucasus	*One Day in the Life of Ivan Denisovich* (1962); *The First Circle* (1968); *The Gulag Archipelago* (1973–8)
Spark, Muriel	1918–	Edinburgh	*The Ballad of Peckham Rye* (1960); *The Prime of Miss Jean Brodie* (1961); *The Girls of Slender Means* (1963)
Stein, Gertrude	1874–1946	Allegheny, Pennsylvania	*Three Lives* (1908); *Tender Buttons* (1914)
Steinbeck, John (Ernst)	1902–68	Salinas, California	*Of Mice and Men* (1937); *The Grapes of Wrath* (1939); *East of Eden* (1952)
Stendhal (Marie Henri Beyle)	1788–1842	Grenoble	*The Red and The Black* (1830); *The Charterhouse of Parma* (1839)
Sterne, Lawrence	1713–68	Clonmel, Tipperary	*Tristram Shandy* (1759–67); *A Sentimental Journey* (1768)
Stevenson, Robert Louis (Balfour)	1850–94	Edinburgh	*Treasure Island* (1883); *Kidnapped* (1886); *The Strange Case of Dr Jekyll and Mr Hyde* (1886)
Stoker, Bram	1847–1912	Dublin	*Dracula* (1897)
Stowe, Harriet Beecher	1811–96	Litchfield, Connecticut	*Uncle Tom's Cabin* (1852)
Süskind, Patrick	1949–		*Perfume* (1985)
Swift, Graham	1949–	London	*The Sweet Shop Owner* (1980); *Waterland* (1984)
Swift, Jonathan	1667–1745	Dublin	*Gulliver's Travels* (1726)
Thackeray, William Makepeace	1811–63	Calcutta	*Vanity Fair* (1847–8); *Pendennis* (1848–50); *The History of Henry Esmond* (1852)
Theroux, Paul	1941–	Medford, Massachusetts	*The Mosquito Coast* (1981); *Doctor Slaughter* (1984); *My Secret History* (1989)
Thomas, D(onald) M(ichael)	1935–	Redruth, Cornwall	*The White Hotel* (1981); *Ararat* (1983); *Lying Together* (1990)
Tolkien, J(ohn) R(onald) R(euel)	1892–1973	Bloemfontein, S Africa	*The Hobbit* (1937); *The Lord of the Rings* (1954–5)
Tolkin, Michael			*The Player* (1988); *Among the Dead* (1993)
Tolstoy, Count Leo Nikolayevich	1828–1910	Yasnaya Polyana, Central Russia	*War and Peace* (1865–9); *Anna Karenina* (1875–7)
Toole, John Kennedy	1937–69	New Orleans	*A Confederacy of Dunces* (1980); *The Neon Bible* (1989)
Townsend, Sue	1946–	Leicester	*The Secret Diary of Adrian Mole* (1982); *The Queen and I* (1992)
Tremain, Rose	1943–	London	*The Cupboard* (1981); *Restoration* (1989); *Sacred Country* (1992)
Trollope, Anthony	1815–82	London	*Barchester Towers* (1857); *The Way We Live Now* (1875)
Turgenev, Ivan (Sergeyevich)	1818–83	Orel province, Russia	*Fathers and Sons* (1862)
Tutola, Amos	1920–	Abeokuta, Nigeria	*The Palm-Wine Drinkard* (1952)

Name	Dates	Place of birth	Selected works
Twain, Mark (Samuel Longhorn Clemens)	1835–1910	Florida, Missouri	*The Adventures of Tom Sawyer* (1876); *The Prince and the Pauper* (1882); *The Adventures of Huckleberry Finn* (1884); *A Connecticut Yankee in King Arthur's Court* (1889)
Tyler, Anne	1941–	Minneapolis	*The Accidental Tourist* (1985); *Breathing Lessons* (1989); *Saint Maybe* (1991)
Updike, John (Hoyer)	1932–	Shillington, Pennsylvania	*Rabbit, Run* (1960); *The Centaur* (1963); *Couples* (1968); *Rabbit Redux* (1971); *Roger's Version* (1986)
van der Post, Sir Laurens	1906–	Philippolis, S Africa	*Flamingo Feather* (1955); *Journey into Russia* (1964); *A Far Off Place* (1974)
Verne, Jules	1828–1905	Nantes	*Voyage to the Centre of the Earth* (1864); *Twenty Thousand Leagues Under the Sea* (1870)
Vidal, Gore (Eugene Luther Vidal, Jr)	1925–	West Point, New York	*The Season of Comfort* (1949); *Myra Breckenridge* (1968); *Kalki* (1978)
Vonnegut, Kurt	1922–	Indianapolis, Indiana	*Cat's Cradle* (1963); *Slaughterhouse-Five* (1969); *Hocus Pocus* (1990)
Walker, Alice	1944–	Eatonville, Georgia	*The Color Purple* (1982)
Warner, Marina	1946–	London	*In A Dark Wood* (1977); *The Skating Party* (1982); *The Lost Father* (1988)
Warner, Rex	1905–86	Birmingham	*The Wild Goose Chase* (1937); *The Professor* (1938); *The Aerodrome* (1941)
Waugh, Evelyn (Arthur St John)	1903–66	Hampstead	*Decline and Fall* (1928); *A Handful of Dust* (1934); *Brideshead Revisited* (1945)
Weldon, Fay	1933–	Alvechurch, Worcestershire	*Down Among Women* (1971); *Female Friends* (1975); *Life and Loves of a She-Devil* (1983)
Wells, H(erbert) G(eorge)	1866–1946	Bromley, Kent	*The Time Machine* (1895); *The Invisible Man* (1897); *The War of the Worlds* (1898); *The History of Mr Polly* (1910)
Welty, Eudora	1909–	Jackson, Mississippi	*A Curtain of Green* (1941); *The Golden Apples* (1949); *The Ponder Heart* (1954); *The Optimist's Daughter* (1972)
Wesley, Mary	1912–	Englefield Green, Berkshire	*The Camomile Lawn* (1984); *A Sensible Life* (1990)
Wharton, Edith	1862–1937	New York	*The House of Mirth* (1905); *Ethan Frome* (1911); *The Age of Innocence* (1920)
White, Antonia (Eirene Adeline Botting)	1899–1980	London	*Frost in May* (1933)
White, Edmund	1940–	US	*A Boy's Own Story* (1982); *The Beautiful Room is Empty* (1988)
White, Patrick (Victor Martindale)	1912–90	London	*Voss* (1957); *The Vivisector* (1970); *A Fringe of Leaves* (1976)
Wilde, Oscar	1854–1900	Dublin	*The Picture of Dorian Gray* (1891)
Wilder, Thornton (Niven)	1897–1975	Madison, Wisconsin	*The Bridge Of San Luis Rey* (1927); *The Woman of Andros* (1930); *Heaven's My Destination* (1935)
Wilson, A(ndrew) N(orman)	1950–	London	*Kindly Light* (1979); *Wise Virgin* (1982); *Daughters of Albion* (1991)
Wilson, Sir Angus (Frank Johnstone)	1913–91	Bexhill, Sussex	*Anglo-Saxon Attitudes* (1956); *The Old Men At The Zoo* (1961)
Winterson, Jeanette	1959–	Lancashire	*Oranges Are Not The Only Fruit* (1987); *The Passion* (1987); *Sexing The Cherry* (1989); *Written on the Body* (1992)
Wodehouse, P(elham) G(renville)	1881–1975	Guildford, Surrey	*My Man Jeeves* (1919); *The Inimitable Jeeves* (1923); *Carry On, Jeeves* (1925)
Wolfe, Tom (Thomas Kennerley)	1931–	Richmond, Virginia	*The Right Stuff* (1979); *The Bonfire of the Vanities* (1988)
Woolf, Virginia	1882–1941	London	*Mrs Dalloway* (1925); *To The Lighthouse* (1927); *Orlando* (1928); *A Room of One's Own* (1929); *The Waves* (1931)
Wright, Richard	1908–60	Natchez, Mississippi	*Native Son* (1940)
Wyndham, John (John Wyndham Parkes Lucas Beynon Haris)	1903–69	Knowle, Warwickshire	*The Day of the Triffids* (1951); *The Midwich Cuckoos* (1957)
Zola, Emile	1840–1902	Paris	*Thérèse Raquin* (1867); *Les Rougon-Macquart* (1871–93); *Germinal* (1885)

Literature

Booker Prize

1971	V S Naipaul *In a Free State*	1983	J M Coetzee *Life and Times of Michael K*
1972	John Berger *G*	1984	Anita Brookner *Hotel du Lac*
1973	J G Farrell *The Siege of Krishnapur*	1985	Keri Hulme *The Bone People*
1974	Nadine Gordimer *The Conservationist*	1986	Kingsley Amis *The Old Devils*
	Stanley Middleton *Holiday*	1987	Penelope Lively *Moon Tiger*
1975	Ruth Prawer Jhabvala *Heat and Dust*	1988	Peter Carey *Oscar and Lucinda*
1976	David Storey *Saville*	1989	Kazuo Ishiguro *The Remains of the Day*
1977	Paul Scott *Staying On*	1990	A S Byatt *Possession*
1978	Iris Murdoch *The Sea, The Sea*	1991	Ben Okri *The Famished Road*
1979	Penelope Fitzgerald *Offshore*	1992	Barry Unsworth *Sacred Hunger*
1980	William Golding *Rites of Passage*		Michael Ondaatje *The English Patient*
1981	Salman Rushdie *Midnight's Children*	1993	Roddy Doyle *Paddy Clarke–Ha ha ha*
1982	Thomas Keneally *Schindler's Ark*		

Nobel Prize in literature

1901	René François Armand Sully-Prudhomme	1930	(Harry) Sinclair Lewis	1964	Jean-Paul Sartre, *declined*
1902	Theodor Mommsen	1931	Erik Axel Karlfeldt	1965	Mikhail (Alexandrovich) Sholokhov
1903	Bjørnsterne Martinius Bjørnson	1932	John Galsworthy	1966	Shmuel Yosef Agnon
		1933	Ivan Alexeievich Bunin		Nelly (Leonie) Sachs
1904	Frédéric Mistral	1934	Luigi Pirandello	1967	Miguel Angel Asturias
	José Echegaray y Eizaguirre	1935	*No award*	1968	Kawabata Yasunari
		1936	Eugene Gladstone O'Neill	1969	Samuel Beckett
1905	Henryk Sienkiewicz	1937	Roger Martin du Gard	1970	Alexander (Isayevich) Solzhenitsyn
1906	Giosuè Carducci	1938	Pearl Buck		
1907	Rudyard Kipling	1939	Frans Eemil Sillanpää	1971	Pablo (Neftali Reyes) Neruda
1908	Rudolf Christoph Eucken	1943	*No award*		
		1944	Johannes Vilhelm (JV) Jensen	1972	Heinrich Böll
1909	Selma Ottiliana Lovisa Lagerlöf			1973	Patrick White
		1945	Gabriela Mistral	1974	Eyvind Johnson
1910	Paul Johann von Heyse	1946	Hermann Hesse		Harry (Edmund) Martinson
1911	Count Maurice Maeterlinck	1947	André (Paul Guillaume) Gide		
				1975	Eugenio Montale
1912	Gerhart Hauptmann	1948	T S (Thomas Stearns) Eliot	1976	Saul Bellow
1913	Rabindranath Tagore			1977	Vicente Aleixandre
1914	*No award*	1949	William Faulkner	1978	Isaac Bashevis Singer
1915	Romain Rolland	1950	Bertrand (Arthur William, 3rd Earl) Russell	1979	Odysseus Elytis
1916	(Karl Gustav) Verner von Heidenstam			1980	Czeslaw Milosz
		1951	Pär (Fabian) Lagerkvist	1981	Elias Canetti
1917	Karl Gjellerup	1952	François Mauriac	1982	Gabriel García Márquez
	Henrik Pontoppidan	1953	Winston (Leonard Spencer) Churchill	1983	William (Gerald) Golding
1918	*No award*				
1919	Carl Friedrich Georg Spitteler	1954	Ernest (Miller) Hemingway	1984	Jaroslav Seifert
				1985	Claude (Eugène Henri) Simon
1920	Knut Hamsun	1955	Halldór Laxness		
1921	Anatole France	1956	Juan Ramón Jiménez	1986	Wole Soyinka
1922	Jacinto Benavente	1957	Albert Camus	1987	Joseph Brodsky
1923	William Butler Yeats	1958	Boris (Leonidovich) Pasternak	1988	Naguib Mahfouz
1924	Władysław Stanisław Reymont			1989	Camilo José Cela
		1959	Salvatore Quasimodo	1990	Octavio Paz
1925	George Bernard Shaw	1960	Saint-John Perse	1991	Nadine Gordimer
1926	Grazia Deledda	1961	Ivo Andrić	1992	Derek Walcott
1927	Henri Bergson	1962	John (Ernest) Steinbeck	1993	Toni Morrison
1928	Sigrid Undset	1963	George Seferis		
1929	Thomas Mann				

Arts and culture

Pulitzer Prize in fiction

1917	*No award*	1956	MacKinlay Kantor *Andersonville*
1918	Ernest Poole *His Family*	1957	*No award*
1919	Booth Tarkington *The Magnificent Ambersons*	1958	James Agee *A Death in the Family*
1920	*No award*	1959	Robert Lewis Taylor *The Travels of Jaime McPheeters*
1921	Edith Wharton *The Age of Innocence*		
1922	Booth Tarkington *Alice Adams*	1960	Allen Drury *Advise and Consent*
1923	Willa Cather *One of Ours*	1961	Harper Lee *To Kill a Mockingbird*
1924	Margaret Wilson *The Able McLaughlins*	1962	Edwin O'Connor *The Edge of Sadness*
1925	Edna Ferber *So Big*	1963	William Faulkner *The Reivers*
1926	Sinclair Lewis *Arrowsmith*	1964	*No award*
1927	Louis Bromfield *Early Autumn*	1965	Shirley Ann Grau *The Keepers of the House*
1928	Thornton Wilder *The Bridge of San Luis Rey*	1966	Katherine Anne Porter *The Collected Stories*
1929	Julia Peterkin *Scarlet Sister Mary*	1967	Bernard Malamud *The Fixer*
1930	Oliver LaFarge *Laughing Boy*	1968	William Styron *The Confessions of Nat Turner*
1931	Margaret Ayre Barnes *Years of Grace*	1969	Navarre Scott Momaday *House Made of Dawn*
1932	Pearl S Buck *The Good Earth*	1970	Jean Stafford *Collected Stories*
1933	T S Stribling *The Store*	1972	Wallace Stegner *Angle of Repose*
1934	Caroline Miller *Lamb in His Bosom*	1973	Eudora Welty *The Optimist's Daughter*
1935	Josephine Winslow Johnson *Now in November*	1975	Michael Shaara *The Killer Angels*
1936	Harold L Davis *Honey in the Horn*	1976	Saul Bellow *Humboldt's Gift*
1937	Margaret Mitchell *Gone with the Wind*	1978	James Alan McPherson *Elbow Room*
1938	John Phillips Marquand *The Late George Apley*	1979	John Cheever *The Stories of John Cheever*
1939	Marjorie Kinnan Rawlings *The Yearling*	1980	Norman Mailer *The Executioner's Song*
1940	John Steinbeck *The Grapes of Wrath*	1981	John Kennedy Toole *A Confederacy of Dunces*
1941	*No award*	1982	John Updike *Rabbit is Rich*
1942	Ellen Glasgow *In This Our Life*	1983	Alice Walker *The Color Purple*
1943	Upton Sinclair *Dragon's Teeth*	1984	William Kennedy *Ironweed*
1944	Martin Flavin *Journey in the Dark*	1985	Alison Lurie *Foreign Affairs*
1945	John Hersey *A Bell for Adano*	1986	Larry McMurtry *Lonesome Dove*
1946	*No award*	1987	Peter Taylor *A Summons to Memphis*
1947	Robert Penn Warren *All the King's Men*	1988	Toni Morrison *Beloved*
1948	James Michener *Tales of the South Pacific*	1989	Anne Tyler *Breathing Lessons*
1949	James Gould Cozzens *Guard of Honor*	1990	Oscar Hijuelos *The Mambo Kings Play Songs of Love*
1950	A B Guthrie Jr *The Way West*		
1951	Conrad Richter *The Town*	1991	John Updike *Rabbit at Rest*
1952	Herman Wouk *The Caine Mutiny*	1992	Jane Smiley *A Thousand Acres*
1953	Ernest Hemingway *The Old Man and the Sea*	1993	Robert Olen Butler *A Good Scent from a Strange Mountain*
1954	*No award*		
1955	William Faulkner *A Fable*		

Poets

Name	Dates	Place of birth	Selected works
Adcock, Fleur	1934–	Papakura, New Zealand	*The Eye of the Hurricane* (1964); *The Incident Book* (1986)
Apollinaire, Guillaume	1880–1918	Rome	*Les Alcools* (1913); *Calligrammes* (1918)
Arnold, Matthew	1822–88	Laleham, Surrey	*The Strayed Reveller* (1849); *Poems: A New Edition* (1853–4); *Merope* (1858); *New Poems* (1867)
Auden, W(ystan) H(ugh)	1907–73	York	*Another Time* (1940); *The Sea and the Mirror* (1944); *The Age of Anxiety* (1947)
Baudelaire, Charles	1821–67	Paris	*Les Fleurs du Mal* (1857)
Belloc, Hilaire	1870–1953	St Cloud, France	*Cautionary Tales* (1907); *Sonnets and Verse* (1923)
Betjeman, John	1906–84	Highgate	*Mount Zion* (1933); *New Bats in Old Belfries* (1945); *A Nip in the Air* (1972)
Blake, William	1757–1827	London	*The Marriage of Heaven and Hell* (1791); *The Vision of the Daughter of Albion* (1793); *Songs of Innocence and Experience* (1794); *Milton* (1810)
Blunden, Edmund	1896–1974	London	*The Waggoner and Other Poems* (1920); *The Shepherd and Other Poems of Peace and War* (1922); *English Poems* (1929); *Collected Poems* (1930); *After the Bombing and Other Short Poems* (1950); *A Hong Kong House* (1962)

Literature

Poets (continued)

Name	Dates	Place of birth	Selected works
Blunt, Wilfrid Scawen	1840–1922	Petworth, Sussex	Sonnets and Songs by Proteus (1875); In Vinculis (1899)
Boccaccio, Giovanni	1313–75	Florence	The Decameron; Filostrato
Brooke, Rupert	1887–1915	Rugby	Poems (1911); 1914 and Other Poems (1915); Complete Poems (1946)
Browning, Elizabeth Barrett	1806–61	Coxhoe Hall, Durham	Sonnets from the Portuguese (1850); Aurora Leigh (1855)
Browning, Robert	1812–89	Camberwell	Bells and Pomegranates (1841–6); Dramatic Lyrics (1842); Men and Women (1855); The Ring and the Book (1868-9)
Burns, Robert	1759–96	Alloway, Ayr	Poems Chiefly in the Scottish Dialect (1786); Tam O'Shanter (1790)
Byron, George Gordon	1788–1824	London	Hours of Idleness (1807); Childe Harolde (1817); Don Juan (1819–24)
Chaucer, Geoffrey	1343–1400	London	Troilus and Criseyde (c.1385); The Canterbury Tales (1387–1400)
Coleridge, Samuel Taylor	1722–1834	Ottery St Mary, Devon	Kubla Khan (1797); The Rime of the Ancient Mariner (1798); Christabel (1798); Sybylline Leaves (1817); Collected Poems (1817)
Cowper, William	1731–1800	Great Berkhampstead, Hertfordshire	The Task (1785)
cummings, e(dward) e(estlin)	1894–1962	Cambridge, Massachusetts	Tulips and Chimneys (1923); XLI Poems (1925); is 5 (1926)
Dante, Alighieri	1265–1321	Florence	Divine Comedy (1321)
Day Lewis, Cecil	1904–72	Ballintubber, Co Kildare	Overtures to Death (1938); The Aeneid of Virgil (1952)
De la Mare, Walter	1873–1956	Charlton, Kent	The Listeners (1912); The Burning Glass and Other Poems (1945)
Dickinson, Emily	1830–86	Amherst, Massachusetts	Poems (1891–6)
Donne, John	1572–1631	London	Satires and Elegies (1590s); Holy Sonnets (1610–11)
Dryden, John	1631–1700	Aldwincle All Saints, Northamptonshire	Astrea Redux (1660); Absalom and Achitophel (1681); MacFlecknoe (1684)
Dunn, Douglas	1942–	Inchinnann	Love or Nothing (1974); Elegies (1985)
Eliot, T(homas) S(tearns)	1888–1965	St Louis, Missouri	Prufrock and Other Observations (1917); The Waste Land (1922); Ash Wednesday (1930); Four Quartets (1944)
Éluard, Paul (Eugene Grindal)	1895–1952	Saint-Denis	La Vie Immediate (1934); Poesie et Verité (1942)
Emerson, Ralph Waldo	1803–82	Boston	Complete Works (1903–4)
Fitzgerald, Edward	1809–83	Bredfield, Suffolk	The Rubáiyát of Omar Khayyám (1859)
Frost, Robert	1874–1963	San Francisco	North of Boston (1914); Mountain Interval (1916); New Hampshire (1923); In The Clearing (1962)
Ginsberg, Allen	1926–	Newark, New Jersey	Howl and Other Poems (1956); Empty Mirror (1961); The Fall of America (1973)
Goethe, Johann Wolfgang von	1749–1832	Frankfurt	Römische Elegien (1795); Der west-östliche Divan (1819)
Graham, W(illiam) S(ydney)	1918–86	Greenock, Renfrewshire	Cage Without Grievance (1942); The Seven Journeys (1944), The White Threshold (1949); The Nightfishing (1955); Implements in their Place (1977); Collected Poems (1979); Aimed at Nobody (1993)
Graves, Robert (von Ranke)	1895–1985	London	Fairies and Fusiliers (1917)
Hardy, Thomas	1840–1928	Higher Bockhampton, Dorset	Wessex Poems (1898); Poems of the Past and Present (1902); Satires of Circumstance, Lyrics and Reveries (1914); Moments of Vision and Miscellaneous Verse (1917); Human Shows, Far Phantasies, Songs and Trifles (1925)
Harrison, Tony	1937–	Leeds	Mysteries (1985); V (1985); The Gaze of the Gorgon (1992)
Heaney, Seamus	1939–	County Derry	Death of a Naturalist (1966); Door into the Dark (1969); Field Work (1979)
Heine, Henrich	1797–1856	Düsseldorf	Das Buch der Lieder (1827)
Herbert, George	1593–1633	Montgomery	The Temple (1633)
Hopkins, Gerard Manley	1844–89	London	The Wreck of the Deutschland (1876)
Hughes, Ted	1930–	Mytholmroyd, Yorkshire	The Hawk in the Rain (1957); Lupercal (1960); Seasons Songs (1976); Moortown (1979)
Keats, John	1795–1821	London	Endymion (1818); Lamia and Other Poems (1820)

Name	Dates	Place of birth	Selected works
Lamartine, Alphonse de	1790–1869	Mâcon	*Meditations Poétiques* (1820); *Harmonies Poétiques et Religieuses* (1830); *Recueillements Poétiques* (1839)
Langland, William	1332–1400	Ledbury, Hertfordshire	*Piers Plowman* (1362–99)
Larkin, Philip	1922–1985	Coventry	*The North Ship* (1945); *The Whitsun Weddings* (1964); *High Windows* (1974)
Lear, Edward	1812–88	London	*A Book of Nonsense* (1846); *Laughable Lyrics* (1876); *Queery Leary Nonsense* (1911); *Teapots and Quails* (1953)
Longfellow, Henry	1807–82	Portland, Maine	*Voices and the Night* (1839); *Ballads and Other Poems* (1841); *Hiawatha* (1855); *Divina Comedia* (1872)
MacDiarmid, Hugh (Christopher Murray Grieve)	1892–1978	Langholm, Dumfriesshire	*A Drunk Man Looks at the Thistle* (1926)
MacNeice, (Frederick) Louis	1907–63	Belfast	*Blind Fireworks* (1929); *Solstices* (1961)
Mallarmé, Stéphane	1842–98	Paris	*Herodiade* (1864); *Prélude à L'Apres-midi d'un Faune* (1865); *Poésies* (1887)
Marvell, Andrew	1621–78	Yorkshire	*Elegy* (1649); *Upon Appleton House* (c. 1652-3); *To His Coy Mistress* (pre-1653)
Masefield, John	1878–1967	Ledbury, Herefordshire	*The Everlasting Mercy* (1911); *Dauber* (1913); *Collected Poems* (1923)
Millay, Edna St Vincent	1892–1950	Rockland, Maine	*Renascence and Other Poems* (1917); *A Few Figs From Thistles* (1920); *The Harp-Weaver and Other Poems* (1923)
Milton, John	1608–74	London	*Paradise Lost* (1667)
Moore, Marianne	1887–1972	St Louis, Missouri	*Poems* (1921); *Observations* (1924); *Collected Poems* (1951); *O, to be a Dragon* (1959); *Tell Me, Tell Me: Granite, Steel and Other Topics* (1966)
Muir, Edwin	1887–1959	Deerness, Orkney	*First Poems* (1925); *Chorus of the Newly Dead* (1926); *Variations on a Time Theme* (1934); *The Labyrinth* (1949); *New Poems* (1949–51)
Muldoon, Paul	1951–	County Armagh	*New Weather* (1973); *Mules* (1977); *Why Brownlee Left* (1980); *Quoof* (1984); *Madoc: A Mystery* (1990)
Nash, (Frederick) Ogden	1902–71	New York	*Free Wheeling* (1931)
Nerval, Gérard de	1808–55	Paris	*Les Chimères* (1854)
O'Hara, Frank (Francis Russell)	1926–66	Baltimore	*A City Winter and Other Poems* (1952); *Lunch Poems* (1964)
Owen, Wilfred (Edward Salter)	1893–1918	Oswestry, Shropshire	*Poems* (1920, 1931); *Collected Poems* (1963)
Parker, Dorothy	1893–1967	New Jersey	*Enough Rope* (1926); *Sunset Gun* (1928); *Death and Taxes* (1931); *Not so Deep as a Well* (1936)
Paulin, Tom	1949–	Leeds	*A Sense of Justice* (1977); *The Strange Museum* (1980); *Liberty Tree* (1983); *Fivemiletown* (1987)
Paz, Octavio	1914–	Mexico City	*Salamander* (1958–61); *Collected Poems* (1988)
Petrarch (Francesco Petrarca)	1304–74	Arezzo	*Rime Sparse*
Plath, Sylvia	1932–63	Boston	*The Colossus and Other Poems* (1960); *Ariel* (1965); *Crossing the Water* (1971); *Winter Trees* (1972)
Pound, Ezra (Weston Loomis)	1885–1972	Hailey, Idaho	*The Cantos* (1917, 1948, 1959)
Pushkin, Aleksandr	1799–1837	Moscow	*Eugen Onegin* (1828); *Ruslan and Lyudmila* (1820)
Raine, Craig	1944–	Shildon, Essex	*A Martian Sends a Postcard Home* (1979); *Rich* (1984)
Raine, Kathleen	1908–	London	*Stone and Flower* (1943)
Rilke, Rainer Maria	1875–1926	Prague	*Die Sonette an Orpheus* (1923)
Rimbaud, Arthur	1854–91	Charleville, Ardennes	*Les Illuminations* (1872)
Rossetti, Christina	1830–94	London	*Goblin Market* (1862); *The Prince's Progress* (1872); *A Pageant and Other Poems* (1881)
Sassoon, Siegfried	1886–1967	Kent	*Counter-Attack and Other Poems* (1918); *The Road to Ruin* (1933)
Schiller, Johann Christoph Friedrich von	1759–1805	Marbach	*Die Künstler* (The Artists); *An die Freude* (Ode to Joy)
Shelley, Percy Bysshe	1792–1822	Sussex	*Prometheus Unbound* (1820); *The Mask of Anarchy* (1819); *Ode to the West Wind* (1819); *The Triumph of Life*
Sitwell, Dame Edith	1887–1964	Scarborough	*Facade* (1922); *Colonel Fantock* (1926)

Arts and culture

Literature

Poets (continued)

Name	Dates	Place of birth	Selected works
Smith, Stevie (Florence Margaret Smith)	1902–71	Hull	*Not Waving But Drowning* (1957)
Spender, Stephen	1909–	London	*Poems* (1933)
Spenser, Edmund	1552–99	London	*The Shepheardes Calender* (1579); *The Faerie Queene* (1590)
Stevens, Wallace	1879–1955	Reading, Pennsylvania	*Harmonium* (1923); *Transport to Summer* (1947)
Tate, James	1943–	Kansas City	*The Lost Pilot* (1967); *The Oblivion Ha-Ha* (1970); *Absences* (1971); *Distance From Loved Ones* (1990)
Tennyson, Alfred, Lord	1809–92	Somersby Rectory, Lincolnshire	*Poems* (1832); *The Princess* (1847); *In Memoriam* (1850); *Idylls of the King* (1859); *Maud* (1885)
Thomas, Dylan	1914–53	Swansea	*Twenty-five Poems* (1936); *Deaths and Entrances* (1946); *In Country Sleep and Other Poems* (1952); *Under Milk Wood* (1954)
Valéry, Paul	1871–1945	Sete	*La Jeune Parque* (1917); *Charmes* (1922)
Vega, Lope de	1562–1635	Madrid	*La Dragentea* (1598)
Verlaine, Paul	1844–96	Metz	*Fêtes Galantes* (1869); *Sagesse* (1881)
Walcott, Derek	1930–	Castries, St Lucia	*In a Green Night* (1962); *The Castaway* (1965); *The Gulf* (1969); *Another Life* (1973); *The Odyssey* (1989) *Omeros* (1990);
Warren, Robert Penn	1905–89	Guthrie, Kentucky	*Brother to Dragons* (1953); *Promises: Poems 1954-56* (1957); *Now and Then: Poems 1976–78* (1978); *Portrait of a Father* (1988)
Whitman, Walt	1819–92	New York	*Leaves of Grass* (1855–89)
Williams, William Carlos	1883–1963	New Jersey	*The Tempers* (1913); *Sour Grapes* (1921); *The Desert Music and Poems* (1954); *Journey to Love* (1955); *Pictures from Breughel and Other Poems* (1962)
Wordsworth, William	1770–1850	Cockermouth	*Lyrical Ballads* (1798); *The Prelude* (1799, 1805, 1850); *The Excursion* (1814)
Yeats W(illiam) B(utler)	1865–1939	County Dublin	*The Wanderings of Oisin and Other Poems* (1888); *The Wind Among the Reeds* (1892); *The Wild Swans at Coole* (1917); *Michael Robartes and the Dancer* (1921); *The Winding Stair and Other Poems* (1933)

Poets laureate

1617	Ben Jonson[a]	1730	Colley Cibber	1896	Alfred Austin
1638	Sir William Davenant[a]	1757	William Whitehead	1913	Robert Bridges
1668	John Dryden	1785	Thomas Warton	1930	John Masefield
1689	Thomas Shadwell	1790	Henry Pye	1968	Cecil Day Lewis
1692	Nahum Tate	1813	Robert Southey	1972	Sir John Betjeman
1715	Nicholas Rowe	1843	William Wordsworth	1984	Ted Hughes
1718	Laurence Eusden	1850	Alfred, Lord Tennyson		

[a]The post was not officially established until 1668.

Pulitzer Prize in poetry

1917	*No award*	1927	Leonora Speyer *Fiddler's Farewell*
1918	Sara Teasdale *Love Songs*	1928	Edwin Arlington Robinson *Tristram*
1919	Carl Sandburg *Corn Huskers*	1929	Stephen Vincent Benét *John Brown's Body*
	Margaret Widdemer *Old Road to Paradise*	1930	Conrad Aiken *Selected Poems*
1920	*No award*	1931	Robert Frost *Collected Poems*
1921	*No award*	1932	George Dillon *The Flowering Stone*
1922	Edwin Arlington Robinson *Collected Poems*	1933	Archibald MacLeish *Conquistador*
1923	Edna St Vincent Millay *The Harp Weaver and Other Poems*	1934	Robert Hillyer *Collected Verse*
		1935	Audrey Wurdemann *Bright Ambush*
1924	Robert Frost *New Hampshire: a Poem with Notes and Grace Notes*	1936	R P Tristram Coffin *Strange Holiness*
		1937	Robert Frost *A Further Range*
1925	Edwin Arlington Robinson *The Man Who Died Twice*	1938	Marya Zaturenska *Cold Morning Sky*
		1939	John Gould Fletcher *Selected Poems*
1926	Amy Lowell *What's O'Clock?*	1940	Mark Van Doren *Collected Poems*

1941	Leonard Bacon *Sunderland Capture*	1967	Ann Sexton *Live or Die*
1942	William Benét *The Dust Which is God*	1968	Anthony Hecht *The Hard Hour*
1943	Robert Frost *A Witness Tree*	1969	George Oppen *Of Being Numerous*
1944	Stephen Vincent Benét *Western Star*	1970	Richard Howard *Untitled Subjects*
1945	Karl Shapiro *V–Letter and Other Poems*	1971	W S Merwin *The Carrier of Ladders*
1946	*No award*	1972	James Wright *Collected Poems*
1947	Robert Lowell *Lord Weary's Castle*	1973	Maxine Winokur Kumin *Up Country*
1948	W H Auden *The Age of Anxiety*	1974	Robert Lowell *The Dolphin*
1949	Peter Viereck *Terror and Decorum*	1975	Gary Snyder *Turtle Island*
1950	Gwendolyn Brooks *Annie Allen*	1976	John Ashbery *Self-Portrait in a Convex Mirror*
1951	Carl Sandburg *Complete Poems*	1977	James Merrill *Divine Comedies*
1952	Marianne Moore *Collected Poems*	1978	Howard Nemerov *Collected Poems*
1953	Archibald MacLeish *Collected Poems 1917–1952*	1979	Robert Penn Warren *Now and Then*
1954	Theodore Roethke *The Waking*	1980	Donald Justice *Selected Poems*
1955	Wallace Stevens *Collected Poems*	1981	James Schuyler *The Morning of the Poem*
1956	Elizabeth Bishop *Poems – North & South*	1982	Sylvia Plath *The Collected Poems*
1957	Richard Wilbur *Things of This World*	1983	Galway Kinnell *Selected Poems*
1958	Robert Penn Warren *Promises: Poems 1954–56*	1984	Mary Oliver *American Primitive*
1959	Stanley Kunitz *Selected Poems 1928–1958*	1985	Carolyn Kizer *Yin*
1960	W D Snodgrass *Heart's Needle*	1986	Henry Taylor *The Flying Change*
1961	Phyllis McGinley *Times Three: Selected Verse from Three Decades*	1987	Rita Dove *Thomas and Beulah*
1962	Alan Dugan *Poems*	1988	William Meredith *Partial Accounts; New and Selected Poems*
1963	William Carlos Williams *Pictures from Breughel*	1989	Richard Wilbur *New and Selected Poems*
		1990	Charles Simic *The World Doesn't End*
1964	Louis Simpson *At the End of the Open Road*	1991	Mona van Duyn *Near Changes*
1965	John Berryman *77 Dream Songs*	1992	James Tate *Selected Poems*
1966	Richard Eberhart *Selected Poems*	1993	Louise Glück *The Wild Iris*

THEATRE

Playwrights

Name	Dates	Place of birth	Selected works
Aeschylus	c.525–426 BC	Eleusis, nr Athens	*Persians* (c.472 BC); *Seven Against Thebes* (c.467 BC); *Oresteia* (458 BC)
Albee, Edward	1928–	Washington DC	*The American Dream* (1960); *Who's Afraid of Virginia Woolf?* (1962)
Anouilh, Jean	1910–87	Bordeaux	*Antigone* (1944); *L'Alouette* (1953); *Beckett* (1959)
Arden, John	1930–	Barnsley	*All Fall Down* (1955); *The Waters of Babylon* (1957); *Serjeant Musgrave's Dance* (1959)
Aristophanes	c.448–380 BC	Athens	*Clouds* (c.423 BC); *Wasps* (c.422 BC); *Birds* (c.414 BC); *Lysistrata* (c.411 BC); *Frogs* (c.405 BC)
Ayckbourn, Alan	1939–	London	*Absurd Person Singular* (1973); *The Norman Conquests* (1974); *A Chorus of Disapproval* (1985); *A Woman in Mind* (1986); *Man of the Moment* (1990)
Barnes, Peter	1931–	Stroud	*The Bewitched* (1974); *Laughter* (1978); *Red Noses* (1985)
Barrie, Sir J(ames) M(atthew)	1860–1937	Kirriemuir, Angus	*Peter Pan* (1904); *What Every Woman Knows* (1908)
Beckett, Samuel	1906–89	Foxrock, nr Dublin	*Waiting for Godot* (1954); *Endgame* (1956); *Happy Days* (1961)
Bennett, Alan	1934–	Yorkshire	*Beyond the Fringe* (1960); *Forty Years On* (1968); *Getting On* (1971); *Habeas Corpus* (1973); *The Madness of George III* (1991)
Berkoff, Steven	1937–	London	*East* (1975); *Greek* (1979); *Decadence* (1981)
Bond, Edward	1934–	London	*Saved* (1965); *Lear* (1971); *The Sea* (1973); *The Fool* (1975)
Brecht, Bertolt	1898–1956	Augsburg	*Galileo* (1938–9); *Mother Courage* (1938); *The Good Person of Setzuan* (1943); *Caucasian Chalk Circle* (1955)
Brenton, Howard	1942–	Portsmouth	*Christie in Love* (1969); *Revenge* (1969); *The Romans in Britain* (1980); *Pravda* (with David Hare) (1985)
Čapek, Karel	1890–1938	Bohemia	*RUR* (1920); *The Makropulos Affair* (1923)
Chekhov, Anton	1860–1904	Taganrog	*The Seagull* (1896); *Uncle Vanya* (1900); *Three Sisters* (1901); *The Cherry Orchard* (1904)
Churchill, Caryl	1938–		*Cloud Nine* (1979); *Top Girls* (1982); *Serious Money* (1987)

Playwrights (continued)

Name	Dates	Place of birth	Selected works
Cocteau, Jean	1889–1963	Maisons-Lafitte, nr Paris	*Orphée* (1926); *La Machine Infernale* (1934)
Congreve, William	1670–1729	Bardsey, nr Leeds	*The Way of the World* (1700)
Corneille, Pierre	1606–84	Rouen	*Le Cid* (1636); *Horace* (1639); *Cinna* (1639); *Polyeucte* (1640)
Coward, Noel	1899–1973	Teddington, Middlesex	*Hay Fever* (1925); *Private Lives* (1930); *Blithe Spirit* (1941)
Delaney, Shelagh	1939–	Salford	*A Taste of Honey* (1958)
Eliot, T S	1888–1965	St Louis, Missouri	*Murder in the Cathedral* (1935); *The Cocktail Party* (1950); *The Family Reunion* (1939)
Euripides	c.480–406 BC (c.	Phyla, Attica	*Medea* (c. 431 BC); *Electra* (c. 422–416 BC); *Iphigenia in Tauris* 414 BC); *Bacchae* (?, produced posthumously)
Fo, Dario	1926–	Lombardy	*Accidental Death of an Anarchist* (1970); *Can't Pay, Won't Pay* (1974)
Ford, John	1586–1640	Devonshire	*'Tis Pity She's a Whore'* (1633)
Frayn, Michael	1933–	London	*The Two of Us* (1970); *Donkey's Years* (1976); *Noises Off* (1982)
Friel, Brian	1929–	Omagh	*Philadelphia, Here I Come!* (1964); *Lovers* (1967); *The Freedom of the City* (1973); *Translations* (1980); *Dancing at Lughnasa* (1991)
Fry, Christopher	1907–		*The Lady's Not for Burning* (1949)
Fugard, Athol	1932–	Middleburg, Cape Province	*Sizwe Bansi is Dead* (1972); *Statement After an Arrest Under the Immortality Act* (1972); *A Lesson From Aloes* (1979); *Master Harold... and the Boys* (1982); *The Road to Mecca* (1984)
Genet, Jean	1910–86	Paris	*Les Bonnes (The Maids)* (1947); *Le Balcon (The Balcony)* (1956)
Giraudoux, Jean	1882–1944	Bellac	*Amphitryon 38* (1929); *La Guerre de Troie n'aura pas Lieu* (1935)
Goethe, Johann Wolfgang von	1749–1832	Frankfurt	*Faust I* (1808); *Faust II* (1832)
Goldsmith, Oliver	1728–74	Pallas, Ireland	*She Stoops to Conquer* (1773)
Gray, Simon	1936–	Hampshire	*Butley* (1971)
Griffiths, Trevor	1935–	Manchester	*Occupations* (1970); *The Party* (1974); *Comedians* (1976)
Hampton, Christopher	1946–	Fayal, Azores	*The Philanthropist* (1970), *Savages* (1973); *Tales from Hollywood* (1982); *Les Liaisons Dangereuses* (1985)
Hare, David	1947–	Bexhill	*Teeth 'n' Smiles* (1975), *Plenty* (1978); *Pravda* (with Howard Brenton) (1985); *The Secret Rapture* (1988); *Racing Demon* (1990)
Hauptmann, Gerhart	1862–1946	Obersalzbrunn	*Vor Sonnenaufgang (Before Sunrise)* (1889); *The Weavers* (1892)
Hellman, Lillian	1907–84	New Orleans	*The Little Foxes* (1939)
Ibsen, Henrik	1828–1906	Skien, Norway	*Peer Gynt* (1867); *A Doll's House* (1879); *Hedda Gabler* (1890); *The Master Builder* (1892)
Ionesco, Eugène	1912–94	Romania	*La Cantatrice Chauve (The Bald Prima Donna)* (1950); *Rhinoceros* (1960)
Jonson, Ben	1572–1637	Westminster	*Every Man His Humour* (1598); *Sejanus* (1603); *Volpone* (1606); *The Alchemist* (1610); *Bartholomew Fair* (1614)
Lorca, Federico Garcia	1899–1936	Fuente Vaqueros, Spain	*Blood Wedding* (1933); *The House of Bernarda Alba* (1936)
Mamet, David	1947–	Chicago	*Sexual Perversity in Chicago* (1974); *American Buffalo* (1976); *Glengarry Glen Ross* (1983)
Marlowe, Christopher	1564–1593	Canterbury	*Tamburlaine the Great* (1587); *Dr Faustus* (1588); *The Jew of Malta* (1589); *Edward II* (1592)
Middleton, Thomas	c.1570–1627	London	*Women Beware Women* (c.1621); *The Changeling* (1622)
Miller, Arthur	1915–	New York	*All My Sons* (1947); *Death of a Salesman* (1949); *The Crucible* (1953); *View From the Bridge* (1955); *The Misfits* (1961)
Molière (Jean-Baptiste Poquelin)	1622–73	Paris	*Tartuffe* (1664); *Le Misanthrope* (1666); *Le Bourgeois Gentilhomme* (1670); *Le Malade Imaginaire* (1673)
Musset, Alfred de	1810–57	Paris	*Fantasio* (1834); *On Ne Badine Pas Avec L'Amour* (1834); *Lorenzaccio* (1834)
Nichols, Peter (Richard)	1927–	Bristol	*A Day In the Death of Joe Egg* (1967); *Privates on Parade* (1977)
O'Casey, Sean	1880–1964	Dublin	*Juno and the Paycock* (1924); *The Plough and the Stars* (1926)
O'Neill, Eugene	1888–1953	New York	*Long Day's Journey into Night* (1956)
Orton, Joe	1933–67	Leicester	*Entertaining Mr Sloane* (1964); *Loot* (1965); *What the Butler Saw* (1969)
Osborne, John	1929–	London	*Look Back in Anger* (1956); *The Entertainer* (1957); *A Patriot for Me* (1965); *Déjàvu* (1991)

Name	Dates	Place of birth	Selected works
Pinero, Arthur Wing	1855–1934	London	*The Second Mrs Tanqueray* (1893); *Trelawny of the Wells* (1898)
Pinter, Harold	1930–	London	*The Birthday Party* (1958); *The Caretaker* (1960); *The Homecoming* (1965); *No Man's Land* (1975); *Betrayal* (1978)
Pirandello, Luigi	1867–1936	Agrigento, Sicily	*Six Characters in Search of an Author* (1920); *Henry IV* (1922)
Poliakoff, Stephen	1952–	London	*The Carnation Gang* (1973); *Hitting Town* (1975); *City Sugar* (1975); *Breaking the Silences* (1984)
Priestley, J(ohn) B(oynton)	1894–1984	Bradford	*Dangerous Corner* (1932); *Time and the Conways* (1937); *When We Are Married* (1938); *An Inspector Calls* (1947);
Racine, Jean (Baptiste)	1639–99	La Ferté-Milon	*Andromaque* (1667); *Bérénice* (1670); *Phèdre* (1677)
Rattigan, Terence	1911–77	London	*French Without Tears* (1936); *The Winslow Boy* (1946); *The Browning Version* (1948); *The Deep Blue Sea* (1952); *Ross* (1960)
Rostand, Edmond de	1868–1918	Marseilles	*Cyrano de Bergerac* (1897)
Sartre, Jean-Paul	1905–80	Paris	*Les Mouches (The Flies)* (1943); *Huis Clos* (1944); *Les Séquestrés D'Altona (The Condemned of Altona)* (1961)
Schiller, Johann Christoph Friedrich von	1759–1805	Marbach	*The Robbers* (1781); *Wallenstein* (1799); *Maria Stuart* (1800)
Shaffer, Peter Levin	1926–	Liverpool	*Five Finger Exercise* (1958); *The Royal Hunt of the Sun* (1964); *Equus* (1973); *Amadeus* (1979); *Yonadab* (1985); *Lettuce and Lovage* (1987)
Taylor, Cecil P(hilip)	1928–81	Glasgow	*Good* (1981)
Shakespeare, William	1564–1616	Stratford-Upon-Avon	For complete list of plays see box on p 550.
Shaw, George Bernard	1856–1950	Dublin	*Arms and the Man* (1894); *Man and Superman* (1903); *Pygmalion* (1913); *Heartbreak House* (1919); *Saint Joan* (1923)
Shepherd, Sam	1943–	Sheridan, Illinois	*La Turista* (1966); *The Tooth of Crime* (1972); *Fool For Love* (1979); *A Lie of the Mind* (1985); *The States of Shock* (1991)
Sheridan, Richard Brinsley	1751–1816	Dublin	*The Rivals* (1775); *The School for Scandal* (1777)
Sherrif, R(obert) C(ederic)	1896–1973	Kingston-upon-Thames	*Journey's End* (1929)
Simon, Neil	1927–	New York	*Barefoot in the Park* (1963); *The Odd Couple* (1965); *Plaza Suite* (1968); *The Last of the Red Hot Lovers* (1969); *California Suite* (1976); *Lost in Yonkers* (1991)
Sophocles	c.496–406 BC	Colonus, nr Athens	*Antigone* (c.442 BC); *Oedipus Tyrannus* (c.420 BC); *Electra* (c.409 BC); *Philoctetes* (c.409 BC)
Soyinka, Wole	1934–	Abeskata, Nigeria	*The Swamp Dwellers* (1958); *The Bacchae of Euripedes* (1973)
Stoppard, Tom	1937–	Zlin, Czechoslovakia	*Rosencrantz and Guildenstern are Dead* (1966); *The Real Inspector Hound* (1968); *Jumpers* (1972); *Travesties* (1974); *Arcadia* (1993)
Storey, David	1933–	Wakefield	*The Contractor* (1970); *Home* (1970); *The Changing Room* (1972)
Strindberg, August	1849–1912	Stockholm	*Miss Julie* (1888); *Master Olof* (1877); *The Dance of Death* (1901)
Synge J(ohn), M(illington)	1871–1909	Dublin	*The Playboy of the Western World* (1907)
Terson, Peter	1932–	Tyneside	*A Night to Make the Angels Weep* (1964); *Zigger, Zagger* (1967); *Strippers* (1984)
Travers, Ben	1886–1980	Hendon	*Rookery Nook* (1926); *Thark* (1927)
Webster, John	1578–1632	London	*The White Devil* (1612); *The Duchess of Malfi* (c.1613)
Wesker, Arnold	1932–	London	*Chicken Soup With Barley* (1958); *Roots* (1959); *I'm Talking About Jerusalem* (1960); *Chips With Everything* (1962)
Wilde, Oscar (Fingal O'Flahertie Wills)	1854–1900	Dublin	*Lady Windermere's Fan* (1892); *The Importance of Being Earnest* (1895); *Salomé* (1896)
Wilder, Thornton	1897–1975	Wisconsin	*Our Town* (1938); *The Merchant of Yonkers* (1938); *The Skin of Our Teeth* (1942)
Williams, Tennessee (Thomas Lanier Williams)	1911–83	Mississippi	*The Glass Menagerie* (1944); *A Streetcar Named Desire* (1947); *Cat on a Hot Tin Roof* (1955); *Sweet Bird of Youth* (1959)
Wycherley, William	1641–1716	Clive, nr Shrewsbury	*The Country Wife* (1675); *The Plain Dealer* (1676)

Arts and culture

Shakespeare: the plays

Early comedies	Written	Well-known characters
The Comedy of Errors	1590–4	Antipholus, Dromio, Adriana
Love's Labour's Lost	1590–4	Armado, Berowne, Costard
The Two Gentlemen of Verona	1592–3	Proteus, Valentine, Julia, Sylvia
The Taming of the Shrew	1592	Petruchio, Katharina, Sly

Histories		
Henry VI Part I	1589–90	Henry, Talbot, Joan of Arc
Henry VI Part II	1590–1	Henry, Margaret, Jack Cade
Henry VI Part III	1590–1	Henry, Margaret, Richard of Gloucester
Richard III	1592–3	Richard, Margaret, Clarence, Anne
King John	1595–7	John, Constance, Arthur, Bastard
Richard II	1595	Richard, John of Gaunt, Bolingbroke
Henry IV Part I	1596	Henry, Hal, Hotspur, Falstaff
Henry IV Part II	1597	Henry, Hal, Falstaff, Mistress Quickly
Henry V	1599	Henry (formerly Hal), Pistol, Nym, Katherine
Henry VIII	1613	Henry, Katherine, Wolsey

Middle comedies		
A Midsummer Night's Dream	1595	Oberon, Titania, Puck, Bottom
The Merchant of Venice	1596–8	Bassanio, Portia, Shylock, Jessica
The Merry Wives of Windsor	1597	Falstaff, Mistress Quickly, Shallow
As You Like It	1599	Rosalind, Orlando, Touchstone, Jaques
Twelfth Night	1600–2	Orsino, Olivia, Viola, Malvolio, Feste, Sir Andrew Aguecheek

Dark comedies		
Much Ado About Nothing	1598	Beatrice, Benedick, Dogberry, Verges
All's Well That Ends Well	1602–3	Bertram, Helena, Parolles
Measure for Measure	1604–5	Duke, Angelo, Isabella, Mariana

Tragedies		
Romeo and Juliet	1595–6	Romeo, Juliet, Mercutio, the Nurse
Hamlet	1600–1	Hamlet, Ophelia, the Ghost, the Grave-Digger
Othello	1604	Othello, Desdemona, Iago, Cassio
King Lear	1605–6	Lear, Cordelia, the Fool, Kent, Edgar/Poor Tom
Macbeth	1605–6	Macbeth, Lady Macbeth, Banquo/Ghost, the Three Witches

Greek and Roman plays		
Titus Andronicus	1590–4	Andronicus, Aaron, Lavinia
Julius Caesar	1599	Caesar, Brutus, Cassius, Antony
Troilus and Cressida	1601–2	Troilus, Cressida, Pandarus
Timon of Athens	1605–9	Timon, Apemantus
Antony and Cleopatra	1606–7	Antony, Cleopatra, Enobarbus
Coriolanus	1607–8	Coriolanus, Volumnia

Late comedies		
Pericles	1607–8	Pericles, Marina
Cymbeline	1609–10	Imogen, Iachimo
The Winter's Tale	1611	Leontes, Perdita, Florizel, Autolycus
The Tempest	1613	Prospero, Miranda, Ferdinand, Ariel, Caliban

Theatre personalities

Name	Dates	Place of birth	Occupation
Abbott, George	1887–	New York	Director/playwright/producer
Abington, Frances	1737–1815	London	Actress
Ackerman, Robert Allan	1945–	na	Director
Agate, James (Evershed)	1877–1947	Manchester	Critic
Aitken, Maria	1945–	Dublin	Actress/director
Alexander, Bill	1948–	Hunstanton	Actor/director
Alleyn, Edward	1566–1626	London	Actor
Allgood, Sara	1883–1950	Dublin	Actress
Anderson, Dame Judith (originally Frances Margaret Anderson)	1898–1992	Adelaide	Actress

Name	Dates	Place of birth	Occupation
Antoine, André	1858–1943	Limoges	Actor
Appia, Adolphe	1862–1928	Geneva	Designer
Arliss, George (originally Augustus George Andrews)	1868–1946	London	Actor
Arnaud, Yvonne Germaine	1892–1958	Boredeaux	Actress
Artaud, Antonin	1896–1948	Marseilles	Dramatist/actor/director/theorist
Ashcroft, Dame Peggy (properly Edith Margaret Emily)	1907–91	London	Actress
Attenborough, Sir Richard	1923–	Cambridge	Actor
Aylmer, Sir Felix Edward	1889–1979	na	Actor
Bancroft, Sir Squire	1841–1926	London	Actor/manager
Barber, Frances	1957–	Wolverhampton	Actress
Barrymore, Ethel	1879–1959	Philadelphia	Actress
Barton, John	1928–	London	Director
Baylis, Lilian	1874–1937	London	Theatrical manager
Benson, Sir Frank Robert	1858–1939	Alresford, Hampshire	Actor/manager
Bergman, Ingmar	1918–	Stockholm	Director
Berkoff, Steven	1937–	London	Dramatist/actor/director
Bernhardt, Sarah (properly Henriette Rosine Bernard)	1844–1923	Paris	Actress
Bjornson, Maria	1949–	Paris	Stage designer
Blakely, Colin	1930–87	Bangor, Co Down	Actor
Blin, Roger	1907–84	Neuilly, Paris	Director
Bloom, Claire	1931–	London	Actress
Bogdanov, Michael	1938–	London	Director
Booth, Edwin Thomas	1833–93	Harford County, Maryland	Actor
Bracegirdle, Anne	c.1663–1748	London	Actress
Branagh, Kenneth	1960–	Belfast	Actor/director
Briers, Richard	1934–	Croydon, Surrey	Actor
Bron, Eleanor	na	Stanmore, Middlesex	Actress/director
Brook, Peter (Stephen Paul)	1925–	London	Director
Brustein, Robert	1927–	New York	Critic/director
Burbage, Richard	c.1567–1619	London	Actor; builder of the Globe Theatre, 1599
Callow, Simon	1949–	London	Actor/director
Campbell, Mrs Patrick (née Beatrice Stella Tanner)	1865–1940	Kensington	Actress
Carte, Richard D'Oyly	1844–1901	London	Impresario
Casson, Sir Lewis	1875–1969	Birkenhead	Actor/manager
Chaikin, Joseph	1935–	Brooklyn	Director/actor/producer
Charleson, Ian	1949–90	Edinburgh	Actor
Cheeseman, Peter	1932–	Portsmouth	Director/artistic director
Chereau, Patrice	1944–	France	Director
Chevalier, Albert	1862–1923	London	Actor
Cibber, Colley	1671–1757	London	Actor /dramatist
Cibber, Mrs (née Susannah Maria Arne)	1714–66	London	Actress
Clements, Sir John Selby	1911–88	London	Actor/director
Clurman, Harold Edgar	1901–80	New York City	Director/critic
Cochran, Sir Charles Blake	1872–1951	Lindfield, Sussex	Producer
Compton, Fay	1894–1978	London	Actress
Cooney, Ray	1932–	London	Dramatist/director/producer
Copeau, Jacques	1879–1949	France	Director/manager
Copley, John (Michael Harold)	1933–	Birmingham	Producer
Cornell, Katharine	1893–1974	Berlin	Actress/producer/manager
Courtenay, Tom	1937–	Hull	Actor
Courtneidge, Dame Cicely (Esmerelda)	1883–1980	Sydney	Actress
Coward, Sir Noel (Pierce)	1899–1973	Teddington	Actor/director/dramatist
Craig, Edward Gordon	1872–1966	Stevenage	Actor/stage designer
Crawford, Michael	1942–	Salisbury, Wiltshire	Actor

Theatre personalities (continued)

Name	Dates	Place of birth	Occupation
Croft, Michael	1922–	Manchester	Director
Crowley, Bob	1954–	na	Stage designer
Cusack, Cyril	1910–93	Durban	Actor/director
Cusack, Sinead	1948–	Dublin	Actress
Cushman, Robert	1943–	London	Critic/director
Daubeny, Sir Peter	1921–75	na	Impresario/theatre manager
Davies, Howard	1945–	Reading	Director
Debureau, Jean Gaspard	1796–1846	Bohemia	Actor
De La Tour, Frances	1944–	Bovingdon, Hertfordshire	Actress
Dench, Judi	1934–	York	Actress
Devine, George	1910–65	na	Actor/stage director
Dexter, John	1925–90	Derby	Director
Draper, Ruth	1884–1956	New York	Monologist and diseuse
Dudley, William	1947–	London	Stage designer
Du Maurier, Sir Gerald	1873–1934	London	Actor-manager
Dunlop, Frank	1927–	Leeds	Stage director
Duse, Eleonora	1859–1924	Venice	Actress
Eddington, Paul	1927–	London	Actor
Egan, Peter	1946–	London	Actor/director
Espert, Nuria	1935–	Spain	Actress/director
Evans, Dame Edith	1888–1976	London	Actress
Eyre, Richard	1943–	Barnstaple	Director
Finlay, Frank	1926–	Farnworth, Lancashire	Actor
Finney, Albert	1936–	Salford	Actor
Forbes-Robertson, Sir Johnston	1853–1937	London	Actor
Forrest, Edwin	1806–72	Philadelphia	Actor
Gambon, Michael	1940–	Dublin	Actor
Garrick, David	1717–79	Hereford	Actor
Gielgud, Sir John	1904–	London	Actor
Grotowski, Jerzy	1933–	Rzeszów, Poland	Stage director
Guinness, Sir Alec	1914–	Southborne	Actor
Guthrie, Sir William Tyrone	1900–71	Tunbridge Wells	Producer
Gwyn, Eleanor (known as Nell)	c.1650–87	Hereford	Actress
Hall, Sir Peter	1930–	Bury St Edmund's	Director
Hancock, Sheila	1933–	Blackgang, Isle of Wight	Actress
Hands, Terry	1941–	Aldershot	Stage director
Hardwicke, Sir Cedric (Webster)	1893–1964	Lye, Worcestershire	Actor
Hare, Robertson	1891–1979	London	Actor
Harewood, George Henry Hubert Lascelles, 7th Earl of	1923–	Harewood, nr Leeds	Arts patron
Harris, Julie	1925–	Michigan	Actress
Harris, Rosemary	1930–	Ashby, Suffolk	Actress
Harvey, Sir John Martin	1863–1944	Wivenhoe, Essex	Actor-manager
Hawthorne, Nigel	1929–	Coventry	Actor
Hayes, Helen	1900–	Washington	Actress
Higgins, Clare	1957–	Yorkshire	Actress
Hijikata, Tatsumi	1928–86	Akita province	Performance artist
Hiller, Dame Wendy	1912–	Bramhall, Cheshire	Actress
Holm, Ian	1931–	Ilford, Essex	Actor
Hordern, Sir Michael	1911–	Berkhampsted	Actor
Horniman, Anne Elizabeth Fredericka	1860–1937	Forest Hall, London	Theatre manager
Houseman, John (originally Jaques Haussmann)	1902–89	Bucharest	Actor/stage director
Irving, Sir Henry (John Henry Brodribb)	1838–1905	Keinton-Mandeville, Somerset	Actor
Jackson, Glenda	1936–	Birkenhead	Actress
Jacobi, Sir Derek	1938–	London	Actor
Jacobs, Sally	1932–	London	Designer
Jefferson, Joseph	1829–1905	Philadelphia	Actor
Johnson, Dame Celia	1908–82	Richmond, Surrey	Actress

Name	Dates	Place of birth	Occupation
Jouvet, Louis	1887–1951	Finistère	Director/actor
Kazan, Elia	1909–	Constantinople	Director
Kean, Edmund	1789–1833	London	Actor
Kemble, Frances ('Fanny')	1809–93	London	Actress
Kemp, Lindsay	1939–	Lewis, Hebrides	Mime artist/actor/director
Kendal, Felicity	1946–	Olton, Warwickshire	Actress
Kendal, Dame Madge	1848–1935	Cleethorpes	Actress
Kerr, Walter Francis	1913–	Evanston, Illinois	Critic
Kingsley, Ben	1943–	Snaiton, Yorkshire	Actor
Langtry, Lilly (properly Emilie Charlotte Le Breton)	1853–1929	Jersey	Actress
Lapotaire, Jane	1944–	Ipswich	Actress
Lawrence, Gertrude	1898–1952	London	Actress
Lecoq, Jacques	1921–	Paris	Mime artist/director
Lehmann, Beatrix	1903–79	Bourne End, Buckinghamshire	Actress/director-producer
Lenya, Lotte (originally Karoline Wilhelmine Blamauer)	1900–1981	Hitzing, Vienna	Actress
Littlewood, Joan	1914–91	London	Stage director
Lloyd, Marie	1870–1922	London	Actress
Lloyd Webber, Sir Andrew	1948–	London	Musicals composer
Lunt, Alfred	1892–1977	Milwaukee	Actor
Lyubimov, Yuri	1917–	Russia	Stage director
Mackintosh, Cameron	1946–	Enfield, Middlesex	Producer
Macrae, John Duncan	1905–67	na	Actor
Macready, William Charles	1793–1873	London	Actor
Marceau, Marcel	1923–	Strasbourg	Mime artist
McCowen, Alec	1925–	Tunbridge Wells	Actor
McEwan, Geraldine	1932–	Old Windsor	Actress
McKellen, Sir Ian	1939–	Burnley	Actor
McKenzie, Julia	1941–	na	Actress
Menken, Adah Isaacs (Adah Berthe Theodore)	1835–68	New Orleans	Actress
Merman, Ethel	1909–84	Long Island, New York	Actress
Meyerhold, Vsevolod Emilievich	1874–1940	Penza	Actor/director
Miles, Bernard, Baron	1907–91	Uxbridge	Actor/stage director
Miller, Jonathan Wolfe	1934–	London	Director
Mirren, Helen	1946–	na	Actress
Mnouchkine, Arianne	1938–	France	Stage director
Morley, Sheridan	1941–	Ascot	Critic
Noble, Adrian	1950–	Chichester	Director
Nunn, Trevor	1940–	Ipswich	Director
Olivier, Laurence	1907–89	Dorking	Actor/director
Papp, Joseph (originally Papirofsky)	1921–91	Brooklyn, New York	Stage director/producer
Pennington, Michael	1943–	na	Actor
Perry, Antoinette	1888–1946	Denver	Actress/director
Piscator, Erwin	1893–1966	Ulm, Germany	Stage director
Plowright, Joan	1929–	Brigg, Lincolnshire	Actress
Porter, Eric	1928–	London	Actor
Prince, Hal (Harold Smith)	1928–	New York City	Stage director/producer
Prowse, Philip	1937–	Worcester	Director
Quayle, Sir Anthony	1913–89	Ainsdale	Actor
Redgrave, Sir Michael	1908–85	Bristol	Actor
Redgrave, Vanessa	1937–	London	Actress
Rees, Roger	1944–	Aberystwyth	Actor
Reinhardt, Max	1873–1943	Baden, nr Vienna	Theatre manager
Richardson, Ian	1934–	Edinburgh	Actor
Richardson, Sir Ralph	1902–83	Cheltenham	Actor
Rix, Sir Brian	1924–	Cottingham	Actor
Robson, Dame Flora	1902–84	South Shields	Actress
Rossiter, Leonard	1926–84	Liverpool	Actor
Routledge, Patricia	1929–	Birkenhead	Actress
Scofield, Paul	1922–	Hurstpierpoint, Sussex	Actor

Theatre personalities (continued)

Name	Dates	Place of birth	Occupation
Sher, Antony	1949–	South Africa	Actor
Smith, Dame Maggie	1934–	Ilford, Essex	Actress
Sondheim, Stephen	1930–	New York City	Musicals composer
Speaight, Robert William	1904–76	na	Actor
Stafford-Clark, Max	1941–	Cambridge	Director
Stanislavsky (Konstantin Sergeyevich Alexeyev)	1863–1938	Moscow	Actor/producer/teacher
Stapleton, Maureen	1925–	New York	Actress
Steadman, Alison	1946–	Liverpool	Actress
Stein, Peter	1937–	Berlin	Director
Stevenson, Juliet	1956–	na	Actress
Strasberg, Lee (originally Israel Strassberg)	1901–82	Budzanow	Actor/director/teacher
Strehler, Giorgio	1921–	Italy	Director
Suzman, Janet	1939–	S Africa	Actress
Terry, Dame Ellen	1847–1928	Coventry	Actress
Thacker, David	1950–	na	Actor
Thorndike, Dame Cybil	1882–1976	Gainsborough	Actress
Threlfell, David	1953–	Manchester	Actor
Tinker, Jack	1938–	Oldham	Critic
Tree, Sir Herbert Beerbohm	1853–1917	London	Actor-manager
Tutin, Dorothy	1931–	London	Actress
Tynan, Kenneth	1927–1980	Birmingham	Critic
Wall, Max (Maxwell George Lorimer)	1908–90	London	Actor
Walter, Harriet	1950–	na	Actress
Wanamaker, Sam	1919–93	Chicago	Actor/director
Wardle, Irving	1929–	Bolton	Critic
Warner, Deborah	1959–	Avon	Director
Weigel, Helene	1900–71	Austria	Actress; founded the Berliner Ensemble, 1948, with husband Bertolt Brecht
Whitelaw, Billie	1932–	Coventry	Actress
Wilson, Snoo	1948–	Reading	Director
Wilton, Penelope	1946–	Scarborough	Actress
Wood, John	na	Derbyshire	Actor
Wood, Peter Lawrence	1927–	Colyton, Devon	Director
Zeffirelli, Franco	1923–	Florence	Director
Ziegfeld, Florenz	1869–1932	Chicago	Theatre manager/producer

na = not available

Pulitzer Prize in drama

1918	No award
1919	Jesse Lynch Williams *Why Marry?*
1920	No award
1921	Eugene O'Neill *Beyond the Horizon*
1922	Zona Gale *Miss Lulu Bett*
1923	Eugene O'Neill *Anna Christie*
1924	Owen Davis *Icebound*
1925	Hatcher Hughes *Hell-Bent for Heaven*
1926	Sidney Howard *They Knew What They Wanted*
1927	George Kelly *Craig's Wife*
1928	Paul Green *In Abraham's Bosom*
1929	Eugene O'Neill *Strange Interlude*
1930	Elmer Rice *Street Scene*
1931	Marc Connelly *The Green Pastures*
1932	Susan Glaspell *Alison's House*
1933	George S Kaufman *Morris Ryskind and Ira Gershwin: Of Thee I Sing*
1934	Maxwell Anderson *Both Your Houses*
1935	Sidney Kingsley *Men in White*
1936	Zöe Akins *The Old Maid*
1937	Robert E Sherwood *Idiot's Delight*
1938	George S Kaufman and Moss Hart *You Can't Take It With You*
1939	Thornton Wilder *Our Town*
1940	Robert E Sherwood *Abe Lincoln in Illinois*
1941	William Saroyan *The Time of Your Life*
1942	Robert E Sherwood *There Shall Be No Night*
1943	No award
1944	Thornton Wilder *The Skin of Our Teeth*
1945	No award
1946	Mary Chase *Harvey*
1947	Russell Crouse and Howard Lindsay *State of the Union*
1948	No award
1949	Tennessee Williams *A Streetcar Named Desire*
1950	Arthur Miller *Death of a Salesman*
1951	Richard Rodgers, Oscar Hammerstein II, and Joshua Logan *South Pacific*

1952	*No award*	1974	Jason Miller *The Championship Season*
1953	Joseph Kramm *The Shake*	1975	*No award*
1954	William Inge *Picnic*	1976	*No award*
1955	John Patrick *Teahouse of the August Moon*	1977	Michael Bennett, James Kirkwood, Nicholas
1956	Tennessee Williams *Cat on a Hot Tin Roof*		Dante, Marvin Hamlisch, and Edward
1957	Frances Goodrich and Albert Hackett *The*		Kleban *A Chorus Line*
	Diary of Anne Frank	1978	Michael Cristofer *The Shadow Box*
1958	Eugene O'Neill *Long Day's Journey into Night*	1979	Donald L Coburn *The Gin Game*
1959	Ketti Frings *Look Homeward Angel*	1980	Sam Shepard *Buried Child*
1960	Archibald Macleish *JB*	1981	Lanford Wildon *Talley's Folly*
1961	George Abbott, Jerome Weidman, Sheldon		Beth Henley *Games of the Heart*
	Harnick, and Jerry Bock *Fiorello*	1982	Charles Fuller *A Soldier's Play*
1962	Tad Mosel *All the Way Home*	1983	Marsha Norman *'Night, Mother*
1963	Frank Loesser and Abe Burrows *How to*	1984	David Mamet *Glengarry Glen Ross*
	Succeed in Business Without Really Trying	1985	Stephen Sondhiem and James Lapine
1964	*No award*		*Sunday in the Park with George*
1965	*No award*	1986	*No award*
1966	Frank D Gilroy *The Subject Was Roses*	1987	August Wilson *Fences*
1967	*No award*	1988	Alfred Uhry *Driving Miss Daisy*
1968	Edward Albee *A Delicate Balance*	1989	Wendy Wasserstein *The Heidi Chronicles*
1969	*No award*	1990	August Wilson *The Piano Lesson*
1970	Howard Sackler *The Great White Hope*	1991	Neil Simon *Lost in Yonkers*
1971	Charles Gordone *No Place to Be Somebody*	1992	Robert Schenkkan *The Kentucky Cycle*
1972	Paul Zindel *The Effect of Gamma Rays on Man-*	1993	Tony Kushner *Angels in America: Millennium*
	in-the-Moon Marigolds		*Approaches*
1973	*No award*		

Musicals

Show	Date	Composer(s)	Lyricist(s)	Librettist(s)
A Chorus Line	1975	Marvin Hamlisch	Edward Kleban	James Kirkwood and Nicholas Dante
A Funny Thing Happened on the Way to the Forum	1962	Stephen Sondheim	Stephen Sondheim	Bert Shevelove and Larry Gelbart
A Little Night Music	1973	Stephen Sondheim	Stephen Sondheim	Hugh Wheeler
Annie	1976	Charles Strouse	Martin Charnin	Thomas Meehan
Annie Get Your Gun	1946	Irving Berlin	Herbert and Dorothy Fields	Herbert and Dorothy Fields
Anyone Can Whistle	1964	Stephen Sondheim	Stephen Sondheim	Arthur Laurents
Anything Goes	1934	Cole Porter	Cole Porter	Guy Bolton and PG Wodehouse
Blood Brothers	1983	Willy Russell	Willy Russell	Willy Russell
Brigadoon	1947	Frederick Loewe	Alan Jay Lerner	Alan Jay Lerner
Cabaret	1966	John Kander	Freb Ebb	Joe Masteroff
Camelot	1960	Frederick Loewe	Alan Jay Lerner	Alan Jay Lerner
Candide	1956	Leonard Bernstein	Richard Wilbur	Lillian Hellman
Carmen Jones	1943	George Bizet, adapted by Meilhac and Halevy	Oscar Hammerstein II	Oscar Hammerstein II
Carousel	1945	Richard Rodgers	Oscar Hammerstein II	Oscar Hammerstein II
Cats	1981	Andrew Lloyd Webber	TS Eliot, adapted by Trevor Nunn	TS Eliot, adapted by Trevor Nunn
Chess	1986	Bjorn Ulvaeus and Benny Anderson	Tim Rice	Tim Rice
Chicago	1975	John Kander	Fred Ebb	Fred Ebb and Bob Fosse
Company	1970	Stephen Sondheim	Stephen Sondheim	George Furth
Do I Hear a Waltz?	1965	Richard Rodgers	Stephen Sondheim	Arthur Laurents
Evita	1978	Andrew Lloyd Webber	Tim Rice	Tim Rice
Fiddler on the Roof	1964	Jerry Bock	Sheldon Harnick	Joseph Stein
Follies	1971	Stephen Sondheim	Stephen Sondheim	James Goldman
42nd Street	1980	Harry Warren	Al Dubin	Michael Stewart and Mark Bramble
Funny Girl	1964	Jule Styne	Bob Merrill	Isobel Lennart
Godspell	1971	Stephen Schwartz	Stephen Schwartz	John-Michael Tebelak
Grease	1972	Jim Jacobs and Warren Casey	Jim Jacobs and Warren Casey	Jim Jacobs and Warren Casey

Arts and culture

Literature

Musicals (continued)

Show	Date	Composer(s)	Lyricist(s)	Librettist(s)
Guys and Dolls	1950	Frank Loesser	Frank Loesser	Abe Burrows and Jo Swerling
Gypsy	1959	Jule Styne	Stephen Sondheim	Arthur Laurents
Hair	1967	Galt MacDermot	Galt MacDermot	Gerome Ragni and James Rado
Half a Sixpence	1963	David Heneker	David Heneker	Beverley Cross
Hello Dolly	1964	Jerry Herman	Jerry Herman	Michael Stewart
How to Succeed in Business Without Really Trying	1961	Frank Loesser	Frank Loesser	Abe Burrows, Jack Weinstock, and Willie Gilbert
Into the Woods	1987	Stephen Sondheim	Stephen Sondheim	James Lapine
Irma La Douce	1956	Margaret Monnot	Margaret Monnot	Alexandre Breffort
Jesus Christ Superstar	1971	Andrew Lloyd Webber	Tim Rice	Tim Rice
Joesph and the Amazing Technicolor Dreamcoat	1968	Andrew Lloyd Webber	Tim Rice	Tim Rice
Kismet	1953	Aleksandr Borodin, arr by Robert Wright and George Forrest	Robert Wright and George Forrest	Charles Lederer and Luther Davis
Kiss Me Kate	1947	Cole Porter	Cole Porter	Samuel and Bella Spewack
La Cage aux Folles	1983	Jerry Herman	Jerry Herman	Harvey Fierstein
Lady Be Good	1924	George Gershwin	Ira Gershwin	Guy Bolton and Fred Thompson
Lady in the Dark	1941	Kurt Weill	Ira Gershwin	Moss Hart
Les Misérables	1980 (1985)	Claude-Michel Schönburg	Alain Boublil and Jean-Marc Natel (English lyrics: Herbert Kretzmer)	Alain Boublil and Jean-Marc Natel
Little Shop of Horrors	1982	Alan Menken	Howard Ashman	Howard Ashman
Mame	1966	Jerry Herman	Jerry Herman	Jerome Lawrence and Robert E Lee
Me and My Girl	1937	Noel Gay	L Arthur Rose and Douglas Farber	L Arthur Rose and Douglas Farber
Miss Saigon	1990	Claude-Michel Schönburg	Alain Boublil and Richard Maltby Jr	Alain Boublil and Richard Maltby Jr
My Fair Lady	1956	Frederick Loewe	Alan Jay Lerner	Alan Jay Lerner
Of Thee I Sing	1931	George Gershwin	Ira Gershwin	George S Kaufman and Murray Ryskind
Oh, Kay!	1926	George Gershwin	Ira Gershwin	Guy Bolton and PG Wodehouse
Oklahoma	1943	Richard Rodgers	Oscar Hammerstein II	Oscar Hammerstein II
Oliver!	1960	Lionel Bart	Lionel Bart	Lionel Bart
On The Town	1944	Leonard Bernstein	Betty Comden and Adolph Green	Betty Comden and Adolph Green
On the Twentieth Century	1978	Cy Coleman	Betty Comden and Adolph Green	Betty Comden and Adolph Green
On Your Toes	1936	Richard Rodgers	Lorenz Hart	Richard Rogers, Lorenz Hart, and George Abbott
Paint Your Wagon	1951	Frederick Loewe	Alan Jay Lerner	Alan Jay Lerner
Pal Joey	1940	Richard Rodgers	Lorenz Hart	John O'Hara
Phantom of the Opera	1987	Andrew Lloyd Webber	Charles Hart	Andrew Lloyd Webber and Richard Stilgoe
Salad Days	1954	Julian Slade	Julian Slade and Dorothy Reynolds	Julian Slade and Dorothy Reynolds
Show Boat	1927	Jerome Kern	Oscar Hammerstein II	Oscar Hammerstein II
South Pacific	1949	Richard Rodgers	Oscar Hammerstein II	Oscar Hammerstein II and Joshua Logan
Starlight Express	1984	Andrew Lloyd Webber	Richard Stilgoe	Andrew Lloyd Webber and Richard Stilgoe
Stop the World – I Want to Get Off	1961	Leslie Bricuse and Anthony Newley	Leslie Bricuse and Anthony Newley	Leslie Bricuse and Anthony Newley
Sunday in the Park with George	1984	Stephen Sondheim	Stephen Sondheim	James Lapine
Sweeney Todd	1979	Stephen Sondheim	Stephen Sondheim	Hugh Wheeler

Arts and culture

Show	Date	Composer(s)	Lyricist(s)	Librettist(s)
Sweet Charity	1966	Cy Coleman	Dorothy Fields	Neil Simon
The Boyfriend	1953	Sandy Wilson	Sandy Wilson	Sandy Wilson
The King and I	1951	Richard Rodgers	Oscar Hammerstein II	Oscar Hammerstein II
The Most Happy Fella	1956	Frank Loesser	Frank Loesser	Frank Loesser
The Music Man	1957	Meredith Wilson	Meredith Wilson	Meredith Wilson
The Rocky Horror Show	1973	Richard O'Brien	Richard O'Brien	Richard O'Brien
The Sound of Music	1959	Richard Rogers	Oscar Hammerstein II	Howard Lindsey and Russell Crouse
West Side Story	1957	Leonard Bernstein	Stephen Sondheim	Arthur Laurents
Wonderful Town	1953	Leonard Bernstein	Betty Comden and Adolph Green	Joseph Fields and Jerome Chadarov

FILM AND TELEVISION

Film and television personalities

Name	Dates	Place of birth	Selected works
Adjani, Isabelle	1955–	Paris	*The Story of Adele H* (1975); *Nosferatu* (1978); *Possession* (1980); *Quartet* (1981), *One Deadly Summer* (1983); *Subway* (1985); *Ishtar* (1987); *Camille Claudel* (1988); *La Reine Margot* (1992)
Agutter, Jenny	1952–	Taunton	*The Railway Children* (1970); *Walkabout* (1970); *Logan's Run* (1976); *Equus* (1977); *An American Werewolf in London* (1981); *Child's Play 2* (1990)
Aimée, Anouk (Françoise Sorya)	1934–	Paris	*Les Amants de Verone* (1949); *La Dolce Vita* (1960); *Lola* (1961); *Un Homme et Une Femme* (1966); *Justine* (1969)
Alda, Alan	1936–	New York City	*Paper Lion* (1968); *Catch 22* (1970); *M*A*S*H* (TV, 1972–83); *California Suite* (1978); *Same Time Next Year* (1978); *The Four Seasons* (1981); *Sweet Liberty* (1985); *A New Life* (1988); *Crimes and Misdemeanours* (1990); *Betsy's Wedding* (1990)
Allen, Woody (Allen Stewart Konigsberg)	1935–	Brooklyn, New York	Director/screenplay writer/actor: *Play it Again Sam* (1972); *Sleeper* (1973); *Love and Death* (1975); *Annie Hall* (1977); *Manhattan* (1979); *Broadway Danny Rose* (1984); *Purple Rose of Cairo* (1985); *Hannah and Her Sisters* (1986); *Crimes and Misdemeanours* (1990); *Husbands and Wives* (1992)
Almodovar, Pedro	1951–	Calzada de Calatrava	Director: *Women on the Verge of a Nervous Breakdown* (1988); *Tie Me Up! Tie Me Down!* (1990); *High Heels* (1991)
Altman, Robert	1925–	Kansas City	Director: *The James Dean Story, McCabe and Mrs Miller* (1971); *The Long Goodbye* (1973); *Popeye* (1980); *Vincent and Theo* (1990); *The Player* (1991)
Andress, Ursula	1936–	Berne	*Dr No* (1963); *She* (1965); *What's New Pussycat?* (1965); *Casino Royale* (1967); *The Clash of the Titans* (1981)
Andrews, Julie (Julia Elizabeth Wells)	1935–	Walton-on-Thames, Surrey	*Mary Poppins* (1964); *The Sound of Music* (1965); *Star!* (1968); *Victor/Victoria* (1982); *Duet for One* (1987)
Anderson, Lindsay	1923–	Bangalore, India	*This Sporting Life* (1963); *If...* (1968); *O Lucky Man* (1973); *Britannia Hospital* (1982)
Antonioni, Michelangelo	1912–	Ferrara	Director: *L'Avventura* (*The Adventure*, 1959); *La Notte* (*The Night*, 1961); *Blow-up* (1966); *Zabriskie Point* (1969); *The Oberwald Mystery* (1979)
Ashcroft, Dame Peggy	1907–91	Croydon	*The Thirty-Nine Steps* (1935); *Quiet Wedding* (1940); *A Passage to India* (1984); *The Jewel in the Crown* (TV, 1984); *Madame Sousatzka* (1988)
Astaire, Fred (Fred Austerlitz)	1899–1987	Omaha, Nebraska	*Top Hat* (1935); *Follow the Fleet* (1936); *Easter Parade* (1948)

Film and television personalities (continued)

Name	Dates	Place of birth	Selected works
Atkinson, Rowan	1955–	Northumberland	*Blackadder* (TV, 1984); *Blackadder II* (TV, 1985); *Blackadder III* (1986); *Blackadder Goes Forth* (TV, 1989); *The Tall Guy* (1989)
Attenborough, Sir Richard	1923–	Cambridge	*In Which We Serve* (1942); *Brighton Rock* (1947). Directed: *Oh What A Lovely War* (1969); *A Bridge Too Far* (1977); *Gandhi* (1982); *A Chorus Line* (1985); *Cry Freedom* (1987); *Chaplin* (1992)
August, Bille	1948–	Denmark	Director: *Pelle The Conqueror* (1987); *The Best Intentions* (1992)
Akroyd, Dan	1952–	Ottawa	*The Blues Brothers* (1980); *Ghostbusters* (1984); *Spies Like Us* (1986); *My Stepmother is an Alien* (1989); *Driving Miss Daisy* (1989)
Bacall, Lauren (Betty Perske)	1924–	New York City	*The Big Sleep* (1946); *Dark Passage* (1947); *Key Largo* (1948)
Ball, Lucille	1911–89	Celaron, New York	*Ziegfield Follies* (1946); *I Love Lucy* (TV, 1951–5)
Bancroft, Anne (Anna Maria Italiano)	1931–	Bronx, New York	*The Miracle Worker* (1962); *The Graduate* (1968); *Silent Movie* (1976); *The Elephant Man* (1980); *84 Charing Cross Road* (1986); *Torch Song Trilogy* (1988)
Bankhead, Tallulah	1903–68	Huntsville, Texas	*Tarnished Lady* (1931); *Lifeboat* (1944); *A Royal Scandal* (1945)
Bardot, Brigitte	1934–	Paris	*Et Dieu Créa La Femme* (*And God Created Woman*, 1956); *Si Don Juan Était Une Femme* (*If Don Juan Were A Woman*, 1973)
Barrault, Jean-Louis	1910–93	Le Vesinet	*Les Enfants du Paradis* (*The Children of Paradise*, 1945); *La Ronde* (1950); *The Longest Day* (1962)
Barrymore, Ethel	1879–1959	Philadelphia	*Rasputin and the Empress* (1932); *None But the Lonely Heart* (1944)
Barrymore, John	1882–1942	Philadelphia	*Grand Hotel* (1932); *Dinner At Eight* (1933); *Midnight* (1939)
Basinger, Kim	1953–	Athens, Georgia	*Never Say Never Again* (1983); *9¹/₂ Weeks* (1985); *Blind Date* (1987); *Batman* (1989); *My Stepmother is an Alien* (1989)
Bates, Alan	1934–	Allestree, Derbyshire	*A Kind of Loving* (1962); *Whistle Down the Wind* (1962); *Zorba the Greek* (1965); *Far From the Madding Crowd* (1967); *Women in Love* (1969); *Hamlet* (1990)
Beatty, Warren	1937–	Richmond, Virginia	*Splendour in the Grass* (1961); *All Fall Down* (1962); *Bonnie and Clyde* (1967); *Reds* (1981); *Dick Tracy* (1990); *Bugsy* (1991)
Belmondo, Jean-Paul	1933–	Neuilly-sur-Seine	*A Bout de Souffle* (*Breathless*, 1959); *Un Singe en Hiver* (1962); *That Man From Rio* (1964)
Bergman, Ingmar	1918–	Uppsala	Director: *Smiles of a Summer Night* (1955); *The Seventh Seal* (1957); *Wild Strawberries* (1957); *Herbsonate* (1978); *Fanny and Alexander* (1983)
Bergman, Ingrid	1915–82	Stockholm	*Intermezzo* (1939); *Casablanca* (1942); *For Whom The Bell Tolls* (1943); *Gaslight* (1944); *Anastasia* (1956); *Autumn Sonata* (1978); *A Woman Called Golda* (TV, 1982)
Besson, Luc	1959–	Paris	Director: *Subway* (1985); *The Big Blue* (1988); *Nikita* (1990)
Bloom, Claire	1931–	London	*Look Back In Anger* (1959); *The Haunting* (1963); *The Spy Who Came in From the Cold* (1966)
Bertolucci, Bernardo	1940–	Parma	Director: *Last Tango in Paris* (1972); *The Last Emperor* (1987); *The Sheltering Sky* (1990)
Bogarde, Dirk (Derek van den Bogaerde)	1921–	London	*Victim* (1961); *The Servant* (1963); *The Damned* (1969); *Death in Venice* (1971)
Bogart, Humphrey	1899–1957	New York City	*The Maltese Falcon* (1941); *Casablanca* (1942); *The Big Sleep* (1946); *The Treasure of the Sierra Madre* (1948); *The African Queen* (1951)
Bogdanovich, Peter	1939–	Kingston, New York	Director: *The Last Picture Show* (1971); *Paper Moon* (1973); *What's Up Doc?* (1972); *Nickelodeon* (1976); *Mask* (1985); *Noises Off* (1992)

Name	Dates	Place of birth	Selected works
Bonham-Carter, Helena	1966–	London	*A Room With a View* (1985); *Hamlet* (1990); *Howard's End* (1992)
Boorman, John	1933–	Shepperton	Director: *Deliverance* (1972); *Excalibur* (1981); *Hope and Glory* (1987)
Bow, Clara	1905–65	New York City	*Mantrap* (1926); *It* (1927); *Wings* (1927)
Boyer, Charles	1899–1978	Figeac	*Mayerling* (1936); *The Garden of Allah* (1936); *The Mad Woman of Chaillot* (1969); *Stavisky* (1974)
Branagh, Kenneth	1960–	Belfast	*A Month in the Country* (1988); *Henry V* (1989); *Dead Again* (1991); *Peter's Friends* (1992)
Brandauer, Klaus Maria von	1944–	Alt Aussee	*Mephisto* (1980); *Out of Africa* (1985); *The Russia House* (1990)
Brando, Marlon	1924–	Omaha, Nebraska	*A Streetcar Named Desire* (1951); *The Wild One* (1953); *On The Waterfront* (1954); *Guys and Dolls* (1955); *Mutiny on the Bounty* (1962); *The Godfather* (1972); *Last Tango in Paris* (1972); *Apocalypse Now* (1979); *The Freshman* (1990)
Bresson, Robert	1907–	Auvergne	Director: *Anges du Péché* (Angels of Sin, 1943); *Le Journal d'un Curé de Campagne* (Diary of a Country Priest, 1951); *Un Condamné à Mort s'est Échappé* (A Man Condemned, 1956)
Bridges, Jeff	1949–	Los Angeles	*The Last Picture Show* (1971); *Against All Odds* (1983); *Jagged Edge* (1985); *The Fabulous Baker Boys* (1989); *The Fisher King* (1991); *The Vanishing* (1992)
Broderick, Matthew	1963–	New York City	*Biloxi Blues* (1988); *Torch Song Trilogy* (1988); *The Freshman* (1990)
Bronson, Charles (Charles Buchinski)	1920–	Ehrenfield, Pennsylvania	*The Magnificent Seven* (1960); *This Property is Condemned* (1966); *The Dirty Dozen* (1967); *Death Wish* (1974)
Brooks, Louise (Leslie Gettman)	1906–85	Cherryvale, Kansas	*Pandora's Box* (1929); *Diary of a Lost Girl* (1930)
Brooks, Mel (Melvin Kaminski)	1926–	New York City	Director: *Blazing Saddles* (1974); *Silent Movie* (1976); *High Anxiety* (1977); *History of the World Part One* (1980)
Buñuel, Luis	1900–83	Calanda	Director: *Un Chien Andalou* (An Adalusian Dog, 1928); *L'Age D'Or* (The Golden Age, 1930); *Los Olvidados* (The Young and the Damned, 1950); *That Obscure Object of Desire* (1977)
Burton, Richard	1925–84	Pontrhydfen, Wales	*My Cousin Rachel* (1952); *Look Back in Anger* (1959); *Cleopatra* (1962); *The Night of the Iguana* (1964); *Who's Afraid of Virginia Woolf?* (1966); *Where Eagles Dare* (1969); *1984* (1984)
Cage, Nicholas (Nicholas Coppola)	1964–	Long Beach, California	*Rumblefish* (1983); *The Cotton Club* (1984); *Birdy* (1985); *Peggy Sue Got Married* (1986); *Raising Arizona* (1987); *Moonstruck* (1987); *Wild At Heart* (1990)
Cagney, James	1899–1986	New York City	*Public Enemy* (1931); *Lady Killer* (1933); *A Midsummer Night's Dream* (1935); *Yankee Doodle Dandee* (1942)
Caine, Michael (Maurice Micklewhile)	1933–	London	*Zulu* (1963); *The Ipcress File* (1965); *Alfie* (1966); *The Man Who Would Be King* (1975); *The Eagle Has Landed* (1976); *Dressed to Kill* (1980); *Educating Rita* (1983); *Hannah and Her Sisters* (1986)
Callow, Simon	1945–	London	*Amadeus* (1984); *A Room With A View* (1985); *Maurice* (1987)
Capra, Frank	1897–1991	Palermo	Director: *It Happened One Night* (1934); *Mr Deeds Goes to Town* (1936); *You Can't Take It With You* (1938); *Arsenic and Old Lace* (1942); *It's A Wonderful Life* (1946)
Carné, Marcel	1909–	Paris	Director: *Quai des Brumes* (Port of Shadows, 1938); *Le Jour se Lève* (Daybreak, 1939); *Les Enfants du Paradis* (Children of Paradise, 1944)
Cassavetes, John	1929–89	New York City	Director: *The Dirty Dozen* (1967); *Rosemary's Baby* (1969); *The Fury* (1978); *Whose Life is it Anyway?* (1981); *Tempest* (1983)

Arts and culture

Film and television personalities (continued)

Name	Dates	Place of birth	Selected works
Chabrol, Claude	1930–	Paris	*Le Beau Serge* (Handsome Serge, 1958); *Les Cousins* (1959); *Les Biches* (The Does, 1968); *Le Boucher* (The Butcher, 1970); *Les Noces Rouges* (Blood Wedding, 1973)
Chaney, Lon	1883–1930	Colorado Springs	*The Hunchback of Notre Dame* (1923); *The Phantom of the Opera* (1925)
Chaplin, Charlie (Sir Charles Spencer Chaplin)	1889–1977	London	*The Kid* (1921); *The Goldrush* (1925); *City Lights* (1931); *Modern Times* (1936); *The Great Dictator* (1940)
Chevalier, Maurice	1888–1972	Paris	*The Innocents of Paris* (1929); *One Hour With You* (1932); *Gigi* (1958)
Christie, Julie	1940–	Assam, India	*Billy Liar* (1963); *Doctor Zhivago* (1965); *Fahrenheit 451* (1966); *Far From the Madding Crowd* (1967); *The Go-Between* (1971); *Don't Look Now* (1974); *Heat and Dust* (1982)
Clair, René (René Lucien Chomette)	1898–1981	Paris	Director: *Sous les Toits de Paris* (1930); *And Then There Were None* (1945); *Les Belles de Nuit* (1952); *Porte des Lilas* (1956)
Cleese, John	1939–	Weston-Super-Mare	*Monty Python's Flying Circus* (TV, 1969–74); *Monty Python and the Holy Grail* (1974); *Fawlty Towers* (TV, 1975 & 1979); *The Life of Brian* (1979); *The Time Bandits* (1982); *The Meaning of Life* (1983); *Clockwise* (1985); *A Fish Called Wanda* (1988)
Clift, Montgomery	1920–66	Omaha, Nebraska	*Red River* (1946); *A Place in the Sun* (1951); *From Here To Eternity* (1953); *Suddenly Last Summer* (1968)
Close, Glenn	1947–	Greenwich, Connecticut	*The World According to Garp* (1982); *The Big Chill* (1983); *Jagged Edge* (1985); *Fatal Attraction* (1987); *Dangerous Liaisons* (1988); *Reversal of Fortune* (1990); *Hamlet* (1990)
Cohen, Ethan and Joel	1958– 1955–	St Louis Park, Minnesota	Directors, screenplay writers, and producers: *Blood Simple* (1984); *Raising Arizona* (1987); *Miller's Crossing* (1990); *Barton Fink* (1991)
Colbert, Claudette (Lily Claudette Chaucoin)	1903–	Paris	*It Happened One Night* (1934); *Tovarich* (1937); *The Palm Beach Story* (1942)
Connery, Sean	1930–	Edinburgh	*Dr No* (1963); *From Russia With Love* (1964); *Goldfinger* (1965); *You Only Live Twice* (1967); *Diamonds Are Forever* (1971); *The Man Who Would Be King* (1975); *The Name of the Rose* (1986); *The Untouchables* (1987); *Indiana Jones and The Last Crusade* (1989); *Hunt for Red October* (1990); *The Russia House* (1991)
Cooper, Gary (Frank)	1901–61	Helena, Montana	*The Winning of Barbara Worth* (1926); *A Farewell to Arms* (1932); *For Whom the Bell Tolls* (1943); *High Noon* (1952)
Coppola, Francis Ford	1939–	Detroit	Director: *The Godfather* (1972); *Apocalypse Now* (1979); *The Cotton Club* (1984); *Peggy Sue Got Married* (1987)
Courtenay, Tom	1937–	Hull	*The Loneliness of the Long Distance Runner* (1962); *Billy Liar* (1963); *Dr Zhivago* (1965); *The Dresser* (1983)
Crawford, Joan (Lucille Le Sueur)	1904–77	San Antonio, Texas	*Our Dancing Daughters* (1928); *Mildred Pierce* (1945); *Possessed* (1947); *Whatever Happened to Baby Jane?* (1962)
Cronenberg, David	1943–	Toronto	*The Dead Zone* (1983); *The Fly* (1986); *Dead Ringers* (1988); *Naked Lunch* (1991)
Crosby, Bing (Harry Lillis Crosby)	1904–77	Tacoma, Washington	*Anything Goes* (1936); *Road to Singapore* (1940), *Road to Morocco* (1942); *A Connecticut Yankee in King Arthur's Court* (1949); *White Christmas* (1954); *High Society* (1956)
Cruise, Tom	1962–	Syracuse, New York	*Risky Business* (1984); *Top Gun* (1985); *The Colour of Money* (1986); *Rain Man* (1988); *Born on the Fourth of July* (1989); *Days of Thunder* (1990); *Far and Away* (1992); *A Few Good Men* (1992)

Name	Dates	Place of birth	Selected works
Crystal, Billy	1947–	Long Beach, New York	Throw Momma From the Train (1987); The Princess Bride (1988); When Harry Met Sally (1989); City Slickers (1991)
Cukor, George D(ewey)	1899–1983	New York City	Director: Girls About Town (1931); Little Women (1933); Gaslight (1944); A Star is Born (1954); My Fair Lady (1964)
Curtis, Tony (Bernard Schwarz)	1925–	New York City	Some Like it Hot (1959); Spartacus (1960); The Boston Strangler (1968)
Curtiz, Michael (Mihály Kertész) Light	1888–1962	Budapest	Director: Captain Blood (1935); Charge of the Brigade (1936); The Adventures of Robin Hood (1938); Yankee Doodle Dandee (1942); Casablanca (1943); Mildred Pierce (1945); White Christmas (1954)
Cushing, Peter	1913–	Kenley, Surrey	The Man in the Iron Mask (1939); The Curse of Frankenstein (1956); Dracula (1958); The Hound of the Baskervilles (1959)
Dafoe, Willem	1955–	Appleton, Wisconsin	Heaven's Gate (1980); Platoon (1986); The Last Temptation of Christ (1988); Mississippi Burning (1989); Born on the Fourth of July (1989); Wild at Heart (1990); Light Sleeper (1992); Body of Evidence (1992)
Dalton, Timothy	1946–	Wales	Wuthering Heights (1970); Mary Queen of Scots (1971); The Living Daylights (1987); Licence to Kill (1989)
Dance, Charles	1946–	Rednal, Worcestershire	The Jewel in the Crown (TV, 1984); Plenty (1985); Good Morning Babylon (1987); White Mischief (1987); Pascali's Island (1988)
Davis, Bette	1908–89	Lowell, Massachusetts	Bad Sister (1931); Dangerous (1935); Jezebel (1938); Whatever Happened to Baby Jane? (1962)
Davis, Geena	1957–	Wareham, Massachusetts	Tootsie (1982); The Fly (1986); The Accidental Tourist (1989); Earth Girls Are Easy (1989); Thelma and Louise (1991)
Davis, Judy	1956–	Perth	My Brilliant Career (1979); A Passage To India (1987); Barton Fink (1991); Husbands and Wives (1992)
Day, Doris (Doris von Kappelhoff)	1924–	Cincinnati, Ohio	Calamity Jane (1953); Young at Heart (1954); The Pyjama Game (1957); Pillow Talk (1959)
Day-Lewis, Daniel	1958–	London	Gandhi (1983); My Beautiful Launderette (1985); Room With A View (1985); The Unbearable Lightness of Being (1988); My Left Foot (1989); The Last of the Mohicans (1992); Age of Innocence (1992)
Dean, James	1931–55	Marion, Indiana	East of Eden (1955); Rebel Without A Cause (1955); Giant (1956)
De Havilland, Olivia	1916–	Tokyo	Midsummer Night's Dream (1955); The Adventures of Robin Hood (1938); Gone With The Wind (1939); The Dark Mirror (1946); The Heiress (1949)
Delon, Alain	1935–	Paris	The Leopard (1962); Swann in Love (1984)
De Mille, Cecil B(lount)	1881–1959	Ashfield, Massachusetts	Director: The Squaw Man (1913); The Ten Commandments (1923); The Plainsman (1937); The Greatest Show On Earth (1952)
Demme, Jonathan	1944–	Long Island, New York	Director: Something Wild (1987); Married To The Mob (1988); The Silence of the Lambs (1991)
Dench, Dame Judy	1934–	York	Four in the Morning (1966); A Fine Romance (TV, 1981–4); A Room With A View (1985); 84 Charing Cross Road (1987); A Handful of Dust (1987); Henry V (1989)
Deneuve, Catherine	1943–	Paris	Repulsion (1965); Belle de Jour (1967); Tristana (1970); The Hunger (1983); Indochine (1992)
De Niro, Robert	1943–	New York City	Mean Streets (1973); Taxi Driver (1976); The Deer Hunter (1978); Raging Bull (1980); Angel Heart (1987); Midnight Run (1988); Goodfellas (1990); Awakenings (1990); Cape Fear (1991); Night and the City (1992); This Boy's Life (1992)

Film and television personalities (continued)

Name	Dates	Place of birth	Selected works
Dennehy, Brian	1940–	Bridgeport, Connecticut	*First Blood* (1982); *Gorky Park* (1983); *Legal Eagles* (1986); *Belly of An Architect* (1987); *Presumed Innocent* (1990)
De Palma, Brian	1940–	Newark, New Jersey	Director: *Dressed To Kill* (1980); *Scarface* (1983); *Body Double* (1984); *The Untouchables* (1987)
Depardieu, Gerard	1948–	Chateauroux	*Loulou* (1980); *The Last Metro* (1980); *The Return of Martin Guerre* (1981); *Danton* (1982); *Jean de Florette* (1986); *Under the Sun of Satan* (1987); *Cyrano de Bergerac* (1990); *Green Card* (1990); *Merci La Vie* (1991); *Mon Père, Ce Héros* (1991); *Tous Les Matins du Monde* (1991); *Germinal* (1992)
Dietrich, Marlene (Maria Magdelena von Losch)	1901–92	Berlin	*Der Blaue Engel* (*The Blue Angel*, 1930); *Blond Venus* (1932); *Shanghai Express* (1932); *The Devil is A Woman* (1935); *Desire* (1936); *Notorious* (1956); *Judgement at Nuremberg* (1961)
Dillon, Matt	1964–	Larchmont, New York	*Rumblefish* (1983); *The Flamingo Kid* (1984); *Target* (1985); *Kansas* (1988); *Drugstore Cowboy* (1989); *Singles* (1992)
Disney, Walt	1901–66	Chicago	Artist and film producer: *Snow White and the Seven Dwarfs* (1937); *Pinocchio* (1940); *Fantasia* (1940); *Dumbo* (1941)
Donat, Robert	1905–58	Withington	*The Count of Monte Cristo* (1934); *The Thirty-Nine Steps* (1935); *The Citadel* (1938); *Goodbye Mr Chips* (1939); *Inn of the Sixth Happiness* (1958)
Douglas, Kirk (Issur Danielovitch Demsky)	1916–	Amsterdam, New York	*The Strange Love of Martha Ivers* (1946); *Lust for Life* (1956); *Gunfight at the OK Corral* (1957); *Paths of Glory* (1957); *Spartacus* (1960); *The Man From Snowy River* (1982)
Douglas, Michael	1944–	New Jersey	*The China Syndrome* (1980); *Romancing the Stone* (1984); *The Jewel of the Nile* (1985); *Fatal Attraction* (1987); *Wall Street* (1987); *War of the Roses* (1989); *Basic Instinct* (1992); *Falling Down* (1992)
Dreyfuss, Richard	1947–	Brooklyn, New York	*The Apprenticeship of Duddy Kravitz* (1974); *Jaws* (1975); *Close Encounters of the Third Kind* (1977); *Whose Life is it Anyway?* (1981); *Down and Out in Beverly Hills* (1986); *Stakeout* (1987); *Tin Men* (1987); *Moon Over Parador* (1988); *Always* (1989)
Dunaway, Faye	1941–	Bascom, Florida	*Bonnie and Clyde* (1967); *Chinatown* (1974); *The Towering Inferno* (1974); *The Eyes of Laura Mars* (1978); *The Champ* (1979); *Mommie Dearest* (1981); *Barfly* (1987); *The Handmaid's Tale* (1990)
Eastwood, Clint	1930–	San Francisco	*A Fistful of Dollars* (1964); *The Good, The Bad and the Ugly* (1966); *Play Misty For Me* (1971); *Dirty Harry* (1971). Director: *Bird* (1987); *Unforgiven* (1992)
Eisenstein, Sergei (Mikhailovich)	1898–1948	Riga	Director: *The Battleship Potemkin* (1925); *October* (1927); *Alexander Nevski* (1938); *Ivan The Terrible* (1944)
Elliott, Denholm	1922–92	London	*A Bridge Too Far* (1977); *Raiders of the Lost Ark* (1981); *Trading Places* (1983); *A Private Function* (1984); *A Room With A View* (1985); *Defence of the Realm* (1985); *Maurice* (1987); *Indiana Jones and the Last Crusade* (1989)
Everett, Rupert	1960–	Norfolk	*Another Country* (1984); *Dance With A Stranger* (1985); *The Comfort of Strangers* (1990)
Fairbanks, Douglas Sr (Douglas Elton Ulman)	1883–1939	Denver, Colorado	*The Mark of Zorro* (1920); *The Three Musketeers* (1921); *Robin Hood* (1922); *The Thief of Baghdad* (1924)
Fairbanks, Douglas Jr	1909–	New York City	*Catherine the Great* (1934); *The Prisoner of Zenda* (1937); *Sinbad the Sailor* (1947)

Name	Dates	Place of birth	Selected works
Farrow, Mia	1945–	Los Angeles	*Rosemary's Baby* (1968); *The Great Gatsby* (1973); *A Midsummer Night's Sex Comedy* (1982); *The Purple Rose of Cairo* (1985); *Hannah and Her Sisters* (1986); *New York Stories* (1989); *Alice* (1991); *Husbands and Wives* (1992)
Fassbinder, Rainer Werner	1945–82	Bad Wörishofen, Germany	Director: *Die Bitteren Tränen der Petra von Kant* (*The Bitter Tears of Petra von Kant*, 1972); *Die Ehe der Maria Braun* (*The Marriage of Maria Braun*, 1978)
Fellini, Federico	1920–93	Rimini	Director: *La Strada* (*The Road*, 1954); *Fellini's Roma* (1972); *Amarcord* (*I Remember*, 1974); *La Dolce Vita* (*The Sweet Life*, 1960)
Fields, W C (William Claude Dunkenfield)	1880–1946	Philadelphia	*It's A Gift* (1934); *The Old-Fashioned Way* (1934); *David Copperfield* (1935); *My Little Chickadee* (1940); *Never Give A Sucker An Even Break* (1941)
Finney, Albert	1936–	Salford	*Saturday Night and Sunday Morning* (1960); *Tom Jones* (1963); *Shoot the Moon* (1981); *Annie* (1982); *The Dresser* (1983); *The Green Man* (TV, 1990); *Miller's Crossing* (1990); *The Playboys* (1992)
Firth, Peter	1953–	Bradford	*Equus* (1983); *A Letter To Breshnev* (1985)
Flaherty, Robert	1884–1951	Iron Mountain, Michigan	Documentary film-maker: *Nanook of the North* (1922); *Moana* (1924); *Tabu* (1930). Director: *Elephant Boy* (1937); *Louisiana Story* (1948)
Flynn, Errol	1909–59	Hobart, Tasmania	*In the Wake of the Bounty* (1933); *Captain Blood* (1935); *The Charge of the Light Brigade* (1936); *The Adventures of Robin Hood* (1938)
Fonda, Henry	1905–82	Grand Island, Nebraska	*Young Mr Lincoln* (1939); *The Grapes of Wrath* (1940); *Twelve Angry Men* (1957); *On Golden Pond* (1981)
Fonda, Jane	1937–	New York City	*Barbarella* (1968); *They Shoot Horses, Don't They?* (1969); *Coming Home* (1978); *The Electric Horseman* (1979); *The China Syndrome* (1980); *Nine To Five* (1981); *On Golden Pond* (1981); *The Morning After* (1986); *Old Gringo* (1989)
Ford, Harrison	1942–	Chicago	*Star Wars* (1977); *The Empire Strikes Back* (1980); *Raiders of the Lost Ark* (1981); *Blade Runner* (1982); *Indiana Jones and the Temple of Doom* (1984); *Witness* (1985); *Mosquito Coast* (1986); *Frantic* (1988); *Working Girl* (1988); *Indiana Jones and the Last Crusade* (1989); *Presumed Innocent* (1990); *Regarding Henry* (1991); *Patriot Games* (1992); *The Fugitive* (1993)
Ford, John	1895–1973	Cape Elizabeth, Maine	Director: *Stagecoach* (1935); *The Grapes of Wrath* (1940); *How Green was my Valley* (1941); *The Quiet Man* (1952)
Forman, Milos	1932–	Caslav	*Lásky Jedné Plavovlásky* (*A Blonde in Love*, 1965); *Horí Mà Panenko* (*The Fireman's Ball*, 1967); *One Flew Over the Cuckoo's Nest* (1975); *Amadeus* (1983)
Forsyth, Bill	1947–	Glasgow	Director: *That Sinking Feeling* (1979); *Gregory's Girl* (1981); *Local Hero* (1983)
Foster, Jodie (Ariane Munker)	1962–	Bronx, New York	*Alice Doesn't Live Here Anymore* (1974); *Bugsy Malone* (1976); *Taxi Driver* (1976); *The Little Girl Who Lives Down the Lane* (1976); *The Accused* (1988); *The Silence of the Lambs* (1991); *Little Man Tate* (1991); *Shadows and Fog* (1992); *Somersby* (1992)
Gabin, Jean (Jean-Alexis Moncorgé)	1904–76	Paris	*Pépé le Moko* (1936); *Quai des Brumes* (*Port of Shadows*, 1938); *Le Jour Se Lève* (*Daybreak*, 1939)
Gable, Clark	1901–60	Cadiz, Ohio	*It Happened One Night* (1934); *Mutiny on the Bounty* (1935); *Gone With the Wind* (1939); *The Misfits* (1961)

Film and television personalities (continued)

Name	Dates	Place of birth	Selected works
Gambon, Michael	1940–	Dublin	Turtle Diary (1985); The Singing Detective (TV, 1986); Paris By Night (1989); The Cook, The Thief, His Wife and Her Lover (1989)
Garbo, Greta (Greta Lovisa Gustafsson)	1905–90	Stockholm	Grand Hotel (1932), Anna Karenina (1935); Camille (1936); Ninotchka (1939)
Gardner, Ava (Lucy Johnson)	1922–90	Smithfield, North Carolina	The Barefoot Contessa (1954); The Sun Also Rises (1957); The Night of the Iguana (1964)
Garland, Judy (Frances Gumm)	1922–69	Grand Rapids, Minnesota	The Wizard of Oz (1939); Babes in Arms (1939); Meet Me in St Louis (1944); Easter Parade (1948); A Star is Born (1954)
Gere, Richard	1949–	Philadelphia	American Gigolo (1980); An Officer and a Gentleman (1982); Breathless (1983); The Cotton Club (1984); No Mercy (1985); Pretty Woman (1990); Somersby (1992)
Gibson, Mel	1956–	Peekskill, New York	Tim (1979); Mad Max (1979); Gallipoli (1981); The Year of Living Dangerously (1982); Lethal Weapon (1987); Hamlet (1990); Forever Young (1992)
Gielgud, Sir John	1904–	London	Oh What A Lovely War (1969); Brideshead Revisited (TV, 1981); Gandhi (1982); Prospero's Books (1991)
Gilliam, Terry	1940–	Minneapolis	Director: Jabberwocky (1977); The Time Bandits (1980); Brazil (1985); The Adventures of Baron Munchausen (1988); The Fisher King (1991)
Gish, Lillian (Lillian de Guiche)	1896–1993	Springfield, Ohio	Birth of A Nation (1915); Intolerance (1916); Orphans of the Storm (1922)
Godard, Jean-Luc	1930–	Paris	Director: A Bout de Souffle (Breathless, 1960); Vivre Sa Vie (My Life to Live, 1962); Weekend (1968); Sauve Qui Peut (Slow Motion, 1980); Detective (1984)
Goldberg; Whoopi Johnson)	1955–	Manhattan, New York	The Color Purple (1985); Jumping Jack Flash (Caryn (1986); Ghost (1990); Sister Act (1992); The Player (1992)
Goldblum, Jeff	1952–	Pittsburgh	Death Wish (1974); Invasion of the Bodysnatchers (1978); The Right Stuff (1983); The Big Chill (1983); The Fly (1985); The Tall Guy (1989); Earth Girls Are Easy (1989); Jurassic Park (1993)
Goodman, John	1953–	St Louis, Missouri	True Stories (1986); The Big Easy (1987); Sea of Love (1990); Always (1990); Barton Fink (1991)
Granger, Stewart (James Lablanche Stewart)	1913–93	London	The Man in Grey (1943); Love Story (1944); King Solomon's Mines (1950); Beau Brummell (1954); The Wild Geese (1977)
Grant, Cary (Archibald Alexander Leech)	1904–86	Bristol	The Awful Truth (1937); His Girl Friday (1940); Arsenic and Old Lace (1944); Notorious (1946); To Catch A Thief (1955); North by Northwest (1959)
Greenaway, Peter	1942–	London	Director: The Draughtsman's Contract (1982); The Belly of An Architect (1987); Drowning By Numbers (1988); The Cook, The Thief, His Wife and Her Lover (1989); Prospero's Books (1991)
Grenfell, Joyce	1910–79	London	The Happiest Days of Your Life (1949); Laughter in Paradise (1951); The Bells of St Trinians (1954)
Griffith, D(avid) W(ark)	1875–1948	Floydsfork, Kentucky	Director: The Birth of a Nation (1915); Intolerance (1916)
Griffith, Melanie	1957–	New York City	Something Wild (1987); Working Girl (1988); Pacific Heights (1990); Bonfire of the Vanities (1990)
Guinness, Sir Alec	1914–	London	Oliver Twist (1948); Kind Hearts and Coronets (1949); The Lavender Hill Mob (1951); The Man in the White Suit (1951); The Ladykillers (1955); The Bridge on the River Kwai (1957); Our Man in Havana (1960); Tunes of Glory (1962); Lawrence of Arabia (1962); Doctor Zhivago (1966); Tinker, Tailor, Soldier, Spy (TV, 1979); Smiley's People (TV, 1981); A Passage to India (1984); Little Dorrit (1987); A Handful of Dust (1988); Kafka (1991)

Name	Dates	Place of birth	Selected works
Hackman, Gene	1931–	San Bernadino, California	Bonnie and Clyde (1967); French Connection (1971); The Poseidon Adventure (1972); Young Frankenstein (1974); A Bridge Too Far (1978); Superman (1978); Mississippi Burning (1989); Postcards From the Edge (1990); Unforgiven (1992)
Hancock, Tony	1924–68	Birmingham	Educating Archie (Radio, 1951); Hancock's Half Hour (TV, 1954–61)
Hanks, Tom	1957–	Oakland, California	Splash! (1984); Big (1988); The Burbs (1989); Turner and Hooch (1990); Bonfire of the Vanities (1991)
Harlow, Jean (Harlean Carpentier)	1911–37	Kansas City	Hell's Angels (1930); Platinum Blonde (1931); Bombshell (1933)
Harris, Richard	1930–	County Limerick	The Guns of Navarone (1961); Mutiny on the Bounty (1962); This Sporting Life (1963); Camelot (1967); A Man Called Horse (1969); The Wild Geese (1978); The Field (1990)
Harrison, Sir Rex (Reginald Carey Harrison)	1908–90	Houghton, Lancashire	Storm in a Teacup (1937); Blithe Spirit (1945); The Constant Husband (1958); My Fair Lady (1964); Dr Doolittle (1967)
Hauer, Rutger	1944–	Amsterdam	Blade Runner (1982); The Osterman Weekend (1983); The Hitcher (1985)
Hawks, Howard	1896–1977	Goshen, Indiana	Director: The Road to Glory (1926); The Dawn Patrol (1930); The Big Sleep (1946)
Hawn, Goldie (Jeanne)	1945–	Washington DC	Cactus Flower (1969); There's A Girl in my Soup (1970); Private Benjamin (1980); Bird on a Wire (1990); Housesitter (1992); Death Becomes Her (1992)
Hayworth, Rita (Margarita Carmen Cansino)	1918–87	New York City	Gilda (1946); Separate Tables (1958)
Hepburn, Audrey	1929–93	Brussels	Roman Holiday (1953); Funny Face (1957); The Nun's Story (1959); Breakfast at Tiffany's (1961); My Fair Lady (1964); Wait Until Dark (1967); Robin and Marian (1976); Always (1991)
Hepburn, Katharine	1909–	Hartford, Connecticut	Morning Glory (1933); The Philadelphia Story (1940); The African Queen (1951); Long Day's Journey into Night (1962); Guess Who's Coming to Dinner? (1967); The Lion in Winter (1968); Suddenly Last Summer (1968); On Golden Pond (1981)
Hershey, Barbara	1948–	Hollywood, California	The Right Stuff (1983); The Natural (1984); Hannah and Her Sisters (1986); The Last Temptation of Christ (1988); Beaches (1988); Naked Lunch (1991)
Herzog, Werner (Walter Stipetic)	1942–	Sachrang	Director: Aguirre, der Zorn Gottes (Aguirre, Wrath of God, 1973); Jeder Für Sich und Gott Gegen Alle (The Mystery of Kaspar Hauser, 1974); Nosferatu, The Vampyre (1979)
Heston, Charlton (John Charles Carter)	1923–	Evanston, Illinois	Dark City (1950); The Greatest Show on Earth (1951); The Ten Commandments (1956); Ben Hur (1959); The Awakening (1980)
Hill, George Roy	1922–	Minneapolis	Director: Butch Cassidy and the Sundance Kid (1969); Slaughterhouse 5 (1972); The Sting (1973); The World According to Garp (1982)
Hitchcock, Sir Alfred (Joseph)	1899–1980	London	Director: The Thirty-Nine Steps (1935); The Lady Vanishes (1938); Rebecca (1940); Psycho (1960); The Birds (1963); Frenzy (1972)
Hoffman, Dustin	1937–	Los Angeles	The Graduate (1967); Midnight Cowboy (1969); Marathon Man (1976); All The President's Men (1976); Kramer vs Kramer (1979); Tootsie (1982); Rain Man (1988); Dick Tracy (1990); Billy Bathgate (1991); Hook (1991)
Holden, William	1918–82	O'Fallon, Illinois	Sunset Boulevard (1950); The Bridge on the River Kwai (1957); Casino Royale (1967); The Wild Bunch (1969)

Film and television personalities (continued)

Name	Dates	Place of birth	Selected works
Hope, Bob (Leslie Townes Hope)	1903–	Eltham, London	*Road to Singapore* (1940); *My Favourite Blonde* (1942); *Road to Morocco* (1942); *Road to Hong Kong* (1961)
Hopkins, Sir Anthony	1941–	Port Talbot, Wales	*The Elephant Man* (1980); *The Bounty* (1983); *84 Charing Cross Road* (1986); *The Silence of the Lambs* (1991); *Howard's End* (1992); *Dracula* (1992)
Hopper, Denis	1936–	Dodge City, Kansas	*Rebel without a Cause* (1955); *Giant* (1956); *Cool Hand Luke* (1967); *Easy Rider* (1969); *Apocalypse Now* (1979); *Blue Velvet* (1986); *River's Edge* (1986)
Hordern, Sir Michael	1911–	Berkhampsted	*The Constant Husband* (1955); *A Funny Thing Happened on the Way to the Forum* (1966); *The Missionary* (1982); *Paradise Postponed* (TV, 1986); *The Fool* (1990)
Hoskins, Bob	1942–	Bury St Edmunds, Suffolk	*Pennies from Heaven* (TV, 1978); *The Long Good Friday* (1980); *The Honorary Consul* (1983); *The Cotton Club* (1984); *Brazil* (1985); *Sweet Liberty* (1985); *Mona Lisa* (1986); *Who Framed Roger Rabbit?* (1988); *Shattered* (1991); *Hook* (1991)
Howard, Leslie (Leslie Howard Stainer)	1893–1943	London	*The Scarlet Pimpernel* (1935); *Gone With The Wind* (1939)
Howard, Trevor	1916–88	Cliftonville, Kent	*Brief Encounter* (1946); *The Third Man* (1949); *Mutiny on the Bounty* (1962); *The Charge of the Light Brigade* (1968); *Ryan's Daughter* (1970); *Gandhi* (1982); *White Mischief* (1987)
Hudson, Rock (Roy Scherer, Jr)	1925–85	Winnetka, Illinois	*Magnificent Obsession* (1954); *Giant* (1956); *Pillow Talk* (1959); *Ice Station Zebra* (1968)
Hurt, John	1940–	Chesterfield, Derbyshire	*A Man for All Seasons* (1966); *The Naked Civil Servant* (TV, 1975); *Midnight Express* (1978); *Alien* (1979); *The Elephant Man* (1980); *1984* (1984); *White Mischief* (1987); *Scandal* (1989)
Hurt, William	1950–	Washington DC	*The Janitor* (1981); *Body Heat* (1981); *The Big Chill* (1983); *Gorky Park* (1983); *Kiss of the Spider Woman* (1985); *Children of a Lesser God* (1986); *Broadcast News* (1987); *The Accidental Tourist* (1989); *Alice* (1990); *The Doctor* (1991)
Huston, Angelica	1952–	Ireland	*The Last Tycoon* (1976); *Prizzi's Honour* (1985); *The Dead* (1987); *A Handful of Dust* (1988); *The Witches* (1990); *The Grifters* (1990); *The Adams Family* (1991); *Bitter Moon* (1992)
Huston, John	1906–87	Nevada, Missouri	Director: *The Maltese Falcon* (1941); *The African Queen* (1951); *Moby Dick* (1956); *The Dead* (1987)
Irons, Jeremy	1948–	Cowes	*The French Lieutenant's Woman* (1981); *Brideshead Revisited* (TV, 1981); *Swann in Love* (1984); *The Mission* (1985); *Dead Ringers* (1988); *Reversal of Fortune* (1990); *Kafka* (1991); *Waterland* (1992); *Damage* (1992)
Ivory, James (Francis)	1928–	Berkeley, California	Director: *Heat and Dust* (1982); *The Bostonians* (1984); *A Room With A View* (1985); *Maurice* (1987); *Mr and Mrs Bridge* (1990); *Howard's End* (1992)
Jackson, Glenda	1936–	Liverpool	*Women in Love* (1969); *Sunday Bloody Sunday* (1971); *A Touch of Class* (1973); *Turtle Diary* (1985); *Business As Usual* (1986); *The Rainbow* (1989)
Jackson, Gordon	1923–89	Glasgow	*Whisky Galore* (1948); *The Great Escape* (1962); *The Ipcress File* (1965); *The Prime of Miss Jean Brodie* (1969); *Upstairs, Downstairs* (TV, 1970–5); *The Medusa Touch* (1977); *The Professionals* (TV, 1977–81); *A Town Like Alice* (TV, 1980); *The Shooting Party* (1980)
Jarman, Derek	1942–94	Northwood, Middlesex	*Jubilee* (1977); *Caravaggio* (1985); *Edward II* (1991); *Wittgenstein* (1993)

Name	Dates	Place of birth	Selected works
Johnson, Dame Celia	1908–82	Richmond, Surrey	*In Which We Serve* (1942); *This Happy Breed* (1944); *Brief Encounter* (1945); *The Prime of Miss Jean Brodie* (1968)
Jordan, Neil	1950–	Sligo	Director: *Angel* (1982); *Company of Wolves* (1984); *Mona Lisa* (1986); *High Spirits* (1988); *The Crying Game* (1992)
Karloff, Boris (William Pratt)	1887–1969	London	*Frankenstein* (1931)
Kasdan, Lawrence	1949–	Miami Beach, Florida	Director: *Body Heat* (1981); *The Big Chill* (1983); *Silverado* (1985); *The Accidental Tourist* (1989); *Love You to Death* (1990); *Grand Canyon* (1991)
Kaufman, Philip	1936–	Chicago	Director: *Invasion of the Body Snatchers* (1978); *The Right Stuff* (1983); *The Unbearable Lightness of Being* (1988); *Henry and June* (1990)
Kaye, Danny (Daniel Kominski)	1913–87	New York City	*Up In Arms* (1943); *Wonder Man* (1944); *The Secret Life of Walter Mitty* (1946); *Hans Christian Andersen* (1952)
Kazan, Elia (Elia Kazanjoglous)	1909–	Constantinople	*Gentleman's Agreement* (1948); *On the Waterfront* (1954)
Keaton, Buster (Joseph Francis Keaton)	1895–1966	Piqua, Kansas	*The Butcher Boy* (1917); *The Navigator* (1924); *The General* (1926); *It's A Mad, Mad, Mad, Mad World* (1963)
Keaton, Diane	1946–	Los Angeles	*The Godfather* (1972); *Sleeper* (1973); *Annie Hall* (1977); *Manhattan* (1979); *Reds* (1981); *Mrs Soffel* (1984); *Baby Boom* (1987)
Keaton, Michael	1951–	Carapolis, Pennsylvania	*Beetlejuice* (1988); *Batman* (1989); *The Dream Team* (1989); *Pacific Heights* (1990); *Batman Returns* (1992)
Kelly, Gene	1912–	Pittsburgh	*For Me and My Gal* (1942); *An American in Paris* (1951); *Singin' in the Rain* (1952)
Kelly, Grace	1929–82	Philadelphia	*High Noon* (1952); *Dial M for Murder* (1954); *Rear Window* (1954); *To Catch a Thief* (1955); *High Society* (1956)
Kerr, Deborah (Deborah Jane Kerr Trimmer)	1921–	Helensburgh, Scotland	*The Life and Death of Colonel Blimp* (1943); *Perfect Strangers* (1945); *Black Narcissus* (1947); *The King and I* (1956); *Separate Tables* (1958); *The Night of the Iguana* (1964); *Casino Royale* (1967)
Kingsley, Ben (Krishna Banji)	1943–	Snaiton, Yorkshire	*Gandhi* (1982); *Turtle Diary* (1985); *Pascali's Island* (1988)
Kinski, Klaus (Claus Gunther Nakszynski)	1926–91	Sopot, Gdańsk	*For A Few Dollars More* (1965); *Dr Zhivago* (1965); *Nosferatu* (1979); *Fitzcarraldo* (1982)
Kinski, Natassja	1960–	Berlin	*Tess* (1979); *Cat People* (1982); *One from the Heart* (1982); *Paris Texas* (1984)
Kline, Kevin	1947–	St Louis, Missouri	*Sophie's Choice* (1983); *The Big Chill* (1983); *Cry Freedom* (1987); *A Fish Called Wanda* (1988); *Love You to Death* (1990); *Chaplin* (1992)
Korda, Sir Alexander (Sándor Laszlo Korda)	1893–1956	Turkeye, Hungary	Director: *The Private Life of Henry VIII* (1932); *The Thief of Baghdad* (1940); *The Third Man* (1949); *Richard III* (1956)
Kubrick, Stanley	1928–	New York City	Director: *Spartacus* (1960); *Lolita* (1962); *Dr Strangelove* (1964); *2001: A Space Odyssey* (1965); *A Clockwork Orange* (1971); *The Shining* (1980); *Full Metal Jacket* (1987)
Kurosawa, Akira	1910–	Tokyo	Director: *Rashomon* (1950); *The Seven Samurai* (1954); *Kagemusha* (1980); *Ran* (1985)
Lambert, Christopher	1957–	New York City	*Greystoke* (1984); *Subway* (1985); *Highlander* (1985); *The Sicilian* (1987)
Lancaster, Burt (Stephen Burton)	1913–	New York City	*From Here To Eternity* (1953); *Gunfight at the OK Corral* (1957); *Birdman of Alcatraz* (1962); *Local Hero* (1983); *Field of Dreams* (1989)
Lang, Fritz	1890–1976	Vienna	Director: *Metropolis* (1926); *Fury* (1936)
Lange, Jessica	1949–	Cloquet, Minnesota	*King Kong* (1976); *The Postman Always Rings Twice* (1981); *Tootsie* (1982); *Music Box* (1989); *Cape Fear* (1991); *Night and the City* (1991)
Laughton, Charles	1899–1962	Scarborough	*The Private Life of Henry VIII* (1932); *Mutiny on the Bounty* (1935); *Hobson's Choice* (1954)

Arts and culture

Film and television personalities (continued)

Name	Dates	Place of birth	Selected works
Laurel and Hardy			
Oliver Hardy	1892–1957	Atlanta, Georgia	*Putting Pants on Philip* (1927); *The Battle of the*
Stan Laurel	1890–1965	Ulverston, Lancashire	*Century* (1927); *Two Tars* (1928); *The Perfect Day* (1929); *The Music Box* (1932); *Babes in Toyland* (1934); *Way out West* (1937); *The Flying Deuces* (1939); *Atoll K* (1950)
Laurie, Piper (Rosetta Jacobs)	1932–	Detroit	*The Hustler* (1961); *Carrie* (1976); *Tender is the Night* (TV, 1985); *Children of a Lesser God* (1986); *Twin Peaks* (TV, 1991)
Lean, David	1908–91	Croydon, Greater London	Director: *Blithe Spirit* (1945); *Brief Encounter* (1945); *Great Expectations* (1946); *Oliver Twist* (1948); *The Bridge on the River Kwai* (1957); *Lawrence of Arabia* (1962); *Doctor Zhivago* (1965); *A Passage to India* (1984)
Lee, Christopher	1922–	London	*The Curse of Frankenstein* (1956); *Dracula* (1958); *The Mummy* (1959); *The Three Musketeers* (1973); *The Man with the Golden Gun* (1974); *Howling II* (1985)
Lee, Spike	1957–	Atlanta, Georgia	Director: *She's Gotta Have it* (1986); *Do the Right Thing* (1989); *Mo Better Blues* (1990); *Malcolm X* (1992)
Leigh, Vivien (Vivien Mary Hartley)	1913–67	Darjeeling, India	*Fire Over England* (1937); *Gone With the Wind* (1939); *Lady Hamilton* (1941); *Anna Karenina* (1941); *A Streetcar Named Desire* (1951)
Lemmon, Jack (John Uhler Lemmon III)	1925–	Boston	*Some Like it Hot* (1959); *The Great Race* (1965); *The Odd Couple* (1968); *The China Syndrome* (1979); *JFK* (1991); *The Player* (1992); *Glengarry Glen Ross* (1992)
Levinson, Barry	1942–	Baltimore	Director: *Diner* (1982); *The Natural* (1984); *Tin Men* (1987); *Good Morning Vietnam* (1987); *Rain Man* (1988); *Bugsy* (1991)
Lloyd, Harold (Clayton)	1893–1971	Burchard, Nebraska	*High and Dizzy* (1920); *Safety Last* (1923); *The Freshman* (1925); *Welcome Danger* (1929)
Lockwood, Margaret (Margaret Day)	1916–90	Karachi, India	*Lorna Doone* (1934); *The Lady Vanishes* (1938); *The Wicked Lady* (1945)
Loren, Sophia (Sofia Scicolone)	1934–	Rome	*The Pride and the Passion* (1957); *Two Women* (1961)
Losey, Joseph (Walton)	1909–84	La Crosse, Wisconsin	Director: *The Boy with the Green Hair* (1945); *The Servant* (1963); *The Go-Between* (1971)
Lubitsch, Ernst	1892–1947	Berlin	Director: *The Love Parade* (1929); *Ninotchka* (1939)
Lynch, David	1946–	Missoula, Montana	Director: *Eraserhead* (1977); *The Elephant Man* (1980); *Blue Velvet* (1986); *Wild at Heart* (1990); *Twin Peaks* (TV 1990–1); *Twin Peaks: Fire Walk With Me* (1992)
MacLaine, Shirley (Shirley Beaty)	1934–	Richmond, Virginia	*The Trouble with Harry* (1955); *Irma La Douce* (1963); *Sweet Charity* (1969); *Terms of Endearment* (1983); *Madame Sousatzka* (1988); *Postcards From the Edge* (1990)
Malkovich, John	1953–	Christopher, Illinois	*The Killing Fields* (1984); *Places in the Heart* (1984); *Empire of the Sun* (1987); *Dangerous Liaisons* (1988); *The Sheltering Sky* (1990)
Malle, Louis	1932–	Thumeries, France	Director, producer, screenwriter: *Les Amants* (*The Lovers*, 1958); *Zazie dans le Métro* (1960); *Lacômbe Lucien* (1974); *Pretty Baby* (1978); *Atlantic City* (1990); *My Dinner with André* (1981); *Au revoir, Les enfants* (1987)
Mankiewicz, Joseph Leo	1909–93	Wilkes-Barre, Pennsylvania	Director: *All About Eve* (1950); *The Barefoot Contessa* (1954); *Guys and Dolls* (1954); *Suddenly Last Summer* (1959)
Mansfield, Jayne (Vera Jayne Palmer)	1933–67	Bryn Mawr, Pennsylvania	*The Girl Can't Help It* (1957); *Too Hot to Handle* (1960)

Name	Dates	Place of birth	Selected works
Martin, Steve	1945–	Waco, Texas	*Dead Men Don't Wear Plaid* (1982); *The Man With Two Brains* (1983); *The Little Shop of Horrors* (1986); *Planes, Trains and Automobiles* (1987); *Roxanne* (1987); *Dirty Rotten Scoundrels* (1989); *Parenthood* (1989); *LA Story* (1991); *Grand Canyon* (1991)
Marx Brothers, The			*The Cocoanuts* (1929); *Monkey Business*; (1931);
Chico (Leonard Marx)	1886–1961	New York City	*Horse Feathers* (1932); *Duck Soup* (1933) *A Day*
Harpo (Adolph Marx)	1888–1964		*at the Races* (1937)
Groucho (Julius Henry Marx)	1890–1977		
Zeppo (Herbert Marx)	1901–77		
Mason, James	1909–84	Huddersfield	*Fanny by Gaslight* (1944); *The Wicked Lady* (1946); *A Star is Born* (1954); *Lolita* (1962); *Georgy Girl* (1966); *Heaven Can Wait* (1978); *The Boys From Brazil* (1978); *The Shooting Party* (1984)
Mastroianni, Marcello	1924–	Fontana Liri	*White Nights* (1957); *La Dolce Vita* (1960); *Otto e Mezzo* (1963); *Dark Eyes* (1987)
Matthau, Walter	1920–	New York City	*The Odd Couple* (1968); *Hello Dolly* (1969); *Cactus Flower* (1969); *Pirates* (1986)
Maura, Carmen	1945–	Madrid	*Dark Habits* (1983); *What Have I Done to Deserve This?* (1964); *Law of Desire* (1987); *Women on the Verge of a Nervous Breakdown* (1988)
McQueen, Steve (Terence Steve McQueen)	1930–80	Slater, Missouri	*The Magnificent Seven* (1960); *The Great Escape* (1963); *The Cincinnati Kid* (1965); *Getaway* (1972); *Papillon* (1973); *Towering Inferno* (1974)
Mercouri, Melina (Anna Amalia Mercouri)	1923–	Athens	*Never on Sunday* (1960); *Topkapi* (1964); *Gaily, Gaily* (1969)
Midler, Bette	1945–	Honolulu, Hawaii	*Down and Out in Beverly Hills* (1986); *Ruthless People* (1986); *Outrageous Fortune* (1987); *Beaches* (1988); *Scenes From the Mall* (1991)
Mills, Hayley	1946–	London	*Tiger Bay* (1959); *Whistle Down the Wind* (1961)
Mills, Sir John	1908–	Felixstowe, Suffolk	*In Which We Serve* (1942); *Great Expectations* (1946); *The History of Mr Polly* (1972); *Ryan's Daughter* (1970)
Minnelli, Liza	1946–	Los Angeles	*Cabaret* (1972); *Stepping Out* (1991)
Mirren, Helen	1945–	London	*Cal* (1984); *Heavenly Pursuits* (1985); *Mosquito Coast* (1986); *The Cook, The Thief, His Wife and Her Lover* (1989); *The Comfort of Strangers* (1990)
Mitchum, Robert	1917–	Bridgeport, Connecticut	*Cape Fear* (1962); *Ryan's Daughter* (1970); *Farewell My Lovely* (1975); *The Big Sleep* (1978); *War and Remembrance* (TV, 1987); *Cape Fear* (1991)
Monroe, Marilyn (Norma Jean Mortensen or Baker)	1926–62	Los Angeles	*Gentlemen Prefer Blondes* (1953); *The Seven Year Itch* (1955); *Some Like it Hot* (1959); *The Misfits* (1961)
Montand, Yves (Ivo Levi)	1921–91	Monsumagno, Italy	*The Wages of Fear* (1953); *Let's Make Love* (1960); *Jean de Florette* (1986); *Manon des Sources* (1986)
Moore, Demi (Demi Guines)	1962–	Roswell, New Mexico	*St Elmo's Fire* (1986); *Ghost* (1990); *The Butcher's Wife* (1991); *A Few Good Men* (1992); *Indecent Proposal* (1992)
Moore, Roger	1927–	London	*The Saint* (TV, 1962–9); *Live and Let Die* (1973); *The Man with the Golden Gun* (1974); *The Spy Who Loved Me* (1977); *The Wild Geese* (1978); *For Your Eyes Only* (1981); *Octopussy* (1983); *A View to a Kill* (1985)
Moreau, Jeanne	1928–	Paris	*Les Amants* (1958); *Jules et Jim* (1961); *Journal d'une Femme de Chambre* (1964); *Nikita* (1990)
Murphy, Eddie	1961–	Brooklyn, New York	*48 Hours* (1982); *Trading Places* (1983); *Beverly Hills Cop* (1985); *Coming to America* (1988); *Another 48 Hours* (1990)
Neeson, Liam	1952–	Ballymena, Northern Ireland	*Excalibur* (1981); *Suspect* (1987); *The Dead Pool* (1988); *Husbands and Wives* (1992)
Neill, Sam	1948–	New Zealand	*The Final Conflict* (1981); *Reilly Ace of Spies* (TV, 1983); *Plenty* (1985); *Kane and Abel* (TV, 1988); *A Cry in the Dark* (1988); *The Hunt for Red October* (1990); *Jurassic Park* (1993)

Film and television

Film and television personalities (continued)

Name	Dates	Place of birth	Selected works
Newman, Paul	1925–	Cleveland, Ohio	*The Long Hot Summer* (1958); *Cat on a Hot Tin Roof* (1958); *The Hustler* (1961); *Butch Cassidy and the Sundance Kid* (1969); *The Sting* (1973); *The Verdict* (1982); *The Color of Money* (1986); *Mr and Mrs Bridge* (1990)
Nicholson, Jack	1937–	Neptune, New Jersey	*Easy Rider* (1969); *Chinatown* (1974); *One Flew Over the Cuckoo's Nest* (1975); *The Shining* (1980); *The Postman Always Rings Twice* (1981); *Terms of Endearment* (1983) *Prizzi's Honour* (1985); *The Witches of Eastwick* (1987); *Batman* (1989); *A Few Good Men* (1992)
Niven, David (James David Graham Nevins)	1910–83	London	*Wuthering Heights* (1939); *Raffles* (1940); *Around the World in Eighty Days* (1956); *Separate Tables* (1958); *The Guns of Navarone* (1961); *The Pink Panther* (1964); *Casino Royale* (1967); *Trail of the Pink Panther* (1982); *Curse of the Pink Panther* (1982)
Nolte, Nick	1940–	Omaha, Nebraska	*48 Hours* (1982); *Down and Out in Beverly Hills* (1986); *Cape Fear* (1991); *Prince of Tides* (1991); *The Player* (1992)
O'Neal, Ryan (Patrick Ryan O'Neal)	1941–	Los Angeles	*Love Story* (1970); *What's Up Doc?* (1972); *Paper Moon* (1973); *Nickelodeon* (1976)
O'Toole, Peter	1932–	Kerry, Connemara	*Lawrence of Arabia* (1962); *Goodbye Mr Chips* (1969); *The Stunt Man* (1980); *The Last Emperor* (1987)
Oldman, Gary	1959–	New Cross, London	*Sid and Nancy* (1986); *Prick up Your Ears* (1987); *Track 29* (1988); *JFK* (1991); *Dracula* (1992)
Olivier, Sir Laurence	1907–89	Dorking	*Wuthering Heights* (1939); *Rebecca* (1940); *Henry V* (1944); *Hamlet* (1948); *Richard III* (1956); *The Prince and the Showgirl* (1958); *The Entertainer* (1960); *Marathon Man* (1976); *A Bridge Too Far* (1977); *Brideshead Revisited* (TV, 1982)
Ophuls or Opüls, Max (Max Oppenheimer)	1902–57	Saarbrücken	Director: *La Ronde* (1950); *Lola Montez* (1955)
Pabst, G(eorg) W(ilhelm)	1895–1967	Raudnitz	Director: *Die Liebe der Jeanne Ney* (*The Love of Jeanne Ney*, 1927); *Westfront 1918* (1930); *Der Letzte Akt* (*The Last Act*, 1955)
Pacino; Al (Alfredo Pacino)	1940–	New York City	*The Godfather* (1972); *Scarface* (1983); *Sea of Love* (1990); *Dick Tracy* (1990); *Frankie and Johnny* (1991); *Glengarry Glen Ross* (1992); *Scent of a Woman* (1992)
Palin, Michael	1943–	Sheffield	*Monty Python's Flying Circus* (TV, 1969–74); *Monty Python and the Holy Grail* (1974); *The Life of Brian* (1978); *The Meaning of Life* (1982); *A Private Function* (1984); *A Fish Called Wanda* (1988); *Around the World in 80 Days* (TV, 1989); *Pole to Pole* (TV, 1992)
Parker, Alan	1944–	London	Director: *Bugsy Malone* (1976); *Midnight Express* (1978); *Birdy* (1985); *Angel Heart* (1987); *Mississippi Burning* (1988); *The Commitments* (1991)
Pasolini, Pier Paulo	1922–75	Bologna	Director: *The Gospel According to St Matthew* (1964); *The Decameron* (1971); *The Canterbury Tales* (1973)
Peck, Gregory (Eldred)	1916–	La Jolla, California	*Spellbound* (1945); *The Man in the Grey Flannel Suit* (1956); *Cape Fear* (1962); *To Kill a Mockingbird* (1962); *The Omen* (1976); *Old Gringo* (1989); *Cape Fear* (1991)
Peckinpah, Sam	1925–84	Fresno, California	Director: *The Deadly Companions* (1961); *Major Dundee* (1965); *The Wild Bunch* (1969)

Arts and culture

Name	Dates	Place of birth	Selected works
Pfeiffer, Michelle	1957–	Santa Ana, California	*Sweet Liberty* (1982); *The Witches of Eastwick* (1987); *Dangerous Liaisons* (1988); *The Fabulous Baker Boys* (1989); *The Russia House* (1990); *Frankie and Johnny* (1991); *Batman Returns* (1992)
Phoenix, River	1970–93	Madras, Oregon	*Mosquito Coast* (1986); *Running on Empty* (1988); *Indiana Jones and the Last Crusade* (1989); *Love You to Death* (1990); *My Own Private Idaho* (1991)
Pickford, Mary (Gladys Mary Smith)	1893–1979	Toronto	*Rebecca of Sunnybrook Farm* (1917); *Poor Little Rich Girl* (1917); *Pollyanna* (1919); *Little Lord Fauntleroy* (1921)
Plowright, Joan	1929–	Scunthorpe Brigg, Lincolnshire	*The Entertainer* (1960); *Drowning By Numbers* (1988); *Love You to Death* (1990)
Plummer, Christopher	1927–	Toronto	*The Sound of Music* (1965); *The Man Who Would be King* (1975); *The Return of the Pink Panther* (1975); *Where the Heart Is* (1990)
Poitier, Sidney	1924–	Miami, Florida	*Cry, The Beloved Country* (1952); *The Blackboard Jungle* (1955); *Porgy and Bess* (1959); *Lilies of the Field* (1963); *In The Heat of the Night* (1967); *To Sir With Love* (1967)
Polanski, Roman	1933–	Paris	Director: *Nóz w Wodzie (Knife in the Water*, 1962); *Rosemary's Baby* (1968); *Repulsion* (1965); *Macbeth* (1971); *Tess* (1979); *Frantic* (1988); *Bitter Moon* (1992)
Pollack, Sydney	1934–	South Bend, Indiana	Director: *They Shoot Horses Don't They?* (1969); *The Electric Horseman* (1979); *Tootsie* (1982); *Out of Africa* (1985)
Powell, Michael	1905–90	Canterbury	Director: *The Thief of Baghdad* (1940); *Black Narcissus* (1947); *The Tales of Hoffman* (1951); *Peeping Tom* (1960); *The Boy Who Turned Yellow* (1972)
Powell, Robert	1944–	Salford, Lancashire	*Jesus of Nazareth* (TV, 1977); *The 39 Steps* (1978); *Pygmalion* (TV, 1981)
Preminger, Otto	1906–86	Vienna	Director: *Laura* (1944); *Carmen Jones* (1954); *Bonjour Tristesse* (1959); *Porgy and Bess* (1959); *Exodus* (1960); *The Human Factor* (1979)
Pudovkin, Vsevoled (Ilarionovich)	1893–1953	Penza, Russia	Director: *Konets Sankt-Peterburga (The End of St Petersburg*, 1927); *Potomok Chingis-Khan (Storm over Asia*, 1928); *Dezetir (Deserter*, 1933)
Quaid, Dennis	1954–	Houston, Texas	*The Big Easy* (1986); *Suspect* (1987); *Great Balls of Fire* (1989); *Postcards From the Edge* (1990)
Rampling, Charlotte	1946–	Sturmer, Essex	*Georgy Girl* (1966); *Angel Heart* (1987); *Paris By Night* (1988)
Rathbone, Basil (Philip St John)	1892–1967	Johannesburg	*David Copperfield* (1935); *Anna Karenina* (1935); *Captain Blood* (1935); *The Hound of the Baskervilles* (1939); *The Adventures of Sherlock Holmes* (1939)
Ray, Satyajit	1921–92	Calcutta	Director: *Pather Panchali (On The Road*, 1954); *Aparajito (The Unvanquished*, 1956); *Apu Sansar (The World of Apu*, 1959); *The Kingdom of Diamonds* (1980); *Pickoo* (1982); *The Home and the World* (1984)
Redford, Robert	1937–	Santa Barbara, California	*Barefoot in the Park* (1968); *Butch Cassidy and the Sundance Kid* (1969); *The Sting* (1973); *All the President's Men* (1976); *Out of Africa* (1985); *Indecent Proposal* (1993). Director: *Ordinary People* (1980); *A River Runs Through It* (1993)
Redgrave, Sir Michael	1908–85	Bristol	*The Lady Vanishes* (1938); *The Dam Busters* (1955); *The Quiet American* (1958); *The Innocents* (1961)
Redgrave, Vanessa	1937–	London	*The Bostonians* (1983); *Wetherby* (1985); *Prick Up Your Ears* (1987); *The Ballad of the Sad Café* (1991); *Howard's End* (1992)
Reed, Sir Carol	1906–76	London	Director: *The Fallen Idol* (1948); *The Third Man* (1949)

Arts and culture

Film and television personalities (continued)

Name	Dates	Place of birth	Selected works
Reed, Oliver	1938–	London	*The Damned* (1962); *Women in Love* (1969); *Castaway* (1987)
Reeve, Christopher	1952–	New York City	*Superman* (1978); *Superman II* (1980); *Superman III* (1983); *The Bostonians* (1984)
Reeves, Keanu	1965–	Beirut, Lebanon	*Dangerous Liaisons* (1988); *Bill and Ted's Excellent Adventure* (1989); *Parenthood* (1989); *Love You to Death* (1990); *My Own Private Idaho* (1991); *Dracula* (1992)
Reiner, Rob	1945–	The Bronx, New York	Director: *This is Spinal Tap* (1984); *Stand By Me* (1987); *The Princess Bride* (1988); *When Harry Met Sally* (1989); *Misery* (1990); *A Few Good Men* (1992)
Renoir, Jean	1894–1979	Paris	Director: *La Grande Illusion* (*Grand Illusion*, 1937), *La Règle du Jeu* (*The Rules of the Game*, 1939)
Resnais, Alain	1922–	Vannes, France	*Van Gogh* (1948); *Guernica* (1950); *Hiroshima, Mon Amour* (*Hiroshima My Love*, 1959); *L'Année Dernière à Marienbad Last Year at Marienbad*, 1961); *Mon Oncle d'Amérique* (*My American Uncle*, 1980); *La Vie est un Roman* (*Life is a Novel*, 1983); *Melo* (1986)
Richardson, Miranda	1958–	Liverpool	*Dance With a Stranger* (1984); *Blackadder II* (TV, 1986); *Empire of the Sun* (1987); *A Month in the Country* (1988); *Damage* (1992)
Richardson, Sir Ralph	1902–83	Cheltenham	*Anna Karenina* (1948); *The Fallen Idol* (1948); *Richard III* (1956); *Long Day's Journey Into Night* (1962); *Dr Zhivago* (1966)
Riefenstahl, Leni	1902–	Berlin	Film-maker: *Triumph des Willens* (*Triumph of the Will*, 1935); *Olympia* (1938)
Robbins, Tim	1958–	New York City	*Bull Durham* (1988); *Jacob's Ladder* (1990); *The Player* (1992); *Bob Roberts* (1992)
Roberts, Julia	1967–	Smyrna, Georgia	*Mystic Pizza* (1988); *Pretty Woman* (1990); *Sleeping With the Enemy* (1991); *Dying Young* (1991); *Hook* (1991); *The Player* (1992)
Robinson, Edward G (Emmanuel Goldberg)	1893–1973	Bucharest	*Little Caesar* (1930); *Double Indemnity* (1944); *All My Sons* (1948); *The Cincinnati Kid* (1965)
Roeg, Nicholas Jack	1928–	London	Director: *Walkabout* (1971); *Don't Look Now* (1973); *The Man Who Fell to Earth* (1976); *Bad Timing* (1980); *Castaway* (1986); *Black Widow* (1988); *Track 29* (1988)
Rogers, Ginger (Virginia Katherine McMath)	1911–	Missouri	*Flying Down to Rio* (1933); *The Gay Divorcee* (1934); *Top Hat* (1935); *Follow The Fleet* (1936)
Rooney, Mickey (Joe Yule, Jr)	1920–	Brooklyn, New York	*A Midsummer Night's Dream* (1935); *Babes in Arms* (1939); *Summer Holiday* (1948); *Breakfast at Tiffany's* (1961); *It's a Mad, Mad, Mad, Mad World* (1963)
Rossellini, Isabella	1952–	Rome	*White Nights* (1985); *Blue Velvet* (1985); *Cousins* (1989); *Wild at Heart* (1990)
Rossellini, Roberto	1906–77	Rome	Director: *Roma, città aperta* (*Rome, Open City*, 1945); *Paisà* (*Paisan*, 1946); *Germania, anno zero* (*Germany, Year Zero*, 1947); *Il Generale della Rovere* (*General della Rovere*, 1959)
Rourke, Mickey	1956–	Schenectady, New York	*Rumble Fish* (1983); *9¹/₂ weeks* (1985); *Angel Heart* (1987); *Wild Orchid* (1990)
Russell, Jane	1921–	Bernidji, Minnesota	*The Outlaw* (1943); *The Paleface* (1948); *Gentlemen Prefer Blondes* (1953)
Russell, Ken	1927–	Southampton	Director: *Women in Love* (1969); *The Music Lovers* (1971); *The Devils* (1971); *Gothic* (1987); *The Rainbow* (1989)
Russell, Kurt	1951–	Springfield, Massachusetts	*Silkwood* (1983); *Tequila Sunrise* (1988); *Backdraft* (1991)
Rutherford, Dame Margaret	1892–1972	London	*Blithe Spirit* (1945); *The Happiest Days of Your Life* (1950); *Murder She Said* (1961); *Murder Most Foul* (1964)

Name	Dates	Place of birth	Selected works
Ryan, Meg	1962–	Fairfield, Connecticut	*Top Gun* (1985); *El Presidio* (1988); *When Harry Met Sally* (1989); *The Doors* (1991)
Ryder, Winona	1971–	Winona, Michigan	*Beetlejuice* (1988); *Heathers* (1989); *Great Balls of Fire* (1989); *Dracula* (1992)
Saint, Eva Marie	1924–	Newark, New Jersey	*On the Waterfront* (1954); *North by Northwest* (1959)
Sarandon, Susan (Susan Abigail Tomalin)	1946–	New York City	*The Hunger* (1983); *The Witches of Eastwick* (1987); *Bull Durham* (1988); *White Palace* (1991); *Thelma and Louise* (1991); *Light Sleeper* (1991)
Schlesinger, John	1926–	London	Director: *A Kind Of Loving* (1962); *Billy Liar* (1963); *Far From the Madding Crowd* (1967); *Midnight Cowboy* (1969); *Sunday, Bloody Sunday* (1971); *Marathon Man* (1976); *Yanks* (1979); *Madame Sousatzka* (1989)
Schwarzenegger, Arnold	1947–	Graz, Austria	*Conan the Barbarian* (1982); *Conan the Destroyer* (1984); *The Terminator* (1984); *Total Recall* (1990); *Kindergarten Cop* (1990); *Teminator 2: Judgement Day* (1991); *Last Action Hero* (1992)
Scofield, Paul	1922–	Hurstpierpoint, Sussex	*A Man For All Seasons* (1966); *Hamlet* (1990)
Scorcese, Martin	1942–	Queens, New York	Director: *Mean Streets* (1973); *Taxi Driver* (1976); *Raging Bull* (1980); *The Mission* (1986); *The Last Temptation of Christ* (1988); *Goodfellas* (1990); *Cape Fear* (1991); *Age of Innocence* (1992)
Scott, George C(ampbell)	1927–	Wise, Virginia	*Anatomy of a Murder* (1959); *The Hustler* (1962); *Dr Strangelove* (1963); *Patton* (1970); *The Changeling* (1980); *Oliver Twist* (1982); *The Exorcist III* (1990)
Scott, Ridley	1937–	South Shields	Director. *Alien* (1979); *Blade Runner* (1982); *No Way Out* (1989); *Thelma and Louise* (1991)
Segal, George	1934–	New York City	*Who's Afraid of Virginia Woolf?* (1966); *The Owl and the Pussycat* (1979); *The Last Married Couple in America* (1979); *Look Who's Talking* (1989)
Sellers, Peter	1925–80	Southsea	*The Ladykillers* (1955); *I'm Alright Jack* (1959); *Dr Strangelove* (1963); *The Pink Panther* (1963); *A Shot in the Dark* (1964); *Return of The Pink Panther* (1975); *The Pink Panther Strikes Again* (1976); *Revenge of The Pink Panther* (1978)
Sennett, Mack (Michael Sinott)	1880–1960	Richmond, Quebec	Producer: *The Keystone Cops* (1912); *Sennett Bathing Beauties* (1920)
Sharif, Omar (Michael Shalhouz)	1932–	Alexandria, Egypt	*Lawrence of Arabia* (1962); *Doctor Zhivago* (1965); *Funny Girl* (1968); *The Tamarind Seed* (1974); *Return to Eden* (1982)
Sheen, Charlie (Carlos Irwin Estevez)	1965–	Santa Monica, California	*Wall Street* (1987); *Platoon* (1987)
Sheen, Martin (Ramon Estevez)	1940–	Dayton, Ohio	*Catch 22* (1970); *The Little Girl Who Lives Down the Lane* (1976); *Apocalypse Now* (1979); *Gandhi* (1982); *The Dead Zone* (1983); *Wall Street* (1987)
Shepherd, Cybil	1950–	Memphis, Tennessee	*The Last Picture Show* (1971); *Taxi Driver* (1976); *The Lady Vanishes* (1979); *Moonlighting* (TV, 1985–9); *Alice* (1991)
Signoret, Simone (Simone Henriette Charlotte Kaminker)	1921–85	Wiesbaden	*La Ronde* (1950); *Les Diaboliques* (1954); *Room at the Top* (1959); *Ship of Fools* (1965)
Sim, Alistair	1900–76	Edinburgh	*The Happiest Days of Your Life* (1950); *Scrooge* (1951); *Laughter in Paradise* (1951); *The Belles of St Trinians* (1954)
Simmons, Jean	1929–	London	*Great Expectations* (1946); *Black Narcissus* (1946); *Hamlet* (1948); *The Blue Lagoon* (1948); *Spartacus* (1960)
Sinatra, Frank (Francis Albert Sinatra)	1915–	Hoboken, New Jersey	*From Here to Eternity* (1953); *The Man With the Golden Arm* (1957); *The Manchurian Candidate* (1962)

Arts and culture

Film and television

Film and television personalities (continued)

Name	Dates	Place of birth	Selected works
Slater, Christian	1969–	New York City	The Name of the Rose (1986); Heathers (1989); Pump up the Volume (1990); Robin Hood, Prince of Thieves (1991); True Romance (1993)
Smith, Dame Maggie	1934–	Ilford, Essex	The Prime of Miss Jean Brodie (1969); Travels with my Aunt (1972); A Private Function (1984); A Room With a View (1985); The Lonely Passion of Judith Hearne (1987)
Spader, James	1960–	Boston, Massachusetts	Pretty in Pink (1986); Sex, Lies and Videotape (1989); The Rachel Papers (1989); Bad Influence (1990); White Palace (1991); The Music of Chance (1993)
Spielberg, Steven	1947–	Cincinnati, Ohio	Director: Duel (1971); Jaws (1975); Close Encounters of the Third Kind (1977); Raiders of the Lost Ark (1981); ET (1982); The Color Purple (1985); Indiana Jones and the Temple of Doom (1984); Empire of the Sun (1987); Indiana Jones and the Last Crusade (1989); Hook (1992); Jurassic Park (1993)
Stallone, Sylvester	1946–	New York City	Rocky (1976); Part II (1979); III (1982); IV (1985); V (1990); First Blood (1981); Rambo (1985); Over the Top (1987); Rambo III (1988); Tango and Cash (1990); Cliffhanger (1992)
Stamp, Terence	1939–	Stepney	The Collector (1965); Far From the Madding Crowd (1967); Superman (1978); Superman II (1980); Company of Wolves (1985); Legal Eagles (1986); Wall Street (1987)
Stanton, Harry Dean	1926–	Kentucky	Cool Hand Luke (1967); The Godfather – Part II (1974); Alien (1979); Repo Man (1984); Paris, Texas (1984)
Steiger, Rod (Rodney Stephen Steiger)	1925–	Westhampton, New York	On the Waterfront (1954); Oklahoma! (1955); Al Capone (1958); Dr Zhivago (1965); In the Heat of the Night (1967); American Gothic (1988)
Sternberg, Josef von (Jonas Stern)	1894–1969	Vienna	Der Blaue Engel (The Blue Angel, 1930); The Devil is a Woman (1935)
Stewart, James	1908–	Indiana, Pennsylvania	You Can't Take it With You (1938); The Philadelphia Story (1940); It's a Wonderful Life (1946); Rear Window (1954); Vertigo (1958); Anatomy of a Murder (1959)
Stone, Oliver	1946–	New York City	Director: Platoon (1987); Wall Street (1987); Born on the Fourth of July (1989); The Doors (1991); JFK (1991)
Streep, Meryl (Mary Louise Streep)	1949–	Summit, New Jersey	The Deer Hunter (1978); Kramer vs Kramer (1979); The French Lieutenant's Woman (1981); Sophie's Choice (1982); Silkwood (1983); Plenty (1985); Out of Africa (1986); A Cry in the Dark (1989); Postcards From the Edge (1990)
Streisand, Barbra	1942–	Brooklyn, New York	Funny Girl (1968); Hello Dolly (1969); What's up Doc? (1972); The Way We Were (1973); A Star Is Born (1976); Yentl (1983); Nuts (1987); Prince of Tides (1991)
Stroheim, Erich (Oswald) von	1886–1957	Vienna	Director: Blind Husbands (1919); Greed (1923); La Grande Illusion (1930); Sunset Boulevard (1955)
Sutherland, Donald	1934–	St John, New Brunswick	The Dirty Dozen (1967); The Eagle Has Landed (1977); Invasion of the Body Snatchers (1978); Ordinary People (1980); Backdraft (1991)
Suzman, Janet	1939–	Johannesburg	Nicholas and Alexandra (1972); Voyage of the Damned (1976); The Draughstman's Contract (1982); Leon, the Pig Farmer (1992)
Swanson, Gloria (Gloria May Josephine Svensson)	1897–1983	Chicago	Male and Female (1919); Manhandled (1924); The Trespasser (1929); Sunset Boulevard (1950)
Tandy, Jessica	1909–	London	The Birds (1963); The World According to Garp (1982); Still of the Night (1982); The Bostonians (1984); Cocoon (1985); The House on Carroll Street (1988); Driving Miss Daisy (1989)

Name	Dates	Place of birth	Selected works
Tati, Jacques (Jacques Tatischeff)	1908–82	Pecq	Director: *Jour de Fête* (*The Big Day*, 1947); *Les Vacances de Mr Hulot* (*Mr Hulot's Holiday*, 1953); *Mon Oncle* (*My Uncle*, 1958)
Taylor, Elizabeth (Rosemond)	1932–	London	*The Father of the Bride* (1950); *Cat on a Hot Tin Roof* (1958); *Butterfield 8* (1960); *Cleopatra* (1962); *Who's Afraid of Virginia Woolf?* (1966); *Suddenly Last Summer* (1968); *The Mirror Crack'd* (1980); *Young Toscanini* (1988)
Temple, Shirley	1928–	Santa Monica, California	*Stand Up and Cheer* (1934); *Bright Eyes* (1934); *Heidi* (1937); *The Little Princess* (1939)
Thomas, Terry (Thomas Terry Hoar Stevens)	1911–90	Finchley, London	*Private's Progress* (1956); *I'm All Right Jack* (1959); *It's a Mad, Mad, Mad, Mad World* (1963); *Those Magnificent Men in Their Flying Machines* (1965); *Don't Look Now* (1968)
Tracy, Spencer (Bonadventure)	1900–67	Milwaukee	*Up The River* (1930); *Captains Courageous* (1937); *Boys' Town* (1938); *Woman of the Year* (1942); *State of the Union* (1948); *Father of the Bride* (1950); *Bad Day at Black Rock* (1955); *Judgement at Nuremberg* (1961); *Guess Who's Coming to Dinner* (1967)
Travolta, John	1954–	Englewood, New Jersey	*Saturday Night Fever* (1977); *Grease* (1978); *Staying Alive* (1983); *Perfect* (1985); *Look Who's Talking* (1989)
Truffaut, François	1932–84	Paris	Director: *Les Quatres Cents Coups* (1959, *The 400 Blows*); *Tirez sur le Pianiste* (*Shoot the Pianist*, 1960); *Jules et Jim* (1962); *La Nuit Américaine* (*Day for Night*, 1972); *L'Enfant Sauvage* (1969); *Le Dernier Metro* (1980); *Vivement Dimanche* (*Lively Sunday*, 1983)
Turner, Kathleen	1954–	Springfield, Missouri	*Body Heat* (1981); *Romancing the Stone* (1984); *The Jewel of the Nile* (1985); *Prizzi's Honour* (1985); *Peggy Sue Got Married* (1986); *The Accidental Tourist* (1989); *The War of the Roses* (1989)
Turturro, John	1957–	Brooklyn, New York	*Raging Bull* (1980); *Hannah and Her Sisters* (1986); *Do the Right Thing* (1989); *Miller's Crossing* (1990); *Barton Fink* (1991)
Ustinov, Peter (Alexander)	1921–	London	*Quo Vadis* (1951); *Spartacus* (1960); *Topkapi* (1964); *Death on the Nile* (1978); *Appointment with Death* (1988)
Vadim, Roger (Roger Vadim Plemiannikov)	1928–	Paris	Director: *Et Dieu Créa La Femme* (*And God Created Woman*, 1956); *Les Liaisons Dangereuses* (1959); *Barbarella* (1968); *La Vice et la Vertue* (1962)
Valentino, Rudolph (Rodolpho Alfonso di Valentino d'Antonguolla)	1895–1926	Castellaneta	*The Four Horsemen of the Apocalypse* (1919); *The Sheikh* (1921); *Blood and Sand* (1922)
Vidor, King	1894–1982	Galveston, Texas	Director: *The Turn of the Road* (1919); *The Big Parade* (1925); *Hallelujah* (1929); *Northwest Passage* (1940); *War and Peace* (1956); *Solomon and Sheba* (1959)
Visconti, Count Luchino	1906–76	Milan	Director: *Ossessione* (*Obsession*, 1942); *La Terra Trema* (*The Earth Trembles*, 1947); *Il Gattopardo* (*The Leopard*, 1963); *Morte a Venezia* (*Death in Venice*, 1971)
Von Sydow, Max	1929–	Lund	*The Seventh Seal* (1957); *The Greatest Story Ever Told* (1965); *Hannah and Her Sisters* (1986); *Pelle the Conqueror* (1988); *The Father* (1990); *Awakenings* (1991); *The Ox* (1991); *The Touch* (1992)
Wajda, Andrzej	1926–	Suwalki, Poland	Director: *Pokolenie* (*A Generation*, 1954); *Czlowiek z marmary* (*Man of Marble*, 1977); *Czlowiek z Zelaza* (*Man of Iron*, 1981)
Walken, Christopher	1943–	Astoria, New York	*The Deer Hunter* (1978); *The Dogs of War* (1981); *The Dead Zone* (1983); *A View to a Kill* (1984); *Biloxi Blues* (1988); *The Comfort of Strangers* (1990); *Batman Returns* (1992); *True Romance* (1993)

Arts and culture

Film and television

Film and television personalities (continued)

Name	Dates	Place of birth	Selected works
Walters, Julie	1950–	Birmingham	*Educating Rita* (1983); *Prick up Your Ears* (1987); *Personal Services* (1987); *Just Like A Woman* (1991)
Washington, Denzel	1954–	Mt Vernon, New York	*Cry Freedom* (1987); *Mo' Better Blues* (1990); *Mississippi Masala* (1991); *Malcolm X* (1992)
Wayne, John (Marion Michael Morrison)	1907–79	Winterset, Iowa	*Stagecoach* (1939); *Red River* (1948); *She Wore a Yellow Ribbon* (1949); *The Quiet Man* (1952); *True Grit* (1969)
Weaver, Sigourney	1949–	New York City	*Alien* (1979); *The Janitor* (1981); *The Year of Living Dangerously* (1982); *Ghostbusters* (1984); *Aliens* (1986); *Gorillas in the Mist* (1988); *Working Girl* (1988); *Aliens III* (1992)
Weir, Peter	1944–	Sydney	Director: *Picnic at Hanging Rock* (1975); *Gallipoli* (1980); *The Year of Living Dangerously* (1982); *Witness* (1985); *Mosquito Coast* (1986); *Dead Poet's Society* (1989); *Green Card* (1990)
Welles, Orson	1915–85	Kenosha, Wisconsin	Director, screenplay writer, actor: *Citizen Kane* (1941); *The Magnificent Ambersons* (1942); *Lady from Shanghai* (1948); *Macbeth* (1948); *The Third Man* (acting only, 1949); *Othello* (1952); *Touch of Evil* (1958); *Chimes at Midnight* (1966)
West, Mae	1893–1980	New York City	*Night After Night* (1932); *I'm No Angel* (1933); *My Little Chickadee* (1940); *Myra Breckinridge* (1970)
Wilder, Billy (Samuel Wilder)	1906–	Vienna	Director: *The Major and The Minor* (1942); *The Lost Weekend* (1945); *Sunset Boulevard* (1955); *The Apartment* (1960); *The Private Life of Sherlock Holmes* (1970); *Fedora* (1978)
Wilder, Gene (Jerome Silberman)	1935–	Milwaukee	*Bonnie and Clyde* (1967); *Blazing Saddles* (1974); *Young Frankenstein* (1974); *The Frisco Kid* (1979); *Stir Crazy* (1982); *Haunted Honeymoon* (1986)
Williams, Robin	1952–	Chicago	*Popeye* (1980); *The World According to Garp* (1982); *Good Morning Vietnam* (1987); *Dead Poets Society* (1989); *Awakenings* (1990); *The Fisher King* (1991); *Hook* (1991); *Toys* (1992); *Mrs Doubtfire* (1993)
Winger, Deborah	1955–	Columbus, Ohio	*An Officer and a Gentleman* (1982); *Terms of Endearment* (1983); *Legal Eagles* (1985); *Betrayed* (1988); *The Sheltering Sky* (1990)
Winters, Shelley (Shirley Schrift)	1922–	St Louis, Missouri	*A Double Life* (1948); *The Night of the Hunter* (1955); *Lolita* (1962)
Wood, Natalie (Natasha Gurdin)	1938–81	San Francisco	*Rebel Without a Cause* (1955); *Splendour in the Grass* (1961); *West Side Story* (1961); *This Property is Condemned* (1966); *Bob and Carol and Ted and Alice* (1969)
Woodward, Joanne	1930–	Thomasville, Georgia	*The Long Hot Summer* (1958); *The Glass Menagerie* (1987); *Mr and Mrs Bridge* (1990)
Wyler, William	1902–81	Mulhausen, Alsace	Director: *Mrs Miniver* (1942); *The Best Years of our Lives* (1946); *Friendly Persuasion* (1956); *Ben Hur* (1959); *Funny Girl* (1968)
Zeffirelli, Franco	1923–	Florence	Director: *Romeo and Juliet* (1968); *La Traviata* (1983); *Othello* (1986); *Hamlet* (1990)
Zinnemann, Fred	1907–	Vienna	Director: *High Noon* (1952); *From Here to Eternity* (1953); *A Man for All Seasons* (1966)

Motion picture Academy Awards (Oscars)

1928
Picture *Wings*, Paramount
Director Frank Borzage, *Seventh Heaven*;
Lewis Milestone, *Two Arabian Nights*
Actress Janet Gaynor, *Seventh Heaven, Street Angel, Sunrise*
Actor Emil Jannings, *The Way of All Flesh, The Last Command*

1929
Picture *The Broadway Melody*, MGM
Director Frank Lloyd, *The Divine Lady*
Actress Mary Pickford, *Coquette*
Actor Warner Baxter, *In Old Arizona*

1930
Picture *All Quiet on the Western Front*, Universal
Director Lewis Milestone, *All Quiet on the Western Front*
Actress Norma Shearer, *The Divorcee*
Actor George Arliss, *Disraeli*

1931
Picture *Cimarron*, RKO Radio
Director Norman Taurog, *Skippy*
Actress Marie Dressler, *Min and Bill*
Actor Lionel Barrymore, *A Free Soul*

1932
Picture *Grand Hotel*, MGM
Director Frank Borzage, *Bad Girl*
Actress Helen Hayes, *The Sin of Madelon Claudet*
Actor Fredric March, *Dr Jekyll and Mr Hyde*,
and Wallace Beery, *The Champ*

1933
Picture *Cavalcade*, Fox
Director Frank Lloyd, *Cavalcade*
Actress Katharine Hepburn, *Morning Glory*
Actor Charles Laughton, *The Private Life of Henry VIII*

1934
Picture *It Happened One Night*, Columbia
Director Frank Capra, *It Happened One Night*
Actress Claudette Colbert, *It Happened One Night*
Actor Clark Gable, *It Happened One Night*

1935
Picture *Mutiny on the Bounty*, MGM
Director John Ford, *The Informer*
Actress Bette Davis, *Dangerous*
Actor Victor McLaglen, *The Informer*

1936
Picture *The Great Ziegfeld*, MGM
Director Frank Capra, *Mr. Deeds Goes to Town*
Actress Luise Rainer, *The Great Ziegfeld*
Actor Paul Muni, *The Story of Louis Pasteur*
Supporting actress Gale Sondergaard, *Anthony Adverse*
Supporting actor Walter Brennan, *Come and Get It*

1937
Picture *The Life of Emile Zola*, Warner Bros
Director Leo McCarey, *The Awful Truth*
Actress Luise Rainer, *The Good Earth*
Actor Spencer Tracy, *Captains Courageous*
Supporting actress Alice Brady, *In Old Chicago*
Supporting actor Joseph Schildkraut, *The Life of Emile Zola*

1938
Picture *You Can't Take it With You*, Columbia
Director Frank Capra, *You Can't Take it With You*
Actress Bette Davis, *Jezebel*
Actor Spencer Tracy, *Boys Town*
Supporting actress Fay Bainter, *Jezebel*
Supporting actor Walter Brennan, *Kentucky*

1939
Picture *Gone with the Wind*, Selznick MGM
Director Victor Flemming, *Gone with the Wind*
Actress Vivien Leigh, *Gone with the Wind*
Actor Robert Donat, *Goodbye Mr Chips*
Supporting actress Hattie McDaniel, *Gone with the Wind*
Supporting actor Thomas Mitchell, *Stagecoach*

1940
Picture *Rebecca*, Selznick UA
Director John Ford, *The Grapes of Wrath*
Actress Ginger Rogers, *Kitty Foyle*
Actor James Stewart, *The Philadelphia Story*
Supporting actress Jane Darwell, *The Grapes of Wrath*
Supporting actor Walter Brennan, *The Westerner*

1941
Picture *How Green Was My Valley*, 20th Century Fox
Director John Ford, *How Green Was My Valley*
Actress Joan Fontaine, *Suspicion*
Actor Gary Cooper, *Sergeant York*
Supporting actress Mary Astor, *The Great Lie*
Supporting actor Donald Crisp, *How Green Was My Valley*

1942
Picture *Mrs Miniver*, MGM
Director William Wyler, *Mrs Miniver*
Actress Greer Garson, *Mrs Miniver*
Actor James Cagney, *Yankee Doodle Dandy*
Supporting actress Teresa Wright, *Mrs Miniver*
Supporting actor Van Heflin, *Johnny Eager*

1943
Picture *Casablanca*, Warner Bros
Director Michael Curtiz, *Casablanca*
Actress Jennifer Jones, *The Song of Bernadette*
Actor Paul Lukas, *Watch on the Rhine*
Supporting actress Katina Paxinou, *For Whom the Bell Tolls*
Supporting actor Charles Coburn, *The More the Merrier*

1944
Picture *Going My Way*, Paramount
Director Leo McCarey, *Going My Way*
Actress Ingrid Bergman, *Gaslight*
Actor Bing Crosby, *Going My Way*
Supporting actress Ethel Barrymore, *None But the Lonely Heart*
Supporting actor Barry Fitzgerald, *Going My Way*

1945
Picture *The Lost Weekend*, Paramount
Director Billy Wilder, *The Lost Weekend*
Actress Joan Crawford, *Mildred Pierce*
Actor Ray Milland, *The Lost Weekend*
Supporting actress Anne Revere, *National Velvet*
Supporting actor James Dunn, *A Tree Grows in Brooklyn*

1946
Picture *The Best Years of Our Lives*, Goldwyn-RKO Radio
Director William Wyler, *The Best Years of Our Lives*
Actress Olivia de Havilland, *To Each His Own*
Actor Fredric March, *The Best Years of Our Lives*

Motion picture Academy Awards (Oscars) (continued)

Supporting actress Anne Baxter, *The Razor's Edge*
Supporting actor Harold Russell, *The Best Years of Our Lives*

1947
Picture *Gentleman's Agreement*, 20th Century Fox
Director Elia Kazan, *Gentleman's Agreement*
Actress Loretta Young, *The Farmer's Daughter*
Actor Ronald Colman, *A Double Life*
Supporting actress Celeste Holm, *Gentleman's Agreement*
Supporting actor Edmund Gwenn, *Miracle on 34th Street*

1948
Picture *Hamlet*, Rank-Two Cities-UI
Director John Huston, *Treasure of the Sierra Madre*
Actress Jane Wyman, *Johnny Belinda*
Actor Laurence Olivier, *Hamlet*
Supporting actress Claire Trevor, *Key Largo*
Supporting actor Walter Huston, *Treasure of the Sierra Madre*

1949
Picture *All the King's Men*, Rossen-Columbia
Director Joseph L Mankiewicz, *A Letter to Three Wives*
Actress Olivia de Havilland, *The Heiress*
Actor Broderick Crawford, *All the King's Men*
Supporting actress Mercedes McCambridge, *All the King's Men*
Supporting actor Dean Jagger, *Twelve O'Clock High*

1950
Picture *All About Eve*, 20th Century Fox
Director Joseph L Mankiewicz, *All About Eve*
Actress Judy Holliday, *Born Yesterday*
Actor José Ferrer, *Cyrano de Bergerac*
Supporting actress Josephine Hull, *Harvey*
Supporting actor George Sanders, *All About Eve*

1951
Picture *An American in Paris*, MGM
Director George Stevens, *A Place in the Sun*
Actress Vivien Leigh, *A Streetcar Named Desire*
Actor Humphrey Bogart, *The African Queen*
Supporting actress Kim Hunter, *A Streetcar Named Desire*
Supporting actor Karl Malden, *A Streetcar Named Desire*

1952
Picture *The Greatest Show on Earth*, DeMille-Paramount
Director John Ford, *The Quiet Man*
Actress Shirley Booth, *Come Back, Little Sheba*
Actor Gary Cooper, *High Noon*
Supporting actress Gloria Grahame, *The Bad and the Beautiful*
Supporting actor Anthony Quinn, *Viva Zapata*

1953
Picture *From Here to Eternity*, Columbia
Director Fred Zinnemann, *From Here to Eternity*
Actress Audrey Hepburn, *Roman Holiday*
Actor William Holden, *Stalag 17*
Supporting actress Donna Reed, *From Here to Eternity*
Supporting actor Frank Sinatra, *From Here to Eternity*

1954
Picture *On the Waterfront*, Horizon-American Corp, Columbia
Director Elia Kazan, *On the Waterfront*
Actress Grace Kelly, *The Country Girl*
Actor Marlon Brando, *On the Waterfront*

Supporting actress Eva Marie Saint, *On the Waterfront*
Supporting actor Edmond O'Brien, *The Barefoot Contessa*

1955
Picture *Marty*, Hecht and Lancaster, United Artists
Director Delbert Mann, *Marty*
Actress Anna Magnani, *The Rose Tattoo*
Actor Ernest Borgnine, *Marty*
Supporting actress Jo Van Fleet, *East of Eden*
Supporting actor Jack Lemmon, *Mister Roberts*

1956
Picture *Around the World in 80 Days*, Michael Todd Co, Inc-UA
Director George Stevens, *Giant*
Actress Ingrid Bergman, *Anastasia*
Actor Yul Brynner, *The King and I*
Supporting actress Dorothy Malone, *Written on the Wind*
Supporting actor Anthony Quinn, *Lust for Life*

1957
Picture *The Bridge on the River Kwai*, Horizon Picture, Columbia
Director David Lean, *The Bridge on the River Kwai*
Actress Joanne Woodward, *The Three Faces of Eve*
Actor Alec Guinness, *The Bridge on the River Kwai*
Supporting actress Miyoshi Umeki, *Sayonara*
Supporting actor Red Buttons, *Sayonara*

1958
Picture *Gigi*, Arthur Freed Productions Inc, MGM
Director Vincente Minnelli, *Gigi*
Actress Susan Hayward, *I Want to Live!*
Actor David Niven, *Separate Tables*
Supporting actress Wendy Hiller, *Separate Tables*
Supporting actor Burl Ives, *The Big Country*

1959
Picture *Ben Hur*, MGM
Director William Wyler, *Ben Hur*
Actress Simone Signoret, *Room at the Top*
Actor Charlton Heston, *Ben Hur*
Supporting actress Shelley Winters, *The Diary of Anne Frank*
Supporting actor Hugh Griffith, *Ben Hur*

1960
Picture *The Apartment*, Mirisch Co Inc, United Artists
Director Billy Wilder, *The Apartment*
Actress Elizabeth Taylor, *Butterfield 8*
Actor Burt Lancaster, *Elmer Gantry*
Supporting actress Shirley Jones, *Elmer Gantry*
Supporting actor Peter Ustinov, *Spartacus*

1961
Picture *West Side Story*, Mirisch Pictures Inc, and B and P Enterprises Inc, United Artists
Director Robert Wise and Jerome Robbins, *West Side Story*
Actress Sophia Loren, *Two Women*
Actor Maximillian Schell, *Judgment at Nuremberg*
Supporting actress Rita Moreno, *West Side Story*
Supporting actor George Chakiris, *West Side Story*

1962
Picture *Lawrence of Arabia*, Horizon Pictures Ltd, Columbia
Director David Lean, *Lawrence of Arabia*
Actress Anne Bancroft, *The Miracle Worker*

Arts and culture

Actor Gregory Peck, *To Kill a Mockingbird*
Supporting actress Patty Duke, *The Miracle Worker*
Supporting actor Ed Begley, *Sweet Bird of Youth*

1963
Picture *Tom Jones*, A Woodfall Production, UA-Lopert Pictures
Director Tony Richardson, *Tom Jones*
Actress Patricia Neal, *Hud*
Actor Sidney Poitier, *Lilies of the Field*
Supporting actress Margaret Rutherford, *The VIPs*
Supporting actor Melvyn Douglas, *Hud*

1964
Picture *My Fair Lady*, Warner Bros
Director George Cukor, *My Fair Lady*
Actress Julie Andrews, *Mary Poppins*
Actor Rex Harrison, *My Fair Lady*
Supporting actress Lila Kedrova, *Zorba the Greek*
Supporting actor Peter Ustinov, *Topkapi*

1965
Picture *The Sound of Music*, Argyle Enterprises Production, 20th Century Fox
Director Robert Wise, *The Sound of Music*
Actress Julie Christie, *Darling*
Actor Lee Marvin, *Cat Ballou*
Supporting actress Shelley Winters, *A Patch of Blue*
Supporting actor Martin Balsam, *A Thousand Clowns*

1966
Picture *A Man for All Seasons*, Highland Films Ltd Production, Columbia
Director Fred Zinnemann, *A Man for All Seasons*
Actress Elizabeth Taylor, *Who's Afraid of Virginia Woolf?*
Actor Paul Scofield, *A Man for All Seasons*
Supporting actress Sandy Dennis, *Who's Afraid of Virginia Woolf?*
Supporting actor Walter Matthau, *The Fortune Cookie*

1967
Picture *In the Heat of the Night*, Mirisch Corp Productions, United Artists
Director Mike Nichols, *The Graduate*
Actress Katharine Hepburn, *Guess Who's Coming to Dinner?*
Actor Rod Steiger, *In the Heat of the Night*
Supporting actress Estelle Parsons, *Bonnie and Clyde*
Supporting actor George Kennedy, *Cool Hand Luke*

1968
Picture *Oliver!* Columbia Pictures
Director Sir Carol Reed, *Oliver!*
Actress Katharine Hepburn, *The Lion in Winter* and Barbra Streisand, *Funny Girl*
Actor Cliff Robertson, *Charly*
Supporting actress Ruth Gordon, *Rosemary's Baby*
Supporting actor Jack Albertson, *The Subject Was Roses*

1969
Picture *Midnight Cowboy*, Jerome Hellman-John Schlesinger Production, United Artists
Director John Schlesinger, *Midnight Cowboy*
Actress Maggie Smith, *The Prime of Miss Jean Brodie*
Actor John Wayne, *True Grit*
Supporting actress Goldie Hawn, *Cactus Flower*
Supporting actor Gig Young, *They Shoot Horses Don't They?*

1970
Picture *Patton*, Frank McCarthy-Franklin J Schaffner Production, 20th Century Fox
Director Franklin J Schaffner, *Patton*
Actress Glenda Jackson, *Women in Love*
Actor George C Scott, *Patton*
Supporting actress Helen Hayes, *Airport*
Supporting actor John Mills, *Ryan's Daughter*

1971
Picture *The French Connection*, D'Antoni Productions, 20th Century Fox
Director William Friedkin, *The French Connection*
Actress Jane Fonda, *Klute*
Actor Gene Hackman, *The French Connection*
Supporting actress Cloris Leachman, *The Last Picture Show*
Supporting actor Ben Johnson, *The Last Picture Show*

1972
Picture *The Godfather*, Albert S Ruddy Production, Paramount
Director Bob Fosse, *Cabaret*
Actress Liza Minnelli, *Cabaret*
Actor Marlon Brando, *The Godfather*
Supporting actress Eileen Heckart, *Butterflies Are Free*
Supporting actor Joel Gray, *Cabaret*

1973
Picture *The Sting*, Universal/Bill Phillips/George Roy Hill Production, Universal
Director George Roy Hill, *The Sting*
Actress Glenda Jackson, *A Touch of Class*
Actor Jack Lemmon, *Save the Tiger*
Supporting actress Tatum O'Neal, *Paper Moon*
Supporting actor John Houseman, *The Paper Chase*

1974
Picture *The Godfather, Part II*, Coppola Co Production, Paramount
Director Francis Ford Coppola, *The Godfather, Part II*
Actress Ellen Burstyn, *Alice Doesn't Live Here Anymore*
Actor Art Carney, *Harry and Tonto*
Supporting actress Ingrid Bergman, *Murder on the Orient Express*
Supporting actor Robert De Niro, *The Godfather, Part II*

1975
Picture *One Flew Over the Cuckoo's Nest*, Fantasy Films Production, United Artists
Director Milos Forman, *One Flew Over the Cuckoo's Nest*
Actress Louise Fletcher, *One Flew Over the Cuckoo's Nest*
Actor Jack Nicholson, *One Flew Over the Cuckoo's Nest*
Supporting actress Lee Grant, *Shampoo*
Supporting actor George Burns, *The Sunshine Boys*

1976
Picture *Rocky*, Robert Chartoff-Irwin Winkler Production, United Artists
Director John G Avildsen, *Rocky*
Actress Faye Dunaway, *Network*
Actor Peter Finch, *Network*
Supporting actress Beatrice Straight, *Network*
Supporting actor Jason Robards, *All the President's Men*

1977
Picture *Annie Hall*, Jack Rollins-Charles H Joffe Production, United Artists
Director Woody Allen, *Annie Hall*
Actress Diane Keaton, *Annie Hall*
Actor Richard Dreyfuss, *The Goodbye Girl*
Supporting actress Vanessa Redgrave, *Julia*
Supporting actor Jason Robards, *Julia*

Film and television

Motion picture Academy Awards (Oscars) (continued)

1978
Picture *The Deer Hunter*, Michael Cimino Film Production, Universal
Director Michael Cimino, *The Deer Hunter*
Actress Jane Fonda, *Coming Home*
Actor Jon Voight, *Coming Home*
Supporting actress Maggie Smith, *California Suite*
Supporting actor Christopher Walken, *The Deer Hunter*

1979
Picture *Kramer vs Kramer*, Stanley Jaffe Production, Columbia Pictures
Director Robert Benton, *Kramer vs Kramer*
Actress Sally Field, *Norma Rae*
Actor Dustin Hoffman, *Kramer vs Kramer*
Supporting actress Meryl Streep, *Kramer vs Kramer*
Supporting actor Melvyn Douglas, *Being There*

1980
Picture *Ordinary People*, Wildwood Enterprises Production, Paramount
Director Robert Redford, *Ordinary People*
Actress Sissy Spacek, *Coal Miner's Daughter*
Actor Robert De Niro, *Raging Bull*
Supporting actress Mary Steenburgen, *Melvin and Howard*
Supporting actor Timothy Hutton, *Ordinary People*

1981
Picture *Chariots of Fire*, Enigma Productions, Ladd Company/Warner Bros
Director Warren Beatty, *Reds*
Actress Katharine Hepburn, *On Golden Pond*
Actor Henry Fonda, *On Golden Pond*
Supporting actress Maureen Stapleton, *Reds*
Supporting actor John Gielgud, *Arthur*

1982
Picture *Gandhi*, Indo-British Films Production/Columbia
Director Richard Attenborough, *Gandhi*
Actress Meryl Streep, *Sophie's Choice*
Actor Ben Kingsley, *Gandhi*
Supporting actress Jessica Lange, *Tootsie*
Supporting actor Louis Gossett Jr, *An Officer and a Gentleman*

1983
Picture *Terms of Endearment*, Paramount
Director James L Brooks, *Terms of Endearment*
Actress Shirley MacLaine, *Terms of Endearment*
Actor Robert Duvall, *Tender Mercies*
Supporting actress Linda Hunt, *The Year of Living Dangerously*
Supporting actor Jack Nicholson, *Terms of Endearment*

1984
Picture *Amadeus*, Orion Pictures
Director Milos Forman, *Amadeus*
Actress Sally Field, *Places in the Heart*
Actor F Murray Abraham, *Amadeus*
Supporting actress Dame Peggy Ashcroft, *A Passage to India*
Supporting actor Haing S Ngor, *The Killing Fields*

1985
Picture *Out of Africa*, Universal
Director Sydney Pollack, *Out of Africa*
Actress Geraldine Page, *The Trip to Bountiful*

Actor William Hurt, *Kiss of the Spider Woman*
Supporting actress Anjelica Huston, *Prizzi's Honor*
Supporting actor Don Ameche, *Cocoon*

1986
Picture *Platoon*, Orion Pictures
Director Oliver Stone, *Platoon*
Actress Marlee Matlin, *Children of a Lesser God*
Actor Paul Newman, *The Color of Money*
Supporting actress Dianne Wiest, *Hannah and Her Sisters*
Supporting actor Michael Caine, *Hannah and Her Sisters*

1987
Picture *The Last Emperor*, Columbia Pictures
Director Bernardo Bertolucci, *The Last Emperor*
Actress Cher, *Moonstruck*
Actor Michael Douglas, *Wall Street*
Supporting actress Olympia Dukakis, *Moonstruck*
Supporting actor Sean Connery, *The Untouchables*

1988
Picture *Rain Man*, United Artists
Director Barry Levington, *Rain Man*
Actress Jodie Foster, *The Accused*
Actor Dustin Hoffman, *Rain Man*
Supporting actress Geena Davis, *The Accidental Tourist*
Supporting actor Kevin Kline, *A Fish Called Wanda*

1989
Picture *Driving Miss Daisy*, Warner Brothers
Director Oliver Stone, *Born on the Fourth of July*
Actress Jessica Tandy, *Driving Miss Daisy*
Actor Daniel Day-Lewis, *My Left Foot*
Supporting actress Brenda Fricker, *My Left Foot*
Supporting actor Denzel Washington, *Glory*

1990
Picture *Dances With Wolves*, Orion
Director Kevin Costner, *Dances With Wolves*
Actress Kathy Bates, *Misery*
Actor Jeremy Irons, *Reversal of Fortune*
Supporting actress Whoopi Goldberg, *Ghost*
Supporting actor Joe Pesci, *Goodfellas*

1991
Picture *The Silence of the Lambs*, Orion
Director Jonathan Demme, *The Silence of the Lambs*
Actress Jodie Foster, *The Silence of the Lambs*
Actor Anthony Hopkins, *The Silence of the Lambs*
Supporting actress Mercedes Ruehl, *The Fisher King*
Supporting actor Jack Palance, *City Slickers*

1992
Picture *Unforgiven*
Director Clint Eastwood, *Unforgiven*
Actress Emma Thompson, *Howard's End*
Actor Al Pacino, *Scent of a Woman*
Supporting actress Marisa Tomei, *My Cousin Vinny*
Supporting actor Gene Hackman, *Unforgiven*

1993
Picture *Schindler's List*
Director Steven Spielberg, *Schindler's List*
Actress Holly Hunter, *The Piano*
Actor Tom Hanks, *Philadelphia*
Supporting actress Anna Paquin, *The Piano*
Supporting actor Tommy Lee Jones, *The Fugitive*

International film festivals

Exact dates of these festivals may vary but the months indicated remain generally the same.

*Denotes a festival recognized by the International Federation of Film Producers Association.

Country	Festival	Time of year
Australia	Australian International Film Festival	September
	Melbourne	June
	Sydney*	June
Austria	Austrian Film Days	September
	Viennale (Vienna)	March
Belgium	Antwerp	March
	Belgian Film Festival (Brussels)	January
	Flanders (Ghent)	October
Brazil	Rio de Janeiro	November
	São Paulo	October
Bulgaria	Varna	June
Burkina Faso	Pan African Film Festival	February–March
Canada	Banff TV Festival	June
	Montreal World Film Festival	August
	Toronto	September
	Vancouver	September–October
Colombia	Cartagena	April
Cuba	New Latin American Cinema	December
Czech Republic	Karlovy Vary*	July
	Prague Television Festival	June
Egypt	Cairo	December
England	Birmingham Film and Television Festival	October–November
	Bristol Film and Television Festival	September
	Cambridge	July
	London Film Festival	November–December
Finland	Midnight Sun	June
	Tampere Film Festival	February
France	Amiens	November
	Annecy (animation)	May–June (alternate years)
	Avoriaz (fantasy and horror)	January
	Biarritz (Iberian, Latin American)	September
	Cannes*	May
	Cherbourg	October
	Clermont-Ferrand (shorts)	February
	Cognac	April
	Deauville (American films)	September
	Grenoble (thrillers)	October
	Paris	March–April
	Rouen	March
	Strasbourg	March
Germany	Berlin*	February
	Hof	October
	Munich	June
Greece	Thessaloniki	October
India	Indian International Film Festival	January
Ireland	Cork*	September–October
	Dublin	October
Israel	Jerusalem	June–July
Italy	Bergamo (horror)	July
	Pesaro International Festival of New Cinema	June
	Pordenone (silents)	October
	Festival dei Popoli, Florence	November–December
	San Remo	March
	Trieste Science-Fiction Festival	July
	Venice Film Festival	September
Japan	Tokyo	September
Monaco	Monte Carlo Film Festival	January–February
Netherlands	Dutch Film Days and Film Market	September
	Rotterdam Film International	March
New Zealand	Wellington	July

Arts and culture

Film and television

International film festivals (continued)

Country	Festival	Time of year
Poland	Gdańsk	September
	Katowice (scientific/technical)	November
	Krakow* (shorts)	June
Portugal	Porto Fantasy Film Festival	February
Russia	Moscow	July
	Teleforum, Moscow	September
Scotland	Edinburgh	August–September
Spain	Barcelona	November
	Madrid (Imagfic)	March–April
	San Sebastian*	September
	Sitges (horror)	September–October
Sweden	Gothenburg	January–February
	Malmo	September
Switzerland	Locarno*	August
	Nyon* (documentaries)	October
	Vevey	August
Taiwan	Taipei	October
United States	AFI/European Community Film Festival, Los Angeles	June
	AFI/LA Film Festival	April
	American Film Market, LA	February–March
	Boston	September
	Chicago	October
	Cinetex, Las Vegas	September
	Filmfest DC, Washington	April–May
	Hawaii, Honolulu	November
	Miami	February
	Mill Valley Film and Video Festival	October
	NATPE, New Orleans	January
	New York*	September–October
	Palm Springs	January
	Portland	February
	Santa Barbara International Film Festival	March
	San Francisco International Film Festival*	April–May
	Seattle International Film Festival	May–June
	Sundance Film Festival, Park City Utah	January
	Women in Film, LA	October
Yugoslavia	Belgrade	January–February
	Pula (national)	July
	Zagreb* (animation)	June

MUSIC

Musical symbols, terms, and abbreviations

SYMBOLS

The staff or stave

staff / stave; additional ('leger') lines are added above or below as required

bar-line   double bar-line   double bar-line (conclusion)

brace, joining staves; read staves simultaneously

Clefs

These are in-common use (the note Middle C is shown in each case):

treble(G) clef   bass (F) clef   alto or viola (C) clef   tenor (C) clef

In older music the C clef is found on any of the five lines of the staff

Accidentals

♯	sharp, raising the pitch of a note by a semitone
×	double sharp, raising the pitch of a note by two semitones
♭	flat, lowering the pitch of a note by a semitone
♭♭	double flat, lowering the pitch of a note by two semitones
♮	natural, cancelling the effect of a previous accidental

Note lengths

▭ (or ⊨)	breve (double whole note)
o	semibreve (whole note)
♩	minim (half-note)
♩	crotchet (quarter-note)
♪	quaver (eighth-note)
♬	semiquaver (1/16 note)
	demisemiquaver (1/32 note)
	hemidemisemiquaver (1/64 note)
	chord: two or more notes sounded simultaneously

Ties (⌢, ⌣) are used to combine the lengths of two or more notes of the same pitch; dots are used to extend the length of a note by one-half, eg:

 =

Beams are often used to group together quavers (eighth-notes) or shorter notes into larger units, eg:

♫ = ♪ ♪   ♫♫ = ♪♪♪   ♫♫♫ = ♪♪♪♪

Time signatures

The lower figure indicates the unit of measurement, the upper figure the number of these units in a bar, eg:

2/2 (or ¢)	two minims (half-notes) or their equivalent in a bar
4/4 (or c)	four crotchets (quarter-notes) or their equivalent in a bar
3/8	three quavers (eighth-notes) or their equivalent in a bar
9/16	nine semiquavers (sixteenth-notes) or their equivalent in a bar

RESTS

breve (double whole)	semibreve (whole), or whole bar	minim (half)

crotchet (quarter)   quaver (eighth)   semiquaver (1/16)

demisemiquaver (1/32)   hemidemisemiquaver (1/64)

A dot placed after a rest increases its length by one-half

Articulation and expression

staccato: the notes to be short and detached

staccatissimo: a more pronounced and accented staccato

non legato: the notes to be detached but not staccato

slur: the notes to be played legato, or smoothly

pause, fermata: the note to be sounded beyond its written value at the discretion of the performer

accent: the note to be stressed

crescendo: becoming louder

decrescendo, diminuendo: becoming quieter

♩ = 84   placed at the beginning of a piece or section, an indication of the tempo (in this case, 84 crotchet beats per minute); often preceded by 'M.M.' (Metronom Maelzel)

Ornaments

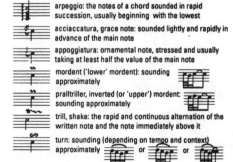

arpeggio: the notes of a chord sounded in rapid succession, usually beginning with the lowest

acciaccatura, grace note: sounded lightly and rapidly in advance of the main note

appoggiatura: ornamental note, stressed and usually taking at least half the value of the main note

mordent ('lower' mordent): sounding approximately

pralltriller, inverted (or 'upper') mordent: sounding approximately

trill, shake: the rapid and continuous alternation of the written note and the note immediately above it

turn: sounding (depending on tempo and context) approximately   or   or

Musical scales and keys

Key signatures
(Major keys: capital letters: minor keys: lower-case letters)

Repetition
In instrumental music repeated notes, figures and even whole sections are often shown in abbreviated form, eg:

repeat signs, indicating that the passage between them is to be performed twice

Tempo and expression marks

Italian terms placed at the head of a piece or section to indicate its tempo and general expression have changed in meaning over the years and are rarely precise. The following list gives some indication of how the more common terms are generally understood today.

adagio slow
agitato agitated
allegro lively, fast
allegretto rather lively
andante 'going'; at a moderate pace
andantino a little quicker than *andante*
animato animated, lively
appassionato impassioned
assai 'very' (*allegro assai* very fast)
brio 'spirit', 'fire' (*allegro con brio* fast energetic)
cantabile in a singing style
dolente sadly
energico energetic, vigorous
espressivo expressive
feroce fierce
fuoco 'fire' (*con fuoco* with fire)
furioso furious
giocoso light, humorous
grave slow, solemn
grazioso graceful
larghetto fairly slow
largo slow, broad
legato smoothly
leggiero light
lento slow

maestoso majestic
marciale in the style of a march
marziale in a military style
meno 'less' (*meno mosso* slower)
moderato moderate, at a moderate pace
molto 'much', 'very' (*molto lento* very slow)
moto 'motion' (*con moto* quickly)
pesante heavy, ponderous
piacevole pleasant, agreeable
più 'more' (*più mosso* faster)
poco 'little' (*poco adagio* rather slowly)
presto very fast
prestissimo faster than *presto*
quasi 'as if', 'almost' (*andante, quasi allegretto*)
risoluto resolute, in a determined manner
scherzando in a jocular style
semplice simple, in an unforced style
sotto voce extremely quiet
strepitoso loud, noisy, boisterous
tanto, troppo 'so much', 'too much' (*allegro non tanto* fast but not very fast; *lento ma non troppo* slow, but not becoming too slow)
veloce rapid
vivace lively, very fast
vivo vigorous, brisk

Other terms and abbreviations

This section lists only those symbols and terms that might be found in a musical score.

a tempo in time (ie reverting to the original speed)
accel. (accelerando) getting gradually faster
alla breve in a time signature where minims or semibreves are the metrical units
allarg. (allargando) broadening, getting slower and (usually) louder
arco with the bow
cal. (calando) dying away
colla voce 'with the voice', follow closely the singer's tempo
col legno 'with the wood', play a string instrument with the stick of the bow
con sordino with the mute
cresc. (crescendo) becoming louder
D C, da capo (al fine) return to the start of the piece or movement (and play to the end marked *fine*)
decresc. (decrescendo) becoming quieter
dim. (diminuendo) becoming quieter
dol (dolce) sweetly
D S, dal segno return to and repeat from the sign (usually $)
f (forte) loud; *ff (fortissimo)*, *fff* increasing degrees of loudness
fine see *D C* above
fz (forzato) accented
gliss. (glissando) slide quickly from one note to another
GP 'General pause', a rest for the whole ensemble
MM metronom maelzel
marc. (marcato) stressed, accented
mf (mezzo forte) moderately loud

mp (mezzo piano) moderately quiet
ossia 'or', 'alternatively'
ottava, 8va, 8 play a passage an octave higher or lower, *coll ottava, col 8va, col 8:* play the written notes together with their octaves
p (piano) quiet, soft; *pp (pianissimo)*, *ppp* increasing (but imprecise) degrees of softness
ped. depress the sustaining (loud) pedal on a piano, release indicated by *
pizz. (pizzicato) 'plucked' with the finger, rather than bowed
rall. (rallentando) getting slower
rinf., rfz, rf (rinforcando, sforzando) getting suddenly louder
rit., ritard. (ritardando) getting slower
rubato with a freedom of tempo, but not impairing the overall flow of the music
segno see *D S* above
senza sordino without the mute
sf, sfz (sforzando, sforzato) strongly accented
simile play in the same manner as before
smorz. (smorzando) fading away
sost. (sostenuto) sustained
stacc. (stoccato) short and detached
string. (stringendo) getting much faster
ten. (tenuto) linger slightly on the note
tre corde see *una corda* below
una corda depress the soft pedal on the piano, release indicated by *tre corde*
V S (volti subito) turn the page quickly

World orchestras

Name	Date founded	Location	Name	Date founded	Location
Academy of Ancient Music	1973	London	NBC Symphony	1937	New York
Academy of St Martin-in-the Fields	1959	London	National Symphony	1931	Washington DC
Berlin Philharmonic	1882	Germany	New Orleans Philharmonic Symphony	1936	New Orleans
Boston Symphony	1881	Boston	New York Philharmonic	1842	New York
BBC Scottish Symphony	1935	Glasgow	New York Symphony	1878	New York
BBC Symphony	1930	London	Northern Sinfonia	1958	Newcastle-Upon-Tyne
BBC Welsh Symphony	1935	Cardiff			
Bournemouth Symphony	1893	Bournemouth	Orchestre Symphonique de Montréal	1842	Montreal
Chicago Symphony	1891	Chicago	Oslo Philharmonic	1919	Oslo
City of Birmingham Symphony	1920	Birmingham	The Philharmonia	1945	London
City of Glasgow Philharmonic		Glasgow	Pittsburgh Symphony	1926	Pittsburgh
			Royal Liverpool Philharmonic	1840	Liverpool
Cleveland Symphony	1918	Cleveland	Royal Philharmonic	1946	London
Concertgebouw	1888	Amsterdam	San Francisco Symphony	1911	San Francisco
Detroit Symphony	1914	Detroit	Santa Cecelia Academy	1895	Rome
English Chamber	1948	London	Scottish Chamber	1974	Edinburgh
Hallé	1858	Manchester	Scottish National	1891	Glasgow
Israel Philharmonic	1936	Tel Aviv	Seattle Symphony	1903	Seattle
Leningrad Philharmonic	1921	St Petersburg	Staatskapelle	1923	Dresden
London Philharmonic	1932	London	Sydney Symphony	1934	Sydney
London Symphony	1904	London	Vienna Philharmonic	1842	Vienna
Los Angeles Philharmonic	1919	Los Angeles	Vienna Symphony	1900	Vienna
Melbourne Symphony	1906	Melbourne			
La Scala, Milan	1778	Milan			

Arts and culture

Brass instruments

French horn   trumpet   cornet   trombone   tuba

Percussion instruments

timpani   side drum   bass drum   cymbals

triangle   tam-tam   tubular bells   xylophone

String instruments

violin   viola

violoncello   double bass

Woodwind instruments

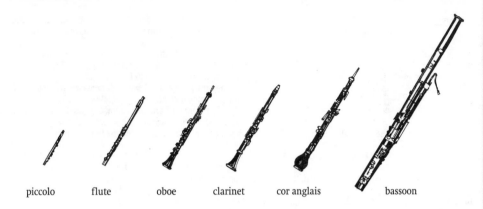

| piccolo | flute | oboe | clarinet | cor anglais | bassoon |

Composers

Name	Dates	Place of birth	Selected works
Albinoni, Tommaso	1671–1751	Venice	String concertos; concerti grossi; Adagio for organ and strings in G minor.
Bach, Johann Sebastian	1685–1750	Eisenach, Germany	Oratorios: *St John Passion*; *St Matthew Passion*; *Christmas Oratorio*. Mass in B Minor. Brandenburg Concertos: Nos.1–6. Keyboard: *The Well-Tempered Clavier*; *Goldberg Variations*. Organ: Toccata and Fugue in D minor.
Barber, Samuel	1910–81	West Chester, Pennsylvania	*Dover Beach* (for voice and strings). *Adagio for Strings*.
Bartók, Béla	1881–1945	Nagyszentmiklos, Hungary (now Sinnicolau Mare, Romania)	Opera: *Duke Bluebeard's Castle*. Ballet: *The Wooden Prince*; *The Miraculous Mandarin*. Orchestral: *Kossuth*; *Dance Suite*; *Concerto for Orchestra*; *Music for Strings, Percussion and Celesta*. Piano concertos: 3. String quartets: 6.
Beethoven, Ludwig van	1770–1827	Bonn	Symphonies: No.3 in E Flat Major (Eroica); No.5 in C Minor; No.6 in F Major (Pastoral); No. 9 in D Minor (Choral). Piano concertos: No.5 in E Flat Major (Emperor). Violin Concerto in D Major. Triple Concerto in C Major. Overtures: *Leonora*, Nos.1,2, and 3; *Egmont*; *Ruins of Athens*. Opera: *Fidelio*. Mass in D Major *(Missa Solemnis)*. Piano Sonatas: No.8 (Pathétique); No.14 (Moonlight); No.23: (Appassionata); No.29 (Hammerklavier). String Quartets: Nos.7–9 (Rasumowsky), Nos.12–16; *Grosse Fuge*.
Bellini, Vincenzo	1801–35	Catania, Sicily	Opera: *La Sonnambula*; *Norma*.
Bennett, Richard Rodney	1936–	Broadstairs, Kent	Opera: *The Mines of Sulphur*; *Penny for a Song*. Spells (for voice and orchestra). Saxophone Concerto.
Berg, Alban	1885–1935	Vienna	Opera: *Wozzeck*; *Lulu*. Orchestral: *Three Pieces*. Chamber Concerto. Violin Concerto.
Berio, Luciano	1925–	Oneglia, Italy	*Sinfonia* (for voice and orchestra). *Sequenza* (pieces for various instruments).
Berlioz, Hector	1803–69	La Cote-St-André, Isere	Opera: *Les Troyens*; *Béatrice et Benedict*. Orchestral: *Harold in Italy*; *Symphonie Fantastique*. For voice and orchestra: *Requiem*; *Roméo et Juliette*; *La Damnation de Faust*; *Les Nuits d'Été*.
Birtwistle, Sir Harrison	1934–	Accrington, Lancashire	Opera: *Punch and Judy*; *The Mask of Orpheus*; *Gawain*. Orchestral: *Earth Dances*.
Bizet, Georges (Alexandre Cesar Leopold Bizet)	1838–75	Paris	Opera: *The Pearl Fishers*; *The Fair Maid of Perth*; *Carmen*. Orchestral: *L'Arlésienne*.
Bloch, Ernst	1880–1959	Geneva	Opera: *Macbeth*. Orchestral: *Israel Symphony*; *Shelomo*. For voice and orchestra: *Sacred Service*.
Borodin, Alexander Porphiryevich	1833–87	St Petersburg	Opera: *Prince Igor*. Orchestral: Symphony No.2 in B Minor; *In the Steppes of Central Asia*.
Boulez, Pierre	1925–	Montbrison, France	*Pli selon pli* (for voice and orchestra). *Éclats* (for chamber orchestra).

Arts and culture

Composers (continued)

Name	Dates	Place of birth	Selected works
Brahms, Johannes	1833–97	Hamburg	Orchestral: Violin Concerto; Concerto for Violin and Cello; Chamber music: Piano Quintet in F; Clarinet Quintet. Choral: *Ein Deutsches Requiem*.
Bridge, Frank	1879–1941	Brighton	Song: *Love Went a-Riding*. Orchestral: *The Sea*; *Oration*.
Britten, Benjamin, Baron Britten of Aldeburgh	1913–76	Lowestoft	Opera: *Peter Grimes*; *Albert Herring*; *Billy Budd*; *The Turn of the Screw*; *A Midsummer Night's Dream*; *Death in Venice*. Orchestral: *Simple Symphony*; *Variations on a Theme of Frank Bridge*; *Sinfonia da Requiem*; *Young Persons Guide to the Orchestra*. For voice and orchestra: *Cantata Academica*; *War Requiem*; *Our Hunting Fathers*.
Bruch, Max	1838–1920	Cologne	Violin concertos: 3. *Scottish Fantasy* (for violin and orchestra).
Bruckner, Anton	1824–96	Ansfelden, Austria	Symphonies: No. 4 in E Flat Major (Romantic); No.7 in E Major; No.8 in C Minor; No.9 in D Minor (unfinished).
Busoni, Ferruccio	1866–1924	Empoli, Italy	Opera: *Arlecchino*; *Turandot*; *Doktor Faust*. Orchestral: *Berceuse élégiaque*. Piano: *Indian Diary*.
Byrd, William	1543–1623	Lincoln (probably)	Masses: 3. Keyboard: *My Ladye Nevells Booke*.
Cage, John	1912–92	Los Angeles	Variations I–VI (for any number of performers and objects). 4'33" (silent: for any instrument(s)).
Carter, Elliott	1908–	New York	String quartets: 4. Orchestral: Double Concerto for Harpsichord and Piano; *A Symphony of Three Orchestras*.
Chopin, Frédéric	1810–49	Zelazowa Wola, Poland	Piano concertos: 2. For solo piano: 3 piano sonatas, numerous Ballades, Scherzos, Études, Nocturnes, Préludes, Valses, Polonaises, Mazurkas.
Copland, Aaron	1900–90	Brooklyn, New York	Ballets: *Billy the Kid*; *Rodeo*; *Appalachian Spring*. Orchestral: *A Lincoln Portrait*; *Fanfare for the Common Man*.
Couperin, François	1668–1733	Paris	For harpsichord: *Pièces de Clavecin* (Books I–IV).
Debussy, Claude	1862–1918	St Germain-en-Laye, France	Opera: *Pelléas et Mélisande*. Ballet: *Jeux*. Orchestral: *Prélude à l'après-midi d'un faune*; *Nocturnes*; *La Mer*. Chamber: String quartet; cello sonata; violin sonata. Piano: *Préludes* (Books I and II).
Delibes, Léo	1836–91	St Germain-du-Val, France	Ballet: *Coppélia*; *Sylvia*. Opera: *Lakmé*.
Delius, Frederick	1862–1934	Bradford, Yorkshire	Opera: *A Village Romeo and Juliette*. Orchestral: *Brigg Fair*; *In a Summer Garden*; *On Hearing the First Cuckoo in Spring*. For voice, chorus, and orchestra: *Sea Drift*; *A Mass of Life*.
Donizetti, Gaetano	1797–1848	Bergamo, Italy	Opera: *L'Elisir d'Amore*; *Lucia di Lammermoor*.
Dukas, Paul	1865–1935	Paris	Orchestral: *The Sorcerer's Apprentice*.
Dvořák, Antonín	1841–1904	Nelahozeves, Czechoslovakia	Symphonies: (No.6 in D Major; No.8 in G Major; No.9 in E Minor (From the New World). *Slavonic Dances*. Concertos: violin concerto; cello concerto.
Elgar, Sir Edward	1857–1934	Broadheath, nr Worcester	Orchestral: *Variations on an Original Theme (Enigma Variations)*; *Pomp and Circumstance Marches*; *Cockaigne*; *Falstaff*. Concertos: violin concerto; cello concerto. Symphony No.1. For voice, chorus, and orchestra: *Dream of Gerontius*.
Falla, Manuel de	1876–1946	Cadiz	Ballet: *The Three-Cornered Hat*. Orchestral: *Nights in the Gardens of Spain*.
Fauré, Gabriel	1845–1924	Pamiers	Opera: *Pénélope*. For voice, chorus, and orchestra: *Requiem*. Songs (*Après un rêve*; *Les Roses d'Ispahan*; *Clair de Lune*)
Franck, César	1822–90	Liège	Orchestral: *Symphonic Variations*; Symphony in D Minor. For chorus and orchestra: *Psyché*.
Gershwin, George	1898–1937	Brooklyn, New York	Opera: *Porgy and Bess*. Orchestral: *Rhapsody in Blue*; *An American in Paris*.
Glass, Philip	1937–	Baltimore	Opera: *Einstein on the Beach*; *Akhnaten*. Film soundtrack: *Koyaanisqatsi*.
Glazunov, Alexander	1865–1936	St Petersburg	Orchestral: Symphony No.1; *The Seasons*.
Glinka, Mikhail	1804–57	Smolensk	Opera: *A Life for the Tsar*; *Ruslan and Lyudmila*.
Gluck, Christoph	1714–87	Erasbach	Opera: *Orfeo*; *Alceste*; *Iphigénie en Aulide*; *Iphigénie en Tauride*.
Górecki, Henryk	1933–	Czernica, Poland	Orchestral: Symphony No.3 (Symphony of Sorrowful Songs). Chamber: *Genesis*.
Gounod, Charles	1818–93	Paris	Opera: *Faust*; *Roméo et Juliette*. Songs *Ave Maria*.
Grieg, Edvard	1843–1907	Bergen	Orchestral: Piano Concerto in A Minor; *Peer Gynt* (Suites 1 and 2).

Name	Dates	Place of birth	Selected works
Handel, George Frideric	1685–1759	Halle	Orchestral: *Water Music*; *Music for Royal Fireworks*. Oratorios: *Saul*; *Messiah*; *Belshazzar*; *Solomon*.
Haydn, Franz Joseph	1732–1809	Rohrau, Austria	Oratorios: *The Creation*; *The Seasons*. Symphonies: Nos.82–7 (Paris); Nos.93–104 (London). String quartets: Nos.50–6 (*Seven Last Words from the Cross*); No.61 (Razor).
Hindemith, Paul	1895–1963	Hanau, Germany	Orchestral: *Mathis der Maler* (symphony); *Trauermusik* (for viola and strings); *Symphonic Metamorphosis of Themes by Carl Maria von Weber*.
Holst, Gustav	1874–1934	Cheltenham	Orchestral: *The Planets* (suite); *Egdon Heath*.
Honegger, Arthur	1892–1955	Le Havre	Oratorio: *Jeanne d'Arc au Bûcher*. Orchestral: *Pacific 231*.
Ives, Charles	1874–1954	Danbury, Connecticut	Orchestral: *Holidays Symphony*; *The Unanswered Question*; *Central Park in the Dark*; Symphonies 1–3; *Variations on 'America'*.
Janáček, Leoš	1854–1928	Hukvaldy, Czechoslovakia	Opera: *Jenufa*; *Kata Kabanova*; *The Cunning Little Vixen*; *From the House of the Dead*. Orchestral: *Sinfonietta*; *Taras Bulba*. For voice, chorus, organ, and orchestra: *Glagolitic Mass*. String quartets: 2. Piano sonata (*I.X.1905*).
Khachaturian, Aram	1903–78	Tbilisi	Ballet: *Gayane*; *Spartacus*.
Kodály, Zoltan	1882–1967	Kecskemét, Hungary	Opera: *Háry János*; For voice, chorus, and orchestra: *Psalmus Hungaricus*.
Léhar, Franz	1870–1948	Komarom, Hungary	Operetta: *The Merry Widow*; *The Land of Smiles*.
Ligeti, György	1923–	Discöszentmáron, Hungary	Opera: *Le Grand Macabre*. Orchestral: *Atmosphères*; *Melodien*.
Liszt, Franz	1811–86	Raiding, Hungary	Orchestral: *A Faust Symphony*; *Mazeppa*. Piano: *Années de Pèlerinages* (Books I–III); *Mephisto Waltz No.2*; *Sonata in B Minor*; *Hungarian Rhapsodies*.
Lully, Jean-Baptiste	1632–87	Florence	*Le Bourgeois Gentilhomme* (comedy-ballet, after Molière). Many operas.
Mahler, Gustav	1860–1911	Kalist, Austria (later Czechoslovakia)	Symphonies: No.2 in C Minor (Resurrection); No.3 in D Minor; No.5 in C Sharp Minor; No.6 in A Minor (*Tragic*); No.8 in E Flat Major (Symphony of a Thousand); No.9 in D Major. Song symphony: *Das Lied von der Erde*. Song cycles: *Lieder eines fahrenden Gesellen*; *Kindertotenlieder*. Songs: *Des Knaben Wunderhorn*.
Mascagni, Pietro	1863–1945	Livorno, Italy	Opera: *Cavalleria Rusticana*.
Maxwell Davies, Sir Peter	1934–	Salford	Opera: *Taverner*; *The Martyrdom of St Magnus*. For the Theatre: *Eight Songs for a Mad King*. Orchestral: *1st Fantasia on In Nomine of John Taverner*, *Sinfonia*.
Mendelssohn, Felix	1809–47	Hamburg	Symphonies: No.3 in A Minor (*Scottish*); No.4 in A Major (*Italian*). Piano concertos: 2. Violin Concerto in E Minor, Overtures: *A Midsummer Night's Dream*; *Hebrides* (*Fingal's Cave*). Piano: *Songs Without Words* (Books I–VIII).
Messiaen, Olivier	1908–92	Avignon	Orchestral: *Turangalîla-symphonie*; *Oiseaux Exotiques*. Piano: *Vingt Regards sur l'enfant Jésus*. Organ: *Nativité du Seigneur*. Chamber: *Quatuor pour la fin du temps*.
Milhaud, Darius	1892–1974	Aix-en-Provence	Opera: *Christophe Colomb*. Ballet: *Le Boeuf sur le Toit*; *La Création du Monde*. Orchestral: *Saudades do Brazil*; *Suite Provençal*.
Monteverdi, Claudio	1567–1643	Cremona, Italy	Opera: *Orfeo*. Church Music: *Vespers of 1610* (*Vespro della Beata Vergine*).
Mozart, Wolfgang Amadeus	1756–91	Salzburg	Opera: *Die Entführung aus dem Serail*; *Le Nozze di Figaro*; *Don Giovanni*; *Così fan tutte*; *Die Zauberflöte*. Orchestral: Symphonies (Nos.35–41), Serenades (*Gran Partita, Eine Kleine Nachtmusik*). Concertos: (No.21 for piano: *Elvira Madigan* for viola and violin: *Sinfonia Concertante* for clarinet in A major, and flute and harp in C major). Church music: *Coronation Mass*; *Requiem*.
Mussorgsky, Modest	1839–81	Karevo, Russia	Opera: *Boris Godunov*. Orchestral: *Night on the Bare Mountain*. Piano: *Pictures at an Exhibition*
Nielsen, Carl	1865–1931	Norre-Lyndelse, Denmark	Opera: *Saul and David*. Symphonies: No.1 in G Minor, No.3 (Sinfonia Espansiva); No.4 (The Inextinguishable); No.5.
Offenbach, Jacques	1819–80	Cologne	Opera: *Orpheus in the Underworld*; *The Tales of Hoffmann*.
Orff, Carl	1895-1982	Munich	*Carmina Burana* (for voice, boy's choir, chorus, and orchestra).

Music

Composers (continued)

Name	Dates	Place of birth	Selected works
Palestrina, Giovanni Pierluigi da	c.1525–94	Palestrina, nr Rome	Many masses and motets.
Poulenc, Francis	1899–1963	Paris	Opera: *Les Dialogues des Carmélites*; *La Voix humaine*. Ballet: *Les Biches*. Concerto in G minor for organ, strings and timpani. Chamber: violin sonata; cello sonata. Choral: *4 Motets pour un temps de pénitence*.
Prokofiev, Sergei Sergeyevitch	1891–1953	Sontsovka, Ukraine	Opera: *Love for Three Oranges*. Ballet: *The Age of Steel*, *Romeo and Juliet*; *Cinderella*. Symphonies: No.1 in D Major (Classical); No.5 in B Flat Major; No.7 in C Sharp Minor. *Peter and the Wolf* (for narrator and orchestra). Film scores: *Lieutenant Kijé*; *Alexander Nevsky*. Piano concertos: 5.
Puccini, Giacomo	1858–1924	Lucca, Italy	Opera: *Manon Lescaut*; *La Bohème*; *Tosca*; *Madama Butterfly*; *Turandot*.
Purcell, Henry	1659–95	London	Opera: *Dido and Aeneas*. Choral: *Come ye sons of art, away*; *Ode on St Cecilia's Day*; *Thou knowest, Lord, the Secrets of our Hearts*.
Rachmaninov, Sergei Vasileyevich	1873–1943	Semyonovo, Russia	Orchestral: 4 piano concertos, 3 symphonies; *The Isle of the Dead*; *Rhapsody on a Theme of Paganini*; *Symphonic Dances*
Rameau, Jean-Philippe	1683–1764	Dijon	Opera: *Castor et Pollux*. Many pieces for harpsichord.
Ravel, Maurice	1875–1937	Ciboure, France	Opera: *L'Heure Espagnole*; *L'Enfant et les Sortilèges*. Ballet: *Daphnis et Chloé*; *Boléro*. Orchestral: *Alborada del gracioso, Rapsodie Espagnole*; *Ma Mère l'Oye*; *La Valse*; Piano Concerto for Left Hand; Piano Concerto in G Major. Chamber: String Quartet; *Introduction and Allegro* (for harp, flute, clarinet and string quartet). Piano: *Pavane pour une infante défunte*; *Miroirs*; *Valses nobles et sentimentales*; *Le Tombeau de Couperin*.
Reich, Steve	1936–	New York	*Drumming* (for percussion instruments and voices). Orchestral: *Four Sections*.
Rimsky-Korsakov, Nikolai	1844–1908	Tikhvin-Novgorod, Russia	Opera: *The Golden Cockerel*. Orchestral: *Capriccio Espagnol*; *Scheherazade*.
Rodrigo, Joáquin	1902–	Sagunto, Spain	*Concierto de Aranjuez* (for guitar and orchestra).
Rossini, Gioacchino	1792–1868	Pesaro, Italy	Opera: *The Barber of Seville*; *Otello*; *William Tell*.
Saint-Saëns, Camille	1835–1921	Paris	Opera: *Samson et Dalila*. Orchestral: Symphony No.3 (Organ); 3 piano concertos; *Carnaval des Animaux* (for piano and orchestra).
Satie, Erik	1866–1925	Honfleur, France	Ballet: *Parade*. Solo piano: 3 *Gymnopédies*; 6 *Gnossiennes*; *Morceaux en forme de poire*.
Scarlatti, Alessandro	1660–1725	Palermo	Many operas, oratorios, and masses.
Schoenberg, Arnold	1874–1951	Vienna	Opera: *Moses und Aron*. Orchestral: 5 *Orchestral Pieces*; Chamber Symphony No.1. For voice, chorus, and orchestra: *Gurrelieder*. For voice and chamber orchestra: *Pierrot Lunaire*. Chamber: *Verklärte Nacht* (for string sextet).
Schubert, Franz	1797–1828	Vienna	Symphonies: No.5 in B Flat Major; No.8 in B minor (Unfinished); No.9 in C Major (Great). Chamber: String Quartet No.14 in D Minor (Death and the Maiden); Piano Quintet in A Major (Trout); Octet in F Major. Song-cycles: *Winterreise*; *Schwanengesang*. Many songs.
Schumann, Robert	1810–56	Zwickau, Germany	Orchestral: Symphony No.1 (Spring); No.3 (Rhenish); Piano Concerto in A Minor; Cello Concerto in A Minor. Solo piano: *Fantasiestücke*; *Études Symphoniques*; *Kinderscenen*; *Waldscenen*; *Albumblätter*.
Shostakovich, Dmitri	1906–75	St Petersburg	Opera: *The Nose*; *Lady Macbeth of Mtsensk*. Ballet: *The Age of Gold*. Symphonies: No.1 in F Minor; No.4 in C Minor; No.5 in D Minor; No.7 in C Major (Leningrad); No.10 in E Minor; No.13 in B Flat Minor (Babi-Yar); No.15 in A Major. Orchestral: 2 piano concertos; 2 violin concertos; 2 cello concertos. String quartets: No.8 in C Minor; No.10 in A Flat Major. Solo piano: *24 Preludes and Fugues*.
Sibelius, Jean	1865–1957	Hameenlinna, Finland	Symphonies: No.1 in E Minor; No.2 in D Major; No.5 in E Flat Major; *Finlandia* (symphonic piece); *Karelia Overture*.

Arts and culture

Name	Dates	Place of birth	Selected works
Smetana, Bedřich	1824–84	Litomyšl, Czechoslovakia	Opera: *The Bartered Bride*; *Dalibor.* Orchestral: *Má Vlast.*
Sousa, John Philip	1854–1932	Washington DC	Marches: *Stars and Stripes*; *Liberty Bell*; *Hands across the Sea.*
Stockhausen, Karlheinz	1928–	Burg Modrath	Opera: *Donnerstag aus Licht.* Orchestral: *Spiel*; *Punkte*; *Gruppen.* Instrumental: *Kontra-Punkte*; *Zeitmasze*; *Zyklus.* Electronic: *Gesang der Jünglinge.*
Strauss, Johann II	1825–99	Vienna	Opera: *Die Fledermaus.* Many waltzes: *Blue Danube*; *Roses from the South*; *Tales from the Vienna Woods.*
Strauss, Richard	1864–1949	Munich	Opera: *Salomé*; *Elektra*; *Der Rosenkavalier*; *Ariadne auf Naxos*; *Capriccio.* Orchestral: *Symphonia Domestica*; *An Alpine Symphony.* Symphonic Poems: *Don Juan*; *Death and Transfiguration*; *Till Eulenspiegels lustige Streiche*; *Also Sprach Zarathustra*; *Don Quixote*; *Ein Heldenleben*; *Metamorphosen.* Song-cycle: *Four Last Songs.*
Stravinsky, Igor	1882–1971	Oranienbaum (now Lomonosov, Russia)	Opera: *Oedipus Rex*; *The Rake's Progress.* Ballet: *The Firebird*; *Petrushka*; *The Rite of Spring*; *Pulcinella*; *Jeu de cartes*; *Orpheus.* Theatre: *The Soldier's Tale.* Orchestral: Symphony in C; *Symphony in Three Movements*; *Symphonies of Wind Instruments*; violin concerto; *Ebony Concerto* (for clarinet). Liturgical: *Symphony of Psalms*; *Mass*; *Canticum Sacrum.*
Suk, Joseph	1874–1935	Krecovice, Czechoslovakia	*Asrael Symphony.*
Sullivan, Sir Arthur	1842–1900	London	Operetta: *HMS Pinafore*; *The Pirates of Penzance*; *Iolanthe*; *The Mikado*; *The Yeomen of the Guard*; *The Gondoliers.*
Szymanowski, Karol	1882–1937	Tymoshovka, Ukraine	Orchestral: Symphony No.2 in B Flat; Symphony No.3 *(Song of the Night)*; *Symphonie Concertante* (for piano and orchestra); 2 violin concertos; *Stabat Mater* (for voice, women's chorus and orchestra).
Tallis, Thomas	c.1505–85	Greenwich	Liturgical music: *Spem in alium* (40-part motet).
Tchaikovsky, Peter Ilyich	1840–93	Kamsko-Votkinsk, Russia	Opera: *Eugene Onegin*; *Queen of Spades.* Ballet: *Swan Lake*; *Sleeping Beauty*; *Nutcracker.* Orchestral: Symphony No.4 in F Minor; Symphony No.5 in E Minor; Symphony No.6 in B Minor *(Pathetic)*; *Manfred Symphony*; *Romeo and Juliet* (overture).
Telemann, Georg Philipp	1681–1767	Magdeburg, Germany	c.600 overtures; also many operas, oratorios, and concertos.
Tippett, Sir Michael	1905–	London	Opera: *The Midsummer Marriage*; *The Ice Break.* Oratorio: *A Child of Our Time.* Orchestral: *Fantasia Concertante on a Theme of Corelli.*
Vaughan Williams, Ralph	1872–1958	Down Ampney, Gloucestershire	Opera: *The Pilgrim's Progress*; Orchestral: *A Sea Symphony*; *A London Symphony*; *A Pastoral Symphony*; Symphony No.4 in F Minor; *Sinfonia Antartica*; *The Wasps* (overture); *Fantasia on a Theme by Thomas Tallis*; *The Lark Ascending* (for violin and orchestra).
Verdi, Giuseppe	1813–1901	Roncole	Opera: *Nabucco*; *Macbeth*; *Rigoletto*; *Il Trovatore*; *La Traviata*; *Simon Boccanegra*; *A Masked Ball*; *The Force of Destiny*; *Don Carlos*; *Aida*; *Otello*; *Falstaff.* Orchestral: *Requiem.*
Villa-Lobos, Heitor	1887–1959	Rio de Janeiro	*Bachianas Brasileiras* (9 chamber pieces).
Vivaldi, Antonio	1678–1741	Venice	c.230 violin concertos: *Le quattro stagioni (The Four Seasons)*; orchestral concertos; bassoon, cello, oboe and flute concertos. Many operas and cantatas.
Wagner, Richard	1813–83	Leipzig	Opera: *Rienzi*; *Der fliegende Holländer*; *Tannhäuser*; *Lohengrin*; *Der Ring des Nibelungen (Das Rheingold, Die Walküre, Siegfried, Götterdämmerung)*; *Tristan und Isolde*; *Die Meistersinger von Nürnberg*; *Parsifal.* Orchestral: *Siegfried Idyll.*
Walton, Sir William	1902–83	Oldham	*Façade* (for reciter and chamber orchestra). Orchestral: Symphony No.1 in B Flat Major; Viola Concerto in B Minor; Coronation marches *(Crown Imperial, Orb and Sceptre)*. For chorus and orchestra: *Belshazzar's Feast.* Film scores: *Henry V*; *Hamlet*; *Battle of Britain*; *Richard III.*
Weber, Carl Maria von	1786–1826	Eutin, in Oldenburg, Germany	Opera: *Der Freischütz*; *Euryanthe*; *Die drei Pintos*; *Oberon.*
Webern, Anton von	1883–1945	Vienna	Orchestral: *Passacaglia*; *6 Pieces*; *5 Pieces.* Choral: *Das Augenlicht.*

Composers (continued)

Name	Dates	Place of birth	Selected works
Weill, Kurt	1900–50	Dessau, Germany	Opera: *The Threepenny Opera*; *Rise and Fall of the City of Mahagonny*; *Happy End*. Ballet: *Seven Deadly Sins*. Orchestral: 2 symphonies; violin concerto; *The Berlin Requiem*.
Wolf, Hugo	1860–1903	Windischgraz, Austria	Opera: *Der Corregidor*. Orchestral: *Italian Serenade*. Songs: *Spanish Songbook*; *Italian Songbook*.
Zemlinsky, Alexander von	1871–1942	Vienna	Opera: *Eine florentinische Tragödie*. Ballet: *Das gläserne Herz*. Orchestral: *Lyric Symphony*.

Operatic works

Name of work	Date	Composer	Librettist
Aida	1871	Verdi	Ghislanzoni
Alceste	1767	Gluck	Calzabigi
Arabella	1933	Richard Strauss	Hofmannsthal
Barber of Seville	1816	Rossini	Sterbini
Bartered Bride, The	1866	Smetana	Sabini
Beggar's Opera	1728	Gay	Gay
Billy Budd	1951	Britten	Forster/Crozier
Bohème, La	1896	Puccini	Giacosa/Illica
Boris Godunov	1974	Mussorgsky	Mussorgsky
Carmen	1875	Bizet	Meilhac/Halevy
Cavalleria Rusticana	1890	Mascagni	Menasci/Targioni-Tozetti
Clemenza di Tito, La	1791	Mozart	Mazzolà
Coronation of Poppea	1642	Monteverdi	Busenello
Cosi Fan Tutte	1790	Mozart	Da Ponte
Cunning Little Vixen, The	1924	Janáček	Janáček
Damnation of Faust, The	1846	Berlioz	Berlioz
Death in Venice	1973	Britten	Piper
Dido and Aeneas	1689	Purcell	Tate
Don Giovanni	1787	Mozart	Da Ponte
Duke Bluebeard's Castle	1918	Bartók	Balasz
Elektra	1909	Richard Strauss	Hofmannsthal
Eugene Onegin	1879	Tchaikovsky	Tchaikovsky/Shilovsky
Falstaff	1893	Verdi	Wagner
Faust	1859	Gounod	Barbier/Carré
Fidelio	1805	Beethoven	Sonnleithner
Fledermaus, Die	1874	Johann Strauss II	Haffner/Genee
Flying Dutchman, The	1843	Wagner	Wagner
Freischütz, Der	1821	Weber	Kind
Golden Cockerel, The	1909	Rimsky-Korsakov	Byelsky
Idomeneo	1781	Mozart	Varesco
Jenufa	1904	Janáček	Janáček
Julius Caesar in Egypt	1724	Handel	Haym
Kátya Kabanová	1921	Janàcek	Janàcek
King Priam	1962	Tippett	Tippett
Les Huguenots	1836	Meyerbeer	Scribe
Lohengrin	1850	Wagner	Wagner
Love for Three Oranges, The	1920	Prokofiev	Prokofiev
Lucia di Lammermoor	1835	Donizetti	Cammarano
Lulu	1937	Berg	Berg
Macbeth	1847	Verdi	Piave
Madame Butterfly	1904	Puccini	Giacoso/Illica
Magic Flute, The	1791	Mozart	Schikaneder
Manon Lescaut	1893	Puccini	Giacoso/Illica
Marriage of Figaro, The	1786	Mozart	Da Ponte
Mask of Orpheus, The	1986	Birtwistle	Zinovieff
Meistersinger, Die	1868	Wagner	Wagner
Midsummer Marriage	1955	Tippett	Duncan
Midsummer Night's Dream, A	1960	Britten	Britten/Pears
Mikado, The	1885	Sullivan	Gilbert
Nabucco	1842	Verdi	Solera
Oedipus Rex	1927	Stravinsky	Cocteau
Orfeo	1607	Monteverdi	Striggio
Orpheus and Eurydice	1762	Gluck	Calzabigi
Orpheus in the Underworld	1858	Offenbach	Cremeux/Halevy
Otello	1887	Verdi	Boito
Pagliacci	1892	Leoncavallo	Leoncavallo
Paradise Lost	1978	Penderecki	Fry
Parsifal	1882	Wagner	Wagner
Pelléas et Mélissande	1902	Debussy	Maeterlinck
Peter Grimes	1945	Britten	Slater
Pilgrim's Progress, The	1951	Vaughan Williams	Vaughan Williams/Wood
Porgy and Bess	1935	Gershwin	Ira Gershwin/Heyward
Prince Igor	1890	Borodin	Borodin
Rake's Progress, The	1951	Stravinsky	Auden/Kallman
Rape of Lucretia, The	1946	Britten	Duncan
Rigoletto	1851	Verdi	Piave
Ring of the Nibelung, The	1876	Wagner	Wagner
Rosenkavalier, Der	1911	Richard Strauss	Hofmannsthal
Rossignol, Le	1914	Stravinsky	Stravinsky/Mitusov

Name of work	Date	Composer	Librettist	Name of work	Date	Composer	Librettist
Salomé	1905	Richard Strauss	Wilde/Lachmann	Tristan and Isolde	1865	Wagner	Wagner
Samson and Delilah	1877	Saint-Saëns	Lemaire	Trojans, The (Les Troyens)	1863	Berlioz	Berlioz
Tales of Hoffman, The	1881	Offenbach	Barbier	Trovatore, Il	1853	Verdi	Cammarano
Tannhäuser	1845	Wagner	Wagner	Turandot	1926	Puccini	Adami/Simoni
Threepenny Opera, The	1928	Weill	Brecht/ Hauptmann	Turn of the Screw, The	1954	Britten	Piper
Tosca	1900	Puccini	Giacosa/Illica	William Tell	1829	Rossini	De Jouy/Bis/ Marrast
Traviata, La	1853	Verdi	Piave	Wozzeck	1925	Berg	Berg

Opera singers

Name	Dates	Place of birth	Range	Name	Dates	Place of birth	Range
Allen, Thomas	1944–	Seaham	Baritone	Flagstad, Kirsten	1895–1962	Hamar, Norway	Soprano
Ameling, Elly	1938–	Rotterdam	Soprano	Forrester, Maureen	1930–	Montreal	Contralto
Anderson, Marian	1902–93	Philadelphia	Contralto	Freni, Mirella	1936–	Modena, Italy	Soprano
Austral, Florence	1894–1968	Richmond, Melbourne	Soprano	Gedda, Nicolai	1925–	Stockholm	Tenor
Bailey, Norman	1933–	Birmingham	Baritone	Gigli, Beniamino	1890–1957	Recanati, Italy	Tenor
Baker, Dame Janet	1933–	Hatfield, Yorkshire	Mezzo-soprano	Gobi, Tito	1913–84	Bassano del Grappa, Italy	Baritone
Barstow, Josephine	1940–	Sheffield	Soprano	Hendricks, Barbara	1948–	Stephens, Arizona	Soprano
Bartolio, Cecilia	1966–	Rome	Mezzo-soprano	Hotter, Hans	1909–	Offenbach-am-Main, Germany	Bass-baritone
Battistini, Mattia	1856–1928	Contigliano, Italy	Baritone	Kollo, René	1937–	Berlin	Tenor
Bergonzi, Carlo	1924–	Polisene, Italy	Tenor	Kraus, Alfredo	1927–	Las Palmas	Tenor
Berganza, Teresa	1935–	Madrid	Mezzo-soprano	Lehmann, Lotte	1888–1976	Perleberg, Germany	Soprano
Björling, Jussi	1911–60	Stora Tuna, Sweden	Tenor	Lind, Jenny	1820–87	Stockholm	Soprano
Borgatti, Giuseppe	1871–1950	Cento, Italy	Tenor	Ludwig, Christa	1924–	Berlin	Mezzo-soprano
Borgioli, Dino	1891–1960	Florence	Tenor	Luxon, Benjamin	1937–	Camborne, Cornwall	Baritone
Bowman, James	1941–	Oxford	Counter-tenor	Martinelli, Giovanni	1885–1969	Montagnana, Italy	Tenor
Butt, Dame Clara	1872–1936	Southwick, Sussex	Contralto	McCormack, John	1884–1945	Athlone, Ireland	Tenor
Caballé, Montserrat	1933–	Barcelona	Soprano	Melba, Dame Nellie	1861–1931	Richmond, nr Melbourne	Soprano
Callas, Maria (Maria Ann Sofia Cecelia Kalogeropoulos)	1923–77	New York	Soprano	Migenes-Johnson Julia	1945–	New York	Soprano
Carreras, José	1946–	Barcelona	Tenor	Milanov, Zinka	1906–89	Zagreb	Soprano
Caruso, Enrico	1873–1921	Naples	Tenor	Nilsson, Birgit	1922–	Karup, Sweden	Soprano
Chaliapin, Fyodor	1873–1938	Kazan, Russia	Bass	Norman, Jessye	1945–	Augusta, Georgia	Soprano
Deller, Alfred	1912–79	Margate	Counter-tenor	Patti, Adelina	1843–1919	Madrid	Soprano
De Los Angeles, Victoria	1923–	Barcelona	Soprano	Pavarotti, Luciano	1935–	Modena, Italy	Tenor
Domingo, Placido	1941–	Madrid	Tenor	Pears, Sir Peter	1910–86	Farnham, Surrey	Tenor
Evans, Sir Geraint	1922–92	Pontypridd, S Wales	Baritone	Pinza, Ezio	1892–1957	Rome	Bass
Ewing, Maria	1950–	Detroit	Mezzo-soprano	Ponselle, Rosa	1897–1981	Meriden, Connecticut	Soprano
Farrar, Geraldine	1882–1967	Ridgefield, Connecticut	Soprano	Popp, Lucia	1939–	Lihorska, Czechoslovakia	Soprano
Ferrier, Kathleen	1912–53	Higher Walton, Lancashire	Contralto	Prey, Hermann	1929–	Berlin	Baritone
Fischer-Dieskau, Dietrich	1925–	Berlin	Baritone	Price, Leontyne	1927–	Laurel, Mississippi	Soprano

Opera singers (continued)

Name	Dates	Place of birth	Range	Name	Dates	Place of birth	Range
Schumann, Elisabeth	1885–1952	Merseburg, Germany	Soprano	Tauber, Richard	1892–1948	Linz	Tenor
Schwarzkopf, Elisabeth	1915–	Janotschin, nr Poznań	Soprano	Tear, Robert	1939–	Barry, Glamorgan	Tenor
Scotto, Renata	1933–	Savona, Italy	Soprano	Tebaldi, Renata	1922–	Pesaro, Italy	Soprano
Shirley-Quirk, John	1931–	Liverpool	Baritone	Te Kanawa, Dame Kiri	1944–	Gisborne, New Zealand	Soprano
Söderström, Elisabeth	1927–	Stockholm	Soprano	Tetrazzini, Luisa	1871–1938	Milan	Soprano
				Teyte, Dame Maggie	1888–1976	Wolverhampton	Soprano
Stratas, Teresa	1938–	Toronto	Soprano	Turner, Dame Eva	1892–1990	Oldham	Soprano
Studer, Cheryl	1955–	Midland, Michigan	Soprano	Van Dam, José	1940–	Brussels	Baritone
				Vickers, Jon	1926–	Prince Albert, Saskatchewan	Tenor
Sutherland, Dame Joan	1926–	Sydney	Soprano				

Jazz personalities

Name	Dates	Place of birth	Instrument
Armstrong, Louis	1900–71	New Orleans	Trumpet, cornet, vocal
Baker, Chet	1929–88	Yale, Oklahoma	Trumpet, flugelhorn, vocal
Barber, Chris	1930–	Hertfordshire	Trombone, bass trumpet, vocal
Basie, William 'Count'	1904–84	Red Bank	Piano, organ
Bechet, Sidney	1897–1959	New Orleans	Soprano, tenor, and bass saxophones, clarinet, piano
Beiderbecke, Bix	1903–31	Davenport	Cornet
Blakey, Art	1919–90	Pittsburgh	Drums
Bley, Carla	1938–	Oakland, California	Piano
Braxton, Anthony	1945–	Chicago	Alto saxophone, clarinet, flute
Brubeck, Dave	1920–	Concord, California	Piano
Calloway, Cab	1907–	New York	Vocal
Charles, Ray	1930–	Albany	Vocal, piano
Cherry, Don	1936–	Oklahoma City	Trumpet, flute
Christian, Charlie	1916–42	Dallas	Guitar
Clark, Kenny	1914–85	Pittsburgh	Drums
Coleman, Ornette	1930–	Fort Worth	Alto and soprano saxophones, vocal
Coltrane, John	1926–67	Hamlet	Soprano, alto, and tenor saxophones, flute
Corea, Chick	1941–	Chelsea (US)	Piano, keyboards
Dankworth, John	1927–	London	Alto saxophone
Davis, Miles	1926–91	Alton	Trumpet
Desmond, Paul	1924–77	San Francisco	Alto saxophone
Dolphy, Eric	1928–64	Los Angeles	Flute, alto saxophone, bass clarinet, clarinet
Eldridge, Roy	1911–89	Pittsburgh	Trumpet
Ellington, Duke	1899–1974	Washington	Piano
Evans, Bill	1929–80	Plainfield	Piano
Evans, Gil (Ian Ernest Gilmore Green)	1912–88	Toronto	Piano
Fitzgerald, Ella	1918–	Newport News	Vocal
Gabarek, Jan	1947–	Mysen, Norway	Soprano, tenor, and bass saxophones, flute
Gaillard, Slim	1916–91	Detroit	Vocal
Garner, Errol	1923–77	Pittsburgh	Piano
Getz, Stan	1927–91	Philadelphia	Soprano, tenor, and baritone saxophones
Gillespie, Dizzy	1917–93	Cheraw	Trumpet, piano, vocal
Goodman, Benny	1909–86	Chicago	Clarinet
Gordon, Dexter	1923–89	Los Angeles	Soprano and tenor saxophones
Grappelli, Stephane	1908–	Paris	Violin
Hamilton, Chico	1921–	Los Angeles	Drums
Hamilton, Scott	1954–	Providence, Rhode Island	Tenor saxophone
Hampton, Lionel	1909–	Louisville	Vibraphone
Hancock, Herbie	1940–	Chicago	Piano

Name	Dates	Place of birth	Instrument
Hawkins, Coleman	1904–69	Saint Joseph	Tenor saxophone, vocal
Herman, Woody	1913–87	Milwaukee	Alto saxophone, clarinet, vocal
Hines, Earl	1905–83	Duquesne	Piano, vocal
Hodges, Johnny	1906–70	Massachusetts	Soprano and alto saxophone
Holliday, Billie	1915–59	Baltimore	Vocal
Ibrahim, Abdullah (Dollar Brand)	1934–	Cape Town	Piano
Jackson, Milt	1923–	Detroit	Vibraphone
Jarrett, Keith	1945–	Allentown	Piano, organ, soprano saxophone
Johnson, J J	1924–	Indianapolis	Trombone
Jones, Elvin	1927–	Pontiac	Drums
Kenton, Stan	1912–79	Wichita, Kansas	Piano, vocal
Konitz, Lee	1927–	Chicago	Soprano and alto saxophones
Lacy, Steve	1934–	New York	Soprano saxophone
Lyttleton, Humphrey	1921–	Eton	Trumpet, cornet, clarinet
Marsalis, Wynton	1961–	New Orleans	Trumpet
McLaughlin, John	1942–	Yorkshire	Guitar
Merrill, Helen	1930–	New York	Vocal
Metheny, Pat	1954–	Lee's Summit	Guitar
Mingus, Charles	1922–79	Nogales	Double bass, piano
Monk, Thelonious	1917–82	Rocky Mount	Piano
Montgomery, Wes	1925–68	Indianapolis	Guitar, bass guitar
Moreton, Jelly Roll (Frederick LaMenthe)	1885-1941	Gulfport	Piano
Mulligan, Gerry	1927–	New York	Soprano and baritone saxophone, piano
Navarro, Theodore 'Fats'	1923–50	Key West, Florida	Trumpet
O'Day, Anita	1919–	Chicago	Vocal
Oliver, King	1885–1938	Abend, LA	Cornet, trumpet
Parker, Charlie	1920–55	Kansas City	Alto and tenor saxophones
Pepper, Art	1925–82	Gardena, California	Alto and tenor saxophones, clarinet
Peterson, Oscar	1925–	Montreal	Piano
Pettiford, Oscar	1922–60	Okmulgee, Oklahoma	Double bass, cello
Powell, Bud	1924–66	New York	Piano
Rheinhardt, Django	1910–53	Liverchies, Belgium	Guitar
Rich, Buddy	1917–87	New York	Drums, vocal
Roach, Max	1925–	New York	Drums
Rollins, Sonny	1930–	New York	Soprano and tenor saxophones
Shaw, Artie	1910–	New York	Clarinet
Shepp, Archie	1937–	Fort Lauderdale	Soprano, alto, and tenor saxophones
Shorter, Wayne	1933–	Newark	Soprano and tenor saxophones
Simone, Nina	1933–	North Carolina	Vocal
Smith, Bessie	1894–1937	Chattanooga	Vocal
Smith, Tommy	1967–	Luton	Tenor saxophone
Solal, Martial	1927–	Algiers	Piano
Surman, John	1944–	Tavistock	Soprano and baritone saxophones, bass clarinet, piano
Tatum, Art	1910–56	Toledo	Piano
Taylor, Cecil	1933–	New York	Piano, vocal
Terry, Clark	1920–	St Louis	Trumpet, flugelhorn
Thielmans, Jean-Baptiste 'Toots'	1922–	Brussels	Harmonica
Tracey, Stan	1926–	London	Piano
Tristano, Lennie	1919–78	Chicago	Piano
Tyner, McCoy	1938–	Philadelphia	Piano, flute
Vaughan, Sarah	1924–90	Newark	Vocal
Walker, T-Bone	1910–75	Linden	Guitar
Waller, Thomas 'Fats'	1904–43	New York	Piano, organ, vocal
Washington, Dinah	1924–63	Alabama	Vocal
Weber, Eberhard	1940–	Stuttgart	Double bass
Webster, Ben	1909–73	Missouri	Tenor saxophone
Williams, Tony	1945–	Chicago	Drums
Young, Lester	1909–59	Woodville	Tenor saxophone

Classic pop and rock groups/singers

*Group members are given for the best-known line-up.

Name	Country of origin	Group members*	Period	Major hits
Abba	Sweden	Benny Anderson (keyboards, vocals) Bjorn Ulvaeus (guitar, vocals) Agnetha Faltskog (vocals) Frida Lyngstad (vocals)	1970s–80s	Waterloo; Mamma Mia; Fernando; Knowing Me Knowing You; Dancing Queen; The Name of the Game; Take a Chance on Me; I Have a Dream; Super Trouper; The Winner Takes it All
Animals, The	Britain	Eric Burden (vocals) Alan Price (keyboards) Hilton Valentine ((guitar) Chas Chandler (bass) John Steel (drums)	1960s	House of the Rising Sun; I'm Crying; Don't Let Me Be Misunderstood; Bring it on Home to Me; We've Gotta Get Out of This Place; It's My Life; Don't Bring Me Down
Band, The	Canada	Robbie Robertson (guitar, vocals) Richard Manuel (piano, vocals) Garth Hudson (organ) Rick Danko (bass, vocals) Levon Helm (drums, vocals)	1960s–70s	Up on Cripple Creek; Rag Mama Rag; Stage Fright. Albums: The Band; Cahoots; Before the Flood; The Last Waltz
Beach Boys, The	USA	Brian Wilson (bass, keyboards, vocals) Mike Love (vocals) Carl Wilson (guitar, vocals) Al Jardine (guitar, vocals) Denis Wilson (drums, vocals)	1960s–70s	Get Around; When I Grow Up; Do You Wanna Dance; Help Me Rhonda; California Girls; Barbara Ann; Surfin' USA; God Only Knows; Wouldn't It Be Nice; Good Vibrations; Then I Kissed Her; Heroes and Villains; Darlin'; Do It Again; I Can Hear Music; Rock and Roll Music; Lady Lynda
Beatles, The	Britain	John Lennon (vocals, rhythm guitar) Paul McCartney (vocals, bass) George Harrison (vocals, lead guitar) Ringo Starr (vocals, drums)	1960s	Please Please Me; From Me to You; She Loves You; I Want to Hold Your Hand; Can't Buy Me Love; A Hard Day's Night; I Feel Fine; Eight Days A Week; Ticket to Ride; Help!; Yesterday; Day Tripper; We Can Work it Out; Paperback Writer; Yellow Submarine; Eleanor Rigby; Penny Lane; Strawberry Fields Forever; All You Need is Love; Hello Goodbye; Lady Madonna; Hey Jude; Get Back; The Ballad of John and Yoko; Let it Be. Albums: Sergeant Pepper's Lonely Hearts Club Band
Bee Gees, The	Britain	Barry Gibb (vocals, guitar) Maurice Gibb (vocals, bass) Robin Gibb (vocals)	1950s– present	To Love Somebody; I've Gotta Get a Message to You; How Deep is Your Love; Stayin' Alive; Saturday Night Fever; Tragedy; You Win Again
Berry, Chuck	USA		1950s– present	Maybellene; Roll over Beethoven; School Day; Rock and Roll Music; Sweet Little Sixteen; Johnny Be Good; Carol; No Particular Place to Go; My Ding-A-Ling
Black Sabbath	Britain	Tony Iommi (guitar) 'Geezer' Butler (bass) Ozzy Osbourne (vocals) Bill Ward (drums)	1970s	Paranoid; Never Say Die; Neon Knights. Albums: Paranoid; Black Sabbath Vol. 4; Sabbath Bloody Sabbath; Master of Reality; Sabotage; Technical Ecstasy; Heaven and Hell; Mob Rules; Born Again
Blondie	USA	Debbie Harry (vocals) Chris Stein (guitar) Jimmy Destri (keyboards) Gary Valentine (bass) Clem Burke (drums)	1970s–80s	Denis; (I'm Always Touched by Your) Presence Dear; Picture This; Hanging on the Telephone; Heart of Glass; Sunday Girl; Dreaming; Atomic; Call Me; The Tide is High; Rapture; French Kissin' in the USA

Name	Country of origin	Group members*	Period	Major hits
Bowie, David	Britain		1970s–present	Space Oddity; Aladdin Sane; The Jean Genie; Time; Sound and Vision; Ashes to Ashes; Fashion; Let's Dance; China Girl; Modern Love; Absolute Beginners
Brown, James	USA		1950s–present	Papa's Got a Brand New Bag; I Got You (I Feel Good); It's a Man's Man's Man's World; I Got the Feelin'; Say it; Loud – I'm Back and I'm Proud; Give it Up or Turn it Loose; Mother Popcorn; Get Up; I Feel Like Being a Sex Machine; Super Bad; Get on the Good Foot
Byrds, The	USA	Roger (Jim) McGuinn (vocals, guitar) Gene Clark (vocals, percussion) David Crosby (vocals, guitar) Chris Hillman (vocals, bass) Michael Clarke (drums)	1960s–70s	Mr Tambourine Man; All I Really Want to Do; Turn! Turn! Turn!; Eight Miles High; Chestnut Mare
Carpenters, The	USA	Richard Carpenter (vocals, drums) Karen Carpenter (vocals, keyboards)	1970s–80s	Close to You; We've Only Just Begun; For All We Know; Rainy Days and Mondays; Hurting Each Other; It's Going to Take Some Time; Goodbye to Love; Sing; Please Mr Postman; Only Yesterday; Calling Occupants of Interplanetary Craft
Clapton, Eric	Britain		1960s–present	Layla; I Shot the Sheriff; Lay Down Sally; Wonderful Tonight; Forever Man; Cocaine; Knocking on Heaven's Door; Behind the Mask; Tears in Heaven
Clash, The	Britain	Joe Strummer (vocals, guitar) Mick Jones (guitar) Paul Simonon (bass) Nicky 'Topper' Headon (drums)	1970s–80s	Tommy Gun; Bankrobber; Rock the Casbah; Should I Stay or Should I Go?
Cochran, Eddie	USA		1950s	Sittin' in the Balcony; Summertime Blues; C'Mon Everybody; Somethin' Else; Three Steps to Heaven; Hallelujah I Love Her So
Collins, Phil	Britain		1980s–present	In the Air Tonight; I Missed Again; You Can't Hurry Love; Against All Odds; Easy Lover; Sussudio; One More Night; Separate Lives; Take Me Home; Groovy Kind of Love; Two Hearts; Another Day in Paradise; I Wish it Would Rain
Commodores, The	USA	Lionel Richie (vocals, keyboards) William King (trumpet) Thomas McClary (lead guitar) Milan Williams (keyboards, trombone, guitar, drums) Ronald La Praed (bass, trumpet) Walter (Clyde) Orange (vocals, drums)	1970s–80s	Machine Gun; Slippery When Wet; Sweet Love; Just To Be Close To You; Easy; Brickhouse; Three Times A Lady; Sail On; Still; Nightshift
Cream	Britain	Eric Clapton (vocals, guitar) Jack Bruce (vocals, bass) Ginger Baker (drums)	1960s	I Feel Free; Strange Brew; Sunshine of Your Love; White Room; Badge
Diamond, Neil	USA		1960s–present	Cherry Cherry; I Got the Feelin'; You Got to Me; Girl You'll Be A Woman Soon; Sweet Caroline; Holly Holy; Cracklin' Rosie; I Am ... I Said; Stones; Song Sung Blue; Longfellow Serenade; Beautiful Noise; You Don't Bring Me Flowers; Forever in Blue Jeans; Love on the Rocks

Classic pop and rock groups/singers (continued)

Name	Country of origin	Group members*	Period	Major hits
Diddley, Bo	USA		1950s–60s	Bo Diddley; I'm a Man; Who Do You Love; Road Runner; Hey Good Lookin'
Dire Straits	Britain	Mark Knopfler (guitar, vocals) John Illsley (bass) Hal Lindes (guitar) Pick Withers (drums) Alan Clark (keyboards)	1970s–80s	Sultans of Swing; Romeo and Juliet; Telegraph Road; Private Investigations; Money for Nothing; Walk of Life
Doors, The	USA	Jim Morrison (vocals) Ray Manzarek (keyboards) Robbie Krieger (guitar) John Densmore (drums)	1960s–70s	Light My Fire; Love Me Two Times; Hello I Love You; Touch Me; Love Her Madly; Riders on the Storm
Dylan, Bob	USA		1960s–present	Blowin' in the Wind; The Times They Are a-Changin'; Subterranean Homesick Blues; Like a Rollin' Stone; Positively 4th Street; Can You Please Crawl Out Your Window; Rainy Day Woman; Just Like a Woman; Lay Lady Lay; Knockin' on Heaven's Door; Baby Stop Crying
Eagles, The	USA	Glenn Frey (guitar, vocals) Bernie Leadon (guitar, vocals) Randy Meisner (bass, vocals) Don Henley (drums, vocals)	1970s	Take it Easy; Witchy Woman; The Best of My Love; One of These Nights; Lyin' Eyes; Hotel California; New Kid in Town; Life in the Fast Lane; Life's Been Good; Heartache Tonight
Eurythmics, The	Britain	Annie Lennox (vocals) Dave Stewart (keyboards, guitar)	1980s	Sweet Dreams; Love is a Stranger; Right By Your Side; Here Comes The Rain Again; Who's That Girl; Would I Lie To You? There Must Be An Angel; Sisters Are Doing It For Themselves; It's Alright; Thorn In My Side
Everley Brothers, The	USA	Don Everley (vocals, guitar) Phil Everley (vocals, guitar)	1950s–60s	Bye Bye Love; Wake Up Little Susie; All I Have to Do is Dream; Devoted to You; Bird Dog; Problems; A Message to Mary; I Kissed You; Let It Be Me; Cathy's Clown; When Will I Be Loved; Like Strangers; Walk Right Back; Ebony Eyes; Temptation; Crying in the Rain; That's Old-Fashioned; That'll Be The Day; Love is Strange
Fleetwood Mac	UK/USA	Mick Fleetwood (drums) John McVie (bass) Christine McVie (keyboards, vocals) Lindsey Buckingham (guitars, vocals) Stevie Nicks (vocals)	1960s–80s	Albatross; Man of the World; Oh Well; The Green Manalishi; Over My Head; Go Your Own Way; Don't Stop; Dreams; You Make Loving Fun; Tusk; Sara; Trouble; Hold Me; Oh Diane; Big Love; Seven Wonders; Little Lies; Everywhere
Four Tops, The	USA	Levi Stubbs (vocals) Renaldo 'Obie' Benson (vocals) Abdul 'Duke' Fakir (vocals) Lawrence Paynton (vocals)	1960s–80s	I Can't Help Myself; It's the Same Old Song; Loving You is Sweeter Than Ever; Reach Out I'll Be There; Bernadette; Seven Rooms of Gloom; Walk Away Renée; If I Were A Carpenter; What is a Man; Do What You Gotta Do; I Can't Help Myself; River Deep Mountain High; So Deep Within You; Ain't No Woman; When She was My Girl; Don't Walk Away; Loco in Acapulco

Arts and culture

Name of origin	Country	Group members*	Period	Major hits
Franklin, Aretha	USA		1960s–80s	I Never Loved a Man; Do Right Woman – Do Right Man; Respect; Baby I Love You; Natural Woman; Since You've Been Gone; I Say A Little Prayer; The House That Jack Built; Chain of Fools; Don't Play That Song; Bridge Over Troubled Water; A Brand New Me; Spanish Harlem; Rock Steady; Who's Zoomin' Who; Sisters Are Doing it For Themselves; I Knew You Were Waiting
Gabriel, Peter	Britain		1980s	Games Without Frontiers; Sledgehammer; In Your Eyes; Don't Give Up
Gaye, Marvin	USA		1960s–80s	How Sweet It Is; Ain't That Peculiar; It Takes Two; You're All I Need To Get By; I Heard It Through The Grapevine; Too Busy Thinking About My Baby; The Onion Song; Abraham; Martin and John; What's Going On? Mercy Mercy Mercy; Let's Get It On; You Are Everything; Sexual Healing
Genesis	Britain	Tony Banks (keyboards) Mike Rutherford (guitars) Phil Collins (drums, vocals)	1960s–present	Follow You; Follow Me; Turn It On Again; Paperlate; Mama; That's All; In Too Deep; Throwing It All Away; Land of Confusion; Tonight Tonight Tonight
Grateful Dead, The	USA	Jerry Garcia (lead guitar) Bob Weir (rhythm guitar) Ron 'Pigpen' McKernan (organ, harmonica) Phil Lesh (bass) Bill Kreutzmann (drums)	1960s–present	Touch of Grey. Albums: Grateful Dead; Workingman's Dead; Europe '72; Wake of the Flood; Blues for Allah; Terrapin Station; Dead Set; In the Dark
Haley, Bill, and his Comets	USA	Bill Haley (vocals, guitar) Frannie Beecher (lead guitar) Al Pompilli (bass) Rudi Pompilli (saxophone) Ralph Jones (drums)	1950s	Shake; Rattle and Roll; Rock Around the Clock; Rock-a-Beatin' Boogie; See You Later Alligator; The Saints Rock'n'Roll; Rockin' Through The Rye; Razzle Dazzle; Rip it Up
Hendrix, Jimi	USA		1960s	Hey Joe; Purple Haze; The Wind Cries Mary; Burning of the Midnight Lamp; Axis: Bold As Love; All Along The Watchtower; Voodoo Chile
Hollies, The	Britain	Allan Clarke (vocals) Graham Nash (guitar) Tony Hicks (guitar) Erick Haydock (bass) Bobby Elliott (drums)	1960s–70s	Just Like Me; Searchin'; Stay; Here I Go Again; We're Through; Yes I Will; I'm Alive; Look Through Any Window; I Can't Let Go; Bus Stop; Stop Stop Stop; On a Carousel; Carrie-Anne; Jennifer Eccles; Listen To Me; Sorry Suza; He Ain't Heavy He's My Brother; I Can't Tell the Bottom From the Top; The Air That I Breathe
Holly, Buddy, and the Crickets	USA	Buddy Holly (vocals, guitar) Sonny Curtis (guitar) Joe B. Mauldin (bass) Jerry Allison (drums)	1950s	That'll Be The Day; Peggy Sue; Oh Boy! ; Listen to Me; Maybe Baby

Classic pop and rock groups/singers (continued)

Name	Country of origin	Group members*	Period	Major hits
Houston, Whitney	USA		1980s	Saving All My Love for You; How Will I Know; Greatest Love of All; I Wanna Dance With Somebody; Didn't We Almost Have It All; So Emotional; One Moment in Time; I'm Your Baby Tonight; I'll Always Love You; I Have Nothing
Jackson, Michael	USA		1970s–present	Don't Stop 'Til You Get Enough; Rock With You; She's Out of My Life; One Day in Your Life; The Girl is Mine; Billie Jean; Beat It; Wanna Be Startin' Somethin'; Say Say Say; Thriller; PYT; I Just Can't Stop Loving You; Bad; The Way You Make Me Feel; Dirty Diana; Another Part of Me; Smooth Criminal; Leave Me Alone
Jacksons, The	USA	Jackie Jackson (vocals) Tito Jackson (vocals) Jermaine Jackson (vocals) Marlon Jackson (vocals) Michael Jackson (vocals)	1960s–80s	I Want You Back; ABC; The Love You Save; I'll Be There; Mama's Pearl; Never Can Say Goodbye; Dancing Machine; Enjoy Yourself; Show You the Way to Go; Blame It on the Boogie; Shake Your Body; Can You Feel It; State of Shock; Torture
Jam, The	Britain	Paul Weller (vocals, bass) Bruce Foxton (guitar) Rick Buckler (drums)	1970s–80s	In the City; All Around the World; Down in the Tube Station at Midnight; Eton Rifles; Going Underground; Start; Funeral Pyre; Absolute Beginners; Town Called Malice; Just Who is the Five O'Clock Hero?; The Bitterest Pill; Beat Surrender
Jefferson Airplane /Starship	USA	Grace Slick (vocals) Marty Balin (vocals) Paul Kantner (guitar) Jorma Kaukonen (guitar) Jack Casady (bass guitar) Spencer Dryden (drums)	1960s–70s	White Rabbit; Miracles; With Your Love; Count on Me; Runaway; Jane; Hearts
Jethro Tull	Britain	Ian Anderson (vocals, flute) Mick Abrahams (guitar) Glen Connick (bass) Clive Bunker (drums)	1960s–present	Living in the Past; The Witch's Promise/Teacher; Life Is A Long Song; Bungle in the Jungle; Thick as a Brick; Too Old To Rock and Roll – Too Young to Die
Joel, Billy	USA		1970s–present	New York State of Mind; Say Hollywood; Just The Way You Are; Goodbye to She's Always a Woman; My Life; It's Still Rock'n'Roll to Me; Tell Her About It; Uptown Girl; An Innocent Man; The Longest Time; We Didn't Start the Fire
John, Elton	Britain		1970s–present	Your Song; Rocket Man; Crocodile Rock; Daniel; Saturday Night's Alright for Fighting; Goodbye Yellow Brick Road; Candle in the Wind; Don't Let the Sun Go Down on Me; Don't Go Breaking My Heart; Sorry Seems to be the Hardest Word; Song for Guy; Blue Eyes; I Guess That's Why They Call It The Blues; I'm Still Standing; Sad Songs; Nikita; Sacrifice

Name of origin	Country	Group members*	Period	Major hits
Jones, Tom	Britain		1960s–present	*It's Not Unusual; What's New; Pussycat? Green Green Grass of Home; Detroit City; Funny Familiar Forgotten Feelings; I'll Never Fall in Love Again; I'm Coming Home; Delilah; Help Yourself; Love Me Tonight; Daughter of Darkness; A Boy From Nowhere; Kiss*
King, B.B.	USA		1950s–80s	*Three O'Clock Blues; You Didn't Want Me; The Thrill is Gone; Hold On*
King, Carole	USA		1960s–80s	*It Might As Well Rain Until September; It's Too Late/I Feel the Earth; Sweet Seasons; Jazzman; Nightingale*
Kinks, The	Britain	Roy Davies (vocals, guitar) Dave Davies (vocals, guitar) Pete Quaire (bass) Mick Avory (drums)	1960s–80s	*You Really Got Me; All Day and All of the Night; Tired of Waiting for You; See My Friend; Till the End of the Day; Sunny Afternoon; Dead End Street; Waterloo Sunset; Autumn Almanac; Lola; Come Dancing*
Knight, Gladys, and the Pips	USA	Gladys Knight (vocals) Merald 'Bubba' Knight (vocals) William Guest (vocals) Edward Pattern (vocals)	1960s–80s	*Every Beat of My Heart; Take Me in Your Arms and Love Me; I Heard It Through the Grapevine; Just Walk in My Shoes; Help Me Make It Through the Night; Neither One of Us; Midnight Train to Georgia; I've Got to Use My Imagination; On and On; The Way We Were; Best Thing That Ever Happened To Me; Come Back and Finish What You Started*
Led Zeppelin	Britain	Robert Plant (vocals) Jimmy Page (guitar) John Paul Jones (bass) John Bonham (drums)	1960s–1980s	*Whole Lotta Love; Stairway to Heaven; Black Dog; Kashmir; Dazed and Confused; Delta Blues*
Lennon, John	Britain		1960s–80s	*Give Peace A Chance; Instant Karma; Power to the People; Imagine; Whatever Gets You Through the Night; Dream; Starting Over; Woman; Jealous Guy*
Lewis, Jerry Lee	USA		1950s–present	*Whole Lotta Shakin'; Great Balls of Fire; Breathless; High School Confidential; What'd I Say; Good Golly Miss Molly; Chantilly Lace*
Little Richard	USA		1950s–present	*Tutti Frutti; Long Tall Sally; Rip it Up; She's Got It; The Girl Can't Help It; Lucille; Jenny Jenny; Keep a-Knockin'; Good Golly Miss Molly; Baby Face; Bama Lama Bama Loo*
McCartney, Paul	Britain		1970s–present	Songs with Wings: *Another Day; Mary Had a Little Mamb; Hi Hi Hi; My Love; Live and Let Die; Helen Wheels; Jet; Band on the Run; Listen to What The Man Said; Silly Love Songs; Let 'Em In; Mull of Kintyre; With a Little Luck.* McCartney's solo songs: *Wonderful Christmastime; Ebony and Ivory; The Girl Is Mine; Say Say Say; Pipes of Peace; No More Lonely Nights; We All Stand Together; My Brave Face*

Classic pop and rock groups/singers (continued)

Name	Country of origin	Group members*	Period	Major hits
Madness	Britain	Graham 'Suggs' McPherson (vocals) Mike Barson (keyboards) Chris Foreman (guitar) Mark Bedford (bass) Lee Thompson (saxophone, vocals) Dan Woodgate (drums) Carl 'Chas Smash' Smyth (horns)	1980s	*One Step Beyond; My Girl; Night Train to Cairo; Baggy Trousers; Embarrassment; Return of the Los Palmas Seven; Grey Day; It Must Be Love; House of Fun; Driving in My Car; Our House; Tomorrow; Wings of a Dove; The Sun and the Rain*
Madonna	USA		1980s–present	*Like a Virgin; Material Girl; Holiday; Crazy for You; Angel; Dress You Up; Live To Tell; True Blue; Papa Don't Preach; Open Your Heart; La Isla Bonita; Who's That Girl; Express Yourself; Like a Prayer; Cherish; Dear Jessie; Vogue; I'm Breathless; Hanky Panky; Justify My Love*
Mamas and Papas, The	USA	John Phillips (vocals) Denny Doherty (vocals) Cass Elliot (vocals) Michelle Gilliam (vocals)	1960s	*California Dreamin'; Monday Monday; I Saw Her Again; Dedicated to the One I Love; San Francisco; Dream a Little Dream of Me*
Marley, Bob, and the Wailers	Jamaica	Bob Marley (vocals, guitar) Peter Tosh (vocals, guitar) Bunny Wailer (vocals, percussion) Carlton Barrett (drums) Aston 'Family Man' Barrett (bass)	1970s	*No Woman No Cry; Exodus; Jamming; Is This Love; Satisfy My Soul; Could You Be Loved; Buffalo Soldier*
Michael, George	Britain		1980s–present	*Careless Whisper; I Knew You Were Waiting; I Want Your Sex; Faith; Father Figure; One More Try; Praying for Time; Freedom!; Too Funky; Somebody to Love*
Monkees, The	USA	Davy Jones (vocals, guitar) Mike Nesmith (vocals, guitar) Peter Tork (vocals, keyboards, bass guitar) Micky Dolenz (drums)	1960s	*Hey Hey We're the Monkees; Last Train to Clarksville; I'm a Believer; A Little Bit of Me; A Little Bit of You; Alternate Title; Pleasant Valley Sunday; Valleri*
Morrison, Van	Ireland		1960s–present	*Brown Eyed Girl; Domino; Blue Money; Wild Night; Jackie Wilson Said*
Newman, Randy	USA		1960s–present	*Short People. Albums: Little Criminals; Born Again*
Orbison, Roy	USA		1950s–60s, 1980s	*Pretty Woman; Only the Lonely; Blue Angel; I'm Hurtin'; Running Scared; Cryin'; Dream By; Falling; Blue Bayou; It's Over; Pretty Paper; Too Soon To Know; You Got It*
Osmonds; The	USA	Alan Osmond (vocals) Wayne Osmond (vocals) Merrill Osmond (vocals) Jay Osmond (vocals) Donny Osmond (vocals)	1970s	*One Bad Apple; Yo-Yo; Down By the Lazy River; Let Me In; I Can't Stop; Love Me for a Reason; The Proud One; Crazy Horses*
Pink Floyd	Britain	Roger Waters (vocals, bass) Rick Wright (keyboards) David Gilmour (vocals, guitar) Nick Mason (drums)	1960s–present	*Arnold Layne; See Emily Play; Another Brick in the Wall; Not Now John. Albums: The Piper at the Gates of Dawn; A Saucerful of Secrets; Ummagumma; Dark Side of the Moon; Wish You Were Here; Animals; The Wall; The Final Cut*

Name of origin	Country	Group members*	Period	Major hits
Pitney, Gene	USA		1960s–80s	24 Hours From Tulsa; Something's Gotten Hold of My Heart; Backstage; A Town Without Pity; 24 Sycamore; Maria Elena
Pogues, The	Britain	Shane McGowan (vocals, guitar) Jem Finer (banjo) James Fearnley (accordian) Spider Stacy (tin whistle) Caitlin O'Riordan (bass) Andrew Ranken (drums)	1980s–present	A Pair of Brown Eyes; Dirty Old Town; The Irish Rover; A Fairytale of New York
Police, The	Britain	Sting (vocals, bass) Andy Summers (vocals, guitar) Stewart Copeland (drums, percussion, vocals)	1970s–80s	Roxanne; Can't Stand Losing You; Message In a Bottle; Walking on the Moon; So Lonely; Don't Stand So Close To Me; Invisible Sun; Every Little Thing She Does is Magic; Every Breath You Take
Presley, Elvis	USA		1950s–70s	Baby Let's Play House; Heartbreak Hotel; Blue Suede Shoes; Hound Dog; I Want You I Need You I Love You; Don't Be Cruel; Love Me Tender; All Shook Up; Teddy Bear; Jailhouse Rock; Don't; Hard-Headed Woman; A Big Hunk of Love; Stuck On You; It's Now or Never; Are You Lonesome Tonight? Surrender; His Latest Flame; Can't Help Falling In Love; Good Luck Charm; She's Not You; Return to Sender; Devil in Disguise; Crying in the Chapel; Suspicious Minds; Don't Cry Daddy; The Wonder of You; I Just Can't Help Believing American Trilogy; In the Ghetto
Pretenders, The	Britain	Chrissie Hynde (vocals) Pete Farndon (bass) James Honeyman-Scott (guitar) Martin Chambers (drums)	1970s–present	Stop Your Sobbing; Brass in Pocket (I'm Special); Talk of the Town; Message of Love; I Go to Sleep; Back on the Chain Gang; Don't Get Me Wrong; Learning to Crawl; Packed
Prince	USA		1980s–present	Little Red Corvette; 1999; When Doves Cry; Purple Rain; Let's Go Crazy; Kiss; Girls and Boys; Sign of the Times; U Got The Look; Alphabet St; Batdance
Queen	Britain	Freddie Mercury (vocals) Brian May (guitar) John Deacon (bass) Roger Taylor (drums)	1970s–90s	Seven Seas of Rye; Killer Queen; Now I'm Here; Bohemian Rhapsody; You're My Best Friend; Somebody To Love; We Are The Champions; We Will Rock You; Fat Bottomed Girls; Don't Stop Me Now; Crazy Little Thing Called Love; Another One Bites the Dust; Flash; Under Pressure; Radio GaGa; I Want To Break Free; A Kind of Magic; The Great Pretender; I Want It All; Innuendo
Redding, Otis	USA		1960s	I've Been Loving You Too Long; Mr Pitiful; Pain in My Heart; My Girl; Try a Little Tenderness; The Dock of the Bay
Reed, Lou	USA		1970s	Walk on the Wild Side; Soul Man
REM	USA	Michael Stipe (vocals) Peter Buck (guitar) Mike Mills (bass) Bill Berry (drums)	1980s–present	Radio Free Europe; It's the End of the World As We Know It; The One I Love; Stand; Losing My Religion; The Greenhouse Effect

Classic pop and rock groups/singers (continued)

Name	Country of origin	Group members*	Period	Major hits
Richard, Cliff	Britain		1950s–present	Move It; Livin' Lovin' Doll; Mean Streak; Living Doll; A Voice in the Wilderness; Fall In Love With You; Please Don't Tease; Nine Times Out of Ten; I Love You; Theme For A Dream; A Girl Like You; When The Girl In Your Arms Is The Girl In Your Heart; It'll Be Me; The Next Time; Batchelor Boy; Summer Holiday; Lucky Lips; Don't Talk To Him; I'm The Lonely One; On The Beach; I Could Easily Fall; The Minute You're Gone; Wind Me Up; Vision; In the Country; The Day I Met Marie; All My Love; Congratulations; Big Ship; Goodbye Sam Hello Samantha; Power To All Our Friends; Devil Woman; We Don't Talk Anymore; Carrie; Dreaming; Wired for Sound; Daddy's Home; Silhouette; Saviour's Day
Richie, Lionel	USA		1980s–present	Endless Love; Truly; All Night Long; Running in the Night; Hello; Stuck On You; Penny Lover; Say You Say Me; Dancing on the Ceiling; Ballerina Girl
Robinson, Smokey	USA		1950s–present	Smokey Robinson and The Miracles songs: Sheree Baby; Shop Around; You've Really Got A Hold On Me; I Second That Emotion; Tracks of my Tears; The Tears of a Clown; I Don't Blame You At All. Smokey Robinson solo songs: Love Machine; Being with You
Rolling Stones, The	Britain	Mick Jagger (vocals, harmonica) Keith Richard (rhythm guitar) Brian Jones (lead guitar) Bill Wyman (bass) Charlie Watts (drums) Mick Taylor (lead guitar 1969–74) Ron Wood (lead guitar 1974–present)	1960s–present	Come On; I Wanna Be Your Man; Not Fade Away; It's All Over Now; Little Red Rooster; Time Is On My Side; The Last Time; Satisfaction; Get Off Of My Cloud; 19th Nervous Breakdown; Paint It Black; Out of Time; Have You Seen Your Mother Baby Standin' In The Shadows?; Let's Spend the Night Together; Jumpin' Jack Flash; Honky Tonk Woman; Brown; Sugar; Fool To Cry; Miss You; Emotional Rescue; Start Me Up; Harlem Shuffle; Under Cover of the Night
Ross, Diana	USA		1970s–present	Ain't No Mountain High Enough; I'm still Waiting; Touch Me in The Morning; All of My Life; You Are Everything; Theme from Mahogany; One Love In My Lifetime; Upside Down; My Old Piano; It's My Turn; Endless Love; Chain Reaction

Name	Country of origin	Group members*	Period	Major hits
Roxy Music	Britain	Bryan Ferry (vocals) Andy MacKay (saxophone, woodwind) Phil Manzanera (guitar) Brian Eno (keyboards) Rik Kenton (bass) Paul Thompson (drums)	1970s–90s	Virginia Plain; Pyjamarama; Street Life; Love Is The Drug; Dance Away; Angel Eyes; Over You; Oh Yeah; Avalon; The Same Old Scene; The Same Old Scene; Jealous Guy; More Than This
Sex Pistols, The	Britain	Johnny Rotten (vocals) Steve Jones (guitar) Sid Vicious (bass) Paul Cook (drums)	1970s	God Save The Queen; Pretty Vacant; Holidays in the Sun; Something Else; C'Mon Everybody; Silly Thing
Shadows, The	Britain	Hank Marvin (lead guitar) Bruce Welch (rhythm guitar) Brian Bennett (drums) Jet Harris (bass 1958–62, left band) Tony Meehan (drums 1958–61, replaced by Bennett)	1960s–present	Apache; Man of Mystery; The Stranger; The Frightened City; Kon-Tiki; Wonderful Land; Guitar Tango; Dance On; Foot Tapper; Atlantis; Shindig; The Rise and Fall of Angel Bunt; Don't Make My Baby Blue; Riders in the Sky
Simon and Garfunkel	USA	Paul Simon (vocals, guitar) Art Garfunkel (vocals)	1960s–70s	The Sound of Silence; Homeward Bound; I am a Rock; Scarborough Fair; 58th Street Bridge Song; Mrs Robinson; The Boxer; Bridge Over Troubled Water
Simon, Paul	USA		1970s–present	Kodachrome; Loves Me Like A Rock; Slip Slidin' Away; Late in the Evening; Fifty Ways to Leave Your Lover; American Theme; You Can Call Me Al
Simple Minds	Britain	Jim Kerr (vocals) Charlie Burchill (guitar) Mike McNeil (keyboards) John Giblin (bass) Mel Gaynor (drums)	1980s–present	Promised You a Miracle; Waterfront; Don't You Forget About Me; Sanctify Yourself; All the Things She Said; Belfast Child
Simply Red	Britain	Mick Hucknall (vocals) Sylvan Richardson (guitar) Fritz McIntyre (keyboards) Tony Bowers (bass) Chris Joyce (drums) Tim Kellett (horns)	1980s–present	Holding Back The Years; Money's Too Tight To Mention; The Right Thing; If You Don't Know Me By Now
Smiths, The	Britain	Morrissey (vocals) Johnny Marr (guitar) Andy Rourke (bass) Mike Joyce (drums)	1980s	What Difference Does It Make?; Heaven Knows I'm Miserable Now; William It Was Really Nothing; Panic; Shoplifters of the World Unite; Sheila Take a Bow; Girlfriend in a Coma
Springfield, Dusty	Britain		1960s–present	I Only Want To Be With You; I Just Don't Know What To Do With Myself; Wishin' and Hopin'; You Don't Have To Say You Love Me; Island of Dreams; Say I Won't Be There; Losing You; In the Middle of Nowhere; Some of Your Lovin'; All I See Is You; I Close My Eyes and Count to Ten; Son of a Preacher Man; What Have I Done To Deserve This; In Private
Springsteen, Bruce	USA		1970s–present	The River; Hungry Heart; Fire; Dancing in the Dark; Cover Me; Born in the USA; I'm On Fire; Born to Run

Arts and culture

Classic pop and rock groups/singers (continued)

Name	Country of origin	Group members*	Period	Major hits
Status Quo	Britain	Francis Rossi (guitar, vocals) Rick Parfitt (guitar, vocals) Alan Lancaster (bass) John Coghlan (drums)	1960s–present	*Pictures of Matchstick Men; Ice in the Sun; Paper Plane; Caroline; Break the Rules; Down Down; Roll Over Lay Down; Rain; Mystery Song; Wild Side of Life; Again and Again; Whatever You Want; Lies; Somethin' 'Bout You Baby I Like; Dear John; The Wanderer; Rockin' All Over The World; Rollin' Home; In The Army Now; Burning Bridges*
Stewart, Rod	Britain		1970s–present	*Maggie May; You Wear It Well; Oh No Not My Baby; Sailing; Tonight's The Night; The Killing of Georgie; I Don't Want to Talk About It; You're In My Heart; Hotlegs; D'Ya Think I'm Sexy? Tonight I'm Yours; Young Turks; Baby Jane; What Am I Gonna Do? Infatuation; Some Guys Have All the Luck; Every Beat of My Heart; Downtown Train; It Takes Two; Rhythm of the Heart*
Sting	Britain		1980s–present	*Spread a Little Happiness; Russians; We'll Be Together; An Englishman in New York*
Stranglers, The	Britain	Hugh Cornwell (vocals, guitar) Dave Greenfield (keyboards) Jean-Jacques Burnel (bass) Jet Black (drums)	1970s–present	*Peaches; Something Better Change; No More Heroes; Five Minutes; Nice'n'Sleazy; Golden Brown; European Female; Skin Deep; All Day and All of the Night*
Summer, Donna	USA		1970s–present	*Love to Love You Baby; I Feel Love; I Remember Yesterday; Down Deep; Last Dance; MacArthur Park; Heaven Knows; Hot Stuff; Bad Girls; Dim All the Lights; No More Tears; On The Radio; The Wanderer; State of Independence; She Works Hard for the Money; This Time I Know It's For Real; I Don't Wanna Get Hurt*
Supremes, The	USA	Diana Ross (vocals) Mary Wilson (vocals) Florence Ballard (vocals)	1960s–70s	*Where Did Our Love Go?; Baby Love; Come See About Me; Stop! In The Name of Love; Back In My Arms Again; I Hear a Symphony; You Can't Hurry Love; You Keep Me Hangin' On; Love Is Here And Now You're Gone; The Happening; In And Out Of Love; Love Child; I'm Gonna Make You Love Me; I Second That Emotion; Someday We'll Be Together; Up The Ladder to the Roof; Stoned Love; Floy Joy; River Deep Mountain High*
T-Rex	Britain	Marc Bolan (vocals, guitar) Steve Peregrine Took (percussion)	1960s–70s	*Ride a White Swan; Hot Love; Get It On; Jeepster; Telegram Sam; Metal Guru; Children of the Revolution; Solid Gold Easy Action; Twentieth Century Boy; The Groover; Truck On; Teenage Dream; I Love to Boogie*

Name	Country of origin	Group members*	Period	Major hits
Talking Heads	USA	David Byrne (guitar, vocals) Tina Weymouth (bass) Jerry Harrison (keyboards) Chris Frantz (drums)	1970s–present	*Psycho Killer; Once in a Lifetime; Burning Down the House; Road to Nowhere; And She Was*
Temptations, The	USA	Eddie Kendricks (vocals) Otis Williams (vocals) Paul Williams (vocals) Melvin Franklin (vocals) David Ruffin (vocals)	1960s–present	*The Way You Do The Things You Do; My Girl; Ain't Too Proud to Beg; Beauty is Only Skin Deep; You're My Everyhng; Get Ready; Papa Was a Rollin' Stone; Treat Her Like a Lady*
10CC	Britain	Graham Gouldman (vocals, guitar) Eric Stewart (vocals, guitar) Lol Creme (vocals, guitar) Kevin Godley (vocals, drums)	1970s	*Rubber Bullets; The Dean and I; Wall Street Shuffle; Life Is A Minestrone; I'm Not In Love; Art For Art's Sake; I'm Mandy Fly Me; Things We Do For Love; Good Morning Judge; Dreadlock Holiday*
Turner, Tina	USA		1960s–present	Ike and Tina Turner songs: *It's Gonna Work Out Fine; River Deep Mountain High; Proud Mary* Tina Turner solo songs: *Let's Stay Together; What's Love Got To Do With It?; Better Be Good To Me; We Don't Need Another Hero; The Best; I Don't Wanna Lose You; Steamy Windows; Private Dancer*
U2	Ireland	Bono (vocals) The Edge (guitar) Adam Clayton (bass) Larry Mullen, Jr (drums)	1980s–present	*New Year's Day; Sunday Bloody Sunday; Two Hearts Beat As One; Pride; The Unforgettable Fire; The Streets Have No Name; With or Without You; I Still Haven't Found What I'm Looking For; Desire; Angel of Harlem; When Love Comes to Town; All I Want Is You*
Waits, Tom	USA		1970s–present	*Ol' 55; Downtown Train; Sea of Love*
Warwick, Dionne	USA		1960s–present	*Anyone Who Had a Heart; Walk On By; A Message to Martha; I Say a Little Prayer; Do You Know The Way To San José?; This Girl's In Love With You; You've Lost That Lovin' Feeling; I'll Never Fall In Love Again; Then Came You; I'll Never Love This Way Again; Déjà Vu; Heartbreaker; All The Love In The World; That's What Friends Are For*
White, Barry	USA		1970s–present	*I'm Gonna Love You Just A Little More; Baby; Never Gonna Give You Up; I'm Under the Influence of Love; Can't Get Enough of Your Love Babe; You're The First The Last My Everything; What Am I Gonna Do With You?; Let The Music Play; You See The Trouble With Me; It's Ecstasy When You Lay Down Next To Me*
Who, The	Britain	Pete Townshend (guitar) Roger Daltrey (vocals) John Entwhistle (bass) Keith Moon (drums)	1960s–80s	*Can't Explain; Anyway Anyhow Anywhere; My Generation; Substitute; I'm A Boy; Happy Jack; Pictures of Lily; I Can See For Miles; Pinball Wizard; Won't Get Fooled Again; Squeeze Box; Who Are You? You Better You Bet*

Music

Classic pop and rock groups/singers (continued)

Name	Country of origin	Group members*	Period	Major hits
Wonder, Stevie	USA		1960s–present	Fingertips – Pt 2; Uptight; A Place in the Sun; I Was Made to Love Her; For Once in My Life; My Cherie Amour; Yester-Me, Yester-You, Yesterday; Never Had A Dream Come True; Signed Sealed Delivered I'm Yours; You Are the Sunshine of My Life; Superstition; Living for the City; He's Misstra Know It All; I Wish; Sir Duke; Master Blaster; I Ain't Gonna Stand For It; Lately; Happy Birthday; Jammin'; Ebony and Ivory; I Just Called to Say I Love You; Part-Time Lover
Young, Neil	Canada		1960s–	Albums: After The Goldrush; Harvest; Time Fades Away; Rust Never Sleeps; American Stars'n'Bars; Comes A Time; Live Rust; Trans
Zappa, Frank	USA		1960s–present	Memories of El Monte Albums: Absolutely Free; Hot Rats; Burnt Weeny Sandwich; Weasels Ripped My Flesh; Over-Nite Sensation; Apostrophe; Sheik Yerbouti

International music festivals

Festival	Date founded	Location	Time of year
Aldeburgh Festival	1948	Aldeburgh, Suffolk	Summer
Aspen Music Festival	1949	Aspen, Colorado	Summer
Bayreuth Festival (Richard Wagner Festival)	1876	Bayreuth, Bavaria	Summer
Berkshire Festival	1937	Stockbridge, Massachusetts	Summer
Glyndebourne Festival	1934	nr Lewes, East Sussex	Summer
Llangollen International Music Eisteddfod	1947	Llangollen, Clwyd, N Wales	Summer
Marlboro Music Festival	1951	Malboro, Vermont	Summer
Montreux International Jazz Festival	1967	Montreux, Switzerland	Summer
Newport Jazz Festival	1954	Newport, Rhode Island (until 1971, then in NYC)	Summer
Salzburg Festival	1920	Salzburg	Summer
Santa Fe Opera	1957	Santa Fe, New Mexico	Summer
Spoleto Festival (Festival of the Two Worlds)	1958	Spoleto, Italy	Summer

Pulitzer Prize in music

1943	Secular Cantata No 2, A Free Song William Schuman	1954	Concerto for Two Pianos and Orchestra Quincy Porter
1944	Symphony No 4 (Op. 34) Howard Hanson	1955	The Saint of Bleecker Street Gian Carlo Menotti
1945	Appalachian Spring Aaron Copland	1956	Symphony No 3 Ernest Toch
1946	The Canticle of the Sun Leo Sowerby	1957	Meditations on Ecclesiastes Norman Dello Joio
1947	Symphony No 3 Charles Ives	1958	Vanessa Samuel Barber
1948	Symphony No 3 Walter Piston	1959	Concerto for Piano and Orchestra John La Montaine
1949	Louisiana Story music Virgil Thomson		
1950	The Consul Gian Carlo Menotti	1960	Second String Quartet Elliott Carter
1951	Music for opera Giants in the Earth Douglas Stuart Moore	1961	Symphony No 7 Walter Piston
		1962	The Crucible Robert Ward
1952	Symphony Concertante Gail Kubik	1963	Piano Concerto No 1 Samuel Barber

1966	*Variations for Orchestra* Leslie Bassett	1981	*No award*
1967	*Quartet No 3* Leon Kirchner	1982	*Concerto for Orchestra* Roger Sessions
1968	*Echoes of Time and the River* George Crumb	1983	*Three Movements for Orchestra* Ellen T Zwilich
1969	*String Quartet No 3* Karel Husa	1984	*Canti del Sole* Bernard Rands
1970	*Time's Encomium* Charles Wuorinen	1985	*Symphony River Run* Stephen Albert
1971	*Synchronisms No 6 for Piano and Electronic Sound* Mario Davidowsky	1986	*Wind Quintet IV* George Perle
		1987	*The Flight into Egypt* John Harbison
1972	*Windows* Jacob Druckman	1988	*12 New Etudes for Piano* William Bolcom
1973	*String Quartet No 3* Elliott Carter	1989	*Whispers Out of Time* Roger Reynolds
1974	*Notturno* Donald Martino	1990	*Duplicates: A Concerto for Two Pianos and Orchestra* Mel Powell
1975	*From the Diary of Virginia Woolf* Dominick Argento	1991	*Symphony* Shulamit Ran
1976	*Air Music* Ned Rorem	1992	*The Face of the Night, The Heart of the Dark* Wayne Peterson
1977	*Visions of Terror and Wonder* Richard Wernick		
1978	*Déjà Vu for Percussion Quartet and Orchestra* Michael Colgrass		SPECIAL AWARD
		1992	*Maus* Art Spiegelmann
1979	*Aftertones of Infinity* Joseph Schwantner	1993	*Trombone Concerto* Christopher Rouse
1980	*In Memory of a Summer Day* David Del Tredici		

National anthems/songs

Country	Title	Composer	Adopted
Australia	*Advance Australia Fair*[a]	Peter Dodds McCormick	1977
Canada	*O Canada*	Calixa Lavallée	1980
France	*La Marseillaise*	Claude-Joseph Rouget de Lisle	1795
Japan	*Kimigayo ('His Majesty's Reign')*	Hayashi Hiromori	not offically adopted
Russian Federation	*State Hymn of the Russian Federation*	Mikhail Glinka	adopted 1991
West Germany	*Deutschland-lied ('Song of Germany')*	Haydn	1950
UK	*God Save the Queen/King*	not known	18th-c
US	*The Star Spangled Banner*	John Stafford Smith	1931

[a]National tune. The official anthem is *God Save the Queen/King* played when a regal or vice-regal personage is present.

DANCE

Dance personalities

Name	Dates	Place of birth	Occupation
Ailey, Alvin	1931–89	Texas	Dancer, choreographer (ballet); formed the Alvin Ailey American Dance Theatre in 1958
Ailian, Dai	1916–	Trinidad	Dancer, choreographer (ballet); 1959 cofounder of Central Ballet of China
Alonso, Alicia	1921–	Havana	Dancer, choreographer; founder of Ballet de Cuba; formed the Alicia Alonso Company, 1948
Alston, Richard	1948–	Sussex	Choreographer (modern dance)
Amagatsu, Yushio	1948–		Choreographer (modern dance)
Argentina, La (Antonia Mercé)	1890–1936	Buenos Aires	Dancer (Spanish dance)
Armitage, Karole	1954–	Madison, Wisconsin	Dancer, choreographer (ballet)
Ashton, Sir Frederick (Wiliam Mallandaine)	1906–88	Guayaquil, Ecuador	Dancer, choreographer (ballet)
Babilée Jean (Jean Gutman)	1923–	Paris	Dancer, choreographer (ballet)
Balanchine, George (Georgi Melitonovich Balanchivadze)	1904–83	St Petersburg	Dancer, choreographer
Baryshnikov, Mikhail Nikolayevich	1948–	Riga	Dancer (ballet)
Bausch, Pina	1940–	Solingen, Germany	Dancer, choreographer, director (ballet)
Beauchamp, Pierre	1637–1705	Versailles	Dancer, choreographer, ballet master
Béjart, Maurice	1927–	Marseilles	Founder of Ballet Béjart, 1954 (modern ballet)
Benesh, Rudolph	1916–75	London	Dance notator
Bennett, Michael	1943–87	Buffalo, New York	Dancer, choreographer (musical)
Berkeley, Busby	1895–1976	Los Angeles	Choreographer (film)
Bessmertnova, Natalia	1941–	Moscow	Ballerina

Dance personalities (continued)

Name	Dates	Place of birth	Occupation
Bolm, Adolph	1884–1951	St Petersburg	Dancer, choreographer, teacher (ballet)
Borovansky, Edouard	1902–59	Prerov	Dancer, choreographer, ballet director
Bournonville, August	1805–79	Copenhagen	Choreographer
Brown, Trisha	1936–	Aberdeen, Washington	Choreographer; cofounder of Judson Dance Company, 1962 (experimental dance)
Bruce, Christopher	1945–	Leicester	Choreographer (ballet/modern dance)
Bruhn, Erik	1928–86	Copenhagen	Dancer, ballet director
Bujones, Fernando	1955–	Florida	Dancer (ballet)
Butcher, Rosemary	1947–	Bristol	Choreographer (experimental dance)
Camargo, Maria Anna de	1710–70	Brussels	Ballerina
Clark, Michael	1962–	Aberdeen	Dancer, choreographer (ballet/modern dance)
Cohan, Robert	1925–	Brooklyn, New York	Choreographer, dancer, director (modern dance)
Cranko, John	1927–73	Rustenburg, S Africa	Dancer, choreographer director (ballet)
Culberg, Birgit Ragnhild	1908–	Nyköping, Sweden	Dancer, choreographer director (ballet)
Cunningham, Merce	1919–	Centralia, Washington	Dancer, choreographer, director, teacher (modern dance)
Danilova, Alexandra (Dionysievna)	1904–	Peterhof	Dancer (ballet)
Dantzig, Rudi von	1933–	Amsterdam	Dancer, choreographer, ballet director
Davies, Siobhan	1950–	London	Choreographer, dancer; formed Siobhan Davies Company, 1988 (contemporary dance)
Dean, Laura	1945–	New York	Dancer, choreographer, teacher (ballet/modern dance)
De Basil, Colonel Wassili	1881–1951	Kaunas	Ballet impresario
DeMille, Agnes	1909–93	New York City	Choreographer (ballet)
Diaghilev, Sergei (Pavlovich)	1872–1929	Novgorod	Ballet impresario and founder of Ballets Russes
Dolin, Anton (Patrick Healey-Kay)	1904–83	Slinfold, Sussex	Dancer, choreographer; cofounder of the Markova–Dolin Ballet
Dowell, Anthony	1943–	London	Dancer (ballet); director of the Royal Ballet
Duncan, Isadora	1877–1927	San Francisco	Dancer, choreographer (ballet)
Dunham, Katherine	1910–	Chicago	Dancer (ballet)
Dunn, Douglas	1942–	Palo, Alto, California	Dancer, choreographer (experimental dance)
Dupond, Patrick	1959–	Paris	Dancer (ballet)
Falco, Louis	1942–	New York City	Dancer, choreographer (contemporary dance)
Farrell, Suzanne	1945–	Cincinatti, Ohio	Dancer (ballet)
Feld, Eliot	1942–	Brooklyn, New York	Dancer, choregrapher (ballet/modern dance)
Fokine, Michel (Mikhail Mikhaylovich Fokine)	1880–1942	St Petersburg	Dancer, choreographer (creator of modern ballet)
Fonteyn, Dame Margot (Margaret Hookham)	1919–91	Reigate	Ballerina
Forsythe, William	1949–	New York City	Dancer, choreographer (contemporary dance)
Fosse, Bob	1927–87	Chicago	Choreographer (film and theatre)
France, Celia	1921–	London	Dancer (ballet); National Ballet of Canada founded under her directorship, 1951
Franklin, Frederic	1914–	Liverpool	Dancer, teacher, ballet director
Fuller, Loie	1862–1928	Illinois	Dancer, choreographer (performance art)
Gable, Christopher	1940–	London	Dancer (ballet)
Gielgud, Maina	1945–	London	Dancer, artistic director, teacher (modern dance)
Gilpin, John	1930–83	Southsea	Dancer (ballet)
Gordon, David	1936–	Brooklyn, New York	Choreographer (experimental dance)
Graham, Martha	1849–91	Pittsburgh, Pennsylvania	Dancer, teacher, choreographer (modern dance)
Grahn, Lucile	1819–1907	Copenhagen	Ballerina
Grant, Alexander	1925–	Wellington, New Zealand	Dancer (ballet)
Grey, Dame Beryl (Mrs Beryl Svenson)	1927–	London	Ballerina
Grigorovich, Yuri (Nikolayevich)	1927–	St Petersburg	Dancer, teacher, choreographer (ballet)
Hawkins, Erick	1909–	Colorado	Dancer, choreographer, teacher (ballet/modern dance)

Name	Dates	Place of birth	Occupation
Haydée, Marcia (Marcia Salavery Pereira de Silva)	1939–	Niteroi, Brazil	Ballerina
Helpmann, Sir Robert (Murray)	1909–86	Mount Gambier, Australia	Dancer, choreographer (ballet)
Hightower, Rosella	1920–	Ardmore, Oklahoma	Dancer, teacher (ballet)
Holm, Hanya (Johanna Eckert)	1893–1992	Worms	Dancer, choreographer, teacher (modern dance)
Humphrey, Doris	1895–1958	Oak Park, Illinois	Dancer, choreographer, teacher (modern dance)
Ivanov, Lev (Ivanovich)	1834–1901	Moscow	Choreographer (ballet)
Jamison, Judith	1943–	Philadelphia	Dancer
Joffrey, Robert (Abdullah Jaffa Anver Bey Khan)	1930–88	Seattle	Dancer, choreographer, teacher, ballet director
Jooss, Kurt	1901–79	Waaseralfingen	Choreographer (ballet)
Kain, Karen	1951–	Hamilton, Ontario	Ballerina
Karsavina, Tamara (Platonovna)	1885–1978	St Petersburg	Ballerina
Kaye, Nora	1920–87	New York	Ballerina
Kidd, Michael	1949–	Brooklyn, New York	Dancer, choreographer, director (modern ballet/musical)
Kirkland, Gelsey	1952–	Bethlehem, Pennsylvania	Dancer (ballet)
Kirstein, Lincoln	1907–	Rochester, New York	Impresario and ballet director
Kylian, Jiri	1947–	Prague	Dancer, choreographer (ballet)
Laban, Rudolf von	1879–1958	Pozsony, Hungary (now Bratislava, Slovakia)	Dancer, choreographer, dance theoretician (modern dance)
Lander, Harald	1905–71	Copenhagen	Dancer, choreographer, teacher (modern ballet)
Larrieu, Daniel	1957–	Marseilles	Dancer, choreographer (modern ballet)
Legat, Nicolai	1869–1937	St Petersburg	Dancer, choreographer, teacher, ballet master
Lifar, Serge	1905–86	Kiev	Dancer, choreographer (ballet)
Limon, Jose	1908–72	Culiacan, Mexico	Dancer, choreographer, teacher (modern dance)
Lophukov, Fyodor	1886–1973	St Petersburg	Dancer, choreographer, teacher (modern ballet/modern dance)
MacDonald, Elaine	1943–	Tadcaster	Ballerina
MacMillan, Sir Kenneth	1929–92	Dunfermline	Dancer, choreographer, ballet company director; artistic director of Royal Ballet from 1970 and principal choreographer from 1977
Makarova, Nataliya (Romanovna)	1940–	St Petersburg	Ballerina
Manen, Hans van	1932–	Amstel, Netherlands	Dancer, choreographer, director (ballet)
Marin, Maguy	1951–	Toulouse	Dancer, choreographer (modern ballet)
Markova, Dame Alicia (Lilian Alicia Marks)	1910–	London	Prima ballerina
Martins, Peter	1946–	Copenhagen	Dancer (ballet)
Massine, Leonide	1896–1979	Moscow	Dancer, choreographer (ballet)
Messerer, Asaf	1903–	Vilnius	Dancer, teacher, choreographer (ballet)
Mitchell, Arthur	1934–	New York	Dancer, choreographer, director; founder of Dance Theater of Harlem, 1971 (ballet/modern dance)
Moiseyev, Igor Alexandrovich	1906–	Kiev	Dancer, choreographer, ballet director; founded the State Ensemble of Classical Ballet, 1967
Mordkin, Mikhail	1880–1944	Moscow	Dancer, teacher (ballet)
Morris, Mark	1956–	Seattle	Dancer, choreographer; founded Mark Morris Dance Group, 1980 (modern dance)
Murphy, Graeme	1951–	Melbourne	Dancer, choreographer, ballet director (ballet/contemporary dance)
Nijinska, Bronislava	1891–1972	Minsk	Dancer, choreographer (ballet)
Nijinsky, Vaslav	1890–1950	Kiev	Dancer, choreographer (ballet/modern ballet)
North, Robert	1945–	Charleston, S Carolina	Dancer, choreographer (contemporary dance)
Noverre, Jean-Georges	1727–1810	Paris	Dancer, choreographer, ballet master
Nureyev, Rudolf (Hametovich)	1938–93	Irkutsk, Siberia	Dancer (ballet); director at Paris Opera from 1983

Dance personalities (continued)

Name	Dates	Place of birth	Occupation
Panov, Valeri	1938–	Vitebsk	Dancer (ballet)
Pavlova, Anna	1881–1931	St Petersburg	Ballerina
Paxton, Steve	1939–	Tucson, Arizona	Dancer, choreographer (experimental dance)
Petipa, Marius	1818–1910	Marseilles	Dancer, choreographer, ballet master; created *The Sleeping Beauty* and *Swan Lake*
Petit, Roland	1924–	Paris	Choreographer and dancer; founded Ballets de Paris de Roland Petit, 1948, and Ballet de Marseille, 1972
Petronio, Stephen	1956–	New Jersey	Dancer, choreographer (experimental dance)
Plisetskaya, Maya (Mikhaylovna)	1925–	Moscow	Ballerina
Praagh, Peggy van	1910–90	London	Dancer, teacher, ballet director
Rainer, Yvonne	1934–	San Francisco	Dancer, choreographer (experimental dance)
Rambert, Dame Marie (Cyvia Rambam)	1888–1982	Warsaw	Dancer, teacher; founded Ballet Rambert, 1935 (ballet/modern dance)
Reitz, Dana	1948–	New York	Dancer, choreographer (ballet)
Robbins, Jerome	1918–	New York City	Dancer, choreographer, director (musical)
Saint-Leon, (Charles Victor) Arthur	1821–70	Paris	Choreographer (ballet)
Sallé, Marie	1707–56	Paris	Ballerina
Schaufuss, Peter	1949–	Copenhagen	Dancer (ballet)
Seymour, Lynn	1939–	Wainright, Canada	Ballerina
Shearer, Moira (Moira King)	1926–	Dunfermline	Ballerina
Sibley, Dame Antoinette	1939–	Bromley	Ballerina
Sokolow, Anna	1912–	Hartford, Connecticut	Dancer, choreographer, teacher (modern dance)
Spoerli, Heinz	1941–	Basel	Dancer, choreographer, ballet director
Takei, Kei	1939–	Tokyo	Post-modern dancer and choreographer
Taylor, Paul (Belville)	1930–	Pittsburgh	Choreographer (modern dance)
Tetley, Glen	1926–	Cleveland, Ohio	Dancer, choreographer (contemporary ballet)
Tharp, Twyla	1942–	Portland, Indiana	Dancer, choreographer (modern dance)
Tudor, Antony (William Cook)	1908–87	London	Choreographer (ballet)
Ulanova, Galina (Sergeyevna)	1910–	St Petersburgh	Ballerina
Valois, Dame Ninette (Edris Stannus) de	1898–	Co. Wicklow, Ireland	Ballerina; founder of Sadler's Wells Ballet, 1931
Villella, Edward	1936–	New York	Dancer (ballet)
Wagoner, Dan	1932–	Springfield, W Virginia	Dancer, choreographer (modern dance)
Wigman, Mary (Marie Wiegmann)	1886–1973	Hanover	Dancer, choreographer, teacher (modern dance)
Zakharov, Rostislav	1907–84	Astrakhan	Dancer, choreographer, teacher, ballet director

Ballets

Ballet	Composer	Choreographer	First performed	Ballet	Composer	Choreographer	First performed
Anastasia	Tchaikovsky	MacMillan	1971	Chant du Rossignol, Le	Stravinsky	Massine	1920
Apollon Musagète	Stravinsky	Bolm	1928				
Appalachian Spring	Copland	Graham	1944	Cinderella	Prokofiev	Zakharov	1945
				Concerto Barocco	Bach	Balanchine	1941
L' Après-midi d'un Faune	Debussy	Nijinsky	1912	Coppélia	Delibes	Saint-Leon	1870
				Don Quixote	Minkus	Petipa	1869
Bayadère, La	Minkus	Petipa	1877	Elite Syncopations	Joplin	MacMillan	1974
Biches, Les	Poulenc	Nijinska	1924	Enigma Variations	Elgar	Ashton	1968
Billy the Kid	Copland	Loring	1938	Fille Mal Gardée, La	Various (traditional French songs)	Dauberval	1789
Bolero	Ravel	Nijinska	1928				
Boutique Fantastique, La	Rossini	Massine	1919				
				Firebird, The	Stravinsky	Fokine	1910
Burrow, The	Martin	MacMillan	1958	Four Seasons, The	Verdi	MacMillan	1975
Cain and Abel	Panufnik	MacMillan	1968	Giselle	Adam	Coralli/Perrot	1841
Carmen	Bizet	Petit	1949				

Ballet	Composer	Choreographer	First performed	Ballet	Composer	Choreographer	First performed
Gods Go A-Begging, The	Handel	Balanchine	1928	Prince of the Pagodas, The	Britten	Cranko	1957
Hamlet	Tchaikovsky	Helpmann	1942	Prodigal Son, The	Prokofiev	Balanchine	1929
Harlequinade	Drigo	Balanchine	1965	Rake's Progress, The	Gordon	De Valois	1935
Hermanas, Las	Martin	MacMillan	1963				
Illuminations	Britten	Ashton	1950	Rendez-Vous, Les	Auber	Ashton	1933
Invitation, The	Seiber	MacMillan	1960	Rhapsody	Rachman-inov	Ashton	1980
Isadora	Rodney Bennett	MacMillan	1981	Rite of Spring, The	Stravinsky	Nijinsky	1913
Ivan The Terrible	Prokofiev	Grigorovich	1975	Rituals	Bartok	MacMillan	1975
Jeune Homme et La Mort, Le	Bach	Petit	1946	Romeo and Juliet	Prokofiev	Psota	1938
				Rooms	Hopkins	Sokolow	1955
Knight Errant	Strauss (Richard)	Tudor	1968	Russian Soldier, The	Prokofiev	Fokine	1942
Judas Tree, The	Elias	MacMillan	1992	Saisons, Les	Glazunov	Petipa	1900
Labyrinth	Schubert	Massine	1941	Scènes de Ballet	Stravinsky	Dolin	1944
Lady and the Fool, The	Verdi	Cranko	1954	Scotch Symphony	Mendelssohn	Balanchine	1952
				Serenade	Tchaikovsky	Balanchine	1934
Lady of the Camellias	Chopin	Neumeier	1978	Seven Deadly Sins	Weill	Balanchine	1933
Lament of the Waves	Masson	Ashton	1970	Scheherezade	Rimsky-Korsakov	Fokine	1910
Legend of Joseph	Strauss (Richard)	Fokine	1914	Sleeping Beauty, The	Tchaikovsky	Petipa	1890
Luna, La	Bach	Béjart	1991	Song of the Earth	Mahler	MacMillan	1965
Malade Imaginaire, Le	Rota	Béjart	1976	Spectre de la Rose, Le	Weber	Fokine	1911
Manon	Massenet	MacMillan	1974	Stoics Quartet	Mendelssohn	Burrows	1991
Masques, Les	Poulenc	Ashton	1933	Summerspace	Feldman	Cunningham	1958
Mathilde	Wagner	Béjart	1965	Swan Lake	Tchaikovsky	Reisinger	1877
Mayerling	Liszt	MacMillan	1978	Sylphides, Les	Chopin	Fokine	1907
Midsummer Night's Dream	Mendelssohn	Balanchine	1962	Symphonic Variations	Franck	Ashton	1946
Month in the Country, A	Chopin	Ashton	1976	Symphonie Fantastique	Berlioz	Massine	1936
Night Journey	Schumann	Graham	1947	Symphony in C	Bizet	Balanchine	1991
Night Shadow	Rieti	Balanchine	1946	Tales of Hoffmann	Offenbach	Darrell	1972
Nocturne	Delius	Ashton	1936	Taming of the Shrew	Scarlatti-Stolze	Cranko	1969
Nutcracker, The	Tchaikovsky	Ivanov	1892	Three-Cornered Hat, The	De Falla	Massine	1919
Ondine	Henze	Ashton	1958				
Onegin	Tchaikovsky	Cranko	1965	Vainqueurs, Les	Wagner	Béjart	1969
Orpheus	Stravinsky	Balanchine	1948	Valse, La	Ravel	Nijinska	1929
Papillons, Les	Schumann	Fokine	1913	Variations	Stravinsky	Balanchine	1966
Parade	Satie	Massine	1917	Voluntaries	Poulenc	Tetley	1973
Patineurs, Les	Meyerbeer	Ashton	1937	Walk to the Paradise Garden, The	Delius	Ashton	1972
Petrushka	Stravinsky	Fokine	1911				
Pineapple Poll	Sullivan	Cranko	1951				
Present Histories	Schubert	Tuckett	1991				
Prince Igor	Borodin	Ivanov	1890				

Dance companies

Name	Date founded	Location	Name	Date founded	Location
Alvin Ailey Dance Company	1958	New York	Ballets de Paris	1948	France
American Ballet Theater	1940	New York	Ballet Rambert	1926	London
Australian Ballet, The	1962	Melbourne	Ballet Russe de Monte Carlo	1938	Monte Carlo
Australian Dance Theatre	1965	Adelaide	Ballets Russes de Sergei Diaghilev (now known as Kirov Ballet)	1909–29	St Petersburg
Ballet des Champs-Elysées	1944	Paris			
Ballet Jooss	1933	Cambridge, UK	Ballets Suedois	1920	France

Dance companies (continued)

Name	Date founded	Location
Ballet Théâtre Contemporain	1968	Amiens
Ballet du Xième Siecle (formerly Ballet Béjart, 1953)	1960	Brussels moved to Lausanne, 1988)
Ballet West	1968	Salt Lake City, Utah
Birmingham Royal Ballet (formerly the Sadler's Wells Royal Ballet)	1946	Birmingham
Bolshoi Ballet	1776	Moscow
Borovansky Ballet	1942	Melbourne
Boston Ballet	1964	Boston
Dance Theater of Harlem	1971	New York
English National Ballet (originally London Festival Ballet)	1950	London
Feld Ballet NY	1974	New York
Grands Ballets Canadiens, Les	1956	Montreal
Houston Ballet	1968	Houston
Joffrey Ballet	1954	New York
Jose Limon Dance Company	1946	New York
Kirov Ballet	1935	St Petersburg
Lar Lubovitch Dance Company	1968	New York
London City Ballet	1978	London
London Contemporary Dance Theatre	1967	London
Maly Ballet	1915	St Petersburg
Martha Graham Dance Company	1927	New York

Name	Date founded	Location
Merce Cunningham Dance Company	1952	New York
Miami City Ballet	1986	Miami
National Ballet	1962	Washington
National Ballet of Canada	1951	Toronto
National Ballet of Cuba	1948	Havana
National Ballet of Mexico	1949	Mexico City
Netherlands Dance Theatre	1959	The Hague
New York City Ballet	1948	USA
Nikolais Dance Theatre	1951	New York
Northern Ballet	1969	Manchester
Pennsylvania Ballet	1963	Philadelphia
Pilobolus Dance Theatre	1971	Vermont
Pittsburgh Ballet Theater	1970	Pittsburgh
Royal Ballet	1931	Covent Garden, London
Royal Danish Ballet	16th-c	Copenhagen
Royal New Zealand Ballet Company (as from 1984)	1961	Wellington
Royal Swedish Ballet	17th-c	Stockholm
Royal Winnipeg Ballet	1938	Canada
San Francisco Ballet	1933	USA
School of American Ballet (now the American Ballet)	1933	New York
Scottish Ballet	1956	Glasgow
Stanislavsky Ballet	1929	Moscow
Stuttgart Ballet	17th-c	Germany
Washington Ballet	1962	Washington
Western Theatre Ballet	1957	Bristol

DESIGN

Design personalities

Name	Dates	Nationality	Field of work
Aalto, Alvar	1898–1976	Finnish	Furniture, particularly bentwood designs
Ashbee, Charles Robert	1863–1942	British	Arts and crafts designer, particularly jewellery, also wallpaper, pottery, and carpets; founded the Guild of Handicraft, 1888
Baillie Scott, Mackay Hugh	1865–1945	British	Stained glass, ironwork, mosaics, furniture, wallpaper
Barnsley, Sidney	1865–1926	British	Furniture
Behrens, Peter	1868–1940	Austrian	Furniture, glass, cutlery, fabrics
Bell, Vanessa	1879–1961	British	Murals and interiors
Berlage, Hendrik Petrus	1856–1934	Dutch	Interior design, furniture, ironwork
Bindesboll, Thorvald	1846–1908	Danish	Ceramics
Brandt, Edgar	1880–1960	French	Metalwork
Brandt, Marianne	1893–	German	Metalwork and lighting; designed the Kandem bedside table light
Brangwyn, Frank	1867–1956	British	Graphics
Breuer, Marcel	1902–81	Hungarian	Furniture
Bugatti, Carlo	1855–1940	Italian	Furniture
Burges, William	1827–81	British	Furniture (Yatman cabinet, Great Bookcase) and interior design
Burne-Jones, Sir Edward	1833–98	British	Stained glass and tapestries
Charpentier, Alexandre	1856–1909	French	Posters, furniture, metalwork, ceramics, interiors

Arts and culture

Name	Dates	Nationality	Field of work
Chermayeff, Serge	1900–	Russian	Furniture, carpets, decorative work
Cliff, Clarice	1899–1972	British	Ceramics
Cooper, John Paul	1869–1933	British	Silversmith and jeweller
Crane, Walter	1845–1915	British	Illustrator and book designer
Czeschka, Carl Otto	1878–1960	Austrian	Jewellery, embroidery, stained glass
Daum, Auguste and Antonin	1853–1909 1864–1930	French	Glasswork
Day, Lewis F	1845–1910	British	Stained glass, wallpaper, textiles, jewellery, furniture
Deck, Theodore	1823–91	French	Pottery
Decoeur, Emile	1876–1953	French	Ceramics
Delaherche, Auguste	1857–1940	French	Ceramics
Doat, Taxile	1851–1938	French	Ceramics
Dorn, Marion	1900–64	American	Textiles
Dresser, Christopher	1834–1904	British	Silver plate, ceramics, glass, furniture, textiles
Dufrene, Maurice	1876–1955	French	Interior design
Dufy, Raoul	1877–1953	French	Textiles
Dunand, Jean	1877–1942	Swiss	Furniture, metalwork, lacquerwork
Eames, Charles	1907–78	American	Furniture
Eastlake, Charles	1836–1906	British	Furniture
Elmslie, George Grant	1871–1952	Scottish	Furniture, metalwork, stained glass, embroidery
Erp, Dirk van	1860–1933	American	Metalworker
Erté (Romain de Tirtoff)	1892–	Russian	Graphics
Fabergé, Carl	1846–1920	Russian	Jewellery
Farge, John La	1835–1910	American	Stained glass
Feure, Georges De	1869–1928	French	Interiors, furniture, porcelain, glass
Finch, Alfred William	1854–1930	Belgian	Ceramics
Fisher, Alexander	1864–1936	British	Enamelling
Follot, Paul	1877–1941	French	Jewellery, textiles, interiors, furniture, ceramics; designed the 'Pomone' dinner service for Wedgwood
Frankl, Paul	1886–1958	Austrian	Furniture
Fry, Roger	1866–1934	British	Founder of the Omega workshop, producing furniture, textiles, stained glass, pottery
Gaillard, Eugene	1862–1933	French	Textiles, furniture, interiors
Gallé, Emile	1846–1904	French	Glass and furniture
Gate, Simon	1883–1943	Swedish	Glass
Gaudi, Antonio	1852–1926	Spanish	Metalwork and furniture
Gill, Eric	1882–1940	British	Sculpture and typography
Gimson, Ernest	1864–1919	British	Furniture
Gomperz, Lucie Marie	1902–	Austrian	Pottery
Grant, Duncan	1885–1978	British	Murals
Grasset, Eugène	1841–1917	Swiss	Textiles, wallpapers, stained glass, ceramics, jewellery
Gray, Eileen	1879–1976	British	Lacquerwork
Greene, Charles Sumner	1868–1957	American	Furniture
Gropius, Walter	1883–1969	German	Furniture; director of Bauhaus
Grueby, William H	1867–1925	American	Pottery
Guimard, Hector	1867–1942	French	Ironwork, decorative work; designed the Paris metro entrance signs
Gulberg, Elsa	1886–na	Swedish	Textiles
Hald, Edward	1883–na	Swedish	Glass
Hansen, Frieda	1855–1931	Norwegian	Textiles
Heal, Ambrose	1872–1959	British	Furniture
Hoffmann, Josef	1870–1956	Austrian	Furniture (Kubus chair), metalwork, textiles, jewellery; founder of the Wiener Werkstatte, 1903
Holiday, Henry	1839–1927	British	Stained glass
Horta, Victor	1861–1947	Belgian	Interiors
Jensen, Georg	1866–1935	Danish	Silver and jewellery
Joel, Betty	1896–na	British	Furniture and textiles
Knox, Archibald	1864–1933	British	Silver
Koehler, Florence	1861–1944	American	Jewellery
Krog, Arnold	1856–1931	Danish	Ceramics
Lalique, Réné	1860–1945	French	Goldsmith; jewellery and glass
Leach, Bernard	1887–1979	British	Ceramics
Lethaby, William	1857–1931	British	Furniture
Livemont, Privat	1861–1936	Belgian	Graphics

Design personalities (continued)

Name	Dates	Nationality	Field of work
Lurcat, Jean	1892–1966	French	Ceramics and tapestry
Mackintosh, Charles Rennie	1868–1928	British	Interiors, furniture, cutlery, stained glass, jewellery
Mackmurdo, Arthur	1851–1942	British	Metalwork, furniture, wallpaper, embroidery; founder of the Century Guild, 1884
Mathews, Arthur and Lucia	1860–1945 1870–1955	American	Murals; founded the Furniture Shop and Philopolis magazine
Morgan, William de	1839–1917	British	Ceramics
Morris, William	1834–96	British	Wallpaper, textiles, carpets, tapestry, typography; leader of the Arts and Crafts Movement
Moser, Koloman	1868–1918	Austrian	Graphics
Mucha, Alphonse	1860–1939	Czech	Art and poster design
Munthe, Gerhard	1849–1929	Norwegian	Furniture
Muthesius, Hermann	1861–1927	German	Interiors and furniture; founder of the Deutscher Werkbund, 1907
Nash, Paul	1889–1946	British	Textiles, upholstery, posters
Nilsson, Wiven	1870–1942	Swedish	Silver
Nordstrom, Patrick	1870–1929	Swedish	Pottery
Obseiger, Robert	1884–1940	Austrian	Pottery
Olbrich, Josef Maria	1867–1908	Austrian	Cofounder of the Vienna Secession
Pabst, Daniel	1826–1910	American	Furniture and cabinet making
Parrish, Maxfield	1870–1966	American	Graphics and poster design
Peche, Dagobert	1887–1923	Austrian	Art, metalwork
Pick, Frank	1878–1941	British	Poster design and typography; responsible for design for the London Underground
Poiret, Paul	1879–1944	French	Interior design, costume design
Ponti, Gio	1891–1979	Italian	Furniture
Prutscher, Otto	1880–1949	Austrian	Furniture and jewellery
Puiforcat, Jean	1897–1945	French	Silversmith
Quarti, Eugenio	1867–1931	Italian	Furniture
Redon, Odilon	1840–1916	French	Lithography, etching
Riegel, Ernst	1871–1946	German	Goldsmith and silversmith
Riemerschmied, Richard	1868–1957	German	Interiors, furniture, porcelain, glass, cutlery; founder member of Deutscher Werkbund
Rietveld, Gerritt Thomas	1888–1964	Dutch	Furniture
Robineau, Adelaide	1865–1929	American	Ceramics; edited the *Keramic Studio*
Rohe, Ludwig Mies van der	1886–1969	German	Furniture; last head of Bauhaus
Rohlfs, Charles	1853–1936	American	Furniture
Rousseau, Clement	1872–na	French	Furniture
Ruskin, John	1819–1900	British	Social critic and inspiration for the Arts and Crafts Movement
Russell, Gordon	1892–1980	British	Furniture
Ryggen, Hannah	1894–1970	Norwegian	Textiles
Serrurier-Bovy, Gustave	1858–1910	Belgian	Ironwork, furniture, wallpaper, stained glass
Staite-Murray, William	1861–1910	British	Ceramics
Stam, Mart	1899–na	Dutch	Designed the first cantilever chair
Stickley, Gustav	1858–1942	American	Furniture; founded *The Craftsman* magazine, 1901
Taylor, William Howson	1876–1935	British	Ceramics; founded the Ruskin Pottery, 1898
Tiffany, Louis Comfort	1848–1933	American	Jewellery, stained glass, art glass, interiors
Voysey, Charles Annesley	1857–1941	British	Wallpaper and textile pattern design, furniture, tableware, lighting
Wagenfeld, Wilhelm	1900–	German	Goldsmith; metalwork, glass, porcelain
Webb, Philip	1831–1915	British	Furniture
Wilson, Henry	1864–1934	British	Silversmith
Wimmer, Joseph Eduard	1882–1961	Austrian	Metalwork; codirector of the Wiener Werkstatte
Wolfe, Elsie de	1865–1950	American	Interior design
Wolfers, Philippe	1858–1929	Belgian	Jewellery
Zen, Carlo	1851–1918	Italian	Cabinet maker
Zen, Pietro	1879–1950	Italian	Furniture

na = not available.

FASHION

Fashion designers

Name	Dates	Place of birth
Alaia, Azzedine	na	Busto Arsizio
Amies, Sir (Edwin) Hardy	1909–	London
Armani, Giorgio	1935–	Piacenza
Ashley, Laura	1925–85	Merthyr Tydfil
Azagury, Jacques	1958–	Casablanca
Balenciaga, Cristobal	1895–1972	Guetaria, Spain
Balmain, Pierre (Alexandre Claudius)	1914–82	St Jean de Maurienne
Banks, Jeff	1943–	Ebbw Vale, Wales
Beene, Geoffrey	1927–	Haynesville, Louisiana
Beretta, Anne-Marie	1937–	Beziers, France
Blass, Bill	1922–	Fort Wayne, Indiana
Bohan, Marc (Roger Maurice Louis)	1926–	Paris
Cacharel, Jean (Louis Henri Bousquet)	1932–	Nîmes
Capucci, Roberto	1929–	Rome
Cardin, Pierre	1922–	Venice
Cerruti, Nino (Antonio)	1930–	Biella, Italy
Chanel, Gabrielle (Coco)	1883–1971	Saumur
Conran, Jasper	1959–	London
Courrèges, André	1923–	Pau, France
De la Renta, Oscar	1932–	Santo Domingo
Desses, Jean (Jean Dimitrie Verginie)	1904–70	Alexandria
Dior, Christian	1905–57	Granville, Normandy
Erté (Romain de Tirtoff)	1892–	St Petersburg
Fiorucci, Elio	1935–	Milan
Fortuny, Mariano (Mariano Fortuny y Madrazo)	1871–1949	Granada
Galliano, John (Charles)	1960–	Gibraltar
Gaultier, Jean-Paul	1952–	Paris
Givenchy, Hubert James Marcel Taffin de	1927–	Beauvais
Halston (Roy Halston Frowick)	1932–	Des Moines, Iowa
Hamnett, Katharine	1948–	Gravesend, Kent
Hartnell, Sir Norman	1901–78	Honiton, Devon
Hechter, Daniel	1938–	Paris
Herrera, Caroline	1939–	Venezuela
Jackson, Betty	1940–	Backup, Lancashire
Karan, Donna	1948–	Forest Hills, New York
Kenzo, Takada	1940–	Kyoto
Klein, Anne Hannah (Hannah Golofski)	1921–74	New York
Klein, Calvin (Richard)	1942–	New York
Lacroix, Christian	1951–	Arles
Lagerfeld, Karl	1939–	Hamburg
Lanvin, Jeanne	1867–1946	Brittany

Name	Dates	Place of birth
Lapidus, Ted	1929–	Paris
Laroche, Guy	1923–89	La Rochelle, nr Bordeaux
Lauren, Ralph (Ralph Lifschitz)	1939–	New York City
Lelong, Lucien	1889–1958	Paris
Mainbocher (Main Rousseau Bocher)	1891–1976	Chicago
Maxwell, Vera (Vera Huppe)	1901–	New York
Michiko, Koshino	1950–	Osaka
Missoni, Tai Otavio	1921–	Yugoslavia
Miyake, Issey	1938–	Hiroshima
Molyneux, Edward Henry	1891–1974	London
Montana, Claude	1949–	Paris
Moschino, Franco	1950–	Italy
Mugler, Thierry	1948–	Strasbourg
Muir, Jean (Elizabeth)	1933–	London
Oldfield, Bruce	1950–	London
Ozbek, Rifat	1955–	Istanbul
Patou, Jean	1880–1936	Normandy
Poiret, Paul	1879–1944	Paris
Pucci, Emilio, Marchese di Barsento	1914–93	Naples
Quant, Mary	1934–	London
Rabanne, Paco (Francisco de Rabaneda-Cuervo)	1934–	San Sebastian
Reger, Janet	1935–	London
Rhodes, Zandra	1940–	Chatham, Kent
Ricci, Nina (Maria Nielli)	1883–1970	Turin
Rochas, Marcel	1902–55	Paris
Saint-Laurent, Yves (Henri Donat Mathieu)	1936–	Oran, Algeria
Scherrer, Jean-Louis	1936–	Paris
Schiaparelli, Elsa	1896–1973	Rome
Simonetta (Duchesa Simonetta Colonna di Cesaro)	1922–	Rome
Stavropoulos, George	1920–	Tripolis, Greece
Stiebel, Victor	1907–76	Durban
Strauss, Levi	na	Bavaria
Tarlazzi, Angelo	1945–	Ascoli Piceno, Italy
Ungaro, Emmanuel (Maffeolti)	1933–	Aix-en-Provence
Valentino (Valentino Garavani)	1933–	Voghera, Italy
Versace, Gianni	1946–	Calabria
Von Furstenburg, Diane (Diane Michelle Halfin)	1946–	Brussels
Westwood, Vivienne	1941–	Tintwistle
Worth, Charles Frederick	1825–95	Bourn, Lincolnshire
Yamamoto, Yohji	1943–	Tokyo

na = not available.

Clothes care

⊠ Do not iron

⊿ Can be ironed with *cool* iron (up to 110°C)

⊿ Can be ironed with *warm* iron (up to 150°C)

⊿ Can be ironed with *hot* iron (up to 200°C)

⊯ Hand wash only

⊟ Can be washed in a washing machine; the number shows the most effective washing temperature (in °C)

⊟ Reduced (medium) washing conditions

⊟ Much reduced (minimum) washing conditions (for wool products)

⊠ Do not wash

⊙ Can be tumble-dried (one dot within the circle means a low temperature setting; two dots for higher temperatures)

⊠ Do not tumble-dry

⊗ Do not dry-clean

Ⓐ Dry-cleanable (letter indicates which solvents can be used) A: all solvents

Ⓕ Dry-cleanable F: white spirit and solvent 11 can be used

Ⓟ Dry-cleanable P: perchloroethylene (tetrachloroethylene), white spirt, solvent 113 and solvent 11 can be used

Ⓟ Dry-cleanable, if special care taken

△ Chlorine bleach may be used with care

⊠ Do not use chlorine bleach

International clothing sizes

Size equivalents are approximate, and may display some variation between manufacturers.

Women's suits/dresses

UK	US	UK/Continent
8	6	36
10	8	38
12	10	40
14	12	42
16	14	44
18	16	46
20	18	48
22	20	50
24	22	52

Women's hosiery

UK/US	UK/Continent
8	0
$8^1/_2$	1
9	2
$9^1/_2$	3
10	4
$10^1/_2$	5

Adults' shoes

UK	US/(ladies)	UK/Continent
4	$5^1/_2$	37
$4^1/_2$	6	38
5	$6^1/_2$	38
$5^1/_2$	7	39
6	$7^1/_2$	39
$6^1/_2$	8	40
7	$8^1/_2$	41
$7^1/_2$	$8^1/_2$	42
8	$9^1/_2$	42
$8^1/_2$	$9^1/_2$	43
9	$10^1/_2$	43
$9^1/_2$	$10^1/_2$	44
10	$11^1/_2$	44
$10^1/_2$	$11^1/_2$	45
11	12	46

Children's shoes

UK/US	UK/Continent
0	15
1	17
2	18
3	19
4	20
5	22
6	23
7	24
8	25
$8^1/_2$	26
9	27
10	28
11	29
12	30
13	32

Men's suits and overcoats

UK/US	Continental
36	46
38	48
40	50
42	52
44	54
46	56

Men's shirts

UK/US	UK/Continent
12	30–1
$12^1/_2$	32
13	33
$13^1/_2$	34–5
14	36
$14^1/_2$	37
15	38
$15^1/_2$	39–40
16	41
$16^1/_2$	42
17	43
$17^1/_2$	44–5

Men's socks

UK/US	UK/Continent
$9^1/_2$	38–9
10	39–40
$10^1/_2$	40–1
11	41–2
$11^1/_2$	42–3

International pattern sizes

Young junior/teenage

Size	Bust cm	in	Waist cm	in	Hip cm	in	Back waist length cm	in
5/6	71	28	56	22	79	31	34.5	13½
7/8	74	29	58	23	81	32	35.5	14
9/10	78	30½	61	24	85	33½	37	14½
11/12	81	32	64	25	89	35	38	15
13/14	85	33½	66	26	93	36½	39	15⅜
15/16	89	35	69	27	97	38	40	15¾

Half-size

Size	Bust cm	in	Waist cm	in	Hip cm	in	Back waist length cm	in
10½	84	33	69	27	89	35	38	15
12½	89	35	74	29	94	37	39	15¼
14½	94	37	79	31	99	39	39.5	15½
16½	99	39	84	33	104	41	40	15¾
18½	104	41	89	35	109	43	40.5	15⅞
20½	109	43	96	37½	116	45½	40.5	16
22½	114	45	102	40	122	48	41	16⅛
24½	119	47	108	42½	128	50½	41.5	16¼

Misses

Size	Bust cm	in	Waist cm	in	Hip cm	in	Back waist length cm	in
6	78	30½	58	23	83	32½	39.5	15½
8	80	31½	61	24	85	33½	40	15¾
10	83	32½	64	25	88	34½	40.5	16
12	87	34	67	26½	92	36	41.5	16¼
14	92	36	71	28	97	38	42	16½
16	97	38	76	30	102	40	42.5	16¾
18	102	40	81	32	107	42	43	17
20	107	42	87	34	112	44	44	17¼

Women's

Size	Bust cm	in	Waist cm	in	Hip cm	in	Back waist length cm	in
38	107	42	89	35	112	44	44	17¼
38	107	42	89	35	112	44	44	17¼
42	117	46	99	39	122	48	44.5	17½
44	122	48	105	41½	127	50	45	17⅝
46	127	50	112	44	132	52	45	17¾
48	132	52	118	46½	137	54	45.5	17⅞
50	137	54	124	49	142	56	46	18

ARCHITECTURE

The orders of architecture

Composite   Corinthian   (Greek) Doric   Ionic   Tuscan

Architects

Name	Dates	Place of birth	Selected works
Aalto, Alvar	1898–1976	Kuortane, Finland	Designed public and industrial buildings, and some furniture.
Abercrombie, Sir (Leslie) Patrick	1879–1957	Ashton-upon-Mersey	Pioneer of town planning. His major work was the replanning of London – County of London Plan (1943) and Greater London Plan (1944).
Adam, Robert	1728–92	Kirkcaldy, Fife	Architect of the King's works in 1761–9. Examples of his work are Home House in London's Portland Square, Landsdown House, Derby House, and Register House in Edinburgh.
Alberti, Leon Battista	1404–72	Genoa	One of the most brilliant figures of the Renaissance, who worked in Florence from 1428.
Alessi, Galeazzo	1512–72	Perugia	Gained recognition in Europe for his designs for churches and palaces in Genoa.
Ammanti, Bartolommeo	1511–92	Settignano	Designed the Ducal Palace at Lucca and part of the Pitti palace and the Ponte Sta Trinita in Florence.
Archer, Thomas	1668–1743	Tanworth	Baroque architect responsible for the churches of St John's, Westminster (1714) and St Paul's, Deptford (1712). He also designed part of Chatsworth House.
Arnolfo di Cambio	1245–1302	Colle di Valdelsa, Tuscany	Major work is the design of Florence Cathedral.
Asplund, Erik Gunnar	1885–1940	Stockholm	Major works are concentrated in Stockholm: the Stockholm City Library (1924–7), the Woodland Chapel, Skandia Cinema. He was responsible for most of the exhibits in the Stockholm Exhibition of 1930.
Baker, Sir Herbert	1862–1946	Kent	Designed Groote Schur, near Cape Town, the Union Government buildings in Pretoria, and worked with Edward Lutyens on the design of New Delhi, India. In Britain he designed the new Bank of England and South Africa House, and Rhodes House in Oxford.
Barry, Sir Charles	1795–1860	London	Palace of Westminster (1840).
Basevi, George	1794–1845	London	In classic revivalist style he designed the Fitzwilliam Museum, Cambridge; laid out part of Belgravia; and designed a number of country houses and Gothic churches.
Behrens, Peter	1868–1940	Hamburg	Designed the AEG turbine assembly works in glass and steel. Also designed workers houses in Stuttgart and Vienna, and the German embassy in St Petersburg.
Berlage, Hendrick Petrus	1856–1934	Amsterdam	Designed the Amsterdam Bourse (1903); Holland House, London (1914); and the Gemeente Museum in the Hague (1934).
Blacket, Edmund Thomas	1817–83	Southwark	Government architect for New South Wales in 1849, but returned to private practice in 1854 and designed the New South Wales University. He adopted Victorian Gothic style for his work on ecclesiastical buildings, including Sydney and Perth cathedrals, but classical forms for his commercial projects, such as banks and hotels.
Borromini, Francesco	1599–1667	Bissone, Lake Lugano	San Carlo alle Quattro Fontane (1637–41), Rome.
Boullée, Etienne-Louis	1728–99	Paris	He became architect to the King of Prussia in 1762. His pre-Revolution Neo-Classical work includes the Hotel de Brunoy, Paris (1772).
Boyd, Robin Penleigh	1919–71	Melbourne	Influential critical works which shaped the future direction of Australian architecture.
Bramante, Donato	c.1444–1514	nr Urbino	Renovation of the Vatican and St Peter's (1505–6).
Breuer, Marcel (Lajos)	1902–81	Pécs	Student of the Bauhaus from 1921 and took charge of the furniture workshop in 1924. His architectural works were designed with Bernard Zehrfuss and Pier Luigi Nervi, and include the UNESCO building in Paris.

Name	Dates	Place of birth	Selected works
Brosse, Salomon de	1565–1626	Verneuil-sur-Oise	Designed the Luxembourg Palace, Paris (1615–20), and Louis XIII's hunting lodge at Versailles (1624–26).
Brunelleschi, Filippo	1377–1446	Florence	Dome of Florence Cathedral (1417–34).
Burges, William	1827–81	London	Architecture employed strong mediaeval style. Designed Castell Coch (1876–81) as a hunting lodge for the third marquess of Bute; Cardiff Castle (1876–81); Cork Cathedral (1862–76); and a house in Park Place (1870s).
Burton, Decimus	1800–81	London	Planned the Regent's Park colosseum and in 1825 designed the new layout of Hyde Park and the Triumphal Arch at Hyde Park Corner. Also designed the Palm House at Kew Gardens (1844–8).
Butterfield, William	1814–1900	London	Leading exponent of the Gothic revival and the architect of Keble College, Oxford; St Augustine's College, Canterbury; the chapel and quad at Rugby and St Albans, Holborn.
Campen, Jacob van	1595–1657	Haarlem	Built the first classical building in Holland. Most celebrated work was the Mauritshuis in The Hague (1633). Other works include the Amsterdam Theatre (1637) and Amsterdam Town Hall (1647–55).
Candela, Felix	1910–	Spain	One of the world's foremost designers of reinforced concrete hyperbolic paraboloid shell roofs. His works include the Sports Palace for the Olympic Games in Mexico City (1968).
Casson, Sir Hugh	1910–	London	Directed the architecture of the Festival of Britain (1948).
Chambers, Sir William	1726–96	Stockholm	Designed Somerset House (1776) and the pagoda in Kew Gardens.
Chermayeff, Serge	1900–	Caucasus	Designed De La Warr Pavilion at Bexhill-on-Sea (1933–5).
Churriguera, Done Jose	1650–1725	Salamanca	Royal architect to Charles II and developed the Churrigueresque style. Designed Salamanca Cathedral.
Coates, Wells Wintemute	1895–1958	Tokyo	Leading figure in the modern movement of architecture. Responsible for the design of the BBC studios and the EKCO laboratories as well as many other buildings in Britain and Canada.
Cockerell, Charles Robert	1788–1863	London	Designed the Taylorian Institute and Ashmolean Museum at Oxford.
Costa, Lucio	1902–	Toulouse	Designed the award-winning Eduardo Gunile apartments. Drew up plans for city of Brasilia.
Dance, George	1695–1768	London	Newgate Prison (1770–83).
Doshi, Balkrishna Vithaldas	1927–	Poona, India	Worked as a senior designer with Le Corbusier. Works include the City Hall, Toronto (1958); the Indian Institute of Management (1962–74) in Ahmedabad; and Vidyadhar Nagar New Town, Jaipur.
Dudok, Willem Marinus	1884–1974	Amsterdam	Became city architect of Hilversum in 1915. His most famous works are the Hilversum Town Hall (1928–30) and the Bijenkorf department store in Rotterdam.
Erickson, Arthur Charles	1924–	Vancouver	His work on the Simon Fraser University buildings (1963) in British Columbia brought him international recognition. He also designed the Lethbridge University (1971) in Alberta; the Museum of Anthropology, British Columbia (1971–7); and the Roy Thomson Hall, Toronto (1976–80).
Fischer von Erlach, Johann Bernard	1656–1723	Graz, Austria	Designer of churches and palaces, notably the Karlskirche in Vienna and the University Church at Salzburg.
Fontana, Carlo	1638–1714	Rancate, nr Como	Worked as a papal architect in Rome where he designed many major works such as the fountain in the Piazza di San Petro. He also designed Loyola College in Spain and the Palazzo Durazzo at Genoa.

Architecture

Architects (continued)

Name	Dates	Place of birth	Selected works
Fontana, Domenico	1543–1607	Melide, nr Lugano	Papal architect in Rome, employed on the Lateran Palace, the Vatican Library, and St Peter's Dome.
Foster, Norman	1935–	Manchester	Works include the Willis Faber Dumas building, Ipswich (1979); Sainsbury Centre, University of East Anglia (1977); Hong Kong and Shanghai Bank, Hong Kong (1979–85).
Fowke, Albert	1823–65	Belfast	Planned the Albert Hall, London, and produced the original designs for the Victoria and Albert. Museum. Also planned the Royal Scottish Museum in Edinburgh.
Francesco di Giorgio	1439–1502	Siena	Chief architect of Siena Cathedral.
Gabriel, Jacques Ange	1698–1782	Paris	Court architect to Louis XV, he designed the Petit Trianon (1768) and also laid out the Place de la Concorde (1753).
Garnier, Tony	1869–1948	Lyon	His theoretical work, *Une Cité Industrielle*, made a major contribution to the development of 20th-c urban architecture. His works include the Grange Blanche hospital (1911–27) and the Stadium (1913–18) in Lyon; and the Hôtel de Ville in Boulogne-Bilancourt (1931–3).
Gaudi, (I Cornet) Antonio	1852–1926	Riudoms, Catalonia	Exponent of Catalan 'modernism'; also famous for the Church of the Holy Family in Barcelona.
Gilbert, Cass	1859–1934	Zanesville, Ohio	Remembered as the architect of the first skyscraper, the 60-storey Woolworth Building in New York (1912). Designed many public buildings, including the US Customs House in New York City (1907); the Supreme Court building in Washington DC (1935); and the campuses of the universities of Minnesota (Minneapolis) and Texas (Austin).
Griffin, Walter Burley	1876–1937	Maywood, Illinois	Director of design and construction of the city of Canberra. His plans for the design of the city were adopted in 1925. Designed a number of notable buildings and Castlecrag Estate in north Sydney
Gropius, Walter	1883–1969	Berlin	Founder of Bauhaus movement.
Guarini, Guarino	1624–83	Modena	Designed several churches in Turin: San Lorenzo (1668–80) and Capella della SS Sindone (1668); also the Palazzo Carignano (1679), as well as palaces for Bavaria and Baden.
Guimard, Hector Germain	1867–1942	Lyon	The most important Art Nouveau architect in Paris before World War 1. Designed the Castel Béranger apartment block (1894–8) and is famous for the Paris Metro signs of the 1900s.
Hamilton, Thomas	1784–1858	Glasgow	Designs include the Burns Monument, Galloway (1820); Royal High School, Edinburgh (1823–29); Royal College of Physicians Hall (1844–45), Edinburgh.
Hardwick, Philip	1792–1870	London	Designer of Euston station, Lincoln's Inn Hall and Library, Goldsmith's Hall, and Limerick Cathedral.
Haussmann, Georges Eugene, Baron	1809–91	Paris	Restructured Paris by widening streets, laying out boulevards and parks, and building bridges.
Hawksmoor, Nicholas	1661–1736	East Drayton, Nottinghamshire	Work includes the London churches St Mary Woolnoth, St George's (Bloomsbury), and Christ Church (Spitalfields).
Hoffmann, Josef	1870–1956	Pirnitz, Austria	Leader of the Vienna Secession and founded the Wiener Werkstatte in 1903. His architectural achievements include the Purkersdorf Sanatorium (1903–5) and Stoclet House in Brussels (1905–11). He was city architect for Vienna from 1920.
Holland, Henry	1746–1806	Ledbury	Designed old Carlton House in London, the original Brighton Pavilion and Brook's Club.

Name	Dates	Place of birth	Selected works
Hood, Raymond Mathewson	1881–1934	Rhode Island	The leading designer of skyscrapers in the 1930s. Designed the American Radiator building, New York (1924), the Daily News building (1929–30), the Rockefeller Center (1930–40), and the McGraw-Hill building (1931).
Horta, Victor, Baron	1861–1947	Ghent	Regarded as the originator of Art Nouveau. In Brussels his works include the Maison Tassel (1892–3), the Maison Solray (1894–1900) and the Maison du Peuple (1895–99). He also designed the first department store there, L'Innovation (1901)
Howard, Sir Ebenezer	1850–1928	London	Founder of the Garden City movement.
Jacobsen, Arne	1902–71	Copenhagen	Main public building in Copenhagen was the SAS skyscraper (1955). He also designed St Catherine's College, Oxford.
Johnson, Philip Cortelyou	1906–	Cleveland, Ohio	Designed the Seagram building, New York City (1945); New York State Theater, Lincoln Center (1964); Amon Carter Museum of Western Art, Texas (1961); and the American Telephone and Telegraph Company (1978–84).
Jones, Inigo	1573–1652	London	Introduced the Palladian style to England. His designs include the Queen's House at Greenwich (1616) and the Banqueting House in Westminster (1619–22).
Kahn, Louis Isadore	1901–74	Saaremaa, Estonia	Pioneer of functionalist architecture. Designed the Richards Medical Research Building in Pennsylvania (1957–61); the City Tower Municipal Building in Philadelphia; Yale University Art Gallery (1953); Salk Institute, La Jolla, California (1959–65); the Indian Institute of Management, Ahmedabad (with Doshi); and the Paul Mellon Center, Yale (1969–72).
Kent, William	1685–1748	Bridlington	Designed many public buildings in London, including the Royal Mews, Trafalgar Square, the Treasury buildings, and the Horse Guards block in Whitehall.
Larsen, Henning	1925–		His buildings include the University of Trondheim, institutes of the Freie Universität and the Danish Embassy in Riadh.
Lasdun, Sir Denys	1914–	London	His best-known buildings include the Royal College of Musicians (1958–64); the University of East Anglia (1962–8); the National Theatre, London (1965–76); European Investment Bank, Luxembourg (1975); and the Institute of Education (1970–8).
Le Corbusier (Charles Edouard Jeanneret)	1887–1965	La-Chaux-de-Fonds	First building was the Unité d'Habitation, Marseilles (1945–50). Designed the plans for the city of Chandigarh, the capital of the Punjab. First use of piloti (stilts) in his designs was the Swiss Pavilion on the campus of the Cité Universitaire, Paris.
Ledoux, Claude Nicolas	1736–1806	Dormans, Champagne	Architect to Louis XVI, his major works include the Chateau at Louveciennes; the Saltworks at Arc-et-Senans (1775–80); theatre at Besançon (1771–3).
Lescot, Pierre	c.1515–78	Paris	Major work is the Louvre, Paris.
Loos, Adolf	1870–1933	Brno	One of the major architects of the 'Modern Movement'. He settled in Vienna in 1896.
Lutyens, Sir Edwin	1869–1944	London	His best-known projects are Castle Drogo (1910–30); the Cenotaph in Whitehall; and the laying out of New Delhi, India (1912–30).
Mackintosh, Charles Rennie	1868–1928	Glasgow	Became a leader of the 'Glasgow style', a movement related to Art Nouveau. As well as interiors and furniture, his designs include the Glasgow School of Art (1896–9 and 1906–9).
Maderno, Carlo	1556–1629	Capalgo, Italy	Appointed architect to St Peter's in 1603, where he added a large façade (1606–12). Other important works are Sta Susanna (1597–1603) and the Palazzo Barberini (1628–38).

Architects (continued)

Name	Dates	Place of birth	Selected works
Mansard or Mansart, François	1598–1666	Paris	He brought a simplified adaptation of the Baroque style into France and made fashionable the high-pitched type of roof which bears his name.
Mendelsohn, Erich	1887–1953	Allenstein, Germany	Designed the Einstein Tower in Potsdam, and various hospitals and stores, also the Hebrew University in Jerusalem. From 1941 he worked in the United States, designing synagogues and hospitals.
Mies van der Rohe, Ludwig	1886–1969	Aachen	His designs include the German pavilion for the Barcelona Exhibition (1928), and the Seagram Building, New York (1956–9).
Nash, John	1752–1835	London	Designed Regent's Park and Marble Arch, recreated Buckingham Palace, and laid out Trafalgar Square and St James Park.
Nervi, Pier Luigi	1891–1979	Sondrio, Italy	Designed the Stadium for the Olympic games in Rome (1960) and San Francisco Cathedral (1970).
Neumann, Balthasar	1687–1753	Eger, Germany	Designed many outstanding examples of the Baroque style, notably Würzburg Palace and Schloss Bruchsal.
Niemeyer, Oscar	1907–	Rio de Janeiro	Works include the Church of São Francisco, Pampulha (1942–44); the Exhibition Hall, São Paulo (1953); and in Brasilia the President's Palace, the Cathedrals, and Law Courts.
Oud, Jacobus Johannes Pieter	1890–1963	Purmerend, Netherlands	Launched the review *de Stijl* and became a pioneer of modern architecture based on simplified forms. He became city architect to Rotterdam in 1918.
Palladio, Andrea	1508–80	Vicenza	Developed the style now known as 'Palladian', based on classical Roman principles. He remodelled the basilica at Vicenza and designed many villas, palaces, and churches, particularly in Venice.
Pei, Ieoh Meng	1917–	Canton	Major projects include Mile High Center, Denver; the John Hancock Tower, Boston; and the glass pyramid at the Louvre.
Peruzzi, Baldassare Tommaso	1481–1536	Ancajano	Designed the Villa Farnesina, the Ossoli Palace, and the Palazzo Massimo in Rome.
Piranesi, Giovanni Battista	1720–78	Venice	Major influence on Neo-Classicism.
Playfair, William Henry	1789–1857	London	Designed most of Edinburgh's most important buildings, including the National Gallery of Scotland, the Royal Scottish Academy, and Donaldson's Hospital.
Poelzig, Hans	1869–1936	Berlin	Expressionist architect who served as the city architect for Dresden between 1916 and 1920. Early projects included the Luban Chemical Works, Posen, and the Water Tower and Exhibition Hall, Posen (1911–12). Later works were the remodelling of the Grosses Schauspielhaus, Berlin (1919); Salzburg Festival Theatre (1920–2); and the I G Farben Headquarters, Frankfurt (1928–31).
Pugin, Augustus	1812–52	London	Designed a large part of the decorations and sculpture for the new Houses of Parliament (1836–7) and did much to revive Gothic architecture in Britain.
Rietveld, Gerrit Thomas	1888–1964	Utrecht	Works include the Schroder House, Utrecht (1924), and the Van Gogh Museum, Amsterdam (completed posthumously 1973).
Rogers, Richard	1933–	Florence	Architect of often controversial works, examples of which include the Centre Pompidou, Paris (1971–9), and Lloyds of London (1979–85).
Saarinnen, Eero	1910–61	Kirkonnumi, Finland	His designs for Expressionist buildings include the Trans-World Airline Kennedy Terminal, New York.
Sangallo, Antonio Giamberti da	1485–1546	Florence	Leading architect of the High Renaissance in Rome, designing the Palazzo Palma-Baldassini, Rome (c.1520), and the Palazzo Farnese, Rome (1534–46).

Name	Dates	Place of birth	Selected works
Scott, Sir George Gilbert	1811–78	Gawcott, Buckinghamshire	The leading practical architect of the British Gothic Revival, as seen in the Albert Memorial (1862–3), St Pancras Station and Hotel (1865); and Glasgow University (1865).
Scott, Sir Giles Gilbert	1880–1960	London	Designed the Anglican cathedral in Liverpool (1924); the new buildings at Clare College, Cambridge, and Cambridge University Library (1931–4); the new Bodleian Library, Oxford (1936–46). He designed the new Waterloo Bridge (1939–45); and was responsible for the rebuilding of the House of Commons after World War 2.
Shaw, (Richard) Norman	1831–1912	Edinburgh	Major works include the Old Swan House, Chelsea (1876); New Scotland Yard (1888); the Gaiety Theatre, Aldwych (1902); and the Piccadilly Hotel (1905).
Smirke, Sir Robert	1781–1867		Significant buildings include Covent Garden Theatre (1809) and the British Museum (1823–47). He also designed the General Post Office (1824–9) and the College of Physicians (1825).
Soane, Sir John	1753–1837	Goring, Oxfordshire	His designs include The Bank of England (1792–1833) and Dulwich College Art Gallery (1811–14).
Soufflot, Jacques	1713–80	Irancy	Leading exponent of Neo-Classicism, designing the Panthéon and École de Droit, Paris; the Hotel Dieu, Lyon; and Rennes Cathedral.
Spence, Sir Basil	1907–76	Bombay	The leading post-war architect; examples of his work include the pavilion for the Festival of Britain (1951) and the new Coventry Cathedral (1951).
Sullivan, Louis	1856–1924	Boston	His experimental, functional skeleton constructions of skyscrapers and office blocks, particularly the Gage Building and stock exchange, earned him the title of the 'Father of Modernism'.
Tait, Thomas Smith	1882–1954		Prominent architect of the inter-war period, designing Adelaide House (1921–4) and the Daily Telegraph offices (1927) in London, and St Andrew's House, Edinburgh (1934).
Tange, Kenzo	1913–	Tokyo	Works include the Hiroshima Peace Centre (1949–55), the Shizoka Press and Broadcasting Centre (1966–7), and the National Gymnasium for the 1964 Olympic Games.
Utzon, Jørn	1918–	Copenhagen	Designer of the Sydney Opera House; the Kuwait House of Parliament; Copenhagen's Bagsuaerd Church and Paustian's House of Furniture.
Vignola, Giacomo da	1507–73	Vignola	In Rome he designed the Villa di Papa Giulio and the Church of the Gesù.
Viollet-le-Duc, Eugene	1814–79	Paris	Restored the cathedrals of Notre Dame, Amiens, and Laon; and the Chateau de Pierrefonds.
Vitruvius (Marco Vitruvius Pollio)	1st-c AD	Rome	Architect and engineer. He wrote the *De Architectura*, the only extant Roman treatise on this subject.
Wagner, Otto	1841–1918	Vienna	Considered the founder of the 'modern movement'. His most influential works include Karlsplatz station (1898–9) and Am Steinhof Church (1905–7). His main hall of the K K Sportsparkasse (1904–6) was regarded as the first example of modern architecture in the 20th-c.
Waterhouse, Alfred	1830–1905	Liverpool	Built the romanesque Natural History Museum in London (1873–81); from his great use of red brick came the name 'red-brick university'.
Webb, Sir Aston	1849–1930	London	Designed the Admiralty Arch, Imperial College of Science, and many other buildings in London.
Wood, John (the Elder)	1705–54	Yorkshire	Responsible for many of the well-known streets and buildings of Bath – North and South Parades, Queen Square, the Circus, and Prior Park.

Arts and culture

Architects (continued)

Name	Dates	Place of birth	Selected works
Wren, Sir Christopher	1632–1723	East Knoyle, Wiltshire	After the Great Fire of London he drew up plans for rebuilding the whole city, but the plans were never implemented. He designed the new St Paul's Cathedral in 1669 and then many other public buildings, such as the Greenwich Observatory; the Ashmolean Library, Oxford; part of Hampton Court; The Sheldonian Theatre, Oxford; the Royal Exchange, the Temple Bar, and Greenwich Hospital.
Wright, Frank Lloyd	1869–1959	Richland Center, Wisconsin	One of the leading designers of private dwellings, planned in conformity with the natural features of the land. Among his larger works is the Guggenheim Museum of Art in New York.
Wyatt, James	1746–1813	Burton Constable, Staffordshire	Designed the London Pantheon (1772), but his best known work is the Gothic-Revival Fonthill Abbey (1796–1807).

PAINTING

Artists

Name	Dates	Place of birth	Selected works
Albani, Francesco	1578–1660	Bologna	Altarpieces in the Chapel of the Annunciation, Quirinal Palace, and the choir of St Maria della Pace; frescoes in the chapel of St Diego, church of St Giacomo degli Spagnuoli; *Dance of the Amorini*
Angelico, Fra (Guido di Petro)	c.1400–1455	Vicchio, Tuscany	San Marco frescoes, Florence; *Last Judgement; Orvieto; Coronation of the Virgin; Glory; Pietas*
Antonello da Messina	1430–79	Sicily	San Cassiano altarpiece; *Annunciation*
Bacon, Francis	1909–92	Dublin	*Studio of Velazquez*
Bassano, Jacopo da	c.1510–92	Bassano	*Adoration of the Magi; Crucifixion*
Beardsley, Aubrey	1872–98	Brighton	*Isolde; Salome; Morte d'Arthur*
Bellini, Giovanni	c.1430–1516	Venice	San Giobbe altarpiece; *Madonna with Baptist and another Saint; Bacchanale; Pieta; The Doge Loredano*
Blake, William	1757–1827	London	Illustrations to the Book of Job
Bonnard, Pierre	1867–1947	Paris	*Nude in the Bath; Skating Rink; Red Bodice; La Toilette; Woman in Black Stockings*
Bosch, Hieronymus	1450–1516	Hertogenbosch	*The Garden of Earthly Delights; The Last Judgement*
Botticelli, Sandro	1445–1510	Florence	*Birth of Venus; Primavera; Nativity; Mars and Venus*
Boucher, François	1703–70	Paris	*Birth of Venus*
Boudin, Eugene	1824–98	Honfleur	*Deauville; Harbour at Trouville; Corvette Russe*
Braque, Georges	1882–1963	Argenteuil-sur-Seine	*Piano and Lute; House at L'Estaque; Still Life*
Breughel, Pieter (the Elder)	1520–69	Breda	*Massacre of the Innocents; Peasant Wedding; Hunters in the Snow; The Triumph of Death*
Bronzino, Agnolo Filippo	1503–72	Monticelli	*Venus; Cupid; Folly and Time; Portrait of Lucrezia Panciatichi*
Canaletto (Giovanni Antonio Canal)	1697–1768	Venice	*The Stonemason's Yard; Venice: Piazza San Marco and the Colonnade of the Procuratie Nuove; Scene in Venice; The Piazzetta Entrance to the Grand Canal*
Caravaggio (Michelangelo Merisi)	1573–1610	Caravaggio	*Madonna of the Rosary; Death of the Virgin; Christ at Emmaus; Deposition of Christ; The Conversion of St Paul; The Entombment; The Calling of St Matthew*
Carpaccio, Vittore	c.1460–c.1525	Venice	*Young Knight in a Landscape; Stories of St Ursula; The Presentation in the Temple*
Cézanne, Paul	1839–1906	Aix-en-Provence	*The Bathers; La Maison du Pendu; Les Grandes Baigneuses; The Blue Vase; Man Standing with Hands on Hips*
Chagall, Marc	1887–1985	Vitebsk	*Self-Portrait with Seven Fingers; The Newspaper Seller; Paris Through the Window*
Constable, John	1776–1837	East Bergholt, Suffolk	*The Haywain; Weymouth Bay; Borrowdale; White Horse; Valley Farm; Cornfield*

Name	Dates	Place of birth	Selected works
Corot, Jean-Baptiste-Camille	1796–1875	Paris	*The Bridge at Nantes; The Studio; Chartres Cathedral; Danse des Nymphes; Le Bûcheron; Orphée; Homère et les Bergers; Joueur de Flûte*
Correggio, Antonio	1494–1534	Correggio	*Adoration of the Shepherds; Madonna of St Francis; Madonna of St Sebastian; Jupiter and Io; Nativity; Jupiter and Antiope; Education of Cupid; Danae; Ecce Homo*
Courbet, Gustave	1819–77	Ornans	*The Painter's Studio; Funeral at Ornans; Girls on the Banks of the Seine; Peasants of Flazey*
Dali, Salvador	1904–89	Figueras	*Persistence of Memory; Christ of St John of the Cross*
Daumier, Honoré	1808–79	Marseilles	*La Rue Transnonain; The Washerwoman; Ecce Homo; Third-Class Carriage*
David, Jacques Louis	1748–1825	Paris	*Oath of the Horatii; The Death of Socrates; Portrait of Madame Recamier*
Degas, Edgar	1834–1917	Paris	*Absinthe Drinker; Bellelli Family; Miss Lola at the Cirque Fernando; Dancer at the Bar; Cotton-brokers Office*
Delacroix, Eugène	1798–1863	Charenton-Saint-Maurice	*Women of Algiers; Liberty Guiding the People; The Massacre at Chios*
Delaunay, Robert	1885–1941	Paris	*Eiffel Tower; Fenêtres*
Dix, Otto	1891–1969	Gera	*The Hall of Mirrors; The Artist's Parents; Pimp and Girls; Two Sacrifices of Capitalism; Saul and David; Crucifixion*
Dufy, Raoul	1877–1953	Le Havre	*Nice; Bois de Boulogne; Deauville*
Dürer, Albrecht	1471–1528	Nuremburg	*Self-Portrait; Lamentation on the Dead Christ; Melancolia*
Ernst, Max	1891–1976	Bruhl	*The Elephant Celebes; The Hat Makes the Man; Two Children are Threatened By a Nightingale; Oedipus; Une Semaine de Bonté*
Fantin-Latour, Henri	1836–1904	Grenoble	*Hommage à Delacroix; Still Life; L' Anniversaire*
Fragonard, Jean-Honoré	1732–1806	Grasse	*La Belle Serveuse; The Swing; Bacchante Endormie; La Chemise Enlevée*
Francesca, Piero della	1420–92	Borgo San Sepolcro	*Annunciation; Flagellation; Brera Madonna*
Gainsborough, Thomas	1727–88	Sudbury, Suffolk	*The Morning Walk; Lady Brisco; Lord and Lady Howe; Mrs Portman; Blue Boy*
Gauguin, Paul	1848–1903	Paris	*The Moon and the Earth; La Belle Angele; Whence do we come? What are we? Where do we go?; The Yellow Christ; Vision after the Sermon; Nevermore*
Gentile da Fabriano	c.1370–c.1427	Fabriano	*Adoration of the Magi*
Giotto	1267–1337	Vespignano	*Stefaneschi Triptych; The Lamentation; Death of the Knight of Celano; The Betrayal; The Lives of Christ and the Virgin*
Goya, Francisco	1746–1828	Saragossa	*The Execution of the Rebels; Stilt Walkers; Blind Guitarist; Baptism; Pentecost; Resurrection; Assumption of the Virgin*
Greco, El (Domenikos Theotokopoulos)	1541–1614	Crete	
Grünewald, Mathias	1480–1528	Würzburg	*Crucifixion;* Isenheim altarpiece
Hals, Frans	c.1580–1666	Antwerp	*Portrait of a Married Couple; Merry Drinkers; Banquet of the Officers of St George; The Laughing Cavalier; Gypsy Girl*
Hiroshige, Ando	1797–1858	Edo, Japan	*Ukiyo-e (Pictures of the Floating World); Fifty-three Stages on the Tōkaidō Progress; Portrait of an Artist*
Hodler, Ferdinand	1853–1918	Berne	*Night; The Elect; Eurhythmy; Day; The Battle of Nafels*
Hogarth, William	1697–1764	London	*Marriage à la Mode; Harlot's Progress; Rake's Progress*
Hokusai, Katsushika	1760–1849		*The Great Wave of Kanagawa; Hundred Views of Mount Fuji*
Holbein, Hans (the Younger)	1497–1543	Augsburg	*Portrait of Erasmus of Rotterdam; The Ambassadors*
Hopper, Edward	1882–1967	New York	*Window at Night; Early Sunday Morning; House by the Railroad; Room in Brooklyn; Nighthawks; Second Story Sunlight*
Hunt, William Henry	1790–1864	London	*Peaches and Grapes; Old Pollard; Wild Flowers*
Ingres, Jean Auguste Dominique	1780–1867	Montauban	*Napoleon on the Imperial Throne; Oedipus and the Sphinx; The Dream of Ossian; La Grande Odalisque; Apotheosis of Homer*
John, Augustus	1878–1961	Tenby	*Smiling Woman;* portraits of James Joyce, G B Shaw, Mme Suggia, and Dylan Thomas
Kandinsky, Wasily	1866–1944	Moscow	*Landscape with Red Spot; Painting with a Black Arch; Improvisation V; The Abstract Watercolour; White Line; Blue Segment; Dominant Curve; Affirmed Pink*

Painting

Artists (continued)

Name	Dates	Place of birth	Selected works
Kirchner, Ernst	1880–1938	Aschaffenburg	*Five Women in the Street; Self-Portrait with Model; Woman at the Mirror*
Klee, Paul	1879–1940	Munchenbuchsee	*Red-Green Gardens; Around the Fish; Goldfish Wife; Twittering Machine*
Klein, Yves	1928–62	Nice	*Anthropometries*
Klimt, Gustav	1862–1918	Baumgarten, Austria	*The Kiss; Frau Fritza Riedler; Frau Adele Bloch-Bauer; Beethoven Frieze; Jurisprudence*
Klinger, Max	1857–1920	Leipzig	*The Judgement of Paris; Pietà; Christ in Olympus; Fantasy on Brahms; Eve of the Future; A Life; Of Death*
Kokoschka, Oskar	1886–1980	Pochlarn, Austria	*The Tempest; Knight Errant; Portrait of Dr Tietze and his Wife; Ambassador Maysky*
Laurencin, Marie	1883–1956	Paris	*The Assembly*
Leonardo da Vinci	1452–1519	Vinci, Florence	*Madonna Benois; Madonna Litta; Mona Lisa; The Virgin of the Rocks; Last Supper*
Lichtenstein, Roy	1923–	New York	*M-Maybe; Hopeless; New York City*
Lippi, Fra Filippo	c.1406–69	Florence	*Annunciation; Tarquinia Madonna; The Virgin and the Saints; The Vision of St Bernard; The Adoration of the Magi*
Lorenzetti, Pietro	c.1280/90 –c.1348	Siena	*Deposition; Birth of the Virgin*
Lowry, Lawrence Stephen	1887–1976	Manchester	*Coming from the Mill*
Macke, August	1887–1914	Meschede	*The Storm; Woman with a Green Jacket; The Zoo*
Magritte, René	1898–1967	Lessines	*Ceci n'est pas une Pipe; Duration Knifed; Le Plaisir; The Wind and the Song; The Human Condition*
Manet, Edouard	1832–83	Paris	*Déjeuner sur L'Herbe; Olympia; Portrait of Emile Zola; A Bar at the Folies-Bergères*
Mantegna, Andrea	1431–1506	Vicenza	*Agony in the Garden; Dead Christ; Martyrdom of St Sebastian; San Zeno altarpiece*
Masson, André	1896–1987	Balagny	*Fish in Sand; Dead Horses*
Matisse, Henri	1869–1954	Cateau-Cambresis	*The Yellow Curtain; Girl Swimming in the Aquarium; The Red Room; Portrait of Madame Matisse with a Green Streak; The Snail; Woman with the Hat*
Michelangelo (Buonarotti)	1475–1564	Caprese	*Tondo Doni; Birth of Eve; Universal Judgement; Holy Family of the Tribune; The Last Judgement*
Millais, Sir John Everett	1829–96	Southampton	*Ophelia; Gambler's Wife; The Boyhood of Raleigh; Bubbles*
Millet, Jean-Francois	1814–75	Gruchy	*The Winnower; The Sower; Angelus*
Miró, Joán Stone	1893–1983	Barcelona	*Dutch Interior; The Ploughed Field; Person Throwing a at a Bird*
Modigliani, Amedeo	1884–1920	Livorno	*Red Nude; Portrait of Madame Anna Zborowska; Reclining Nude*
Mondrian, Piet	1872–1944	Amersfoort	*Composition with Red; Yellow and Blue; Tree*
Monet, Claude	1840–1926	Giverny	*Rouen Cathedral; Waterlilies; Women in the Garden; Impression: Sunrise*
Morisot, Berthe	1841–95	Bourges	*The Artist's Sister; Madame Pontillon; Seated on the Grass; The Artist's Sister Edma and their Mother*
Moroni, Giovanni Battista	1525–78	Bondo	*The Tailor*
Munch, Edvard	1863–1944	Loten	*The Scream; Angst; Girls on the Bridge; The Dance of Life; White Night; Marat's Death; Inttell–Self-Portrait*
Nicholson, Ben	1894–1982	Denham	*White Relief*
Nolan, Sir Sidney	1917–92	Melbourne	*Boy and the Moon; Kelly; Leda and the Swan*
Noland, Kenneth	1924–	Asheville, Carolina	*Gift*
Nolde, Emil (Emil Hansen)	1867–1956	Nolde, Germany	*Dance Round the Golden Calf; Red and Yellow Roses; The Life of Christ; Marsh Landscape*
O'Keefe, Georgia	1887–1986	Sun Prairie, Wisconsin	*Blue and Green Music; Black Iris; 'Near Abiquiu; New Mexico'*
Pechstein, Max	1881–1955	Zwickau	*Still Life with African Mask; Indian and Woman*
Picasso, Pablo	1881–1973	Malaga	*The Accordian Player; Les Demoiselles d'Avignon; Bottle of Vieux Marc; Guernica; Girl with a Mandolin; Two Women Running on the Beach*
Pisanello, Antonio	1395–1455	San Visilio	*Vision of St Eustache; The Madonna with Saints Anthony and George; Margherita Gonzaga; Lionello d'Este*

Name	Dates	Place of birth	Selected works
Pissarro, Camille	1830–1903	St Thomas, W Indies	*Entrance to the Village of Voisins; Boulevard Montmartre; Place du Théâtre Français; Bridge at Bruges; 'Orchard with Flowering Fruit Trees, Springtime, Pontoise'; Peasant Girl with a Stick*
Pollock, Jackson	1912–56	Cody, Wyoming	*Number 1; Convergence; Number 12; Lucifer*
Poussin, Nicolas	1594–1665	Les Andelys	*Triumph of Neptune; Autumn; The Adoration of the Golden Calf*
Raphael (Raffaello Sanzio)	1483–1520	Urbino	*Conestabile Madonna; Holy Family; Sistine Madonna; Madonna of the Meadow; The Three Graces; Madonna and Child Enthroned with Saints; La Belle Jardinière; Coronation of the Virgin; Transfiguration; Madonna of Foligno; School of Athens*
Rembrandt (Harmenszoon) van Rijn	1606–69	Leyden	*Self-Portrait with Saskia; Self-Portrait; Flora; The Night Watch; The Jewish Bride; Syndics of the Cloth Drapers' Guild; Dr Tulp's Anatomy Lesson*
Renoir, Pierre Auguste	1841–1919	Limoges	*Le Moulin de la Galette; La Grenouillère; The Two Sisters; Luncheon of the Boating Party*
Roberti, Ercole de	1450–96	Ferrara	*Santa Maria in Porto altarpiece; Madonna; Pietà*
Rossetti, Dante Gabriel	1828–82	London	*Beata Beatrix; The Annunciation; The Girlhood of Mary Virgin; Ecce Ancilla Domini*
Rothko, Mark	1903–70	Dvinsk, Russia	*Number 10; Light Red Over Black*
Rousseau, Henri (le Douanier)	1844–1910	Laval	*The Sleeping Gypsy; Carnival Evening; Myself : Portrait Landscape; Yadivigha's Dream; The Hungry Lion*
Rousseau, Théodore	1812–67	Paris	*Path through the Forest of L'Isle Adam; Effet d'Orage; Forest of Compiègne*
Rubens, Peter Paul	1577–1640	Siegen	*Deposition; Henry IV Receiving the Portrait of Maria de' Medici; Allegory of War; Descent from the Cross; The Crucifixion of St Peter*
Sargent, John Singer	1856–1925	Florence	*Madame Gautreau; Madam X; The Wyndham Sisters; 'Carnation, Lily, Lily, Rose'; Mountain Fire*
Schiele, Egon	1890–1918	Tulln	*Self-Portrait; The Self-Seer; The Cardinal and the Nun; Embrace*
Schwitters, Kurt	1887–1948	Hanover	*The Constellation; Picture with Light Centers; Merzbilden*
Seurat, Georges	1859–91	Paris	*Bathers at Asnières; Sunday Afternoon on the Island of La Grande Jatte; La Baignade; Les Poseuses; Le Cirque*
Signac, Paul	1863–1935	Paris	*The Seine at Asnières; View of the Port of Marseilles*
Signorelli, Luca	c.1441–1523	Cortona	*The Preaching of the Anti-Christ; Last Judgement*
Sisley, Alfred	1839–99	Paris	*Flood at Port Marley; The Boat During the Flood*
Spencer, Sir Stanley	1891–1959	Cookham, Berkshire	*Resurrection: Port Glasgow; Shipbuilding on the Clyde; The Resurrection*
Steer, Philip Wilson	1860–1942	Birkenhead	*Self-Portrait; The Music Room; Portrait of Mrs Hammersley*
Tanguy, Yves	1900–55	Paris	*Fear; Mama Papa is Wounded*
Tiepolo, Giovanni Battista	1696–1770	Venice	*Thetis Comforting Achilles; The Sacrifice of Isaac; Madonna of Carmelo and the Souls of Purgatory; The Banquet of Cleopatra; The Martyrdom of St Sebastian; Time Revealing Truth*
Tintoretto (Jacopi Robusti)	1518–94	Venice	*Miracles of St Mark; Discovery of the Body of St Mark; The Last Supper; The Miracle of the Loaves and Fishes; The Golden Calf; Entombment*
Titian (Tiziano Vecelli)	1490–1576	Pieve di Cadore	*Pietà; Presentation of the Virgin in the Temple; Isabella d'Este; The Gypsy Madonna; Madonna of Frari; Assumption of the Virgin*
Toulouse-Lautrec, Henri	1864–1901	Albi	*Au Moulin Rouge; Les Deux Amis; The Bar; At the Races*
Turner, Joseph Mallord William	1775–1851	London	*Calais Pier; Fall of an Avalanche in the Grisons; Norham Castle; Hannibal Crossing the Alps; Burning of the Houses of Parliament*
Utrillo, Maurice	1883–1955	Paris	*Church at Chatillon; Sacré-Coeur de Montmartre*
Van Dyck, Sir Anthony	1599–1641	Antwerp	*Iconographica; The Deposition; Le Roi à la Chasse*
Van Eyck, Jan	1390–1441	Maastricht	*Arnolfini Wedding Portrait; Adoration of the Lamb*
Van Gogh, Vincent	1853–90	Groot Zundert	*The Night Café; Starry Night; The Potato Eaters; Sunflowers; The Bridge; The Chair and the Pipe*
Velazquez, Diego	1599–1660	Seville	*The Drinkers; Christ in the House of Martha; The Coronation of the Virgin; The Toilet of Venus*
Vermeer, Jan	1632–75	Delft	*A Girl Asleep; Young Woman Reading a Letter; The Letter; The Kitchen Maid; View of Delft; The Love Letter; The Lacemaker*

Sculpture

Artists (continued)

Name	Dates	Place of birth	Selected works
Veronese, Paolo	c.1528–88	Verona	*Feast in the House of Levi; Mars and Venus United by Love; Venice Crowned Queen of the Sea; The Marriage Feast at Cana; The Adoration of the Magi*
Vuillard, Edouard	1868–1940	Cuiseaux	*Under the Trees; Jardin de Paris; Woman Sweeping*
Warhol, Andy	1927–87	Pittsburgh, Pennsylvania	*Campbell's Soup; Marilyn Monroe; Dick Tracy; 100 Soup Cans*
Watteau, Antoine	1684–1721	Valenciennes	*L'Indifférente; Enseigne de Gersaint; Fêtes Galantes; Embarquement pour Cythère*
Whistler, James Abbott McNeill	1834–1903	Lowell, Massachusetts	*Portrait of the Artist's Mother; Old Battersea Bridge; The White Girl; Cremorne Gardens; No.2; Three Figures: Pink and Grey*
Witz, Konrad	1400–46	Rottweil	*Annunciation; Christ Walking on the Water; Miraculous Draft of Fishes*

SCULPTURE

Sculptors

Name	Dates	Place of birth	Selected works
Agostino di Duccio	1418–81	Florence	Tempio Malatestiano decorations, oratory of St Bernadino, Perugia
Andre, Carl	1935–	Massachusetts	*Equivalents; Cedar Piece*
Arp, Hans (Jean)	1887–1966	Strasbourg	*Shell and Head*
Barlach, Ernst	1870–1938	Wedel	*The Avenger; Death*
Bernini, Gian Lorenzo	1598–1680	Naples	*Fontana dei Quattro Fiumi;* Rome, dome of San Carlo alle Quattro Fontane; *Appollo and Daphne; Conaro Chapel*
Brancusi, Constantin	1876–1957	Hobitza	*Bird in Space; The Kiss; Torso of a Young Man*
Brunelleschi, Filippo	1377–1446	Florence	Dome of Florence cathedral; *Sacrifice of Isaac*
Calder, Alexander	1898–1976	Philadelphia	*Joesphine Baker; Romulus and Remus; The Horse; Spring; A Universe; Hanging Mobile; Lobster Trap and Fish Tail; Constellation with Red Object*
Canova, Antonio	1757–1822	Possagno	*Cupid and Psyche; Winged Cupid; Venus and Adonis; Psyche Holding a Butterfly; Penitent Magdalen; Perseus with the Head of the Medusa*
Cellini, Benvenuto	1500–71	Florence	*Perseus with the Head of the Medusa; Nymph; Neptune and Ceres*
Donatello (Donato) di Niccolo	c.1386–1466	Florence	*David; Judith and Holofernes; Cantoria; Magdalen; Gattamelata*
Duchamp, Marcel	1887–1968	Blainville	*The Bride Stripped Bare by her Bachelors; Fountain; Bicycle Wheel*
Duchamp Villon, Ramond	1876–1918	Damville	*Horse; Baudelaire; Maggy; The Seated Woman*
Epstein, Sir Jacob	1880–1959	New York	*Rima; Genesis; Ecce Homo; Christ in Majesty; St Michael and the Devil*
Ghiberti, Lorenzo	c.1378–1455	Florence	*Sacrifice of Isaac; John the Baptist; St Matthew; The Gates of Paradise*
Giacommetti, Alberto	1901–66	Stampo	*Suspended Square; Observing Head; Torso; Cubist Composition; Three Figures Outdoors; Tall Figures; City Square; Chariot*
Giambologna, Jean de Boulogne	1529–1608	Douai	*Rape of the Sabine Women; Mercury; Fountain of Neptune; Samson and a Philistine; Altar of Liberty*
Gill, Eric (Arthur Eric Rowton Gill)	1882–1940	Brighton	*Stations of the Cross; Mankind; Mother and Child; Prospero and Ariel; The Creation of Adam*
Hepworth, Dame Barbara	1903–75	Wakefield	*Figure of a Woman; Large and Small Forms; Reclining Figure; Wave; Four Squares; Orpheus*
Judd, Donald	1928–	Excelsior Springs	*Eight Modular Unit V-Channel Piece*
Laurens, Henri	1885–1954	Paris	*The Farewell; Head of a Young Girl; Still Life*
Leonardo da Vinci	1452–1519	Vinci	*St John the Baptist*
Leoncillo (Leoncillo Leonardi)	1915–1968	Spoleto	*St Sebastian*

Name	Dates	Place of birth	Selected works
Lipchitz, Jacques	1891–1973	Druskininkai	*Sailor with a Guitar; Harpist; The Couple; Prayer; Prometheus Strangling the Vulture II*
Maitani, Lorenzo	c.1275–1330	Orvieto	*Creation of the Animals; Eagle of St John; Angel of St Matthew*
Marini, Marino	1901–80	Pistoia	*The Dancer; Horse and Rider; Portrait of Igor Stravinsky*
Martini, Arturo	1889–1947	Treviso	*Water Drinker; Moonlight; Thirst; Girl Swimming Under Water; Corporate Justice*
Michelangelo (Buonarroti)	1475–1564	Caprese	*Pietà; Madonna of the Steps; Victory*
Moore, Henry	1898–1986	Castleford	*Recumbent Figure; Fallen Warrior; Mother and Child; Family Group; Reclining Figure; King and Queen; Seated Figure Against Curved Wall*
Morris, Robert	1931–	Kansas City	*Untitled; In the Realm of the Carceral*
Parmiggiani, Claudio	1943–	Luzzara	*Sineddoche*
Pisano, Andrea	1270–1349	Pontedera	*The Baptism of Christ; Bell Tower of Florence Cathedral*
Pisano, Giovanni	1245–1317	Pisa	*Annunciation; Nativity; Annunciation to the Shepherds; tomb sculpture for Margaret of Luxembourg*
Rodin, Auguste	1840–1917	Paris	*L'Homme au Nez Cassé; Le Baiser; Le Penseur; Les Bourgeois de Calais; The Vanquished; The Age of Bronze*
Rossellino, Antonio	1427–79	Florence	*Bust of Florentine Matteo Palmieri; bust of Giovanni Chellini; Madonna and Child; Shrine of the Marcolino de Forli*
Schlemmer, Oskar	1888–1943	Stuttgart	*Triadic Ballet; Abstrakte Rindplastik*
Segal, George	1925–	New York	*Rock'n Roll Combo; The Truck; The Laundromat; Hot Dog Stand*
Sluter, Claus	1350–1405	Haarlem	*Bust of Christ; Well of Moses;* chapel of Chartreuse de Champnol, Dijon, tomb of Philip the Bold, Duke of Burgundy
Tinguely, Jean	1925–91	Fribourg	*Machines à Peindre; Study for an End of the World; Metamécanique No.; Homage to New York*

PHOTOGRAPHY

Photographers

Name	Dates	Place of birth	Name	Dates	Place of birth
Adams, Ansel	1902–84	San Francisco	Fenton, Roger	1819–69	Lancashire
Arbus, Diane	1923–71	New York City	Firth, Francis	1822–98	Chesterfield
Bailey, David	1938–	London	Godwin, Fay Simmonds	1931–	Berlin
Beaton, Sir Cecil	1904–80	London	Hardy, Bert	1913–	London
Bourke-White, Margaret	1906–71	New York City	Hill, David Octavius	1802–70	Perth, Scotland
Brady, Matthew	1823–96	Lake George, New York	Hine, Lewis	1874–1940	Oshkosh, Wisconsin
Brandt, Bill	1904–83	London	Karsh, Yousuf	1908–	Mardin (Turkey)
Brassaï (Gyula Halasz)	1899–1984	Brasso, Transylvania	Kertész, André	1894–1985	Budapest
			Lange, Dorothea	1895–1965	Hoboken, New Jersey
Cameron, Julia Margaret	1815–79	Calcutta	Lartigue, Jacques-Henri	1894–1986	Curbevoie, France
Capa, Robert (André Friedmann)	1913–54	Budapest	Martin, Paul	1864–1942	Herbenville, France
			McBean, Angus Rowland	1904–90	Newbridge, Monmouth
Cartier-Bresson, Henri	1908–	Paris	Moholy-Nagy, László	1895–1946	Bacsbarsod, Hungary
Cunningham, Imogen	1883–1976	Portland, Oregon	Muybridge, Eadweard (Edward James Muggeridge)	1830–1904	Kingston-on-Thames
Curtis, Edward Sheriff	1868–1952	Madison, Wisconsin			
Daguerre, Louis Jacques Mandé	1789–1851	Cormeilles	Nadar (Gaspard-Felix Tournachon)	1820–1910	Paris
Eisenstaedt, Alfred	1898–	Tczew, Poland (formerly Dirschau)	Nilsson, Lennart	1922–	Strängnäs, Sweden
			Parer, Damien	1912–44	Malvern, Victoria
Evans, Frederick	1853–1943	Whitechapel, London	Parkinson, Norman (Ronald William Parkinson Smith)	1913–90	London
Evans, Walker	1903–75	St Louis, Missouri			

Arts and culture

Photographers (continued)

Name	Dates	Place of birth	Name	Dates	Place of birth
Ray, Man (Emanuel Rabinovitch)	1870–1976	Philadelphia	Stieglitz, Alfred	1864–1946	Hoboken, New Jersey
Robinson, Henry Peach	1830–1901	Ludlow	Strand, Paul	1890–1976	New York City
Saint Joseph, John Kenneth Sinclair	1912–	Worcestershire	Sutcliffe, Frank Meadow	1853–1941	Whitby, Yorkshire
Sander, August	1876–1964	Herdorf, Germany	Weston, Edward	1886–1958	Highland Park, Illinois
Sheeler, Charles	1883–1965	Philadelphia	White, Minor	1908–76	Minneapolis
Steichen, Edward Jean	1879–1973	Luxembourg			

KNOWLEDGE

ACADEMIC STUDY

Museums and art galleries of the world

Country	Location	Museum	Date established
Afghanistan	Kabul	Kabul Museum	1922
Albania	Tiranë	Albanian National Culture Museum	na
Argentina	Buenos Aires	National History Museum	1889
Algeria	Algiers	National Museum of Algiers	1930
Armenia	Yerevan	Armenian State Historical Museum	
		Armenian State Picture Gallery	1921
Australia	Sydney	Australian Museum	1827
	Canberra	Australian National Gallery	1975
	Melbourne	Museum of Victoria	1854
Austria	Salzburg	Residence Gallery	1789
	Vienna	Kunsthistorisches Museum	1891
		Belvedere Gallery	18th-c
		Schönbrunn Palace	1569, museum in 1922
Bahamas	Nassau	Bahamia Museum	na
Bahrain	Manama	Bahrain Museum	1970
Bangladesh	Dhaka	Bangladesh National Museum	1913
Barbados	St Ann's Garrison	Barbados Museum and Historical Society	1933
Belarus	Minsk	Belarussian State Art Museum	1939
Belgium	Antwerp	Ruben's House	17th-c
		Royal Museum of Fine Art	1890
	Brussels	Erasmus House	1515
Bhutan	Paro	National Museum	1968
Bolivia	La Paz	National Museum	1846
Brazil	Rio de Janerio	National Museum	1818
Brunei	Kota Batu	Brunei Museum	1965
Bulgaria	Sofia	National Art Gallery	1948
Canada	Quebec	McCord Museum of Canadian History	1919
	Montreal	Montreal Museum of Fine Arts	1860
	Vancouver	Vancouver Art Gallery	1931
Chile	Santiago	National Historical Museum	1911
China	Beijing	Museum of Chinese History	1920
Colombia	Carrera	National Museum	1823
Costa Rica	San Jose	National Museum of Costa Rica	1887
Croatia	Zagreb	Croatian Historical Museum	1844
Cuba	Havana	National Museum	1913
Cyprus	Nicosia	The Cyprus Museum	1883
Czech Republic	Prague	National Museum	1818
		National Gallery	1796
Denmark	Copenhagen	National Museum	1807
Dominican Republic	Santo Domingo	National Fine Arts Gallery	1943
Ecuador	Quito	Civic Museum of Arts and History	1930
Egypt	Cairo	Egyptian Museum	1857
El Salvador	San Salvador	National Museum	1976
Estonia	Tallinn	Art Museum of Estonia	1919
		Estonian History Museum	1864
Ethiopia	Addis Abbaba	Museum of the Institute of Ethiopian Studies	1963
Finland	Helsinki	Museum of Applied Arts	1873
France	Beauvais	National Tapestry Gallery	1964
	Fontainebleau	The Royal Palace of Fontainebleau	12th-c
	Paris	Auguste Rodin Museum	1915
		The Louvre	1791
		Museé d'Orsay	1986
		Museum of Modern Art at the Pompidou centre	1976
		Museum of Technology	1794
		Picasso Museum	1985
	Saint-Germain-en-Laye	Museum of National Antiquities	16th-c
	Versailles	Château de Versailles	1837
Georgia	Tbilisi	Georgian State Museum	1852

Museums and art galleries of the world (continued)

Country	Location	Museum	Date established
Germany	Berlin	Bauhaus Archives and Museum of Design	1969
		Berlin Museum	1962
		Deutsches Historisches Museum	1987
		Haus der Wannsee-Konferenz	1992
	Frankfurt	Goethe Museum	1859
	Hamburg	Altona Museum	1863
		Hamburg Art Gallery	1869
	Mainz	Roman-Germanic Central Museum	1852
	Munich	Deutsches Museum	1925
		Bavarian National Museum	1859
Greece	Athens	National Archaeological Museum	1866
		Museum of Cycladic Art	1986
		Acropolis Museum	1865
	Heraklion (Crete)	Archaeological Museum	1904
	Olympia	Museum of Ancient Olympia	1888
Grenada	St George's	Grenada National Museum	1976
Guatemala	Guatemala City	National Museum of History	1975
Guyana	George Town	Guyana Museum	1853
Haiti	Port-au-Prince	National Museum	1983
Hong Kong	Tsimshatsui	Hong Kong Museum of History	1975
Hungary	Budapest	Hungarian National Museum	1802
Iceland	Reykjavik	National Museum	1863
India	New Delhi	National Museum of India	1949
Indonesia	Jakarta	National Museum	1778
Iran	Teheran	Iran Bastan Museum	1946
Iraq	Baghdad	Archaeological Museum of Iraq	na
Ireland	Dublin	National Museum of Ireland	1731
		National Gallery of Ireland	1864
Israel	Tel Aviv	Eretz-Israel Museum	1948
	Jerusalem	Israel Museum	1965
Italy	Bologna	Archaeological Museum	1881
		Museum of the Middle Ages and Renaissance	1985
		National Art Gallery	1882
	Florence	Accademia Gallery	1784
		Museum of the History of Science	1929
		Bardini Museum	1924
		Bargello Museum	1857
		Uffizi Gallery	1581
	Milan	Brera Art Gallery	1776
		Leonardo da Vinci Museum of Science and Technology	1953
	Naples	National Archaeological Museum	18th-c
	Rome	Borghese Gallery	1902
		Vatican Museums	na
		National Museum of Popular Art	1923
	Siena	Siena Museum	na
	Turin	Sabauda Gallery	1832
	Venice	Accademia Gallery	1807
		Peggy Guggenheim Collection	1980
		Treasury of St Mark's	na
Japan	Tokyo	National Museum	1871
Jordan	Amman	Folklore Museum	1972
		Popular Life Museum	1973
Kazakhstan	Alma Ata	Central State Museum of Kazakhstan	na
Kyrgyzstan	Bishkek	State Historical Museum of Kyrgyzstan	na
Korea, North	Pyongyang	Korean Central Historical Museum	na
Korea, South	Seoul	National Museum of Korea	1908
Kuwait	Kuwait City	Kuwait National Museum	1957
Laos	Vientiane	National Museum	1965
Latvia	Riga	Latvian Historical Museum	1869
		State Museum of Latvian and Russian Art	
Lebanon	Beirut	National Museum of Lebanon	1920
Liechtenstein	Vaduz	Liechtenstein Museum	1954

Country	Location	Museum	Date established
Lithuania	Vilnius	Museum of History and Ethnography of Lithuania	1855
		Art Museum of Lithuania	1941
Luxembourg	Luxembourg-Ville	Luxembourg Museum	1845
Malaysia	Kuala Lumpur	National Museum of Malaysia	1963
Maldives	Dhivehi	National Museum	1952
Mexico	Mexico City	National Museum of Archaeology	1964
Monaco	Monaco-Ville	Oceanographic Museum	1910
Morocco	Rabat	Museum of Antiquities	1917
Nepal	Katmandu	National Museum of Nepal	1928
Netherlands	Amsterdam	Rijksmuseum	1817
		Rijksmuseum Vincent Van Gogh	1973
		Stedelijk Museum	1893
	Utrecht	Catherine Convent State Museum	1921
New Zealand	Auckland	Auckland City Art Gallery	1888
		Auckland Institute and Museum	1852
	Wellington	Museum of New Zealand Te Papa Tongarewa	1992
Nicaragua	Managua	National Museum of Nicaragua	1896
Norway	Bergen	Bergen Art Gallery	1925
	Oslo	Edvard Munch Museum	1963
		National Gallery	1836
		National Museum of Contemporary Art	1902
Oman	Muscat	Oman Natural History Museum	1983
Pakistan	Islamabad	National Museum of Pakistan	1950
Panama	Apdo	Museum of the History of Panama	1977
Paraguay	Asuncion	National Museum of Fine Arts	1887
Peru	Lima	National Museum of History	1836
Philippines	Manila	National Museum of the Philippines	1901
Poland	Warsaw	National Museum	1862
Portugal	Lisbon	National Museum of Natural History	1859
		Museum of Popular Art	1948
Qatar	Doha	Qatar National Museum	1975
Romania	Bucharest	National History Museum of Romania	1968
		National Museum of Art	1950
Russia	Moscow	Pushkin Museum of Fine Arts	1912
	St Petersburg	Hermitage Museum	1764
		State Russian Museum	1898
Saudi Arabia	Riyadh	Museum of Archaeology and Ethnography	1978
Singapore	Singapore City	National Museum	1849
Spain	Barcelona	Catalan Museum of Art	1929
		Ethnological Museum	1948
		Picasso Museum	1963
	Bilbao	Museum of Fine Art	1914
	Madrid	Prado Museum	1819
		National Museum of Ethnology	1940
	Seville	Museum of the Alcazar of Seville	na
		Museum of Fine Art	1835
	Valencia	Museum of Fine Art	1839
Sri Lanka	Colombo	Colombo National Museum	1877
Surinam	Paramaribo	Stichting Suranaams Museum	1947
Sweden	Stockholm	National Museum of Antiquities	1647
		Nordic Museum	1873
Switzerland	Basle	Basle Historical Museum	1894
	Geneva	Museum of Art and History	1910
	Zürich	Swiss National Museum	1898
		House of Art	1910
Syria	Damascus	National Museum	1919
Tajikistan	Dushanbe	Tajik Historical State Museum	na
Thailand	Bangkok	National Museum	1926
Trinidad and Tobago	Port of Spain	National Museum and Art Gallery	1898
Tunisia	Tunis	National Museum of Bardo	1888
Turkey	Istanbul	Topkapi Palace Museum	na
		Hagia Sophia Museum	1934
		Museum of the Ancient Orient	na
		Archaeological Museum	1891

Knowledge

Museums and art galleries of the world (continued)

Country	Location	Museum	Date established
Turkmenistan	Ashkhabad	Turkmen State United Museum of History and Ethnography	1899
Ukraine	Kiev	Kiev State Historical Museum	1934
United Arab Emirates	Abu Dhabi	Al-Ain Museum	1971
United Kingdom	Bradford	National Museum of Photography, Film and Television	1983
	Cambridge	Fitzwilliam Museum	1848
	Cardiff	National Museum of Wales	1907
	Edinburgh	National Gallery of Scotland	1859
		Royal Museum of Scotland	1854
		Scottish National Portrait Gallery	1882
	Glasgow	Kelvingrove Art Gallery and Museum	1902
		Burrell Collection	1944
	London	British Museum	1824
		Imperial War Museum	1815
		National Gallery	1838
		National Maritime Museum	1934
		National Portrait Gallery	1896
		Natural History Museum	1963
		Tate Gallery	1897
		Victoria & Albert Museum	1850
	Oxford	Ashmolean Museum	1683
Uruguay	Montevideo	National Historical Museum	1900
USA	Boston	Museum of Fine Arts	1924
	Chicago	Field Museum of Natural History	1893
	Dallas	Dallas Museum of Fine Arts	1903
	Detroit	Henry Ford Museum	1929
	Los Angeles (Malibu)	John Paul Getty Museum	1953
	New York	Solomon R Guggenheim Museum	1937
		Metropolitan Museum of Art	1870
		Museum of Modern Art	1929
	Philadelphia	Philadelphia Museum of Art	1876
	San Francisco	MH de Young Memorial Museum	1895
	Washington	National Air and Space Museum	1946
	Smithsonian	National Museum of American Art	1846
	Institution	National Museum of American History	na
Uzbekistan	Tashkent	Tashkent Historical Museum of the People of Uzbekistan	1876
Venezuela	Los Caobos	Museum of Fine Arts	1938
Vietnam	Hanoi	Vietnam History Museum	1958

na = not available

Presidents of the Royal Academy

1768–92	Joshua Reynolds
1792–1805	Benjamin West
1805–6	James Wyatt
1806–20	Benjamin West
1820–30	Thomas Lawrence
1830–50	Martin Archer Shee
1850–66	Charles Eastlake
1866–78	Francis Grant
1878–96	Frederick, 1st Baron Leighton
1896	John Millais
1896–1919	Edward Poynter
1919–24	Aston Webb
1924–8	Frank Dicksee
1928–33	William Llewellyn
1938–44	Edwin Lutyens
1944–9	Alfred Munnings
1949–54	Gerald Festus Kelly
1954–6	Albert Edward Richardson
1956–66	Charles Wheeler
1966–76	Thomas Monnington
1976–84	Hugh Casson
1984–	Roger de Grey

Presidents of the Royal Society

1662–77	William, 2nd Viscount Brouncker
1677–80	Joseph Williamson
1680–2	Christopher Wren
1682–3	John Hoskins
1683–4	Cyril Wyche
1684–6	Samuel Pepys
1686–9	John, Earl of Carbery
1689–90	Thomas Herbert, Earl of Pembroke
1690–5	Robert Southwell
1695–8	Charles Montagu, 1st Earl of Halifax
1698–1703	John, 1st Baron Somers
1703–27	Isaac Newton
1727–41	Hans Sloane
1741–52	Martin Folkes
1752–64	George, Earl of Macclesfield
1764–8	Lord Morton
1768–72	James West
1772–8	John Pringle
1778–1820	Joseph Banks
1820–7	Humphrey Davy
1827–30	Davies Gilbert
1830–8	Augustus Frederick, Duke of Sussex
1838–47	Marquis of Northampton
1847–54	William Parsons, 3rd Earl of Rosse
1854–8	Lord Wrothesley
1858–61	Benjamin Brodie
1861–71	Edward Sabine
1871–3	George Airy
1873–8	Joseph Hooker
1878–83	William Spottiswoode
1883–5	Thomas H Huxley
1885–90	George Stokes
1890–5	William Thomson, 1st Baron Kelvin
1895–1900	Joseph, Lord Lister
1900–5	William Huggins
1905–8	John William Strutt, 3rd Baron Rayleigh
1908–13	Archibald Geikie
1913–15	William Crookes
1915–20	Joseph Thomson
1920–5	Charles Sherrington
1925–30	Ernest, 1st Baron Rutherford
1930–5	Frederick Hopkins
1935–40	William Bragg
1940–5	Henry Dale
1945–50	Robert Robinson
1950–5	Edgar, 1st Baron Adrian
1955–60	Cyril Hinshelwood
1960–5	Howard, Baron Florey
1965–70	Patrick Stuart, Baron Blackett
1970–5	Alan Hodgkin
1975–80	Alexander, Baron Todd
1980–5	Andrew Huxley
1985–90	George, Lord Porter
1990–	Michael Atiyah

Nobel prizes 1981–93

Year	Peace	Literature	Economic science	Chemistry	Physics	Physiology/Medicine
1981	Office of the UN High Commissioner for Refugees	Elias Canetti	James Tobin	Kenrichi Fukui Roald Hoffman	Nicolaas Bloembergen Arthur L Schawlow Kai M Siegbahn	Roger W Sperry David H Hubel Torsten N Wiesel
1982	Alfonso García Robles Alva Myrdal	Gabriel García Márquez	George J Stigler	Aaron Klug	Kenneth G Wilson	Sune K Bergström Bengt I Samuelsson John R Vane
1983	Lech Wałęsa	William Golding	Gerard Debreu	Henry Taube	Subrahmanyan Chandrasekhar William A Fowler	Barbara McClintock
1984	Desmond Tutu	Jaroslav Seifert	Richard Stone	Robert B Merrifield	Carlo Rubbia Simon van der Meer	Niels K Jerne Georges J F Köhler César Milstein
1985	International Physicians or the Prevention of Nuclear War	Claude Simon	Franco Modigliani	Herbert Hauptman Jerome Karle	Klaus von Klitzing	Joseph L Goldstein Michael S Brown
1986	Elie Wiesel	Wole Soyinka	James M Buchanan	Dudley R Herschbach Yuan Tseh Lee John C Polanyi	Gerd Binnig Heinrich Rohrer Ernst Ruska	Stanley Cohen Rita Levi-Montalcini
1987	Oscar Arias Sánchez	Joseph Brodsky	Robert M Solow	Charles Pedersen Donald Cram Jean-Marie Lehn	George Bednorz Alex Müller	Susumu Tonegawa
1988	UN Peacekeeping Forces	Naguib Mahfouz	Maurice Allais	Johann Deisenhofer Robert Huber Hartmut Michel	Leon Lederman Melvin Schwartz Jack Steinberger	James Black Gertrude Elion George Hitchings
1989	Tenzin Ciyatso (Dalai Lama)	Camilo José Cela	Trygve Haavelmo Thomas Cech	Sydney Altman Wolfgang Paul Norman Ramsay	Hans Dehmelt Harold E Varmus	J Michael Bishop
1990	Mikhail Gorbachev	Octavio Paz	Harry M Markovitz Merton Miller William Sharpe	Elias James Corey	Jerome Friedman Henry Kendall Richard Taylor	Joseph E Murray E Donnall Thomas
1991	Aung San Suu Kyi	Nadine Gordimer	Ronald Coase	Richard Ernst	Pierre-Gilles de Gennes	Erwin Nehrer Bert Sakmann
1992	Rigoberta Menchú	Derek Walcott	Gary S Becker	Rudolph A Marcus	George Charpak	Edmond H Fisher Edward G Krebs
1993	Nelson Mandela F W de Klerk	Toni Morrison	Douglass C North Robert W Fogel	Kary Mullis Michael Smith	Joseph Taylor Russell Hulse	Richard J Roberts Phillip A Sharp

Universities of the world

Country	City	University	Date founded	Approximate number of students
Austria	Graz	Karl-Franzens-Universität	1585	27 300
		Technische Universität Graz	1811	12 300
		Hochschule für Musik und Darstellende Kunst in Graz (University of Music and Dramatic Art in Graz)	1963	1 600
	Innsbruck	Leopold-Franzens Universität Innsbruck	1669	24 700
	Klagenfurt	Universität Klagenfurt	1970	5 000
	Linz	Johannes Kepler Universität Linz	1966	12 000
		Hochschule für Künstlerische und Industrielle Gestaltung (University of Art and Industrial Design)	1947	500
	Leoben	Montanuniversität Leoben (Leoben University of Mining and Metallurgy)	1840	2 000
	Salzburg	Universität Salzburg	1622; closed 1810, reconstituted 1962	12 000
		Hochschule für Musik und Darstellende Kunst 'Mozarteum' in Salzburg ('Mozarteum' University of Music and Dramatic Art in Salzburg)	1841	1 500
	Vienna	Universität Wien	1365	68 000
		Technische Universität Wien	1815	18 500
		Universität für Bodenkultur Wien (Vienna Agricultural University)	1872	6 500
		Wirtschaftsuniversität Wien (Vienna University of Economics and Business Administration)	1898	19 000
		Veterinärmedizinische Universität Wien	1767	2 700
		Akademie der Bildende Künste (Academy of Fine Arts)	1692	560
		Hochschule für Angewandte Kunst in Wien (University of Applied Arts in Vienna)	1868	1 100
		Hochschule für Musik und Darstellende Kunst (University of Music and Dramatic Art)	1909	3 000
Belgium	Brussels	Catholic University of Brussels	1991	911
		Free University of Brussels (Flemish)	1834, present status 1970	7 500
		Free University of Brussels (French)	1834, present status 1970	17 300
	Ghent	University of Ghent	1817	16 000
	Liège	University of Liège	1817	12 200
	Louvain	Catholic University of Louvain (Flemish)	1970	25 200
	Louvain-le-Neuve	Catholic University of Louvain (French)	1425, present status 1970	19 900
	Mons	University of Mons	1965	3 500
Czech Republic	Brno	Univerzita Masarykova (Masaryk University)	1919	11 300
		Vysoká Škola Veterinární A Farmaceutická v Brně (University of Veterinary Science and Pharmacy in Brno)	1918	1 100
		Vysoké Učení Technické v Brně (Technical University of Brno)	1899	14 600
		Vysoká Škola Zemědělska (University of Agriculture)	1919	3 300
	Liberec	Vysoká Škola Strojní a Textilní Liberci (Technical University of Mechanical and Textile Engineering in Liberec)	1953	2 900
	Olomouc	Univerzita Palackého v Olomouci (Palacky University)	1573, reopened 1946	5 600
	Ostrava	Vysoká Škola Báňská v Ostravě (Technical University of Mining and Metallurgy of Ostrava)	1716	6 500
	Pardubice	Vysoká Škola Chemicko-Technologická v Pardubicích (Institute of Chemical Technology in Pardubice)	1950	975

Universities of the world (continued)

Country	City	University	Date founded	Approximate number of students
	Plzen	Západočeská Univerzita (University of West Bohemia)	1949, present name 1991	4 100
	Prague	České Vysoké Učení Technické v Praze (Czech Technical University)	1707, reorganized 1960	15 000
		Univerzita Karlova (Charles University)	1348	30 000
		Vysoká Škola Chemicko-Technologická v Praze (University of Chemistry and Technology, Prague)	1807	2 500
		Vysoká Škola Ekonomická (Prague University of Economics)	1953	11 000
		Vysoká Škola Zemědělska v Praze (Prague Agricultural University)	1906	4 900
	Nitra	Vysoka Skola Pol'Nohospodarska (College of Agriculture)	1946	4 000
	Zvolen	Vysoka Skola Lesnicka a Drevarska (College of Forestry and Wood Technology)	1807, reorganized 1952	1 200
Denmark	Aalborg	Aalborg Universitets Center	1974	9 000
	Aarhus	University of Aarhus	1928	13 000
		Jutland Open University	1982	864
	Copenhagen	University of Copenhagen	1479	26 300
		Technical University of Denmark	1829	5 600
	Fredericksburg	Royal Veterinary and Agricultural University	1856	3 200
	Odense	University of Odense	1964	5 600
Finland	Åbo	Åbo Akademi (Finland-Swedish University of Åbo)	1918	5 200
	Helsinki	Helsingin Yliopisto/Helsingfors Universitet	1911	26 600
		Teknillinen Korkeakoulu (Helsinki University of Technology)	1908	11 500
	Joensuu	Jeonsuun Yliopisto (Jeonsuu University)	1969	5 700
	Jyväskylä	Jyväskylän Yliopisto	1966	8 600
	Kuopio	Kuopion Yliopisto (University of Kuopio)	1966	2 300
	Rovaniemi	Lapin Yliopisto (University of Lapland)	1979	1 700
	Lappeenranta	Lappeenrannan Teknillinen Korkeakoulu (Lappeenranta University of Technology)	1969	2 500
	Oulu	Oulun Yliopisto	1958	10 000
	Tampere	Tampereen Tenknillinen Korkeakoulu (Tampere University of Technology)	1965	5 500
		Tampereen Yliopisto (University of Tampere)	1925	15 200
	Turku	Turun Yliopisto (Turka University)	1920	11 800
	Vaasa	Vaasan Yliopisto (University of Vaasa)	1968	2 300
France	Aix-en-Provence	Université d'Aix-Marseille III (Université de Droit, d'Economie et des Sciences)	1973	19 200
	Angers	Université d'Angers	1971	14 000
	Amiens	Université de Picardie	1965	18 000
	Avignon	Université d'Avignon	1973	5 200
	Besançon	Université de Franche-Comté	1423 at Dôle, 1691 at Besançon	19 300
	Bordeaux	Université de Bordeaux II	na	14 500
	Brest	Université de Bretagne Occidentale	na	16 600
	Caen	Université de Caen	1432, reorganized 1985	23 000
	Chambéry	Université de Savoie (Chambéry)	1970	7 900
	Clermont-Ferrand	Université de Clermont-Ferrand I	1976, present status 1985	9 600
		Université de Clermont-Ferrand II (Université Blaise Pascal)	1810, present status 1984	14 800
	Corti	Université de Corse 1	1976, opened 1981	
		Università de Corsica		
	Créteil	Université de Paris XII (Paris-Val-de-Marne)	1970	18 000
	Dijon	Université de Bourgogne		24 000
	Grenoble	Université de Grenoble I (Université Joseph Fourier)		15 000

Country	City	University	Date founded	Approximate number of students
	Grenoble	Université de Grenoble II (Université Pierre Mendès-France)	1970	18 500
	Grenoble	Université de Grenoble III (Université Stendhal)	1810	6 800
	Le Havre	Université du Havre	1984	4 400
	Le Mans	Université du Maine	1969	8 600
	Lille	Université de Lille II (Droit et Santé)	1969	17 400
	Limoges	Université de Limoges	1808, reopened 1965	11 600
	Lyons	Université Lyon II		19 900
		Université Lyon III (Université Jean Moulin)	1973	16 000
	Marseilles	Université d'Aix-Marseille I (Université de Provence)	1970	18 700
		Université d'Aix-Marseille II	1973	19 100
	Metz	Université de Metz	1971	12 100
	Montpellier	Université de Montpellier I	1970	18 000
		Université de Montpellier II (Université des Sciences et Techniques de Languedoc)	na	11 000
		Université de Montpellier III (Université Paul Valéry)	1970	15 500
	Mont-Saint-Aignan	Université de Rouen	1966	21 300
	Mulhouse	Université de Haute-Alsace	1975	2 000
	Nancy	Université de Nancy I	1970	16 300
		Université de Nancy II	1970	18 500
	Nanterre	Université de Paris X (Paris-Nanterre)	na	32 500
	Nantes	Université de Nantes	1962	28 000
	Nice	Université de Nice	1971	22 500
	Orléans	Université d'Orléans	1961	13 200
	Orsay	Université de Paris XI (Paris-Sud)	1970	28 000
	Paris	Université de Paris I (Panthéon-Sorbonne)	1971	36 800
		Université de Paris II (Université Panthéon-Assas)	1970	18 600
		Université de Paris III (Sorbonne-Nouvelle)	1970	
		Université de Paris IV (Paris-Sorbonne)	1970	23 700
		Université de Paris V (René Descartes)	1970	32 300
		Université de Paris VI (Pierre et Marie Curie)	na	
		Université de Paris VII	1970	30 000
		Université de Paris IX (Paris-Dauphine)	1968	6 700
	Pau	Université de Pau et des Pays de l'Adour	1970	12 100
	Perpignan	Université de Perpignan	1971	4 500
	Poiters	Université de Poitiers	1432	25 000
	Reims	Université de Reims Champagne-Ardenne	1548	23 500
	Rennes	Université de Rennes I	na	23 500
		Université de Rennes II (Université de Haute Bretagne)	na	13 000
	St Denis	Université de Paris VIII (Vincennes à St-Denis)	1969	23 500
	St-Étienne	Université Jean Monnet (Université de St-Étienne)	1969, present name 1991	12 600
	Strasbourg	Université de Strasbourg I (Université Louis Pasteur)	1971	17 500
		Université de Strasbourg II (Sciences Humaines)	1538	11 000
		Université de Strasbourg III (Université Robert Schumann)		8 300
	Talence	Université de Bordeaux I	na	18 600
		Université de Bordeaux III	na	14 800
	Toulon/La Garde	Université de Toulon et du Var	1970	5 200
	Toulouse	Université de Toulouse I (Sciences Sociales)	1229	16 400
		Université de Toulouse II (Le Mirail)	na	21 300
		Université de Toulouse III (Université Paul Sabatier)	1969	26 800
	Tours	Université de Tours (Université François Rabelais)	1970	22 000
	Valenciennes	Université de Valenciennes et du Hainaut-Cambresis	1964	9 000
	Versailles	Université Versailles/Saint Quentin-en-Yvelines	1991	4 400

Universities of the world (continued)

Country	City	University	Date founded	Approximate number of students
France	Villeneuve d'Ascq	Université de Lille I (Université des Sciences et Techniques de Lille Flandres Artois)	1855 as Faculty of Sciences, present status 1971	19 100
		Université de Lille III (Sciences Humaines, Lettres et Arts)	1560, present status 1985	23 900
	Villetaneuse	Université de Paris XIII (Pais-Nord)	1970	13 400
	Villeurbanne	Université Lyon I (Université Claude-Bernard)	1970	23 000
Germany	Aachen	Rheinisch-Westfälische Technische Hochschule Aachen	1870, university status 1880	37 000
	Augsburg	Universität Augsburg	1970	14 700
	Bamberg	Otto Friedrich Universität Bamberg	1647	7 500
	Bayreuth	Universität Bayreuth	1972	8 500
	Berlin	Humboldt-Universität zu Berlin	1809	21 000
		Freie Universität Berlin	1948	62 000
		Technische Universität Berlin	Bauakademie (f.1799) and Gewerbeakademie (f.1821), amalgamated 1879 as Technische Hochschule; opened under present title 1946	38 000
	Bielefeld	Universität Bielefeld	1969	16 000
	Bochum	Ruhr-Universität Bochum	1961	37 000
	Bonn	Rheinische Friedrich-Wilhelms-Universität Bonn	founded 1786; refounded 1818	38 000
	Braunschweig	Technische Universität Carolo Wilhelmina zu Braunschweig	1745, present title 1968	17 000
	Bremen	Universität Bremen	1971	15 600
	Chemnitz	Technische Universität (Karl-Marx-Stadt) Chemnitz	1836	6 200
	Clausthal-Zellerfeld	Technische Universität Clausthal	1775, university status 1968	4 200
	Darmstadt	Technische Hochschule Darmstadt	1836, university status 1895	18 400
	Dortmund-Eichlinghafen	Universität Dortmund	1966	22 300
	Dresden	Technische Universität Dresden	1828, university status 1961	12 000
	Duisburg	Universität Duisburg Gesamthochschule	1972	14 500
	Düsseldorf	Heinrich-Heine-Universität Düsseldorf	1965 (formerly Medizinische Akademie f.1907)	17 800
	Eichstätt	Katholische Universität Eichstätt	1972 (founded originally 1574)	3 000
	Erlangen	Friedrich-Alexander-Universität Erlangen-Nürnberg	1743	28 000
	Essen	Universität Essen-Gesamthochschule	1972	20 500
	Frankfurt am Main	Johann Wolfgang Goethe-Universität Frankfurt	1914	34 300
	Freiburg	Albert Ludwigs Universität	1457	23 600
	Giessen	Justus-Liebig-Universität Giessen	1607	20 500
	Göttingen	George-August-Universität Göttingen	1737	30 000
	Greifswald	Ernst Moritz Arndt Universität	1456	4 000
	Freiburg	Albert-Ludwigs-Universität Freiburg	1457	23 600
	Halle	Martin Luther-Universität Halle-Wittenberg	1502 Wittenberg; 1694 Halle; 1817 Halle-Wittenberg	
	Hamburg	Universität Hamburg	na	43 000
	Hannover	Universität Hannover	1831	29 900
	Heidelberg	Ruprecht-Karls-Universität Heidelberg	1386	27 500
	Hohenheim (Stuttgart)	Universität Hohenheim	1818	6 200
	Jena	Friedrich-Schiller Universität	1558	6 500

Country	City	University	Date founded	Approximate number of students
	Kaiserslautern	Universität Kaiserslautern	1975	10 000
	Karlsruhe	Universität Fridericiana Karlsruhe	1825	21 200
	Kassel	Gesamthochschule Kassel	1970	14 900
	Kiel	Christian-Albrechts Universität zu Kiel	1665	20 000
	Konstanz	Universität Konstanz	1966	8 900
	Köln	Universität zu Köln	1388	54 000
	Leipzig	Universität Leipzig	1409	na
	Lüneburg	Universität Lüneburg	1946	5 400
	Mainz	Johannes Gutenburg-Universität Mainz	1477; closed 1816; reopened 1946	27 000
	Mannheim	Universität Mannheim	1907, university status 1967	13 000
	Marburg	Philipps-Universität Marburg	1527	16 900
	Munich	Ludwig-Maximilians-Universität München	1472	60 000
		Technische Universität München	1868	24 100
	Münster	Westfälische Wilhelms-Universität Münster	1780	45 900
	Oldenburg	Universität Carl von Ossietzky Oldenburg	1974	11 000
	Osnabruck	Universität Osnabrück	1973	13 000
	Hagen	Open University	1974	50 000
	Paderborn	Universität-Gesamthochschule Paderborn	1972	16 300
	Passau	Universität Passau	1972	8 500
	Regensburg	Universität Regensburg	1962	13 000
	Rostock	Universität Rostock	1419	7 900
	Saarbrücken	Universität des Saarlandes	1948	20 000
	Siegen	Universität-Gesamthochschule Siegen	1972	12 500
	Stuttgart	Universität Stuttgart	1829, university status 1967	21 400
	Trier	Universität Trier	1970	10 300
	Tübingen	Eberhard-Karls-Universität Tübingen	1477	24 800
	Ulm	Universität Ulm	1967	6 100
	Wuppertal	Bergische Universität-Gesamthochschule Wuppertal	1972	17 700
	Würzburg	Bayerische-Julius-Maximilians-Universität Würzburg	1582	18 200
Greece	Athens	National and Capodistrian University of Athens	1837	45 000
		National Technical University of Athens	1836	8 000
		University of the Aegean	1984	1 400
	Crete	University of Crete	1973	1 000
		Technical University of Crete	1977	850
	Ioannina	University of Ioannina	1964, independent status 1970	9 100
	Komotini	'Demokritos' University of Thrace	1973	6 000
	Patras	University of Patras	1964	8 900
	Thessaloniki	University of Macedonia	1957	6 200
		Aristotelian University of Thessaloniki	1925	65 000
Hungary	Budapest	Eötvös Loránd Tudományegyetem (Loránd Eötvös University)	1635	11 000
		Semmelweis Orvostudományi Egyetem	1769, independent 1951	5 000
		Budapesti Közgazdaságtudományi Egyetem (Budapest University of Economic Sciences)	1948	4 600
		Orvostovábbképzö Egyetem (Postgraduate Medical University)	1987	10 000
		Állatorvostudományi Egyetem (University of Veterinary Sciences)	1787	550
		Budapesti Müszaki Egyetem (Technical University of Budapest)	1871	9 300
		Kertészeti És Élelmiszeripari Egyetem (University of Horticulture and Food Technology)	1853	1 800
	Debrecen	Kossuth Lajos Tudományegyetem	1912	2 600
		Debreceni Orvostudományi Egyetem (University Medical School of Debrecen)	1951	1 100

Knowledge

Universities of the world (continued)

Country	City	University	Date founded	Approximate number of students
		Debreceni Agrártudományi Egyetem (Debrecen University of Agrarian Sciences)	1868	1400
	Gödollö	Agrártudományi Egyetem (University of Agricultural Sciences)	1945	3500
	Keszthely	Pannon Agrártudományi Egyetem (Pannon University of Agricultural Sciences)	1797	1400
	Miskolc	Miskolci Egyetem (Miskolc University)	1949	2800
	Pécs	Pécsi Jannus Pannonius Tudományegyetem (Janus Pannonius University of Pécs)	1367	3800
		Pécsi Orvostudományi Egyetem (Medical University of Pecs)	1951	1500
	Szeged	Szent-Györgi Albert Orvostudományi Egyetem (Albert Szent-Györgi Medical University)	1951	2100
		József Attila Tudományegyetem (Attila József University)	1872	4300
	Sopron	Erdészeti És Faipari Egyetem (University of Forestry and Wood Science)	1808	840
	Veszprém	Veszprémi Egyetem (Veszprem University)	1949	1500
Ireland	Cork	University College Cork[a]	1845 as Queen's College; 1908	7100
	Dublin	University of Dublin Trinity College	1592	9800
		National University of Ireland	1908	
		University College Dublin[a]	1909	12500
		Dublin City University	1975, university status 1989	4500
	Galway	University College Galway[a]	1845 as Queen's College; 1908	6100
	Limerick	University of Limerick	1970, university status 1989	6200
Italy	Ancona	Università degli Studi di Ancona	1969	7900
	L'Aquila	Università degli Studi dell' Aquila	1952	8200
	Bari	Università degli Studi di Bari	1924	42400
	Bologna	Università degli Studi di Bologna	11th-c	59100
	Brescia	Università degli Studi di Brescia	1982	7800
	Cagliari, Sardinia	Università di Cagliari	1606	18000
	Camerino	Università di Camerino	1336, university status 1727	6000
	Commenda di Rende	Università di Calabria	1972	11000
	Campobasso	Università degli Studi del Molise	1982	na
	Cassino	Università degli Studi di Cassino	1982	na
	Catania	Università di Catania	1434	45500
	Ferrara	Università degli Studi di Ferrara	1391	6000
	Florence	Università degli Studi di Firenze	1321	46300
	Fisciano (Salerno)	Università degli Studi di Salerno	1970	na
	Genoa	Università degli Studi di Genova	1471	30400
	Lecce	Università degli Studi di Lecce	1956	13000
	Macerata	Università degli Studi di Macerata	1290	7100
	Messina	Università degli Studi di Messina	1548	28000
	Milan	Università degli Studi di Milano	1924	89200
		Catholic University of the Sacred Heart	1920, present status 1924	28200
		Università Commerciale Luigi Bocconi	1902	10900
	Modena	Università degli Studi di Modena	1175	8100
	Naples	Università degli Studi di Napoli	1224	100000
	Padua	Università degli Studi di Padova	1222	53800
	Palermo	Università degli Studi di Palermo	1777	20000
	Parma	Università degli Studi	962	22600

[a]The National University of Ireland has three constituent Colleges.

Country	City	University	Date founded	Approximate number of students
	Pavia	Università degli Studi di Pavia	1361	26 600
	Perugia	Università degli Studi di Perugia	1200	19 200
		Università Italiana per Stranieri	1921	7 000
	Pisa	Università degli Studi di Pisa	1343	28 000
	Reggio Calabria	Università di Reggio Calabria	1982	na
	Rome	Università degli Studi di Roma 'La Sapienza'	1303	180 000
		Università degli Studi di Roma 'Tor Vergata'	1970	na
	Sassari	Università degli Studi di Sassari	1562	9 500
	Siena	Università degli Studi di Siena	1240	11 000
	Trento	Università degli Studi di Trento	1962	10 200
	Trieste	Università degli Studi di Trieste	1938	18 500
	Turin	Università degli Studi di Torino	1404	42 500
		Politecnico di Torino	1859	18 200
	Udine	Università degli Studi di Udine	1977	8 000
	Urbino	Università degli Studi di Urbino	1506	16 500
	Venice	Università degli Studi di Venezia	1868	18 000
	Verona	Università degli Studi di Verona	1982	13 800
	Viterbo	Università degli Studi della Tuscia	1981	na
Netherlands	Amsterdam	University of Amsterdam	1632	27 000
		Free University, Amsterdam	1880	12 000
	Delft	Delft University of Technology	1842	14 500
	Eindhoven	Eindhoven University of Technology	1956	7 000
	Enschede	Twente University of Technology	1961	7 000
	Groningen	University of Groningen	1614	18 000
	Heerlen	Open University	1984	50 000
	Leiden	Leiden University	1575	17 900
	Maastricht	University of Limburg	1976	7 000
	Nijmegen	Catholic University, Nijmegen	1923	13 000
	Rotterdam	Erasmus University, Rotterdam	1973	18 000
	Tilburg	Tilburg University	1927	9 000
	Utrecht	Utrecht University	1636	23 000
	Wageningen	Agricultural University	1918	6 000
Norway	Bergen	Universitetet I Bergen	1948	13 600
	Oslo	Universitetet I Oslo	1811	32 000
	Tromsø	Universitetet I Tromsø	1968	3 800
	Trondheim	Universitetet I Trondheim	1968	14 500
Poland	Białystok	Politechnika Białostocka (Białystok Technical University)	1949	2 600
	Częstochowa	Politechnika Częstochowska (Częstochowa Technical University)	1949	2 000
	Gdańsk	Uniwersytet Gdański (University of Gdańsk)	1970	12 300
		Politechnika Gdańska (Technical University of Gdańsk)	1945	5 700
	Gliwice	Politechnika Slaska Im. W. Pstrowskiego (Silesian Technical University)	1945	8 000
	Katowice	Uniwerystet Słaski (Silesian University)	1968	13 400
	Kielce	Politechnika Świętokrzyska (Kielce University of Technology)	1965	2 100
	Kraków	Uniwersytet Jagielloński (Jagiellonian University)	1364	9 600
		Akademia Gorniczo-Hutnicza Im. Stanisława Staszica W Krakowie (Stanisław Staszic Academy of Mining and Metallurgy)	1919	7 500
		Politechnika Krakowska Im. Tadeusza Kościuszki (Kraków Technical University)	1945	5 100
	Łódz	Uniwersytet Łódzki (University of Łódz)	1945	14 200
		Politechnika Łódzka (Łódz Technical University)	1945	8 200
	Lublin	Katolicki Uniwersytet Lubelski (Catholic University of Lublin)	1918	7 100
		Uniwersytet Marii Curie-Skłodowskiej (Marie-Curie Skłodowska University)	1944	15 800
		Politechnika Lubelska (Technical University of Lublin)	1953	3 300

Universities of the world (continued)

Country	City	University	Date founded	Approximate number of students
	Poznań	Uniwersytet Im Adama Mickiewicza w Poznaniu (Adam Mickiewicz University in Poznań)	1919	15 300
		Politechnika Poznańska (Poznań Technical University)	1919	4 200
	Rzeszów	Politechnika Rzeszowska (Rzeszów Technical University)	1974	3 700
	Szczecin	Uniwersytet Szczeciński (Szczecin University)	1985	9 500
		Politechnika Szczecinska (Szczecin Technical University)	1946	2 400
	Toruń	Uniwersytet Mikołaja Kopernika w Toruniu (Nicholas Copernicus University in Toruń)	1945	10 000
	Warsaw	Uniwersytet Warszawski (University of Warsaw)	1818	25 400
		Politechnika Warszawska (Warsaw University of Technology)	1826	12 500
	Wrocław	Uniwersytet Wrocławski	1702, rebuilt 1945	14 600
		Politechnika Wrocławska (Wrocław Technical University)	1945	6 800
Portugal	Braga	Universidade de Minho	1973	7 800
	Coímbra	Universidade de Coímbra	1290	13 000
	Corvilla	Universidade de Beira Interior	1986	3 000
	Évora	Universidade de Évora	1973, university status 1979	2 200
	Lisbon	Universidade Autónoma de Lisboa 'Luis de Camões'	1977	5 000
		Universidade Católica Portuguesa	1968	9 200
		New University of Lisbon	1973	9 100
		Universidade Técnica de Lisboa	1930	15 900
		Universidade Lusíada	1986	8 900
	Porto	Universidade de Porto	1911	18 000
Slovak Republic	Bratislava	Univerzita Komenského Bratislava (Comenius University of Bratislava)	1919	15 900
		Slovenská Technická Univerzita v Bratislave (Slovak Technical University)	1938	12 100
		Vysoká Ekonomicka v Bratislave (School of Economics in Bratislava)	1940	7 400
	Košice	Univerzita Pavla Jozefa Šafárika (Safarik University)	1959	6 100
		Vysoká Škola Veterinárská Košiciach (University of Veterinary Medicine in Košice)	1949	750
		Technická Univerzita v Košiciach (Košice Technical University)	1952	6 400
	Žilina	Vysoká Škola Dopravy a Spojov (University of Transport and Telecommunications)	1953	4 900
Spain	Alcalá de Henares (Madrid)	Universidad de Alcalá de Henares	1977	15 700
	Alicante	Universidad de Alicante	1979	19 500
	Barcelona	Universitat de Barcelona	1450	80 500
	Bellaterra	Universitat Autónoma de Barcelona	1968	33 400
	Bilbao	Universidad de Deusto	1886	15 000
		University of the Basque Country	1968, reorganized 1980	50 500
	Cáceres	Universidad de Extremadura	1973	12 300
	Cádiz	Universidad de Cádiz	1979	14 900
	Ciudad Real	Universidad de Castilla-la-Mancha	1982	18 600
	Córdoba	Universidad de Córdoba	1972	14 000
	Granada	Universidad de Granada	1526	56 200
	La Laguna, Canary Is	Universidad de La Laguna	1792	21 200
	León	Universidad de León	1979	10 300
	Madrid	Universidad Complutense de Madrid	1508	24 150

Country	City	University	Date founded	Approximate number of students
		Universidad Pontificia 'Comillas'	1890 in Santander; moved to Madrid 1960	16 800
		Universidad Autónoma de Madrid	1968	28 000
		Open University	1972	88 000
		Universidad Carlos III de Madrid	1989	4 000
	Málaga	Universidad de Málaga	1972	23 000
	Murcia	Universidad de Murcia	1915	26 400
	Palma de Mallorca	Universitat de Les Illes Balears	1978	9 500
	Las Palmas, Canary Is	Universidad de Las Palmas de Gran Canaria	1980	10 000
	Pamplona	Universidad de Navarra	1952	15 300
	Oviedo	Universidad de Oviedo	1608	36 900
	Salamanca	Universidad Pontificia de Salamanca	1134 as Ecclesiastical School, university status 1219; defunct by end 18th-c, restored 1940	8 500
		Universidad de Salamanca	1218, reorganized 1254	27 600
	Santander	Universidad de Cantabria	1972, as Universidad de Santander	12 000
	Seville	Universidad de Sevilla	1502	56 900
	Valencia	Universitat de València	1510	55 300
	Valladolid	Universidad de Valladolid	13th-c	42 500
	Zaragoza	Universidad de Zaragoza	1583	40 000
Sweden	Gothenburg	Chalmers Tekniska Högskola (Chalmers University of Technology)	1829	4 500
		Göteborgs Universitet	1891	22 000
	Karlstad	Högskolan Karlstad (Karlstad University)	1977	4 300
	Linköping	Universitet Linköping	1970	11 000
	Luleå	Högskolan I Luleå	1971	5 200
	Lund	Lunds Universitet	1666	30 000
	Örebro	Högskolan I Örebro	1967	5 000
	Stockholm	Kungliga Tekniska Högskolan (Royal Institute of Technology)	1827	8 500
		Stockholms Universitet	1877, state university 1960	26 000
	Uppsala	Sveriges Lantbruksuniversitet (Swedish University of Agricultural Sciences)	1977	2 500
		Uppsala Universitet	1477	18 000
	Umeå	Umeå Universitet	1963	10 000
	Växjö	Högskolan Växjö (Växjö University)	1967	3 600
Switzerland	Basel	Universität Basel	1460	6 800
	Bern	Universität Bern	1834	8 000
	Fribourg	Université de Fribourg	1889	5 900
	Geneva	Université de Genève	1559	12 900
	Lausanne	Université de Lausanne	1537	6 700
		École Polytechnique Fédérale de Lausanne	1853	3 900
	Neuchâtel	Université de Neuchâtel	1909	2 900
	Zürich	Universität Zürich	1833	21 100
		Eidgenössische Technische Hochschule Zürich (Swiss Federal Institute of Technology)	1855	11 200
United Kingdom	Aberdeen	University of Aberdeen	1495	8 000
		Robert Gordon University	1885[a]	4 600 full-time, 1 300 part-time
	Aberystwyth	University College of Wales	1872	4 000
	Bangor	University College of North Wales	1884	4 200
	Bath	University of Bath	1966	5 000
	Bedford	Cranfield Institute of Technology	1969	2 091
	Belfast	The Queen's University of Belfast	1908	7 867
	Birmingham	Aston University	1966	4 700
		The University of Birmingham	1900	9 700

Universities of the world (continued)

Country	City	University	Date founded	Approximate number of students
		University of Central England in Birmingham	1971[a]	7800 full-time; 7000 part-time
	Bradford	University of Bradford	1966[a]	5300
	Brighton	University of Brighton	1970[a]	7500
		The University of Sussex	1961	6600
	Bristol	The University of Bristol	1909	9200
		University of the West of England	1969[a]	7000 full-time; 5000 part-time
	Buckingham	University of Buckingham	1983[a]	900
	Chelmsford and Cambridge	Anglia Polytechnic University	1905[a] as Chelmsford School of Science and Art	10700, incl. part-time
	Cambridge	The University of Cambridge		14000
		Christ's College	1505	
		Churchill College	1960	
		Clare College	1326	
		Clare Hall College	1966	
		Corpus Christi College	1352	
		Darwin College	1964	
		Downing College	1800	
		Emmanuel College	1584	
		Fitzwilliam College	1966	
		Girton College	1869	
		Gonville & Caius College	1348	
		Homerton College	1824	
		Hughes Hall College	1885	
		Jesus College	1496	
		King's College	1441	
		Lucy Cavendish College	1965	
		Magdalene College	1542	
		New Hall College	1954	
		Newnham College	1871	
		Pembroke College	1347	
		Peterhouse College	1284	
		Queens' College	1448	
		Robinson College	1977	
		St Catharine's College	1473	
		St Edmund's College	1896	
		St John's College	1511	
		Selwyn College	1882	
		Sidney Sussex College	1596	
		Trinity College	1546	
		Trinity Hall College	1350	
		Wolfson College	1965	
	Canterbury	University of Kent at Canterbury	1965	5500
	Cardiff	The University of Wales	1893	24450
		University of Wales College of Cardiff	1988	11000
		University of Wales	1931	1300
		College of Medicine	1984	
	Colchester	The University of Essex	1964	4600
	Coleraine	University of Ulster	1985	11140
	Coventry	Coventry University	1970[a]	8300
		The University of Warwick	1965	11000
	Dundee	University of Dundee	1967	5500
	Durham	The University of Durham	1832	5500
	Edinburgh	University of Edinburgh	1583	14000
		Heriot-Watt University	1966	8000
		Napier University	1964[a]	5500 full-time; 3500 part-time
	Exeter	The University of Exeter	1955	6800

Country	City	University	Date founded	Approximate number of students
	Glasgow	University of Glasgow	1451	13 460
		Caledonia University	Queen's College 1875; Glasgow Polytechnic 1971[a]; merged 1992	4 000 full-time; 2 700 part-time
		University of Strathclyde	1964	8 500
	Guildford	University of Surrey	1966	5 000
	Hatfield	University of Hertfordshire	1952[a]	8 000
	Huddersfield	University of Huddersfield	1841[a]	6 800 full-time; 2 900 part-time
	Hull	The University of Hull	1954	7 000
		University of Humberside	1978[a]	8 000
	Kingston-upon-Thames	Kingston University	1970[a]	12 700
	Lampeter	St David's College, Lampeter	1827, present status 1971	1 100
	Lancaster	The University of Lancaster	1964	4 500
	Leeds	The University of Leeds	1904	11 500
		Leeds Metropolitan University	1970[a]	9 000 full-time; 7 200 part-time
	Leicester	The University of Leicester	1957	6 800
		De Montfort University	1969[a]	6 300 full-time; 2 300 part-time
	Liverpool	The University of Liverpool	1903	12 100
		Liverpool John Moores University	1970[a]	15 500
	London	City University	1966	5 000
		City of London University	1970[a]	15 000
		University of East London	1970[a]	6 500 full-time; 3 000 part-time
		The University of London	1836	66 000 internal; 22 400 external
		Birkbeck College	1823	
		Goldsmiths' College	1904	
		Imperial College of Science, Technology, and Medicine	1907	
		Institute of Education	1902; controlled by London University since 1932; School of London University since 1987	
		King's College London	1829	
		London School of Economics and Political Science	1895	
		Queen Mary and Westfield College	Queen Mary 1887; Westfield 1882; merged 1989	
	(Egham)	Royal Holloway and Bedford New College	Royal Holloway 1886; Bedford 1849; merged 1985	
		Royal Veterinary College	1791	
		School of Oriental and African Studies	1916	
		School of Pharmacy	1842	
		University College London	1826	
	(Ashford)	Wye College	1447	
		Middlesex University	1973[a]	5 000 full-time; 4 000 sandwich; 2 000 part-time
		University of North London	1971[a]	10 800
		South Bank University	1970[a]	11 000
		University of Westminster	1970[a]	5 000 full-time; 6 500 part-time; 18 000 short course
	Loughborough	Loughborough University of Technology	1966	5 900

Academic study

Universities of the world (continued)

Country	City	University	Date founded	Approximate number of students
	Manchester	Victoria University of Manchester	1851	16 500
		University of Manchester Institute of Science and Technology	1824	
		Manchester Metropolitan University	1970[a]	10 700 full-time; 2 800 sandwich; 7 000 part-time
	Middlesbrough	University of Teesside	1929[a]	7 800
	Milton Keynes	The Open University	1969	195 000
	Newcastle under Lyme	The University of Keele	1962	3 100
	Newcastle upon Tyne	The University of Newcastle upon Tyne	1851	8 500
	Newcastle	University of Northumbria at Newcastle	1969[a]	9 200 full-time; 4 400 part-time
	Norwich	The University of East Anglia	1964	5 800
	Nottingham	City University Nottingham	1970[a]	11 000 full-time; 4 700 part-time
		The University of Nottingham	1948	10 500
	Oxford	The University of Oxford		14 000
		All Souls College	1438	
		Balliol College	1263	
		Brasenose College	1509	
		Christ Church College	1546	
		Corpus Christi College	1517	
		Exeter College	1314	
		Green College	1979	
		Hertford College	1874	
		Jesus College	1571	
		Keble College	1868	
		Lady Margaret Hall College	1878	
		Linacre College	1962	
		Lincoln College	1427	
		Magdalen College	1458	
		Merton College	1263	
		New College College	1379	
		Nuffield College	1937	
		Oriel College	1326	
		Pembroke College	1624	
		Queen's College	1340	
		Rewley House College	1990	
		St Anne's College	1952	
		St Antony's College	1950	
		St Catherine's College	1962	
		St Cross College	1965	
		St Edmund Hall College	c.1278	
		St Hilda's College	1938	
		St Hugh's College	1886	
		St John's College	1555	
		St Peter's College	1929	
		Somerville College	1879	
		Trinity College	1554	
		University College	1249	
		Wadham College	1612	
		Wolfson College	1966	
		Worcester College	1714	
		Oxford Brookes University	1970[a]	6 400 full-time; 2 900 part-time
	Paisley	University of Paisley	1897	4 000 full-time; 1 000 part-time
	Plymouth	University of Plymouth	1970[a]	7 700 full-time; 1 100 part-time

Country	City	University	Date founded	Approximate number of students
	Pontypridd	University of Glamorgan	1913[a] as mining college	4 900 full-time; 1 600 part-time
	Poole	Bournemouth University	1961 as Dorset Institute of Higher Education[a]	8 300
	Portsmouth	University of Portsmouth	1870[a]	8 700 full-time; 1 800 part-time
	Preston	University of Central Lancashire	1956[a]	7 500 full-time; 4 800 part-time
	Reading	The University of Reading	1926	9 600
	Salford	University of Salford	1967	4 300
	Sheffield	The University of Sheffield	1905	9 600
		Sheffield Hallam University	1969[a]	12 200 full-time; 4 800 part-time
	Southampton	The University of Southampton	1952	7 800
	St Andrews	University of St Andrews	1411	4 600
	Stirling	University of Stirling	1967	4 000
	Stoke-on-Trent	Staffordshire University	1970[a]	3 700 full-time; 1 900 sandwich; 2 400 part-time
	Sunderland	University of Sunderland	1969[a]	4 400 full-time; 1 400 part-time
	Swansea	University College, Swansea	1920	5 800
	Uxbridge	Brunel University	1966	4 800
	West London	Thames Valley University	1991[b]	5 900 full-time; 9 000 part-time
	Wolverhampton	University of Wolverhampton	1969[a]	7 362 full-time; 4 885 part-time
	Woolwich	University of Greenwich	1890[a]	12 000
	York	The University of York	1963	4 600

[a]Founded as a polytechnic or other college; university status applied for in 1992; 1991–2 enrolment figures
[b]Formerly Ealing College of Higher Education
na = not available

Country	State	University	Location	Date founded
United States	Alabama	Auburn University	Auburn University	1856
		Tuskegee University	Tuskegee	1881
		University of Alabama	Tuscaloosa	1831
		University of Alabama at Birmingham	Birmingham	1969
		University of Alabama in Huntsville	Huntsville	1950
		University of South Alabama	Mobile	1963
	Alaska	University of Alaska Anchorage	Anchorage	1954
		University of Alaska Fairbanks	Fairbanks	1917
	Arizona	Arizona State University	Tempe	1885
		Northern Arizona University	Flagstaff	1899
		University of Arizona	Tucson	1885
	Arkansas	University of Arkansas	Fayetteville	1871
		University of Arkansas at Little Rock	Little Rock	1927
		University of Arkansas at Pine Bluff	Pine Bluff	1873
	California	California Institute of Technology	Pasadena	1891
		California Polytechnic State University	San Luis Obispo	1901
		California Polytechnic State University	Pomona	1938
		California State University	Bakersfield	1970
		California State University	Chico	1887
		California State University, Dominguez Hills	Carson	1960
		California State University	Fresno	1911
		California State University	Fullerton	1957
		California State University	Hayward	1957
		California State University	Long Beach	1949
		California State University	Los Angeles	1847
		California State University	Northridge	1958
		California State University	Sacramento	1947
		California State University	San Bernardino	1965

Universities of the world (continued)

Country	State	University	Location	Date founded
		Loyola Marymount University	Los Angeles	1911
		National University	San Diego	1971
		Pomona College	Claremont	1887
		San Diego State University	San Diego	1897
		San Francisco State University	San Francisco	1899
		San Jose State University	San Jose	1857
		Santa Clara University	Santa Clara	1851
		Stanford University	Stanford	1891
		University of California at Berkeley	Berkeley	1868
		University of California, Davis	Davis	1906
		University of California, Irvine	Irvine	1965
		University of California, Los Angeles	Los Angeles	1919
		University of California, Riverside	Riverside	1954
		University of California, San Diego	La Jolla	1959
		University of California, Santa Barbara	Santa Barbara	1891
		University of California, Santa Cruz	Santa Cruz	1965
		University of Southern California	Los Angeles	1880
	Colorado	Colorado School of Mines	Golden	1874
		Colorado State University	Fort Collins	1862
		Metropolitan State College	Denver	1965
		University of Colorado at Boulder	Boulder	1876
		University of Northern Colorado	Greeley	1890
	Connecticut	Central Connecticut State University	New Britain	1849
		Fairfield University	Fairfield	1942
		Southern Connecticut State University	New Haven	1893
		University of Connecticut	Storrs	1881
		Wesleyan University	Middletown	1831
		Yale University	New Haven	1701
	Delaware	University of Delaware	Newark	1743
	District of Columbia	American University	Washington	1893
		Catholic University of America	Washington	1887
		Gallaudet University	Washington	1856
		Georgetown University	Washington	1789
		George Washington University	Washington	1821
		Howard University	Washington	1867
		University of the District of Columbia	Washington	1976
	Florida	Florida Atlantic University	Boca Raton	1961
		Florida International University	Miami	1965
		Florida State University	Tallahassee	1857
		Nova University	Fort Lauderdale	1964
		University of Central Florida	Orlando	1963
		University of Florida	Gainsville	1853
		University of Miami	Coral Gables	1925
		University of South Florida	Tampa	1956
	Georgia	Emory University	Atlanta	1836
		Georgia Institute of Technology	Atlanta	1885
		Georgia Southern University	Statesboro	1906
		Georgia State University	Atlanta	1913
		University of Georgia	Athens	1785
	Hawaii	University of Hawaii at Hilo	Hilo	1970
		University of Hawaii at Manoa	Honolulu	1907
	Idaho	Boise State University	Boise	1932
		University of Idaho	Moscow	1889
	Illinois	DePaul University	Chicago	1898
		Eastern Illinois University	Charleston	1895
		Illinois State University	Normal	1857
		Loyola University Chicago	Chicago	1870
		Northern Illinois University	De Kalb	1895
		Northeastern Illinois University	Chicago	1961
		Northwestern University	Evanston	1851
		Southern Illinois University of Carbondale	Carbondale	1869
		Southern Illinois University at Edwardsville	Edwardsville	1957
		University of Chicago	Chicago	1891
		University of Illinois at Chicago	Chicago	1965
		University of Illinois at Urbana – Champaign	Urbana	1867

Country	State	University	Location	Date founded
		Western Illinois University	Macomb	1899
	Indiana	Ball State University	Muncie	1918
		Indiana State Univesity	Terre Haute	1865
		Indiana State University Kokomo	Kokomo	1945
		Indiana University at Bloomington	Bloomington	1820
		Indiana University at South Bend	South Bend	1922
		Indiana University Northwest	Gary	1959
		Indiana University of Pennsylvania	Indiana	1875
		Indiana University – Purdue University at Fort Wayne	Fort Wayne	1917
		Indiana University – Purdue University at Indianapolis	Indianapolis	1969
		Indiana University Southeast	New Albany	1941
		Purdue University	West Lafayette	1869
		Purdue University Calumet	Hammond	1951
		Purdue University North Central	Westville	1967
		University of Notre Dame	Notre Dame	1842
		Valparaiso University	Valparaiso	1859
	Iowa	Drake University	Des Moines	1881
		Grinnell College	Grinnell	1846
		Iowa State University of Science and Technology	Ames	1858
		University of Iowa	Iowa City	1947
		University of Northern Iowa	Cedar Falls	1876
	Kansas	Kansas State University	Manhattan	1863
		University of of Kansas	Lawrence	1866
		Wichita State University	Wichita	1895
	Kentucky	Bellarmine College	Louisville	1950
		University of Kentucky	Lexington	1865
		University of Louisville	Louisville	1798
		Western Kentucky University	Bowling Green	1906
	Louisiana	Louisiana State University and A&M College	Baton Rouge	1860
		Louisiana Technical University	Ruston	1894
		Loyola University New Orleans	New Orleans	1912
		Northeast Louisiana University	Monroe	1931
		Southern University and A&M College	Baton Rouge	1880
		Tulane University	New Orleans	1834
		University of New Orleans	New Orleans	1958
		University of Southwestern Louisiana	Lafayette	1898
	Maine	Bowdoin College	Brunswick	1794
		University of Maine	Orono	1865
		University of Southern Maine	Portland	1878
	Maryland	Johns Hopkins University	Baltimore	1876
		Towson State University	Towson	1866
		University of Maryland Baltimore County	Baltimore	1966
		University of Maryland College Park	College Park	1856
		University of Maryland University College	College Park	1947
		Washington College	Chestertown	1782
	Massachusetts	Amherst College	Amherst	1821
		Boston College	Chestnut Hill	1863
		Boston University	Boston	1839
		Brandeis University	Waltham	1948
		College of the Holy Cross	Worcester	1843
		Harvard University	Cambridge	1636
		Massachusetts Institute of Technology	Cambridge	1861
		Northeastern University	Boston	1898
		Smith College	Northampton	1871
		Tufts University	Medford	1852
		University of Lowell	Lowell	1894
		University of Massachusetts at Amherst	Amherst	1863
		University of Massachusetts at Boston	Boston	1964
		Wellesley College	Wellesley	1870
		Wheaton College	Norton	1834
		Williams College	Williamstown	1793
	Michigan	Central Michigan University	Mount Pleasant	1892
		Eastern Michigan University	Ypsilanti	1849
		Ferris State University	Big Rapids	1884

Universities of the world (continued)

Country	State	University	Location	Date founded
		Grand Valley State University	Allendale	1960
		Michigan State University	East Lansing	1855
		Oakland University	Rochester	1957
		University of Michigan	Ann Arbor	1817
		University of Michigan – Dearborn	Dearborn	1959
		University of Michigan – Flint	Flint	1956
		Wayne State University	Detroit	1868
		Western Michigan University	Kalamazoo	1903
	Minnesota	Mankato State University	Mankato	1867
		St Cloud State University	St Cloud	1869
		University of Minnesota, Twin Cities Campus	Minneapolis	1851
	Mississippi	Mississippi State University	Mississippi State	1878
		University of Mississippi	University	1844
		University of Southern Mississippi	Hattiesburg	1910
	Missouri	Central Missouri State University	Warrensburg	1871
		Saint Louis University	St Louis	1818
		Southwest Missouri State University	Springfield	1905
		Stephens College	Columbia	1833
		University of Missouri – Columbia	Columbia	1839
		University of Missouri – Kansas City	Kansas City	1933
		University of Missouri – Rolla	Rolla	1870
		University of Missouri – St Louis	St Louis	1963
		Washington University	St Louis	1853
	Montana	Montana State University	Bozeman	1893
		University of Montana	Missoula	1893
	Nebraska	Creighton University	Omaha	1878
		University of Nebraska at Kearney	Kearney	1903
		University of Nebraska at Omaha	Omaha	1908
		University of Nebraska – Lincoln	Lincoln	1869
	Nevada	University of Nevada, Las Vegas	Las Vegas	1957
		University of Nevada, Reno	Reno	1874
	New Hampshire	Dartmouth College	Hanover	1769
		University of New Hampshire	Durham	1866
		Drew University	Madison	1866
	New Jersey	Fairleigh-Dickinson University, Teaneck-Hackensack Campus	Teaneck	1954
		Kean College of New Jersey	Union	1855
		Montclair State College	Upper Montclair	1908
		Princeton University	Princeton	1746
		Rutgers, State University of New Jersey		
		Douglas College	New Brunswick	1918
		Livingston College	New Brunswick	1969
		Newark College of Arts and Science	Newark	1946
		Rutgers College	New Brunswick	1766
		University College – New Brunswick	New Brunswick	1934
		Seton Hall University	South Orange	1856
		William Paterson College of New Jersey	Wayne	1855
	New Mexico	New Mexico State University	Las Cruces	1888
		University of New Mexico	Albuquerque	1889
	New York	Adelphi University	Garden City	1896
		Barnard College	New York	1889
		Baruch College of the City University of New York	New York	1968
		Brooklyn College of the City University of New York	New York	1930
		City College of the City University of New York	New York	1847
		Clarkson University	Potsdam	1896
		Colgate University	Hamilton	1819
		College of Staten Island of the City University of New York	New York	1955
		Columbia College	New York	1754

Country	State	University	Location	Date founded
		Columbia University School of Engineering and Applied Science	New York	1864
		Columbia University School of General Studies	New York	1754
		Cooper Union for the Advancement of Science and Art	New York	1859
		Cornell University	Ithaca	1865
		Fashion Institute of Technology	New York	1944
		Fordham University	New York	1841
		Hamilton College	Clinton	1812
		Hartwick College	Oneonta	1797
		Hofstra University	Hempstead	1935
		Hunter College of the City University of New York	New York	1870
		Ithaca College	Ithaca	1892
		Juilliard School	New York	1905
		Long Island University, Brooklyn Campus	Brooklyn	1926
		Long Island University, CW Post Campus	Brookville	1954
		New York Institute of Technology	Old Westbury	1955
		New York University	New York	1831
		Pace University	New York	1906
		Parsons School of Design, New School for Social Research	New York	1896
		Pratt Institute	Brooklyn	1887
		Queens College of the City University of New York	Flushing	1937
		Rensselaer Polytechnic Institute	Troy	1824
		Rochester Institute of Technology	Rochester	1829
		Sarah Lawrence College	Bronxville	1926
		Skidmore College	Saratoga Springs	1903
		St John's University	Jamaica	1870
		State University of New York at Albany	Albany	1844
		State University of New York at Binghamton	Binghamton	1946
		State University of New York at Buffalo	Buffalo	1946
		State University of New York at Stony Brook	Brook	1957
		State University of New York, College at Brockport	Brockport	1867
		State University of New York, College at Buffalo	Buffalo	1867
		State University of New York, College at Cortland	Cortland	1868
		State University of New York, College at Fredonia	Fredonia	1826
		State University of New York, College at Geneseo	Geneseo	1867
		State University of New York, College at New Paltz	New Paltz	1828
		State University of New York, College at Old Westbury	Old Westbury	1965
		State University of New York, College at Oneonta	Oneonta	1889
		State University of New York, College at Oswego	Oswego	1861
		State University of New York, College at Plattsburgh	Plattsburgh	1889
		State University of New York, College at Potsdam	Potsdam	1816
		State University of New York, Empire State College	Saratoga Springs	1971
		Syracuse University	Syracuse	1870
		Union College	Schenectady	1795
		State University of New York, Regents College	Albany	1971
		Vassar College	Poughkeepsie	1861
		Yeshiva University	New York	1886
	North Carolina	Appalachian State University	Boone	1899
		Duke University	Durham	1838
		East Carolina University	Greenville	1907
		North Carolina State University	Raleigh	1887
		University of North Carolina at Asheville	Asheville	1927
		University of North Carolina at Chapel Hill	Chapel Hill	1795
		University of North Carolina at Charlotte	Charlotte	1946
		University of North Carolina at Greensboro	Greensboro	1891
		University of North Carolina at Wilmington	Wilmington	1947
		Wake Forest University	Winston-Salem	1834

Knowledge

Universities of the world (continued)

Country	State	University	Location	Date founded
	North Dakota	University of North Dakota	Grand Forks	1883
	Ohio	Bowling Green State University	Bowling Green	1910
		Case Western Reserve University	Cleveland	1826
		Cleveland State University	Cleveland	1964
		John Carroll University	University Heights	1886
		Kent State University	Kent	1910
		Miami University	Oxford	1809
		Oberlin College	Oberlin	1833
		Ohio State University	Columbus	1870
		Ohio University	Athens	1804
		University of Akron	Akron	1870
		University of Cincinnati	Cincinnati	1819
		University of Dayton	Dayton	1850
		University of Toledo	Toledo	1872
		Wright State University	Dayton	1964
		Xavier University	Cincinnati	1831
		Youngstown State University	Youngstown	1908
	Oklahoma	Central State University	Edmond	1890
		Oklahoma State University	Stillwater	1890
		Oral Roberts University	Tulsa	1963
		University of Oklahoma	Norman	1890
	Oregon	Oregon State University	Corvallis	1868
		Portland State University	Portland	1946
		University of Oregon	Eugene	1872
	Pennsylvania	Bryn Mawr College	Bryn Mawr	1885
		Bucknell University	Lewisburg	1846
		Carnegie Mellon University	Pittsburgh	1900
		Dickinson College	Carlisle	1773
		Drexel University	Philadelphia	1891
		Duquesne University	Pittsburgh	1878
		Haverford College	Haverford	1833
		La Salle University	Philadelphia	1863
		Lehigh University	Bethlehem	1865
		Moravian College	Bethlehem	1742
		Pennsylvania State University, University Park Campus	University Park	1855
		Swarthmore College	Swarthmore	1864
		Temple University	Philadelphia	1884
		Temple University, Ambler Campus	Ambler	1910
		University of Pennyslvania	Philadelphia	1740
		University of Pittsburgh	Pittsburgh	1787
		University of Pittsburgh at Johnstown	Johnstown	1927
		Villanova University	Villanova	1842
		Washington and Jefferson College	Washington	1781
		West Chester University of Pennsylvania	West Chester	1871
	Rhode Island	Brown University	Providence	1764
		Rhode Island School of Design	Providence	1877
		University of Rhode Island	Kingston	1892
	South Carolina	The Citadel, The Military College of South Carolina	Charleston	1842
		Clemson University	Clemson	1889
		Converse College	Spartanburg	1889
		University of South Carolina	Columbia	1801
		University of South Carolina at Spartanburg	Spartanburg	1967
		University of South Carolina – Coastal Carolina College	Conway	1954
	Tennessee	East Tennessee State University	Johnson City	1911
		Memphis State University	Memphis	1912
		Middle Tennessee State University	Murfreesboro	1911
		University of Tennessee at Chattanooga	Chattanooga	1886
		University of Tennessee at Martin	Martin	1927
		University of Tennessee, Knoxville	Knoxville	1794
		Vanderbilt University	Nashville	1873
	Texas	Abilene Christian University	Abilene	1906

Country	State	University	Location	Date founded
		Baylor University	Waco	1845
		Lamar University	Beaumont	1923
		Rice University	Houston	1912
		Sam Houston State University	Huntsville	1879
		Southern Methodist University	Dallas	1911
		Southwest Texas State University	San Marcos	1899
		Stephen F Austin State University	Nacogdoches	1923
		Texas A&M University	College Station	1876
		Texas Technical University	Lubbock	1923
		Trinity University	San Antonio	1869
		University of Houston	Houston	1927
		University of Houston – Clear Lake	Houston	1971
		University of Houston – Downtown	Houston	1974
		University of North Texas	Denton	1890
		University of Texas at Arlington	Arlington	1895
		University of Texas at Austin	Austin	1883
		University of Texas at Dallas	Richardson	1969
		University of Texas at El Paso	El Paso	1913
		University of Texas at San Antonio	San Antonio	1969
		University of Texas at Tyler	Tyler	1972
		University of Texas – Pan American	Edinburg	1927
	Utah	Brigham Young University	Provo	1875
		University of Utah	Salt Lake City	1850
		Utah State University	Logan	1888
		Weber State College	Ogden	1889
	Vermont	University of Vermont	Burlington	1791
	Virginia	College of William and Mary	Williamsburg	1693
		George Mason University	Fairfax	1957
		Hampden-Sydney College	Hampden-Sydney	1776
		James Madison University	Harrisonburg	1908
		Liberty University	Lynchburg	1971
		Old Dominion University	Norfolk	1930
		University of Virginia	Charlottesville	1810
		Virginia Commonwealth University	Richmond	1838
		Virginia Polytechnic Institute and State University	Blacksburg	1872
		Washington and Lee University	Lexington	1749
	Washington	Gonzaga University	Spokane	1887
		University of Washington	Seattle	1861
		Washington State University	Pullman	1892
	West Virginia	Marshall University	Hungtinton	1837
		West Virginia University	Morgantown	1867
	Wisconsin	Marquette University	Milwaukee	1881
		University of Wisconsin – Eau Claire	Eau Claire	1916
		University of Wisconsin – Green Bay	Green Bay	1968
		University of Wisconsin – La Crosse	La Crosse	1909
		University of Wisconsin – Madison	Madison	1848
		University of Wisconsin – Milwaukee	Milwaukee	1956
		University of Wisconsin – Oshkosh	Oshkosh	1871
		University of Wisconsin – Parkside	Kenosha	1968
		University of Wisconsin – Platteville	Platteville	1866
		University of Wisconsin – River Falls	River Falls	1874
		University of Wisconsin – Stevens Point	Stevens Point	1894
		University of Wisconsin – Stout	Menomonie	1891
		University of Wisconsin – Whitewater	Whitewater	1868
	Wyoming	University of Wyoming	Laramie	1886

Knowledge

SPORTS AND GAMES

OLYMPIC GAMES

The first modern Olympic Games took place in 1896, founded by the Frenchman Baron de Coubertin. They are held every four years. Women first competed in 1900. The first separate Winter Games celebration was in 1924; beginning in 1994, the Winter Games will take place between Summer Games celebrations.

Venues

	Summer Games	Winter Games
1896	Athens, Greece	–
1900	Paris, France	–
1904	St Louis, USA	–
1908	London, UK	–
1912	Stockholm, Sweden	–
1920	Antwerp, Belgium	–
1924	Paris, France	Chamonix, France
1928	Amsterdam, Netherlands	St Moritz, Switzerland
1932	Los Angeles, USA	Lake Placid, NY, USA
1936	Berlin, Germany	Garmisch-Partenkirchen, Germany
1948	London, UK	St Moritz, Switzerland
1952	Helsinki, Finland	Oslo, Norway
1956	Melbourne, Australia	Cortina, Italy
1960	Rome, Italy	Squaw Valley, CA, USA
1964	Tokyo, Japan	Innsbruck, Austria
1968	Mexico City, Mexico	Grenoble, France
1972	Munich, West Germany	Sapporo, Japan
1976	Montreal, Canada	Innsbruck, Austria
1980	Moscow, USSR	Lake Placid, NY, USA
1984	Los Angeles, USA	Sarajevo, Yugoslavia
1988	Seoul, South Korea	Calgary, Canada
1992	Barcelona, Spain	Albertville, France
1994	–	Lillehammer, Norway
1996	Atlanta, USA	–

Olympic Games were also held in 1906 in Athens, Greece, to commemorate the 10th anniversary of the birth of the modern Games.

The 1956 equestrian events were held at Stockholm, Sweden, due to quarantine laws in Australia.

Leading medal winners (including 1992)

	Summer Games	Gold	Silver	Bronze	Total
1	USA	783	594	512	1889
2	Germany[a]	343	357	362	1062
3	USSR	395	323	299	1017
	Unified Team (1992)	45	38	29	112
4	Great Britain	178	225	218	621
5	France	161	172	193	526
6	Sweden	132	146	173	451
7	Italy	153	126	132	411
8	Hungary	135	124	143	402
9	Finland	98	77	112	287

	Winter Games	Gold	Silver	Bronze	Total
1	Germany[a]	75	72	64	211
2	USSR	79	57	59	195
	Unified Team (1992)	9	6	8	23
3	Norway	63	66	59	188
4	USA	47	51	36	134
5	Austria	34	45	40	119
6	Finland	36	44	37	117
7	Sweden	37	25	34	96
8	Switzerland	24	25	27	76
9	Canada	16	15	20	51

The USSR dissolved in 1991. The newly formed Unified Team, consisting of competitors from 12 of the former soviet republics, gained the most medals in the 1992 Summer Games and the second highest number of medals in the 1992 Winter Games.

[a]This figure includes East Germany's total (shown below) for the years 1968–88 when West and East Germany competed as two nations.

	Gold	Silver	Bronze	Total
Summer	153	129	127	409
Winter	39	36	35	110

COMMONWEALTH GAMES

First held as the British Empire Games in 1930. They take place every four years and between Olympic celebrations. They became the British Empire and Commonwealth Games in 1954; the current title was adopted in 1970.

Venues

1930	Hamilton, Canada
1934	London, England
1938	Sydney, Australia
1950	Auckland, New Zealand
1954	Vancouver, Canada
1958	Cardiff, Wales
1962	Perth, Australia
1966	Kingston, Jamaica
1970	Edinburgh, Scotland
1974	Christchurch, New Zealand
1978	Edmonton, Canada
1982	Brisbane, Australia
1986	Edinburgh, Scotland
1990	Auckland, New Zealand
1994	Victoria, Canada

Leading medal winners (including 1990)

	Nation	Gold	Silver	Bronze	Total
1	England	420	368	368	1156
2	Australia	397	374	382	1153
3	Canada	287	301	299	887
4	New Zealand	94	121	161	376
5	Scotland	56	74	109	239
6	South Africa	60	44	47	151
7	Wales	32	39	60	131
8	India	37	36	31	104
9	Kenya	35	24	33	92
10	Northern Ireland	15	20	34	69

Sports and games

ANGLING

World freshwater championship

First held in 1957; takes place annually.

Recent winners: individual
1979 Gérard Heulard (France)
1980 Wolf-Rüdiger Kremkus (W Germany)
1981 David Thomas (England)
1982 Kevin Ashurst (England)
1983 Wolf-Rüdiger Kremkus (W Germany)
1984 Bobby Smithers (Ireland)
1985 David Roper (England)
1986 Lud Wever (Netherlands)
1987 Clive Branson (Wales)
1988 Jean-Pierre Fouquet (France)
1989 Tom Pickering (England)
1990 Bob Nudd (England)
1991 Bob Nudd (England)
1992 David Wesson (Australia)
1993 (Portugal)

Recent winners: team
1979 France
1980 W Germany
1981 France
1982 Netherlands
1983 Belgium
1984 Luxembourg
1985 England
1986 Italy
1987 England
1988 England
1989 Wales
1990 France
1991 England
1992 Italy
1993 Italy

Most wins: Individual (3), Robert Tesse (France): 1959–60, 1965. Team (12), France: 1959, 1963–4, 1966, 1968, 1972, 1974–5, 1978–9, 1981, 1990.

World fly-fishing championship

First held in 1981; takes place annually.

Winners: individual
1981 C. Wittkamp (Netherlands)
1982 Viktor Diez y Diez (Spain)
1983 Segismondo Fernandez (Spain)
1984 Tony Pawson (England)
1985 Lesław Frasik (Poland)
1986 Slivoj Svoboda (Czechoslovakia)

1987 Brian Leadbetter (England)
1988 John Pawson (England)
1989 Władysław Trzebuinia (Poland)
1990 Franciszek Szajnik (Poland)
1991 Brian Leadbetter (England)
1992 Pierluigi Cocito (Italy)
1993 Russell Owen (Wales)

Winners: team
1981 Netherlands
1982 Italy
1983 Italy
1984 Italy
1985 Poland
1986 Italy
1987 England
1988 England
1989 Poland
1990 Czechoslovakia
1991 New Zealand
1992 Italy
1993 England

Most wins: Individual (2), Brian Leadbetter (England): 1987, 1991. Team (5), Italy: 1982–84, 1986, 1992.

ARCHERY

World championships

First held in 1931; took place annually until 1959; since then, every two years.

Recent winners: individual – men
1969 Hardy Ward (USA)
1971 John Williams (USA)
1973 Vikto Sidoruk (USSR)
1975 Darrell Pace (USA)
1977 Richard McKinney (USA)
1979 Darrell Pace (USA)
1981 Kysti Laasonen (Finland)
1983 Richard McKinney (USA)
1985 Richard McKinney (USA)
1987 Vladimir Yesheyev (USSR)
1989 Stanislav Zabrodsky (USSR)
1991 Simon Fairweather (Australia)
1993 Kim Park (Korea)

Recent winners: team – men
1969 USA
1971 USA
1973 USA
1975 USA
1977 USA
1979 USA
1981 USA
1983 USA
1985 South Korea
1987 South Korea

1989 USSR
1991 South Korea
1993 France

Most wins: Individual (4), Hans Deutgen (Sweden): 1947–50. Team (14), USA: 1957–83.

Recent winners: individual – women
1969 Dorothy Lidstone (Canada)
1971 Emma Gapchenko (USSR)
1973 Linda Myers (USA)
1975 Zebiniso Rustamova (USSR)
1977 Luann Ryon (USA)
1979 Kim Jin-ho (South Korea)
1981 Natalia Butuzova (USSR)
1983 Kim Jin-ho (South Korea)
1985 Irina Soldatova (USSR)
1987 Ma Xiaojun (China)
1989 Kim Soo-nyung (South Korea)
1991 Kim Soo-nyung (South Korea)
1993 Kim Hyo Jung (Korea)

Recent winners: team – women
1969 USSR
1971 Poland
1973 USSR
1975 USSR
1977 USA
1979 South Korea
1981 USSR
1983 South Korea
1985 USSR
1987 USSR
1989 South Korea
1991 South Korea
1991 Korea

Most wins: Individual (7), Janina Kurkowska (Poland): 1931–4, 1936, 1939, 1947. Team (8), USA: 1952, 1957–9, 1961, 1963, 1965, 1977.

Olympic Games

Gold medal winners: 1992
Individual (men)
Sebastien Flute (France)

Team (men)
Spain

Individual (women)
Cho Youn Jeong (South Korea)

Team (women)
South Korea

ATHLETICS

Performance times are given in seconds, or minutes:seconds, or hours:minutes:seconds. Distances are given in metres. Performances in the decathlon, pentathlon, and heptathlon are given in points.

World championships

First held in Helsinki, Finland, in 1983; then in Rome, Italy, in 1987; Tokyo, Japan, in 1991, and Stuttgart, Germany in 1993.

Event winners: men

100 m
1987   Carl Lewis (USA) 9.93[a]
1991   Carl Lewis (USA) 9.86
1993   Linford Christie (Great Britain) 9.87

200 m
1987   Calvin Smith (USA) 20.16
1991   Michael Johnson (USA) 20.01
1993   Frankie Fredericks (Namibia) 19.85

400 m
1987   Thomas Schlönlebe (E Germany) 44.33
1991   Antonio Pettigrew (USA) 44.57
1993   Michael Johnson (USA) 43.65

800 m
1987   Billy Konchellah (Kenya) 1:43.06
1991   Billy Konchellah (Kenya) 1:43.99
1993   Paul Ruto (Kenya) 1:44.71

1500 m
1987   Abdi Bile (Somalia) 3:36.80
1991   Noureddine Morceli (Algeria) 3:32.84
1993   Noureddine Morceli (Algeria) 3:34.24

5000 m
1987   Saïd Aouita (Morocco) 13:26.44
1991   Yobes Ondieki (Kenya) 13:14.45
1993   Ismael Kurui (Kenya) 13:02.75

10000 m
1987   Paul Kipkoech (Kenya) 27:38.63
1991   Moses Tanui (Kenya) 27:38.74
1993   Haile Gebresilassie (Ethiopia) 27:46.02

Marathon
1987   Douglas Wakiihuri (Kenya) 2:11:48
1991   Hiromi Taniguchi (Japan) 2:14:57
1993   Mark Plaatjes (USA) 2:13:57

3000 m steeplechase
1987   Francesco Panetta (Italy) 8:08.57
1991   Moses Kiptanui (Kenya) 8:12.59
1993   Moses Kiptanui (Kenya) 8:06.36

110 m hurdles
1987   Greg Foster (USA) 13:21
1991   Greg Foster (USA) 13:06
1993   Colin Jackson (Great Britain) 12.91

400 m hurdles
1987   Edwin Moses (USA) 47:46
1991   Samuel Matete (Zambia) 47:64
1993   Kevin Young (USA) 47:18

High jump
1987   Patrik Sjöberg (Sweden) 2.38
1991   Charles Austin (USA) 2.38
1993   Javier Sotomayor (Cuba) 2.40

Pole vault
1987   Sergey Bubka (USSR) 5.85
1991   Sergey Bubka (USSR) 5.92
1991   Sergey Bubka (Ukraine) 6.00

Long jump
1987   Carl Lewis (USA) 8.67
1991   Mike Powell (USA) 8.95
1993   Mike Powell (USA) 8.59

Triple jump
1987   Khristo Markov (Bulgaria) 17.92
1991   Kenny Harrison (USA) 17.78
1993   Mike Conley (USA) 17.86

Shot
1987   Werner Günthör (Switzerland) 22.23
1991   Werner Günthör (Switzerland) 21.67
1993   Werner Günthör (Switzerland) 21.97

Discus
1987   Jürgen Schult (E Germany) 68.74
1991   Lars Riedel (Germany) 66.20
1993   Lars Riedel (Germany) 67.72

Hammer
1987   Sergey Litvinov (USSR) 83.06
1991   Yuriy Sedykh (USSR) 81.70
1993   Andrey Abdu Valeyiv (Tajikistan) 81.64

Javelin
1987   Seppo Räty (Finland) 83.54
1991   Kimmo Kinnunen (Finland) 90.82
1993   Jan Zelezny (Czech Republic) 85.98

Decathlon
1987   Torsten Voss (E Germany) 8680
1991   Dan O'Brien (USA) 8812
1993   Dan O'Brien (USA) 8817

4 × 100 m relay
1987   USA 37.90
1991   USA 37.50
1993   USA 37.48

4 × 400 m relay
1987   USA 2:57.29
1991   Great Britain 2:57.53
1993   USA 2:54.29

20 km walk
1987   Maurizio Damilano (Italy) 1:20:45
1991   Maurizio Damilano (Italy) 1:19:37
1993   Valentin Massana (Spain) 1:22.31

50 km walk
1987   Hartwig Gauder (E Germany) 3:40:53
1991   Aleksandr Potashov (USSR) 3:53:09
1993   Jesús Angel Garcia (Spain) 3:41.41

[a]Ben Johnson (Canada) stripped of this title following IAAF ruling on illegal drug-taking.

Sports and games

Event winners: women

100 m
1987   Silke Gladisch (E Germany) 10.90
1991   Katrin Krabbe (Germany) 10.99
1993   Gail Devers (USA) 10.82

200 m
1987   Silke Gladisch (E Germany) 21.74
1991   Katrin Krabbe (Germany) 22.09
1993   Merlene Ottey (Jamaica) 21.98

400 m
1987   Olga Bryzgina (USSR) 49.38
1991   Marie-José Pérec (France) 49.13
1993   Jearl Miles (USA) 49.82

800 m
1987   Sigrun Wodars (E Germany) 1:55.26
1991   Lilia Nurutdinova (USSR) 1:57.50
1993   Maria Mutola (Mozambique) 1:55.43

1500 m
1987   Tatyana Samolenko (USSR) 3:58.56
1991   Hassiba Boulmerka (Algeria) 4:02.21
1993   Liu Dong (China) 4:00.50

3000 m
1987   Tatyana Samolenko (USSR) 8:38.73
1991   Tatyana Dorovskikh (USSR) 8:35.82
1993   Qu Yunxia (China) 8:28.71

10000 m
1987   Ingrid Kristiansen (Norway) 31:05.85
1991   Liz McColgan (Great Britain) 31:14.31
1993   Wang Junxia (China) 30:39.30

Marathon
1987   Rosa Mota (Portugal) 2:25:17
1991   Wanda Panfil (Poland) 2:29:53
1993   Junko Asari (Japan) 2:30.03

100 m hurdles
1987   Ginka Zagorcheva (Bulgaria) 12.34
1991   Lyudmila Narozhilenko (USSR) 12.59
1993   Gail Devers (USA) 12.46

400 m hurdles
1987   Sabine Busch (E Germany) 53.62
1991   Tatyana Ledovskaya (USSR) 53.11
1993   Sally Gunnell (Great Britain) 52.74

High jump
1987   Stefka Kostadinova (Bulgaria) 2.09
1991   Heike Henkel (Germany) 2.05
1993   Ioamnet Quintero (Cuba) 1.99

Long jump
1987   Jackie Joyner-Kersee (USA) 7.36
1991   Jackie Joyner-Kersee (USA) 7.32
1993   Heike Drechsler (Germany) 7.11

Shot
1987   Natalya Lisovskaya (USSR) 21.24
1991   Huang Zhihong (China) 20.83
1993   Huang Zhihong (China) 20.57

Discus
1987   Martina Hellmann (E Germany) 71.62
1991   Tsvetanka Khristova (Bulgaria) 71.02
1993   Olga Burova (Russia) 67.40

Javelin
1987   Fatima Whitbread (Great Britain) 76.64
1991   Xu Demei (China) 68.78
1993   Trine Hattestool (Norway) 69.18

Heptathlon
1987   Jackie Joyner-Kersee (USA) 7128
1991   Sabine Braun (Germany) 6672
1993   Jackie Joyner-Kersee (USA) 6837

10 km walk
1991   Alina Ivanova (USSR) 42:57
1993   Sari Essayah (Finland) 42:59

4 × 100 m relay
1987   USA 41.58
1991   Jamaica 41.94
1993   Russia 41.49

4 × 400 m relay
1987   E Germany 3:18.63
1991   USSR 3:18.43
1993   USA 3:16.71

Olympic Games

Event winners: men
100 m
1896   Thomas Burke (USA) 12.0
1900   Francis Jarvis (USA) 11.0
1904   Archie Hahn (USA) 11.0
1906   Archie Hahn (USA) 11.2
1908   Reginald Walker (S Africa) 10.8
1912   Ralph Craig (USA) 10.8
1920   Charles Paddock (USA) 10.8
1924   Harold Abrahams (Great Britain) 10.6
1928   Percy Williams (Canada) 10.8
1932   Eddie Tolan (USA) 10.3
1936   Jesse Owens (USA) 10.3
1948   Harrison Dillard (USA) 10.3
1952   Lindy Remigino (USA) 10.4
1956   Bobby Morrow (USA) 10.5
1960   Armin Hary (W Germany) 10.2
1964   Bob Hayes (USA) 10.06
1968   James Hines (USA) 9.95
1972   Valeriy Borzov (USSR) 10.14
1976   Hasely Crawford (Trinidad) 10.06
1980   Allan Wells (Great Britain) 10.25
1984   Carl Lewis (USA) 9.99
1988   Carl Lewis (USA) 9.92
1992   Linford Christie (Great Britain) 9.96

200 m
1900   John Walter Tewksbury (USA) 22.2
1904   Archie Hahn (USA) 21.6
1908   Robert Kerr (Canada) 22.6
1912   Ralph Craig (USA) 21.7
1920   Allen Woodring (USA) 22.0
1924   Jackson Scholz (USA) 21.6
1928   Percy Williams (Canada) 21.8
1932   Eddie Tolan (USA) 21.2
1936   Jesse Owens (USA) 20.7
1948   Melvin Patton (USA) 21.1
1952   Andrew Stanfield (USA) 20.7
1956   Bobby Morrow (USA) 20.5
1960   Livio Berruti (Italy) 20.6

1964 Henry Carr (USA) 20.36
1968 Tommie Smith (USA) 19.83
1972 Valeriy Borzov (USSR) 20.00
1976 Donald Quarrie (Jamaica) 20.3
1980 Pietro Mennea (Italy) 20.19
1984 Carl Lewis (USA) 19.80
1988 Joe DeLoach (USA) 19.75
1992 Michael Marsh (USA) 20.01

400 m
1896 Thomas Burke (USA) 54.2
1900 Maxey Long (USA) 49.4
1904 Harry Hillman (USA) 49.2
1906 Paul Pilgrim (USA) 53.2
1908 Wyndham Halswelle (Great Britain) 50.0
1912 Charles Reidpath (USA) 48.2
1920 Bevil Rudd (S Africa) 49.6
1924 Eric Liddell (Great Britain) 47.6
1928 Ray Barbuti (USA) 47.8
1932 Bill Carr (USA) 46.28
1936 Archie Williams (USA) 46.66
1948 Arthur Wint (Jamaica) 46.2
1952 George Rhoden (Jamaica) 46.09
1956 Charles Jenkins (USA) 46.86
1960 Otis Davis (USA) 45.07
1964 Michael Larrabee (USA) 45.15
1968 Lee Evans (USA) 43.86
1972 Vincent Matthews (USA) 44.66
1976 Alberto Juantoreno (Cuba) 44.26
1980 Viktor Markin (USSR) 44.60
1984 Alonzo Babers (USA) 44.27
1988 Steve Lewis (USA) 43.87
1992 Quincy Watts (USA) 43.50

800 m
1896 Edwin Flack (Australia) 2:11.0
1900 Alfred Tycoe (Great Britain) 2:01.2
1904 James Lightbody (USA) 1:56.0
1906 Paul Pilgrim (USA) 2:01.5
1908 Mel Sheppard (USA) 1:52.8
1912 James Meredith (USA) 1:51.9
1920 Albert Hill (Great Britain) 1:53.4
1924 Douglas Lowe (Great Britain) 1:52.4
1928 Douglas Lowe (Great Britain) 1:51.8
1932 Tom Hampson (Great Britain) 1:49.70
1936 John Woodruff (USA) 1:52.9
1948 Malvin Whitfield (USA) 1:49.2
1952 Malvin Whitfield (USA) 1:49.34
1956 Thomas Courtney (USA) 1:47.75
1960 Peter Snell (New Zealand) 1:46.48
1964 Peter Snell (New Zealand) 1:45.1
1968 Ralph Doubell (Australia) 1:44.40
1972 David Wottle (USA) 1:45.86
1976 Alberto Juantorena (Cuba) 1:43.50
1980 Steven Ovett (Great Britain) 1:45.40
1984 Joaquim Cruz (Brazil) 1:43.00
1988 Paul Ereng (Kenya) 1:43.45
1992 William Tanui (Kenya) 1:43.66

1500 m
1896 Edwin Flack (Australia) 4:33.2
1900 Charles Bennett (Great Britain) 4:06.2
1904 James Lightbody (USA) 4:05.4
1906 James Lightbody (USA) 4:12.0
1908 Mel Sheppard (USA) 4:03.4
1912 Arnold Jackson (Great Britain) 3:56.8
1920 Albert Hill (Great Britain) 4:01.8
1924 Paavo Nurmi (Finland) 3:53.6
1928 Harri Larva (Finland) 3:53.2

1932 Luigi Beccali (Italy) 3:51.20
1936 Jack Lovelock (New Zealand) 3:47.8
1948 Henry Eriksson (Sweden) 3:49.8
1952 Josef Barthel (Luxembourg) 3:45.28
1956 Ron Delany (Ireland) 3:41.49
1960 Herbert Elliott (Australia) 3:35.6
1964 Peter Snell (New Zealand) 3:38.1
1968 Kipchoge Keino (Kenya) 3:34.91
1972 Pekkha Vasala (Finland) 3:36.33
1976 John Walker (New Zealand) 3:39.17
1980 Sebastian Coe (Great Britain) 3:38.40
1984 Sebastian Coe (Great Britain) 3:32.53
1988 Peter Rono (Kenya) 3:35.96
1992 Fermin Cacho (Spain) 3:40.12

5000 m
1912 Hannes Kolehmainen (Finland) 14.36.6
1920 Joseph Guillemot (France) 14:55.6
1924 Paavo Nurmi (Finland) 14.31.2
1928 Ville Ritola (Finland) 14:38.0
1932 Lauri Lehtinen (Finland) 14:29.91
1936 Gunnar Höckert (Finland) 14:22.2
1948 Gaston Reiff (Belgium) 14:17.6
1952 Emil Zátopek (Czechoslovakia) 14:06.72
1956 Vladimir Kuts (USSR) 13:39.86
1960 Murray Halberg (New Zealand) 13:43.4
1964 Robert Schul (USA) 13:48.8
1968 Mohamed Gammoudi (Tunisia) 14:05.0
1972 Lasse Viren (Finland) 13:26.42
1976 Lasse Viren (Finland) 13:24.76
1980 Miruts Yifter (Ethiopia) 13:20.91
1984 Saïd Aouita (Morocco) 13:05.59
1988 John Ngugi (Kenya) 13:11.70
1992 Dieter Baumann (Germany) 13:12.52

10 000 m
1912 Hannes Kolehmainen (Finland) 31:20.8
1920 Paavo Nurmi (Finland) 31:45.8
1924 Ville Ritola (Finland) 30:23.1
1928 Paavo Nurmi (Finland) 30:18.8
1932 Janusz Kusocinski (Poland) 30:11.4
1936 Ilmari Salminen (Finland) 30:15.4
1948 Emil Zátopek (Czechoslovakia) 29:59.6
1952 Emil Zátopek (Czechoslovakia) 29:17.0
1956 Vladimir Kuts (USSR) 28:45.60
1960 Pyotr Bolotnikov (USSR) 28:32.18
1964 William Mills (USA) 28:24.4
1968 Naftali Temu (Kenya) 29:27.45
1972 Lasse Viren (Finland) 27:38.35
1976 Lasse Viren (Finland) 27:40.38
1980 Miruts Yifter (Ethiopia) 27:42.69
1984 Alberto Cova (Italy) 27:47.54
1988 Brahim Boutayeb (Morocco) 27:21.46
1992 Khalid Skah (Morocco) 27:46.70

Marathon*
1896 Spyridon Louis (Greece) 2:58:50.0 *(40 km)*
1900 Michel Théato (France) 2:59:45.0 *(40.26 km)*
1904 Thomas Hicks (USA) 3:28:35.0 *(40 km)*
1906 William Sherring (Canada) 2:51:23.6 *(41.86 km)*
1908 John Hayes (USA) 2:55:18.4
1912 Kenneth McArthur (S Africa) 2:36:54.8 *(40.2 km)*
1920 Hannes Kolehmainen (Finland) 2:32:35.8 *(42.75 km)*
1924 Albin Stenroos (Finland) 2:41:22.6
1928 Mohamed Boughéra El Ouafi (France) 2:32:57.0
1932 Juan Carlos Zabala (Argentina) 2:31:36.0
1936 Kitei Son (Japan) 2:29:19.2[a]
1948 Delfo Cabrera (Argentina) 2:34:51.6

Athletics

Athletics, Olympic games (continued)

1952	Emil Zátopek (Czechoslovakia) 2:23:03.2
1956	Alain Mimoun (France) 2:25:00.0
1960	Abebe Bikila (Ethiopia) 2:15:16.2
1964	Abebe Bikila (Ethiopia) 2:12:11.2
1968	Mamo Wolde (Ethiopia) 2:20:26.4
1972	Frank Shorter (USA) 2:12:19.8
1976	Waldemar Cierpinski (E Germany) 2:09:55
1980	Waldemar Cierpinski (E Germany) 2:11:03
1984	Carlos Lopes (Portugal) 2:09:21
1988	Gelindo Bordin (Italy) 2:10:32
1992	Hwang Young-jo (S Korea) 2:13:23

*Unless shown as otherwise above, the Marathon is run over a distance of 42 km 195 m/26 mi 385 yd.

110 m hurdles

1896	Thomas Curtis (USA) 17.6
1900	Alvin Kraenzlein (USA) 15.4
1904	Fred Schule (USA) 16.0
1906	Robert Leavitt (USA) 16.2
1908	Forrest Smithson (USA) 15.0
1912	Fred Kelly (USA) 15.1
1920	Earl Thomson (Canada) 14.8
1924	Daniel Kinsey (USA) 15.0
1928	Sydney Atkinson (S Africa) 14.8
1932	George Saling (USA) 14.57
1936	Forrest Towns (USA) 14.2
1948	William Porter (USA) 13.9
1952	Harrison Dillard (USA) 13.91
1956	Lee Calhoun (USA) 13.70
1960	Lee Calhoun (USA) 13.98
1964	Hayes Jones (USA) 13.67
1968	Willie Davenport (USA) 13.33
1972	Rodney Milburn (USA) 13.24
1976	Guy Drut (France) 13.30
1980	Thomas Munkelt (E Germany) 13.39
1984	Roger Kingdom (USA) 13.20
1988	Roger Kingdom (USA) 12.98
1992	Mark McKoy (Canada) 13.12

400 m hurdles

1900	Walter Tewksbury (USA) 57.6
1904	Harry Hillman (USA) 53.0
1908	Charles Bacon (USA) 55.0
1920	Frank Loomis (USA) 54.0
1924	Morgan Taylor (USA) 52.6
1928	Lord Burghley (Great Britain) 53.4
1932	Robert Tisdall (Ireland) 51.67
1936	Glenn Hardin (USA) 52.4
1948	Roy Cochran (USA) 51.1
1952	Charles Moore (USA) 51.06
1956	Glenn Davis (USA) 50.29
1960	Glenn Davis (USA) 49.51
1964	Rex Cawley (USA) 49.69
1968	David Hemery (Great Britain) 48.12
1972	John Akii-Bua (Uganda) 47.82
1976	Edwin Moses (USA) 47.63
1980	Volker Beck (E Germany) 48.70
1984	Edwin Moses (USA) 47.75
1988	Andre Phillips (USA) 47.19
1992	Kevin Young (USA) 46.78

Steeplechase*

1900	George Orton (Canada) 7:34.4 *(2500 m)*
1900	John Rimmer (Great Britain) 12:58.4 *(4000 m)*
1904	James Lightbody (USA) 7:39.6 *(2590 m)*
1908	Arthur Russell (Great Britain) 10:47.8 *(3200 m)*
1920	Percy Hodge (Great Britain) 10:00.4

1924	Ville Ritola (Finland) 9:33.6
1928	Toivo Loukola (Finland) 9:21.8
1932	Volmari Iso-Hollo (Finland) 10:33.4**
1936	Volmari Iso-Hollo (Finland) 9:03.8
1948	Tore Sjöstrand (Sweden) 9:04.6
1952	Horace Ashenfelter (USA) 8:45.68
1956	Christopher Brasher (Great Britain) 8:41.35
1960	Zdzislaw Kryszkowiak (Poland) 8:34.31
1964	Gaston Roelants (Belgium) 8:30.8
1968	Amos Biwott (Kenya) 8:51.0
1972	Kipchoge Keino (Kenya) 8:23.64
1976	Anders Gärderud (Sweden) 8:08.02
1980	Bronislaw Malinowski (Poland) 8:09.70
1984	Julius Korir (Kenya) 8:11.80
1988	Julius Kariuki (Kenya) 8:05.51
1992	Matthew Birir (Kenya) 8:08.94

*Unless shown otherwise above, distance is 3000 m.
**Athletes ran an extra lap in error – distance 3460 m.

High jump

1896	Ellery Clark (USA) 1.81
1900	Irving Baxter (USA) 1.90
1904	Samuel Jones (USA) 1.80
1906	Con Leahy (Ireland)[b] 1.77
1908	Harry Porter (USA) 1.90
1912	Alma Richards (USA) 1.93
1920	Richard Landon (USA) 1.94
1924	Harold Osborn (USA) 1.98
1928	Robert King (USA) 1.94
1932	Duncan McNaughton (Canada) 1.97
1936	Cornelius Johnson (USA) 2.03
1948	John Winter (Austrialia) 1.98
1952	Walter Davis (USA) 2.04
1956	Charles Dumas (USA) 2.12
1960	Robert Shavlakadze (USSR) 2.16
1964	Valeriy Brumel (USSR) 2.18
1968	Dick Fosbury (USA) 2.24
1972	Jüri Tamak (USSR) 2.23
1976	Jacek Wszola (Poland) 2.25
1980	Gerd Wessig (E Germany) 2.36
1984	Dietmar Mögenburg (W Germany) 2.35
1988	Gennadiy Avdeyenko (USSR) 2.38
1992	Javier Sotomayor (Cuba) 2.34

Pole vault

1896	William Hoyt (USA) 3.30
1900	Irving Baxter (USA) 3.30
1904	Charles Dvorak (USA) 3.50
1906	Fernand Gonder (France) 3.40
1908	Edward Cooke & Alfred Gilbert (USA) 3.71
1912	Harry Babock (USA) 3.95
1920	Frank Foss (USA) 4.09
1924	Lee Barnes (USA) 3.95
1928	Sabin Carr (USA) 4.20
1932	Bill Miller (USA) 4.31
1936	Earle Meadows (USA) 4.35
1948	Guinn Smith (USA) 4.30
1952	Robert Richards (USA) 4.55
1956	Robert Richards (USA) 4.56
1960	Donald Bragg (USA) 4.70
1964	Frederick Hansen (USA) 5.10
1968	Bob Seagren (USA) 5.40
1972	Wolfgang Nordwig (E Germany) 5.50
1976	Tadeusz Slusarski (Poland) 5.50
1980	Wladyslaw Kozakiewicz (Poland) 5.78
1984	Pierre Quinon (France) 5.75
1988	Sergey Bubka (USSR) 5.90
1992	Maksim Tarassov (Unified Team) 5.80

Long jump

1896	Ellery Clark (USA)	6.35
1900	Alvin Kraenzlein (USA)	7.18
1904	Myer Prinstein (USA)	7.34
1906	Myer Prinstein (USA)	7.20
1908	Francis Irons (USA)	7.48
1912	Albert Gutterson (USA)	7.60
1920	William Pettersson (Sweden)	7.15
1924	William De Hart Hubbard (USA)	7.44
1928	Edward Hamm (USA)	7.73
1932	Edward Gordon (USA)	7.64
1936	Jesse Owens (USA)	8.06
1948	William Steele (USA)	7.82
1952	Jerome Biffle (USA)	7.57
1956	Gregory Bell (USA)	7.83
1960	Ralph Boston (USA)	8.12
1964	Lynn Davies (Great Britain)	8.07
1968	Bob Beamon (USA)	8.90
1972	Randy Williams (USA)	8.24
1976	Arnie Robinson (USA)	8.35
1980	Lutz Dombrowski (E Germany)	8.54
1984	Carl Lewis (USA)	8.54
1988	Carl Lewis (USA)	8.72
1992	Carl Lewis (USA)	8.67

Triple jump

1896	James Connolly (USA)	13.71
1900	Myer Prinstein (USA)	14.47
1904	Myer Prinstein (USA)	14.35
1906	Peter O'Connor (Ireland)[b]	14.07
1908	Tim Ahearne (Ireland)[b]	14.91
1912	Gustaf Lindblom (Sweden)	14.76
1920	Viho Tuulos (Finland)	14.50
1924	Anthony Winter (Australia)	15.52
1928	Mikio Oda (Japan)	15.21
1932	Chuhei Nambu (Japan)	15.72
1936	Naoto Tajima (Japan)	16.00
1948	Arne Åhman (Sweden)	15.40
1952	Adhemar Ferreira da Silva (Brazil)	16.22
1956	Adhemar Ferreira da Silva (Brazil)	16.35
1960	Jozef Schmidt (Poland)	16.81
1964	Jozef Schmidt (Poland)	16.85
1968	Viktor Saneyev (USSR)	17.39
1972	Viktor Saneyev (USSR)	17.35
1976	Viktor Saneyev (USSR)	17.29
1980	Jaak Uudmäe (USSR)	17.35
1984	Al Joyner (USA)	17.26
1988	Khristo Markov (Bulgaria)	17.61
1992	Mike Conley (USA)	18.17[c]

Shot

1896	Robert Garrett (USA)	11.22
1900	Richard Sheldon (USA)	14.10
1904	Ralph Rose (USA)	14.80
1906	Martin Sheridan (USA)	12.32
1908	Ralph Rose (USA)	14.21
1912	Patrick McDonald (USA)	15.34
1920	Ville Pörhölä (Finland)	14.81
1924	Clarence Houser (USA)	14.99
1928	John Kuck (USA)	15.87
1932	Leo Sexton (USA)	16.00
1936	Hans Woellke (Germany)	16.20
1948	Wilbur Thompson (USA)	17.12
1952	Parry O'Brien (USA)	17.41
1956	Parry O'Brien (USA)	18.57
1960	William Nieder (USA)	19.68
1964	Dallas Long (USA)	20.33
1968	Randy Matson (USA)	20.54
1972	Wladyslaw Komar (Poland)	21.18

1976	Udo Beyer (E Germany)	21.05
1980	Vladimir Kiselyov (USSR)	21.35
1984	Alessandro Andrei (Italy)	21.26
1988	Ulf Timmermann (E Germany)	22.47
1992	Mike Stulce (USA)	21.70

Discus

1896	Robert Garrett (USA)	29.15
1900	Rudolf Bauer (Hungary)	36.04
1904	Martin Sheridan (USA)	39.28
1906	Martin Sheridan (USA)	41.46
1904	Martin Sheridan (USA)	40.89
1912	Armas Taipale (Finland)	45.21
1920	Elmer Niklander (Finland)	44.68
1924	Clarence Houser (USA)	46.15
1928	Clarence Houser (USA)	47.32
1932	John Anderson (USA)	49.49
1936	Ken Carpenter (USA)	50.48
1948	Adolfo Consolini (Italy)	52.78
1952	Sim Iness (USA)	55.03
1956	Al Oerter (USA)	56.36
1960	Al Oerter (USA)	59.18
1964	Al Oerter (USA)	61.00
1968	Al Oerter (USA)	64.78
1972	Ludvik Danek (Czechoslovakia)	64.40
1976	Mac Wilkins (USA)	67.50
1980	Viktor Rashchupkin (USSR)	66.64
1984	Rolf Danneberg (W Germany)	66.60
1988	Jürgen Schult (E Germany)	68.82
1992	Romas Ubartas (Lithuania)	65.12

Hammer

1900	John Flanagan (USA)	49.73
1904	John Flanagan (USA)	51.23
1908	John Flanagan (USA)	51.92
1912	Matt McGrath (USA)	54.74
1920	Patrick Ryan (USA)	52.87
1924	Fred Tootell (USA)	53.29
1928	Patrick O'Callaghan (Ireland)	51.39
1932	Patrick O'Callaghan (Ireland)	53.92
1936	Karl Hein (Germany)	56.49
1948	Imre Németh (Hungary)	56.07
1952	József Csermak (Hungary)	60.34
1956	Harold Connolly (USA)	63.19
1960	Vasiliy Rudenkov (USSR)	67.10
1964	Romuald Klim (USSR)	69.74
1968	Gyula Zsivótzky (Hungary)	73.36
1972	Anatoliy Bondarchuk (USSR)	75.50
1976	Yuriy Sedykh (USSR)	77.52
1980	Yuriy Sedykh (USSR)	81.80
1984	Juha Tiainen (Finland)	78.08
1988	Sergey Litvinov (USSR)	84.80
1992	Andrey Abduyvaliyev (Unified Team)	82.54

Javelin*

1906	Erik Lemming (Sweden)	53.90
1908	Erik Lemming (Sweden)	54.82
1912	Erik Lemming (Sweden)	60.64
1920	Jonni Myyrä (Finland)	65.78
1924	Jonni Myyrä (Finland)	62.96
1928	Erik Lundkvist (Sweden)	66.60
1932	Matti Järvinen (Finland)	72.71
1936	Gerhard Stöck (Germany)	71.84
1948	Tapio Rautavaara (Finland)	69.77
1952	Cyrus Young (USA)	73.78
1956	Egil Danielsen (Norway)	85.71
1960	Viktor Tsibulenko (USSR)	84.64
1964	Pauli Nevala (Finland)	82.66
1968	Janis Lusis (USSR)	90.10

Athletics, Olympic games (continued)

1972 Klaus Wolfermann (W Germany) 90.48
1976 Miklós Németh (Hungary) 94.58
1980 Dainis Kula (USSR) 91.20
1984 Arto Harkönen (Finland) 86.76
1988 Tápio Korjus (Finland) 84.28
1992 Jan Zelezny (Czechoslovakia) 89.66

*New javelin specification introduced in 1984.

Decathlon*

1904 Thomas Kiely (Ireland) 6036
1912 Jim Thorpe (USA) 6564
1920 Helge Lövland (Norway) 5804
1924 Harold Osborn (USA) 6476
1928 Paavo Yrjölä (Finland) 6587
1932 James Bausch (USA) 6735
1936 Glenn Morris (USA) 7254
1948 Robert Mathias (USA) 6628
1952 Robert Mathias (USA) 7592
1956 Milton Campbell (USA) 7614
1960 Rafer Johnson (USA) 7926
1964 Willi Holdorf (W Germany) 7794
1968 Bill Toomey (USA) 8144
1972 Nikolay Avilov (USSR) 8466
1976 Bruce Jenner (USA) 8634
1980 Daley Thompson (Great Britain) 8522
1984 Daley Thompson (Great Britain) 8847
1988 Christian Schenk (E Germany) 8488
1992 Robert Zmelik (Czechoslovakia) 8611

*All points given here are rescored using 1984 tables.

20 000 m walk

1956 Leonid Spirin (USSR) 1:31:27.4
1960 Vladimir Golubnichiy (USSR) 1:34:07.2
1964 Kenneth Matthews (Great Britain) 1:29:34.0
1968 Vladimir Golubnichiy (USSR) 1:33:58.4
1972 Peter Frenkel (E Germany) 1:26:42.4
1976 Daniel Bautista (Mexico) 1:24:40.6
1980 Maurizio Damilano (Italy) 1:23:35.5
1984 Ernesto Canto (Mexico) 1:23:13
1988 Jozef Pribilinec (Czechoslovakia) 1:19:57
1992 Daniel Plaza (Spain) 1:21:45

50 000 m walk

1932 Thomas Green (Great Britain) 4:50:10.0
1936 Harold Whitlock (Great Britain) 4:30:41.1
1948 John Ljunggren (Sweden) 4:41:52.0
1952 Giuseppe Dordoni (Italy) 4:28:07.8
1956 Norman Read (New Zealand) 4:30:42.8
1960 Don Thompson (Great Britain) 4:25:30.0
1964 Abdon Pamich (Italy) 4:11:12.4
1968 Christophe Höhne (E Germany) 4:20:13.6
1972 Bernd Kannenberg (E Germany) 3:56:11.6
1980 Hartwig Gauder (E Germany) 3:49:24
1984 Raúl Gonzales (Mexico) 3:47:26
1988 Vyacheslav Ivanenko (USSR) 3:38:29
1992 Andrei Perlov (Unified Team) 3:50:13

4 × 100 m relay

1912 Great Britain 42.4
1920 USA 42.2
1924 USA 41.0
1928 USA 41.0
1932 USA 40.1
1936 USA 39.8
1948 USA 40.6
1952 USA 40.26
1956 USA 39.59
1960 W Germany 39.66
1964 USA 39.06
1968 USA 38.23
1972 USA 38.19
1976 USA 38.83
1980 USSR 38.26
1984 USA 37.83
1988 USSR 38.19
1992 USA 37.40

4 × 400 m relay

1912 USA 3:16.6
1920 Great Britain 3:22.2
1924 USA 3:16.0
1928 USA 3:14.2
1932 USA 3:08.14
1936 Great Britain 3:09.0
1948 USA 3:10.4
1952 Jamaica 3:04.04
1956 USA 3:04.80
1960 USA 3:02.37
1964 USA 3:00.71
1968 USA 2:56.16
1972 Kenya 2:59.83
1976 USA 2:58.66
1980 USSR 3:01.08
1984 USA 3:57.91
1988 USA 2:56.16
1992 USA 2:55.74

Event winners: women

100 m

1928 Elizabeth Robinson (USA) 12.2
1932 Stanislawa Walasiewicz (Poland) 11.9
1936 Helen Stephens (USA) 11.5
1948 Fanny Blankers-Koen (Netherlands) 11.9
1952 Marjorie Jackson (Australia) 11.65
1956 Betty Cuthbert (Australia) 11.82
1960 Wilma Rudolph (USA) 11.08
1964 Wyomia Tyus (USA) 11.49
1968 Wyomia Tyus (USA) 11.08
1972 Renate Stecher (E Germany) 11.07
1976 Annegret Richter (W Germany) 11.08
1980 Lyudmila Kondratyeva (USSR) 11.06
1984 Evelyn Ashford (USA) 10.97
1988 Florence Griffith-Joyner (USA) 10.54ᶜ
1992 Gail Devers (USA) 10.82

200 m

1948 Fanny Blankers-Koen (Netherlands) 24.4
1952 Marjorie Jackson (Australia) 23.89
1956 Betty Cuthbert (Australia) 23.55
1960 Wilma Rudolph (USA) 24.03
1964 Edith Maguire (USA) 23.05
1968 Irena Szewinska (Poland) 22.58
1972 Renate Stecher (E Germany) 22.40
1976 Bärbel Eckert (E Germany) 22.37
1980 Bärbel Wöckel (E Germany) 22.03
1984 Valerie Brisco-Hooks (USA) 21.81
1988 Florence Griffith-Joyner (USA) 21.34
1992 Gwen Torrence (USA) 21.81

400 m

1964 Betty Cuthbert (Australia) 52.01
1968 Colette Besson (France) 52.03
1972 Monika Zehrt (E Germany) 51.08
1976 Irena Szewinska (Poland) 49.29
1980 Marita Koch (E Germany) 48.88
1984 Valerie Brisco-Hooks (USA) 48.83

1988   Olga Bryzgina (USSR) 48.65
1992   Marie-José Pérec (France) 48.83

800 m
1960   Lyudmila Shevtsova (USSR) 2:04.50
1964   Ann Packer (Great Britain) 2:01.1
1968   Madeline Manning (USA) 2:00.92
1972   Hilde Falck (W Germany) 1:58.55
1976   Tatyana Kazankina (USSR) 1:54.94
1980   Nadezhda Olizarenko (USSR) 1:53.43
1984   Doina Melinte (Romania) 1:57.60
1988   Sigrun Wodars (E Germany) 1:56.10
1992   Ellen van Langen (Netherlands) 1:55.54

1500 m
1972   Lyudmila Bragina (USSR) 4:01:38
1976   Tatyana Kazankina (USSR) 4:05.48
1980   Tatyana Kazankina (USSR) 3:56.56
1984   Gabriella Doria (Italy) 4:03.25
1988   Paula Ivan (Romania) 3:53.96
1992   Hassiba Boulmerka (Algeria) 3:55:30

3000 m
1984   Maricica Puica (Romania) 8:35.96
1988   Tatyana Samolenko (USSR) 8:26.53
1992   Yelena Romanova (Unified Team) 8:46.04

10000 m
1988   Olga Bondarenko (USSR) 31:05.21
1992   Derartu Tulu (Ethiopia) 31:06.02

Marathon
1984   Joan Benoit (USA) 2:24:62
1988   Rosa Mota (Portugal) 2:25:40
1992   Valentina Yegorova (Unified Team) 2:32:41

80 m hurdles
1932   Mildred Didrikson (USA) 11.7
1936   Trebisonda Valla (Italy) 11.75
1948   Fanny Blankers-Koen (Netherlands) 11.2
1952   Shirley Strickland (Australia) 11.03
1956   Shirley Strickland (Australia) 10.96
1960   Irina Press (USSR) 10.94
1964   Karin Balzer (E Germany) 10.54
1968   Maureen Caird (Australia) 10.39

100 m hurdles
1972   Annelie Ehrhardt (E Germany) 12.59
1976   Johanna Schaller (E Germany) 12.77
1980   Vera Komisova (USSR) 12.56
1984   Benita Fitzgerald-Brown (USA) 12.84
1988   Yordanka Donkova (Bulgaria) 12.38
1992   Paraskevi Patoulidou (Greece) 12.64

400 m hurdles
1984   Nawal El Moutawakil (Morocco) 54.61
1988   Debbie Flintoff-King (Australia) 53.17
1992   Sally Gunnell (Great Britain) 53.23

High jump
1928   Ethel Catherwood (Canada) 1.59
1932   Jean Shiley (USA) 1.65
1936   Ibolya Csák (Hungary) 1.60
1948   Alice Coachman (USA) 1.68
1952   Esther Brand (S Africa) 1.67
1956   Mildred McDaniel (USA) 1.76
1960   Iolanda Balas (Romania) 1.85
1964   Iolanda Balas (Romania) 1.90
1968   Miloslava Rezková (Czechoslovakia) 1.82
1972   Ulrike Meyfarth (W Germany) 1.92

1976   Rosemarie Ackermann (E Germany) 1.93
1980   Sara Simeoni (Italy) 1.97
1984   Ulrike Meyfarth (W Germany) 2.02
1988   Louise Ritter (USA) 2.03
1992   Heike Henkel (Germany) 2.02

Long jump
1948   Olga Gyarmati (Hungary) 5.69
1952   Yvette Williams (New Zealand) 6.24
1956   Elzbieta Krzesinska (Poland) 6.35
1960   Vyera Krepkina (USSR) 6.37
1964   Mary Rand (Great Britain) 6.76
1968   Viorica Viscopoleanu (Romania) 6.82
1972   Heide Rosendahl (W Germany) 6.78
1976   Angela Voigt (E Germany) 6.72
1980   Tatyana Kolpakova (USSR) 7.06
1984   Anisoara Stanciu (Romania) 6.96
1988   Jackie Joyner-Kersee (USA) 7.40
1992   Heike Drechsler (Germany) 7.14

Shot
1948   Micheline Ostermeyer (France) 13.75
1952   Galina Zybina (USSR) 15.28
1956   Tamara Tishkyevich (USSR) 16.59
1960   Tamara Press (USSR) 17.32
1964   Tamara Press (USSR) 18.14
1968   Margitta Gummel (E Germany) 19.61
1972   Nadezhda Chizhova (USSR) 21.03
1976   Ivanka Khristova (Bulgaria) 21.16
1980   Ilona Slupianek (E Germany) 22.41
1984   Claudia Losch (W Germany) 20.48
1988   Natalya Lisovskaya (USSR) 22.24
1992   Svetlana Krivelyova (Unified Team) 21.06

Discus
1928   Helena Konopacka (Poland) 39.62
1932   Lillian Copeland (USA) 40.58
1936   Gisela Mauermayer (Germany) 47.63
1948   Micheline Ostermeyer (France) 41.92
1952   Nina Ponomaryeva (USSR) 51.42
1956   Olga Fikotová (Czechoslovakia) 53.69
1960   Nina Ponomaryeva (USSR) 55.10
1964   Tamara Press (USSR) 57.27
1968   Lia Manoliu (Romania) 58.28
1972   Faina Melnik (USSR) 66.62
1976   Evelin Schlaak (E Germany) 69.00
1980   Evelin Jahl (E Germany) 69.96
1984   Ria Stalmach (Netherlands) 65.36
1988   Martina Hellmann (E Germany) 72.30
1992   Maritza Marten (Cuba) 70.06

Javelin
1932   Mildred Didrikson (USA) 43.68
1936   Tilly Fleischer (Germany) 45.18
1948   Herma Bauma (Australia) 45.57
1952   Dana Zátopková (Czechoslovakia) 50.47
1956   Inese Jaunzeme (USSR) 53.86
1960   Elvira Ozolina (USSR) 55.98
1964   Mihaela Penes (Romania) 60.54
1968   Angéla Németh (Hungary) 60.36
1972   Ruth Fuchs (E Germany) 63.88
1976   Ruth Fuchs (E Germany) 65.94
1980   Maria C. Colón (Cuba) 68.40
1984   Tessa Sanderson (Great Britain) 69.56
1988   Petra Felke (E Germany) 74.68
1992   Silke Renk (Germany) 68.34

Sports and games

Athletics, Olympic games (continued)

Pentathlon

1964	Irina Press (USSR) 4702
1968	Ingrid Becker (W Germany) 4559
1972	Mary Peters (Great Britain) 4801
1976	Sigrun Siegl (E Germany) 4745
1980	Nadezhda Tkachenko (USSR) 5083

Heptathlon

1984	Glynis Nunn (Australia) 6387
1988	Jackie Joyner-Kersee (USA) 7291
1992	Jackie Joyner-Kersee (USA) 7044

10 km walk

1992	Chen Yueling (China) 44:32

4 × 100 m relay

1928	Canada 48.4
1932	USA 46.86
1936	USA 46.9
1948	Netherlands 47.5
1952	USA 46.14
1956	Australia 44.65
1960	USA 44.72
1964	Poland 43.69
1968	USA 42.87
1972	W Germany 42.81
1976	E Germany 42.55
1980	E Germany 41.60
1984	USA 41.65
1988	USA 41.98
1992	USA 42.11

4 × 400 m relay

1972	E Germany 3:22.95
1976	E Germany 3:19.23
1980	USSR 3:20.12
1984	USA 3:18.29
1988	USSR 3:15.18
1992	Unified Team 3:20.20

[a] Real name: Sohn Kee-chung, of Korea.
[b] Competing as a member of the Great Britain team.
[c] Wind-assisted.

Marathon

Run over 42 km 195 m/26 mi 385 yd; a distance which became standard from 1924. Women first competed officially in 1972.

Boston

The world's oldest annual race; first held in 1897.

Men

1981	Toshihiko Seko (Japan)
1982	Alberto Salazar (USA)
1983	Greg Meyer (USA)
1984	Geoff Smith (Great Britain)
1985	Geoff Smith (Great Britain)
1986	Rob de Castella (Australia)
1987	Toshihiko Seko (Japan)
1988	Ibrahim Hussein (Kenya)
1989	Abebe Mekonnen (Ethiopia)
1990	Gelindo Bordin (Italy)
1991	Ibrahim Hussein (Kenya)
1992	Ibrahim Hussein (Kenya)
1993	Cosmas N'deli (Kenya)

Most wins: (7) Clarence De Mar (USA): 1911, 1922–4, 1927–8, 1930.

Women

1981	Allison Roe (New Zealand)
1982	Charlotte Teske (W Germany)
1983	Joan Benoit (USA)
1984	Lorraine Moller (New Zealand)
1985	Lisa Weidenbach (USA)
1986	Ingrid Kristiansen (Norway)
1987	Rosa Mota (Portugal)
1988	Rosa Mota (Portugal)
1989	Ingrid Kristiansen (Norway)
1990	Rosa Mota (Portugal)
1991	Wanda Panfil (Poland)
1992	Olga Markova (Russia)
1993	Olga Markova (Russia)

Most wins: (3) Rosa Mota (Portugal): as above.

London

First run in 1981.

Men

1981	Dick Beardsley (USA) and Inge Simonsen (Norway)
1982	Hugh Jones (Great Britain)
1983	Mike Gratton (Great Britain)
1984	Charlie Spedding (Great Britain)
1985	Steve Jones (Great Britain)
1986	Toshihiko Seko (Japan)
1987	Hiromi Taniguchi (Japan)
1988	Henrik Jørgensen (Denmark)
1989	Douglas Wakihuri (Kenya)
1990	Allister Hutton (Great Britain)
1991	Yakov Tolstikov (USSR)
1992	António Pinto (Portugal)
1993	Eamonn Martin (Great Britain)

Most wins: (No one more than 1).

Women

1981	Joyce Smith (Great Britain)
1982	Joyce Smith (Great Britain)
1983	Grete Waitz (Norway)
1984	Ingrid Kristiansen (Norway)
1985	Ingrid Kristiansen (Norway)
1986	Grete Waitz (Norway)
1987	Ingrid Kristiansen (Norway)
1988	Ingrid Kristiansen (Norway)
1989	Véronique Marot (Great Britain)
1990	Wanda Panfil (Poland)
1991	Rosa Mota (Portugal)
1992	Katrin Dörre (Germany)
1993	Katrin Dörre (Germany)

Most wins: (4) Ingrid Kristiansen (Norway): as above.

New York

First run in 1970.

Men

1981	Alberto Salazar (USA)
1982	Alberto Salazar (USA)
1983	Rod Dixon (New Zealand)
1984	Orlando Pizzolato (Italy)

Sports and games

1985 Orlando Pizzolato (Italy)	1983 Grete Waitz (Norway)
1986 Gianni Poli (Italy)	1984 Grete Waitz (Norway)
1987 Ibrahim Hussein (Kenya)	1985 Grete Waitz (Norway)
1988 Steve Jones (Great Britain)	1986 Grete Waitz (Norway)
1989 Juma Ikangaa (Tanzania)	1987 Priscilla Welch (Great Britain)
1990 Douglas Wakihuri (Kenya)	1988 Grete Waitz (Norway)
1991 Salvador Garcia (Mexico)	1989 Ingrid Kristiansen (Norway)
1992 Willie Mtolo (South Africa)	1990 Wanda Panfil (Poland)
1993 Andreas Espinosa (Mexico)	1991 Liz McColgan (Great Britain)
	1992 Liz McColgan (Great Britain)
	1993 Uta Pippig (Germany)

Most wins: (4) Bill Rodgers (USA): 1976–9.

Women
1981 Allison Roe (New Zealand)
1982 Grete Waitz (Norway)

Most wins: (9) Grete Waitz (Norway): 1978–80, 1982–6, 1988.

BADMINTON

World championships

First held in 1977; initially took place every three years, since 1983 every two years.

Singles winners: men
1980 Rudo Hartono (Indonesia)
1983 Icuk Sugiarto (Indonesia)
1985 Han Jian (China)
1987 Yang Yang (China)
1989 Yang Yang (China)
1991 Zhao Jianhua (China)
1993 Joko Suprianto (Indonesia)

Singles winners: women
1980 Wiharjo Verawaty (Indonesia)
1983 Li Lingwei (China)
1985 Han Aiping (China)
1987 Han Aiping (China)
1989 Li Lingwei (China)
1991 Tang Jiuhong (China)
1993 Susi Susanti (Indonesia)

Most titles: (4) Park JooBong (South Korea): men's doubles 1985, 1991; mixed doubles 1989, 1991.

Thomas cup

An international event for men's teams: inaugurated in 1949, now held every two years.

Recent winners
1967 Malaysia
1970 Indonesia
1973 Indonesia
1976 Indonesia
1979 Indonesia
1982 China
1984 Indonesia
1986 China
1988 China
1990 China
1992 Malaysia

Most wins: (8) Indonesia: 1958, 1961, 1964, 1970, 1973, 1976, 1979, 1984.

Uber cup

An international event for women's teams; first held in 1957, now held every two years.

Recent winners
1966 Japan
1969 Japan
1972 Japan
1975 Indonesia
1978 Japan
1981 Japan
1984 China
1986 China
1988 China
1990 China
1992 China

Most wins: (5) Japan and China: as above.

All-England championship

Badminton's premier event prior to the inauguration of the World Championships; first held in 1899.

Recent winners: singles – men
1982 Morten Frost (Denmark)
1983 Luan Jin (China)
1984 Morten Frost (Denmark)
1985 Zhao Jianhua (China)
1986 Morten Frost (Denmark)
1987 Morten Frost (Denmark)
1988 Ib Frederikson (Denmark)
1989 Yang Yang (China)
1990 Zhao Jianhua (China)
1991 Ardi Wiranata (Indonesia)
1992 Liu Jun (China)
1993 Heryanto Arbi (Indonesia)

Recent winners: singles – women
1982 Zang Ailing (China)
1983 Zang Ailing (China)
1984 Li Lingwei (China)
1985 Han Aiping (China)
1986 Yun-Ja Kim (Korea)
1987 Kirsten Larsen (Denmark)
1988 Gu Jiaming (China)
1989 Li Lingwei (China)
1990 Susi Susanti (Indonesia)
1991 Susi Susanti (Indonesia)
1992 Tang Jiuhong (China)
1993 Susi Susanti (Indonesia)

Most titles: (21; 4 singles, 9 men's doubles, 8 mixed doubles), George Thomas (England): 1903–28.

Olympic Games

Gold medal winner: 1992
Singles (men)
Alan Budi Kusuma (Indonesia)

Singles (women)
Susi Susanti (Indonesia)

BASEBALL

There are two leagues in the North American Major League – the National League (NL) and the American League (AL). Each league consists of two divisions (Eastern and Western), and each league championship is settled in a best-of-seven series between the leaders of these divisions.

World Series

First held in 1903; takes place each October, the best of seven games; professional baseball's leading event, the end-of-season meeting between the 'Pennant' winners of the National League and the American League.

1903 Boston (AL) 5, Pittsburgh (NL) 3
1904 *No series*
1905 New York (NL) 4, Philadelphia (AL) 1
1906 Chicago (AL) 4, Chicago (NL) 2
1907 Chicago (NL) 4, Detroit (AL) 0; 1 tie
1908 Chicago (NL) 4, Detroit (AL) 1
1909 Pittsburgh (NL) 4, Detroit (AL) 3
1910 Philadelphia (AL) 4, Chicago (NL) 1
1911 Philadelphia (AL) 4, New York (NL) 2
1912 Boston (AL) 4, New York (NL) 3; 1 tie
1913 Philadelphia (AL) 4, New York (NL) 1
1914 Boston (NL) 4, Philadelphia (AL) 0
1915 Boston (AL) 4, Philadelphia (NL) 1
1916 Boston (AL) 4, Brooklyn (NL) 1
1917 Chicago (AL) 4, New York (NL) 2
1918 Boston (AL) 4, Chicago (NL) 2
1919 Cincinnati (NL) 5, Chicago (AL) 3
1920 Cleveland (AL) 5, Brooklyn (NL) 2
1921 New York (NL) 5, New York (AL) 3
1922 New York (NL) 4, New York (AL) 0; 1 tie
1923 New York (AL) 4, New York (NL) 2
1924 Washington (AL) 4, New York (NL) 3
1925 Pittsburgh (NL) 4, Washington (AL) 3
1926 St Louis (NL) 4, New York (AL) 3
1927 New York (AL) 4, Pittsburgh (NL) 0
1928 New York (AL) 4, St Louis (NL) 0
1929 Philadelphia (AL) 4, Chicago (NL) 1
1930 Philadelphia (AL) 4, St Louis (NL) 2
1931 St Louis (NL) 4, Philadelphia (AL) 3
1932 New York (AL) 4, Chicago (NL) 0
1933 New York (NL) 4, Washington (AL) 1

1934 St Louis (NL) 4, Detroit (AL) 3
1935 Detroit (AL) 4, Chicago (NL) 2
1936 New York (AL) 4, New York (NL) 2
1937 New York (AL) 4, New York (NL) 1
1938 New York (AL) 4, Chicago (NL) 0
1939 New York (AL) 4, Cincinnati (NL) 0
1940 Cincinnati (NL) 4, Detroit (AL) 3
1941 New York (AL) 4, Booklyn (NL) 1
1942 St Louis (NL) 4, New York (AL) 1
1943 New York (AL) 4, St Louis (NL) 1
1944 St Louis (NL) 4, St Louis (AL) 2
1945 Detroit (AL) 4, Chicago (NL) 3
1946 St Louis (NL) 4, Boston (AL) 3
1947 New York (AL) 4, Brooklyn (NL) 3
1948 Cleveland (AL) 4, Boston (NL) 2
1949 New York (AL) 4, Brooklyn (NL) 1
1950 New York (AL) 4, Philadelphia (NL) 0
1951 New York (AL) 4, New York (NL) 2
1952 New York (AL) 4, Brooklyn (NL) 3
1953 New York (AL) 4, Brooklyn (NL) 2
1954 New York (NL) 4, Cleveland (AL) 0
1955 Brooklyn (NL) 4, New York (AL) 3
1956 New York (AL) 4, Brooklyn (NL) 3
1957 Milwaukee (NL) 4, New York (AL) 3
1958 New York (AL) 4, Milwaukee (NL) 3
1959 Los Angeles (NL) 4, Chicago (AL) 2
1960 Pittsburgh (NL) 4, New York (AL) 3
1961 New York (AL) 4, Cincinnati (NL) 1
1962 New York (AL) 4, San Francisco (NL) 3
1963 Los Angeles (NL) 4, New York (AL) 0
1964 St Louis (NL) 4, New York (AL) 3
1965 Los Angeles (NL) 4, Minnesota (AL) 3

1966 Baltimore (AL) 4, Los Angeles (NL) 0
1967 St Louis (NL) 4, Boston (AL) 3
1968 Detroit (AL) 4, St Louis (NL) 3
1969 New York (NL) 4, Baltimore (AL) 1
1970 Baltimore (AL) 4, Cincinnati (NL) 1
1971 Pittsburgh (NL) 4, Baltimore (AL) 3
1972 Oakland (AL) 4, Cincinnati (NL) 3
1973 Oakland (AL) 4, New York (NL) 3
1974 Oakland (AL) 4, Los Angeles (NL) 1
1975 Cincinnati (NL) 4, Boston (AL) 3
1976 Cincinnati (NL) 4, New York (AL) 0
1977 New York (AL) 4, Los Angeles (NL) 2
1978 New York (AL) 4, Los Angeles (NL) 2
1979 Pittsburgh (NL) 4, Baltimore (AL) 3
1980 Philadelphia (NL) 4, Kansas City (AL) 2
1981 Los Angeles (NL) 4, New York (AL) 2
1982 St Louis (NL) 4, Milwaukee (AL) 3
1983 Baltimore (AL) 4, Philadelphia (NL) 1
1984 Detroit (AL) 4, San Diego (NL) 1
1985 Kansas City (AL) 4, St Louis (NL) 3
1986 New York (NL) 4, Boston (AL) 3
1987 Minnesota (AL) 4, St Louis (NL) 3
1988 Los Angeles (NL) 4, Oakland (AL) 1
1989 Oakland (AL) 4, San Francisco (NL) 0
1990 Cincinnati (NL) 4, Oakland (AL) 0
1991 Minnesota (AL) 4, Atlanta (NL) 3
1992 Toronto (AL) 4, Atlanta (NL) 2
1993 Toronto (AL) 4, Philadelphia (NL) 2

Most wins: (22) New York Yankees (AL): 1923, 1927–8, 1932, 1936–9, 1941, 1943, 1947, 1949–53, 1956, 1958, 1961–2, 1977–8.

World amateur championship

Instituted in 1938; since 1974 held every two years.

Recent winners

1973	Cuba & USA (shared)
1974	USA
1976	Cuba
1978	Cuba
1980	Cuba
1982	South Korea
1984	Cuba
1986	Cuba
1988	Cuba
1990	Cuba
1992	Cuba

Most wins: (21) Cuba: 1939–40, 1942–3, 1950, 1952–3, 1961, 1969–73, 1976, 1978, 1980, 1984, 1986, 1988, 1990, 1992.

Olympic Games

Became an Olympic event in 1992.

1992   Cuba

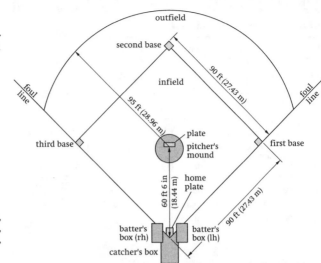

Minimum distance along each foul line is 250 ft (72.2 m)
Distance to the farthest point in centre field is at least 400 ft (122 m)

Baseball diamond

BASKETBALL

In the USA the game's governing body is the National Basketball Association (NBA), which comprises two 'conferences': Eastern (Atlantic Division and Central Division) and Western (Midwest Division and Pacific Division). At the end of the season (currently played over 82 games), each conference title is decided in a series of play-offs involving the divisional leaders and the next six best teams; the two conference title-holders compete in a best-of-seven series for the NBA Championship.

National Basketball Association championship

First held in 1947; the major competition in professional basketball in the USA.

1947	Philadelphia 4, Chicago 1
1948	Baltimore 4, Philadelphia 2
1949	Minneapolis 4, Washington 2
1950	Minneapolis 4, Syracuse 2
1951	Rochester 4, New York 3
1952	Minneapolis 4, New York 3
1953	Minneapolis 4, New York 1
1954	Minneapolis 4, Syracuse 3
1955	Syracuse 4, Ft Wayne 3
1956	Philadelphia 4, Ft Wayne 4
1957	Boston 4, St Louis 3
1958	St Louis 4, Boston 2
1959	Boston 4, Minneapolis 0
1960	Boston 4, St Louis 3
1961	Boston 4, St Louis 1
1962	Boston 4, LA Lakers 3
1963	Boston 4, LA Lakers 2

1964	Boston 4, San Francisco 1
1965	Boston 4, LA Lakers 1
1966	Boston 4, LA Lakers 3
1967	Philadelphia 4, San Francisco 2
1968	Boston 4, LA Lakers 2
1969	Boston 4, LA Lakers 3
1970	New York 4, LA Lakers 3
1971	Milwaukee 4, Baltimore 0
1972	LA Lakers 4, New York 1
1973	New York 4, LA Lakers 1
1974	Boston 4, Milwaukee 3
1975	Golden State 4, Washington 0
1976	Boston 4, Phoenix 2
1977	Portland 4, Philadelphia 2
1978	Washington 4, Seattle 3
1979	Seattle 4, Washington 1

1980	LA Lakers 4, Philadelphia 2
1981	Boston 4, Houston 2
1982	LA Lakers 4, Philadelphia 2
1983	Philadelphia 4, LA Lakers 0
1984	Boston 4, LA Lakers 3
1985	LA Lakers 4, Boston 2
1986	Boston 4, Houston 2
1987	LA Lakers 4, Boston 2
1988	LA Lakers 4, Detroit 3
1989	Detroit 4, LA Lakers 0
1990	Detroit 4, Portland 1
1991	Chicago 4, LA Lakers 1
1992	Chicago 4, Portland 1
1993	Chicago 4, Phoenix 2

Most wins: (16) Boston Celtics: 1967, 1959–66, 1968–9, 1974, 1976, 1981, 1984, 1986.

Sports and games

Basketball (continued)

World championship

First held 1950 for men, 1953 for women; generally now takes place every four years.

Winners (men)		Winners (women)	
1954	USA	1957	USA
1959	Brazil	1959	USSR
1963	Brazil	1964	USSR
1967	USSR	1967	USSR
1970	Yugoslavia	1971	USSR
1974	USSR	1975	USSR
1978	Yugoslavia	1979	USA
1982	USSR	1983	USSR
1986	USA	1987	USA
1990	Yugoslavia	1991	USA

Most wins: (3) USSR and Yugoslavia: as above.

Most wins: (6) USSR: as above.

Olympic Games

Became an Olympic event for men in 1936, for women in 1976.

Winners (men)		Winners (women)	
1936	USA	1976	USSR
1948	USA	1980	USSR
1952	USA	1984	USA
1956	USA	1988	USA
1960	USA	1992	Unified Team
1964	USA		
1968	USA	*Most wins:* (2) USA and
1972	USSR	USSR: as above.
1976	USA	
1980	Yugoslavia	
1984	USA	
1988	USSR	
1992	USA	

Most wins: (10) USA: as above.

BIATHLON

World championships

First held in 1958; take place annually; the Olympic champion is the automatic world champion in Olympic years; women's championship first held in 1984.

Recent winners: individual – men

15 km (10 km before 1988)
1979	Frank Ullrich (E Germany)
1980	Frank Ullrich (E Germany)
1981	Frank Ullrich (E Germany)
1982	Eirik Kvalfoss (Norway)
1983	Eirik Kvalfoss (Norway)
1984	Eirik Kvalfoss (Norway)
1985	Frank-Peter Rötsch (E Germany)
1986	Valeriy Medvetsev (USSR)
1987	Frank-Peter Rötsch (E Germany)
1988	Frank-Peter Rötsch (E Germany)
1989	Frank Luck (E Germany)
1990	Mark Kirchner (E Germany)
1991	Mark Kirchner (Germany)
1992	Mark Kirchner (Germany)
1993	Mark Kirchner (Germany)

20 km
1979	Klaus Siebert (E Germany)
1980	Anatoliy Alyabyev (USSR)
1981	Heikki Ikola (Finland)
1982	Frank Ullrich (E Germany)
1983	Frank Ullrich (E Germany)
1984	Peter Angerer (W Germany)
1985	Yuriy Kashkarov (USSR)
1986	Valeriy Medevetsev (USSR)
1987	Frank-Peter Rötsch (E Germany)
1988	Frank-Peter Rötsch (E Germany)
1989	Eric Kvalfoss (Norway)
1990	Valeriy Medvetsev (USSR)
1991	Mark Kirchner (Germany)
1992	Yevgeniy Redkine (Unified Team)
1993	Franz Zingerle (Austria)

Most individual titles: (6): Frank Ullrich (E Germany) 1978 10 km, and as above.

4 x 7.5 km relay (first held 1965)
1979	E Germany	1987	E Germany
1980	USSR	1988	USSR
1981	E Germany	1989	E Germany
1982	E Germany	1990	Italy
1983	USSR	1991	Germany
1985	USSR	1992	Germany
1986	USSR		

Most wins (including Olympic years): (15) USSR: 1968–74, 1976–77, 1980, 1983–6, 1988.

Recent winners: individual – women

7.5 km (5 km before 1988)
1984	Venera Cherhyshova (USSR)
1985	Sanna Gronlid (Norway)
1986	Kaya Parva (USSR)
1987	Yelena Golovina (USSR)
1988	Petra Schaaf (W Germany)
1989	Anne-Elinor Elvebakk (Norway)
1990	Anne-Elinor Elvebakk (Norway)
1991	Grete Ingeborg Nykkelmo (Norway)
1992	Anfissa Restzova (Unified Team)
1993	Bedard (Canada)

15 km (10 km before 1988)
1984	Venera Chernyshova (USSR)
1985	Kaya Parva (USSR)
1986	Eva Korpela (Sweden)
1987	Sanna Gronlid (Norway)
1988	Anne-Elinor Elvebakk (Norway)
1989	Petra Schaaf (W Germany)
1990	Svetlana Davydova (USSR)
1991	Petra Schaaf (Germany)
1992	Antje Misersky (Germany)
1993	Petra Schaaf (Germany)

Most individual titles: (3) Anne-Elinor Elvebakk (Norway) and Petra Schaaf (Germany): as above.

3 x 7.5 km relay (3 x 5 km before 1989)
1984	USSR	1987	USSR	1990	USSR
1985	USSR	1988	USSR	1991	USSR
1986	USSR	1989	USSR	1992	France

Most wins: (8) USSR: as above.

BILLIARDS

World professional championship

First held in 1870, organized on a challenge basis. Became a knockout event in 1909; discontinued in 1934; revived in 1951 as a challenge system; reverted to a knockout event in 1980.

Recent winners

1982	Rex Williams (England)
1983	Rex Williams (England)
1984	Mark Wildman (England)
1985	Ray Edmonds (England)
1986	Robbie Foldvari (Australia)
1987	Norman Dagley (England)
1988	Norman Dagley (England)
1989	Mike Russell (England)
1990	*Not held*
1991	Mike Russell (England)
1992	Geet Sethi (India)
1993	Geet Sethi (India)

Most wins: Knockout (6) Tom Newman (England): 1921–2, 1924–7. Challenge (8) John Roberts, Jnr (England): 1870–85.

BOBSLEIGHING AND TOBOGGANING/LUGE

World championships

First held in 1930 (four-man) and in 1931 (two-man). Olympic champions automatically become world champions.

Recent winners: two-man

1981	Bernard Germeshausen/Hans-Jürgen Gerhardt (E Germany)
1982	Erich Schärer/Josef Benz (Switzerland)
1983	Ralf Pichler/Urs Leuthold (Switzerland)
1984	Wolfgang Hoppe/Dietmar Schauerhammer (E Germany)
1985	Wolfgang Hoppe/Dietmar Schauerhammer (E Germany)
1986	Wolfgang Hoppe/Dietmar Schauerhammer (E Germany)
1987	Ralf Pichler/Celest Poltera (Switzerland)
1988	Janis Kipurs/Vladimir Kozlov (USSR)
1989	Wolfgang Hoppe/Bogdan Musiol (E Germany)
1990	Gustav Weber/Bruno Gerber (Switzerland)
1991	Rudi Lochner/Markus Zimmermann (Germany)
1992	Gustav Weber/Donat Acklin (Switzerland)
1993	Christoph Langan/Peer Joechel (Switzerland)
1994	Gustav Weber/Donat Acklin (Switzerland)

Recent winners: four-man

1980	E Germany	1987	Switzerland
1981	E Germany	1988	Switzerland
1982	Switzerland	1989	Switzerland
1983	Switzerland	1990	Switzerland
1984	E Germany	1991	Germany
1985	E Germany	1992	Austria
1986	Switzerland	1993	Switzerland

Most wins: Two-man (8) Eugenio Monti (Italy): 1957–61, 1963, 1966, 1968. Four-man (15), Switzerland: 1939, 1947, 1954–5, 1957, 1971, 1973, 1975, 1982–3, 1986–90.

Luge world championships

First held in 1955; annually until 1981, then every two years. The Olympic champion automatically becomes the world champion.

Recent winners: men's single-seater

1977	Hans Rinn (E Germany)
1978	Paul Hildgartner (Italy)
1979	Detlef Günther (E Germany)
1980	Bernhard Glass (E Germany)
1981	Sergey Danilin (USSR)
1983	Miroslav Zajonc (Canada)
1985	Michael Walter (E Germany)
1987	Markus Prock (Austria)
1989	Georg Hackl (W Germany)
1990	Georg Hackl (W Germany)
1991	Arnold Huber (Italy)
1993	Werdel Suckow (USA)
1994	Georg Hackl (W Germany)

Most wins: (3) Thomas Köhler (E Germany): 1962, 1964, 1967; Georg Hackl, as above.

Recent winners: women's single-seater

1977	Margrit Schumann (E Germany)
1978	Vera Sosulya (USSR)
1979	Melitta Sollmann (E Germany)
1980	Vera Sosulya (USSR)
1981	Melitta Sollman (E Germany)
1983	Steffi Martin (E Germany)
1985	Steffi Martin (E Germany)
1987	Cerstin Schmidt (E Germany)
1989	Susi Erdmann (E Germany)
1990	Gabriele Kohlisch (E Germany)
1991	Susi Erdmann (Germany)
1993	Gerda Weissensteiner (Italy)
1994	Gerda Weissensteiner (Italy)

Most wins: (5) Margrit Schumann (E Germany): 1973–7.

Olympic Games, luge

Winners: men's single-seater

1984	Paul Hildgartner (Italy)
1988	Jens Müller (E Germany)
1992	Georg Hackl (Germany)

Winners: pairs (men)

1984	W Germany	1988	E Germany
1992	Germany		

Most wins: Singles (no one more than 1). Pairs (5) E Germany: 1968, 1972, 1976, 1980, 1988.

Winners: women's single-seater

1984	Steffi Martin (E Germany)
1988	Steffi Martin Walter (E Germany)
1992	Doris Neuner (Austria)

Most wins: (2) Steffi Martin Walter (E Germany): as above.

BOWLS

World championships

Instituted for men in 1966 and for women in 1969; held every four years.

Men's singles
1966 David Bryant (England)
1972 Malwyn Evans (Wales)
1976 Doug Watson (South Africa)
1980 David Bryant (England)
1984 Peter Bellis (New Zealand)
1988 David Bryant (England)
1992 Tony Allcock (England)

Men's pairs
1966 Australia
1972 Hong Kong
1976 South Africa
1980 Australia
1984 USA
1988 New Zealand
1992 Scotland

Men's triples
1966 Australia
1972 USA
1976 South Africa
1980 England
1984 Ireland
1988 New Zealand
1992 Israel

Men's fours
1966 New Zealand
1972 England
1976 South Africa
1980 Hong Kong
1984 England
1988 Ireland
1992 Scotland

Leonard Trophy
Team award, given to the nation with the best overall performances in the men's world championship.

Winners
1966 Australia
1972 Scotland
1976 South Africa
1980 England
1984 Scotland
1988 England
1992 Scotland

Most wins: (5) David Bryant (singles: as above; triples: 1988; team: 1980).

Women's singles
1969 Gladys Doyle (Papua New Guinea)
1973 Elsie Wilke (New Zealand)
1977 Elsie Wilke (New Zealand)
1981 Norma Shaw (England)
1985 Merle Richardson (Australia)

1988* Janet Ackland (Wales)
1992 Margaret Johnston (Ireland)

Women's pairs
1969 South Africa
1973 Australia
1977 Hong Kong
1981 Ireland
1985 Australia
1988* Ireland
1992 Ireland

Women's triples
1969 South Africa
1973 New Zealand
1977 Wales
1981 Hong Kong
1985 Australia
1988* Australia
1992 Scotland

Women's fours
1969 South Africa
1973 New Zealand
1977 Australia
1981 England
1985 Scotland
1988* Australia
1992 Scotland

Women's team
1969 South Africa
1973 New Zealand
1977 Australia
1981 England
1985 Australia
1988* England
1992 Scotland

Most wins: (3) Merle Richardson (fours: 1977; singles and pairs: 1985).

*The women's event was advanced to December 1988 (Australia).

World indoor championships

First held in 1979; takes place annually.

Winners
1981 David Bryant (England)
1982 John Watson (Scotland)
1983 Bob Sutherland (Scotland)
1984 Jim Baker (Ireland)
1985 Terry Sullivan (Wales)
1986 Tony Allcock (England)
1987 Tony Allcock (England)
1988 Hugh Duff (Scotland)
1989 Richard Corsie (Scotland)
1990 John Price (Wales)
1991 Richard Corsie (Scotland)
1992 Ian Schuback (Australia)
1993 Richard Corsie (Scotland)

Most wins: (3) David Bryant (England): 1979, 1980, 1981.

Waterloo Handicap

First held in 1907 and annually at Blackpool's Waterloo Hotel; the premier event of Crown Green Bowling.

Recent winners
1981 Roy Nicholson
1982 Dennis Mercer
1983 Stan Frith
1984 Steve Ellis
1985 Tommy Johnstone
1986 Brian Duncan
1987 Brian Duncan
1988 Ingham Gregory
1989 Brian Duncan
1990 John Bancroft
1991 John Eccles
1992 Brian Duncan
1993 Alan Broadhurst

Most wins: (5) Brian Duncan: 1979 and as above.

BOXING

World heavyweight champions

Undisputed
1882 John L Sullivan (USA)
1892 James J Corbett (USA)*
1897 Bob Fitzsimmons (Great Britain)
1899 James J Jefferies (USA)
1905 Marvin Hart (USA)
1906 Tommy Burns (Can)
1908 Jack Johnson (USA)
1915 Jess Willard (USA)
1919 Jack Dempsey (USA)
1926 Gene Tunney (USA)
1930 Max Schmeling (Germany)
1932 Jack Sharkey (USA)
1933 Primo Carnera (Italy)
1934 Max Baer (USA)
1935 James J Braddock (USA)
1937 Joe Louis (USA)
1949 Ezzard Charles (USA)
1951 Jersey Joe Walcott (USA)
1952 Rocky Marciano (USA)
1956 Floyd Patterson (USA)
1959 Ingemar Johansson (Sweden)
1960 Sonny Liston (USA)
1964 Cassius Clay (USA)[a]
1970 Joe Frazier (USA)
1973 George Foreman (USA)
1974 Muhammad Ali (USA)[a]
1978 Leon Spinks (USA)
1987 Mike Tyson (USA)

*The first world heavyweight champion under Queensberry rules with gloves.

World heavyweight champions (continued)

In recent years, 'world champions' have been recognized by up to four different governing bodies.

Champions since 1978		Recognizing body
1978	Muhammad Ali (USA)[a]	WBA
1978	Larry Holmes (USA)	WBC
1979	John Tate (USA)	WBA
1980	Mike Weaver (USA)	WBA
1982	Mike Dokes (USA)	WBA
1983	Gerry Coetzee (South Africa)	WBA
1984	Larry Holmes (USA)	IBF
1984	Tim Witherspoon (USA)	WBC
1984	Pinklon Thomas (USA)	WBC
1984	Greg Page (USA)	WBA
1985	Michael Spinks (USA)	IBF
1985	Tony Tubbs (USA)	WBA
1986	Tim Witherspoon (USA)	WBA
1986	Trevor Berbick (Canada)	WBC
1986	Mike Tyson (USA)	WBC
1986	James Smith (USA)	WBA
1987	Tony Tucker (USA)	IBF
1987	Mike Tyson (USA)	WBA/WBC
1987	Mike Tyson (USA)	UND
1989	Francesco Damiani (Italy)	WBO
1990	James (Buster) Douglas (USA)	WBA/WBC/IBF
1990	Evander Holyfield (USA)	WBA/WBC/IBF
1991	Ray Mercer (USA)	WBO
1992	Riddick Bowe (USA)	WBA/WBC/IBF
1992	Michael Mourer (USA)	WBO
1992	Lennox Lewis (Great Britain)	WBC
1993	Tommy Morrison (USA)	WBO

[a]Cassius Clay changed his name to Muhammad Ali upon joining the Black Muslims.

IBF = International Boxing Federation
UND = Undisputed Champion
WBA = World Boxing Association
WBC = World Boxing Council
WBO = World Boxing Organization

The weight divisions in professional boxing

Name	Maximum weight
Heavyweight	any weight
Cruiserweight/junior-heavyweight	88 kg/195 lb
Light-heavyweight	79 kg/175 lb
Super-middleweight	77 kg/170 lb
Middleweight	73 kg/160 lb
Light-middleweight/junior-middleweight	70 kg/154 lb
Welterweight	67 kg/147 lb
Light-welterweight/junior-welterweight	64 kg/140 lb
Lightweight	61 kg/135 lb
Junior-lightweight/super-featherweight	59 kg/130 lb
Featherweight	57 kg/126 lb
Super-bantamweight/junior-featherweight	55 kg/122 lb
Bantamweight	54 kg/118 lb
Super-flyweight/junior-bantamweight	52 kg/115 lb
Flyweight	51 kg/112 lb
Light-flyweight/junior-flyweight	49 kg/108 lb
Mini-flyweight/straw-weight/minimum weight	under 48 kg/105 lb

CANOEING

Olympic Games

Single kayak: 1000 m – men
1936	Gregor Hradetzky (Austria)
1948	Gert Fredriksson (Sweden)
1952	Gert Fredriksson (Sweden)
1956	Gert Fredriksson (Sweden)
1960	Erik Hansen (Denmark)
1964	Rolf Peterson (Sweden)
1968	Mihaly Hesz (Hungary)
1972	Aleksandr Shaparenko (USSR)
1976	Rüdiger Helm (E Germany)
1980	Rüdiger Helm (E Germany)
1984	Alan Thompson (New Zealand)
1988	Greg Barton (USA)
1992	Clint Robinson (Australia)

Single kayak: 500 m – women
1948	Keren Hoff (Denmark)
1952	Sylvi Saimo (Finland)
1956	Elisaveta Dementyeva (USSR)
1960	Antonina Seredina (USSR)
1964	Lyudmila Khvedosyuk (USSR)
1968	Lyudmila Pinayeva (USSR)
1972	Yulia Ryabchinskaya (USSR)
1976	Carola Zirzow (E Germany)
1980	Birgit Fischer (E Germany)
1984	Agneta Andersson (Sweden)
1988	Vania Gecheva (USSR)
1992	Brigit Schmidt (Germany)

Most wins: Men (3) Gert Fredriksson: as above. No woman has won more than one title.

CHESS

World champions

World champions have been recognized since 1886; first women's champion recognized in 1927.

Recent champions: men

1948-57	Mikhail Botvinnik (USSR)
1957-8	Vassiliy Smyslov (USSR)
1958-60	Mikhail Botvinnik (USSR)
1960-1	Mikhail Tal (USSR)
1961-3	Mikhail Botvinnik (USSR)
1963-9	Tigran Petrosian (USSR)
1969-72	Boris Spassky (USSR)
1972-5	Bobby Fischer (USA)
1975-85	Anatoliy Karpov (USSR)
1985-	Gary Kasparov (USSR/Azerbaijan)

Longest reigning champion: 27 years, Emanuel Lasker (Germany): 1894–1921.

Champions: women

1927-44	Vera Menchik-Stevenson (UK)
1950-3	Lyudmila Rudenko (USSR)
1953-6	Elizaveta Bykova (USSR)
1956-8	Olga Rubtsova (USSR)
1958-62	Elizaveta Bykova (USSR)
1962-78	Nona Gaprindashvili (USSR)
1978-92	Maya Chiburdanidze (USSR)
1992-	Xie Jun (China)

Longest reigning champion: 17 years, Vera Menchik-Stevenson (UK): as above.

Chess notation

The opening position

Abbreviations

B	Bishop
K	King
KB	King's bishop
KN	King's knight
KR	King's rook
N	Knight
P	Pawn
Q	Queen
QB	Queen's bishop
QN	Queen's knight
QR	Queen's rook
R	Rook

Descriptive notation

Each file is named by the piece on the first rank; ranks are numbered 1-8 away from the player.

x	captures (Q x P = Queen takes Pawn)
–	moves to (Q–KB4)
ch	check (R–QB3 ch)
dis ch	discovered check
dbl ch	double check
e.p.	en passant
mate	checkmate
0-0	castles, King's side
0-0-0	castles, Queen's side
!	good move (P x R!)
!!	very good move
!!!	outstanding move
?	bad move
!?	good or bad move (depends on response of the other player)

Algebraic notation

Each square is named by a combination of file letter and rank number.

Chess pieces in other languages

French
B	fou (fool)
K	roi (king)
N	cavalier (horseman)
P	pion (pawn)
Q	dame, reine (lady), (queen)
R	tour (tower)

German
B	Läufer (runner)
K	König (king)
N	Springer (jumper)
P	Bauer (peasant)
Q	Königin (queen)
R	Turm (tower)

Sports and games

CONTRACT BRIDGE

World team championship

The game's biggest championship; men's contest (The Bermuda Bowl) first held in 1951, and now takes place every two years; women's contest (The Venice Cup) first held in 1974, and since 1985 is concurrent with the men's event.

Bermuda Bowl winners: men
1973	Italy	1981	USA
1974	Italy	1983	USA
1975	Italy	1985	USA
1976	USA	1987	USA
1977	USA	1989	Brazil
1979	USA	1991	Iceland

Most wins: (13) Italy: 1957–9, 1961–3, 1965–7, 1969, 1973–5.

Venice Cup winners: women
1974	USA	1985	UK
1976	USA	1987	Italy
1978	USA	1989	USA
1981	UK	1991	USA
1983	*Not held*		

Most wins: (5) USA: as above.

World team olympiad

First held in 1960; takes place every four years.

Winners: men
1960	France	1980	France
1964	Italy	1984	Poland
1968	Italy	1988	USA
1972	Italy	1992	France
1976	Brazil		

Winners: women
1960	United Arab Emirates	1976	USA
		1980	USA
1964	UK	1984	USA
1968	Sweden	1988	Denmark
1972	Italy	1992	Austria

Most wins: Men (3) Italy and France: as above. Women (3) USA: as above.

CRICKET

World cup

First played in England in 1975; held every four years. The 1987 competition was the first to be played outside England, in India and Pakistan.

Winners
1975	West Indies	1987	Australia
1979	West Indies	1992	Pakistan
1983	India		

County championship

The oldest cricket competition in the world; first won by Sussex in 1827. Not officially recognized until 1890, when a proper points system was introduced.

Recent winners
1981	Nottinghamshire
1982	Middlesex
1983	Essex
1984	Essex
1985	Middlesex
1986	Essex
1987	Nottinghamshire
1988	Worcestershire
1989	Worcestershire
1990	Middlesex
1991	Essex
1992	Essex
1993	Middlesex

Most outright wins: (29) Yorkshire: 1893, 1896, 1898, 1900–2, 1905, 1908, 1912, 1919, 1922–5, 1931–3, 1935, 1937–9, 1946, 1959–60, 1962–3, 1966–8.

Benson and Hedges cup

First held in 1972.

Recent winners
1981	Somerset
1982	Somerset
1983	Middlesex
1984	Lancashire
1985	Leicestershire
1986	Middlesex
1987	Yorkshire
1988	Hampshire
1989	Nottinghamshire
1990	Lancashire
1991	Worcestershire
1992	Hampshire
1993	Derbyshire

Most wins: (3) Kent: 1973, 1976, 1978; Leicestershire: 1972, 1975, 1985.

NatWest Bank trophy

First held in 1963; known as the Gillette Cup until 1981.

Recent winners
1981	Derbyshire
1982	Surrey
1983	Somerset
1984	Middlesex
1985	Essex
1986	Sussex
1987	Nottinghamshire
1988	Middlesex
1989	Warwickshire
1990	Lancashire
1991	Hampshire
1992	Northamptonshire
1993	Warwickshire

Most wins: (5) Lancashire: 1970–2, 1975, 1990.

AXA Equity and Law League

First held in 1969; known as the John Player League 1969–86 and as the Refuge Assurance League until 1991.

Recent winners
1981	Essex
1982	Sussex
1983	Yorkshire
1984	Essex
1985	Essex
1986	Hampshire
1987	Worcestershire
1988	Worcestershire
1989	Lancashire
1990	Derbyshire
1991	Nottinghamshire
1992	Middlesex
1993	Glamorgan

Most wins: (3) Kent: 1972–3, 1976; Essex: as above; Lancashire: 1969–70, 1989; Hampshire: 1975, 1978, 1986; Worcestershire: 1971, 1987, 1988.

Sports and games

Cricket (continued)

Sheffield Shield

Australia's leading domestic competition; contested inter-state since 1891.

Recent winners
1982 South Australia
1983 New South Wales
1984 Western Australia
1985 New South Wales
1986 New South Wales
1987 Western Australia
1988 Western Australia
1989 Western Australia
1990 New South Wales
1991 Victoria
1992 Western Australia
1993 New South Wales

Most wins: (41) New South Wales, 1896–7, 1900, 1902–7, 1909, 1911–12, 1914, 1920–1, 1923, 1926, 1929, 1932–3, 1938, 1940, 1949–50, 1952, 1954–62, 1965–6, 1983, 1985–6, 1990.

Cricket field positions

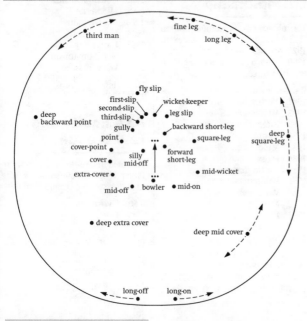

McRobertson Shield

Croquet's leading tournament; held spasmodically since 1925; contested by teams from Great Britain, New Zealand, and Australia.

Winners
1925 Great Britain
1928 Australia
1930 Australia
1935 Australia
1937 Great Britain
1950 New Zealand
1956 Great Britain
1963 Great Britain
1969 Great Britain
1974 Great Britain
1979 New Zealand
1982 Great Britain
1986 New Zealand
1990 Great Britain
1993 Great Britain

Most wins: (9) Great Britain: as above.

World singles championships

Inaugurated in 1989; held at Hurlingham.

Winners
1989 Joe Hogan (New Zealand)
1990 Robert Fulford (Great Britain)
1991 John Walters (Great Britain)
1992 Robert Fulford (Great Britain)
1993 *Not held*

Most wins: (2) Robert Fulford (UK): as above.

CROSS-COUNTRY RUNNING

World championships

First international championship held in 1903, but only included runners from England, Ireland, Scotland, and Wales. Recognized as an official world championship from 1973; first women's race in 1967.

Recent winner: individual – men
1982 Mohamed Kedir (Ethiopia)
1983 Bekele Debele (Ethiopia)
1984 Carlos Lopes (Portugal)
1985 Carlos Lopes (Portugal)
1986 John Ngugi (Kenya)
1987 John Ngugi (Kenya)
1988 John Ngugi (Kenya)
1989 John Ngugi (Kenya)
1990 Khalid Skah (Morocco)
1991 Khalid Skah (Morocco)
1992 John Ngugi (Kenya)
1993 William Sigei (Kenya)

Recent winners: team – men

1982	Ethiopia	1988	Kenya
1983	Ethiopia	1989	Kenya
1984	Ethiopia	1990	Kenya
1985	Ethiopia	1991	Kenya
1986	Kenya	1992	Kenya
1987	Kenya	1993	Kenya

Most wins: Individual (5) John Ngugi (Kenya): as above. Team (45), England: between 1903 and 1980.

Recent winners: individual – women
1982 Maricica Puica (Romania)
1983 Grete Waitz (Norway)
1984 Maricica Puica (Romania)
1985 Zola Budd (England)
1986 Zola Budd (England)
1987 Annette Sergent (France)
1988 Ingrid Kristiansen (Norway)
1989 Annette Sergent (France)
1990 Lynn Jennings (USA)
1991 Lynn Jennings (USA)
1992 Lynn Jennings (USA)
1993 Albertina Dias (Portugal)

Recent winners: team – women

1982	USSR	1988	USA
1983	USA	1989	USSR
1984	USA	1990	USSR
1985	USA	1991	Kenya
1986	England	1992	Kenya
1987	USA	1993	Kenya

Most wins: Individual (5) Doris Brown (USA): 1967–71; Grete Waitz (Norway): 1978–81, 1983. Team (8), USA: 1968–9, 1975, 1979, 1983–5, 1987, 1988–9.

CURLING

World championships

First men's championship held in 1959; first women's championship in 1979. Takes place annually.

Recent winners: men

1979	Norway	1987	Canada
1980	Canada	1988	Norway
1981	Switzerland	1989	Canada
1982	Canada	1990	Canada
1983	Canada	1991	Scotland
1984	Norway	1992	Switzerland
1985	Canada	1993	Canada
1986	Canada		

Recent winners: women

1979	Switzerland	1987	Canada
1980	Canada	1988	W Germany
1981	Sweden	1989	Canada
1982	Denmark	1990	Norway
1983	Switzerland	1991	Norway
1984	Canada	1992	Switzerland
1985	Canada	1993	Germany
1986	Canada		

Most wins: Men (20) Canada: 1959–64, 1966, 1968–72, 1980, 1982–3, 1985–7, 1989, 1990. Women (6) Canada: as above.

CYCLING

Tour de France

World's premier cycling event; first held in 1903.

Recent winners

1981	Bernard Hinault (France)
1982	Bernard Hinault (France)
1983	Laurent Fignon (France)
1984	Laurent Fignon (France)
1985	Bernard Hinault (France)
1986	Greg LeMond (USA)
1987	Stephen Roche (Ireland)
1988	Pedro Delgado (Spain)
1989	Greg LeMond (USA)
1990	Greg LeMond (USA)
1991	Miguel Induráin (Spain)
1992	Miguel Induráin (Spain)
1993	Miguel Induráin (Spain)

Most wins: (5) Jacques Anquetil (France): 1957, 1961–4; Eddy Merckx (Belgium): 1969–72, 1974; Bernard Hinault (France): 1978–9, 1981–2, 1985.

World road race championships

Men's race first held in 1927; takes place annually. First women's race in 1958; takes place annually, but not in Olympic years.

Recent winners: professional men

1981	Freddy Maertens (Belgium)
1982	Giuseppe Saroni (Italy)
1983	Greg LeMond (USA)
1984	Claude Criquielion (Belgium)
1985	Joop Zoetemelk (Netherlands)
1986	Moreno Argentin (Italy)
1987	Stephen Roche (Ireland)
1988	Maurizio Fondriest (Italy)
1989	Greg LeMond (USA)
1990	Rudy Dhaemens (Belgium)
1991	Gianni Bugno (Italy)
1992	Gianni Bugno (Italy)
1993	Gianni Bugno (Italy)

Recent winners: women

1981	Ute Enzenauer (W Germany)
1982	Mandy Jones (Great Britain)
1983	Marianne Berglund (Sweden)
1985	Jeannie Longo (France)
1986	Jeannie Longo (France)
1987	Jeannie Longo (France)
1989	Jeannie Longo (France)
1990	Catherine Marsal (France)
1991	Leontein van Moorseel (Netherlands)
1992	Kathryn Watt (Australia)
1993	Leontein van Moorsel (Netherlands)

Most wins: Men (3) Alfredo Binda (Italy): 1927, 1930, 1932; Rik Van Steenbergen (Belgium): 1949, 1956–7; Eddy Merckx (Belgium): 1967, 1971, 1974. Women (4) Yvonne Reynders (Belgium): 1959, 1961, 1963, 1966; Jeannie Longo (France): as above.

Olympic Games

Gold medal winners: 1992 – men

Individual road race
Fabio Casartelli (Italy)

Sprint
Jens Fiedler (Germany)

4000 m individual pursuit
Chris Boardman (Great Britain)

Gold medal winners: 1992 – women

Individual road race
Kathryn Watt (Australia)

Sprint
Erika Salumyae (Estonia)

3000 m individual pursuit
Petra Rossner (Germany)

CYCLO-CROSS

World championships

First held in 1950 as an open event; separate professional and amateur events since 1967.

Recent winners: professional

1980	Roland Liboton (Belgium)
1981	Johannes Stamsnijder (Netherlands)
1982	Roland Liboton (Belgium)
1983	Roland Liboton (Belgium)
1984	Roland Liboton (Belgium)
1985	Klaus-Peter Thaler (W Germany)
1986	Albert Zweifel (Switzerland)
1987	Klaus-Peter Thaler (W Germany)
1988	Pascal Richard (Switzerland)
1989	Danny De Bie (Belgium)
1990	Henk Baars (Netherlands)
1991	Radomir Simunek (Czechoslovakia)
1992	Mike Kluge (Germany)
1993	Dominique Arnaud (France)

Recent winners: amateur

1980	Fritz Saladin (Switzerland)
1981	Milos Fisera (Czechoslovakia)
1982	Milos Fisera (Czechoslovakia)
1983	Radomir Simunek (Czechoslovakia)
1984	Radomir Simunek (Czechoslovakia)
1985	Mike Kluge (W Germany)
1986	Vito di Tano (Italy)
1987	Mike Kluge (W Germany)
1988	Karol Camrola (Czechoslovakia)
1989	Ondrej Glaja (Czechoslovakia)
1990	Andreas Buesser (Switzerland)
1991	Thomas Frischknecht (Switzerland)
1992	Daniele Pontoni (Italy)
1993	Henrik Djemis (Denmark)

Most wins: Professional (7) Eric de Vlaeminck (Belgium): 1966, 1968–73. Amateur (5) Robert Vermiere (Belgium): 1970–1, 1974–5, 1977.

DARTS

World professional championship

First held at Nottingham in 1978.

Winners

1979	John Lowe (England)
1980	Eric Bristow (England)
1981	Eric Bristow (England)
1982	Jocky Wilson (Scotland)
1983	Keith Deller (England)
1984	Eric Bristow (England)
1985	Eric Bristow (England)
1986	Eric Bristow (England)
1987	John Lowe (England)
1988	Bob Anderson (England)
1989	Jocky Wilson (Scotland)
1990	Phil Taylor (England)
1991	Dennis Priestley (England)
1992	Phil Taylor (England)
1993	John Lowe (England)
1994	John Part (Canada)

Most wins: (5) Eric Bristow: as above.

World cup

A team competition first held at Wembley in 1977; takes place every two years.

Winners: team

1979	England
1981	England
1983	England
1985	England
1987	England
1989	England
1991	England
1993	England

Winners: individual

1979	Nicky Virachkul (USA)
1981	John Lowe (England)
1983	Eric Bristow (England)
1985	Eric Bristow (England)
1987	Eric Bristow (England)
1989	Eric Bristow (England)
1991	John Lowe (England)
1993	Roland Schollen (Denmark)

Most wins: Team (7) England: as above. Individual (4) Eric Bristow (England): as above.

DRAUGHTS

World championship

Held on a challenge basis. The champion since 1979 has been M Tinsley (USA); he has defended the title five times.

British Open championship

The leading championship in Britain. First held in 1926; now takes place every two years.

Recent winners

1970	I Edwards (Great Britain)
1972	G Davies (Great Britain)
1974	J McGill (Great Britain)
1976	A Huggins (Great Britain)
1978	J McGill (Great Britain)
1980	T Watson (Great Britain)
1982	T Watson (Great Britain)
1984	A Long (USA)
1986	H Devlin (Great Britain)
1988	De Oldbury (Great Britain)
1990	T Watson (Great Britain)
1992	H Devlin (Great Britain)

EQUESTRIAN EVENTS

World championships

Show-jumping championships first held in 1953 (for men) and 1965 (for women); since 1978 men and women have competed together and on equal terms. Team competition introduced in 1978; three-day event and dressage championships introduced in 1966. All three now held every four years.

Winners: show jumping – men

1953	Francisco Goyoago (Spain)
1954	Hans-Günter Winkler (W Germany)
1955	Hans-Günter Winkler (W Germany)
1956	Raimondo D'Inzeo (Italy)
1960	Raimondo D'Inzeo (Italy)
1966	Pierre d'Oriola (France)
1970	David Broome (Great Britain)
1974	Hartwig Steenken (W Germany)

Winners: show jumping – women

1965	Marion Coakes (Great Britain)
1970	Janou Lefèbvre (France)
1974	Janou Tissot (France)

Winners: individual

1978	Gerd Wiltfang (W Germany)
1982	Norbert Koof (W Germany)
1986	Gail Greenough (Canada)
1990	Eric Navet (France)

Winners: team

1982	France
1986	USA
1990	France

Winners: three-day event – individual

1970	Mary Gordon-Watson (Great Britain)
1974	Bruce Davidson (USA)
1978	Bruce Davidson (USA)
1982	Lucinda Green (Great Britain)
1986	Virginia Leng (Great Britain)
1990	Blyth Tait (New Zealand)

Winners: three-day event – team

1970	Great Britain
1974	USA
1978	Canada
1982	Great Britain
1986	Great Britain
1990	New Zealand

Winners: dressage – individual

1970	Yelene Petouchkova (USSR)
1974	Reiner Klimke (W Germany)
1978	Christine Stückelberger (Switzerland)
1982	Reiner Klimke (W Germany)
1986	Anne Grethe Jensen (Denmark)
1990	Nicole Uphoft (W Germany)

Winners: dressage – team

1970	USSR	1982	W Germany
1974	W Germany	1986	W Germany
1978	W Germany	1990	W Germany

Olympic Games

Gold medal winners: 1992 – individual

Three-day event
Matthew Ryan (Australia)

Dressage
Nicole Uphoff (Germany)

Jumping
Ludger Beerbaum (Germany)

Gold medal winners: 1992 – team

Three-day event	Australia
Dressage	Germany
Jumping	Netherlands

FENCING

World championships

Held annually since 1921 (between 1921–35, known as European Championships). Not held in Olympic years.

Recent winners

Foil: individual – men

1975	Christian Noel (France)
1977	Alexander Romankov (USSR)
1978	Didier Flament (France)
1979	Alexander Romankov (USSR)
1981	Vladimir Smirnov (USSR)
1982	Alexander Romankov (USSR)
1983	Alexander Romankov (USSR)
1985	Mauro Numa (Italy)
1986	Andrea Borella (Italy)
1987	Mathias Gey (W Germany)
1989	Alexander Koch (W Germany)
1990	Philippe Omnes (France)
1991	Ingo Weissenborn (Germany)
1993	Alexander Koch (Germany)

Foil: team – men

1975	France
1977	W Germany
1978	Poland
1979	USSR
1981	USSR
1982	USSR
1983	W Germany
1985	Italy
1986	Italy
1987	USSR
1989	USSR
1990	Italy
1991	Cuba
1993	Germany

Most wins: Individual (5) Alexander Romankov (USSR): 1974, 1977, 1979, 1982–3. Team (15) USSR: during 1959–89.

Foil: individual – women

1975	Ecaterina Stahl (Romania)
1977	Valentina Sidorova (USSR)
1978	Valentina Sidorova (USSR)
1979	Cornelia Hanisch (W Germany)
1981	Cornelia Hanisch (W Germany)
1982	Naila Giliazova (USSR)
1983	Dorina Vaccaroni (Italy)
1985	Cornelia Hanisch (W Germany)
1986	Anja Fichtel (W Germany)
1987	Elisabeta Tufan (Romania)
1989	Olga Velitschko (USSR)
1990	Anja Fichtel (W Germany)
1991	Giovanna Trillini (Italy)
1993	Francesca Bortolozzi (Italy)

Foil: team – women

1975	USSR	1985	W Germany
1977	USSR	1986	USSR
1978	USSR	1987	Hungary
1979	USSR	1989	W Germany
1981	USSR	1990	Italy
1982	Italy	1991	Cuba
1983	Italy	1993	Germany

Most wins: Individual (3) Helène Mayer (Germany): 1929, 1931, 1937; Ilona Elek (Hungary): 1934–5, 1951; Ellen Müller-Preiss (Austria): 1947, 1949, 1950; Cornelia Hanisch: as above. Team (15) USSR: during 1956–86.

Epée: individual – men

1975	Alexander Pusch (W Germany)
1977	Johan Harmenberg (Sweden)
1978	Alexander Pusch (W Germany)
1979	Philippe Riboud (France)
1981	Zoltan Szekely (Hungary)
1982	Jenö Pap (Hungary)
1983	Ellmar Bormann (W Germany)
1985	Philippe Boisse (France)
1986	Philippe Riboud (France)
1987	Volker Fischer (W Germany)
1989	Manuel Pereira (Spain)
1990	Thomas Gerull (W Germany)
1991	Andrei Shuvalov (USSR)
1993	Ivan Kolobov (Russia)

Epée: team – men

1975	Sweden	1985	W Germany
1977	Sweden	1986	W Germany
1978	Hungary	1987	W Germany
1979	USSR	1989	Italy
1981	USSR	1990	Italy
1982	France	1991	USSR
1983	France	1993	Italy

Most wins: Individual (3) Georges Buchard (France): 1927, 1931, 1933; Alexei Nikanchikov (USSR): 1966–7, 1970. Team (11) Italy: during 1931–58 and 1989–90; France: during 1934–83.

Epée: individual – women

1989	Anja Straub (Switzerland)
1990	Anja Straub (Switzerland)
1991	Taime Chappe (Cuba)
1992	Mariann Horváth (Hungary)
1993	Oksana Emakova (Estonia)

Epée: team – women

1989	Hungary
1990	W Germany
1991	Hungary
1993	Hungary

Sabre: individual – men

1975	Vladimir Nazlimov (USSR)
1977	Pal Gerevich (Hungary)
1978	Viktor Krovopuskov (USSR)
1979	Vladimir Nazlimov (USSR)
1981	Mariusz Wodke (Poland)
1982	Viktor Krovopuskov (USSR)
1983	Vasiliy Etropolski (Bulgaria)
1985	György Nebald (Hungary)
1986	Sergey Mindirgassov (USSR)
1987	Jean-François Lamour (France)
1989	Grigoriy Kirienko (USSR)
1990	György Nébald (Hungary)
1991	Grigoriy Kirienko (USSR)
1993	Grigoriy Kirienko (Russia)

Sabre: team – men

1975	USSR
1977	USSR
1978	Hungary
1979	USSR
1981	Hungary
1982	Hungary
1983	USSR
1985	USSR
1986	USSR
1987	USSR
1989	USSR
1990	USSR
1991	Hungary
1993	Hungary

Most wins: Individual (3) Aladar Gerevich (Hungary): 1935, 1951, 1955; Jerzy Pawlowski (Poland): 1957, 1965–6; Yokov Rylsky (USSR): 1958, 1961, 1963. Team (18) Hungary: during 1930–91.

Olympic Games

Gold medal winners: 1992 – men

Individual foil
Philip Omnes (France)

Team foil
Germany

Individual epée
Eric Srecki (Hungary)

Team epée
Germany

Individual sabre
Bence Szabo (Hungary)

Team sabre
Unified Team

Gold medal winners: 1992 – women

Individual foil
Giovanna Tullini (Italy)

Team foil
Italy

FOOTBALL (AMERICAN)

National Football League (NFL)

In its existing form since 1970, the NFL consists of two 'conferences': the American Football Conference (AFC) and the National Football Conference (NFC). Each of these comprises three divisions (Eastern, Central, and Western), which are made up of either four or five teams. The season is played over sixteen games, with the championship of each conference being decided by two rounds of play-offs involving the three winners of the divisions, plus a number of 'wild cards', ie the best of the rest.

Superbowl

First held in 1967 between champions of the National Football league (NFL) and the American Football League (AFL). Takes place each January; since 1971 an end of season meeting between the champions of the AFC and the NFC.

1967 Green Bay Packers (NFL) 35, Kansas City Chiefs (AFL) 10
1968 Green Bay Packers (NFL) 33, Oakland Raiders (AFL) 14
1969 New York Jets (AFL) 16, Baltimore Colts (NFL) 7
1970 Kansas City Chiefs (AFL) 23, Minnesota Vikings (NFL) 7
1971 Baltimore Colts (AFC) 16, Dallas Cowboys (NFC) 13
1972 Dallas Cowboys (NFC) 24, Miami Dolphins (AFC) 3
1973 Miami Dolphins (AFC) 14, Washington Redskins (NFC) 7
1974 Miami Dolphins (AFC) 24, Minnesota Vikings (NFL) 7
1975 Pittsburgh Steelers (AFC) 16, Minnesota Vikings (NFC) 6
1976 Pittsburgh Steelers (AFC) 21, Dallas Cowboys (NFC) 17
1977 Oakland Raiders (AFC) 32, Minnesota Vikings (NFC) 14
1978 Dallas Cowboys (NFC) 27, Denver Broncos (AFC) 10
1979 Pittsburgh Steelers (AFC) 35, Dallas Cowboys (NFC) 31
1980 Pittsburgh Steelers (AFC) 31, Los Angeles Rams (NFC) 19
1981 Oakland Raiders (AFC) 27, Philadelphia Eagles (NFC) 10
1982 San Francisco 49ers (NFC) 26, Cincinnati Bengals (AFC) 21
1983 Washington Redskins (NFC) 27, Miami Dolphins (AFC) 17
1984 Los Angeles Raiders (AFC) 38, Washington Redskins (NFC) 9
1985 San Francisco 49ers (NFC) 38, Miami Dolphins (AFC) 16
1986 Chicago Bears (NFC) 46, New England Patriots (AFC) 10
1987 New York Giants (NFC) 39, Denver Broncos (AFC) 20

1988 Washington Redskins (NFC) 42, Denver Broncos (AFC) 10
1989 San Francisco 49ers (NFC) 20, Cincinnati Bengals (AFC) 16
1990 San Francisco 49ers (NFC) 55, Denver Broncos (AFC) 10
1991 New York Giants (NFC) 20, Buffalo Bills (AFC) 19
1992 Washington Redskins (NFC) 37, Buffalo Bills (AFC) 24
1993 Dallas Cowboys (NFC) 52, Buffalo Bills (AFC) 17

Most wins: (4) Pittsburgh Steelers: 1975–6, 1979–80; (2) San Francisco 49ers: 1982, 1985, 1989–90.

American football field

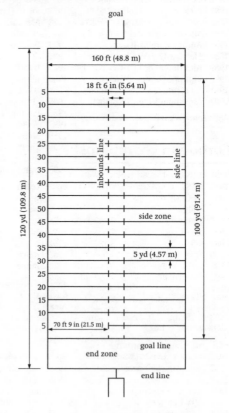

goal

160 ft (48.8 m)

18 ft 6 in (5.64 m)

inbounds line

side line

120 yd (109.8 m)

100 yd (91.4 m)

side zone

5 yd (4.57 m)

70 ft 9 in (21.5 m)

goal line

end zone

end line

FOOTBALL (ASSOCIATION FOOTBALL/SOCCER)

FIFA World Cup

Association Football's premier event. First contested for the Jules Rimet Trophy in 1930; Brazil won it outright after winning for the third time in 1970. Since then teams have competed for the FIFA (*Fédération Internationale de Football Association*) World Cup; held every four years.

	Winner	Score	Runner-up	Final held in
1930	Uruguay	4–2	Argentina	Montevideo
1934	Italy	2–1	Czechoslovakia	Rome
1938	Italy	4–2	Hungary	Paris
1950	Uruguay	2–1	Brazil	Rio de Janeiro
1954	W Germany	5–2	Sweden	Stockholm
1958	Brazil	5–2	Hungary	Berne
1962	Brazil	3–1	Czechoslovakia	Santiago
1966	England	4–2	W Germany	London
1970	Brazil	4–1	Italy	Mexico City
1974	W Germany	2–1	Netherlands	Munich
1978	Argentina	3–1	Netherlands	Buenos Aires
1982	Italy	3–1	W Germany	Madrid
1986	Argentina	3–2	W Germany	Mexico City
1990	W Germany	1–0	Argentina	Rome

Most wins: (3) Brazil, Italy, and W Germany: as above.

European championship

Held every four years since 1960; qualifying group matches held over the two years preceding the final.

	Winner	Score	Runner-up	Final held in
1960	USSR	2–1	Yugoslavia	Paris
1964	Spain	2–1	USSR	Madrid
1968[a]	Italy	2–1	Yugoslavia	Rome
1972	W Germany	3–0	USSR	Brussels
1976[b]	Czechoslovakia	2–2	W Germany	Belgrade
1980	W Germany	2–1	Belgium	Rome
1984	France	2–0	Spain	Paris
1988	Netherlands	2–0	USSR	Munich
1992	Denmark	2–0	Germany	Gothenburg

[a] Replay after 1–1 draw.
[b] Czechoslovakia won 5–2 on penalties.

Most wins: (2) W Germany: as above.

Association football field

South American championship

First held in 1916, for South American national sides. Discontinued in 1967, but revived eight years later; now played every two years.

Recent winners

1956	Uruguay	1975	Peru
1957	Argentina	1979	Paraguay
1959[a]	Argentina	1983	Uruguay
1959[a]	Uruguay	1987	Uruguay
1963	Bolivia	1989	Brazil
1967	Uruguay	1991	Argentina
		1993	Denmark

[a]There were two tournaments in 1959.

Most wins: (13) Uruguay: 1916–17, 1920, 1923–4, 1926, 1935, 1942, 1956, 1959, 1967, 1983, 1987.

European Champions Cup

The leading club competition in Europe. Open to the League champions of countries affiliated to UEFA (Union of European Football Associations); commonly known as the 'European Cup'. Anaugurated in the 1955-6 season; played annually.

Recent winners

	Winner	Score	Runner-up
1975	Bayern Munich	2-0	Leeds United
1976	Bayern Munich	1-0	St Etienne
1977	Liverpool	3-1	BM/Gladbach
1978	Liverpool	1-0	FC Bruges
1979	Nottingham Forest	1-0	Malmo
1980	Nottingham Forest	1-0	SV Hamburg
1981	Liverpool	1-0	Real Madrid
1982	Aston Villa	1-0	Bayern Munich
1983	SV Hamburg	1-0	Juventus
1984[a]	Liverpool	1-1	AS Roma
1985	Juventus	1-0	Liverpool
1986[b]	Steaua Bucharest	0-0	Barcelona
1987	FC Porto	2-1	Bayern Munich
1988[c]	PSV Eindhoven	0-0	Benfica
1989	AC Milan	4-0	Steaua Bucharest
1990	AC Milan	1-0	Benfica
1991[d]	Red Star Belgrade	0-0	Olympique Marseilles
1992	Barcelona	1-0	Sampdoria
1993	Olympique Marseilles	1-0	AC Milan

[a] Liverpool won 4-2 on penalties.
[b] Steaua won 2-0 on penalties.
[c] Eindhoven won 6-5 on penalties.
[d] Red Star won 5-3 on penalties.

Most wins: (6) Real Madrid (Spain): 1956-60, 66.

European Cup-Winners' Cup

Annual club competition, open to the main cup winners from all the UEFA countries; inaugurated in 1961, when the final was played over two legs. Since 1962 there has been a single game final.

Recent winners

1981	Dynamo Tbilisi	1988	Mechelen
1982	Barcelona	1989	Barcelona
1983	Aberdeen	1990	Sampdoria
1984	Juventus	1991	Manchester United
1985	Everton	1992	Werder Bremen
1986	Dynamo Kiev	1993	Parma
1987	Ajax		

Most wins: (3) Barcelona: 1979, 1982, 1989.

UEFA Cup

Originally the International Industries Fairs Inter-Cities Cup (more commonly the 'Fairs Cup'). It was first contested in 1955, and became the UEFA Cup in 1971. Each participating nation is allotted a certain number of team places. The final is played over two legs.

Recent winners

1981	Ipswich Town	1988	Bayer Leverskusen
1982	IFK Gothenburg	1989	Napoli
1983	Anderlecht	1990	Juventus
1984	Tottenham Hotspur	1991	Inter-Milan
1985	Real Madrid	1992	Ajax
1986	Real Madrid	1993	Juventus
1987	IFK Gothenburg		

Most wins: (3) Barcelona: 1958, 1960, 1966.

Football League

The oldest league in the world, founded in 1888; consists of four divisions; the current complement of 92 teams achieved in 1950. Prior to the start of the 1992-93 season, the 22 teams of the 1st division voted to form the FA Premier League, divisions 2, 3 and 4 becoming League divisions 1, 2 and 3 respectively; the system of promotion and relegation remained unchanged.

League champions

1888-89	Preston North End
1889-90	Preston North End
1890-91	Everton
1891-92	Sunderland
1892-93	Sunderland
1893-94	Aston Villa
1894-95	Sunderland
1895-96	Aston Villa
1896-97	Aston Villa
1897-98	Sheffield United
1898-99	Aston Villa
1899-1900	Aston Villa
1900-01	Liverpool
1901-02	Sunderland
1902-03	Sheffield Wednesday
1903-04	Sheffield Wednesday
1904-05	Newcastle United
1905-06	Liverpool
1906-07	Newcastle United
1907-08	Manchester United
1908-09	Newcastle United
1909-10	Aston Villa
1910-11	Manchester United
1911-12	Blackburn Rovers
1912-13	Sunderland
1913-14	Blackburn Rovers
1914-15	Everton
1919-20	West Bromwich Albion
1920-21	Burnley
1921-22	Liverpool
1922-23	Liverpool
1923-24	Huddersfield Town
1924-25	Huddersfield Town
1925-26	Huddersfield Town
1926-27	Newcastle United
1927-28	Everton
1928-29	Sheffield Wednesday
1929-30	Sheffield Wednesday
1930-31	Arsenal
1931-32	Everton
1932-33	Arsenal
1933-34	Arsenal
1934-35	Arsenal
1935-36	Sunderland
1936-37	Manchester City
1937-38	Arsenal
1938-39	Everton
1946-47	Liverpool
1947-48	Arsenal
1948-49	Portsmouth
1949-50	Portsmouth
1950-51	Tottenham Hotspur
1951-52	Manchester United
1952-53	Arsenal
1953-54	Wolverhampton Wanderers
1954-55	Chelsea
1955-56	Manchester United
1956-57	Manchester United
1957-58	Wolverhampton Wanderers
1958-59	Wolverhampton Wanderers
1959-60	Burnley
1960-61	Tottenham Hotspur

Sports and games

1961–62	Ipswich Town
1962–63	Everton
1963–64	Liverpool
1964–65	Manchester United
1965–66	Liverpool
1966–67	Manchester United
1967–68	Manchester City
1968–69	Leeds United
1969–70	Everton
1970–71	Arsenal
1971–72	Derby County
1972–73	Liverpool
1973–74	Leeds United
1974–75	Derby County
1975–76	Liverpool
1976–77	Liverpool
1977–78	Nottingham Forest
1978–79	Liverpool
1979–80	Liverpool
1980–81	Aston Villa
1981–82	Liverpool
1982–83	Liverpool
1983–84	Liverpool
1984–85	Everton
1985–86	Liverpool
1986–87	Everton
1987–88	Liverpool
1988–89	Arsenal
1989–90	Liverpool
1990–91	Arsenal
1991–92	Leeds United
1992–93	Manchester United
1993–94	Manchester United

Most wins: (18) Liverpool: 1901, 1906, 1922–3, 1947, 1964, 1966, 1973, 1976–7, 1979–80, 1982–4, 1986, 1988, 1990.

Football Association Challenge Cup

The world's oldest club knockout competition (the 'FA cup'), held annually, it is open to both League and non-League teams; first contested in the 1871–2 season; first final at the Kennington Oval on 16 March 1872; first winners were the Wanderers. Played at Wembley since 1923.

	Winners	*Score*	*Runner-up*
1871–72	Wanderers	1–0	Royal Engineers
1872–73	Wanderers	2–0	Oxford University
1873–74	Oxford University	2–0	Royal Engineers
1874–75	Royal Engineers	1–1, 2–0	Old Etonians
1875–76	Wanderers	1–1, 3–0	Old Etonians
1876–77	Wanderers	2–1	Oxford University
1877–78	Wanderers	3–1	Royal Engineers
1878–79	Old Etonians	1–0	Clapham Rovers
1879–80	Clapham Rovers	1–0	Oxford University
1880–81	Old Carthusians	3–0	Old Etonians
1881–82	Old Etonians	1–0	Blackburn Rovers
1882–83	Blackburn Olympic	2–1	Old Etonians
1883–84	Blackburn Rovers	2–1	Queen's Park Rangers
1884–85	Blackburn Rovers	2–0	Queen's Park Rangers
1885–86	Blackburn Rovers	0–0, 2–0	West Bromwich Albion
1886–97	Aston Villa	2–0	West Bromwich Albion
1887–88	West Bromwich Albion	2–1	Preston North End
1888–89	Preston North End	3–0	Wolverhampton Wanderers
1889–90	Blackburn Rovers	6–1	Sheffield Wednesday
1890–91	Blackburn Rovers	3–1	Notts County
1891–92	West Bromwich Albion	3–0	Aston Villa
1892–93	Wolverhampton Wanderers	1–0	Everton
1893–94	Notts County	4–1	Bolton Wanderers
1894–95	Aston Villa	1–0	West Bromwich Albion
1895–96	Sheffield Wednesday	2–1	Wolverhampton Wanderers
1896–97	Aston Villa	3–2	Everton
1897–98	Nottingham Forest	3–1	Derby County
1898–99	Sheffield United	4–1	Derby County
1899–1900	Bury	4–0	Southampton
1900–01	Tottenham Hotspur	2–2, 3–1	Sheffield United
1901–02	Sheffield United	1–1, 2–1	Southampton
1902–03	Bury	6–0	Derby County
1903–04	Manchester City	1–0	Bolton Wanderers
1904–05	Aston Villa	2–0	Newcastle United
1905–06	Everton	1–0	Newcastle United
1906–07	Sheffield Wednesday	2–1	Everton
1907–08	Wolverhampton Wanderers	3–1	Newcastle United
1908–09	Manchester United	1–0	Bristol City
1909–10	Newcastle United	1–1, 2–0	Barnsley
1910–11	Bradford City	0–0, 1–0	Newcastle United
1911–12	Barnsley	0–0, 1–0	West Bromwich Albion
1912–13	Aston Villa	1–0	Sunderland
1913–14	Burnley	1–0	Liverpool
1914–15	Sheffield United	3–0	Chelsea
1919–20	Aston Villa	1–0	Huddersfield Town
1920–21	Tottenham Hotspur	1–0	Wolverhampton Wanderers
1921–22	Huddersfield Town	1–0	Preston North End
1922–23	Bolton Wanderers	2–0	West Ham United
1923–24	Newcastle United	2–0	Aston Villa
1924–25	Sheffield United	1–0	Cardiff City
1925–26	Bolton Wanderers	1–0	Manchester City
1926–27	Cardiff City	1–0	Arsenal
1927–28	Blackburn Rovers	3–1	Huddersfield Town
1928–29	Bolton Wanderers	2–0	Portsmouth
1929–30	Arsenal	2–0	Huddersfield Town
1930–31	West Bromwich Albion	2–1	Birmingham City
1931–32	Newcastle United	2–1	Arsenal

Football (Association football/soccer)

Football Association Challenge Cup (continued)

	Winners	Score	Runner-up
1932–33	Everton	3–0	Manchester City
1933–34	Manchester City	2–1	Portsmouth
1934–35	Sheffield Wednesday	4–2	West Bromwich Albion
1935–36	Arsenal	1–0	Sheffield United
1936–37	Sunderland	3–1	Preston North End
1937–38	Portsmouth	4–1	Wolverhampton Wanderers
1945–46	Derby County	4–1	Charlton Athletic
1946–47	Charlton Atheltic	1–0	Burnley
1947–48	Manchester United	4–2	Blackpool
1948–49	Wolverhampton Wanderers	3–1	Leicester City
1949–50	Arsenal	2–0	Liverpool
1950–51	Newcastle United	2–0	Blackpool
1951–52	Newcastle United	1–0	Arsenal
1952–53	Blackpool	4–3	Bolton Wanderers
1953–54	West Bromwich Albion	3–2	Preston North End
1954–55	Newcastle United	3–1	Manchester City
1955–56	Manchester City	3–1	Birmingham City
1956–57	Aston Villa	2–1	Manchester United
1957–58	Bolton Wanderers	2–0	Manchester United
1958–59	Nottingham Forest	2–1	Luton Town
1959–60	Wolverhampton Wanderers	3–0	Blackburn Rovers
1960–61	Tottenham Hotspur	2–0	Leicester City
1961–62	Tottenham Hotspur	3–1	Burnley
1962–63	Manchester United	3–1	Leicester City
1963–64	West Ham United	3–2	Preston North End
1964–65	Liverpool	2–1	Leeds United
1965–66	Everton	3–2	Sheffield Wednesday
1966–67	Tottenham Hotspur	2–1	Chelsea
1967–68	West Bromwich Albion	1–0	Everton
1968–69	Manchester City	1–0	Leicester City
1969–70	Chelsea	2–2, 2–1	Leeds United
1970–71	Arsenal	2–1	Liverpool
1971–72	Leeds United	1–0	Arsenal
1972–73	Sunderland	1–0	Leeds United
1973–74	Liverpool	3–0	Newcastle United
1974–75	West Ham United	2–0	Fulham
1975–76	Southampton	1–0	Manchester United
1976–77	Manchester United	2–1	Liverpool
1977–78	Ipswich Town	1–0	Arsenal
1978–79	Arsenal	3–2	Manchester United
1979–80	West Ham United	1–0	Arsenal
1980–81	Tottenham Hotspur	1–1, 3–2	Manchester City
1981–82	Tottenham Hotspur	1–1, 1–0	Queen's Park Rangers
1982–83	Manchester United	2–2, 4–0	Brighton & Hove Albion
1983–84	Everton	2–0	Watford
1984–85	Manchester United	1–0	Everton
1985–86	Liverpool	3–1	Everton
1986–87	Coventry City	3–2	Tottenham Hotspur
1987–88	Wimbledon	1–0	Liverpool
1988–89	Liverpool	3–2	Everton
1989–90	Manchester United	3–3, 1–0	Crystal Palace
1990–91	Tottenham Hotspur	2–1	Nottingham Forest
1991–92	Liverpool	2–0	Sunderland
1992–93	Arsenal	1–1, 2–1	Sheffield Wednesday
1993–94	Manchester United	4–0	Chelsea

Most wins: (8) Tottenham Hotspur: 1901, 1921, 1961–2, 1967, 1981–2, 1991.

Football League Cup

Inaugurated in 1961, it is competed for by the 92 clubs of the Football League. From 1982 to 1986 it was known as the Milk Cup; during 1986–90 as, the Littlewoods Cup; during 1990–92 as the Rumbelows Cup; and from 1992–3 as the Coca-Cola Cup.

Recent winners
1981	Liverpool
1982	Liverpool
1983	Liverpool
1984	Liverpool
1985	Norwich City
1986	Oxford United
1987	Arsenal
1988	Luton Town
1989	Nottingham Forest
1990	Nottingham Forest
1991	Sheffield Wednesday
1992	Manchester United
1993	Arsenal

Most wins: (4) Liverpool: as above; Nottingham Forest 1978–9, 1989–90.

Sports and games

Clubs of the English Football League

Team	Nickname	Ground	Team	Nickname	Ground
Arsenal	Gunners	Highbury	Preston North End	Lillywhites	Deepdale
Aston Villa	Villa	Villa Park	Queens Park Rangers	'R's	Loftus Road
Barnet	–	Underhill	Reading	Royals	Elm Park
Barnsley	–	Oakwell	Rochdale	–	Spotland
Birmingham City	Blues	St Andrews	Rotherham United	Millers	Millmoor
Blackburn Rovers	–	Ewood Park	Scarborough	–	Seamer Road
Blackpool	Tangerines	Bloomfield Road	Scunthorpe United	Irons	Glanford Park
Bolton Wanderers	Trotters	Burnden Park	Sheffield United	Blades	Bramall Lane
Bournemouth	Cherries	Dean Court	Sheffield Wednesday	Owls	Hillsborough
Bradford City	Bantams	Valley Parade	Shrewsbury Town	Shrews	Gay Meadow
Brentford	Bees	Griffin Park	Southampton	Saints	The Dell
Brighton and Hove Albion	Seagulls	Goldstone Ground	Southend United	Shrimpers	Roots Hall
			Stockport County	–	Edgeley Park
Bristol City	Robins	Ashton Gate	Stoke City	Potters	Victoria Ground
Bristol Rovers	Pirates	Twerton Park	Sunderland	Black Cats	Roker Park
Burnley	Clarets	Turf Moor	Swansea City	Swans	Vetch Field
Bury	Shakers	Gigg Lane	Swindon Town	Robins	County Ground
Cambridge United	'U's	Abbey Stadium	Torquay United	Gulls	Plainmoor
Cardiff City	Bluebirds	Ninian Park	Tottenham Hotspur	Spurs	White Hart Lane
Carlisle United	–	Brunton Park	Transmere Rovers	–	Prenton Park
Charlton Athletic	Valiants	The Valley	Walsall	Saddlers	Bescot Stadium
Chelsea	Blues	Stamford Bridge	Watford	Hornets	Vicarage Road
Chester City	–	Moss Rose	West Bromwich Albion	Baggies	The Hawthorns
Chesterfield	Spireites	Saltergate	West Ham United	Hammers	Upton Park
Colchester United	'U's	Layer Road	Wigan Athletic	Latics	Springfield Park
Coventry City	Sky Blues	Highfield Road	Wimbledon	Dons	Plough Lane
Crewe Alexandra	Railwaymen	Gresty Road	Wolverhampton Wanderers	Wolves	Molineux
Crystal Palace	Eagles	Selhurst Park			
Darlington	Quakers	Feethams	Wrexham	Robins	Racecourse Ground
Derby County	Rams	Baseball Ground			
Doncaster Rovers	–	Belle Vue	Wycombe Wanderers	Blues	Adams Park
Everton	Toffeemen	Goodison Park	York City	–	Bootham Crescent
Exeter City	Grecians	St James Park			
Fulham	Cottagers	Craven Cottage			
Gillingham	Gills	Priestfield			
Grimsby Town	Mariners	Blundell Park			
Halifax Town	Shaymen	The Shay			
Hartlepool United	Pool	Victoria Ground			
Hereford United	–	Edgar Street			
Huddersfield Town	Terriers	Leeds Road			
Hull City	Tigers	Boothferry Park			
Ipswich Town	–	Portman Road			
Leeds United	Peacocks	Elland Road			
Leicester City	–	Filbert Street			
Leyton Orient	'O's	Brisbane Road			
Lincoln City	Imps	Sincil Bank			
Liverpool	Reds	Anfield			
Luton Town	Hatters	Kenilworth Road			
Manchester City	Blues	Maine Road			
Manchester United	Reds	Old Trafford			
Mansfield Town	Stags	Field Mill			
Middlesbrough	Boro	Ayresome Park			
Millwall	Lions	The Den			
Newcastle United	Magpies	St James' Park			
Northampton Town	Cobblers	County Ground			
Norwich City	Canaries	Carrow Road			
Nottingham Forest	Reds	City Ground			
Nottingham County	Magpies	Meadow Lane			
Oldham Athletic	Latics	Boundary Park			
Oxford United	'U's	Manor Ground			
Peterborough United	Posh	London Road			
Plymouth Argyle	Pilgrims	Home Park			
Portsmouth	Pompey	Fratton Park			
Port Vale	–	Vale Park			

Scottish Football League

Formed in 1890, with a second division added in 1893. The present format (Premier Division, Division 1, Division 2) was arrived at in 1975.

Recent winners

1981–82	Celtic		1987–88	Celtic
1982–83	Dundee United		1988–89	Rangers
1983–84	Aberdeen		1989–90	Rangers
1984–85	Aberdeen		1990–91	Rangers
1985–86	Celtic		1991–92	Rangers
1986–87	Rangers		1992–93	Rangers

Most wins: (43) Rangers.

Scottish FA Cup

First played in 1874; held at Hampden Park.

Recent winners

1981	Rangers	1988	Celtic
1982	Aberdeen	1989	Celtic
1983	Aberdeen	1990	Aberdeen
1984	Aberdeen	1991	Motherwell
1985	Celtic	1992	Rangers
1986	Aberdeen	1993	Rangers
1987	St Mirren		

Most wins: (29) Celtic.

FOOTBALL (AUSTRALIAN)

Australian Football League

Known as the Victoria Football League until 1987, when teams from Western Australia and Queensland joined the league. The top prize is the annual VFL Premiership Trophy.

Premiership Trophy

First contested in 1897 and won by Essendon.

Recent winners

1981	Carlton
1982	Carlton
1983	Hawthorn
1984	Essendon
1985	Essendon
1986	Hawthorn
1987	Carlton
1988	Hawthorn
1989	Hawthorn
1990	Collingwood
1991	Hawthorn
1992	West Coast Eagles
1993	Essendon

Most wins: (15) Carlton: 1906–8, 1914–15, 1938, 1945, 1947, 1968, 1970, 1972, 1979, 1981–2, 1987.

Australian football field

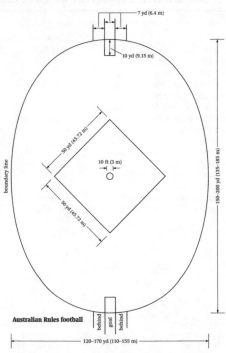

Australian Rules football

FOOTBALL (GAELIC)

All-Ireland championship

First held in 1887. Takes place in Dublin on the third Sunday in September each year.

Recent winners

1979	Kerry
1980	Kerry
1981	Kerry
1982	Offaly
1983	Dublin
1984	Kerry
1985	Kerry
1986	Kerry
1987	Meath
1988	Meath
1989	Cork
1990	Cork
1991	Down
1992	Donegal

Most wins: (30) Kerry: 1903–4, 1909, 1913-14, 1924, 1926, 1929–32, 1937, 1939–41, 1946, 1953, 1955, 1959, 1962, 1969–70, 1975, 1978–81, 1984–6.

GLIDING

World championships

First held in 1937. Current classes are Open, Standard, and 15 metres. The Open class is the principal event, held every two years until 1978 and again since 1981.

Recent winners: open category

1968	Harro Wödl (Austria)
1970	George Moffat (USA)
1972	Göran Ax (Sweden)
1974	George Moffat (USA)
1976	George Lee (Great Britain)
1978	George Lee (Great Britain)
1981	George Lee (Great Britain)
1983	Ingo Renner (Australia)
1985	Ingo Renner (Australia)
1987	Ingo Renner (Australia)
1989	Claude Lopitaux (France)
1991	Janusz Centka (Poland)
1993	Andy Davis (Great Britain)

Most wins: (3) George Lee and Ingo Renner: as above.

GOLF

British Open

First held at Prestwick in 1860, and won by Willie Park. Takes place annually; regarded as the world's leading golf tournament.

Recent winners

1981	Bill Rogers (USA)
1982	Tom Watson (USA)
1983	Tom Watson (USA)
1984	Severiano Ballesteros (Spain)
1985	Sandy Lyle (Great Britain)
1986	Greg Norman (Australia)
1987	Nick Faldo (Great Britain)
1988	Severiano Ballesteros (Spain)
1989	Mark Calcavecchia (USA)
1990	Nick Faldo (Great Britain)
1991	Ian Baker-Finch (Australia)
1992	Nick Faldo (Great Britain)
1993	Greg Norman (Australia)

Most wins: (6) Harry Vardon (Great Britain): 1896, 1898–9, 1903, 1911, 1914.

Sports and games

United States Open

First held at Newport, Rhode Island, in 1895, and won by Horace Rawlins. Takes place annually.

Recent winners
1981 David Graham (Australia)
1982 Tom Watson (USA)
1983 Larry Nelson (USA)
1984 Fuzzy Zoeller (USA)
1985 Andy North (USA)
1986 Ray Floyd (USA)
1987 Scott Simpson (USA)
1988 Curtis Strange (USA)
1989 Curtis Strange (USA)
1990 Hale Irwin (USA)
1991 Payne Stewart (USA)
1992 Tom Kite (USA)
1993 Lee Janzen (USA)

Most wins: (4) Willie Anderson (USA): 1901, 1903–5; Bobby Jones (USA): 1923, 1926, 1929–30; Ben Hogan (USA): 1948, 1950–1, 1953; Jack Nicklaus (USA): 1962, 1967, 1972, 1980.

US Masters

First held in 1934. Takes place at the Augusta National course in Georgia every April.

Recent winners
1981 Tom Watson (USA)
1982 Craig Stadler (USA)
1983 Severiano Ballesteros (Spain)
1984 Ben Crenshaw (USA)
1985 Bernhard Langer
         (W Germany)
1986 Jack Nicklaus (USA)
1987 Larry Mize (USA)
1988 Sandy Lyle (Great Britain)
1989 Nick Faldo (Great Britain)
1990 Nick Faldo (Great Britain)
1991 Ian Woosnam (Great Britain)
1992 Fred Couples (USA)
1993 Bernard Langer (Germany)

Most wins: (6) Jack Nicklaus (USA): 1963, 1965–6, 1972, 1975, 1986.

United States PGA championship

The last of the season's four 'Majors'; first held in 1916, and a match-play event until 1958. Takes place annually.

Recent winners
1981 Larry Nelson (USA)
1982 Ray Floyd (USA)
1983 Hal Sutton (USA)
1984 Lee Trevino (USA)
1985 Hubert Green (USA)
1986 Bob Tway (USA)

1987 Larry Nelson (USA)
1988 Jeff Sluman (USA)
1989 Payne Stewart (USA)
1990 Wayne Grady (USA)
1991 John Daly (USA)
1992 Nick Price (South Africa)
1993 Paul Azinger (USA)

Most wins: (5) Walter Hagen (USA): 1921, 1924–7; Jack Nicklaus (USA): 1963, 1971, 1973, 1975, 1980.

Ryder Cup

The leading international team tournament, first held at Worcester, Massachusetts, in 1927. Takes place every two years between teams from the USA and Europe (Great Britain 1927–71; Great Britain and Ireland 1973–7).

Recent winners

1971	USA	$18^1/_2$–$13^1/_2$
1973	USA	19–13
1975	USA	21–11
1977	USA	$12^1/_2$–$7^1/_2$
1979	USA	17–11
1981	USA	$18^1/_2$–$9^1/_2$
1983	USA	$14^1/_2$–$13^1/_2$
1985	Europe	$16^1/_2$–$11^1/_2$
1987	Europe	15–13
1989	Drawn	14–14
1991	USA	$14^1/_2$–$13^1/_2$
1993	USA	15–13

Wins: (22) USA: during 1927–91. (3), Great Britain: 1929, 1933, 1957. (2), Europe: 1985, 1987. (2), Drawn: 1969, 1989.

GREYHOUND RACING

Greyhound Derby

The top race of the British season, first held in 1927. Run at the White City every year (except 1940) until its closure in 1985; since then all races run at Wimbledon.

Recent winners
1979 Sarah's Bunny
1980 Indian Joe
1981 Parkdown Jet
1982 Laurie's Panther
1983 I'm Slippy
1984 Whisper Wishes
1985 Pagan Swallow
1986 Tico
1987 Signal Spark
1988 Hit the Lid
1989 Lartigue Note

1990 Slippy Blue
1991 Ballinderry Ash
1992 Farloe Melody
1993 Ringa Hustle

Most wins: (2) Mick the Miller: 1929–30; Patricia's Hope: 1972–3.

GYMNASTICS

World championships

First held in 1903. Took place every four years, 1922–78; since 1979, every two years.

Recent winners: individual combined exercises – men
1966 Mikhail Voronin (USSR)
1970 Eizo Kenmotsu (Japan)
1974 Shigeru Kasamatsu (Japan)
1978 Nikolai Adrianov (USSR)
1979 Aleksandr Ditiatin (USSR)
1981 Yuriy Korolev (USSR)
1983 Dmitri Belozerchev (USSR)
1985 Yuriy Korolev (USSR)
1987 Dmitri Belozerchev (USSR)
1989 Igor Korobichensky (USSR)
1991 Grigoriy Misutin (USSR)
1993 Vitaly Scherbo (Belarus)

Recent winners: team – men
1966	Japan	1983	China
1970	Japan	1985	USSR
1974	Japan	1987	USSR
1978	Japan	1989	USSR
1979	USSR	1991	USSR
1981	USSR	1993	Belarus

Most wins: Individual (2) Marco Torrès (France): 1909, 1913; Peter Sumi (Yugoslavia): 1922, 1926; Yuriy Korolev and Dmitri Belozerchev: as above. Team (8) USSR: 1954, 1958, and as above.

Recent winners: individual combined exercises – women
1966 Vera Caslavska
         (Czechoslovakia)
1970 Ludmila Tourischeva (USSR)
1974 Ludmila Tourischeva (USSR)
1978 Yelena Mukhina (USSR)
1979 Nelli Kim (USSR)
1981 Olga Bitcherova (USSR)
1983 Natalia Yurchenko (USSR)
1985 Yelena Shoushounova (USSR)
         and Oksana Omeliantchuk
         (USSR)
1987 Aurelia Dobre (Romania)
1989 Svetlana Boginskaya (USSR)
1991 Kim Zmeskal (USA)
1993 Shannon Miller (USA)

Gymnastics (continued)

Recent winners team – women

1966 Czechoslovakia
1970 USSR
1974 USSR
1978 USSR
1979 Romania
1981 USSR
1983 USSR
1985 USSR
1987 Romania
1989 USSR
1991 USSR
1993 USA

Most wins: Individual (2) Vlasta Dekanová (Czechoslovakia): 1934, 1938; Larissa Latynina (USSR): 1958, 1962; Ludmila Tourischeva: as above. Team (10) USSR: 1954, 1958, and as above.

Olympic Games

Gold medal winners: 1992

Combined exercises: men
Individual
Vitally Sheherbo (Unified Team)

Team
Unified Team

Gold medal winners: 1992

Combined exercises: women
Individual
Tatjana Gutsu (Unified Team)

Team
Unified Team

HANDBALL

World championships

First men's championships held in 1938, both indoors and outdoors (latter discontinued in 1966). First women's outdoor championships in 1949 (discontinued in 1960); first women's indoor championships in 1957.

Winners: indoors – men
1938 Germany
1954 Sweden
1958 Sweden
1961 Romania
1964 Romania
1967 Czechoslovakia
1970 Romania
1974 Romania
1978 W Germany
1982 USSR
1986 Yugoslavia
1990 Sweden

Winners: outdoors – men
1938 Germany
1948 Sweden
1952 W Germany
1955 W Germany
1959 E/W Germany (combined)
1963 E Germany
1966 W Germany

Most wins: Indoors (4) Romania: as above. Outdoors (4) W Germany (including 1 as combined E/W German team): as above.

Winners: indoors – women
1957 Czechoslovakia
1962 Romania
1965 Hungary
1971 E Germany
1973 Yugoslavia
1975 E Germany
1979 E Germany
1982 USSR
1986 USSR
1990 USSR

Winners: outdoors – women
1949 Hungary
1956 Romania
1960 Romania

Most wins: Indoors (3) E Germany: as above. Outdoors (2) Romania: as above.

Olympic Games

Gold medal winners: 1992
Men   Unified Team
Women   South Korea

HANG GLIDING

World championships

First held officially in 1976; since 1979, take place every two years.

Winners: individual – class 1
1976 Christian Steinbach (Austria)
1979 Josef Guggenmose (W Germany)
1981 Pepe Lopez (Brazil)
1983 Steve Moyes (Australia)
1985 John Pendry (Great Britain)
1987 Rich Duncan (Australia)
1989 Robert Whittall (Great Britain)
1991 Tomás Suchanek (Czechoslovakia)
1993 Tomás Suchanek (Czech Republic)

Winners: team
1976 Austria
1979 France
1981 Great Britain
1983 Australia
1985 Great Britain
1987 Australia
1989 Great Britain
1991 Great Britain
1993 USA

Most wins: Individual: no person has won more than once. Team (4) Great Britain: as above.

HOCKEY

World Cup

Men's tournament first held in 1971, and every four years since 1978. Women's tournament first held in 1974, and now takes place every three years.

Recent winners: men

1973	Netherlands
1975	India
1978	Pakistan
1982	Pakistan
1986	Australia
1990	Netherlands

Most wins: (3) Pakistan: 1971, and as above.

Recent winners: women

1976	W Germany
1978	Netherlands
1981	W Germany
1983	Netherlands
1986	Netherlands
1990	Netherlands
1993	Netherlands

Most wins: (5) Netherlands: 1974, and as above.

Olympic Games

Regarded as hockey's leading competition. First held in 1908; included at every celebration since 1928; women's competition first held in 1980.

Recent winners: men

1948	India
1952	India
1956	India
1960	Pakistan
1964	India
1968	Pakistan
1972	W Germany
1976	New Zealand
1980	India
1984	Pakistan
1988	Great Britain
1992	Germany

Recent winners: women

1980	Zimbabwe
1984	Netherlands
1988	Australia
1992	Spain

Most wins: Men (8) India: 1928, 1932, 1936, and as above. Women: no nation has won the title more than once.

Hockey field

HORSE RACING

The English Classics are five races run from April to September each year for three-year-olds: The Derby; The Oaks; One Thousand Guineas; Two Thousand Guineas; and St Leger.

The Derby

The 'Blue Riband' of the Turf; run at Epsom over 1¹/₂ miles. First run in 1780.

Recent winners

Horse (Jockey)

1981	Shergar (Walter Swinburn)
1982	Golden Fleece (Pat Eddery)
1983	Teenoso (Lester Piggott)
1984	Secreto (Christy Roche)
1985	Slip Anchor (Steve Cauthen)
1986	Shahrastani (Walter Swinburn)
1987	Reference Point (Steve Cauthen)
1988	Kahyasi (Ray Cochrane)
1989	Nashwan (Willie Carson)
1990	Quest for Fame (Pat Eddery)
1991	Generous (Alan Munro)
1992	Dr Devious (John Reid)
1993	Commander-In-Chief (Michael Kinane)

Most wins: Jockey (9) Lester Piggott: 1954, 1957, 1960, 1968, 1970, 1972, 1976–7, 1983.

The Oaks

Raced at Epsom over 1¹/₂ miles; for fillies only. First run in 1779.

Recent winners

1981	Blue Wind (Lester Piggott)
1982	Time Charter (Billy Newnes)
1983	Sun Princess (Willy Carson)
1984	Circus Plume (Lester Piggott)
1985	Oh So Sharp (Steve Cauthen)
1986	Midway Lady (Ray Cochrane)
1987	Unite (Walter Swinburn)
1968	Diminuendo (Steve Cauthen)
1989	Aliysa (Walter Swinburn)
1990	Salsabil (Willie Carson)
1991	Jet Ski Lady (Christy Roche)
1992	User Friendly (George Duffield)
1993	Intrepidity (Michael Roberts)

Most wins: Jockey (9) Frank Buckle: 1797–9, 1802–3, 1805, 1817–18, 1823.

Horse racing (continued)

One Thousand Guineas

Run over 1 mile at Newmarket; for fillies only. First run in 1814.

Recent winners

1981 Fairy Footsteps (Lester Piggott)
1982 On the House (John Reid)
1983 Ma Biche (Freddy Head)
1984 Pebbles (Philip Robinson)
1985 Oh So Sharp (Steve Cauthen)
1986 Midway Lady (Ray Cochrane)
1987 Miesque (Freddy Head)
1988 Ravinella (Gary Moore)
1989 Musical Bliss (Walter Swinburn)
1990 Salsabil (Willie Carson)
1991 Shadayid (Willie Carson)
1992 Hatoof (Walter Swinburn)
1993 Sayyedati (Walter Swinburn)

Most wins: Jockey (7) George Fordham: 1859, 1861, 1865, 1868–9, 1881, 1883.

Two Thousand Guineas

Run at Newmarket over 1 mile. First run in 1809.

Recent winners

1981 To-Agori-Mou (Greville Starkey)
1982 Zino (Freddy Head)
1983 Lomond (Pat Eddery)
1984 El Gran Senor (Pat Eddery)
1985 Shadeed (Lester Piggott)
1986 Dancing Brave (Greville Starkey)
1987 Don't Forget Me (Willie Carson)
1988 Doyoun (Walter Swinburn)
1989 Nashwan (Willie Carson)
1990 Tirol (Michael Kinane)
1991 Mystiko (Michael Roberts)
1992 Rodrigo de Triano (Lester Piggott)
1993 Zafonic (Pat Eddery)

Most wins: Jockey (9) Jem Robinson: 1825, 1828, 1831, 1833, 1847–8.

St Leger

The oldest of the five English classics, first run in 1776. Raced at Doncaster annually over 1 mile 6 furlongs 127 yards.

Recent winners

1981 Cut Above (Joe Mercer)
1982 Touching Wood (Paul Cook)
1983 Sun Princess (Willie Carson)
1984 Commanche Run (Lester Piggott)
1985 Oh So Sharp (Steve Cauthen)
1986 Moon Madness (Pat Eddery)
1987 Reference Point (Steve Cauthen)
1988 Minster Son (Willie Carson)
1989 Michelozzo (Steve Cauthen)
1990 Snurge (Richard Quinn)
1991 Toulon (Pat Eddery)
1992 User Friendly (George Duffield)
1993 Bob's Return (Philip Robinson)

Most wins: Jockey (9) Bill Scott: 1821, 1825, 1828–9, 1938–41, 1846.

Grand National

Steeplechasing's most famous race. First run at Maghull in 1836; at Aintree since 1839; war-time races at Gatwick, 1916–18.

Recent winners

1981 Aldaniti (Bob Champion)
1982 Grittar (Mr Dick Saunders)*
1983 Corbiere (Ben De Haan)
1984 Hallo Dandy (Neale Doughty)
1985 Last Suspect (Hywel Davies)
1986 West Tip (Richard Dunwoody)
1987 Maori Venture (Steve Knight)
1988 Rhyme 'N' Reason (Brendan Powell)
1989 Little Polveir (Jimmy Frost)
1990 Mr Frisk (Marcus Armytage)
1991 Seagram (Nigel Howke)
1992 Party Politics (Carl Llewellyn)
1993** *Void*
1994 Minnehoma (Richard Dunwoody)

**'Mr' denotes that the jockey is an amateur rider.
**After a 2nd false start, the field was not called back.

Most wins: Jockey (5) George Stevens: 1856, 1863–4, 1869–70. Horse (3) Red Rum: 1973–4, 1977.

Prix de l'Arc de Triomphe

The leading end-of-season race in Europe; raced over 2 400 metres at Longchamp, France. First run in 1920.

Recent winners

1981 Gold River (Gary Moore)
1982 Akiyda (Yves Saint-Martin)
1983 All Along (Walter Swinburn)
1984 Sagace (Yves Saint-Martin)
1985 Rainbow Quest (Pat Eddery)
1986 Dancing Brave (Pat Eddery)
1987 Trempolino (Pat Eddery)
1988 Tony Bin (John Reid)
1989 Caroll House (Michael Kinane)
1990 Saumarez (Gerald Mosse)
1991 Suave Dancer (Cash Asmussen)
1992 Subotica (Thierry Jarnet)
1993 Urban Sea (Eric Saint-Martin)

Most wins: Jockey (4) Jacko Doyasbère: 1942, 1944, 1950–1; Freddy Head: 1966, 1972, 1976, 1979; Yves Saint-Martin: 1970, 1974, and as above. Horse (2) Ksar: 1921–2; Motrico: 1930, 1932; Corrida: 1936–7; Tantième: 1950–1; Ribot: 1955–6; Alleged: 1977–8.

The American Triple Crown comprises three races for three-year olds; The Kentucky Derby, the Preakness Stakes, and the Belmont Stakes.

Kentucky Derby

Raced at Churchill Downs, Louisville, over 1 mile 2 furlongs. First run in 1875.

Recent winners

1981 Pleasant Colony (Jorge Velasquez)
1982 Gato Del Sol (Eddie Delahoussaye)
1983 Sunny's Halo (Eddie Delahoussaye)
1984 Swale (Laffit Pincay, Jr)
1985 Spend A Buck (Angel Cordero, Jr)
1986 Ferdinand (Willie Shoemaker)
1987 Alysheba (Chris McCarron)
1988 Winning Colors (Gary Stevens)
1989 Sunday Silence (Pat Valenzuela)
1990 Unbridled (Craig Perret)
1991 Strike The Gold (Chris Antley)
1992 Lil E Tee (Pat Day)
1993 Sea Hero (J Bailey)

Most wins: Jockey (5) Eddie Arcaro: 1938, 1941, 1945, 1948, 1952; Bill Hartack: 1957, 1960, 1962, 1964, 1969.

Preakness Stakes

Raced at Pimlico, Baltimore, Maryland, over 1 mile 1^1/$_2$ furlongs. First run in 1873.

Recent winners

1981	Pleasant Colony (Jorge Velasquez)
1982	Aloma's Ruler (Jack Kaenel)
1983	Deputed Testimony (Don Miller, Jr)
1984	Gate Dancer (Angel Cordero, Jr)
1985	Tank's Prospect (Pat Day)
1986	Snow Chief (Alex Solis)
1987	Alysheba (Chris McCarron)
1988	Risen Star (Eddie Delahoussaye)
1989	Sunday Silence (Pat Valenzuela)
1990	Summer Squall (Pat Day)
1991	Hansel (Jerry Bailey)
1992	Pine Bluff (Chris McCarron)
1993	Prairie Bayou (Mike Smith)

Most wins: Jockey (6) Eddie Arcaro: 1941, 1948, 1950–1, 1955, 1957.

Belmont Stakes

Raced at Belmont Park, New York, over 1 mile 4 furlongs. First run in 1867, at Jerome Park.

Recent winners

1981	Summing (George Martens)
1982	Conquistador Cielo (Laffit Pincay, Jr)
1983	Caveat (Laffit Pincay, Jr)
1984	Swale (Laffit Pincay, Jr)
1985	Creme Fraiche (Eddie Maple)
1986	Danzig Connection (Chris McCarron)
1987	Bet Twice (Craig Perrett)
1988	Risen Star (Eddie Delahoussaye)
1989	Easy Goer (Pat Day)
1990	Go And Go (Michael Kinane)
1991	Hansel (Jenny Bailey)
1992	A.P. Indy (Eddie Delahoussaye)
1993	Colonial Affair (Julie Krone)

Most wins: Jockey (6) Jimmy McLaughlin: 1882–4, 1886–8; Eddie Arcaro: 1941–2, 1945, 1948, 1952, 1955.

HURLING

All-Ireland championship

First contested in 1887. Played on the first Sunday in September each year.

Recent winners

1979	Kilkenny
1980	Galway
1981	Offaly
1982	Kilkenny
1983	Kilkenny
1984	Cork
1985	Offaly
1986	Cork
1987	Galway
1988	Galway
1989	Tipperary
1990	Cork
1991	Tipperary
1992	Limerick

Most wins: (27) Cork: 1890, 1892–4, 1902–3, 1919, 1926, 1928–9, 1931, 1941–4, 1946, 1952–4, 1966, 1970, 1976–8, 1984, 1986, 1990.

ICE HOCKEY

World championship

First held in 1930; takes place annually (except 1980). Up to 1968, the Olympic champions were also regarded as world champions.

Recent winners

1981	USSR
1982	USSR
1983	USSR
1984	USSR
1985	Czechoslovakia
1986	USSR
1987	Sweden
1988	USSR
1989	USSR
1990	USSR
1991	Sweden
1992	Sweden
1993	Russia

Most wins: (24) USSR: 1954, 1956, 1963–71, 1973–5, 1978–9, and as above.

Stanley Cup

The most sought-after trophy at club level; the end-of-season meeting between the winners of the two conferences in the National Hockey League in the USA and Canada.

Recent winners

1981	New York Islanders
1982	New York Islanders
1983	New York Islanders
1984	Edmonton Oilers
1985	Edmonton Oilers
1986	Montreal Canadiens
1987	Edmonton Oilers
1988	Edmonton Oilers
1989	Calgary Flames
1990	Edmonton Oilers
1991	Pittsburgh Penguins
1992	Pittsburgh Penguins
1993	Montreal Canadiens

Most wins: (24) Montreal Canadiens: 1916, 1924, 1930–1, 1944, 1946, 1953, 1956–60, 1965–6, 1968–9, 1971, 1973, 1976–9, 1986, 1993.

Olympic Games

Gold medal winners

1972	USSR
1976	USSR
1980	USA
1986	USSR
1988	USSR
1992	Unified Team

ICE SKATING

World championships

First men's championships in 1896; first women's event in 1906; pairs first contested in 1908. Ice dance officially recognized in 1952.

Recent winners: men

1982	Scott Hamilton (USA)
1983	Scott Hamilton (USA)
1984	Scott Hamilton (USA)
1985	Alexander Fadayev (USSR)
1986	Brian Boitano (USA)
1987	Brian Orser (Canada)
1988	Brian Boitano (USA)
1989	Kurt Browning (Canada)
1990	Kurt Browning (Canada)
1991	Kurt Browning (Canada)
1992	Viktor Petrenko (Unified Team)
1993	Kurt Browning (Canada)

Most wins: (10) Ulrich Salchow (Sweden): 1901–5, 1907–11.

Recent winners: women

1982	Elaine Zayak (USA)
1983	Rosalynn Sumners (USA)
1984	Katarina Witt (E Germany)
1985	Katarina Witt (E Germany)
1986	Debbie Thomas (USA)
1987	Katarina Witt (E Germany)
1988	Katarina Witt (E Germany)
1989	Midori Ito (Japan)
1990	Jill Trenany (USA)
1991	Kristi Yamaguchi (USA)
1992	Kristi Yamaguchi (USA)
1993	Oksana Baiul (Ukraine)

Most wins: (10) Sonja Henie (Norway): 1927–36.

Recent winners (pairs)

1982	Sabine Baess/Tassilo Thierbach (E Germany)
1983	Yelena Valova/Oleg Vasiliev (USSR)
1984	Barbara Underhill/Paul Martini (Canada)
1985	Yelena Valova/Oleg Vasiliev (USSR)
1986	Yekaterina Gordeeva/Sergey Grinkov (USSR)
1987	Yekaterina Gordeeva/Sergey Grinkov (USSR)
1988	Yelena Valova/Oleg Vasiliev (USSR)
1989	Yekaterina Gordeeva/Sergey Grinkov (USSR)
1990	Yekaterina Gordeeva/Sergey Grinkov (USSR)
1991	Natalya Mishkutienko/Artur Dmitriev (USSR)
1992	Natalya Mishkutienko/Artur Dmitriev (Unified Team)
1993	Natalya Mishkutienko/Artur Dmitriev (Unified Team)
1994	Yekaterina Gordeyeva/Sergey Grinkov (Russia)

Most wins: (10) Irina Rodnina (USSR): 1969–72 (with Aleksey Ulanov), 1973–8 (with Aleksander Zaitsev).

Recent winners: ice dance

1982	Jayne Torvill/Christopher Dean (Great Britain)
1983	Jayne Torvill/Christopher Dean (Great Britain)
1984	Jayne Torvill/Christopher Dean (Great Britain)
1985	Natalya Bestemianova/Andrey Bukin (USSR)
1986	Natalya Bestemianova/Andrey Bukin (USSR)
1987	Natalya Bestemianova/Andrey Bukin (USSR)
1988	Natalya Bestemianova/Andrey Bukin (USSR)
1989	Marina Klimova/Sergey Ponomarenko (USSR)
1990	Marina Klimova/Sergey Ponomarenko (USSR)
1991	Maia Usova/Alexandr Zhulin (USSR)
1992	Marina Klimova/Sergey Ponomarenko (Unified Team)
1993	Maia Usova/Alexandr Zhulin (Unified Team)
1994	Oksana Grichtchuk/Yevgery Platov (Russia)

Most wins: (6) Aleksander Gorshkov and Lyudmila Pakhomova (USSR): 1970–4, 1976.

JUDO

World championships

First held in 1956, now contested every two years. Current weight categories established in 1979; women's championship instituted in 1980.

Recent winners: open – men

1981	Yasuhiro Yamashita (Japan)
1983	Hitoshi Saito (Japan)
1985	Yoshimi Masaki (Japan)
1987	Naoya Ogawa (Japan)
1989	Naoya Ogawa (Japan)
1991	Naoya Ogawa (Japan)
1993	Rafael Kubacki (Poland)

Recent winners: over 95 kg – men

1981	Yasuhiro Yamashita (Japan)
1983	Yasuhiro Yamashita (Japan)
1985	Yung-chul Cho (Korea)
1987	Grigori Vertichev (USSR)
1989	Naoya Ogawa (Japan)
1991	Sergey Kosorotow (USSR)
1993	David Douillet (France)

Recent winners: under 95 kg – men

1981	Tengiz Khubuluri (USSR)
1983	Valeriy Divisenko (USSR)
1985	Hitoshi Sugai (Japan)
1987	Hitoshi Sugai (Japan)
1989	Koba Kurtanidze (Japan)
1991	Stéphane Traineau (France)
1993	Antal Kovacs (Hungary)

Recent winners: under 85 kg – men

1981	Bernard Tchoullouyan (France)
1983	Detlef Ultsch (E Germany)
1985	Peter Seisenbacher (Austria)
1987	Fabien Canu (France)
1989	Fabien Canu (France)
1991	Hirotaka Okada (Japan)
1993	Yoshio Nakamura (Japan)

Recent winners: under 78 kg – men

1981	Neil Adams (Great Britain)
1983	Nobutoshi Hikage (Japan)
1985	Nobutoshi Hikage (Japan)
1987	Hirotaka Okada (Japan)
1989	Kim Byung-ju (S Korea)
1991	Daniel Lascau (Germany)
1993	Ki-young Chun (Korea)

Recent winners: under 71 kg – men

1981	Chon-hak Park (Korea)
1983	Kidetoshi Nakanishi (Japan)
1985	Byeong-keun Ahn (Korea)
1987	Mike Swain (USA)
1989	Toshihiko Koga (Japan)
1991	Toshihiko Koga (Japan)
1993	Hoon Chung (Korea)

Recent winners: under 65 kg – men

1981	Katsuhiko Kashiwazaki (Japan)
1983	Nikolai Soludkhin (USSR)

Sports and games

1985 Yuriy Sokolov (USSR)
1987 Yosuke Yamamoto (Japan)
1989 Drago Becanovic (Yugoslavia)
1991 Udo Quellmalz (Germany)
1993 Yoshio Nakamura (Japan)

Recent winners: under 60 kg – men

1981 Yasuhiko Moriwaki (Japan)
1983 Khazret Tletseri (USSR)
1985 Shinji Hosokawa (Japan)
1987 Kim Jae-yup (S Korea)
1989 Amiran Totikashvili (USSR)
1991 Tadanori Koshino (Japan)
1993 Ryudi Sanoda (Japan)

Most titles: (4) Yashiro Yamashita (Japan): 1981 (Open), 1979, 1981, 1983 (over 95 kg); Shozo Fujii (Japan): 1971, 1973, 1975 (under 80 kg), 1979 (under 78 kg).

Recent winners: open – women

1982 Ingrid Berghmans (Belgium)
1984 Ingrid Berghmans (Belgium)
1986 Ingrid Berghmans (Belgium)
1987 Gao Fengliang (China)
1989 Estella Rodriguez (Cuba)
1991 Zhuang Xiaoyan (China)
1993 Beata Maksymow (Poland)

Recent winners: over 72 kg – women

1982 Natalina Lupino (France)
1984 Maria-Teresa Motta (Italy)
1986 Gao Fengliang (China)
1987 Gao Fengliang (China)
1989 Gao Fengliang (China)
1991 Moon Ji-yoon (S Korea)
1993 Johanna Hagen (Germany)

Recent winners: under 72 kg – women

1982 Barbara Classen
      (W Germany)
1984 Ingrid Berghmans (Belgium)
1986 Irene de Kok (Netherlands)
1987 Irene de Kok (Netherlands)
1989 Ingrid Berghmans (Belgium)
1991 Kim Mi-jeono (S Korea)
1993 Chun Huileng (China)

Recent winners: under 66 kg (women)

1982 Brigitte Deydier (France)
1986 Brigitte Deydier (France)
1987 Alexandra Schreiber
      (W Germany)
1989 Emanuela Pierantozzi (Italy)
1991 Emanuela Pierantozzi (Italy)
1993 Cha Min-sun (Korea)

Recent winners: under 61 kg (women)

1982 Martine Rotheir (France)
1984 Natasha Hernandez
      (Venezuela)
1986 Diane Bell (Great Britain)
1987 Diane Bell (Great Britain)
1989 Catherine Fleury (France)

1991 Frauke Eickhoff (Germany)
1993 Caveye de Van (Belgium)

Recent winners: under 56 kg – women

1982 Béatrice Rodriguez (France)
1984 Ann-Maria Burns (USA)
1986 Ann Hughes (Great Britain)
1987 Catherine Arnaud (France)
1989 Catherine Arnaud (France)
1991 Miriam Blasco Soto (Spain)
1993 Nicola Fairbrother (Great
      Britain)

Recent winners: under 52 kg – women

1982 Loretta Doyle (Great Britain)
1984 Kaori Yamaguchi (Japan)
1986 Dominique Brun (France)
1987 Sharon Rendle
      (Great Britain)
1989 Sharon Rendle
      (Great Britain)
1991 Alessandra Giungi (Italy)
1993 Rodriguez Verdecia (Cuba)

Recent winners: under 48 kg – women

1980 Jane Bridge (Great Britain)
1982 Karen Briggs (Great Britain)
1984 Karen Briggs (Great Britain)
1986 Karen Briggs (Great Britain)
1987 Zhangyun Li (China)
1989 Karen Briggs (Great Britain)
1991 Cécille Nowak (France)
1993 Ryoko Tamura (Japan)

Most titles: (6) Ingrid Berghmans (Belgium): 1980, 1982, 1984, 1986 (open), 1984, 1989 (under 72 kg).

KARATE

World championships

First held in Tokyo 1970; have taken place every two years since 1980, when women first competed; there is a team competition plus individual competitions – Kumite (seven weight categories for men and three for women) and Kata.

Team winners

1970 Japan
1972 France
1975 Great Britain
1977 Netherlands
1980 Spain
1982 Great Britain
1984 Great Britain
1986 Great Britain
1988 Great Britain
1990 Great Britain

Most wins: (6) Great Britain: as above.

LACROSSE

World championships

First held for men in 1967; and for women in 1969. Have taken place every four years since 1974; since 1982 the women's event has been called the World Cup.

Winners: men

1967 USA
1974 USA
1978 Canada
1982 USA
1986 USA
1990 USA

Most wins: (5) USA: as above.

Winners: women

1969 Great Britain
1974 USA
1978 Canada
1982 USA
1986 Australia
1989 USA

Most wins: (3) USA: as above.

Iroquois Cup

The sport's best-known trophy; contested by English club sides annually since 1890.

Recent winners

1979 Cheadle
1980 South Manchester
1981 Cheadle
1982 Sheffield University
1983 Sheffield University
1984 Cheadle
1985 Cheadle
1986 Heaton Mersey
1987 Stockport
1988 Mellor
1989 Stockport
1990 Cheadle
1991 Cheadle
1992 Cheadle
1993 Heaton Mersey

Most wins: (17) Stockport: 1897–1901, 1903, 1905, 1911–13, 1923–4, 1926, 1928, 1934, 1987, 1989.

MODERN PENTATHLON

World championships

Held annually since 1949 with the exception of Olympic years, when the Olympic champions automatically become world champions.

Recent winners: individual

1979 Robert Nieman (USA)
1980 Anatoliy Starostin (USSR)
1981 Janusz Pyciak-Peciak (Poland)
1982 Daniele Masala (Italy)
1983 Anatoliy Starostin (USSR)
1984 Daniele Masala (Italy)
1985 Attila Mizser (Hungary)
1986 Carlo Massullo (Italy)
1987 Joel Bouzou (France)
1988 Janos Martinek (Hungary)
1989 László Fábián (Hungary)
1990 Gianluca Tiberti (Italy)
1991 Arkadiusz Skrzypasjek (Poland)
1992 Arkadiusz Skrzypasjek (Poland)
1993 Richard Phelps (Great Britain)

Recent winners: team

1979	USA	1987	Hungary
1980	USSR	1988	Hungary
1981	Poland	1989	Hungary
1982	USSR	1990	USSR
1983	USSR	1991	USSR
1984	Italy	1992	Poland
1985	USSR	1993	Hungary
1986	Italy		

Most wins: Individual (6) Andras Balczo (Hungary): 1963, 1965–9, 1972. Team (18) USSR: 1956–9, 1961–2, 1964, 1969, 1971–4, 1980, 1982–3, 1985, 1990, 1991.

MOTOR CYCLING

World championships

First organized in 1949; current titles for 500 cc, 250 cc, 125 cc, 80 cc and Sidecar. Formula One and Endurance world championships also held annually. The most prestigious title is the 500 cc category.

Recent winners: 500 cc

1981 Marco Lucchinelli (Italy)
1982 Franco Uncini (Italy)
1983 Freddie Spencer (USA)
1984 Eddie Lawson (USA)
1985 Freddie Spencer (USA)
1986 Eddie Lawson (USA)
1987 Wayne Gardner (Australia)
1988 Eddie Lawson (USA)
1989 Eddie Lawson (USA)
1990 Wayne Rainey (USA)
1991 Wayne Rainey (USA)
1992 Wayne Rainey (USA)
1993 Kevin Schwantz (USA)

Most wins: (8) Giacomo Agostini (Italy): 1966–72, 1975.

Most world titles: (15) Giacomo Agostini (Italy): 350 cc 1968–74, 500 cc as above.

Isle of Man TT races

The most famous of all motor-cycle races; first held 1907; takes place each June. Principal race is the Senior TT.

Recent winners: senior TT

1981 Mick Grant (Great Britain)
1982 Norman Brown (Great Britain)
1983 Rob McElnea (Great Britain)
1984 Rob McElnea (Great Britain)
1985 Joey Dunlop (Ireland)
1986 Roger Burnett (Great Britain)
1987 Joey Dunlop (Ireland)
1988 Joey Dunlop (Ireland)
1989 Steve Hislop (Great Britain)
1990 Carl Fogarty (Great Britain)
1991 Steve Hislop (Great Britain)
1992 Steve Hislop (Great Britain)
1993 Nigel Davies (Great Britain)

Most senior TT wins: (7) Mike Hailwood (Great Britain): 1961, 1963–7, 1979.

MOTOR RACING

World championship

A Formula One drivers' world championship instituted in 1950; constructor's championship instituted in 1958.

Recent winners

1981 Nelson Piquet (Brazil); Brabham
1982 Keke Rosberg (Finland); Williams
1983 Nelson Piquet (Brazil); Brabham
1984 Niki Lauda (Austria); McLaren
1985 Alain Prost (France); McLaren
1986 Alain Prost (France); McLaren
1987 Nelson Piquet (France); Williams
1988 Ayrton Senna (Brazil); McLaren
1989 Alain Prost (France); McLaren
1990 Ayrton Senna (Brazil); McLaren
1991 Ayrton Senna (Brazil); McLaren
1992 Nigel Mansell (Great Britain); Williams
1993 Alain Prost (France); McLaren

Most wins: Driver (5) Juan Manuel Fangio (Argentina): 1951, 1954–7. Constructor (8) Ferrari: 1964, 1975–7, 1979, 1982–3.

Le Mans 24-Hour Race

The greatest of all endurance races. First held in 1923.

Recent winners

1981 Jacky Ickx (Belgium)
     Derek Bell (Great Britain)
1982 Jacky Ickx (Belgium)
     Derek Bell (Great Britain)
1983 Vern Schuppan (Austria)
     Al Holbert (USA)
     Hurley Haywood (USA)
1984 Klaus Ludwig (W Germany)
     Henri Pescarolo (France)
1985 Klaus Ludwig (W Germany)
     'John Winter'* (W Germany)
     Paolo Barilla (Italy)
1986 Hans Stück (W Germany)
     Derek Bell (Great Britain)
     Al Holbert (USA)
1987 Hans Stück (W Germany)
     Derek Bell (Great Britain)
     Al Holbert (USA)
1988 Jan Lammers (Netherlands)
     Johnny Dumfries (Great Britain)
     Andy Wallace (Great Britain)
1989 Jochen Mass (W Germany)
     Manuel Reuter (W Germany)
     Stanley Dickens (Sweden)
1990 John Neilsen (Denmark)
     Price Cobb (USA)
     Martin Brundle (Great Britain)
1991 Volker Weidler (Germany)
     Johnny Herbert (Great Britain)
     Bertrand Gochot (Belgium)
1992 Derek Warwick (Great Britain)
     Mark Blundell (Great Britain)
     Yannick Dalmas (France)
1993 Geoff Brabham (Australia)
     Christophe Bouchut (France)
     Eric Helary (France)

*Pseudonym.

Most wins: (6) Jacky Ickx (Belgium): 1969, 1975–7, 1981–2.

Sports and games

Indianapolis 500

First held in 1911. Raced over the Indianapolis Raceway as part of the Memorial Day celebrations at the end of May each year.

Recent winners
1981   Bobby Unser (USA)
1982   Gordon Johncock (USA)
1983   Tom Sneva (USA)
1984   Rick Mears (USA)
1985   Danny Sullivan (USA)
1986   Bobby Rahal (USA)
1987   Al Unser (USA)
1988   Rick Mears (USA)
1989   Emerson Fittipaldi (Brazil)
1990   Arie Luyendyk (Netherlands)
1991   Rick Mears (USA)
1992   Al Unser Jr (USA)
1993   Emerson Fittipaldi (Brazil)

Most wins: (4) A J Foyt (USA): 1961, 1964, 1967, 977; Al Unser (USA): 1970–1, 1978, 1987; Rick Mears (USA): 1979, 1984, 1988, 1991.

Monte Carlo rally

The world's leading rally; first held in 1911.

Recent winners
1980   Walter Röhrl/Christian Geistdorfer (W Germany)
1981   Jean Ragnotti/Jean-Marc André (France)
1982   Walter Röhrl/Christian Geistdorfer (W Germany)
1983   Walter Röhrl/Christian Geistdorfer (W Germany)
1984   Walter Röhrl/Christian Geistdorfer (W Germany)
1985   Ari Vatanen (Finland)/Terry Harryman (Great Britain)
1986   Henri Toivonen (Finland)/ Sergio Cresto (Italy)
1987   Mikki Biasion/Tigiano Siviero (Italy)
1988   Bruno Saby/Jean-Francois Fauchille (France)
1989   Mikki Biasion/Tigiano Siviero (Italy)
1990   Didier Auriol/Bernard Occelli (France)
1991   Carlos Sainz/Luis Moya (Spain)
1992   Didier Auriol/Bernard Occelli (France)
1993   Didier Auriol/Bernard Occelli (France)

Most wins: (4) Sandro Munari (Italy): 1972, 1975–7; Walter Röhrl (W Germany): as above. Most successful co-driver: (4) Christian Geistdorfer (all with Walter Röhrl).

NETBALL

World championships

First held in 1963, then every four years.

Winners
1963   Australia
1967   New Zealand
1971   Australia
1975   Australia
1979   Australia, New Zealand, Trinidad & Tobago (*shared*)
1983   Australia
1987   New Zealand
1991   Australia

Most wins: (6) Australia: as above.

ORIENTEERING

World championships

First held in 1966. Take place every two years (to 1978, and since 1979).

Winners: individual – men
1966   Age Hadler (Norway)
1968   Karl Johansson (Sweden)
1970   Stig Berge (Norway)
1972   Age Hadler (Norway)
1974   Bernt Frilen (Sweden)
1976   Egil Johansen (Norway)
1978   Egil Johansen (Norway)
1979   Oyvin Thon (Norway)
1981   Oyvin Thon (Norway)
1983   Morten Berglia (Norway)
1985   Kari Sallinen (Finland)
1987   Kent Olsson (Sweden)
1989   Peter Thoresen (Norway)
1991   Jörgen Mårtensson (Sweden)
1993   Allan Mogensen (Denmark)

Winners: individual – women
1966   Ulla Lindqvist (Sweden)
1968   Ulla Lindqvist (Sweden)
1970   Ingrid Hadler (Norway)
1972   Sarolta Monspart (Finland)
1974   Mona Norgaard (Denmark)
1976   Lia Veijalainen (Finland)
1978   Anne Berit Eid (Norway)
1979   Outi Bergonstrom (Finland)
1981   Annichen Kringstad (Norway)
1983   Annichen Kringstad Svensson (Norway)
1985   Annichen Kringstad Svensson (Norway)
1987   Arja Hannus (Sweden)
1989   Marita Skogum (Sweden)
1991   Katalin Olah (Hungary)
1993   Marita Skogurn (Sweden)

Most wins: Men (2), Age Hadler (Norway): as above; Egil Johansen (Norway): as above; Oyvin Thon (Norway): as above. Women (3), Annichen Kringstad (Norway): as above.

Winners: relay – men

1966	Sweden	1981	Norway
1968	Sweden	1983	Norway
1970	Norway	1985	Norway
1972	Sweden	1987	Norway
1974	Sweden	1989	Norway
1976	Sweden	1991	Switzerland
1978	Norway	1993	Switzerland
1979	Sweden		

Winners: relay – women

1966	Sweden	1981	Sweden
1968	Norway	1983	Sweden
1970	Sweden	1985	Sweden
1972	Finland	1987	Norway
1974	Sweden	1989	Sweden
1976	Sweden	1991	Sweden
1978	Finland	1993	Sweden
1979	Finland		

Most wins: Men (7) Norway: as above. Women (9) Sweden: as above.

POLO

Cowdray Park Gold Cup

First held in 1956, replacing the Champion Cup. The British Open Championship for club sides; so named because it is played at Cowdray Park, Sussex.

Recent winners
1979   Songhai
1980   Stowell Park
1981   Falcons
1982   Southfield
1983   Falcons
1984   Southfield
1985   Maple Leafs
1986   Tramontona
1987   Tramontona
1988   Tramontona
1989   Tramontona
1990   Hildon
1991   Tramontona
1992   Black Bears
1993   Maple Leafs

Most wins: (5) Stowell Park: 1973–4, 1976, 1978, 1980; Tramontona: as above.

POWERBOAT RACING

World championships

Instituted in 1982; held in many categories, with Formula One and Formula Two being the principal competitions. Formula Two, known as Formula Grand Prix, was discontinued in 1989.

Winners: Formula One
1982 Roger Jenkins (Great Britain)
1983 Renato Molinari (Italy)
1984 Renato Molinari (Italy)
1985 Bob Spalding (Great Britain)
1986 Gene Thibodaux (USA)
1987 Ben Robertson (USA)
1990 John Hill (Great Britain)
1991 Jonathan Jones (Great Britain)
1992 Fabrizio Bacca (Italy)
1993 Guido Capellina (Italy)

Most wins: (2) Renato Molinari (Italy): as above.

Winners: Formula Two/Formula Grand Prix
1982 Michael Werner (W Germany)
1983 Michael Werner (W Germany)
1984 John Hill (Great Britain)
1985 John Hill (Great Britain)
1986 Jonathan Jones (Great Britain) and Buck Thornton (USA) (*shared*)
1987 Bill Seebold (USA)
1988 Chris Bush (USA)
1989 Jonathan Jones (Great Britain)

Most wins: (2) Michael Werner (W Germany): as above; John Hill (Great Britain): as above; Jonathan Jones (Great Britain): as above.

RACKETS

World championship

Organized on a challenge basis, the first champion in 1820 was Robert Mackay (Great Britain).

Recent winners
1929–37 Charles Williams (Great Britain)
1937–47 Donald Milford (Great Britain)
1947–54 James Dear (Great Britain)
1954–72 Geoffrey Atkins (Great Britain)
1972–3 William Surtees (USA)
1973–4 Howard Angus (Great Britain)
1975–1 William Surtees (USA)
1981–4 John Prenn (Great Britain)
1984–6 William Boone (Great Britain)
1986–8 John Prenn (Great Britain)
1988– James Male (Great Britain)

Longest-reigning champion: 18 years, Geoffrey Atkins: as above.

REAL TENNIS

World championship

The first world champion was M Clerge (France), c. 1740, regarded as the first world champion of any sport. Held on a challenge basis; first held for women in 1985, and then every two years.

Recent winners: men
1916–28 Fred Covey (Great Britain)
1928–55 Pierre Etchebaster (France)
1955–7 James Dear (Great Britain)
1957–9 Albert Johnson (Great Britain)
1959–69 Northrup Knox (USA)
1969–72 Pete Bostwick (USA)
1972–5 Jimmy Bostwick (USA)
1976–81 Howard Angus (Great Britain)
1981–7 Chris Ronaldson (Great Britain)
1987– Wayne Davis (Australia)

Longest-reigning champion: 33 years, Edmond Barre (France): 1829–62.

Winners – women
1985 Judy Clarke (Australia)
1987 Judy Clarke (Australia)
1989 Penny Fellows (Great Britain)
1991 Penny Fellows Lumley (Great Britain)

ROLLER SKATING

World championships

Figure-skating world championships were first organized in 1947.

Recent winners: combined – men
1981   Michael Butzke (E Germany)
1982   Michael Butzke (E Germany)
1983   Joachim Helmle (W Germany)
1984   Michele Biserni (Italy)
1985   Michele Biserni (Italy)
1986   Michele Tolomini (Italy)
1987   Sandro Guerra (Italy)
1988   Sandro Guerra (Italy)
1989   Sandro Guerra (Italy)
1990   Samo Kokorovec (Italy)
1991   Sandro Guerra (Italy)
1992   Sandro Guerra (Italy)
1993   Samo Kokorovec (Italy)

Most wins: (5) Karl-Heinz Losch (W Germany): 1958–9, 1961–2, 1966.

Recent winners: combined – women
1981   Petre Schneider (W Germany)
1982   Claudia Bruppacher (W Germany)
1983   Claudia Bruppacher (W Germany)
1984   Claudia Bruppacher (W Germany)
1985   Chiara Sartori (Italy)
1986   Chiara Sartori (Italy)
1987   Chiara Sartori (Italy)
1988   Rafaella Del Vinaccio (Italy)
1989   Rafaella Del Vinaccio (Italy)
1990   Rafaella Del Vinaccio (Italy)
1991   Rafaella Del Vinaccio (Italy)
1992   Rafaella Del Vinaccio (Italy)
1993   Letitia Tinghi (Italy)

Most wins: (4) Astrid Bader (W Germany): 1965–8; Rafaella Del Vinaccio (Italy): as above.

Recent winners: pairs
1981   Paul Price/Tina Kniesley (USA)
1982   Paul Price/Tina Kniesley (USA)
1983   John Arishita/Tammy Jeru (USA)
1984   John Arishita/Tammy Jeru (USA)
1985   John Arishita/Tammy Jeru (USA)
1986   John Arishita/Tammy Jeru (USA)
1987   Fabio Trevisani/Monica Mezzardi (Italy)
1988   Fabio Trevisani/Monica Mezzardi (Italy)
1989   David De Motte/Nicky Armstrong (USA)
1990   Larry McGrew/Tammy Jeru (USA)
1991   Larry McGrew/Tammy Jeru (USA)
1992   Patrick Venerucci/Maura Ferri (Italy)
1993   Patrick Venerucci/Maura Ferri (Italy)

Most wins: (6) Tammy Jeru (USA): as above (4 with John Arishita).

Recent winners: dance
1981   Mark Howard/Cindy Smith (USA)
1982   Mark Howard/Cindy Smith (USA)
1983   David Golub/Angela Famiano (USA)
1984   David Golub/Angela Famiano (USA)
1985   Martin Hauss/Andrea Steudte (W Germany)
1986   Scott Myers/Anna Danks (USA)

1987   Rob Ferendo/Lori Walsh (USA)
1988   Peter Wulf/Michela Mitzlaf (W Germany)
1989   Greg Goody/Jodee Viola (USA)
1990   Greg Goody/Jodee Viola (USA)
1991   Greg Goody/Jodee Viola (USA)
1992   Doug Wait/Deanna Monaham (USA)
1993   Doug Wait/Deanna Monaham (USA)

Most wins: (3) Jane Puracchio (USA): 1973, 1975–6; Dan Littel and Florence Arsenault (USA): 1977–9; Greg Goody and Jodee Viola (USA): as above.

ROWING

World championships

First held for men in 1962 and for women in 1974; Olympic champions assume the role of world champion in Olympic years. Principal events are the single sculls.

Recent winners: single sculls – men
1981   Peter-Michael Kolbe (W Germany)
1982   Rudiger Reiche (E Germany)
1983   Peter-Michael Kolbe (W Germany)
1984   Perrti Karppinen (Finland)
1985   Perrti Karppinen (Finland)
1986   Peter-Michael Kolbe (W Germany)
1987   Thomas Lange (E Germany)
1988   Thomas Lange (E Germany)
1989   Thomas Lange (E Germany)
1990   Yuri Janson (USSR)
1991   Thomas Lange (Germany)
1992   Thomas Lange (Germany)
1993   Derek Porter (Canada)

Most wins: (5) Thomas Lange (Germany): as above.

Recent winners: sculls – women
1981   Sanda Toma (Romania)
1982   Irina Fetissova (USSR)
1983   Jutta Hampe (E Germany)
1984   Valeria Racila (Romania)
1985   Cornelia Linse (E Germany)
1986   Jutta Hampe (E Germany)
1987   Magdelena Georgieva (Bulgaria)
1988   Jutta Behrendt (E Germany)
1989   Elisabeta Lipa (Romania)
1990   Brigit Peter (E Germany)
1991   Silke Laumann (Canada)
1992   Elisabeta Lipa (Romania)
1993   Jana Phieme (Germany)

Most wins: (5) Christine Hahn (née Scheiblich) (E Germany): 1974–8.

University Boat Race

An annual contest between the crews from the Oxford and Cambridge University rowing clubs, first contested in 1829. The current course is from Putney to Mortlake.

Recent winners
1981 Oxford	1986 Cambridge	1988 Oxford
1982 Oxford	1987 Oxford	1991 Oxford
1983 Oxford	1988 Oxford	1992 Oxford
1984 Oxford	1989 Oxford	1993 Cambridge
1985 Oxford	1990 Oxford	1994 Cambridge

Wins: 71 Cambridge; 68 Oxford; 1 dead-heat (1877).

Diamond Sculls

Highlight of Henley Royal Regatta held every July; first contested in 1884.

Recent winners

1981	Chris Baillieu (Great Britain)
1982	Chris Baillieu (Great Britain)
1983	Steve Redgrave (Great Britain)
1984	Chris Baillieu (Great Britain)
1985	Steve Redgrave (Great Britain)
1986	Bjarne Eltang (Denmark)
1987	Peter-Michael Kolbe (W Germany)
1988	Hamish McGlashan (Australia)
1989	Vaclav Chalupa (Czechoslovakia)
1990	Eric Verdonk (New Zealand)
1991	Wim van Belleghem (Belgium)
1992	Rorie Henderson (Great Britain)
1993	Thomas Lange (Germany)

Most wins: (6) Stuart Mackenzie (Great Britain): 1957–62.

RUGBY LEAGUE

World Cup/International championship

First contested in 1954 between Great Britain, France, New Zealand, and Australia. In 1975, England and Wales replaced Great Britain. The competition was discontinued after the 1977 World Cup, but was revived in 1988.

Winners

1954	Great Britain	1972	Great Britain
1957	Australia	1975	Australia
1960	Great Britain	1977	Australia
1968	Australia	1988	Australia
1970	Australia	1992	Australia

Most wins: (7) Australia: as above.

League championship

The original Northern Union was formed in 1895–6, and was won by Manningham. Since then there have been many changes to the rules and structure of the league, which from 1906 to 1973 featured a Championship Play-off. The present structure, with Divisions One and Two, dates from the 1973–4 season.

Recent winners

1981–82	Leigh	1987–88	Widnes
1982–83	Hull	1988–89	Widnes
1983–84	Hull Kingston Rovers	1989–90	Wigan
1984–85	Hull Kingston Rovers	1990–91	Wigan
1985–86	Halifax	1991–92	Wigan
1986–87	Wigan	1992–93	Wigan
		1993–94	Wigan

Challenge Cup final

First contested in 1897 and won by Batley; first final at Wembley Stadium in 1929.

Recent winners

1981	Widnes	1988	Wigan
1982	Hull	1989	Wigan
1983	Featherstone Rovers	1990	Wigan
1984	Widnes	1991	Wigan
1985	Wigan	1992	Wigan
1986	Castleford	1993	Wigan
1987	Halifax	1994	Wigan

Most wins: (14) Wigan: 1924, 1929, 1948, 1951, 1958–9, 1965, and as above.

Premiership trophy

End-of-season knockout competition involving the top eight teams in the first division. First contested at the end of the 1974–5 season.

Recent winners

1981	Hull Kingston Rovers	1988	Widnes
1982	Widnes	1989	Widnes
1983	Widnes	1990	Widnes
1984	Hull Kingston Rovers	1991	Hull
1985	St Helens	1992	Wigan
1986	Warrington	1993	Wigan
1987	Wigan		

Most wins: (6) Widnes, 1980: and as above.

Regal trophy

A knockout competition, first held in 1971–2. Formerly known as the John Player Special Trophy, it adopted its current name/title in 1989–90.

Recent winners

1982	Hull	1988	St Helens
1983	Wigan	1989	Wigan
1984	Leeds	1990	Wigan
1985	Hull Kingston Rovers	1991	Warrington
1986	Wigan	1992	Widnes
1987	Wigan	1993	Wigan
		1994	Castleford

Most wins: (6) Wigan: as above.

Sydney Premiership

The principal competition in Australia, first held in 1908. The culmination of the competition is the Grand Final; the winning team receives the Winfield Cup.

Recent winners

1980	Canterbury-Bankstown
1981	Parramatta
1982	Parramatta
1983	Parramatta
1984	Canterbury-Bankstown
1985	Canterbury-Bankstown
1986	Parramatta
1987	Manly-Warringah
1988	Canterbury-Bankstown
1989	Canberra
1990	Canberra
1991	Penrith
1992	Brisbane Broncos
1993	Brisbane Broncos

Sports and games

RUGBY UNION

World Cup

The first Rugby Union World Cup was staged in 1987; New Zealand were crowned the first champions after beating France in the final. Australia beat England in the final of the second competition, in 1991.

Five Nations championship

A round-robin competition involving England, Ireland, Scotland, Wales and France; first contested in 1884.

Recent winners

1982	Ireland	1988	France and Wales
1983	France and Ireland		(Shared)
	(Shared)	1989	France
1984	Scotland	1990	Scotland
1985	Ireland	1991	England
1986	France and Scotland	1992	England
1987	France	1993	France
		1994	Wales

Most outright wins: (22) Wales: 1893, 1900, 1902, 1905, 1908–9, 1911, 1922, 1931, 1936, 1950, 1952, 1956, 1965–6, 1969, 1971, 1975–6, 1978–9, 1994.

County championship

First held in 1889.

Recent winners

1982	Lancashire	1988	Lancashire
1983	Gloucestershire	1989	Durham
1984	Gloucestershire	1990	Lancashire
1985	Middlesex	1991	Cornwall
1986	Warwickshire	1992	Lancashire
1987	Yorkshire	1993	Lancashire
		1994	Yorkshire

Most wins: (15) Gloucestershire: 1910, 1913, 1920–2, 1930–2, 1937, 1972, 1974–6, 1983–4.

Pilkington Cup

An annual knockout competition for English club sides; first held in the 1971–2 season. Known as the John Player Special Cup until 1988.

Recent winners

1982	Gloucester and	1988	Harlequins
	Moseley (shared)	1989	Bath
1983	Bristol	1990	Bath
1984	Bath	1991	Harlequins
1985	Bath	1992	Bath
1986	Bath	1993	Leicester
1987	Bath	1994	Bath

Most wins: (8) Bath: as above.

Rugby Union football field

Schweppes Welsh Cup

The knockout tournament for Welsh clubs; first held in 1971–2.

Recent winners

1982	Cardiff	1988	Llanelli
1983	Pontypool	1989	Neath
1984	Cardiff	1990	Neath
1985	Llanelli	1991	Llanelli
1986	Cardiff	1992	Llanelli
1987	Cardiff	1993	Llanelli

Most wins: (9) Llanelli: 1973–6, 1985, 1988, 1991–3.

Sports and games

SHOOTING

Olympic Games

The Olympic competition is the highlight of the shooting calendar; winners in all categories since 1980 are given below.

Free pistol: men
1980   Aleksander Melentyev (USSR)
1984   Xu Haifeng (China)
1988   Sorin Babil (Romania)
1992   Konstantine Loukachik
         (Unified Team)

Rapid fire pistol: men
1980   Corneliu Ion (Romania)
1984   Takeo Kamachi (Japan)
1988   Afanasi Kouzmine (USSR)
1992   Ralf Shumann (Germany)

Small-bore rifle: three position – men
1980   Viktor Vlasov (USSR)
1984   Malcolm Cooper (Great
         Britain)
1988   Malcolm Cooper (Great
         Britain)
1992   Gratchia Petrikiane (Unified
         Team)

Running game target: men
1980   Igor Sokolov (USSR)
1984   Li Yuwei (China)
1988   Tor Heiestad (Norway)
1992   Michael Jakositz (Germany)

Trap: mixed
1980   Luciano Giovanetti (Italy)
1984   Luciano Giovanetti (Italy)
1988   Dmitri Monakov (USSR)
1992   Peter Hrdlicka
         (Czechoslovakia)

Skeet: mixed
1980   Hans Rusmussen (Denmark)
1984   Matthew Dryke (USA)
1988   Axel Wegner (E Germany)
1992   Zhang Shan (China)

Small-bore rifle: prone – men
1980   Karoly Varga (Hungary)
1984   Edward Etzel (USA)
1988   Miroslav Varga
         (Czechoslovakia)
1992   Lee Eun Chul (S Korea)

Air rifle: men
1984   Philippe Heberle (France)
1988   Goran Maksimovic
         (Yugoslavia)
1992   Iouri Fedkine (Unified Team)

Air pistol: men
1988   Taniou Kiriakoy (USSR)
1992   Wang Yifu (China)

Sport pistol: women
1984   Linda Thom (Canada)
1988   Nino Saloukvadze (USSR)
1992   Marina Logvinenko (Unified
         Team)

Air rifle: women
1984   Pat Spurgin (USA)
1988   Irina Chilova (USSR)
1992   Yeo Kab-Soon (S Korea)

Small-bore rifle: women
1984   Wu Xiaoxuan (China)
1988   Silvia Sperber (W Germany)
1992   Lauri Melli (USA)

Air pistol: women
1988   Jasna Sekuric (Yugoslavia)
1992   Marina Logrinenko (Unified
         Team)

SKIING

World Cup

A season-long competition first organized in 1967. Champions are declared in downhill, slalom, giant slalom, and super-giant slalom, as well as the overall champion; points are obtained for performances in each category.

Recent overall winners: men
1982   Phil Mahre (USA)
1983   Phil Mahre (USA)
1984   Pirmin Zurbriggen
         (Switzerland)
1985   Marc Girardelli
         (Luxembourg)
1986   Marc Girardelli
         (Luxembourg)
1987   Pirmin Zurbriggen
         (Switzerland)
1988   Pirmin Zurbriggen
         (Switzerland)
1989   Marc Girardelli
         (Luxembourg)
1990   Pirmin Zurbriggen
         (Switzerland)
1991   Marc Girardelli
         (Luxembourg)
1992   Paul Accola (Switzerland)
1993   Marc Girardelli
         (Luxembourg)

Recent overall winners: women
1982   Erika Hess (Switzerland)
1983   Tamara McKinney (USA)
1984   Erika Hess (Switzerland)
1985   Michela Figini (Switzerland)
1986   Maria Walliser (Switzerland)
1987   Maria Walliser (Switzerland)
1988   Michela Figini (Switzerland)
1989   Vreni Schneider
         (Switzerland)
1990   Petra Kronberger (Austria)
1991   Petra Kronberger (Austria)
1992   Petra Kronberger (Austria)
1993   Anita Wachter (Austria)

Most wins: Men (4) Gustavo Thoeni (Italy): 1971–3, 1975; Pirmin Zurbriggen (Switzerland): as above; Marc Girardelli (Luxembourg): as above. Women (6) Annemarie Moser-Pröll (Austria): 1971–5, 1979.

Olympic Games

Gold medal winners
Men's Alpine combination
1992   Josef Polig (Italy)
1994   Lasse Kjus (Norway)

Women's Alpine combination
1992   Petra Kronberger (Austria)
1994   Pernille Wiberg (Sweden)

SNOOKER

World Professional championship

Instituted in the 1926–7 season. A knockout competition open to professional players who are members of the World Professional Billiards and Snooker Association; played at the Crucible Theatre, Sheffield.

Recent winners
1981   Steve Davis (England)
1982   Alex Higgins (N Ireland)
1983   Steve Davis (England)
1984   Steve Davis (England)
1985   Dennis Taylor (N Ireland)
1986   Joe Johnson (England)
1987   Steve Davis (England)
1988   Steve Davis (England)
1989   Steve Davis (England)
1990   Stephen Hendry (Scotland)
1991   John Parrott (England)
1992   Stephen Hendry (Scotland)
1993   Stephen Hendry (Scotland)
1994   Stephen Hendry (Scotland)

Most wins: (15) Joe Davis (England): 1927–40, 1946.

Rothmans Grand Prix

Originally the Professional Players Tournament; under present name since 1984. A ranking tournament.[a]

Winners
1982 Ray Reardon (Wales)
1983 Tony Knowles (England)
1984 Dennis Taylor (N Ireland)
1985 Steve Davis (England)
1986 Jimmy White (England)
1987 Stephen Hendry (Scotland)
1988 Steve Davis (England)
1989 Steve Davis (England)
1990 Stephen Hendry (Scotland)
1991 Stephen Hendry (Scotland)
1992 Jimmy White (England)
1993 Jimmy White (England)

Most wins: (3) Steve Davis (England): as above; Stephen Hendry (Scotland): as above; Jimmy White (England): as above.

British Open

Became a ranking tournament[a] in 1985.

Recent winners
1980 Alex Higgins (N Ireland)
1981 Steve Davis (England)
1982 Steve Davis (England)
1983 Ray Reardon (Wales)
1984 Steve Davis (England)
1985 Silvino Francisco (S Africa)
1986 Steve Davis (England)
1987 Jimmy White (England)
1988 Stephen Hendry (Scotland)
1989 Tony Meo (England)
1990 Bob Chaperon (Canada)
1991 Stephen Hendry (Scotland)
1992 Jimmy White (England)
1993 Steve Davies (England)

Most wins: (4) Steve Davis (England): as above.

Benson & Hedges Masters

First contested in 1975 and won by John Spencer. Held at the Wembley Conference Centre, it is the most prestigious non-ranking tournament of the season.

Recent winners
1982 Steve Davis (England)
1983 Cliff Thorburn (Canada)
1984 Jimmy White (England)
1985 Cliff Thorburn (Canada)
1986 Cliff Thorburn (Canada)
1987 Dennis Taylor (N Ireland)
1988 Steve Davis (England)
1989 Stephen Hendry (Scotland)

1990 Stephen Hendry (Scotland)
1991 Stephen Hendry (Scotland)
1992 Stephen Hendry (Scotland)
1993 Stephen Hendry (Scotland)

Most wins: (5) Stephen Hendry (Scotland): as above.

World Amateur championship

First held in 1963. Originally took place every two years, but annual since 1984.

Recent winners
1976 Doug Mountjoy (Wales)
1978 Cliff Wilson (Wales)
1980 Jimmy White (England)
1982 Terry Parson (Wales)
1984 O. B. Agrawal (India)
1985 Paul Mifsud (Malta)
1986 Paul Mifsud (Malta)
1987 Darren Morgan (Wales)
1988 James Wattana (Thailand)
1989 Ken Doherty (Ireland)
1990 Steven O'Connor (Ireland)
1991 Noppodol Noppachorn (Thailand)
1992 Neil Moseley (England)
1993 Neil Moseley (England)

Most wins: (2) Gary Owen (England): 1963, 1966; Ray Edmonds (England): 1972, 1974; Paul Mifsud (Malta): as above.

[a]A ranking tournament ia a tournament at which players may gather world-ranking points.

SOFTBALL

World championships

First held for women in 1965 and for men the following year; now held every four years.

Winners: men
1966 USA
1968 USA
1972 Canada
1976 Canada, New Zealand, USA (shared)
1980 USA
1984 New Zealand
1988 USA
1992 Canada

Most wins: (5) USA: as above.

Winners: women
1965 Australia
1970 Japan
1974 USA
1978 USA
1982 New Zealand

1986 USA
1990 USA

Most wins: (3) USA: as above.

SPEEDWAY

World championships

Individual championships inaugurated in 1936; team championship instituted in 1960; first official pairs world championship in 1970 (threes from 1991).

Recent winners: individual
1981 Bruce Penhall (USA)
1982 Bruce Penhall (USA)
1983 Egon Muller (W Germany)
1984 Erik Gundersen (Denmark)
1985 Erik Gundersen (Denmark)
1986 Hans Nielsen (Denmark)
1987 Hans Nielsen (Denmark)
1988 Erik Gundersen (Denmark)
1989 Hans Nielsen (Denmark)
1990 Per Jonsson (Sweden)
1991 Jan Pedersen (Denmark)
1992 Gary Havelock (England)
1993 Sam Ermolenko (USA)

Most wins: (6) Ivan Mauger (New Zealand): 1968–70, 1972, 1977, 1979.

Recent winners: pairs
1981 Bruce Penhall/Bobby Schwartz (USA)
1982 Dennis Sigalos/Bobby Schwartz (USA)
1983 Kenny Carter/Peter Collins (England)
1984 Peter Collins/ Chris Morton (England)
1985 Erik Gundersen/Tommy Knudsen (Denmark)
1986 Erik Gunderson/Hans Nielsen (Denmark)
1987 Erik Gundersen/Hans Nielsen (Denmark)
1988 Erik Gundersen/Hans Nielsen (Denmark)
1989 Erik Gundersen/Hans Nielsen (Denmark)
1990 Hans Nielsen/Jan Pedersen (Denmark)
1991 Hans Nielsen/Jan Pedersen/ Tommy Knudsen (Denmark)
1992 Greg Hancock/Sam Ermolenko/Ronnie Correy (USA)
1993 Tony Richardson/Per Jonsson/ Henrik Gustafsson (Sweden)

Most wins: (6) Hans Nielsen (Denmark): as above.

Squash

Speedway (continued)

Recent winners: team
1981	Denmark
1982	USA
1983	Denmark
1984	Denmark
1985	Denmark
1986	Denmark
1987	Denmark
1988	Denmark
1989	England
1990	USA
1991	Denmark
1992	USA

Most wins: (9) Great Britain/England: 1968, 1971–5, 1977, 1980, 1989.

SQUASH

World Open championship

First held in 1976; held annually for men, every two years for women, until 1990, since when it has been annual.

Recent winners: men
1981	Jahangir Khan (Pakistan)
1982	Jahangir Khan (Pakistan)
1983	Jahangir Khan (Pakistan)
1984	Jahangir Khan (Pakistan)
1985	Jahangir Khan (Pakistan)
1986	Ross Norman (New Zealand)
1987	Jansher Khan (Pakistan)
1988	Jahangir Khan (Pakistan)
1989	Jansher Khan (Pakistan)
1990	Jansher Khan (Pakistan)
1991	Rodney Martin (Australia)
1992	Jansher Khan (Pakistan)
1993	Jansher Khan (Pakistan)

Most wins: (6) Jahangir Khan (Pakistan): as above.

Recent winners: women
1979	Heather McKay (Australia)
1981	Rhonda Thorne (Australia)
1983	Vicky Cardwell (Australia)
1985	Sue Devoy (New Zealand)
1987	Sue Devoy (New Zealand)
1989	Martine Le Moignan (Great Britain)
1990	Sue Devoy (New Zealand)
1991	Sue Devoy (New Zealand)
1992	Sue Devoy (New Zealand)
1993	Michelle Martin (Australia)

Most wins: (5) Sue Devoy (New Zealand): as above.

SURFING

World professional championship

A season-long series of Grand Prix events. First held in 1970.

Recent winners: men
1979	Mark Richards (Australia)
1980	Mark Richards (Australia)
1981	Mark Richards (Australia)
1982	Mark Richards (Australia)
1983	Tom Carroll (Australia)
1984	Tom Carroll (Australia)
1985	Tommy Curren (USA)
1986	Tommy Curren (USA)
1987	Damien Hardman (Australia)
1988	Barton Lynch (Australia)
1989	Martin Potter (Great Britain)
1990	Tommy Curren (USA)
1991	Damien Hardman (Australia)
1992	Kelly Slater (USA)
1993	Derek Ho (Hawaii)

Recent winners: women
1979	Margo Oberg (Hawaii)
1980	Lyne Boyer (Hawaii)
1981	Margo Oberg (Hawaii)
1982	*Not held*
1983	Margo Oberg (Hawaii)
1984	Kim Mearig (USA)
1985	Frieda Zamba (USA)
1986	Frieda Zamba (USA)
1987	Wendy Botha (S Africa)
1988	Frieda Zamba (USA)
1989	Wendy Botha (S Africa)
1990	Pam Burridge (Australia)
1991	Wendy Botha (Australia)
1992	Wendy Botha (Australia)
1993	Pauline Menczer (Australia)

Most wins: Men (5) Mark Richards (Australia): 1975, 1979–82. Women (4) Wendy Botha (Australia, ex-S Africa): as above.

SWIMMING AND DIVING

World championships

First held in 1973, the World Championships have since taken place in 1975, 1978, 1982, 1986, and 1991.

World champions: 1991 – men
50 m freestyle	Tom Jager (USA)
100 m freestyle	Matt Biondi (USA)
200 m freestyle	Giorgio Lamberti (Italy)
400 m freestyle	Jörg Hoffmann (Germany)
1500 m freestyle	Jörg Hoffmann (Germany)
100 m backstroke	Jeff Rouse (USA)
200 m backstroke	Martin López-Zubero (Spain)
100 m breaststroke	Norbert Rosza (Hungary)
200 m breaststroke	Mike Barrowman (USA)
100 m butterfly	Anthony Nesty (Surinam)
200 m butterfly	Melvin Stewart (USA)
200 m individual medley	Tamás Darnyi (Hungary)
400 m individual medley	Tamás Darnyi (Hungary)
4 x 100 m freestyle medley	USA
4 x 200 m freestyle medley	Germany
4 x 100 m medley relay	USA
1 m springboard diving	Edwin Jongejans (Netherlands)
Platform diving	Sun Shewei (China)

World champions: 1991 – women

50 m freestyle	Zhuang Yong (China)
100 m freestyle	Nicola Haislett (USA)
200 m freestyle	Hayley Lewis (Australia)
400 m freestyle	Janet Evans (USA)
800 m freestyle	Janet Evans (USA)
100 m backstroke	Krisztina Egerszegi (Hungary)
200 m backstroke	Krisztina Egerszegi (Hungary)
100 m breaststroke	Linley Frame (Australia)
200 m breaststroke	Elena Volkova (USSR)
100 m butterfly	Qian Hong (China)
200 m butterfly	Summer Sanders (USA)
200 m individual medley	Lin Li (China)
400 m individual medley	Lin Li (China)
4 x 100 m freestyle medley	USA
4 x 200 m freestyle medley	Germany
4 x 100 m medley relay	USA
1 m springboard diving	Gao Min (China)
Platform diving	Fu Mingxia (China)
Synchronized swimming	
Solo	Silvie Frechette (Canada)
Duet	USA
Team	USA

Olympic Games

Gold medal winners: 1992 – men

50 m freestyle	Aleksandr Popov (Unified Team)
100 m freestyle	Aleksandr Popov (Unified Team)
200 m freestyle	Yevgeniy Sadoviy (Unified Team)
400 m freestyle	Yevgeniy Sadoviy (Unified Team)
1 500 m freestyle	Kieren Perkins (Australia)
100 m breaststroke	Nelson Diebel (USA)
200 m breaststroke	Mike Barrowman (USA)*
100 m butterfly	Pablo Moralos (USA)
200 m butterfly	Mel Stewart (USA)
100 m backstroke	Mark Tewksbury (Canada)
200 m backstroke	Martin López-Zubero (Spain)
200 m individual medley	Tamás Darnyi (Hungary)
400 m individual medley	Tamás Darnyi (Hungary)
400 m freestyle relay	USA
800 m freestyle relay	Unified Team
400 m medley relay	USA

Gold medal winners: 1992 – women

50 m freestyle	Yang Wenyl (China)
100 m freestyle	Zhuang Yong (China)
200 m freestyle	Nicole Haislett (USA)
400 m freestyle	Dagmar Hase (Germany)
800 m freestyle	Janet Evans (USA)
100 m breaststroke	Yelena Rudkovskaya (Unified Team)
200 m breaststroke	Kyoko Iwasaki (Japan)
100 m backstroke	Krisztina Egerszegi (Hungary)
200 m backstroke	Krisztina Egerszegi (Hungary)
100 m butterfly	Qian Hong (China)
200 m butterfly	Summer Sanders (USA)
200 m individual medley	Lin Li (China)
400 m individual medley	Krisztina Egerszegi (Hungary)
400 m freestyle relay	USA
400 m medley relay	USA

TABLE TENNIS

World championships

First held in 1926 and every two years since 1957.

Recent winners: Swaythling Cup – men's team

1971	China	1983	China
1973	Sweden	1985	China
1975	China	1987	China
1977	China	1989	Sweden
1979	Hungary	1991	Sweden
1981	China	1993	Sweden

Recent winners: Corbillon Cup – women's team

1971	Japan	1983	China
1973	S Korea	1985	China
1975	China	1987	China
1977	China	1989	China
1979	China	1991	China
1981	China	1993	China

Most wins: Swaythling Cup (12) Hungary: 1926, 1928–31, 1933 (twice), 1935, 1938, 1949, 1952, 1979. Corbillon Cup (9) China: 1965, 1975, 1977, 1979, 1981, 1983, 1985, 1987, 1989.

Recent winners: men

1971	Stellan Bengtsson (Sweden)
1973	Hsi En-Ting (China)
1975	Istvan Jonyer (Hungary)
1977	Mitsuru Kohno (Japan)
1979	Seiji Ono (Japan)
1981	Guo Yuehua (China)
1983	Guo Yuehua (China)
1985	Jiang Jialiang (China)
1987	Jiang Jialiang (China)
1989	Jan-Ove Waldner (Sweden)
1991	Jörgen Persson (Sweden)
1993	Jean-Philippe Gatien (France)

Most wins: (5) Viktor Barna (Hungary): 1930, 1932–5.

Table tennis, world championships (continued)
Recent winners: women
1971 Lin Hui-Ching (China)
1973 Hu Yu-Lan (China)
1975 Pak Yung-Sun (N Korea)
1977 Pak Yung-Sun (N Korea)
1979 Ge Xinai (China)
1981 Ting Ling (China)
1983 Cao Yanhua (China)
1985 Cao Yanhua (China)
1987 He Zhili (China)
1989 Qiao Hong (China)
1991 Deng Yaping (China)
1993 Hyun Jung-hwa (S Korea)

Most wins: (6) Angelica Rozeanu (Romania): 1950–5.

Recent winners: doubles – men
1971 Istvan Jonyer/Tiber Klampar
      (Hungary)
1973 Stellan Bengtsson/Kjell Johansson (Sweden)
1975 Gabor Gergely/Istvan Jonyer (Hungary)
1977 Li Zhenshi/Liang Geliang (China)
1979 Dragutin Surbek/Anton Stipancic (Yugoslavia)
1981 Cai Zhenhua/Li Zhenshi (China)
1983 Dragutin Surbek/Zoran Kalinic (Yugoslavia)
1985 Mikael Applegren/Ulf Carlsson (Sweden)
1987 Chen Longcan/Wei Quinguang (China)
1989 Joerg Rosskopf/Stefen Fetzner (W Germany)
1991 Peter Karlson/Thomas von Scheele (Sweden)
1993 Wang Tao/Lu Lin (China)

Most wins: (8) Viktor Barna (Hungary/England): 1929–33 (won two titles 1933), 1935, 1939.

Recent winners: doubles – women
1971 Cheng Min-Chih/Lin Hui-Ching (China)
1973 Maria Alexandru (Romania)/
      Miho Hamada (Japan)
1975 Maria Alexandru (Romania)/
      Shoko Takashima (Japan)
1977 Pak Yong Ok (N Korea)/Yang Yin (China)

1979 Zhang Li/Zhang Deying (China)
1981 Zhang Deying/Cao Yanhua (China)
1983 Shen Jianping/Dai Lili (China)
1985 Dai Lili/Geng Lijuan (China)
1987 Yang Young-Ja/Hyun Jung-Hwa (Korea)
1989 Quio Hong/Deng Yaping (China)
1991 Chen Zhie/Gao Jun (China)
1993 Liu Wen/Qiao Yunping (China)

Most wins: (7) Maria Mednyanszky (Hungary): 1928, 1930–5.

Recent winners: mixed doubles
1971 Chang Shih-Ling/Lin Hui-Ching (China)
1973 Liang Geliang/Li Li (China)
1975 Stanislav Gomozkov/Anna Ferdman (USSR)
1977 Jacques Secretin/Claude Bergeret (France)
1979 Liang Geliang/Ge Xinai (China)
1981 Xie Saike/Huang Junqun (China)
1983 Guo Yuehua/Ni Xialian (China)
1985 Cai Zhenua/Coa Yanhua (China)
1987 Hui Jun/Geng Lijuan (China)
1989 Yoo Nam-Kyu/Hyun Jung-Hwa (S Korea)
1991 Wang Tao/Liu Wei (China)
1993 Wang Tao/Liu Wei (China)

Most wins: (6) Maria Mednyanszky (Hungary): 1927–8, 1930–1, 1933 (two titles).

Olympic Games

Gold medal winners: 1992
Men's singles
Jan-Ove Waldner (Switzerland)

Men's doubles
Lu Lin/Wang Tao (China)

Women's singles
Deng Yaping (China)

Women's doubles
Deng Yaping/Qiao Hong (China)

TENNIS (LAWN)

Wimbledon Championships

The All-England Championships at Wimbledon are lawn tennis's most prestigious championships. First held in 1877.

Recent winners: men's singles
1981 John McEnroe (USA)
1982 Jimmy Connors (USA)
1983 John McEnroe (USA)
1984 John McEnroe (USA)
1985 Boris Becker (W Germany)
1986 Boris Becker (W Germany)
1987 Pat Cash (Australia)
1988 Stefan Edberg (Sweden)
1989 Boris Becker (W Germany)
1990 Stefan Edberg (Sweden)
1991 Michael Stich (Germany)
1992 Andre Agassi (USA)
1993 Pete Sampras (USA)

Most wins: (7) William Renshaw (Great Britain): 1881–6, 1889.

Recent winners: women's singles
1981 Chris Evert-Lloyd (USA)
1982 Martina Navratilova (USA)
1983 Martina Navratilova (USA)
1984 Martina Navratilova (USA)
1985 Martina Navratilova (USA)
1986 Martina Navratilova (USA)
1987 Martina Navratilova (USA)
1988 Steffi Graf (W Germany)
1989 Steffi Graf (W Germany)
1990 Martina Navratilova (USA)
1991 Steffi Graf (Germany)
1992 Steffi Graf (Germany)
1993 Steffi Graf (Germany)

Most wins: (9) Martina Navratilova (Czechoslovakia/USA): 1978, 1979, and as above.

Recent winners: men's doubles

1981	Peter Fleming/John McEnroe (USA)
1982	Peter McNamara/Paul McNamee (Australia)
1983	Peter Fleming/John McEnroe (USA)
1984	Peter Fleming/John McEnroe (USA)
1985	Heinz Gunthardt (Switzerland)/Balazs Taroczy (Hungary)
1986	Joakim Nystrom/Mats Wilander (Sweden)
1987	Ken Flach/Robert Seguso (USA)
1988	Ken Flach/Robert Seguso (USA)
1989	John Fitzgerald (Australia)/Anders Jarryd (Sweden)
1990	Rick Leach/Jim Pugh (USA)
1991	John Fitzgerald (Australia)/Anders Jarryd (Sweden)
1992	John McEnroe (USA)/Michael Stich (Germany)
1993	Todd Woodbridge/Mark Woodforde (Australia)

Most wins: (8) Lawrence Doherty/Reg Doherty (Great Britain): 1897–1901, 1903–5.

Recent winners: women's doubles

1981	Martina Navratilova/Pam Shriver (USA)
1982	Martina Navratilova/Pam Shriver (USA)
1983	Martina Navratilova/Pam Shriver (USA)
1984	Martina Navratilova/Pam Shriver (USA)
1985	Kathy Jordan/Elizabeth Smylie (Australia)
1986	Martina Navratilova/Pam Shriver (USA)
1987	Claudia Kohde-Kilsch (W Germany)/ Helena Sukova (Czechoslovakia)
1988	Steffi Graf (W Germany)/Gabriela Sabatini (Argentina)
1989	Jana Novotna/Helena Sukova (Czechoslovakia)
1990	Jana Novotna/Helena Sukova (Czechoslovakia)
1991	Larissa Savchenko/Natalya Zvereva (USSR)
1992	Gigi Fernandez (USA)/Natalya Zvereva (Belarus)
1993	Gigi Fernandez (USA)/Natalya Zvereva (Belarus)

Most wins: (12) Elizabeth Ryan (USA): 1914, 1919–23, 1925–7, 1930, 1933–4.

Recent winners: mixed doubles

1981	Betty Stove (Netherlands)/Frew McMillan (S Africa)
1982	Anne Smith (USA)/Kevin Curren (S Africa)
1983	Wendy Turnbull (Australia)/John Lloyd (Great Britain)
1984	Wendy Turnbull (Australia)/John Lloyd (Great Britain)
1985	Martina Navratilova (USA)/Paul McNamee (Australia)
1986	Kathy Jordan/Ken Flach (USA)
1987	Jo Durie/Jeremy Bates (Great Britain)
1988	Sherwood Stewart/Zina Garrison (USA)
1989	Jim Pugh (USA)/Jana Novotna (Czechoslovakia)
1990	Rick Leach/Zina Garrison (USA)
1991	John Fitzgerald/Elizabeth Smylie (Australia)
1992	Cyril Suk (Czech Republic)/Lavisa Savchenko (Latvia)
1993	Mark Woodforde (Australia)/Martina Navratilova (USA)

Most wins: (7) Elizabeth Ryan (USA): 1919, 1921, 1923, 1927–8, 1930, 1932.

Tennis court

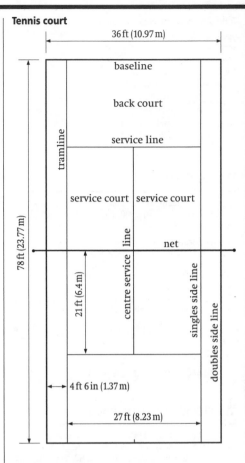

United States Open

First held in 1891 as the United States Championship; became the United States Open in 1968.

Recent winners: men's singles

1981	John McEnroe (USA)
1982	Jimmy Connors (USA)
1983	Jimmy Connors (USA)
1984	John McEnroe (USA)
1985	Ivan Lendl (Czechoslovakia)
1986	Ivan Lendl (Czechoslovakia)
1987	Ivan Lendl (Czechoslovakia)
1988	Mats Wilander (Sweden)
1989	Boris Becker (W Germany)
1990	Peter Sampras (USA)
1991	Stefan Edberg (Sweden)
1992	Stefan Edberg (Sweden)
1993	Pele Sameras (USA)

Recent winners: women's singles

1981	Tracy Austin (USA)
1982	Chris Evert-Lloyd (USA)
1983	Martina Navratilova (USA)
1984	Martina Navratilova (USA)
1985	Hana Mandlikova (Czechoslovakia)
1986	Martina Navratilova (USA)
1987	Martina Navratilova (USA)
1988	Steffi Graf (W Germany)

Tennis (lawn) (continued)

1989 Steffi Graf (W Germany)
1990 Gabriela Sabatini (Argentina)
1991 Monica Seles (Yugoslavia)
1992 Monica Seles (Yugoslavia)
1993 Steffi Graf (Germany)

Most wins: Men (7) Richard Sears (USA): 1881–7; Bill Larned (USA), 1901–2, 1907–11; Bill Tilden (USA): 1920–5, 1929. Woen (7) Molla Mallory (née Bjurstedt) (USA): 1915–16, 1928, 1920–2, 1926; Helen Wills-Moody (USA): 1923–5, 1927–9, 1931.

Davis Cup

International team competition organized on a knock-out basis. First held in 1900; contested on a challenge basis until 1972.

Recent winners

1981	USA	1987	Sweden
1982	USA	1988	W Germany
1983	Australia	1989	W Germany
1984	Sweden	1990	USA
1985	Sweden	1991	France
1986	Australia	1992	USA

Most wins: (29) USA: 1900, 1902, 1913, 1920–6, 1937–8, 1946–9, 1954, 1958, 1963, 1968–72, 1978–9, 1981–2, 1990.

TENPIN BOWLING

World championships

First held in 1923 by the International Bowling Association; since 1954 organized by the Fédération Internationale des Quillieurs (FIQ). Since 1963, when women first competed, held every four years.

Recent winners: individual – men

1954 Göska Algeskog (Sweden)
1955 Nils Bäckström (Sweden)
1958 Kaarlo Asukas (Finland)
1960 Tito Reynolds (Mexico)
1963 Les Zikes (USA)
1967 David Pond (Great Britain)
1971 Ed Luther (USA)
1975 Bud Staudt (USA)
1979 Ollie Ongtawco (Philippines)
1983 Armando Marino (Colombia)
1987 Rolland Patrick (France)
1991 Ma Ying-chei (Taiwan)

Recent winners: individual – women

1963 Helen Shablis (USA)
1967 Helen Weston (USA)
1971 Ashie Gonzales (Puerto Rico)
1975 Annedore Haefker (W Germany)
1979 Lita de la Roas (Philippines)
1983 Lena Sulkanen (Sweden)
1987 Edda Piccini (Italy)
1991 Martha Beckel (Germany)

Most wins: No one has won more than once.

TRAMPOLINING

World championships

First held in 1964 and annually until 1968; since then, every two years.

Recent winners: individual – men

1970 Wayne Miller (USA)
1972 Paul Luxon (Great Britain)
1974 Richard Tison (France)
1976 Richard Tison (France)/Yevgeni Yanes (USSR) (*shared*)
1978 Yevgeni Yanes (USSR)
1980 Stewart Matthews (Great Britain)
1982 Carl Furrer (Great Britain)
1984 Lionel Pioline (France)
1986 Lionel Pioline (France)
1988 Vadim Krasnoshapka (USSR)
1990 Aleksandr Moskalenko (USSR)
1992 Aleksandr Moskalenko (Russia)

Most wins: (2) David Jacobs (USA): 1967–8; Wayne Miller (USA): 1966, 1970; Richard Tison (France): as above; Yevgeni Yanes (USSR): as above; Lionel Pioline (France): as above; Aleksandr Moskalenko (Russia): as above.

Recent winners: individual – women

1970 Renee Ransom (USA)
1972 Alexandra Nicholson (USA)
1974 Alexandra Nicholson (USA)
1976 Svetlana Levina (USSR)
1978 Tatyana Anisimova (USSR)
1980 Ruth Keller (Switzerland)
1982 Ruth Keller (Switzerland)
1984 Sue Shotton (Great Britain)
1986 Tatyana Lushina (USSR)
1988 Rusadan Khoperia (USSR)
1990 Yelena Merkulova (USSR)
1992 Yelena Merkulova (Russia)

Most wins: (5) Judy Wills (USA): 1964–8.

TUG OF WAR

World championships

Instituted in 1975. Held every two years; contested at 560 kg from 1982.

Winners

	720 kg	640 kg	560 kg	Catchweight (no specification)
1975	England	England	–	–
1976	England	England	–	–
1977	England	Wales	–	–
1978	England	England	–	–
1980	England	England	–	–
1982	England	Ireland	Switzerland	–
1984	Ireland	Ireland	England	England
1985	Switzerland	Switzerland	Switzerland	–
1986	Ireland	Ireland	England	–
1988	Ireland	England	England	–
1990	Ireland	Ireland	Switzerland	–
1992	Switzerland	Switzerland	Spain	

Most titles: (15) England: as above.

VOLLEYBALL

World championships

Inaugurated in 1949; first women's championships in 1952. Now held every four years, but Olympic champions are also world champions in Olympic years.

Recent winners: men
1970	E Germany	1982	USSR
1972	Japan	1984	USA
1974	Poland	1986	USA
1976	Poland	1988	USA
1978	USSR	1990	Italy
1980	USSR	1992	Brazil

Recent winners: women
1970	USSR	1982	China
1972	USSR	1984	China
1974	Japan	1986	China
1976	Japan	1988	USSR
1978	Cuba	1990	USSR
1980	USSR	1992	Cuba

Most wins: Men (9), USSR: 1949, 1952, 1960, 1962, 1964 1968, 1978, 1980, 1982. Women (8) USSR: 1952, 1956, 1960, 1968, 1970, 1972, 1980, 1988.

WALKING

Lugano Trophy

The principal road-walking trophy. Contested every two years by men's national teams; first held in 1961.

Recent winners
1973	E Germany	1985	E Germany
1975	USSR	1987	USSR
1977	Mexico	1989	USSR
1979	Mexico	1991	Italy
1981	Italy	1993	Mexico
1983	Italy		

Most wins: (5) E Germany: 1965, 1967, 1970, 1973, 1985.

Eschborn Cup

The women's equivalent of the Lugano Trophy; first held in 1979; takes place every two years.

Winners
1981	USSR	1989	USSR
1983	China	1991	USSR
1985	China	1993	Italy
1987	USSR		

Most wins: (4) USSR: as above.

WATER POLO

World championship

First held in 1973, and every four years since 1978. It used to be included in the world swimming championships; since 1991 it has been held separately. First women's event held in 1986.

Winners: men
1973	Hungary	1982	USSR
1975	USSR	1986	Yugoslavia
1978	Italy	1991	Yugoslavia

Winners: women
1986	Australia
1991	Netherlands

Most wins: Men (2) USSR: Yugoslavia: as above.

World Cup

Inaugurated in 1979 and held every two years. Women's event unofficial until 1989.

Winners: men
1979	Hungary	1987	Yugoslavia
1981	USSR	1989	Yugoslavia
1983	USSR	1991	USA
1985	W Germany		

Most wins: (2) USSR: as above; Yugoslavia; as above.

Winners: women
1979	USA
1981	Canada
1988	Netherlands
1989	Netherlands
1991	Netherlands

Most wins: (3) Netherlands: as above.

WATER SKIING

World championships

First held in 1949; take place very two years. Competitions for slalom, tricks, jumps, and the overall individual title.

Recent winners: overall – men
1971	George Athans (Canada)
1973	George Athans (Canada)
1975	Carlos Suarez (Venezuela)
1977	Mike Hazelwood (Great Britain)
1979	Joel McClintock (Canada)
1981	Sammy Duvall (USA)
1983	Sammy Duvall (USA)
1985	Sammy Duvall (USA)
1987	Sammy Duvall (USA)
1989	Patrice Martin (France)
1991	Patrice Martin (France)
1993	Patrice Martin (France)

Most wins: (4) Sammy Duvall (USA): as above.

Recent winners: overall – women
1971	Christy Weir (USA)
1973	Lisa St John (USA)
1975	Liz Allan-Shetter (USA)
1977	Cindy Todd (USA)
1979	Cindy Todd (USA)
1981	Karin Roberge (USA)
1983	Ana-Maria Carrasco (Venezuela)
1985	Karen Neville (Australia)
1987	Deena Brush (USA)
1989	Deena Mapple (USA)
1991	Karen Neville (Australia)
1993	Natalia Rumiantseva (Russia)

Most wins: (3) Willa McGuire (USA): 1949–50, 1955; Liz Allan-Shetter (USA): 1965, 1969, 1975.

WEIGHTLIFTING

World championships

First held in 1898. 11 weight divisions; the most prestigious is the 110 kg plus category (formerly known as Super Heavyweight). Olympic champions are automatically world champions in Olympic years.

Recent champions: over 110 kg
1981	Anatoliy Pisarenko (USSR)
1982	Anatoliy Pisarenko (USSR)
1983	Anatoliy Pisarenko (USSR)
1984	Dean Lukin (Australia)
1985	Antonio Krastev (Bulgaria)
1986	Antonio Krastev (Bulgaria)
1987	Aleksandr Kurlovich (USSR)
1988	Aleksandr Kurlovich (USSR)
1989	Aleksandr Kurlovich (USSR)
1990	Leonid Taranenko (USSR)
1991	Aleksandr Kurlovich (USSR)
1992	Aleksandr Kurlovich (Unified Team)

Most titles (all categories): (8) John Davies (USA): 1938 (82.5 kg), 1946–50 (over 82.5 kg), 1951–2 (over 90 kg), Tommy Kono (USA): 1952 (67.5 kg), 1953, 1957–9 (75 kg), 1954–6 (82.5 kg) Vasiliy Alexseyev (USSR): 1970–7 (over 110 kg).

Sports and games

WRESTLING

World championships

Graeco-Roman world championships first held in 1921. First freestyle championships in 1951; each style contests 10 weight divisions, the heaviest being the 130 kg (formerly over 100 kg) category. Olympic champions become world champions in Olympic years.

Recent winners: freestyle – super-heavyweight/over 100 kg
1981   Salman Khasimikov (USSR)
1982   Salman Khasimikov (USSR)
1983   Salman Khasimikov (USSR)
1984   Bruce Baumgartner (USA)
1985   David Gobedzhishvilli (USSR)
1986   Bruce Baumgartner (USA)
1987   Khadartsv Aslam (USSR)
1988   David Gobedzhishvilli (USSR)
1989   Ali Reiza Soleimani (Iran)
1990   David Gobedzhishvilli (USSR)
1991   Andreas Schroder (Germany)
1992   Bruce Baumgartner (USA)
1993   Mikael Ljunberg (Sweden)

Recent winners: Graeco-Roman – super-heavyweight/over 100 kg
1981   Refik Memisevic (Yugoslavia)
1982   Nikolai Denev (Bulgaria)
1983   Jevgeniy Artiochin (USSR)
1984   Jeffrey Blatnick (USA)
1985   Igor Rostozotskiy (USSR)
1986   Thomas Johansson (Sweden)
1987   Igor Rostozotskiy (USSR)
1988   Aleksandr Karelin (USSR)
1989   Aleksandr Karelin (USSR)
1990   Aleksandr Karelin (USSR)
1991   Aleksandr Karelin (USSR)
1992   Aleksandr Karelin (Unified Team)
1993   Aleksandr Karelin (Russia)

Most titles (all weight divisions): Freestyle (10) Aleksander Medved (USSR): 1962–4, 1966 (90 kg), 1967–8 (100 kg), 1969–72 (over 100 kg). Graeco-Roman (7) Valeriy Rezantsev (USSR): 1970–6 (90 kg).

YACHTING

America's Cup

One of sport's famous trophies, first won by the schooner *Magic* in 1870. Now held approximately every four years, when challengers compete in a series of races to find which of them races against the holder. All 25 winners up to 1983 were from the United States.

Recent winners
1958   *Columbia* (USA) (Briggs Cunningham)
1962   *Weatherly* (USA) (Emil Mosbacher)
1964   *Constellation* (USA) (Bob Bavier)
1967   *Intrepid* (USA) (Emil Mosbacher)
1970   *Intrepid* (USA) (Bill Ficker)
1974   *Courageous* (USA) (Ted Hood)
1977   *Courageous* (USA) (Ted Turner)
1980   *Freedom* (USA) (Dennis Conner)
1983   *Australia II* (Australia) (John Bertrand)
1987   *Stars & Stripes* (USA) (Dennis Conner)
1988   *Stars & Stripes* (USA) (Dennis Conner)[a]
1992   *America 3* (USA) (Bill Koch)

[a]*Stars & Stripes* won a special challenge match but on appeal the race was awarded to *New Zealand*, skippered by Davis Barnes. However, after much legal wrangling, the cup was retained by *Stars & Stripes*.

Most wins: (Skipper) (3) Charlie Barr (USA): 1899, 1901, 1903; Harold Vanderbilt (USA): 1930, 1934, 1937; Dennis Conner (USA): as above.

Admiral's Cup

A two-yearly series of races in the English Channel, around Fastnet rock and at Cowes; national teams of three boats per team. First held in 1957.

Recent winners
1969	USA	1981	Great Britain
1971	Great Britain	1983	W Germany
1973	W Germany	1985	W Germany
1975	Great Britain	1987	New Zealand
1977	Great Britain	1989	Great Britain
1979	Australia	1991	France
		1993	Australia

Most wins: (9) Great Britain: 1957, 1959, 1963, 1965, 1971, 1975, 1977, 1981, 1989.

International racing yacht classes

Class	Crew	Type of craft
Finn	1	Centre-board dinghy
Flying Dutchman	2	Centre-board dinghy
International 470	2	Centre-board dinghy
International Soling	3	Keel boat
International Star	2	Keel boat
International Tornado	2	Catamaran
Windglider	1	Single board

GOVERNING BODIES IN SPORT

AAA	Amateur Athletic Association
AAU	Amateur Athletic Union (USA)
ACU	Auto Cycle Union
AIBA	International Amateur Boxing Federation
ASA	Amateur Swimming Association
BDO	British Darts Organization
FA	Football Association
FEI	International Equestrian Federation
FIA	International Automobile Association
FIAC	International Amateur Cycling Federation
FIBA	International Basketball Federation
FIBT	International Bobsleigh and Tobogganing Federation
FIC	International Canoeing Federation
FIDE	International Chess Federation
FIE	International Fencing Federation
FIFA	International Football Association Federation
FIG	International Gymnastic Federation
FIH	International Hockey Federation
FILA	International Amateur Wrestling Federation
FIM	International Motorcycling Federation
FINA	International Amateur Swimming Federation
FIQ	International Bowling Federation
FIRA	International Amateur Rugby Federation
FIS	International Ski Federation
FIT	International Trampoline Federation
FITA	International Archery Federation
FIVB	International Volleyball Federation
GAA	Gaelic Athletic Association
IAAF	International Amateur Athletic Federation
IBA	International Baseball Association
IBF	International Badminton Federation
IBF	International Boxing Federation
IBSF	International Billiards and Snooker Federation Association
ICF	International Curling Federation
IHF	International Handball Federation
IIHF	International Ice Hockey Federation
IJF	International Judo Federation
IOC	International Olympic Committee
IRFB	International Rugby Football Board
ISRF	International Squash Rackets Federation
ISU	International Skating Union
ITF	International Tennis Federation
ITTF	International Table Tennis Federation
IWF	International Weightlifting Federation
IWSF	International Water Ski Federation
IYRU	International Yacht Racing Union
LPGA	Ladies' Professional Golfers' Association
LTA	Lawn Tennis Association
MCC	Marylebone Cricket Club
NBA	National Basketball Association (USA)
NCAA	National Collegiate Athletic Association (USA)
NFL	National Football League (USA)
NHL	National Hockey League (USA)
PGA	Professional Golfers' Association
RFU	Rugby Football Union
RL	Rugby League
TCCB	Test and County Cricket Board
UEFA	Union of European Football Associations
UIPMB	International Union of Modern Pentathlon and Biathlon
UIT	International Shooting Union
USGA	United States Golf Association
USPGA	United States Professional Golfers' Association
WBA	World Boxing Association
WBC	World Boxing Council
WBO	World Boxing Organisation
WPBSA	World Professional Billiards and Snooker Association
WWSU	World Water Skiing Union

INDEX

Guide to the Index

The alphabetical arrangement of this index is letter-by-letter. The order follows the English alphabet, ignoring capital letters, accents, diacritics, and apostrophes.

In cases where a series of headwords have the same spelling, general topics are ordered before people, and people precede places.

Rulers are listed chronologically, ordering them by country if their names are the same (eg *Charles I of England* would precede *Charles I of Spain*, and these would be followed by *Charles II*).

When a number of people have the same name, monarchs are given before saints and popes, and these are followed by lay people. Compound names (eg *John of Gaunt*) appear later than single-element surnames (eg *John, Elton*), and are taken in strict letter-by-letter order, including grammatical words (eg *John of Gaunt* precedes *John the Baptist*).

Entries involving numbers are located on the basis of their spoken form (eg *10* will be found under 'ten').

Names beginning with *St* are ordered under *Saint*, and all *Mc* prefixes are ordered as if they were *Mac*. Cross-references between index entries are shown with the symbol >>.

Conventional abbreviations are used for American states; these are explained on pp. 345–6.

Most of the entries consist of a single reference to a page in the first part of this book. In a few cases, sets of references have been compiled on points of possible interest.

Index

Index

Index

Index

Index

Index

world heritage sites
46
Lebanon Mts 272
Lebowa 315
Lebowakgom 315
Le Breton, Emilie
Charlotte 553
Lebrun, Albert 190
Le Carré, John 538
Lecce University 646
lecithins 134
Lecoq, Jacques 553
Le Corbusier 621, 623
lector 406
Lecythis species 110
Leda 7
Lederer, Charles 556
Lederman, Leon 640
Ledoux, Claude
Nicolas 623
Ledovskaya, Tatyana
666
Le Duc Anh 353
Led Zeppelin 601
Lee, Christopher 568
Lee, George 692
Lee, Harper 538, 543
Lee, Laurie 538
Lee, Robert E 178, 556
Lee, Spike 568
Lee, Yuan Tseh 640
leech 78
Leech, Archibald
Alexander 564
Leeds
Festival 552
football team 688,
689, 690, 691
rugby league team
704
universities 651
Lee Eun Chul 706
Lee Huan 323
Lee Jeng-hui 323
leek 108
Leekpai, Chuan 326
leeks 131
Lee Kuan Yew 312
Lee Teng-hui 323
Leeward Is 204, 291,
307, 338, 340, 342
Lefebvre, Janou 684
leg 119
Legat, Nicolai 611
Legend of Joseph 613
Leger, St 408
Leghan, Farooq Ahmed
297
Legion d'Honneur 372
Legionella 123
legionnaires' disease
123
Legion of Merit 373
Legislative Assembly
(France) 186
legumes 109, 132, 133
Leguminosae 107–8

Léhar, Franz 589
Le Havre University, PA
643
Lehigh University 658
Lehmann, Beatrix 553
Lehmann, Lotte 593
Lehmann, Rosamond
538
Lehn, Jean-Marie 640
Lehtinen, Lauri 667
lei 304
Leicester 334
football team 690,
691
rugby union team
705
universities 651
Leicestershire 334
cricket team 681
Leiden University 647
Leigh, Vivien 568, 577,
578
Leigh, rugby league
team 704
Leighton, Frederick,
Baron 639
Leiopelmatidae 94
Leipzig 188
university 645
Leitrim 260
Lek 201, 361
Lekhanya, Justin
Metsing 273
Lelong, Lucien 617
Lemaire, Ferdinand
593
Leman, L 62
Le Mans, university
643
Le Mans 24-hour race
700
Le Mesnil-sur-Oger
(wine) 139
Lemland 38
lemming 82
Lemming, Erik 669
Lemmon, Jack 568,
579
Le Moignan, Martine
708
lemon 107
LeMond, Greg 683
lempira 254, 362
lemur, types of 83, 84
Lemuridae 83
Lena, R 42, 304
drainage basin 43
Lendl, Ivan 711
Leng, Virginia 684
length, conversion
tables 504–5
Lenin 159, 187, 305
Leningrad 179
Philarmonic
Orchestra 585
Lenin Peak 324
Lennart, Isobel 555

Lennon, John 161, 596,
601
Lennox, Earl of 168
Lennox, Annie 598
lens (optics) 516, 525
lens (of eye) 121
Lens culinaris 109
Lent 403, 412
lentils 109, 131
Lenya, Lotte 553
Leo (constellation) 3, 5
Leo (zodiac) 151
Leo I 164
Leo I, the Great (pope)
404, 406, 408
Leo II 164
Leo II (pope) 404
Leo III, St (pope) 404,
407
Leo IV (pope) 404, 407
Leo V–VIII (popes) 404
Leo IX (pope) 404, 407
Leo X–XIII (popes)
405–6
Leoben University 641
Leodegar, St 408
Leo Minor 3, 4
Léon Carpio, Ramiro
de 251
León, Kingdom of 316
León University 648
Leonard, St 408
Leonard Trophy
(bowls) 678
Leonardi, Leoncillo
630
Leonardo da Vinci 46,
154, 628, 630
Leoncavallo, Ruggiero
592
Leoncillo 630
leone 311, 365
Leonids 6
Leopold (Emperor) 172
Leopold II (Belgium)
356
Leopold II (Emperor)
173
Leopold (son of Queen
Victoria) 170
Leopold of Austria 182
Leopold of Saxe-
Coburg 213
Lepanto, Battle of 155
Lepidoptera 101
Lepilmuridae 84
Leporidae 83
leprosy 123
leptac 249
leptae 362
Leptis Magna 46
Leptodactylidae 95
Leptosomatidae 88
Lepus 3, 4
Lerner, Alan Jay 555,
556
lev 361

Levi, Tribe of 410
Lerwick 336
Lesage, Georges Louis
525
Lesbos 249
Lescot, Pierre 623
Lesh, Phil 599
Les Huguenots 592
Lesotho **272–3**, 363
area ranking 197
Commonwealth
membership 382
government
information 471
population ranking
198
UN membership 380
Lesotho (language) 272
Lessing, Doris 538
Le Sueur, Lucille 560
Lethaby, William 615
Lethbridge University
(Alberta) 621
Leto 399
Letotyphlopidae 93
Letsie III 273
letter frequencies in
English 451–2
lettuce 107, 131
types of 107
Letzeburgesch 276, 363
leu 284, 304, 364, 365
leucine 118
leukaemia 125
leukocytes 121
Leuthold, Urs 677
lev 219
Level (constellation) 3
Levi, Ivo 569
Levi, Priom 538
Levi-Montalcini, Rita
640
Levina, Svetlana 712
Levinson, Barry 568,
580
Levisticum officinale 111
Leviticus 402
Levkas 39
Lewes 334, 608
Lewis, Carl 665,
666, 667, 669
Lewis, Hayley 709
Lewis, Jerry Lee 601
Lewis, Lennox 679
Lewis, Sinclair 538,
542, 543
Lewis, Steve 667
Lewis (island) 39
lexan 523
Lexington 187
Leygues, Georges 190
Leyton Orient football
team 691
Lhotse 42
Liang, Geliang 710
Lias epoch 18
Liban, Jebel 272

Index

Index

Index

Index

Index

Index

Index

Index

Index

ACKNOWLEDGEMENTS

We would like to thank the following for their help in the preparation of this book:

Geoffrey Briggs, NASA; British Rail; British Standards Institution; British Telecom; Dr Michael Brooke, Cambridge; Professor A. Brown and Mrs P. Brown, Oxford; Calmann and King; Carol-June Cassidy; Central Statistical Office; Civil Aviation Authority; Department of Health; Food and Agriculture Organization; Dr J.T. Houghton, Hadley Climate Centre; International Monetary Fund; International Phonetic Association; Organization for Economic Co-operation and Development; Maureen Storey; World Health Organization; UNESCO.

The following Cambridge University Press titles were used in the preparation of data for this book:

M. Brooke and T. Birkhead (eds) *The Cambridge Encyclopedia of Ornithology* (Cambridge University Press, 1991)
D. Crystal (ed.) *The Cambridge Encyclopedia* (Cambridge University Press, 1992)
D. Crystal *The Cambridge Encyclopedia of Language* (Cambridge University Press, 1991)
D. Crystal (ed.) *The Cambridge Paperback Encyclopedia* (Cambridge University Press, 1993)
J.T. Houghton, G.J. Jenkins, and J.J. Ephraums (eds) *Climate Change The Scientific Assessment* (Cambridge University Press, 1990)
S. Jones, R. Martin, and D. Pilbeam (eds) *The Cambridge Encyclopedia of Human Evolution* (Cambridge University Press, 1992)
R.J. Lincoln and G.A. Boxhall *The Cambridge Illustrated Dictionary of Natural History* (Cambridge University Press, 1990)
K. Nicholls and A. Nicholls (eds) *The Cambridge Guide to the Museums of Europe* (Cambridge University Press, 1991)
A. Sherratt (ed.) *The Cambridge Encyclopedia of Archaeology* (Cambridge University Press, 1980)
N. Smart *The World's Religions* (Cambridge University Press, 1992)
D. Smith (ed.) *The Cambridge Encyclopedia of Earth Sciences* (Cambridge University Press, 1982)

Thank you also to the following for their work on the index:

Hilary Crystal; Geoff Leeming; Teresa Regan; Ann Rowlands